# Western Civilization

# Western Civilization

## THE CONTINUING EXPERIMENT

### THIRD EDITION

## Volume II
## Since 1560

**Thomas F. X. Noble**
University of Notre Dame

**Barry S. Strauss**
Cornell University

**Duane J. Osheim**
University of Virginia

**Kristen B. Neuschel**
Duke University

**William B. Cohen**
Indiana University

**David D. Roberts**
University of Georgia

Houghton Mifflin Company    Boston    New York

Editor-in-Chief: Jean L. Woy
Sponsoring Editor: Nancy Blaine
Senior Development Editor: Jennifer E. Sutherland
Editorial Associate: Gillie Jones
Senior Project Editor: Christina M. Horn
Editorial Assistant: Marie Bernard-Jackson
Senior Designer: Henry Rachlin
Senior Production/Design Coordinator: Sarah Ambrose
Senior Manufacturing Coordinator: Sally Culler
Senior Marketing Manager: Sandra McGuire

Volume II cover image: Aria Ipatuescu at head of the first group of revolutionaries in Transylvania against Russia, 1848. Painting by D. Stoica. Photograph: Dagli Ori/The Art Archive, London.

Text credits begin on page A-17, which constitutes an extension of the copyright page.

Printed in the U.S.A.

Library of Congress Control Number: 2001131390

ISBN: 0-618-10211-6

1 2 3 4 5 6 7 8 9-WEB-05 04 03 02 01

# Brief Contents

# Contents

# CHAPTER 18

# Europe on the Threshold of Modernity, ca. 1715–1789   603

# CHAPTER 19

# An Age of Revolution, 1789–1815   643

# CHAPTER 23

# The Age of Optimism, 1850–1880   775

# CHAPTER 24

# Escalating Tensions, 1880–1914   809

# MAPS

# DOCUMENTS

# Weighing the Evidence

# Information Technology

# PREFACE

In the days devoted to writing this preface in February 2001, the British prime minister visited the president of the United States, and the American secretary of state visited the Middle East. American and British aircraft bombed Iraq, and U.S. officials made vigorous representation to the Chinese government about reports that they had furnished the Iraqis with radar technology and components. An American submarine on maneuvers in the Pacific surfaced without due caution and sank a Japanese fishing boat. Taliban militants in Afghanistan destroyed ancient Buddhist statues on the grounds that they offended Islam's strict prohibition of idolatry. The pope named forty-four cardinals from all over the world. With these kinds of subjects in the news in the dawning third millennium, one might well ask: Why study Western Civilization any longer?

For some five thousand years, a Western civilization has been growing, changing, reflecting on itself, and sharing ideas with its neighbors. The West alone is not civilized, of course, for there were ancient civilizations in China, India, and Africa. But the West is uniquely civilized in the sense that its ideas and institutions are distinctive. This is not to imply that the West is better or worse than the other civilizations with which it shares the earth. It is simply to emphasize the persistence of one ancient tradition alongside others. But does antiquity alone constitute a claim on the efforts of teachers and students?

We begin to answer that question by pointing out that everyone alive today has been influenced by Western Civilization. The West deserves to be studied because its tale is old and compelling but *demands* to be studied because its story has been central to the development of the world in which we live. Western institutions—most notably representative democracy and commercial capitalism—have spread to every corner of the world. Even capitalism's greatest rival, communism, is fundamentally Western. Western styles in architecture dominate the skylines of every major city in the world. Western popular culture, from movies and music to fast food, are found absolutely everywhere. Communications technologies, from cell phones to e-mail, are as global in spread as they are Western in origin.

Some people, inside and outside the West, have grave reservations about the extent of Western influence in the modern world. Some critics challenge Western religious, philosophical, political, and economic ideas at their core. Others have no quarrel with Western ideas but regret that local cultures all over the globe are vanishing before a relentless Western onslaught. Still others wonder why Western achievements in political stability and economic prosperity cannot be more widely shared. In other words, to say that the West is dominant is only to state the obvious, not to insist that such domination is inevitable or desirable. But the sheer, unassailable fact of that domination makes the careful study of the West essential for informed, responsible participation in the modern world.

However ancient Western Civilization may be, and however pervasive its influence, the definition of the term itself is controversial. The "West" is sometimes understood in terms of geography and sometimes in terms of culture. Each understanding invites misunderstanding. For most people today, the "West" means western Europe. And yet western Europe was the heir of the peoples and cultures of antiquity. These included Mesopotamians and Egyptians, who were the ancestors of the West, as well as Greeks, Romans, Jews, and Christians, who were the founders of the West. These peoples all lived around the Mediterranean world, and it was those who came after them, who lived in Europe proper, who built the West. Within Europe, some might take the West to mean Paris, London, Vienna, Berlin, and Rome. Others would include Madrid, Dublin, St. Petersburg, Stockholm, Warsaw, and Budapest. Moreover, through exploration, war, and commerce, the "West" gradually imposed its influence on the whole globe. One thinks immediately of the Westernization of the North and South American continents, but Tokyo and Hong Kong, although undeniably Eastern, are strongly marked by Western influences. In short, the West has never been, and is not now, neatly confined to one area or people.

As a cultural phenomenon, "Western" implies many things: freedom and free, participatory political institutions; economic initiative and opportunity; monotheistic religious faiths; rationalism and ordered thought in the social, political, and philosophical realms; an aesthetic sensibility that aspires to a universal sense of truth and beauty. But westerners have felt free to evoke tradition as their guiding light and also to innovate brilliantly; to accommodate slavery and freedom simultaneously; to esteem original thought and to persecute people who deviate from the norm. "Western" indeed has meant many things in various places at different times.

More than a decade ago, the six authors of *Western Civilization: The Continuing Experiment* set out to create a textbook for a course that informs students about a tradition that has powerfully, although not always positively, affected everyone in the contemporary world. Although each of us found something to admire in all of the existing textbooks, none of us was fully happy with any of them. Convinced of both the inherent interest of Western Civilization and the importance of teaching the subject, we were nevertheless disconcerted by the celebratory tone of some books, which portrayed the West as resting on its laurels instead of creatively facing its future. We were disappointed with books that claimed "balance" but actually stressed a single kind of history. We regretted that so many texts were uneven in their command of recent scholarship. We aimed to address the full range of subjects that a Western Civilization book needs to address and to provide the student reader with interesting, timely material in a book that is handsome to look at—in short, a book that helps the instructor to teach and the student to learn.

In preparing the Third Edition, we profited from the experience of using the book, the advice and criticism of dozens of colleagues, and the reactions of thousands of students. We are pleased that fellow teachers have found our vision and approach to be sound and that students have found our material accessible. In this new edition we have incorporated many changes, but we have not abandoned our approach to the subject, our commitment to its importance (and interest!), and our dedication to the students and teachers who share the adventure of learning the subject.

## BASIC APPROACH

Western Civilization is a story. Therefore, we aimed for a strong chronological narrative line. Our experience as teachers tells us that students appreciate this clear but gentle orientation. Our experience tells us, too, that an approach that is broadly chronological will leave instructors plenty of room to adapt our narrative to their preferred organization, or to supplement our narrative with one of their own.

Although we maintain the familiar, large-scale divisions of a Western Civilization book, we also present some innovative adjustments in arrangement. For instance, Chapter 2 treats early Greece together with the whole eastern Mediterranean region in the period from about 1500 to 750 B.C. This approach links kindred cultures and respects chronological flow better than customary treatments, which take western Asia to a certain point and then backtrack to deal with early Greece. We present a single chapter on Late Antiquity, the tumultuous and fascinating period from A.D. 284 to 600 that witnessed the transformation of the Roman Empire into three successors: Byzantine, Islamic, and European. One chapter studies those three successors, thereby permitting careful comparisons. But we do assign chapters to some of the greatest issues in Western Civilization, such as the Renaissance, the age of European exploration and conquest, the Scientific Revolution, and the industrial transformation. Our twentieth-century chapters reflect an understanding of the last century formed in its closing years rather than in its middle decades. What is new in our organization represents adjustments grounded in the best scholarship, and what is old represents time-tested approaches.

In fashioning our picture of the West, we take two unusual steps. First, our West is bigger than the one found in most textbooks. We treat the Celtic world, Scandinavia, and the Slavic world as integral parts of the story. We look often at the lands that border the West—Anatolia/Turkey, western Asia, North Africa, the Eurasian steppes—in order to show the to-and-fro of peoples, ideas, technologies, and products.

Second, we continually situate the West in its global context. This is not a world history book. But just as we recognize that the West has influenced the rest of the world, so too we carefully acknowledge how the rest of the world has influenced the West. Silks and spices, algebra and pointed arches, poetic forms and religious ideas have all entered the West from Asia and Africa and left deep marks. We begin this story of mutual interaction with the Greeks and Romans, carry it through the European Middle Ages, focus on it in the age of European exploration and conquest, and analyze it closely in the modern world of industry, diplomacy, empire, and immigration.

Another approach that runs like a ribbon throughout this textbook involves balance and integration. Teachers and students, just like the authors of this book, have their particular interests and emphases. In the large and diverse American academy, that is as it should be. But a textbook, if it is to be helpful and useful, should incorporate as many interests and emphases as possible. For a long time, some said, Western Civilization books devoted excessive coverage to high politics—"the public deeds of great men," as an ancient Greek writer defined the historian's subject. Others felt that high culture—all the Aristotles and Mozarts—were included to the exclusion of supposedly lesser figures and ordinary men and women. In the 1970s books began to emphasize social history. Many applauded this new emphasis even as they debated fiercely what to include under this heading. We capture the Western tradition in its full contours, listening to the voices of all of those who have made durable contributions. Naturally, we have had to make choices about how and where to array key topics within our narrative. We have used two basic rules to guide our writing.

First, we deal with topics when they were historically significant, when they commanded a great deal of attention in the historical past, or when modern historians have been able to discover a lot of information about them. Our approach to the history of women is an instructive example. A glance at this book's table of contents and then at its index is revealing. The former reveals very few sections devoted explicitly and exclusively to women. The latter shows that women appear constantly in every section of this book. Is there a contradiction here? Not at all. Women have not experienced history in complete separation from men. We do not assume that Western Civilization is a male or a female story. But we do recognize that men have been seen as the dominant historical actors, and so, again and again, we turn to *gender* as a tool of historical analysis. This permits us to ask why, in certain political, economic, or social circumstances, either men or women were assigned or denied roles or opportunities.

Second, we have tried to be integrative. For example, when we talk about power we present the institutional structures through which power was exercised, the people who possessed power as well as the people who did not, the ideological foundations for the use of power, and the material conditions that fostered or hindered the truly or the would-be powerful. Similarly, when we talk of great ideas we describe the antecedent ideas from which seemingly new ones were built up, and we ask about the consequences of those ideas. We explore the social position of the authors of those ideas to see if this helps explain the ideas themselves or to gauge their influence. We try to understand how ideas in one field of human endeavor proved to be influential in other fields.

We invite the reader to look at our narrative as if it were a mosaic. Taken as a whole, our narrative, like a mosaic, contains a coherent picture. Viewed more closely, our narrative, like a mosaic, is made up of countless tiny bits that may have their individual interest but that do not even hint at the larger picture. Finally, just as the viewer of a mosaic may find his or her eye drawn especially to one area, feature, color, or style, so too the reader of this book will find some parts more engaging or compelling than others. But it is only because there is, in this book as in a mosaic, a complete picture that the individual sections make sense, command our attention, excite our interest.

We ask, finally, that you note the subtitle of the book: "The Continuing Experiment." It was carefully chosen to convey our resolve to avoid a deterministic approach. For students and teachers, an appreciation of continuity and change, of unity and diversity, can foster sympathetic participation in our often bewildering world. We try to give individual actors, moments, and movements the sense of drama, possibility, and contingency that they actually possessed. We, with faultless hindsight, always know how things came out. Contemporaries often hadn't a clue. We respect them. Much of the fascination, and the reward, of studying Western Civilization lies precisely in its richness, diversity, changeability, and unpredictability. Moreover, and just as important, the experiment continues.

## CHANGES IN THE THIRD EDITION

In preparing our Third Edition, we thought hard about our own experiences in using the book and we paid close attention to the advice given us by many instructors, both those who had used the book and those who had not. The authors of this book have always been attentive to how we organized its contents. But just as our understanding of great historical issues is not static, so too our thinking on the matter of how to present this history undergoes constant revision.

### ■ New Organization and Content

For this edition the most dramatic organizational changes will be found in the sections dealing with the Middle Ages, the nineteenth century, and the twentieth century. Chapters 9 and 10, on the period from 900 to 1300, have been completely reorganized and heavily rewritten. In the first two editions, each of these chapters was comprehensive in thematic coverage, and they split the period at the year 1150. In the Third Edition, each chapter treats the whole period from 900 to 1300. Chapter 9 covers economic and political history and includes the Crusades. Chapter 10 covers social, religious, and cultural developments.

Chapters 20 and 21 have been reversed. By presenting "The Industrial Transformation of Europe, 1750–1850" (formerly 21 and now 20) before "Restoration, Reform, and Revolution, 1814–1848," it has been possible to resolve some tensions that persisted through the first two editions. As but one example, our former discussion of workers and the working class in Chapter 20 suffered from a lack of economic, industrial background. Chapters 29 and 30 have been reorganized to accommodate both the inclusion of recent events and the altered perspectives that inevitably attend the unpredictable course of history's march. Chapter 29 now covers the years from 1949 to 1989, and Chapter 30 treats the years from 1989 to the present.

Chapters 1–6 contain new discussions of archaeological evidence, revised treatment of Judaism, expanded material on Spartan and Roman women, and new coverage of Roman law. Discussions of the social, political, and military struggles of late medieval Europe in Chapter 11 have been reorganized. There is new material on humanism in Chapter 12. Chapter 14 has a revised treatment of John Calvin and of the Reformation in Scandinavia and eastern Europe. Seventeenth-century Europe's complicated political history has been streamlined. Several aspects of the Scientific Revolution in Chapter 17 have been revised, and there is new material on Galileo and Newton. The treatment of France in Chapters 18 and 19 has been revised, with new material added on eastern Europe. The discussions of socialism and Marxism in Chapter 21 have been reorganized. Chapter 22 has a new treatment of the Canadian Confederation. All of the chapters on the twentieth century contain new material, and Chapter 30 incorporates contemporary coverage, for instance on the Russian regime of Vladimir Putin and the new parity laws for elections in France. In highlighting these changes, it is important to add that *every single chapter* finds new material inserted, old material deleted, and existing material reorganized.

## ■ New Approaches to Teaching and Learning

To make this book as accessible as possible to students, we have constantly been aware of its place in a program of teaching and learning. Each chapter begins with a vignette that is directly tied to an accompanying picture. The vignettes introduce the reader to one or more of the key aspects of the chapter. Then the reader encounters a thematic introduction that points clearly and in some detail to what will follow.

To make our chapter introductions even more effective, which means to give students greater confidence as they proceed through the book, we took four steps. First we placed on the first page of each chapter a succinct outline that immediately and dramatically tells the student reader what he or she is going to encounter in the following pages. Second, we put at the end of each chapter's introduction a list of three or four Questions to Consider designed to work with the introduction and outline to give the student a clear orientation to what will follow. Third, we added a list of Terms to Know—generally ten or twelve—that alert the student to people, events, or developments demanding special attention. As a complement to text coverage, a ready reference, and a potential study guide, all of the Terms to Know are defined in a Glossary at the back of the book. Fourth, as the reader begins to read the chapter proper, he or she will meet a general chapter chronology that serves as yet another orientation to the material contained in the chapter.

In addition to this fundamental attention to the opening of each chapter, we also sought to improve the book's teachability by adding a pronunciation guide. Whenever we use an unfamiliar name or term, we show the reader how to pronounce it. Instead of using the intricate rules of phonetics, we provided commonsense guides to pronunciation at the foot of the page.

Careful chapter summaries draw together major topics and themes and link the present chapter to the one that follows. To encourage students to strike out on their own historical discoveries, each chapter offers a few carefully selected suggestions for further reading. This book's website (discussed later) contains a lengthy, searchable list of additional readings.

## ■ New and Revised Features

In preparing this Third Edition, we paid particular attention to the book's features. Beginning with its first edition, this book has presented the two-page feature Weighing the Evidence at the end of each chapter. These features introduce students to the fascinating array of sources that historians use and invite them to think critically about the nature of historical information and inquiry. Each opens with a description of the evidence presented in the feature—sources such as images of Cleopatra, the Ravenna mosaics, a Renaissance painting, eighteenth-century political symbols, the layout of the British Museum, and pop art—and then permits the students to look over the shoulder of the historian to become active participants in the interpretive process. The sources examined are interesting and instructive in their own right, but the Weighing the Evidence features also contribute to the teaching program of the book. There are references to the features at appropriate points in the narrative, they contain cross-references to other sections or illustrations, and they support ongoing discussions.

Our Weighing the Evidence essays have been both distinctive and well received since the First Edition. Feeling no complacency about them, however, the authors prepared eight new ones, including "Gladiators," "Stained Glass," "The Modern City and Photography," and "Advertising."

Many textbooks have boxed documents. In four different respects we have taken special care with our documents for this edition. First, we have added forty-seven new documents. Second, we have included in every chapter at least one document that permits a gendered analysis of a key historical person or problem. Third, each chapter also includes a Global Encounters box, quoting either a Western person commenting on the non-Western world, or vice versa. These boxes further our intention to situate our story in its global context. Fourth, and finally, because some documents cry out for more discussion or context, the website for the book provides exercises to help students analyze one key document per chapter, as well as twelve of the Weighing the Evidence features.

To this edition we have added a distinctive new feature: an Information Technology box with an accompanying image. The book has six of these, detailing papyrus, paper, printing, newspapers, the telegraph, and the Internet. These boxes provide readers with interesting examples of how communication technology affected people's lives. For example, the box on printing discusses how the new technology dramatically reduced the price of books and helped promote literacy across Europe.

We have been conscious of how the book *looks* to the reader from the very beginning. In keeping with our desire to integrate the components of the book into a coherent whole, we carefully anchor the maps and photographs. The authors developed the maps in this book and wrote their captions. Moreover, for this edition there are eight new maps, including European Resources and Trade Routes, ca. 1100; Dominion of Canada, 1873; GDP per Capita in Europe, 2000; and Foreign-Born Population in Western Europe. In addition, nearly twenty of the carry-over maps have been significantly revised. The same is true of the pictures: the authors selected them and wrote all the captions. As part of our continuing quest to make all of the elements of the book work together, the authors replaced about one-third of the photos for the Third Edition and revised the captions of many others. All of the maps in the book are cross-referenced in the text, some several times, and many of the photos are also referred to directly. Our diverse array of boxed documents—five per chapter—are referred to and

tightly anchored in the text, and they support their surrounding discussion. As with the maps, familiar documents are blended with pleasing newcomers.

## ■ Formats

This book is flexible in format as well as substantive organization. Because schools use different academic calendars, organize Western Civilization courses according to different chronologies, and require or recommend different parts of the course, we issue this book in three formats:

- **One-volume hardcover edition** (Chapters 1–30)
- **Two-volume paperback:** Volume I: To 1715 (Chapters 1–17); Volume II: Since 1560 (Chapters 15–30)
- **Three-volume paperback:** Volume A: To 1500 (Chapters 1–12); Volume B: 1300–1815 (Chapters 11–19); Volume C: Since 1789 (Chapters 19–30)

Volume II begins with a comprehensive Introduction designed for students who did not take the first semester of the course or who are new to this book. It provides a survey of the course of Western Civilization from ancient times to the early centuries of the modern era. This Introduction has been streamlined, organized along more strictly chronological lines, and illustrated for the Third Edition.

## SUPPLEMENTS

We have assembled with care an array of text supplements to aid students in learning and instructors in teaching. These supplements, including the website, *HM ClassPrep* instructor CD-ROM, *Test Items, Computerized Test Items, GeoQuest* interactive maps CD-ROM, and *Transparencies,* are tied closely to the text to provide a tightly integrated and comprehensive program. Student study aids and instructor course management materials are also available in WebCT E-Packs and Blackboard Course Cartridges.

The text-specific website contains a wealth of resources for students and instructors. For students, there are over forty web exercises, written by Christopher Carlsmith of Stanford University, relating to the boxed documents and Weighing the Evidence features in the text. Icons in the textbook direct students to the corresponding activities on the Houghton Mifflin website. Students can also test their knowledge of chapter content using *ACE* self tests and a comprehensive on-line study guide. To visit the site, begin at the Houghton Mifflin Company home page (**college.hmco.com**) and select the text and/or discipline.

Instructors will find a complete *Instructor's Resource Manual*, written by Sharon Arnoult of Midwestern State University, on the website, including learning objectives, annotated outlines, suggested lecture topics, discussion questions, classroom activities, and paper topics for each chapter of the text. The *Instructor's Resource Manual* also features suggestions for integrating the web exercises into your teaching.

Other website features include an extensive searchable bibliography to aid in student and instructor research, primary source selections, web links, and class presentation maps.

Each chapter of the *Test Items*, prepared by Diane Moczar of Northern Virginia Community College, offers a list of 10 to 20 key terms, 5 to 10 short-answer and essay questions, 2 or 3 map questions, and 40 to 50 multiple-choice questions. Answers to the multiple-choice questions are located at the end of the *Test Items.* We also offer a computerized version of the *Test Items,* enabling instructors to alter, replace, or add questions.

The full package of instructor materials is also available on an *HM ClassPrep* CD-ROM. The *Instructor's Resource Manual* and *Test Items* appear on the CD-ROM in their entirety, in addition to Powerpoint slides of the textbook maps and selected art images. The CD-ROM will function on either a PC or Macintosh platform. In addition, a set of overhead map *Transparencies* for the Western Civilization course is available on adoption.

The *GeoQuest* CD-ROM features thirty interactive maps and thirty presentation maps that illuminate the history of Western Civilization from ancient times to the present. Each of the interactive maps is accompanied by exercises with answers and essay questions. Different types of interactivity allow students to move at their own pace through each section. Four sample maps can be viewed on the Houghton Mifflin history website.

WebCT E-Packs and Blackboard Course Cartridges provide text-specific student study aids in customizable, Internet-based education platforms. Both platforms provide a full array of content delivery and course management features for instructors who wish to incorporate educational technology in their traditional classrooms or for those who are creating distance-learning courses.

# ACKNOWLEDGMENTS

The authors have benefited throughout the process of revision from the acute and helpful criticisms of numerous colleagues. We thank in particular: **Sharon L. Arnoult,** Midwestern State University; **Pierre Cagniart,** Southwest Texas State University; **Eleanor A. Congdon,** Plymouth State College; **David Dean,** Carleton University; **Maribel Dietz,** Louisiana State University; **George Drake,** Grinnell College; **Janusz Duzinkiewicz,** Purdue University North Central; **Alan Fisher,** Michigan State University; **Peter A. Goddard,** University of Guelph; **Aaron Goldman,** San Jose State University; **Robert W. Hayman,** Providence College; **Charles J. Herber,** Emeritus, George Washington University; **W. Robert Houston,** University of South Alabama; **Gerald E. Kadish,** Binghamton University (SUNY); **Laurie Koloski,** College of William and Mary; **Lawrence N. Langer,** University of Connecticut; **Thomas F. Madden,** Saint Louis University; **Donald M. McKale,** Clemson University; **Shannon McSheffrey,** Concordia University; **Isabel Moreira,** University of Utah; **Mark Munn,** The Pennsylvania State University; **Christopher Oldstone-Moore,** Wittenberg University; **Mary R. O'Neil,** University of Washington; **Ron Palmer,** Jefferson Community College; **Joseph F. Patrouch,** Florida International University; **Craig Pepin,** Western Carolina University; **Thomas Lynwood Powers,** University of South Carolina, Sumter; **Carole Putko,** San Diego State University; **Paul Lawrence Rose,** The Pennsylvania State University; **John Rosser,** Boston College; **Raffael Scheck,** Colby College; **Bernard Schlager,** University of New Hampshire; **Thomas P. Schlunz,** University of New Orleans; **Eileen Soldwedel,** Edmonds Community College; **Alan E. Steinweis,** University of Nebraska, Lincoln; **Charles R. Sullivan,** University of Dallas; **Timothy M. Thibodeau,** Nazareth College of Rochester; **Kevin Uhalde,** Northern Illinois University; and **Leigh Whaley,** Acadia University.

Each of us has also benefited from the close readings and careful criticisms of our coauthors, although we all assume responsibility for our own chapters. Barry Strauss has written Chapters 1–6; Thomas Noble, 7–10; Duane Osheim, 11–14; Kristen Neuschel, 15–19; William Cohen, 20–24; and David Roberts, 25–30.

Many colleagues, friends, and family members have helped us develop this work as well. Thomas Noble wishes to thank Linda Noble for her patience and good humor. He is also grateful to John Contreni, Wendy

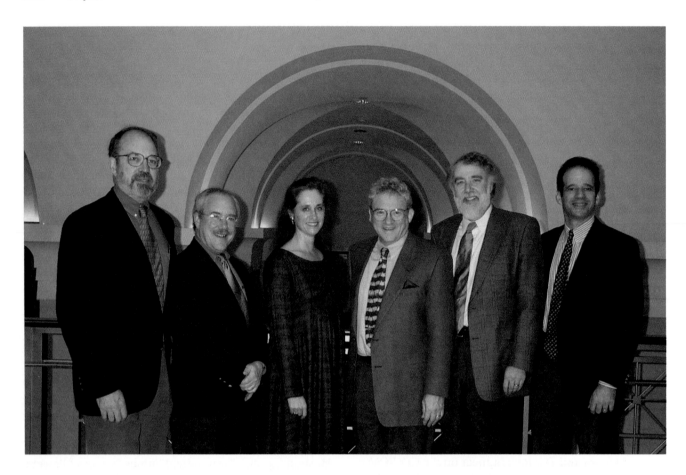

**The Authors:  Duane Osheim, Tom Noble, Kristen Neuschel, Bill Cohen, David Roberts, Barry Strauss**

Davies, Thomas Head, Elizabeth Meyer, Julia Smith, Richard Sullivan, John Van Engen, Robert Wilken, and Ian Wood.

Barry Strauss is grateful to colleagues at Cornell and at other universities who offered advice and encouragement and responded to scholarly questions. He would also like to thank the people at Cornell who provided technical assistance and support. Most important have been the support and forbearance of his family. His daughter Sylvie, his son Michael, and, above all, his wife, Marcia, have truly been sources of inspiration.

Duane Osheim wishes to thank his family for support during the writing and revising of this book. He is also grateful to colleagues at the University of Virginia, who helped to clarify the many connections between Western Civilization and the wider world. He would specifically like to thank Erik Midelfort, Arthur

Field, Janis Gibbs, and Beth Plummer for comments and advice.

Kristen Neuschel thanks her colleagues at Duke University for sharing their expertise. She is especially grateful to Sy Mauskopf, Bill Reddy, John Richards, Tom Robisheaux, and Alex Roland. She also thanks her husband and fellow historian, Alan Williams, for his wisdom about Western Civilization and his support throughout the project, and her children, Jesse and Rachel, for their patience, joy, and curiosity.

William Cohen thanks his wife, Christine Mathieu, and his daughters Natalie, Leslie, and Laurel for their support and encouragement over the many years that this project has matured.

David Roberts wishes to thank Bonnie Cary, Linda Green, and Nancy Heaton for their able assistance and Joshua Cole, Karl Friday, Thomas Ganschow, John Haag,

Michael Kwass, John Morrow, Douglas Northrup, Miranda Pollard, William Stueck, Eve Trout Powell, and Kirk Willis, colleagues at the University of Georgia, for sharing their expertise in response to questions. He also thanks Beth Roberts for her constant support and interest and her exceedingly critical eye, and Ellen, Trina, and Anthony for their college-age perspective and advice.

The first plans for this book were laid in 1988, and over the course of thirteen years there has been remarkable stability in the core group of people who have been responsible for its growth and development. The author team remains intact. Our original Sponsoring Editor, Jean Woy, has become Editor-in-Chief for History, Political Science, and Economics but has never missed a meeting with us or weakened in her interest in and commitment to this book. Christina Horn, our Senior Project Editor, has been the wizard behind the curtain for all three editions. She understood from the beginning our desire to have maps, pictures, and boxes closely integrated with their pertinent text and she has never let us down. Our photo researcher, Carole Frolich, has been with us from the start, and she has always understood the spirit of this book and the wishes of its authors. When the Second Edition was in preparation, a Brief Edition was planned and produced. Our work on that version introduced us to Jennifer Sutherland, who then served as Senior Development Editor for the Third Edition. She

entered quickly into the spirit of our book, but by casting a fresh eye on it she helped us see it again as if for the first time. Elizabeth Welch, our Senior Basic Book Editor for the first two editions, helped us to turn six voices into one and taught us how to write a textbook. We have now worked for several years with Nancy Blaine, our Sponsoring Editor, and we are most appreciative of her tireless energy and her faith in this book and its authors.

Although stability has been the hallmark of this project for years now, we are nevertheless delighted to acknowledge some people who came on board with the Third Edition. Sandra McGuire, Senior Marketing Manager, helped us to understand the many audiences for which we were writing. Gillie Jones, Editorial Associate, was masterful in managing the flow of manuscripts, disks, and e-mail attachments. Penny Peters designed the page layouts and created a pleasing visual effect. Henry Rachlin, Senior Designer, assembled diverse components into a book whose beauty truly facilitates its academic purpose.

Producing a successful textbook is hard work that makes high demands in terms of confidence, good humor, honesty, respect, and understanding. The authors of this book have been fortunate in their long and maturing relationship with their publishers.

Thomas F. X. Noble

# ABOUT THE AUTHORS

**Thomas F. X. Noble**   After receiving his Ph.D. from Michigan State University, Thomas Noble taught at Albion College, Michigan State University, Texas Tech University, and the University of Virginia. In 1999 he received the University of Virginia's highest award for teaching excellence. In 2001 he became Robert M. Conway Director of the Medieval Institute at the University of Notre Dame. He is the author of *The Republic of St. Peter: The Birth of the Papal State, 680–825; Religion, Culture and Society in the Early Middle Ages; Soldiers of Christ: Saints and Saints' Lives from Late Antiquity and the Early Middle Ages;* and *Images and the Carolingians: Tradition, Order, and Worship.* Noble's articles and reviews have appeared in many leading journals, including the *American Historical Review, Byzantinische Zeitschrift, Catholic Historical Review, Revue d'histoire ecclésiastique, Speculum,* and *Studi medievali.* He has also contributed chapters to several books and articles to three encyclopedias. He was a member of the Institute for Advanced Study in 1994 and the Netherlands Institute for Advanced Study in 1999–2000. He has been awarded fellowships by the National Endowment for the Humanities (twice) and the American Philosophical Society.

**Barry S. Strauss**   Professor of history and Classics at Cornell University, where he is also Director of the Peace Studies Program, Barry Strauss holds a Ph.D. from Yale in history. He has been awarded fellowships by the National Endowment for the Humanities, the American School of Classical Studies at Athens, and the Killam Foundation of Canada. He is the recipient of the Clark Award for excellence in teaching from Cornell. His many publications include *Athens After the Peloponnesian War: Class, Faction, and Policy, 403–386 B.C.; Fathers and Sons in Athens: Ideology and Society in the Era of the Peloponnesian War; The Anatomy of Error: Ancient Military Disasters and Their Lessons for Modern Strategists* (with Josiah Ober); *Hegemonic Rivalry from Thucydides to the Nuclear Age* (co-edited with R. Ned Lebow); *War and Democracy: A Comparative Study of the Korean War and the Peloponnesian War* (co-edited with David R. McCann); and *Rowing Against the Current: On Learning to Scull at Forty.*

**Duane J. Osheim**   A Fellow of the American Academy in Rome with a Ph.D. in history from the University of California, Davis, Duane Osheim is a professor of history at the University of Virginia. A specialist in late medieval and Renaissance social and institutional history, he is the author of *A Tuscan Monastery and Its Social World* and *An Italian Lordship: The Bishopric of Lucca in the Late Middle Ages,* as well as numerous studies of religious values and rural life in late medieval Italy.

**Kristen B. Neuschel**   Associate professor of history at Duke University, Kristen Neuschel received her Ph.D. from Brown University. She is a specialist in early modern French history and is the author of *Word of Honor: Interpreting Noble Culture in Sixteenth-Century France* and articles on French social history and European women's history. She has received grants from the National Endowment for the Humanities and the American Council of Learned Societies. In 1988 she received the Alumni Distinguished Undergraduate Teaching Award, which is awarded annually on the basis of student nominations for excellence in teaching at Duke.

**William B. Cohen**   After receiving his Ph.D. at Stanford University, William Cohen taught at Northwestern University and Indiana University, where he is now professor of history. At Indiana, he served as chairman of the West European Studies and History Departments; he is currently Director of Graduate Studies for the History Department. A previous president of the Society of French Historical Studies, Cohen has received several academic fellowships, including a National Endowment for the Humanities and a Fulbright fellowship. Among his many publications are *Rulers of Empire; The French Encounter with Africans; European Empire Building; Robert Delavignette and the French Empire; The Transformation of Modern France;* and *Urban Government and the Rise of the City.* His current research is on the Algerian war and French memory.

**David D. Roberts**   After taking his Ph.D. in modern European history at the University of California, Berkeley, David Roberts taught at the Universities of Virginia and Rochester before becoming professor of history at the University of Georgia in 1988. At Rochester he chaired the Humanities Department of the Eastman School of Music, and he chaired the History Department at Georgia from 1993 to 1998. A recipient of Woodrow Wilson and Rockefeller Foundation fellowships, he is the author of *The Syndicalist Tradition and Italian Fascism; Benedetto Croce and the Uses of Historicism;* and *Nothing but History: Reconstruction and Extremity After Metaphysics,* as well as numerous articles and reviews.

# The West Before 1560

HISTORIANS sometimes say that "History begins at Sumer," a region of ancient Mesopotamia located in the south of modern Iraq. For the reader of Volume II of *Western Civilization: The Continuing Experiment,* history begins forty-five hundred years after Sumer, in the last decades of the sixteenth-century European world. Some orientation may therefore be helpful to situate the start of this volume in time and place.

"Western civilization" is the traditional name for the history you will encounter in these pages. Before we go back to Sumer, let us reflect a little on these two words. The "West" is sometimes understood geographically and sometimes culturally. Each understanding is complex. For most people, the "West" means western Europe. And yet, western Europe was itself the heir of the peoples and cultures of the Mediterranean world of antiquity. These included Mesopotamians—people such as the Sumerians—and Egyptians, Greeks and Romans, Jews and Christians. Moreover, through exploration, war, and commerce, the "West" gradually imposed its influence on the whole globe. Concerning Europe itself, one view might encompass Rome, Paris, and London whereas another might stretch from Dublin to Moscow.

As a cultural phenomenon, "western" implies many things: freedom and free, participatory political institutions; economic initiative and opportunity; monotheistic religious faiths (Judaism, Christianity, and Islam); rationalism and ordered thought in the social, political, and philosophical realms; an aesthetic sensibility that aspires to a universal sense of truth and beauty. But the West has felt free both to evoke tradition as its guiding light *and* to innovate brilliantly; to accommodate slavery and freedom simultaneously; to esteem original thought and to persecute people who deviate from the norm. "Western" has different meanings depending on time, place, and circumstance.

What, then, is civilization? No definition has won universal acceptance, but certain elements are seen in almost every civilization.

Cities are crucial. Cities require complex social organizations that involve at least a minimal division of labor: Some people work in the fields, some in the home. Soldiers defend the city, and artisans provide its handcrafted goods. Governing institutions have a wide measure of acceptance and the wherewithal to enforce their wills. Cultures grow more complex and exhibit such traits as religious ideas and authorities; a literature and law that may be oral or written; monumental architecture, especially fortifications, palaces, and temples; and arts such as music, painting, and sculpture.

Civilization emerged in the West over a long time after about 3500 B.C. It appears that a slowly but steadily increasing population made it imperative to secure a predictable food supply. This need led to agriculture and animal husbandry, the taming of fields and flocks to the needs of a human community. The many processes involved in agriculture led to specialization of labor. The sharper definition of social and economic roles led to the delineation of gender roles. Communities defined certain tasks—government and war, for example—as essentially male, while reserving domestic responsibilities and some religious duties for women. The interests of self-sufficiency became subordinated to the needs of the community.

# THE ANCIENT WORLD, CA. 3500–323 B.C.

ISTORIANS usually begin their accounts of Western civilization with the Sumerians and Egyptians because they were, between about 3500 and 3000 B.C., the first peoples to attain civilization within the orbit of the West.

## ◼ Western Asia

Sumer lies in *Mesopotamia*, the land "between the rivers" Tigris and Euphrates. After the Sumerians, a succession of peoples in Mesopotamia itself—Akkadians, Babylonians, and Assyrians, for example—and many other peoples in the lands bordering Mesopotamia—Medes and Persians to the east, Hittites to the north, Phoenicians, Canaanites, and Hebrews to the west—also crossed the line that marks the beginnings of civilization.

All of these peoples are interesting and important in their own rights, but they concern the continuing course of Western civilization in one particularly important way: they were the cultural ancestors of the founders of the West, the Greeks and the Romans. The Greeks were a millennium behind them in developing civilization; the Romans were another millennium behind the Greeks. Western Asia (often called "the Middle East") contributed religious ideas, artistic norms, mathematical concepts, ways of reckoning time, and even the alphabet. Ideas, technologies, and practices from western Asia radiated far beyond the Greek and Roman worlds and helped spark the rise of civilization in Europe, where the Neolithic period (the "new stone" age, the time of carefully fashioned stone tools) gave way to civilization more slowly than in the Mediterranean world.

## ◼ Egypt

The Greek historian Herodotus (480–425 B.C.) called Egypt "the gift of the Nile." Historical Egypt is a fertile strip of land, ranging from 5 to 15 miles wide, that hugs the Nile River along its 750-mile course. Whereas the Tigris and Euphrates flood irregularly, sometimes violently, the Nile usually floods annually and beneficently. Efforts to manage irrigation, grain production, and storage along the course of the river led to an early (just before 3000 B.C.) replacement of local autonomy by a unified monarchy under god-kings called pharaohs.

Under the pharaohs of the period that historians now call the "Old Kingdom" (2695–2160 B.C.), Egypt faced no foreign threats and built up its central institutions. The great monuments of this time, the pyramids—pharaonic tombs—symbolize the power, wealth, and security of Egypt. An invasion brought an end to the Old Kingdom, but the eventual overthrow of the invaders ushered in the Middle Kingdom (1963–1786 B.C.), a time of political innovation—pharaohs had to share power with aristocrats—and cultural stimulation from Mesopotamian sources. The Middle Kingdom yielded in turn to the New Kingdom (1550–1070 B.C.), when Egypt became an imperial state whose reach extended all the way to Mesopotamia. The treasures of Tutankhamon ("King Tut") exemplify the wealth and sophistication of this age. Imperial Egypt was eventually ground down in a series of wars with the Hittites, an Indo-European-speaking people who settled in Anatolia (present-day Turkey).

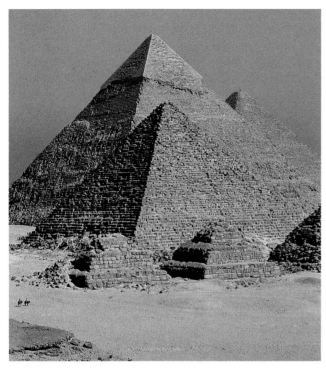

**Great Pyramids of Giza**    Royal funerary monuments of three Egyptian kings of the twenty-sixth century B.C., the pyramids symbolize the power and ambition of the Old Kingdom.
*(Michael Holford)*

## ■ Small Kingdoms and Great Empires

After the Egyptians and Hittites wore each other out, western Asia experienced a time of smaller, independent states. Phoenicia (roughly today's Lebanon) emerged as a major commercial power. The Phoenicians gathered up goods bought from Asia and Arabia via long-established overland trade routes and exchanged them for products acquired in their colonies all over the Mediterranean. Phoenician commerce thus initiated the cultural unification of the Mediterranean world.

Another small state of immense importance was the kingdom created by the Hebrews. Oral traditions and much later writings suggest that as early as 2000 B.C. a band of Hebrews under their tribal leader Abraham migrated from Mesopotamia to Palestine, on the eastern shore of the Mediterranean. Neither numerous nor united nor powerful, the Hebrews were often victimized by stronger neighbors. Around 1200 B.C. a group of Hebrews, slaves and workers in Egypt, cast off their bondage and returned to Palestine. This formative experience, remembered as the Exodus ("journey out" in Greek), forged a nation. For a century after 1000 B.C.,

Kings Saul, David, and Solomon built a state that was a match for its neighbors. Later, fierce rivalries among the Hebrews led to the disintegration of the unified monarchy, and the fragmented Hebrew communities were eventually conquered by powerful enemies.

The unique religious vision of the Hebrews makes them key founders of the Western tradition. The Jewish faith is very much alive today and serves as the basis for two other major religious traditions: Christianity and Islam.

The Hebrew religious vision is revealed to us in the Hebrew Bible, a large collection of writings that Christians call the Old Testament. The Hebrew Bible consists of historical writings on the unfolding relationship of the Hebrews with their God, legal books that lay down rules for personal conduct and social organization, prophetic books that express some of humanity's deepest spiritual insights, and wisdom literature that is full of humane guidance for daily life.

The central truth revealed by these Scriptures is exclusive monotheism. There is only one God. With this God the Hebrews have a covenant, a special pact. As long as the Hebrews do God's will by observing the Law and heeding His prophets, they will enjoy God's blessings and protection.

The period of small states was concluded by the creation, one after another, of ever larger states culminating in the Persian Empire (ca. 550–334 B.C.), which was centered in modern Iran. The Persians spread ideas and institutions through their vast empire, the largest the world had yet seen. The Persians were finally conquered by the armies of Alexander the Great (r. 336–323 B.C.), from Macedon in the northern Balkans.

This long succession of states and peoples led to the diffusion of many ideas and practices. We have remarked on one example already: the religious vision of the Hebrews. Another is a style of rulership that we call "theocratic." In a "theocracy," rulers are placed in office by, and are answerable only to, a god. In Mesopotamia rulers were generally believed to be the agents of the gods; in Egypt rulers were believed to *be* gods. In Alexander and his successors, notably Roman emperors, theocratic rulership had a long run. Egyptian ideas of a last judgment and of life after death circulated widely. Scientific and mathematical advances are another legacy of the ancient kingdoms and empires. In building huge monuments such as pyramids, in preserving human remains by mummification, in measuring fields, in observing the heavens, people in Mesopotamia and Egypt laid up a huge store of practical information from which later peoples, especially the Greeks, drew enthusiastically.

# CLASSICAL ANTIQUITY, CA. 1000 B.C.– A.D. 284

*LASSICAL* means normative, a standard by which to judge. In the nineteenth century, intellectuals were fond of saying to one another, "You were born in Greece." Such an assertion insisted that many cultural and aesthetic standards still prevalent in their own day had arisen in ancient Greece. So powerful has been the hold of Greece over architecture and sculpture, for example, that some modern movements have been deliberately "anticlassical." The Romans were the great interpreters of Greek culture, but they also added their own distinctive contributions to Western civilization.

## ■ Ancient Greece

The Greeks made fundamental—classical—contributions in two areas: political ideas and institutions, and culture. Homer's epic poems, the *Iliad* and the *Odyssey,* probably composed not long after 800 B.C. but the products of a long oral development, open before us the course of Greek political development. The poems purport to tell of Greece in the days of the Trojan Wars. Greek memory fixed those wars in about 1200 B.C., when undoubtedly the Greeks engaged in some nasty commercial squabbles with their neighbors in the Aegean basin. It is grand to imagine, with Homer, that the beauty of Helen of Troy launched a thousand Greek ships. It is unlikely, however, that it is historically accurate to think so.

The *Iliad* and the *Odyssey* profess to describe actual events in the Greek world in the Mycenaean period, so called because Mycenae was the greatest city of that time. Between about 1500 and 1200 B.C., several remarkable cities were built in the Greek lands by peoples who were the ancestors of the Greeks of the classical period. Before the Mycenaeans a remarkable culture had flourished, then faded, on the island of Crete. Historians call this culture "Minoan" after the legendary King Minos. But there is nothing legendary about the spectacular Minoan palaces, whose ruins are still impressive, or about the exquisite artistic remains of Minoan culture. The Minoan and Mycenaean periods played a key role in connecting the Greeks with the realms of western Asia and Egypt. The *Iliad,* after all, is a tale about a Greek expedition to Anatolia.

Homer sings of a world of kings and aristocrats. Huge armies are mustered on his pages; individual warriors are described in minute detail. A common soldier could be flogged for speaking in the presence of his betters. This regal, aristocratic society, whose leaders were *Eupatrids,* "well-fathered men," dominated Greece for centuries.

Slowly the polis, the city-state, the basic Greek political institution, began to emerge. The people of rugged, craggy Greece clustered in small territories; as a result, many independent poleis arose in a land smaller than most American states. Each polis had a central urban zone and an agricultural hinterland. Often the urban zone featured an easily fortified hill: an *acropolis.* The acropolis sheltered people in times of attack and served as a meeting place for the conduct of civic and religious affairs.

Many poleis outstripped the locally available food supplies and looked enviously at their neighbors' provisions. Weaker poleis had to see to their defenses just as stronger ones had to beef up their capacity for attack. This competition resulted in the expansion of political and social participation in the public life of the polis. The infantryman, known as the hoplite, gained a role in defending his city and then insisted on a role in its government. Some cities, most notably Athens, moved toward greater and greater participation until *demokratia,* the rule of the people, was achieved. In Athens, all adult male citizens could vote and hold any of the key offices in the city. Sparta, however, became a military juggernaut in which the rights of all were subordinated to the dictates of a small number of the oldest, most conservative citizens. Corinth, where large landowners invested in trade, became a commercial oligarchy. In all cases, expanded or redefined participation belonged only to men. Women were excluded from participation in political life. Yet in Sparta women exercised effective daily control over the private lands allotted to soldiers, and in Athens women played leading roles in public religious celebrations.

As their populations exceeded the available resources of their tiny homelands, many Greek cities exported surplus population to colonies all over the Mediterranean world. As well as defusing Greek tensions, these colonies spread Greek culture far and wide.

While they were creating their basic political institutions between about 750 and 500 B.C., the Greeks also began to reflect systematically on political organization. Indeed, much of our political vocabulary is Greek in origin. Politics, after all, is what people do publicly in a polis.

Although Athens invented democracy, most Greek political thinkers were hostile to democratic ideas. They argued that democracy elevated the rabble over the best citizens and permitted the masses to satisfy their imme-

**The Parthenon**
The temple of Athena Parthenos ("the Maiden") on the Athenian Acropolis, the Parthenon was dedicated in 438 B.C. The partially restored ruins symbolize the wealth, power, and greatness of classical Greece. *(William Katz/Photo Researchers)*

diate desires, cast aside restraint, and neglect the long-term needs of the community. In one way or another, every Greek political thinker addressed an issue that has been critical in Western political discourse ever since: How can a person reconcile personal interests with the needs of the community?

The second Greek achievement lies in the realm of culture—in art, architecture, literature, science, and philosophy. Generalizations are difficult, but it may be fair to say that the Greeks, or at least the elite among them, set out very early to pursue truth and beauty. The Greeks were not unique in this quest. What sets them apart is the way they defined their objectives.

To a Greek thinker, beauty existed in the balance, order, and harmony that seemed to underlie everything really good. Greek scientific writers looked for a single, unchanging substance behind everything in existence. Failing in this search, they looked for overarching theories capable of explaining everything. Failing in this, they explored the nature of thought and language to see what could be known and communicated. In relative terms, the Greeks added rather few concrete details to the huge fund of Mesopotamian and Egyptian discoveries. What the Greeks contributed was a vast mental framework designed to systematize and explain what is known. In Classical Greece we see the birth of both science and philosophy.

Greek literature is full of memorable characters who present the reader, or the theater audience, with dilemmas of conscience. Oedipus, the main character of *Oedipus the Tyrant* by Sophocles (ca. 495–406 B.C.), whom Shakespeare called "the most tragic of poets," kills his father and marries his mother. He has absolutely no idea that he has done so. Is he nevertheless guilty of a hideous offense? It is to Greek literature that we must turn for in-

sights into the roles of women, for they were excluded from formal, public positions. Antigone, the central character in Sophocles' *Antigone*, is one of the most memorable women in literature. She struggles courageously to reconcile the conflicting demands of political allegiance and family ties. What is justice; what does it mean to be just; is it possible to be just? Can a rule apply to one person alone, or must it apply to everyone? Do rules exist at all? Reading the best of Greek literature today evokes the same feelings it did then: gut-wrenching agony over life choices.

To look at a fine Greek statue or building is, first of all, to admire the astonishing technical skill that went into making it. Second, the viewer is moved by its beauty. Another look will usually prove disconcerting. The object in our gaze is *too* perfectly executed, *too* beautiful. It is like nothing we have ever seen, although it is vaguely like everything we see all the time. It is as if the object is meant less to remind us of things in this world than to provide a glimpse of a better, purer world.

Greek art opens up a vista on the greatest Greek philosophers. Plato (427–348 B.C.) distrusted the senses as guides to truth or reality. He believed that we are all prisoners of the world and of our human limitations. According to Plato, ultimate reality exists not here and now but in a transcendent world. In our world, and in this life, we can gain only hints of what really exists. His greatest pupil was Aristotle (384–322 B.C.), whose mania for classification has been the despair of many a biology student. Aristotle reminds us of the technical artistry of the Greek sculptor. For Aristotle, knowledge was possible in this world. But knowledge was the result of knowing what you wanted to find out, of working immensely hard to discover truth, and of living with the consequences of the truths you found.

Fame and success are not the same. Greek political ideas, institutions, and terminology have been famous for ages, but the Greeks were, finally, unsuccessful at politics. Only during the Persian Wars (490–479 B.C.) were the Greeks able to rally together, and even then they quarreled over strategy and leadership. Individual Greek states were notoriously unstable and violent, and most of the time the poleis of Greece found themselves forced to accept membership in leagues and alliances. Between 431 and 404 B.C., Sparta's Peloponnesian League and the Athenian Empire—an involuntary association of the Greek states that had fought against Persia—convulsed the whole Greek world in the Peloponnesian War.

Philip II of Macedon, an increasingly powerful and well-organized kingdom to the north of Greece, conquered the Greeks in 338 B.C. and bequeathed his prize to his remarkable son, Alexander the Great. After securing the Balkans, Alexander set off on a tour of military conquest unrivaled before his time. He conquered the Persian Empire and much more besides. His conquests ushered in a period that historians call "Hellenistic."

*Hellenistic,* the customary name for the period following Alexander's death, roughly 323 to 30 B.C., when Greek language and culture dominated the Mediterranean world, means "Greeklike," as opposed to *Hellenic,* "purely Greek," the term applied to the preceding period from about 750 to 323 B.C. Alexander's generals carved his vast empire into many smaller states that survived despite many struggles, until one by one they fell to Rome. Greek leaders and elites mixed with local populations of many traditions to produce a rich, international culture that was everywhere recognizably, but nowhere purely, Greek.

The expanding, fluid nature of Hellenistic culture and states provided unprecedented opportunities for women in commerce and in government. Unlike cities, which reserved offices to men, monarchies had courts in which women could be influential advisers and sometimes actual rulers. Cleopatra of Egypt (r. 51–30 B.C.) is the most famous but by no means the only powerful Hellenistic woman.

### ■ The Roman Republic and Empire

The Roman poet Horace (65–8 B.C.) once said that "Captive Greece took her captor captive." His clever epigram is an apt transition from Greek to Roman history. But what did he mean? First, to be sure, the Romans conquered Greece—and many more lands. Second, Greek culture deeply influenced the Romans, who in general were not as original and creative as the Greeks.

The Romans considered their history to have begun with the founding of Rome itself, an event that they dated to what we call 753 B.C. Actually, the historical Romans were in Rome's neighborhood long before that date, and Rome's familiar society and institutions arose long after it.

From 509 B.C., when the Romans believed that their Republic had been instituted, until 27 B.C., when that Republic was definitively transformed into a military monarchy, Rome was remarkably stable. That stability was partly institutional. Rome had several magistrates with differing degrees of power, responsibility, and prestige, and several representative institutions with varying areas of authority. All adult men participated in important but very different ways. In addition, Rome's stability was partly cultural. In society and politics, Rome was hierarchical and deferential in equal measure. Rome accorded responsibility for running the Republic to a small number of men. As in Greece, women in Rome were systematically excluded from public life. Roman literature depicts women as domestic and submissive.

Prominent Romans ruled through office and assembly and also through patronage and private influence. Leading Romans were firmly opposed to innovation. The only good ways were the old ways, they believed. A Roman speech almost always began with an appeal to the "way our ancestors would have done things." Thus, it took a long time for the Roman system to emerge, and it seemed unchanged and unchanging.

Slowly the Romans conquered their neighbors in Italy (509–265 B.C.). Then victory in wars (264–146 B.C.) against Carthage, an old Phoenician colony, gave Rome dominance in the western Mediterranean. Finally, a series of wars against the Hellenistic monarchies (200–31 B.C.) left Rome in control of the whole Mediterranean world. It is easy to appreciate the old saying, "All roads lead to Rome."

Rome's wars came at a high price. Political and social stability was destroyed as personal and imperial ambition became regular weapons in domestic politics. Generals came to count for more than statesmen. Vast wealth, new and unevenly distributed, fractured the old structures of social deference that had long organized Roman society. Great fortunes and shifting social realities also created unprecedented opportunities for women to influence public life through family politics and artistic patronage. The culture of the Hellenistic world, as Horace correctly saw, overwhelmed the earnest Romans, who were less bumpkinish than they pretended but less sophisticated than most of their neighbors.

The Republic collapsed in a century of civil wars. Augustus Caesar (r. 31 B.C.–A.D. 14) created a dramatically changed regime. He inaugurated a two-century-long period, the *pax Romana* (the Roman peace), that brought the Mediterranean world as close as it has ever come to unity. Peace and prosperity, good government, spectacular building projects, and a process of cultural diffusion now called "Romanization" also characterized the pax Romana.

Augustus took the title *Princeps* ("First Citizen"). The Augustan Principate rested on a few basic notions. Rome's ruler was now an emperor whose power depended on his control of the military. The Roman Empire was now less and less an exclusively Roman entity: People from all over Italy and from the provinces shared in the benefits of empire. Augustus and the emperors who succeeded him forged a partnership with local elites everywhere. For instance, the Herods of Judea are villains in the Christian Scriptures, but from the Roman point of view, they were loyal, pliable, competent servants. And they were hardly alone. One of the ways in which such people showed their loyalty to Rome was by adopting the trappings of Roman culture—that is, by Romanizing.

Although the Romans were less innovative than the Greeks, they were by no means uncreative. Roman architecture achieved heights of complexity and sophistication. Roman law remains influential to this day. Cities from England to Mesopotamia still reveal their Roman street plans, and highway systems all over Europe lie atop Roman roads. Roman writers were learned, technically expert, verbally adroit, and at their best they ranged from moving to hilarious. Virgil's *Aeneid,* the story of Aeneas, one of the defeated at Troy and the legendary founder of Rome, presents the archetypal Roman hero: strong, familial, humble, loyal, and, above all else, perseverant.

The third century A.D. brought the Augustan Principate and the classical order to a close. From one end of the Roman Empire to the other, both the forms and the feelings of classical literature vanished. Large-scale building ceased. New religions, perhaps capable of explaining the difficulties of the age, proliferated. One prominent historian speaks of an "age of anxiety." What happened?

First, as the Roman historian Tacitus dryly observed in the first century A.D., "the army made the emperor." And, we might add, unmade him too, with alarming frequency. Civil wars between military commanders competing for the imperial office became endemic. Civil strife undermined the empire's ability to meet military threats along its exposed frontiers. Military and civil unrest contributed to a loosening of the old ties between the imperial government and the provincial elites. The economy was disrupted by political turmoil and was fur-

**The Appian Way**    Rome's first great road was built in 312 B.C. It originally ran 132 miles from Rome to Capua and was extended an additional 234 miles, probably by 244 B.C. *(F. H. C. Birch/Sonia Halliday Photographs)*

ther weakened by uncontrollable inflation. At the end of the third century, Rome's prospects looked grim.

# THE WORLD OF LATE ANTIQUITY, 284–CA. 600

HE years from about 284 to 600, now usually called Late Antiquity, witnessed changes in the structure of Roman institutions, alterations in the composition and functions of the social and political elite, and the elaboration of a Christian culture and an undivided, universal—that is, catholic—church.

## ■ The Transformation of the Roman Empire

To preserve the empire, Diocletian (r. 284–305) and Constantine (r. 306–337) radically expanded the imperial bureaucracy and army. Constantine established a second capital for the empire at Byzantium on the Bosphorus, which he renamed after himself: Constantinople. These reforms were costly in several senses. They necessitated higher taxes and more vigilant tax collecting. Roman officials seemed more intrusive and, quite often, less honest. A larger army solved neither border problems nor political ones. The armies themselves were increasingly recruited from Germanic peoples living along the frontiers. Some of these people were loyal to Rome; others sought to profit from its weakness. Not only the legions but the military leaders in the fourth and fifth centuries were likely to be Germanic. These men were usually loyal and competent, but divided allegiance could be a problem for them in ways unknown to the sturdy Romans of old.

The greatest change in the political landscape of Late Antiquity can be seen on a map. In 300 the western half of the Roman Empire consisted of a number of provinces governed by a hierarchy of Roman officials. In 600 a number of Germanic kingdoms had replaced those provinces. One might suppose that Rome had "fallen," that the ancient world had ended. It is true that after 476 there were no more emperors in the western half of the empire. But a closer look at those supplanting kingdoms reveals some interesting continuities.

The earliest kingdoms were actually founded by Roman-Germanic collaboration, and their kings continued to cultivate close relations with the eastern Roman Empire headquartered at Constantinople. Kings covered themselves with Roman titles, adapted Roman public ceremonies, and acted like imperial magistrates. They issued laws and recorded documents in Latin and maintained, under their own authority, features of Roman local administration. Given that most Germanic kings were the descendants of late antique Roman military officers, it is unlikely that most people detected much difference between Roman and Germanic rule.

Who were these Germanic kings and their followers? The lands beyond the Rhine and Danube, the two rivers that formed Rome's northern frontier, held innumerable peoples with whom the Romans had long, complex relationships. Rome traded with, fought against, allied with, and recruited many Germanic peoples at one time or another. The Germanic peoples were confederations, not ethnic groups. "Frank," the name of one Germanic people, applies not only to persons who were Frankish but also to their relatives by marriage, clients, allies, defeated foes, and hangers-on. Such peoples created kingdoms by violent encounters and by peaceful settlement, by usurpation and by delegation. One might say that the kingdoms were Germanized and militarized versions of formerly Roman provinces. In other words, Rome provided the framework within which its own transformation took place.

## ■ The Triumph of Christian Culture

Continuity and change are also evident in the most important cultural transformation of Late Antiquity: the triumph of Christianity. Christianity arose in first-century Palestine among a dedicated band of followers of Jesus of Nazareth. Jesus, a Jewish teacher of great charisma and compassion, preached an uncompromising morality, a need for repentance, and preparation for a coming kingdom of God. Jesus's teachings were intimately connected to venerable strains in Jewish thought and life. His followers believed him to be the Son of God.

From unpromising beginnings among a minority sect of Jews in a small, poor province, Christianity rose by the end of the fourth century to become the dominant religion in the Roman world. Fundamental teachings, the basic message of Jesus as related in the New Testament books of Matthew, Mark, Luke, and John—four accounts of Jesus's life and teachings written a generation or two after his death—were critical to this success. Jesus's teachings were universal, addressed to men and women, people of every land, persons of every status.

Christianity spread initially through towns. In each town, communities of believers installed officials whose customary titles in English are *bishop, priest,* and *deacon.* Bishops—the word means "overseers"—gradually came to have administrative, moral, and intellectual responsibilities in their towns. They controlled the local church and its property, recruited and trained priests and deacons, disciplined heretics (dissenters from official doctrine), and preached. A growing Christian church adapted the administrative geography of the Roman Empire. Bishops from towns and provinces began to meet in councils to decide complex matters of theology and ordinary matters of Christian living.

Christians were at times persecuted, but in 314 Constantine granted Christianity legal equality with all other religions. By 400 the most eminent local personage in almost every town of the empire was the bishop. Bishops came from the same families that had long given Rome its greatest citizens. Following the lead of the bishops was not difficult for local populations. Leading people from the pulpit was easy for men accustomed to authority and respect.

Christians were invited both to change the world around themselves and also to flee that world and its temptations. The church's public institutions represented an effort to respond to the first of these invitations. Another institution, monasticism, responded to the second. All over the Roman world, groups of men and women settled as monks or nuns in communities dedicated to prayer, study, self-denial, and work. Monasticism attracted people from every region, class, and level of education. This powerful spiritual force was one of Late Antiquity's most enduring legacies.

Christianity touched the lives of women in a variety of ways. Church teachings held out two models to women. There was Eve, the eternal temptress, who had tricked Adam and cost humanity the joys of paradise. Then there was Mary, the holy, obedient, and exemplary mother of Jesus. Women were gradually denied clerical positions in the church but gained great prominence in monasticism. Generally, Christian teachings accorded women more respect and dignity than secular laws did.

The bishop of Rome attained special prominence. This status owed something to the doctrine of apostolic succession, according to which all bishops inherited the teaching authority of the apostles, the twelve most prominent original followers of Jesus. In the Roman version of this doctrine, Peter had been the leader of the apostles and Peter's successors, the bishops of Rome—they began to be called popes in the third century—were the leaders of the church as a whole. Roman prominence is also attributable to the connection between the popes and the city of Rome itself, the capital of the empire to which all roads led. Finally, papal leadership matured during bitter theological struggles in the Christian community. Popes routinely intervened on behalf of, or entertained appeals from, persons they supported. As the popes attained leadership and defined dogmas, they laid the foundations for the Roman Catholic Church.

The quarrels were many but tended to focus on two key issues: the problem of the Trinity and the person of Jesus. The majority of Christian thinkers argued that God was triune, three persons—Father, Son, and Holy Spirit—in one. Christian tradition also maintained that the second person of the Trinity, Jesus Christ, was true God and true man.

Between about 350 and 450, Christian thinkers all over the Mediterranean world addressed themselves to solving such theological problems, to explaining both the Jewish and the Christian Scriptures (which Christians call the Old and the New Testaments), and to defining practical rules for living. We call such thinkers "Church Fathers" and their age "patristic" (from *pater*, the Latin word for "father"). The most famous of the Latin Church Fathers was Augustine (354–430), a North African who became a professor of rhetoric and converted to Christianity as an adult. Augustine's writings chronicled his own spiritual quest and commented on the religious issues of his day.

The Church Fathers are among the most learned, prolific, accomplished, and influential writers in all of history. They were products of the Roman world, but they did not suppose, as Virgil had, that time would last only as long as Rome. For them, the source and goal of human existence was in heaven, not on earth.

# MEDIEVAL CIVILIZATIONS, 600–1300

 HE Roman world left not one but three heirs. The first comprised the Germanic kingdoms that replaced Rome's western provinces. The second was the eastern Roman Empire centered in Constantinople. The third was a surprising development that no one in Late Antiquity could have predicted: the emergence of the Islamic faith and the Muslim empire.

## ■ Islam and the Arabs

Islam arose in Arabia, a large, barren land in western Asia deeply influenced by all the currents of ancient culture but never wholly conquered by any ancient people. In 570 Islam's pivotal figure, Muhammad, was born in Mecca, a great commercial city. Tradition holds that when Muhammad was a young man, his spiritual sensibilities were awakened by visits from the archangel Gabriel, who commanded him to "recite" a holy text. That text revolved around one great truth: "There is no God but Allah, and Muhammad is his prophet."

Like many religious leaders, Muhammad gained both followers and foes. Enemies forced Muhammad to flee in 622 to Medina, a city about 200 miles from Mecca. There he gave full force to his religious and social vision. Before he died in 632, Muhammad saw that vision triumph in Mecca and throughout Arabia.

The faith of Muhammad is revealed in the Quran, a collection of Allah's revelations to the prophet. Muhammad's religion demands absolute surrender to Allah: *al-Islam,* "the surrender," whence the name of the faith. Like Judaism, Islam has two central components: faith and community. The faith is simple, direct, uncompromising. There is no God but Allah, the creator and ruler of all. Islam had no creeds, no statements of religious belief, and no hierarchical clergy. The community, the *umma muslima,* was the totality of those who had surrendered to Allah. Class, status, occupation, gender, ethnicity—none of these mattered at all.

After Muhammad's death, his followers rallied to the standard of the caliph, the successor to the prophet and commander of the faithful, and in a century created an empire that extended from France to the frontiers of China. That empire, the caliphate, centering on Arabia plus the ancient lands of Mesopotamia and Egypt, hugged the Mediterranean. Over time Muslim scholars reflected on the Judeo-Christian and the Greco-Roman heritages, and their writings proved influential when western Europeans discovered them in the twelfth and thirteenth centuries. As it expanded, the caliphate also absorbed rich cultural ingredients from Persia, India, Africa, and Asia.

Internal rivalries and external threats eventually pulled the caliphate apart. Spain broke away first, then a series of small states across North Africa, then Egypt, then parts of Anatolia. Caliphs sat on their jeweled thrones until 1258 while a succession of foreigners dominated the state. Byzantines, Italian merchants, and Turkish mercenaries were among the most prominent of the caliphate's external foes until the Mongols over-

**Justinian and His Courtiers**    This magnificent mosaic from Ravenna depicts Emperor Justinian in all his power and majesty.    *(Scala/Art Resource, NY)*

whelmed the caliphate in that year in their bid for world domination. A collection of peoples from the frontiers of Mongolia and China, the Mongols turned the Islamic world so that its back was to the Mediterranean and its face to Asia. Until then, the Islamic world had been very much a part of the West. Since that time, neither the Islamic world nor the West has been quite sure about their relationship.

## ■ The Byzantine Empire

As the western Roman Empire was being parceled into kingdoms, the eastern half survived almost intact. In the sixth century, the Roman emperor Justinian (r. 527–565), based in Constantinople, regained several of Rome's former western provinces, reformed the imperial administration, issued a major codification of Roman law, and regulated ecclesiastical affairs. In the next two centuries his successors created new military and administrative institutions to address Muslim threats in the east and Slavic threats in the Balkans.

In 726 Emperor Leo III (r. 717–741) issued the first major revision of Roman law since Justinian's. Leo's code, a drastically abbreviated version of Justinian's, provided a simplified, unified body of law for provincial judges in the empire. In religion, the Orthodox tradition of Christianity began clearly to emerge, based on the writings of the Greek Church Fathers, Greek forms of worship and church discipline, and a close partnership between the emperors and the patriarchs of Constantinople, the highest religious officers. For almost a thousand years this eastern incarnation of the Roman Empire, usually called the Byzantine Empire, preserved the Roman legacy.

In 867 a new and highly talented dynasty, the Macedonian, came to the throne in the person of Basil I (r. 867–886). Until 1025, rulers from this family expanded the empire's frontiers, carried out impressive legal and government reforms, and continued a close partnership with the Orthodox Church. This period proved the high point of Byzantine political, military, and diplomatic influence.

The years after 1025 brought short reigns, disputed successions, aristocratic and ecclesiastical factionalism, a bitter feud with the papacy in Rome over theology and worship, and, worst of all, military threats from the Turks. In 1071 the Byzantines suffered a devastating defeat by the Turks at Manzikert in central Anatolia. Appeals to western Europe for assistance brought not mercenaries to recapture Anatolia from the Turks but Crusaders intent on liberating the Holy Land—the Palestine of Jesus—from the Muslims. In 1204 a crusading army conquered Constantinople, and until 1261 a "Latin Empire" held sway in the east. The Byzantines eventually rallied, expelled the Latins, and restored independent rule. Down to the fall of Constantinople to the Turks in 1453, however, Byzantium was a shadow of its former self.

## ■ Western Europe

In Late Antiquity the Roman West had been divided among several Germanic kingdoms. Those that did not confront more powerful neighbors, that experienced reasonable religious harmony, and that had room to expand managed to succeed. Thus, the late antique heritage fell to the Franks in Gaul and the Anglo-Saxons in Britain.

By the middle of the eighth century, continental Europe was dominated by a single family whom we call "Carolingian" from *Carolus Magnus,* Charles the Great (or Charlemagne). Charlemagne's dynasty united France, the Low Countries, most of Germany, northern Italy, and northeastern Spain into a single empire that lasted in reality for a few generations—and in memory for a millennium—as "Christendom." In 800 Charlemagne was crowned emperor in Rome by the pope. By force of will the Carolingians imposed standards of worship, education, law, and institutions throughout Christendom. Their success was very uneven, but much of the similarity in the later history of the western European countries derives from their common Carolingian past.

In Britain, Germanic Anglo-Saxons from continental Europe jostled with local Celts, especially in Wales and Scotland. Anglo-Saxon, or English, Britain was moving toward unity, as were Wales and Scotland, until attacks by the Vikings. These seaborne raiders from Scandinavia provoked a crisis of authority in Britain that was resolved to the advantage of the central government only in Scotland. In 1013 and again in 1066, bands of Northmen conquered England. Bands of Vikings called Varangians founded the beginnings of a new state near Kiev in Ukraine. Vikings attacked the Continent too, but so did Muslims in the south and Magyars, the ancestors of the Hungarians, in the east. The Carolingian Empire, already weakened by struggles among Charlemagne's descendants, succumbed to these attacks and crumbled into a number of kingdoms and smaller political entities.

For more than two centuries social and political development was more creative at the local than at the central level. Powerful men (lords) forced lesser men (vassals) into bonds of dependence that we usually refer to as feudalism. Vassals pledged homage (honor), fealty (fidelity), and service; lords promised maintenance and protection. To maintain their vassals, lords sometimes gave them fiefs—estates consisting of farms and peasants.

Between the collapse of the Carolingian Empire around 900 and the renewal of central authority around 1150, Europe experienced effective government only at the local level. In fact, counties, duchies, principalities, and cities displayed an amazing institutional creativity. The population of Europe expanded dramatically, perhaps doubling in two and a half centuries. Trade expanded everywhere. In a sense, Europe grew physically. New states emerged in the Celtic world (Ireland, Scotland, Wales), in Scandinavia (Denmark, Norway, Sweden), and in the Slavic regions (Poland, Bohemia, Serbia, Hungary, Bulgaria, Kievan Rus). The Crusades extended Europe's frontier to Muslim Palestine. People everywhere felled forests, drained marshes, and brought new land into cultivation.

Twelfth- and thirteenth-century Europe was marked by a series of struggles for authority between secular and religious rulers. If, as all seemed to agree, government existed to promote eternal salvation, who was to have final authority: the pope and the ecclesiastical hierarchy or the emperor and other secular rulers? No land in Europe escaped these battles between 1050 and 1300. The Catholic Church, with its elaborate administration, its sophisticated canon law, and its command of people's spiritual loyalties, won most of the early battles. Then, slowly, secular governments began to define their responsibilities in nonreligious terms and to treat churches as subordinate institutions. By 1300 the church was exhausted from decades of struggles with a variety of rulers, European society had become more secular, and public institutions were growing more effective. The advantageous position the church had enjoyed in, say, 1100 or 1200 had been reversed by 1300.

Central governments gained strength as kings promoted themselves through ceremonies, built up their financial resources, won key military victories, reduced great aristocrats to submission, and allied themselves to rising urban and commercial movements. But Europe was a complex place, and the governments were fragile. England, France, and Spain were headed toward centralization by 1300 but then suffered reverses and differed sharply in their basic institutional structures. Imperial and royal power collapsed in Germany. Italy remained disunited but its many urban communes produced regimes of infinite variety and robust creativity. In 1300 Europe was teeming in its political complexity.

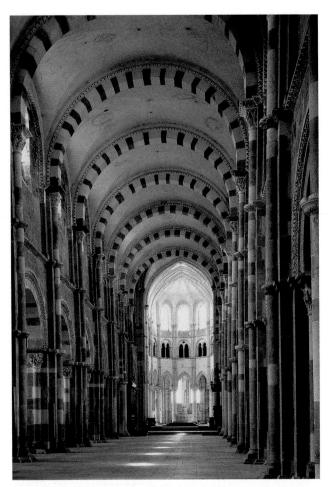

**Nave of Vezelay, 1104–1132**    The basilica of Sainte-Madeleine is a crowning achievement of French Romanesque architecture, featuring height and a sense of airy spaciousness.    *(Éditions Gaud)*

European culture was likewise rich and complex. Latin culture was primarily religious culture, fostered by the church. The church needed educated clergy to carry out its tasks of preaching and teaching. Moreover, religious leaders were conscious of belonging to a rich intellectual tradition that needed to be mastered and transmitted.

Schools and libraries were found in cathedrals, bishops' churches, and monasteries. Monasteries preserved books and learning while serving as witnesses to a holy way of living. Many convents of nuns were also intellectual centers and places where women could attain a control over their lives that was denied them in the male world of lords and vassals. Gradually a new kind of religious intellectual establishment, the university, achieved prominence. Though changed in important

ways since its twelfth-century origins, the university has never lost its position as the paramount intellectual institution in the West.

Although medicine and law were important courses of study in some places, university teaching and research were focused primarily on the key texts of the Christian tradition. The approach to those texts was increasingly through the logic of the Greek philosopher Aristotle. Scholasticism is the name for this encounter between Greek logic and Christian revelation. Thomas Aquinas (1225–1274), prolific author, immensely learned scholar, and Paris professor, was the greatest of the Scholastics.

A vernacular culture flourished alongside the Latin culture of the Catholic Church. Literature in Welsh and Irish had appeared already in the seventh century; Old English literature, capped by the epic poem *Beowulf,* came only a little later. French literature produced an epic—*The Song of Roland*—around 1100, then romances and adventures. German literature preceded French but took longer to reach a high standard. Italian emerged last but was the first to produce a true masterpiece, Dante's *Divine Comedy* of the early fourteenth century. More and more literatures appeared, especially in Scandinavian and Slavic lands. In addition to imaginative literature, lawbooks, ordinary legal documents, and commercial texts were written in languages other than Latin.

Architecture produced two stunning leaps forward. In Romanesque (after 1050) and Gothic (after 1150) cathedrals, all existing forms were recombined in buoyant new styles that have lost none of their power to move and inspire. Romanesque façades saw the reappearance of large-scale sculpture, lost since antiquity, and free-standing sculpture reappeared. Gothic stained glass was one of medieval Europe's crowning achievements.

Medieval Europe remained a challenging place for women. Public power was generally reserved for men in a society that prized military qualities. Except in convents, church offices were confined to men, as were student and teaching positions in schools and universities. Nevertheless, on Europe's many expanding frontiers, where old conventions were observed less strictly, women had opportunities for social and political power. Bustling, innovative cities accorded women a wide range of occupations. Some women, such as the gifted theologian Hildegard of Bingen (1098–1179), made distinguished contributions to Latin literature, and a number of women, such as Marie de France (active ca. 1170), became prominent as vernacular authors. Women played key roles in the many new religious movements of the Middle Ages. The thirteenth-century Beguines made up the first religious movement created by and only for women in the history of Christianity.

# FROM MEDIEVAL TO RENAISSANCE EUROPE, 1300–1500

THE biblical Book of Revelation depicts Four Horsemen of the Apocalypse: war, slaughter, famine, and death. Those grim riders trod hard on fourteenth-century Europe.

## ■ Crisis and Recovery

Old hostilities dragged France and England into the conflict now known as the "Hundred Years' War" (1337–1453), which, before it ended, drained the talent and treasure of many parts of Europe. This conflict was only one of the age's struggles. Trade wars rocked the Baltic and North Seas, religious and ethnic battles flared in the Holy Roman Empire (as the German Empire came to be called), Christian-Muslim struggles continued in Spain, peasants rebelled in France and England, and workers staged revolts in Flanders and Italy. Violence seemed to be the norm.

To all this slaughter must be added economic dislocation. Several problems combined to produce economic and social crisis. Population began leveling off in the thirteenth century. The weather turned foul. And in 1348 Europe was visited by an outbreak of bubonic plague that carried off perhaps one-third of the population and worked its cruelest ravages on the cities that were Europe's most creative, productive areas. The epidemic of 1348–1349 was only the first of many recurrences of the plague.

A sense of despair fell over a Christian society convinced that God was punishing it. But for what? Moralists complained about dissolute living, and ecclesiastical powers worried about heresy. Jews sometimes became scapegoats as people sought to blame others for their own misfortunes.

The church could not salve Europe's wounds because it too was going through deep struggles. By the end of the thirteenth century the papacy seemed focused more on political power than on spiritual leadership. From 1305 to 1378 the popes resided not in Rome but in Avignon, in the south of what is now France. They had settled there temporarily to settle some outstanding controversies with the French monarchy but scandal-

ized people all over Europe by staying for three-quarters of a century. When the popes tried to return to Rome, the college of cardinals, the aristocrats of the church, split into factions. From 1378 to 1417 the Catholic Church suffered the Great Schism, as two or more men claimed to be the legitimate pope. The schism was healed and the pope restored to Rome only after a council proclaimed a new vision of church government: "conciliarism" maintained that the church was not a monarchy under the pope but a collegial body of all bishops. Churchmen argued for years over the implications of this pronouncement.

After surmounting these trials, western Europe began to recover in the fifteenth and early sixteenth centuries. France emerged from its long war with England with a greatly strengthened royal government that could raise armies, collect taxes, and control nobles. England suffered through a civil war after the Hundred Years' War but then, after 1485, began a long, steady process of political consolidation under the Tudor dynasty. Major compromises in 1356 provided the Holy Roman Empire with a formula not for unity but at least for stability. The Spanish monarchies grew stronger by the year. In Italy a profusion of independent cities deferred, by choice or by force, to Florence, Milan, or Venice.

## ■ The Renaissance

The years from 1300 to about 1550 were both constructive and destructive in the political and material realms but were boundlessly creative in the cultural realms. This was the Renaissance (from a French word meaning "rebirth"). Its pioneers were Italians, who believed that they were calling back to life the spirit, the ideals, of classical Greece and Rome. They sought out works of classical literature and combed through them for models of style and for long-lost gems of practical wisdom and guidance. Though by no means irreligious, Renaissance writers were more concerned with the ancient world, and their own world, than they were the next. We call them "humanists" because of their interest in the humane disciplines. The "study of humanity" (*studia humanitatis*) that was central to the Renaissance was grounded in the seven so-called liberal arts—grammar, rhetoric, logic, arithmetic, astronomy, geometry, and music—that had formed the core of Western education since antiquity. The "arts" were the skills or methods used by the "liberal"—literally, the free—in the conduct of their affairs in society. Armed with the liberal arts, the humanists sought beauty and harmony; they cultivated elegance in the spoken and written word. Their achievements in lit-

**The Doors of Paradise**    In his representations of scenes from the Old Testament, Lorenzo Ghiberti combined a love of ancient statuary with the new Florentine interest in linear perspective.    *(Alinari/Art Resource, NY)*

erature, art, and architecture represent for many the dawn of a new age.

"They," however, were mostly men. A great historian has asked whether women had a Renaissance at all. Some women humanists have come to light, and the importance of vernacular writers such as Christine de Pizan (1364–1430) and Marguerite de Navarre (1492–1549) has long been acknowledged. But women's daily lives do not seem to have changed much during the Renaissance.

The Renaissance was disseminated from Italy—first by northerners who had studied in the south and then, after 1454, by printing, which made books and ideas more accessible than ever before. In northern Europe, Renaissance scholars turned to the sources of the Christian tradition—to the Scriptures and the Church Fathers—with the same zeal and scholarship that the Italians had applied to classical sources. Such study led some figures to harsh criticism of the institutional, intellectual, and moral failings of the late medieval Catholic Church.

# GLOBALIZATION, RELIGIOUS REFORMATION, POLITICAL TRANSFORMATION, 1500–1560

**A**S the Renaissance was wending its way through European space and consciousness, other momentous changes began to appear. Spanish and Portuguese explorers and conquerors had begun building vast overseas empires in North and South America and in the Indian Ocean basin. The whole globe was being brought within the orbit of Western civilization. The European world was riven by religious differences that reflected old political and cultural divisions and generated new tensions. The late medieval state system was marked by ever larger empires and ever more intricate, and fickle, alliances.

## ■ Europe and the Wider World

A glance at a map of the world today will show that Europe is not especially well placed for global domination. It is smaller than other continents, its population is modest, and its material resources are unexceptional. One of the important questions in world history is why it was Europeans, of all peoples, who succeeded in exploring and exploiting the rest of the world.

Europeans long had had contacts with non-Europeans. From ancient times, trade routes running across Africa and Asia had brought the products of the whole world to Europe's markets. Occasional bursts of crusading ferocity or missionary zeal carried Europeans beyond their own frontiers. Travelers, such as the renowned Italian Marco Polo (1254–1324), were sometimes drawn by an irresistible urge to know what lay beyond the horizon. Nevertheless, most Europeans traveled little and knew almost nothing about the world.

In the fifteenth century an accumulation of factors changed forever Europe's place on earth. Travel literature aroused some people's curiosity. Real and imagined threats from the Turks fanned the remaining embers of crusading and missionary zeal. Above all, the Italian stranglehold on Mediterranean trade encouraged other nations to seek alternative commercial routes. New technologies for sailing and navigation made possible long voyages beyond the security of familiar coastlines. Better maps and charts and improved ship and sail designs—some of the latter borrowed from the non-European world—gave Europeans distinct advantages. The consolidation of powerful states such as Spain and, a century later, France and England put financial

**The Holy Household**    One of the most popular ideas among Protestants was that true religion should be taught and preserved in the Christian family, presided over by the father.    *(The Shakespeare Birthplace Trust)*

resources at the disposal of brave and ambitious seamen.

From modest explorations of the West African coast sponsored by the Portuguese royal family, European involvement with the rest of the world expanded to the creation of vast empires. By 1560 the Spanish had conquered southwestern North America, Central America, and South America, except for Brazil, which fell to Portugal. The Portuguese had established military and commercial bases in the Indian Ocean and the South China Sea. The Dutch would eventually contest Portuguese control of the seas and islands lying to the south of China, as well as land colonists in southern Africa and North America. Yet the Dutch presence in North America would pale into insignificance before the territorial acquisitions of France and England.

Did Europeans bring real benefits to the rest of the world, or were they merely cruel exploiters? How did the non-Western world influence the West? People continue to argue over these questions. What cannot be denied is that during the 1500s, Western civilization assumed a role in world history that it had never held before.

■ **Religious Divisions**

For hundreds of years after Charlemagne (r. 768–814), many people held up the ideal of Europe as "Christendom." Christianity was seen as a badge of citizenship in a world where the purpose of governments—indeed of organized societies—was to assist people in their quest for eternal salvation.

A truly Christian political order that transcended national boundaries never existed in the Middle Ages, but a fundamentally Christian society certainly did. The beliefs of ordinary people were not their own affair. Deviation from official beliefs brought swift punishment. "Correct" belief was nurtured, imposed, and reinforced in countless ways. Most schools were run by the church to promote religious learning and culture. The major turning points of life—birth, baptism, marriage, death—were attended by religious ceremonies. Celebrations, from royal feasts to humble village revels, were held on saints' days. Christianity, and churchmen, were literally and figuratively inescapable.

In the sixteenth century western Europe's religious life was sundered in unprecedented ways by a series of developments that are usually called the Protestant Reformation. The reformers shared fundamental beliefs. The first was that everything necessary for salvation had been revealed by God in the Bible; thus, the teachings of the Catholic Church were as nothing compared to the word of God. The second was that salvation resulted from faith in God and from God's grace; thus, good works and upright behavior were no guarantees of salvation. The name *Protestant* was coined in 1529 and has become a common designation for many groups of people who both dissented from the Catholic Church and embraced devout views of their own.

Protestant reformers such as the German Martin Luther (1483–1546) and the French-born John Calvin (1509–1564) sought to restore Christianity to the form they believed it had possessed in the first centuries of its existence. Royal reformers such as Henry VIII of England (r. 1509–1547) decreed the reform of the church in their lands. Fiery radicals wished to cast down the existing order of society in the name of a purified religion, and humble pietists sought to withdraw from all social and political entanglements. The Catholic Church corrected many of the abuses that had offended its critics but reaffirmed its basic teachings at the Council of Trent (1545–1563). There was no longer a possibility of attaining or enforcing a single pattern of belief. The Roman Catholic Church and Catholic rulers had permanently lost their control of England and Scotland, Scandinavia, the Netherlands, Switzerland, and northern Germany.

Many of the political and diplomatic controversies of the sixteenth century were related to religious issues. The English crown vastly strengthened itself by promoting religious reform, while bitter religious quarrels threatened more than once to destroy the French monarchy. Spain set itself up as the guardian of Catholic orthodoxy but usually lacked the power to impose its will in matters of religion. Since the Holy Roman emperors were Catholic, and most northern German rulers were Protestant, religious divisions worsened old antagonisms and generated new ones.

The Protestant Reformation did not dramatically alter the roles of women in European society or in the Christian churches. From the beginning, ambivalence marked women's participation in the Christian religion. On the one hand, the teachings of Jesus proclaimed the essential equality of women and men and opened heaven equally to both. On the other hand, both Protestant and Catholic Churches denied official and educational roles to women. The reformers were not social revolutionaries. They said, for example, that a housewife was as pleasing to God as a nun, but they refused to suppose that a woman could be a minister. And the Protestants' closing of convents denied some women the intellectual and administrative opportunities long available in those houses.

### ■ States and Empires

Europe's state system was dominated by two multiethnic empires. Through marriage alliances, the Habsburg family, originally from Switzerland, had established extensive claims: to Spain and its overseas empire, to parts of Italy and much of Austria, to the crown of the Holy Roman Empire, to Burgundy, and to the Netherlands. The Habsburg dominions literally surrounded France. The chief dynamic in western Europe was continuing rivalry between the Habsburgs and the Valois rulers of France. At the opposite end of Europe, the empire of the Muslim Ottoman Turks reached from central Asia to the gates of Vienna.

Other states in Europe sought a place alongside the greater ones. Scandinavia was dominated by Sweden, whose rulers continually entered the complicated politics of northern Germany. Those complications, and Sweden's opportunities, were directly tied to the fluctuating influence of the Holy Roman emperors. Prussia, a small Baltic state founded by German knights and adventurers, was hemmed in by other German states, Sweden, Lithuania, and, on occasion, Russia. In the fifteenth century, the Russians threw off the yoke of the Mongols and began expanding to the east, without ever losing sight of their western frontier with Germanic and Slavic Europe or their southern frontier with the Turks. The Turks threatened, or at least contemporaries perceived them to threaten, the Holy Roman Empire in the northern Balkans, Russia in the Black Sea region, and Italian merchants all over the Mediterranean. The traders of Venice and Genoa, in particular, were anxious about their old commercial superiority after the Portuguese and the Spanish opened vast new economic opportunities as a result of their commercial exploitation of the Americas, Africa, and the Indian Ocean basin.

In the fourteenth century the Florentine man of letters Francesco Petrarch (1304–1374) and his contemporaries, the earliest humanists, explicitly stated their feeling that they were unlike the people and times that had just preceded them and were instead similar to the ancient Romans. Petrarch and the others created the traditional tripartite division of Western history into ancient, modern, and the part in the middle—the so-called Middle Ages, or Dark Ages.

Scholars today do not think Petrarch was right either in his dismissal of the medieval period as the "Dark Ages" or in his claim that he and his contemporaries resembled the Romans. His argument reveals more about how people thought in his period than about the realities of the past. Modern historians do not see sharp breaks between historical periods. Historians now talk about continuity and change operating in tandem. Nevertheless, the old three-part division persists because it represents the major way in which we in the West have reflected on our history and because broad chronological divisions accommodate academic programs of study. In this volume, you will explore the possibilities and paradoxes, triumphs and tragedies, indeed the *Continuing Experiment*, of the modern phase of Western civilization.

THOMAS F. X. NOBLE

# CHAPTER 15

# Europe in the Age of Religious Wars 1560–1648

THREE well-dressed gentlemen stand over a mutilated body; one of them holds up the severed head. Elsewhere sword-wielding men engage in indiscriminate slaughter, even of babies. Corpses are piled up in the background. This painting memorializes the grisly events of August 24, 1572. A band of Catholic noblemen accompanied by the personal guard of the king of France had hunted down a hundred Protestant nobles, asleep in their lodgings in and around the royal palace, and murdered them in cold blood. The king and his counselors had planned the murders as a preemptive political strike because they feared that other Protestant nobles were gathering an army outside Paris. But the calculated attack became a general massacre when ordinary Parisians, overwhelmingly Catholic and believing they were acting in the king's name, turned on their neighbors. About three thousand Protestants were slain in Paris over the next three days.

This massacre came to be called the Saint Bartholomew's Day Massacre for the Catholic saint on whose feast day it fell. Though particularly horrible in its scope, the slaughter was not unusual in the deadly combination of religious and political antagonisms it reflected. Religious conflicts were by definition intractable political conflicts since virtually every religious group felt that all others were heretics who could not be tolerated and must be eliminated. Rulers of all faiths looked to divine authority and religious institutions to uphold their power.

In the decades after 1560, existing political tensions contributed to instability and violence, especially when newly reinforced by religious differences. Royal governments continued to consolidate authority, but resistance to royal power by provinces, nobles, or towns accustomed to independence now might have a religious sanction.

The Saint Bartholomew's Day Massacre.
(Musée Cantonal des Beaux-Arts, Lausanne)

**Economic Change and Social Tensions**

**Imperial Spain and the Limits of Royal Power**

**Religious and Political Conflict in France and England**

**The Holy Roman Empire and the Thirty Years' War, 1555–1648**

**Writing, Drama, and Art in an Age of Upheaval**

Warfare over these issues had consumed the Holy Roman Empire in the first half of the sixteenth century. The conflict had now spilled over into France and the Netherlands, and threatened to erupt in England. In the early seventeenth century, the Holy Roman Empire once again was wracked by a war simultaneously religious and political in origin. Regardless of its roots, warfare itself had become more destructive than ever before thanks to innovations in military technology and campaign tactics. Tensions everywhere were also worsened by economic changes, especially soaring prices and grinding unemployment.

A period of tension, even extraordinary violence, in political and social life, the era of the late sixteenth and early seventeenth centuries was also distinguished by great creativity in some areas of cultural and intellectual life. The plays of Shakespeare, for example, mirrored the passions but also reflected on the dilemmas of the day and helped to analyze Europeans' circumstances with a new degree of sophistication.

---

### QUESTIONS TO CONSIDER

- How did ordinary people cope with the economic stresses of these decades?

- In what ways was the most powerful state of the era—Spain—exceptional among western European monarchies, and in what ways typical of them?

- Why did war break out again in the Holy Roman Empire, and what was the significance of the conflict?

- In what ways do the literature and art of this period reflect the political, social, and religious tensions of the age?

---

### TERMS TO KNOW

| | |
|---|---|
| price revolution | Edict of Nantes |
| gentry | Elizabeth I |
| Philip II | Puritans |
| The Armada | Thirty Years' War |
| Huguenots | Peace of Westphalia |
| Henry IV | baroque |

---

## ECONOMIC CHANGE AND SOCIAL TENSIONS

 RELIGIOUS strife, warfare, and economic change disrupted the everyday lives of whole communities as well as individuals in the late sixteenth and early seventeenth centuries. Wars were devastating to many areas of western Europe and contributed to especially severe economic decline in parts of the Low Countries (the Netherlands), France, and the Holy Roman Empire. But other factors, most notably a steady rise in prices, also played a role in the dramatic economic and social changes of the century after 1550. A series of economic changes altered power relations in cities, in the countryside, and in the relationship of both to central governments. Ordinary people managed their economic difficulties in a variety of ways: they sought new sources of work; they protested against burdensome taxes; sometimes, they found scapegoats for their distress among their neighbors.

### ■ Economic Transformation and the New Elites

The most obvious economic change was an unrelenting rise in prices, which resulted in the concentration of wealth in fewer and fewer hands. Sixteenth-century observers attributed rising prices to the inflationary effects of the influx of precious metals from Spanish territories in the New World. Historians now believe that European causes may also have helped trigger this "price revolution." Steady population growth caused a relative shortage of goods, particularly food, and the result was higher prices. Both the amount and the effect of price changes were highly localized, depending on factors such as the structure of local economies and the success of harvests. Between 1550 and 1600, however, the price of grain may have risen between 50 and 100 percent, and sometimes more, in cities throughout Europe—including eastern Europe, the breadbasket for growing urban areas to the west. Wages did not keep pace with prices; historians estimate that wages lost between one-tenth and one-fourth of their value by the end of the century. The political and religious struggles of the era thus took place against a background of increasing want, and economic distress was often expressed in both political and religious terms.

These economic changes affected the wealthy as well as the poor. During this period, monarchs were making new accommodations with the hereditary aristocracy—with the Crown usually emerging stronger, if only through concessions to aristocrats' economic interests. Underlying this new symbiosis of monarchy and traditional warrior-nobles were the effects of the widespread economic changes. These changes would eventually blur lines between the old noble families and the new elites and would simplify power relationships within the state. Conditions in the countryside, where there were fewer resources to feed more mouths, grew less favorable. But at the same time more capital became available to wealthy urban or landholding families to invest in the countryside, by buying land outright on which to live like gentry or by making loans to desperate peasants. This capital came from profits from expanded production and trade and was also an effect of the scarcity of land as population and prices rose. Enterprising landholders raised ground rents wherever they could, or they converted land to the production of wool, grain, and other cash crops destined for distant markets.

As a result, a stratum of wealthy, educated, and socially ambitious "new gentry," as these families were called in England, began growing and solidifying. Many of the men of these families were royal officeholders. Where the practice existed, many bought titles outright or were granted nobility as a benefit of their offices. They often lent money to royal governments. The monumental expense of wars made becoming a lender to government, as well as to individuals, an attractive way to live off personal capital.

No one would have confused this up-and-coming gentry with warrior-aristocrats from old families, but the social distinctions between them are less important (to us) than what they had in common: legal privilege, the security of landownership, a cooperative relationship with the monarchy. Monarchs deliberately favored the new gentry as counterweights to independent aristocrats.

City governments also changed character as wealth accumulated in the hands of formerly commercial families. Town councils became dominated by successive generations of privileged families, now more likely to live from landed than from commercial wealth. By the beginning of the seventeenth century, traditional guild control of government had been subverted in many

| CHRONOLOGY | |
|---|---|
| 1558–1603 | Reign of Elizabeth I |
| 1559 | Act of Supremacy (England) |
| 1562–1598 | Religious wars in France |
| 1565 | Netherlands city councils and nobility ignore Philip's law against heresy |
| 1566 | Calvinist "iconoclastic fury" begins |
| 1567 | Duke of Alba arrives in the Netherlands |
| 1571 | Defeat of Turkish navy at Lepanto |
| 1576 | Sack of Antwerp |
| 1579 | Union of Utrecht |
| 1588 | Defeat of Spanish Armada |
| 1589–1610 | Reign of Henry IV |
| 1598 | Edict of Nantes |
| 1609 | Truce is declared between Spain and the Netherlands |
| 1618–1648 | Thirty Years' War |
| 1620 | Catholic victory at Battle of White Mountain |
| 1621 | Truce between Spain and the Netherlands expires; war between Spain and the Netherlands begins |
| 1629 | Peace of Alais |
| 1631 | Swedes under Gustav Adolf defeat imperial forces |
| 1632 | Death of Gustav Adolf |
| 1635 | Peace of Prague |
| 1640–1653 | "Long Parliament" in session in England |
| 1648 | Peace of Westphalia |

places. Towns became more closely tied to royal interests by means of the mutual interests of Crown and town elites. The long medieval tradition of towns serving as independent corporate bodies had come to an end.

### ■ Economic Change and the Common People

The growth of markets around Europe and in Spanish possessions overseas, as well as population growth within Europe, had a marked effect on patterns of production and the lives of artisans and laborers. Production of cloth on a large scale for export, for example, now required huge amounts of capital—much more than a typical guild craftsman could amass. Cloth production was increasingly controlled by new investor-producers with enormous resources and access to distant markets. These entrepreneurs bought up large amounts of wool and hired it out to be cleaned, spun into thread, and woven into cloth by wage laborers in urban workshops or by pieceworkers in their homes. Thousands of women and men in the countryside around urban centers helped to support themselves and their families in this way.

The new entrepreneurs had sufficient capital entirely to bypass guild production. In towns, guilds still regulated most trades but could not accommodate the numbers of artisans who sought to join them. Fewer and fewer apprentices and journeymen could expect to become master artisans. The masters began to treat apprentices virtually as wage laborers, at times letting them go during slow periods. The household mode of production, in which apprentices and journeymen had worked and lived side by side with the master's family, also began to break down, with profound economic, social, and political consequences.

One of the first reflections of the dire circumstances faced by artisans was an attempt to reduce competition at the expense of the artisans' own mothers, sisters, daughters, and sons. Increasingly, widows were forbidden to continue practicing their husbands' enterprises, though they headed from 10 to 15 percent of households in many trades. Women had traditionally learned and practiced many trades but rarely followed the formal progress from apprenticeship to master status. A woman usually combined work of this kind with household production, with selling her products and those of her husband, and with bearing and nursing children. Outright exclusion of women from guild organization appears as early as the thirteenth century but now began regularly to appear in guild statutes. In addition, town governments tried to restrict women's participation in work such as selling in markets, which they had long dominated. Even midwives had to defend their practices, even though as part of housewifery women were expected to know about herbal remedies and practical medicine. (See the box "Reading Sources: A Woman Defends Her Right to Practice Healing.") Working women thus began to have difficulty supporting themselves if single or widowed and difficulty supporting their children. In the changing position of such women, we can see the distress of the entire stratum of society that they represent.

Wealth in the countryside was also becoming more stratified. Population growth caused many peasant farms to be subdivided for numerous children, creating tiny plots that could not support the families who lived on them. Countless peasants lost what lands they had to wealthy investors—many of them newly wealthy gentry—who lent them money for renting more land or for purchasing seed and tools, and then reclaimed the land when the peasants failed to repay. Other peasants were simply unable to rent land as rents rose. To survive, some sought work as day laborers on the land of rich landlords or more prosperous farmers. But with the shrinking opportunities for farming, this option became less feasible. Many found their way to cities, where they swelled the ranks of the poor. Others, like some of their urban counterparts, coped by becoming part of the newly expanding network of cloth production, combining spinning and weaving with subsistence farming. However, one bad harvest might send them out on the roads begging or odd-jobbing; many did not long survive such a life.

In eastern Europe, peasants faced other dilemmas, for their lands had a different relationship to the wider European economy. The more densely urbanized western Europe, whose wealth controlled the patterns of trade, sought bulk goods, particularly grain, from eastern Germany, Poland, and Lithuania. Thus, there was an economic incentive for landowners in eastern Europe to bind peasants to the land just as the desire of their rulers for greater cooperation had granted the landlords more power. Serfdom now spread in eastern Europe when precisely the opposite condition—a more mobile labor force—grew in the West.

### ■ Coping with Poverty and Violence

The common people of Europe did not submit passively to either the economic difficulties or the religious and political crises of their day. Whatever their religion, common people took the initiative in attacking members of other faiths to rid their communities of them. Heretics were considered to be spiritual pollution that might provoke God's wrath, and ordinary citizens believed that they had to eliminate heretics if the state failed to do so. Common people, as well as elites and governments, were thus responsible for the violence that sometimes occurred in the name of religion.

## ❧ READING SOURCES

## A Woman Defends Her Right to Practice Healing

*In this document, Katharine Carberiner testifies to the city council of Munich in defense of her right to her livelihood. Notice that she insists she does not deliberately compete with male doctors. Rather, she has skills that might lead women to choose her over male practitioners. How else does she justify her right to practice healing? Do you think the members of the city government were persuaded by her appeal?*

I use my feminine skills, given by the grace of God, only when someone entreats me earnestly, and never advertise myself, but only when someone has been left for lost. . . . I do whatever I can possibly do . . . using only simple and allowable means that should not be forbidden or proscribed in the least. Not one person who has come under my care has a complaint or grievance against me. If the doctors, apothecaries or barber-surgeons have claimed this, it is solely out of spite.

At all times, as is natural, women have more trust in other women to discover their secrets, problems and illnesses, than they have in men—but perhaps this jealousy came from that. Undoubtedly as well, husbands who love and cherish their wives will seek any help and assistance they can, even that from women, if the wives have been given up (by the doctors) or otherwise come into great danger.

Because I know that I can help in my own small way, I will do all I can, even, as according to the Gospel, we should help pull an ox out of a well it has fallen into on Sunday.

*Source:* Quoted in Merry Wiesner, "Women's Defense of Their Public Role," in Mary Beth Rose, ed., *Women in the Middle Ages and the Renaissance* (Syracuse: Syracuse University Press, 1986), p. 9.

---

Ordinary people fought in wars not only from conviction but also from the need for self-defense and from economic choice. It was ordinary people who defended the walls of towns, dug siege works, and manned artillery batteries. Although nobles remained military leaders, armies consisted mostly of infantry made up of common people, not mounted knights. Women were part of armies, too. Much of the day-to-day work of finding food and firewood, cleaning guns, and endlessly repairing inadequate clothing was done by women looking after their husbands and lovers among the troops.

Many men joined the armies and navies of their rulers because, given the alternatives, the military seemed a reasonable way of life. Landless farm hands, day laborers, and out-of-work artisans found the prospect of employment in the army attractive enough to outweigh the dangers of military life. Desertion was common; nothing more than the rumor that a soldier's home village was threatened might prompt a man to abandon his post. Battle-hardened troops could threaten their commanders not only with desertion but

with mutiny. A mutiny of Spanish soldiers in 1574 was a well-organized affair, for example, somewhat like a strike. Occasionally, mutinies were brutally suppressed; more often, they were successful and troops received some of their back wages.

Townspeople and country people participated in riots and rebellions to protest their circumstances when the situation was particularly dire or when other means of action had failed. The devastation of religious war led to both peasant rebellions and urban uprisings. Former soldiers, prosperous farmers, or even noble landlords whose economic fortunes were tied to peasant profits might lead rural revolts. Urban protests could begin spontaneously when new grievances worsened existing problems. In Naples, in 1585, food riots were provoked not simply by a shortage of grain but by a government decision to raise the price of bread during the shortage. Rebels sometimes seized property—for example, they might distribute looted bread among themselves—and occasionally killed officials. Their protests rarely generated lasting political change and were usually brutally quashed.

Governments at all levels tried to cope with the increasing problem of poverty by changing the administration and scale of poor relief. In both Catholic and Protestant Europe, caring for the poor became more institutionalized and systematic, and more removed from religious impulses. In the second half of the sixteenth century, governments established public almshouses and poorhouses to dispense food or to care for orphans or the destitute in towns throughout Catholic and Protestant Europe. Initially, these institutions reflected an optimistic vision of an ideal Christian community attentive to material want. But by 1600, the charitable distribution of food was accompanied by attempts to distinguish "deserving" from "undeserving" poor, by an insistence that the poor work for their ration of food, and even by an effort to compel the poor to live in almshouses and poorhouses.

These efforts were not uniformly successful. Begging was outlawed by Catholic and Protestant city governments alike, but never thoroughly suppressed. Catholic religious orders and parishes often resisted efforts at regulating their charitable work—even when they were imposed by Catholic governments. Nonetheless, the trend was clear. From viewing poverty as a fact of life and as an occasional lesson in Christian humility, European elites were beginning to see it as a social problem. And they saw the poor as people in need of control and institutional discipline.

**Publicizing Witch Trials**   Printed pamphlets, such as this one describing the execution of three women in Essex, England, spread the news of local "outbreaks" of witchcraft. One of the women, Joan Prentis, is also depicted surrounded by her animal familiars. The ferret in Joan's lap, the pamphlet relates, was the Devil himself in animal form.   *(Lambeth Palace Library)*

## ■ The Hunt for Witches

Between approximately 1550 and 1650, Europe saw a dramatic increase in the persecution of women and men for witchcraft. Approximately one hundred thousand people were tried and about sixty thousand executed. The surge in witch-hunting was closely linked to communities' religious concerns and also to the social tensions that resulted from economic difficulties.

Certain types of witchcraft had long existed in Europe. So-called black magic of various kinds—one peasant casting a spell on another peasant's cow—had been common since the Middle Ages. What now made the practice seem particularly menacing, especially to elites, were theories linking black magic to Devil worship. Catholic leaders and legal scholars began to advance such theories in the fifteenth century, and by the late sixteenth century both Catholic and Protestant elites viewed a witch not only as someone who might cast harmful spells but also as a heretic.

The impetus for most individual accusations of witchcraft came from within the communities where the "witch" lived—that is, from common people. Usually targeted were solitary or unpopular people whose difficult relationships with fellow villagers made them seem likely sources of evil. Often, such a person had practiced black magic (or had been suspected of doing so) for years, and the villagers took action only when faced with a community crisis, such as an epidemic.

A majority of accused witches were women. Lacking legal, social, and political resources, women may have been more likely than men to use black magic for self-protection or advancement. Women's work often made them vulnerable to charges of witchcraft since families' food supplies and routine medicines passed through women's hands. The deaths of young children or of domestic animals, such as a milk cow, were among the most common triggers for witchcraft accusation. The increase in poverty during the late sixteenth and early seventeenth centuries made poor women frequent targets of witch-hunts. It was easier to find such a woman menacing—and to accuse her of wrongdoing—than to feel guilty because of her evident need.

Both Christian dogma and humanistic writing portrayed women as morally weaker than men and thus more susceptible to the Devil's enticements. Writings on witchcraft described Devil worship in sexual terms, and the prosecution of witches had a voyeuristic, sexual dimension. The bodies of accused witches were searched for the "Devil's mark"—a blemish thought to be Satan's imprint. In some regions, women accounted for 80 percent of those prosecuted and executed. A dynamic of gender stereotyping was not always at work, however; in other regions, prosecutions were more evenly divided between men and women, and occasionally men made up the majority of those accused.

Because they were often prompted by village disasters or tragedies, individual accusations of witchcraft increased in these decades in response to the crises that beset many communities. In addition, isolated accusations often started localized frenzies of active hunting for other witches. Dozens of "witches" might be identified and executed before the whirlwind subsided. These more widespread hunts were driven, in part, by the anxieties of local elites about disorder and heresy and were facilitated by contemporary legal procedures that they applied. These procedures permitted lax rules of evidence and the use of torture to extract confessions. Torture or the threat of torture led most of those accused of witchcraft to "confess," and to name accomplices or other "witches." In this way, a single initial accusation could lead to dozens of prosecutions. In regions where procedures for appealing convictions and sentences were fragile or nonexistent, witch-hunts could expand with alarming speed. Aggressive hunts were common, for example, in the small principalities and imperial cities of the Holy Roman Empire, which were largely independent of higher political authority.

The widespread witch-hunts virtually ended by the late seventeenth century, in part because the intellectual energies of elites shifted from religious to scientific thought. The practice of witchcraft continued among common folk, although accusations of one neighbor by another never again reached the level of these crisis-ridden decades.

# IMPERIAL SPAIN AND THE LIMITS OF ROYAL POWER

**T**O contemporary observers, no political fact of the late sixteenth century was more obvious than the ascendancy of Spain. Philip II (r. 1556–1598) ruled Spanish conquests in the New World as well as wealthy territories in Europe, including the Netherlands and parts of Italy. Yet imperial Spain did not escape the political, social, and religious turmoil of the era. Explosive combinations of religious dissent and political disaffection led to revolt against Spain in the Netherlands. This conflict revealed the endemic tensions of sixteenth-century political life: nobles, towns, and provinces trying to safeguard remnants of medieval autonomy against efforts at greater centralization—with the added complications of economic strain and religious division. The revolt also demonstrated the material limits of royal power, since even with treasure from the American conquests pouring in, Philip could at times barely afford to keep armies in the field. As American silver dwindled in the seventeenth century, Philip's successors faced severe financial and political strains even in their Spanish domains.

## ■ The Revolt of the Netherlands

Philip's power stemmed in part from the far-flung territories he inherited from his father, the Habsburg king of Spain and Holy Roman emperor Charles V: Spain, the Low Countries (the Netherlands), the duchy of Milan, the kingdom of Naples, the conquered lands in the Americas, and the Philippine Islands in Asia. (Control of Charles's Austrian lands had passed to his brother, Ferdinand, Philip's uncle; see Map 15.1.) Treasure fleets bearing precious metals from the New World began to reach Spain regularly during Philip's reign. Spain was now the engine powering a trading economy unlike any that had existed in Europe before. To supply its colonies, Spain needed timber and other shipbuilding materials from the hinterlands of the Baltic Sea. Grain from the Baltic fed the urban populations of Spain (where wool was the principal cash crop) and the Netherlands, while the Netherlands, in turn, was a source of finished goods, such as cloth. The major exchange point for all of these goods was the city of Antwerp in the Netherlands, the leading trading center of all of Europe by 1550.

The Netherlands were the jewel among Philip's European possessions. These seventeen provinces (constituting mostly the modern nations of Belgium and the

**Map 15.1** **The Spanish Habsburgs and Europe, ca. 1556** Philip II's control of territories in northern Italy permitted the overland access of Spanish troops to the Netherlands and heightened the Spanish threat to France. Lands bordering the western Mediterranean made the sea a natural sphere of Spanish influence as well. Habsburg lands in central Europe were controlled after 1556 by Charles V's brother Ferdinand and his descendants.

Lands ruled by the Spanish Habsburgs

Lands ruled by the Austrian Habsburgs

Boundary of the Holy Roman Empire

Spanish military corridor ("Spanish Road")

Major battles

**The City of Antwerp**     Antwerp, in the southern Netherlands, was the point of sale for Portuguese spices brought around Africa from India, the selling and transshipping center for Baltic goods, including timber, fur, and grain, and the source for manufactured goods such as cloth.     *(Musées royaux des Beaux-Arts de Belgique)*

Netherlands) had been centers of trade and manufacture since the twelfth century and, in the fourteenth and fifteenth centuries, had enjoyed political importance and a period of cultural innovation under the control of the dukes of Burgundy. By the time Philip inherited the provinces from his father, a sort of federal system of government had evolved to accommodate the various centers of power. Each province had an assembly (Estates) in which representatives of leading nobility and towns authorized taxation, but each also acknowledged a central administration in Brussels that represented Philip. Heading the council of state in Brussels was a governor-general, Philip's half-sister, Margaret of Parma.

Philip's clumsy efforts to adjust this distribution of power in his favor pushed his subjects in the Netherlands into revolt. Though conscientious to a fault, Philip was a rigid, unimaginative man. Born and raised in Spain, he had little real familiarity with the densely populated, linguistically diverse Netherlands, and he never visited there after 1559. Early in Philip's reign, tensions in the Netherlands arose over taxation and over Spanish insistence on maintaining tight control. Bad harvests and commercial disruptions occasioned by wars in the Baltic region in the 1560s depressed the Netherlands' economy and made it difficult for the provinces to pay taxes demanded by Spain. When the Peace of Cateau-Cambrésis° of 1559 brought an end to the long struggle between the Habsburgs and the Valois° kings of France, the people of the Netherlands had reason to hope for lower taxes and reduced levels of Spanish control, yet neither was forthcoming. Indeed, Philip had named to the council of state officials who were Spaniards themselves or had close ties to the Spanish court, bypassing local nobles who had fought for Philip and his father before 1559 and who expected positions of influence in his government.

**Cateau-Cambrésis** (kah-toe kam-bray-SEE)     **Valois** (val-WAH)

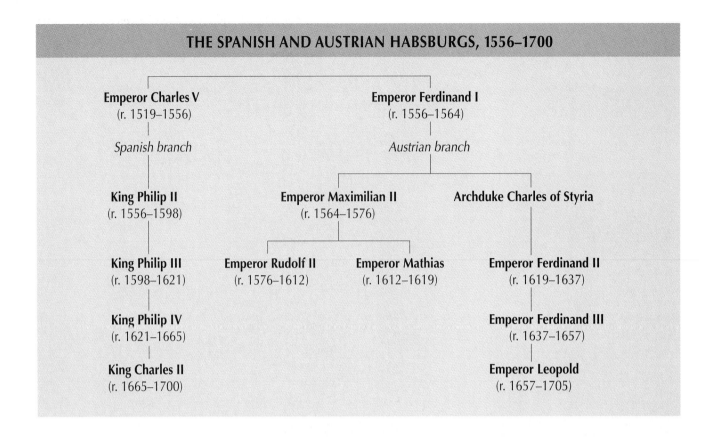

## THE SPANISH AND AUSTRIAN HABSBURGS, 1556–1700

**Emperor Charles V** (r. 1519–1556)

*Spanish branch*

**Emperor Ferdinand I** (r. 1556–1564)

*Austrian branch*

**King Philip II** (r. 1556–1598)

**Emperor Maximilian II** (r. 1564–1576)

**Archduke Charles of Styria**

**King Philip III** (r. 1598–1621)

**Emperor Rudolf II** (r. 1576–1612)

**Emperor Mathias** (r. 1612–1619)

**Emperor Ferdinand II** (r. 1619–1637)

**King Philip IV** (r. 1621–1665)

**Emperor Ferdinand III** (r. 1637–1657)

**King Charles II** (r. 1665–1700)

**Emperor Leopold** (r. 1657–1705)

Philip only added to the economic and political discontent by unleashing an invigorated repression of heresy. Unlike his father, Philip directed the hunt for heretics not just at lower-class dissenters but also at well-to-do Calvinists—followers of the French Protestant religious reformer John Calvin—whose numbers were considerable. Punishment for heresy now included confiscation of family property not just execution of the individual. By 1565 municipal councils in the Netherlands were routinely refusing to enforce Philip's religious policies, believing that urban prosperity—as well as their personal security—depended on restraint in the prosecution of heresy. Leading nobles also stopped enforcing the policies on their estates.

Encouraged by greater tolerance, by 1566 Protestants had begun to hold open-air meetings and attracted new converts in many towns. In a series of actions called the "iconoclastic fury," townsfolk around the provinces stripped Catholic churches of the relics and statues deemed idolatrous by Calvinist doctrine. At the same time, reflecting the economic strain of these years, some townsfolk rioted to protest the price of bread. One prominent nobleman warned Philip, "All trade has come to a standstill, so that there are 100,000 men begging for their bread who used to earn it . . . which is [important] since poverty can force people to do things which otherwise they would never think of doing."[1]

In early 1567 armed bands of Calvinist insurgents seized two towns in the southern Netherlands by force of arms in hopes of stirring a general revolt that would secure freedom of worship. Margaret of Parma quelled the uprisings by rallying city governments and loyal nobles, now fearful for their own property and power. But by then, far away in Spain, a decision had been made to send in the Spanish duke of Alba with an army of ten thousand men.

Alba arrived in August 1567 and, to bolster his own shaky standing at the Spanish court, acted more like a conqueror than a peacemaker. He billeted troops in friendly cities, established new courts to try rebels, arrested thousands of people, executed about a thousand rebels (including Catholics as well as prominent Protestants), and imposed heavy new taxes to support his army. Thus, Alba repeated every mistake of Spanish policy that had triggered rebellion in the first place.

Margaret of Parma resigned in disgust and left the Netherlands. Protestants from rebellious towns escaped into exile, where they were joined by nobles who had been declared traitors for resisting Alba's extreme policies. The most important of these was William of Nassau°, prince of Orange (1533–1584), whose lands outside the Netherlands, in France and the empire, lay beyond

**Nassau** (NAS-saw)

**Philip II in 1583**   Dressed in the austere black in fashion at the Spanish court, Philip holds a rosary and wears the Order of the Golden Fleece, an order of knighthood, around his neck. At age 56 Philip has outlived four wives and most of his children.   *(Museo del Prado, Madrid)*

Spanish reach and so could be used to finance continued warfare against Spain. A significant community with military capability began to grow in exile.

In 1572 ships of exiled Calvinist privateers known as the "Sea Beggars" began preying on Spanish shipping and coastal fortresses from bases in the northern provinces. The northern provinces, increasingly Calvinist, became the center of opposition to the Spanish, who concentrated their efforts against rebellion in the wealthier southern provinces. Occasionally the French and English lent aid to the rebels.

The war in the Netherlands was a showcase for the new and costly technology of warfare in this period. Many towns in the Netherlands were (or came to be, as a consequence of the revolt) equipped with "bastions,"

newly designed walled defenses that could resist artillery fire; such cities could not be taken by storm. Where bastions had been built, military campaigns consisted of grueling sieges, skirmishes in surrounding areas for control of supplies, and occasional pitched battles between besiegers and forces attempting to break the siege. Vast numbers of men were required both for effective besieging forces and for garrisoning the many fortresses that controlled the countryside and defended access to major towns.

In an attempt to supply the Netherlands with seasoned veterans and materiel from Spain and Spanish territories in Italy, the Spanish developed the "Spanish Road," an innovative string of supply depots where provisions could be gathered in advance of troops marching

**Bastioned Fortress** This fortress in the Netherlands was protected by five bastions—the five pentagonal projections around the buildings in the center. The bastions enabled defenders to fire from all angles on besiegers and created a smaller expanse of wall on which besiegers could direct artillery fire. The walls were also lower than those of a medieval fortress and were reinforced with earth. The Dutch took this fortress from the Spanish in 1592—a rare successful attack on a bastioned fortress—by tunneling to the outer wall (*lower right*) and mining it with huge explosive charges. (*From Christopher Duffy,* Siege Warfare: The Fortress in the Early Modern World, 1494–1660 *[London: Routledge]. Reproduced with permission.*)

**Map 15.2 The Netherlands, 1559–1609** The seventeen provinces of the Netherlands were strikingly diverse politically, economically, and culturally. Like his father, Philip was, technically, the ruler of each province separately—that is, he was count of Flanders, duke of Brabant, and so forth.

to the Netherlands (see Map 15.1). Maintaining its large armies, however, taxed Spain's resources to the breaking point. Even with American silver at hand, Philip could at times barely afford to keep armies in the field. Inevitably, large numbers of troops also exhausted the countryside, and both soldiers and civilians suffered great privations. On occasion, Spanish troops reacted violently to difficult conditions and to delayed pay (American treasure dwindled badly between 1572 and 1578). In 1576 Spanish troops sacked the hitherto loyal city of Antwerp and massacred about eight thousand people. This event was bitterly remembered afterward as the "Spanish Fury."

The massacre prompted leaders in the southern provinces to raise their own armies to protect themselves against the Spanish. Late in 1576, they concluded an alliance with William of Orange and the northern rebels. But the northern and southern provinces were increasingly divided by religion, and their differences were skillfully exploited by Philip's new commander, Margaret's son Alexander Farnese°, duke of Parma. With galleons from America filling the king's coffers again, Parma wooed the Catholic elites of the southern provinces back into loyalty to Philip, in return for promises to respect their provincial liberties and safeguard their property from troops.

In 1579 the northern provinces united in a defensive alliance, the Union of Utrecht°, against the increasingly unified south. Parma's forces could not surmount the natural barrier of the Rhine River that bisects the Low Countries (see Map 15.2) or meet the increasing costs of

**Farnese** (far-NAY-zee)  **Utrecht** (OO-trekt)

siege warfare in waterlogged terrain, particularly as Spain diverted money to conflicts with England, in 1588, and France, after 1589. In 1609 a truce was finally concluded between Spain and the northern provinces. This truce did not formally recognize the "United Provinces" as an independent entity, though in fact they were. The modern nations of Belgium (the Spanish provinces) and the Netherlands are the distant result of this truce.

The independent United Provinces (usually called, simply, the Netherlands) was a fragile state, an accident of warfare at first. But commercial prosperity began to emerge as its greatest strength. Much of the economic activity of Antwerp had shifted north to Amsterdam in the province of Holland because of fighting in the south and a naval blockade of Antwerp by rebel ships. Philip's policies had created a new enemy nation and had enriched it at his expense.

## ■ The Failure of the Invincible Armada

The revolt of the Netherlands had lured Spain into wider strategic involvement, particularly against England. England and Spain had a common foe in France and common economic interests, and Philip had married Mary Tudor, the Catholic queen of England (r. 1553–1558). Even after Mary's death and the accession of her Protestant half-sister, Queen Elizabeth (r. 1558–1603), Spanish-English relations remained cordial. Relations started to sour, however, when Elizabeth began tolerating the use of English ports by the rebel Sea Beggars and authorizing attacks by English privateers on Spanish treasure fleets. In response, Spain supported Catholic resistance to Elizabeth within England, including plots to replace Elizabeth on the throne with her Catholic cousin Mary, Queen of Scots. Greater Spanish success in the Netherlands, raids by the Spanish and English on each other's shipping, and Elizabeth's execution of Mary in 1587 prompted Philip to order an invasion of England. A fleet (*armada*) of Spanish warships sailed in 1588.

"The enterprise of England," as the plan was called in Spain, represented an astounding logistical effort. The Armada was supposed to clear the English Channel of English ships in order to permit an invading force—troops under Parma in the Netherlands—to cross on barges. The sheer number of ships required for the undertaking—about 130—meant that some, inevitably, were slower supply ships, or vessels designed for the more protected waters of the Mediterranean. The English also had the advantage in arms, since they had better long-range artillery and better-trained gunners.

When the Armada entered the Channel on July 29, the English harassed the Spanish with artillery from a distance without sustaining much damage themselves. Parma could not get his men readied on their barges quickly enough once the fleet's presence in the Channel had been confirmed by messenger, nor could the fleet protect itself while waiting offshore. On the night of August 7, the English launched eight fire ships—burning vessels set adrift to deliver arson—into the anchored Spanish fleet. At dawn on the next day, they attacked the weakened fleet off Gravelines°, sank many ships, and dispersed what remained. (See the box "Reading Sources: Secret Dispatches from the Venetian Ambassador in Spain.")

The Battle at Gravelines was the first major artillery battle by sailing ships and helped set the future course of naval warfare. It was a disaster for Philip's hopes, and for thousands of sailors and soldiers in Spanish pay. Many of the surviving ships sank in bad weather, or were forced into hostile harbors, as the Armada sailed for home around the northern tip of the British Isles (see Map 15.1). Less than half of Philip's great fleet made it back to Spain.

## ■ Successes at Home and Around the Mediterranean

Despite his bountiful overseas empire and his preoccupation with the Netherlands, many of Philip's interests still centered on the Mediterranean. Spain and the kingdom of Naples had exchanged trade for centuries. Newer ties had been forged with the duchy of Milan and the city-state of Genoa, whose bankers were financiers to the Spanish monarchy. It was in his kingdoms of Spain and their Mediterranean sphere of interest that Philip made his power felt more effectively, though not without effort.

Philip's father, Charles V, had tried to secure the western Mediterranean against the Turks and their client states along the African coast, but it was under Philip that the Turkish challenge in the western Mediterranean receded. The Spanish allied temporarily with the papacy and Venice—both were concerned with the Turkish naval power in the Mediterranean—and their combined navies inflicted a massive defeat on the Turkish navy at Lepanto, off the coast of Greece, in October 1571 (see Map 15.1). The Turks remained the leading power in the eastern Mediterranean, but their ability to threaten Spain and Spanish possessions in the west was over.

To Philip and his advisers, the Turks represented a potential internal threat as well, since it was feared they might incite rebellion among his Muslim subjects. These

**Gravelines** (grahv-LEEN)

## READING SOURCES

# Secret Dispatches from the Venetian Ambassador in Spain

*Because it so heavily depended on its trading empire, Venice closely monitored developments at foreign courts. The Venetian ambassador at the Spanish court sent these reports back about the Spanish Armada. Note that the most sensitive material (here, in italics) was sent in code. What differences do you notice between the encoded and other dispatches? What seems to be the ambassador's attitude toward Philip and his invincible fleet? What can you learn from these dispatches about how fast and how accurately news traveled in sixteenth-century Europe?*

**April 30, 1588**

Day by day we are expecting news that the Armada has sailed. It has drawn down the river to Belem at the mouth of the port, three miles from Lisbon. The blessing of the standard [flag] was performed with great pomp and many salvos of artillery. . . . Here in all the churches they make constant prayers; and the king himself is on his knees two or three hours every day before the sacrament. Everyone hopes that the greater the difficulties, humanly speaking, the greater will be the favor of God.

**June 4, 1588**

The Armada set sail from Lisbon at length on the twenty-ninth of last month, a Sunday. . . . They are now waiting the news of its arrival at Corunna to embark more troops, and then to sail. I have from time to time reported the great preparations which have been made; but we here must expect news of its progress from other quarters now, unless the peace is effected in Flanders.

**July 12, 1588**

*The wiser wonder what can induce the king to insist, quite against his natural temper, that the Armada shall give battle to the English, who are known to be awaiting the attack with eager courage, and so they surmise that, over and above the belief that God will be on his side, two motives urge the king to this course; first, that he has some secret understandings which will fail if there is any delay; secondly, that these expenses of a million of gold a month cannot be supported for long, and so he has resolved to try his fortune. . . .*

**August 20, 1588**

Don Bernardino de Mendoza [the Spanish ambassador in France] announces from France, in letters of the second of August, that the Armada has given battle to the English, sunk some of their ships, won a great victory and passed on to join the duke of Parma; but the report is so confused, and that ambassador is so accustomed to deceive himself, that they are waiting confirmation of the news. . . .

**September 6, 1588**

*The bad news received in dispatches from the duke of Parma, and dated the tenth of August . . . pain the king and the court all the more that they were unexpected, and moreover quite contrary to the news sent by [Mendoza], who by three different couriers had confirmed . . . that [the Armada] had sunk many of the enemy and was on the point of effecting a junction with the Duke of Parma. . . . It is a blessing that the bad news did not reach Spain while the king was suffering from fever, for though His Majesty professes to allow no occurrence to disturb his equanimity, yet this war moves him in such a way as to prove clearly that on other occasions he was only acting and that now he is unable to do so, perhaps because this war is entirely conducted by himself alone and that it should not succeed brings to light all his anxiety.*

*Source:* James C. Davis, ed., *Pursuit of Power: Venetian Ambassadors' Reports on Turkey, France and Spain in the Age of Philip II, 1560–1600* (New York: Harper and Row, 1970), pp. 110–113.

 **For additional information on this topic, go to http://college.hmco.com.**

were the nominally Christian descendants of the Muslims of Granada who had been conquered by the Spanish in 1492. Called *moriscos*, they had been forced to convert to Christianity in 1504 or be expelled from Spain, but no serious effort had been made to teach them Christian beliefs in their own language (Arabic) and they had not been assimilated into Spanish society. Philip inaugurated a new wave of persecution and provoked a massive rebellion by the moriscos that began on Christmas Day in 1568. The revolt took two years to suppress. After it was crushed, the moriscos of Granada were forcibly exiled and dispersed farther north in Spain.

Philip's power in each of his Spanish kingdoms was limited by the traditional privileges of towns, nobility, and clergy. In Aragon, for example, he could raise revenues only by appealing to local assemblies, the cortes°. Philip made significant inroads into Aragonese independence by the end of his reign, however. Noble feuds and peasant rebellions in Aragon during the 1580s provided a pretext for sending in veteran troops from the Netherlands campaigns to establish firmer royal control. Philip was successful in the long run in Aragon, as he had not been in the Netherlands, because he used adequate force but tempered it afterward with constitutional changes that were cleverly moderate. He cemented the peace by appearing in Aragon in person, in the words of a contemporary, "like a rainbow at the end of a storm."[2]

In Castile, the arid kingdom in the center of the Iberian Peninsula, the king was able to levy taxes with greater ease but only because of concessions that gave nobles undisputed authority over their peasants. Philip established his permanent capital, Madrid, and his principal residence, the Escorial, there. The Spanish Empire became more and more Castilian as the reign progressed, with royal advisers and counselors increasingly drawn only from the Castilian elite. Yet the rural economy of Castile was stunted by the dual oppression of landholders and royal tax collectors.

Philip also invaded and annexed Portugal in 1580, temporarily unifying the Iberian Peninsula. The annexation was ensured by armed force but had been preceded by careful negotiation to guarantee that Philip's claim to the throne—through his mother—would find some support within the country. When Philip died in 1598, he was old and ill, a man for whom daily life had become a painful burden. His Armada had been crushed; the Netherlands had slipped through his fingers. Yet he had learned from his mistakes and had been more successful, by his own standards, in other regions that he ruled.

## ■ Spain in Decline, 1600–1648

Spain steadily lost ground economically and strategically after the turn of the century. Imports of silver declined. The American mines were exhausted, and the natives forced to work in them were decimated by European diseases and brutal treatment. Spain's economic health was further threatened by the very success of its colonies: local industries in the Americas began to produce goods formerly obtained from Spain. The increasing presence of English, French, and Dutch shipping in the Americas provided colonists with rival sources for the goods they needed. Often, these competitors could offer their goods more cheaply than Spaniards could for Spanish productivity was low and prices were high because of the inflationary effects of the influx of precious metals.

Spain renewed hostilities with the United Provinces in 1621, after the truce of 1609 had expired. Philip IV (r. 1621–1645) also aided his Habsburg cousins in the Thirty Years' War in the Holy Roman Empire (see page 523). Squeezed for troops and revenue for these commitments, other Spanish territories revolted. The uprisings reflected both economic distress and unresolved issues of regional autonomy. Castile bore the brunt of the financial support of the state. The chief minister to Philip IV, Gaspar de Guzmán, Count Olivares° (1587–1645), was an energetic Castilian aristocrat determined to distribute the burdens of government more equitably among the various regions of Spain. His policies provoked rebellions in Catalonia and Portugal.

In Catalonia, a province of the kingdom of Aragon, the revolt began as a popular uprising against the billeting of troops. At one point Catalan leaders invited French troops to defend them and solemnly transferred their loyalty to the French king in the hope that he would respect their autonomy. Spain resumed control only in 1652, after years of military struggle and promises to respect Catalan liberties.

In Portugal, a war of independence began in 1640, also launched by popular revolt. The Spanish government tried to restore order with troops under the command of a leading Portuguese prince, John, duke of Braganza. The duke, however, was the nearest living relative to the last king of Portugal, and he seized this opportunity to claim the crown of Portugal for himself. Although war dragged on until 1668, the Portuguese under John IV (r. 1640–1656) succeeded in winning independence from Spain.

---

**cortes** (core-TEZ)

**Olivares** (oh-lih-VAR-ez)

As a result of these uprisings, Count Olivares resigned in disgrace in 1643. In 1647 upheaval would shake Spain's Italian possessions of Sicily and Naples. By mid-century, Spain had lost its position as the pre-eminent state in Europe.

# RELIGIOUS AND POLITICAL CONFLICT IN FRANCE AND ENGLAND

N the second half of the sixteenth century, France was convulsed by civil war that had both religious and political causes. Though a temporary resolution was achieved by 1598, the kingdom was still divided by religion and by military and political challenges to royal authority. England, in contrast, was spared political and religious upheaval in the second half of the century, in part because of the talents and long life of its ruler, Elizabeth I. But in the seventeenth century, constitutional and religious dissent began to reinforce each other in new ways and dramatically threatened royal power.

## ■ The French Religious Wars, 1562–1598

Civil war wracked France from 1562 until 1598. As in the Netherlands, the conflicts in France had religious and political origins, and international ramifications. The French monarch, like Philip, was unable to monopolize military power. In 1559 the king of France, Henry II (r. 1547–1559), had concluded the Peace of Cateau-Cambrésis with Philip II, ending the Habsburg-Valois Wars, but had died in July of that year from wounds suffered at a tournament held to celebrate the new treaty. His death was a political disaster. Great noble families vied for influence over his 15-year-old son, Francis II (r. 1559–1560). The queen mother, Catherine de' Medici° (1519–1589), worked carefully and intelligently to balance the nobles' interests. She gained greater authority when, in late 1560, the sickly Francis died and was succeeded by his brother, Charles IX—a 10-year-old for whom Catherine was officially the regent. But keeping the conflicts among the great courtiers from boiling over into civil war proved impossible.

In France, as elsewhere, noble conflict invariably had a violent component. Noblemen carried swords and daggers and were accompanied by armed entourages. Although they relied on patronage and army commands from the Crown, the Crown depended on their services. Provincial landholdings, together with the royal offices they enjoyed, afforded enough resources to support private warfare, and the nobles assumed a right to wage it.

In addition, religious tension was rising throughout France. (Henry II had welcomed the 1559 treaty in part because he wanted to turn his attention to "heresy.") Public preaching by, and secret meetings of, Protestants (known as "Huguenots°" in France) were causing unrest in towns. At court, members of leading noble families—including the Bourbons, who were princes of royal blood—had converted to Protestantism and worshiped openly in their rooms in the palace. In 1561 Catherine convened a national religious council, known as the Colloquy of Poissy°, to reconcile the two faiths. When it failed, she chose provisional religious toleration as the only practical course and issued a limited edict of toleration in the name of the king in January 1562.

The edict led only to further unrest. Ignoring its restrictions, Protestants armed themselves, while townspeople of both faiths insulted and attacked one another at worship sites and religious festivals. In March 1562 the armed retainers of a Catholic duke killed a few dozen Protestants gathered in worship at Vassy° near one of the duke's estates. The killing, in bringing the military power of the nobility to bear on the broader problem of religious division, sparked the first of six civil wars. In some ways, the initial conflict was decisive. The Protestant army lost the principal pitched battle of the war in December 1562. This defeat checked the growth of the Protestant movement by reducing the appeal of the movement to nobles. The peace edict granted in 1563 curtailed the reach of the Huguenot movement; the limited rights granted to Protestants in the Crown's edict made it difficult for Protestants in towns—where the vast majority of them lived—to worship. But if the Protestants were not powerful enough to win, neither were they weak enough to be decisively beaten.

The turning point most obvious to contemporaries came a decade later. The Protestant faction was still represented at court by the Bourbon princes and by the very able and influential nobleman Gaspard de Coligny°, related to the Bourbons by marriage. Coligny was pressing the king for a war against Spain in order to aid Protestant rebels in the Netherlands. Opposed to entanglement in another war against Spain and alarmed by rumors of Huguenot armies massing outside Paris,

---

**de' Medici** (day MAY-di-chi)

**Huguenots** (HEW-guh-nots)   **Poissy** (pwa-SEE)   **Vassy** (vah-SEE)   **Gaspard de Coligny** (gas-PAR duh koh-leen-YEE)

**ᴥ READING SOURCES**

## A Justification for Rebellion Against the King

*This is an excerpt from* A Defense of Liberty Against Tyrants, *the most important work of Protestant political theory in France, published in 1579. It was probably written by Philippe Duplessis-Mornay, a Huguenot nobleman and confidant of Henry of Navarre who narrowly escaped death in the Saint Bartholomew's Day Massacre. In his tract, the author argues that a contract exists between the sovereign and his people. If the king violates that contract, he thereby becomes a tyrant, and his subjects are no longer obligated to obey him.*

[Must we] always obey God's commandments without any exception, and men's ever with limitation? As there are many princes in these days, calling themselves Christians, which arrogantly assume an unlimited power, over which God himself hath no command, and that they have no want of flatterers, which adore them as gods upon earth, many others also, which for fear or by constraint, either seem or else do believe, that princes ought to be obeyed in all things by all men. And withal, seeing the unhappiness of these times is such that there is nothing so firm, certain or pure which is not shaken, disgraced or polluted; I fear that whosoever shall . . . consider these things will confess this question to be not only most profitable, but also, the times considered, most necessary. . . . Princes exceed their bounds, not contenting themselves with that authority which the almighty and all good God hath given them, but seek to usurp that sovereignty, which he hath reserved to himself over all men, being not content to command the bodies and goods of their subjects . . . but assume

license to themselves to enforce the consciences, which appertains chiefly to Jesus Christ. . . .

Now for that we see that God invests kings into their kingdoms, almost in the same manner that vassals are invested into their [fiefs] by their sovereign, we must needs conclude that kings are the vassals of God, and deserve to be deprived of the benefit they receive from their lord if they commit a felony, in the same fashion as rebellious vassals are of their estates. These premises being allowed, this question may easily be resolved; for if God hold the place of the sovereign lord, and the king as vassal, who dare deny but that we must rather obey the sovereign than the vassal? If God commands one thing, and the king commands the contrary, what is that proud man that would term him a rebel who refuses to obey the king, when else he must disobey God?

*Source:* Harold J. Laski, ed., *A Defense of Liberty Against Tyrants* (Gloucester, Mass.: Peter Smith, 1963), pp. 65–66, 79.

---

Charles IX (r. 1560–1574) and his mother authorized royal guards to murder Coligny and other Protestant leaders on August 24, 1572—Saint Bartholomew's Day. Coligny's murder touched off a massacre of Protestants throughout Paris and, once news from Paris had spread, throughout the kingdom.

The Saint Bartholomew's Day Massacre revealed the degree to which religious differences had strained the fabric of community life. Neighbor murdered neighbor in an effort to rid the community of heretical pollution; bodies of the dead, including Coligny's, were torn apart,

mutilated. Gathered in the south of France, the remaining Huguenot forces vowed "never [to] trust those who have so often and so treacherously broken faith and the public peace."[3] Huguenot writers published tracts arguing that royal power was by nature limited and that rebellion was justified against tyrants who overstepped their legitimate authority. (See the box "Reading Sources: A Justification for Rebellion Against the King.")

Further war produced the inevitable truces and limited toleration, but many Catholics also renounced reconciliation. Some noblemen formed a Catholic league to fight in place of the weakened monarchy. Charles's brother, Henry III (r. 1574–1589), was another king of limited abilities. Middle-aged, Henry had no children. The heir to his throne was the Protestant Henry of Navarre, and the assumption of the throne by a Protestant was unimaginable to the zealous Catholic faction at court and to many ordinary Catholics. By the end of Henry III's reign, the king had almost no royal authority left to wield. He was forced to cooperate with first one of the warring parties and then with another. In December 1588 he resorted to murdering two courtiers who led the ultra-Catholic faction; in turn, he was murdered by a priest in early 1589.

Henry of Navarre, the Bourbon prince who became Henry IV (r. 1589–1610), had to fight for his throne. He faced Catholic armies now subsidized by Philip II of Spain, an extremist Catholic city government in Paris, and subjects who were tired of war but mainly Catholic, and could count on only meager support from Protestants abroad. Given these obstacles, the politically astute Henry agreed to convert to Catholicism.

After his conversion in 1593, the wars continued for a time, but after thirty years of civil strife, many of Henry's subjects believed that only rallying to the monarchy could save France from chaos. Nobles grew increasingly disposed, for both psychological and practical reasons, to cooperate with the Crown. Service to a successful king could be a source of glory, and Henry was personally esteemed because he was a talented general and brave, gregarious, and charming. The nobility forced the citizens of Paris and other cities to accept Henry's authority. The civil war period thus proved to be an impor-

**The Entry of Henry IV into Paris After the Religious Wars**    The king is depicted here as the magnanimous victor and the residents of the city as both submissive and grateful.    *(Louvre © R.M.N.)*

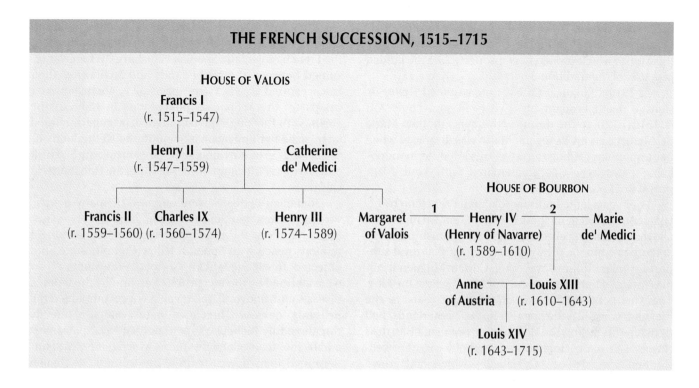

## THE FRENCH SUCCESSION, 1515–1715

HOUSE OF VALOIS

Francis I
(r. 1515–1547)

Henry II ——— Catherine
(r. 1547–1559)    de' Medici

HOUSE OF BOURBON

Francis II    Charles IX    Henry III    Margaret ——1—— Henry IV ——2—— Marie
(r. 1559–1560) (r. 1560–1574)  (r. 1574–1589)  of Valois    (Henry of Navarre)    de' Medici
                                                              (r. 1589–1610)

Anne ——— Louis XIII
of Austria    (r. 1610–1643)

Louis XIV
(r. 1643–1715)

tant phase in the incremental accommodation of the nobility to the power of the state.

In April 1598 Henry granted toleration for the Huguenot minority in a royal edict proclaimed in the city of Nantes°. The Edict of Nantes was primarily a repetition of provisions from the most generous edicts that had ended the various civil wars. Nobles were allowed to practice the Protestant faith on their estates; townspeople were granted more limited rights to worship in selected towns in each region. Protestants were guaranteed access to schools, hospitals, royal appointments, and separate judicial institutions to ensure fair treatment. They were also guaranteed rights of self-defense—specifically, the right to maintain garrisons in about two hundred towns. About half of these garrisons would be paid for by the Crown.

The problem was that the Edict of Nantes, like any royal edict, could be revoked by the king at any time. Moreover, the provision allowing Protestants to keep garrisoned towns reflected concessions to Protestant aristocrats who could support their followers by paid garrison duty. These concessions also meant that living peacefully amid religious diversity was not yet thought to be possible. Thus, although Henry IV ended the French religious wars, he had not solved the problem of religious and political division within France.

### ■ The Consolidation of Royal Authority in France, 1598–1643

During Henry IV's reign, France recovered from the long years of civil war. Population and productivity began to grow; the Crown encouraged internal improvements to facilitate commerce. Henry's chief minister, Maximilien de Béthune°, duke of Sully° (1560–1641), increased royal revenue by nibbling away at traditional local self-government and control of taxation. He succeeded in creating a budget surplus and in extending mechanisms of centralized government.

Yet Henry's regime was stable only in comparison with the preceding years of civil war. The power of the great nobility had not been definitively broken. Moreover, the king had agreed to a provision, known as the *paulette* (named for the functionary who first administered it), that allowed royal officeholders not merely to own their offices but also to pass on those offices to their heirs in return for the payment of an annual fee. Primarily a device to raise revenue after decades of civil war, the paulette also helped cement the loyalty of royal bureaucrats at a critical time, particularly that of the royal judges of the supreme law court, the Parlement of Paris, who had recently agreed to register the Edict of Nantes

---

**Nantes** (NAHNT)

**Béthune** (bay-TOON)    **Sully** (soo-LEE)

only under duress. However, the paulette made royal officeholders largely immune from royal control since their posts were now, in effect, property, like the landed property of the traditional nobility.

In 1610 a fanatical Catholic assassinated Henry IV. Henry's death brought his 9-year-old son, Louis XIII (r. 1610–1643), to the throne with Louis's mother, Marie de' Medici, serving as regent. Marie was disgraced when her unpopular leading minister—resented for monopolizing patronage—was assassinated with Louis's approval in 1617.

Four years later, Louis faced a major rebellion by his Huguenot subjects in southwestern France. Huguenots felt that Louis's recent marriage to a Spanish princess, and other ominous royal policies, meant that royal support for toleration was wavering. Certain Huguenot nobles initiated fighting as a show of force against the king. The wars persisted, on and off, for eight years, as the French troops, like the Spanish in the Netherlands, had difficulty breeching the defenses of even small fortress towns. The main Huguenot stronghold was the well-fortified port city of La Rochelle—which had grown wealthy from European and overseas trade. Not until the king took the city, after a siege lasting more than a year and costing thousands of lives, did the Protestants accept a peace on royal terms.

The Peace of Alais° (1629) reaffirmed the policy of religious toleration but rescinded the Protestants' military and political privileges. It was a political triumph for the Crown because it deprived French Protestants of the means for further rebellion while reinforcing their dependence on the Crown for religious toleration. Most of the remaining great noble leaders began to convert to Catholicism.

The Peace of Alais was also a personal triumph for the king's leading minister, who crafted the treaty and who had directed the bloody siege that made it possible: Armand-Jean du Plessis° (1585–1642), Cardinal Richelieu°. From a provincial noble family, Richelieu had risen in the service of the queen mother. He was admired and feared for his skill in the political game of seeking and bestowing patronage—a crucial skill in an age when elites received offices and honors through carefully cultivated relationships at court. His control of many lucrative church posts gave him the resources to build up a large network of clients. He and the king—whose sensitive temperament Richelieu handled adeptly—formed a lasting partnership that had a decisive impact not only on French policy but also on the entire shape of the French state.

Richelieu favored an aggressive foreign policy to counter what he believed still to be the greatest threat to the French crown: the Spanish Habsburgs. When war resumed between the Netherlands and Spain after their truce expired in 1621 (see page 525), Richelieu sent troops to attack Spanish possessions in Italy. In the 1630s, with the king's full confidence, he superintended large-scale fighting against Spain in the Netherlands itself, as well as in Italy, and he began subsidizing Swedish and German Protestant armies fighting the Habsburgs in Germany.

Richelieu's policies were opposed by many people, who saw taxes double, then triple, in just a few years. Many courtiers and provincial elites favored keeping a tenuous peace with Spain, a fellow Catholic state, and objected to alliances with German Protestants. They were alarmed by the increasing taxes and by the famine, disease, and, above all, the revolts that accompanied the peasants' distress. Their own status was also directly threatened by Richelieu's monopoly of royal patronage and by his creation of new offices, which diluted and undermined their power. In 1632, for example, Richelieu created the office of *intendant*. Intendants had wide powers for defense and administration in the provinces that overrode the established bureaucracy.

By 1640 Richelieu's ambitious foreign policy seemed to be bearing fruit. The French had won territory along their northern and eastern borders by their successes against Habsburg forces. But when Richelieu and Louis XIII died within five months of each other, in December 1642 and May 1643, Richelieu's legacy was tested. Louis XIII was succeeded by his 5-year-old son, and the warrior nobility as well as royal bureaucrats would waste little time before challenging the Crown's new authority.

## ■ Precarious Stability in England: The Reign of Elizabeth I, 1558–1603

England experienced no civil wars during the second half of the sixteenth century, but religious dissent challenged the stability of the monarchy. In Elizabeth I (r. 1558–1603), England—in stark contrast to France—possessed an able and long-lived ruler. Elizabeth was well educated in the humanistic tradition and was already an adroit politician at the age of 25, when she acceded to the throne at the death of her Catholic half-sister, Mary Tudor (r. 1553–1558).

Elizabeth faced the urgent problem of reaching a policy of consensus in religious matters. Her father, Henry VIII (r. 1509–1547), had broken away from the Catholic Church for political reasons but had retained many Catholic doctrines and practices. A Calvinist-

---

**Alais** (ah-LAY)    **du Plessis** (doo pleh-SEE)
**Richelieu** (RISH-el-yeuh)

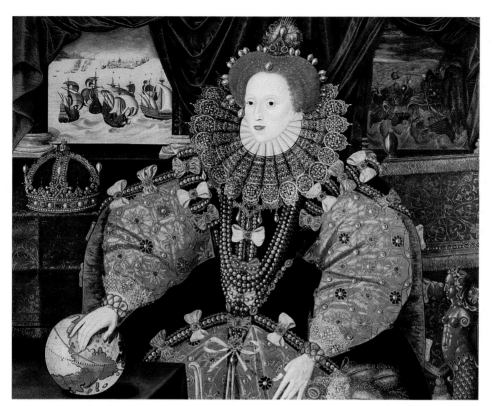

**Elizabeth I: The Armada Portrait**
Both serene and resolute, Elizabeth is flanked by "before" and "after" glimpses of the Spanish fleet; her hand rests on the globe in a gesture of dominion that also memorializes the circumnavigation of the globe by her famous captain, Sir Francis Drake, some years before.
*(By kind permission of Marquess of Tavistock and Trustees of Bedford Estate)*

inspired Protestantism had been prescribed for the Church of England by the advisers of Henry's successor, Elizabeth's young half-brother, Edward VI (r. 1547–1553). True Catholicism, such as Mary had tried to reimpose, was out of the question. The Roman Church had never recognized Henry VIII's self-made divorce and thus regarded Elizabeth as a bastard with no right to the throne.

Elizabeth adopted a cleverly moderate solution and used force, where necessary, to maintain it. In 1559 Parliament passed a new Act of Supremacy, which restored the monarch as head of the Church of England. Elizabeth dealt with opposition to the act by arresting bishops and lords whose votes would have blocked its passage by Parliament. Elizabeth and most of her ministers, moderate realists as was she, were willing to accept some flexibility for personal belief. For example, the official prayer book in use in Edward's day was revised to include elements of both traditional and radical interpretations of communion. But church liturgy, clerical vestments, and, above all, the hierarchical structure of the clergy closely resembled Catholic practices. The Act of Uniformity required all worship to be conducted according to the new prayer book. Yet although uniformity was required in worship, Elizabeth was careful, in her words, not to "shine beacons into her subjects' souls."

Catholicism continued to be practiced, especially by otherwise loyal nobility and gentry in the north of England who worshiped privately on their estates. But priests returning from exile beginning in the 1570s, most newly imbued with the proselytizing zeal of the Counter-Reformation (the Catholic response to the Protestant Reformation), practiced it more visibly, and were zealously prosecuted for their boldness. In the last twenty years of Elizabeth's reign, approximately 180 Catholics were executed for treason, two-thirds of them priests. (By 1585, being a Catholic priest in itself was a crime.)

In the long run, the greater threat to the English crown came from the most radical Protestants in the realm, known (by their enemies initially) as Puritans. Puritanism was a broad movement for reform of church practice along familiar Protestant lines: emphasis on Bible reading, preaching, private scrutiny of conscience, and a de-emphasis on institutional ritual and clerical authority. Most Puritans had accepted Elizabeth's religious compromise for practical reasons but grew increasingly alienated by her insistence on clerical authority and her refusal to change any elements of the original religious settlement. A significant Presbyterian underground movement began to form among them.

Presbyterians wanted to dismantle the episcopacy, the hierarchy of priests and bishops, and govern the church instead with councils, called "presbyteries," that included lay members of the congregation. Laws were passed late in the queen's reign to enable the Crown more easily to prosecute, and even to force into exile, anyone who attended "nonconformist" (non-Anglican) services.

The greatest challenge Elizabeth faced from Puritans came in Parliament, where they were well represented by many literate gentry. Parliament met only when called by the monarch, and in theory members could merely voice opinions and complaints. Initiating legislation and prescribing policy were beyond its purview. However, only Parliament could vote taxes. Further, since it had in effect helped constitute royal authority by means of the two Acts of Supremacy, Parliament's supposedly consultative role had been expanded by the monarchy itself. During Elizabeth's reign, Puritans capitalized on Parliament's enlarged scope, using meetings to press for further religious reform. In 1586 they went so far as to introduce bills calling for an end to the episcopacy and the Anglican prayer book. Elizabeth had to resort to imprisoning one Puritan leader to end debate on the issue and on Parliament's right to address it.

In Elizabeth's reign, efforts at English expansion in the New World began, in the form of unsuccessful attempts at colonization and successful raids on Spanish possessions. However, the main focus of her foreign policy remained Europe itself. Elizabeth, like all her forebears, felt her interests tightly linked to the independence of the Netherlands, whose towns were a major outlet for English wool. Philip II's aggressive policy in the Netherlands increasingly alarmed her, especially in view of France's weakness. She began to send small sums of money to the rebels and allowed their ships access to southern English ports, from which they could raid Spanish-held towns on the Netherlands' coast. In 1585, in the wake of the duke of Parma's successes against the rebellions, she committed troops to help the rebels.

Her decision was a reaction not only to the threat of a single continental power dominating the Netherlands but also to the threat of Catholicism. From 1579 to 1583, the Spanish had helped the Irish fight English domination and were involved in several plots to replace Elizabeth with her Catholic cousin, Mary, Queen of Scots. These threats occurred as the return of Catholic exiles to England peaked. The victory over the Spanish Armada in 1588 was quite rightly celebrated for it ended any Catholic threat to Elizabeth's rule.

The success against the Armada has tended to overshadow other aspects of Elizabeth's foreign policy, particularly with regard to Ireland. Since the twelfth century, an Anglo-Irish state dominated by great princely families had been loosely supervised from England, but most of Ireland remained under the control of Gaelic chieftains. Just as Charles V and Philip II attempted to tighten their governing mechanisms in the Netherlands, so in England did Henry VIII's minister, Thomas Cromwell, streamline control of outlying areas such as Wales and Anglo-Ireland. Cromwell proposed that the whole of Ireland be brought under English control partly by the established mechanism of feudal ties: the Irish chieftains were to pay homage as vassals to the king of England.

Under Elizabeth, this legalistic approach gave way to virtual conquest. Elizabeth's governor, Sir Henry Sidney, appointed in 1565, inaugurated a policy whereby Gaelic lords, by means of various technicalities, could be entirely dispossessed of their lands. Any Englishman capable of raising a private force could help enforce these dispossessions and settle his conquered lands as he saw fit. This policy provoked stiff Irish resistance, which was viewed as rebellion and provided the rationale for further military action, more confiscations of land, and more new English settlers. Eventually, the Irish, with Spanish assistance, mounted a major rebellion, consciously Catholic and aimed against the "heretic" queen. The rebellion gave the English an excuse for brutal suppression and massive transfers of land to English control. The political domination of the Irish was complete with the defeat, in 1601, of the Gaelic chieftain Hugh O'Neill, lord of Tyrone, who had controlled most of the northern quarter of the island. Although the English were unable to impose Protestantism on the conquered Irish, to Elizabeth and her English subjects the conquests in Ireland seemed as significant as the victory over the Spanish Armada.

The English enjoyed relative peace at home during Elizabeth's reign. However, her reign ended on a note of strain. The foreign involvements, particularly in Ireland, had been very expensive. Taxation granted by Parliament more than doubled during her reign, and local taxes further burdened the people. Price inflation related to government spending, social problems caused by returned unemployed soldiers, and a series of bad harvests heightened popular resentment against taxation. Despite her achievements, therefore, Elizabeth passed two problems on to her successors: unresolved religious tensions and financial instability. Elizabeth's successors would also find in Parliament an increasing focus of opposition to their policies.

## ■ Rising Tensions in England, 1603–1642

In 1603 Queen Elizabeth died and James VI of Scotland, the Protestant son of Mary, Queen of Scots, ascended to the English throne as James I (r. 1603–1625). Religious tensions between Anglicans and Puritans were temporarily quieted under James because of a plot, in 1605, by Catholic dissenters. The Gunpowder Plot, as it was called, was a conspiracy to blow up the palace housing both king and Parliament at Westminster. Protestants of all stripes once again focused not on their differences but on their common enemy, Catholicism.

Financial problems were James's most pressing concern. Court life became more elaborate and an increasing drain on the monarchy's resources. James's extravagance was partly to blame for his financial problems, but so were pressures for patronage from courtiers. Added to the debts left from the Irish conflicts and wars with Spain were new military expenses as James helped defend the claims of his daughter and her husband, a German prince, to rule Bohemia (see page 525).

To raise revenue without Parliament's consent, James relied on sources of income that the Crown had enjoyed since medieval times: customs duties, wardship (the right to manage and liberally borrow from the estates of minor nobles), and the sale of monopolies, which conveyed the right to be sole agent for a particular kind of goods. To rebuild his treasury, James increased the number of monopolies for sale and even created a new noble title—baronet—which he sold to socially ambitious commoners.

The monopolies were widely resented. Merchants objected to the arbitrary restriction of production and trade; common people found that they could no longer afford certain ordinary commodities, such as soap. Resentments among the nobility were sharpened, and general criticism of the court escalated, as James indulged in extreme favoritism of certain courtiers, including the corrupt George Villiers° (1592–1628), duke of Buckingham, who served as the king's first minister.

When James summoned Parliament to ask for funds in 1621, Parliament used the occasion to protest court corruption and the king's financial measures. The members revived the medieval procedure of impeachment and removed two royal ministers from office. In 1624, still faced with expensive commitments to Protestants abroad and in failing health, James again called Parliament, which voted new taxes but also openly debated the wisdom of the king's foreign policy.

---

**Villiers** (VIL-yerz)

**Criticism of Monopolies**    Holders of royally granted monopolies were bitterly resented by English consumers and tradespeople alike, as this contemporary print reveals. The greedy beast pictured here controls even ordinary commodities such as pins, soap, and butter. *(Courtesy of the Trustees of the British Museum)*

Tensions between Crown and Parliament increased under James's son, Charles I (r. 1625–1649). One reason was the growing financial strain of foreign policy as well as the policies themselves. Charles declared war on Spain and supported the Huguenot rebels in France. Many wealthy merchants opposed this aggressive foreign policy because it disrupted trade. In 1626 Parliament was dissolved without granting any monies in order to stifle its objections to royal policies. Instead, Charles levied a forced loan and did not hesitate to imprison gentry who refused to lend their money to the government.

Above all, Charles's religious policies were a source of controversy. Charles was personally inclined toward "high church" practices: an emphasis on ceremony and sacrament reminiscent of Catholic ritual. He also was a believer in Arminianism, a school of thought that rejected the Calvinist notion that God's grace cannot be earned, and hence emphasized the importance of the sacraments and the authority of the clergy. Charles's attempt to fashion the Church of England into an instrument that would reflect and justify royal claims to power put him on a collision course with gentry and aristocrats who leaned toward Puritanism.

Charles's views were supported by William Laud° (1573–1645), archbishop of Canterbury from 1633 and thus leader of the Church of England. He tried to impose changes in worship, spread Arminian ideas, and censor opposing views. He also challenged the redistribution of church property, which had occurred in the Reformation of the sixteenth century, and thereby alienated the gentry on economic as well as religious grounds.

Charles's style of rule worsened religious, political, and economic tensions. Cold and intensely private, he did not inspire confidence or have the charm or the political skills to disarm his opponents. His court was ruled by formal protocol, and access to the king himself was highly restricted—a serious problem in an age when proximity to the monarch was a guarantee of political power.

Revenue and religion dominated debate in the Parliament of 1628–1629, which Charles had called, once again, to get funds for his foreign wars. In 1628 the members of Parliament presented the king with a document called the Petition of Right, which protested his financial policies as well as arbitrary imprisonment. (Seventeen members of Parliament had been imprisoned for refusing loans to the Crown.) Though couched conservatively as a restatement of customary practice, the petition in fact claimed a tradition of expanded parliamentary participation in government. Charles dissolved the Parliament in March 1629, having decided that the money he might extract was not worth the risk.

For eleven years, Charles ruled without Parliament. When he was forced by necessity to summon it again, in 1640, the kingdom was in crisis. Royal finances were in desperate straits even though Charles had pressed collection of revenues far beyond traditional bounds. In 1634, for example, he had revived annual collection of "ship money"—a medieval tax levied on coastal districts to help support the navy during war. England, however, was not at war at that time, and the tax was levied not only on seaports but on inland areas, too.

The immediate crisis in 1640—and the reason for Charles's desperate need for money—was a rebellion in Scotland. Like Philip II in the Netherlands, Charles tried to rule in Scotland through a small council of men who did not represent the local elite. Worse, he also tried to

force his "high church" practices on the Scots. The Scottish Church had been more dramatically reshaped during the Reformation and now was largely Presbyterian in structure. The result of Charles's politics was riots—and rebellion. Unable to suppress the revolt in a first campaign in 1639, Charles was forced to summon Parliament to obtain funds to raise a more effective army.

But the Parliament that assembled in the spring of 1640 provided no help. Instead, members questioned the war with the Scots and other royal policies. Charles's political skills were far too limited for him to re-establish a workable relationship with Parliament under the circumstances. Charles dissolved this body, which is now known as the "Short Parliament," after just three weeks. Even more stinging than Charles's dissolution of the Parliament was the lack of respect he had shown the members: a number of them were harassed or arrested. Mistrust fomented by the eleven years in which Charles had ruled without Parliament thus increased.

Another humiliating and decisive defeat at the hands of the Scots later in 1640 made summoning another Parliament imperative. Members of the "Long Parliament" (it sat from 1640 to 1653) took full advantage of the king's predicament. Charles was forced to agree not to dissolve or adjourn Parliament without the members' consent and to summon Parliament at least every three years. Parliament abolished many of his unorthodox and traditional sources of revenue and impeached and removed from office his leading ministers, including Archbishop Laud. The royal commander deemed responsible for the Scottish fiasco, Thomas Wentworth, earl of Strafford, was executed without trial in May 1641.

The execution of Strafford shocked many aristocrats in the House of Lords (the upper house of Parliament) as well as some moderate members of the House of Commons. Meanwhile, Parliament began debating the perennially thorny religious question. A bare majority of members favored abolition of Anglican bishops as a first step in thoroughgoing religious reform. Working people in London, kept apprised of the issues by the regular publication of parliamentary debates, demonstrated in support of that majority. Moderate members of Parliament, in contrast, favored checking the king's power but not upsetting the Elizabethan religious compromise.

An event that unified public and parliamentary opinion at a crucial time—a revolt against English rule in Ireland in October 1641—temporarily eclipsed these divisions and once again focused suspicion on the king. The broad consensus of anti-Catholicism once again became the temporary driving force in politics. Fearing that Charles would use Irish soldiers against his English

---

**Laud** (LAWD)

subjects, Parliament demanded that it have control of the army to put down the rebellion. In November, the Puritan majority introduced a document known as the "Grand Remonstrance," an appeal to the people and a long catalog of parliamentary grievances against the king. It was passed by a narrow margin, further setting public opinion in London against Charles. The king's remaining support in Parliament eroded in January 1642 when he attempted to arrest five leading members on charges of treason. The five escaped and the stage was set for wider violence. The king withdrew from London, unsure he could defend himself there, and began to raise an army. In mid-1642 the kingdom stood at the brink of civil war.

## THE HOLY ROMAN EMPIRE AND THE THIRTY YEARS' WAR, 1555–1648

 HE Holy Roman Empire enjoyed a period of comparative quiet after the Peace of Augsburg halted religious and political wars in 1555. The 1555 agreement, which permitted rulers of the various states within the empire to impose either Catholicism or Lutheranism in their lands, proved to be a workable solution, for a time, to the problem of religious division. By the early seventeenth century, however, fresh causes of instability brought about renewed fighting. One factor was the rise of Calvinism, for which no provision had been necessary in 1555. Especially destabilizing was the drive by the Austrian Habsburgs to reverse the successes of Protestantism both in their own lands and in the empire at large and to solidify their control of their diverse personal territories.

In the Thirty Years' War (1618–1648), as it is now called, we can see the continuation of conflicts from the sixteenth century—religious tensions, regionalism versus centralizing forces, dynastic and strategic rivalries between rulers. The war was particularly destructive because of the size of the armies and the degree to which army commanders evaded control by the states for which they fought. As a result of the war, the empire was eclipsed as a political unit by the regional powers that composed it.

### ■ Peace Through Diversity, 1556–ca. 1618

The Austrian Habsburgs ruled over a diverse group of territories in the Holy Roman Empire, as well as northwestern Hungary (see Map 15.3). On his abdication in 1556, Emperor Charles V had granted Habsburg lands in central Europe to his brother Ferdinand (see the chart on page 508), who had long been the actual ruler there in Charles's stead. On Charles's death in 1558, Ferdinand was duly crowned emperor.

Though largely contiguous, Ferdinand's territories comprised independent duchies and kingdoms, each with its own institutional structure, and included speakers of Italian, German, and Czech, plus a few other languages. The non-German lands of Bohemia (the core of the modern Czech Republic) and Hungary had been distinct kingdoms since the High Middle Ages. Both states bestowed their crowns by election and had chosen Ferdinand, the first Habsburg to rule them, in separate elections in the 1520s and 1530s. Most of Hungary was now under Ottoman domination, but Bohemia, with its rich capital, Prague, was a wealthy center of population and culture.

Unlike the Netherlands, these linguistically and culturally diverse lands were still governed by highly decentralized institutions. Moreover, unlike their Spanish cousins, the Austrian Habsburgs made no attempt to impose religious uniformity in this period. Ferdinand was firmly Catholic but tolerant of reform efforts within the church, including clerical marriage and allowing the laity to receive both wine and bread at communion. Both he and his son, Maximilian II (r. 1564–1576), believed an eventual reunion of the Catholic and Protestant faiths might be possible. During his reign, Maximilian worked to keep religious peace in the empire as a whole and granted limited rights of worship to Protestant subjects within his ancestral lands (separate territories more or less equivalent to modern Austria in extent). Catholicism and many strands of Protestantism flourished side by side in Maximilian's domain, above all in Hungary and Bohemia.

Maximilian's son, Rudolf II (r. 1576–1612), shared the religious style of his father and grandfather. He was an energetic patron of the arts and sponsored the work of scientists. During his reign, as under Maximilian, education, printing, and humanistic intellectual life flourished. Yet Rudolf, a weak leader politically, was challenged for control of the Habsburg lands and the empire itself by his brother and ambitious cousins. Political rivalries as well as renewed religious conflict would soon end the period of relative peace in Habsburg lands and in the empire.

The resurgence of Catholicism in the wake of the Council of Trent (1545–1563) had begun to shift the religious balance. Members of the Jesuit order arrived in Habsburg lands in the reign of Maximilian. Tough-minded and well trained, they established Catholic

**Map 15.3   Territories of the Austrian Habsburgs, ca. 1556** In addition to the lands constituting modern Austria, Austrian Habsburg lands comprised the Tyrol (modern west Austria and northeast Italy), Carniola (modern Slovenia), part of Croatia, Bohemia (the core of the modern Czech Republic and southern Poland), and Hungary. Most of Hungary had been in Ottoman hands since the Battle of Mohács in 1526.

schools and became confessors and preachers to the upper classes. Self-confident Catholicism emerged as one form of cultural identity among the German-speaking ruling classes and thus as a religious impetus to further political consolidation of all the Habsburg territories.

Resurgent Catholicism was evident, too, in the empire as a whole, where certain princes were confident they might now eliminate Protestantism, as their ancestors had failed to do. In the face of this challenge, certain Protestant princes formed a defensive pact known as the Evangelical Union in 1608; in response, Catholic princes formed an alliance, the Holy League, the next year. A major war between the two alliances over a disputed territory was narrowly averted the following year. Like the

English under Elizabeth, Habsburg subjects and peoples in the empire had enjoyed a period of calm in political and religious matters. Now, as in England, the stage was set for conflict of both kinds.

### ■ The Thirty Years' War, 1618–1648

The Thirty Years' War was touched off in 1618 by a revolt against Habsburg rule in the kingdom of Bohemia. Bohemia was populous and prosperous; Rudolf II had made its bustling capital, Prague, his imperial capital. The powerful and diverse Protestant community had wrested formal recognition of its rights to worship from Rudolf and from his younger brother, Matthias (r. 1612–1618).

Matthias was quickly succeeded by his cousin Ferdinand II (r. 1619–1637), who was the ideal Counter-Reformation prince, and unlikely to honor these agreements. Educated by the Jesuits, he sincerely believed that reimposing Catholicism was his Christian duty. He once stated that he would "sooner beg than rule over heretics";[4] he had virtually eliminated Protestantism, by persuasion as well as by compulsion, in the small duchy in southern Austria he had governed before assuming the throne.

Ferdinand would not tolerate the political independence of nobles and towns in Bohemia or the religious pluralism that independence defended. As Philip II had done in the Netherlands, Ferdinand appointed a regency council to govern in his name that enforced unpopular policies: the right to build new Protestant churches was denied; Bohemian crown lands were given to the Catholic Church; non-Catholics were barred from serving in government.

On May 23, 1618, delegates to a Protestant assembly that had unsuccessfully petitioned Ferdinand to end his violations of earlier guarantees marched to the palace in Prague where the hated royal officials met. After a confrontation over their demands, the delegates "tried" the officials on the spot for treason and, literally, threw them out the palace window. The incident became known as the Defenestration of Prague (from the Latin *fenestra*, "window"). (The officials' lives were saved only because they fell into a pile of refuse in the moat.) The rebels proceeded to set up their own government.

This upstart Bohemian government officially deposed Ferdinand and elected a new king in 1619: a Protestant, Frederick, elector of the Palatinate, and a Calvinist prince. His selection had implications for the empire as a whole because his territories in west central Germany (called the Lower Palatinate and the Upper Palatinate) conveyed the right to be one of the seven electors who chose the emperor.

Emboldened by these events, Protestant subjects in other Habsburg lands asked for guarantees of freedom of worship similar to those enjoyed by Protestants in Bohemia. Other princes saw their chance to make political gains. For example, rival claimants to Habsburg rule in Hungary took up arms against Ferdinand.

The revolt in Bohemia set off a wider war because foreign rulers also felt their interests to be involved. The English king, James I, supported Frederick because Frederick was married to his daughter. Spain's supply routes north from Italy to the Netherlands passed next to Frederick's lands in western Germany. France's first interest was its rivalry with Spain; thus, France kept its eye on the border principalities that were strategically important to Spain. In addition, France desired to keep Protestant as well as Catholic princes within the empire strong enough to thwart Austrian Habsburg ambitions. Thus, from the outset, the war was a conflict not only over the Habsburgs' power in their own lands but also over the balance of religious and political power in the empire and in Europe (see Map 15.4).

Ferdinand secured aid from the Catholic duke of Bavaria and from his cousin, King Philip III of Spain, by promising them Frederick's lands in the Palatinate. By the fall of 1620 a Catholic army was closing in on Bohemia. On November 8, on a hillside near Prague, the Catholic force faced a Bohemian army that had received little aid from Protestant allies. The Battle of White Mountain was a complete Catholic victory.

Despite the rout, fighting did not cease but became more widespread. The truce between Spain and the Netherlands, established in 1609, expired in 1621, and the nearby Lower Palatinate, now in Spanish hands, offered a staging point for Spanish forces and thus threatened the peace in that corner of the empire. Claiming to be a Protestant champion, the Protestant king of Denmark, Christian IV (r. 1588–1648), who was also duke of Holstein in northern Germany, sought to conquer additional German territory. His goals were to gain greater control over profitable German Baltic seaports and to defend himself against any Catholic attempt to seize northern German territory. Christian received little help from fellow Protestants, however. The Dutch were busy with Spain, the English were wary of fighting after Frederick's defeat, and Denmark's regional rivals, the Swedish, were uninterested in furthering Danish ambitions in the Baltic.

The confusing blend of politics and religion that motivated the Protestant rulers was also evident on the Catholic side. When imperial forces defeated Christian's armies in 1626, Catholic princes became alarmed at the possibility of greater imperial power in northern Germany. Led by the duke of Bavaria, they arranged a truce that led to Denmark's withdrawal from the fighting on relatively generous terms. At the same time, Protestants outside Bohemia learned some of the consequences of imperial victory, and took up arms. As his armies defeated Christian, Ferdinand issued new edicts that in effect voided the religious settlement in place since 1555. His victorious armies brutally enforced his edicts wherever they passed.

Christian's rival, Gustav Adolf, king of Sweden (r. 1611–1632), now assumed the role of Protestant leader. Gustav Adolf hoped to gain territory along the Baltic

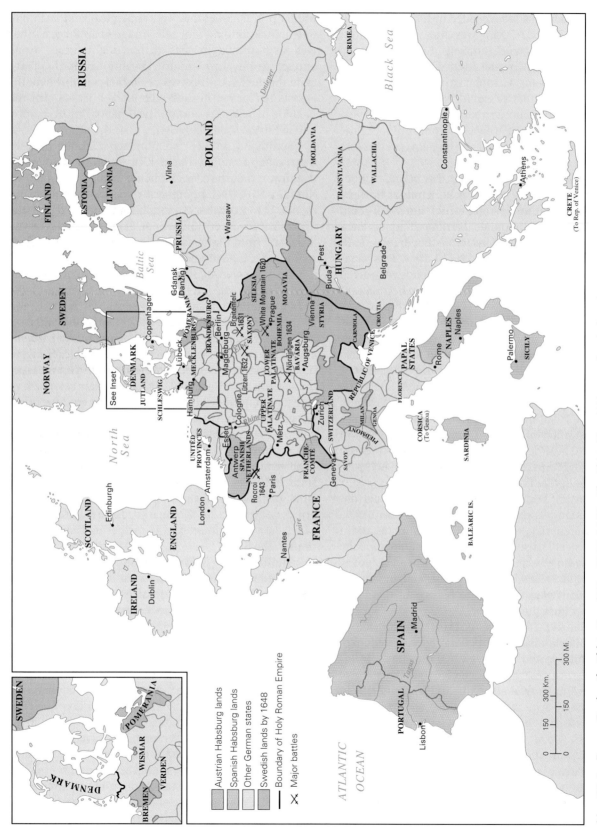

**Map 15.4  Europe During the Thirty Years' War, 1618–1648**  The Thirty Years' War was fought largely within the borders of the Holy Roman Empire. It was the result of conflicts within the empire as well as the meddling of neighbors for their own strategic advantages.

seacoast, but personal aggrandizement also was one of his goals. An innovative military leader, his campaigns were capped by a victory over an imperial army at Breitenfeld° in Saxony in 1631. After Gustav Adolf was killed in battle in 1632, however, the tide turned in the favor of Ferdinand's forces. A decisive imperial victory over a combined Swedish and German Protestant army, at Nördlingen° in 1634, led to a general peace treaty favorable to the Catholics: the Peace of Prague (1635).

The Peace of Prague brought only a temporary peace, however, because Ferdinand died shortly thereafter, and because French involvement increased now that other anti-Habsburg forces had been eclipsed. France tried to seize imperial territory along its own eastern border and generously subsidized continued fighting within the empire by channeling monies to Protestant princes and mercenaries there. Fighting dragged on. By the end of the Thirty Years' War, order had disintegrated so completely in the wake of the marauding armies that both staunchly Catholic rulers and firmly Protestant ones allied with religious enemies to safeguard their states.

A comprehensive peace treaty became possible when France withdrew its sponsorship of the fighting in order to concentrate on its conflict with Spain. The French wanted only a workable balance of power in the empire, which was achieved once they and their allies convincingly defeated imperial forces in 1645. More urgent to the French was the continued rivalry with the Spanish Habsburgs for control of territory along France's eastern and northern borders and in Italy. A defeat by France in the Spanish Netherlands in 1643 had convinced Spain to concentrate on that rivalry too, and fighting between them continued separately until 1659. Negotiations for peace had begun in 1643 among warweary states of the empire and resulted in a group of agreements known as the Peace of Westphalia° in 1648.

## ■ The Effects of the War

The Thirty Years' War ruined the economy and decimated the population in many parts of the empire and had long-term political consequences for the empire as a whole. One reason for the war's devastation was a novel application of firepower to warfare that increased both the size of armies and their deadly force in battle. This was the use of volley fire, the arrangement of foot soldiers in parallel lines so that one line of men could fire

while another reloaded. This tactic, pioneered in the Netherlands around the turn of the century, was further refined by Gustav Adolf of Sweden. Gustav Adolf amassed large numbers of troops and increased the rate of fire so that a virtually continuous barrage was maintained; he also used maneuverable field artillery to protect the massed infantry from cavalry charges.

Following Gustav Adolf's lead, armies of all the major states adopted these tactics. Despite these new offensive tactics, defensive expertise—as in holding fortresses—remained important, and pitched battles, such as at Nördlingen in 1634, still tended to be part of sieges. The costs in resources and human life of this kind of warfare reached unheard-of dimensions. Popular printed literature and court drama both condemned the horrors of the war.

Where fighting had been concentrated, as in parts of Saxony, between a third and half of the inhabitants of rural villages and major towns may have disappeared. Many starved, were caught in the fighting, or were killed by marauding soldiers. The most notorious atrocity occurred in the aftermath of the siege of Magdeburg° in 1631. After the city surrendered to besieging Catholic forces, long-deprived soldiers ate and drank themselves into a frenzy, raped and killed indiscriminately, and set fires that destroyed the town. Some victims of war migrated to other regions in search of peaceful conditions and work. Some joined the armies in order to survive. Others formed armed bands to fight off the soldiers or to steal back enough goods to live on.

Compounding these effects of war were the actions of armies hired by enterprising mercenary generals for whom loyalty to the princes who paid them took a back seat to personal advancement. They contracted to provide, supply, and lead troops and thus were more willing than the princes would have been to allow troops to live "economically" on plunder. States thus managed to field large armies but had not yet evolved the mechanisms fully to fund, and thus control, them.

The Peace of Westphalia, which ended fighting in the empire, was one of the most important outcomes of the war. The various treaties composing the peace effectively put an end to religious war in the empire. Calvinism was recognized as a tolerated religion. The requirement that all subjects must follow their rulers' faith was retained, but some leeway was allowed for those who now found themselves under new rulers.

In political matters, the treaties reflected some of the recent successes of the Swedish by granting them Baltic

---

**Breitenfeld** (BRIGHT-un-feld)   **Nördlingen** (NERD-ling-un)
**Westphalia** (west-FAIL-yuh)

**Magdeburg** (MAHG-duh-boorg)

coast territory. France gained the important towns of Metz, Toul, and Verdun on its eastern border. Spain formally recognized the independence of the Netherlands.

The most important political outcome of the peace was a new balance of power in the empire. Most of the major Catholic and Protestant rulers extended their territories at the expense of smaller principalities and cities. The son of Frederick, king of Bohemia, received back the smaller of the two Palatine territories that his father had held. The Upper Palatinate—as well as the right to be a new elector of the emperor—was given to the powerful duke of Bavaria. The principalities within the empire were acknowledged, in the peace, to be virtually autonomous, both from the emperor and from one another. In addition, the constitution of the empire was changed to make it very difficult for one prince or a group of princes to disrupt the peace in their own interests. As a result, the agreements at Westphalia were the beginning of one hundred years of peace within the Holy Roman Empire.

Another outcome was that the Habsburgs, though weakened as emperors, were strengthened as rulers of their own hereditary lands on the eastern fringes of the empire. Except in Hungary, Protestantism—and its contrary political baggage—had been eliminated early in the wars, and the peace did not alter these circumstances. The Habsburgs moved their capital back to Vienna from Prague, and the government of their hereditary lands gained in importance as administration of the empire waned.

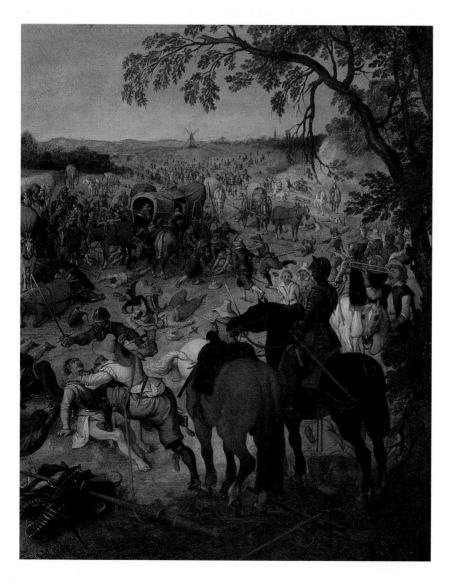

**The Horrors of War** This painting by a seventeenth-century artist depicts an attack on a supply convoy by opposing troops. Control of supplies to feed and equip the increasing numbers of troops was one of the most important aspects of warfare. *(Staatsgalerie Aschaffenburg [Schloss], Bayerische Staatsgemäldesammlungen/Godwin Alfen-ARTOTHEK)*

# WRITING, DRAMA, AND ART IN AN AGE OF UPHEAVAL

OTH imaginative literature and speculative writing, such as political theory, bear the stamp of their times. In the late sixteenth and early seventeenth centuries, political speculation often concerned questions of the legitimacy of rulers and of the relationship of political power to divine authority—urgent problems in an age when religious division threatened the very foundations of states. Authors and rulers alike often relied on still-prevalent oral modes of communication to convey their ideas. Indeed, some of the greatest literature and some of the most effective political statements of the period were presented as drama and not conveyed in print. Nevertheless, literacy continued to spread and led to greater opportunities for knowledge and reflection. The medium of print became increasingly important to political life. In the visual arts, the dramatic impulse was wedded to religious purposes to create works that conveyed both power and emotion.

## ■ Literacy and Literature

Traditional oral culture changed slowly under the impact of the spread of printing, education, and literacy. Works of literature from the late sixteenth and early seventeenth century incorporate material from traditional folktales, consciously reflecting the coexistence of oral and literature culture. In *Don Quixote*°, by Spain's Miguel de Cervantes° (1547–1616), the title character and his companion, Sancho Panza, have a long discussion about oral and literate traditions. The squire Panza speaks in the style that was customary in oral culture—a rather roundabout and repetitive style, by our standards, that enabled the speaker and listener to remember what was said. Much of the richness of Don Quixote is due to the interweaving of prose styles and topical concerns from throughout Cervantes' culture—from the oral world of peasants to the refined world of court life. Yet the perspective that enabled Cervantes to accomplish this rich portrayal came about from his own highly developed literacy and the awareness of language that literacy made possible.

The spread of education and literacy in the late sixteenth century had a dramatic impact on attitudes toward literature and on literature itself. The value of education—particularly of the continuing humanist recovery of ancient wisdom—was reflected in much of the literature of the period. Writers found in humanistic education a vision of what it meant to be cultivated and disciplined men of the world. This vision provided the beginnings of a new self-image for members of the warrior class.

It is customary to regard the French author Michel de Montaigne° (1533–1592) as the epitome of the reflective and—more important—the *self*-reflective gentleman. Montaigne was a judge in the parlement (law court) of Bordeaux; he resigned from the court in 1570, however, and retired to his small château, where he wrote his *Essais* (from which we derive the word *essays*), a collection of short reflections that were revolutionary in both form and content. Montaigne invented writing in the form of a sketch, a "try" (the literal meaning of *essai*), which enabled him to combine self-reflection with formal analysis.

Montaigne's reflections ranged from the destructiveness of the French civil wars to the consequences of European exploration of the New World. Toward all of these events and circumstances, Montaigne was able to achieve an analytic detachment remarkable for his day. For example, he noted an irony in Europeans labeling New World peoples "savage," given Europeans' seemingly endless and wanton violence against those "savages" and against one another. (See the box "Global Encounters: Montaigne Discusses Barbarity in the New World and the Old.") Owing to the spread of printing and literacy, Montaigne had—in addition to his own effort and the resources of leisure—a virtually unparalleled opportunity to reflect on the world through reading the wide variety of printed texts available to him. For the first time, it was possible for a leisured lay reader to consider and compare different events, values, and cultures.

His essays also reveal a distancing from himself, and this distancing is another result of literacy—not simply the ability to read and write but the capacity to enjoy long periods of solitude and reflection in the company of other solitary, book-bound, voices. Montaigne's works mark the beginning of what we know as the "invention" of private life, in which an individual is known more by internal character and personality traits than by social role and past behavior.

The works of the great English poet and playwright William Shakespeare (1564–1616) are still compelling to us because of the profundity of the questions he asked about love, honor, and political legitimacy, but he asked

---

**Quixote** (key-HO-tay)    **Cervantes** (sair-VAHN-tayz)      **Montaigne** (mon-TEN-yuh)

## ⊕ GLOBAL ENCOUNTERS

### Montaigne Discusses Barbarity in the New World and the Old

*In one of his most famous essays, Michel de Montaigne ironically compares the customs of Native Americans, about whom he has heard, with the customs of his own society.*

They have their wars with [other] nations, to which they go quite naked, with no other arms than bows or wooden spears. . . . It is astonishing that firmness they show in their combats, which never end but in slaughter and bloodshed; for, as to routs and terror, they know nothing of either.

Each man brings back as his trophy the head of the enemy he has killed. . . . After they have treated their prisoner well for a long time with all the hospitality they can think of . . . they kill him with their swords. This done, they roast him and eat him in common and send some pieces to their absent friends.

I am not sorry that we notice the barbarous horror of such acts, but am heartily sorry that . . . we should be so blind to our own. I think there is more barbarity . . . in tearing by tortures and the rack a body still full of feeling, in roasting a man bit by bit, having him bitten and mangled by dogs (as we have not only read but seen within fresh memory . . .

among neighbors and fellow citizens, and what is worse, on the pretext of piety and religion).

Three of these men (were brought to France) . . . and [someone] wanted to know what they had found most amazing. . . . They said that in the first place they thought it very strange that so many grown men, bearded, strong and armed who were around the king . . . should submit to obey a child [the young French king]. . . . Second (they have a way in their language of speaking of men as halves of one another), they had noticed that there were among us men full and gorged with all sorts of good things, and that their other halves were beggars at their doors, emaciated with hunger and poverty; and they thought it strange that these needy halves could endure such injustice.

*Source:* Donald M. Frame, trans., *The Complete Essays of Montaigne* (Stanford, Calif.: Stanford University Press, 1948), pp. 153, 155–159.

these questions in terms appropriate to his own day. One of his favorite themes—evident in *Hamlet* and *Macbeth*—is the legitimacy of rulers. He was at his most skilled, perhaps, when exploring the contradictions in values between the growing commercial world he saw around him and the older, seemingly more stable world of feudal society. Subtle political commentary distinguishes Shakespeare's later plays, written near and shortly after the death of Queen Elizabeth in 1603, when political and economic problems were becoming increasingly visible and troublesome. Shakespeare explored not only the duties of rulers but also the rights of their subjects. In *Coriolanus* he portrays commoners as poor but neither ignorant nor wretched; they are in fact fully rational and capable of analyzing their situation—

perhaps more capable, Shakespeare hints, than their ruler is. The play is safely set in ancient Rome, but the social and political tensions it depicts clearly applied to the Elizabethan present.

Shakespeare, Cervantes, and other writers of their day were also representatives of what were starting to be self-consciously distinct national literatures. The spread of humanism added a historical dimension to their awareness of their own languages and to their distinct subject matter: their own society and its past. This kind of self-consciousness is evident in Shakespeare's historical plays, such as *Henry V* and *Richard II*. In *Richard II* he depicts the kingdom in terms that reflect the Elizabethan sense of England as a separate and self-contained nation:

This royal throne of kings, this scept'red isle,
This earth of majesty, this seat of Mars,
This other Eden, demi-paradise,
This fortress built by Nature for herself
Against infection and the hand of war,
This happy breed of men, this little world,
This precious stone set in the silver sea . . .
This blessed plot, this earth, this realm, this
    England . . .
(*Richard II*, act 2, sc. 1, lines 40–50)[5]

### ■ The Great Age of Theater

Shakespeare's extraordinary career was possible because his life coincided with the rise of professional theater. In the capitals of both England and Spain, professional theaters first opened in the 1570s. Some drama was produced at court or in aristocratic households, but most public theaters drew large and very mixed audiences, including the poorest city dwellers. Playwrights, including Shakespeare, often wrote in teams under great pressure to keep acting companies supplied with material. The best-known dramatist in Spain in this period, Lope de Vega° (1562–1635), wrote more than fifteen hundred works on a wide range of topics. Although religious themes remained popular in Spanish theater, as an echo of medieval drama, most plays in England and Spain treated secular subjects and, as in *Coriolanus*, safely disguised political commentary.

Over time, theater became increasingly restricted to aristocratic circles. In England, Puritan criticism of the "immorality" of public performance drove actors and playwrights to seek royal patronage. The first professional theater to open in Paris, in 1629, as political and religious turmoil quieted, quickly became dependent on Cardinal Richelieu's patronage. Inevitably, as court patronage grew in importance, the wide range of subject matter treated in plays began to narrow to those of aristocratic concern, such as family honor and martial glory. These themes were depicted in the works of the Spaniard Pedro Calderón° (1600–1681), who wrote for his enthusiastic patron, Philip IV, and of the Frenchman Pierre Corneille° (1606–1684), whose great tragedy of aristocratic life, *Le Cid*, was one of the early successes of the seventeenth-century French theater.

Drama's significance as an art form is reflected in its impact on the development of music: the opera, which weds drama to music, was invented in Italy in the early seventeenth century. The first great work in this genre is generally acknowledged to be *Orfeo* (*Orpheus*, 1607) by Claudio Monteverdi° (1567–1643). Opera, like drama, reflected the influence of humanism in its secular themes and in its emulation of Greek drama, which had used both words and music. The practice of music itself changed under the dramatic impulse. Monteverdi was the first master of a new musical style known as monody, which emphasized the progression of chords. Monodic music was inherently dramatic, creating a sense of forward movement, expectation, and resolution.

### ■ Sovereignty in Ceremony, Image, and Word

Whether produced on a public stage or at court or in a less formal setting, drama was a favored method of communication in this era because people responded to and made extensive use of oral communication. Dramatic gesture and storytelling to get a message across were commonplace and were important components of politics.

What we might call "street drama" was an ordinary occurrence: when great noble governors entered major towns, such as when Margaret of Parma entered Brussels, a solemn yet ostentatious formal "entry" was often staged. The dignitary would ride through the main gate, usually beneath a canopy made of luxurious cloth. The event might include staged tableaux in the town's streets, with costumed townspeople acting out brief symbolic vignettes such as David and Goliath, and it might end in an elaborate banquet. A remnant of these proceedings survives today in the ceremony by which distinguished visitors are given "the keys to the city," which, in the sixteenth century, really were functional.

Royalty made deliberate and careful use of dramatic ceremony. Royal entries into towns took on an added weight, as did royal funerals and other such occasions. These dramas reinforced political and constitutional assumptions in the minds of witnesses and participants. Thus, over time, we can see changes in the representations of royal power. In France, for example, the ritual entry of the king into Paris had originally stressed the participation of the leading guilds, judges, and administrators, symbolizing their active role in governing the city and the kingdom. But in the last half of the sixteenth century, the procession began to glorify the king alone.

The very fact that rulers experimented self-consciously with self-representation suggests that issues pertaining to the nature and extent of royal power were

---

**Lope de Vega** (LOW-pah day VAY-guh)    **Pedro Calderón** (PAY-dro kall-day-ROHN)    **Corneille** (kore-NAY)

**Monteverdi** (mon-tay-VAIR-dee)

## ᘒ R E A D I N G   S O U R C E S

### Elizabeth I Addresses Her Troops

*The day after English ships dispersed the Spanish Armada in 1588, Elizabeth addressed a contingent of her troops. She used the opportunity to fashion an image of herself as a warrior above all but also as the beloved familiar of her people, unafraid of potential plots against her. Note her willingness to portray herself as androgynous—that is, embodying both female and male qualities.*

My loving people, we have been persuaded by some that are careful of our safety, to take heed how we commit ourselves to armed multitudes, for fear of treachery. But I assure you, I do not desire to live to distrust my faithful and loving people. Let tyrants fear. I have always so behaved myself that, under God, I have placed my chiefest strength in the loyal hearts and good will of my subjects; and therefore I am come amongst you, as you see, at this time, not for my reaction or disport, but being resolved, in the midst and heat of the battle, to live or die amongst you all, to lay down for my God, and for my kingdom, and for my people, my honor and my blood, even in the dust. I know I have the body of a weak and feeble woman, but I have the heart and the stomach of a king, and of a king of England too, and think foul scorn that Parma or Spain, or any prince of Europe should dare to invade the borders of my realm; to which, rather than any dishonor shall grow by me, I myself will take up arms, I myself will be your general, judge, and rewarder of every one of your virtues in the field.

*Source:* J. E. Neale, *Queen Elizabeth I* (New York: Anchor, 1957), pp. 308–309.

profoundly important and far from settled. Queen Elizabeth had the particular burden of assuming the throne in a period of great instability. Hence, she paid a great deal of attention to the image of herself that she conveyed in words and authorized to be fashioned in painting. Elizabeth styled herself variously as mother to her people and as a warrior-queen (drawing on ancient myths of Amazon women). She made artful use of the image of her virginity to buttress each of these images—as the wholly devoted, self-sacrificing mother (which, of course, had religious tradition behind it) or as an androgynous ruler, woman but doing the bodily work of man. (See the box "Reading Sources: Elizabeth I Addresses Her Troops.")

More formal speculation about constitutional matters also resulted from the tumult of the sixteenth and seventeenth centuries. As we have seen, the Protestant faction in France advanced an elaborate argument for the limitation of royal power. Alternative theories enhancing royal authority were offered, principally in support of the Catholic position though also simply to buttress the beleaguered monarchy itself. The most famous of these appeared in *The Six Books of the Republic* (1576), by the legal scholar Jean Bodin° (1530–1596). Bodin was a Catholic but offered a fundamentally secular perspective on the purposes and source of power within a state. His special contribution was a vision of a truly sovereign monarch. Bodin offered a theoretical understanding that is essential to states today and is the ground on which people can claim rights and protection from the state—namely, that there is a final sovereign authority. For Bodin, that authority was the king. He recognized that in practice royal power was constrained by limitations; but he was more intrigued with the theoretical grounding for royal authority, not its practical application.

Contract theory devised by French Protestants to legitimize resistance to the monarchy had to be abandoned when Henry IV granted toleration to the Huguenots in 1598. In England, theoretical justification of resistance to Charles I was initially limited to invoking tradition and precedent. Contract theory as well as other

**Bodin** (bo-DAHN)

sweeping claims regarding subjects' rights would be more fully developed later in the century.

Bodin's theory of sovereignty, however, was immediately echoed in other theoretical works, most notably that of Hugo Grotius° (1583–1645). A Dutch jurist and diplomat, Grotius developed the first principles of modern international law. He accepted the existence of sovereign states that owed no loyalty to higher authority (such as the papacy) and thus needed new principles to govern their interactions. His major work, *De Jure Belli ac Pacis (On the Law of War and Peace)* (1625), was written in response to the turmoil of the Thirty Years' War.

Grotius argued that relations between states could be based on respect for treaties voluntarily reached between them. In perhaps his boldest move, he argued that war must be justified and developed criteria to distinguish just from unjust wars.

### ■ Baroque Art and Architecture

Speculation about and celebration of power, as well as of dramatic emotion, also occurred in the visual arts—most notably in painting and architecture, in the style now known as "baroque°." (See the feature "Weighing

---

**Grotius** (GROW-shus)

**baroque** (ba-ROKE)

the Evidence: Art at Court" on pages 536–537.) The word *baroque* comes from the Portuguese *barroco,* used to describe irregularly shaped pearls; the term as applied to the arts was initially derogatory, describing illogic and irregularity. Baroque architecture modified the precision, symmetry, and orderliness of Renaissance architecture to produce a sense of greater dynamism in space. Façades and interiors were both massive and, through clever use of architectural and decorative components, suggestive of movement. Hence baroque churches, for example, were impressively grand and emotionally engaging at the same time. Baroque techniques were pioneered in Italy, first in church design, in the late sixteenth century and spread slowly, with many regional variations, especially throughout Catholic Europe, during the seventeenth century.

One of the primary purposes of baroque architecture and painting was to encourage piety that was not only emotionally involved but also awe-inspired. Italian baroque painting made use of the realism developed in Renaissance art but added dynamism and emotional energy—such as by painting throngs of people or by using light to create direction and energy in the scene portrayed. Dramatic illusion was also a common device, such as painting a chapel ceiling with figures receding as if ascending to heaven. The faithful were emotionally engaged through their senses, yet always aware of divine majesty.

In Italy baroque sculpture and architecture were dominated by the work of Gianlorenzo Bernini° (1598–1680), who designed the sweeping portico outside Saint Peter's Basilica in Rome. He is perhaps best known for his moving sculpture of the sixteenth-century mystic Saint Theresa, known as "St. Theresa in Ecstasy." The most influential baroque painter was Peter Paul Rubens (1577–1640), a native of the southern Netherlands. Rubens's early training in Italy shaped him as an artist and established his secondary career as a diplomat, trusted by princely patrons. Throughout his life, he undertook diplomatic missions for the Habsburg viceroys in the Spanish Netherlands, gaining artistic commissions wherever he traveled. Rubens's subject matter varied widely, including church design and decoration, portraiture, and landscape painting. Baroque technique, of which he was a master, is distinguished by the dramatic use of color and shading and by the dynamic energy of his figures.

**Bernini** (bare-NEE-nee)

# SUMMARY

THE late sixteenth and early seventeenth centuries were an era of intense struggle over political and religious authority. Rulers everywhere, through a variety of expedients, tried to buttress and expand royal power. They were resisted by traditional centers of power, such as independent-minded nobles. But they were also resisted by the novel challenge of religious dissent, which empowered subjects both to claim a greater right to question authority and to risk more in their attempts to oppose it. In some areas of Europe, such as the Holy Roman Empire, the struggles reached some resolution. In other areas, such as England, decades of bloody conflict still lay ahead.

On the whole, these conflicts did little to improve the lives of ordinary people since for the most part victorious elites decided matters of religion and governance in their own interests. In addition, the difficult economic circumstances of these decades meant that working people, desperate for a secure livelihood, rioted or took up arms out of economic as well as religious concerns.

Yet however grim the circumstances people faced, the technology of print and the spread of literacy helped spur speculative and creative works by providing the means for reflection and the audiences to receive and appreciate it. Ironically, the increased importance and grandeur of court life, although a cause of political strain, resulted in a new wave of patronage for art, literature, and drama. Some of the works we still value, such as Rubens's paintings, portray the splendid ambience of royal courts. Other works, such as Shakespeare's plays, both reflect and reflect on the tensions and contradictions in the society of the day: for example, the importance of the stability provided by royal authority as opposed to the dignity and wisdom of ordinary people, who had no claim to power at all.

## ■ Notes

1. Geoffrey Parker, *The Dutch Revolt* (London: Penguin Books, 1985), p. 288, n. 5.
2. Quoted in A. W. Lovett, *Early Habsburg Spain, 1517–1598* (Oxford: Oxford University Press, 1986), p. 212.
3. Quoted in R. J. Knecht, *The French Wars of Religion, 1559–1598* (London: Longman, 1989), p. 109.
4. Quoted in Jean Berenger, *A History of the Habsburg Empire, 1273–1700,* trans. C. A. Simpson (London and New York: Longman, 1990), p. 239.

5. *The Riverside Shakespeare*, 2d ed. (Boston: Houghton Mifflin, 1997), p. 855.

## ■ Suggested Reading

Bonney, Richard. *The European Dynastic States, 1494–1660.* 1991. A recent, rich survey of the period that is solid on eastern as well as western Europe; however, written from an English point of view, it does not consider England as part of Europe.

Eagleton, Terry. *William Shakespeare.* 1986. A brief and highly readable interpretation of Shakespeare that emphasizes the tensions in the plays caused by language and by ideas from the new world of bourgeois commercial life.

Hale, J. R. *War and Society in Renaissance Europe.* 1985. An analysis of war as a function of government and as a part of the social, economic, and intellectual life of the sixteenth century.

Holt, Mack P. *The French Wars of Religion, 1562–1629.* 1995. An up-to-date synthesis that evaluates social and political context while not slighting the importance of religion.

Lynch, John. *Spain, 1516–1598: From Nation-State to World Empire.* 1991. A survey covering the reign of Philip II by a leading scholar of Spanish history.

Parker, Geoffrey. *The Military Revolution.* 1988; and Black, Jeremy. *A Military Revolution?* 1991. Two works that disagree about the nature and extent of the changes in military practices and their significance for military, political, and social history. Black tries to refute claims for a dramatic military "revolution."

———. *The Dutch Revolt.* 2d ed. 1985. The best survey of the revolt available in English.

Smith, A. G. R. *The Emergence of a Nation-State: The Commonwealth of England, 1529–1660.* 1984. A good place to start in the immense bibliography on the Elizabethan period.

Wiesner, Merry. *Women and Gender in Early Modern Europe.* 1993. Discusses all aspects of women's experience, including their working lives.

 **For a searchable list of additional readings for this chapter, go to http://college.hmco.com.**

# Art at Court

The painting you see reproduced here (at less than ⅟₂₅ of its original size) is a portrait of the English king Charles I painted by the Flemish painter Anthony Van Dyck about the year 1638. Van Dyck was a pupil of the great baroque painter Peter Paul Rubens. Like Rubens, he enjoyed international fame. Among his greatest works are portraits completed during a long sojourn at the English court in the 1630s. This large portrait was designed to be hung at the end of a long corridor or a similar place so that, from a distance, the observer would have the illusion of actually seeing the king outdoors on horseback. This effect was similar to that achieved by baroque artists who painted church ceilings with receding angels and cherubs, giving the faithful the illusion of gazing up toward heaven.*

How are we meant to interpret and respond to Charles's portrait? What visual cues did Van Dyck include for his contemporaries that we might miss, or misinterpret? Charles's suit of armor was, by itself, a complex image. Aristocrats no longer wore full body armor onto the battlefield since it had been designed for fighting against lances, not guns. Indeed, although his body is fully armored, Charles wears riding boots rather than armor on his shins and feet. The fact that he is about to be handed a magnificently decorated helmet by his attendant further complicates the image. This kind of headgear was worn for a festive mock battle, a typical entertainment at courts throughout Europe. Thus, the king is not portrayed in the unbelievable role of a medieval knight; instead, he is dressed in a costume that any courtier could have identified as "pretend." Both Charles and the artist, Van Dyck, could count on the fact that his courtiers would have *expected* Charles to manipulate images of himself; indeed, they would have expected him to be skillful at it. The mock battles, staged entries, and courtly theatricals that they regularly witnessed or participated in were all vehicles for dramatically displaying royal power.

Although courtiers were familiar with the image of a heroic knight on horseback, it was not commonplace or banal. Van Dyck here drew on a tradition, dating back to

---

*This discussion draws on the work of Roy Strong, *Van Dyck: Charles I on Horseback* (New York: Viking Press, Inc., 1972).

the Roman Empire and recently revived by Renaissance sculptors and painters, of depicting a ruler, particularly the emperor, as a heroic mounted warrior. Equestrian statues of Renaissance generals and princes, aping ancient ones of Roman emperors, were among the great achievements of fifteenth- and sixteenth-century art. The most immediate influence on Van Dyck was a painting of the Holy Roman emperor Charles V by the Renaissance master Titian: to celebrate Charles's victory over Protestant forces, the emperor is portrayed as an armored warrior on horseback. In later decades (see pages 538 and 554), the theme would be overused and this kind of image would be constantly reused, but in the early seventeenth century it was still novel and fresh and must have retained particular force on the imagination.

What use to Charles was a heroic image borrowed from antiquity? Note that behind Charles, fastened to the tree, is a plaque with a Latin inscription. This writing would have been easily legible to anyone viewing the actual, 12-foot-high painting. It reads: *Carolus I Rex Magnae Britaniae*, or Charles I, King of Great Britain. Any courtier viewing the painting would have known of the recent political wrangling about the king's claim to that title. "Great Britain" was a newly coined term referring to the combined kingdoms of England and Scotland. James I, Charles's father, had been king of Scotland when he acceded to the English throne and had referred to himself as "King of Great Britain." But Parliament insisted that his titles be listed separately until the institutions of the two kingdoms had been united to create a truly integrated state—a process Parliament intended to oversee. James used the title "King of Great Britain" anyway, one of the many ways he asserted his prerogative against the power of Parliament. Charles, however, had actually begun to force the integration of the two kingdoms by forcing Anglican Church structure on the Scots. Thus, Van Dyck cleverly reinforces Charles's claim to this quasi-imperial title of King of Great Britain by depicting him as emperor, complete with label.

Van Dyck added yet another symbolic prop to Charles's majesty and authority: the medallion around his neck. This medallion (which carried the image of Saint George and the dragon) identifies him as the leader of the Order of the Knights of the Garter, an

**Van Dyck: Charles I on Horseback**
*(© The National Gallery, London)*

English order of knights founded in the Middle Ages. This symbol of the loyalty and valor of ideal knights, and the ceremonies such as celebration of the feast day of Saint George, had a variety of symbolic possibilities. Elizabeth I had used the Garter Festival (on Saint George's day) as an occasion to celebrate the chivalrous loyalty of her subjects for their lady fair—that is, Elizabeth herself. During his reign so far, Charles had emphasized a different aspect of the order's symbolic potential: its religious symbolism. In the Middle Ages, knighthood had always been imbued with religious values. Under Charles, the Garter Festival included a formal procession of magnificently attired knights, clergy, and courtiers, followed by a religious service that was almost unchanged from the days of Catholicism. In other words, Charles used the trappings of the Order of the Garter to sponsor religious services reminiscent of Rome at the court and to help craft an identity as a warrior fighting on God's behalf.

Van Dyck's portrayal of Charles I was thus a highly charged, contentious one. It laid claim symbolically to the powers Charles was trying to exercise in practice, including wider authority over his two kingdoms and the stature of divine agent on earth. Unlike us, the courtiers of his day would have known how to "read" the symbolic references in the painting because the painting borrowed images from court life and ceremony, and from other art forms with which they were familiar. By trying to re-enter the world in which this painting once made symbolic sense, we can appreciate how uncertain were the boundaries of royal power in this epoch and how high were the stakes in representing the king. Van Dyck's extraordinary skill made this particular representation both daring in its claims for royal power and compelling to the viewer.

 **For additional information on this topic, go to http://college.hmco.com.**

# CHAPTER 16

# Europe in the Age of Louis XIV

## ca. 1640–1715

T HE portrait of King Louis XIV of France as a triumphant warrior, to the left, was one of hundreds of such images of the king that decorated his palace at Versailles and other sites around his kingdom—where they made his subjects aware of his presence, regardless of whether he was in residence. Louis is dressed as a Roman warrior, and his power is represented by a mixture of other symbols—Christian and pagan, ancient and contemporary. An angel crowns him with a victor's laurel wreath and carries a banner bearing the image of the sun. In his hand, Louis holds a marshal's baton—a symbol of military command—covered with the royal emblem of the fleur-de-lys°. In the background, behind the "Roman" troops following Louis, is an idealized city.

These trappings symbolized the significant expansion of royal power during Louis's reign. He faced down the challenges of warrior-nobles, suppressed religious dissent, and tapped the nation's wealth to wage a series of wars of conquest. A period of cultural brilliance early in his reign and the spectacle of an elaborate court life crowned his achievements. In his prime, his regime was supported by a consensus of elites; such harmony was made possible by the lack of institutional brakes on royal authority. However, as his attention to symbolism suggests, Louis's power was not unchallenged. By the end of the Sun King's reign, the glow was fading: France was struggling under economic distress brought on by the many wars fought for his glory and had missed opportunities for commercial success abroad. Elites throughout France who had once accepted, even welcomed, his rule became trenchant critics, and common people outright rebels.

**fleur-de-lys** (flur–duh–LEE)

**France in the Age of Absolutism**

**English Civil War and Its Aftermath**

**New Powers in Central and Eastern Europe**

**The Expansion of Overseas Trade and Settlement**

Louis XIV in Roman armor, by the contemporary artist Charles Le Brun. (Scala/Art Resource, NY)

After the Thirty Years' War, vigorous rulers in central and eastern Europe undertook a program of territorial expansion and state building that led to the dominance in the region of Austria, Brandenburg-Prussia, and Russia. The power of these states derived, in part, from the economic relationship of their lands to the wider European economy. In all the major states of continental Europe, princely governments were able to monopolize military power for the first time, in return for economic and political concessions to noble landholders. In England, by contrast, the Crown faced rebellion by subjects claiming religious authority and political legitimacy for their causes. Resistance to the expansion of royal authority, led by Parliament, resulted in the execution of the king and the establishment of a short-lived republic, the Commonwealth. Although the monarchy was restored, the civil war had long-term consequences for royal power in England.

The seventeenth century also witnessed a dynamic phase of European expansion overseas, following on the successes of the Portuguese and the Spanish in the fifteenth and sixteenth centuries. Eager migrants settled in the Americas in ever increasing numbers, while forced migrants—enslaved Africans—were transported by the thousands to work on the profitable plantations of European colonizers. Aristocrats, merchants, and peasants back in Europe jockeyed to take advantage of—or to mitigate the effects of—the local political and economic impact of Europe's expansion.

### QUESTIONS TO CONSIDER

- How did Louis XIV successfully expand royal power in France?
- What were the long-term consequences of the English civil war?
- What economic and political interests led to war in eastern Europe?
- How did the expansion of international trade and colonization affect European states and communities?

### TERMS TO KNOW

| | |
|---|---|
| Louis XIV | Brandenburg-Prussia |
| absolutism | Treaty of Carlowitz |
| mercantilism | Great Northern War |
| Oliver Cromwell | Peter the Great |
| Interregnum | Dutch East India Company |
| Glorious Revolution | plantation system |

## FRANCE IN THE AGE OF ABSOLUTISM

*BSOLUTISM* is a term often used to describe the extraordinary concentration of power in royal hands achieved by the kings of France, most notably Louis XIV (r. 1643–1715), in the seventeenth century. Louis continued the expansion of state power begun by his father's minister, Cardinal Richelieu (see page 518). The extension of royal power, under Louis as well as his predecessor, was accelerated by the desire to sustain an expensive and aggressive foreign policy. The policy itself was partly traditional—fighting the perpetual enemy, the Habsburgs, and seeking military glory—and partly new—expanding the borders of France. Louis XIV's successes in these undertakings made him both envied and emulated by other rulers; the French court became a model of culture and refinement. But increased royal authority was not accepted without protest: common French people as well as elites dug in their heels.

### ■ The Last Challenge to Absolutism: The Fronde, 1648–1653

Louis came to the throne as a 5-year-old child in 1643. Acting as his regent, his mother, Anne of Austria (1601–1666), had to defuse a serious challenge to royal authority during her son's minority. Together with her chief minister and personal friend, Cardinal Jules Mazarin° (1602–1661), she faced opposition from royal bureau-

**Mazarin** (mah-zah-RAHN)

crats and the traditional nobility as well as the common people.

Revolts against the concentration of power in royal hands and against the exorbitant taxation that had prevailed under Louis's father began immediately. In one province, a group of armed peasants cornered the intendant and forced him to agree to lower taxes; elsewhere, provincial parlements tried to abolish special ranks of officials, especially the intendants, created by Richelieu. In 1648, after several more years of foreign war and of financial expedients to sustain it, the most serious revolt began, led by the Parlement° of Paris and the other sovereign law courts in the capital.

The source of the Parlement's leverage over the monarchy was its traditional right to register laws and edicts, which amounted to judicial review. Now, the Parlement, as a guardian of royal authority, attempted to extend this power by debating and even initiating government policy: the sovereign courts sitting together drew up a reform program abolishing most of the machinery of government established under Richelieu and calling for consent to future taxation. The citizens of Paris rose to defend the courts when royal troops were sent against them in October.

Mazarin was forced to accept the proposed reform of government, at least in theory. He also had to avert challenges by great nobles for control of the young king's council. Civil war waxed and waned around France from 1648 until 1653. The main combatants were conventionally ambitious great nobles, but reform-minded urban dwellers often made common cause with them, to benefit from their military power. Meanwhile, middling nobles in the region around Paris began to devise a thoroughgoing reform program and to prepare for a meeting of the Estates General—a representative assembly—to enact it.

These revolts begun in 1648 were derided with the name "Fronde°," which was a popular children's game. However, the Fronde was not child's play: it constituted a serious challenge to the legacy of royal government as it had developed under Richelieu. It ended without a noteworthy impact on the growth of royal power for several reasons. First, Mazarin methodically regained control of the kingdom through armed force and artful concessions to individual aristocrats, who were always eager to trade their loyalty for the fruits of royal service. Meanwhile, the Parlement of Paris, as well as many citizens of the capital, welcomed a return to royal authority when civil war caused starvation as well as political unrest.

Moreover, the Parlement of Paris was a law court, not a representative assembly. Its legitimacy derived

**Parlement** (par-luh-MAWNH)    **Fronde** (FRAWND)

| CHRONOLOGY | |
|---|---|
| **1602** | Dutch East India Company formed |
| **1607** | Jamestown colony founded in Virginia |
| **1608** | Champlain founds Quebec City |
| **1613** | Michael becomes first Romanov tsar in Russia |
| **1620** | Pilgrims settle at Plymouth (Massachusetts) |
| **1643** | Louis XIV becomes king of France |
| **1642–1648** | Civil war in England |
| **1648–1653** | Fronde revolts in France |
| **1649** | Execution of Charles I |
| **1649–1660** | English Commonwealth |
| **1659** | Peace of the Pyrenees |
| **1660** | Monarchy restored in England |
| **1661** | Louis XIV assumes full control of government |
| **1672–1678** | Dutch War |
| **1682** | Peter the Great becomes tsar of Russia |
| **1685** | Edict of Nantes revoked |
| **1688** | Glorious Revolution |
| **1699** | Treaty of Carlowitz |
| **1700–1721** | Great Northern War |
| **1701–1714** | War of the Spanish Succession |
| **1713** | Peace of Utrecht |
| **1715** | Death of Louis XIV |

from its role as upholder of royal law, and it could not, over time, challenge the king on the pretext of upholding royal tradition in his name. Parlementaires tended to see the Estates General as a rival institution and helped quash the proposed meeting of representatives. Above all, they wanted to avert such reforms as the abolition of the paulette, a fee guaranteeing the hereditary right to royal office (see page 517).

Unlike in England, there was in France no single institutional focus for resistance to royal power. A strong-willed and able ruler, such as Louis XIV proved to be, could obstruct or override challenges to royal power, particularly when he satisfied the ambitions of aristocrats and those bureaucrats who profited from the expansion of royal power. Moreover, the young Louis had been traumatized by the uprisings of the Fronde and grew up determined never to allow another such challenge to his absolute sovereignty.

## ■ France Under Louis XIV, 1661–1715

Louis XIV fully assumed control of government at Mazarin's death in 1661. It was a propitious moment. The Peace of the Pyrenees in 1659 had ended in France's favor the wars with Spain that had dragged on since the end of the Thirty Years' War. As part of the peace agreement, Louis married a Spanish princess, Maria Theresa. In the first ten years of his active reign, Louis achieved a degree of control over the mechanisms of government unparalleled in the history of monarchy in France or anywhere else in Europe. Louis was extremely vigorous and proved a diligent king. He put in hours a day at a desk while sustaining the ceremonial life of the court with its elaborate hunts, balls, and other public events.

Louis did not invent any new bureaucratic devices but rather used existing ranks of officials in new ways that increased government efficiency and further centralized control. He radically reduced the number of men in his High Council, the advisory body closest to the king, to include only three or four great ministers of state affairs. This intimate group, with Louis's active participation, handled all policymaking. The ministers of state, war, and finance were chosen exclusively from non-noble men of bourgeois backgrounds whose training and experience fitted them for such positions. Jean-Baptiste Colbert° (1619–1683), perhaps the greatest of them, served as minister of finance and supervised most domestic policy from 1665 until his death; he was from a merchant family and had served for years under Mazarin.

Several dozen other officials, picked from the ranks of up-and-coming lawyers and administrators, drew up laws and regulations and passed them to the intendants for execution at the provincial level. Sometimes, these officials at the center were sent to the provinces on short-term supervisory missions. The effect of this system was to bypass many entrenched provincial bureaucrats, particularly those known as tax farmers. Tax farmers were freelance businessmen who bid for the right to collect taxes in a region in return for a negotiated fee they paid to the Crown. The Crown, in short, did not control its own tax revenues. The money Louis's regime saved by the more efficient collection of taxes (revenues almost doubled in some areas) enabled the government to streamline the bureaucracy: dozens of the offices created over the years to bring cash in were bought back by the Crown from their owners.

The system still relied on the bonds of patronage and personal service, political bonds borrowed from aristocratic life. Officials rose through the ranks by means of service to the great, and family connection and personal loyalty still were essential. Of the seventeen different men who were part of Louis XIV's High Council during his reign, five were members of the Colbert family, for example. In the provinces, important local families vied for minor posts, which at least provided prestige and some income.

Further benefits of centralized administration can be seen in certain achievements of the early years of Louis's regime. Colbert actively encouraged France's economic development. He reduced the internal tolls and customs barriers, which were relics of medieval decentralization—for example, the right of a landholder to charge a toll on all boats along a river under his control. He encouraged industry with state subsidies and protective tariffs. He set up state-sponsored trading companies—the two most important being the East India Company and the West India Company, established in 1664.

*Mercantilism* is the term historians use to describe the theory behind Colbert's efforts. This economic theory stressed self-sufficiency in manufactured goods, tight control of trade to foster the domestic economy, and the absolute value of bullion. Both capital for development—in the form of hard currency, known as bullion—and the amount of world trade were presumed to be limited in quantity. Therefore, state intervention in the form of protectionist policies was believed necessary to guarantee a favorable balance of payments.

This static model of national wealth did not wholly fit the facts of growing international trade in the seventeenth century. Nevertheless, mercantilist philosophy was helpful to France. France became self-sufficient in the all-important production of woolen cloth, and French industry expanded notably in other sectors. Colbert's greatest success was the systematic expansion of the navy and merchant marine. By 1677 the navy had increased almost sixfold, to 144 ships. By the end of Louis XIV's reign, the French navy was virtually the equal of the English navy.

Colbert and the other ministers began to develop the kind of planned government policymaking that we now take for granted. Partly by means of their itinerant supervisory officials, they tried to formulate and execute

---

**Colbert** (coal-BEAR)

policy based on carefully collected information. How many men of military age were available? How abundant was this year's harvest? Answers to such questions enabled not only the formulation of economic policy but the deliberate management of production and services to achieve certain goals—above all, the recruitment and supply of the king's vast armies.

Beginning in 1673, Louis tried to bring the religious life of the realm more fully under royal control, claiming for himself—with mixed success—some of the church revenues and powers of ecclesiastical appointment that still remained to the pope. Partly to bolster his position with the pope, he also began to attack the Huguenot community in France. First, he offered financial inducements for conversions to Catholicism. Then he took more drastic steps such as destroying Protestant churches and quartering troops in Huguenots' households to force them to convert. In 1685 he declared that France would no longer abide any Protestant community, and he revoked the Edict of Nantes. A hundred thousand Protestant subjects—including some six hundred army and navy officers—refused even nominal conversion to Catholicism and chose to emigrate.

Meanwhile, Louis faced resistance to his claims against the pope from within the ranks of French clergy. These churchmen represented a movement within French Catholicism known as Jansenism, after the professor of theology named Cornelius Jansen, whose writings were its inspiration. Jansenists practiced an austere style of Catholic religiosity that, in its notions about human will and sinfulness, was akin to some Protestant doctrine. Louis was suspicious of Jansenism, because its adherents included many of his political enemies, particularly among families of parlementary officials. Louis was wary of any threat to the institutional—or symbolic—unity of his regime, such as Protestants and, now, Jansenists represented. At the end of Louis's long reign, another pope obligingly declared many Jansenist doctrines to be heretical as part of a compromise agreement with Louis on matters of church governance and finance. Louis's efforts to exert greater control over the church had brought him modest practical gains, but at the price of weakening the religious basis of his authority in the eyes of many sincere Catholics.

By modern standards, the power of the Crown was still greatly limited. The "divine right" of kingship, a notion formulated by Louis's chief apologist, Bishop Jacques Bossuet° (1627–1704), did not mean unlimited power to rule; rather it meant that hereditary monarchy was the divinely ordained form of government, best

suited to human needs. *Absolutism* was not iron-fisted control of the realm but rather the successful focusing of energy, loyalties, and symbolic authority in the Crown. The government functioned well in the opening decades of Louis's reign because his role as the focal point of power and loyalty was both logical, after the preceding years of unrest, and skillfully exploited. Much of the glue holding together the absolutist state lay in informal mechanisms such as patronage and court life, as well as in the traditional hunt for military glory—all of which Louis amply supplied.

## ■ The Life of the Court

An observer comparing the lives of prominent noble families in the mid-sixteenth and mid-seventeenth centuries would have noticed striking differences. By the second half of the seventeenth century, most sovereigns or territorial princes had the power to crush revolts, and the heirs of the feudal nobility had to accommodate themselves to the increased power of the Crown. The nobility relinquished its former independence but retained economic and social supremacy and, as a consequence, considerable political clout. Nobles also developed new ways to symbolize their privilege by means of cultural refinement. This process was particularly dramatic in France as a strong Crown won out over a proud nobility.

One sign of Louis's success in marshaling the loyalty of the aristocracy was the brilliant court life that his regime sustained. No longer able to wield independent political power, aristocrats lived at court whenever they could. There, they endlessly jostled for patronage and prestige—for commands in the royal army and for honorific positions at court itself. (See the box "Reading Sources: A Courtier Criticizes the King.") A favored courtier might, for example, participate in the elaborate daily *lever* (arising) of the king; he might be allowed to hand the king his shirt—a demeaning task, yet a coveted one for the attention by the king that it implied and guaranteed. Courtiers now defended their honor with private duels, not warfare, and more routinely relied on elegant ceremonial, precise etiquette, and clever conversation to demarcate their political and social distinctiveness. (See the feature "Weighing the Evidence: Table Manners" on pages 571–572.)

As literacy became more widespread, and the power of educated bureaucrats of even humble origin became more obvious, nobles from the traditional aristocracy began increasingly to use reading and writing as a means to think critically about their behavior—in the case of men, to re-imagine themselves as gentlemen rather than warriors. Noblewomen and noblemen alike began to

---

**Bossuet** (BOS-soo-way)

## ❧ READING SOURCES

### A Courtier Criticizes the King

*Louis de Rouvroy, duke of Saint-Simon (1675–1755), was a favored courtier but one critical of Louis XIV on a number of counts. In this excerpt from his memoirs, Saint-Simon evaluates the character of the king and criticizes his reliance on men of bourgeois backgrounds for his leading ministers. As a member of the traditional aristocracy, Saint-Simon certainly had a reason for disliking this policy. However, this testimony does have the ring of unbiased authenticity in some important respects.*

[The king's] ministers, general, mistresses and courtiers learned soon after he became their master that glory, to him, was a foible rather than an ambition. They therefore flattered him to the top of his bent, and in so doing, spoiled him. Praise, or better, adulation . . . were the only road to his favour and those whom he liked owed his friendship to choosing their moments well and never ceasing in their attentions. That is what gave his ministers their power, for they had endless opportunities of flattering his vanity, especially by suggesting that he was the source of all their ideas. . . .

He was well aware that though he might crush a nobleman with the weight of his displeasure, he could not destroy him or his line, whereas a secretary of state or other such minister could be reduced together with his whole family to those depths of nothingness from which he had been elevated. . . . Therein lay the reason for the watchful, jealous attitude of his ministers, who made it difficult for the King to hear any but themselves, although he pleased to think that he was an easy man to approach.

Nevertheless, in spite of the fact that the King had been so spoiled with false notions of majesty and power, that every other thought was stifled in him, there was much to be gained from a private audience, if it might be obtained, and if one knew how to conduct oneself with all the respect due to his dignity and habits. Once in his study, however prejudiced he might be . . . he would listen patiently, good-naturedly, and with a real desire to be informed. You could see that he had a sense of justice and a will to get at the truth. . . . It is therefore enough to make one weep to think of the wickedness of an education designed solely to suppress the . . . intelligence of that prince, and the insidious poison of barefaced flattery which make him a kind of god in the very heart of Christendom.

*Source:* Louis, duc de Saint-Simon, *Versailles, the Court and Louis XIV,* Lucy Norton, ed. (New York: Harper and Row, 1966), pp. 248–251.

reflect on their new roles in letters, memoirs, and the first novels. A prominent theme of these works is the increasing necessity for a truly private life of affection and trust, with which to counterbalance the public façade necessary to an aspiring courtier. The most influential early French novel was *The Princess of Cleves* by Marie-Madeleine Pioche de la Vergne (1634–1693), best known by her title, Madame de Lafayette. Mme. de Lafayette's novel treats the particular difficulties faced by aristocratic women who, without military careers to bring glory and provide distraction, were more vulnera-ble than men to gossip and slander at court and more trapped by their arranged marriages.

Louis XIV's court is usually associated with the palace he built at Versailles°, southwest of Paris. Some of the greatest talent of the day worked on the design and construction of Versailles from 1670 through the 1680s. It became a masterpiece of luxurious but restrained baroque styling—a model for royal and aristocratic palaces throughout Europe for the next one hundred years.

**Versailles** (vare-SIGH)

**The Château of Versailles**    This view of the central section of the palace is taken from the gardens. The reflecting pools you see here are on the first level of an immense terraced garden that, to someone exiting the château, seems to stretch to the horizon. The apparent openness of the king's residence (notice the rows of floor-length windows on the ground floor) is in stark contrast to a fortified castle, and was a dramatic statement of a new kind of royal power.    *(Château de Versailles, France/Peter Willi/The Bridgeman Art Library)*

Before Louis's court in his later years withdrew to Versailles, it traveled among the king's several châteaux around the kingdom, and in this itinerant period of the reign, court life was actually at its most creative and productive. These early years of Louis's personal reign were the heyday of French drama. The comedian Jean-Baptiste Poquelin, known as Molière° (1622–1673), impressed the young Louis with his productions in the late 1650s and was rewarded with the use of a theater in the main royal palace in Paris. Like Shakespeare earlier in the century, Molière explored the social and political tensions of his day. He satirized the pretensions of the aristocracy, the social climbing of the bourgeoisie, the self-righteous piety of clerics. Some of his plays were banned from performance, but most were not only tolerated but extremely popular with the elite audiences they mocked—their popularity

is testimony to the confidence of Louis's regime in its early days.

Also popular at court were the tragedies of Jean Racine° (1639–1699), who was to the French theater what Shakespeare was to the English: the master of poetic language. His plays, which treated familiar classical stories, focused on the emotional and psychological lives of the characters and often stressed the unpredictable, usually unhappy, role of fate, even among royalty. The pessimism in Racine foreshadowed the less successful second half of Louis's reign.

## ■ The Burdens of War and the Limits of Power

Wars initiated by Louis XIV dominated the attention of most European states in the second half of the seventeenth century. Louis's wars sprang from traditional

**Molière** (mole-YARE)

**Racine** (rah-SEEN)

causes: the importance of the glory and dynastic aggrandizement of the king and the preoccupation of the aristocracy with military life. But if Louis's wars were spurred by familiar concerns about territorial and economic advantage, they were far more demanding on state resources than any previous wars.

In France and elsewhere, the size of armies grew markedly. And with the countryside still smarting from the rampaging armies of the Thirty Years' War, so did the need for greater management of troops. Louis XIV's victories in the second half of the century are partly traceable to his regime's attention to the bureaucratic tasks of recruitment, training, and supply, which together constituted another phase of the "military revolution." The new offensive tactics developed during the Thirty Years' War (see page 527) changed the character of armies in ways that demanded more resources for training. A higher proportion of soldiers became gunners, and their effectiveness lay in how well they operated as a unit. Armies began to train seriously off the field of battle because drill and discipline were vital to success. France was the first to provide its soldiers with uniforms, which boosted morale and improved discipline. The numbers of men on the battlefield increased somewhat as training increased the effectiveness of large numbers of infantry, but the total numbers of men in arms supported by the state at any time increased dramatically once the organization to support them was in place. Late in the century, France kept more than 300,000 men in arms when at war (which was most of the time).

Louis's first war, in 1667, reflected the continuing French preoccupation with Spanish power on French frontiers. Louis invoked rather dubious dynastic claims to demand, from Spain, lands in the Spanish Netherlands and the large independent county on France's eastern border called the Franche-Comté° (see Map 16.1). After a brief conflict, the French obtained only some towns in the Spanish Netherlands by the terms of the Treaty of Aix-la-Chapelle. Louis had already begun to negotiate with the Austrian Habsburgs over the eventual division of Spanish Habsburg lands, for it seemed likely that the Spanish king, Charles II (r. 1665–1700), would die without an heir. So, for the moment, Louis was content with modest gains at Spain's expense, confident that he would get much more in the future.

Louis's focus then shifted to a new enemy: the Dutch. The Dutch had been allied with France since the beginning of their existence as provinces in rebellion against Spain. The French now turned against the Dutch

for reasons that reflect the growth of the international trading economy: the Dutch dominance of seaborne trade. The French at first tried to offset the Dutch advantage in trade with tariff barriers against Dutch goods. But confidence in the French army led Louis's generals to urge action against the vulnerable Dutch lands. "It is impossible that his Majesty should tolerate any longer the insolence and arrogance of that nation," rationalized the usually pragmatic Colbert in 1670.[1]

The Dutch War began in 1672, with Louis personally leading one of the largest armies ever fielded in Europe—perhaps 120,000 men. At the same time, the Dutch were challenged at sea by England. The English had fought the Dutch over trade in the 1650s; now Louis secretly sent the English king, Charles II, a pension to secure an alliance against the Dutch.

At first, the French were spectacularly successful against the tiny Dutch army. However, the Dutch opened dikes and flooded the countryside, and what had begun as a rout became a soggy stalemate. Moreover, the Dutch were beating combined English and French forces at sea and were gathering allies who felt threatened by Louis's aggression. The French soon faced German and Austrian forces along their frontier, and, by 1674, the English had joined the alliance against France as well.

Nonetheless, the French managed to hold their own, and the Peace of Nijmegen°, in 1678, gave the illusion of a French victory. Not only had the French met the challenge of an enemy coalition, but Spain ceded them further border areas in the Spanish Netherlands as well as control of the Franche-Comté.

Ensconced at Versailles since 1682, Louis seemed to be at the height of his powers. Yet the Dutch War had in fact cost him more than he had gained. Meeting the alliance against him had meant fielding ever increasing numbers of men. Internal reforms in government and finance ended under the pressure of paying for war, and old financial expedients of borrowing money and selling privileges were revived. Other government obligations, such as encouraging overseas trade, were neglected. Colbert's death in 1683 dramatically symbolized the end of an era of innovation in the French regime.

Louis's unforgiving Dutch opponent, William of Orange, king of England from 1689 to 1702, renewed and stirred up anti-French alliances. The war, now known as the Nine Years' War, or King William's War, was touched off late in 1688 by French aggression—an invasion of Germany to claim an inheritance there. In his ongoing dispute with the pope, Louis seized the papal territory of

---

**Franche-Comté** (FRAWNSH–con-TAY)

**Nijmegen** (NIME-ay-gehn)

**Map 16.1   Territorial Gains of Louis XIV, 1667–1715**   Louis's wars, though enormously expensive for France, produced only modest gains of territory along France's eastern and northern frontiers.

Avignon° in southern France. Boldest of all, he helped the exiled Catholic claimant to the English crown mount an invasion to reclaim his throne.

A widespread war began with all the major powers—Spain, the Netherlands, England, Austria, the major German states—ranged against France. The French also carried the fighting abroad by seizing English territory in Canada. As with the Dutch War, the Nine Years' War was costly and, on most fronts, inconclusive. This time, though, there was no illusion of victory for Louis. In the Treaty of Ryswick (1697), Louis had to give up most of the territories in Germany, the Spanish Netherlands, and northern Spain that he managed to occupy by war's end. Avignon went back to the pope, and Louis gave up his contentious claim to papal revenues. The terrible burden of war taxes combined with crop failures in 1693 and

1694 caused widespread starvation in the countryside. French courtiers began to criticize Louis openly.

The final major war of Louis's reign, called the War of the Spanish Succession, broke out in 1701. In some ways it was a straightforward dynastic clash between France and its perennial nemesis, the Habsburgs. Both Louis and Habsburg Holy Roman emperor Leopold I (r. 1657–1705) hoped to claim for their heirs the throne of Spain, left open at the death in 1700 of the last Spanish Habsburg, Charles II. Leopold represented the Austrian branch of the Habsburg family (see the genealogy, page 508), but Charles II bequeathed the throne to Louis's grandson, Philip of Anjou°, by reason of Louis's marriage to the Spanish princess, Maria Theresa. Philip quickly proceeded to enter Spain and claim his new kingdom. War was made inevitable when Louis renounced one of

---

**Avignon** (ah-veen-YOHN)

**Anjou** (ahn-ZHOO)

the conditions of Charles's will: Philip's accession to the throne of Spain, Louis insisted, did not preclude his becoming king of France as well. This declaration was an act of sheer belligerence, for Philip was only third in line for the French throne. The Dutch and the English responded to the prospect of so great a disruption of the balance of power in Europe by joining the emperor in a formal Great Alliance in 1701. The Dutch and English also wanted to defend their colonial interests since the French had already begun to profit from new trading opportunities with the Spanish colonies.

Again the French fought a major war on several fronts on land and at sea. Again the people of France felt the cost in crushing taxes worsened by harvest failures. Major revolts inside France forced Louis to divert troops from the war. For a time it seemed that the French would be soundly defeated, but they were saved by the superior organization of their forces and by dynastic accident: unexpected deaths in the Habsburg family meant that the Austrian claimant to the Spanish throne suddenly was poised to inherit rule of Austria and the empire as well. The English, more afraid of a revival of unified Habsburg control of Spain and Austria than of French domination of Spain, quickly called for peace negotiations.

The Peace of Utrecht in 1713 resolved long-standing political conflicts and helped to set the agenda of European politics for the eighteenth century. Philip of Anjou was recognized as Philip V, the first Bourbon king of Spain, but on the condition that the Spanish and French crowns would never be worn by the same monarch. To maintain the balance of power against French interests, the Spanish Netherlands and Spanish territories in Italy were ceded by a second treaty in 1714 to Austria, which for many decades would be France's major continental rival. The Peace of Utrecht also marked the beginning of England's dominance of overseas trade and colonization. The French gave to England lands in Canada and the Caribbean and renounced any privileged relationship with Spanish colonies. England was allowed to control the highly profitable slave trade with Spanish colonies.

Louis XIV had added small amounts of strategically valuable territory along France's eastern border (see Map 16.1), and a Bourbon ruled in Spain. But the costs in human life and resources were great for the slim results achieved. Moreover, the army and navy had swallowed up capital that might have fueled investment and trade; strategic opportunities overseas were lost, never to be regained. Louis's government had been innovative in its early years but remained constrained by traditional ways of imagining the interest of the state.

# ENGLISH CIVIL WAR AND ITS AFTERMATH

 N England, unlike in France, a representative institution—Parliament—became an effective, permanent brake on royal authority. The process by which Parliament gained a secure role in governing the kingdom was neither easy nor peaceful, however. As we saw in Chapter 15, conflicts between the English crown and its subjects, culminating in the Crown-Parliament conflict, concerned control over taxation and the direction of religious reform. Beginning in 1642, England was beset by civil war between royal and parliamentary forces. The king was eventually defeated and executed, and a period followed during which the monarchy was abolished altogether. It was restored in 1660, but Parliament retained a crucial role in governing the kingdom, a role that was confirmed when, in 1688, it again deposed a monarch whose fiscal and religious policies became unacceptable to its members.

## ■ Civil War and Regicide, 1642–1649

Fighting broke out between the armies of Charles I and parliamentary armies in the late summer of 1642. The Long Parliament (see page 522) continued to represent a broad coalition of critics and opponents of the monarchy, ranging from aristocrats concerned primarily with the abuses of royal prerogative to radical Puritans eager for thorough religious reform and determined to defeat the king. Fighting was halfhearted initially, and the tide of war at first favored Charles.

In 1643, however, the scope of the war broadened. Charles made peace with Irish rebels and brought Irish troops to England to bolster his armies. Parliament, in turn, sought military aid from the Scots in exchange for promises that Presbyterianism would become the religion of England. Meanwhile, Oliver Cromwell (1599–1658), a Puritan member of the Long Parliament and a cavalry officer, helped reorganize parliamentary forces. The eleven-hundred-man cavalry trained by Cromwell and known as the "Ironsides," supported by parliamentary and Scottish infantry, defeated the king's troops at Marston Moor in July 1644. The victory made Cromwell famous.

Shortly afterward, Parliament further improved its forces and created the New Model Army, rigorously trained like Cromwell's Ironsides. Sitting Members of Parliament were barred from commanding troops;

hence upper-class control of the army was reduced. This army played a decisive role not only in the war but also in the political settlement that followed the fighting.

The New Model Army won a convincing victory over royal forces at Naseby in 1645. In the spring of 1646, Charles surrendered to a Scottish army in the north. In January 1647 Parliament paid the Scots for their services in the war and took the king into custody. In the negotiations that followed, Charles tried to play his opponents off against each other, and, as he had hoped, divisions among them widened.

Most members of Parliament were Presbyterians, Puritans who favored a strongly unified and controlled state church along Calvinist lines. They wanted peace with the king in return for acceptance of the new church structure and parliamentary control of standing militias for a specified period. They did not favor expanding the right to vote or other dramatic constitutional or legal change. These men were increasingly alarmed by the rise of sectarian differences and the actual religious freedom that many ordinary people were claiming for themselves. With the weakening of royal authority and the disruption of civil war, censorship was relaxed, and public preaching by ordinary men and even women who felt divinely inspired was becoming commonplace.

Above all, Presbyterian gentry in Parliament feared more radical groups in the army and in London who had supported them up to this point but who favored more thoroughgoing reform. Most officers of the New Model Army, such as Cromwell, were Independents, Puritans who favored a decentralized church, a degree of religious toleration, and a wider sharing of political power among men of property, not just among the very wealthy gentry. In London, a well-organized artisans' movement known as the Levellers favored universal manhood suffrage, law reform, better access to education, and decentralized churches—in short, the separation of political power from wealth and virtual freedom of religion. Many of the rank and file of the army were deeply influenced by Leveller ideas.

In May 1647 the majority in Parliament voted to offer terms to the king and to disband the New Model Army— without first paying most of the soldiers' back wages. This move provoked the first direct intervention by the army in politics. Representatives of the soldiers were chosen to present grievances to Parliament; when this failed, the army seized the king and, in August, occupied Westminster, Parliament's meeting place. Independent and Leveller elements in the army debated the direction of possible reform to be imposed on Parliament. (See the box "Reading Sources: The Putney Debates.")

**Oliver Cromwell**   Cromwell had seen his own family's income decline under the weight of Charles I's exactions. Elected to Parliament in 1628 and again in 1640, he also brought a long-standing religious zeal to his public life. His opposition to the "tyranny and usurpation" of the Anglican Church hierarchy first prompted him to criticize royal government.   *(In the collection of the Duke of Buccleuch and Queensberry KT)*

However, in November, Charles escaped from his captors and raised a new army among his erstwhile enemies, the Scots, who were also alarmed by the growing radicalism in England. Civil war began again early in 1648. Although it ended quickly with a victory by Cromwell and the New Model Army in August, the renewed war further hardened political divisions and enhanced the power of the army. The king was widely blamed for the renewed bloodshed, and the army did not trust him to keep any agreement he might now sign. When Parliament, still dominated by Presbyterians, once again voted to negotiate with the king, army troops under a Colonel Thomas Pride prevented members who favored Presbyterianism or the king from attending sessions. The "Rump" Parliament that remained after "Pride's Purge" voted to try the king. A hasty trial ensued, and Charles I was executed for "treason, tyranny and bloodshed" against his people on January 30, 1649.

## ❧ READING SOURCES

### The Putney Debates

*In October 1647, representatives of the Leveller movement in the army ranks confronted Independents—largely comprising the officer corps—in formally staged debates in a church at Putney, outside London. The debates reflected the importance of the army in deciding the shape of change. In this exchange the Leveller representative, Thomas Rainsborough, advocates universal manhood suffrage, whereas Cromwell's fellow officer, Henry Ireton, argues for a franchise more restricted to men of some means.*

**Rainsborough:** . . . Really I think that the poorest he that is in England hath a life to live as the greatest he; and therefore truly, sir, I think it's clear, that every man that is to live under a government ought first by his own consent to put himself under that government; and I do think that the poorest man in England is not at all bound in a strict sense to that government that he hath not had a voice to put himself under; and I am confident that, when I have heard the reasons against it, that something will be said to answer those reasons, insomuch that I should doubt whether I was an Englishman or no, that should doubt of these things.

**Ireton:** . . . I think that no person hath a right to an interest or share in the disposing of the affairs of the kingdom, and in determining or choosing those that shall determine what laws we shall be ruled by here, no person hath a right to this that hath not a permanent fixed interest in this kingdom, and those persons together are properly the represented of this kingdom, who taken together, and consequently are to make up the representers of this kingdom, are the representers, who taken together do comprehend whatsoever is of real or permanent interest in the kingdom, and I am sure there is otherwise (I cannot tell what), otherwise any man can say why a foreigner coming in amongst us, or as many as will be coming in amongst us, or by force or otherwise settling themselves here, or at least by our permission having a being here, why they should not as well lay claim to it as any other. We talk of birthright. Truly birthright there is thus much claim: men may justly have by birthright, by their very being born in En-

gland, that we should not seclude them out of England. That we should not refuse to give them air and place and ground, and the freedom of the highways and other things, to live amongst us, not any man that is born here, though he in birth, or by his birth there come nothing at all that is part of the permanent interest of this kingdom to him. That I think is due to a man by birth. But that by a man's being born here he shall have a share in that power that shall dispose of the lands here, and of all things here, I do not think it a sufficient ground, but I am sure if we look upon that which is the utmost, within man's view, of what was originally the constitution of this kingdom, upon that which is most radical and fundamental, and which if you take away, there is no man hath any land, any goods, you take away any civil interest, and that is this: that those that choose the representers for the making of laws by which this state and kingdom are to be governed, are the persons who taken together, do comprehend the local interest of this kingdom; that is, the persons in whom all land lies, and those in corporations in whom all trading lies. This is the most fundamental constitution of this kingdom, and which if you do not allow, you allow none at all.

---

*Source:* G. E. Aylmer, ed., *The Levellers in the English Revolution* (Ithaca: Cornell University Press, 1975), pp. 100–101.

## ■ The Interregnum, 1649–1660

A Commonwealth—a republic—was declared. Executive power resided in a council of state. The House of Lords having been abolished, legislative power resided in a one-chamber Parliament, the Rump Parliament. Declaring a republic proved far easier than running one, however. The execution of the king shocked most English and Scots people and alienated many elites from the new regime. The legitimacy of the Commonwealth government would always be in question.

The tasks of making and implementing policy were hindered by the narrow political base on which the government now rested. Excluded were the majority of the reformist gentry who had been purged from Parliament. Also excluded were the more radical Levellers; Leveller leaders in London were arrested when they published tracts critical of the new government. Within a few years, many disillusioned Levellers would join a new religious movement called the Society of Friends, or Quakers, which espoused complete religious autonomy. Quakers declined all oaths or service to the state, and they refused to acknowledge social rank.

Above all, the new government was vulnerable to the power of the army, which had created it. In 1649 and 1650 Cromwell led expeditions to Ireland and Scotland, partly for sheer revenge and partly to put down resistance to Commonwealth authority. In Ireland, Cromwell's forces acted with shameful ruthlessness. English control there was strengthened by more dispossession of Irish landholders, which also served to pay off the army's wages. Meanwhile, Parliament could not agree on systematic reforms, particularly the one reform Independents in the army insisted on: more broadly based elections for a new Parliament. Fresh from his victories, Cromwell led his armies to London and dissolved Parliament in the spring of 1652.

In 1653 a cadre of army officers drew up the "Instrument of Government," England's first and only written constitution. It provided for an executive, the Lord Protector, and a Parliament to be based on somewhat wider male suffrage. Cromwell was the natural choice for Lord Protector, and whatever success the government of the Protectorate had was due largely to him.

Cromwell was an extremely able leader who was not averse to compromise. Although he had used force against Parliament in 1648, he had worked hard to reconcile the Rump Parliament and the army before marching on London in 1652. He believed in a state church, but one that allowed for control, including choice of minister, by local congregations. He also believed in toleration

**Popular Preaching in England** Many women took advantage of the collapse of royal authority to preach in public—a radical activity for women at the time. This print satirizes the Quakers, a religious movement that attracted many women. *(Mary Evans Picture Library)*

for other Protestant sects, as well as for Catholics and Jews, as long as no one disturbed the peace.

As Lord Protector, Cromwell oversaw impressive reforms in law that testify to his belief in the limits of governing authority. For example, contrary to the practice of his day, he opposed capital punishment for petty crimes. The government of the Protectorate, however, accomplished little given Parliament's internal divisions and opposition to Cromwell's initiatives. The population at large still harbored royalist sympathizers; after a royalist uprising in 1655, Cromwell divided England into military districts and vested governing authority in army generals.

In the end, the Protectorate could not survive the strains over policy and the challenges to its legitimacy. When Cromwell died of a sudden illness in September

1658, the Protectorate did not long survive him. In February 1660 the decisive action of one army general enabled all the surviving members of the Long Parliament to rejoin the Rump. The Parliament summarily dissolved itself and called for new elections. The newly elected Parliament recalled Charles II, son of Charles I, from exile abroad and restored the monarchy. The chaos and radicalism of the late civil war and *interregnum*—the period between reigns, as the years from 1649 to 1660 came to be called—now spawned a conservative reaction.

## ■ The Restoration, 1660–1685

Charles II (r. 1660–1685) claimed his throne at the age of 30. He had learned from his years of uncertain exile and from the fate of his father. He did not seek retribution but rather offered a general pardon to all but a few rebels (mostly those who had signed his father's death warrant), and he suggested to Parliament a relatively tolerant religious settlement that would include Anglicans as well as Presbyterians. He was far more politically adept than his father and far more willing to compromise.

That the re-established royal government was not more tolerant than it turned out to be was not Charles's doing but Parliament's. During the 1660s, the "Cavalier" Parliament, named for royalists in the civil war, passed harsh laws aimed at religious dissenters. Anglican orthodoxy was reimposed, including the re-establishment of bishops and the Anglican *Book of Common Prayer*. All officeholders and clergy were required to swear oaths of obedience to the king and to the established church. As a result, hundreds were forced out of office and pulpits. Holding nonconformist religious services became illegal, and Parliament passed a "five-mile" act to prevent dissenting ministers from traveling near their former congregations. Property laws were tightened and the criminal codes made more severe.

The king's behavior, in turn, began to mimic prerevolutionary royalist positions. Charles II began to flirt with Catholicism, and his brother and heir, James, openly converted. Charles promulgated a declaration of tolerance that would have included Catholics as well as nonconformist Protestants, but Parliament would not accept it. Anti-Catholic feeling still united all Protestants. In 1678 Charles's secret treaties with the French became known (see page 546), and rumors of a Catholic plot to murder Charles and reimpose Catholicism became widespread. No evidence of any plot was ever unearthed, though thirty-five people were executed for alleged participation. Parliament focused its attention on anti-Catholicism, passing the Test Act, which barred all but Anglicans from public office. As a result, the Catholic James was forced to resign as Lord High Admiral.

When Parliament moved to exclude James from succession to the throne, Charles dissolved it. A subsequent Parliament, worried by the specter of a new civil war, backed down. But the legacy of the civil war was a potent one. First, despite the harsh laws, to silence all dissent was not possible. After two decades of religious pluralism and broadly based political activity, it was impossible to reimpose conformity; well-established communities of various sects and a self-confidence bred vigorous resistance. The clearest reflection of the legacy of events was the power of Parliament. Though reluctant to press too far, Parliament had tried to assert its policies against the desires of the king.

Nevertheless, by the end of his reign, Charles was financially independent of Parliament thanks to increased revenue from overseas trade and to secret subsidies from France, his recent ally against Dutch trading rivals. This financial independence and firm political tactics enabled Charles to regain, and retain, a great deal of power. If he had been followed by an able successor, Parliament might have lost a good measure of its confidence and independence. But his brother James's reign and its aftermath further enhanced Parliament's power.

## ■ The Glorious Revolution, 1688

When James II (r. 1685–1689) succeeded Charles, Parliament's royalist leanings were at first evident. James was granted customs duties for life and was also given funds to suppress a rebellion by one of Charles's illegitimate sons. James did not try to impose Catholicism on England as some had feared, but he did try to achieve toleration for Catholics in two declarations of indulgence in 1687 and 1688. However admirable his goal—toleration—he had essentially changed the law of the realm without Parliament's consent and further undermined his position with heavy-handed tactics. When several leading Anglican bishops refused to read the declarations from their pulpits, he had them imprisoned and tried for seditious libel. However, a sympathetic jury acquitted them.

James also failed because of the coincidence of other events. In 1685, at the outset of James's reign, Louis XIV in France had revoked the Edict of Nantes. The possibility that subjects and monarchs in France and, by extension, elsewhere could be of different faiths seemed increasingly unlikely. Popular fears of James's Catholicism were thus heightened early in his reign, and his later declarations of tolerance, though benefiting Protestant dissenters, were viewed with suspicion. In 1688 not only were the Anglican bishops acquitted but the king's second wife, who was Catholic, gave birth to a son. The birth raised the specter of a Catholic succession.

In June 1688, to put pressure on James, leading Members of Parliament invited William of Orange, husband of James's Protestant daughter, Mary, to come to England. William mounted an invasion that became a rout when James refused to defend his throne. James simply abandoned England and went to France. William called Parliament, which declared James to have abdicated and offered the throne jointly to William and Mary. With French support James eventually invaded Ireland in 1690—bound for Westminster—but was defeated by William at the Battle of Boyne that year.

The substitution of William (r. 1689–1702) and Mary (r. 1689–1694) for James, known as the "Glorious Revolution," was engineered by Parliament and confirmed its power. Parliament presented the new sovereigns with a Declaration of Rights upon their accession and, later that year, with a Bill of Rights that defended freedom of speech, called for frequent Parliaments, and required subsequent monarchs to be Protestant. The effectiveness of these documents was reinforced by Parliament's power of the purse. Parliament's role in the political process was ensured by William's interests in funding his ambitious military efforts, particularly the Netherlands' ongoing wars with France.

The issues that had faced the English since the beginning of the century were common to all European states: religious division and elite power, fiscal strains and resistance to taxation. Yet the cataclysmic events in England—the interregnum, the Commonwealth, the Restoration, the Glorious Revolution—had set it apart from the experience of other states. Consequently, the incremental assumption of authority by a well-established institution, Parliament, made challenge of the English monarchy more legitimate and more effective.

# NEW POWERS IN CENTRAL AND EASTERN EUROPE

**B**Y the end of the seventeenth century, three states dominated central and eastern Europe: Austria, Brandenburg-Prussia, and Russia. After the Thirty Years' War, the Habsburgs' dominance in the splintering empire waned, and they focused on expanding and consolidating their power in their hereditary possessions. Brandenburg-Prussia, in northeastern Germany, emerged from obscurity to rival the Habsburg

state. The rulers of Brandenburg-Prussia had gained lands in the Peace of Westphalia, and astute management transformed their relatively small and scattered holdings into one of the most powerful states in Europe. Russia's new stature in eastern Europe resulted in part from the weakness of its greatest rival, Poland, and the determination of one leader, Peter the Great, to assume a major role in European affairs. Sweden controlled valuable Baltic territory through much of the century but eventually was also eclipsed by Russia as a force in the region.

The internal political development of these states was dramatically shaped by their relationship to the wider European economy: they were sources of grain and raw materials for the more densely urbanized west. The development of and the competition among states in central and eastern Europe were closely linked to developments in western Europe.

## ■ The Consolidation of Austria

The Thirty Years' War (see pages 523–528) weakened the Habsburgs as emperors but strengthened them in their own lands. The main Habsburg lands in 1648 were a collection of principalities comprising modern Austria, the kingdom of Hungary (largely in Turkish hands), and the kingdom of Bohemia (see Map 16.2). In 1714 Austria acquired the Spanish Netherlands, which were renamed the "Austrian Netherlands." Although language and ethnic differences prevented an absolutist state along French lines, Leopold I (r. 1657–1705) instituted political and institutional changes that enabled the Habsburg state to become one of the most powerful in Europe through the eighteenth century.

Much of the coherence that already existed in Leopold's lands had been achieved by his predecessors in the wake of the Thirty Years' War. The lands of rebels in Bohemia had been confiscated and redistributed among loyal, mostly Austrian, families. In return for political and military support for the emperor, these families were given the right to exploit their newly acquired land and the peasants who worked it. The desire to recover population and productivity after the destruction of the Thirty Years' War gave landlords further incentive to curtail peasants' autonomy sharply, particularly in devastated Bohemia. Austrian landlords throughout the Habsburg domains provided grain and timber for the export market and foodstuffs for the Austrian armies, while elite families provided the army with officers. This political-economic arrangement provoked numerous serious peasant revolts, but the peasants were not able to force changes in a system that suited both the elites and the central authority.

**Celebrating Habsburg Power**   Leopold I is depicted here trampling a Turkish soldier, wearing armor and a medieval order of knighthood around his neck—appropriate garb with which to represent a victory over "the Infidel." Compare this sculpture with the painting of Louis XIV in Roman armor on page 538.   *(Kunsthistorisches Museum, Vienna)*

Although Leopold had lost much influence within the empire itself, an imperial government made up of various councils, a war ministry, financial officials, and the like still functioned in his capital, Vienna. Leopold worked to extricate the government of his own lands from the apparatus of imperial institutions, which were staffed largely by Germans more loyal to imperial than to Habsburg interests. In addition, Leopold used the Catholic Church as an institutional and ideological support for the Habsburg state.

Leopold's personal ambition was to re-establish devout Catholicism throughout his territories. Acceptance of Catholicism became the litmus test of loyalty to the Habsburg regime, and Protestantism vanished among elites. Leopold encouraged the work of Jesuit teachers and members of other Catholic orders. These men and women helped staff his government and administered religious life down to the most local levels.

Leopold's most dramatic success, as a Habsburg and as a religious leader, was his reconquest of the kingdom of Hungary from the Ottoman Empire. Since the mid-sixteenth century, the Habsburgs had controlled only a narrow strip of the kingdom. Preoccupied with countering Louis XIV's aggression, Leopold did not himself choose to begin a reconquest. His centralizing policies, however, alienated nobles and townspeople in the portion of Hungary he did control, as did his repression of Protestantism, which had flourished in Hungary. Hungarian nobles began a revolt, aided by the Turks, aiming for a reunited Hungary under Ottoman protection.

The Habsburgs emerged victorious in part because they received help from the Venetians, the Russians, and especially the Poles, whose lands in Ukraine were threatened by the Turks. The Turks overreached their supply lines to besiege Vienna in 1683. When the siege failed, Habsburg armies slowly pressed east and south, recovering Buda, the capital of Hungary, in 1686 and Belgrade in 1688. The Danube basin lay once again in Christian hands. The Treaty of Carlowitz ended the fighting in 1699, after the first conference where European allies jointly dictated terms to a weakening Ottoman Empire. Austria's allies had also gained at the Ottomans' expense: the Poles recovered the threatened Ukraine, and the Russians gained a vital foothold on the Black Sea.

Leopold gave land in the reclaimed lands to Austrian officers who he believed were loyal to him. The traditions of Hungarian separatism, however, were strong, and the great magnates—whether they had defended the Habsburgs against Turkish encroachment or guarded the frontier for Turkish overlords—retained their independence. The peasantry, as elsewhere, suffered a decline in status as a result of the Crown's efforts to ensure the loyalty of elites. In the long run, Hungarian independence weakened the Habsburg state, but in the short run Leopold's victory over the Turks and the recovery of Hungary itself were momentous events, confirming the Habsburgs as the pre-eminent power in central Europe.

## ■ The Rise of Brandenburg-Prussia

Three German states, in addition to Austria, gained territory and stature after the Thirty Years' War: Bavaria, Saxony, and Brandenburg-Prussia. By the end of the seventeenth century, the strongest was Brandenburg-Prussia, a conglomeration of small territories held, by dynastic accident, by the Hohenzollern family. The two principal territories were electoral Brandenburg, in northeastern Germany, with its capital, Berlin, and the duchy of Prussia, a fief of the Polish crown along the Baltic coast east of Poland proper (see Map 16.2). In addition the Hohenzollerns ruled a handful of small principalities near the Netherlands. The manipulation of resources and power that enabled these unpromising lands to become a powerful state was primarily the work of Frederick William, known as "the Great Elector" (r. 1640–1688).

Frederick William used the occasion of a war to effect a permanent change in the structure of government. He took advantage of a war between Poland and its rivals, Sweden and Russia (described in the next section), to win independence for the duchy of Prussia from Polish overlordship. When his involvement in the war ended in 1657, he kept intact the general war commissariat, a combined civilian and military body that had efficiently directed the war effort, bypassing traditional councils and representative bodies. He also used the standing army to force the payment of high taxes. Most significantly, he established a positive relationship with the *Junker*°, hereditary landholders, which ensured him both revenue and loyalty. He agreed to allow the Junkers virtually total control of their own lands in return for their agreement to support his government—in short, they surrendered their accustomed political independence in exchange for greater economic and social power over the peasants who worked their lands.

Peasants and townspeople were taxed, but nobles were not. The freedom to control their estates led many nobles to invest in profitable agriculture for the export market. The peasants were serfs who received no benefits from the increased productivity of the land. Frederick William further enhanced his state's power by sponsoring state industries. These industries did not have to fear competition from urban producers because the towns had been frozen out of the political process and saddled with heavy taxes. Although an oppressive place for many Germans, Brandenburg-Prussia attracted many skilled refugees, such as Huguenot artisans fleeing Louis XIV's France.

Bavaria and Saxony, in contrast to Brandenburg-Prussia, had vibrant towns, largely free peasantries, and weaker aristocracies but were relative nonentities in international affairs. Power on the European stage depended on military force. Such power, whether in a large state like France or in a small one like Brandenburg-Prussia, usually came at the expense of the people.

## ■ Competition Around the Baltic: The Demise of Poland and the Zenith of Swedish Power

The rivers and port cities of the Baltic coast were conduits for the growing trade between the Baltic hinterland and the rest of Europe. Tolls assessed on the passage of

*Junker* (YUNG-kur)

timber, grain, naval stores, and furs were an important source of local income, and the commodities themselves brought profits to their producers. This trading system had profound social and political consequences for all of the states bordering the Baltic Sea in the seventeenth century.

First, it was a spur to war: Sweden and Denmark fought over control of the sea-lanes connecting the Baltic and North Seas. Sweden, Poland, and Russia fought for control of the eastern Baltic coastline in the sixteenth and seventeenth centuries. In the seventeenth century, Poland and Russia fought over grain- and timber-producing lands comprising modern Belarus, parts of modern Russia, and Ukraine. Second, profits from the production of grain for export in such volume reinforced the power of large landholders, particularly within Poland, where most of the grain was produced.

In 1600 a large portion of the Baltic hinterland lay under the control of Poland-Lithuania, a dual kingdom at the height of its power, but one that would prove an exception to the pattern of expanding royal power in the seventeenth century (see Map 16.2). A marriage in 1386 had brought the duchy of Lithuania under a joint ruler with Poland; earlier in the fourteenth century, Lithuania had conquered Belarus and Ukraine. Poland-Lithuania commanded considerable resources, including the Vistula and Nieman Rivers and the ports of Gdansk and Riga on the Baltic coast. Like the neighboring Habsburg lands, it was a multi-ethnic state, particularly in the huge duchy of Lithuania, where Russian-speakers predominated. Poland was Catholic but had large minorities of Protestants and Jews. Owing to ties with Poland, Lithuanians themselves were mostly Catholic (and some were Protestant), but Russian-speakers were Orthodox. German-speaking families dominated trade in most coastal cities.

Internal strains and external challenges began to mount in Poland-Lithuania in the late sixteenth century. The commercial power of Polish landlords gave them considerable political clout; the king was forced to grant concessions that weakened urban freedoms and bound impoverished peasants to the nobles' estates. In 1572 the sudden death of the very able but childless king, Sigismund II (r. 1548–1572), only enhanced the nobles' position. Sigismund's successors would be elected, which dramatically limited their power: they would have no control over succession to the throne and would be closely supervised by noble counselors.

The spread of the Counter-Reformation, encouraged by the Crown, created tensions with both Protestant and Orthodox subjects in the diverse kingdom. In Ukraine, communities of Cossacks, nomadic farmer-warriors,

**Map 16.2    New Powers in Central and Eastern Europe, to 1725**    The balance of power in central and eastern Europe shifted with the strengthening of Austria, the rise of Brandenburg-Prussia, and the expansion of Russia at the expense of Poland and Sweden.

grew as Polish and Lithuanian peasants fled harsh conditions to join them. The Cossacks had long been tolerated because they served as a military buffer against the Ottoman Turks to the south, but now Polish landlords wanted to reincorporate the Cossacks into the profitable political-economic system that they controlled. Meanwhile, the Crown was involved in several wars. From 1609 to 1612 Polish armies tried but failed to impose a Polish king on the Russians during a dispute over the succession. While aiding Austria in the Thirty Years' War against the Turks, their common enemy, the Poles lost Livonia (modern Latvia) and other bits of northern territory to the aggressive Gustav Adolf of Sweden.

In 1648 the Polish crown faced revolt and invasion that it could not counter. The Cossacks, with the Crimean Tatars and their Ottoman overlords as allies, staged a major uprising, defeated Polish armies, and established an independent state. In 1654 the Cossacks transferred their allegiance to Moscow and became part of a Russian invasion of Poland that, by the next year, had engulfed much of the eastern half of the dual kingdom. At the same time, the Swedes seized central Poland and competed with the Russians for control elsewhere; the Swedes were helped by Polish and Lithuanian aristocrats acting like independent warlords.

Polish royal armies managed to recover much territory—most important, the western half of Ukraine. But the invasions and subsequent fighting were disastrous. The population of Poland may have declined by as much as 40 percent, and vital urban economies were in ruins. The Catholic identity of the Polish heartland had been a rallying point for resistance to the Protestant Swedes and the Orthodox Russians, but the religious tolerance that had distinguished the Polish kingdom and had been mandated in its constitution was now abandoned. In addition, much of its recovery of territory was only nominal. In parts of Lithuania inhabited by Russian-speaking peoples, the Russian presence during the wars had achieved local transfers of power from Lithuanian to Russian landlords loyal to Moscow.

The elective Polish crown passed in 1674 to the brilliant military commander Jan Sobieski° (r. 1674–1696), known as "Vanquisher of the Turks" for his role in raising the siege of Vienna in 1683. Given Poland's internal weakness, however, Sobieski's victories in the long run helped the Ottomans' other foes—Austria and Russia—more than they helped the Poles. His successor, Augustus II of Saxony (r. 1697–1704, 1709–1733), dragged Poland back into war, from which Russia would emerge the clear winner in the power struggle in eastern Europe.

On the Baltic coast, however, Sweden remained the dominant player through most of the seventeenth century. Swedish efforts to control Baltic territory began in the sixteenth century, first to counter the power of its perennial rival, Denmark, in the western Baltic. It then competed with Poland to control Livonia, whose principal city, Riga°, was an important trading center for goods from both Lithuania and Russia. By 1617, under Gustav Adolf, the Swedes gained the lands to the north surrounding the Gulf of Finland (the most direct outlet for Russian goods) and in 1621 displaced the Poles in Livonia itself. Swedish intervention in the Thirty Years' War came when imperial successes against Denmark both threatened the Baltic coast and created an opportunity to strike at Sweden's old enemy. The Treaty of Westphalia (1648) confirmed Sweden's earlier gains and added control of further coastal territory, mostly at Denmark's expense.

The port cities held by Sweden were profitable but simply served to pay for the costly wars necessary to seize and defend them. Indeed, Sweden's efforts to hold Baltic territory were driven by dynastic and strategic needs as much as economic objectives. The ruling dynasty struggled against Denmark's control of western Baltic territory in order to safeguard its independence from the Danes, who had ruled the combined kingdoms until 1523. Similarly, competition with Poland for the eastern Baltic was part of a dynastic struggle after 1592. Sigismund Vasa, son of the king of Sweden, had been elected king of Poland in 1587 but also inherited the Swedish throne in 1592. Other members of the ruling Swedish Vasa family fought him successfully to regain rule over Sweden and extricate Swedish interests from Poland's continental preoccupations. Sigismund ruled Poland until his death in 1632, but a Vasa uncle replaced him on the Swedish throne in 1604.

The one permanent gain that Sweden realized from its aggression against Poland at mid-century was the renunciation of the Polish Vasa line to any claim to the Swedish crown. Owing to its earlier gains, Sweden reigned supreme on the Baltic coast until the end of the century, when it was supplanted by the powerful Russian state.

## ■ The Expansion of Russia

The Russian state expanded dramatically through the sixteenth century. Ivan IV (r. 1533–1584) was proclaimed "Tsar of All the Russias" in 1547. This act was the culmination of the accumulation of land and authority by the princes of Moscow through the late Middle Ages, when

**Sobieski** (so-BYESS-key)

**Riga** (REE-guh)

**Peter the Great** This portrait by a Dutch artist captures the tsar's "Westernizing" mission by showing Peter in military dress according to European fashions of the day.

(*Rijksmuseum-Stichting, Amsterdam*)

Moscow had vied for pre-eminence with other Russian principalities. Ivan IV's grandfather, Ivan III (r. 1462–1505), the first to use the title *tsar,* had absorbed neighboring Russian principalities and ended Moscow's subservience to Mongol overlords.

Ivan IV, also known as Ivan "the Terrible" (in Russian, *groznyi,* more accurately translated as "awe-inspiring"), was the first actually to be crowned tsar and routinely to use the title. His use of the title aptly reflected his imperial intentions, as he continued Moscow's push westward and, especially, eastward against the Mongol states of central Asia. Two of the three Mongol states to the east and south fell, and Russian hegemony edged eastward over the Ural Mountains to Siberia for the first time.

Within this expanding empire, Ivan IV ruled as an autocrat. Part of his authority stemmed from his own personality. He was willing—some suggest because of mental imbalance—to use ruthless methods, including the torture and murder of thousands of subjects, to enforce his will. The practice of gathering tribute for Mon-

gol overlords had put many resources in the hands of Muscovite princes. Ivan IV was able to bypass noble participation and intensify the centralization of government by creating ranks of officials, known as the service gentry, loyal only to him.

A period of disputed succession known as the Time of Troubles followed Ivan's death in 1584, not unlike similar crises in other European states, where jealous aristocrats vied for power during periods of royal weakness. In this case, aristocratic factions fought among themselves as well as against armies of Cossacks and other common people who disputed nobles' ambitions and desired less oppressive government. Nonetheless, the foundations of the large and cohesive state laid by Ivan enabled Michael Romanov° to rebuild autocratic government with ease after being chosen tsar in 1613.

The Romanovs were an eminent aristocratic family related to Ivan's. Michael (r. 1613–1645) was selected to rule by an assembly of aristocrats, gentry, and commoners who were more alarmed at the civil wars and recent Polish incursions than at the prospect of a return to strong tsarist rule. Michael was succeeded by his son, Alexis (r. 1645–1676), who presided over the extension of Russian control to eastern Ukraine in 1654 and developed interest in cultivating relationships with the West.

Shifting the balance of power in eastern Europe and the Baltic in Russia's favor was also the work of Alexis's son, Peter I, "the Great" (r. 1682–1725). Peter accomplished this by military successes against his enemies and by forcibly reorienting Russian government and society toward involvement with the rest of Europe.

Peter was almost literally larger than life. Nearly 7 feet tall, he towered over most of his contemporaries and had physical and mental energy to match his size. He set himself to learning trades and studied soldiering by rising through the ranks of the military like a common soldier. He traveled abroad to learn as much as he could about western European economies and governments. He wanted the revenue, manufacturing output, technology and trade, and, above all, the up-to-date army and navy that other rulers enjoyed. In short, Peter sought for Russia a more evolved state system because of the strength it would give him.

Immediately on his accession to power, Peter initiated a bold series of changes in Russian society. His travels had taught him that European monarchs coexisted with a privileged but educated aristocracy and that a brilliant court life symbolized and reinforced the rulers' authority. So he set out to refashion Russian society in what amounted to an enforced cultural revolution. He

**Romanov** (ROH-man-off)

## Resistance to Peter the Great

*Many of his subjects resisted Peter's policies, including nobles who despised the enforced cultural changes and peasants who chafed under Peter's more traditional demand of heavy taxes. This letter, from July 1705, reflects the efforts of one group of resisters, city dwellers from Astrakhan, a port on the Caspian Sea, to join forces with another, the Cossacks of the Don River region, to their west. Many citizens of Astrakhan had been at odds with the tsars since the seventeenth century over church reforms. Note that their objections to Peter's cultural reforms, which included European dress and other matters of style (such as being clean-shaven and using tobacco), are thus couched in religious terms. What other concerns does this document reveal? Why might the citizens of Astrakhan have forged an alliance with the Cossacks?*

To [the Chief] and to all the Don Cossack Host, we . . . all the city folk of Astrakhan . . . send our greetings. We wish to inform you of what has happened in Astrakhan on account of our Christian faith, because of beard-shaving, German dress, and tobacco; how we, our wives and our children were not admitted into churches in our old Russian dress; how men and women who entered the holy church had their clothes shorn and were expelled and thrown out. . . . Moreover, in the last year, they imposed on us and collected a [new] tax: one ruble "bath money" apiece; and they also ordered us to pay [a certain tax] per seven feet of cellar space. . . . The [local governor] together with other men in authority, colonels and captains, took away all of our firearms and wanted to kill us. . . . They also took away from us, without orders, our bread allowance and forbade that it be issued to us. We endured all this for a long time. [At last,] after taking counsel among ourselves . . . moved by our great distress, for we could endure it no more to be in danger of losing our Christian faith, we resisted: we killed some of them and have put some others in prison. You, the Cossack [Chief] and all the Host of the Don, please deliberate among yourselves and stand up together with us to defend the Christian faith, and send a message about your decision to us at Astrakhan. We are awaiting you . . . and we rely upon you.

*Source:* Alfred J. Andrea and James H. Overfield, *The Human Record: Sources of Global History*, vol. 2: *Since 1500*, 2d ed. (Boston: Houghton Mifflin, 1994), pp. 168–169.

provoked a direct confrontation with Russia's traditional aristocracy over everything from education to matters of dress. He elevated numerous new families to the ranks of gentry and created an official ranking system for the nobility to encourage and reward service to his government.

Peter's effort to reorient his nation culturally, economically, and politically toward Europe was most apparent in the construction of the city of St. Petersburg on the Gulf of Finland, which provided access to the Baltic Sea (see Map 16.2). In stark contrast to Moscow, dominated by the medieval fortress of the Kremlin and churches in the traditional Russian style, St. Petersburg was a modern European city with wide avenues and palaces designed for a sophisticated court life.

But although Peter was highly intelligent, practical, and determined to create a more productive and better-governed society, he was also cruel and authoritarian. Peasants already were bearing the brunt of taxation, but their tax burden worsened when they were assessed arbitrarily by head and not by output of the land. The building of St. Petersburg cost staggering sums in money and in workers' lives. Peter's entire reform system was carried out tyrannically; resistance was brutally suppressed. Victims of Peter's oppression included his son, Alexis, who died after torture while awaiting execution for questioning his father's policies.

Peter faced elite as well as populist rebellions against the exactions and the cultural changes of his regime. The most serious challenge, in 1707, was a revolt of Cossacks of the Don River region against the regime's tightened controls. (See the box "Reading Sources: Resistance to Peter the Great.") A major reason for the high cost of Peter's government to the Russian people was his ambition for territorial gain—hence his emphasis on an improved, and costly, army and navy. Working side by side with workers and technicians, many of whom he had recruited while abroad, Peter created the Russian navy from scratch. At first, ships were built in the south to contest Turkish control of the Black Sea; later, they were built in the north to secure and defend the Baltic. Peter also modernized the Russian army by employing tactics, training, and discipline he had observed in the West. He introduced military conscription and munitions plants. By 1709 Russia was able to manufacture most of the up-to-date firearms its army needed.

Russia waged war virtually throughout Peter's reign. Initially with some success, he struck at the Ottomans and their client state in the Crimea. Later phases of these conflicts brought reverses, however. Peter was spectacularly successful against his northern competitor, Sweden, for control of the weakened Polish state and the Baltic Sea. The conflicts between Sweden and Russia, known as the Great Northern War, raged from 1700 to 1709 and, in a less intense phase, lasted until 1721. By the Treaty of Nystadt in 1721, Russia gained its present-day territory in the Gulf of Finland near St. Petersburg, plus Livonia and Estonia. These acquisitions gave Russia a secure window on the Baltic and, in combination with its gains of Lithuanian territory earlier in the century, made Russia the pre-eminent Baltic power, at Sweden's and Poland's expense.

# THE EXPANSION OF OVERSEAS TRADE AND SETTLEMENT

**B**Y the beginning of the seventeenth century, competition from the Dutch, French, and English was disrupting the Spanish and Portuguese trading empires in Asia and the New World. During the seventeenth century, European trade and colonization expanded and changed dramatically. The Dutch not only became masters of the spice trade but broadened the market to include many other commodities. In the Americas, a new trading system linking Europe, Africa, and the New World came into being with the expansion of tobacco and, later, sugar production. French and English colonists began settling in North America in increasing numbers. By the end of the century, trading and colonial outposts around the world figured regularly as bargaining chips in disagreements between European states. More important, overseas trade had a crucial impact on life within Europe: on patterns of production and consumption, on social stratification, and on the distribution of wealth.

## ■ The Growth of Trading Empires: The Success of the Dutch

By the end of the sixteenth century, the Dutch and the English were making incursions into the Portuguese-controlled spice trade with areas of India, Ceylon, and the East Indies. Spain had annexed Portugal in 1580, but the drain on Spain's resources from its wars with the Dutch and French prevented Spain from adequately defending its enlarged trading empire in Asia. The Dutch and, to a lesser degree, the English rapidly supplanted Portuguese control of this lucrative trade (see Map 16.3).

The Dutch were particularly well placed to be successful competitors in overseas trade. They already dominated seaborne trade within Europe, including the most important long-distance trade, which linked Spain and Portugal—with their wine and salt, as well as spices, hides, and gold from abroad—with the Baltic seacoast, where these products were sold for grain and timber produced in Germany, Poland-Lithuania, and Scandinavia. The geographic position of the Netherlands and the fact that the Dutch consumed more Baltic grain than any other area, because of their large urban population, help to explain their dominance of this trade. In addition, the Dutch had improved the design of their merchant ships to maximize their profits. By 1600 they were building the *fluitschip* (flyship) to transport cargo economically; it was a vessel with a long, flat hull, simple rigging, and cheap construction.

The Dutch were successful in Asia because of institutional as well as technological innovations. In 1602 the Dutch East India Company was formed. The company combined government management of trade, typical of the period, with both public and private investment. In the past, groups of investors had funded single voyages or small numbers of ships on a one-time basis. The formation of the Dutch East India Company created a permanent pool of capital to sustain trade. After 1612 investments in the company were negotiable as stock. These greater assets allowed proprietors to spread the risks and delays of longer voyages among larger numbers of investors. In addition, more money was available for warehouses, docks, and ships. The English East India Company, founded in 1607, also supported trade, but more modestly. It had one-tenth the capital of the Dutch company and did not use the same system of permanent

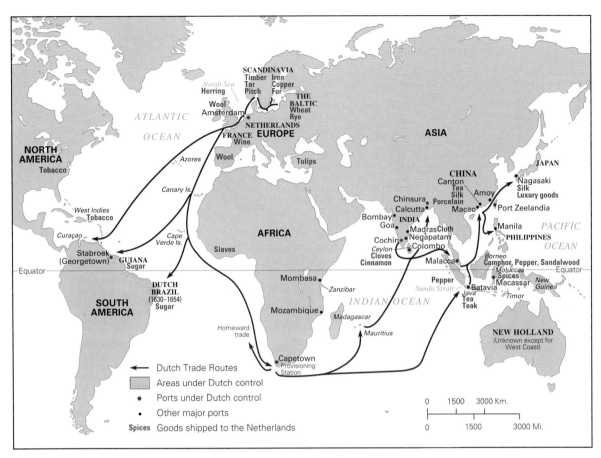

**Map 16.3    Dutch Commerce in the Seventeenth Century**    The Dutch supplanted
Portuguese control of trade with Asia and dominated seaborne trade within Europe.

capital held as stock by investors until 1657. The Bank of
Amsterdam, founded in 1609, became the depository for
the bullion that flowed into the Netherlands with the
flood of trade. The bank established currency exchange
rates and issued paper money and instruments of credit
to facilitate commerce.

A dramatic expansion of trade with Asia resulted
from the Dutch innovations, so much so that by 1650
the European market for spices was glutted, and traders'
profits had begun to fall. To control the supply of spices,
the Dutch seized some of the areas where they were produced. The Dutch and English further responded to the
oversupply of spices by diversifying their trade. The proportion of spices in cargoes from the East fell from
about 70 percent at midcentury to just over 20 percent
by the century's end. New consumer goods such as tea,
coffee, silks, and cotton fabrics took their place. The demand of ordinary people for inexpensive yet serviceable
Indian cottons grew steadily. Eventually, the Dutch and

the English, alert for fresh opportunities in the East, entered the local carrying trade among Asian states. Doing
so enabled them to make profits even without purchasing goods, and it slowed the drain of hard currency from
Europe—currency in increasingly short supply as silver
mines in the Americas were depleted.

## ■ The "Golden Age" of the Netherlands

The prosperity occasioned by the Netherlands' "mother
trade" within Europe and its burgeoning overseas commerce helped to foster social and political conditions
unique among European states. The concentration of
trade and shipping sustained a healthy merchant oligarchy and also an extensive and prosperous artisanal
sector. Disparities of wealth were smaller here than anywhere else in Europe. The shipbuilding and fishing
trades, among others, supported large numbers of workers with a high standard of living for the age.

**Dutch Strength at Sea**    This painting by Dutch artist Van der Velde the Younger celebrates a Dutch victory over a combined French and English fleet in 1673. The Dutch had fought their primary commercial rivals, the English, during the 1650s and had built up their fleet of warships in response. Like most major sea battles of the era, this one was fought close to home, off the Dutch coast near the sea-lanes to Amsterdam. *(HarperCollins Publishers/The Art Archive)*

The Netherlands appeared to contemporaries to be an astonishing exception to the normal structures of politics. Political decentralization in the Netherlands persisted. The Estates General (representative assembly) for the Netherlands as a whole had no independent powers of taxation. Each of the seven provinces retained considerable autonomy. Wealthy merchants in the Estates of the province of Holland in fact constituted the government for the entire nation for long periods because of Holland's economic dominance. The head of government was the executive secretary, known as the pensionary, of Holland's Estates.

Holland's only competition in the running of affairs came from the House of Orange, aristocratic leaders of the revolt against Spain (see pages 505–511). They exercised what control they had by means of the office of *stadholder°*—a kind of military governorship—to which they were elected in individual provinces. Their principal interest was the traditional one of military glory and self-promotion. Therein lay a portion of their influence, for they continued to lead the defense of the Netherlands against Spanish attempts at reconquest until the Peace of Westphalia in 1648, and against French aggres-

sion after 1672. Their power also came from their status as the only counterweight within the Netherlands to the dominance of Amsterdam's (in Holland) mercantile interests. Small towns dependent on land-based trade or rural areas dominated by farmers and gentry looked to the stadholders of the Orange family to defend their interests.

As elsewhere, religion was a source of political conflict. The stadholders and the leading families of Holland, known as regents, vied for control of the state church. Pensionaries and regents of Holland generally favored a less rigid and austere form of Calvinism than did the stadholders. Their view reflected the needs of the diverse urban communities of Holland, where thousands of Jews as well as Catholics and various kinds of Protestants lived. Foreign policy was also disputed: Hollanders desired peace in order to foster commerce, whereas stadholders willingly engaged in warfare for territory and dynastic advantage.

These differences notwithstanding, Dutch commercial dominance involved the Netherlands in costly wars throughout the second half of the century. Between 1657 and 1660 the Dutch defended Denmark against Swedish ambitions in order to safeguard the sea-lanes and port cities of the Baltic. More costly conflicts arose because of

**stadholder** (STAHT-hole-der)

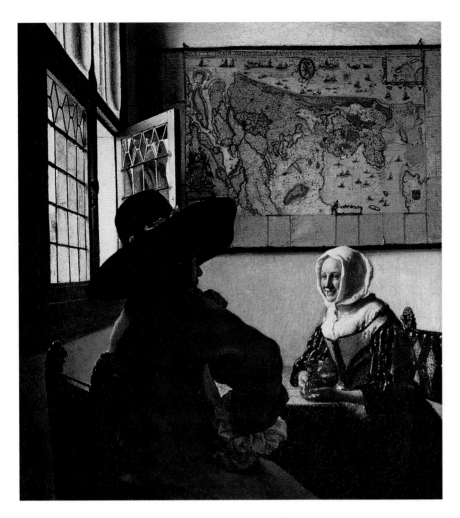

**Vermeer: The Soldier and the Laughing Girl** This is an early work by one of the great artists of the Dutch "Golden Age." Dutch art was distinguished by its treatment of common, rather than heroic, subjects. The masterful use of light and perspective in paintings such as this one would not be equaled until the invention of photography.

*(Copyright The Frick Collection, New York)*

rivalry with the more powerful England and France. Under Cromwell, the English attempted to close their ports to the Dutch carrying trade. In 1672 the English under Charles II allied with the French, assuming that together they could destroy Dutch power and perhaps even divide the Netherlands' territory between them. The Dutch navy, rebuilt since Cromwell's challenge, soon forced England out of the alliance.

Owing largely to the land war with France, the Estates in Holland lost control of policy to William of Nassau (d. 1702), prince of Orange after 1672. William drew the Netherlands into his family's long-standing close relationship with England. Like other members of his family before him, William had married into the English royal family: his wife was Mary, daughter of James II.

Ironically, after William and Mary assumed the English throne, Dutch commerce suffered more in alliance with England than in its previous rivalry. William used Dutch resources for the land war against Louis XIV and reserved for the English navy the fight at sea. By the end of the century, Dutch maritime strength was being eclipsed by English sea power.

## ◼ The Growth of Atlantic Colonies and Commerce

In the seventeenth century, the Dutch, the English, and the French joined the Spanish as colonial and commercial powers in the Americas. The Spanish colonial empire, in theory a trading system closed to outsiders, was in fact vulnerable to incursion by other European traders. Spanish treasure fleets were themselves a glittering attraction. In 1628, for example, a Dutch captain seized the entire fleet. But by then Spain's goals and those of its competitors had begun to shift. The limits of an economy based on the extraction, rather than the production, of wealth became clear with the declining output of the Spanish silver mines during the 1620s. In response, the Spanish and their Dutch, French, and English competitors expanded the production of the cash crops of tobacco, dyestuffs, and, above all, sugar.

The European demand for tobacco and sugar, both addictive substances, grew steadily in the seventeenth century. The plantation system—the use of forced labor to produce cash crops on vast tracts of land—had been

**Sugar Manufacture in Caribbean Colonies**    Production of sugar required large capital outlays, in part because the raw cane had to be processed quickly, on site, to avoid spoilage. This scene depicts enslaved workers operating a small sugar mill on the island of Barbados in the seventeenth century. In the background a press crushes the cane; in the foreground, the juice from the cane is boiled down until sugar begins to crystallize.    *(Mary Evans Picture Library)*

developed on Mediterranean islands in the Middle Ages by European entrepreneurs, using slaves procured in Black Sea ports by Venetian and Genoese traders. Sugar production by this system had been established on Atlantic islands, such as the Cape Verde Islands, using African labor, and then in the Americas by the Spanish and Portuguese. Sugar production in the New World grew from about 20,000 tons in 1600 to about 200,000 tons by 1770.

In the 1620s, while the Dutch were exploiting Portuguese weakness in the eastern spice trade, they were also seizing sugar regions in Brazil and replacing the Portuguese in slaving ports in Africa. The Portuguese were able to retake most of their Brazilian territory in the 1650s. But the Dutch, because they monopolized the carrying trade, were able to become the official supplier of slaves to Spanish plantations in the New World and the chief supplier of slaves as well as other goods to most other regions. (See the box "Global Encounters: Journal of a Dutch Slave Ship.") The Dutch were able to make handsome profits dealing in human cargo until the end of the seventeenth century, when they were supplanted by the British.

The Dutch introduced the techniques of sugar cultivation to the French and English after learning it themselves in Brazil. Sugar plantations began to supplant tobacco cultivation as well as subsistence farming on the Caribbean islands the English and the French controlled. Beginning late in the sixteenth century, English and French seamen had seized island territories to serve as provisioning stations and staging points for raids against or commerce with Spanish colonies. Some island outposts had expanded into colonies and attracted European settlers—some, as in North America, coming as indentured servants—to work the land. Sugar cultivation, though potentially more profitable than tobacco, demanded huge outlays of capital and continual supplies of unskilled labor, and it drastically transformed the settlements' characters. Large plantations owned by wealthy, often absentee landlords and dependent on slave labor replaced smaller-scale independent farming. The most profitable sugar colonies were, for the French, the islands of Martinique° and Guadeloupe°, and for the English, Barbados° and Jamaica.

---

**Martinique** (mar-tih-NEEK)    **Guadeloupe** (gwah-dah-LOO-puh)    **Barbados** (bar-BAY-dose)

## ⊕ GLOBAL ENCOUNTERS

### Journal of a Dutch Slave Ship

*These excerpts from a journal kept by the captain of the Dutch ship* St. Jan *record a 1659 slave-trading voyage that began in Africa and ended on Curaçao, a Dutch island colony in the Caribbean. A companion document reveals that 110 of the 219 captive men, women, and children died during the voyage across the Atlantic. Note the fate of those who were still alive by journey's end: why was a pirate able to escape with so many of the slaves?*

The 8th [of March]. We arrived with our ship on Saturday before Arda [in modern Benin] to take on board the surgeon's mate, and tamarinds as refreshment for the slaves. We set sail the next day to continue our voyage to Rio Reael.

The 22nd [of May]. We weighed anchor again and sailed out of the Rio Reael. . . . We acquired there in trade two hundred and nineteen slaves, men and women, boys as well as girls; and we set our course for [islands in the Gulf of Biafra] in order to seek food for the slaves, because nothing was to be had in Rio Reael.

The 26th ditto. On Monday we arrived [on the islands]. We spent seven days there looking but barely obtained enough for the slaves' daily consumption; therefore we decided to sail [up a nearby river] to see whether any food could be found there.

The 29th [of June]. On Sunday we decided to continue our voyage because there was also little food [up the river mouth] for the slaves because of the heavy rain which we had daily and because many slaves were suffering from dysentery caused by the bad food supplied to us at [St. George del Mina, a Dutch fort established to serve the slave trade]. . . .

The 11th [of August]. We lay sixteen days at Cape Lopez [modern Gabon] in order to take on water and firewood. Among the water barrels some forty were taken apart to be repaired because our cooper died . . . [and] we had no one who could repair them.

The 24th [of September]. On Friday we arrived at the island of Tobago [in the Caribbean] where we took on water and also bought some bread for our crew because for three weeks they have had no rations.

The 1st of November. We lost our ship on the reef [east of Curaçao] and our crew fled in the boat immediately. There was no chance to save the slaves because we had to abandon the ship on account of heavy surf.

The 4th ditto. We arrived with the boat at . . . Curaçao. The [governor] dispatched two sloops to retrieve the slaves from the shipwreck. One of the sloops was taken by a pirate together with eighty-four slaves.

*Source:* Charles T. Gehring and J. A. Schiltkamp, eds., *New Netherlands Documents*, vol. 17 (Interlaken, N.Y.: Heart of the Lakes Publishing, 1987), pp. 128–131.

 **For additional information on this topic, go to http://college.hmco.com.**

---

Aware of the overwhelming Spanish territorial advantage in the New World, and yet still hoping for treasures such as the Spanish had found, the English, French, and Dutch were also eager to explore and settle North America. From the early sixteenth century, French, Dutch, English, and Portuguese seamen had fished and traded off Newfoundland. By 1630 small French and Scottish settlements in Acadia (near modern Nova Scotia) and on the St. Lawrence River and English settlements in Newfoundland were established to systematically exploit the timber, fish, and fur of the north Atlantic coasts.

In England rising unemployment as well as religious discontent created a large pool of potential colonists,

## ✿ READING SOURCES

### The Disappointments of the Virginia Colony

*In this letter sent to the Virginia Company back in London in 1608, Captain John Smith (1580–1631) explains somewhat angrily that the colony cannot produce the profits that the investors had hoped for. He notes the folly of carrying boats west over the fall line of the Virginia rivers—where, it had been assumed, they might sight the Pacific Ocean as the Spaniards had done in Panama. He reports no sign of the colony of Sir Walter Raleigh, which vanished after being planted in North Carolina in 1585. He also notes the difficulties of mere survival, let alone extracting wealth.*

I have received your letter, wherein you write that . . . we feed you but with ifs and ands and hopes, and some few proofs . . . and that we must expressly follow your instructions sent by Captain Newport [the commander of the supply ship], the charge of whose voyage . . . we cannot defray.

For the quartered boat to be borne by the soldiers over the falls, Newport had 120 of the best men. . . . If he had burned her to ashes, one might have carried her in a bag, but as she is, five hundred cannot, to a navigable place above the falls. And for him, at that time to find in the South Sea a mine of gold, or any of them sent by Sir Walter Raleigh, at our consultation I told them was as likely as the rest. . . . In their absence I followed the new begun works of pitch and tar, glass, [potash, and lumber],

whereof some small quantities we have sent you. But if you rightly consider, what an infinite toil it is in Russia and [Sweden], where the woods are proper for naught else [and where] there be the help of both man and beast . . . yet thousands of those poor people can scarce get necessaries to live. . . .

From your ship we had not provision in victuals worth twenty pound, and we are more than two hundred to live upon this. . . . Though there be fish in the sea, fowls in the air, and beasts in the woods . . . they are so wild and we so weak and ignorant, we cannot much trouble them.

*Source:* Philip L. Barbour, ed., *The Complete Works of Captain John Smith* (1580–1631), vol. 2 (Chapel Hill: University of North Carolina Press, 1986), pp. 187–189.

some of whom were initially attracted to the Caribbean. The first of the English settlements to endure in what was to become the United States was established at Jamestown, named for James I, in Virginia in 1607. ("Virginia," named for Elizabeth I, the "Virgin Queen," was an extremely vague designation for the Atlantic coast of North America and its hinterland.)

The Crown encouraged colonization, but a private company similar to those that financed long-distance trade was established to organize the enterprise. The directors of the Virginia Company were London businessmen. Investors and would-be colonists purchased shares. Shareholders among the colonists could participate in a colonial assembly, though the governor appointed by the company was the final authority.

The colonists arrived in Virginia with ambitious and optimistic instructions. They were to open mines, establish profitable cultivation, and search for sea routes to Asia. But at first the colonists struggled merely to survive. (See the box "Reading Sources: The Disappointments of the Virginia Colony.") The indigenous peoples in Virginia, unlike those in Spanish-held territory, were not organized in urbanized, rigidly hierarchical societies that, after conquest, could provide the invaders with a labor force. Indeed, much of the local native population was quickly wiped out by European diseases. The introduction of tobacco as a cash crop a few years later saved the colonists economically—though the Virginia Company had already gone bankrupt and the Crown had assumed control of the colony. With the cultivation of tobacco, the

Virginia colony, like the Caribbean islands, became dependent on forced, eventually slave, labor.

Among the Virginia colonists were impoverished men and women who came as servants indentured to those who had paid their passage—that is, they were bound by contract to pay off their debt by several years of labor. Colonies established to the north, in what was called "New England," also drew people from the margins of English society. Early settlers there were religious dissidents. The first to arrive were the Pilgrims, who arrived at Plymouth (modern Massachusetts) in 1620. They were a community of religious Separatists who had originally immigrated to the Netherlands from England for freedom of conscience.

Following the Pilgrims came Puritans escaping escalating persecution under Charles I. The first, in 1629, settled under the auspices of another royally chartered company, the Massachusetts Bay Company. Among their number were many prosperous Puritan merchants and landholders. Independence from investors in London allowed them an unprecedented degree of self-government once the Massachusetts Bay colony was established.

Nevertheless, the colonies in North America were disappointments to England because they generated much less wealth than expected. Shipping timber back to Europe proved too expensive, though New England forests did supply some of the Caribbean colonists' needs. The fur trade became less lucrative as English settlement pushed westward the Native Americans who did most of the trapping and as French trappers to the north encroached on the trade. Certain colonists profited enormously from the tobacco economy, but the mother country did so only moderately because the demand in Europe for tobacco never grew as quickly as the demand for sugar. The English settlements did continue to attract more migrants than other colonizers' outposts. By 1640 Massachusetts had some fourteen thousand European inhabitants. Through most of the next century, the growth of colonial populations in North America would result in an English advantage over the French in control of New World territory.

The French began their settlement of North America at the same time as the English, in the same push to compensate for their mutual weakness vis-à-vis the Spanish (see Map 16.4). The French efforts, however, had very different results, owing partly to the sites of their settlements but mostly to the relationship between the mother country and the colonies. The French hold on territory was always tenuous because of the scant number of colonists who could be lured from home. There

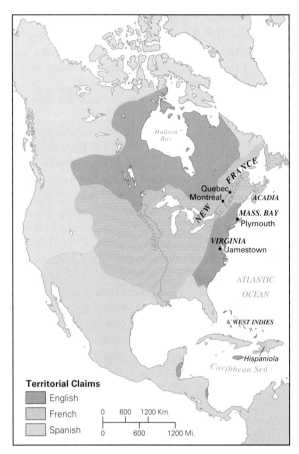

**Map 16.4    English and French in North America, ca. 1700**    By 1700 a veritable ring of French-claimed territory encircled the coastal colonies of England. English-claimed areas, however, were more densely settled and more economically viable.

seems to have been less economic impetus for colonization from France than from England. And, after the French crown took over the colonies, any religious impetus evaporated, for only Catholics were allowed to settle in New France. Moreover, control by the Crown forced a traditional hierarchical political organization on the French colonies. A royal governor directed the colony, and large tracts of land were set aside for privileged investors. Thus, North America offered little to tempt French people of modest means who were seeking a better life.

The first successful French colony was established in Acadia in 1605. This settlement was an exception among the French efforts because it was founded by Huguenots, not by Catholics. A few years later, the explorer Samuel de Champlain (1567?–1635) navigated the

St. Lawrence River and founded Quebec City (1608). He convinced the royal government, emerging from its pre-occupations with religious wars at home, to promote the development of the colony. French explorers went on to establish Montreal, farther inland on the St. Lawrence (1642), and to explore the Great Lakes and the Mississippi River basin (see Map 16.4).

Such investment as the French crown was able to attract went into profitable trade, mainly in furs, and not into the difficult business of colonization. French trappers and traders who ventured into wilderness areas were renowned for their hardiness and adaptability, but they did not bring their families and establish settled, European-style towns. Quebec remained more of a trading station, dependent on shipments of food from France, than a growing urban community. Added to the commercial dimension of New France was the church's interest: much of the energy of French colonization was expended by men and women of religious orders—the "Black Robes"—bringing their zeal to new frontiers. By the middle of the seventeenth century, all of New France had only about three thousand European inhabitants.

The seeming weakness of the French colonial effort in North America was not much noticed at the time. French and English fishermen, trappers, and traders competed intensely, and the French often reaped the greater share of profits, owing to their closer ties with native American trading systems. Outright battles occasionally erupted between English and French settlements. But for both England and France, the major profits and strategic interests in the New World lay to the south, in the Caribbean. The Dutch experience reveals the degree to which North America was of secondary importance, for all colonial powers, to the plantation profits farther south. In 1624 the Dutch founded a trading center, New Amsterdam, at the site of modern-day New York City. Fifty years later they relinquished New Amsterdam—the cornerstone of their northern enterprise—to the English in return for recognition of the Dutch claims to sugar-producing Guiana (modern Suriname°) in South America.

Consequently, by far the largest group of migrants to European-held territories in the Americas were forced migrants: African men and women sold into slavery and transported across the Atlantic to work the plantations established by Europeans. A conservative estimate is that approximately 1,350,000 Africans were forcibly transported as slave labor to the New World during the seventeenth century.

---

**Suriname** (SIR-ih-nam)

## ◼ The Beginning of the End of Traditional Society

Within Europe, the economic impact of overseas trade was profound. Merchants and investors in a few of Europe's largest cities reaped great profits. Mediterranean ports such as Venice, once the heart of European trade, did not share in the bonanza from the new trade with Asia or the Americas. Atlantic ports such as Seville, through which most Spanish commerce with the New World flowed, and, above all, Amsterdam began to flourish. The population of Amsterdam increased from about 30,000 to 200,000 in the course of the seventeenth century.

All capital cities, however, not just seaports, grew substantially during the 1600s. Increasing numbers of government functionaries, courtiers and their hangers-on, and people involved in trade lived and worked in capital cities. These cities also grew indirectly from the demand such people generated for services and products, ranging from fashionable clothing to exotic foodstuffs. For the first time, cities employed vast numbers of country people. Perhaps as much as one-fifth of the population of England passed through London at one time or another, creating the mobile, volatile community so active in the English civil war and its aftermath.

The economy became more productive and flexible as it expanded, but social stratification intensified. Patterns of consumption in cities reflected the economic gulfs between residents. Most people could not afford to buy imported pepper or sugar. Poverty increased in cities, even in vibrant Amsterdam, because cities attracted people fleeing rural unemployment with few skills and fewer resources. As growing central governments heaped up tax burdens on peasants, many rural people were caught in a cycle of debt; the only escape was to abandon farming and flock to cities.

Peasant rebellions occurred throughout the century as a result of depressed economic conditions and heavy taxation, reflecting expansion of royal power and expensive royal military ambitions. Some small-scale revolts involved direct action, such as seizing the tax collector's grain or stopping the movement of grain to the great cities. Urban demand often caused severe food shortages in rural areas in western Europe, despite the booming trade in grain with eastern Europe via the Baltic.

The typical peasant revolt in western Europe during the seventeenth century, however, was directed against escalating taxation. Tax rebellions often formed spontaneously, perhaps as tax officials passed through a village, but they were not mere chaotic gatherings of rabble. Countryfolk were accustomed to defending themselves as communities—against brigands and marauding soldiers, for example. Local gentry or prosperous farmers who ordinarily fulfilled the function of local constable led such revolts from time to time, convinced that they represented the legitimate interests of the community against rapacious officials higher up. The scale of peasant violence meant that thousands of troops sometimes had to be diverted from a state's foreign wars. As a matter of routine, soldiers accompanied tax officials and enforced collection all over Europe. Thus, as the ambitions of rulers grew, so too did resistance of ordinary people to the exactions of the state.

# Summary

HE beginning of the seventeenth century was marked by religious turmoil and by social and political upheaval. By the end of the century, the former had faded as a source of collective anxiety, and the latter was largely resolved. States troubled by religious and political turmoil or on the political margins early in the century had evolved into secure and dynamic centers of power: the Netherlands, the Habsburg domains, Brandenburg-Prussia, and Russia. Following the most powerful monarchy in Europe, France, most states had moved from internal division—with independent provinces and aristocrats going their own way—to greater coherence. This stability was both cause and consequence of rulers' desires to make war on an ever larger scale. By the end of the century, only those states able to field massive armies were competitive on the European stage. The Netherlands, a stark exception to the pattern of centralized royal control, began more closely to resemble other states under the pressure of warfare by century's end.

At the beginning of the century, overseas trade and colonization had been the near monopoly of Spain and Portugal; at the century's end, the English, French, and Dutch had supplanted the Iberian states in controlling trade with Asia and were reaping many profits in the Americas, especially from the extension of plantation agriculture. Beneath all these developments lay subtle but significant economic, social, and cultural shifts. One effect of the increased wealth generated by overseas trade and the increased power of governments to tax their subjects was a widening gulf between rich and poor. New styles of behavior and patterns of consumption highlighted differences between social classes. Long-term effects of overseas voyages on Old World attitudes, as well as fundamental changes in world-views that were paving the way for modern science, would have a revolutionary impact on Europeans and their cultures.

## ■ Notes

1. Quoted in D. H. Pennington, *Europe in the Seventeenth Century,* 2d ed. (London: Longman, 1989), p. 508.

## ■ Suggested Reading

Collins, James B. *The State in Early Modern France.* 1995. An up-to-date synthesis by one of the leading scholars of French absolutism.

De Vries, Jan. *The Economy of Europe in an Age of Crisis, 1600–1750.* 1976. The single most important work on the development of the European economy in this period, integrating European developments with the growth of overseas empires.

Howard, Michael. *War in European History.* 1976. A general study of warfare emphasizing the relationship between war making and state development.

Kishlansky, Mark. *A Monarchy Transformed.* 1996. The most recent, full scholarly treatment of political events in England.

Oakley, Stewart P. *War and Peace in the Baltic, 1560–1790.* 1992. An excellent survey of the Baltic region in the early modern period.

Pennington, D. H. *Europe in the Seventeenth Century.* 2d ed. 1989. A general history of the century.

Riasanovsky, Nicolas V. *A History of Russia.* 6th ed. 2000. A reliable and readable survey of Russian history from medieval times; includes an extensive bibliography of major works available in English.

Schama, Simon. *The Embarrassment of Riches: An Interpretation of Dutch Culture in the Golden Age.* 1997. An innovative study of Dutch culture that explores the social and psychological tensions created by its growing wealth in the seventeenth century.

Wolf, Eric R. *Europe and the People Without History.* 1982. A survey of European contact with and conquest of peoples after 1400; includes extensive treatments of non-European societies and detailed explanations of the economic and political interests of the Europeans.

 **For a searchable list of additional readings for this chapter, go to http://college.hmco.com.**

# Table Manners

If you were to sit down in a fancy restaurant, order a juicy steak, and then eat it with your bare hands, other diners would undoubtedly stare, shocked by your bad manners. It has not always been the case that table manners meant very much—were able to signal social status, for example. It was not always the case that table manners existed at all in the sense that we know them. How did they evolve? How did they come to have the importance that they do? And why should historians pay any attention to them?

Imagine that you have been invited to dinner at a noble estate in the year 1500. As you sit down, you notice that there are no knives, forks, and spoons at your place at the table, and no napkins either. A servant (a young girl from a neighboring village) sets a roast of meat in front of you and your fellow diners. The lords and ladies on either side of you hack off pieces of meat with the knives that they always carry with them, and then they eat the meat with their fingers. Hunks of bread on the table in front of them catch the dripping juices.

One hundred fifty years later, in 1650, dinner is a much more "civilized" meal. Notice the well-to-do women dining in this engraving by the French artist Abraham Bosse (1602–1676). The table setting, with tablecloths, napkins, plates, and silverware, is recognizable to us. The lady at the extreme right holds up her fork and napkin in a somewhat forced and obvious gesture. These diners have the utensils that we take for granted, but the artist does not take them for granted: they are intended to be noticed by Bosse's elite audience.

In the seventeenth century, aristocrats and gentry signaled their political and social privilege with behavior that distinguished them from the lower classes in ways their more powerful ancestors had found unnecessary. Historians have called this the invention of civility. As we have seen, proper courtesy to one's superiors at court was considered essential. It marked the fact that rituals of honor and deference were increasingly taking the place of armed conflict as the routine behavior of the upper classes. Also essential, however, were certain standards of physical privacy and delicacy. Something as seemingly trivial as the use of a fork became charged with symbolic significance. As the actual power of the aristocrats was circumscribed by the state, they found new expressions of status. Since the sixteenth century, new kinds of manners had been touted in handbooks, reflecting changes that already had occurred at Italian courts. During the seventeenth century, these practices became more widespread and opened up a gulf between upper- and lower-class behavior.

Some of the new behaviors concerned bodily privacy and discretion. A nobleman now used a handkerchief instead of his fingers or coat sleeve, and he did not urinate in public. The new "rules" about eating are particularly interesting. Why did eating with a fork seem refined and desirable to aristocrats trying to buttress their own self-images? As any 3-year-old knows, eating with a fork is remarkably inefficient.

Using a fork kept you at a distance—literal and symbolic—from the animal you were eating. Napkins wiped away all trace of bloody juices from your lips. Interestingly, as diners began to use utensils, other eating arrangements changed in parallel ways. Sideboards had been in use for a long time, but pieces of meat were now discreetly carved on the sideboard and presented to diners in individual portions. The carcass was brought to the sideboard cut into roasts instead of unmistakably whole, and it was often decorated—as it is today—to further disguise it.

The new aristocrat was increasingly separated from the world of brute physical force, both in daily life and on the battlefield. In warfare, brute force was no longer adequate. Training, discipline, and tactical knowledge were more important and heightened the significance of rank, which separated officers from the vast numbers of common soldiers (see page 546). Aristocrats now lived in a priviledged world where violence—except for an occasional duel—was no longer a fact of life. Their new behavior codes signaled their new invulnerability to others. Above all, they worked to transform a loss—of the independence that had gone hand in hand with a more violent life—into a gain: a privileged immunity to violence.

Specific manners became important, then, because they were symbols of power. The symbolic distance be-

**Table Manners of the Upper Class in the Seventeenth Century** *(Courtesy of the Trustees of the British Museum)*

tween the powerful and the humble was reinforced by other changes in habits and behavior. A sixteenth-century warrior customarily traveled on horseback and often went from place to place within a city on foot, attended by his retinue. A seventeenth-century aristocrat was more likely to travel in a horse-drawn carriage. The presence of special commodities from abroad—such as sugar—in the seventeenth century created further possibilities for signaling status.

It is interesting to note that other personal habits still diverged dramatically from what we would consider acceptable today. Notice the large, stately bed in the same room as the dining table in Bosse's engraving. Interior space was still undifferentiated by our standards, and it was common for eating, talking, sleeping, and estate management all to go on in a single room. The grand bed is in the picture because, like the fork, it is a mark of status. Like virtually everything else, what is "proper" varies with historical circumstance.

# CHAPTER 17

# A Revolution in World-View

PRESERVED in the Museum of Science in Florence, Italy, are two narrow cylinders mounted on an ornate stand. They are two of the telescopes built in the seventeenth century by the astronomer Galileo. Galileo's telescopes permitted the first enhanced views of heavenly bodies in human history. They seem very simple instruments to our eyes, but the twenty-fold magnification provided by the smaller instrument enabled Galileo to make celestial observations that would help revolutionize humans' understanding of their physical world. These telescopes were also enormously popular devices. Galileo made dozens of them in his lifetime and gave many away to interested colleagues and would-be patrons. The Scientific Revolution, as we now label the dramatic shifts in scientific explanation that occurred in this era, was a complex cultural movement that included both the specialized work of individuals such as Galileo and the involvement and support of patrons, other scholars, and learned amateurs.

By the end of the seventeenth century, a vision of an infinite but orderly cosmos appealing to human reason had, among educated Europeans, largely replaced the medieval vision of a closed universe centered on earth and suffused with Christian purpose. Religion became an increasingly subordinate ally of science as confidence in an open-ended, experimental approach to knowledge came to be as strongly held as religious conviction. It is because of this larger shift in world-view, not simply because of particular scientific discoveries, that the seventeenth century may be labeled the era of the scientific *revolution.*

The revolution was initiated within the sciences in the sixteenth century by the astronomical calculations and hypotheses of Nicholas Copernicus, who posited that the earth moves around the sun.

### The Revolution in Astronomy, 1543–1632

### The Scientific Revolution Generalized, ca. 1600–1700

### The New Science: Society, Politics, and Religion

Lens and telescopes of Galileo.
(Scala/Art Resource, NY)

Galileo and others eventually proved this hypothesis true, overturning principles of physics and philosophy that had held sway since ancient times. Later generations of scientists and philosophers labored to construct new principles to explain the way the physical universe behaves. The readiness of scientists, their patrons, and educated lay people to push Copernicus's hypothesis to these conclusions came from several sources: their exposure to the intellectual innovations of Renaissance thought; the intellectual challenges and material opportunities represented by the discovery of the New World; and the challenge to authority embodied in the Reformation. Also, the new science offered prestige and technological advances to the rulers who sponsored it.

Because religious significance had been attached to previous explanations, and religious authority defended them, the new astronomy automatically led to an enduring debate about the compatibility of science and religion. But the revolution in world-view was not confined to astronomy or even to science generally. As philosophers gained confidence in human reason and the intelligibility of the world, they turned to new speculation about human af-fairs. They began to challenge traditional justifications for the hierarchical nature of society and the sanctity of authority just as energetically as Copernicus and his followers had overthrown old views about the cosmos.

## QUESTIONS TO CONSIDER

- Why did new theories about astronomy lead to a broader Scientific Revolution?

- What were some of the features of the new "mechanistic" world-view?

- How did religious, political, and social conditions shape the work of scientists?

- What were the implications for political thought of the new scientific approach to the world?

## TERMS TO KNOW

Nicholas Copernicus
heliocentrism
Johannes Kepler
Galileo Galilei
René Descartes
mechanistic world-view

Francis Bacon
empirical reasoning
Isaac Newton
laws of motion
Thomas Hobbes
John Locke

## THE REVOLUTION IN ASTRONOMY, 1543–1632

**T**HE origins of the seventeenth-century revolution in world-view lie, for the most part, in developments in astronomy. Because of astronomy's role in the explanations of the world and of human life that had been devised by ancient and medieval scientists and philosophers, any advances in astronomy were bound to have widespread intellectual repercussions. By the early part of the seventeenth century, fundamental astronomical beliefs had been successfully challenged. The consequence was the undermining of both the material (physics) and the philosophical (metaphysics) explanations of the world that had been standing for centuries.

## ■ The Inherited World-View and the Sixteenth-Century Context

Ancient and medieval astronomy accepted the perspective on the universe that unaided human senses support—namely, that the earth is fixed at the center of the universe and the celestial bodies rotate around it. The regular movements of heavenly bodies and the obvious importance of the sun for life on earth made astronomy a vital undertaking for both scientific and religious purposes in many ancient societies. Astronomers in ancient Greece carefully observed the heavens and learned to calculate and to predict the seemingly circular motion of the stars and the sun about the earth. The orbits of the planets were more difficult to explain, for the planets seemed to travel both east and west across the sky at various times and with no regularity that could be mathematically understood. Indeed, the very word *planet* comes from a Greek word meaning "wanderer."

We now know that all the planets simultaneously orbit the sun at different speeds in paths that are at different distances from the sun. The relative positions of the planets thus constantly change; sometimes other planets are "ahead" of the earth and sometimes "behind." In the second century A.D. the Greek astronomer Ptolemy° attempted to explain the planets' occasional "backward" motion by attributing it to "epicycles"—small circular orbits within the larger orbit. Ptolemy's mathematical explanations of the imagined epicycles were extremely complex, but neither Ptolemy nor medieval mathematicians and astronomers were ever able fully to account for planetary motion.

Ancient physics, most notably the work of the Greek philosopher Aristotle° (384–322 B.C.), explained the fact that some objects (such as cannonballs) fall to earth but others (stars and planets) seem weightless relative to the earth because of their composition: different kinds of matter had different inherent tendencies and properties. In this view, all earthbound matter (like cannonballs) falls because it is naturally attracted to earth—heaviness being a property of earthbound things.

In the Christian era, the Aristotelian explanation of the universe was infused with Christian meaning and purpose. The heavens were said to be made of different, pure, matter because they were the abode of the angels. Both earth and the humans who inhabited it were changeable and corruptible. Yet God had given human beings a unique and special place in the universe. The universe was thought to be literally a closed world with the stationary earth at the center. Revolving around the earth in circular orbits were the sun, the moon, the stars, and the planets. The motion of all lesser bodies was caused by the rotation of all the stars together in the vast crystal-like sphere in which they were embedded.

A few ancient astronomers theorized that the earth moved about the sun. Some medieval philosophers also adopted this heliocentric thesis (*helios* is the Greek word for "sun"), but it remained a minority view because it seemed to contradict both common sense and observed data. The sun and stars *appeared* to move around the earth with great regularity. Moreover, how could objects fall to earth if the earth was moving beneath them? Also, astronomers detected no difference in angles from which observers on earth viewed the stars at different times. Such differences would exist, they thought, if the earth changed positions by moving around the sun. It

---

Ptolemy (TOL-eh-mee)    Aristotle (AIR-is-tot-il)

| | CHRONOLOGY |
|---|---|
| **1543** | Copernicus, *De Revolutionibus Orbium Caelestium*; Vesalius, *On the Fabric of the Human Body* |
| **1576** | Construction of Brahe's observatory begins |
| **1603** | Accadèmia dei Lincei founded in Rome |
| **1609** | Kepler's third law of motion |
| **1610** | Galileo, *The Starry Messenger* |
| **1620** | Bacon, *Novum Organum* |
| **1628** | Harvey, *On the Motion of the Heart* |
| **1632** | Galileo, *Dialogue on the Two Chief Systems of the World* |
| **1633** | Galileo condemned and sentenced to house arrest |
| **1637** | Descartes, *Discourse on Method* |
| **1651** | Hobbes, *Leviathan* |
| **1660** | Boyle, *New Experiments Physico-Mechanical* |
| **1660** | Royal Society of London founded |
| **1666** | Académie Royale des Sciences founded in France |
| **1686** | Fontenelle, *Conversations on the Plurality of Worlds* |
| **1687** | Newton, *Principia (Mathematical Principles of Natural Philosophy)* |
| **1690** | Locke, *Two Treatises on Government* and *Essay on Human Understanding* |
| **1702** | Bayle, *Historical and Critical Dictionary* |

was inconceivable that the universe could be so large and the stars so distant that the earth's movement would produce no measurable change in the earth's position with respect to the stars.

Several conditions of intellectual life in the sixteenth century encouraged new work in astronomy and led to revision of the earth-centered world-view. The most important was the work of Renaissance humanists in recovering and interpreting ancient texts. Now able to work with new Greek versions of Ptolemy, mathematicians and astronomers noted that his explanations for

**The Traditional Universe**    In this print from around 1600, heavenly bodies are depicted orbiting the earth in perfectly circular paths. In fact, the ancient astronomer Ptolemy believed that the planets followed complex orbits-within-orbits, known as *epicycles,* moving around the stationary earth.
*(Hulton-Getty/Liaison)*

the motions of the planets were imperfect and not simply inadequately transmitted, as they had long believed. Also, the discovery of the New World dramatically undercut the assumption that ancient knowledge was superior. The existence of the Americas specifically undermined Ptolemy's authority once again, for it disproved many of the assertions in his *Geography,* which had just been recovered in Europe the previous century.

The desire to explain heavenly motions better was still loaded with religious significance in the sixteenth century and was heightened by the immediate need for reform of the Julian calendar (named for Julius Caesar). Ancient observations of the movement of the sun, though remarkably accurate, could not measure the precise length of the solar year. By the sixteenth century, the cumulative error of this calendar had resulted in a change of ten days: the spring equinox fell on March 11 instead of March 21. An accurate and uniform system of dating was necessary for all rulers and their tax collec-

tors and recordkeepers. And because the calculation of the date of Easter was at stake, a reliable calendar was the particular project of the church.

Impetus for new and better astronomical observations and calculations arose from other features of the intellectual and political landscape as well. Increasingly as the century went on, princely courts became important sources of patronage for and sites of scientific activity. Rulers eager to buttress their own power by symbolically linking it to dominion over nature sponsored investigations of the world, as Ferdinand and Isabella had so successfully done, and displayed the marvels of nature at their courts. Sponsoring scientific inquiry also yielded practical benefits: better mapping of the ruler's domains and better technology for mining, gunnery, and navigation.

Finally, schools of thought fashionable at the time, encouraged by the humanists' critique of received tradition, hinted at the possibilities of alternative physical and metaphysical systems. The ancient doctrine of Hermeticism (named for the mythical originator of the ideas, Hermes Trismegistos), revived since the Renaissance, claimed that matter is universally imbued with divine (or magical) spirit. Drawing on Hermeticism was Paracelsianism, named for the Swiss physician Philippus von Hohenheim (1493–1541), who called himself Paracelsus° (literally "beyond Celsus," an acclaimed Roman physician whose works had just been recovered). Paracelsus scoffed at the notion that ancient authorities were the final word on the workings of nature. "He who is born in imagination," he wrote, "discovers the latent forces of nature."[1] Paracelsus offered an alternative to accepted medical theory, put forth by the physician Galen° (ca. 131–201), the premier medical authority of antiquity, now as revered as Aristotle. Galen believed that an imbalance of bodily "humors" caused illness. Paracelsus substituted a theory of chemical imbalance that was a forerunner of modern understandings of pathology. He was wildly popular wherever he taught because of the success of his treatments of illness and his willingness to lecture openly to laymen.

Neo-Platonism, another school of thought, had a more systematic and far-reaching impact. Neo-Platonism was a revival, primarily in Italian humanist circles, of certain aspects of Plato's thought. It contributed directly to innovation in science because it emphasized the abstract nature of true knowledge and thus encouraged mathematical investigation. This provided a spur to astronomical studies, which, since ancient times, had been concerned more with mathematical analysis of heavenly movements than with physical explanations for them. Also, like Hermeticism and Paracelsianism, Neo-Platonism had a mystical dimension that fostered creative speculation about the nature of matter and the organization of the universe. Neo-Platonists were particularly fascinated by the sun as a symbol of the one divine mind or soul at the heart of all creation.

## ■ The Copernican Challenge

Nicholas Copernicus° (1473–1543), son of a German merchant family in Poland, pursued wide-ranging university studies in philosophy, law, astronomy, mathematics, and medicine—first in Cracow in Poland and then in Bologna and Padua in Italy. In Italy he was exposed to Neo-Platonic ideas. He took a degree in canon (church) law in 1503 and became a cathedral canon (a member of the cathedral staff) in the city of Frauenburg

(modern Poland), where he pursued his own interests in astronomy while carrying out administrative duties. When the pope asked Copernicus to assist with the reform of the Julian calendar, he replied that reform of the calendar required reform in astronomy. His major work, *De Revolutionibus Orbium Caelestium* (*On the Revolution of Heavenly Bodies,* 1543), was dedicated to the pope in the hopes that it would help with the task of calendar reform—as indeed it did. The Gregorian calendar, issued in 1582 during the pontificate of Gregory XIII (r. 1572–1585), was based on Copernicus's calculations.

Copernicus postulated that the earth and all the other planets orbit the sun. He did not assert that the earth does in fact move around the sun but offered the heliocentric system as a mathematical construct, useful for predicting the movements of planets, stars, and the sun. However, he walked a thin line between making claims for a mathematical construct on the one hand and physical reality on the other. Scholars now believe Copernicus was himself persuaded that the heliocentric theory was correct. He had searched in ancient sources for thinkers who believed the earth did move. Other astronomers familiar with his work and reputation urged him to publish the results of his calculations. But not until 1542, twelve years after finishing the work, did he send *De Revolutionibus* to be published; he received a copy just before his death the next year. (See the box "Reading Sources: Copernicus Justifies His Work to the Pope.")

By affirming the earth's movement around the sun while also salvaging features of the old system, Copernicus faced burdens of explanation not faced by Ptolemy. For example, Copernicus still assumed that the planets traveled in circular orbits, so he was forced to retain some epicycles in his schema to account for the circular motion. In general, however, the Copernican account of planetary motion was simpler than the Ptolemaic account. It appealed to other astronomers of the age because it was useful and because it highlighted the harmony of heavenly motion, which remained a fundamental physical and metaphysical principle. Inaccessible except to other astronomers, Copernicus's work only slowly led to conceptual revolution, as scientists worked with his calculations and assembled other evidence to support the heliocentric theory.

The most important reason why fundamental conceptual change followed Copernican theory so gradually was that Copernicus did not resolve the physical problems his ideas raised. If Copernicus were right, the earth would have to be made of the same material as other planets. How, then, would Copernicus explain the motion of objects on earth—the fact that they fall to the

Paracelsus (pair-uh-SEL-sus)    Galen (GAY-len)
Copernicus (kuh-PURR-nih-kus)

## ❧ READING SOURCES

### Copernicus Justifies His Work to the Pope

*In this dedicatory letter to the pope that prefaced* On the Revolution of Heavenly Bodies, *Copernicus expresses his desire to assist with calendar reform. Principally, however, he seeks to justify his novel conclusions. Note that he not only cites ancient authority for the movement of the earth but also stresses the mathematical (not metaphysical) nature of the problem and of his solution to it.*

To the Most Holy Lord, Pope Paul III

I may well presume, most Holy Father, that certain people, as soon as they hear that in this book about the Revolutions of the Spheres of the Universe I ascribe movement to the earthly globe, will cry out that, holding such views, I should at once be hissed off the stage. . . . How I came to dare to conceive such motion of the Earth, contrary to the received opinion of the Mathematicians and indeed contrary to the impression of the senses, is what your Holiness will rather expect to hear. So I should like your Holiness to know that I was induced to think of a method of computing the motions of the spheres by nothing else than the knowledge that the Mathematicians are inconsistent in these investigations. . . . Mathematicians are so unsure of the movements of the Sun and the Moon that they cannot even explain . . . the constant length of the seasonal year.

. . . I pondered long upon this uncertainty of mathematical tradition. I . . . read again the works of all the philosophers on whom I could lay a hand to seek out whether any of them had ever supposed that the motions of the spheres were other[wise]. I found first in Cicero that Hicetas [of Syracuse, fifth century B.C.] had realized that the earth moved. . . . Mathematics are for mathematicians, and they, if I be not wholly deceived, will hold that my labors contribute somewhat . . . to the Church. . . . For under Leo X, the question of correcting the ecclesiastical calendar was . . . left undecided.

*Source:* Thomas S. Kuhn, *The Copernican Revolution* (Cambridge, Mass.: Harvard University Press, 1985), pp. 137–143.

---

earth—if it was not in their nature to fall toward the heavy, stationary earth? In Copernicus's system, the movement of the earth caused the *apparent* motion of the stars. But if the stars did not rotate in their crystalline sphere, what made all other heavenly bodies move?

Copernicus was not as troubled by these questions as we might expect him to be. Since ancient times, mathematical astronomy—the science of measuring and predicting the movement of heavenly bodies—had been far more important than, and had proceeded independently of, physical explanations for observed motion. Nevertheless, as Copernicus's own efforts to support his hypothesis reveal, his theories directly contradicted many of the supposed laws of motion. The usefulness of his theories to other astronomers meant that the contradictions between mathematical and physical models for the universe would have to be resolved. Copernicus himself might be best understood as the last Ptolemaic astronomer, working within inherited questions and with known tools. His work itself did not constitute a revolution, but it did initiate one.

### ■ The First Copernican Astronomers

In the first generation of astronomers after the publication of *De Revolutionibus* in 1543 we can see the effects of Copernicus's work. His impressive computations rapidly won converts among fellow astronomers. Several particularly gifted astronomers continued to develop the Copernican system. Thus, by the second quarter of the seventeenth century, they and many others accepted the heliocentric theory as a reality and not just as a useful mathematical fiction. The three most important astronomers to build on Copernican assumptions, and on the work of one another, were the Dane Tycho Brahe (1546–1601), the German Johannes Kepler (1571–1630), and the Italian Galileo Galilei (1564–1642).

Like generations of observers before him, Tycho Brahe° had been stirred by the majesty of the regular movements of heavenly bodies. After witnessing a partial eclipse of the sun, he abandoned a career in government befitting his noble status and became an astronomer. Brahe was the first truly post-Ptolemaic astronomer because he was the first to improve on the data that the ancients and all subsequent astronomers had used. Ironically, *no* theory of planetary motion could have reconciled the data that Copernicus had used: they were simply too inaccurate, based as they were on naked-eye observations, even when errors of translation and copying, accumulated over centuries, had been corrected.

In 1576 the king of Denmark showered Brahe with properties and pensions enabling him to build an observatory, Uraniborg, on an island near Copenhagen. At Uraniborg, Brahe improved on ancient observations with large and very finely calibrated instruments that permitted precise measurements of celestial movements by the naked eye. His attention to precision and frequency of observation produced results that were twice as accurate as any previous data had been.

As a result of his observations, Brahe agreed with Copernicus that the various planets did rotate around the sun, not around the earth. He still could not be persuaded that the earth itself moved, for none of his data supported such a notion. Brahe's lasting and crucial contribution was his astronomical data. They would become obsolete as soon as data from telescopic observations were accumulated about a century later. But in the meantime, they were used by Johannes Kepler to further develop Copernicus's model and arrive at a more accurate heliocentric theory.

Kepler was young enough to be exposed to Copernican ideas from the outset of his training, and he quickly recognized in Brahe's data the means of resolving the problems in Copernican analysis. Though trained in his native Germany, Kepler went to Prague, where Brahe spent the last years of his life, at the court of the Holy Roman emperor after a quarrel with the Danish king. There, Kepler became something of an apprentice to Brahe. After Brahe's death in 1601, Kepler kept his mentor's records of astronomical observation and continued to work at the imperial court as Rudolf II's court mathematician.

Kepler's contribution to the new astronomy, like that of Copernicus, was fundamentally mathematical. In it,

we can see the stamp of the Neo-Platonic conviction about the purity of mathematical explanation. Kepler spent ten years working to apply Brahe's data to the most intricate of all the celestial motions—the movement of the planet Mars—as a key to explaining all planetary motion. Mars is close to the earth but its orbital path is farther from the sun. This combination produces very puzzling and dramatic variations in the apparent movement of Mars to an earthly observer.

The result of Kepler's work was laws of planetary motion that, in the main, are still in use. First, Kepler eliminated the need for epicycles by correctly asserting that planets follow elliptical and not circular orbits. Elliptical orbits could account, both mathematically and visually, for the motions of the planets when combined with Kepler's second law, which described the *rate* of a planet's motion around its orbital path. Kepler noted that the speed of a planet in its orbit slows proportionally as the planet's distance from the sun increases. A third law demonstrated that the distance of each planet from the sun and the time it takes each planet to orbit the sun are in a constant ratio.

Kepler's work was a breakthrough because it mathematically confirmed the Copernican heliocentric hypothesis. In so doing, the work directly challenged the ancient world-view, in which heavenly bodies constantly moved in circular orbits around a stationary earth. Hence, Kepler's laws invited speculation about the properties and motion of heavenly and terrestrial bodies alike. A new physics would be required to explain the novel motions that Kepler had posited. Kepler himself, in Neo-Platonic fashion, attributed planetary motion to the sun: "[The sun] is a fountain of light, rich in fruitful heat, most fair, limpid and pure . . . called king of the planets for his motion, heart of the world for his power. . . . Who would hesitate to confer the votes of the celestial motions on him who has been administering all other movements and changes by the benefit of the light which is entirely his possession?"[2]

## ■ Galileo and the Triumph of Copernicanism

Galileo Galilei° holds a pre-eminent position in the development of astronomy because, first, he provided compelling new evidence to support Copernican theory and, second, he contributed to the development of a new physics—or, more precisely, mechanics—that could account for the movement of bodies in new terms. In short, he began to close the gap between the new astronomy and new explanations for the behavior of matter.

---

**Brahe** (BRAH)

**Galileo Galilei** (gal-ih-LAY-oh gal-ih-LAY-ee)

F. Villamoena Feat.

**Galileo** This portrait of Galileo appeared as the frontispiece in two of his publications. He is identified as "philosopher and mathematician of the Grand Duke of Tuscany." The cherubs above the portrait hold a military compass and a telescope—both Galileo's inventions that he gave to his patrons. *(Ann Ronan Picture Library)*

Just as important, his efforts to publicize his findings and his condemnation by the church spurred popular debate about Copernican ideas in literate society and helped to determine the course science would take.

Galileo's career also illustrates, in dramatic fashion, the dependence of scientists on and their vulnerability to patronage relationships. Born to a minor Florentine noble family, Galileo began studying medicine at the University of Pisa at the age of 17 but became intrigued by problems of mechanics and mathematics. He began studying those disciplines at Pisa under the tutelage of a Tuscan court mathematician and himself became a lecturer in mathematics there in 1589, at 25, after publishing promising work in mechanics. Three years later, well-connected fellow mathematicians helped him secure a more lucrative and prestigious professorship at the University of Padua, where Copernicus had once studied. Galileo skillfully cultivated the learned Venetian aristocrats (Venice ruled Padua at this time) who controlled academic appointments and secured renewals and salary raises over the next eighteen years.

During his years at Pisa and Padua, Galileo pursued his revolutionary work in mechanics, although he did not publish the results of his experiments until much later. Galileo's principal contribution to mechanics lay in his working out of an early theory of inertia. As a result of a number of experiments with falling bodies (balls rolling on carefully constructed inclines—not free-falling objects that, according to myth, he dropped from the Leaning Tower of Pisa), Galileo ventured a new view of what is "natural" to objects. Galileo's view was that uniform motion is as natural as a state of rest. In the ancient and medieval universe, all motion needed a cause, and all motion could be explained in terms of purpose. "I hold," Galileo countered, "that there exists nothing in external bodies . . . but size, shape, quantity and motion."[3] Galileo retained the old assumption that motion was somehow naturally circular. Nevertheless, his theory was a crucial step in explaining motion according to new principles and in fashioning a world-view that accepted a mechanical universe devoid of metaphysical purpose.

The results of this work were, for the most part, not published until the end of his life. In the meantime, Galileo became famous for his astronomical observations, which he began in 1609 and which he parlayed into a position at the Florentine court. Early that year, Galileo learned of the invention of a primitive telescope (which could magnify distant objects only three times) and quickly improved on it to make the first astronomically useful instrument. In *Sidereus Nuncius* (*The Starry Messenger*, 1610) he described his scrutiny of the heavens with his telescope in lay language. He documented sighting previously undetectable stars as well as moons orbiting the planet Jupiter. In another blow to ancient descriptions of the universe, he also noted craters and other "imperfections" on the surface of the moon. Three years later he published his solar observations in *Letters on Sunspots*. Sunspots are regions of relatively cool gaseous material that appear as dark spots on the sun's surface. For Galileo sunspots and craters on the moon proved that the heavens were not perfect and changeless but rather were like the supposedly "corrupt" and changeable earth. His telescopic observations also provided further support for Copernican heliocentrism. Indeed, Galileo's own acceptance of Copernicanism can be dated to this point because magnification revealed that each heavenly body rotated on its axis: sunspots, for example, could be tracked across the visible surface of the sun as the sun rotated.

## ❧ READING SOURCES

## Galileo Reassures a Patron

*After Galileo's work on sunspots was released, many learned followers grew anxious about the implications of the new science. In the letter excerpted here, published in 1615 and widely circulated, Galileo reassures the mother of Cosimo, the dowager grand duchess, that the new science does not contradict Christianity. The confident, almost arrogant tone is typical of Galileo's writing. The fact that he presumed to judge the work of theologians as well as to interpret Scripture would be used against him by the Inquisition.*

But I do not feel obliged to believe that the same God who has endowed us with senses, reason and intellect has intended to forgo their use and by some other means to give us knowledge which we can attain by them. He would not require us to deny sense and reason in physical matters which are set before our eyes and minds by direct experience or demonstrations. This must be especially true in those sciences of which but the faintest trace . . . is to be found in the Bible. Of astronomy, for instance, so little is found that none of the planets except Venus are so much as mentioned. . . .

Now, if the Holy Spirit has purposely neglected to teach us propositions of this sort as irrelevant to the highest goal (that is, to our salvation), how can anyone affirm that it is obligatory to take sides on them, and that one belief is required by faith, while another side is erroneous? . . . I would assert here something that was heard from [a respected cleric]: . . . "the intention of the Holy Ghost is to teach us how to go to heaven, not how heaven goes."

But let us again consider the degree to which necessary demonstrations and sense experience ought to be respected in physical conclusions, and the authority they have enjoyed at the hands of . . .

learned theologians. [For example] in St. Augustine we read: "If anyone shall set the authority of Holy Writ against clear and manifest reason, . . . he opposes to the truth not the meaning of the Bible, which is beyond his comprehension, but rather his own interpretation. . . ."

Moreover, we are unable to affirm that all interpreters of the Bible speak with divine inspiration, for if that were so there would exist no differences between them about the sense of a given passage. Hence [it would be wise] not to permit anyone to usurp scriptural texts and force them in some way to maintain any physical conclusion to be true, when at some future time the senses . . . may show the contrary. Who indeed will set bounds to human ingenuity? Who will assert that everything in the universe capable of being perceived is already discovered and known?

*Source:* Stillman Drake, *The Discoveries and Opinions of Galileo* (New York: Doubleday, 1957), pp. 183–187.

 **For additional information on this topic, go to http://college.hmco.com.**

Galileo had already been approached by various Italian princes and in turn sought to woo their support with gifts of some of his earlier inventions, such as a military compass. He aimed his *Starry Messenger* at the Medici dukes of Florence, naming Jupiter's moons the "Medicean Stars" and publishing the work to coincide with the accession of the young Cosimo II, whom he had tutored as a youth. In 1610 he returned in triumph to his native Tuscany as court philosopher to the grand

duke. Soon, however, his own fame and the increasing acceptance of Copernicanism, especially vindicated by his work on sunspots, aroused opposition. In 1615 Galileo was denounced to the Inquisition by a Florentine friar. (See the box "Reading Sources: Galileo Reassures a Patron.") After an investigation, the geokinetic theory (that the earth moves) was declared heretical, but Galileo himself was not condemned. He could continue to use Copernican theory, but only as a theory.

Indeed, a number of the most fervent practitioners of the new science continued to be clergymen who followed Galileo's work with interest. A new pope, elected in 1623, was a Tuscan aristocrat and an old friend of Galileo's; Galileo dedicated his work on comets, *The Assayer* (1624), to Urban VIII in honor of his election.

Now in his sixties, Galileo began to work on a book that summarized his life's work: *Dialogue on the Two Chief Systems of the World* (1632), structured as a conversation among three characters debating the merits of Copernican theory. Given the work's sensitive subject matter, Galileo obtained explicit permission from the pope to write it and cleared some portions with censors before publication. The work was the most important single source in its day for the popularization of Copernican theory, but it led to renewed concerns in Rome. Galileo had clearly overstepped the bounds of discussing Copernicanism in theory only and indeed appeared to advocate it: Simplicio, the character representing the old world-view, was, as his name suggests, an example of ignorance not wisdom.

Moreover, the larger political context affecting Galileo's patrons and friends had changed. The pope was being threatened by the Spanish and Austrian Habsburgs for his tepid support in the Thirty Years' War, in which Catholic forces were now losing to Protestant armies and he could no longer be indulgent with his friend Galileo. (The pope tended to favor French foreign policy as a counterweight to the enormous power of the Habsburgs.) Galileo was forced to stand trial for heresy in Rome in 1633. When, in a kind of plea-bargain arrangement, he pled guilty to a lesser charge of inadvertently advocating Copernicanism, Pope Urban intervened to insist on a weightier penalty. Galileo's book was banned, he was forced to formally renounce his "error," and he was sentenced to house arrest. Galileo lived confined and guarded, continuing his investigations of mechanics, until his death seven years later.

## THE SCIENTIFIC REVOLUTION GENERALIZED, CA. 1600–1700

GALILEO'S work found such a willing audience in part because Galileo, like Kepler and Brahe, was not working alone. Dozens of other scientists were examining old problems from the fresh perspective offered by the breakthroughs in astronomy. Some analyzed the nature of matter, now that it appeared that all matter in the universe was somehow the same despite its varying appearances. Many of these thinkers addressed the metaphysical issues that their investigations inevitably raised. They began the complex intellectual and psychological journey toward a new world-view, one that accepted the existence of an infinitely large universe of undifferentiated matter with no obvious place in it for humans.

### ■ The Promise of the New Science

No less a man than Francis Bacon (1561–1626), lord chancellor of England during the reign of James I, wrote a utopian essay extolling the benefits of science for a peaceful society and for human happiness. In *New Atlantis,* published one year after his death, Bacon argued that science would produce "things of use and practice for man's life."[4] In *New Atlantis* and in *Novum Organum* (1620), Bacon revealed his faith in science by advocating patient, systematic observation and experimentation to accumulate knowledge about the world. He argued that the proper method of investigation "derives axioms from . . . particulars, rising by gradual and unbroken ascent, so that it arrives at the most general axioms of all. This is the true way but untried."[5]

Bacon himself did not undertake experiments, though his widely read works were influential in encouraging both the empirical method (relying on observation and experimentation) and inductive reasoning (deriving general principles from particular facts). Indeed, Bacon was a visionary. Given the early date of his writings, it might even seem difficult to account for his enthusiasm and confidence. In fact, Bacon's writings reflect the widespread interest and confidence in science within his elite milieu, an interest actively encouraged by the state. In another of his writings he argued that a successful state should concentrate on effective "rule in religion *and nature,* as well as civil administration."[6]

Bacon's pronouncements reflected the fact that an interest in exploring nature's secrets and exercising "dominion over nature" had become an indispensable part of princely rule. Princely courts were the main source of financial support for science and a primary site of scientific work during Bacon's lifetime. Part of the impetus for this development had come from the civic humanism of the Italian Renaissance, which had celebrated the state and service to it and had provided models both for educated rulers and for cultivated courtiers. Attention to science and to its benefits for the state also reflected the scope, and pragmatism, of princely resources and ambitions: the desire of rulers for technical expertise in armaments, fortification, construction, navigation, and mapmaking. (See the feature "Weighing the Evidence: Modern Maps" on pages 600–601.)

The promise of the New World and the drive for overseas trade and exploration especially encouraged princely support of scientific investigation. A renowned patron of geographic investigation, from mapmaking to navigation, was Henry, prince of Wales (d. 1612), eldest son of James I. Prince Henry patronized technical experts such as experienced gunners and seamen as well as those with broader and more theoretical expertise. One geographer at his court worked on the vital problem of calculating longitude, sketched the moon after reading and emulating Galileo's work with the telescope, and—in a spirit of empiricism often associated with Bacon—compiled information about the new territory Virginia, including the first dictionary of any Native American language.

Science was an ideological as well as a practical tool for power. Most courts housed collections of marvels, specimens of exotic plants and animals, and mechanical contrivances. These demonstrated the ruler's interest in investigation of the world—in other words, his or her status as an educated individual. These collections and the work of court experts also enhanced the ruler's reputation as a patron and person of power. Galileo was playing off such expectations when he named his newly discovered moons of Jupiter "Medicean Stars." Like all patronage relationships, the status was shared by both partners; indeed, the attention of a patron was a guarantor of the researcher's scientific credibility.

By the beginning of the seventeenth century, private salons and academies where investigators might meet on their own were another significant milieu of scientific investigation. These, too, had their roots in the humanist culture of Italy, where circles of scholars without university affiliations had formed. Though also dependent on private resources, these associations were an important alternative to princely patronage, since a ruler's funds

**A Collection of Naturalia**    Displays of exotica, such as these specimens in Naples, symbolized the ruler's authority by suggesting his or her power over nature.    *(From Ferrante Imperato,* Dell' Historia Naturale *[Naples, 1599]. By permission of the Houghton Library, Harvard University)*

might wax and wane according to his or her other commitments. Private organizations could avoid the stark distinctions of rank that were inevitable at courts, yet mimicked courts in the blend of scholars and educated courtiers they embraced. This more collegial but still privileged environment also fostered a sense of legitimacy for the science pursued there: legitimacy came from the recognition of fellow members and, in many cases, from publication of work by the society itself.

The earliest academy dedicated to scientific study was the *Accadèmia Segreta* (Secret Academy) founded in Naples in the 1540s. The members pursued experiments together, in order, in the words of one member, "to make a true anatomy of the things and operations of nature itself."[7] During the remainder of the sixteenth century and on into the seventeenth, such academies sprang up in many cities. The most celebrated was the *Accadèmia dei Lincei*, founded in Rome by an aristocrat in 1603. Its most famous member, Galileo, joined in 1611. The name "Lincei," from *lynx*, was chosen because of the legendary keen sight of that animal, an appropriate mascot for "searchers of secrets."

Galileo's notoriety and the importance of his discoveries forced all such learned societies to take a stand for or against Copernicanism. Throughout the seventeenth century, specific investigation of natural phenomena would continue in increasingly sophisticated institutional settings. The flowering of scientific thought in the seventeenth century occurred because of the specific innovations in astronomy and the general spread of scientific investigation that had been achieved by the end of Bacon's life.

### ■ Scientific Thought in France: Descartes and a New Cosmology

Philosophers, mathematicians, and educated elites engaged in lively debate and practical investigation throughout Europe in the first half of the seventeenth century. In France the great questions about cosmic order were being posed, ironically, at a time of political disorder. The years following the religious wars saw the murder of Henry IV, another regency, and further civil war in the 1620s (see pages 517–518). In this environment, questions about order in the universe and the possibilities of human knowledge took on particular urgency. It is not surprising that a Frenchman, René Descartes° (1596–1650), created the first fully articulated alternative world-view.

Descartes's thinking was developed and refined in dialogue with a circle of other French thinkers. His work became more influential among philosophers and lay people than the work of some of his equally talented contemporaries because of its thoroughness and rigor, grounded in Descartes's mathematical expertise, and because of his graceful, readable French. His system was fully presented in his *Discours de la méthode* (*Discourse on Method*, 1637). Descartes described some of his intellectual crises in his later work, *Meditations* (1641).

Descartes accepted Galileo's conclusion that the heavens and the earth are made of the same elements. In his theorizing about the composition of matter, he drew on ancient atomic models that previously had not been generally accepted. His theory that all matter is made up of identical bits, which he named "corpuscles," is a forerunner of modern atomic and quantum theories. Descartes believed that all the different appearances and behaviors of matter (for example, why stone is always hard and water is always wet) could be explained solely by the size, shape, and motion of these "corpuscles." Descartes's was an extremely mechanistic explanation of the universe. It nevertheless permitted new, more specific observations and hypotheses and greater understanding of inertia. For example, because he reimagined the universe as being filled with "corpuscles" free to move in any direction, "natural" motion no longer seemed either circular (Galileo's idea) or toward the center of the earth (Aristotle's idea). The new understanding of motion would be crucial to Isaac Newton's formulations later in the century.

In his various works, Descartes depicts and then firmly resolves the crisis of confidence that the new discoveries about the universe had produced. The collapse of the old explanations about the world made Descartes and other investigators doubt not only what they knew but also their capacity to know anything at all. Their physical senses—which denied that the earth moved, for example—had been proved untrustworthy. Descartes's solution was to re-envision the human rational capacity, the mind, as completely distinct from the world—that is, as distinct from the human body—and the unreliable perceptions it offers the senses. In a leap of faith, Descartes presumed that he could count on the fact that God would not have given humans a mind if that mind consistently misled them. For Descartes, God became the guarantor of human reasoning capacity, and humans, in Descartes's view, were distinguished by that capacity. This is the significance of his famous claim, "I think, therefore I am." (See the box "Reading Sources: Descartes: 'I think, therefore I am.'")

---

**Accadèmia dei Lincei** (ack-uh-DAY-mee-uh day-ee lin-CHAY-ee)  **Descartes** (day-KART)

**Descartes at the Swedish Court**   In 1649 René Descartes (shown here pointing to the drawing on the table) accepted an invitation from Queen Christina to reside at the Swedish Court. He discovered that the queen was an eager but demanding patron, requiring him to lecture on scientific topics at 5 A.M. each day. Descartes died in Stockholm of pneumonia after a few short months of residence. *(Versailles/Bulloz)*

Descartes thus achieved a resolution of the terrifying doubt about the world, a resolution that exalted the role of the human knower. The Cartesian universe was one of mechanical motion, not purpose or mystical meaning, and the Cartesian human being was pre-eminently a mind that could apprehend that universe. In what came to be known as "Cartesian dualism," Descartes was proposing the human mind is detached from the world yet at the same time can objectively analyze the world.

Descartes's ambitious view of human reason emphasized deductive reasoning (a process of reasoning in which the conclusion follows necessarily from the stated premises), a natural consequence of his philosophical rejection of sense data. The limits of deductive reasoning

for scientific investigation would be realized and much of Cartesian physics itself supplanted by the end of the century. Nevertheless, Descartes's assumption about the objectivity of the observer would become an enduring part of scientific practice. In Descartes's day, the most radical aspect of his thought was the reduction of God to the role of guarantor of knowledge. Many fellow scientists and interested lay people were fearful of Descartes's system because it seemed to encourage "atheism." In fact, a profound faith in God was necessary for Descartes's creativity in imagining his new world system—but the system did work without God.

Although Descartes would have been surprised and offended by charges of atheism, he knew that his work

## ℛ READING SOURCES

### Descartes: "I think, therefore I am"

*In the passages leading up to this one in his* Discourse on Method, *Descartes has made it clear that he does not advocate, or anticipate, any social or political upheaval as a consequence of his search for truth. On the contrary, he acknowledges his duty to abide by the tenets of religion and the laws of his country. The only status quo he wants to challenge is the habits of his own mind, in order to build a sure foundation for reasoning. Notice that he assumes his senses may deceive him and therefore sure knowledge cannot be based on sensory data.*

For a long time I had remarked that it is sometimes requisite in common life to follow opinions which one knows to be most uncertain, as [I have stated] above. But because in this case I wished to give myself entirely to the search for Truth, I thought that it was necessary for me to take an apparently opposite course, and to reject as absolutely false everything as to which I could imagine the least ground of doubt, in order to see afterwards if there remained anything in my belief that was entirely certain. Thus, because our senses sometimes deceive us, I wished to suppose that nothing is just as they cause us to imagine . . . and judging that I was as subject to error as was any other [man], I rejected as false all the reason formerly accepted by me as demonstrations. . . . I resolved to assume that everything that ever entered into my mind was no more true than the illusions of my dreams. But immediately afterwards I noticed that whilst I thus wished to think all things false, it was absolutely essential that the "I" who thought this should be somewhat, and remarking that this truth, "I think, therefore I am" was so certain and so assured that all the most extravagant suppositions brought forward by the skeptics were incapable of shaking it, I came to the conclusion that I could receive it without scruple as the first principle of the Philosophy for which I was seeking.

*Source: Discourse on the Method of Rightly Conducting the Reason,* trans. Elizabeth S. Haldane and G. R. T. Ross, in Mortimer Adler, ed., *Great Books of the Western World,* vol. 28 (Chicago: Encyclopaedia Britannica, 1990), p. 275.

would antagonize the church. He moved to the Netherlands to study in 1628, and his *Discourse* was first published there. He had lived in the Netherlands and in Germany earlier in his life; fearful of the tense atmosphere during the renewed war against French Protestants, he now left France virtually for good. Unlike Galileo, Descartes enjoyed personal wealth that enabled him to travel widely, work in solitude, and sample the intellectual environment of courts and universities without depending on powerful patrons. Long residence in the Netherlands led him to advocate religious toleration late in his life.

A contemporary of Descartes, fellow Frenchman Blaise Pascal° (1623–1662), drew attention in his writings

---

**Pascal** (pahss-KAHL)

and in his life to the limits of scientific knowledge. Son of a royal official, Pascal was perhaps the most brilliant mind of his generation. A mathematician like Descartes, he stressed the importance of mathematical representations of phenomena, built one of the first calculating machines, and invented probability theory. He also carried out experiments to investigate air pressure, the behavior of liquids, and the existence of vacuums.

Pascal's career alternated between periods of intense scientific work and religious retreat. Today he is well known for his writings that justified the austere Catholicism known as Jansenism and explored the human soul and psyche. His *Pensées* (*Thoughts*, 1657) consists of the published fragments of his defense of Christian faith, which remained unfinished at the time of his early death. Pascal's appeal for generations after him may lie in his attention to matters of faith and of feeling. His most famous statement, "The heart has its reasons which reason knows not," can be read as a declaration of the limits of the Cartesian world-view.

## ■ Science and Revolution in England

The new science had adherents and practitioners throughout Europe by 1650. Dutch scientists in the commercial milieu of the Netherlands, for example, had the freedom to pursue practical and experimental interests. The Dutch investigator Christiaan Huygens° (1629–1695) worked on a great variety of problems, including air pressure and optics. He invented and patented the pendulum clock in 1657, the first device accurately to measure small units of time, essential for a variety of measurements.

England proved a unique environment for the development of science in the middle of the century. In a society torn by civil war, differing positions on science became part and parcel of disputes over Puritanism, church hierarchy, and royal power. Scientific investigation and speculation were spurred by the urgency of religious and political agendas. Scientific, along with political and religious, debate was generally encouraged by the collapse of censorship beginning in the 1640s.

In the 1640s natural philosophers with Puritan leanings were encouraged in their investigations by dreams that science, of the practical Baconian sort, could be the means by which the perfection of life on earth could be brought about and the end of history, the reign of the saints preceding the return of Christ, accelerated. Their concerns ranged from improved production of gunpowder (for the armies fighting against Charles I) to surveying and mapmaking. Perhaps the best-known member of this group was Robert Boyle (1627–1691). In his career we can trace the evolution of English science through the second half of the seventeenth century.

Boyle and his colleagues were theoretically eclectic, drawing on Cartesian mechanics and even Paracelsian chemical theories. They attacked the English university system, still under the sway of Aristotelianism, and proposed widespread reform of education. They were forced to moderate many of their positions, however, as the English civil wars proceeded. Radical groups such as the Levellers used Hermeticism and the related Paracelsianism as part of their political and religious tenets. The

**Huygens** (HI-ghenz)

Levellers and other radical groups drew on the hermetic notion that matter is imbued with divine spirit; they believed that each person was capable of divine knowledge and a godly life without the coercive hierarchy of church and state officials.

Boyle and his colleagues responded to these challenges. They gained institutional power, accepting positions at Oxford and Cambridge. They formed the core of the Royal Society of London, which they persuaded Charles II to recognize and charter on his accession to the throne in the Restoration of 1660. They worked to articulate a theoretical position that combined the orderliness of mechanism, a continued divine presence in the world, and a Baconian emphasis on scientific progress. This unwieldy set of notions was attractive to the educated elite of their day, who embraced the certainties of science but also clung to certain authoritarian aspects of the old Christian world-view.

Their most creative contribution, both to their own cause and to the advancement of science, was their emphasis on and refinement of experimental philosophy and practice. In 1660 Boyle published *New Experiments Physico-Mechanical.* The work described the results of his experiments with an air pump he had designed, and it laid out general rules for experimental procedure. Descartes had accounted for motion by postulating that "corpuscles" of matter interact, thereby eliminating the possibility of a vacuum in nature. Recent experiments on air pressure suggested otherwise, however, and Boyle tried to confirm their findings with his air pump.

Boyle's efforts to demonstrate that a vacuum could exist—by evacuating a sealed chamber with his pump—were not successes by modern standards because they could not readily be replicated. Boyle tied the validity of experimental results to the agreement of witnesses to the experiment—a problematic solution, for only investigators sympathetic to his hypothesis and convinced of his credibility usually witnessed the results. In response to a Cambridge scholar who criticized his interpretation of one of his experiments, Boyle replied that he could not understand his critic's objections, ". . . the experiment having been tried both before our whole society [the Royal Society of London], and very critically, by its royal founder, his majesty himself."[8] Rather than debate differing interpretations, Boyle appealed to the authority and prestige of the participants themselves. In English science of the mid-seventeenth century, therefore, we have a further example of the fact that new truths, new procedures for determining truth, and new criteria for practitioners were all being established simultaneously.

**Isaac Newton** Pictured here about fifteen years after the publication of the *Principia,* Newton was also one of the developers of calculus. The cumbersome mathematics he still relied on, however, has led one scholar to ponder: "What manner of man he was who could use as a weapon what we can scarcely lift as a burden."[9] *(By courtesy of the National Portrait Gallery, London)*

### ■ The Newtonian Synthesis: The Copernican Revolution Completed

The Copernican revolution reached its high point with the work of the Englishman Isaac Newton (1643–1727), born one year almost to the day after Galileo died. Newton completed the new explanation for motion in the heavens and on earth that Copernicus's work had initiated and that Kepler, Galileo, and others had sought.

After a difficult childhood and an indifferent education, Newton entered Cambridge University as a student in 1661. Copernicanism and Cartesianism were being hotly debated, though not yet officially studied. Newton made use of Descartes's work in mathematics to develop his skill on his own and, by 1669, he had invented calculus. (He did not publish his work at the time and another mathematician, Gottfried von Leibniz°, later independ-

Leibniz (LIBE-nits)

ently developed calculus and vied with Newton for credit.)

Newton was elected to a fellowship at Cambridge in 1667 and, in 1669, was made professor of mathematics at the recommendation of a retiring professor with whom Newton had shared his work on calculus. With less demanding teaching assignments, he was able to devote much of the next decade to work on optics—an important area of study for testing Descartes's corpuscular theory of matter.

In the 1680s, Newton experienced a period of self-imposed isolation from other scientists after a particularly heated exchange with one colleague, provoked by Newton's difficult temperament. During this decade, he returned to the study of alternative theories about matter. As a student at Cambridge he had been strongly influenced by the work of a group of Neo-Platonists who were critical of Cartesian dualism. This controversial theory posited God as a cause of all matter and motion but removed God, or any other unknown or unknowable force, as an explanation for the behavior of matter. Their concerns were both religious and scientific. As Newton says in some of his early writing while a student, "However we cast about we find almost no other reason for atheism than this [Cartesian] notion of bodies having . . . a complete, absolute and independent reality."[10]

Newton now read treatises in alchemy and hermetic tracts and began to imagine explanations for the behavior of matter (such as for bits of cloth fluttered from a distance by static electricity) that Cartesian corpuscular theory could not readily explain. Precisely what the forces were that caused such behavior he was not sure, but his eclectic mind and his religious convictions enabled him to accept their existence.

It was this leap that allowed him to propose the existence of gravity—a mysterious force that accounts for the movement of heavenly bodies in the vacuum of space. Others had speculated about the existence of gravity; indeed, the concept of inertia as so far elaborated by Galileo, Descartes, and others suggested the need for the concept of gravity. Otherwise, if a planet were "pushed" (say, in Kepler's view, by the "motive force" of the sun), it would continue along that course forever unless "pulled back" by something else.

Newton's extraordinary contribution to a new mechanistic understanding of the universe was the mathematical computation of the laws of gravity and planetary motion, which he combined with a fully developed concept of inertia. In 1687 Newton published *Philosophia Naturalis Principia Mathematica* (*Mathematical Principles of Natural Philosophy*; usually called *Principia*). In this mathematical treatise—so intricate that it was baffling to lay people, even those able to read Latin—Newton laid out his laws of motion and expressed them as mathematical theorems that can be used to test future observations of moving bodies. Then he demonstrated that these laws also apply to the solar system, confirming the data already gathered about the planets and even predicting the existence of an as-yet-unseen planet. His supreme achievement was his law of gravitation, with which he could predict the discovery of the invisible planet. This law states that every body, indeed every bit of matter, in the universe exerts over every other body an attractive force proportional to the product of their masses and inversely proportional to the square of the distance between them. Newton not only accounted for motion but definitively united heaven and earth in a single scheme and created a convincing picture of an orderly nature.

Neither Newton nor anyone else claimed that his theorems resolved all questions about motion and matter. Exactly what gravity is and how it operates were not clear, as they still are not. Newton's laws of motion are taught today because they still adequately account for most problems of motion. The fact that so fundamental a principle as gravity remains unexplained in no way diminishes Newton's achievement but is clear evidence about the nature of scientific understanding: science provides explanatory schemas that account for many—but not all—observed phenomena. No schema explains everything, and each schema contains open doorways that lead both to further discoveries and to blind alleys. Newton, for example, assumed that the forces that accounted for gravity would mysteriously work on metals so that, as alchemists predicted, they might "quickly pass into gold."[11]

After the publication of the *Principia,* Newton was more of a celebrated public figure than a practicing scientist. He helped lead resistance to James II's Catholicizing policies in the university, and he became the familiar of many other leading minds of his day, such as John Locke (see page 596). In 1703 Newton became the president of the Royal Academy of Sciences and was knighted in 1705, the first scientist to be so distinguished. By the end of Newton's life, universities in England were dominated by men who acclaimed and built on his work: the transformation of the institutional structure of science in England was complete.

## ■ Other Branches of Science

The innovations in astronomy that led to the new mechanistic view of the behavior of matter did not automatically spill over to other branches of science. In astronomy, innovation came after the ancient and medieval inheritance had been fully assimilated and its errors disclosed. Other branches of science followed their own paths, though all were strongly influenced by the mechanistic world-view.

In chemistry, the mechanistic assumption that all matter was composed of small, equivalent parts was crucial to understanding the properties and behavior of compounds (combinations of elements). But knowledge of these small units of matter was not yet detailed enough to be of much use in advancing chemistry conceptually. Nevertheless, the flawed conceptual schema did not hold back all chemical discovery and development. Lack of understanding of gases, and of the specific elements in their makeup, for example, did not prevent the development and improvement of gunpowder. Indeed, unlike the innovations in astronomy, eventual conceptual innovation in chemistry and biology owed a great deal to the results of plodding experiment and the slow accumulation of data.

A conceptual leap forward was made in biology in the sixteenth and seventeenth centuries. Because biological knowledge was mostly a byproduct of the practice of medicine, biological studies remained very practical and experimental. The recent discovery of *On Anatomical Procedures,* a treatise by the ancient physician Galen, encouraged dissection and other practical research. Andreas Vesalius° (1514–1564), in particular, made important advances by following Galen's exhortation to anatomical research. Born in Brussels, Vesalius studied at the nearby University of Louvain, and then at Padua, where he was appointed professor of surgery. He ended his career as physician to Emperor Charles V and his son, Philip II of Spain. In his teaching at Padua Vesalius acted on the newly recovered Galenic teachings by doing dissections himself rather than giving the work to technicians. In 1543 he published versions of his lectures as an illustrated compendium of anatomy, *De Humani Corporis Fabrica* (*On the Fabric of the Human Body*).

The results of his dissections of human corpses, revealed in this work, demonstrated a number of errors in Galen's knowledge of human anatomy, much of which had been derived from dissection of animals. Neither Vesalius nor his immediate successors, however, questioned overall Galenic theory about the functioning of the human body, any more than Copernicus had utterly rejected Aristotelian physics.

The slow movement from new observation to changed explanation is clearly illustrated in the career of

---

**Vesalius** (vuh-SAY-lee-us)

the Englishman William Harvey (1578–1657). Much like Vesalius, Harvey was educated first in his own land and then at Padua, where he benefited from the tradition of anatomical research. He also had a career as a practicing physician in London and at the courts of James I and Charles I.

Harvey postulated the circulation of the blood—postulated rather than discovered because, owing to the technology of the day, he could not observe the tiny capillaries where the movement of arterial blood into the veins occurs. After conducting vivisectional experiments on animals that revealed the actual functioning of the heart and lungs, he reasoned that circulation must occur. He carefully described his experiments and his conclusions in *Exercitatio Anatomica de Motu Cordis et Sanguinis in Animalibus* (1628), usually shortened to *De Motu Cordis* (*On the Motion of the Heart*).

Harvey's work challenged Galenic anatomy and, like Copernicus's discoveries, created new burdens of explanation. According to Galenic theory, the heart and the lungs helped each other to function. The heart sent nourishment to the lungs through the pulmonary artery, and the lungs provided raw material for the "vital spirit," which the heart gave to the blood to sustain life. The lungs also helped the heart sustain its "heat." This heat was understood to be an innate property of organs, just as "heaviness," in traditional physics, had been considered an innate property of earthbound objects.

From his observations, Harvey came to think of the heart in terms consonant with the new mechanistic notions about nature: as a pump to circulate the blood. But he adjusted, rather than abandoned, Galenic theories concerning "heat" and "vital spirit." The lungs had been thought to "ventilate" the heart by providing air to maintain "heat," just as a bellows aerates a fire. In light of his discovery of the pulmonary transit (that all of the blood is pumped through the lungs and back through the heart), Harvey suggested instead that the lungs carried out some of these functions for the blood, helping it to concoct the "vital spirit." Only in this sense did he think of the heart as a machine, circulating this life-giving material throughout the body.

Harvey's explanation of bodily functions in light of his new knowledge thus did not constitute a rupture with Galenic tradition. But by the end of his life, Harvey's own adjustments of Galenic theory were suggesting new conceptual possibilities. His work inspired additional research in physiology, chemistry, and physics. Robert Boyle's efforts to understand vacuums can be traced in part to questions Harvey raised about the function of the lungs and the properties of air.

# THE NEW SCIENCE: SOCIETY, POLITICS, AND RELIGION

**S**CIENTISTS wrestled with questions about God and human capacity every bit as intently as they attempted to find new explanations for the behavior of matter and the motion of the heavens. Eventually, the profound implications of the new scientific world-view would affect thought and behavior throughout society. Once people no longer thought of the universe in hierarchical terms, they could question the hierarchical organization of society. Once people questioned the authority of traditional knowledge about the universe, the way was clear for them to begin to question traditional views of the state, the social order, and even the divine order. Such profound changes of perspective took hold very gradually, however. The advances in science did lead to revolutionary cultural change, but until the end of the seventeenth century, traditional institutions and ideologies limited its extent.

## ■ The Beginnings of Scientific Professionalism

Institutions both old and new supported the new science developing in the sixteenth and seventeenth centuries. Some universities were the setting for scientific breakthroughs, but court patronage, a well-established institution, also sponsored scientific activity. The development of the Accadèmia dei Lincei, to which Galileo belonged, and other academies was a step toward modern professional societies of scholars, although these new organizations depended on patronage.

In both England and France, royally sponsored scientific societies were founded in the third quarter of the century. The Royal Society of London, inaugurated in 1660, received royal recognition but no money and remained an informal institution sponsoring amateur scientific interests as well as specialized independent research. The Académie Royale des Sciences in France, established in 1666 by Jean-Baptiste Colbert, Louis XIV's minister of finance (see page 542), sponsored research and supported chosen scientists with pensions. These associations were extensions to science of traditional kinds of royal recognition and patronage. Thus, the French Académie was well funded but tightly controlled by the government of Louis XIV, and the Royal Society of London received little of Charles II's scarce resources or precious political capital. Like the earlier academies, these royally sponsored societies published their fellows' work; in England, the *Philosophical Transactions of the Royal Society* began in 1665.

The practice of seventeenth-century science took place in so many diverse institutions—academies, universities, royal courts—that neither *science* nor *scientist* was rigorously defined. Science as a discipline was not yet detached from broad metaphysical questions. Boyle, Newton, Pascal, and Descartes all concerned themselves with questions of religion, and all thought of themselves not as scientists but, like their medieval forebears, as natural philosophers. These natural philosophers were still members of an elite who met in aristocratic salons to discuss literature, politics, or science with equal ease and interest. Nevertheless, the beginnings of a narrowing of the practice of science to a tightly defined, truly professional community are evident in these institutions.

The importance of court life and patronage to the new science had at first enabled women to be actively involved. Women ran important salons in France; aristocratic women everywhere were indispensable sources of patronage for scientists; and women themselves were scientists, combining, as did men, science with other pursuits. Noblewomen and daughters of gentry families had access to education in their homes, and a number of such women were active scientists—astronomers, mathematicians, and botanists. The astronomer Maria Cunitz° (1610–1664), from Silesia (a Habsburg-controlled province, now in modern Poland), learned six languages with the encouragement of her father, who was a medical doctor. Later, she published a useful simplification of some of Kepler's mathematical calculations. Women from artisanal families might also receive useful training at home. Such was the case of the German entomologist Maria Sibylla Merian (1647–1717). Merian learned the techniques of illustration in the workshop of her father, an artist in Frankfurt. She later used her artistic training and her refined powers of observation to study and record the features and behavior of insects and plants in the New World.

Margaret Cavendish, duchess of Newcastle (1623–1673), wrote several major philosophical works, including *Grounds of Natural Philosophy* (1668). She was a Cartesian but was influenced by Neo-Platonism. She believed matter to have "intelligence" and thus disagreed with Cartesian dualism, but she criticized fellow English philosophers on the grounds that, like Descartes, she distrusted sensory knowledge as a guide to philosophy.

Women were routinely accepted as members of Italian academies, but they were excluded from formal

Cunitz (KOO-nits)

**Astronomers Elisabetha and Johannes Hevelius**    The Heveliuses were one of many collaborating couples among the scientists of the seventeenth century. Women were usually denied pensions and support for their research when they worked alone, however.    *(From Hevelius,* Machinae coelestis. *By permission of the Houghton Library, Harvard University)*

membership in the academies in London and Paris, though they could use the academies' facilities and received prizes from the societies for their work. One reason that women were barred was the purse: the amount of available patronage was limited, and coveted positions automatically went to men. Moreover, the hierarchical distinction signified by gender made the exclusion of women a useful way to define the academies as special and privileged.

Margaret Cavendish was aware of the degree to which her participation in scientific life depended on informal networks and on the resources available to her

## ✒ R E A D I N G   S O U R C E S

### Margaret Cavendish Challenges Male Scientists

*In her preface to her earliest scientific work,* The Philosophical and Physical Opinions *(1655), Cavendish addresses scholars at Oxford and Cambridge Universities with deceptive humility. She implies that the seeming limitations of women's abilities are in fact the consequence of their exclusion from education and from participation in worldly affairs.*

Most Famously Learned,

I here present to you this philosophical work, not that I can hope wise school-men and industrious laborious students should value it for any worth, but to receive it without scorn, for the good encouragement of our sex, lest in time we should grow irrational as idiots, by the dejectedness of our spirits, through the careless neglects and despisements of the masculine sex to the female, thinking it impossible we should have either learning or understanding, wit or judgment, as if we had not rational souls as well as men, and we out of a custom of dejectedness think so too, which makes us quit all industry towards profitable knowledge, being imployed only in low and petty imployments which take away not only our abilities towards arts but higher capacities in speculations, so that we are become like worms, that only live in the dull earth of ignorance, winding ourselves sometimes out by the help of some refreshing rain of good education, which seldome is given us, for we are kept like birds in cages, to hop up and down in our houses . . . ; thus by an opinion, which I hope is but an erroneous one in men, we are shut out of all power and authority by reason we are never imployed either in civil or martial affairs, our counsels are despised and laughed at and the best of our actions are trodden down with scorn, by the over-weening conceit men have of themselves and through a despisement of us.

*Source:* Moira Ferguson, ed., *First Feminists: British Women Writers, 1578–1799* (Bloomington and New York: Indiana University Press and The Feminist Press, 1985), pp. 85–86.

because of her aristocratic status. (See the box "Reading Sources: Margaret Cavendish Challenges Male Scientists.") Women scientists from more modest backgrounds, without Cavendish's resources, had to fight for the right to employment as public institutions gained importance as settings for the pursuit of science. The German astronomer Maria Winkelman° (1670–1720), for example, tried to succeed her late husband in an official position in the Berlin Academy of Sciences in 1710, after working as his unofficial partner during his tenure as astronomer to the academy. The academy withheld an official position from Winkelman after her husband's death, however, despite her experience and accomplishments (she had discovered a new comet, for example, in 1702). The secretary of the academy stated: "That she be kept on in an official capacity to work on the calendar or to continue with observations simply will not do. Already during her husband's lifetime the society was burdened with ridicule because its calendar was prepared by a woman. If she were now to be kept on in such a capacity, mouths would gape even wider."[12]

Winkelman worked in private observatories, but was able to return to the Berlin Academy only as the unofficial assistant to her own son, whose training she herself had supervised. As the new science gained in prestige, women scientists often found themselves marginalized.

### ■ The New Science, the State, and the Church

The new natural philosophy had implications for traditional notions about the state. The new world-view that all matter was identical and answerable to discernible natural laws gradually undermined political systems resting on a belief in the inherent inequality of persons

**Winkelman** (VINK-el-mahn)

and on royal prerogative. By the middle of the eighteenth century, a fully formed alternative political philosophy would argue for more "rational" government in keeping with the rational, natural order of things. But the change came slowly, and while it was coming, traditional rulers found much to admire and utilize in the new science.

Technological possibilities of the new science were very attractive to governments. Experiments with vacuum pumps had important applications in the mining industry, for example. Governments also sponsored pure, and not only applied, scientific research. A French naval expedition to Cayenne, in French Guiana, led to refinements of the pendulum clock but had as its main purpose progressive observations of the sun to permit the calculation of the earth's distance from the sun.

Members of the elite saw the opportunity not only for practical advances but also for prestige and, most important, confirmation of the orderliness of nature. It is hard to overestimate the psychological impact and intellectual power of this fundamental tenet of the new science—namely, that nature is an inanimate machine that reflects God's design not through its purposes but simply by its orderliness. Thus, in the short run, the new science supported a vision of order that was very pleasing even to a monarch of absolutist pretensions such as Louis XIV.

As we have seen, scientists themselves flourished in close relationships with princes and actively sought their patronage for its many benefits. Christiaan Huygens left the Netherlands to accept the patronage of Louis XIV, producing in France some of his most important work in

**Science and Royal Power**    This painting memorializes the founding of the French Académie des Sciences and the building of the royal observatory in Paris. Louis himself is at the center of the painting, reflecting the symbolic importance of royal power in the sponsorship of science. *(Château de Versailles/Laurie Platt Winfrey, Inc.)*

optics and mechanics. Huygens had learned from his father, secretary to the princes of Orange in the Netherlands, that a princely court not only offered steady support, but also opened doors to other royal academies and salons. Huygens published some of his early research through the Royal Society in London, thanks to contacts his father had established. When Galileo left his position at Padua for the Medici court in Florence, he wrote to a friend, "It is not possible to receive a salary from a Republic [Venice] . . . without serving the public, because to get something from the public one must satisfy it and not just one particular person; . . . no one can exempt me from the burden while leaving me the income; and in sum I cannot hope for such a benefit from anyone but an absolute prince."[13]

Scientists and scientific thought also remained closely tied to religion in both practical and institutional ways during the seventeenth century. Both religion and the Catholic Church as an institution were involved with scientific advancement from the time of Copernicus. Copernicus himself was a cleric, as were many philosophers and scientists active after him. This is not surprising, for most research in the sciences to this point had occurred within universities sponsored and staffed by members of religious orders, who had the education, time, and resources necessary for scientific investigation. Some of Descartes's closest collaborators were clerics, as were certain of Galileo's aristocratic patrons and his own protégés. Moreover, religious and metaphysical concerns were central to the work of virtually every scientist. The entire Cartesian edifice of reasoning about the world, for example, was grounded in Descartes's certainty about God. Copernicus, Kepler, Newton, and others perceived God's purpose in the mathematical regularity of nature.

The notion that religion was the opponent of science in this era is a result of Galileo's trial, and represents a distortion even of that event. It is true that the new astronomy and mechanics challenged traditional interpretations of Scripture as well as the fundamentals of physics and metaphysics that were taught in universities. Thus, in its sponsorship of universities, the church was literally invested in the old view, even though individual clerics investigated and taught Copernican ideas.

The rigid response of the church hierarchy to Galileo is partially explained by the aftermath of the Protestant Reformation, which, in the minds of many churchmen—including Galileo's accusers and some of his judges—had demonstrated the need for a firm response to any challenge to the church's authority. Galileo seemed particularly threatening because he was well known, wrote for a wide audience, and, like the Protestants, presumed on the church's right to interpret the Scriptures. Galileo may well have escaped punishment entirely had it not been for the political predicament faced by the pope coincident with his trial, however.

The condemnation of Galileo shocked many clerics, including the three who had voted for leniency at his trial. Clerics who were also scientists continued to study and teach the new science where and when they could. Copernicanism was taught by Catholic missionaries abroad. (See the box "Global Encounters: Jesuits and Astronomy in China.") To be sure, Galileo's trial did have a chilling effect on scientific investigation in most Catholic regions of Europe. Investigators could and did continue their research, but many could publish results only by smuggling manuscripts to Protestant lands. Many of the most important empirical and theoretical innovations in science occurred in Protestant regions after the middle of the seventeenth century.

Protestant leaders, however, were also not initially receptive to Copernican ideas because they defied scriptural authority as well as common sense. In 1549 one of Martin Luther's associates wrote: "The eyes are witnesses that the heavens revolve in the space of twenty-four hours. But certain men, either from love of novelty or to make a display of ingenuity, have concluded that the earth moves. . . . Now it is want of honesty and decency to assert such notions publicly and the example is pernicious. It is part of a good mind to accept the truth as revealed by God and to acquiesce in it."[14]

Protestant thinkers were also as troubled as Catholics by the metaphysical dilemmas that the new theories seemed to raise. In 1611, one year after Galileo's *Starry Messenger* appeared, the English poet John Donne (1573–1631) reflected on the confusion that now reigned in human affairs, with the heavenly hierarchy dismantled:

> [The] new Philosophy calls all in doubt,
> The Element of fire is quite put out;
> The Sun is lost, and th'earth, and no man's wit
> Can well direct him where to look for it.
>
> . . . . . . . . . . . . . . . .
>
> Tis all in pieces, all coherence gone;
> All just supply, and all Relation:
> Prince, Subject, Father, Son, are things forgot,
> For every man alone thinks he hath got
> To be a Phoenix, and that then can be
> None of that kinde, of which he is, but he.[15]

## ⊕ GLOBAL ENCOUNTERS

### Jesuits and Astronomy in China

*The Italian Matteo Ricci (1552–1610) was one of the first Jesuit missionaries to establish himself at the imperial court in China. He was appreciative as well as critical of Chinese science, but his remarks are more interesting to us because they reveal that Ricci himself regarded expertise in mathematics and astronomy as worthy of esteem. Ricci's own scientific knowledge was crucial to his acceptance at court; Jesuit missionaries who followed Ricci in the seventeenth century found their scientific expertise equally valued, and several openly taught Copernican theory in the East. Chinese interest in European knowledge was itself new; in previous centuries, Europeans had eagerly borrowed from China—including knowledge of papermaking and printing.*

The Chinese have not only made considerable progress in moral philosophy but in astronomy and in many branches of mathematics as well. At one time they were quite proficient in arithmetic and geometry, but in the study and teaching of these branches of learning they labored with more or less confusion. They divide the heavens into constellations in a manner somewhat different from that which we employ. Their count of the stars outnumbers the calculations of our astronomers by fully four hundred, because they include in it many of the fainter stars which are not always visible. And yet with all this, the Chinese astronomers take no pains whatever to reduce the phenomena of celestial bodies to the discipline of mathematics. Much of their time is spent in determining the moment of eclipses and the mass of the planets and the stars, but here, too, their deductions are spoiled by innumerable errors. Finally they center their whole attention on that phase of astronomy which our scientists term astrology, which may be accounted for the fact that they believe that everything happening on this terrestrial globe of ours depends upon the stars.

Some knowledge of the science of mathematics was given to the Chinese by the Saracens [Mongols], who penetrated into their country from the West, but very little of this knowledge was based upon definite mathematical proofs. What the Saracens left them, for the most part, consisted of certain tables of rules by which the Chinese regulated their calendar and to which they reduced their calculations of planets and the movements of the heavenly bodies in general. The founder of the family which at present regulates the study of astrology prohibited anyone from indulging in the study of this science unless he were chosen for it by hereditary right. The prohibition was founded upon fear, lest he who should acquire a knowledge of the stars might become capable of disrupting the order of the empire and seek an opportunity to do so.

*Source:* Louis J. Gallagher, trans., *China in the Sixteenth Century: The Journals of Matthew Ricci: 1583–1610* (New York: Random House, 1953), pp. 30–31.

The challenge of accounting in religious terms for the ideas of Copernicus and Descartes became more urgent for Protestants as the ideas acquired an anti-Catholic status after the trial of Galileo in 1633, and as they became common scientific currency by about 1640. A religious certainty about divine force that could account for the motion of bodies in a vacuum enabled Newton to develop his theories on motion and gravity. In short, religion did not merely remain in the scientists' panoply of explanations; it remained a fundamental building block of scientific thought and central to most scientists' lives, whether they were Catholic or Protestant.

## ■ The New Science and Human Affairs at the End of the Seventeenth Century

Traditional institutions and ideologies checked the potential effects of the new science for a time, but by the middle of the seventeenth century, political theory was beginning to reflect the impact of the mechanistic world-view. Political philosophers began to doubt that either the world or human society was an organic whole in which each part was distinguished in nature and function from the rest. Thomas Hobbes, John Locke, and others recast the bonds that link citizens to each other and to their rulers.

Because of the political turmoil in England, Thomas Hobbes (1588–1679) spent much of his productive life on the Continent. After the beginnings of the parliamentary rebellion, he joined a group of royalist émigrés in France. He met Galileo and lived for extended periods in Paris, in contact with the circle of French thinkers that included Descartes. Like Descartes, he theorized about the nature and behavior of matter and published a treatise on his views in 1655.

Hobbes is best known today for *Leviathan*° (1651), his treatise on political philosophy. *Leviathan* applies to the world of human beings his mostly Cartesian view of nature as composed of "self-motivated," atomlike structures. Hobbes viewed people as mechanistically as he viewed the rest of nature. In his view, people were made up of appetites of various sorts—the same kind of innate forces that drove all matter. The ideal state, concluded Hobbes, is one in which a strong sovereign controls the disorder that inevitably arises from the clash of desires. Unlike medieval philosophers, Hobbes did not draw analogies between the state and the human body (the king as head, judges and magistrates as arms, and so forth). Instead, Hobbes compared the state to a machine that "ran" by means of laws and was kept in good working order by a skilled technician—the ruler.

Hobbes's pessimism about human behavior and his insistence on the need for restraint imposed from above reflect, as does the work of Descartes, a concern for order in the wake of political turmoil. This concern was one reason he was welcomed into the community of French philosophers, who were naturally comfortable with royalty as a powerful guarantor of order. But Hobbes's work, like theirs, was a radical departure because it envisioned citizens as potentially equal and constrained neither by morality nor by natural obedience to authority.

---

**Leviathan** (luh-VIE-uh-thun)

Another Englishman, John Locke (1632–1704), offered an entirely different vision of natural equality among people and, consequently, of social order. Locke's major works, *Essay on Human Understanding* (1690) and *Two Treatises on Government* (1690), reflect the experimentalism of Robert Boyle, the systematizing rationality of Descartes, and other strands of the new scientific thought. In the *Essay*, Locke offered a view of human knowledge more pragmatic and utilitarian than the rigorous mathematical model of certainty used by many other philosophers. He argued that human knowledge is largely the product of experience. He agreed with Descartes that reason orders and explains human experience but, unlike Descartes, doubted that human reason had unlimited potential to comprehend the universe. Locke, however, offered a more optimistic vision of the possible uses of reason. Whereas Descartes was interested in mentally ordering and understanding the world, Locke was interested in actually functioning *in* the world.

Locke's treatises on government reflect his notion of knowledge based on experience as well as his particular experiences as a member of elite circles following the Restoration of monarchy in England. Trained in medicine, he served as personal physician and general political assistant to one of the Members of Parliament most opposed to Charles II's pretensions to absolutist government. When James II acceded to the throne in 1685, Locke remained in the Netherlands, where he had fled to avoid prosecution for treason. He became an adviser to William of Orange and returned to England with William and Mary in 1688. Locke's view of the principles of good government, then, came to reflect the pro-parliamentary stance of his political milieu.

Unlike Hobbes, Locke argued that people are capable of self-restraint and mutual respect in their pursuit of self-interest. The state arises, he believed, from a contract that individuals freely enter into to protect themselves, their property, and their happiness from possible aggression by others. They can invest the executive and legislative authority to carry out this protection in monarchy or any other governing institution, though Locke believed the English Parliament was the best available model. Because sovereignty resides with the people who enter into the contract, rebellion against abuse of power is justified. At the core of Locke's schema was thus a revolutionary vision of political society based on human rights.

Locke's experience as an English gentleman is apparent in his emphasis on private property, which he considered a fundamental human right. Nature, he believed, could not benefit humankind unless it was worked by human hands, as in a farm, for example; private ownership of property guaranteed its productivity and entitled the owner to participate in his imagined contract. Indeed, his political vision is unequivocal, and unbending, on the nature of property. Locke even found a justification for slavery. He also did not consider women to be political beings in the same way as men. The family, he felt, was a separate domain from the state, not bound by the same contractual obligations.

Locke and many other seventeenth-century thinkers were unable to imagine a new physical or political reality without invoking a notion of gender as a "natural" principle of order and hierarchy. Although Margaret Cavendish (see page 591) and other women disputed the validity of such gender distinctions, men frequently used them. Locke's use of gender as an arbitrary organizing principle gave his bold new vision of rights for certain men a claim to being "natural." The use of gender-specific vocabulary to describe nature itself had the effect of making the new objective attitude toward the world seem "natural." Works by seventeenth-century scientists are filled with references to nature as a woman who must be "conquered," "subdued," or "penetrated."

Traditional gender distinctions limited and reinforced most facets of political thought, but in other areas the fact of uncertainty and the need for tolerance were embraced. Another of Locke's influential works was the impassioned *Letter on Toleration* (1689). In it he argued that religious belief is fundamentally private and that only the most basic Christian principles need be accepted by everyone. Others went further than Locke by entirely removing traditional religion as necessary to morality and public order. Fostering this climate of religious skepticism were religious pluralism in England and the self-defeating religious intolerance of Louis XIV's persecution of Protestants.

Pierre Bayle (1647–1706), a Frenchman of Protestant origins, argued that morality can be wholly detached from traditional religion. Bayle cited as an example of morality the philosopher Baruch Spinoza° (1632–1677). Spinoza believed the state to have a moral purpose and human happiness to have spiritual roots. Yet he was not a Christian at all but a Dutch Jew who had been ejected from his local synagogue for supposed atheism! One need hardly be a Christian of any sort in order to be a moral being, Bayle concluded.

Bayle's skepticism toward traditional knowledge was more wide ranging than his views on religion. His

**Spinoza** (spin-OH-za)

**Gentleman Surveying a Town**    This illustration appeared in a seventeenth-century book on surveying by a mathematician who helped design the gardens at Versailles. The book aimed to teach elites the math necessary for precise measurements of landscapes—for example, for the purpose of siege warfare. The presence of the gentleman in the foreground, estimating the proportions of the town by sight, reveals that the author expected his audience to be interested in the mathematical computations he sought to teach them.    *(Bibliothèque Nationale de France)*

best-known work, *Dictionnaire historique et critique* (*Historical and Critical Dictionary,* 1702), was a compendium of observations about and criticisms of virtually every thinker whose works were known at the time, including such recent and lionized figures as Descartes and Newton. Bayle was the first systematic skeptic, and he relentlessly exposed errors and shortcomings in all received knowledge. His works were very popular with elite lay readers.

**Science Gains an Audience**   This illustration from Bernard de Fontenelle's major work popularized the new science. It reveals the audience for which the work was intended. A gentleman, sitting with a lady in a formal garden, gestures to a depiction of the solar system as it was now understood; the lady is presumed to understand and to be interested in the information.   *(By permission of Houghton Library, Harvard University)*

Bayle's fellow countryman Bernard de Fontenelle° (1657–1757), secretary to the Académie des Sciences from 1699 to 1741, was the greatest popularizer of the new science of his time. His *Entretiens sur la Pluralités des Mondes* (*Conversations on the Plurality of Worlds*, 1686) was, as the title implies, an informally presented description of the infinite universe of matter. A great success, it went through numerous editions and transla-

---

**Fontenelle** (fon-tuh-NEL)

tions. As secretary to the Académie, Fontenelle continued his work as popularizer by publishing descriptions of the work of the Académie's scientists. At his death (at age 99) in 1757 it was said that "the Philosophic spirit, today so much in evidence, owes its beginnings to Monsieur de Fontenelle."[16]

## Summary

FONTENELLE is a fitting figure with whom to end a discussion of the Scientific Revolution because he represents, and worked to accomplish, the transference of the new natural philosophy into political and social philosophy—a movement we know as the "Enlightenment." The Scientific Revolution began, as innovation in scientific thinking often does, with a specific research problem whose answer led in unexpected directions. Copernicus's response to traditional astronomical problems led to scientific and philosophical innovation because of his solution and because of the context into which it was received. Recent recoveries of new ancient texts in the Renaissance and the discovery of previously unknown lands in the New World made it possible to imagine challenging ancient scientific authority. The interest of princes in both the prestige and the practical use of science helped support the work of scientists.

Other scientists, following Copernicus, built on his theories, culminating in the work of Galileo, who supported Copernican theory with additional data and widely published his findings. The Frenchman Descartes was the first to fashion a systematic explanation for the operations of nature to replace the medieval view. The political and intellectual climate in England, meanwhile, encouraged the development of experimental science and inductive reasoning. Isaac Newton provided new theories to explain the behavior of matter and expressed them in mathematical terms that could apply to either the earth or the cosmos; with his work, traditional astronomy and physics were overturned. In their place was a vision of the universe of matter that behaved, not according to higher purposes, but rather as a machine. New institutions in the form of private as well as officially sponsored scientific societies rose up to support scientists' work. These were particularly important before the new science became accepted in universities; they excluded some practitioners of the new science, however, particularly women.

Rulers made use of the new science for the practical results it offered despite the ideological challenge it presented to their power. The relationship of religion to the new science was equally complex and contrary. Some religious leaders scorned the new science; most scientists, whether Catholic or Protestant, worked to accommodate both the new science and their religious beliefs. Indeed, religious faith, in the case of Newton, for example, was a spur to innovation. By the end of the seventeenth century, the hierarchical Christian world-view grounded in the old science was being challenged on many fronts, most notably in the work of political philosophers Hobbes and Locke. A fully articulated secular world-view would be the product of the Enlightenment in the next century.

## ■ Notes

1. Quoted in *The New Encyclopaedia Britannica*, 15th ed., vol. 9 (Chicago, 1992), p. 135.
2. Quoted in Thomas S. Kuhn, *The Copernican Revolution* (Cambridge, Mass.: Harvard University Press, 1985), p. 131.
3. Quoted in Margaret C. Jacob, *The Cultural Meaning of the Scientific Revolution* (Philadelphia: Temple University Press, 1988), p. 18.
4. Quoted ibid., p. 33.
5. Quoted in Alan G. R. Smith, *Science and Society in the Sixteenth and Seventeenth Centuries* (New York: Science History Publications, 1972), p. 72.
6. Quoted in Jacob, p. 32 (emphasis added).
7. Quoted in Bruce T. Moran, ed., *Patronage and Institutions: Science, Technology and Medicine at the European Court* (Rochester, N.Y.: Boyden Press, 1991), p. 43.
8. Quoted in Steven Shapin, *A Social History of Truth* (Chicago: University of Chicago Press, 1994), p. 298.
9. Quoted in Smith, p. 130.
10. Quoted in Jacob, p. 89.
11. Quoted ibid., p. 25.
12. Quoted in Londa Schiebinger, *The Mind Has No Sex?* (Cambridge, Mass.: Harvard University Press, 1989), p. 92.
13. Quoted in Richard S. Westfall, "Science and Patronage," *ISIS* 76(1985): 16.
14. Quoted in Kuhn, p. 191.
15. *Complete Poetry and Selected Prose of John Donne*, ed. John Hayward (Bloomsbury, England: Nonesuch Press, 1929), p. 365, quoted in Kuhn, p. 194.
16. Quoted in Paul Edwards, ed., *The Encyclopedia of Philosophy*, vol. 3 (New York: Macmillan, 1967), p. 209.

## ■ Suggested Reading

Biagioli, Mario. *Galileo, Courtier.* 1993. A new study that stresses the power of patronage relations to shape scientific process.

Kuhn, Thomas. *The Copernican Revolution.* 1985. A classic treatment of the revolution in astronomy that lucidly explains the Aristotelian world-view; to understand the Copernican revolution, start here.

Schiebinger, Londa. *The Mind Has No Sex?* 1989. An examination of the participation of women in the practice of science and an explanation of how science began to reflect the exclusion of women in its values and objects of study—above all, in its claims about scientific "facts" about women themselves.

Shapin, Steven. *The Scientific Revolution.* 1996. An elegant short introduction with a lengthy bibliography; emphasizes the intellectual, social, and political contexts that shaped the development of the new science.

———, and Simon Schaffer. *Leviathan and the Air-Pump.* 1985. One of the most important studies of seventeenth-century science: traces the conflict between Cartesian science, as represented by Hobbes, and experimental science, in the work of Boyle; and shows the relationship of Hobbes and Boyle to their respective contexts and the widespread philosophical implications of each school of thought.

Westfall, R. *Never at Rest: A Biography of Isaac Newton.* 1993. A biography by one of the best-known historians of science.

 **For a searchable list of additional readings for this chapter, go to http://college.hmco.com.**

# Modern Maps

We take for granted that contemporary maps will provide accurate representations of geography and present information in standardized ways we can easily read. But how did these standards of clarity and accuracy come about?

Modern mapping was developed during the Scientific Revolution. Like most of the changes we have labeled the "Scientific Revolution," changes in mapping were the result of several influences: innovations in Renaissance art, knowledge gleaned from voyages of exploration, the impact of new astronomical discoveries, and the interest and support of princely patrons. All of these factors enabled Europeans of this era to have a literally new view of their world.

Let us look at Christopher Saxton's map of Somerset, a county in England. This map was printed in 1579 in one of the first atlases ever published. We might be struck by how different this map appears from contemporary maps; many of its features seem decorative or even quaint. Ships, not drawn to scale, ride at anchor or sail off the coast. Towns are represented not by dots of various sizes but by miniature town buildings. Relief in the landscape is depicted with hills drawn, like the town buildings, from a side view inconsistent with the aerial perspective of the map as a whole. The large royal coat of arms that occupies the upper left quadrant of the map seems the most antiquated and irrelevant feature.

But is it irrelevant? Let us try to appreciate what a striking and powerful image this map must have been for its original viewers. Because the features are represented in ways that we consider decorative, it is easy for us to overlook the fact that this map illustrates a revolutionary method of depicting space. Saxton provides an aerial view of an entire county, with all locales arrayed in accurate spatial relationship to one another. This accurate rendering of space was, first, the result of the discovery of linear perspective by Renaissance artists. This discovery, which enabled space to be imagined from the perspec-

**Map of the County of Somerset, England, 1579** *(British Library)*

**Map of the French Coastline, 1693**
*(Bibliothèque Nationale de France)*

tive of a distanced observer, created the illusion of three-dimensional space in Renaissance paintings. Saxton's maps—and the few others published at about the same time—represented the first time Europeans could take "visual possession" of the land they lived in, in the way we now take for granted whenever we buy a road map.*

Precise measurement of land forms—the location of hills in this map, for example—still relied on the established craft of systematic surveying. And here is where the royal coat of arms enters the picture, literally. Saxton's surveying and the production of his atlas were sponsored by the government of Queen Elizabeth. Thus, just as this map enabled contemporary observers to envision for the first time, in its entirety, the land they lived in, it simultaneously marked royal power over that land.

Now let us look at a 1693 map of the coastline of France. We immediately note that most decorative elements are gone: no ships sail the abundant seas, for example. The figure of a compass marks the Paris meridian—the site of the city, we are shown, has been precisely determined by means of its longitude and latitude. More accurate calculation of longitude had been made possible by the work of Kepler and Galileo, whose mapping of heavenly bodies provided known points in

the night sky from which to calculate the longitude of the observer's position on earth. (Calculation of latitude had always been easier, since it involved only determining the angle of the sun above the horizon, but it was also improved by better instrumentation in the seventeenth century.) After 1650, French cartographers, among others, systematically collected astronomical observations from around the world so they could map all known lands more precisely.

This map superimposes a corrected view (the darker line) of the coastline of France over an older rendering. The power of this coastline map, then, lies in the way it dramatically advertises the progress of mapmaking itself. Royal power remains connected to scientific effort: the title reads, "Map of France, corrected by order of the King by the observations of Messieurs of the Academy of Sciences."

Thus, both of these maps glorify royal power: one by linking it with a new visualization of the land it ruled, the other by presenting royalty as a patron and guarantor of knowledge. But in the second map, royal identity is no longer pictured along with the land it claims. Instead, the king is mentioned discreetly, in what came to be a standardized label.

Like all innovations of the Scientific Revolution, those in mapmaking had unintended consequences. Claims to royal power articulated on maps lost their force as the information the maps conveyed was increasingly valued for itself. Royal power had many practical and ideological uses for the new science but, in the end, would be undermined by the world-view the new science made possible.

---

*Richard Helgerson, "The Land Speaks: Cartography, Chorography, and Subversion in Renaissance England," *Representations* 16 (Fall 1986): 51. This discussion of Saxton's map and the evolution of mapmaking is drawn from Helgerson and from Norman J. W. Thrower, *Maps and Civilization* (Chicago: University of Chicago Press, 1996), chaps. 5 and 6.

# CHAPTER 18

# Europe on the Threshold of Modernity ca. 1715–1789

**D**RINKS are set before these gentlemen on their table, but something tells us this is more than just a social gathering. The men are absorbed in intense conversation. One man raises his hand, perhaps to emphasize his point, while another listens with a skeptical smirk. Several others eagerly follow their conversation. Other animated discussions go on at nearby tables. The setting depicted here was altogether new in the eighteenth century, when this picture was made, and a caption that originally accompanied the illustration speaks to its importance: "Establishment of the new philosophy: our cradle was the café."

Cafés were one of the new settings in which literate elites could discuss the "new philosophy"—what we now call Enlightenment philosophy—and could explore its implications for social and political life. Men gathered in clubs and cafés; women directed private gatherings known as salons. Both men and women read more widely than ever before. The Enlightenment was the extension into political and social thought of the intellectual revolution that had already occurred in the physical sciences. Hence, it constituted a revolution in political philosophy, but it was also much more. The era witnessed the emergence of an informed body of public opinion, critical of the prevailing political system. The relationship between governments and the governed had begun to change: subjects of monarchs were becoming citizens of nations.

The notion that human beings, using their rational faculties, could not only understand nature but might also transform their societies

---

**The Enlightenment**

---

**European States in the Age of Enlightenment**

---

**The Widening Scope of Warfare**

---

**Economic Expansion and Social Change**

---

Café society in the eighteenth century.
(The Art Archive/Musée Carnavalet, Paris/Dagli Orti)

was appealing to rulers as well, in part for the traditional reason—strengthening state power. Frederick the Great of Prussia, Catherine the Great of Russia, and other monarchs self-consciously tried to use Enlightenment precepts to guide their efforts at governing. They had mixed success because powerful interests opposed their efforts at reform and because, ultimately, their own hereditary and autocratic power was incompatible with Enlightenment perspectives.

Profound changes in economic and social life accompanied this revolution in intellectual and political spheres. Economic growth spurred population growth, which in turn stimulated industry and trade. The increasing economic and strategic importance of overseas colonies made them important focal points of international conflict. As the century closed, Europe was on the threshold of truly revolutionary changes in politics and production that had their roots in the intellectual, economic, and social ferment of eighteenth-century life.

### QUESTIONS TO CONSIDER

■ What were the most important notions in Enlightenment thought, and what were some of the intellectual, social, and political conditions that favored its development?

■ To what extent did the activities of "enlightened despots" reflect Enlightenment precepts, and to what extent did they reflect traditional concerns of state power?

■ How did warfare itself, and the causes of war, change in the eighteenth century?

■ How was European agriculture transformed in this era, and what further transformations did it bring in its wake?

### TERMS TO KNOW

| | |
|---|---|
| **philosophes** | **Frederick the Great** |
| **Voltaire** | **Maria Theresa** |
| **Adam Smith** | **Catherine the Great** |
| **Jean-Jacques Rousseau** | **agricultural revolution** |
| **salon, salonnière** | **putting-out system** |
| **enlightened despotism** | |

# THE ENLIGHTENMENT

 HE Enlightenment was an intellectual movement that applied to political and social thought the confidence in the intelligibility of natural law that Newton and other scientists had recently achieved. Following Descartes and Locke, Enlightenment thinkers believed that human beings could discern and work in concert with the laws of nature for the betterment of human life. Perhaps the most significant effect of this confidence was the questioning of traditional social and political bonds. A belief grew that society must be grounded on rational foundations to be determined by humans, not arbitrary foundations determined by tradition and justified by religious authority.

The Enlightenment was a social and cultural movement: Enlightenment thought was received and debated in the context of increasingly widespread publications and new opportunities for exchanging views in literary societies, salons, and cafés. This context shaped the potential radicalism of the Enlightenment by helping to ensure that informed public opinion would become a new force in political and cultural life. Given this broad base, Enlightenment thinking was certain to challenge the very foundations of social and political order.

### ■ Voltaire: The Quintessential *Philosophe*

A wide range of thinkers participated in the Enlightenment. In France they were known as *philosophes°*, a term meaning not a formal philosopher but rather a thinker and critic. The most famous of the philosophes was Voltaire (1694–1778). A prolific writer, critic, and reformer, Voltaire was lionized by admirers throughout Europe, including several rulers. Born François-Marie Arouet to a middle-class family, he took the pen name Voltaire in 1718, after one of his early plays was a critical success. Like many philosophes, Voltaire moved in courtly circles but

---

**philosophes** (fee-low-ZOHFS)

was often on its margins. His mockery of the regent for the young French king earned him a year's imprisonment in 1717, and an exchange of insults with a leading courtier some years later led to enforced exile in Great Britain for two years.

After returning from Britain, Voltaire published his first major philosophical work. *Lettres philosophiques* (*Philosophical Letters*, 1734) revealed the influence of his British sojourn and helped to popularize Newton's achievement. To confidence in the laws governing nature Voltaire added cautious confidence in humans' attempts to discern truth. From Locke's work (see page 596) he was persuaded to trust human educability tempered by awareness of the finite nature of the human mind. These elements gave Voltaire's philosophy both its passionate conviction and its sensible practicality.

Voltaire portrayed Great Britain as a more rational society than France. He was particularly impressed with the relative religious and intellectual toleration evident across the Channel. The British government had a more workable set of institutions; the economy was less crippled by the remnants of feudal privilege; and education was not in the hands of the church. (See the box "Reading Sources: Voltaire on Britain's Commercial Success.") Voltaire was one of many French thinkers who singled out the Catholic Church as the archenemy of progressive thought. Philosophes constantly collided with the church's negative views of human nature and resented its control over most education and its still strong sway in political life. Typical of Voltaire's castigation of the church is his stinging satire of the clerics who condemned Galileo: "I desire that there be engraved on the door of your holy office: Here seven cardinals assisted by minor brethren had the master of thought of Italy thrown into prison at the age of seventy, made him fast on bread and water, because he instructed the human race."

After the publication of his audacious *Lettres,* Voltaire was again forced into exile from Paris, and he resided for some years in the country home of a woman with whom he shared a remarkable intellectual and emotional relationship: Emilie, marquise du Châtelet° (1706–1749). Châtelet was a mathematician and a scientist. She prepared a French translation of Newton's *Principia* while Voltaire worked at his accustomed variety of writing, which included a commentary on Newton's work. Because of Châtelet's tutelage, Voltaire became more knowledgeable about the sciences and more serious in his efforts to apply scientific rationality to human affairs. He was devastated by her sudden death in 1749.

Châtelet (shot-uh-LAY)

## CHRONOLOGY

| | |
|---|---|
| 1715–1774 | Reign of Louis XV in France |
| 1722–1741 | Walpole first British "prime minister" |
| 1734 | Voltaire, *Philosophical Letters* |
| 1740–1748 | War of the Austrian Succession |
| 1740–1780 | Reign of Maria Theresa of Austria |
| 1740–1786 | Reign of Frederick the Great of Prussia |
| 1746 | Battle of Culloden |
| 1748 | Montesquieu, *The Spirit of the Laws* |
| 1748 | Hume, *Essay on Human Understanding* |
| 1751–1765 | Diderot, editor, *The Encyclopedia* |
| 1756–1763 | Seven Years' War |
| 1758 | Voltaire, *Candide* |
| 1762 | Rousseau, *The Social Contract* |
| 1762–1796 | Reign of Catherine the Great of Russia |
| 1772 | First partition of Poland |
| 1776 | Smith, *The Wealth of Nations* |
| 1780–1790 | Reign of Joseph II of Austria |
| 1792 | Wollstonecraft, *A Vindication of the Rights of Woman* |

Shortly afterward, he accepted the invitation of the king of Prussia, Frederick II, to visit Berlin. His stay was stormy and brief because of disagreements with other court philosophers. He resided for a time in Geneva, until his criticisms of the city's moral codes forced yet another exile on him. He spent most of the last twenty years of his life at his estates on the Franco-Swiss border, where he could be relatively free from interference by any government. These were productive years. He produced his best-known satirical novelette, *Candide,* in 1758. It criticized aristocratic privilege and the power of clerics as well as the naiveté of philosophers who took "natural law" to mean that the world was already operating as it should.

**Voltaire Visits Frederick the Great of Prussia**    Voltaire leans forward, at left, to discuss a point of philosophy with Frederick. Skill at witty conversation enabled philosophes such as Voltaire to advance fundamental criticisms of society even to elite audiences.    *(Bildarchiv Preussischer Kulturbesitz)*

Voltaire's belief that only by struggle are the accumulated habits of centuries overturned is also reflected in his political activity. Voltaire became involved in several celebrated legal cases in which individuals were pitted against the authority of the church, which was still backed by the authority of the state. In pursuit of justice in these cases and in relentless criticism of the church, Voltaire added a stream of straightforward political pamphlets to his literary output. He also worked closer to home, initiating agricultural reform on his estates and working to improve the status of peasants in the vicinity.

Voltaire died in Paris in May 1778, after a triumphal welcome for the staging of one of his plays. By then, he was no longer leader of the Enlightenment in strictly intellectual terms. Thinkers and writers more radical than he had earned prominence during his long life and had dismissed some of his beliefs, such as the notion that a monarch could introduce reform. But Voltaire had provided a crucial stimulus to French thought with his *Lettres philosophiques*. His importance lies also in his embodiment of the critical spirit of eighteenth-century rationalism: its confidence, its increasingly practical bent, its wit and sophistication. Until the end of his life, Voltaire remained a bridge between the increasingly diverse body of Enlightenment thought and the literate elite audience.

## ❧ READING SOURCES

### Voltaire on Britain's Commercial Success

*In this excerpt from* Philosophical Letters, *Voltaire compares British trade and sea power with the commercial activities of the German and French elites, who scorned trade in order to engage in aristocratic pretentiousness and court politics. Voltaire's admiration for England and his penchant for criticizing irrationalities of all sorts are evident, as is his famed wit. Wit and irony were important tools, enabling Voltaire to advance trenchant criticism when seeming only to poke fun.*

Commerce, which has brought wealth to the citizenry of England, has helped to make them free, and freedom has developed commerce in its turn. By means of it the nation has grown great; it is commerce that little by little has strengthened the naval forces that make the English the masters of the seas. . . . Posterity may learn with some surprise that a little island with nothing of its own but a bit of lead, tin . . . and coarse wool became, by means of its commerce, powerful enough to send three fleets at one time to three different ends of the earth.

All this makes the English merchant justly proud; moreover, the younger brother of a peer of the realm does not scorn to enter into trade. . . . [In Germany], they are unable to imagine how [an aristocrat could enter trade since they have] as many as thirty Highnesses of the same name, with nothing to show for it but pride and a coat of arms.

In France anybody who wants to can [act the part of marquis] and whoever arrives in Paris with money to spend and a [plausible name] may indulge in such phrases as "a man of my rank and quality" and with sovereign eye look down upon a wholesaler. . . . Yet I don't know which is the more useful to a state, a well-powdered lord who knows precisely what time the king gets up in the morning . . . and who gives himself airs of grandeur while playing the role of slave in a minister's antechamber, or a great merchant who enriches his country.

*Source:* Ernest Dilworth, trans. and ed., *Voltaire: Philosophical Letters* (New York: Bobbs-Merrill, 1961), pp. 39–40.

---

### ■ The Variety of Enlightenment Thought

Differences among philosophes grew as the century progressed. In the matter of religion, for example, there was virtual unanimity of opposition to the Catholic Church among French thinkers, but no unanimity about God. Voltaire was a theist—believing firmly in God, creator of the universe, but not a specifically Christian God. To some later thinkers, God was irrelevant—the creator of the world, but a world that ran continuously according to established laws. Some philosophes were atheists, arguing that a universe operating according to discoverable laws needs no higher purpose and no divine presence to explain, run, or justify its existence. In Protestant areas of Europe, in contrast to France, Enlightenment thought was often less hostile to Christianity.

Questions about social and political order, as well as about human rationality itself, were also pondered. Charles de Secondat (1689–1755), baron of Montesquieu°, a French judge and legal philosopher, combined the belief that human institutions must be rational with Locke's assumption of human educability. Montesquieu's treatise *De L'Esprit des lois* (*The Spirit of the Laws*, 1748) was published in twenty-two printings within two years. In it Montesquieu maintained that laws were not meant to be arbitrary rules but derived naturally from human society: the more evolved a society was, the more liberal were its laws. This notion that progress is possible within society and government deflated Europeans' pretensions with regard to other

---

**Montesquieu** (mawn-tess-KYUH)

societies, for a variety of laws could be equally "rational" given differing conditions. Montesquieu is perhaps best known to Americans as the advocate of the separation of legislative, executive, and judicial powers that later became enshrined in the U.S. Constitution. To Montesquieu, this scheme seemed to parallel in human government the balance of forces observable in nature; moreover, the arrangement seemed best to guarantee liberty.

Enlightenment philosophers also investigated the "laws" of economic life. In France economic thinkers known as *physiocrats* proposed ending "artificial" control over land use in order to free productive capacity and permit the flow of produce to market. Their target was traditional forms of land tenure, including collective control of village lands by peasants and seigneurial rights over land and labor by landlords. The freeing of restrictions on agriculture, manufacture, and trade was proposed by the Scotsman Adam Smith in his treatise *An Inquiry into the Nature and Causes of the Wealth of Nations* (1776).

Smith (1723–1790), a professor at the University of Glasgow, is best known in modern times as the originator of "laissez-faire" economics. *Laissez faire,* or "let it run on its own," assumes that an economy will regulate itself, without interference by government and, of more concern to Smith, without the monopolies and other economic privileges common in his day. Smith's schema for economic growth was not merely a rigid application of natural law to economics. His ideas grew out of an optimistic view of human nature and rationality that was heavily indebted to Locke. Humans, Smith believed, have drives and passions that they can direct and govern by means of reason and inherent mutual sympathy. Thus, Smith suggested, in seeking their own achievement and well-being, people are often "led by an invisible hand" simultaneously to benefit society as a whole.

Throughout the century, philosophers of various stripes disagreed about the nature and the limits of human reason. Smith's countryman and friend David Hume (1711–1776) was perhaps the most radical in his critique of the human capacity for knowing. He was the archskeptic, taking Locke's view of the limitations on pure reason to the point of doubting the efficacy of any sensory data. His major exposition of these views, *Essay Concerning Human Understanding* (1748), led to important innovations later in the century in the work of the German philosopher Immanuel Kant. At the time, though, Hume's arguments were almost contrary to the prevailing spirit that embraced empirical knowledge. Hume himself separated this work from his other efforts in moral,

political, and economic philosophy, which were more in tune with contemporary views.

Mainstream confidence in empirical knowledge and in the intelligibility of the world is evident in the production of the *Encyclopédie* (*Encyclopedia*). This seventeen-volume compendium of knowledge, criticism, and philosophy was assembled by leading philosophes in France and published there between 1751 and 1765. The volumes were designed to contain state-of-the-art knowledge about arts, sciences, technology, and philosophy. The guiding philosophy of the project, set forth by its chief editor, Denis Diderot° (1713–1784), was a belief in the advancement of human happiness through the advancement of knowledge. The *Encyclopédie* was a history of the march of knowledge as well as a compendium of known achievements. It was revolutionary in that it not only intrigued and inspired intellectuals but assisted thousands of government officials and professionals.

The encyclopedia project illustrates the political context of Enlightenment thought as well as its philosophical premises. The Catholic Church placed the work on the *Index of Prohibited Books,* and the French government might have barred its publication but for the fact that the official who would have made the decision was himself drawn to Enlightenment thinking. Many other officials, however, worked to suppress it. By the late 1750s, losses in wars overseas had made French officials highly sensitive to political challenges of any kind. Thus, like Voltaire, the major contributors to the *Encyclopédie* were admired by certain segments of the elite and persecuted by others in their official functions.

The *Encyclopédie* reflects the complexities and limitations of Enlightenment thought on another score—the position of women. One might expect that the Enlightenment penchant for challenging received knowledge and traditional hierarchies would lead to revised views of women's abilities and rights. Indeed, some contributors blamed women's inequality with men not on inherent gender differences but rather on the customs and laws that had kept women from education and the development of their abilities. However, other contributors blamed women, and not society, for their plight, or they argued that women had talents that fit them only for the domestic sphere.

Both positions were represented in Enlightenment thought as a whole. The assumption of the natural equality of all people provided a powerful ground for arguing the equality of women with men. Some thinkers, such as Mary Astell (1666–1731), challenged Locke's sep-

---

**Diderot** (DEED-uh-row)

## ❧ READING SOURCES

### An Enlightenment Thinker Argues for the Equality of Women

*In these passages from* A Vindication of the Rights of Woman, *Mary Woll-stonecraft argues that just as living as aristocratic courtiers corrupts men, so too does dependence on men corrupt women. Wollstonecraft argued, in a move very radical for her day, that even to be good wives and mothers women must be economically independent. She was extending to women the connection between independence and virtue that Locke and Rousseau, among others, applied to men.*

It is vain to expect virtue from women till they are in some degree independent from men; nay, it is vain to expect that strength of natural affection which would make them good wives and mothers. Whilst they are absolutely dependent on their husbands, they will be cunning, mean and selfish. . . . Yet whilst wealth enervates men, and women live, as it were, by their personal charms, how can we expect them to discharge those ennobling duties which equally require exertion and self-denial? . . . the society is not properly organized which does not compel men and women to discharge their respective duties, by making it the only way to acquire that countenance [respect] from their fellow creatures which every human being wishes some way to attain. . . .

But to render [woman] really virtuous and useful, she must not . . . want, individually, the protection of civil laws; she must not be dependent on her husband's bounty for her subsistence during his life or support after his death—for how can a being be generous who has nothing of its own? Or virtuous, who is not free? . . .

Business of various kinds they might likewise pursue, if they were educated in a more orderly manner. . . . Women would not then marry for a support, as men accept of places under government, and neglect the implied duties; nor would an attempt to earn their own subsistence . . . sink them almost to the level of those poor abandoned creatures who live by prostitution.

*Source:* Moira Ferguson, ed., *First Feminists: British Women Writers, 1578–1799* (Bloomington: Indiana University Press, 1985), pp. 423–429.

 **For additional information on this topic, go to http://college.hmco.com.**

aration of family life from the public world of free, contractual relationships. "If absolute authority be not necessary in a state," she reasoned, "how comes it to be so in a family?" Most such thinkers advocated increased education for women, if only to make them more fit to raise enlightened children. By 1800 the most radical thinkers were advocating full citizenship rights for women and equal rights to property, along with enhanced education.

The best-known proponent of those views was an Englishwoman, Mary Wollstonecraft (1759–1797), who authored *A Vindication of the Rights of Woman* (1792). She assumed that most elite women would devote themselves to domestic duties, but she argued that without the responsibilities of citizenship, the leavening of education, and economic independence, women could be nei-

ther fully formed individuals nor worthy of their duties. Working women, she concluded, needed these rights simply to survive. (See the box "Reading Sources: An Enlightenment Thinker Argues for the Equality of Women.")

A more limited view of women's capacities was one element in the influential work of Jean-Jacques Rousseau° (1712–1778). Like Locke, Rousseau could conceive of the free individual only as male, and he grounded his scorn of the old order and his novel political ideas in an arbitrary division of gender roles. Rousseau's view of women was linked to a critique of the artificiality of elite, cosmopolitan society in which Enlightenment thought was then flourishing, and in which aristocratic women

**Rousseau** (roo-SO)

## ❧ READING SOURCES

### Rousseau Discusses the Benefits of Submitting to the General Will

*In this excerpt from his* Social Contract, *Rousseau describes the relationship of individuals to the general will. Notice the wider-ranging benefits Rousseau believes men will enjoy in society as he envisions it; Rousseau is clearly interested in intellectual, moral, and emotional well-being.*

I assume that men reach a point where the obstacles to their preservation in a state of nature prove greater than the strength that each man has to preserve himself in that state. Beyond this point, the primitive condition cannot endure, for then the human race will perish if it does not change its mode of existence. . . .

"How to find a form of association which will defend the person and goods of each member with the collective force of all, and under which each individual, while uniting himself with the others, obeys no one but himself, and remains as free as before." This is the fundamental problem to which the social contract holds the solution. . . .

The passing from the state of nature to the civil society produces a remarkable change in man; it puts justice as a rule of conduct in the place of instinct, and gives his actions the moral quality they previously lacked. . . . And although in civil society man surrenders some of the advantages that belong to the state of nature, he gains in return far greater ones; his faculties are so exercised and developed, his mind is so enlarged, his sentiments so ennobled, and his whole spirit so elevated that . . . he should constantly bless the happy hour that lifted him for ever from the state of nature and from a stupid, limited animal made a creature of intelligence and a man. . . .

For every individual as a man may have a private will contrary to, or different from, the general will that he has as a citizen. His private interest may speak with a very different voice from that of the public interest; his absolute and naturally independent existence may make him regard what he owes to the common cause as a gratuitous contribution, the loss of which would be less painful for others than the payment is onerous for him; and fancying that the artificial person which constitutes the state is a mere fictitious entity (since it is not a man), he might seek to enjoy the rights of a citizen without doing the duties of a subject. The growth of this kind of injustice would bring about the ruin of the body politic.

Hence, in order that the social pact shall not be an empty formula, it is tacitly implied in that commitment—which alone can give force to all others—that whoever refuses to obey the general will shall be constrained to do so by the whole body, which means nothing other than that he shall be forced to be free; for this is the necessary condition which, by giving each citizen to the nation, secures him against all personal dependence, it is the condition which shapes both the design and the working of the political machine, and which alone bestows justice on civil contracts—without it, such contracts would be absurd, tyrannical and liable to the grossest abuse.

*Source:* Jean-Jacques Rousseau, *The Social Contract,* trans. Maurice Cranston (London: Penguin Books, 1968), pp. 59–60, 63–65.

---

were fully involved. Rousseau believed in the educability of men but was as concerned with issues of character and emotional life as with cognitive knowledge. Society—particularly the artificial courtly society—was corrupting, he believed. The true citizen had to cultivate virtue and sensibility, not manners, taste, or refinement.

Rousseau designated women as guarantors of the "natural" virtues of children and as nurturers of the emotional life and character of men—but not as fully formed beings in their own right.

Rousseau's emphasis on the education and virtue of citizens was the underpinning of his larger political vision, set forth in *Du Contrat social* (*The Social Contract*, 1762). He imagined an egalitarian republic—possible particularly in small states such as his native Geneva—in which men would consent to be governed because the government would determine and act in accordance with the "general will" of the citizens. The "general will" was not majority opinion but rather what each citizen *would* want if he were fully informed and were acting in accordance with his highest nature. The "general will" became apparent whenever the citizens met as a body and made collective decisions, and it could be imposed on all inhabitants. (See the box "Reading Sources: Rousseau Discusses the Benefits of Submitting to the General Will.") This was a breathtaking vision of direct democracy—but one with ominous possibilities, for Rousseau rejected the institutional checks on state authority proposed by Locke and Montesquieu.

Rousseau's emphasis on private emotional life anticipated the romanticism of the early nineteenth century. It also reflected Rousseau's own experience as the son of a humble family, always sensing himself an outcast in the brilliant world of Parisian salons. He had a love-hate relationship with this life, remaining attached to several aristocratic women patrons even as he decried their influence. His own personal life did not match his prescriptions for others. He completely neglected to give his four children the nurture and education that he argued were vital; indeed, he abandoned them all to a foundling home. He was nevertheless influential as a critic of an elite society still dominated by status, patronage, and privilege. Rousseau's work reflects to an extreme degree the tensions in Enlightenment thought generally: it was part of elite culture as well as its principal critic.

## ■ The Growth of Public Opinion

It is impossible to appreciate the significance of the Enlightenment without understanding the degree to which it was a part of public life. Most of the philosophes were of modest origin. They influenced the privileged elite of their day because of the social and political environment in which their ideas were elaborated. Indeed, the clearest distinguishing feature of the Enlightenment may be the creation of an informed body of public opinion that stood apart from court society.

Increased literacy and access to books and other printed materials are an important part of the story. Perhaps more important, the kinds of reading that people favored began to change. We know from inventories made of people's belongings at the time of their deaths (required for inheritance laws) that books in the homes

of ordinary people were no longer just traditional works such as devotional literature. Ordinary people now read secular and contemporary philosophical works. As the availability of such works increased, reading itself evolved from a reverential encounter with old ideas to a critical encounter with new ideas. Solitary reading for reflection and pleasure became more widespread.

Habits of reading and responding to written material changed not only because of these increased opportunities to read but also because of changes in the social environment. In the eighteenth century, forerunners of the modern lending libraries made their debut. In Paris, for a fee, one could join a *salle de lecture* (literally, a "reading room") where the latest works were available to any member. Booksellers, whose numbers increased dramatically, found ways to meet readers' demands for inexpensive access to reading matter. One might pay for the right to read a book in the bookshop itself. In short, new venues encouraged people to see themselves not just as readers but as members of a reading public.

Among the most famous and most important of these venues were the Parisian salons, regular gatherings in private homes, where Voltaire and others read their works in progress aloud and discussed them. Several Parisian women—mostly wealthy, but of modest social status—invited courtiers, bureaucrats, and intellectuals to meet in their homes at regular times each week. The *salonnières*° (salon leaders) themselves read widely in order to facilitate the exchange of ideas among their guests. This mediating function was crucial to the success of the salons. Manners and polite conversation had been a defining feature of aristocratic life since the seventeenth century, but they had largely been means of displaying status and safeguarding honor. The leadership of the salonnières and the protected environment they provided away from court life enabled a further evolution of "polite society" to occur: anyone with appropriate manners could participate in conversation as an equal. The assumption of equality, in turn, enabled conversation to turn away from maintaining the status quo to questioning it.

The influence of salons was extended by the wide correspondence networks the salonnières maintained. Perhaps the most famous salonnière in her day, Marie-Thérèse Geoffrin° (1699–1777) corresponded with Catherine the Great, the reform-minded empress of Russia, as well as with philosophes outside Paris and with interested would-be members of her circle. The ambassador of Naples regularly attended her salon while in Paris and exchanged weekly letters with her when home in Italy. He

**salonnières** (sal-on-YAIR)    **Geoffrin** (zhoh-FRAN)

**The Growth of the Book Trade**  Book ownership dramatically increased in the eighteenth century, and a wide range of secular works—from racy novelettes to philosophical tracts—was available in print. In this rendering of a bookshop, shipments of books have arrived from around Europe. Notice the artist's optimism in the great variety of persons, from the peasant with a scythe to a white-robed cleric, who are drawn to the shop by "Minerva" (the Roman goddess of wisdom).   *(Musée des Beaux-Arts de Dijon)*

reflected on the importance of salon leaders such as Geoffrin when he wrote from Naples lamenting, "[our gatherings here] are getting farther away from the character and tone of those of France, despite all [our] efforts. . . . There is no way to make Naples resemble Paris unless we find a woman to guide us, organize us, *Geoffrinise* us."[1]

Various clubs, local academies, and learned and secret societies, such as Masonic lodges, copied some features of the salons of Paris. Hardly any municipality was without a private society that functioned both as a forum for political and philosophical discussion and as an elite social club. Here mingled doctors, lawyers, local officials—some of whom enjoyed the fruits of the political system in offices and patronage. In Scotland universities were flourishing centers of Enlightenment thought, but political clubs in Glasgow and Edinburgh enriched debate and the development of ideas.

Ideas circulated beyond the membership of the multitude of clubs by means of print. Newsletters reporting the goings-on at salons in Paris were produced by some participants. Regularly published periodicals in Great Britain, France, and Italy also served as important means for the dissemination of enlightened opinion in the form of reviews, essays, and published correspondence. Some of these journals had been in existence since the second half of the seventeenth century, when they had begun as a means to circulate the new scientific work. Now, subscribers included Americans anxious to keep up with intellectual life in Europe. Europeans who could not afford the annual subscriptions could peruse the journals in the newly opened reading rooms and libraries. In addition to newsletters and journals, newspapers, which were regularly published even in small cities throughout western and central Europe, circulated ideas. (See the feature "Information Technology: Newspapers.")

In all these arenas Enlightenment ideas encouraged, and lended legitimacy to, a type of far-reaching political debate that had never before existed, except possibly in England during the seventeenth century. The greatest impact of the Enlightenment, particularly in France, was not

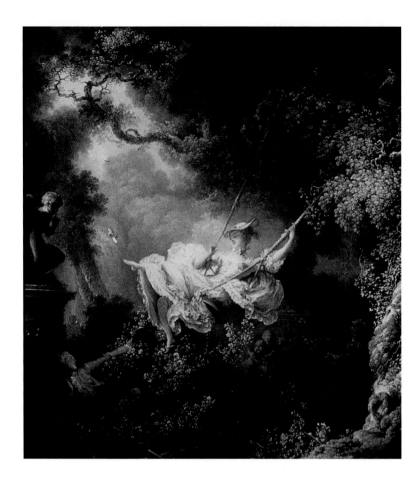

**The Cult of Sensibility in Art**   This painting, *The Swing,* by the Frenchman Fragonard, depicts a moment of playful and sensuous intimacy. This style of painting was an elaboration of baroque style known as *rococo.* It began to be considered too excessive and lighthearted and was replaced by the more serious neoclassical style as the century wore on.   *(Wallace Collection, London/Art Resource, NY)*

the creation of any specific program for political or social change. Rather its supreme legacy was an informed body of public opinion that could generate change.

### ■ Art in the Age of Reason

The Enlightenment reverberated throughout all aspects of cultural life. Just as the market for books and the reading public expanded, so did the audience for works of art in the growing leisured urban circles of Paris and other great cities. The modern cultured public—a public of concert goers and art gallery enthusiasts—began to make its first appearance and constituted another arena in which public opinion was shaped. The brilliant and sophisticated courts around Europe continued to sponsor composers, musicians, and painters by providing both patronage and audiences. Yet some performances of concerts and operas began to take place in theaters and halls outside the courts in venues more accessible to the public.

Beginning in 1737 one section of the Louvre° palace in Paris was devoted annually to public exhibitions of painting and sculpture (though by royally sponsored and

**Louvre** (LOO-vruh)

approved artists). In both France and Britain, public discussion of art began to take place in published reviews and criticisms: the role of art critic was born. Works of art were also sold by public means, such as auctions. As works became more available, demand grew and production increased.

In subject matter and style these various art forms exhibited greater variety than works in preceding centuries had shown. We can nevertheless discern certain patterns and tendencies in both the content and the form of eighteenth-century European art. Late baroque painters contributed to an exploration of private life and emotion sometimes called the "cult of sensibility." Frequently, they depicted private scenes of upper-class life, especially moments of intimate conversation or flirtation.

The cult of sensibility was fostered by literature as well. The private life of emotion was nurtured by increased literacy, greater access to books, and the need to retreat from the elaborate artifice of court life. The novel became an increasingly important genre as a means of exploring social problems and human relationships. In English literature the novels of Samuel Richardson (1689–1761)—*Pamela* (1740) and *Clarissa* (1747–1748)— explored personal psychology and passion. Other novelists,

# Newspapers

The invention of printing in the fifteenth century greatly expanded the kinds of information available to Europeans. In addition to books, thousands of pamphlets and single-page "reports" of startling news appeared, such as the 1513 "Trew Encountre" describing a battle between the English and Scots, and detailing the heroic deeds of the combatants. Along with these other short, occasional publications, the newspaper was born in the seventeenth century. By the eighteenth century newspapers had become firmly established as a means of spreading news of European and world affairs, as well as of local concerns, within European society. Newspapers represented an application of printing technology that, under new conditions and for new purposes, constituted a real innovation in communication—and one with long-term consequences.

News had commercial as well as entertainment value. Even before printing technology had taken hold, the agents of great merchant families dispatched detailed news of products and harvests, as well as of timely political issues. In the sixteenth century, the Venetian government charged citizens a small fee to hear official news of battles against its great rival, the Turks. (A common name for newspaper—gazette—comes from *gazetta,* the coin Venetians used to pay for their news.) One of the first true newspapers was the Dutch paper *Nieuwe Tidjingen.* It began publication early in the seventeenth century about the same time the Dutch East India Company was formed; the same ships that brought goods back from abroad brought news of the world, too.

Dutch publishers had an advantage over many other publishers around Europe since the Netherlands' highly decentralized political system made its censorship laws very difficult to enforce. Throughout Europe in the seventeenth century governments began recognizing the revolutionary potential of the free press and began requiring licenses of newspapers—to control who was able to publish news. Another tactic, in France and elsewhere on the Continent from the 1630s onward, was for governments to sponsor official newspapers. These state publications met the increasing demand for news but always supported the governments' views of the events of the day.

By the eighteenth century new conditions allowed newspapers to flourish as never before. First, demand for news increased as Europe's commercial and political interests spread around the globe. Merchants in London, Liverpool, or Glasgow, for example, depended on early news of Caribbean harvests and gains and losses in colonial wars. Europe's growing commercial strength also increased distribution networks for newspapers; there were more and better roads, and more carters who could deliver newspapers in cities and convey them to outlying towns. Newspaper publishers made use of the many new sites where the public expected to read; newspapers were delivered to cafés and sold or delivered by booksellers.

Second, many European states had established effective postal systems by the eighteenth century. It was through the mails that readers outside major cities and their environs—and virtually all readers in areas where press censorship was firmly in control—received their newspapers. One of the most successful newspapers in Europe was a French-language paper (one of the many known as "la Gazette") published in Leiden in the Netherlands, which boasted a wide readership in France and among elites throughout Europe. Censorship thus had a dwindling effect on well-educated readers anywhere in Europe.

Finally, press censorship faltered in one of the most important markets for news—England—at the turn of the eighteenth century. After the Glorious Revolution, debates raged about whether Parliament or the Crown had the right to control the press, and in the confusion the press flourished. The emergence of political parties further hampered control of the press because political decisions in Parliament now always involved compromise and many members believed an active press was useful to that process. British control of the press was reduced to a tax (one of the Stamp Acts so hated by American colonists) that drove some papers out of business.

such as Daniel Defoe in *Robinson Crusoe* (1717), used realism for purposes of social commentary.

Rousseau followed Richardson's lead in structuring his own novels, *La Nouvelle Héloïse* (1761) and *Emile* (1762). The cult of sensibility was not mere entertainment; it also carried the political and philosophical message that honest emotion was a "natural" virtue and that

courtly manners, by contrast, were irrational and degrading. The enormous popularity of Rousseau's novels, for example, came from the fact that their intense emotional appeal was simultaneously felt to be uplifting.

A revival of classical subjects and styles after the middle of the century evoked what were thought to be the pure and timeless values of classical heroes. This re-

**Producing a Newspaper**    This illustration of the process of typesetting by hand in a newspaper printshop appears in Diderot's *Encyclopedia*. Notice the finished printed sheets drying above the workers' heads.    *(Division of Rare & Manuscript Collections/Cornell University Library)*

Eighteenth-century newspapers were modest products, by our standards. Many were published only once or twice a week instead of every day, in editions of only a few thousand copies. Each newspaper was generally only four pages long. Illustrations were rare, and headlines had not yet been invented. Hand-operated wooden presses were used to print the papers, just as they had been used to print pamphlets and books since the invention of printing in the fifteenth century.

Yet these newspapers had a dramatic impact on their reading public. Regular production of newspapers (especially of many competing newspapers) meant that news was presented to the public at regular intervals and in manageable amounts. Even strange and threatening news from around the world became increasingly easy for readers to absorb and interpret. The more sophisticated reader of the eighteenth century would respond to news more skeptically than had readers of the harrowing "Trew Encountre."

Newspaper readers also felt themselves part of the public life about which they were reading. This was true partly because newspapers, available in public reading rooms and in cafés, were one kind of reading that occupied an increasingly self-aware and literate audience. Newspapers were also uniquely responsive to their readers, however. They began to carry advertisements, which both produced revenue for papers and widened the readers' exposure to their own communities. Even more important was the inauguration of letters to the editor. Newspapers themselves thus became venues for the often rapid exchange of news and opinions. They were a vital tool of Europe's "enlightened" citizenries.

vival revealed the influence of Enlightenment thought because the artists assumed the educability of their audience by means of example. Classical revival architecture illustrated a belief in order, symmetry, and proportion. Americans are familiar with its evocations because it has been the architecture of their republic, but even churches were built in this style in eighteenth-century Europe. The classical movement in music reflected both the cult of sensibility and the classicizing styles in the visual arts. Embodied in the works of Austrians Franz Josef Haydn (1732–1809) and Wolfgang Amadeus Mozart (1756–1791), this movement saw the clarification of musical structures, such as the modern sonata and symphony, and enabled melody to take center stage.

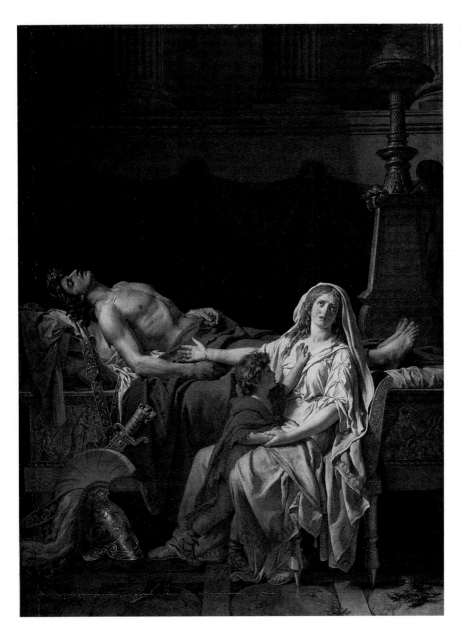

**The Moralizing Message of Neoclassical Art** The French painter Jacques-Louis David portrays the mourning of Trojan hero Hector by his wife, Andromache. David was well known for depicting his subjects with simple gestures—such as the extended arm of Andromache here—that were intended to portray honest and sincere emotion. *(Private Collection/The Stapleton Collection/Bridgeman Art Library)*

Another trend in art and literature was a fascination with nature and with the seemingly "natural" in human culture—less "developed" or more historically distant societies. One of the most popular printed works in the middle of the century was the alleged translation of the poems of Ossian°, a third-century Scots Highland poet. Early English, German, Norse, and other folktales were also "discovered" (in some cases invented) and published, some in several editions during the century. Folk life, other cultures, and untamed nature itself thus be-

gan to be celebrated at the very time they were being more definitively conquered. (See the feature "Weighing the Evidence: Gardens" on pages 638–639.) Ossian, for example, was celebrated just as the Scottish Highlands were being punished and pacified by the English after the clans' support for a rival claimant to the English throne. Once purged of any threat, the exotic image of another culture (even the folk culture of one's own society) could be a spur to the imagination. Thus the remote became romantic, offering a sense of distance from which to measure one's own sophistication and superiority.

---

**Ossian** (AHSH-un)

# EUROPEAN STATES IN THE AGE OF ENLIGHTENMENT

**M**INDFUL of the lessons to be learned from the civil war in England and the achievements of Louis XIV, European rulers in the eighteenth century continued their efforts to govern with greater effectiveness. Some, like the rulers of Prussia and Russia, were encouraged in their efforts by Enlightenment ideas that stressed the need for reforms in law, economy, and government. In the main they, like Voltaire, believed that monarchs could be agents for change. In Austria significant reforms, including the abolition of serfdom, were enacted. The changes were uneven, however, and at times owed as much to traditional efforts at better government as to enlightened persuasion.

In all cases, rulers' efforts to govern more effectively meant continual readjustments in relationships with traditional elites. Whether elites had formal roles in the governing process by means of established institutions such as the English Parliament, royal governments everywhere still depended on their participation. However limited their "enlightened" policies, monarchs were changing their views of themselves and their public images from diligent but self-aggrandizing absolutist to servant of the state. In this way, monarchs actually undermined their dynastic claims to rule by re-founding their regimes on a utilitarian basis. The state was increasingly seen as separate from the ruler, with dramatic consequences for the future.

## ■ France During the Enlightenment

It is one of the seeming paradoxes of the era of the Enlightenment that critical thought about society and politics flourished in France, an autocratic state. Yet France was blessed with a well-educated elite, a tradition of scientific inquiry, and a legacy of cultured court life that, since the early days of Louis XIV, had become the model for all Europe (see pages 543–545). French was the international intellectual language, and France was the most fertile center of cultural life. Both Adam Smith and David Hume, for example, spent portions of their careers in Paris and were welcomed into Parisian salons. In fact, the French capital was an environment that encouraged debate and dissent precisely because of the juxtaposition of the new intellectual climate with the difficulties the French state was facing and the institutional rigidities of its political system. In France, access to power was wholly through patronage and privilege, a system that excluded many talented and productive members of the elite.

The French state continued to embody fundamental contradictions. As under Louis XIV, the Crown sponsored scientific research, subsidized commerce and exploration, and tried to rationalize the royal administration. Royal administrators tried to chip away at the privileges, accrued since the Middle Ages, that hampered effective government—such as the exemption most nobles enjoyed from taxation. However, the Crown also continued to claim the right to govern autocratically, and the king was supported both ideologically and institutionally by the Catholic Church. A merchant in the bustling port of Bordeaux might be glad of the royal navy's protection of the colonies, and of the Crown's efforts to build better roads for the movement of goods within France. However, with his fellow Masons, he would fume when church officials publicly burned the works of Rousseau and be continually frustrated over his exclusion from any formal role in the political process.

The problems facing the French government were made worse by two circumstances: first, the strength of the privileged elites' defense of the old order, and second, mounting state debt from foreign wars that made fiscal reform increasingly urgent. Louis XIV was followed on the throne by his 5-year-old great-grandson, Louis XV (r. 1715–1774). During the regency early in his reign, the supreme law courts, the parlements, reclaimed the right of remonstrance—that is, the right to object to royal edicts and thus to exercise some control over the enactment of law. Throughout Louis XV's reign, his administration often locked horns with the parlements, particularly as royal ministers tried various expedients to cope with financial crises.

The power of the parlements came not only from their routine role in government but also from the fact that parlementaires were all legally noble and owned their offices just as a great nobleman owned his country estate. In addition, the parlements were the only institutions that could legitimately check royal power. As such, the parlements were often supported in their opposition to royal policies by the weight of public opinion. On the one hand, enlightened opinion believed in the rationality of doing away with privileges such as the ownership of offices. On the other hand, the role of consultative bodies and the separation of powers touted by Montesquieu, himself a parlementaire, were much prized. And even our Bordeaux merchant, who had little in common with privileged officeholders, might nevertheless see the parlementaires' resistance as his best protection from royal tyranny. The parlementaires, however, usually used their power for protecting the status quo.

Further hampering reform efforts was the character of the king himself. Louis XV displayed none of the kingly qualities of his great-grandfather. He was neither pleasant nor affable, and he was lazy. By the end of his reign, he was roundly despised. He did not give the "rationality" of royal government a good name. By the late 1760s, the weight of government debt from foreign wars finally forced the king into action. He threw his support behind the reforming schemes of his chancellor, Nicolas de Maupeou°, who dissolved the parlements early in 1771 and created new law courts whose judges would not enjoy independent power.

The Crown lost control of reform when Louis died soon after, in 1774. His 20-year-old grandson, Louis XVI, well-meaning but insecure, allowed the complete restoration of the parlements. Further reform efforts, sponsored by the king and several talented ministers, came to naught because of parlementary opposition. Not surprisingly, from about the middle of the century, there had been calls to revive the moribund Estates General, the representative assembly last convened in 1614, as well as for the establishment of new councils—local, decentralized representative assemblies. By the time an Estates General was finally called in the wake of further financial problems in 1788, the enlightened elites' habit of carrying on political analysis and criticism outside the actual corridors of power, and their accumulated mistrust of the Crown, had given rise to a volatile situation.

## ■ Monarchy and Constitutional Government in Great Britain

After the deaths of William (d. 1702) and Mary (d. 1694), the British crown passed to Mary's sister, Anne (r. 1702–1714), and then to a collateral line descended from Elizabeth Stuart (d. 1662), sister of the beheaded Charles I. Elizabeth had married Frederick, elector of the Palatinate (and had reigned with him briefly in Bohemia at the outset of the Thirty Years' War; see page 525), and her descendants were Germans, now electors of Hanover. The new British sovereign in 1714, George I (r. 1714–1727), was both a foreigner and a man of mediocre abilities. Moreover, his claim to the throne was immediately contested by Catholic descendants of James II, who attempted to depose him in 1715 and later his son, George II (r. 1727–1760), in 1745.

The 1745 attempt to depose the Hanoverian kings was more nearly successful. The son of the Stuart claimant to the throne, Charles (known in legend as Bonnie Prince Charlie), landed on the west coast of Scotland, with French assistance, and marched south into England. Most of the British army, and George II himself, was on the Continent, fighting in the War of the Austrian Succession (see page 626). Scotland had been formally united with England in 1707 (hence the term *Great Britain* after that time), and Charles found some support among Scots dissatisfied with the economic and political results of that union.

But the vast majority of Britons did not want the civil war that Charles's challenge inevitably meant, especially on behalf of a Catholic pretender who relied on support from Britain's great rival, France. Charles's army, made up mostly of poor Highland clansmen, was destroyed at the Battle of Culloden° in April 1746 by regular army units returned from abroad. Charles fled back to France, and the British government used the failed uprising as justification for the brutal and forceful integration of the still remote Highlands into the British state.

Traditional practices, from wearing tartans to playing bagpipes, were forbidden. Control of land was redistributed to break the social and economic bonds of clan society. Thousands of Highlanders died at the battle itself, in prisons or deportation ships, or by deliberate extermination at the hands of British troops after the battle.

Despite this serious challenge to the new dynasty and the harsh response it occasioned, the British state, overall, enjoyed a period of relative stability as well as innovation in the eighteenth century. The events of the seventeenth century had reaffirmed both the need for a strong monarchy and the role of Parliament in defending elite interests. The power of Parliament had recently been reinforced by the Act of Settlement, by which the Protestant heir to Queen Anne had been chosen in 1701. By excluding the Catholic Stuarts from the throne and establishing the line of succession, this document reasserted that Parliament determined the legitimacy of the monarchy. In addition, the act claimed greater parliamentary authority over foreign and domestic policy in the wake of the bellicose William's rule (see page 563).

Noteworthy in the eighteenth century were the ways in which cooperation evolved between monarchy and Parliament as Parliament became a more sophisticated and secure institution. Political parties—that is, distinct groups within the elite favoring certain foreign and domestic policies—came into existence. Two groups, the Whigs and the Tories, had begun to form during the

---

**Maupeou** (mo-POO)

**Culloden** (cull-AH-dun)

reign of Charles II (d. 1685). The Whigs (named derisively by their opponents with a Scottish term for horse thieves) had resisted Charles's pro-French policies and his efforts to tolerate Catholicism and had wholly opposed his brother and successor, James II. Initially, the Whigs favored an aggressive foreign policy against continental opponents, particularly France. The Tories (whose name was also a taunt, referring to Irish cattle rustlers) tended to be staunch Anglicans uninterested in Protestant anti-Catholic agitation. They leaned toward a conservative view of their own role, favoring isolationism in foreign affairs and deference toward monarchical authority. Whigs generally represented the interests of the great aristocrats or wealthy merchants or gentry. Tories more often represented the interests of provincial gentry and the traditional concerns of landholding and local administration.

The Whigs were the dominant influence in government through most of the century to 1770. William and Mary as well as Queen Anne favored Whig religious and foreign policy interests. The loyalty of many Tories was called into question by their support for a Stuart, not Hanoverian, succession at Anne's death in 1714. The long Whig dominance of government was also ensured by the talents of Robert Walpole, a Member of Parliament who functioned virtually as a prime minister from 1722 to 1742.

Walpole (1676–1745) was from a minor gentry family and was brought into government in 1714 with other Whig ministers in George I's new regime. An extremely talented politician, he took advantage of the mistakes of other ministers over the years and, in 1722, became both the first lord of the treasury and chancellor of the exchequer. No post or title of "prime minister" yet existed, but the great contribution of Walpole's tenure was to create that office in fact, if not officially. He chose to maintain peace abroad when and where he could and thus presided over a period of recovery and relative prosperity that enhanced the stability of government.

Initially, Walpole was helped in his role as go-between for king and Parliament by George I's own limitations. The king rarely attended meetings of his own council of ministers and, in any case, was hampered by his limited command of English. Gradually, the Privy Council of the king became something resembling a modern cabinet dominated by a prime minister. By the end of the century the notions of "loyal opposition" to the Crown within Parliament and parliamentary responsibility for policy had taken root.

In some respects, the maturation of political life in Parliament resembled the lively political debates in the

**Political Satire in England**    This gruesome image, showing England being disemboweled by members of the government, criticizes the government's acceptance of a treaty with France. Satirical images such as this one were increasingly part of the lively and more open political life in eighteenth-century England.    *(Courtesy of the Trustees of the British Museum)*

salons of Paris. In both cases, political life was being legitimized on a new basis. In England, however, that legitimation was enshrined in a legislative institution, which made it especially effective and resilient.

Parliament was not yet in any sense representative of the British population, however. Because of strict property qualifications, only about 200,000 adult men could vote. In addition, representation was very uneven, heavily favoring traditional landed wealth. Some constituencies with only a few dozen voters sent members to Parliament. Many of these "pocket boroughs" were under the control of (in the pockets of) powerful local families who could intimidate the local electorate, particularly in the absence of secret ballots.

Movements for reform of representation in Parliament began in the late 1760s as professionals, such as doctors and lawyers, with movable (as opposed to landed) property and merchants in booming but underrepresented cities began to demand the vote. As the burden of taxation grew—the result of the recently concluded Seven Years' War (discussed below)—these groups felt increasingly deprived of representation. Indeed, many felt kinship and sympathy with the American colonists who opposed increased taxation by the British government on these same grounds and revolted in 1775.

However, the reform movement faltered over the issue of religion. In 1780 a tentative effort by Parliament to extend some civil rights to British Catholics provoked rioting in London (known as the Gordon Riots, after one of the leaders). The riots lasted for eight days and claimed three hundred lives. Pressure for parliamentary reform had been building as Britain met with reversals in its war against the American rebels, but this specter of a popular movement out of control temporarily ended the drive for reform by disenfranchised elites.

## ■ "Enlightened" Monarchy

Arbitrary monarchical power might seem antithetical to Enlightenment thought. After all, the Enlightenment stressed the reasonableness of human beings and their capacity to discern and act in accord with natural law. Yet monarchy seemed an ideal instrument of reform to Voltaire and to many of his contemporaries. The work of curtailing the influence of the church, reforming legal codes, and eliminating barriers to economic activity might be done more efficiently by a powerful monarch than by other available means. Historians have labeled a number of rulers of this era "enlightened despots" because of the arbitrary nature of their power and the enlightened or reformist uses to which they put it.

"Enlightened despotism" aptly describes certain developments in the Scandinavian kingdoms in the late eighteenth century. In Denmark the Crown had governed without significant challenge from the landholding nobility since the mid-seventeenth century. The nobility, however, like its counterparts in eastern Europe, had guaranteed its supremacy by means of ironclad domination of the peasantry. In 1784 a reform-minded group of nobles, led by the young crown prince Frederick (governing on behalf of his mentally ill father), began to apply Enlightenment remedies to the kingdom's economic problems. The reformers encouraged freer trade and sought, above all, to improve agriculture by elevating the status of the peasantry. With improved legal status and

with land reform, which enabled some peasants to own the land they worked for the first time, agricultural productivity in Denmark rose dramatically. These reforms constitute some of the clearest achievements of any of the "enlightened" rulers.

In Sweden, in 1772, Gustav III (r. 1771–1796) staged a coup with army support that overturned the dominance of the Swedish parliament, the Diet. In contrast to Denmark, Sweden had a relatively unbroken tradition of noble involvement in government, stemming in part from its marginal economy and the consequent interest of the nobility in participation in the Crown's aggressive foreign policy. Since Sweden's eclipse as a major power after the Great Northern War (see page 560), factions of the Diet, not unlike the rudimentary political parties in Great Britain, had fought over the reins of government. After reasserting his control, Gustav III began an ambitious program of reform of the government. Bureaucrats more loyal to parliamentary patrons than to the Crown were replaced; restrictions on trade in grain and other economic controls were liberalized; the legal system was rationalized; the death penalty was strictly limited; and legal torture was abolished.

Despite his abilities, Gustav III suffered the consequences of the contradictory position of advancing reform by autocratic means in a kingdom with a strong tradition of representative government. Gustav eventually tried to deflect the criticisms of the nobility by reviving grandiose—but completely untenable—schemes for the reconquest of Baltic territory. However, in 1796 he was mortally wounded by an assassin hired by disgruntled nobles.

Another claimant to the title "enlightened despot" was Frederick II of Prussia (r. 1740–1786), "the Great." Much of the time, Frederick resided in his imperial electorate of Brandenburg, near its capital, Berlin. His scattered states, which he extended by seizing new lands, are referred to as Prussia rather than as Brandenburg-Prussia because members of his family were now kings of Prussia thanks to their ambitions and the weakness of the Polish state, of which Prussia had once been a dependent duchy. In many ways, the Prussian state *was* its military victories, for Frederick's bold moves and the policies of his father, grandfather, and great-grandfather committed the state's resources to a military presence of dramatic proportions. Prussia was on the European stage at all only because of that driving commitment.

The institutions that constituted the state and linked the various provinces under one administration were dominated by the needs of the military. Frederick II's father, Frederick William (r. 1713–1740), had added an efficient provincial recruiting system to the state's central institutions, which he also further consolidated. But in many other respects, the Prussian state was in its infancy. There was no tradition of political participation—even by elites—and little chance of cultivating any. Nor was there any political or social room for maneuver at the lower part of the social scale. The rulers of Prussia had long ago acceded to the aristocracy's demand for tighter control over peasant labor on their own lands in return for their support of the monarchy. The rulers relied on nobles for local administration and army commands. Thus, the kinds of social, judicial, or political reforms that Frederick could hope to carry out without undermining his own power were starkly limited.

Frederick tried to modernize agricultural methods and simultaneously to improve the condition of peasants, but he met stiff resistance from noble landholders. He did succeed in abolishing serfdom in some regions. He tried to stimulate the economy by sponsoring state industries and trading monopolies, but too few resources and too little initiative from the tightly controlled merchant communities stymied his plans. Simplifying and codifying the inherited jumble of local laws was a goal of every ruler. A law code published in 1794, after Frederick's death, was partly the product of his efforts.

Frederick's views of the role of Enlightenment thought reflect the limitations of his situation. One doesn't have to lead a frontal assault on prejudices consecrated by time, he thought; instead, one must be tolerant of superstition because it will always have a hold on the masses. Perhaps his most distinctive "enlightened" characteristic was the seriousness with which he took his task as ruler. He was energetic and disciplined to a fault. In his book *Anti-Machiavel* (1741) he argued that a ruler has a moral obligation to work for the betterment of the state. He styled himself as the "first servant" or steward of the state. However superficial this claim may appear, Frederick compares favorably with Louis XV of France who, having a far more wealthy and flexible society to work with, did much less.

### ■ Enlightenment and Tradition: The Case of Austria

One of the most effective rulers of the eighteenth century was the Habsburg ruler Maria Theresa of Austria (r. 1740–1780). A devout Catholic, she was guided more by traditional concerns for effective rule and compassion for her subjects than by Enlightenment ideas. After surviving the near dismemberment of Austrian territories in the War of the Austrian Succession (see page 626), she

embarked on an energetic program of reform to remedy the weaknesses in the state that the war had revealed. "Austria," it must be remembered, is a term of convenience; the state was a very medieval-looking hodge-podge that included present-day Austria, the kingdoms of Bohemia and Hungary, the Austrian Netherlands, and lands in northern Italy. In addition, since the sixteenth century, a male member of the Habsburg family had almost always been elected emperor of the Holy Roman Empire.

Maria Theresa streamlined and centralized administration, finances, and defense, particularly in Bohemia and Austria, where she was able to exercise her authority relatively unchecked, compared with her other domains. Above all, she reformed the assessment and collection of taxes to tap the wealth of her subjects more effectively and thus better defend all her domains. She improved her subjects' access to justice and limited the exploitation of serfs by landlords. She made primary schooling universal and compulsory, in order better to train peasants for the army. Although the policy was far from fully implemented at the time of her death (only about half of Austrian children were in school, and far fewer in Hungary and elsewhere), hers was the first European state with so ambitious an education policy. Maria Theresa accomplished all of this without being particularly "enlightened" personally. For example, she had a traditional fear of freedom of the press and cherished orthodoxy in religious matters.

Maria Theresa's policies were implemented by a group of ministers, bureaucrats, and officers who shared her concern for effective government and defense, and who were well-versed in "enlightened" ideas for reform. The diverse character of the Habsburg lands meant that some members of the governing elite came from the Netherlands and from Italy, where sympathy for the Enlightenment was well rooted by comparison with the relatively poorer and more rural society of the Austrian hinterland. Moreover, the language of the Habsburg court was French (Maria Theresa spoke it fluently), thus no amount of local censorship—which, in any case, Maria Theresa relaxed—could prevent the governing class from reading and absorbing Enlightenment philosophy in its original language.

Maria Theresa was followed on the throne by her two sons Joseph II (r. 1780–1790) and Leopold II (r. 1790–1792). Each son counted himself a follower of the Enlightenment and each, as was the family custom, served a period of "apprenticeship" governing Habsburg territories where he could attempt to implement reform. After his mother's death, Joseph II carried out a variety of bold initiatives that she had not attempted, including freedom of the press, significant freedom of religion, and the abolition of serfdom in Habsburg lands. During his ten-year reign, the political climate in Vienna began to resemble that in Paris, London, and other capitals where political life was no longer confined to the royal court.

Like Frederick the Great, Joseph regarded himself as a servant of the state. Like Frederick, his reform program was limited by the economic and social rigidities of the society he ruled: Austria had but a small middle class to insist on reform, and Joseph could not directly assault the privileges of great landholders, on whose wealth the state depended. In addition, Joseph was by temperament an inflexible autocrat, whose methods antagonized many of these powerful subjects. Joseph's

policies provoked simmering opposition, even open revolt, and some of his reforms were repealed even before his death. His more able brother, Leopold, had implemented many reforms while ruling as grand duke in Tuscany (Italy) before assuming the throne in 1790. Much of his brief two-year reign was spent dexterously saving reforms enacted by his mother and brother in the face of mounting opposition.

### ■ Catherine the Great and the Empire of Russia

Another ruler with a claim to the title "enlightened despot" was Catherine, empress of Russia (r. 1762–1796). Catherine the Great, as she came to be called, was the true heir of Peter the Great in her abilities, policies, and

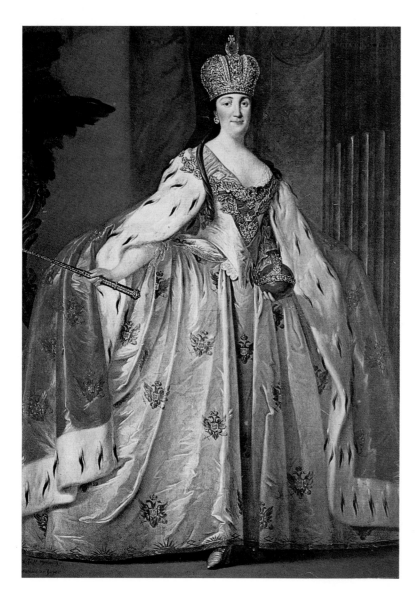

**Catherine the Great**   Catherine was a German princess who had been brought to Russia to marry another German, Peter of Holstein-Gottorp, who was being groomed as heir to the Russian throne. Russia had crowned several monarchs of mixed Russian and German parentage since the time of Peter the Great's deliberate interest in and ties with other European states.
*(The Luton Hoo Foundation)*

**Map 18.1    The Partition of Poland and the Expansion of Russia**    Catherine the Great acquired present-day Lithuania, Belarus, and Ukraine, which had once constituted the duchy of Lithuania, part of the multi-ethnic Polish kingdom.

ambitions. Her determination and political acumen were obvious early in her life at the Russian court, where she had been brought from her native Germany in 1745. Brutally treated by her husband, Tsar Peter III, Catherine engineered a coup in which he was killed, then ruled alone for more than thirty years.

Like any successful ruler of her age, Catherine counted territorial aggrandizement among her chief achievements. With regard to the major European powers, Russia tended to ally with Britain (with which it had important trading connections, including the provision of timber for British shipbuilding) and with Austria

(against their common nemesis, Turkey), and against France, Poland, and Prussia. In 1768 Catherine initiated a war against the Turks from which Russia gained much of the Crimean coast. She also continued Peter's efforts to dominate the weakened Poland. She was aided in this goal by Frederick the Great, who proposed the deliberate partitioning of Poland to satisfy his own territorial ambitions as well as those of his competitors Russia and Austria. In 1772 portions of Poland were gobbled up in the first of three successive "grabs" of territory (see Map 18.1). Warsaw itself eventually landed in Prussian hands, but Catherine gained all of Belarus, Ukraine, and modern Lithuania—which had constituted the duchy of Lithuania.

Nevertheless, Catherine also counted herself a sincere follower of the Enlightenment. While young, she had received an education that bore the strong stamp of the Enlightenment. Like Frederick, she attempted to take an active role in the European intellectual community, corresponding with Voltaire over the course of many years and acting as patron to encyclopedist Diderot. One of Catherine's boldest political moves was the secularization of church lands. Although Peter the Great had extended government control of the Russian Orthodox Church, he had not touched church lands. Catherine also licensed private publishing houses and permitted a burgeoning periodical press. The number of books published in Russia tripled during her reign. This enriched cultural life was one of the principal causes of the flowering of Russian literature that began in the early nineteenth century.

The stamp of the Enlightenment on Catherine's policies is also clearly visible in her attempts at legal reform. In 1767 she convened a legislative commission and provided it with a guiding document, the *Instruction*, which she had penned. The commission was remarkable because it included representatives of all classes, including peasants, and provided a place for the airing of general grievances. Catherine hoped for a general codification of law as well as reforms such as the abolition of torture and capital punishment—reforms that made the *Instruction* radical enough to be banned from publication in other countries. She did not propose changing the legal status of serfs, however, and class differences made the commission unworkable in the end. Most legal reforms were accomplished piecemeal and favored the interests of landed gentry.

Like the Austrian rulers, Catherine undertook far-reaching administrative reform to create more effective local units of government. Here again, political imperatives were fundamental, and reforms in local government strengthened the hand of the gentry. The legal subjection of peasants in serfdom was also extended as a matter of state policy to help win the allegiance of landholders in newly acquired areas—such as Ukrainian territory gained in the partition of Poland. Gentry in general and court favorites in particular, on whom the stability of her government depended, were rewarded with estates and serfs to work them.

In Russia, as in Prussia and Austria, oppression of the peasantry was perpetuated because the monarch wanted to ensure the allegiance of the elites who lived from their labor. Catherine particularly valued the coop-

eration of elites because the Russian state was in a formative stage in another sense as well. It was trying to incorporate new peoples, such as the Tatars in the Crimea, and to manage its relationships with border peoples such as the Cossacks. Catherine's reign was marked by one of the most massive and best-organized peasant rebellions of the century. Occurring in 1773, the rebellion expressed the grievances of the thousands of peasants who joined its ranks and called for the abolition of serfdom. The revolt took its name, however, from its Cossack leader, Emelian Pugachev° (d. 1775), and reflected the dissatisfaction with the Russian government of this semiautonomous people.

The dramatic dilemmas faced by Catherine illustrate both the promise and the costs of state formation throughout Europe. State consolidation permitted the imposition of internal peace, of coordinated economic policy, of reform of justice, but it came at the price of greater—in some cases much greater—control and coercion of the population. Thus, we can see from the alternative perspective of Russia the importance of the political sphere that was opening up in France and was being consolidated in England. It was in that environment, rather than in Russia, that the Enlightenment philosophy could find most fertile ground.

# THE WIDENING SCOPE OF WARFARE

 N the eighteenth century a new constellation of states emerged to dominate politics in Europe. Alongside the traditional powers of England, France, and Austria were Prussia in central Europe and Russia to the east (see Map 18.1); these five states would dominate European politics until the twentieth century. Certain characteristics common to all these states account for their dominance. None is more crucial than their various abilities to field effective armies. In the eighteenth century most wars were launched to satisfy traditional territorial ambitions. Now, however, the increasing significance of overseas trade and colonization also made international expansion an important source of conflict, particularly between England and France. As warfare widened in scope, governments increasingly focused on recruiting and maintaining large navies and armies, with increasingly devastating effects on ordinary people.

---

**Pugachev** (poo-guh-CHOFF)

## ■ A Century of Warfare: Circumstances and Rationales

The large and small states of Europe continued to make war on one another for both strategic and dynastic reasons. States fought over territory that had obvious economic and strategic value. War over the Baltic coastline, for example, absorbed Sweden and Russia early in the century. Dynastic claims, however, were still major causes of war. Indeed, the fundamental instability caused by hereditary rule accounts for many of the major wars of the eighteenth century. The century opened with the War of the Spanish Succession, and later the succession of the Austrian Habsburgs provoked a continent-wide war. Often, these conflicts were carried out in arbitrary ways that reflected a dynastic, rather than wholly strategic, view of territory. Although rational and defensible "national" borders were important, collecting isolated bits of territory was also still the norm. The wars between European powers thus became extremely complex strategically. France, for example, might choose to strike a blow against Austria by invading an Italian state in order to use the conquered Italian territory as a bargaining chip in eventual negotiations. Wars were preceded and carried out with complex systems of alliances and were followed by the adjustments of many borders and the changing control of small scattered territories. Rulers of lesser states in Germany and Italy, particularly, remained important as allies and as potential rivals of the great powers. The rise of Prussia, after all, had demonstrated the benefits of zealous ambition.

The state of military technology, tactics, and organization shaped the outcomes of conflicts as well as the character of the leading states themselves. In the eighteenth century weapons and tactics became increasingly refined. More reliable muskets were introduced. A bayonet that could slip over a musket barrel without blocking the muzzle was invented. Coordinated use of bayonets required even more assured drill of troops than volley fire alone to ensure disciplined action in the face of enemy fire and charges. Artillery and cavalry forces were also subjected to greater standardization of training and discipline in action. Increased discipline of forces meant that commanders could exercise meaningful control over a battle for the first time, but such battles were not necessarily decisive, especially when waged against a comparable force. Indeed, training now was so costly that commanders were, at times, ironically reluctant to hazard their fine troops in battle at all.

Thus, one sure result of the new equipment and tactics was that war became a more expensive proposition than ever before and an ever greater burden on a state's resources and administration. It became increasingly difficult for small states such as Sweden to compete with the forces that others could mount. Small and relatively poor states, such as Prussia, that were able to support large forces did so by means of an extraordinary bending of civil society to the economic and social needs of the army. In Prussia twice as many people were in the armed forces, proportionally, as in other states, and a staggering 80 percent of meager state revenue went to sustain the army.

Most states introduced some form of conscription in the eighteenth century. In all regions, the very poor often volunteered for army service to improve their lives. However, conscription of peasants, throughout Europe but particularly in Prussia and Russia, imposed a significant burden on peasant communities and a sacrifice of productive members to the state. Governments everywhere supplemented volunteers and conscripts with mercenaries and even criminals, as necessary, to fill the ranks without tapping the wealthier elements of the community. Thus, common soldiers were increasingly seen not as members of society but as its rejects. Said Frederick II, "Useful hardworking people should [not be conscripted but rather] be guarded as the apple of one's eye," and a French war minister agreed that armies had to consist of the "scum of people and of all those for whom society has no use."[2] Brutality became an accepted tool for governments to use to manage such groups of men. From the eighteenth century, the army increasingly became an instrument of social control used to contain and make use of individuals who otherwise might disrupt their own communities.

But the costs of maintaining these forces had other outcomes as well. Wars could still be won or lost not on the battlefield but on the supply line. Incentive still existed to bleed civilian populations and to exploit the countryside. Moreover, when supply lines were disrupted and soldiers not equipped or fed, the armies of a major power could be vulnerable to smaller, less disciplined armies of minor states. Finally, even supplies, training, and sophisticated tactics could not guarantee success. Not until 1746, at Culloden, could the British army decisively defeat the fierce charge and hand-to-hand fighting of Highland clansmen by holding its position and using disciplined volley fire. Warfare became increasingly professional but was still an uncertain business with unpredictable results, despite its staggering cost.

### ■ The Power of Austria and Prussia

Major wars during the mid-eighteenth century decided the balance of power in German-speaking Europe for the next hundred years: Prussia emerged as the equal of Austria in the region. The first of these wars, now known as the War of the Austrian Succession, began shortly after the death of the Emperor Charles VI in 1740. Charles died without a male heir, and his daughter, Maria Theresa, succeeded him. Charles VI had worked to shore up his daughter's position as his heir (versus other female relatives who also had claims) by means of an act called the Pragmatic Sanction, which he had painstakingly persuaded allies and potential opponents to accept. When Charles VI died, rival heiresses and their husbands challenged Maria Theresa for control of her various lands. They were supported by France, the Habsburgs' perennial rival.

The Austrian lands were threatened with dismemberment. Indeed, Charles himself had negotiated away the wealthy Bohemian province of Silesia°, promising it to Prussia in return for acceptance of his heir (see Map 18.1), and had not left his armies or his treasury well equipped to fight such a war. When Frederick the Great's troops marched into Silesia in 1740, Maria Theresa's rivals saw their chance and invaded other Habsburg territories.

Maria Theresa proved a more tenacious opponent than anyone had anticipated, and she was helped by Great Britain, which saw the possibility of gains against its colonial rival, France. Fighting eventually spread throughout Habsburg territories, including the Netherlands and in Italy, as well as abroad to British and French colonies. In a preliminary peace signed in 1745, Frederick the Great was confirmed in possession of Silesia, but the throne of the Holy Roman Empire was returned to the Habsburgs—given to Maria Theresa's husband, Francis (Franz) I (r. 1745–1765). A final treaty in 1748 ended all the fighting that had continued since 1745, mostly by France and Britain overseas. The Austrian state had survived dismemberment, but Maria Theresa now embarked on the administrative and military reforms necessary to make her state less vulnerable in the future. Prussia, because of the annexation of Silesia and the psychological imprint of victory, emerged as a power of virtually equal rank to the Habsburgs.

The unprecedented threat that Austria now felt from Prussia led to a revolution in alliances across Europe. In order to isolate Prussia, Maria Theresa agreed to an alliance with France, the Habsburgs' long-standing enemy.

**Silesia** (sigh-LEE-zhee-uh)

Sweden and Russia, with territory to gain at Prussia's expense, joined as well.

Frederick the Great himself initiated what came to be known as the Seven Years' War in 1756, hoping to prevent consolidation of the new alliances. Instead, he found that he had started a war against overwhelming odds. What saved him, in part, was limited English aid. The English, engaged with France in the overseas conflict that Americans call the French and Indian War, wanted France to be heavily committed on the Continent. Prussia managed to emerge intact—though strained economically and demographically. Prussia and Austria were confirmed as the two states of European rank in German-speaking Europe. Their rivalry would dominate German history until the late nineteenth century. Austria's and Prussia's narrow escapes from being reduced to second-class status reveal how fragile even successful states could be; Prussia's emergence as a major power was by no means ensured.

### ■ The Atlantic World: Trade, Colonization, Competition

The importance of international trade and colonial possessions to the states of western Europe grew enormously in the eighteenth century. Between 1715 and 1785, Britain's trade with North America rose from 19 to 34 percent of its total trade, and its trade with Asia and Africa rose from 7 to 19 percent of the total. By the end of the century, more than half of all British trade was carried on outside Europe; for France, the figure was more than a third.

European commercial and colonial energies were concentrated in the Atlantic world in the eighteenth century because there the profits were greatest. The population of British North America grew from about 250,000 in 1700 to about 1.7 million by 1760. The densely settled New England colonies provided a market for manufactured goods from the mother country, though they produced little by way of raw materials or bulk goods on which traders could make a profit. The colonies of Maryland and Virginia produced tobacco, the Carolinas rice and indigo (a dyestuff). England re-exported all three throughout Europe at considerable profit.

The French in New France, only 56,000 in 1740, were vastly outnumbered by the British colonists. Nevertheless, the French had successfully expanded their control of territory in Canada. Settlements sprang up between the outposts of Montreal and Quebec on the St. Lawrence River. Despite resistance, the French extended their fur trapping—the source of most of the profits New France generated—west and north along the Great

## ⊕ GLOBAL ENCOUNTERS

### An African Recalls the Horrors of the Slave Ship

*Olaudah Equiano (ca. 1750–1797) was one of several Africans sold into slavery in the Americas to leave a written record of his experiences. An Ibo from the Niger region, he first experienced slavery as a boy when kidnapped from his village by other Africans. But nothing prepared him for the brutality of the Europeans who bought and shipped him to Barbados, in the British West Indies. He eventually regained his freedom and received an education.*

The first object which saluted my eyes when I arrived on the [African] coast was the sea and a slave-ship . . . waiting for its cargo. . . . When I was carried on board I was immediately handled, and tossed up, to see if I were sound, by some of the crew. . . . I was soon put down under the decks, and there I received such a salutation in the nostrils as I had never experienced in my life; so that with the loathsomeness of the stench . . . I became so sick and low that I was not able to eat. . . . I now wished for the last friend, death, to relieve me; but soon, to my grief, two of the white men offered me eatables; and, on my refusing to eat, one of them held me fast by the hands and laid me across, I think, the windlass, and tied my feet while the other flogged me severely.

One day, when we had a smooth sea and a moderate wind, two of my wearied countrymen, who were chained together, preferring death to such a life of misery, somehow made through the nettings and jumped into the sea; immediately another dejected fellow who [was ill and so not in irons] followed their example. . . . Two of the wretches were drowned, but they got the other and afterwards flogged him unmercifully for thus attempting to prefer death to slavery. In this manner we continued to undergo more hardships than I can now relate. Many a time we were near suffocation for want of fresh air. . . . This, and the stench of the necessary tubs, carried off many.

*Source:* Philip D. Curtin, *Africa Remembered* (Madison University of Wisconsin Press, 1967), pp. 92–96.

---

Lakes, consolidating their hold by building forts at strategic points. They penetrated as far as the modern Canadian province of Manitoba, where they cut into the British trade run out of Hudson Bay to the north. The French also contested the mouth of the St. Lawrence River and the Gulf of St. Lawrence with the British. The British held Nova Scotia and Newfoundland; the French controlled parts of Cape Breton Island; and both states fished the surrounding waters.

The commercial importance of all of these holdings, as well as those in Asia, was dwarfed by the European states' Caribbean possessions, however. The British held Jamaica and Barbados; the French, Guadeloupe and Martinique; the Spanish, Cuba and San Domingo; and the Dutch, a few small islands. Sugar produced by slave labor was the major source of profits, along with other cash crops such as coffee, indigo, and cochineal (another dyestuff). The concentration of shipping to this region in-

dicates the region's importance. By the 1760s the British China trade occupied seven or eight ships. In the 1730s British trade with Jamaica alone drew three hundred ships. The tiny Dutch possession of Guiana on the South American coast required twice as many visits by Dutch ships as the Dutch East India Company sent into Asia.

The economic dependence of the colonies on slave labor meant that the colonies were tied to their home countries not with a two-way commercial exchange but with a three-way, or "triangle," trade (see Map 18.2). Certain European manufactures were shipped to ports in western Africa, where they were traded for slaves. Captive Africans were transported to South America, the Caribbean, or North America, where planters bought and paid for them with profits from their sugar and tobacco plantations. (See the box "Global Encounters: An African Recalls the Horrors of the Slave Ship.") Sugar and tobacco were then shipped back to the mother country

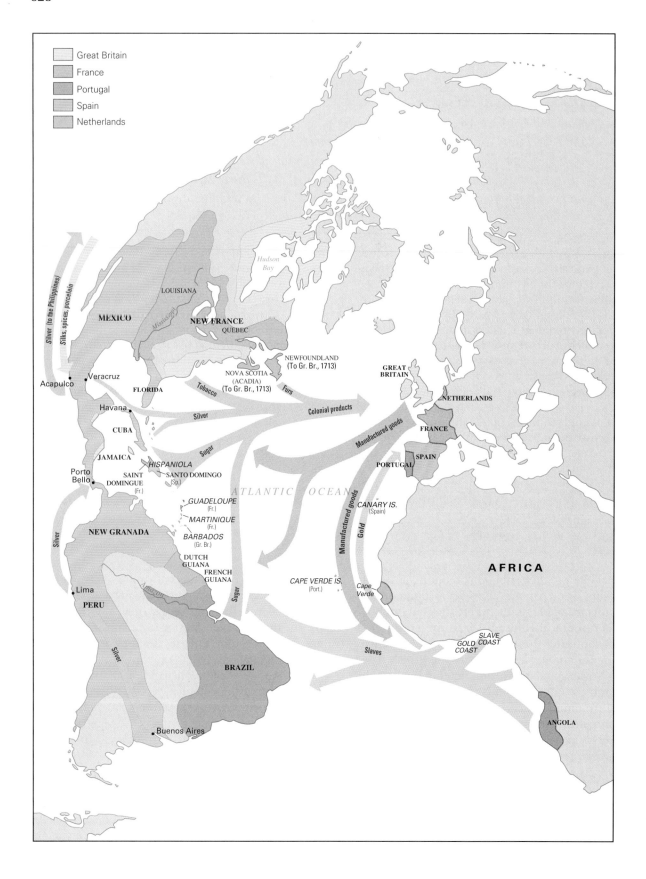

Great Britain
France
Portugal
Spain
Netherlands

Silver (to the Philippines)
Silks, spices, porcelain

*Hudson Bay*

LOUISIANA

MEXICO

NEW FRANCE
QUEBEC

NEWFOUNDLAND
(To Gr. Br., 1713)

NOVA SCOTIA
(ACADIA)
(To Gr. Br., 1713)

Acapulco

Veracruz

FLORIDA

Tobacco

Furs

GREAT
BRITAIN

Havana

Silver

Colonial products

NETHERLANDS

CUBA

Sugar

Manufactured goods

FRANCE

JAMAICA

*HISPANIOLA*

PORTUGAL

SPAIN

Porto
Bello

SAINT
DOMINGUE
(Fr.)

SANTO DOMINGO
(Sp.)

*ATLANTIC OCEAN*

CANARY IS.
(Spain)

*GUADELOUPE*
(Fr.)

*MARTINIQUE*
(Fr.)

Silver

NEW GRANADA

*BARBADOS*
(Gr. Br.)

DUTCH
GUIANA

FRENCH
GUIANA

Manufactured goods

Gold

AFRICA

Lima

*Amazon*

Sugar

CAPE VERDE IS.
(Port.)

Cape
Verde

PERU

Silver

SLAVE
COAST

GOLD
COAST

Slaves

GOLD
COAST

BRAZIL

Buenos Aires

ANGOLA

to be re-exported at great profit throughout Europe. A variety of smaller exchanges also took place. For example, timber from British North America was traded in the Caribbean for sugar or its byproducts, molasses and rum. Individual planters in the colonies were not the only ones whose fortunes and status depended on these networks. Merchants in cities such as Bordeaux in France and Liverpool in England were also heavily invested in the slave trade and the re-export business.

### ■ Great Britain and France: Wars Overseas

The proximity and growth of French and British settlements in North America ensured conflict (see Map 18.3). The Caribbean and the coasts of Central and South America were strategic flashpoints as well. At the beginning of the eighteenth century, several substantial islands remained unclaimed by any power. The British were making incursions along the coastline claimed by Spain and were trying to break into the monopoly of trade between Spain and Spain's vast possessions in the region. Public opinion in both Britain and France became increasingly sensitive to colonial issues. For the first time, tensions abroad would fuel major conflicts between two European states.

During this century England became the dominant naval power in Europe. Its navy protected its far-flung trading networks, its merchant fleet, and the coast of England itself. England's strategic interests on the Continent lay in promoting a variety of powers there, none of which (or no combination of which) posed too great a threat to England or to its widespread trading system. A second, dynastic consideration in continental affairs was the electorate of Hanover, the large principality in western Germany that was the native territory of the Hanoverian kings of England. Early in the century especially, the interests of this German territory were a significant factor in British foreign policy. Unable to field a large army, given their maritime interests, the British sought protection for Hanover in alliances and subsidies for allies' armies on the Continent and paid for these ventures with the profits on trade.

**Map 18.2  The Atlantic Economy, ca. 1750**   The triangle trade linked Europe, Africa, and European colonies in the Americas. The most important component of this trade for Europe was the plantation agriculture of the Caribbean islands, which depended on enslaved Africans for labor.

After the death of Louis XIV in 1715, England's energies centered on colonial rivalries with France, its greatest competitor overseas. Conflict between England and France in colonial regions played out in three major phases. The first two were concurrent with the major land wars in Europe: the War of the Austrian Succession (1740–1748) and the Seven Years' War (1756–1763). The third phase coincided with the rebellion of British colonies in North America—the American Revolution—beginning in the 1770s. France was inevitably more committed to affairs on the Continent than were the British. The French were able to hold their own successfully in both arenas during the 1740s, but by 1763, though pre-eminent on the Continent, they had lost many of their colonial possessions to the English.

In the 1740s France was heavily involved in the War of the Austrian Succession while Britain vied with Spain for certain Caribbean territories. Both France and England also tested each other's strength in scattered colonial fighting, which produced a few well-balanced gains and losses. Their conquests were traded back when peace was made in 1748.

Tension was renewed almost immediately at many of the strategic points in North America. French and British naval forces harassed each other's shipping in the Gulf of St. Lawrence. The French reinforced their encirclement of British colonies with more forts along the Great Lakes and the Ohio River. When British troops (at one point led by the colonial commander George Washington) attempted to strike at these forts, beginning in 1754, open fighting between the French and the English began.

In India, meanwhile, both the French and the British attempted to strengthen their commercial footholds by making military and political alliances with local Indian rulers. The disintegration of the Mogul Empire heightened competition among regional Indian rulers and sparked a new level of ambition on the part of the European powers with interests in Asia. A British attack on a French convoy provoked a declaration of war by France in May 1756, three months before fighting in the Seven Years' War broke out in Europe. For the first time, a major war between European nations had started and would be fought in their empires, signifying a profound change in the relation of these nations to the world.

The French had already committed themselves to an alliance with Austria and were increasingly involved on the Continent after Frederick II initiated war there in August 1756. Slowly, the drain of sustaining war both on the Continent and abroad began to tell, and Britain scored

**Map 18.3  British Gains in North America**  The British colonies on the Atlantic coast were effective staging posts for the armies that ousted the French from North America by 1763. However, taxes imposed on the colonies to pay the costs of the Seven Years' War helped spark revolt—the American Revolution—a decade later.

major victories against French forces after an initial period of balanced successes and failures. The French lost a number of fortresses on the Mississippi and Ohio Rivers and on the Great Lakes and, finally, also lost the interior of Canada with the fall of Quebec and of Montreal in 1759 and 1760, respectively (see Map 18.3).

In the Caribbean, the British seized Guadeloupe, a vital sugar-producing island. Superior resources in India enabled the British to take several French outposts there, including Pondicherry°, the most important. The cost of involvement on so many fronts meant that French troops were short of money and supplies. They were particularly vulnerable to both supply and personnel shortages—especially in North America—because they were

weaker than the British at sea and because New France remained sparsely settled and dependent on the mother country for food.

By the terms of the Peace of Paris in 1763, France regained Guadeloupe; the most profitable of its American colonies—the sugar islands—thus remained in French control. In India, France retained many of its trading stations but lost its political and military clout. British power in India was dramatically enhanced not only by French losses but also by victories over Indian rulers who had allied with the French. In the interior Britain now controlled lands that had never before been under the control of any European power. British political rule in India, as opposed to merely a mercantile presence, began at this time. The British now also held Canada. They emerged from the Seven Years' War as the pre-eminent world power among European states.

---

**Pondicherry** (pon-dih-CHAIR-ee)

**The Death of General Wolfe at Quebec**    General Wolfe commanded British troops that in 1759 defeated the French at Quebec in Canada. Wolfe's death at the battle was memorialized ten years later by American-born artist Benjamin West. This image became widely popular after West sold cheap engraved versions. Notice West's sympathetic treatment of the Native American earnestly focused, like his British allies, on the death of the commander.    *(National Gallery of Canada, Ottawa. Transfer from the Canadian War Memorials)*

# ECONOMIC EXPANSION AND SOCIAL CHANGE

**T**HE eighteenth century was an era of dramatic change, though that change was not always apparent to those who lived through it. The intellectual and cultural ferment of the Enlightenment laid the groundwork for domestic political changes to come, just as British victories in the Seven Years' War shifted the balance of power abroad. More subtle and potentially more profound changes were occurring in the European countryside, however. Population, production, and consumption were beginning to grow beyond the bounds that all preceding generations had lived within and taken for granted.

## ■ More Food and More People

Throughout European history, a delicate balance had existed between available food and numbers of people to feed. Population growth had accompanied increases in the amount of land under cultivation. From time to time, however, population growth surpassed the ability of the land to produce food, and people became malnourished and prey to disease. In 1348 the epidemic outbreak of bubonic plague known as the Black Death struck just such a vulnerable population in decline.

Europeans had few options for increasing the productivity of land. Peasants safeguarded its fertility by alternately cultivating some portions while letting others lie fallow or using them as pasture. Manure provided fertilizer, but during the winter months livestock could not be kept alive in large numbers. Limited food for livestock meant limited fertilizer, which in turn meant limited production of food for both humans and animals.

After devastating decline in the fourteenth century, the European population experienced a prolonged recovery, and in the eighteenth century the balance that had previously been reached began to be exceeded for the first time. Infant mortality remained as high as ever. No less privileged a person than Queen Anne of England outlived every one of the seventeen children she bore, and all but one of them died in infancy. Population growth occurred because of a decline in the death rate for adults and a simultaneous increase in the birthrate in some areas owing to earlier marriages.

Adults began to live longer partly because of a decline in the incidence of plague. However, the primary reason adults were living longer, despite the presence of various epidemic diseases, was that they were better nourished and thus better able to resist disease. More and different kinds of food began to be produced. The increase in the food supply also meant that more new families could be started.

Food production increased because of the introduction of new crops and other changes in agricultural practices. The cumulative effect of these changes was so

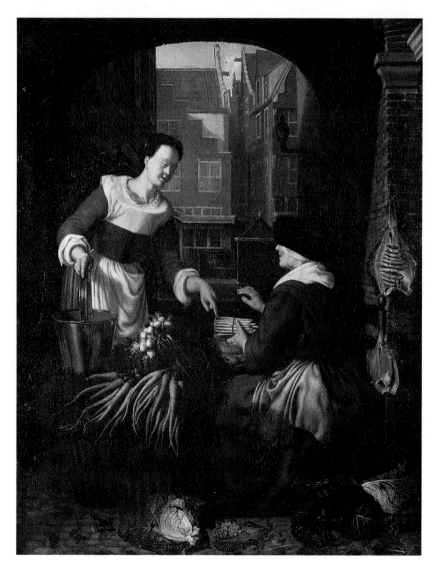

**Gérard Dou: The Vegetable Seller**
The specialization of agriculture meant that a more varied diet was available to increasing numbers of Europeans. *(Musée des Beaux-Arts, Nimes/Giraudon/Art Resource, NY)*

dramatic that historians have called them an "agricultural revolution." The new crops included fodder, such as clover, legumes, and turnips, which did not deplete the soil and could be fed to livestock over the winter. The greater availability of animal manure, in turn, boosted grain production. The potato, introduced from the Americas in the sixteenth century, is nutrient-dense and can feed more people per acre than can grain. In certain areas, farming families produced potatoes to feed themselves while they grew grain to be sold and shipped elsewhere.

More food being produced meant more food available for purchase. The opportunity to buy food freed up land and labor. A family that could purchase food might decide to convert its farm to specialized use, such as raising dairy cattle. In such a case, many families might be supported from a piece of land that had previously supported only one. Over a generation or two, a number of children might share the inheritance of what had previously been a single farm, yet each could make a living from his or her share, and population could grow as it had not done before.

Farmers had known about and experimented with many of the crops used for fodder for centuries. However, the widespread planting of these crops, as well as other changes, was long in coming and happened in scattered areas. A farmer had to have control over land in order to implement change. In the traditional open-field system, peasants had split up all the land in each community so that each family might have a piece of each field. Making effective changes was hard when an entire community had to act together. Most important, changing agriculture required capital for seed and fertilizer and for the greater number of people and animals needed to cultivate the new crops. Only prosperous farmers had spare capital. Few were inclined to take risks with the production of food and to trust the workings of the market. The bad condition of roads alone was reason enough not to rely on distant markets.

Yet where both decent roads and growing urban markets existed, some farmers—even entire villages working together—were willing to produce for urban populations. Capital cities, like London and Amsterdam, and trading centers such as Glasgow and Bordeaux were booming. These growing cities demanded not only grain but also specialized produce such as dairy products and fruits and vegetables. Thus, farmers had an incentive to make changes such as to dairy farming. Urbanization and improved transportation networks also encouraged agriculture because human waste produced by city dwellers—known as "night soil"—could be collected and distributed in the surrounding agricultural regions as fertilizer. By the late eighteenth century, pockets of intensive, diversified agriculture existed in England, northern France, the Rhineland in Germany, the Po Valley in Italy, and Catalonia in Spain.

In other areas, changes in agriculture were often accompanied by a shift in power in the countryside. Wealthy landlords began to invest in change in order to reap the profits of producing for the new markets. Where the traditional authority of the village to regulate agriculture was weak, peasants were vulnerable. In England a combination of weak village structure and the attraction of urban markets created a climate that encouraged landlords to treat land speculatively. To make their holdings more profitable, they raised the rents that farmers paid. They changed cultivation patterns on the land that they controlled directly. They appropriated the village common lands, a process known as "enclosure," and used them for cash crops such as sheep (raised for their wool) or beef cattle. Among other ramifications, the clans of Scotland completely disintegrated as meaningful social units as markets for beef, wool, and other Highland commodities drew chieftains' resources and turned what remained of their traditional clan relationships into exploitative commercial ones.

Thus, although the agricultural revolution increased the food supply to sustain more people in Europe generally, it did not create general prosperity. The growth of population did not mean that most people were better off. Indeed, many rural people were driven off the land or made destitute by the loss of the resources of common lands. Peasants in eastern Europe produced grain for export to the growing urban centers in western Europe, but usually by traditional methods. In both eastern and western Europe, the power and profits of landlords were a major force in structuring the rural economy.

## ■ The Growth of Industry

Agricultural changes fostered change in other areas of economic and social life. As more food was grown with less labor, that labor was freed to take on other productive work. If enough people could be kept employed making useful commodities, then the nonagricultural population could continue to grow. If population grew, more and more consumers would be born, and the demand for more goods would help continue the cycle of population growth, changes in production, and economic expansion. This is precisely what happened in the eighteenth century. A combination of forces increased the numbers of people who worked at producing a few essential materials and products (see Map 18.4).

**Map 18.4    Population and Production in Eighteenth-Century Europe**    The growth of cottage industry helped to support a growing population. With changes in agriculture, more land-poor workers were available in the countryside to accept work as spinners, knitters, and weavers.

Especially significant was the expansion in the putting-out system. Also known as cottage industry, putting out involved the production in the countryside of thread and cloth by spinners and weavers working in their own homes for an entrepreneur who bought raw materials and "put them out" to be finished by individual workers. The putting-out system expanded in the eighteenth century as the agricultural economy was transformed. All agricultural work was seasonal, demanding intensive effort and many hands at certain times but not at others. The labor demands of the new crops meant that an even larger number of people might periodically need nonfarm work in order to make ends meet. Rural poverty, whether as a result of traditional or new agricultural methods, made manufacturing work in the home attractive to more and more people.

Overseas trade also stimulated the expansion of production by spurring the demand in Europe's colonies for cloth and other finished products and increasing the demand at home for manufactured items, such as nails to build the ships that carried the trade. The production of cloth expanded also because heightened demand led to changes in the way cloth was made. Wool was increasingly combined with other fibers to make less expensive fabrics. By the end of the century, wholly cotton fabrics were being made cheaply in Europe from cotton grown in America by slave labor.

**⁊ᱺ READING SOURCES**

---

### A Peasant Protests Forced Labor

*Generally, the condition of agricultural workers was worst in eastern Europe, where political and economic forces kept them bound in serfdom. In* A Journey from St. Petersburg to Moscow *(1790), the reform-minded nobleman Alexander Radishchev (1749–1802) describes an encounter with a Russian serf who, like most serfs, was forced to work the lord's lands at the expense of his own.*

---

A few steps from the road I saw a peasant plowing a field. It was now Sunday, [about midday]. The ploughing peasant, of course, belonged to a landed proprietor, who would not let him pay a commutation tax. The peasant was plowing very carefully. The field . . . was not part of the master's land. He turned the plow with astonishing ease.

"God help you," I said, walking up to the ploughman, who, without stopping, was finishing the furrow he had started. . . . "Have you no time to work during the week, then, and can you not have any rest on Sundays, in the hottest part of the day, at that?"

"In a week, sir, there are six days, and we go six times a week to work on the master's field; in the evening, if the weather is good, we haul to the master's house the hay that is left in the woods. . . . God

grant that it rains this evening. If you have peasants of your own, sir, they are praying for the same thing."

"But how do you manage to get food enough [for your family] if you have only the holidays free?"

"Not only the holidays, the nights are ours too."

"Do you work the same way for your master?"

"No, sir, it would be a sin to work the same way. On his fields there are a hundred hands for one mouth, while I have two for seven mouths: you can figure it out for yourself."

---

*Source:* Alexander Radishchev, *A Journey from St. Petersburg to Moscow,* trans. Leo Wiener, ed. Roderick Page Thaler (Cambridge, Mass.: Harvard University Press, 1958; quoted in Robert and Elborg Forster, eds., *European Society in the Eighteenth Century* (New York: Harper and Row, 1969), pp. 136–139.

---

Steady innovation in textile production allowed woven goods to be aimed at broader markets. In the Middle Ages, weavers produced luxury-quality cloth, and their profits came not from demand, which was relatively low, but from the high price that affluent consumers paid. In the eighteenth century, cloth production became a spur to a transformed industrial economy because cheaper kinds of cloth were made for mass consumption. Producing in great quantities became important, and innovations that promoted productivity were welcomed.

A crucial innovation was increased mechanization. The invention of machines to spin thread in the late eighteenth century brought a marked increase in the rate of production. Machines likewise brought profound changes to the lives of rural workers who had been juggling agricultural and textile work according to season and need. The selected areas of England, France, and the

Low Countries where the new technologies were introduced stood, by the end of the century, on the verge of a massive industrial transformation that would have unprecedented social consequences.

### ■ Control and Resistance

The economic changes of the century produced both resistance and adaptation by ordinary people and, at times, direct action by state authorities. (See the box "Reading Sources: A Peasant Protests Forced Labor.") Sometimes ordinary people coped in ways that revealed their desperation. In many cities numbers of abandoned children rose greatly because urban families, particularly recent immigrants from the countryside, could not support all their offspring. The major cities of Europe put increasing resources into police forces and

**An Idle Apprentice Is Sent to Sea, 1747** In one of a series of moralizing engravings by William Hogarth, the lazy apprentice, Tom, is sent away to a life at sea. The experienced seamen in the boat introduce him to some of its terrors: on the left one dangles a cat-o'-nine-tails—the instrument used for flogging—and on the distant promontory is a gallows, where pirates and mutineers meet their fate. *(From the Collections of Lauinger Library, Georgetown University)*

city lighting schemes. Charitable institutions run by cities, churches, and central governments expanded. By 1789, for example, there were more than two thousand *hôpitaux*°—poorhouses for the destitute and ill—in France. The poor received food and shelter but were forced to work for the city or to live in poorhouses against their will. Men were sometimes taken out of poorhouses and forced to become soldiers.

Resistance and adaptation were particularly visible wherever the needs of common people conflicted with the states' desire for order and revenue. This scenario was evident on the high seas, for example, in the cru-

sade to suppress piracy. Piracy had been a way of life for hundreds of Europeans and colonial settlers since the sixteenth century. From the earliest days of exploration, European rulers had authorized men known as privateers to commit acts of war against specific targets. The Crown took little risk and was spared the cost of arming the ships but shared in the plunder. True piracy—outright robbery on the high seas—was illegal, but in practice the difference between piracy and privateering was negligible. As governments and merchants grew to prefer regular trade over the irregular profits of plunder, and as national navies developed in the late seventeenth century, a concerted effort to eliminate piracy began.

---

**hôpitaux** (op-ee-TOE)

Life on the seas became an increasingly vital part of western European economic life in the eighteenth century; English-speaking seamen alone numbered about thirty thousand around the middle of the century. Sea life began to resemble life on land in the amount of compulsion it entailed. Sailors in port were always vulnerable to forcible enlistment in the navy by impressment gangs, particularly during wartime. A drowsy sailor sleeping off a rowdy night in port could wake up to find himself aboard a navy ship. Press gangs operated throughout England and not just in major ports, for authorities were as interested in controlling "vagrancy" as in staffing the navy. Merchant captains occasionally filled their crews by such means, particularly when sailing unpopular routes.

Like soldiers in the growing eighteenth-century armies, sailors in the merchant marine as well as the navy could be subjected to brutal discipline and appalling conditions. Merchant seamen attempted to improve their lot by trying to regulate their relationship with ships' captains. Contracts for pay on merchant ships became more regularized, and seamen often negotiated their terms very carefully, including, for example, details about how rations were to be allotted. Sailors might even take bold collective action aboard ship. The modern term for a work stoppage, *strike,* comes from the sailing expression "to strike sail," meaning to lower the sails so that they cannot fill with wind. Its use dates from the eighteenth century, from "strikes" of sailors protesting unfair shipboard conditions.

Seafaring men were an unusually large and somewhat self-conscious community of wage workers. Not until industrialization came into full swing a century later would a similar group of workers exist within Europe itself (see Chapter 21). But economic and political protest by ordinary people on the Continent also showed interesting parallel changes. Peasant revolts in the past had ranged from small-scale actions against local tax collectors to massive uprisings that only an army could suppress. The immediate goals of the rebels were usually practical. For example, they aimed not to eliminate taxation altogether but might protest the collection of a particularly burdensome tax. The political rationale behind such actions was not a hope that the system would disappear but rather a hope that it would operate more fairly, as it presumably had in the past. Where there was a revolutionary vision, it was usually a utopian one—a political system with no kings, landlords, taxes, or state of any kind.

Peasant revolts continued to follow those patterns in the eighteenth century. They were also driven by the localized unemployment caused by agricultural reforms or by objections to press gangs. In certain cases, however, peasants, like sailors, began to confront the state in new ways. Peasants often attacked not state power but the remnants of landlords' power, wielded over them in the shape of forced labor and compulsory use of landlords' mills. As weapons, they increasingly marshaled legal devices to maintain control over their land and to thwart landlords' efforts to enclose fields and cultivate cash crops. This change, though subtle, was important because it signaled an effort to bring permanent structural change to the system and was not simply a temporary redress of grievances. In part, the trend toward "enlightened" revolt reflects increased access to information and the circulation of ideas about reform. A major peasant rebellion in 1775 in Austrian lands, for example, followed several years of bad harvests but specifically protested the delay in implementing changes—the subject of earnest debate among elites—in compulsory labor by peasants.

## SUMMARY

T is important not to exaggerate the degree to which circumstances of life changed in the eighteenth century. The economy was expanding and the population growing beyond previous limits, and the system of production was being restructured. But these developments occurred incrementally over many decades and were not recognized for the fundamental changes they were.

Most of the long-familiar material constraints were still in place. Roads, on which much commerce depended, were generally impassable in bad weather. Shipping was relatively dependable and economical— but only relatively. Military life likewise reflected traditional constraints. Despite technological changes and developments of the administrative and economic resources of the state to equip, train, and enforce discipline, the conduct of war was still hampered by problems of transport and supply that would have been familiar to warriors two centuries before.

Similarly, though some rulers were inspired by precepts of the Enlightenment, all were guided by traditional concerns of dynastic aggrandizement and strategic advantage. One new dimension of relations between states was the importance of conflict over colonies abroad, but the full economic and strategic impact of British colonial gains would not be felt until the next century.

*(continued on page 640)*

# Gardens

What is a garden? We first think of intensely culti-vated flower gardens, such as the famous Rose Garden at the White House. We usually don't think of the yards around houses as gardens, yet that is what they are. The landscaping around most ordinary American homes derives from English landscape gardening of the eighteenth century and after—a fact that is reflected in the British custom of calling the "yards" around their homes "gardens." Like most of the art forms that we see habitually, the garden, reproduced in the American backyard, is difficult to analyze or even to think of as an art form. Like the buildings they surround, however, gardens have much to tell us about human habits and values. Let us examine their eighteenth-century ancestors for evidence of contemporaries' attitudes toward nature and their relationship with it.

Look at the two English-style gardens illustrated here. The first is next to the Governor's Mansion in Williamsburg, the capital of the English colony of Virginia. Construction of this garden began at the end of the seventeenth century; the photograph shows the restored gardens that tourists may visit today. The second garden, from the private estate of West Wycombe in England, looks very different—much more like a natural land-scape. The engraving reproduced here dates from the 1770s. The two gardens represent distinct epochs in the development of the garden, hence the differences be-tween them. However, each of these gardens in its own way celebrates human domination of nature.

This symbolic domination of nature is more obvious to us in the Williamsburg garden. The lawns and hedges are trimmed in precise geometrical shapes and are laid out, with the walkways, in straight lines. This "palace gar-den" was a small English variant of the classical garden developed in France—most spectacularly at Versailles Palace—and then imitated throughout Europe during the seventeenth century. At Versailles, the garden is so vast that at many points all of nature visible to the eye is nature disciplined by humans.

We can think of such gardens as pieces of architec-ture, because that is how they were originally conceived: The design originated in the enclosed courtyard gardens of the homes of classical antiquity. The straight lines and squared shapes of these gardens mimic the buildings they are attached to. In fact, these seventeenth- and eigh-teenth-century gardens were usually laid out as an exten-sion of the building itself. Notice the wide staircase that descends from the central axis of the Governor's Mansion into the central walkway of the garden. Other architec-tural details, such as the benches positioned at the ends of various walkways, add to the sense of the garden as an exterior room. Elsewhere, this sense was enhanced by the construction of devices such as grottoes, such as that at Versailles. The garden symbolizes the taming of nature into a pleasing vision of order and regularity.

The later, eighteenth-century garden represents even greater confidence in the human relationship with nature, although it does not appear to do so at first glance. The extensive gardens at first seem to be nature itself plus a few added details, such as the statuary, and a few improvements, such as the grass kept trim by the workers in the foreground. Our familiarity with such landscapes—in our own suburban yards—keeps us from immediately perceiving how contrived such a landscape is. Nature, however, does not intersperse dense stands of trees or clumps of shrubbery with green expanses of lawns. Nor does nature conveniently leave portions of a hillside bare of trees to provide a view of the water from the palatial house, to the left on the hill. Note also that the waterfall cascading over rocks and statuary flows from an artificial lake, neatly bordered by a path.

This kind of garden reflects Enlightenment optimism about humans' ability to understand and work with na-ture. Such gardens were asymmetrical: paths were usu-ally curved, and lakes and ponds were irregularly shaped, as they would be in nature. Trees and shrubs were al-lowed to maintain their natural form. Nevertheless, this landscaping conveys a powerful message of order. Hu-mans cannot bend or distort nature to their own ends, but they can live in harmony with it as they manage it and enjoy its beneficence. People were freed from regarding nature as hostile and needing to be fought. In this garden, one lives with nature but improves on it. The workers cut-ting the grass do not detract from the engraving but rather make the scene more compelling.

This brand of landscape gardening appeared in English colonies across the Atlantic by the end of the eighteenth century. One of the best examples is at Mon-

**The Governor's Mansion and Formal Gardens at Williamsburg, Virginia**
*(© Robert Llewellyn)*

ticello, Thomas Jefferson's Virginia estate, first designed in the 1770s and constructed and improved over the remainder of Jefferson's life (1743–1826). If you tour Monticello, you will notice a curving garden path bordered by flowers in season, with mature trees scattered here and there. Jefferson, we know, planned every inch of this largely random-looking outdoor space, just as he planned the regimented fruit and vegetable garden that borders it. The older, classical style of the Williamsburg garden is partly explained by its earlier date and also because this more aggressively controlling style lasted longer in the American colonies than in Europe, perhaps because "nature" seemed more wild and still more formidable in the New World. You might wish to consider the curious blend of "nature" and order that is evident in the landscapes we create and live with today.

The most visible change would happen first in politics, where goals and expectations nurtured by Enlightenment philosophy clashed with the rigid structure of the French state and triggered the French Revolution. The Enlightenment was not simply an intellectual movement that found fault with society. It also encompassed the public and private settings in which "enlightened" opinion flourished. The revolutionary potential of Enlightenment thought came from belief in its rationality and from the fact that it was both critical of its society and fashionable to practice.

## ■ Notes

1. Quoted in Dena Goodman, *The Republic of Letters: A Cultural History of the French Enlightenment* (Ithaca, N.Y.: Cornell University Press, 1994), p. 89.
2. Quoted in M. S. Anderson, *Europe in the Eighteenth Century, 1713–1783*, 3d ed. (London: Longman, 1987), pp. 218–219.

## ■ Suggested Reading

Anderson, M. S. *Europe in the Eighteenth Century, 1713–1783.* 4th ed. 2000. A general history covering political, economic, social, and cultural developments.

Black, Jeremy. *European Warfare, 1660–1815.* 1994. One of several recent books by this military historian known particularly for his studies of the seventeenth and eighteenth centuries.

Cipolla, Carlo. *Before the Industrial Revolution.* 1976. A comprehensive treatment of the development of the European economy and technology through this period.

Colley, Linda. *Britons: Forging the Nation, 1707–1837.* 1992. A history of the British that emphasizes the interrelationships of political, social, and cultural history.

Goodman, Dena. *The Republic of Letters: A Cultural History of the French Enlightenment.* 1994. Useful for understanding the social context of the Enlightenment, especially the role of women as salon leaders.

Kennedy, Paul. *The Rise and Fall of British Naval Mastery.* 1976. A comprehensive work on the rise of British sea power from the sixteenth century to modern times.

Porter, Roy. *The Enlightenment.* 1990. A brief introduction.

Roche, Daniel. *France in the Enlightenment.* 1998. An indispensable study of state and society in France by an eminent French scholar.

 **For a searchable list of additional readings for this chapter, go to http://college.hmco.com.**

# CHAPTER 19

# An Age of Revolution 1789–1815

THESE militiamen marching off to defend France against the invader in September 1792 appear to be heroes already. Adoring women in the crowd hand them laurel wreaths as they pass; the men march by, resolute and triumphant. Symbols of the ongoing revolution stand out as well: the prominent tricolor flag, the tricolor cockade in each man's hat. In fact, that September, France's citizen armies for the first time defeated the army of a foreign monarch poised to breach its borders and snuff out its revolution. The painting celebrates this triumph about to happen and thereby inspires confidence in the Revolution and pride in its citizen-soldiers.

Today the French Revolution is considered the initiation of modern European as well as modern French history. The most powerful monarch in Europe was forced to accept constitutional limits to his power by subjects convinced of their right to demand them. Eventually, the king was overthrown and executed, and the monarchy abolished. Events in France reverberated throughout Europe because the overthrow of one absolute monarchy threatened fellow royals elsewhere. Revolutionary fervor on the part of ordinary soldiers enabled France's armies unexpectedly to best many of their opponents. By the late 1790s the armies of France would be led in outright conquest of other European states by one of the most talented generals in European history: Napoleon Bonaparte. He brought to the continental European nations that his armies eventually conquered a mixture of imperial aggression and revolutionary change. Europe was transformed both by the shifting balance of power and by the spread of revolutionary ideas.

**The Beginnings of Revolution, 1775–1789**

**The Phases of the Revolution, 1789–1799**

**The Napoleonic Era and the Legacy of Revolution, 1799–1815**

The National Guard of Paris leaves to join the army, September 1792 (detail). (Château de Versailles/Hubert Josse)

Understanding the French Revolution means understanding not only its origins but also its complicated course of events, and their significance. Challenges to the power of the king were not new, but the Revolution overthrew his right to rule at all. The notion that the people constituted the nation, were responsible as citizens, and had some right to representation in government became irresistible. The republican system it conjured up replaced a government by inherited privilege. Louis XVI was transformed from the divinely appointed father of his people to an enemy of the people, worthy only of execution. Central to the Revolution was the complex process by which public opinion was shaped and, in turn, shaped events. Change was driven, in part, by the power of symbols—flags, rallying cries, inspiring art—to challenge an old political order and to legitimize a new one.

**QUESTIONS TO CONSIDER**

■ What factors led to the beginning of revolution in France in 1789?

■ Why did the Revolution take a more radical direction from 1792 until 1794?

■ What was the impact of Napoleon's rule on France?

■ What were the major effects of the French Revolution and Napoleonic rule on the rest of Europe and overseas?

**TERMS TO KNOW**

Third Estate
National Assembly
Tennis Court Oath
Declaration of the
    Rights of Man
    and the Citizen
Jacobins
sans-culottes

Maximilien Robespierre
the Terror
Society of Revolutionary
    Republican Women
Directory
Napoleon Bonaparte
the Civil Code
François Toussaint-Louverture

# THE BEGINNINGS OF REVOLUTION, 1775–1789

 AM a citizen of the world," wrote John Paul Jones, captain in the fledgling United States Navy, in 1778. He was writing to a Scottish aristocrat, apologizing for raiding the lord's estate while marauding along the British coast during the American Revolution. Jones (1747–1792), himself born a Scotsman, was one of the thousands of cosmopolitan Europeans who were familiar with European cultures on both sides of the Atlantic. As a sailor, Jones literally knew his way around the Atlantic world, but he was a "citizen of the world" in another sense as well. When the Scotsman wrote back to Jones, he expressed surprise that his home had been raided because he was sympathetic to the American colonists. Like Jones, he said, he was a man of "liberal sentiments."[1] Both Jones and the Scottish lord felt they belonged to an international society of gentlemen who recognized certain Enlightenment principles regarding just and rational government.

In the Atlantic world of the late eighteenth century, both practical links of commerce and shared ideals about "liberty" were important shaping forces. The strategic interests of the great European powers were also always involved. Thus, when the American colonists actively resisted British rule and then in 1776 declared their independence from Britain, the consequences were widespread and varied: British trading interests were challenged, French appetites for gains at British expense were whetted, and illusive notions about "liberty" seemed more plausible. The victory of the American colonies in 1783, followed by the creation of the U.S. Constitution in 1787, further heightened the appeal of liberal ideas elsewhere. Attempts at liberal reform were mounted in several states, including Ireland, the Netherlands, and Poland. However, the American Revolution had the most direct impact on later events in France because the French had been directly involved in the American effort.

## ■ Revolutionary Movements in Europe

While the British government was facing the revolt of the American colonies, it also confronted trouble closer to home. The war against the American colonies was not firmly supported by Britons. Like many Americans, many Britons had divided loyalties, and many who did favor armed force to subdue the rebellion were convinced that the war was being mismanaged. The prosecution of the war against the American colonies proceeded amid calls for reform of the ministerial government. In this setting, a reform movement sprang up in Ireland in 1779. The reformers demanded greater autonomy from Britain. Like the Americans, Irish elites felt like disadvantaged junior partners in the British Empire. They chafed over British policies that favored British imperial interests over those of the Irish ruling class: for example, the exclusion of Irish ports in favor of English and Scottish trading stops and the granting of political rights to Irish Catholics so that they might fight in Britain's overseas armies.

Protestant Irish landlords, threatened by such policies, expressed their opposition not only in parliamentary debates but also in military defiance. Following the example of the American rebels, middle- and upper-class Anglo-Irish set up a system of locally sponsored voluntary militia to resist British troops if necessary. The Volunteer Movement was neutralized when greater parliamentary autonomy for Ireland was granted in 1782, following the repeal of many restrictions on Irish commerce. Unlike the Americans, the Irish elites faced an internal challenge to their own authority—the Catholic population whom they had for centuries dominated. That challenge forced them to reach an accommodation with the British government.

Meanwhile, a political crisis with constitutional overtones was also brewing in the Netherlands. Tensions between the aristocratic stadholders of the House of Orange and the merchant oligarchies of the major cities deepened during the American Revolution. The Dutch were then engaged in a commercial war against the British, to whom the stadholder was supposed to be sympathetic. The conflict ceased to be wholly traditional for two reasons. First, the representatives of the various cities, calling themselves the Dutch "Patriot" Party, defended their position on the grounds of traditional balance of power within the Netherlands and invoked wider claims to American-style "liberty." Second, the challenge to traditional political arrangements widened when middling urban dwellers, long disenfranchised by these oligarchies, demanded "liberty," too—that is, political enfranchisement within the cities—and briefly took over the Patriot movement. Just as many Irish rebels accepted the concessions of 1782, many Patriot oligarchs in the Netherlands did nothing to resist an invasion in 1787 that restored the power of the stadholder, the prince of Orange, and thereby ended the challenge to their own control of urban government.

Both the Irish volunteers and the Dutch Patriots, though members of very limited movements, echoed

## CHRONOLOGY

| | |
|---|---|
| 1775–1783 | American Revolutionary War |
| 1779–1782 | Irish Volunteer Movement |
| 1788 | United States Constitution ratified<br>Reform movement begins in Poland<br>"Patriot" movement ends in the Netherlands |
| 1789 | French Estates General meets in Versailles (May)<br>Third Estate declares itself the National Assembly (June)<br>Storming of the Bastille (July) |
| 1790 | Polish constitution |
| 1791 | French king Louis XVI captured attempting to flee<br>Slave revolt begins in Saint Domingue |
| 1792 | France declares war on Austria; revolutionary wars begin (April)<br>Louis XVI arrested; France declared a republic (August–September) |
| 1793 | Louis XVI guillotined |
| 1793–1794 | Reign of Terror in France |
| 1799 | Napoleon seizes power in France |
| 1802 | Napoleon declared consul for life |
| 1804 | Napoleon crowned emperor<br>Napoleonic Civil Code<br>Independence of Haiti (Saint Domingue) declared |
| 1805 | Battle of Trafalgar<br>Battle of Austerlitz |
| 1806 | Dissolution of Holy Roman Empire |
| 1812 | French invasion of Russia |
| 1814 | Napoleon abdicates and is exiled<br>French monarchy restored |
| 1815 | Hundred Days (February–June)<br>Battle of Waterloo |

the American rebels in practical and ideological ways. Both were influenced by the economic and political consequences of Britain's relationship with its colonies. Both were inspired by the success of the American rebels and their thoroughgoing claims for political self-determination.

Desire for political reform flared in Poland as well during this period. Reform along lines suggested by Enlightenment precepts was accepted as a necessity by Polish leaders after the first partition of Poland in 1772 had left the remnant state without some of its wealthiest territories (see Map 18.1 on page 623). Beginning in 1788, however, reforming gentry in the *sejm°* (representative assembly) went further; they established a commission to write a constitution, following the American example. The resulting document, known as the May 3 (1791) Constitution, was the first codified constitution in Europe; it was read and admired by George Washington.

Poles thus established a constitutional monarchy in which representatives of major towns as well as gentry and nobility could sit as deputies. The *liberum veto*, which had allowed great magnates to obstruct royal authority at will, was abolished. However, Catherine the Great, empress of Russia, would not tolerate a constitutional government operating so close to her own autocratic regime; she ordered an invasion of Poland in 1792. The unsuccessful defense of Poland was led by a veteran of the American Revolution, Tadeusz Kosciuszko° (1746–1817). The second, more extensive partition of Poland followed, to be answered in turn in 1794 by a widespread insurrection against Russian rule, again spearheaded by Kosciuszko. The uprising was mercilessly suppressed by an alliance of Russian and Prussian troops. Unlike the U.S. Constitution from which they drew inspiration, the Poles' constitutional experiment was doomed by the power of its neighbor.

### ■ The American Revolution and the Kingdom of France

As Britain's greatest commercial and political rival, France naturally was drawn into Britain's struggle with its North American colonies. In the Seven Years' War (1756–1763), the French had lost many of their colonial settlements and trading outposts to the English (see page 630). Stung by this outcome, certain French courtiers and ministers pressed for an aggressive colonial policy that would regain for France some of the riches in trade that Britain now threatened to monopolize. The American Revolution seemed to offer the perfect opportunity. The French extended covert aid to the Americans from the very beginning of the conflict in 1775. After the first major defeat of British troops by the Americans—at the Battle of Saratoga in 1777—France formally recognized the independent United States and established an alliance with them. The French then committed troops as well as funds for the American cause. John Paul Jones's most famous ship, the *Bonhomme Richard°*, was purchased and outfitted in France at French government expense, as were many other American naval vessels during the war. French support was decisive. In 1781 the French fleet kept reinforcements from reaching the British force besieged by George Washington at Yorktown. The American victory at Yorktown effectively ended the war; the colonies' independence was formally recognized by the Treaty of Paris in 1783.

The consequences for France of its American alliance were momentous. Aid for the Americans saddled France with a debt of about 1 billion *livres* (pounds), which represented as much as one-quarter of the total debt that the French government was trying to service. A less tangible impact of the American Revolution derived from the direct participation of about nine thousand French soldiers, sailors, and aristocrats. The best known is the Marquis de Lafayette°, who became an aide to George Washington and helped command American troops. For many humble men, the war was simply employment. For others, it was a quest of sorts. For them, the promise of the Enlightenment—belief in human rationality, natural rights, and universal laws by which society should be organized—was brought to life in America.

Exposure to the American conflict occurred at the French court, too. Beginning in 1775, a permanent American mission to Versailles lobbied hard for aid and later managed the flow of that assistance. The chief emissary of the Americans was Benjamin Franklin (1706–1790), a philosophe by French standards whose writings and scientific experiments were already known to European elites. His talents—among them, a skillful exploitation of a simple, Quaker-like demeanor—succeeded in promoting the idealization of America at the French court.

The U.S. Constitution, the various state constitutions, and the debates surrounding their ratifications were all published in Paris and much discussed in salons and at court, where lively debate about reform of French institutions had been going on for decades. America became the prototype of the rational republic—the embodiment of Enlightenment philosophy. It was hailed as the place where the irrationalities of inherited privilege did not prevail. A British observer, Arthur Young (1741–1820), believed that "the American revolution has laid

---

**sejm** (SAME)
**Tadeusz Kosciuszko** (tah-DAY-oosh kos-USE-ko)

**Bonhomme Richard** (bon-OHM ree-SHARD)
**Marquis de Lafayette** (mar-KEE duh la-fye-ET)

**Marie-Joseph, Marquis de Lafayette**    The marquis is depicted commanding troops during the American Revolution. Called the "hero of two worlds," Lafayette returned to France to become one of the most imortant aristocratic reformers during the French Revolution. He favored a constitutional monarchy and opposed republican rule.    *(Jean-Loup Charmet)*

the foundation of another in France, if [the French] government does not take care of itself."[2]

By the mid-1780s there was no longer a question of whether the French regime would experience reform but rather what form the reform would take. The royal government was almost bankrupt. A significant minority of the politically active elite was convinced of the fundamental irrationality of France's system of government. Nevertheless, a dissatisfied elite and a financial crisis—even fanned by a successful revolt elsewhere—do not necessarily lead to revolution. Why did the French government—the *Ancien Régime*°, or "Old Regime," as it became known after the Revolution—not "take care of itself"?

## ■ The Crisis of the Old Regime

The Old Regime was brought to the point of crisis in the late 1780s by three factors: (1) heavy debts that dwarfed an antiquated system for collecting revenue; (2) institutional constraints on the monarchy that defended privileged interests; and (3) public opinion that envisioned thoroughgoing reform and pushed the monarchy in that direction. Another factor was the ineptitude of the king, Louis XVI (r. 1774–1793).

Louis came to the throne in 1774, a year before the American Revolution began. He was a kind, well-meaning man better suited to carry out the finite responsibilities of a petty bureaucrat than to be king. The queen, the Austrian Marie Antoinette (1755–1793), was unpopular. She was regarded with suspicion by the many who despised the "unnatural" alliance with Austria the marriage had sealed. She, too, was politically inept, unable to negotiate the complexities of court life and widely rumored to be selfishly wasteful of royal resources despite the realm's financial crises.

The fiscal crisis of the monarchy had been a long time in the making and was an outgrowth of the system in which the greatest wealth was protected by traditional privileges. At the top of the social and political pyramid were the nobles, a legal grouping that included warriors and royal officials. In France, nobility conferred exemption from much taxation. Thus, the royal government could not directly tax its wealthiest subjects.

This situation existed throughout much of Europe, a legacy of the individual contractual relationships that had formed the political and economic framework of medieval Europe. Unique to France, however, was the strength of the institutions that defended this system. Of particular importance were the royal law courts, the parlements°, which claimed a right of judicial review over royal edicts. All the parlementaires—well-educated lawyers and judges—were noble and loudly defended the traditional privileges of all nobles. Louis XV (d. 1774), near the end of his life, had successfully undermined the power of the parlements by a bold series of moves. Louis XVI, immediately after coming to the throne, buckled under pressure and restored the parlements to full strength.

Deficit financing had been a way of life for the monarchy for centuries. After early efforts at reform, Louis XIV (d. 1715) had reverted to common fund-raising expedients such as selling offices, which only added to the weight of privileged investment in the old order. England had established a national bank to free its government from the problem, but the comparable French

---

**Ancien Régime** (ahn-SYEN ray-ZHEEM)

**parlements** (par-luh-MAWHN)

**The Common People Crushed by Privilege**    In this contemporary cartoon, a nobleman in military dress and a clergyman crush a commoner under the rock of burdensome taxes and forced labor (*corvées*). The victim's situation reflects that of the peasantry, but his stylish clothes would allow affluent towns-people to identify with him. *(Musée Carnavalet, Paris/Giraudon/Art Resource, NY)*

effort early in the century had been undercapitalized and had failed. Late in the 1780s, under Louis XVI, one-fourth of the annual operating expenses of the government was borrowed, and half of all government expenditure went to paying interest on its debt. Short-term economic crises, such as disastrous harvests, added to the cumulative problem of government finance.

The king employed able finance ministers who tried to institute fundamental reforms, such as replacing the tangle of taxes with a simpler system in which all would pay and eliminating local tariffs, which were stifling commerce. The parlements and many courtiers and aristocrats, as well as ordinary people, resisted these policies. Peasants and townsfolk did not trust the "free market" (free from traditional trade controls) for grain; most feared that speculators would buy up the grain supply and people would starve. Trying to implement such reforms in times of grain shortage almost guaranteed their failure. Moreover, many supported the parlements simply because they were the only institution capable of standing up to the monarchy. Yet not all members of the elite joined the parlements in opposing reform. The imprint of "enlightened" public opinion was apparent in the thinking of some courtiers and thousands of educated commoners who believed that the government and the economy had to change and openly debated the nature and extent of reform needed.

In 1787 the king called an "Assembly of Notables"— an ad hoc group of elites—to support him in facing down the parlements and proceeding with some changes. He found little support even among men known to be sympathetic to reform. Some did not support particular proposals, and many were reluctant to allow the monarchy free rein. Others, reflecting the influence of the American Revolution, maintained that a "constitutional" body such as the Estates General, which had not been called since 1614, needed to make these decisions.

Ironically, nobles and clergy who were opposed to reform supported the call for the Estates General, confident they could control its deliberations. The three Estates met and voted separately by "order"—clergy (First Estate), nobles (Second Estate), and commoners (Third Estate). The combined votes of the clergy and nobles would presumably nullify whatever the Third Estate might propose.

In 1788 popular resistance to reform in the streets of Paris and mounting pressure from his courtiers and bureaucrats induced Louis to summon the Estates General. On Louis's orders, deputies were to be elected by local assemblies, which were chosen, in turn, by wide male suffrage. Louis mistakenly assumed he had widespread support in the provinces, and he wished to tap into it by means of this grass-roots voting. Louis also agreed that

## 🐚 READING SOURCES

## Lists of Grievances for the Estates General

*In preparation for the meeting of an Estates General, communities throughout France prepared lists of grievances that they hoped the deputies would address. Among the following petitions compiled by a town in Normandy in 1789, we can note deference to the king but also radical proposals reflecting the impact of Enlightenment thought. The document denounces certain special privileges associated with nobility, in particular the burdensome remnants of medieval property control, and clearly recognizes the Estates as the legitimate voice of the nation. Note also the initial demand: that, contrary to the king's plans, voting in the Estates should occur by head.*

. . . [T]he inhabitants decreed that their wishes were:

1. That in the assembly of the Estates-General, opinions be counted by head and not by order. . . .

2. That only the assembled nation may consent to taxes, loans and new offices, and no corporation, organization, not even provincial estates will be allowed to represent the nation.

3. That, in keeping with his majesty's promise, the Estates-General will assemble at fixed and determined periods, that taxes may only be consented to by the Estates until the period of their next meeting, and that each new assembly of estates will be preceded by a new choosing of deputies, so that no citizen can perpetually represent the nation. . . .

7. That all privileges and pecuniary exemptions be abolished, and taxes be collected without discrimination in the same proportion from all orders within the province.

8. That, to facilitate commerce, tollgates be removed to the frontiers of the realm, that his majesty be entreated to remedy the obstacles to commerce occasioned by differences in weights and measures. . . .

10. That the right of *franc fief* [fee payable by commoners to the king for the right of holding a noble fief] be suppressed, as humiliating to the Third Estate.

11. That, at the same time, his majesty be humbly entreated to recall that decision . . . which excludes from his majesty's service all citizens who cannot prove four degrees of nobility; that his majesty equally be entreated to bring about a reform of the [Parlement's] decisions whereby a gentleman is sought for an office which confers nobility before a candidate's merits are considered, in consequence of which merit will become sufficient grounds to enter the different estates.

*Source:* Annales du Centre Régional de Documentation Pédagogique de Caen, *Les Cahiers de Doléances de 1789 dans le Calvados.* Nouvelle série #6. Service Éducatif des Archives départementales du Calvados. Translated by Laura Mason. Reprinted in Laura Mason and Tracey Rizzo, eds., *The French Revolution: A Document Collection* (Boston: Houghton Mifflin, 1999), pp. 56–57.

the Third Estate should have twice as many deputies as the other two Estates, but he did not authorize voting by head rather than by order, which would have brought about the dominance of the Third Estate. Nevertheless, the king hoped that the specter of drastic proposals put forth by the Third Estate would frighten the aristocrats and clergy into accepting some of his reforms. (See the box "Reading Sources: List of Grievances for the Estates General.")

Louis's situation was precarious when the Estates General convened in May 1789. As ever, he faced immediate financial crisis. He also faced a constitutional crisis. Already a groundswell of sentiment confirmed the legitimacy of the Estates General, the role of the Third Estate, and the authority of the Third Estate to enact change. Political pamphlets abounded arguing that the Third Estate deserved enhanced power because it carried the mandate of the people. The most important of these was

*What Is the Third Estate?* (1789) by Joseph Emmanuel Sieyès° (1748–1836), a church official from the diocese of Chartres. The sympathies of Abbé Sieyès, as he was known, were with the Third Estate: his career had suffered and stalled because he was not noble. Sieyès argued that the Third Estate represented the nation because it did not reflect special privilege.

Among the deputies of the first two Estates—clergy and nobility—were men, such as the Marquis de Lafayette (1757–1834), who were sympathetic to reform. More important, however, the elections had returned to the Third Estate a large majority of deputies who reflected the most radical political thought possible for men of their standing. Most were lawyers and other professionals who were functionaries in the government but, like Sieyès, of low social rank. They frequented provincial academies, salons, and political societies. They were convinced of the validity of their viewpoints and determined on reform, and they had little stake in the system as it was. When this group convened and met with resistance from the First and Second Estates and from Louis himself, they seized the reins of government and a revolution began.

## ■ 1789: A Revolution Begins

As soon as the three Estates convened at the royal palace at Versailles, conflicts surfaced. The ineptness of the Crown was immediately clear. On the first day of the meetings in May, Louis and his ministers failed to introduce a program of reforms for the deputies to consider. This failure raised doubt about the monarchy's commitment to reform. More important, it allowed the political initiative to pass to the Third Estate. The deputies challenged the Crown's insistence that the three Estates meet and vote separately. Deputies to the Third Estate refused to be certified (that is, to have their credentials officially recognized) as members of only the Third Estate rather than as members of the Estates General as a whole.

For six weeks the Estates General was unable to meet officially, and the king did nothing to break the impasse. During this interlude, the determination of the deputies of the Third Estate strengthened. More and more deputies were won over to the notion that the three Estates must begin in the most systematic way: France must have a written constitution.

By the middle of June, more than thirty reformist members of the clergy were sitting jointly with the Third Estate, which had invited all deputies from all three Estates to meet and be certified together. On June 17 the

Third Estate simply declared itself the National Assembly of France. At first, the king did nothing, but when the deputies arrived to meet on the morning of June 20, they discovered they had been locked out of the hall. Undaunted, they assembled instead in a nearby indoor tennis court and produced the document that has come to be known as the "Tennis Court Oath." It was a collective pledge to meet until a written constitution had been achieved. Only one deputy refused to support it. Sure of their mandate, the deputies had assumed the reins of government.

The king continued to handle the situation with both ill-timed self-assertion and feeble attempts at compromise. As more and more deputies from the First and Second Estates joined the National Assembly, Louis "ordered" the remaining loyal deputies to join it, too. Simultaneously, however, he ordered troops to come to Paris. He feared disorder in the wake of the recent disturbances throughout France and believed that any challenge to the legitimacy of arbitrary monarchical authority would be disastrous.

This appeal for armed assistance stirred unrest in the capital. Paris, with a population of about 600,000 in 1789, was one of the largest cities in Europe. It was the political nerve center of the nation—the site of the publishing industry, salons, the homes of parlementaires and royal ministers. It was also a working city, with thousands of laborers of all trades plus thousands more—perhaps one-tenth of the inhabitants—jobless recent immigrants from the countryside. The city was both extremely volatile and extremely important to the stability of royal power. The king's call for troops aroused Parisians' suspicions. Some assumed a plot was afoot to starve Paris and destroy the National Assembly. Already they considered the Assembly to be a guarantor of acceptable government.

It took little—the announcement of the dismissal of a reformist finance minister—for Paris to erupt in demonstrations and looting. Crowds besieged City Hall and the royal armory, where they seized thousands of weapons. A popular militia formed as citizens armed themselves. Armed crowds assailed other sites of royal authority, including the huge fortified prison, the Bastille, on the morning of July 14. The Bastille now held only a handful of petty criminals, but it still remained a potent symbol of royal power and, it was assumed, held large supplies of arms. Like the troops at the armory, the garrison at the Bastille had received no firm orders to fire on the crowds if necessary. The garrison commander at first mounted a hesitant defense, then decided to surrender after citizens managed to secure cannon and drag them to face the prison. Most of the garrison were

---

**Sieyès** (say-EZ)

**The Tennis Court Oath** It was raining on June 20 when the deputies found themselves barred from their meeting hall and sought shelter in the royal tennis court. Their defiance created one of the turning points of the Revolution; the significance was recognized several years later by this painting's artist. *(Photographie Bulloz)*

allowed to go free, although the commander and several officers were murdered by the crowd.

The citizens' victory was a great embarrassment to royal authority. The king immediately had to embrace the popular movement. He came to Paris and in front of crowds at City Hall donned the red and blue cockade worn by the militia and ordinary folk as a badge of resolve and defiance. This symbolic action signaled the reversal of the Old Regime—politics would now be based on new principles.

Encouraged by events in Paris, inhabitants of cities and towns around France staged similar uprisings. In many areas, the machinery of royal government completely broke down. City councils, officials, and even parlementaires were thrown out of office. Popular militias took control of the streets. A simultaneous wave of uprisings shook the countryside. Most of them were the result of food shortages, but their timing added momentum to the more strictly political protests in cities. These events forced the members of the National Assembly to

work energetically on the constitution and to pass legislation to satisfy popular protests against economic and political privileges.

On August 4 the Assembly issued a set of decrees abolishing the remnants of powers that landlords had enjoyed since the Middle Ages, including the right to co-opt peasant labor and the bondage of serfdom itself. Although largely symbolic, because serfdom and forced labor had been eliminated in much of France, these changes represented a dramatic inroad into the property rights of the elite as they had been traditionally construed. The repeals were hailed as the "end of feudalism." A blow was also struck at established religion by eliminating the tithe. At the end of August, the Assembly issued a Declaration of the Rights of Man and the Citizen. It was a bold assertion of the foundations of a newly conceived government, closely modeled on portions of the U.S. Constitution. Its preamble declared "that [since] the ignorance, neglect or contempt of the rights of man are the sole cause of public calamities and the corruption of governments," the deputies were "determined to set forth in a solemn declaration the natural, inalienable and sacred rights of man. . . ."[3]

In September the deputies debated the king's role in a new constitutional government. Monarchists favored a government rather like England's, with a two-house legislature, including an upper house representing the hereditary aristocracy and a royal right to veto legislation. More radical deputies favored a single legislative chamber and no veto power for the king. After deliberation, the Assembly reached a compromise. The king was given a three-year suspensive veto—the power to suspend legislation for the sitting of two legislatures. This was still a formidable amount of power but a drastic curtailment of his formerly absolute sovereignty.

Again, Louis resorted to troops. This time, he called them directly to Versailles, where the Assembly sat. News of the troops' arrival provoked outrage, which heightened with the threat of another grain shortage. Early on

the morning of October 5, women in the Paris street markets saw the empty grocers' stalls and took immediate collective action. "We want bread!" they shouted at the steps of City Hall. Because they were responsible for procuring their families' food, women often led protests over bread shortages. This protest, however, went far beyond the ordinary. A crowd of thousands gathered and decided to walk all the way to Versailles, accompanied by the popular militia (now called the "National Guard"), to petition the king directly for sustenance.

At Versailles, they presented a delegation to the National Assembly, and a joint delegation of the women and deputies was dispatched to see the king. Some of the women fell at the feet of the king with their tales of hardship, certain that the "father of the people" would alleviate their suffering. He did order stored grain supplies distributed in Paris, and he also agreed to accept the constitutional role that the Assembly had voted for him.

**Storming the Bastille** The crowd was convinced that the Bastille held political prisoners as well as a large supply of arms. In fact, it held neither. Thousands of Parisians—including artisans and shopkeepers and not merely desperate rabble—surrounded the fortress and forced the garrison to surrender. *(Photographie Bulloz)*

That very night members of the National Guard, which had replaced the royal guard around the person of the king, saved Louis's life. A mob broke into the palace and managed to kill two members of the royal guard still in attendance outside the queen's chamber. The king agreed to return to Paris so that he could reassure the people. But the procession back to the city was a curious one. The royal family was escorted by militia and bread protesters, and the severed heads of the dead royal guardsmen were carried on pikes.

The king was now in the hands of his people. Already, dramatic change had occurred as a result of a complex dynamic among the three Estates, the Crown, and the people of Paris. The king was still assumed to be the fatherly guardian of his people's well-being; but his powers were now limited, and his authority was badly shaken. The Assembly had begun to govern in the name of the "nation" and, so far, had the support of the people.

# THE PHASES OF THE REVOLUTION, 1789–1799

HE French Revolution was a complicated affair. It was a series of changes, in a sense a series of revolutions, driven not by one group of people but by several groups. Even among elites convinced of the need for reform the range of opinion was wide. The people of Paris continued to be an important force for change. Country people also became active, primarily in resisting changes forced on them by the central government.

All of the wrangling within France was complicated by foreign reaction. Managing foreign war soon became a routine burden for the fragile revolutionary governments. In addition, they had to cope with the continuing problems that had precipitated the Revolution in the first place: the government's chronic indebtedness, economic difficulties, and recurrent grain shortages. Finally, the Revolution itself was an issue in that, once the traditional arrangements of royal government had been altered, momentum for further change was unleashed.

### ■ The First Phase Completed, 1789–1791

At the end of 1789, Paris was in ferment, but for a time forward progress blunted the threat of disastrous divisions between king and Assembly and between either of those and the people of Paris. The capital continued to be the center of lively political debate. Salons continued

to meet; academies and private societies proliferated. Deputies to the Assembly swelled the ranks of these societies or helped to found new ones. Several would be important throughout the Revolution—particularly the Jacobin° Club, named for the monastic order whose buildings the members used as a meeting hall.

These clubs represented the gamut of revolutionary opinion. Some, in which ordinary Parisians were well represented, focused on economic policies that would directly benefit common people. Women were active in a few of the more radical groups. Monarchists dominated other clubs. At first similar to the salons and debating societies of the Enlightenment era, the clubs quickly became both sites of political action and sources of political pressure on the government. A bevy of popular newspapers also contributed to the vigorous political life in the capital.

The broad front of revolutionary consensus began to break apart as the Assembly forged ahead with decisions about the constitution and with policies necessary to remedy France's still-desperate financial situation. The largest portion of the untapped wealth of the nation lay with the Catholic Church, an obvious target for anticlerical reformers. The deputies did not propose to dismantle the church, but they did make sweeping changes: They kept church buildings intact and retained the clergy as salaried officials of the state. They abolished all monasteries and pensioned the monks and nuns to permit them to continue as nurses and teachers where possible. With the depleted treasury in mind, the Assembly seized most of the vast lands of the church and declared them national property (*biens nationaux*) to be sold for revenue.

Economic and political problems ensued. Revenue was needed faster than the property could be inventoried and sold, so government bonds (*assignats°*) were issued against the eventual sale of church properties. Unfortunately, in the cash-strapped economy, the bonds were treated like money, their value became inflated, and the government never realized the hoped-for profits. A greater problem was the political divisiveness generated by the restructuring of the church. Many members of the lower clergy, living as they did near ordinary citizens, were among the most reform-minded of the deputies. These clergy were willing to go along with many changes, but the required oath of loyalty to the state made a mockery of clerical independence.

The Civil Constitution of the Clergy, as these measures were called, was passed by the Assembly in July 1790 because the clerical deputies opposing it were outvoted.

---

**Jacobin** (JACK-oh-bin)   **assignats** (ah-see-NYAH)

## CHRONOLOGY

### The French Revolution

| | | |
|---|---|---|
| **1789** | **May 5** | Estates General meets in Versailles |
| | **June 17** | Third Estate declares itself the National Assembly |
| | **June 20** | Tennis Court Oath |
| | **July 14** | Storming of the Bastille |
| | **August 27** | Declaration of the Rights of Man and the Citizen |
| | **October 5–6** | Women's march on Versailles Louis XVI returns to Paris |
| **1790** | **July** | Civil Constitution of the Clergy |
| **1791** | **June** | Louis XVI captured attempting to flee |
| | **August** | Declaration of Pillnitz |
| | **September** | New constitution implemented |
| **1792** | **April** | France declares war on Austria |
| | **August 10** | Storming of the Tuileries Louis XVI arrested |
| | **September 21** | National Convention declares France a republic |
| **1793** | **January 21** | Louis XVI guillotined |
| | **May** | First Law of the Maximum |
| | **July** | Terror inaugurated |
| **1794** | **July** | Robespierre guillotined Terror ends |
| **1795** | **October** | Directory established |
| **1799** | **November** | Napoleon seizes power |

More than half of the churchmen did take the oath of loyalty. Those who refused, concentrated among the higher clergy, were in theory thrown out of their offices. A year later (April 1791) the pope declared that clergy who had taken the oath were suspended from their offices. Antirevolutionary sentiment grew among thousands of French people, particularly in outlying regions, to whom the church was still vital as a source of charity and a center of community life. This religious opposition worked to undermine the legitimacy of the new government.

Meanwhile, the Assembly proceeded with administrative and judicial reform. The deputies abolished the medieval provinces as administrative districts and replaced them with uniform *départements* (departments). They declared that local officials would be elected—a revolutionary dispersal of power that had previously belonged to the king.

As work on the constitution drew to a close in the spring of 1791, the king decided that he had had enough. Royal authority, as he knew it, had been virtually dismantled. Louis himself was now a virtual prisoner in the Tuileries° Palace in the very heart of Paris. Afraid for himself and his family, he and a few loyal aides worked out a plan to flee France. The king and the members of his immediate family set out in disguise on June 20, 1791. However, the party missed a rendezvous with a troop escort and was stopped—and recognized—in the town of Varennes°, near the eastern border of the kingdom.

Louis and his family were returned to Paris and held under lightly disguised house arrest. The circumstances of his flight were quickly discovered. He and the queen had sent money abroad ahead of themselves. He had left behind a document condemning the constitution. His intention was to invade France with Austrian troops if necessary. Thus, in July 1791, just as the Assembly was completing its proposal for a constitutional monarchy, the constitution it had created began to seem unworkable because the monarch was not to be trusted.

Editorials and protests against the monarchy increased. In one incident known as the Massacre of the Champ (Field) de Mars°, government troops led by Lafayette fired on citizens at an antimonarchy demonstration that certain Parisian clubs had organized; about fifty men and women died. This inflammatory incident both reflected and heightened tensions between moderate reformers satisfied with the constitutional monarchy, such as Lafayette, and outspoken republicans who wanted to eliminate the monarchy altogether.

On September 14 the king swore to uphold the constitution. He had no choice. The event became an occasion for celebration, but the tension between the interests of the Parisians and the provisions of the new constitution could not be glossed over. Though a liberal document for its day, the constitution reflected the views of the elite deputies who had created it. The right to vote, based on a minimal property qualification, was given to about half of all adult men. However, these men only chose electors, for whom the property qualifications were higher. The electors in turn chose deputies to

---

**Tuileries** (TWEE-lair-ee)    **Varennes** (vah-REN)
**Champ de Mars** (SHOM duh MARSS)

## Declaration of the Rights of Woman

*This retort to the new constitution, in which rights for women were conspicuously absent, was written in 1791 by Olympe de Gouges (1748?–1793), a self-educated butcher's daughter from southwestern France. The document reflects the complexity of political life during the Revolution. Gouges's declaration urges the extension to women of the Revolution's broad-based challenge to tradition. Yet Gouges dedicates the declaration to the queen, Marie-Antoinette, drawing on the tradition of aristocratic patronage. Ironically, given Article 10, Gouges died on the scaffold for her revolutionary sympathies.*

Man, Are you capable of being just? It is a woman who poses the question; at least you will not take away this right. Tell me, what gives you the sovereign empire to oppress my sex? Your strength? Your talents? Observe the Creator in his wisdom; look at nature in all her grandeur, with whom you seem to want to be in harmony, and give me, if you dare, an example of this tyrannical empire. . . . Bizarre, blind, bloated with science and degenerated—in a century of light and wisdom—in the crassest ignorance, he wants to command as a despot a sex which has received all intellectual faculties; he pretends to enjoy the Revolution and reclaim his rights to equality only to say nothing more about it.

1. Woman is born free and lives equal to man in her rights. Social distinctions may be founded only upon common utility.

2. The purpose of any political association is the conservation of the natural and imprescriptible rights of woman and man; these rights are liberty, property, security, and above all resistance to oppression.

3. The principle of all sovereignty resides essentially in the Nation, which is nothing other than the union of woman and man: no body, no individual can exercise authority which does not emanate from it.

4. Liberty and justice consist of rendering all that belongs to others; thus, the exercise of the natural rights of woman has only been limited by the perpetual tyranny that man opposes to them; these limits should be reformed by the laws of nature and reason. . . .

10. No one should be troubled for holding basic opinions; woman has the right to mount the scaffold; she must equally have the right to mount the podium. . . .

*Source:* Olympe de Gouges, *Écrits politiques, 1788–1791* (Paris: Côte-femmes, 1993), pp. 204–210. Translated by Tracey Rizzo. Reprinted in Laura Mason and Tracey Rizzo, eds., *The French Revolution: A Document Collection* (Boston: Houghton Mifflin, 1999), pp. 110–112.

---

national bodies as well as local officials. Although in theory any eligible voter could be an elected deputy or official, the fact that elite electors determined every officeholder meant that few ordinary citizens would become deputies or local administrators. The Declaration of Rights that accompanied the constitution reflected a fear of the masses that had not existed when the Declaration of the Rights of Man and the Citizen was first promulgated in 1789. Freedom of the press and freedom of assembly, for example, were not fully guaranteed.

Further, no political rights were accorded to women. Educated women had joined Parisian clubs such as the *Cercle sociale* (Social Circle), where opinion favored extending rights to women. Through such clubs, these women had tried to influence the National Assembly. But the Assembly granted neither political rights nor legal equality to women, nor did it pass other laws beneficial to women such as legalizing divorce or mandating female education. The prevailing view of women among deputies seemed to reflect those of the Enlightenment philosophe Rousseau, who imagined women's competence to be entirely circumscribed within the family. A Declaration of the Rights of Woman was drafted by a woman named Olympe de Gouges° to draw attention to the treatment of women in the constitution. (See the box "Reading Sources: Declaration of the Rights of Woman.")

**Olympe de Gouges** (oh-LAMP duh GOOZH)

Very soon after the constitution was implemented, the fragility of the new system became clear. The National Assembly declared that its members could not serve in the first assembly to be elected under the constitution. Thus, the members of the newly elected Legislative Assembly, which began to meet in October 1791, lacked any of the cohesiveness that would have come from collective experience. Also, unlike the previous National Assemblymen, they did not represent a broad range of opinion but were mostly republicans.

In fact, the Legislative Assembly was dominated by republican members of the Jacobin Club. They were known as Girondins°, after the region in southwestern France from which many of the club's leaders came. The policies of these new deputies and continued pressure from the ordinary citizens of Paris would cause the constitutional monarchy to collapse in less than a year.

### ■ The Second Phase and Foreign War, 1791–1793

An additional pressure on the new regime soon arose: a threat of foreign invasion and a war to counter the threat. Antirevolutionary aristocratic émigrés, including the king's brothers, had taken refuge in nearby German states and were planning to invade France. The emperor and other German rulers did little actively to aid the plotters. Austria and Prussia, however, in the Declaration of Pillnitz of August 1791, declared, as a concession to the émigrés, that they would intervene if necessary to support the monarchy in France.

The threat of invasion, when coupled with distrust of the royal family, seemed more real to the revolutionaries in Paris than it may actually have been. Indeed, many deputies hoped for war. They assumed that the outcome would be a French defeat, which would lead to a popular uprising that would rid them, at last, of the monarchy. In April 1792, under pressure from the Assembly, Louis XVI declared war against Austria. From this point, foreign war would be an ongoing factor in the Revolution.

At first, the war was a disaster for France. The army had not been reorganized into an effective fighting force after the loss of many aristocratic officers and the addition of newly self-aware citizens. On one occasion, troops insisted on putting an officer's command to a vote. The French lost early battles in the Austrian Netherlands, but the Austrians did not press their advantage and invade France because they were preoccupied with problems in eastern Europe.

Girondins (zhih-ron-DEHN)

**Louis XVI in 1792**    The king, though a kindly man, had neither the character nor the convictions necessary to refashion royal authority symbolically as the Revolution proceeded. When Parisian crowds forced him to wear the "liberty cap," the monarchy was close to collapse.    *(Metropolitan Museum of Art, The Elisha Whittelsey Collection, The Elisha Whittelsey Fund, 1962)*

The defeats emboldened critics of the monarchy, who demanded action. Under the direction of the Girondins, the Legislative Assembly began to press for the deportation of priests who had been leading demonstrations against the government. The Assembly abolished the personal guard of the king and summoned provincial national guardsmen to Paris. The king's resistance to these measures, as well as fears of acute grain shortages owing to a poor harvest and the needs of the armies, created further unrest. Crowds staged boisterous marches near the royal palace, physically confronted the king, and forced him to don the "liberty cap," a symbol of republicanism. The king's authority and prestige were now thoroughly undermined.

By July 1792, tensions had become acute. The grain shortage was severe, Austrian and Prussian troops committed to saving the royal family were threatening to invade, and, most important, the populace was better organized and more determined than ever before. In each of the forty-eight "sections"—administrative wards—of Paris a miniature popular assembly thrashed out all the events and issues of the day just as deputies in the nationwide Legislative Assembly did. Derisively called *sans-culottes*° ("without knee pants") because they could not afford elite fashions, the ordinary Parisians in the section assemblies included shopkeepers, artisans, and laborers. Their political organization enhanced their influence with the Assembly, the clubs, and the newspapers in the capital. By late July most sections of the city had approved a petition calling for the exile of the king, the election of new city officials, the exemption of the poor from taxation, and other radical measures.

In August the sans-culottes took matters into their own hands. On the night of August 9, after careful preparations, representatives of the section assemblies constituted themselves as a new city government with the aim of "saving the state." They then assaulted the Tuileries Palace, where the royal family was living. In the bloody confrontation, hundreds of royal guards and citizens died. After briefly taking refuge in the Legislative Assembly itself, the king and his family were imprisoned in one of the fortified towers in the city, under guard of the popularly controlled city government.

The storming of the Tuileries inaugurated the second major phase of the Revolution: the establishment of republican government in place of the monarchy. By their intimidating numbers, the people of Paris now controlled the Legislative Assembly. Some deputies had fled. Those who remained agreed under pressure to dissolve the Assembly and make way for another body to be elected by universal manhood suffrage. On September 20, that assembly—known as the National Convention—began to meet. The next day, the Convention declared the end of the monarchy and set to work crafting a constitution for the new republic.

Coincidentally, that same September day, French forces won their first genuine victory over the allied Austrian and Prussian invasion forces. Though not a decisive battle, it was a profound psychological triumph. A citizen army had defeated the professional force of a ruling prince. The victory bolstered the republican government and encouraged it to put more energy into the wars. Indeed, maintaining armies in the field became a weighty factor in the delicate equilibrium of revolutionary government. The new republican regime let it be known that

**sans-culottes** (sahn–koo-LOT)

its armies were not merely for self-defense but for the liberation of all peoples in the "name of the French Nation."

The Convention faced the divisive issue of what to do with the king. Louis had not done anything truly treasonous, but some of the king's correspondence, discovered after the storming of the Tuileries, provided the pretext for charges of treason. The Convention held a trial for him, lasting from December 11, 1792, through January 15, 1793. He was found guilty of treason by an overwhelming vote (683 to 39); the republican government would not compromise with monarchy. Less lopsided was the sentence: Louis was condemned to death by a narrow majority, 387 to 334.

The consequences for the king were immediate. On January 21, 1793, Louis mounted the scaffold in a public square near the Tuileries and was beheaded. The execution split the ranks of the Convention and soon resulted in the breakdown of the institution itself.

### ■ The Faltering Republic and the Terror, 1793–1794

In February 1793 the republic was at war with virtually every state in Europe; the only exceptions were the Scandinavian kingdoms and Russia. Moreover, the regime faced massive and widespread counterrevolutionary uprisings within France. Vigilance against internal and external enemies became a top priority. The Convention established an executive body, the Committee of Public Safety. In theory, this executive council was answerable to the Convention as a whole. As the months passed, however, it acted with greater and greater autonomy not only to institute policies but also to eradicate enemies. The broadly based republican government represented by the Convention began to disintegrate.

The first major narrowing of control came in June 1793. Pushed by the Parisian sections, a group of extreme Jacobins purged the Girondin deputies from the Convention, arresting many of them. The Girondins were republicans who favored an activist government in the people's behalf, but they were less radical than the Jacobins, less insistent on central control of the Revolution, and less willing to share power with the citizens of Paris. After the purge, the Convention still met, but most authority lay with the Committee of Public Safety.

New uprisings against the regime began. Added to counterrevolutionary revolts by peasants and aristocrats were new revolts by Girondin sympathizers. As resistance to the government mounted and the foreign threat continued, a dramatic event in Paris led the Committee

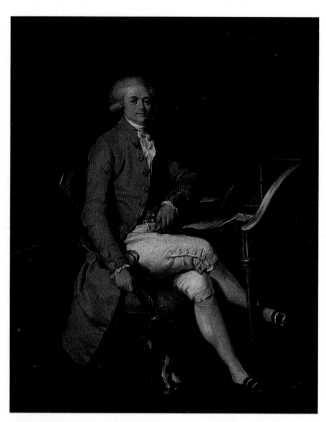

**Robespierre the Incorruptible**    A lawyer who had often championed the poor, Robespierre was elected to the Estates General in 1789 and was a consistent advocate of republican government from the beginning of the Revolution. His unswerving loyalty to his political principles earned him the nickname "the Incorruptible."    *(Musée des Beaux-Arts, Lille)*

of Public Safety officially to adopt a policy of political repression. A well-known figure of the Revolution, Jean Paul Marat (1743–1793), publisher of a radical republican newspaper very popular with ordinary Parisians, was murdered on July 13 by Charlotte Corday (1768–1793), a young aristocratic woman who had asked to meet with him. Shortly afterward, a long-time member of the Jacobin Club, Maximilien Robespierre° (1758–1794), joined the Committee and called for "Terror"—the systematic repression of internal enemies. He was not alone in his views. Members of the section assemblies of Paris led demonstrations to pressure the government into making Terror the order of the day.

Terror meant the use of intimidation to silence dissent. Since the previous autumn, the guillotine had been at work against identified enemies of the regime, but now a more energetic apparatus of terror was instituted. A Law of Suspects was passed that allowed citizens to be arrested simply on vague suspicion of counterrevolutionary sympathies. Revolutionary tribunals and an oversight committee made arbitrary arrests and rendered summary judgments. In October a steady stream of executions began, beginning with the queen, imprisoned since the storming of the Tuileries the year before. The imprisoned Girondin deputies followed, and then the beheadings continued relentlessly. Paris witnessed about 2,600 executions from 1793 to 1794.

Around France the verdicts of revolutionary tribunals led to approximately 14,000 executions. Another 10,000 to 12,000 people died in prison. Ten thousand or more were killed, usually by summary execution, after the defeat of counterrevolutionary uprisings. For example, 2,000 people were summarily executed in Lyon when a Girondin revolt collapsed there in October. The aim of the Terror was not merely to stifle active resistance; it was also to silence simple dissent. The victims in Paris included not only aristocrats or former deputies but also sans-culottes. The radical Jacobins wanted to seize control of the Revolution from the Parisian citizens who had lifted them to power.

Robespierre himself embodied all the contradictions of the policy of Terror. He was an austere, almost prim, man who lived very modestly—a model, of sorts, of the virtuous, disinterested citizen. The policies followed by the government during the year of his greatest influence, from July 1793 to July 1794, included generous, rational, and humane actions to benefit ordinary citizens as well as the atrocities of official Terror. (See the box "Reading Sources: Robespierre Justifies the Terror.") Indeed, the Terror notwithstanding, the government of the Committee of Public Safety was effective in providing direction for the nation at a critical time. In August 1793 it instituted the first mass conscription of citizens into the army (*levée en masse*°), and a consistently effective popular army came into existence. In the autumn of 1793 this army won impressive victories. In May the Convention had instituted a Law of the Maximum, which controlled the price of grain so that city people could afford their staple food—bread. In September the Committee extended the law to apply to other necessary commodities. Extensive plans were made for a system of free and universal primary education. Slavery in the French colonies was abolished in February 1794. Divorce, first legalized in 1792, was made easier for women to obtain.

**Robespierre** (ROBES-pee-air)

**levée en masse** (leh-VAY ohn MAHSS)

## Robespierre Justifies the Terror

*In this excerpt from a speech before the Convention in December 1793, Robespierre justifies the revolutionary government's need to act in an extraconstitutional manner. He echoes Rousseau's notion of a highly abstract sense of the public good. He also warns against challenges to the Revolution within France posed by foreign powers.*

The defenders of the Republic must adopt Caesar's maxim, for they believe that "nothing has been done so long as anything remains to be done." Enough dangers still face us to engage all our efforts. It has not fully extended the valor of our Republican soldiers to conquer a few Englishmen and a few traitors. A task no less important, and one more difficult, now awaits us: to sustain an energy sufficient to defeat the constant intrigues of all the enemies of our freedom and to bring to a triumphant realization the principles that must be the cornerstone of public welfare. . . . Revolution is the war waged by liberty against its enemies; a constitution . . . crowns the edifice of freedom once victory has been won and the nation is at peace. . . . The principal concern of a constitutional government is civil liberty; that of a revolutionary government, public liberty. [A] revolutionary government is obliged to defend the state itself against the factions that assail it from every quarter. To good citizens revolutionary government owes the full protection of the state; to the enemies of the people it owes only death.

Is a revolutionary government the less just and the less legitimate because it must be more vigorous in its actions and freer in its movement than ordinary government? . . . It also has its rules, all based on justice and public order. . . . It has nothing in common with arbitrary rule; it is public interest which governs it and not the whims of private individuals.

Thanks to five years of treason and tyranny, thanks to our credulity and lack of foresight . . . Austria and England, Russia, Prussia, and Italy had time to set up in our country a secret government to challenge the authority of our own. . . . We shall strike terror, not in the hearts of patriots, but in the haunts of foreign brigands.

*Source:* George Rudé, ed., *Robespierre* (Englewood Cliffs, N.J.: Prentice-Hall, 1967), pp. 58–63.

---

In the name of "reason," traditional rituals and rhythms of life were changed. One reform of long-term significance was the introduction of the metric system of weights and measures. Although people continued to use the old, familiar measures for a very long time, the change was eventually accomplished, leading the way for standardization throughout Europe. Equally "rational" but not as successful was the elimination of the traditional calendar; weeks and months were replaced by forty-day months and *decadi* (ten-day weeks with one day of rest), and all saints' days and Christian holidays were eliminated. The years had already been changed—Year I had been declared with the founding of the republic in the autumn of 1792.

Churches were rededicated as "temples of reason." Believing that outright atheism left people with no basis for personal or national morality, Robespierre sought instead to promote a cult of the Supreme Being. The new public festivals were solemn civic ceremonies intended to ritualize and legitimize the new political order. These and other innovations of the regime were not necessarily welcomed. The French people generally resented the elimination of the traditional calendar. In the countryside massive peasant uprisings protested the loss of poor relief, community life, and familiar ritual.

Divorce law and economic regulation were a boon, especially to urban women, but women's participation in sectional assemblies and in all organized political activity—which had been energetic and widespread—was banned in October 1793. The particular target of the regime was the Society of Revolutionary Republican Women, a powerful club representing the interests of female sans-culottes. By banning women from political life, the regime helped to ground its legitimacy, since the seemingly "natural" exclusion of women might make the new system of government appear part of the "natural" order. (See the feature "Weighing the Evidence: Political Symbols" on pages 674–675.) Outlawing women's clubs and barring women from section assemblies also eliminated a source of popular power, from which the regime was now trying to distance itself.

The Committee and the Convention were divided over religious and other policies, but the main policy differences concerned economic matters: how far to go to assist the poor, the unemployed, and the landless. Several of the temperate critics of Robespierre and his allies were guillotined for disagreeing with these policies and for doubting the continuing need for the Terror itself. Their deaths helped precipitate the end of the Terror by causing Robespierre's power base to shrink so much that it had no further legitimacy.

Deputies to the Convention finally dared to move against Robespierre in July 1794. French armies had scored a major victory over Austrian troops on June 26, so there was no longer any need for the emergency status that the Terror had thrived on. In late July the Convention voted to arrest Robespierre, the head of the revolutionary tribunal in Paris, and their closest associates and allies in the city government. On July 28 and 29, Robespierre and the others—about a hundred in all—were guillotined, and the Terror ended.

### ■ Thermidorian Reaction and the Directory, 1794–1799

After the death of Robespierre, the Convention reclaimed many of the executive powers that the Committee of Public Safety had seized. The Convention dismantled the apparatus of the Terror, repealed the Law of Suspects, and forced the revolutionary tribunals to adopt ordinary legal procedures. The Convention also passed into law some initiatives, such as expanded public education, that had been proposed in the preceding year but not enacted. This post-Terror phase of the Revolution is called the "Thermidorian Reaction" because it began in the revolutionary month of Thermidor (July 19–August 17).

Lacking the weapons of the Terror, the Convention was unable to enforce controls on the supply and price of bread. Thus, economic difficulties and a hard winter produced famine by the spring of 1795. The people of Paris tried to retain influence with the new government. In May crowds marched on the Convention chanting "Bread and the Constitution of '93," referring to the republican constitution drafted by the Convention but never implemented because of the Terror. The demonstrations were met with force and were dispersed.

Members of the Convention remained fearful of a renewed, popularly supported Terror, on the one hand, or a royalist uprising, on the other. Counterrevolutionary uprisings had erupted in the fall of 1794, and landings on French territory by émigré forces occurred the following spring. The Convention drafted a new constitution that limited popular participation in government, as had the first constitution of 1791. The new plan allowed fairly widespread (but not universal) male suffrage, but only for electors, who would choose deputies for the two houses of the legislature. The property qualifications for being an elector were very high, so all but elite citizens were effectively disenfranchised. The Convention also decreed, at the last minute, that two-thirds of its members must serve in the new legislature, regardless of the outcome of elections. Though this maneuver enhanced the stability of the new regime, it undermined the credibility of the new ballot.

Governance under the provisions of the new constitution, beginning in the fall of 1795, was called the Directory, for the executive council of five men chosen by the upper house of the new legislature. To avoid the concentration of authority that had produced the Terror, the members of the Convention had tried to enshrine separation of powers in the new system. However, the governments under the Directory were never free from attempted coups or from their own extraconstitutional maneuvering.

The most spectacular external challenge, the Conspiracy of Equals, was led by extreme Jacobins who wanted to restore popular government and aggressive economic and social policy on behalf of the common people. The conspiracy ended with arrests and executions in 1797. When elections in 1797 and 1798 returned many royalist as well as Jacobin deputies, the Directory itself abrogated the constitution to forestall challenges to its authority: many undesirable deputies were arrested, sent into exile, or denied seats.

The armies of the republic did enjoy some spectacular successes during these years, for the first time carrying the fighting—and the effects of the Revolution—onto foreign soil. French armies conquered the Dutch in 1795. In 1796–1797 French armies led by the young general

Napoleon Bonaparte° wrested control of northern Italy from the Austrians. Both regions were transformed into "sister" republics, governed by local revolutionaries but under French protection. By 1799, however, conditions had once again reached a critical juncture. The demands of the war effort, together with rising prices and the continued decline in the value of the assignats, brought the government again to the brink of bankruptcy. The government also seemed to be losing control of the French countryside; there were continued royalist uprisings, local political vendettas between moderates and Jacobins, as well as outright banditry.

Members of the Directory had often turned to sympathetic army commanders to suppress dissent and to carry out arrests and purges of the legislature. They now invited General Bonaparte to help them form a government that they could more strictly control. Two members of the Directory plotted with Napoleon and his brother, Louis Bonaparte, to seize power on November 9, 1799.

# THE NAPOLEONIC ERA AND THE LEGACY OF REVOLUTION, 1799–1815

TALENTED, charming, and ruthless, Napoleon Bonaparte (1769–1821) was the kind of person who gives rise to myths. His audacity, determination, and personal magnetism enabled him to profit from the political instability and confusion in France and to ensconce himself in power. Once in power, he temporarily stabilized the political scene by fixing in law the more conservative gains of the Revolution. He also used his power and his remarkable abilities as a general to continue wars of conquest against France's neighbors, which helped deflect political tensions at home.

Napoleon's troops, in effect, exported the Revolution as they conquered most of Europe. In most states that came under French control, law codes were reformed, governing elites opened to talent, and public works upgraded. Yet French conquest also meant domination, pure and simple, and involvement in France's rivalry with Britain. The Napoleonic era left Europe an ambiguous legacy—war and its complex aftermath yet also revolution and its goad to further change.

---

**Napoleon Bonaparte** (nuh-POLE-ee-un BONE-uh-part)

## ■ Napoleon: From Soldier to Emperor, 1799–1804

Napoleon was from Corsica, a Mediterranean island that had passed from Genoese to French control in the eighteenth century. The second son of a large gentry family, he was educated at military academies in France, and he married the politically well-connected widow Joséphine de Beauharnais (1763–1814), whose aristocratic husband had been a victim of the Terror.

Napoleon steered a careful course through the political turmoil of the Revolution. By 1799 his military victories had won him much praise and fame. He had demonstrated his reliability and ruthlessness in 1795 when he ordered troops guarding the Convention to fire on a Parisian crowd. He had capped his successful Italian campaign of 1796–1797 with an invasion of Egypt in an attempt to strike at British influence and trade connections in the eastern Mediterranean. The Egyptian campaign failed in its goals, but individual spectacular victories during the campaign ensured Napoleon's military reputation. In addition, Napoleon had demonstrated his widening ambitions. He had taken leading scientists and skilled administrators with him to Egypt in order to export the seeming benefits of French civilization—and to install a more lasting bureaucratic authority.

Napoleon's partners in the new government after the November 1799 coup soon learned of his great political ambition and skill. In theory, the new system was to be a streamlined version of the Directory: Napoleon was to be first among equals in a three-man executive—First Consul, according to borrowed Roman terminology. But Napoleon quickly asserted his primacy among them and began not only to dominate executive functions but also to bypass the authority of the regime's various legislative bodies.

Perhaps most important to the success of his increasingly authoritarian rule was his effort to include, among his ministers, advisers, and bureaucrats, men of many political stripes—Jacobins, reforming liberals, even former Old Regime bureaucrats. He welcomed many exiles back to France, including all but the most ardent royalists. He thus stabilized his regime by healing some of the rifts among ruling elites. Napoleon combined toleration with ruthlessness, however. Between 1800 and 1804 he imprisoned, executed, or exiled dozens of individuals for alleged Jacobin agitation or royalist sympathies. His final gesture to intimidate royalist opposition came in 1804 when he kidnapped and coldly murdered a Bourbon prince who had been living in exile in Germany.

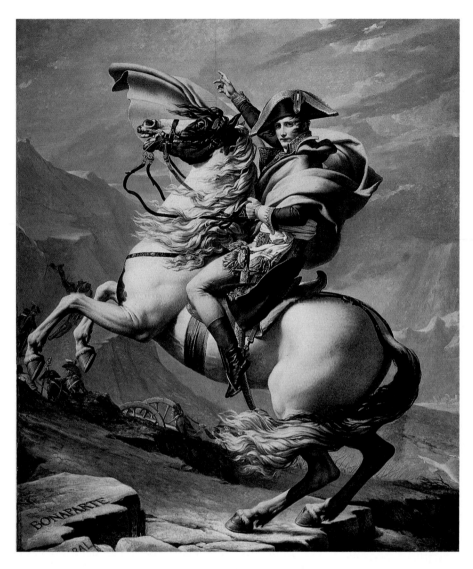

**Napoleon Crossing the Great St. Bernard**   This stirring portrait by the great neoclassical painter Jacques-Louis David memorializes Napoleon's 1796 crossing of the Alps before his victorious Italian campaign, as a general under the Directory. In part because it was executed in 1801–1802, the painting depicts the moment heroically rather than realistically. (In truth, Napoleon wisely crossed the Alps on a sure-footed mule, not a stallion.) Napoleon, as First Consul, wanted images of himself that would justify his increasingly ambitious claims to power.   *(Réunion des Musées Nationaux/Art Resource, NY)*

Under Napoleon's regime, any semblance of free political life ended. Legislative bodies lost all initiative in the governing process, becoming rubber stamps for the consuls' policies. In any case, there were no meaningful elections. Voters chose only candidates for a kind of pool of potential legislators, from which occasional replacements were chosen by sitting legislators! Political clubs were banned; the vibrant press of the revolutionary years wilted under heavy censorship. Napoleon also further centralized the administrative system, set up by the first wave of revolutionaries in 1789, by establishing the office of prefect to govern the départements. All prefects and their subordinates were appointed by Napoleon, thus extending the range of his power and undermining autonomous local government.

Certain administrative changes that enhanced central control, such as for tax collection, were more uniformly positive in their effects. Napoleon oversaw the establishment of the Bank of France, modeled on the Bank of England. The bank provided capital for investment and helped the state stabilize the French currency. Perhaps the most important achievement early in his regime was the Concordat of 1801. The aim of this treaty with the pope was to solve the problem of church-state relations that for years had provoked counterrevolutionary rebellions. The agreement allowed for the resumption of Catholic worship and the continued support of the clergy by the state, but also accepted the more dramatic changes accomplished by the Revolution. Church lands that had been sold were guaranteed to their new owners. Protestant churches were also allowed and their clergy were paid, although Catholicism was recognized as the "religion of the majority of Frenchmen." Later, Napoleon granted new rights to Jews also. Nonetheless, the Concordat removed one of the most important grounds for counterrevolutionary upheaval in the countryside and defused royalist resistance from abroad.

The law code that Napoleon established in 1804 was much like his accommodation with the church in its limited acceptance of revolutionary gains. His Civil Code (also known as the *code napoléon*, or Napoleonic Code) honored the revolutionary legacy in its guarantee of equality before the law and its requirement for the taxation of all social classes; it also enshrined modern forms of property ownership and civil contracts. Neither the code nor Napoleon's political regime fostered individual rights, especially for women. Fathers' control over their families was enhanced. Divorce was no longer permitted except in rare instances. Women lost all property rights when they married, and they generally faced legal domination by fathers and husbands.

Napoleon was careful, though, to avoid heavy-handed displays of power. He cleverly sought ratification of each stage of his assumption of power through national plebiscites (referendums in which all eligible voters could vote for or against proposals)—one plebiscite for a new constitution in 1800 and another when he claimed consulship for life in 1802. He approached his final political coup—declaring himself emperor—with similar dexterity. Long before he claimed the imperial title, Napoleon had begun to sponsor an active court life appropriate to imperial pretensions. The empire was proclaimed in May 1804 with the approval of the Senate; it was also endorsed by another plebiscite. Members of Napoleon's family were given princely status, and a number of his favorites received various titles and honors. The titles brought no legal privilege but signaled social and political distinctions of great importance. Old nobles were allowed to use their titles on this basis.

Many members of the elite, whatever their persuasions, tolerated Napoleon's claims to power because he safeguarded fundamental revolutionary gains yet reconfirmed their own status. War soon resumed against political and economic enemies—principally Britain, Austria, and Russia—and, for a time, Napoleon's success on the battlefield continued. Because military glory was central to the political purpose and self-esteem of elites, Napoleon's early successes as emperor further enhanced his power.

## ■ Conquering Europe, 1805–1810

Napoleon maintained relatively peaceful relations with other nations while he consolidated power at home, but the truces did not last. Tensions with the British quickly re-escalated when Britain resumed aggression against French shipping in 1803, and Napoleon countered by seizing Hanover, the ancestral German home of the English king. England was at war on the high seas with Spain and the Netherlands, which Napoleon had forced to enter the fray. Napoleon began to gather a large French force on the northern coast of France; his objective was to invade England.

The British fleet, commanded by Horatio Nelson (1758–1805), intercepted the combined French and Spanish fleets that were to have been the invasion flotilla and inflicted a devastating defeat off Cape Trafalgar in southern Spain (see Map 19.1) on October 21, 1805. The victory ensured British mastery of the seas and, in the long run, contributed to Napoleon's demise. In the short run, the defeat at Trafalgar paled for the French beside Napoleon's impressive victories on land. Even as the French admirals were preparing for battle, Napoleon had abandoned the plans to invade England and in August had begun to march his army east through Germany to confront the great continental powers, Austria and Russia.

In December 1805, after some preliminary, small-scale victories, Napoleon's army routed a combined Austrian and Russian force near Austerlitz°, north of Vienna (see Map 19.1). The Battle of Austerlitz was Napoleon's most spectacular victory. Austria sued for peace. In further battles in 1806, French forces defeated Prussian as well as Russian armies once again. Prussia was virtually dismembered by the subsequent Treaty of Tilsit (1807), but Napoleon tried to remake Russia into a contented ally. His hold on central Europe would not be secure with a hostile Russia, nor would the anti-British economic system that he envisioned—the Continental System (see page 666)—be workable without Russian participation.

French forces were still trying to prevail in Spain, which had been a client state since its defeat by revolutionary armies in 1795 but was resisting outright rule by a French-imposed king. In 1808, however, Napoleon turned his attention to more fully subduing Austria. Napoleon won the Battle of Wagram° in July 1809, and Austria, like Russia, accepted French political and economic hegemony in a sort of alliance. By 1810 Napoleon had transformed most of Europe into allied or dependent

---

**Austerlitz** (AW-stir-lits)    **Wagram** (VAHG-rahm)

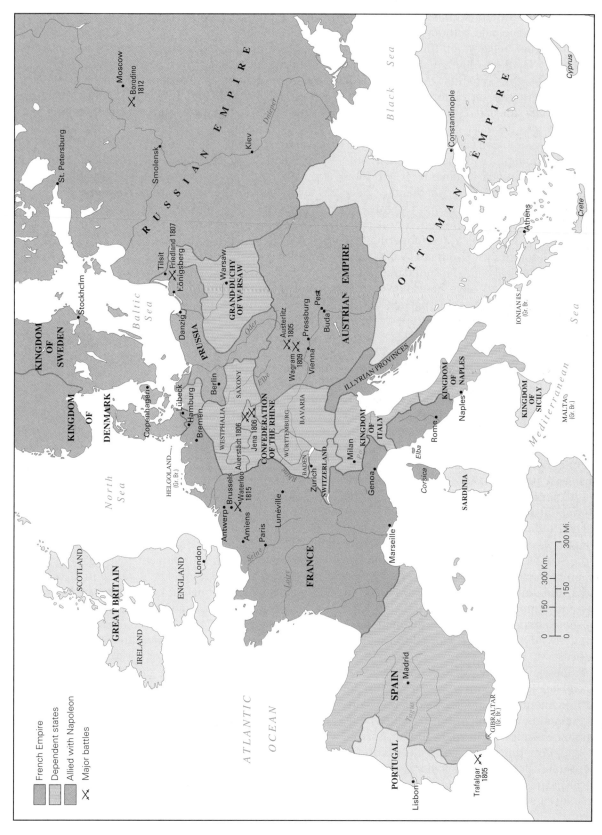

**Map 19.1  Napoleonic Europe, ca. 1810**  France dominated continental Europe after Napoleon's victories.

**"And It Cannot Be Changed"**
This horrifying scene of an execution of rebels against French rule in Spain was one of a series of etchings by Madrid artist Francisco Goya. In the 1810 series, titled "The Disasters of War," Goya was severely critical of French actions as well as of barbarities committed by the British-backed Spaniards.
*(Foto Marburg/Art Resource, NY)*

states (see Map 19.1). The only exceptions were Britain and the parts of Spain and Portugal that continued, with British help, to resist France.

The states least affected by French hegemony were its reluctant allies: Austria, Russia, and the Scandinavian countries. Denmark had allied with France in 1807 only for help in fending off British naval supremacy in the Baltic. Sweden had reluctantly made peace in 1810 after losing control of Finland to Napoleon's ally, Russia, and only minimally participated in the Continental System. At the other extreme were territories that had been incorporated into France. These included the Austrian Netherlands, territory along the Rhineland, and sections of Italy that bordered France. These regions were occupied by French troops and were treated as though they were départements of France itself.

In most other areas, some form of French-controlled government was in place, usually headed by a member of Napoleon's family. In both northern Italy and the Netherlands, where "sister" republics had been established after French conquests under the Directory, Napoleon imposed monarchies. Rulers were also installed in the kingdom of Naples and in Spain. Western German states

of the Holy Roman Empire that had allied with Napoleon against Austria were organized into the Confederation of the Rhine, with Napoleon as its "Protector." After a thousand years, the Holy Roman Empire ceased to exist. Two further states were created, largely out of the defeated Prussia's territory: the kingdom of Westphalia in western Germany and the grand duchy of Warsaw in the east (see Map 19.1).

Napoleon's domination of these various regions had complex, and at times contradictory, consequences. On the one hand, Napoleonic armies essentially exported the French Revolution, in that French domination brought with it the Napoleonic Civil Code, and with it political and economic reform akin to that of the early phases of the Revolution. Equality before the law was decreed following the French example; this meant the end of noble exemption from taxation in the many areas where it existed. In general, the complex snarl of medieval taxes and tolls was replaced with straightforward property taxes that were universally applied. As a consequence, tax revenues rose dramatically—by 50 percent in the kingdom of Italy, for example. Serfdom and forced labor were also abolished, as they had been in France in August 1789.

In most Catholic regions, the church was subjected to the terms of the Concordat of 1801. The tithe was abolished, church property seized and sold, and religious orders dissolved. Though Catholicism remained the state-supported religion in these areas, Protestantism was tolerated and Jews were granted rights of citizenship. Secular education, at least for males, was encouraged.

On the other hand, Napoleon would countenance in the empire only those aspects of France's revolutionary legacy that he tolerated in France itself. Just as he had suppressed any meaningful participatory government in France, so too did he suppress it in conquered regions. This came as a blow in states such as the Netherlands, which had experienced its own democratizing "Patriot" movement and which had enjoyed republican self-government after invasion by French armies during the Revolution itself. Throughout the Napoleonic Empire, many of the benefits of streamlined administration and taxation were offset by the drain of continual warfare; deficits rose three- and fourfold, despite increased revenues. In addition, one of the inevitable costs of empire was political compromise to secure allies. In the duchy of Warsaw, reconstituted from lands Prussia had seized in the eighteenth century, Napoleon tampered little with either noble privileges or the power of the church. And, throughout Europe, Napoleon randomly allotted lands to reward his greatest generals and ministers, thereby exempting those lands from taxation and control by his own bureaucracy.

If true self-government was not allowed, a broad segment of the elite in all regions was nevertheless won over to cooperation with Napoleon by being welcomed into his bureaucracy or into the large multinational army, called the *Grande Armée*. Their loyalty was cemented when they bought confiscated church lands.

The impact of Napoleon's Continental System was equally mixed. Under this system, the Continent was in theory closed to all British shipping and British goods. The effects were widespread but uneven, and smuggling to evade controls on British goods became a major enterprise. Regions heavily involved in trade with Britain or its colonies or dependent on British shipping suffered in the new system, as did overseas trade in general when Britain gained dominance of the seas after Trafalgar. However, the closing of the Continent to British trade, combined with increases in demand to supply Napoleon's armies, spurred the development of continental industries, at least in the short run. This industrial growth, enhanced by the improvement of roads, canals, and the like, formed the basis for further industrial development.

## ■ Defeat and Abdication, 1812–1815

Whatever its achievements, Napoleon's empire was ultimately precarious because of the hostility of Austria and Russia, as well as the belligerence of Britain. Russia was a particularly weak link in the chain of alliances and subject states because Russian landowners and merchants were angered when their vital trade in timber for the British navy was interrupted and when supplies of luxury goods, brought in British ships, began to dwindle. A century of close alliances with German ruling houses made alliance with a French ruler an extremely difficult political option for Tsar Alexander I.

It was Napoleon, however, who ended the alliance by provoking a breach with Russia. He suddenly backed away from an arrangement to marry one of Alexander's sisters and accepted the Austrian princess Marie Louise instead. (He had reluctantly divorced Joséphine in 1809 because their marriage had not produced an heir.) Also, he seized lands along the German Baltic seacoast belonging to a member of Alexander's family. When Alexander threatened rupture of the alliance if the lands were not returned, Napoleon mounted an invasion. Advisers warned him about the magnitude of the task he seemed so eager to undertake—particularly about the preparations needed for winter fighting in Russia—but their alarms went unheard.

Napoleon's previous military successes had stemmed from a combination of strategic innovations and pure audacity. Napoleon divided his forces into independent corps. Each corps included infantry, cavalry, and artillery. Organized in these workable units, his armies could travel quickly by several separate routes and converge in massive force to face the enemy. Leadership on the battlefield came from a loyal and extremely talented officer corps that had grown up since army commands had been thrown open to nonaristocrats during the Revolution. The final ingredient in the success formula was the high morale of French troops. Since the first victory of the revolutionary armies in September 1792, citizen-soldiers had proved their worth. Complicated troop movements and bravery on the battlefield were possible when troops felt they were fighting for their *nation*, not merely their ruling dynasty. Napoleon's reputation as a winning general added a further measure of self-confidence.

The campaign against Russia began in June 1812. It was a spectacular failure. Napoleon had gathered a force of about 700,000 men—about half from France and half from allied states—a force twice as large as Russia's. The strategy of quickly moving independent corps and assembling massive forces could not be implemented: simply mustering so many men along the border was already the equivalent of gathering them for battle. Bold victories had often enabled Napoleon's troops to live off the countryside while they waited for supplies to catch up to the front line. But when the enemy attacked supply lines, when the distances traveled were very great, when the countryside was impoverished, or when battles were not decisive, Napoleon's ambitious strategies proved futile. In varying degrees, these conditions prevailed in Russia.

By the time the French faced the Russians in the principal battle of the Russian campaign—at Borodino°, west of Moscow (see Map 19.1)—the Grande Armée had been on the march for two and a half months and stood at less than half its original strength. After the indecisive but bloody battle, the French occupied and pillaged Moscow but found scarcely enough food and supplies to sustain them. When Napoleon finally led his troops out of Moscow late in October, the fate of the French forces was all but sealed. As they retreated, French and allied soldiers who had not died in battle died of exposure or starvation or were killed by Russian peasants when they wandered away from their units. The talents of generals and the determination of troops were focused on sheer survival. Of the original 700,000 troops of the Grand Armée, fewer than 100,000 made it out of Russia. (See the box "Reading Sources: A Napoleonic Soldier Recounts the Horrors of the Russian Campaign.")

Napoleon left his army before it was fully out of Russia. A coup attempt in Paris prompted him to return to his governing duties before the French people realized the extent of the disaster in the east. The collapse of his reign had begun, spurred by a coincidental defeat in Spain. Since 1808 Spain had been largely under French domination, with Napoleon's brother, Joseph, as king. A rebel cortes (national representative assembly), however, continued to meet in territory that the French did not control, and British troops were never expelled from the Iberian Peninsula. In 1812, as Napoleon was advancing against Russia, the collapse of French control accelerated. By the time Napoleon reached Paris at the turn of the new year, Joseph had been expelled from Spain, and an Anglo-Spanish force led by the duke of Wellington was poised to invade France.

Napoleon lost his last chance to stave off a coalition of all major powers against him when he refused an Aus-

trian offer of peace for the return of conquered Austrian territories. With Britain willing to subsidize the allied armies, Tsar Alexander determined to destroy Napoleon, and the Austrians now anxious to share the spoils, Napoleon's empire began to crumble. Imperial forces—many now raw recruits—were crushed in a massive "Battle of Nations" near Leipzig in October, during which some troops from German satellite states deserted him on the battlefield. The allies invaded France and forced Napoleon to abdicate on April 6, 1814.

Napoleon was exiled to the island of Elba, off France's Mediterranean coast, but was still treated somewhat royally. He was installed as the island's ruler and was given an income drawn on the French treasury. Meanwhile, however, the restored French king was having his own troubles. Louis XVIII (r. 1814–1824) was the brother of the executed Louis XVI; he took the number eighteen out of respect for Louis XVI's son, who had died in prison in 1795. The new monarch had been out of the country and out of touch with its circumstances since the beginning of the Revolution. In addition to the delicate task of establishing his own legitimacy, he faced enormous practical problems, including pensioning off thousands of soldiers now unemployed and still loyal to Napoleon.

Napoleon, bored and almost penniless on his island kingdom (the promised French pension never materialized), took advantage of the circumstances and returned surreptitiously to France on February 26, 1815. His small band of attendants was joined by the soldiers sent by the king to halt his progress. Louis XVIII abandoned Paris to the returned emperor.

Napoleon's triumphant return lasted only one hundred days, however. Though many soldiers welcomed his return, many members of the elite were reluctant to throw in their lot with Napoleon again. Many ordinary French citizens had also become disenchanted with him since the defeat in Russia, and with the high costs, in conscription and taxation, of raising new armies. In any case, Napoleon's reappearance galvanized the divided allies, who had been haggling over a peace settlement, into unity. Napoleon tried to strike first, but he lost against English and Prussian troops in his first major battle, at Waterloo (in modern Belgium; see Map 19.1) on June 18, 1815. When Napoleon arrived in Paris after the defeat, he discovered the government in the hands of an ad hoc committee that included the Marquis de Lafayette. Under pressure, he abdicated once again. This time, he was exiled to the tiny, remote island of St. Helena in the South Atlantic, from which escape would be impossible. He died there in 1821.

---

**Borodino** (bore-uh-DEE-no)

**&a READING SOURCES**

## A Napoleonic Soldier Recounts the Horrors of the Russian Campaign

*Jakob Walter, a stonemason from western Germany, was conscripted in 1806 into the army of a German prince, an ally of Napoleon against Prussia and Austria. In 1812, aged 24, he marched into Russia with the massive Grande Armée and was one of the lucky few to survive the campaign. Some years afterward, Walter recorded his memoirs of military life in the citizen army—including its appalling dehumanization. In this passage, he describes the fleeing army's crossing of the Berezina River (in modern Belarus). Thousands managed to ford the Berezina thanks to the heroic work of French engineers, many of whom died constructing the bridges. But the horror of the crossing, in Walter's experience, almost overshadows the fact that part of the army was saved. This excerpt also provides a glimpse of the extreme privation that the soldiers endured.*

When I had gone somewhat further . . . I met a man who had a sack of raw bran in which there was hardly a dust of flour. I begged him ceaselessly to sell me a little of the bran, pressing a silver ruble into his hand; so he put a few handfuls in my little cloth. . . . When I and my master came closer to the Beresina, we camped on a near-by hill and by contributing wood I obtained a place at the fire. I immediately mixed some snow with my bran . . . [and] allowed it to heat red on the outside in order to obtain something like bread from the inside. . . .

After a time . . . the Russians pressed nearer and nearer from every side, and the murdering and torturing seemed to annihilate everyone. . . . When it became day again, we stood near the stream approximately a thousand paces from the two bridges. . . . However, one could not see the bridges because of the crowd of people, horses and wagons. Everyone crowded together into a solid mass, and nowhere could one see a way out or a means of rescue. From

morning til night we stood unprotected from the cannonballs and grenades which the Russians hurled at us from two sides. . . . I had to kneel on [my horse] in order not to have my feet crushed off, for everything was so closely packed that in a quarter of an hour one could move only four or five steps forward. To be on foot was to lose all hope of rescue. . . . Everyone was screaming under the feet of the horses, and everywhere was the cry, "Shoot me. . . ." Finally, toward four o'clock in the evening, when it was almost dark, I came to the bridge. . . . Now it is with horror, but at that time it was with a dull, indifferent feeling, that I looked at the masses of horses and people that lay dead, piled upon the bridge.

*Source:* Jakob Walter, *The Diary of a Napoleonic Footsoldier,* ed. by Marc Raeff (New York: Penguin Books, 1993), pp. 83–86.

 **For additional information on this topic, go to http://college.hmco.com.**

## ■ The Legacy of Revolution for France and the World

The process of change in France between 1789 and 1815 was so complex that it is easy to overlook the overall impact of the Revolution. Superficially, the changes seemed to come full circle—with first Louis XVI on the throne, then Napoleon as emperor, and then Louis XVIII on the throne. Even though the monarchy was restored, however, the Revolution had discredited absolute monarchy in theory and practice. Louis XVIII had to recognize the right of "the people," however narrowly defined, to participate in government and to enjoy due process of law. Another critical legacy of the Revolution and the Napoleonic era was a centralized political system of départements rather than a patchwork of provinces. For the first time, a single code of law applied to all French people. Most officials—from département administrators to city mayors—were appointed by the central government until the late twentieth century. The conscientious attention of the government, at various stages of the Revolution, to advances for France generally reflects the positive side of this centralization. The government sponsored national scientific societies, a national library and archives, and a system of teachers' colleges and universities. Particularly under Napoleon, a spate of canal- and road-building projects drastically improved transport systems.

Napoleon's legacy, like that of the Revolution itself, was mixed. His self-serving reconciliation of aristocratic pretensions with the opening of careers to men of talent ensured the long-term success of revolutionary principles from which the elite as a whole profited. His reconciliation of the state with the Catholic Church helped to stabilize his regime and cemented some revolutionary gains. The restored monarchy could not renege on these gains. Yet whatever his achievements, Napoleon's overthrow of constitutional principles worsened the problem of political instability. His brief return to power in 1815 reflects the degree to which his power had always been rooted in military adventurism and in the loyalty of soldiers and officers. Similarly, the swiftness of his collapse suggests that although the empire under Napoleon may have seemed an enduring solution to the political instability of the late 1790s, it was no more secure than any of the other revolutionary governments.

Although Louis XVIII acknowledged the principle of constitutionalism at the end of the Revolution, the particular configuration of his regime rested on fragile footing. Indeed, the fragility of new political systems was one of the most profound lessons of the Revolution. There was division over policies, but even greater division over legitimacy—that is, the acceptance by a significant portion of the politically active citizenry of a particular government's right to rule. Before the Revolution started, notions about political legitimacy had undergone a significant shift. The deputies who declared themselves to be the National Assembly in June 1789 already believed that they had a right to do so. In their view, they represented "the nation," and their voice had legitimacy for that reason. The shift reflects not the innate power of ideas but the power of ideas in context. These deputies brought to Versailles not only their individual convictions that "reason" should be applied to the political system but also their experience in social settings where those ideas were well received. In their salons, clubs, and literary societies, they had experienced the familiarity, trust, and sense of community that are essential to effective political action.

The deputies' attempt to transplant their sense of community into national politics was not wholly successful. Factions, competing interests, and clashes of personality can be fatal to an insecure system. The National Assembly had scarcely been inaugurated when its deputies guaranteed its failure by disqualifying themselves from standing for office under the new constitution. The king also actively undermined the system because he disagreed with it in principle. The British parliamentary system, by comparison, though every bit as elitist as the narrowest of the representative systems during the French Revolution, had a long history as a workable institution for lords, commoners, and rulers. This shared experience was an important counterweight to differences over fundamental issues, so that Parliament as an institution both survived political crises and helped resolve them. The Revolution thus left a powerful yet ambiguous legacy for France. Politics was established on new principles, yet still lacking were the practical means to achieve the promise inherent in those principles.

Throughout Europe and overseas, the Revolution left a powerful and equally complex legacy. France's continental conquests were the least enduring of the changes of the revolutionary era. Nevertheless, French domination had certain lasting effects: elites were exposed to modern bureaucratic management, and equality under the law transformed social and political relationships. Although national self-determination had an enemy in Napoleon, the breaking down of ancient political divisions provided important practical grounding for later cooperation among elites in nationalist movements. In Napoleon's kingdom of Italy, for example, a tax collector from Florence for the first time worked side by side with one from Milan. The most important legacy of the revolutionary wars, however, was the change in warfare itself made possible by the citizen armies of the French. Citizen soldiers who identified closely with their nation, even when conscripts, proved able to maneuver and attack on the battlefield in ways that the brutishly disciplined poor conscripts in other armies would not. In response, other states tried to build competing armies; the mass national armies that fought the world wars of the twentieth century were the result.

Naturally, the most important legacy of the French Revolution, as of the American, was the success of the revolution itself. The most powerful absolute monarchy in Europe had succumbed to the demands of its people for dramatic social and political reforms. Throughout

**Haitian Leader Toussaint-Louverture**    Son of an educated slave, Toussaint-Louverture had himself been freed in 1777 but took on a leadership role when the slave revolt began on Saint Domingue in 1791. His military skill and political acumen were vital to the success of the revolt and to ruling the island's diverse population afterward.    *(Stock Montage, Inc.)*

Europe, in the nineteenth century, ruling dynasties faced revolutionary movements that demanded constitutional government, among other changes, and resorted to force to achieve it. European colonies overseas felt the impact of the Revolution and subsequent European wars in several ways. The British tried to take advantage of Napoleon's preoccupation with continental affairs by seizing French colonies and the colonies of the French-dominated Dutch. In 1806 they seized the Dutch colony of Capetown—crucial for support of trade around Africa—as well as French bases along the African coast. In 1811 they grabbed the island of Java. In the Caribbean, the French sugar-producing islands of Martinique and Guadeloupe were particularly vulnerable to English sea power while Napoleon was executing his brilliant victories on the Continent after 1805. On the most productive of the French-controlled Caribbean islands, Saint Domingue°, the Revolution inspired a successful rebellion by the enslaved plantation workers.

The National Assembly in Paris had delayed abolishing slavery in French colonies, despite the moral appeal of such a move, because of pressure from the white planters and out of fear that the financially strapped French government would lose some of its profitable sugar trade. But the example of revolutionary daring in Paris and confusion about ruling authority as the Assembly and the king wrangled did not go unnoticed in the colonies—in either plantation mansions or slave quarters. White planters on Saint Domingue simply hoped for political and economic "liberty" from the French government and its mercantilist trade policies. White planter rule was challenged, in turn, by wealthy people of mixed European and African descent who wanted equal citizenship, hitherto denied them. A civil war broke out between these upper classes and was followed by a full-fledged slave rebellion, beginning in 1791. (See the box "Global Encounters: A Planter's Wife on the Haitian Slave Revolt.") Britain sent aid to the rebels when it went to war against the French revolutionary government in 1793. Only when the republic was declared in Paris and the Convention abolished slavery did the rebels abandon alliances with France's enemies and attempt to govern in concert with the mother country.

Though it recovered other colonies from the British, France never regained control of Saint Domingue. Led by a former slave, François Dominique Toussaint-Louverture° (1743–1803), the new government of the island tried to run its own affairs, though without formally declaring independence from France. Napoleon, early in his rule, decided to tighten control of the profitable colonies by reinstituting slavery and ousting the independent government of Saint Domingue. In 1802 French forces fought their way onto the island. They captured Toussaint-Louverture, who died shortly thereafter in prison. But in 1803 another rebellion provoked by the threat of renewed slavery expelled French forces for good. A former aide of Toussaint's declared the independence of the colony under the name Haiti—the island's Native American name—on January 1, 1804.

The French Revolution and Napoleonic rule, and the example of the Haitian revolution, had a notable impact on Spanish colonies in the Americas also. Like other American colonies, the Spanish colonies wanted to loosen the closed economic ties the mother country tried to impose. In addition, the liberal ideas that had helped

**Saint Domingue** (SAHN dome-ANGUE)
**Toussaint-Louverture** (too-SAHN–loo-ver-TOUR)

## A Planter's Wife on the Haitian Slave Revolt

*The following are excerpts from two letters of Madame de Rouvray, a wealthy planter's wife living in the French colony of Saint Domingue (the western half of the island of Hispaniola), to her married daughter in France. The decree of May 15, 1791, that Madame de Rouvray mentions in her first letter granted civil rights to free persons of mixed race. The decree affected only a few hundred persons on Saint Domingue (many of whom themselves owned slaves), but white planters feared any breach in the barriers between the races. Tensions between white planters, on the one hand, and mulattos and modest white settlers who favored revolutionary changes, on the other, enabled the well-organized slave rebellion to be dramatically successful. It began in late August 1791 and is the backdrop to Madame de Rouvray's second letter. Madame de Rouvray and her husband fled the island for the United States in 1793.*

July 30, 1791

I am writing to you from Cap [a city on the island] where I came to find out what the general mood is here. . . . All the deputies who make up the general assembly [of the colony] left here the day before yesterday to gather at Léogane [another city]. If they conduct themselves wisely their first action should be to send emissaries to all the powers who have colonies with slaves in order to tell them of the decree [of May 15] and of the consequences that will follow from it, and ask for help from them in case it happens that the National Assembly actually abolishes slavery too, which they will surely do. After their decree of May 15, one cannot doubt that that is their plan. And you understand that all the powers who have slave colonies have a common interest in opposing such a crazy plan because the contagion of liberty will soon infect their colonies too, especially in nearby Jamaica. It is said that [the English] will send a ship and troops [which] would be wonderful for us. Your father thinks it won't be long before the English take control here.

September 4, 1791

If news of the horrors that have happened here since the 23rd of last month have reached you, you must have been very worried. Luckily, we are all safe. We can't say whether our fortunes are also safe because we are still at war with the slaves who revolted [and] who have slaughtered and torched much of the countryside hereabouts. . . . All of this will gravely damage our revenues for this year and for the future, because how can we stay in a country where slaves have raised their hands against their masters? . . . You have no idea, my dear, of the state of this colony; it would make you tremble. Don't breathe a word of this to anyone but your father is determined, once the rebels have been defeated, to take refuge in Havanna.

*Source:* M. E. McIntosh and B. C. Weber, *Une Correspondance familiale au temps des troubles de Saint-Domingue* (Paris: Société de l'Histoire des Colonies Françaises et Librairie Larose, 1959), pp. 22–23, 26–28. Trans. by Kristen B. Neuschel.

spawn the French Revolution spurred moves toward independence in Spanish America. Taking advantage of the confusion of authority in Spain, some of these colonies were already governing themselves independently in all but name. Echoes of radical republican ideology and of the Haitian experience resounded in some corners. For example, participants in two major rebellions in Mexico espoused the end of slavery and championed the interests of the poor against local and Spanish elites. The leaders of these self-declared revolutions were executed (in 1811 and 1815), and their movements were crushed by local elites in alliance with Spanish troops. The efforts of local elites to become self-governing—the attempted liberal revolutions—were little more successful. Only Argentina and Paraguay broke away from Spain at this time.

But as in Europe, a legacy remained of both limited and more radical revolutionary activity, and of its risks. Slave rebellions rocked British Caribbean islands in subsequent decades. Other colonies had learned a lesson from the Haitian revolution and were determined to avoid the horrors that had surrounded that struggle for freedom. In some regions dominated by plantations, such as some British possessions and the Spanish island of Cuba, planters were reluctant to disturb the prevailing order with any liberal political demands.

### ■ The View from Britain

Today the city of Paris is dotted with public monuments that celebrate Napoleon's victories. In London another hero and other victories are celebrated. In Trafalgar Square stands a statue of Lord Nelson, the British naval commander whose fleet destroyed a combined French and Spanish navy in 1805. Horatio Nelson was a brilliant tactician, whose innovations in maneuvering ships in

the battle line resulted in stunning victories at Trafalgar and, in 1798, at the Nile Delta, which limited French ambitions in Egypt and the eastern Mediterranean. Trafalgar looms large in British history because it ensured British mastery of the seas, which then forced Napoleon into economic policies that strained French ties to France's allies and satellites. Virtually unchallenged sea power enabled the British to seize colonies formerly ruled by France and its allies.

Britain's maritime supremacy and seizure of French possessions expanded British trading networks overseas—though in some cases only temporarily—and closer to home, particularly in the Mediterranean. As long as the British had been involved in trade with India, the Mediterranean had been important for economic and strategic reasons: it marked the end of the land route for trade from the Indian Ocean. Especially after Napoleon's aggression in Egypt, the British redoubled their efforts to control strategic outposts in the Mediterranean, such as ports in southern Italy and on the island of Malta.

The British economy would expand dramatically in the nineteenth century as industrial production soared. The roots for growth were laid in this period in the coun-

**The Funeral of Lord Nelson, January 8, 1806**  Nelson had been mortally wounded on the deck of his flagship at the Battle of Trafalgar in October. Rather than being buried at sea, as was the custom, his body was returned to London for an impressive state funeral, commemorated here in a contemporary engraving.  *(National Maritime Museum, London)*

tryside of Britain, where changes in agriculture and in production were occurring. These roots were also laid in Britain's overseas possessions as tighter control of foreign sources of raw materials, notably raw Indian cotton, meant rising fortunes back in Britain. In regions of India, the East India Company was increasing its political domination, and hence its economic stranglehold on Indian commodities. The export of Indian cotton rose significantly during the revolutionary period as part of an expanding trading system that included China, the source of tea.

However, economic expansion was not the sole motive for British aggression. In fact, economic expansion was often a by-product of increased British control of particular regions or sea-lanes, and the reasons for it were as much strategic as economic. Not every conquest had direct economic payoffs, but British elites were sure that strategic domination was a desirable step, wherever it could be managed. One Scottish landholder, writing in the opening years of the nineteenth century, spoke for many when he said that Britain needed an empire to ensure its greatness and that an empire of the sea was an effective counterweight to Napoleon's empire on land. Much as the French were at that moment exporting features of their own political system, the British, he said, could export their constitution wherever they conquered territory.

Thus, England and France were engaged in similar phases of expansion in this period. In both, the desire for power and profit drove policy. In each, myths about heroes and about the supposed benefits of domination masked the state's self-interest. For both, the effects of conquest would become a fundamental shaping force in the nineteenth century.

## SUMMARY

THE French Revolution was a watershed in European history because it successfully challenged the principles of hereditary rule and political privilege by which all European states had hitherto been governed. The Revolution began when a financial crisis forced the monarchy to confront the desire for political reform by a segment of the French elite. Political philosophy emerging from the Enlightenment and the example of the American Revolution moved the French reformers to action. In its initial phase, the French Revolution established the principle of constitutional government and ended many of the traditional political privileges of the Old Regime.

Then, because of the intransigence of the king, the threat of foreign invasion, and the actions of republican legislators and Parisian citizens, the Revolution moved in more radical directions. Its most extremist phase, the Terror, produced the most effective legislation for ordinary citizens but also the worst violence of the Revolution. A period of unstable conservative rule that followed the Terror ended when Napoleon seized power.

Though Napoleonic rule solidified some of the gains of the Revolution, it also subjected France and most of Europe to the great costs of wars of conquest. After Napoleon, the French monarchy was restored but henceforth its power would not be absolute—and the people would not be refused a voice in government—as a result of the Revolution. Indeed, hereditary rule and traditional social hierarchies remained in place in much of Europe, but they would not be secure in the future. The legacy of revolutionary change would prove impossible to contain in France or anywhere else.

### ■ Notes

1. Quoted in Samuel Eliot Morrison, *John Paul Jones: A Sailor's Biography* (Boston: Little, Brown, 1959), pp. 149–154.
2. Quoted in Owen Connelly, *The French Revolution and the Napoleonic Era* (New York: Holt, Rinehart and Winston, 1979), p. 32.
3. James Harvey Robinson, *Readings in European History* (Boston: Ginn, 1906), p. 409.

### ■ Suggested Reading

Baker, Keith Michael. *Inventing the French Revolution.* 1990. A series of essays situating the Revolution amid the dramatic changes in eighteenth-century political culture.

Hunt, Lynn. *The French Revolution and Human Rights: A Brief Documentary History.* 1996. A well-presented short collection of documents, useful for a greater understanding of the impact of the Revolution on the development of human rights.

Jordan, D. P. *The King's Trial.* 1979. An engaging study of Louis XVI's trial and its importance for the Revolution.

Landes, Joan. *Women and the Public Sphere in the Age of the French Revolution.* 1988. An analysis of the uses of gender ideology to fashion the new political world of the revolutionaries.

Langley, Lester D. *The Americas in the Age of Revolution, 1750–1850.* 1996. A survey of all the American states and colonies and the impact of the Atlantic revolutions.

Popkin, Jeremy. *A Short History of the French Revolution.* 1995. A compact and readable recent synthesis of research.

 **For a searchable list of additional readings for this chapter, go to http://college.hmco.com.**

# Political Symbols

**An Armed Citizen, ca. 1792**  *(Bibliothèque Nationale de France)*

During the French Revolution, thousands of illustrations in support of various revolutionary (or counterrevolutionary) ideas were reproduced on posters, on handbills, and in pamphlets. Some satirized their subjects, such as Marie Antoinette, or celebrated revolutionary milestones, such as the fall of the Bastille. The etching here of the woman armed with a pike, dating from 1792, falls into this category. Other pictures, such as the representation from 1795 of Liberty as a young woman wearing the liberty cap, symbolized or reinforced various revolutionary ideals.*

Political images like these are an invaluable though problematic source for historians. Let us examine these two images of women and consider how French people during the Revolution might have responded to them. To understand what they meant to contemporaries, we must know something about the other images that these would have been compared to. We must also view the images in the context of the events of the Revolution itself. Immediately, then, we are presented with an interpretive agenda. How ordinary and acceptable was this image of an armed woman? If women were not citizens coequal with men, how could a woman be a symbol of liberty? What, in short, do these political images reveal about the spectrum of political life in their society?

The woman holding the pike stares determinedly at the viewer. Many details confirm what the original caption announced: This is a French woman who has become free. In her hat she wears one of the symbols of revolutionary nationhood: the tricolor cockade. The badge around her waist celebrates a defining moment for the revolutionary nation: the fall of the Bastille. Her pike itself is inscribed with the words "Liberty or death!"

---

*This discussion draws on the work of Joan Landes, "Representing the Body Politic: The Paradox of Gender in the Graphic Politics of the French Revolution," and Darlene Gay Levy and Harriet B. Applewhite, "Women and Militant Citizenship in Revolutionary Paris," in Sara E. Melzer and Leslie W. Rabine, eds., *Rebel Daughters: Women and the French Revolution* (New York: Oxford University Press, 1992), pp. 15–37, 79–101.

The woman appears to be serving not merely as a symbol of free women. She comes close to being the generic image of a free citizen, willing and able to fight for liberty—an astonishing symbolic possibility in a time when women were not yet treated equally under the law or granted the same political rights as the men of their class. Other images prevalent at the time echo this possibility. Many contemporary representations of the women's march on Versailles in 1789 show women carrying arms, active in advancing the Revolution. By the time this image was created (most likely in 1792), many other demonstrations and violent confrontations by ordinary people had resulted in the creation of dozens of popular prints and engravings that showed women acting in the same ways as men.

Repeatedly during 1792, women proposed to the revolutionary government that they be granted the right to bear arms. Their request was denied, but it was not dismissed out of hand. There was debate, and the issue was in effect tabled. Nevertheless, women's actions in the Revolution had created at least the possibility of envisaging citizenship with a female face.

The image of liberty from 1795 does not reflect the actions of women but rather represents their exclusion from political participation. It is one of a number of images of Liberty that portray this ideal as a passive, innocent woman, here garbed in ancient dress, surrounded by a glow that in the past had been reserved for saints. Liberty here is envisaged as a pure and lofty goal, symbolized as a pure young woman.

Late in 1793, during the Terror, women were excluded from formal participation in politics with the disbanding of women's organizations. Nor did they gain political rights under the Directory, which re-established some of the limited gains of the first phase of the Revolution. The justification offered for their exclusion in 1793 was borrowed from Rousseau: it is contrary to nature for women to be in public life (see page 611). Women "belong" in the private world of the family, where they will nurture male citizens. Women embody ideal qualities such as patience and self-sacrifice; they are not fully formed beings capable of action in their own right.

Such notions made it easy to use images of women to embody ideals for public purposes. A woman could represent Liberty precisely because actual women were not able to be political players.

The two images shown here thus demonstrate that political symbols can have varying relationships to "re-

**"Liberty" as a Young Woman, ca. 1795** *(S. P. Avery Collection, Miriam and Ira D. Wallach Division of Art, Prints, and Photographs, The New York Public Library, Astor, Lenox, and Tilden Foundations)*

ality." The pike-bearing citizen is the more "real." Her image reflects the way of thinking about politics that became possible for the first time because of their actions. The other woman reflects not the attributes of actual women but an ideal type spawned by the use of arbitrary gender distinctions to legitimize political power. In these images we can see modern political life taking shape: the sophistication of its symbolic language, the importance of abstract ideas such as liberty and nationhood—as well as the grounding of much political life in rigid distinctions between public and private, male and female.

 **For any additional information on this topic, go to http://college.hmco.com.**

# CHAPTER 20

# The Industrial Transformation of Europe 1750–1850

W ITH fires spewing from factory chimneys, it was hard to distinguish day from night. At night the sky was so lit up it might be daytime. During the day smoke and smog so obscured the sunlight that it might be night. Shropshire, England, a region previously renowned for its natural beauty, was transformed by industrial activity by 1788, when this painting was made. Containing in proximity both coal and iron deposits, Shropshire was the ideal site for establishing ironworks. Here Abraham Darby (1676–1717) and his descendants built one of the largest and most important concentrations of ironworks in Britain. The dramatic rise in the use of new machinery, which led to previously unheard of levels in production of iron and textiles, struck contemporaries. In the 1830s the French socialist Louis Blanqui° (see page 720) would propose a descriptive term, suggesting that just as France had recently experienced a political revolution, so Britain was undergoing an "industrial revolution." Eventually, that expression entered the general vocabulary to describe the advances in production that occurred first in England and then dominated most of western Europe by the end of the nineteenth century. Many economic historians now emphasize how gradual and cumulative the changes were and question the appropriateness of the term. Indeed, it seems best to discuss the changes not as an industrial revolution but as a continuous process of economic transformation.

Industrial development left its mark on just about every sphere of human activity. Scientific and rational methods altered production. Economic activity became increasingly specialized. The unit of production changed from the family to a larger and less personal group. Significant numbers of workers left farming to enter mining and

**Blanqui** (blahn-KEE)

**Setting the Stage for Industrialization**

**Industrialization and European Production**

**The Transformation of Europe and Its Environment**

**Responses to Industrialization**

George Robertson, *Nat-Y-Glo Iron Works.*
(National Museums & Galleries of Wales)

manufacturing, and major portions of the population moved from rural to urban environments. Machines replaced or supplemented manual labor.[1]

The economic changes brought about by industrial development physically transformed Europe. Greater levels of production were achieved, and more wealth was created, than ever before. Factory chimneys belched soot into the air. Miners in search of coal, iron ore, and other minerals cut deep gashes into the earth. Cities, spurred by industrialization, grew quickly, and Europe became increasingly urban.

Industrialization simultaneously created unprecedented advancement and opportunity as well as unprecedented hardships and social problems. Workers, with a growing sense of solidarity, struggled to protect and advance their interests.

---

### QUESTIONS TO CONSIDER

■ Why did Europe industrialize before the rest of the world?

■ Which inventions appear to have been the most important in launching industrialization?

■ What impact did industrialization have on the environment?

■ What did workers gain and what did they lose as a result of industrialization?

### TERMS TO KNOW

| | |
|---|---|
| industrialization | urbanization |
| steam engine | friendly societies |
| entrepreneurship | proletariat |
| factories | Luddite |
| mass production | |

---

## SETTING THE STAGE FOR INDUSTRIALIZATION

NO one can say with certainty what conditions were necessary for the industrialization of Europe. Nevertheless, we do know why industrialization did not spread widely to the rest of the world in the nineteenth century. A certain combination of conditions—geographic, cultural, economic, demographic—helped make industrialization possible in Europe.

### ■ Why Europe?

A unique set of circumstances seems to explain why Europe was the stage for industrial development. With the development of legal due process, rich merchants did not run the risk of having their wealth confiscated—as they did, for instance, in the Ottoman Empire, where sultans and corrupt officials on a whim grabbed wealth. Hence in the West accumulating wealth was a worthwhile endeavor. The unfolding of state power in Europe reduced the frequency of highway robbery—still common in many parts of the world—and thus encouraged trade.

In Europe, disparities of wealth, though serious, were less extreme than in other parts of the world; thus, there was a better market for goods. At the time western Europe industrialized, the average yearly income per person was equivalent to $500—more than the amount in many non-Western societies even today. And nearly half of the population was literate, again a very high proportion compared with non-Western societies.

Although Europe's population grew during the eighteenth century, late marriages and limited family sizes kept its rise in check. European society was therefore rarely overwhelmed by population pressure; because all of its energies were not absorbed feeding its people, Europe could mobilize for other production.

Compared with Asia, Europe enjoyed greater cultural, political, and social diversity. Challenges to dominant religious and political powers had brought some diversity—a rarity in Asia, where large territories tended to be dominated by a single ruler and faith. Diversity encouraged a culture that tolerated and eventually promoted innovation. Competitiveness drove states to try to outdo one another. Governments actively encouraged industries and commerce to enrich their countries and make them more powerful than their neighbors. None of these factors alone explains why industrialization occurred, but their combination seems to have facilitated the process when it did occur.[2]

The industrialization of Europe radically transformed power relationships between the industrial West and nonindustrial Africa, Asia, and South America. By 1900 the West had overwhelmed the other regions with its economic and military power. Within Europe, power shifted to the most industrial nation. Britain, the first to industrialize, was the dominant political power throughout the nineteenth century. The rest of Europe admired Britain and regarded it not only as an economic model but also as a political and cultural one. As France had been the dominant power in the eighteenth century, so Britain dominated the nineteenth, a stellar accomplishment for a small island nation.

## ■ Transformations Accompanying Industrialization

A number of transformations preceded or accompanied and helped define the industrializing era. Changes in commerce, agriculture, transportation, and behavior of the population, if not always creating the preconditions of industrial development directly, were at least the major stimuli making them possible.

Changes in agriculture increased the productivity of the land. Farmers more frequently used fertilizer and improved the rotation of their crops, easing the exhaustion of the soil. New, more efficient plows enabled them to cultivate more land than ever before. In the eighteenth century, new crops that provided high yields even in poor soil were introduced into Europe: maize (corn) and potatoes from the Americas. The wealth created by agriculture allowed for investment in industry and for expenditures on infrastructure, such as roads and canal systems, useful to industry. More prosperous farmers could purchase manufactured goods such as iron plows and even machine-woven textiles, thus providing an impetus for industry. Most important, the new crops and the more efficient cultivation of traditional ones increased the capacity to feed a growing population and freed many people to go to the city and work in the industries.

In the seventeenth and eighteenth centuries, European trade had grown significantly, enriching entrepreneurs and making them aware of the fortunes to be made by marketing high-demand goods not just locally but even far away. A new dynamic ethos inspired entrepreneurs to venture into untried fields of economic endeavor.

During the years of the industrial transformation, population grew, enough to promote industrialization, yet not so much as to put a brake on economic expansion. The first spurt in population growth occurred in the mid-eighteenth century, before the effects of industrialization could be widely felt. Thereafter the population of

### CHRONOLOGY

| | |
|---|---|
| 1712 | Newcomen invents steam-operated water pump |
| 1733 | Kay invents flying shuttle |
| 1750–1800 | 3 million Africans are brought to the Americas as slaves |
| 1753 | First steam engine in the Americas |
| 1760s | Hargreaves invents spinning jenny |
| 1765 | Watt improves steam engine with separate condenser |
| 1769 | Arkwright invents water frame |
| 1777 | Watt and Arkwright build power loom |
| 1793 | Whitney invents cotton gin |
| 1811–1812 | Luddites |
| 1825 | Börsig builds first steam engine in Germany |
| 1832 | Cholera epidemic |
| 1831, 1834 | Workers' uprising in Lyon |
| 1834 | Creation of German Customs Union, the Zollverein |
| 1844 | Workers' uprising in Silesia |
| 1851 | Majority of Britain's population becomes urban |

Europe increased dramatically throughout the industrial era: from 1750 to 1850 it doubled.

This growth was largely due to a lowering of the death rate. Infant mortality had been very high from diseases such as smallpox, diphtheria, and tuberculosis. Although none of these diseases had been medically conquered, improved standards of living after 1750, such as greater food intake, enabled children to better resist killer diseases. Better employment opportunities led to earlier marriages and thus higher fertility. Most of the population increase occurred in the countryside. This growing group of people supplied the labor force for the new industries and provided the large surge in consumers of various industrial goods.

In the countryside industrialization was foreshadowed by a form of production that had developed beginning in the seventeenth century—the putting-out system, or cottage industry. During the winter and at other slack times, peasants took in handwork such as spinning, weaving, or dyeing. Often they were marginal agriculturists, who on a part-time basis were able to augment their incomes. Entrepreneurs discovered that some individuals were better than others at specific tasks. Rather than have one household process the wool through all the steps of production until it was a finished piece, the entrepreneur would buy wool from one family, then take it to another to spin, a third to dye, a fourth to weave, and so on. Some historians believe that this form of production, also called protoindustrialization, laid the basis for industrial manufacture. Both protoindustrialization and industrial manufacture depended on specialization; both of them supplied goods to a market beyond the producers' needs. Although cottage industry was an important contributor to industrialization in some regions, that was not the case everywhere.

A less ambiguous prerequisite for industry was a good transportation network. Transportation improved significantly in the eighteenth century. Better roads were built; new coaches and carriages could travel faster and carry heavier loads. Government and private companies built canals linking rivers to each other or to lakes. Road- and canal-building were important preconditions for industrialization, hastening and cheapening transportation and making possible the movement of raw materials to manufacture and products to market without too great an increase in the price of the finished good. In Great Britain these transformations occurred simultaneously with industrialization; on the Continent they were actual precursors to economic change.

In Britain industrialization preceded the development of railroads; yet once railroad expansion occurred, beginning in the 1830s, the order for iron rails, steam engines, and wagons sustained and advanced industrial growth. (See the box "Global Encounters: A Persian Discovers the British Rail System.") On the Continent rail-building stimulated industrialization, notably in Germany and later in Italy.

**First Railroad, from Manchester to Liverpool**   The engineer George Stephenson (1781–1848) first built engines that could pull coal at mines; then in 1821 he constructed the first "locomotive" for public transportation. Four years later the first regular railroad line, connecting Manchester with Liverpool, was erected.   *(Private Collection/The Bridgeman Art Library, London and New York)*

⊕ G L O B A L   E N C O U N T E R S

# A Persian Discovers the British Rail System

*In 1836 a delegation of three Persian princes visited England. Traveling widely, they had the opportunity to meet important Englishmen and to inspect and experience some of the country's latest technological advances, including the railroad. One of the princes, Najaf-Kuli Mirza, wrote down his observations. In this entry on the new British rail system, he attempts to describe its workings to fellow Persians.*

All the wonderful arts which require strong power are carried on by means of steam, which has rendered immense profits and advantages. The English then began to think of steam coaches, which are especially applicable to their country, because it is small, but contains an enormous population. Therefore, in order to do away with the necessity for horses, and that the land which is sown with horse-corn [rye] should be cultivated with wheat, so as to cause it to become much more plentiful (as it is the most important article of food), and that England might thereby support a much greater population, they have with their ingenious skill invented this miraculous wonder, so as to have railroads from the capital to all parts of the kingdom.

Thus, by geometrical wisdom, they have made roads of iron, and where it was necessary these roads are elevated on arches. The roads on which the coaches are placed and fixed are made of iron bars. The coach is so fixed that no air or wind can do it any harm and twenty or thirty coaches may be fixed to the first in the train, and these one after the other.

All that seems to draw these coaches is a box of iron, in which they put water to boil, as in a fire-place; underneath this iron box is like an urn, and from it rises the steam which gives the wonderful force: when the steam rises up, the wheels take their motion, the coach spreads its wings, and the travellers become like birds. In this way these coaches go the incredible distance of forty miles an hour.

We actually travelled in this coach, and we found it very agreeable, and it does not give more but even less motion than horses; whenever we came to the sight of a distant place, in a second we passed it. The little steam engine possesses the power of eighteen horses.

*Source:* Najaf-Kuli Mirza, *Journal of a Residence in England and of a Journey to and from Syria* II (London: 1839; reprint, Farnborough, England: Gregg International Publishers, 1971), pp. 11–12.

# INDUSTRIALIZATION AND EUROPEAN PRODUCTION

EVERAL important technological advances powered European industry, and breakthroughs in one field often led to breakthroughs in others. The first two industries to be affected by major technological breakthroughs were textiles and iron. New forms of energy drove the machinery; novel methods of directing labor and organizing management further enhanced production. At first limited to the British Isles, industry spread to the Continent, a development that occurred unevenly in various regions and at different times.

## ■ Advances in the Cotton Industry

A series of inventions in the eighteenth century led the way to the mass manufacture of textiles. One of the earliest was the flying shuttle, introduced in Britain in 1733 by John Kay (1704–1764). (A shuttle carries the thread back and forth on a loom.) Kay's flying shuttle accelerated the weaving process to such an extent that it increased the demand for thread. This need was met in the 1760s by James Hargreaves (d. 1778), who invented the

**British Cotton Manufacture**    Machines simultaneously performed various functions. The carding machine (*front left*) separated cotton fibers, readying them for spinning. The roving machine (*front right*) wound the cotton onto spools. The drawing machine (*rear left*) wove patterns into the cloth. Rich in machines, this factory needed relatively few employees; most were women and children. *(The Granger Collection, New York)*

spinning jenny, a device that spun thread from wool or cotton. Improvements, such as the "mule" of Samuel Crompton (1753–1827), made the spinning jenny increasingly efficient, and by 1812 one jenny could produce as much yarn as two hundred hand spinners. In 1769 Richard Arkwright (1732–1792), a barber and wigmaker, invented the water frame. It was installed in a single establishment with three hundred employees, forming the first modern factory. The frame was originally powered by horses or by a waterfall, but in 1777 Arkwright had James Watt construct a steam engine to operate it, the first power loom. With these innovations, cotton manufacturing was fully mechanized; its output increased 130-fold between 1770 and 1841.

The cotton manufacturing industry in Great Britain was an important departure from traditional production. For the first time in history a staple industry was based on a natural resource that was not domestically produced. Grown mainly in the U.S. South, cotton was transformed into cloth in Britain. Manufactured cotton was comfortable to wear and easy to wash; it became so cheap that it competed effectively with all handmade textiles. The popularity of cotton may have improved public health as well, for it enabled people to own several changes of clothing and keep them clean. Everyone was eager to buy British cottons. The higher demand for raw material put pressure on cotton growers in the U.S. South, who opened up new land.

In 1793 the American Eli Whitney (1765–1825) invented the cotton gin, a device that mechanically removed the seeds from cotton, formerly a laborious hand process. The cotton gin meant that more cotton could be processed and thus more could be grown. Almost overnight the machine heightened the profitability of the United States's southern plantation economy, and that situation increased the attractiveness of slave labor.

Between 1750 and 1800 approximately 3 million Africans were forcibly transported to the New World. The demographic loss to Africa was great; at least 10 percent of the captives died in the "middle passage," while being transported to the Americas, and an unknown number died in the wars triggered by slavers. Since predominantly young men were enslaved, villages were often left without their most productive workers and became vulnerable to famine, which also may have decimated the population.

The slave economy in the Americas influenced Britain's economy in several ways. Sugar produced by slave labor in the West Indies and cotton in the American South shifted Britain's trade patterns from Asia to the Atlantic. The sophisticated administrative skills that went into organizing and operating the slave trade provided invaluable management experience to the more conventional sectors of the British economy. Although some historians have argued that Britain's industrialization was founded on the wealth generated by the traffic in humans, the evidence is far from conclusive. Yet, once industrialized, Britain's economy benefited enormously from processing sugar and cotton, staples produced by slaves.

In ways beneficial and not, people were interconnected by the cotton trade; later other products would also link the economies of various nations and peoples. No longer, as in preindustrial trade, were all goods locally made, nor did the consumer meet producers and buy from them. Increasingly, specialization became the norm. Those most skilled performed a particular function efficiently and productively. The results were high production and low prices for the finished products.

## ■ Iron, Steam, and Factories

Industrial production was facilitated by the use of a new energy source, coal. Traditionally, charcoal had fueled the smelting of iron. Britain, however, ran low on wood—the source for charcoal—before other European countries did and needed an alternative fuel. There was plenty of coal, but it contained impurities, particularly sulfur, which contaminated the materials with which it came into contact. In 1708 the English ironmaster Abraham Darby discovered that coal in a blast furnace could smelt iron without these attending complications. His discovery triggered the iron industry's use of coal. In 1777 the introduction of a steam engine to operate the blast furnace considerably increased efficiency. In 1783 a

steam engine was first used to drive a forge hammer to shape the iron; three years later, steam-driven rollers flattened the iron into sheets. With these innovations, the output of the English iron industry doubled between 1788 and 1796 and again in the following eight years.

The greater supply of iron stimulated other changes. Relatively cheap and durable iron machines replaced wooden machines, which wore out rapidly. The new machines opened the door to further advances. Improvements in manufacturing methods and techniques led to the production of ever larger amounts of goods, usually at lower prices. Industrial change started with cotton, but breakthroughs in the use of iron and coal continued and sustained these changes.

Before the age of industry, the basic sources of power were humans, animals, wind, and water. Humans and animals were limited in their capacities to drive the large mills needed to grind grain or cut wood. Wind was unreliable because it was not constant. Water-driven mills depended on the seasons—streams dried up in the summer and froze in the winter. And water mills could be placed only where a downward flow of water was strong enough to drive a watermill. Clearly the infant industries needed a power source that was constant and not confined to riverbanks. The steam engine, invented and improved on in Britain, met that need and stoked the island's industrial growth. As late as the 1860s people, animals, and wind- and water-operated machines still supplied more than half of the energy needs of manufacturing in Great Britain and the United States. But the steam engine was clearly the wave of the future.

The steam engine was first used to pump water out of coal mines. As mining shafts were dug ever deeper through groundwater, drainage became a critical factor. In 1712 Thomas Newcomen (1663–1729) invented a steam-operated water pump. Its use spread rapidly. The first steam engine in the Americas was a Newcomen engine installed in New Jersey in 1753. James Watt (1736–1819) improved on the Newcomen engine considerably, making it twice as efficient in energy output. Eventually, by developing a separate condenser, Watt devised an engine that could convert the reciprocating motion of the piston to the more functional rotary motion. This breakthrough enabled the steam engine to power a variety of machines. (See the box "Reading Sources: James Watt Receives a Patent for the Steam Engine.") Thus, steam engines could operate mills that had previously been powered by water or wind. The high-pressure steam engine was even more powerful and energy-efficient. The use of steam engines spread in Britain, to the Continent, and to the United States.

**Newcomen Engine** Thomas Newcomen, a hardware merchant, produced the first successful operating steam engine in 1712. Steam was introduced into a cylinder that was then cooled, creating a partial vacuum. The pressure of the atmosphere forced the piston down, pulling down one end of the beam and creating a pumping stroke. The engine could make as many as fourteen pumping strokes a minute. *(The Fotomas Index, U.K.)*

The steam engine centralized the workplace. With the machine as a central power source, it became practical and commonplace to organize work in a factory. Locating a manufacturing plant where it was most convenient eliminated the expense of transporting raw materials to be worked on at a natural but fixed power source such as a waterfall. The central factory also reinforced work discipline. These factories were large, austere edifices, sometimes inspired by military architecture and therefore resembling barracks. With the introduction of blast furnaces and other heat-producing manufacturing methods, the tall factory chimney became a common sight on the industrial landscape.

The steam engine powered a dramatic growth in production. It increased the force of blast furnaces and the mechanical power of machinery used to forge iron and to produce equipment for spinning and weaving. Assisted by machines, workers were enormously more productive than when they depended solely on hand-operated tools. In 1700 spinning 100 pounds of cotton took 50,000 worker-hours; by 1825, it took only 135—a 370-fold increase in productivity capacity per worker.

### ■ Inventions and Entrepreneurs

Inventions triggered the industrial age, and the continued flow of new ones sustained it. In the decade 1700–1709, 22 patents had been issued in Britain; between 1840 and 1849, 4,581 were issued. Something revolutionary was occurring. People were seeing in their lifetimes sizable growth in productivity, both in the factory and on the farm. Rather than cling to traditional methods, many entrepreneurs consciously and persistently challenged tradition and attempted to find new ways of improving production. In this age of invention, innovation was prized as never before.

The early industrialists came from a variety of backgrounds. In Britain very few were landed nobles, industrial workers, or artisans. A large number of the early manufacturers were university educated, a fact suggesting that even in the early stages of industry, scientific knowledge was valuable. Most came from the merchant class, since also in these early years the possession of capital was a distinct advantage in launching an industrial enterprise.

Entrepreneurs such as Arkwright and Watt pioneered innovations and became famous, but most who advanced the cause of industrial production were not particularly inventive. They just replicated methods of production that had proved profitable to others. Truly successful entrepreneurs, however, seemed to share one attribute: they were driven by a nearly insatiable appetite for innovation, work, and profit.

Entrepreneurs took the financial risk of investing in new types of enterprises. Most industrialists ran a single plant by themselves or with a partner, but even in the early stages, some ran several plants. In 1788 Richard Arkwright and his partners ran eight mills. Some enterprises were vertically integrated, controlling production at many stages. The Peels in Britain owned operations ranging from spinning to printing and even banking. The entrepreneurs' dynamism and boldness fostered the growth of the British industrial system, making that small nation the "workshop of the world."

## ≥ READING SOURCES

### James Watt Receives a Patent for the Steam Engine

*British laws encouraged innovation by promoting and protecting patents, which guaranteed inventors sole rights to profit from their inventions for a set time. Watt had first received a patent for a fourteen-year period in 1769, but by 1775 after lots of experiments, he was uncertain that his efforts to develop an even more efficient engine would succeed. So he sought and received a twenty-five-year extension. This document, granting the extension, expresses the state's vested interest in industrialization and explains its willing support of men such as Watt.*

And whereas, the said James Watt hath employed many years, and . . . whereas, in order to manufacture these engines with the necessary accuracy, and so that they may be sold at moderate prices, a considerable sum of money must be previously expended in erecting mills, and other apparatus; and as several years, and repeated proofs, will be required before any considerable part of the publick can be fully convinced of the utility of the invention, and of their interest to adopt the same, the whole term granted by the said Letters Patent may probably elapse before the said James Watt can receive an advantage adequate to his labour and invention:

And whereas, by furnishing mechanical powers at much less expense, and in more convenient forms, than has hitherto been done, his engines may be of great utility in facilitating the operations in many great works and manufacturers of this kingdom; yet it will not be in the power of the said James Watt to carry his invention into that complete execution which he wishes, and so as to render the same of the highest utility to the publick of which it is capable, unless the term granted by the said Letters patent be prolonged . . . be it enacted, by the King's Most Excellent Majesty . . . that the said *James Watt*, his executors, administrators, and assigns, shall and lawfully may have and enjoy the whole profit, benefit, commodity and advantage, from time to time coming, growing, accruing, and arising, by reason of these his said inventions, for the said term of twenty-five years, to have, hold, receive and enjoy the same, for and during and to the full end and term of twenty-five years as aforesaid. . . .

*Source:* B. W. Clapp, H. E. S. Fisher, and A. R. J. Jurica, eds. *Documents in English History* (London: G. Bell & Sons, 1976), pp. 147–149.

### ■ Britain's Lead in Industrial Innovation

Britain led the way industrially for many reasons. It was the first European country to have a standard currency, tax, and tariff system. Although Britain was by no means an egalitarian society, it accommodated some movement between the classes. Ideas and experiments were readily communicated among entrepreneurs, workers, and scientists.

In addition, England had gained an increasing share of international trade since the seventeenth century. This trade provided capital for investment in industrial plants. The world trade network also ensured that Britain had a market beyond its borders, and because total demand was relatively high, mass manufacture was feasible. The international trade network also enabled Britain to import raw materials for its industry, the most important of which was cotton.

Earlier than its competitors, Britain had a national banking system that could finance industries in areas where private funding fell short. In addition to numerous London banks lending mainly in the capital, six hundred provincial banks serviced the economy by 1810. The banking system reflected the growth of the economy as much as it contributed to it. Banking could flourish because Britons had wide experience in trade,

**Map 20.1    The Industrial Transformation in England, ca. 1850**    Industry developed in the areas rich in coal and iron fields. Important cities sprang up nearby and were soon linked by a growing rail network.

had accumulated considerable amounts of wealth, and had found a constant demand for credit.

Geographically, Britain was also fortunate. Coal and iron were located close to each other (see Map 20.1). A relatively narrow island, virtually all of Britain has easy access to the sea—no part of the country is more than 70 miles from a seacoast. This was a strategic advantage, for water was by far the cheapest means of transportation. Compared with the Continent, Britain had few tolls, and moving goods was relatively easy and inexpensive.

On the whole, British workers were better off than their continental counterparts. They were more skilled, earned higher wages, and had discretionary income to spend on the manufactured goods now for sale. But because labor was more costly than on the Continent, British business owners had an incentive to find labor-saving devices and reduce the number of workers needed for production.

Population growth in Great Britain—in part the result of industrial growth—increased by 8 percent in each decade from 1750 to 1800. This swelling population expanded the market for goods. The most rapid growth occurred in the countryside, causing a steady movement of people from rural to urban areas. The presence of this work force was another contributing factor in Britain's readiness for change.

Britain was far more open to dissent than were other European countries at the time. The lack of conformity was reflected in religion, and also in a willingness to try new methods of production. In fact, the two often went together. A large proportion of British entrepreneurs were Quakers or belonged to one of the dissenting (non-Anglican) religious groups—for instance, the iron-making Darby family; the engineer of the steam engine, James Watt; and the inventor of the "mule," Samuel Crompton. Perhaps dissenters were accustomed to questioning authority and treading new paths. They were also well educated and, as a result of common religious bonds, inclined to provide mutual aid, including financial support.

The timing of the industrial transformation in Britain was also influenced by plentiful harvests in the years 1715–1750, creating low food prices and thus making possible low industrial wages. The demand for industrial goods was reasonably high. Farmers with good earnings could afford to order the new manufactured iron plows. It is likely that income from farming helped bring about changes associated with industrialization, such as population growth, improvements to the transportation system, and the growing availability of capital for investment. Thus, each change triggered more change; the cumulative effect was staggering.

## ■ The Spread of Industry to the Continent

The ideas and methods that were changing industry in Britain spread to the Continent by direct contact and by emulation. Visitors came to Britain, studied local methods of production, and returned home to set up blast furnaces and spinning works inspired by British design. The German engineer August Börsig° (1804–1854), after studying steam engines in Britain, built the first German steam engine in 1825 and the first German locomotive in 1842. Some visitors even resorted to industrial espionage, smuggling blueprints of machines out of Britain. Although a British law forbade local artisans to emigrate, some did leave, including entrepreneurs who helped set up industrial plants in France and Belgium. By the 1820s

**Börsig** (BEUR-sick)

British technicians were all over Europe—in Belgium, France, Germany, and Austria.

In the eighteenth century France had seemed a more likely candidate for economic growth than Britain. France's overseas trade was growing faster than Britain's. In 1780 France's industrial output was greater than Britain's, though production per person was less. In the nineteenth century, however, while Britain's industry boomed and it became the workshop of the world, France lagged behind. Why?

Historians have suggested several reasons. The wars and revolutions of the late eighteenth century were certainly contributing factors. They slowed economic growth and cut France off from the flow of information and new techniques from Britain. Moreover, in the 1790s, when the French peasants pressured for legislation to ease their situation, the revolutionaries responded positively. Thus, the misery of the peasantry was somewhat relieved, and peasants were comfortable enough to feel no urgency to leave the land and provide the kind of cheap and ready labor that Britain had. Further, the Napoleonic Code of 1804 abolished primogeniture, so that when a peasant died, his younger sons were not forced off the land.

Population figures suggest another reason for France's relatively low economic growth. Between 1800 and 1914, the population of France grew at half the average rate experienced by the rest of the Continent. In Britain during this period, much of the labor that left the land and worked the factories and mills came from the rural population explosion. But no such phenomenon occurred in the French countryside, and thus the labor force in France was not poised for industrial growth.

Traditionally France had produced high-quality luxury goods, and French entrepreneurs who sought to emulate British accomplishments faced serious difficulties.

**The Börsig Ironworks in the 1840s**  August Börsig, an artisan, founded these ironworks in Berlin. The factory expanded to meet the needs of the burgeoning German rail system. By the time of Börsig's death in 1854, his factory had built five hundred locomotives.  *(Bildarchiv Preussischer Kulturbesitz)*

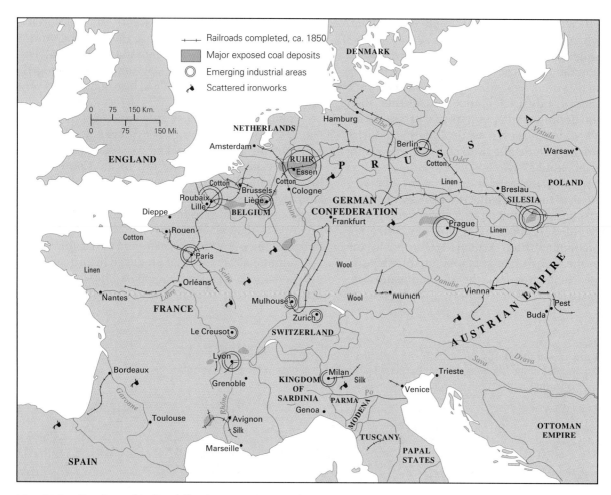

**Map 20.2 Continental Industrialization, ca. 1850** Industry was still sparse on the Continent, but important regions had developed near major coal deposits in Liège, the Ruhr, and Silesia.

Iron and coal deposits in France were not close together (see Map 20.2). Because labor was still quite cheap, many goods could be manufactured inexpensively by hand; thus the incentive to invest in labor-saving devices was absent. Soon, however, French manufacturers found themselves facing British competition. By being the first to industrialize, the British had the advantage of being able to manufacture goods and to corner markets efficiently and relatively cheaply. The French were the first to feel the negative effects of being industrial latecomers.

The invasions of Germany by Napoleon caused considerable destruction, but they also brought some positive economic benefits. The example of the French Revolution led to important socioeconomic changes. Restrictive guilds declined. The French occupiers suppressed the small German states with their many tariffs and taxes, established a single unified legal system—which survived even after 1815—and introduced a single standard of measurement based on the metric system.

Government in Germany played an important role in the adoption of improved methods of manufacturing. The Prussian state, eager for industrial development, sent an official to Britain to observe the puddling process (the method by which iron is freed of carbon) and bring that know-how back home. The Prussian government promoted industrial growth by investing in a transportation network to carry raw materials for processing and finished goods to their markets. To spur both trade and industrial growth, Prussia took the lead in creating a customs union, the *Zollverein°*, which abolished

---

**Zollverein** (TZOLL-fair-eyn)

tariffs among its members. By 1834 a German market embracing eighteen German states with a population of 23 million had been created.

German industrial growth accelerated dramatically in the 1850s. Massive expenditures on railways created a large demand for metal, which pressured German manufacturers to enlarge their plant capacities and increase efficiency. The German states were not yet politically unified, but the German middle classes saw economic growth as the means by which their country could win a prominent place among Europe's nation-states.

Germany's growth was phenomenal. It successfully emulated Britain, overtook France, and toward the end of the nineteenth century pioneered in the electrical engineering and chemical industries. If France experienced the disadvantages of being a latecomer, Germany reaped the benefits of that status. The Germans were able to avoid costly and inefficient early experimentation and to adopt the latest, proven, methods; moreover, Germany entered fields that Britain had neglected.

Even by the end of the century, however, progress remained slow in many areas of Europe. As long as Russia retained serfdom (until 1861), it would lack the mobile labor force needed for industrial growth. And until late in the century, the ruling Russian aristocracy hesitated to adopt an economic system in which wealth was not based on land. In Austria, Bohemia was the only important industrial center; otherwise, Austria remained heavily agrarian (see Map 20.2).

The impoverished southern Mediterranean countries experienced little economic growth. With mostly poor soil, their agriculture yielded only a meager surplus. Spain, lacking coal and access to other energy sources, could not easily diversify its economic base. Some industry emerged in Catalonia, especially around Barcelona, but it was limited in scope and did not have much impact on the rest of the country. The Italian peninsula was still industrially underdeveloped in the middle of the nineteenth century. There were modest advances, but growth was too slow to have a measurable positive impact on the Italian economy. In 1871, 61 percent of the population of Italy was still agrarian.

Although by midcentury only a few European nations had experienced industrialization to any great extent, many more would do so by the end of the century, pressured by vigorous competition from their more advanced neighbors (see Figure 20.1). The potential threat was political and military as well as economic, for the industrialized nations had the backing of military might

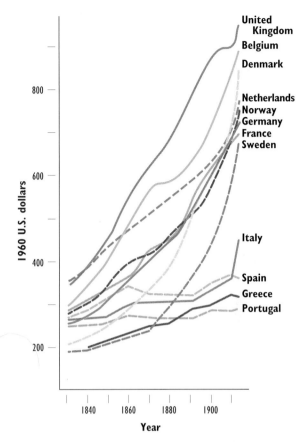

**Figure 20.1    The Increase in Gross National Product per Capita in Principal European Countries, 1830–1913**
The countries that industrialized rapidly—such as the United Kingdom in particular, and also Belgium, France, and Germany—experienced dramatic increase in per capita income during the nineteenth century. Other countries such as Greece and Portugal economically trailed the industrial leaders, and per capita income there remained essentially flat.    *(Source: Norman J. G. Pounds,* An Historical Geography of Europe, *1800–1914 [New York: Cambridge University Press, 1985], p. 32. Used by permission of Cambridge University Press.)*

and superiority. Compared with the rest of the world, the European continent in the nineteenth century had acquired a distinct material culture that was increasingly based on machine manufacture or was in the process of becoming so. The possession of "skillful industry," one Victorian writer exulted, was "ever a proof of superior civilization." Although only some regions of Europe were industrialized, many Europeans came to view themselves as obviously "superior," while deeming all other races "inferior."

# THE TRANSFORMATION OF EUROPE AND ITS ENVIRONMENT

NDUSTRY changed the traditional methods of agriculture, commerce, trade, and manufacture. It also transformed people's lives, individually and collectively. It altered how they made a livelihood, where and how they lived, even how they thought of themselves. Industry's need of people with specialized skills created new occupations. Because industry required specialization, the range of occupations that people adopted expanded dramatically.

The advent of industry transformed the way society functioned. Until the eighteenth century, the basis of influence and power was hereditary privilege, which meant aristocratic birth and land. The aristocracy did not disappear overnight. From the late eighteenth century on, however, it was challenged by a rising class of people whose wealth was self-made and whose influence was based on economic contributions to society rather than on bloodlines. Increased social mobility opened opportunities even for some workers. Industrialization transformed both the social and the natural environment. Cities experienced extraordinary growth as a result of industrialization. Europeans faced not only urban problems but also the dangerous pollution of their air and water.

## ■ Urbanization and Its Discontents

A sociologist at the end of the nineteenth century observed, "The most remarkable social phenomenon of the present century is the concentration of population in cities."[3] The number and size of cities grew as never before. The major impetus for urban growth was the concentration of industry in cities and the resulting need of large numbers of urban workers and their families for goods and services (see Map 20.3).

Industrialization was not the only catalyst. France provides many examples of urban growth with little industry. Increased commercial, trading, and administrative functions led to the growth of cities such as Toulouse, Bordeaux, and Nancy. Neither Holland, Italy, nor Switzerland witnessed much industrial development in the first half of the nineteenth century, yet their cities grew. In general, however, industry transformed people from rural to urban inhabitants. People wanted to live near their work, and as industries concentrated in cities, so did populations.

Urban growth in some places was explosive. In the entire eighteenth century, London grew by only 200,000; but in the first half of the nineteenth century, it grew by 1.4 million, more than doubling its size. Liverpool and Manchester experienced similar growth in the same period. Census figures show that by 1851 Britain was a predominantly urban society, the first country to have as many people living in cities as in the countryside. For Germany that date was 1891, and for France it was not until 1931. Although the proportion of people who were urban varied from place to place, the trend was clear and has continued.

As the pace of industry governed in part urban growth, it was fueled in turn by urbanization. Large cities provided convenient markets for goods and a labor pool for manufacturing. The concentration of people encouraged the exchange of ideas. A large city was likely to have scientific societies and laboratories where engineers and scientists could share new ideas and new inventions that would encourage industrial production. After midcentury, industrialization was driven more and more by scientific and technological breakthroughs made in urban environments.

Cities pulled in people from near and far. Usually, the larger the city, the stronger its ability to attract migrants from great distances. The medium-sized French town of Saint-Etienne° drew resettlers from the nearby mountains, whereas Paris drew from the entire country. Industrial centers even attracted people from beyond the nation's borders. The Irish arrived in large numbers to work in the factories of Lancashire, in northwestern England; Belgians came for mine work in northern France; and Poles sought employment in the Ruhr Valley region of western Germany. Industrial activity stimulated the growth of world trade and shipping across the seas, taking merchant sailors far from home. Many large cities were marked by heterogeneous populations, which included people with different native languages, religions, and national origins, as well as, in some cases, people of different races. Africans and Asians inhabited port cities such as Amsterdam, Marseille, and Liverpool.

With the growth of cities came a multitude of urban ills. In the first half of the nineteenth century, mortality rates were higher in the cities than in the countryside. In the 1840s Britain as a whole had a death rate of 22 per thousand, but Liverpool averaged 39.2 and Manchester 33.1. In France national mortality rates were around 22 per thousand, but in some French cities the rate was as high as 35 per thousand. Social inequality in the face of death was startling. Including the high child mortality rate, the average age at death for members of gentry

**Saint-Etienne** (sen–et-YEN)

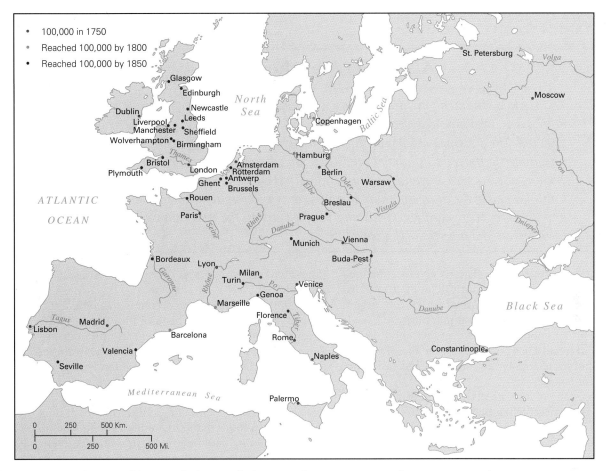

- • 100,000 in 1750
- • Reached 100,000 by 1800
- • Reached 100,000 by 1850

**Map 20.3   Cities Reaching Population Level of 100,000 by 1750, 1800, and 1850**   In 1750 the largest cities owed their existence to factors other than industry, but thereafter the development of industry often determined the growth of cities. England, the leading industrial nation, contained many of the largest cities.   *(Source: Data from Tertius Chandler,* Four Thousand Years of Urban Growth: An Historical Census *[Lewistown, N.Y.: St. David's University Press, 1987], pp. 22–24.)*

families in Liverpool in 1842 was 35; for members of laborers' families it was 15. In 1800 boys living in urban slums were 8 inches shorter than the sons of rich urban dwellers.

The rapid growth of the cities caught local authorities unprepared, and in the early stages of industrialization, city life was particularly severe for the poor. Urban slums developed. The most notorious London slum was St. Giles, which became a tourist attraction because of its squalor. In many cities, large numbers of people were crammed into small areas. The houses were built back to back on small lots and had insufficient lighting and ventilation. Overcrowding was the norm. (See the box "Reading Sources: A Slum in Manchester.")

Sanitation was rudimentary or nonexistent. A single privy in a courtyard was likely to serve dozens of tenants—in some notorious cases in Britain and France, a few hundred. Waste from the privy might drain through open sewers to a nearby river, which was likely to be the local source of drinking water. Or the privy might be connected to a cesspool from which wastewater would seep and contaminate nearby wells. Some tenants lacked toilets and relieved themselves in the streets. In the 1830s people living in the poorest sections of Glasgow stored human waste in heaps alongside their houses and sold it as manure. Water in the cities was scarce and filthy. Piped water was reserved for the rich. The poor had to supply themselves from public fountains or wells and were often obliged to carry water a considerable distance.

In manufacturing towns factory chimneys spewed soot, and everything was covered with dirt and grime.

## ❧ READING SOURCES

### A Slum in Manchester

*The terrible conditions in urban slums were captured by the physician James Philips Kay, who practiced medicine in the newly industrialized city of Manchester, England. The dizzying pace of growth made it impossible for the city to provide basic sanitary facilities for its inhabitants. At the time Kay wrote, in 1832, the causes of many diseases such as typhus and tuberculosis were not known. He attributed the unhealthiness of the city to dirt, and, in a way, he was right. In the dirt, dampness, and darkness of crowded tenements and polluted streets, the fleas that communicated typhus and tuberculosis bacteria thrived.*

Manchester, properly so called, is chiefly inhabited by shopkeepers and the labouring classes. Those districts where the poor dwell are of very recent origin. The rapid growth of the cotton manufacture has attracted hither operatives from every part of the kingdom, and Ireland has poured forth the most destitute of her hordes to supply the constantly increasing demand for labour. . . .

The state of the streets powerfully affects the health of their inhabitants. Sporadic cases of typhus chiefly appear in those which are narrow, ill ventilated, unpaved, or which contain heaps of refuse, or stagnant pools. The confined air and noxious exhalations, which abound in such places, depress the health of the people. And on this account contagious diseases are also most rapidly propagated there. The operation of these causes is exceedingly promoted by their reflex influence on the manners. The houses, in such situations, are unclean, ill provided with furniture; an air of discomfort if not of squalid and loathsome wretchedness pervades them, they are often dilapidated, badly drained, damp; and the habits of their tenants are gross—they are ill-fed, ill-clothed. . . .

A whole family is often accommodated on a single bed, and sometimes a heap of filthy straw and a covering of old sacking hide them in one undistinguished heap, debased alike by penury, want of economy and dissolute habits. Frequently, the inspectors found two or more families crowded into one small house, containing only two apartments, one in which they slept, and another in which they eat; and often more than one family lived in a damp cellar, containing only one room, in whose pestilential atmosphere from twelve to sixteen persons were crowded. To these fertile sources of disease were sometimes added the keeping of pigs and other animals in the house, with other nuisances of the most revolting character.

*Source:* J. P. Kay, *The Moral and Physical Condition of the Working Classes Employed in the Cotton Manufacture in Manchester* (London: James Ridgway, 1832), pp. 6, 14–15, 19.

---

Smoke was a major ingredient of the famous London fog, which not only reduced visibility but posed serious health risks. City streets were littered with refuse; rotting corpses of dogs and horses were common sights. In 1858 the stench from sewage and other rot was so putrid that the British House of Commons was forced to suspend its sessions.

It is not surprising that cholera, a highly infectious disease transmitted through contaminated water, swept London and other European urban centers. In the 1830s one of the first epidemics of modern times struck Europe, killing 100,000 in France, 50,000 in Britain, and 238,000 in Russia. A generation later, the cholera epidemic of 1854 killed 150,000 in France. Typhoid fever, also an acute infectious disease, struck mostly the poor but did not spare the privileged. Queen Victoria of Great Britain nearly died of it; her husband, Prince Albert, did.

**St. Giles**    The most notorious London slum was St. Giles, whose human squalor made it a tourist attraction.    *(From Thomas Beames,* The Rookeries of London. *Courtesy Harvard University Library)*

For most of its denizens, the city provided a crowded and squalid environment. Only in the second half of the nineteenth century would any attempts be made to bring order to the chaos of urban life.

## ■ The Working Classes and Their Lot

In 1842 a middle-class observer traveling in industrial Lancashire noted that around the mills and factories there had developed a "population [that] like the system to which it belongs is NEW . . . hourly increasing in breadth and strength."[4] A French countess, using the pen name Daniel Stern, wrote in her memoirs of France in the 1830s and 1840s of the emergence of "a class apart, as if it were a nation within the nation," working in factories and mines, called "by a new name: the industrial proletariat."[5] Originally used to designate the poorest propertyless wretches in Roman society, the term *proletariat* became synonymous with the class of workers developing in the burgeoning factories. What distinguished this growing class throughout the nineteenth century was that it was relatively unskilled and totally dependent on the factory owners for its livelihood. In earlier eras

apprentices appear to have occupied a similar situation. But guild rules and traditions gave apprentices some protection from arbitrariness, and they could escape their lowly position by eventually becoming master artisans themselves, owning their own tools and being masters of their own time—a possibility denied the members of the working class.

As industry advanced and spread, more and more people depended on it for a livelihood. In the putting-out system, during an agricultural downturn, a cottager could spend more time on hand labor; and when demand for piecework slacked off, the cottager could devote more time to the land. But people living in industrial cities had no such backup. And neither skilled nor unskilled workers were assured of regular employment: any downturn in the economy translated into layoffs or job losses.

In addition, the introduction of new industries often devastated laborers in older forms of production. The mechanization of cotton production reduced the earning power of weavers in England and in Flanders, for instance. The production of linen was mechanized in Belgium by the 1840s, but cotton production was so much cheaper that in order to price their wares competitively, linen producers drastically reduced their workers' wages.

Most factory work was dirty and laborious, in grim plants with heavy, noisy machinery. Sixteen-hour workdays were common. Child labor was widespread. With no safety provisions, the workers were prone to accidents. Few factory owners protected their workers against dangerous substances or circumstances. Mercury used in hat manufacturing gradually poisoned the hatmakers and often led to dementia, hence the term "mad hatters." Lead used in paints and pottery also had a devastating impact on workers' health.

Usually physically lighter than boys and often underfed, young girls were faced with heavy labor that undermined their health. In 1842, 18-year-old Ann Eggley, a mineworker since the age of 7, hauled carriages loaded with ore weighing 800 pounds, for twelve hours a day. She testified to a parliamentary commission that she was so tired from her work that when she came home, she often fell asleep before even going to bed. Isabel Wilson, another mineworker, testified that she had given birth to ten children and had suffered five miscarriages. These women were overworked, exhausted, and vulnerable to disease, and faced premature death.

Did industrialization improve the workers' lot? Perhaps this question is best answered by another question:

What would the workers have done without industrial employment? A population explosion meant that many did not have enough land to make a living, and more efficient farming methods lessened the need for farm hands. It is not clear that these workers could have made a better living, or any at all, if they had remained in the country.

Until the mid-nineteenth century, information on workers' income and expenses is incomplete. The best evidence comes from Britain, where an average family of five needed at least 21 shillings a week to fend off poverty. Skilled workers, who were in demand, might earn as much as 30 shillings a week, but most workers were unskilled. And even skilled workers enjoyed little security: if they became less productive because of illness or old age, their wages fell. If women and children did not always need to work to help the family meet its minimum needs, at some point they usually did have to pitch in. Women, even when they were the main breadwinners, almost never received wages sufficient to meet a family's total needs.

Incomes were so low that workers normally spent between two-thirds and three-fourths of their budget on food. Those who lived in rural areas might raise chickens or pigs or have a plot of potatoes. Bread was the largest single item consumed, varying between one and two pounds a day per person. In Britain and Germany people also ate a lot of potatoes. A little bacon or other meat

**Children Toiling in Mines** Able to crawl in narrow mine shafts, many children were employed underground. In this woodcut, a woman joins a child in his labor. Often, whole families worked together and were paid a fixed price for the amount of coal extracted. *(Hulton Getty/Liaison)*

gave flavor to the soup in which people dipped their bread or potatoes, but meat was rarely consumed as a main course. Because men were the chief breadwinners and tended to have the most strenuous occupations, they received the choice piece of meat and the largest amount of food. Women and children ate what was left.

From the beginning, industrialization increased society's wealth. But did it benefit workers? "Optimist" historians argue that some of the new wealth trickled down to the lower levels of society. "Pessimist" historians say that a downward flow did not necessarily occur. Statistics suggest that by the 1840s workers' lives in Britain did improve. Their real income rose by 40 percent between 1800 and 1850.

Factory workers benefited not only from increased earnings but from the relatively low prices of many basic goods. In London the price of 4 pounds of household bread fell from 15 pennies at the beginning of the nineteenth century to 8½ pennies in the 1830s. As the cost of cloth declined, the dress of working-class people noticeably improved. On the Continent, the lot of workers improved a little later than in Britain, but the process followed the same pattern. (See the feature "Weighing the Evidence: Workers' Wages" on pages 704–705.)

## ■ Industrialization and the Family

Industrialization dramatically changed the character of the working-class family and household. Job segregation reserved the best-paying jobs for men; men were supervisors and ran machinery such as the jenny. Especially in the textile industries, factory owners employed children and women in the lowliest positions. They were thought to be more pliable than men, and their wages were considerably lower. Women generally received from 30 to 50 percent of men's wages, children from 5 to 25 percent. In 1839 Thomas Heath, a weaver in Spitalfields, a London neighborhood, earned 15 shillings a week, his wife but 3 shillings.

Factory work often undermined the ability of women to take care of their children. As farmers or cottagers, women had been able simultaneously to work and to supervise their children; the factory, however, often separated mothers from their children. Many children were given heavy responsibilities at an early age, and it was not uncommon for an older child, sometimes only 5 or 6 years old, to be entrusted with the care of a younger sibling.

Other workers resorted to more dangerous methods of child-care. They might send newborns to "baby-farms," run by individuals in the countryside who were paid to take care of infants. Very often these babies were neglected, and their mortality rate was extremely high. In many cases, babyfarming was no more than a camouflaged form of infanticide. Mothers who kept their children but were obliged to leave them unwatched at home during factory hours sometimes pacified the children by drugging them with mixtures of opium, readily available from the local apothecary.

Working-class women carried an exhausting burden in the family. In addition to sometimes working outside the home, they were responsible for running the household, managing the family income, and taking care of the children, providing most of the nurture and supervision they required.

Because of the many demands on married women, their employment pattern often was affected by the life cycle. Young women might work before marriage, or before giving birth, then stay home until the children were older, and then return to work. Factory work had a harsh impact on women's lives, but it should be remembered that relatively few women were in the wage market—by 1850 only about a quarter in both Britain and France. And of that quarter few worked in factories; far more were in agriculture, crafts industries (which still flourished despite poor working conditions), and domestic service, with many of these women working part-time while their children were small. Some sectors of industry employed a large proportion of women—for instance, textiles. Other sectors, such as the metal and mining industries, were heavily male-dominated.

The textile industry found employment for children once they were over the age of 5 or 6. Their size and agility made them useful for certain jobs, such as reaching under machines to pick up loose cotton. Because of their small hands they were also hired as "doffers," taking bobbins off frames and replacing them. Elizabeth Bentley began work as a doffer in 1815 at the age of 6. At the age of 23, when she testified before a parliamentary commission, she was "considerably deformed . . . in consequence of this labor." (See the box "Reading Sources: The Young Girl in the Factory.") Child labor certainly did not start with the industrial transformation; it had always existed. What was new was the stern industrial discipline imposed on the very young. Children were subject to the clock, closely supervised and prevented from taking long breaks, or mixing work and play—as had been possible in an earlier era.

Although children were common in British textile industries, overall less than 10 percent of working children were in industry. Most were in agriculture or the service sector. In the early stages of industrialization, children were primarily employed in textile mills to pick up waste and repair broken threads. As technological

## The Young Girl in the Factory

*Reformers in Parliament, among them Michael Sadler, denounced the appalling conditions in the factories. Sadler was appointed to head the commission that investigated the matter. Workers who appeared before the panel gave vivid descriptions of their lot. Public and parliamentary outrage at the conditions revealed by these hearings led to the Factory Act of 1833. Among the witnesses was Elizabeth Bentley, a 23-year-old weaving machine operative, who gave the following testimony. Note the extent to which the questions and answers deal with time. Both employers and employees had developed a strong sense of time. As Bentley's testimony shows, employees who ignored the clock risked retribution.*

What age are you?—23. . . .

What time did you begin to work in a factory?—When I was 6 years old. . . .

What were your hours of labor? . . . —From 5 in the morning till 9 at night, when they were thronged [busy].

For how long have you worked that excessive length of time?—For about half a year.

What were your usual hours of labor when they were not so thronged?—From 6 in the morning till 7 at night.

What time was allowed for your meals?—40 minutes at noon. . . .

Your labor is very excessive?—Yes, you have not time for anything.

Suppose you flagged a little, or were too late, what would they do?—Strap us. . . .

Girls as well as boys?—Yes.

Severely?—Yes.

Could you eat your food well in that factory? —No, indeed, I had not much to eat, and the little I had I could not eat it, my appetite was so poor, and being covered with dust; and it was no use taking it home, I could not eat it. . . .

Did you live far from the mill?—Yes, two miles.

Had you a clock?—No, we had not. . . .

Were you generally there in time?—Yes; my mother has been up at four o'clock in the morning and at two o'clock; the colliers used to go to their work at about three or four o'clock, and when she heard them stirring she has got up out of her warm bed, and gone out and asked them the time; and I have sometimes been at Hunslet Car at 2 o'clock when it was steaming down with rain, and we have had to stay till the mill was opened [at 5 A.M.].

*Source:* Great Britain, Sessional Papers, House of Commons, Hearing of June 4, 1832, vol. XV (1831–1832), pp. 195–197.

 **For additional information on this topic, go to http://college.hmco.com.**

advances relieved both problems, the need for children lessened.

Improved technology and the growth of industries other than textiles increased the employment of adult men. In iron and later steel plants, physical strength was essential. Despite the higher labor costs that resulted when men were employed, managers had no choice but to hire them. However, in France, where textiles were still the predominant product after the turn of the nine-teenth century, women made up two-thirds of the textile industry work force as late as 1906.

In some cases, industrialization meant a transformation in the authority structure of workers' households, undermining the influence of the male as head of the household. A woman could make a living independent of her spouse, and children at a reasonably early age could emancipate themselves from their parents and make a go of it working in a factory or a mine. These

### Table 20.1
### Coal Production in Industrializing Nations

| | Millions of Tons | Kilograms per Inhabitant |
|---|---|---|
| 1700 | 4 | 26 |
| 1750 | 7 | 16 |
| 1800 | 16 | 76 |
| 1830 | 30 | 120 |
| 1860 | 129 | 390 |

*Source:* Based on B. R. Mitchell, "Statistical Appendix, 1700–1914," in Carlo Cippola, ed., *The Fontana Economic History of Europe,* vol. 4 (London: Collins, 1973), pp. 747, 770; and Norman J. G. Pounds, *An Historical Geography of Europe, 1500–1840* (New York: Cambridge University Press, 1979), pp. 268–269.

options were not possible in agriculture or in the putting-out system. As in the putting-out system, however, often whole families were hired as a group to perform a specific function. Contemporaries sometimes denounced industry for dissolving family bonds, but the family remained an effective work unit.

If not participating in the wage market, wives and children contributed in other ways to the household budget—by making clothes, raising a pig, tending a potato patch, and performing daily household chores. Grandparents often moved from the country to live with the family and take care of children. When industrial workers married, they frequently settled with their spouses on the same street or in the same neighborhood where their parents lived. Although industry had the potential to break up traditional family structures, the historical evidence is that the family adjusted and survived the challenges posed by the new economic system.

### ■ The Land, the Water, and the Air

Industrialization seriously disturbed the environment, transforming the surface of the earth, the water, and the air. To run the new machinery, coal was mined in increasing amounts (see Table 20.1). Iron and other minerals were also in great demand. The exploitation of coal ushered in the modern age of energy use, in which massive amounts of nonrenewable resources are consumed.

To extract coal and other minerals, miners dug deep tunnels, removing millions of tons of earth, rock, and other debris. This material, plus slag and other waste from the factories, was heaped up in mounds that at times covered acres of land, creating new geological formations.

**A Letter Written with Polluted Water** In 1868 an irate Englishman wrote the health board, using water drawn from the Calder River in northern England to make his point about the condition of the river. As the letter writer points out, readers of the missive will miss one dimension of the situation—the river's stench. *(The British Library)*

With axes and saws people cut down trees, depleting forests to supply the wood needed to build shafts for coal, iron, and tin mines, or to make the charcoal necessary for glassmaking. Between 1750 and 1900, industrial and agricultural needs led to the clearing of 50 percent of all the forests ever cleared. Many of Europe's major forests disappeared or were seriously diminished. Deforestation in turn sped up soil erosion.

Industry changed the physical environment in which people lived. Forests, lakes, rivers, and air—as well as people themselves—showed the harmful effects of industry. Centrifugal pumps drained large marshes in the Fenland in eastern England. A contemporary lamented, "The wind which, in the autumn of 1851 was curling the blue water of the lake, in the autumn of 1853 was blowing in the same place over fields of yellow

**Manchester, England, 1851** A small, unimportant town of 20,000 in the 1750s, Manchester—as a result of industrialization—had 400,000 inhabitants in 1850. In this 1851 painting, the polluted industrial city is contrasted with its idealized pastoral suburb. *(The Royal Collection © 2001 Her Majesty Queen Elizabeth II)*

corn." Factories dumped waste ash into rivers, changing their channels and making them considerably shallower. Because of pollution from industrial and human waste, by 1850 no fish could survive in the lower Thames River. Some rivers were so polluted that their water could be used as ink. Alkali, used for making glass, when released into the atmosphere killed trees for several miles around. Smoke and soot darkened the skies, intensifying the fog over London and other cities. Foul odors from factories could be detected at several miles' distance. Not merely unpleasant, various air pollutants caused cancer and lung diseases, though the connection between pollutants and disease was not yet understood.

### ■ Changing Sense of Time

In agrarian societies time was measured in terms of natural occurrences, such as sunrise and sunset, or the time it might take to milk a cow. With industrialization, punctuality became essential. Shifts of labor had to be rotated to keep the smelters going; they could not stop, or the

molten iron would harden at the bottom of the hearths. The interactive nature of industrial production, in which workers with differing specialties each performed a particular task in finishing a product, made it necessary for employees to be at the factory at an appointed time. They could not be late.

Clocks were installed in church towers and municipal buildings as early as the fourteenth century, but they were not very reliable until the eighteenth century. Watches were commonly owned by men of property and even by some artisans. By the mid-nineteenth century— at least in Britain—as the price of watches came down, many workers could afford them. And even when workers did not own timepieces, they were intensely aware of time. Those who ignored time were fined or fired from their jobs. People listened for the church bell or factory whistle, or asked a neighbor or passer-by for the time. (See the box "Reading Sources: The New Discipline of the Factory System." See also "The Young Girl in the Factory" on page 696.) Western societies increasingly regularized and internalized the sense of time.

## ❧ READING SOURCES

### The New Discipline of the Factory System

*The new factories regimented the work force and were likely to impose stiff penalties for infractions of the rules. This document lists some of the regulations of the Berlin Foundry and Engineering Works of the Royal Overseas Trading Company of 1844. Note how obsessed with efficient use of time the factory rules are. The worker is left little room for personal initiative.*

The normal working day begins at all seasons at 6 A.M. precisely and ends, after the usual break of half an hour for breakfast, an hour for dinner, and half an hour for tea, at 7 P.M., and it shall be strictly observed.

Five minutes before the beginning of the stated hours of work until their actual commencement, a bell shall ring and indicate that every worker employed in the concern has to proceed to his place of work, in order to start as soon as the bell stops.

The doorkeeper shall lock the door punctually at 6 A.M., 8:30 A.M., 1 P.M., and 4:30 P.M.

Workers arriving 2 minutes late shall lose half an hour's wages; whoever is more than 2 minutes late may not start work until after the next break, or at least shall lose his wages until then. . . .

Repeated irregular arrival at work shall lead to dismissal. This shall also apply to those who are found idling by an official or overseer, and refuse to obey their order to resume work. . . .

All conversation with fellow-workers is prohibited. . . .

Smoking in the workshops or in the yard is prohibited during working-hours; anyone caught smoking shall be fined five silver groschen for the sick fund.

Natural functions must be performed at the appropriate places. . . .

It goes without saying that all overseers and officials of the firm shall be obeyed without question, and shall be treated with due deference. Disobedience will be punished by dismissal.

Immediate dismissal shall also be the fate of anyone found drunk in any of the workshops. . . .

The gatekeeper and the watchman, as well as every official, are entitled to search the baskets, parcels, aprons, etc. of the women and children who are taking the dinners into the works, on their departure, as well as search any worker suspected of stealing any article whatever. . . .

A free copy of these rules is handed to every workman, but whoever loses it and requires a new one, or cannot produce it on leaving, shall be fined 2½ silver groschen.

*Source:* S. Pollard and C. Holmes, eds., *Documents of European Economic History*, vol. 1 (New York: St. Martin's Press, 1968), pp. 534–536.

## RESPONSES TO INDUSTRIALIZATION

PEOPLE in the new industrial classes living at subsistence levels were disquieting evidence of the impact of industrialization. What should be done about the working classes—or for them? These new classes developed their own sense of a common interest and fate. The result was a resounding cry for political and social democracy that began in the first half of the nineteenth century and became increasingly insistent. Many solutions were proffered.

### ■ The Growth of Working-Class Solidarity

Hardest hit by economic changes, workers sought to improve their conditions by organizing and articulating their needs. In the preindustrial economy, artisans and craftsmen lived in an accepted hierarchy with prescribed rules. They began by serving for a certain number of years as apprentices to a master, next became journeymen, and finally with hard work and good fortune became masters of their trades. As tradesmen with common interests, they tended to band together into brotherhoods, promising one another help and trying to improve their working conditions.

With industrialization, guilds declined. Unlike the skilled handicrafts that required years of apprenticeship, few aspects of industrial production demanded extensive training. The system of dependence between apprentice and master became irrelevant. Guilds trying to protect their members often resisted new technologies and came to be seen as a hindrance to economic development. Liberals viewed guilds as constraints on trade and the free flow of labor. In France the revolutionaries abolished the guilds and all workers' coalitions. Throughout the eighteenth century the British Parliament passed various acts against "combinations" by workmen.

While guilds faded in importance, the solidarity and language born of the guild continued to shape workers' attitudes throughout much of the nineteenth century. New experiences also reinforced the sense of belonging to a group and sharing common aspirations.

Cultural forces fostered workers' sense of solidarity. The common language of religion and shared religious practice united workers. Religious sects flourished in an environment of despair punctuated by hopes of deliverance. Some historians believe that the growth of Methodism in England in the 1790s (see page 713) was a response to grim economic conditions. Emphasis on equality before God fueled the sense of injustice in a world where a privileged few lived in luxury while others were condemned to work along with their children for a pittance. Joanna, a self-proclaimed prophet active in the 1810s in England, announced both salvation and the coming of a new world of material well-being. In France workers believed the new society would come about by their martyrdom; like Jesus, the workers would suffer, and from their suffering would emerge a new, better society. Ideas of social justice were linked in the countryside with religious broadsides speaking of "Jesus the worker." Religious themes and language continued to be important in labor organization for many years.

Other cultural and social factors created bonds among workers. Housing was increasingly segregated. Workers lived in low-rent areas—in slums in the center

**Leisure Activity for the Working Poor**   Some harsh forms of entertainment turned up in the industrial period. Scores of working-class spectators came to see the celebrated dog "Billy" kill a hundred rats at one time at the Westminster Pit in London in 1822.   *(The British Library)*

of cities or in outlying areas near the factories. Thus, urban workers lived close together, in similar conditions of squalor and hardship. Workers grew close by spending their leisure time together, drinking in pubs, attending theaters and new forms of popular entertainment such as the circus, or watching traditional blood sports such as boxing or cockfights. Sports became popular as both spectator and participatory events in the 1880s. Soccer, which developed in England at this time, drew players and fans overwhelmingly from the working class.

Social institutions also encouraged class unity. In the eighteenth century both husband and wife were usually in the same craft. By 1900 it became more common for workers to marry across their crafts, thereby strengthening the sense of solidarity that encompassed the working classes as a whole.

Faced with the uncertainties of unemployment and job-related accidents, in addition to disease and other natural catastrophes, workers formed so-called friendly societies in which they pooled their resources to provide mutual aid. These societies, descendants of benefit organizations of the Middle Ages and Renaissance, combined business activity with feasts, drinking bouts, and other social functions.

Friendly societies had existed as early as the seventeenth century, but they became increasingly popular and important after industrialization. Their strength in a region often reflected the degree to which the area was industrialized. First started to provide aid for workers in a particular trade, they soon included members in several crafts. In time, they federated into national organizations, so that a worker who moved to a new town could continue membership in the new locale. Connected by common membership in friendly societies, workers expressed a feeling of group solidarity beyond their individual occupations. Though far from solidified, a working class was in the making.

## ■ Collective Action

Militant and in some cases violent action strengthened workers' solidarity. In politics, workers expressed common grievances, and some of their disappointments in the political arena underscored their common situation.

In the face of hardships, artisans organized for collective action. In 1811–1812 British hand weavers, faced with competition from mechanized looms, organized in groups claiming to be led by a mythical General Ned Ludd. In the name of economic justice and to protect their livelihood, the "Luddites," as the general's followers were called, smashed machines or threatened to do so. In Saxony in eastern Germany in the 1830s and 1840s,

weavers went on machine-crushing campaigns. These movements revealed the militance of labor and its willingness to resort to violence.

In Lyon, France, in 1831 and 1834, workers led uprisings demanding fair wages for piecework. Angered when the silk merchants lowered the amount they would pay, the workers marched in the streets bearing banners proclaiming "Live Working or Die Fighting." Troops were brought in to restore order to the riot-torn city. Although conditions of the silk trade had been the immediate impetus for the uprising, the workers appealed for help to their fellow workers in other trades, who joined in the protests.

Labor agitation in much of Europe increased in the 1840s: A major strike wave involving twenty thousand workers broke out in Paris in 1840. In the summer of 1842, an industrial downturn in England led to massive unemployment and rioting. During the summer of 1844 in Silesia, in eastern Prussia, linen handloom weavers, desperate because of worsening conditions brought on by competition from machine-made cotton fabrics, attacked the homes of the wealthy. In 1855 in Barcelona, the government tried to dissolve unions, and fifty thousand workers went on strike carrying placards that warned "Association or Death."

Workers had to conform to severe discipline and rigid rules not only in the workplace but also away from it. Workers in some factories were forbidden to read certain newspapers, had to attend religious services, and could marry only with the owners' permission. Workers resisted these attempts at control and resented employers' intrusiveness.

Workers' actions in the early nineteenth century clearly showed that they wanted both freedom from intrusive regulation by their employers and the security of employment at a decent wage. Unions provided a means to these goals.

Many of the friendly societies struggled to improve their members' working conditions, acting very much as labor unions would. They organized strikes and provided support to members during work stoppages. The advantages offered by unions were well understood—by both sides. Unions were illegal in Britain until 1825, in Prussia until 1859, and in France until the 1860s. As a French workers' paper declared in 1847, "If workers came together and organized . . . nothing would be able to stop them." An organized force could threaten to withhold labor if the employer did not grant decent wages and acceptable conditions. Unions made workers a countervailing force to the factory owners.

The process of unionization was difficult. By 1850 many countries had passed laws supporting employers

**Unionization**    This certificate signifies membership in the first professional union in Britain, the Amalgamated Society of Engineers. With references to classical antiquity, British inventors, and various trades, the document highlights the nobility of the trade.    *(The Art Archive)*

against the workers. Censorship and the use of force against organized strikes were not uncommon. Population growth made it difficult for workers to withhold labor lest they be replaced by others only too willing to take their places. Foreign workers—for example, the Irish who streamed into England and the Belgians and Italians who migrated to France—were often desperate for work and not well informed about local conditions.

In many countries, workers formed unions before unions were legalized. Although there were early attempts in Britain to organize unions on a national basis, most were centered around a single craft or a single industry. Because labor unions originated in the crafts tradition, the earliest members were skilled craftsmen who organized to protect their livelihoods from the challenge that industrialization posed. These craftsmen were usually lit-

erate and long-time residents of their communities. They provided the labor movement with much of its leadership and organization. Skilled craft workers also played a strong role in developing a sense of class-consciousness. The language and institutions that they had developed over decades and sometimes over centuries became the common heritage of workers in general.

Workers looked to political action as the means to improve their situations. In the 1830s and 1840s British and French workers agitated for the right to vote; they saw voting as a way to put themselves on equal footing with the privileged and to win better conditions. Their disappointment at their failure to win political representation strengthened their class solidarity against the wealthy, privileged upper classes. Politically, organized workers played a major role in the revolutions that would rock Europe in 1848 (see pages 732–735), sometimes helping to instigating the uprisings, often influencing their course. However vague their ideas, European workers showed that their organizations were legitimate representatives of the people and that the lot of the worker should be the concern of government. In general, workers upheld the ideal of a moral economy— one in which all who labored got a just wage and every person was assured a minimum level of well-being.

The working classes were never a monolithic group. They consisted of people with varying skills, responsibilities, and incomes. Artisans with valuable skills were the segment that employers most respected and favored in pay and in working conditions. In contrast, unskilled workers were poorly paid, harshly treated, and often given only temporary work. Many skilled workers looked with contempt on the unskilled.

If both sexes worked side by side, it created little solidarity between them. Men worried that women were undermining their earning power by accepting lower wages. They often excluded women from their unions. Men even went on strike to force employers to discharge women.

Nor was there solidarity across nationalities. Foreign workers were heartily despised. British workers were hostile to their Irish colleagues, the French to the Belgians and Italians in their midst. The hostility often led to fisticuffs. In London anti-Irish riots were common. Many forces fostered dissension among the working classes in the nineteenth century, and unity among workers was far from achieved. Nevertheless, various experiences, including the spread of industry, broadened and deepened workers' sense of a shared fate and common goal.

The middle classes came to believe that all workers formed a single class. By the mid-nineteenth century, they had developed a clear fear of workers, not only as individuals but as a group, as a class. It was not unusual for members of the elite to refer to workers as "the swinish multitude" or, as the title of a popular English book put it, *The Great Unwashed* (1868). In France reference was alternately made to "the dangerous classes" and "the laboring classes." Not just workers but even the privileged seemed to see relations between the groups as a form of class war.

## SUMMARY

 TS industrial transformation altered the face of Europe. This process, which started around 1750 in parts of England, spread by 1850 to other states of Europe. Material and cultural factors combined with a number of fortuitous circumstances explain why industrial production originated in England. The proximity of coal and iron, the relative ease of domestic transportation, a culture open to innovation and entrepreneurship, and the existence of an already relatively dynamic economy help explain why Britain was the first nation to industrialize.

Economies based on industry changed power relations within Europe and altered the relationship of Europe to the rest of the world. As a result of the transformation in its economy, Britain became in the nineteenth century the most powerful nation in Europe and achieved worldwide influence. Although Europe was industrialized only in certain areas, many Europeans came to think of their continent as economically and technologically superior to the rest of the world. Being industrial became synonymous for many with Europe's identity.

Industry changed the nature of work for large numbers of Europeans. Machines replaced human energy in the workplace. By the application of science and technology, manufacturing productivity increased significantly. A decreasing number of people worked in agriculture, and more entered manufacturing. Population patterns changed; cities grew dramatically, and for the first time European cities had over a million inhabitants.

The massing of workers in factories and urban areas aggravated their misery but called attention to their potential power. Eager to improve their lives and working conditions, workers began to express their solidarity. They organized into associations that were more broadly based and therefore more powerful than workers' groups of the past. As workers began to think of themselves as a class, the dominant elites within society began to per-

ceive them as such. The new proletarian class, shaped by industrialization, was a growing force that would challenge the existing order throughout the nineteenth century and much of the next.

### ■ Notes

1. Phyllis Deane, *The First Industrial Revolution* (Cambridge: Cambridge University Press, 1965), p. 1.
2. These ideas are provocatively developed in E. L. Jones, *The European Miracle: Environments, Economies and Geopolitics of Europe and Asia* (Cambridge: Cambridge University Press, 1981).
3. Adna Ferrin Weber, *The Growth of Cities in the Nineteenth Century: A Study in Statistics* (New York: Macmillan, 1899; reprint, Ithaca, N.Y.: Cornell University Press, 1963), p. 1.
4. Cooke Taylor, *Notes of a Tour in the Manufacturing Districts of Lancashire, in a Series of Letters to His Grace the Archbishop of Dublin* (London, 1842), pp. 4–6, quoted in E. P. Thompson, *The Making of the English Working Class* (New York: Vintage, 1963), p. 191.
5. Marie de Flavigny d'Agoult [Daniel Stern], *Histoire de la Révolution de 1848*, 2d ed., vol. 1 (Paris, 1862), p. 7, quoted in Theodore S. Hamerow, *The Birth of a New Europe: State and Society in the Nineteenth Century* (Chapel Hill: University of North Carolina Press, 1983), pp. 206–207.

### ■ Suggested Reading

Chinn, Carl. *Poverty Amidst Prosperity: The Urban Poor in England, 1834–1914.* 1995. Concentrates on the harsher aspects of industrialization.

Hopkins, Eric. *Industrialisation and Society.* 2000. A survey that considers the social and political impact of industry on British society.

Jones, E. L. *The European Miracle.* 1981. A broad comparative work that considers the forces leading to the industrialization of the West.

Landes, David S. *The Wealth and Poverty of Nations.* 1999. Explores why Europe industrialized as compared with the rest of the world.

Mokyr, Joel. *The Lever of Riches: Technological Creativity and Economic Progress.* 1990. A comparative study of Western and Chinese technology, emphasizing cultural elements as explanations for the industrialization of the West.

Sylla, Richard, and Gianni Toniolo, eds. *Patterns of European Industrialization.* 1991. A comparative perspective on the patterns of industrialization.

Thompson, E. P. *The Making of the English Working Class.* 1963. Emphasizes the cultural factors that encouraged the development of working-class consciousness in England.

 **For a searchable list of additional readings for this chapter, go to http://college.hmco.com.**

# Workers' Wages

In 1869 the Chamber of Commerce of Verviers°, a town in eastern Belgium, published a report on workers' wages. In the seventeenth century, Verviers, located on the Vesdre° River, had become a major producer of woolens. The river provided water for power, for washing the cloth, and for carrying away industrial waste. Thus, the site was ideal for finishing textiles, and the merchants of Verviers drew on the labor of spinners and weavers in the surrounding farm areas. With a population of 4,500 in the mid-seventeenth century, Verviers had 10,000 inhabitants by the end of the eighteenth.

Two local entrepreneurs brought the Englishman John Cockerill to town. In 1802 he set up the first spinning machine on the Continent and in 1816 the first steam engine in Belgium. Thirty years later, Verviers boasted forty factories and the population had increased to 23,000.

Industrialization transformed the people's lives in many ways. The table of wages reveals the existence of a variegated, hierarchical work force with clear, separate functions and specified salaries. It indicates the uneven ways in which people benefited from industry, depending on their skills, age, and gender.

For example, this list allows us to compare the wages of industrial workers and artisans. Industry made it difficult for the artisans to survive; unable to compete with machine manufacture, many had to give up their trade or tighten their belts to make ends meet. The new machine age, however, created an increased demand for the services of some artisans. Early in the nineteenth century the new machines eliminated hand spinning, for example, but inexpensive yarn at first increased the demand for handloom weavers. Notice that handloom weavers ("hand weavers" in the table) were relatively well paid in 1836. This is due to the uneven introduction of mechanical production. Weaving of high-quality woolens proved to be more difficult to mechanize than cotton goods. Power looms did not become common in Verviers until the 1860s, and we see the relative wages of handloom weavers decline in 1869. Joiners and ironsmiths not only did the work they had traditionally done but found new opportunities building and repairing machines. The ironsmiths, joiners, and carpenters of Verviers were all paid better than other workers.

Even among the factory workers we find some significant wage discrepancies. Compare, for example, the wages of the nonspecialized laborer to the wages of the other, specialized industrial workers.

Changes in technology, productivity, labor supply, and market demand for certain goods increased the relative wages of workers over time. Thus the relative wages of jobs changed between 1836 and 1869. Notice that a wool washer in 1869 was making 174 percent more than a wool washer made in 1836, but in the same period the wages paid to a warper had increased by 300 percent.

Let us next consider women in the labor force. Notice that the list is divided into "male occupations," "female occupations," and finally "children's occupation." Work is divided according to gender and age. Look at the list of women's industrial occupations. The absence of spinning female occupations in this list is significant. Spinning had been a female occupation since antiquity, but the spinning machines in Verviers were tended by men. Notice how little differentiation is evident among women's work; far fewer industrial occupations are listed for women than for men. Also look at the wages. Women's wages were all equally depressed, with the one exception of menders' wages, hovering in 1836 around .7 francs but climbing by 1869 to 2.25 francs, an increase of over 300 percent. Among men's occupations the spread of salaries was far greater. In 1869 the highest-paid women (menders) received 40 percent more than the lowest-paid women in 1836 (scourers), but the highest-paid men (ironsmiths) received 138 percent more than the lowest-paid men (wool washers) in 1836. By 1869 the wage gap had somewhat diminished for both men and women, but it was still far larger for men (72 percent) than for women (28 percent).

Some male artisans—carpenters, for example— consistently received wages higher than the wages of many machine operators. But notice the one female artisan occupation: seamstress. Although a seamstress was probably quite skilled, she was paid no more than the women in the factories. Special crafts, still prized for some men, were not given much monetary value when practiced by women. Note the wage differences overall

---

**Verviers** (ver-VYAY)   **Vesdre** (VEH-druh)

## Wage Differentials in Verviers, Belgium, 1836–1869

| | | Wages (francs per day) | | | | |
|---|---|---|---|---|---|---|
| | | **1836** | **1846** | **1856** | **1863** | **1869** |
| **Male Occupations** | Ironsmith* | 1.73 | 2.25 | 2.50 | 3.00 | 3.87 |
| | Carpenter* | 1.90 | 2.25 | 2.65 | 2.87 | 3.50 |
| | Dyer | 1.40 | 1.46 | 1.60 | 2.60 | 3.37 |
| | Spinner | 1.80 | 1.90 | 2.90 | 3.12 | 3.40 |
| | Carder | 1.47 | 1.75 | 2.30 | 3.25 | 3.30 |
| | Tanner* | 1.83 | 2.00 | 2.25 | 3.00 | 3.25 |
| | Warper | 0.80 | 0.95 | 1.57 | 1.65 | 3.25 |
| | Hand weaver* | 1.97 | 1.70 | 2.85 | 3.00 | 3.00 |
| | Joiner* | 1.98 | 2.00 | 2.25 | 2.75 | 3.00 |
| | Tenterer | — | 1.25 | 1.40 | 2.34 | 3.00 |
| | Presser | 1.47 | 1.78 | 1.78 | 2.15 | 3.00 |
| | Machine weaver | — | — | — | — | 2.75 |
| | Comber | 0.84 | 1.27 | 1.50 | 1.75 | 2.65 |
| | Fuller | 1.40 | 1.50 | 1.75 | 2.30 | 2.67 |
| | Laborer | — | 1.25 | 1.50 | 1.87 | 2.50 |
| | Wool washer | 1.15 | 1.25 | 1.40 | 1.75 | 2.25 |
| **Female Occupations** | Mender | 0.73 | 0.80 | 1.10 | 1.40 | 2.25 |
| | Wool sorter | 0.98 | 1.08 | 1.70 | 1.85 | 2.00 |
| | Gigger | 0.75 | 0.80 | 0.80 | 1.25 | 2.00 |
| | Burler | 0.77 | 1.00 | 1.20 | 1.70 | 1.80 |
| | Seamstress* | 0.73 | 0.80 | 1.10 | 1.40 | — |
| | Scourer | 0.70 | 0.75 | 0.85 | 1.35 | 1.62 |
| **Children's Occupation** | Piecener | — | 0.70 | 0.90 | 1.10 | 1.60 |

*Artisans. (Those not starred were industrial workers.)

*Source:* Chamber of Commerce of Verviers, *Rapport général sur la situation du commerce et de l'industrie en 1868* (Verviers, 1869), p. 69; repr. in George Alter, *Family and the Female Life Course—The Women of Verviers, Belgium, 1849–1880* (Madison: University of Wisconsin Press, 1988), p. 103. © 1988. Reprinted by permission of The University of Wisconsin Press.

between male and female workers. In 1836 the average female worker received wages equivalent to 53.2 percent of the average male worker's wages. By 1869 there was some improvement: the difference had declined by 11 percentage points; still, women earned only 64 percent of men's pay.

The table lists only one occupation for children: piecener. Small and nimble, children were paid to splice broken threads. They worked in many other capacities as well. Some were paid wages by their employers; others helped their parents in a factory or workshop. The wages of some adults probably included compensation for their children's labor.

We can learn much from a statistical table such as this about the impact of industrialization on the labor force. Some workers benefited, and others were harmed by the adoption of industry; over time workers experienced changes in their circumstances. If statistical tables are informative on such issues, they also have their limits. They do not tell us how workers interpreted and understood their experience. As workers suffered daily hardships, they had to try to make sense of their changing world, an effort no table can count.

 **For additional information on this topic, go to** http://college.hmco.com.

# CHAPTER 21

# Restoration, Reform, and Revolution 1814–1848

**R**EVOLUTION struck Berlin in March 1848. King Friedrich Wilhelm IV (r. 1840–1861), who initially opposed the revolutionaries' demands for political liberties and a unified nation, surprised his subjects on March 21 by announcing support for a united, free, constitutional Germany. This print, distributed by the thousands, shows the king, on horseback, being acclaimed by a grateful people. The black, red, and gold flags, the symbol of German unity since the Napoleonic Wars, are prominently displayed. The king is preceded by a businessman he had appointed as chief minister. People from most walks of life appear united in purpose. Notice the depiction of well-dressed middle-class citizens as well as humble artisans. The print captures a moment of hope and great possibilities. Soon, however, the forces that made the revolution possible fell into disunion, and the Prussian king was able to turn back the tide of change. As in Prussia, the first moments of exhilarating possibilities in the rest of Europe nearly always were followed by failure and disappointment as the forces of reaction won the upper hand.

In 1848 Europe experienced a revolutionary wave, unprecedented in over a half century since the heady days of the French Revolution. These revolutions erupted in protest against the reactionary regimes established after the fall of Napoleon. The political order in western Europe started changing by the 1830s; the pace of change was slower, however, in eastern Europe.

Despite European statesmen's dogged attempts to set the clock back, the forces unleashed by the French Revolution proved irrepressible. Conservatism attempted to bolster the old order, but new

King Friedrich Wilhelm IV (*center*) announcing his devotion to German unity (detail). (Germanisches National Museum Nuremberg)

ideologies such as romanticism, nationalism, liberalism, and socialism challenged it. (An ideology is a structured, organized set of ideas that reflects a group's thinking about life or society.) The forces revealing themselves in 1848 suggested the outline of Europe's development in the second half of the century.

At the end of the Napoleonic Wars, in 1815, the victorious Great Powers—Austria, Great Britain, Prussia, and Russia—tried to re-establish as much of the old European state system as possible. The international arrangements they carved out at the Congress of Vienna were soon shaken by outbreaks of nationalist fervor. Nationalists aimed either to create larger political units, as in Italy and Germany, or to win independence from foreign rule, as in Greece.

The attempt to set the clock back had only limited success. The conservatism of European rulers and their opposition to change were at odds with the new dynamism of European society. Between 1800 and 1850, Europe's population increased by nearly 50 percent, from around 190 million to 280 million. Population growth and surging industrialization had turned small towns into large cities. Factory manufacturing was on the rise, promising to reshape class structures and the lives of workers. Romanticism, liberalism, and other systems of thought were redefining the relationship of the individual to society. Sporadic outbreaks of collective violence reached a crescendo when the revolutions of 1848 swept most of Europe, undermining the established order in state after state. Revolutionaries did not win all their goals, and in many cases the forces of order crushed them. Yet by midcentury, major intellectual, social, and political changes had occurred.

## QUESTIONS TO CONSIDER

- **What were the goals of the restorations that followed the Napoleonic era?**

- **What major ideologies developed in the first half of the nineteenth century?**

- **What were the main causes of the revolutions of 1848, and what roles did nationalism and liberalism play in inciting and sustaining revolution?**

- **What new and permanent features were created by the revolutions of 1848?**

## TERMS TO KNOW

| | |
|---|---|
| Congress of Vienna | socialism |
| conservatism | Marxism |
| romanticism | July Revolution |
| nationalism | Decembrists |
| liberalism | Great Reform Bill |
| laissez faire | Chartism |
| utilitarian | Frankfurt Assembly |

## THE SEARCH FOR STABILITY: THE CONGRESS OF VIENNA, 1814–1815

 HE defeat of Napoleon put an end to French dominance in Europe. In September 1814 the victorious Great Powers—Austria, Great Britain, Prussia, and Russia—convened an international conference in Vienna to negotiate the terms of peace. The victors sought to draw territorial boundaries advantageous to themselves and to provide long-term stability on the European continent. Although many small powers attended the Congress of Vienna, their role was reduced to ratifying the large states' decisions. Having faced a powerful France, which had mobilized popular forces with revolutionary principles, the victors decided to erect an international system that would remove such threats. One method was to restore the European order that had existed before the French Revolution. Thus, following principles of "legitimacy and compensation," they redrew the map of Europe (see Map 21.1). Rulers who had been overthrown were restored to their thrones. The eldest surviving brother of Louis XVI of France became King Louis XVIII. In Spain, Ferdinand VII

**Metternich**    The consummate statesman and aristocrat, the Austrian prince Metternich tried to quell revolution at home and abroad. Some called his era the Metternichean age.

*(The Royal Collection © 2001 Her Majesty Queen Elizabeth II)*

## CHRONOLOGY

| | |
|---|---|
| 1808 | Beethoven, *Pastoral* Symphony |
| 1814–1815 | Congress of Vienna |
| 1819 | Peterloo massacre |
| 1819 | Carlsbad Decrees |
| 1821 | Spanish revolt |
| 1821 | Greek revolution |
| 1821–1825 | Spanish colonies in the Americas win independence |
| 1823 | Monroe Doctrine |
| 1824 | Owen establishes New Harmony |
| 1825 | Decembrists in Russia |
| 1830 | July Revolution in France |
| 1830 | Ottoman Empire recognizes Serbian autonomy |
| 1832 | Great Reform Bill in Britain |
| 1833 | Abolition of slavery in British colonies |
| 1834 | Turner, *Fire at Sea* |
| 1838 | "People's charter" in Great Britain |
| 1839 | Anti–Corn Law League |
| 1845–1848 | Hungry '40s |
| 1848 | Marx and Engels, *Communist Manifesto* |
| 1848 | Revolutions of 1848 |

was restored to the throne from which Napoleon had toppled him and his father. The restoration, however, was not so complete as its proponents claimed. After the French Revolution, certain new realities had to be recognized. For example, Napoleon had consolidated the German and Italian states; the process was acknowledged in the former with the creation of a loose German Confederation. In Italy the number of independent states had shrunk to nine. Also, unlike earlier French kings, Louis XVIII could not be an absolute monarch.

Negotiations at the Congress of Vienna strengthened the territories bordering France, enlarged Prussia and created the kingdom of Piedmont-Sardinia, joined Belgium to Holland, and provided the victors with spoils and compensation for territories bartered away. Austria received Venetia and Lombardy in northern Italy to compensate for the loss of Belgium (to the Netherlands) and parts of Poland (to Russia) and to strengthen its position in general. Prussia was also allowed annexations in compensation for giving up parts of Poland. England

acquired a number of colonies and naval outposts. Thus, with one hand these conservative statesmen swore their loyalty to the prerevolutionary past, and with the other they nevertheless changed the map of Europe.

The leading personality at the Congress of Vienna was the Austrian foreign minister, Prince Clemens von Metternich° (1773–1859), who presided over the meetings. An aristocrat in exile from the Rhineland, which had been annexed by revolutionary France, he had gone into the service of the Habsburg Empire and risen to become its highest official. Personal charm, tact, and representation of a state that for the time being was satisfied

**Metternich** (MEH-ter-nick)

**Map 21.1** **Europe in 1815** Intent on regaining the security and stability of prerevolutionary years the Great Powers redrew the map of Europe at the Congress of Vienna.

with its territories made Metternich seem a disinterested statesman. His influence at the congress was great.

Because it was Napoleon's belligerent imperialism that had brought the powers together in Vienna, France was at first treated as an enemy at the conference. By the end, however, France managed to join the other states and be included with them as one of the five Great Powers jointly known as the "Concert of Europe." The Concert continued to function for nearly forty years, meeting and resolving international crises, and preventing any major European war from breaking out. Underlying the states' cooperation was the principle of a common European destiny.

# IDEOLOGICAL CONFRONTATIONS

THE international and domestic political system established in 1815 was modified by a series of challenges, even revolts, culminating in revolutions throughout Europe in 1848. The order established in 1815 was inspired by conservatism. Its challengers advocated competing ideologies: romanticism, nationalism, liberalism, and socialism.

## ■ Conservatism

The architects of the restoration justified their policies with doctrines based on the ideology of conservatism, emphasizing the need to preserve the existing order of monarchies, aristocracy, and an established church. As a coherent movement, conservatism sprang up during and after the French Revolution to resist the forces of change. Before the American and French Revolutions, the existing political institutions appeared to be permanent. When the old order faced serious challenges in the late eighteenth and early nineteenth centuries, an ideology justifying traditional authority emerged.

Edmund Burke (1729–1797), a British statesman and political theorist, launched one of the first intellectual assaults on the French Revolution. The revolutionary National Assembly had asserted that ancient prerogatives were superseded by the rights of man and principles of human equality based on appeals to natural law. In *Reflections on the Revolution in France* (1790), Burke countered that such claims were abstract and dangerous and that the belief in human equality undermined the social order. Government should be anchored in tradition, he argued. No matter how poorly the French monarchy and its institutions had served the nation,

they should be preserved; their very longevity proved their usefulness. Burke's writings were widely read and influential on the Continent.

In the English-speaking world, one of the most popular writers was Hannah More (1745–1833), who with her four sisters ran a prosperous school. More saw piety as a rampart against rebellion. In a series of pamphlets entitled *Cheap Repository Tracts,* she advocated the acceptance of the existing order and the solace of religious faith. Costing but a penny, the moral tracts were often handed out by the rich together with alms or food to the poor. More was the first writer in history to sell over a million copies; within three years her sales doubled. Conservative values thus spread to a very large audience in both Britain and the United States, where one of her works appeared in thirty editions.

A more extreme version of conservatism was the counterrevolutionary or ultraroyalist ideology. Unlike Burke, who was willing to tolerate some change, counterrevolutionaries wanted to restore society to its prerevolutionary condition. The most extreme counterrevolutionaries were those with personal experience of the upheavals of the Revolution. Count Joseph de Maistre° (1753–1821), a Savoyard (from the Franco-Italian border region) nobleman whose estates were occupied by the invading French, described monarchy as a God-given form of government in his *Considerations on France* in 1796. Any attempt to abolish or even limit it was a violation of divine law. According to de Maistre and his fellow reactionaries, the authority of church and state was necessary to prevent human beings from falling into evil ways. De Maistre advocated stern government control, including the generous use of the death penalty, to keep people loyal to throne and altar.

Conservatism was also influenced by romanticism, with its glorification of the past, taste for pageantry, and belief in the organic unity of society. Nor were conservative ideas limited to intellectual circles; at times they had mass appeal. (See the box "Reading Sources: A Spanish Carlist Appeals to the Peasantry.")

## ■ Romanticism

The long-lived romantic movement had emerged in the 1760s as a rebellion against rationalism and persisted until the 1840s. It was primarily a movement in the arts. Writers, painters, composers, and others consciously rebelled against the Enlightenment and its rationalist values. In contrast to the philosophes and their emphasis on reason,

**Maistre** (MESS-treh)

## A Spanish Carlist Appeals to the Peasantry

*The conservatism of political thinkers became current enough that its language was used in a popular appeal to rally support in Spain for Don Carlos, the brother of Ferdinand VII. A conservative, Don Carlos challenged the right of his niece Isabella to the throne and precipitated the Carlist war (1834–1839). Carlism was defeated but its ideas were an influential part of Spanish conservatism. Notice the appeals made to tradition, religion, and history, the underpinnings of conservatism.*

. . . Policies which alter the laws of the state without need or utility are found most often when they are influenced by other nations; there is general agreement to reject these changes, as they shock public opinion; Holy Religion is the ultimate, sublime principle of the people, who desire a pious prince, who will restore the old ways and revive the blessed days of our fathers. . . . Don Carlos, protected by God, will defeat the revolution, and under his paternal rule, we will see the hoped for restoration; the restoration of principles and doctrines, of laws and institutions, of habits, of customs. . . . The Holy Faith in all its dignity and purity; the sovereignty of the king, without the checks that destroy it or hinder his good deeds; . . . the vigour of the old laws and *fueros* [local and provincial privileges]; the extinction of administrative abuses and vices; the noble and honourable independence of the nation and the prosperity of all classes: these are his aims. . . . We turn to religion as the basic foundation of society and we see the legitimate authority of the prince as its powerful and healthy influence on society, the best and most secure guarantee against the fury of popular passion and the degradation of true liberty . . . by tyranny. . . . What is irrational or extremist in this? . . . that the monarchy might be made strong through a united sovereign will of the people rather than by armed force and a mass of civil servants; that the abuses of public administration which enrage the people and the excesses that warp and corrupt the government be destroyed. There is no surer road to these ends than the preservation of old, essentially conservative institutions. . . . [We demand] nothing more than to be left in active possession of our immemorial legitimate rights; and that, in accord with the wise counsel of public law, no innovations be introduced without grave need. . . .

*Source:* A. Bullon de Mendoza, *La primera Guerra Carlista* (Madrid, 1992), pp. 560–562, in Michael Broers, trans. and ed., *Europe After Napoleon: Revolution, Reaction and Romanticism, 1814–1848* (1996), pp. 129–130.

---

romantics praised emotion and feeling. Jean-Jacques Rousseau's strong appeal to sentiment was taken up by the German writer Johann Wolfgang von Goethe° (1749–1832), who declared, "Feeling is everything." Goethe's *Sorrows of Young Werther* (1774), the most widely read book of the era—Napoleon had a copy by his bedside—depicted the passions of the hero, who, depressed over unrequited love, kills himself. Many young men dressed in "Werther clothes"—tight black pants, blue vest, and an open yellow shirt—and in some cases emulated the tragic hero by committing suicide.

Whereas the Enlightenment had studied nature for the principles it could impart, romantics worshiped nature for its inherent beauty. The German composer Ludwig van Beethoven° (1770–1827) wrote his *Pastoral Symphony* in praise of idyllic nature, depicting the passions one might feel in contemplating its loveliness and serenity. The English poets William Wordsworth (1770–1850) and Samuel Taylor Coleridge (1772–1834) treated untamed wilderness as a particular subject of wonder. Fellow Englishman Joseph Mallord William Turner (1775–1851) displayed the raw passions of the sea in such paintings as *Fire at Sea* (1834) and *Snowstorm: Steamboat off a Harbour's Mouth* (1842). Before painting the latter, Turner is said to have tied himself to a ship's mast and braved a snowstorm for four hours.

In pursuit of the authentic and the ancient, of feeling rather than rationality, many romantics rediscovered

---

**Goethe** (GOE-teh)

**Beethoven** (BATE-ho-ven)

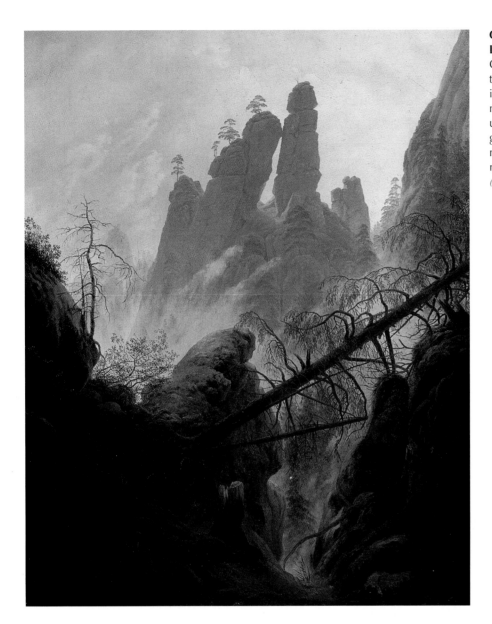

**Caspar David Friedrich: Rocky Landscape (1822–1823)** The German romantic painter evokes the mystery, majesty, and awe-inspiring natural beauty of the mountains. The dead tree reminds us of our mortality, while the young growths on the left remind us of the miracle of life—two themes that the romantics also often evoked.
*(Osterreichische Galerie Belvedere Vienna)*

religion. In some areas of Europe, popular religion had anticipated the artists' and intellectuals' romantic sensibilities. France experienced a revival of Catholicism. In the German states, pietism, which had emerged in the seventeenth and eighteenth centuries, stressed the personal relationship between the individual and God, unimpeded by theological formalities or religious authorities. The influence of pietism, with its emphasis on spirituality and emotion, spread throughout central Europe in schools and churches.

In England, emotionalism in religion expressed itself in the popularity of Methodism. Founded in the 1730s by the English preacher John Wesley (1703–1791), this movement emphasized salvation by a faith made active in one's life, a method of living. Appealing especially to the poor and desperate, Methodism by the 1790s had

gained seventy thousand members; within a generation it quadrupled its flock.

The classicism of the Enlightenment had required an audience well versed in the traditional texts. Since the mid-eighteenth century, however, the reading public had grown to include people without access to elite culture. Appeals to emotion and sentiment were congenial to these new audiences, and a new interest developed in folklore and rustic life. In his short but productive life, Franz Schubert (1797–1828) composed, among other forms of music, over 600 *lieder°*, or songs, that echo the simplicity of folk tunes. Although living in Paris, Frédéric Chopin° (1810–1849) composed works influenced by the peasant music of his native Poland.

**lieder** (LEE-der)  **Chopin** (sho-PEHN)

## 🐾 READING SOURCES

### Franz Liszt, Passionate Piano Virtuoso

*Franz Liszt (1811–1886) was both a composer and virtuoso pianist. With the demise of aristocratic patronage, artists who wanted to make a living had to beguile their audiences and make piano playing a dramatic enough event to woo sponsors and commissions. A Viennese news account vividly describes Liszt's performance, which fulfilled many of the expectations of romanticism, with its emphasis on youth, spontaneity, feeling, and genius.*

Vienna, end of April [1838].—Unusual events require an extraordinary report. The present one is prompted by the wholly unexpected arrival of the famous pianist Franz Liszt, whom Vienna had not seen since his 12th year and who, like a *Deus ex machina* [an unhoped for savior], came to us quite suddenly from the slopes of the Apennines [he had spent the winter in Italy].

We have now heard him, the strange wonder, whom the superstition of past ages, possessed by the delusion that such things could never be done without the help of the Evil One, would undoubtedly have condemned without mercy to the stake—we have heard him, and seen him too, which, of course, makes a part of the affair. Just look at the pale, slender youth in his clothes that signal the nonconformist; the long, sleek, drooping hair, the thin arms, the small, delicately formed hands; the almost gloomy and yet childlike pleasant face—those features so strongly stamped and full of meaning, in this respect. . . .

Liszt knows no rule, no form, no law; he creates them all himself. He remains an inexplicable phenomenon, a compound of such heterogeneous, strangely mixed materials, that an analysis would inevitably destroy what lends the highest charm, the individual enchantment, namely, the inscrutable secret of the chemical mixture of genial coquetry and childlike simplicity, of whimsy and divine nobleness.

After the concert he stands there like a conqueror on the field of battle . . . vanquished pianos lie about him, broken strings flutter . . . the hearers look at each other in mute astonishment as after a storm . . . and he, the Prometheus [the titan in Greek mythology who stole the fire of the gods] who creates a form from every note . . . who now treats his beloved, the piano, tenderly, then tyrannically; caresses, pouts, scolds, strikes, drags by the hair, and then, all the more fervently, with all the fire and glow of love, throws all his arms around her with a shout, and away with her through all the spaces; he stands there bowing his head, leaning languidly on a chair, with a strange smile, like an exclamation mark after the burst of universal admiration: this is Franz Liszt!

*Source: Allgemeine musikalische Zeitung* (May 1838), in Pierro Weiss and Richard Taruskin, eds., *Music in the Western World— A History in Documents* (New York: Schirmer Books, 1984), pp. 363, 365.

---

Whereas the philosophes had decried the Middle Ages, the romantics celebrated the medieval period. Painters frequently took Gothic buildings or ruins as their theme. Architects imitated the Gothic style in both private and public buildings. Sir Walter Scott (1771–1832) in Scotland and Victor Hugo° (1802–1885) in France recaptured chivalry and the age of faith in such popular works as *Ivanhoe* (1819) and *The Hunchback of Notre Dame* (1831). The opera *William Tell* by Gioacchini

Rossini (1792–1868) is based on the legendary tale of a freedom-loving peasant who supposedly lived in thirteenth-century Switzerland. Thus it also had a liberal and nationalistic appeal.

The romantics sought displacement not only in time but also in place. The exotic had great appeal to them. Recently conquered Algeria in North Africa provided exotic scenes for French painters, among them Eugène Delacroix° (1798–1863) and Jean Ingres° (1780–1867).

---

**Hugo** (U-go)

**Delacroix** (de-la-KRWAH)   **Ingres** (AENG-reh)

Senegal in West Africa, which the French recovered from the British in 1815, offered the setting for Théodore Géricault's° powerful *Raft of the "Medusa."* (See the feature "Weighing the Evidence: Raft of the 'Medusa'" on pages 738–739.) In music Franz Liszt (1811–1886) composed Hungarian rhapsodies that were considered exotic since they were based on gypsy music. (See the box "Reading Sources: Franz Liszt, Passionate Piano Virtuoso.")

Romanticism exalted mythical figures as embodiments of human energy and passion. In the dramatic poem *Faust,* Goethe retold the legend of a man who sells his soul to the devil in exchange for worldly success. Several composers set that story to powerful music. In the poetic drama *Prometheus Unbound,* the English romantic poet Percy Bysshe Shelley (1792–1822) celebrated Prometheus°, who, according to Greek mythology stole fire from the gods and gave it to human beings. In much the same spirit, many romantics lionized Napoleon, who had overthrown kings and states. Delacroix, who witnessed the July Revolution of 1830 in Paris (see pages 723–724), celebrated the heroism and passion of the revolutionaries in his huge canvas *Liberty Leading the People* (1830).

Romantics often challenged existing power relations, including relations between the sexes. The French writer Amandine-Aurore Dupin° (1804–1876), better known by her pen name, George Sand°, spoke for the emancipation of women from the oppressive supervision of their husbands, fathers, and brothers. In her personal life, Sand practiced the freedom she preached, dressing like a man, smoking cigars, and openly pursuing affairs with a number of well-known artists. The English writer Mary Ann Evans (1819–1892), like George Sand, adopted a male pseudonym, George Eliot. She conducted her life in a nonconformist manner, living with a married man. The use of male pen names by both writers attests to the hostility that intellectual women still faced.

After the French Revolution, nobles and monarchs ceased sponsoring art on a grand scale and were expected to conduct their lives soberly. Cut off from royal patronage, artists had to depend on members of the new middle classes to buy paintings and books and attend plays and musical performances. If earning a livelihood had often been difficult for artists in the past, it now became even more so. Forced to live marginally, they cultivated the image of the artist as unconventional. In their lifestyles and their work, they deliberately rejected the norms of society. The romantic period gave rise to the

Géricault (jair-ih-KO)    Prometheus (pro-MEETH-ee-us)
Amandine-Aurore Dupin (ah-man-DEEN–oh-ROR du-PAEN)
Sand (SAN)

**Lord Byron in Albanian Costume**    The British romantic poet had himself painted in exotic garb. Romantics were attracted to what were believed to be the mysteries of the East, representing a truer, more authentic existence.    *(Courtesy of the National Portrait Gallery, London)*

notion of the starving genius, alienated from society, loyal only to his all-consuming art.

Romantics of many stripes declared their determination to overthrow the smug present and create a new world. Victor Hugo called for "no more rules, no more models" to constrain the human imagination. Romantic painters and musicians consciously turned their backs on the classical tradition in both subject matter and style. Old methods were discarded for new ones. The English poet George Gordon, Lord Byron (1788–1824), declared war on kings, on established religion, and on the international order; a nationalist as well as a romantic, he died while fighting for the independence of Greece.

## ■ Nationalism

The ideology of nationalism emerged in, and partly shaped, this era. Nationalism is the belief that people derive their identity from their nation and owe it their primary loyalty. A list of criteria for nationhood is likely to include a common language, religion, and political authority, as well as common traditions and shared historical experiences. Some nineteenth-century nationalists found any one of those criteria sufficient. Others insisted that all of them had to be present before a group could consider itself a nation.

In an era that saw the undermining of traditional religious values, nationalism offered a new locus of faith. To people who experienced the social turmoil brought about by the erosion of the old order, nationalism held out the promise of a new community. Nationalism became an ideal espoused as strongly as religion. The Italian nationalist Giuseppe Mazzini° (1805–1872) declared that nationalism was "a faith and mission" ordained by God. The Polish romantic poet and nationalist Adam Mickiewicz° (1798–1855) compared perpetually carved-up Poland to the crucified Christ. The religious intensity of nationalism helps explain its widespread appeal.

Many forces shaped nationalism. Its earliest manifestation, cultural nationalism, had its origins in Rousseau's ideas of the organic nature of a people. Johann Gottfried Herder (1744–1833), Rousseau's German disciple, elaborated on his mentor's ideas, declaring that every people has a "national spirit." To explore the unique nature of this spirit, intellectuals all over Europe began collecting local folk poems, songs, and tales. In an effort to document the spirit of the German people, the Grimm brothers, Jacob (1785–1863) and Wilhelm (1786–1859), compiled fairy tales and published them between 1812 and 1818; among the better known are "Little Red Riding Hood" and "Snow White."

Political nationalism, born in the era of the French Revolution, injected urgency and passion into the new ideology. In the 1770s, French aristocrats resisted attempts by the French monarchy to impose taxes, claiming that they embodied the rights of "the nation" and could not be taxed without its consent. Thus, the concept of nation was given general currency. When revolutionary France was attacked by neighboring countries, which were ruled by kings and dukes, the Legislative Assembly called on the French people to rise and save the nation. The realm of the king of France had become the French nation.

In reaction to the French threat, intellectuals in Germany and Italy embraced the spirit of nationalism. In Germany the philosopher Johann Gottlieb Fichte° (1762–1814) delivered his series of *Addresses to the German Nation* after the Prussian defeat at Jena, calling on all Germans to stand firm against Napoleon. He argued

that Germans were endowed with a special genius that had to be safeguarded for the well-being of all humankind. In Italy the writer Vittorio Alfieri (1749–1803) challenged France's claim to the right to lead the peoples of Europe. That right, Alfieri insisted, properly belonged to Italians, the descendants and heirs of ancient Rome.

For the most part, however, after the French Revolution and the Napoleonic era, early-nineteenth-century nationalism was generous and cosmopolitan in its outlook. Herder and Mazzini believed that each of Europe's peoples was destined to achieve nationhood by forming its own political identity and that the nations of Europe would then live peacefully side by side. The members of dedicated nationalist groups such as Young Germany and Young Italy were also members of Young Europe. Many nationalists in the 1830s and 1840s were likewise committed to the ideal of a "Europe of free peoples." Victor Hugo even envisioned a "European republic" with its own parliament.

It is important to remember, however, that although many intellectuals found nationalism attractive, in the first half of the nineteenth century most people were likely to feel local and regional affinities more than national identities. Only as the result of several decades of propaganda by nationalists and governments was this ideology to win wide support, and only then did it become natural for Europeans to think of dying for their nations.

## ■ Liberalism

Liberalism was a direct descendant of the Enlightenment's critique of eighteenth-century absolutism. Nineteenth-century liberals believed that individual freedom was best safeguarded by reducing government powers to a minimum. They wanted to impose constitutional limits on government, to establish the rule of law, to sweep away all restrictions on individual enterprise—specifically, state regulation of the economy—and to ensure a voice in government for men of property and education. Liberalism was influenced by romanticism, with its emphasis on individual freedom and the imperative of the human personality to develop to its full potential. Liberalism was also affected by nationalism, especially in multinational autocratic states such as Austria, Russia, and the Ottoman Empire, in which free institutions could be established only if political independence were wrested from, respectively, Vienna, St. Petersburg, and Istanbul. (Nationalism challenged the established order in the first half of the century, but in the second half, conservatives were to use nationalism as a means to stabilize their rule.)

---

**Mazzini** (mat-SEE-nee)  **Mickiewicz** (MISS-kyev-ich)
**Fichte** (FISH-te)

### ❧ READING SOURCES

## Adam Smith Describes the Workings of the Market Economy

*In* An Inquiry into the Nature and Causes of the Wealth of Nations, *Adam Smith explained how individuals working to maximize their own interests cause the economy as a whole to expand and society to benefit. Among the various economic activities, trade and specialization particularly contribute to the well-being of both society and the individual. Notice the reciprocal nature of self-interest. Smith is building a model that he believed was true in all societies and at all times. Characterized by a mixture of theory and down-to-earth examples, his writings remain a pleasure to read.*

In almost every other race of animals each individual, when it is grown up to maturity, is entirely independent, and in its state has occasion for the assistance of no other living creature. But man has almost constant occasion for the help of his brethren, and it is in vain for him to expect it from their benevolence only. He will be more likely to prevail, if he can interest their self-love in his favour, and shew them that it is for their advantage to do for him what he requires of them. Whoever offers to another a bargain of any kind, proposes to do this. Give me that which I want, and you shall have this which you want, is the meaning of every such offer; and it is in this manner that we obtain from one another the far greater part of those good offices which we stand in need of. It is not from the benevolence of the butcher, the brewer, or the baker, that we expect our dinner, but from their regard to their own interest. We address ourselves, not to their humanity, but to their self-love, and never talk to them of our own necessities, but of their advantages. Nobody but a beggar chooses to depend chiefly upon the benevolence of his fellow-citizens. . . .

So it is this same trucking [trading] disposition which originally gives occasion to the division of labour. In a tribe of hunters or shepherds a particular person makes bows and arrows, for example, with more readiness and dexterity than any other. He frequently exchanges them for cattle or venison with his companions; and he finds at last that he can in this manner get more cattle and venison, than if he himself went to the field to catch them. From a regard to his own interest, therefore, the making of bows and arrows grows to be his chief business, and he becomes a sort of armourer. Another excels in making the frames and covers of their little huts or moveable houses. He is accustomed to be of use in this way to his neighbours, who reward him in the same manner with cattle and with venison, till at last he finds it in his interest to dedicate himself entirely to this employment, and to become a sort of house-carpenter. In the same manner a third becomes a smith or a brazier, a fourth a tanner or dresser of hides of skin, the principal part of the clothing of savages. And thus the certainty of being able to exchange all that surplus part of the produce of his own labour, which is over and above his own consumption, for such parts of the produce of other men's labour as he may have occasion for, encourages every man to apply himself to a particular occupation. . . .

*Source:* Adam Smith, *An Inquiry into the Nature and Causes of the Wealth of Nations* (London: W. Strahan, 1776), pp. 17–18.

Liberalism was both an economic and a political theory. In 1776 Adam Smith (1723–1790), the influential Scottish economist, published *An Inquiry into the Nature and Causes of the Wealth of Nations,* a systematic study of the economic knowledge of his era. Smith advocated freeing national economies from the fetters of the state. (See the box "Reading Sources: Adam Smith Describes the Workings of the Market Economy.") Under the mercantilist system, prevalent throughout Europe until about 1800, the state regulated the prices and conditions of manufacture. Smith argued for letting the free forces of the marketplace shape economic decisions. He believed that economics was subject to basic unalterable laws that could be discerned and applied in the same fashion as natural laws. Chief among them, in Smith's view, was the compatibility of economic self-interest and the general good. He argued that entrepreneurs who lower prices sell more products, thus increasing their own profits *and* providing the community with affordable wares. In this way, an individual's drive for profit benefits society as a whole. The economy is driven as if "by an invisible hand." This competitive drive for profits, Smith predicted, would expand the "wealth of nations." In France, advocates of nonintervention by government in the economy were called supporters of *laissez faire* (meaning "to leave alone, to let run on its own").

Smith and his disciples formed what came to be known as the school of classical economy, emphasizing the importance of laissez faire. Smith had been relatively optimistic about the capacities of the free market. Those who followed him, and who witnessed more of the negative results of industrialization, were more gloomy. Thomas Malthus (1766–1834), a parson, published in 1798 *An Essay on the Principle of Population*, which suggested that population was outstripping resources. Unless people voluntarily limited their family sizes, they would suffer starvation. By their failure to exercise sexual restraint, the poor, Malthus declared, "are themselves the cause of their own poverty." The laws of economics suggested to Malthus that factory owners could not improve their workers' lot by increasing wages or providing charity because higher living standards would lead to more births, which in turn would depress wages and bring greater misery.

David Ricardo (1772–1823) made his fortune in the stock market, retired young, and wrote on economics, his best-known work being *Principles of Political Economy* (1817). Ricardo argued that capitalists' profits depended on wages paid to workers; to be profitable, industrialists had to compete in limiting the wages they offered. The capitalist offering the lowest wages was likely to be most successful. The "iron law of wages" seemed to provide, as had Malthus, scientific justification for the exploitation of workers.

Even supporters of laissez faire had some reservations about the market economy. In France in the first half of the nineteenth century, commentators on the factory system, including industrialists, expressed fear that factory work would undermine the stability of family life and hence of society itself. Philanthropic intervention, they hoped, would resolve the problems they had identified.

Even some of the British classical economists doubted the wisdom of allowing the market economy to operate entirely without regulation and of trusting it to provide for human happiness. Smith warned that the market tended to form monopolies, and he suggested that government intervene to prevent this occurrence. According to Smith, the marketplace could not provide for all human needs; the government needed to supply education, road systems, and an equitable system of justice.

John Stuart Mill (1806–1873), the leading British economic and political thinker at midcentury, voiced strong support for laissez-faire economics in the first edition of his *Principles of Political Economy* (1848). If left alone, the individual could carry on economic functions better than the government, Mill insisted. In subsequent editions, however, he remarked that the state had an obligation to relieve human misery. Nor could the free market satisfactorily address every human need. Once wealth was produced, he noted, its distribution was subject to traditions and to decisions made by those in power. Thus, presumably, wealth could be shared by society as a whole. Toward the end of his life, Mill seemed to be leaning toward socialism.

Mill's about-face reflected and presaged changing attitudes among the proponents of laissez faire. In the face of unsanitary urban conditions, child labor, stark inequities in wealth, and other alarming results of industrialization, at least some liberals around midcentury called on the state to intervene in areas of concern that would have been unthinkable a half-century earlier.

In their political positions, liberals were firm throughout the century, constant in their support for limiting government power to prevent despotism. Enlightened eighteenth-century monarchs had declared that the purpose of their rule was to promote the public good. In even more ringing terms, the French Revolution had proclaimed that the purpose of government is to ensure the happiness of humankind. As Thomas Jefferson (1743–1826), another child of the Enlightenment, asserted in the Declaration of Independence (1776), among the "unalienable rights" of individuals are "life, liberty, and the pursuit of happiness." The purpose of government is to safeguard and promote those rights.

The Enlightenment had posited natural law as the basis of government. French liberals in the nineteenth century continued to see human liberty as founded on natural law, but their English counterparts were less theoretical in outlook. Jeremy Bentham (1748–1832) argued that the purpose of government is to provide "the greatest happiness of the greatest number" and that governments should be judged on that basis. Bentham and his disciples believed that the test of government is its usefulness; thus they were known as "Utilitarians."

Democracy was implicit in Bentham's philosophy: the greatest number could ensure its own happiness only by voting for its rulers. John Stuart Mill, a disciple of Bentham, was the foremost proponent of liberalism, seeing it as guaranteeing the development of a free society. Individuals could best develop their talents if they were unhampered by state interference. In his essay *On Liberty*, one of the fundamental documents of nineteenth-century liberalism, Mill argued for the free circulation of ideas—even false ideas. For in the free marketplace of ideas, false ideas will be defeated, and truth vindicated, in open debate. Mill also asserted that a free society should be free for all its members. Influenced by Harriet Taylor (1807–1856), who was to become his wife, he wrote in *On the Subjection of Women* (1861) that women should be permitted to vote and should have access to equal educational opportunities and the professions. Such equality not only would be just but also would have the advantage of "doubling the mass of mental faculties available for the higher service of humanity." Mill, the foremost male proponent of women's rights in his generation, helped win a broader audience for the principle of equality between the sexes.

Despite Mill's influence, many liberals, especially in the early nineteenth century, feared the masses and therefore vigorously opposed democracy. They feared that the common people, uneducated and supposedly gullible, would easily be swayed by demagogues who might become despotic or who, in a desire to curry favor with the poor, might attack the privileges of the wealthy. The French liberal Benjamin Constant denounced democracy as "the vulgarization of despotism"; the vote, he declared, should be reserved for the affluent and educated. When less fortunate Frenchmen denounced the property requirements that prevented them from voting, the liberal statesman François Guizot (1787–1874) smugly replied, "Get rich."

In the twelfth and thirteenth centuries, a new wealthy class based on urban occupations emerged; its members were called "burgers" or "bourgeois." This class fully developed in the nineteenth century. If unsympathetic to extending suffrage to the lower classes, the *bourgeoisie*° championed liberalism, which justified its own right to participate in governance. Economic liberalism was also attractive to merchants and manufacturers, who wished to gather wealth without state interference.

If originating in and justifying middle-class interests, the basic tenets of liberalism—the belief in the sanctity of human rights, freedom of speech and freedom to organize, the rule of law and equality before the law—eventually became so widely accepted that even conservative and socialist opponents of liberalism accepted them as fundamental rights.

## ■ Socialism

The notion that human happiness can best be ensured by the common ownership of property had been suggested in earlier times by individuals as different as the Greek philosopher Plato (427?–347 B.C.) and Sir Thomas More (1478–1535), the English author of *Utopia*. Troubled by the harsh condition of the working classes, thinkers in Britain and France came to espouse theories that, beginning in the 1820s, were called "socialist." Socialists believed that the "social" ownership of property, unlike private ownership, would benefit society as a whole. During the first half of the nineteenth century, most workers, even in industrializing England, where manufacturing was increasingly large scale, were artisans. It was in a later era that socialism would address the issues raised by industry.

In 1796, during the French Revolution, Gracchus Babeuf° (1760–1797), a minor civil servant, participated in the Conspiracy of Equals (see page 660). The Revolution, however haltingly, had proclaimed political equality for its citizens, but it had failed to bring economic equality. Babeuf decided to resort to revolution to bring about a "communist" society—a society in which all property would be owned in common and private property would be abolished. Work would be provided for everyone; medical services and education would be free to all. Babeuf's plot was discovered, and he was guillotined, but his theories and example of conspiratorial revolutionary action would influence later socialists.

Several other important French thinkers made contributions to European socialism. Curiously, it was a French aristocrat, Henri de Saint-Simon° (1760–1825), who emphasized the need "to ameliorate as promptly and as quickly as possible the moral and physical existence of the most numerous class." The proper role for the state, Saint-Simon declared, was to ensure the welfare of the masses. The course of history, he suggested, was in the direction of expertise. No longer could people rule solely on the basis of their birth. Rather, Europe

---

**bourgeoisie** (boor-zhwa-ZEE)

**Gracchus Babeuf** (GRAH-kus bah-BOEF)
**Saint-Simon** (saen–see-MON)

should come to be governed by a council of qualified artists and scientists who would oversee the economy and ensure that everyone enjoyed a minimum level of well-being.

Another vital contribution to socialist thought came from thinkers who tried to imagine an ideal world. They were later derisively dismissed as dreamers, as builders of utopias, fantasy worlds (the Greek word *utopia* means "nowhere"). Their schemes varied, but they shared the view that property should be owned in common and used for the common good. They also believed that society should rest on principles of cooperation rather than competitive individualism.

One of the earliest and most notable utopians was the Welsh mill-owner Robert Owen (1771–1859). Beginning in 1800 he ran a prosperous cotton mill in New Lanark, Scotland. He also provided generously for his workers, guaranteeing them jobs and their children decent educations. In his writings Owen suggested the establishment of self-governing communities owning the means of production. Essentials would be distributed to all members according to their needs. Owen's ideas for the new society included equal rights for women.

Owen received little support from fellow manufacturers and political leaders, and his own attempt in 1824 to establish an ideal society in the United States at New Harmony, Indiana, ended in failure after four years.

Another influential contributor to early socialist theory was the Frenchman Charles Fourier° (1772–1837). A clerk and salesman, Fourier wrote out in great detail his vision of the ideal future society. It would consist of cooperative organizations called "phalansteries," each with 1,600 inhabitants who would live in harmony with nature and with one another. Everyone would be assured gainful employment, which would be made enjoyable by rotating jobs. Because cooperative communes often faced the issue of who would carry out the distasteful tasks, everyone would share the pleasant *and* unpleasant work. Fourier thought that because children enjoy playing with dirt, they should be put in charge of picking up garbage.

Fourier had an important female following because of his belief in the equality of the sexes, and some of these women tried to put his ideas into action. In Belgium the activist Zoé Gatti de Gamond° (1806–1854) cofounded a phalanstery for women. She believed that if women could be assured of economic well-being, other rights would follow. Also inspired by Fourier, Flora Tristan (1801–1844) was an effective advocate for workers'

rights. In her book *Union Ouvrière (Workers' Union)*, she suggested that all workers should contribute to establish a "Worker's Palace" in every town. In the palace, the sick and disabled would have shelter, and the workers' children could receive a free education. Crossing France on foot, she spread the word of workers' solidarity and self-help.

There were other approaches. The French socialist journalist Louis Blanc° (1811–1882) saw in democracy the means of bringing into existence a socialist state. By securing the vote, the common people could win control over the state and require it to serve their needs. The state could be induced to buy up banks, insurance companies, and railway systems and set up a commercial and retail chain that would provide jobs for workers and offer goods and services at prices unaffected by the profit motive. Once the workers controlled the state by the ballot, the state in turn would establish social workshops in which the workers would be responsible for production and supervision of business matters. Society should be established according to (from the socialist viewpoint) fundamental fairness: "Let each produce according to his aptitudes and strength; let each consume according to his need."

Blanc's contemporary Louis Blanqui° (1805–1882) suggested a more violent mode of action. He advocated seizure of the state by a small, dedicated band of men who were devoted to the welfare of the working class and who would install communism, for the equality of all. Blanqui was a perpetual conspirator, confined to state prisons for much of his long life. His ideas strengthened the notion of class warfare, and his own life served as a symbol of this struggle. The thought and example of Blanqui and the other socialists would play a major role in shaping the thinking of the most important socialist of the nineteenth century, Karl Marx.

Karl Marx (1818–1883), the son of a lawyer, grew up in the Rhineland, in western Germany, an industrializing area that was particularly open to political ideas and agitation. The Rhineland had been influenced by the ideas of the French Revolution and was primed for political radicalism. As a young man Marx studied philosophy at the University of Berlin and joined a group known as the "Young Hegelians," self-declared disciples of the idealist philosopher G. W. F. Hegel (1770–1831). Hegel taught that reality is mainly based on the ability of the mind to conceive of it. Marx, by contrast, was a materialist, believing that material realities impose themselves on the mind.

---

**Fourier** (foor-YAY)   **Gamond** (gay-MON)

**Blanc** (BLAHN)   **Blanqui** (blahn-KEE)

Marx showed an early interest in political liberty and socialism. In 1842–1843 he edited a newspaper that spoke out for freedom and democracy in Germany. The following year, in Paris, he met several of the French socialist writers. Even when he was a young man, his contemporaries perceived him as bright but unyielding in his determination.

Because of his radical journalism, he was exiled from the Rhineland and lived briefly in Paris, then Brussels. In 1849 he settled in London, where he lived for the rest of his life, dedicated to establishing his ideas on what he viewed as scientific bases. Deriving a modest income from writing for the *New York Daily Tribune* and from funds provided by his friend and collaborator Friedrich Engels (1820–1895), Marx was never able to provide well for his family, which constantly lived on the edge of poverty. Of the six children born to the Marx household, three died in infancy.

In 1848 Marx and Engels published the *Communist Manifesto.* A pamphlet written for the Communist League, a group of Germans living in exile, the manifesto was an appeal to the working classes of the world. The league deliberately called itself "Communist" rather than "Socialist." Communism was a radical program, bent on changing property relations by violence; socialism was associated with more peaceful means of transformation. The pamphlet laid out Marx's basic ideas, calling on the proletariat to rise—"You have nothing to lose but your chains"—and create a society that would end the exploitation of man by man. (See the box "Reading Sources: Karl Marx's *Communist Manifesto*.")

A number of political and polemical works flowed from Marx's pen, but most of them remained unpublished during his lifetime. The first volume of his major work, *Capital*, was published in 1867; subsequent volumes appeared posthumously. Marxism, the body of Marx's thought, is complex and sometimes contradictory. *Capital* is written in an obscure style, difficult to penetrate. But certain basic concepts resound throughout and were embraced by Marx's followers.

Marx agreed with Hegel and many of his contemporaries that human history has a direction and a goal. Hegel believed that the goal was the realization of the world spirit. Marx believed that it was the abolition of capitalism, the victory of the proletariat, the disappearance of the state, and the ultimate liberation of all humankind.

Whereas Hegel thought that ideas govern the world, Marx insisted that material conditions determine it. Hegel said that history evolves by the "dialectic": a principle, say despotism, has within it ideas that oppose it; in

**Karl Marx**　Through his writings and agitation, Marx transformed the socialism of his day and created an ideology that helped shape the nineteenth and twentieth centuries. *(Corbis)*

the struggle between despotism and its opposite, a higher ideal emerges—freedom, the ultimate goal of history. Following Hegel, Marx posited a world of change but insisted that it was embedded in material conditions, not in a clash of ideas. Hence, the process of history was grounded on the notion of "dialectical materialism." Ideas, to Marx, were but a reflection of the material world.

Marx grouped human beings into classes based on their relationship to the means of production. Capitalists were one class because they owned the means of production. Workers were a separate class—the proletariat—because they did not own any of the means of production and their income came only from their own

## ❧ READING SOURCES

### Karl Marx's *Communist Manifesto*

*The* Communist Manifesto *provides a preview of the major themes that would inform Marx and Engels's later writings: the concept of class formation and class antagonism, the privileged role of the proletariat, and the inevitability of the proletariat's success.*

The history of all hitherto existing society is the history of class struggles.

Freeman and slave, patrician and plebeian, lord and serf, guild-master and journeyman, in a word, oppressor and oppressed, stood in constant opposition to one another, carried on an uninterrupted, now hidden, now open fight, that each time ended, either in a revolutionary reconstitution of society at large, or in the common ruin of the contending classes. . . .

In ancient Rome we have patricians, knights, plebeians, slaves; in the Middle Ages, feudal lords, vassals, guild-masters, journeymen, apprentices, serfs; in almost all of these classes, again, subordinate gradations.

The modern bourgeois society that has sprouted from the ruins of feudal society, has not done away with class antagonisms. It has but established new classes, new conditions of oppression, new forms of struggle in place of the old ones. . . .

Society as a whole is more and more splitting up into two great hostile camps, into two great classes directly facing each other: Bourgeoisie and Proletariat. . . .

With the development of industry the proletariat not only increases in number; it becomes concentrated in greater masses, its strength grows and it

feels that strength more. . . . [T]he collisions between individual workmen and individual bourgeois take more and more the character of collisions between two classes. . . .

Of all the classes that stand face to face with the bourgeoisie today, the proletariat alone is a really revolutionary class. The other classes decay and finally disappear in the face of modern industry; the proletariat is its special and essential product.

All previous historical movements were movements of minorities. The proletarian movement is the self-conscious, independent movement of the immense majority. The proletariat, the stratum of our present society, cannot stir, cannot raise itself up, without the whole superincumbent strata of official society being sprung into the air. . . .

. . . The development of modern industry, therefore, cuts from under its feet the very foundation on which the bourgeoisie produces and appropriates products. What the bourgeoisie therefore produces, above all, are its own grave-diggers. Its fall and the victory of the proletariat are equally inevitable.

*Source:* Karl Marx and Friedrich Engels, *Communist Manifesto* (1848; reprint, New York: International Publishers, 1948), pp. 9, 17, 20–21.

hands. Because these two classes had different relationships to the means of production, they had different—in fact, antagonistic—interests and were destined (Marx believed) to engage in a class struggle.

Some of Marx's contemporaries lamented the increasing hostility between workers and capitalists. Marx, however, saw the conflict as necessary to advance human history, and he sought to validate his thesis by the study of the past. In the Middle Ages, he pointed out, the feudal class dominated society but eventually lost

the struggle to the commercial classes. Now, in turn, the capitalists were destined to be overwhelmed by the rising proletariat.

In his study of history and economics, Marx found not only justification for but irrefutable proof of the "scientific" basis of his ideas. Capitalism was itself creating the forces that would supplant it. The large industrial plants necessitated an ever greater work force with a growing sense of class interest. The inherently competitive nature of capitalism would inevitably drive an increasing number of enterprises out of business, and a form of monopoly capitalism would emerge, abusive of both consumers and workers. As a result of ever more savage competition, more businesses would fail, and consequently more workers would become unemployed. Angered and frustrated by their lot, workers would overthrow the system that had abused them for so long: "The knell of private property has sounded. The expropriators will be expropriated." The proletariat would take power and, to solidify its rule, would temporarily exercise the "dictatorship of the proletariat." Once that had taken place, the state would wither away. With the coming to power of the proletariat, the history of class war would end and the ideal society would prevail. Ironically, Marx, who spent his life writing about the nature and history of social change, envisaged a time when change would cease, when history, as it were, would stop.

Many protested the evils of industrialism, but Marx described economic change in dramatic terms as a necessary stage for humankind to traverse on its way to liberation. The suffering of the workers was not in vain. Rather, it was a necessary process, part of the drama that would finally lead to human emancipation. Unlike some of the utopians who deplored industrialism, Marx accepted it and saw it as part of the path that history was fated to follow.

Marx's study of economics and history proved to him that the coming of socialism was not only desirable—as the utopians had thought—but inevitable. The laws of history dictated that capitalism, having created the rising proletariat, would collapse. By labeling his brand of socialism as scientific, Marx gave it the aura it needed to become the faith of millions of people. To declare ideas scientific in the nineteenth century, when science was held in such high esteem, was to ensure their popularity.

# RESTORATION, REFORM, AND REACTION

ESPITE the new ideologies that emerged to challenge the existing order, efforts at restoration appeared successful until at least 1830. Indeed in central and eastern Europe, from the German states to Russia and the Ottoman Empire, the political systems established in 1815 would persist virtually unchanged until midcentury. In western Europe, however, important transformations would occur by the 1830s as reaction gave way to reform. Then in 1848, widespread revolutions would break out on much of the Continent. The language of liberalism and nationalism and even the newer idiom of socialism would be heard on the barricades, in popular assemblies, and in parliamentary halls.

## ■ Western Europe: From Reaction to Liberalism, 1815–1830

Most of Europe until the 1830s experienced the heavy hand of reaction. Then western Europe saw more liberal regimes come into their own. Revolution and the threat of revolution helped dismantle the worst features of the restored regimes. The more liberal western European states faced continuing discontents of various sorts—mainly social and political—which they managed to negotiate with varying degrees of success.

The most dramatic restoration of the older order occurred in France. The restored Bourbons turned the clock back, not to 1789 but closer to 1791, when the country had briefly enjoyed a constitutional monarchy, and it went beyond that in maintaining the Napoleonic Code with its provisions of legal equality. The Bourbon constitution provided for a parliament with an elected lower house, the Chamber of Deputies, and an appointed upper house, the Chamber of Peers. Although suffrage to the Chamber of Deputies was limited to a small elite of men with landed property—100,000 voters, about 0.2 percent of the population—this constitution was a concession to representative government that had not existed in the Old Regime (see page 647). Louis XVIII (r. 1814–1824) stands out among European rulers because he realized that it would be necessary to compromise on the principles of popular sovereignty proclaimed by the French Revolution. His intention was to "popularize the monarchy" and "royalize the nation." A moderate, Louis was succeeded by his ultrareactionary brother, Charles X (r. 1824–1830), who alienated the middle classes. More general disenchantment came with an economic downturn in 1827, marked by poor harvests and increased unemployment in the cities. Discontent brought to Parliament a liberal majority that refused to accept the reactionary ministers the king appointed. On July 26, 1830, after the humiliating defeat of his party at the polls, the king issued a set of decrees suspending freedom of the press, dissolving the Chamber of Deputies, and stiffening property qualifications for voters in subsequent elections. The king appeared to be engineering a coup against the existing political system.

The first to protest were the Parisian journalists and typesetters, directly threatened by the censorship laws. On July 28, others joined the protest and began erecting barricades across many streets. After killing several

**Louis XVIII as Military Leader**    The French king, returned to his throne by France's foreign enemies, had no military glory attached to his reign. But in 1823 France successfully invaded Spain, helping its reactionary king suppress a liberal revolt. This painting celebrates the return of the victorious French troops.    *(Château de Versailles/Laurie Platt Winfrey, Inc.)*

hundred protesters, the king's forces lost control of the city. The uprising, known as "the three glorious days," drove the king into exile.

Alarmed by the crowds' clamor for a republic, the liberal opposition—consisting of some of the leading newspaper editors and sympathetic deputies—quickly drafted the duke of Orléans, Louis Philippe (r. 1830–1848), known for his liberal opinions, to occupy the throne.

Compared with the rest of Europe, Great Britain enjoyed considerable constitutional guarantees and a parliamentary regime. Yet liberals and radicals found their government retrograde and repressive. Traumatized by the French Revolution, the ruling class clung to the past, certain that advocates for change were Jacobins in disguise. Change seemed to invite revolution.

Social unrest beset Britain as it faced serious economic dislocation. The arrival of peace in 1815 led to a sudden drop in government expenditures, the return into the economy of several hundred thousand men who had been away at war, financial disarray, and plummeting prices. The poor and the middle classes were especially incensed over the clear economic advantages that the landed classes, dominating Parliament, had secured for themselves in 1815 in passing the Corn Law. This legislation imposed high tariffs on imported "corn"—that is, various forms of grain. It thus shielded the domestic market from international competition and allowed landowners to reap huge profits at the expense of consumers. All these issues were cause for demonstrations, petitions, protest marches, and other challenges to the authorities.

In August 1819, sixty thousand people gathered in St. Peter's Fields in Manchester to demand universal suffrage for men and women alike, an annual Parliament, and other democratic reforms. The crowd was peaceful and unarmed, yet mounted soldiers charged, killing eleven and wounding four hundred. Using military force against the people as if against the French at Waterloo was seen as wrong, and the confrontation was branded "the battle of Peterloo." The British public was shocked by this use of violence against peaceful demonstrators; Parliament responded by passing the so-called Six Acts, which outlawed freedom of assembly and effectively imposed censorship. Through much of the 1820s Britain appeared resistant to reform until news of revolution across the channel in 1830 brought about change.

The term *liberal* was first coined in Spain, where the fate of liberals prefigured what would happen elsewhere in continental Europe. In 1812 a national parliament, the Cortes, elected during the Napoleonic occupation, issued a democratic constitution that provided for universal manhood suffrage and a unicameral legislature with control over government policy. Supporters and admirers of the constitution in Spain and elsewhere were known as "liberals," or friends of liberty.

Napoleon had ousted the Bourbon king of Spain, Ferdinand VII (r. 1808, 1814–1833). Ferdinand returned to power in 1814, promising to respect the liberal 1812 constitution. But Ferdinand was by temperament hostile to the new order, and he was a believer in the divine right of kings. He drew his support from the aristocracy and from segments of the general population still loyal to the call of throne and altar. Liberals were arrested or driven into exile.

Ferdinand's plan to restore Spain to its earlier prominence included a reassertion of control over its American colonies. The Spanish dominions had grown restless in the eighteenth century, for they had witnessed the advent of an independent United States and the French occupation of Spain itself. Spain's emboldened colonies had refused to recognize the Napoleonic regime in Madrid and became increasingly self-reliant. Their attitude did not change when French control of Spain ended. Ferdinand refused to compromise with the overseas territories. Instead, he gathered an army to subdue them. Some liberal junior officers, declaring the army's loyalty to the constitution of 1812, won support from the rank and file, who balked at going overseas. This military mutiny coincided with a sympathetic provincial uprising to produce the "revolution of 1820," the first major assault on the European order established in 1815 at the Congress of Vienna. Ferdinand appealed to the European powers for help. France intervened on his behalf and crushed the uprising.

Ferdinand restored his reactionary regime but could not regain Spain's American colonies. The British,

**"Peterloo" Massacre**   In August 1819 at St. Peter's Fields in Manchester, a crowd demanding parliamentary reform was charged by government troops, leading to bloodshed. Many English people derided the event and called it "Peterloo."   *(Public Record Office)*

sympathetic to the cause of Latin American independence and eager for commercial access to the region, opposed reconquest, and their naval dominance of the seas kept Spain in its place. The United States, meanwhile, had recognized the independence of the Latin American republics and wished to see their independence maintained. In 1823 President James Monroe issued the statement known as the Monroe Doctrine, prohibiting European colonization or intervention in the affairs of independent republics in the Americas. Of course, the United States had no military muscle to back this proclamation, but the British navy effectively enforced it. By 1825 all of Spain's colonies on the mainland in Central and South America had won their freedom.

The newly independent states patterned their regimes on models of Spanish liberalism; all had constitutions stipulating separation of powers and guaranteeing human rights. Brazil, the Portuguese empire in the Americas, was a monarchy for most of the rest of the nineteenth century, as was Mexico for a short time, but all the other states became republics, opting for what was then an unusual form of government. Although most of the Latin regimes eventually became dictatorships, they continued to pay lip service to liberal values.

### ■ Western Europe, 1830–1848

For the political systems of western Europe, the 1830s marked a time of modification. The threat, and occasionally the sting, of revolt produced more liberal regimes, but except for Britain and Spain, most governments were unable to stem the tide of discontent, which became revolution in 1848.

As a result of the 1830 revolution in Paris, a more liberal regime was installed in France. Louis Philippe proclaimed himself "King of the French," thus acknowledging that he reigned at the behest of the people. Freedom of the press was reinstated. Suffrage was extended to twice as many voters as before, 200,000 men. The July Monarchy, named after the month in which it was established by revolution, justified itself by celebrating the great Revolution of 1789. Louis Philippe commissioned huge canvases glorifying great moments of the Revolution. On the site where the Bastille had been razed in 1789, the government erected a large column with the names of the victims of the July 1830 revolution, thus suggesting a continuity between those who had fought tyranny in 1789 and 1830.

Identification with the Revolution appeared to legitimize the regime but also had the potential to subvert it. Fearful that the cult of revolution would encourage violence against the new monarchy, the regime censored artistic production, promoting only works that extolled the period from 1789 to 1791, when the revolutionaries had attempted to found a constitutional monarchy. Now that the revolution of 1830 had established a constitutional monarchy, the regime was suggesting, any further uprisings were illegitimate. If the July Monarchy turned out not to be as liberal as its founders had hoped, foreign visitors coming from more authoritarian societies were nonetheless impressed by France's apparently liberal institutions. (See the box "Global Encounters: A Moroccan Describes the French Freedom of the Press.") Many French liberals, however, saw the regime as a travesty of the hopes and promises it had represented on coming to power in 1830.

The major political problem facing Britain in the early nineteenth century was the composition of Parliament, which did not reflect the dramatic population shifts that had occurred since the seventeenth century. Industrialization had transformed mere villages into major cities—Manchester, Birmingham, Leeds, Sheffield—but those cities had no representation in Parliament. Localities that had lost population, however, were still represented. In districts known as "pocket boroughs," single individuals owned the right to a seat in Parliament. In districts known as "rotten boroughs," a handful of voters elected a representative.

News of the July 1830 revolution in Paris encouraged British liberals to push for reform. Fearing the same fate as the hapless Charles X, some conservatives silently yielded. The government introduced a reform bill abolishing or reducing representation for sparsely populated areas while granting seats for the populous and unrepresented cities. The bill also widened the franchise by lowering property qualifications to include many middle-class men. Following a prolonged, bitter political battle between the government and middle classes on one side and the aristocracy on the other, the House of Lords finally passed what came to be known as the Great Reform Bill of 1832.

The reform was not particularly radical. Only the upper layers of the middle class were enfranchised, or one in seven adult males. By establishing national criteria for the vote and eliminating local variations, some people, including some women, actually lost the vote. Yet despite its shortcomings, the reform demonstrated the willingness of the political leaders to acknowledge the increasing economic importance of manufacturing. Parliament became a more representative forum whose makeup better reflected the shift of economic power from agricultural landowners to the industrial and commercial classes. The bill passed as a result of nationwide agitation, evidence that the political

⊕ G L O B A L   E N C O U N T E R S

## A Moroccan Describes French Freedom of the Press

*In 1845–1846 a Moroccan diplomatic mission visited Paris; the ambassador's secretary, Muhammad as-Saffar (d. 1881), wrote an account of the visit. Impressed by many aspects of French society, in the following passage he praises France's press. The "Sultan" as-Saffar refers to is King Louis Philippe. To this Moroccan observer, the extent to which the French enjoyed constitutional government was striking.*

The people of Paris, like all the French indeed, like all of [Europe] are eager to know the latest news and events that are taking place in other parts [of the world]. For this purpose they have the gazette. [In] these papers . . . they write all the news that has reached them that day about events in their own country and in other lands both near and far.

This is the way it is done. The owner of a newspaper dispatches his people to collect everything they see or hear in the way of important events or unusual happenings. Among the places where they collect the news are the two Chambers, the Great and the Small, where they come together to make their laws. When the members of the Chamber meet to deliberate, the men of the gazette sit nearby and write down everything that is said, for all debating and ratifying of laws is matter for the gazette and is known to everyone. No one can prevent them from doing this. . . .

. . . [I]f someone has an idea about a subject but he is not a member of the press, he may write about it in the gazette and make it known to others, so that the leaders of opinion learn about it. If the idea is worthy they may follow it, and if its author was out of favor it may bring him recognition.

No person in France is prohibited from expressing his opinion or from writing it and printing it, on condition that he does not violate the law. . . .

In the newspapers they write rejoinders to the men of the two Chambers about the laws they are making. If their Sultan demands gifts from the notables or goes against the law in any way, they write about that too, saying that he is a tyrant and in the wrong. He cannot confront them or cause them harm. Also, if someone behaves out of the ordinary, they write about that too, making it common knowledge among people of every rank. If his deeds were admirable, they praise and delight in him, lauding his example; but if he behaved badly, they revile him to discourage the like.

Moreover, if someone is being oppressed by another, they write about that too, so that everyone will know the story from both sides just as it happened, until it is decided in court. One can also read in it what their courts have decided.

*Source:* Susan Gilson Miller, ed. and trans., *Disorienting Encounters: Travels of a Moroccan Scholar in France in 1845–1846. The Voyage of Muhammad as-Saffar* (Berkeley: University of California Press, 1992), pp. 150–153.

---

system could respond to grievances and bring about reform peacefully.

Parliament justified the population's newfound faith in its efficacy by undertaking several more reforms. In 1835 Parliament passed the Municipal Corporation Act, which provided for more representative municipal councils with increased decision-making powers in local affairs.

A series of colonial reforms also showed Parliament's willingness to adapt to changing circumstances. Opposition to slavery had been voiced since the 1780s. (See the box "Reading Sources: A Plea to Abolish Slavery in the British Colonies.") Slavery, the very opposite of human freedom, was an affront to liberal principles. Moreover, its persistence threatened the empire—in 1831, 60,000 slaves rebelled in Jamaica. Parliament heeded the call for change and in 1833 abolished slavery throughout the British Empire.

In addition, the British began to review their imperial administration. Their control over Canada had been challenged in an uprising in 1837; London sent out a fact-finding mission headed by Lord Durham (1806–1848). As a result of the *Durham Report*, the

## ☙ READING SOURCES

# A Plea to Abolish Slavery in the British Colonies

*Among the causes that British reformers embraced was the abolition of slavery. The slave trade had been abolished in 1807; one more step was left—ending in the colonies the institution of slavery itself. In this petition to Parliament in 1823, the Society for the Mitigation and Gradual Abolition of Slavery Throughout the British Dominions explains the harsh and degrading nature of the institution. Trading in slaves had already been abolished as immoral and unnatural; here the petitioners remind Parliament that holding slaves is no less abhorrent. Under the pressure of this type of agitation, Parliament in 1833 abolished slavery in the British Empire.*

In the colonies of Great Britain there are at this moment upwards of 800,000 human beings in a state of degrading personal slavery.

These unhappy persons, whether young or old, male or female, are the absolute property of their master, who may sell or transfer them at his pleasure, and who may also regulate according to his discretion (within certain limits) the measure of their labour, their food, and their punishment.

Many of the slaves are (and all may be) branded like cattle, by means of a hot iron, on the shoulder or other conspicuous part of the body, with the initials of their master's name; and thus bear about them in indelible characters the proof of their debased and servile state. . . .

It can hardly be alleged that any man can have a right to obtain his fellow creatures in a state so miserable and degrading as has been described. And the absence of such right will be still more apparent, if we consider how these slaves were originally obtained. They, or their parents, were the victims of the Slave Trade. They were obtained, not by lawful means, or under any colourable pretext, but by the most undisguised rapine, and the most atrocious fraud. Torn from their homes and from every dear relation in life, barbarously manacled, driven like herds of cattle to the sea-shore, crowded into the potential holds of slave-ships, they were transported to our colonies and there sold in bondage. . . .

The Government and Legislature of this country have on various occasions, and in the most solemn and unequivocal terms denounced the Slave Trade as immoral, inhuman, and unjust; but the legal perpetuation of that state of slavery, which has been produced by it, is surely, in its principle, no less immoral, inhuman and unjust, than the trade itself. . . .

*Source:* Reprinted in *Circular Letters of the Society for the Mitigation and Gradual Abolition of Slavery Throughout the British Dominions* (April 1823).

 **For additional information on this topic, go to http://college.hmco.com.**

British government promulgated self-government for Canada in 1839 and 1841; eventually all the British colonies with a majority of white settlers were given similar rights of self-rule. The idea of self-government for nonwhites in the colonies was as yet an unimaginable proposition.

Reforms solidified Britain's influence overseas. In Canada they reduced opposition to British rule. The antislavery campaign led to the extension of British power into Africa. Having abolished the slave trade in 1807, the British worked to compel other nations to end the trade. With the largest navy in the world, Britain was well equipped to patrol the coast of West Africa, trying to suppress the traffic in humans and hinder its colonial rivals from benefiting from the trade. Needing bases for these patrols, the British established a number of minor settlements in West Africa, becoming the predominant European power along the coast. Although unimportant when acquired, these possessions foreshadowed the increasing European intrusion into African affairs.

Parliament's reforming zeal stimulated support for Chartism, a movement intended to transform Britain from essentially an oligarchy—rule by a few—into a democracy. In 1838 political radicals with working-class support drew up a "people's charter" calling for universal male suffrage; electoral districts with equal population; salaries and the abolition of property qualifications for members of Parliament; the secret ballot; and annual general elections. The Chartists hoped that giving workers the vote would end the dominance of the much smaller upper classes in Parliament and ensure an improvement in the workers' lot.

Chartism won wide support among men and women in the working class, sparking demonstrations and petition drives of unprecedented size. Women participated to a larger extent than in any other political movement of the day, founding over a hundred female Chartist chapters. Some Chartists, especially female members, asked for women's suffrage, but this demand failed to gain overall adherence from the membership. Winning mass support during particularly hard economic years, Chartism lost followers during a temporary economic upswing. The movement also fell under the sway of advocates of violence, who scared off many artisans and potential middle-class supporters. It lost credibility too by criticizing British institutions for being unresponsive to the needs of the working class, whereas in fact Parliament had introduced a number of significant reforms, including the Factory Act of 1833, which provided some protection to laborers. Lacking popular support, Chartism failed as a political movement; yet it drew public attention to an integrated democratic program whose main provisions (except for yearly elections) would be adopted piecemeal over the next half-century.

In 1839 urban businessmen founded the Anti–Corn Law League for the purpose of abolishing the Corn Law of 1815, which was increasing the price of grain. The Corn Law was unpopular with manufacturers, who knew that low food prices would allow them to pay low wages. It was also unpopular with workers, who wanted bread at a price they could afford. The anti–Corn Law movement proved more effective than Chartism because it had the support of the middle classes. Alarmed by the threat of famine after the poor harvest of 1845, Parliament repealed the Corn Law in 1846.

In the end, this action did not affect the price of grain. Nevertheless, repeal of the Corn Law was a milestone in British history, demonstrating the extent to which organized groups could bring about economic improvements. A popular, mass organization had been able to shape public policy—a far cry from the days of Peterloo, when the government had not only ignored the public but attacked it with bayonets fixed.

## ■ The Absolutist States of Central and Eastern Europe, 1815–1848

Having seen the turmoil unleashed by the French Revolution and suffered at the hands of the Grande Armée, the states of central and eastern Europe were particularly committed to maintaining absolute government. In contrast to many parts of western Europe, which saw important political changes in the 1830s, the absolutist states were able to preserve themselves essentially unchanged until 1848—and in some cases even beyond.

The Austrian Empire's far-flung territories seemed to its Habsburg rulers to require a firm hand (see Map 21.1). Liberalism, which challenged imperial power, could not be countenanced. Nor, in this multinational empire, could nationalism be tolerated. The emperor, Francis I (r. 1792–1835), was opposed to any change; his motto was "Rule and change nothing." Prince Metternich, Francis's chief minister, viewed the French Revolution of 1789 and its aftermath as a disaster and believed his task was to hold the line against the threat of revolution. Quick to interpret protests or the desire for change as a threat to the fundamental order, Metternich established a network of secret police and informers to spy on the imperial subjects and keep them in check.

In most of the German states, the political order was authoritarian and inflexible. The states of Baden and Württemberg in the southwest and Bavaria in the south had granted their subjects constitutions, although effective power remained in the hands of the ruling houses. The king of Prussia had repeatedly promised a constitution, but none had materialized. A central, representative Diet would not meet there until 1847. Prussia was ruled by an alliance of the king and the *Junkers°*, the landowning aristocrats who staffed the officer corps and the bureaucracy. Both the officer corps and the bureaucracy were efficient enough to serve as models for the rest of Europe. Where Prussia lagged by liberal standards was in its political institutions.

Throughout the German states, the urban middle classes, intellectuals, journalists, university professors, and students were frustrated with the existing system. They were disappointed by the lack of free institutions and the failure of the patriotic wars against Napoleon to create a united Germany. University students formed *Burschenschaften°*, or brotherhoods, whose slogan was "Honor, Liberty, Fatherland." Metternich imposed a policy of reaction on the German Confederation and pushed through the Carlsbad Decrees in July 1819, establishing

**Junkers** (YUNG-kurz)
**Burschenschaften** (BOOR-shen-shaft-en)

close supervision over the universities, censorship of the press, and dissolution of the youth groups. Wholesale persecution of liberals and nationalists followed. The Prussian king dismissed his more enlightened officials.

The outbreak of revolution in Paris in 1830 inspired further political agitation and repression in several German states. Mounting opposition to local despots and agitation for national unity led to the prosecution of outspoken liberals. Many associated with the nationalist "Young Germany" movement fled abroad, particularly to Paris.

Renewed nationalist agitation swept the German states in the 1840s. A mass outpouring of patriotic sentiment erupted in response to possible French ambitions on the Rhine during a diplomatic crisis in 1840. Two patriotic songs were penned: "The Watch on the Rhine" and *"Deutschland, Deutschland über alles"* ("Germany, Germany above all"), the latter becoming Germany's national anthem half a century later. German rulers, who in the past had been reluctant to support the national idea, now attempted to co-opt it. In Bavaria the crown prince, who later became King Ludwig I (r. 1825–1848), built Walhalla, named after the hall in which fallen heroes gather in Germanic lore. Ludwig's Walhalla was to be a "sacred monument" to German unity adorned with statues of famous Germans. Cologne's unfinished cathedral became a symbol of German enthusiasm; from all over Germany donations poured in to finish it. These events suggested a broadening base for nationhood, which potentially could replace the existing system of a fragmented Germany. But with minor exceptions, the system established in 1815 prevailed until 1848.

Austria exercised considerable power over Italy through its possession of Italian territory, by dynastic ties to several ruling houses in the central part of the peninsula, and by political alliances with others, including the papacy. The only ruling house free of Austrian ties—and hence eventually looked to by nationalists as a possible rallying point for the independence of the peninsula—was the Savoy dynasty of Piedmont-Sardinia.

Italy consisted of eight political states, and it was in Austria's interest to maintain disunity. Many Italian governments—notably the papacy, the kingdom of Naples, and the central Italian duchies—imposed repressive policies, knowing that they could count on Austrian assistance to squelch any uprising. Indeed, Metternich did crush rebellions that were intended to bring about freer institutions and a unified Italy. His interventions generated hatred of Austria among Italian liberals and nationalists.

By far the most autocratic of the European states was tsarist Russia. Since 1801 Alexander I (r. 1801–1825) had been tsar. An enigmatic character whose domestic policy vacillated between liberalism and reaction and whose foreign policy wavered between brutal power politics and apparently selfless idealism, Alexander puzzled his contemporaries. When the Congress of Vienna gave additional Polish lands to the tsar, establishing the Kingdom of Poland, he demonstrated his liberalism to the world (and curried favor with his new subjects) by granting Poland a liberal constitution. But he offered no such constitution to his own people and within a few years violated the Polish constitution, refusing to call the diet into session. Alexander and his council discussed terms for the abolition of serfdom in Russia in 1803 and again in 1812, but like so many of his plans, this one was not implemented. Although he earnestly desired freedom for the serfs, the tsar was unwilling to impose any policy detrimental to the interests and privileges of the landed gentry.

Toward the end of his rule, Alexander became increasingly authoritarian and repressive, probably in response to growing opposition. Western liberal ideas, including constitutionalism, were adopted by Russian military officers who had served in western Europe, by Russian Freemasons who had corresponded with Masonic lodges in western Europe, and by Russian intellectuals who read Western liberal political tracts. These groups formed secret societies with varying agendas. Some envisioned Russia as a republic, others as a constitutional monarchy, but all shared a commitment to the abolition of serfdom and the establishment of a freer society.

Alexander died in December 1825, without designating which of his brothers would succeed him. Taking advantage of the confusion, the military conspirators declared in favor of the older brother, Constantine, in the belief that he favored a constitutional government. The younger brother, Nicholas, claimed to be the legal heir. The St. Petersburg garrison rallied to the conspirators' cause. Taking their cue from the Spanish uprising of 1820, the officers little doubted that the military could bring about change on its own in a country in which popular participation in governance was unknown.

The "Decembrist uprising," as it is known, quickly failed. The military revolt in the Russian capital was badly coordinated with uprisings planned in the countryside, and Nicholas moved quickly to crush the rebellion. He had the leaders executed, sent to Siberia, or exiled. In spite of its tragic end, throughout the nineteenth century the Decembrist uprising served as an inspiration to Russians resisting tsarist oppression.

Coming to the throne under such circumstances, Nicholas I (r. 1825–1855) was obsessed with the danger of revolution and determined to suppress all challenges to his authority. The declared goal of his rule was to uphold "orthodoxy, autocracy, and nationality." Nicholas created a stern, centralized bureaucracy to control all facets of Russian life. He originated the modern Russian secret police, called the "Third Section"; a state within the state, it was above the law. Believing in the divine right of monarchs, Nicholas refused to accept limits to his imperial powers. The tsar supported the primacy of the Russian Orthodox Church within Russian society; the church in turn upheld the powers of the state. Nicholas also used nationalism to strengthen the state, exalting the country's past and trying to Russify non-Russian peoples. After a nationalist rebellion in 1831 in Poland attempted to shake loose Russian control, Nicholas abrogated the kingdom's constitution and tried to impose the Russian language on its Polish subjects.

Russia's single most overwhelming problem was serfdom. Economically, serfdom had little to recommend it; free labor was far more efficient. Moreover, public safety was threatened by the serfs' dissatisfaction with their lot. Nicholas's thirty-year reign was checkered with over six hundred peasant uprisings, half of them put down by the military. Nicholas understood that serfdom had to be abolished for Russia's own good, but he could envision no clear alternative to it. Emancipation, he believed, would only sow further disorder. Except for a few minor reforms, he did nothing. Nicholas's death, followed by Russia's defeat in the Crimean War (see page 742), eventually brought to an end the institution that had held nearly half of the Russian people in bondage.

In its sheer mass, the Ottoman Empire continued to be a world empire. It extended over three continents. In Africa it ran across the whole North African coast. In Europe it stretched from Dalmatia (on the Adriatic coast) to Istanbul. In Asia it extended from Mesopotamia (present-day Iraq) to Anatolia (present-day Turkey). But it was an empire in decline, seriously challenged from inside by nationalist movements and from outside by foreign threats.

The Ottoman bureaucracy, once the mainstay of the government, had fallen into decay. In the past, officials had been recruited and advanced by merit; now lacking funds, Constantinople sold government offices. Tax collectors ruthlessly squeezed the peasantry. By the eighteenth century, the Janissaries, formerly an elite military force, had become an undisciplined band that menaced the peoples of the Ottoman Empire—especially those located at great distances from the close control of the capital. The reform-minded Sultan Selim III (r. 1789–1807) sought to curb the army, but he was killed by rebellious Janissaries, who forced the new ruler, Mahmud

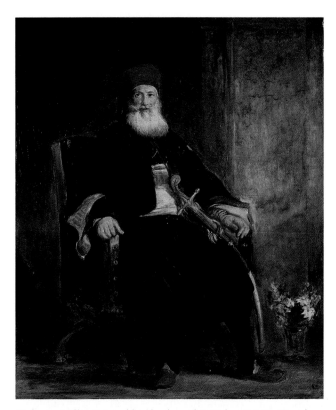

**Mehemet Ali** Painted by the famed British artist Sir David Wilkie, this portrait depicts the Egyptian leader at the height of his powers. Mehemet challenged the Ottoman Empire, winning for Egypt virtual independence and bringing Syria under his control. *(Tate Gallery, London/Art Resource, NY)*

II (r. 1808–1839), to retract most of the previous improvements. The worst features of the declining empire were restored.

Most of the Ottoman Empire was inhabited by Muslims, but in the Balkans Christians were in the majority. Ottoman officials usually treated religious minorities such as Jews and Orthodox with tolerance. But the Christian subject people found in their religion a means of collectively resisting a harsh and at times capricious rule. Some Christian peoples in the Balkans looked back nostalgically to earlier eras—the Greeks to their great Classical civilization or the Serbs to their era of self-rule. The ideas of nationalism and liberty that triggered changes in western Europe also stirred the peoples of the Balkans.

The Serbs were the first people to revolt successfully against Ottoman rule. A poor, mountainous region, Serbia suffered greatly from the rapaciousness of the Janissaries. In protest, a revolt broke out in 1804. At first the Ottomans were able to contain the insurrection, but in 1815 they had to recognize one of its leaders, Milosh Obrenovich (r. 1815–1839), as governor and allow the formation of a national assembly. In 1830, under pressure from Russia, which took an interest in fellow Slavs and members of the Orthodox faith, Constantinople recognized Milosh as hereditary ruler over an autonomous Serbia.

The Greeks' struggle led to complete independence from Ottoman rule. Greeks served as administrators throughout the Ottoman lands and, as merchants and seafarers, traveled widely throughout the Mediterranean world and beyond. They had encountered the ideas of the French Revolution and, in the 1790s, were affected by the nationalism spreading in Europe. Adamantios Koraïs° (1748–1833), an educator living in revolutionary Paris, reformed written Greek to make it more consonant with ancient Greek by removing foreign accretions. Koraïs created a new, more elegant Greek and edited Greek classics to connect his fellow countrymen with their ancient and illustrious past. Greek cultural nationalism found an echo among some intellectuals. The *Philike Hetairia* (Society of Friends), a conspiratorial group, founded in 1814, dedicated itself to restoring Greek independence by political means.

Greek peasants were not particularly interested in politics, but they were hostile to the Ottoman Turks, who had accumulated vast landholdings at their expense. This in part motivated Greek peasants to join the anti-Turkish revolt that began in 1821. Greeks killed large numbers of defenseless Turks in the Morea, a region in central Greece. The Turkish authorities hanged the patriarch, the leader of the Orthodox Church, in Constantinople and massacred or sold into slavery the population of the Aegean island of Chios. The war continued fitfully. By 1827 the Ottomans, aided by their vassal Mehemet Ali (1769–1849) of Egypt, controlled most of the Balkan peninsula. The rest of Europe, excited by the idea of an independent Greece restored to its past greatness, widely supported the Greek movement for freedom. The Great Powers intervened in 1827, sending their navies to intercept supplies intended for the Ottoman forces. At Navarino Bay, in the southwest of the Peloponnesus, the Ottoman navy fired on the allies, who returned fire and sank the Turkish ships. The destruction of Ottoman power ensured the independence of Greece. In 1830 an international agreement spelled out Greek independence.

Losing influence in the Balkans, the Ottoman Empire was also challenged elsewhere. In Egypt, Mehemet Ali, nominally subordinate to Constantinople, actually ruled Egypt as if it were independent. He wrested Syria away in 1831 and threatened to march against his over-

Koraïs (KOOR-ay-iss)

lord, the sultan. Britain and Russia, concerned that an Ottoman collapse would upset the region's balance of power, intervened on the empire's behalf. Constantinople won back Syria but in 1841 had to acknowledge Mehemet Ali as the hereditary ruler of Egypt. The survival of the Ottoman Empire was beginning to depend on the goodwill—or self-interest—of the Great Powers.

# THE REVOLUTIONS OF 1848

FROM France in the west to Poland in the east, at least fifty separate revolts and uprisings shook the Continent in 1848, the most extensive outbreak of popular violence in nineteenth-century Europe (see Map 21.2). The revolt had an impact far beyond Europe's borders. Inspired by the example of the European revolutions, Brazilians rose up against their government. In Bogota, Colombia, church bells rang, and in New York public demonstrations enthusiastically greeted the announcement of a republic in France. And as a result of the Parisian revolution, slaves in French colonies were emancipated.

## ■ Roots of Rebellion

At no time since 1800 had so many Europeans been involved in collective action. Many reasons account for this widespread outbreak of discontent. In the countryside, restrictions in access to land such as enclosure frustrated peasants. Although in the past many had enjoyed free access to village commons, these were coming increasingly under private control, or the peasants faced competition for their use. Formerly a peasant might have grazed sheep in the commons, but now a peasant's two or three animals competed with herds of sometimes hundreds of sheep owned by a rich farmer. Also, the poor once had relatively free access to forests to forage for firewood, but the limitation of this right also now led to frequent conflicts.

Points of friction were made worse by growing populations that put pressure on available resources. In the urban environment a crisis erupted in the handicrafts industry, which dominated city economies. Urban artisans were being undercut by the putting-out system or cottage industry, in which capitalists had goods produced in the countryside by cottagers—part-time artisans who supported themselves partly through agriculture and were thus willing to work for lower wages. Crises in the crafts hurt the journeymen who wanted to be masters; they had to serve far longer apprenticeships and in many cases could never expect promotion. Where the

**Map 21.2   Major Uprisings and Reforms, 1848–1849**   In no other year had as many revolts broken out simultaneously; in many cases the revolutions led to reforms and new constitutions.

guild system still existed, it was in decline, unable to protect the economic interests of artisans anxious about their futures.

These developing concerns came to a crisis point as a result of the economic depression of 1845–1846. In 1845 a crop disaster, including the spread of potato blight, destroyed the basic food of the poor in northern Europe. The most notorious catastrophe was in Ireland. In the last famine in western Europe, 1 million Irish starved to death between 1844 and 1851 as a result of the blight. The poor harvests doubled the price of food from the 1840 level. An industrial downturn accompanied these agricultural disasters, creating massive unemployment. Municipal and national governments seemed unable to deal with the crowding, disease, and unsanitary conditions that were worsening already high tensions in the cities, the sites of national governments. People were ready to heed those who called for the overthrow of the existing regimes. The established political and adminis-

trative elites were disoriented and found they could not count on their traditional sources of support. Revolts were triggered not only by discontent, but also by the hope for change.

The revolutions of 1848 were sparked by the revolution in Paris in February. News of the fall of Louis Philippe triggered a ripple effect, spreading turbulence to over fifty localities in Europe. In France the revolution was for political and social rights. In several other countries, another issue was added to the combustible situation—nationalism. Once the revolution in the Germanies had started, the demands arose for national unification. Throughout the Italian peninsula, national unity was the goal; northern Italians added their desire for independence from the Habsburg Empire. In other Habsburg lands the cry went out for national independence: the Hungarians, Poles, and Czechs all wanted to be masters of their own destinies, and free from Vienna's control.

## ■ Liberals: From Success to Defeat

The revolutions of 1848 went through a number of stages. In the first stage liberal demands for more political liberties joined with popular demands for social justice. In France the victors declared a republic, which provided basic constitutional freedoms and granted universal male suffrage (the first European regime to do so). The provisional government included a working man in the cabinet and instituted national workshops to give work to the urban unemployed. Inspired by the example of Paris, crowds in Vienna demonstrated and petitioned the emperor. Having lost control over the capital, Metternich resigned and fled to England. On March 15, 1848, the Austrian imperial court, faced with continued agitation by students and workers, announced its willingness to issue a constitution. Even more important was Austria's decision to abolish serfdom. Some had feared a serf uprising, but the relatively generous terms of the emancipation mollified the peasantry.

In Germany news of the February uprising in Paris also acted as a catalyst for change in the German states. The forces of change seemed irresistible. As the king of Württemberg observed, "I cannot mount on horseback against ideas." The wisest course appeared to be compromise. He and many of his fellow dukes and princes changed their governments, dismissing their cabinets and instituting constitutions.

Up to this point Prussia was conspicuous for being untouched by the revolutionary wave. But when news of Metternich's fall reached Berlin on March 16, middle-class liberals and artisans demonstrated for reforms. To appease his subjects, King Friedrich Wilhelm IV appointed the liberal Rhenish businessman who in the ceremonial march through Berlin (see the illustration on page 706) walked ahead of the king. Representative government was introduced, and suffrage was extended, though it was still restricted to men of property. No longer the exclusive preserve of the aristocracy, government was opened to men from the liberal professions and the business classes. As in Austria, the German countryside was appeased by reducing some of the feudal arrangements that still existed in many areas.

The second stage of the revolution marked a breakdown in the unity that had initially formed against the old regimes. With the enemy defeated or compliant, the middle classes, peasants, and workers discovered they no longer shared a common goal. In France the peasants, who at least had not opposed the revolution, by April 1848 were hostile to the new republic. They decried the additional taxes that had to be levied to pay for the national workshops supporting unemployed urban workers. Armed with the vote, the peasants elected conservative landowners, lawyers, and notaries—a group nearly identical to the pre-1848 deputies. In June the new parliament decided to terminate the costly national workshops. The workers, in despair, revolted. The government carried out a bloody repression, killing 1,500 and arresting 12,000. The re-election of conservative forces revealed that universal suffrage could serve as a means to mobilize moderate public opinion against radicalism in Paris. The advent of railroads allowed the government to muster military support from outside the city. Thereafter, it would be far more difficult for radical Parisian crowds to dictate policies to the rest of the country.

The propertied classes, feeling menaced by the poor, looked to authority for security. Of the several candidates for president in 1848, Louis Napoleon (1808–1873), a nephew of Napoleon Bonaparte, appealed to the

**Ballots, Not Bullets**    This print of 1848 informs the revolutionary of the barricade to put away his rifle and trust the democratic process. Pointing to the rifle, our French revolutionary announces, "this is for the external enemy." "As for the internal ones," he says, indicating the election urn, "this is how one fairly competes with them."    *(Harlingue-Viollet)*

Ça, c'est pour l'ennemi du dehors, pour le dedans, voici comme l'on combat loyalement les adversaires....

largest cross section of the population. The middle class was attracted by the promise of authority and order. Peasants, disillusioned by the tax policies of the republic, remained loyal to the memory of Napoleonic glory. Workers embittered by the government's repression of the June uprisings were impressed by Louis Napoleon's vaguely socialistic program. Louis Napoleon was elected president; three years later, he dissolved the National Assembly by force and established a personal dictatorship. In 1852 he declared himself Emperor Napoleon III.

In Austria and Germany the middle classes became wary of the lower classes; the class conflict in Paris intensified their concern. Once the peasants had won their freedom from feudal dues in Germany and from serfdom in the Austrian Empire, they were no longer interested in what was occurring in the capital. Thus the alliance in favor of change disappeared, and it could not even serve as a bulwark against the return of conservative forces. In Austria the reactionary forces around the court, led by General Windischgrätz, reconquered Vienna in October 1848 for the emperor and suspended the liberals' constitution. In December the king of Prussia, who had appeared to bow to liberal opinion, regained his courage and dismissed the elected assembly. Most of the liberal forces were spent and overcome by the end of the year.

## ■ The Nationalist Impulse

The revolutions did not break out because of nationalism, but once they erupted, the nationalist cause helped shape the outcome in several regions. Faced with internal turmoil, Prussia and Austria—which both opposed German unification lest it undermine their power— could not prevent the question of a united Germany from coming to the fore. In March 1848 a self-appointed national committee invited five hundred prominent German liberals to convene in Frankfurt to begin the process of national unification. In addition to fulfilling a long-standing liberal dream, a united German nation would consolidate the liberal victory over absolutism. The gathering called for suffrage based on property qualifications, thus excluding most Germans from the political process and alienating them from the evolving new order. The first all-German elected legislature met in May 1848 in Frankfurt to pursue unification. It faced the thorny issue of the shape of this new Germany: which regions should be included and which excluded? The most ambitious plan envisioned a *Grossdeutsch-land*°, or large Germany, consisting of all the members of

the German Confederation, including the German-speaking parts of Austria and the German parts of Bohemia. Such a solution would include many non-Germans, including Poles, Czechs, and Danes. The proponents of *Kleindeutschland*°, or small Germany, which would exclude Austria and its possessions, saw their solution as a more likely scenario, although it would exclude many Germans. They succeeded in the end, largely because the reassertion of Austrian imperial power in the fall of 1848 put the non-German areas under Vienna's control out of reach.

The Prussian reassertion of royal power, though partial, was a signal for other German rulers in late 1848 to dismiss their liberal ministers. The moment for liberalism and national unification to triumph had passed by the time the Frankfurt Assembly drew up a constitution in the spring of 1849. Having opted for the *Kleindeutsch* solution, the parliament offered the throne to Friedrich Wilhelm IV, king of Prussia. Although the king was not a liberal, he ruled the largest state within the designated empire. If power could promote and protect German unity, he possessed it in the form of the Prussian army. But Friedrich Wilhelm feared that accepting the throne would lead to war with Austria. Believing in the principle of monarchy, he also did not want an office offered by representatives of the people, and so he refused the offer. Lacking an alternative plan, most members of the Frankfurt Assembly went home. A rump parliament and a series of uprisings in favor of German unity were crushed by the Prussian army. So German unification failed. Liberalism alone was unable to bring about German unity; other means would be required to do so.

In Italy, too, nationalist aspirations emerged once a revolt triggered by social and economic grievances had broken out. In the years before 1848, nationalists and liberals hoped somehow to see their program of a united and free Italy implemented. News of the Paris uprising in February galvanized revolutions in Italy. Italians under Austrian rule forced the Austrians to evacuate their Italian possessions. Revolts and mass protests in several Italian states led rulers to grant, or at least promise, a constitution. The king of Piedmont, Charles Albert (r. 1831–1849), granted his people a constitution, the Statuto. Charles Albert hoped to play a major part in unifying Italy. In Austrian Italy, the middle classes, although eager to be free of foreign rule, feared radical elements among the laborers. They believed that annexation to nearby Piedmont would provide security from both Austria and the troublesome lower classes. The king of Piedmont decided to unite Italy under his

---

**Grossdeutschland** (Grose-DOYT-shlant)

**Kleindeutschland** (Kline-DOYT-shlant)

**Constitutional Government in Denmark**   On March 21, 1848, fifteen thousand Danes, inspired by the example of Paris, marched on the palace to demand constitutional rights. Unlike in the French capital, however, this event was peaceful and led to the establishment of constitutional government. This painting honors the new parliament that came into being after the liberal constitution was adopted in 1849.   *(Statens Museum for Kunst, Copenhagen)*

throne if doing so would prevent the spread of radicalism to his kingdom. On March 24, 1848, he declared war on Austria but was defeated in July and had to sue for an armistice. The continued spread of nationalist and revolutionary sentiment tempted Charles Albert to declare war on Austria once again, in March 1849. The outcome for Piedmont was even worse than it had been a year earlier. Within six days its army was defeated. Humiliated, Charles Albert resigned his throne to his son, Victor Emmanuel II (r. 1849–1878). The Austrians quickly reconquered their lost provinces and reinstated their puppet governments. The dream of a united Italy was dashed.

In the multinational empire of the Habsburgs, nationalism manifested itself in the form of demands for national independence from foreign rule. With Austria's power temporarily weakened as a result of revolution in Vienna, nationalist revolts broke out not only in Italy, but simultaneously in Hungary, the Czech lands, and Croa-

tia. The Austrian emperor yielded in Hungary, giving it virtual independence; it was joined to the empire solely by personal union to the ruler. Constitutional government was established in Hungary, but participation in the political process was limited to Magyars, who were the single largest ethnic group, constituting 40 percent of the population. The other nationalities in Hungary—Romanians, Slovaks, Croats, and Slovenes—preferred the more distant rule of Austrian Vienna to Magyar authority. The Czech lands also witnessed agitation, but there and elsewhere the tide favoring the nationalists turned. The revolt against the empire was not coordinated, and the nationalisms were often in conflict with one another. Once the emperor re-established his power in Vienna, he could move against his rebellious subjects. The Austrian Empire practiced a policy of divide and rule; it re-established its authority in Italy, bombarded Prague into submission, and with Russian help brought Hungary to heel. If the nationalist fires had been quenched, the dangers nationalism posed to the survival of the Habsburg Empire were also revealed.

In the large sweep of revolutions that washed across Europe, three major countries were spared. In Great Britain the government had proven sufficiently capable of adjusting to some of the major popular demands; revolution seemed unnecessary. In Russia the repressive tsarist system prevented any defiance from escalating into an opposition mass movement. Successive military officers governed in Spain, including General Ramón Narváez° (1799–1868), who brutally ran the country from 1844 to 1851. When he was on his deathbed, the priest asked him whether he forgave his enemies. He answered, "I have no enemies. I have shot them all!" So in 1848, no revolution disturbed Spain.

## SUMMARY

 HE revolutions of 1848 released many of the forces for change that had been gathering strength since 1815. In spite of the Congress of Vienna's effort to restore the old order after Napoleon's fall, the generation after 1815 established a new order. The ideas of change that had powered the French Revolution of 1789 continued to shape an era that claimed to be rolling history back to prerevolutionary times. Liberalism contested authoritarianism.

Reform-minded regimes in Europe improved the lives of people in colonies overseas, abolishing slavery in British and then French colonies and providing self-rule for Canada. Some states even turned away from monarchy and experimented with republicanism, a form of government that until then many had thought fit only for small states. All of the Latin American colonies except Mexico and Brazil became republics on gaining independence. In Europe during 1848–1849, the French, German, Hungarian, and Roman republics were proclaimed. Although they did not last, these experiments suggested new modes of political organization that were to become common in the following century.

The generation after 1815 experienced revolutions frequently and broadly. These uprisings usually failed, and the forces of order in most cases were able to recapture power. Yet the status quo was altered. In many cases absolutist rulers had to grant constitutions and accept ministers who were not their choices. Even though most of these arrangements were temporary, they established an impor-

tant precedent. If unusual in the first half, constitutions became the norm in the second half of the century.

Nationalism arose in these years. The desire for national independence and unity found expression in Italy, Germany, Hungary, Poland, and the land of the Czechs. To free themselves from Madrid's rule, the Spanish colonies in the Americas employed a nationalist discourse borrowed from Europe. In the second half of the century, Europe would have to contend more rigorously with the forces of nationalism that first appeared after 1814.

Socialist ideas challenged private property. In 1848 some might have pointed to the institution of the temporary workshops in Paris as an effort to realize a part of the socialist program. But that was a modest effort; socialist ideas would come into full expression—and their power become formidable—toward the end of the century.

The middle classes found their position strengthened after 1848. They did not dominate the political system, but their influence increased with the growth of entrepreneurship. Middle-class professionals were recruited into the civil services of states determined to streamline their operations in order to withstand revolution more effectively. Revolutionary fervor waned after 1848, but the current of economic and social change continued to transform Europe.

### ■ Suggested Reading

Broers, Michael. *Europe After Napoleon: Revolution, Reaction, and Romanticism, 1815–1848.* 1996. Evaluates the era from the point of view of the participants.

Hobsbawm, E. J. *The Age of Revolution, 1789–1848.* 1962. Presents compelling arguments that the era was dominated by two simultaneous revolutions, the French Revolution and the industrial transformation.

Johnson, Paul. *The Birth of the Modern World Society, 1815–1830.* 1991. A weighty but readable book providing a panoramic view of the era; includes biographical sketches of some of the major figures of the time.

Laven, David, and Lucy Riall, eds. *Napoleon's Legacy: Problems of Government in Restoration Europe.* 2000. Essays on the Restoration experience in different European countries.

Sperber, Jonathan. *The European Revolutions, 1848–1851.* 1994. The best up-to-date synthesis, which includes some new emphases, such as the role of rural and religious discontent in shaping the revolts.

Wheen, Francis. *Karl Marx: A Life.* 2000. A lively biography that, in addition to discussing Marxian thought, emphasizes the man's personal life.

Narváez (NAR-va-yes)

 **For a searchable list of additional readings for this chapter, go to http://college.hmco.com.**

# Raft of the "Medusa"

In September 1816 the French were shocked at the news of the disaster that had befallen the government ship *Méduse* (Medusa) as it headed for Senegal in West Africa the previous July. Including the ship's crew, 400 passengers had boarded the vessel.

The captain of the ship was a nobleman, Duroys de Chaumareys°, whom the restoration government had appointed solely on the basis of his family and political connections. Inexperienced as a seaman, the captain clumsily ran his ship aground on the Mauritanian coast, off West Africa, on July 2. The *Medusa* had only six lifeboats capable of carrying a total of 250 people; for the rest of the passengers a raft was rigged with planks, beams, and ropes. The captain and his officers forcibly took over the lifeboats, abandoning 150 passengers, including one woman, to the less secure raft. With no navigational tools and insufficient food and water, the passengers of the raft were at the mercy of stormy seas and a brutal sun. Anger at officers for having abandoned them led seamen on the raft to murder some of their superiors. By the third day, driven by thirst and hunger, some passengers ate their dead companions—killed by exposure or drowned by huge waves. On the sixth day, the strongest among the survivors, fearing that their rations were dwindling, banded together and murdered the weaker ones. On the thirteenth day, the French frigate *Argus* spotted the raft and rescued fifteen survivors. Five died soon after, leaving only ten survivors out of the raft's original 150 passengers.

Although the government tried to suppress information about the event, the French press exposed the incompetence and cowardice of Captain de Chaumareys. The event was understood to reflect the weakness of the regime that had appointed him. The selfish act of the captain and his fellow officers suggested the narrow class interest of the restoration government, favoring aristocracy at the cost of the common people.

The French painter Théodore Géricault (1791–1824) befriended the ship's surgeon Henri Savigny, one of the lucky ten who survived the harrowing experience on the raft of the *Medusa*. In addition to press reports, Géricault

**Duroys de Chaumareys** (du-RWAH duh sho-mah-RAY)

thus had a direct eyewitness account of the event. The painter shared Savigny's sense of outrage against the government for having appointed the incompetent captain and for having treated the survivors callously—at one point the government arrested Savigny for publicizing the tragedy. The light prison sentence imposed on the captain was another source of grievance.

Since 1815 the French government had sought to bring distinction to itself by displaying art in salon expositions. That of 1819 was intended to be larger, more glorious than any previous one. Among its paintings was Géricault's huge canvas—the largest in that year's exposition—measuring 16 feet high by 24 feet wide, innocently titled "Scene of Shipwreck." Carelessly, the regime had wanted to gain glory for itself by exhibiting this impressive artwork, while at the same time keeping hidden its real subject. But the stratagem failed; everyone recognized the painting to be the *Raft of the "Medusa"* and an attack on the Bourbon regime.

The painting, reproduced here, depicts the moment the survivors have spotted the frigate, the *Argus*, barely visible in the horizon. Notice the figure of an African standing at the fore of the raft, waving a red-and-white cloth to attract the ship's attention. In this painting the nobility and symbol of hope the African symbolizes is an attack on the slave trade, which Britain had abolished but which France was still engaged in. And so by including the African, the painting is implicitly criticizing the restoration regime for sanctioning commerce in humans. Just as the *Argus* is coming to the rescue of the shipwrecked, the painting appears to suggest, so Africans will see the day when their enslavement will be ended.

Historians often regard the *Raft of the "Medusa"* as the most important painting of French romanticism, and it includes nearly all the major themes of the movement. By locating the scene off the coast of Africa, Géricault incorporates an element of exoticism. Nature—cruel and unforgiving—is central to the scene, reflected in the turbulent sea, dark clouds, and imperiled raft. The canvas includes an extraordinary range of passions: Observe, for example, the inconsolable grief of the figure at the bottom left, a father cradling the dead body

**Géricault: Raft of the "Medusa"**   *(Erich Lessing/Art Resource, NY)*

of his son. Other figures express despair and terror, and still others limitless hope. The painting evokes the dark passions lurking in the human heart. Although it does not show the scenes of insanity, murder, and cannibalism that the survivors had witnessed, they undoubtedly came to the mind of the viewers, who were familiar with the tragic events. The painting was a powerful indictment of Enlightenment faith in humans as creatures of reason and balance.

Romantic artists wanted to engage the passions of those viewing, reading, or hearing their works. *Raft of the "Medusa"* purposely stages the events in the foreground in order to pull viewers into the picture and make them participants in the drama; they thus share in the alternating feelings of terror and hope that swept the raft.

The fate of the painting and the artist followed a romantic script. When Géricault started the painting, he intended it as an indictment of the restoration government. He poured energy into it in an effort to take his

mind off a disastrous love affair, and as his work proceeded he came to see the painting as an allegory of larger human passions and concerns. Yet when it was displayed, much to his disappointment, the painting was understood mainly in political terms. Disillusioned by this reaction, Géricault thereafter painted no major works. He grew sickly, rarely bestirred himself, and died of bone tuberculosis in 1824, aged 33. He illustrated the romantics' view of a heroic life—the genius who performs a major feat and then dies young, before realizing his potential. To the romantics, human intent and effort often appeared thwarted by larger forces. This painting, originally meant to criticize the regime, was after Géricault's death purchased by the restoration government and hung in France's national museum, the Louvre.

# CHAPTER 22

# Nationalism and Political Reform 1850–1880

I N 1885, on the occasion of the seventieth birthday of the German Chancellor Otto von Bismarck, Kaiser Wilhelm I gave the chancellor this painting, depicting the proclamation of German unification in the Hall of Mirrors in Versailles in 1871. On the podium, standing just behind the newly declared kaiser, is Crown Prince Friedrich Wilhelm (later Kaiser Friedrich III). To the kaiser's left, with his arm upraised, is the grand duke of Baden. In the middle of the scene, resplendent in his white uniform, is Bismarck, the political architect of German unification, and on the right nearby, Field Marshal Helmuth von Moltke°, the military genius who provided the series of military victories allowing Prussia to unify Germany under its aegis. The new state was proclaimed by the crowned heads of Germany; no popular vote or parliament sanctioned the founding event. By war, Germany had become a united nation. Wars and the threat of wars brought about the emergence of several new states on the European scene: Italy, Romania, and Bulgaria. In the generation after 1850 the contours of European politics were being changed—new states appeared on the map, and within their national borders a good number of states reformed their political institutions. As Europe changed, a much enlarged and more powerful United States and a united Canada also emerged.

To meet the demand for popular participation in government so forcefully expressed in 1848, every European state except the Ottoman and Russian Empires found it necessary to have a parliament. Rare before midcentury, such institutions became common thereafter. No longer was the demand for popular participation seen as a threat to the existing political and social order. In fact, popular participation, or the appearance of it, gave the existing order a legitimacy

**von Moltke** (fon molt-KEH)

**The Changing Nature of International Relations**

**Italian Unification, 1859–1870**

**German Unification, 1850–1871**

**Precarious Empires**

**The Emergence of a Powerful, Democratic United States, 1840–1880**

**The Development of Western Democracies**

Wilhelm I is proclaimed ruler of the German Empire at Versailles, 1871. (Friedrichsruh, Bismarck-Museum/AKG London) it had not enjoyed since before the French Revolution. Nationalism flourished during this period, emerging as a decisive force in European affairs and in the United States, where it promoted territorial expansion and fired a determination to preserve the Union.

These political transformations occurred in an era of unprecedented economic growth and prosperity. Industrial production expanded the economy; the discovery of gold in California in 1848 led to the expansion of credit (since currencies were backed by gold), which led to the founding of new banks and mass investments in growing industries. The standard of living rose significantly in industrializing nations. Industrial production in Great Britain increased by 90 percent, and in France by 50 percent, between 1850 and 1880. The middle classes expanded dramatically.

In the first half of the century, international relations had been dominated by the congress system, in which representatives of the major European states met periodically to refine and preserve the balance of power. This system disappeared in the second half of the century, as political leaders pursued the narrow interests of their respective states. Instead of negotiating with one another, a new generation of leaders employed brute military force—or the threat of its use—to resolve international conflicts. The new age was dominated not by ideals but by force, announced Prussian chancellor Otto von Bismarck, the main practitioner of what became known as *Realpolitik,* a policy in which war became a regular instrument of statecraft.

### QUESTIONS TO CONSIDER

- How did the Crimean War affect international relations?
- How did political leaders in Prussia and Piedmont harness the forces of nationalism to achieve German and Italian national unity?
- Why did Russia abolish serfdom, and what was the impact of this action?
- Why was comprehensive political reform, especially the expansion of democracy, possible in some countries, but only limited reforms in others?

### TERMS TO KNOW

| | |
|---|---|
| Realpolitik | Tanzimat |
| congress system | Young Turks |
| risorgimento | glasnost |
| trasformismo | mir |
| Otto von Bismarck | manifest destiny |
| February Patent | Paris Commune |
| Compromise of 1867 | Second Reform Bill |

# THE CHANGING NATURE OF INTERNATIONAL RELATIONS

THE Crimean War and its aftermath shaped European international relations for several decades. Following the 1815 Congress of Vienna (see Chapter 21), European states attempted to work out their differences by negotiation, avoiding situations in which one state triumphed at the cost of another. The Crimean War and subsequent realignments raised mutual suspicions, leading nations to act in their own self-interests and to ignore the concerns of the other major players in the international system. This reorientation facilitated the emergence of nation-states.

### ■ The Crimean War, 1854–1856

The Crimean War had many causes. Principally, however, it was ignited by the decision of French and British statesmen to contain Russian power in the Balkans and keep it from encroaching on the weakening Ottoman Empire. Russian claims to have the right to intervene on behalf of Ottoman Christians had led to war between the two states in October 1853. The defeat of the Ottoman navy at Sinope° in November left the Ottoman Empire defenseless.

British and French statesmen had considerable interest in the conflict. Britain had long feared that the collapse of the Ottoman Empire would lead Russia to seek territorial gains in the Mediterranean. Such a move would challenge Britain's supremacy. An explosion of public sentiment against Russia also obliged the British government to take an aggressive stance. Meanwhile, the French emperor, Napoleon III, viewed defeat of Russia as a way to eclipse one of the states most dedicated to preserving the current European borders. He wanted to undermine existing power relations, hoping that a new order would lead to increased French power and influence. Napoleon also imagined that fighting side by side with Britain could lay the foundation for Anglo-French friendship. And so England and France rushed to defend the Ottoman Empire and declared war on Russia in March 1854.

The war was poorly fought on all sides. Leadership was woefully inadequate, and five times more casualties resulted from disease than from enemy fire. Although the Russians had a standing army of a million men, their poor communications and supply systems prevented them from ever fielding more than a quarter of their forces. In Britain the press and Members of Parliament denounced their side's inadequate materiel and incompetent leadership. For the first time the press played an active role in reporting war, and photography brought to readers at home the gruesome realities of battle. One of the few heroic figures to emerge from this conflict was the English nurse Florence Nightingale (1820–1910), who organized a nursing service to care for the British sick and wounded. Later, her wartime experience allowed her to pioneer nursing as a professional calling. (See the box "Reading Sources: Florence Nightingale in the Crimean War.")

After almost two years of fighting in the Balkans and the Crimean peninsula, Russia abandoned the key fortress of Sevastopol in September 1855. Militarily defeated, the Russians also were alarmed at Austria's posture. Tsar Nicholas I had expected Austrian assistance in the war in return for his help in crushing the Hungarian rebellion in 1849. Instead, Austria's leaders not only withheld aid but even threatened to join the Western alliance.

The Crimean conflict killed three-quarters of a million people—more than any European war between the

---

**Sinope** (see-NO-pay)

## CHRONOLOGY

| | |
|---|---|
| **1840s** | Tanzimat in the Ottoman Empire |
| **1851** | Louis Napoleon's coup d'état |
| **1854–1856** | Crimean War |
| **1860** | Italy united under Piedmontese rule |
| **1861–1865** | U.S. Civil War |
| **1861** | Great Reforms in Russia |
| **1862** | Bismarck appointed minister president of Prussia |
| **1864** | Austria and Prussia attack Denmark and occupy Schleswig-Holstein |
| **1866** | Austro-Prussian War |
| **1866** | Abolition of estate system in Sweden |
| **1867** | Second Reform Bill in England |
| **1867** | North America Act creates Canadian federation |
| **1867** | Austro-Hungarian compromise |
| **1870** | Franco-Prussian War |
| **1870** | Rome, joined to Italy, becomes its capital |
| **1870** | Declaration of French Third Republic |
| **1871** | Unification of German Empire |
| **1871** | Paris Commune |
| **1876** | Bulgarian horrors |
| **1878** | Congress of Berlin |

end of the Napoleonic Wars and World War I. It was a particularly futile, senseless war whose most important consequence was political: it unleashed dramatic new changes in the international order that allowed for the emergence of the new nation-states.

## ■ The Congress of Paris, 1856

The former combatants met in Paris in February 1856 to work out a peace treaty. Their decisions—which pleased no one—shaped relations among European states for the next half-century. Russian statesmen were especially discontented, as their country was forbidden from

**Crimean War** This photograph shows the interior of the Sevastapol fortress after it had been battered into surrender. The Crimean War was the first conflict to be documented by photographers.
*(Courtesy of the Board of Trustees of the Victoria & Albert Museum)*

having a fleet in the Black Sea. Nor did French leaders feel their nation had benefited. Although holding the congress in Paris flattered the emperor's pride, no other clear advantages emerged for France. The north Italian state of Piedmont°, which had joined the allies, gained from the congress only a vague statement on the unsatisfactory nature of the existing situation in Italy. Prussia was invited to attend the congress only as an afterthought and hence also felt slighted.

Although the war seemed to have sustained the integrity of the Ottoman Empire, the peace settlement weakened it indirectly by dictating reforms in the treatment of its Christian populations. These reforms impaired the empire's ability to repress the growing nationalist movements in the Balkans. British political leaders, galled by the heavy sacrifices of the war, moved toward isolationism in foreign policy. Austrian policymakers, who had hoped to gain the aid of Britain and France in preserving the Habsburg Empire, found them

**Florence Nightingale** This photograph was taken in 1856, shortly after Nightingale returned to England from the Crimean War. Her privileged background provided the official connections that helped the success of her nursing services. *(Courtesy, Florence Nightingale Museum, St. Thomas' Hospital, London. Photo: London Metropolitan Archives)*

---

**Piedmont** (PEED-mont)

## 🕭 READING SOURCES

### Florence Nightingale in the Crimean War

*Nightingale used her influential family connections to win an appointment to the Crimean battlefield. Once there, she organized nursing for the wounded and was able to secure additional personnel and medical supplies for her hospital. Women were supposed to be sheltered from the harsh realities of the outside world, but as this letter indicates, Nightingale was not spared war in its cruelest aspects.*

We have no room for corpses in the wards. The Surgeons pass on to the next, an excision of the shoulder-joint—beautifully performed and going on well—[cannon] ball lodged just in the head of the joint, and fracture starred all round. The next poor fellow has two stumps for arms—and the next has lost an arm and leg. As for the balls, they go in where they like, and do as much harm as they can in passing. That is the only rule they have. The next case has one eye put out, and paralysis of the iris of the other. He can neither see nor understand. But all who can walk come into us for Tobacco, but I tell them that we have not a bit to put into our own mouths. Not a sponge, nor a rag of linen, not anything have I left. Everything is gone to make slings and stump pillows and shirts. These poor fellows have not had a clean shirt nor been washed for two months before they came here, and the state in which they arrive from the transport is literally crawling. I hope in a few days we shall establish a little cleanliness. But we have not a basin nor a towel nor a bit of soap nor a broom—I have ordered 300 scrubbing brushes. But one half the Barrack is so sadly out of repair that it is impossible to use a drop of water on the stone floors, which are all laid upon rotten wood, and would give our men fever in no time. . . .

I am getting a screen now for the Amputations, for when one poor fellow, who is to be amputated tomorrow, sees his comrade today die under the knife it makes impression—and diminishes his chance. But, anyway, among these exhausted frames the mortality of the operations is frightful.

*Source:* Letter to Dr. William Bowman, November 14, 1854, in Sue M. Goldie, ed., *"I Have Done My Duty": Florence Nightingale in the Crimean War, 1854–56* (Iowa City: University of Iowa Press, 1987), pp. 37–38.

---

hostile instead, a stance that encouraged the forces undermining Habsburg hegemony. At the time the peace treaty was signed, few people foresaw the enormous results that would flow from it.

In the first half of the century, the congress system had tried to ensure that no major state was dissatisfied enough to subvert the existing distribution of power. The international order had been upheld in part by the cooperation of the rulers of the conservative Eastern powers: Russia, Austria, and Prussia. Now these powers were rivals, and their competition contributed to growing instability in the international system. By and large, the decisions reached in Paris would be disregarded or unilaterally revised. This new international climate also allowed new states to take shape without international sanction.

## ITALIAN UNIFICATION, 1859–1870

 N Metternich's memorable phrase, Italy at midcentury was nothing but a "geographic expression." The revolution of 1848 (see pages 735–736) had revealed an interest in national unification, but the attempt had failed. Yet within a dozen years what many believed to be impossible would come to pass. Idealists such as Giuseppe Mazzini (see page 716) had preached that Italy would be unified not by its rulers but by its people, who would rise and establish a free republic. Instead, the deed was done by royalty, by war, and with the help of a foreign state. Although ideals were not absent from the process of unification, cynical manipulation and scheming also came into play.

Since the late eighteenth century, some Italians had been calling for a *risorgimento°*, a political and cultural renewal of Italy. By the mid-nineteenth century the idea was actively supported by a small, elite group consisting of the educated middle class, urban property owners, and members of the professions. For merchants, industrialists, and professionals, a unified state would provide a larger stage on which to pursue their ambitions.

## ■ Cavour Plots Unification

After the failed 1848 revolution, most Italian rulers resorted to repression. Only the north Italian kingdom of Piedmont kept the liberal constitution adopted during the 1848 revolution, and it welcomed political refugees from other Italian states. Not only politically but economically, it was a beacon to the rest of Italy, establishing modern banks and laying half the rail lines on the peninsula.

The statesman who was to catapult Piedmont into a position of leadership in the dramatic events leading to Italian unification was Count Camillo di Cavour° (1810–1861). The son of a Piedmontese nobleman and high government official, he grew up speaking French, the language of the royal court and formal education in Piedmont, and mastered Italian only as an adult. Cosmopolitan in his interests, Cavour knew more about Britain and France than about Italy. He was sympathetic to the aspirations of the middle class and saw in Britain and France models of what Italy ought to become, a liberal and economically advanced society.

Short, fat, and near-sighted, Cavour hardly cut a heroic figure. Yet he was ambitious, hard-working, and driven to succeed. A well-known journalist, the editor of the newspaper *Risorgimento,* he joined the government in 1850. Two years later King Victor Emmanuel appointed him prime minister. He shared the enthusiasm of the middle classes for an Italian nation, but his vision did not include the entire Italian peninsula, only its north and center, which then could dominate the rest of the peninsula in a loose federation. One lesson he had learned from the failures of 1848 was that foreign help, especially French assistance, would be necessary to expel the Austrians from the peninsula.

When the Crimean War broke out in 1854, Cavour steered Piedmont to the allied side, hoping to advance his cause. He sent twenty thousand troops to the Crimea, one-tenth of whom died. This act gained him a seat at the Congress of Paris, where his presence boosted the kingdom's prestige—and where he and Napoleon III had an opportunity to meet and size up each other.

Napoleon III favored the cause of Italian liberation from Austrian rule and some form of unification of the peninsula. Austria had been France's traditional opponent; destroying Austria's power in Italy might strengthen France. Thus in July 1858 the French emperor and the Piedmontese prime minister met secretly at Plombières°, a French spa, to discuss how Italian unity could be achieved. They agreed that Piedmont would stir up trouble in one of Austria's Italian territories in an effort to goad the Austrians into war. France would help the Piedmontese expel Austria from the peninsula, and the new Piedmont, doubled in size, would become part of a confederation under the papacy. In exchange, the French emperor demanded the Piedmontese provinces of Nice° and Savoy, which bordered France.

This demand presented difficulties: Savoy was the heartland of the Piedmont kingdom, the ancestral home of the royal family; and Nice had a mostly Italian, not French, population. Napoleon's other condition was that the king of Piedmont, who headed the oldest reigning house in Europe, the Savoy, allow his 15-year-old daughter to marry the emperor's 38-year-old dissipated cousin. To accept these terms seemed a betrayal of national honor and conventional morality. But scruples gave way to political ambition, and Cavour assented. (See the box "Reading Sources: Cavour Outlines a Deal with Napoleon III.")

War between Austria and Piedmont broke out in April 1859. By June the combined Piedmontese and French forces had routed the Austrians at Magenta and Solferino (see Map 22.1). The bloodiness of these battles impressed contemporaries: the color magenta was named after the deep red of the soaked battlefield, and when a Swiss humanitarian, Henri Dunant° (1828–1901), organized emergency services for both French and Austrians wounded at Solferino, he proposed the founding of voluntary relief societies in every nation, called the Red Cross.

Instead of pressing on after these two victories, Napoleon III decided to end the fighting. He was shocked by the bloodshed he had witnessed and alarmed by the Prussian mobilization on the Rhine on behalf of Austria. In addition, his plan for Italy was threatening to develop in unforeseen directions. Several states in central Italy had appealed for annexation to Piedmont, which would have resulted in a larger inde-

---

**risorgimento** (ree-sor-djee-MEN-toe)    **Cavour** (kah-VOOR)

**Plombières** (plom-bee-YAIR)    **Nice** (NEECE)
**Dunant** (dew-NAN)

**Map 22.1   The Unification of Italy, 1859–1870**   Piedmontese leadership and nationalist fervor united Italy.

pendent state than Napoleon III had anticipated. These factors led Napoleon to sign an armistice with the Austrians, allowing Austria to remain in northern Italy and participate in an Italian confederation. Cavour was outraged by Napoleon's betrayal and resigned as prime minister; he returned to office, however, in January 1860.

## ■ Unification Achieved, 1860

Cavour had envisioned no more than a united northern Italy. Unexpected events in the south, however, dramatically expanded that vision. The centuries-old misgovernment of the kingdom of Naples led to an uprising in

## ❧ READING SOURCES

### Cavour Outlines a Deal with Napoleon III

*In July 1858 Cavour and Napoleon III met at Plombières in France to plot war against Austria. In this note written to the military aide of the king of Savoy, Cavour reports on the negotiations. The king's young daughter was to be given in marriage to cement the Piedmontese-French alliance. Notice the lack of concern for the 15-year-old princess; she is to be sacrificed on the altar of Realpolitik.*

The Emperor entered into many particulars on the problems of the war, which it is my duty to tell you about, and which I shall report to you orally. He seemed to me to have studied the matter rather better than his generals, and to have sensible ideas in that regard. He talked of direct command questions—of how to manage the Pope—of the administrative system for stabilizing the occupied countries—of methods of finance. In a word of all the essential things for our grand project. We were in accord on everything.

The only undefined point is that of the marriage of the Princess Clotilde. The King had authorized me to agree to that, but only in the case that the Emperor had made it a condition *sine qua non* of the alliance. The Emperor not having pushed his insistence to that extreme, I did not, as a gentleman, undertake pledges. But I remain convinced that he lays very great importance on the matrimonial question, and that on it depends, if not the alliance, then its final outcome. It would be an error and a very grave error

to commit oneself to the Emperor and at the same time to give him an affront which would never fade. . . . I have written strongly to the King not to risk the finest undertaking of modern times out of sour aristocratic scruples. I beg you, if he consults you, to join your voice to mine. Perhaps this enterprise should not be attempted, in which the crown of our King and the fate of our people are jeopardized; but if it is attempted, then for the love of heaven let nothing be neglected which could decide the final outcome.

I left Plombières in very serene spirits. If the King consents to the marriage I am confident, let me say almost certain, that within two years you will enter Vienna at the head of our victorious columns.

*Source:* Letter from Cavour to La Marmora, 24 July 1858, repr. in Mack Walker, ed., *Plombières: Secret Diplomacy and the Rebirth of Italy* (New York: Oxford University Press, 1968), p. 227.

---

Sicily in April 1860. The revolutionary firebrand Giuseppe Garibaldi° (1807–1882), a rival of Cavour, set sail for Sicily in May 1860, with but a thousand poorly armed, red-shirted followers, to help the island overthrow its Bourbon ruler. Winning that struggle, Garibaldi's forces crossed to the mainland in August. Victory followed victory, and enthusiasm for Garibaldi grew. His army swelled to 57,000 men, and he won the entire kingdom of Naples.

Threatened by the advance of Garibaldi's power and fearing its reach into the Papal States, Cavour sent his army into the area in September 1860. This brutal attack on a weak state that had not harmed Piedmont was viewed by many Catholics as aggression against the

pope and the church. However, as Cavour explained to his parliament, political necessity required it. Morality was less important than the interests of Piedmont and the about-to-be-born Italy. Although Garibaldi was a republican, he was convinced that Italy could best achieve unity under the king of Piedmont, and he willingly submitted the southern part of Italy, which he controlled, to the king, Victor Emmanuel II (r. 1849–1878). Thus by November 1860, Italy had been united under Piedmontese rule (see Map 22.1). The territories that had come under Piedmont's control affirmed their desire to be part of the new Italy in plebiscites based on universal male suffrage. The 1848 constitution of Piedmont became the constitution of the newly united Italy. The statesman who had engineered the nation's unification lived to relish his handiwork only a few months, dying of an undiagnosed

---

**Garibaldi** (gar-ih-BALL-dee)

**Garibaldi Leading His "Red Shirts" to Victory over the Neapolitan Army, May 1860**    Garibaldi's successful conquests in the south and Cavour's in the north opened the way for Italian unification.
*(Museo di Risorgimento, Milan/Scala/Art Resource, NY)*

illness in May 1861; Cavour's last words were "Italy is made—all is safe."

Still to be joined to the new state were Austrian-held Venetia in the northeast and Rome and its environs, held by the pope with the support of a French garrison. But within a decade, a favorable international situation enabled the fledgling country to acquire both key areas. After Austria was defeated in the Austro-Prussian War in 1866, it ceded Venetia to Italy. Then the Franco-Prussian War forced the French to evacuate Rome, which they had occupied since 1849. Rome was joined to Italy and became its capital in 1870. With that event, unification was complete.

### ■ The Problems of Unified Italy

National unity had been achieved, but it was frail. The uprisings in the south that had led to its inclusion in a united Italy were motivated more by hatred of the Bour-

bons than by fervor for national union. And once the union was achieved, the north behaved like a conquering state—sending its officials to the south, raising taxes, and imposing its laws. In 1861 an uprising of disbanded Neapolitan soldiers and brigands broke out. To crush the revolt, half the Italian army was sent south; the civil war lasted five years and produced more casualties than the entire effort of unification.

Other major divisions remained. In 1861 only 2.5 percent of the population spoke the national language, Florentine Italian. The economy also remained divided. The north was far more industrialized than the rural south. In the south, child mortality was higher, life expectancy was lower, and illiteracy was close to 90 percent. The two regions seemed to belong to two different nations. Piedmont imposed strong central control, resolutely refusing a federal system of government, which many Italians in an earlier era had hoped for. This choice reflected the determination of Piedmont to project its power onto the rest of the peninsula, as well as fear that any other form of government might lead to disintegration of the new state. The United States, with its federal system of government, was wracked by secessionism so strident that in early 1861 it led to the Civil War (see page 763). Piedmont wanted to save the new Italian state from such a fate.

Piedmont imposed its constitution on unified Italy, which limited suffrage to men of property and education, less than 2 percent of the population. Further, although parliamentarism was enshrined in the constitution, Cavour's maneuvering as prime minister had kept governments from being answerable to the parliament. Instead of parliamentary majorities designating the government, Cavour created majorities in parliament to support the cabinet. He cajoled and bribed parliamentarians, transforming previous foes into supporters. This system of manipulation, known as *trasformismo*°, would characterize Italian government for the next several decades. Nevertheless, the new unified Italy was a liberal state that guaranteed legal equality and freedom of association, and provided more freedom for its citizens than the Italian people had seen for centuries.

The Catholic Church remained hostile to the new Italian state. The popes, left to rule a tiny domain—a few square blocks around the papal palace known as the Vatican—considered themselves prisoners; they denounced their "captor" and all its supporters, including anyone who participated in elections. Thus many Italian Catholics refused to recognize the new state for decades, thwarting its legitimacy. With its 27 million people in 1870, Italy was the sixth-most-populous European nation. It was too small to be a great power and too large to accept being a small state. Italian statesmen found it difficult to define their country's role in international politics, and they lacked a firm consensus on Italy's future.

# GERMAN UNIFICATION, 1850–1871

 IKE Italy, Germany had long been a collection of states. Since 1815 the thirty-eight German states had been loosely organized in the German Confederation. Like Piedmont in Italy, one German state, powerful Prussia, led the unification movement. And just as Italy had in Cavour a strong leader who imposed his will, so did German unification have a ruthless and cunning champion: Otto von Bismarck, minister

president of Prussia. Cavour, however, for all his wiliness was committed to establishing a liberal state; Bismarck, on the other hand, was wedded to autocratic rule.

The revolutionaries of 1848 had failed in their attempt to achieve German unification when the king of Prussia refused to accept a throne offered by the elected Frankfurt Assembly. As the painting at the beginning of this chapter illustrates, German unification was ratified not by the ballot as it was in Italy, but rather by the acclamation of the crowned heads of Germany. The nation was united by the use of military force and the imposition of Prussian absolutism over the whole country.

## ■ The Rise of Bismarck

Austria under Metternich had always treated Prussia as a privileged junior partner. After Metternich's fall in 1848, however, rivalry erupted between the two German states. Each tried to manipulate for its own benefit the desire for national unity that had become manifest during the revolution of 1848.

In March 1850 a number of German states met in Erfurt to consider unification under Prussian sponsorship. Austria, which had been excluded, insisted that the "Erfurt Union" be dissolved and that Prussia remain in the German Confederation. Austrian leaders, supported by Russia, threatened war. Since the Prussian military was not strong enough to challenge Austria, Prussia agreed to scuttle the Erfurt Union and accept Austrian leadership in Germany. The new Prussian king, Wilhelm I (r. 1861–1888), was determined to strengthen Prussia by expanding the size and effectiveness of the army. He wanted to reduce the reserve army, increase the professional army, and expand the training period from two to three years. These measures needed parliamentary approval, but the parliament, which was dominated by liberals, opposed the increased costs.

When the parliament refused to accept the king's proposals, he dissolved it. But new elections produced an even stronger liberal majority. The issue was not purely military, but rather one of who should govern the country—the king or the elected representatives. To get his way, the king appointed Count Otto von Bismarck as minister president.

Bismarck was a Junker, a Prussian aristocrat known for his reactionary views, who had opposed the liberal movement in 1848. As Prussian emissary to the German Confederation, he had challenged Austrian primacy. Devoted to his monarch, Bismarck sought to heighten Prussian power in Germany and throughout Europe. He faced down the parliament, telling the Budget Commission in 1862, "The position of Prussia in Germany will be

---

**trasformismo** (trass-for-MEES-mo)

## ℰ READING SOURCES

### Bismarck Lectures Parliament on Royal Prerogatives

*In 1862–1863, a showdown pitted the Prussian king against his country's parliament. The latter claimed it had the right to control the budget and, if it wished, to veto the military reforms proposed by the king. The newly appointed minister president, Otto von Bismarck, insisted that the king had the final word. Prussia was not going to submit to parliamentarism, as Britain had.*

If you, gentlemen, had the exclusive right finally to determine the total amount and the particulars of the budget, if you had the right to demand of His Majesty the King the dismissal of those ministers who do not retain your confidence, if you had the right through your resolutions concerning the budget to determine the strength and organization of the army, if you had the right—as constitutionally you do not have, although you claim it in the Address—to control the relationship of the executive power of the government to its officials, then you would in fact possess the complete governmental power in this country (Prussia). Your Address is based upon these claims, if it has any basis at all. I believe, therefore, that its practical significance can be characterized in a few words: "Through this Address the Royal House of Hohenzollern is requested to transfer its constitutional governing rights to the majority of this House.". . .

You know as well as anyone in Prussia that the ministry acts in Prussia in the name of and on behalf of His Majesty the King, and that in this sense it has executed those acts in which you see a violation of the constitution. You know that in this connection a Prussian ministry has a different position from that of the English. An English ministry, call it what you will, is a parliamentary one, a ministry of the parliamentary majority; but we are ministers of His Majesty the King. . . . Theories about what is lawful when no budget is passed have been advanced, and I do not intend to evaluate them here. . . .

It is sufficient for me to recognize the necessity of state and not pessimistically allow to come to pass a situation in which the treasury is closed. Necessity alone is decisive, and we have taken this necessity into account . . . we shall reject, and we shall steadfastly protect the rights of the Crown against your claims.

The Prussian monarchy has not yet fulfilled its mission; it is not yet ripe for becoming a purely ornamental decoration of your constitutional edifice, not yet ready to be integrated like a lifeless, mechanical part into the mechanism of a parliamentary regime.

*Source:* Bismarck Speech to the Prussian Parliament, January 27, 1863, repr. in Eugene N. Anderson, Stanley Pincetl, Jr., and Donald Ziegler, eds. *Europe in the Nineteenth Century—A Documentary Analysis of Change and Conflict*, Vol. I (Indianapolis: Bobbs Merrill, 1961), pp. 261–262, 265–267.

decided not by its liberalism but by its power . . . not through speeches and majority decisions are the great questions of the day decided—that was the mistake of 1848 and 1849—but by iron and blood."[1]

Bismarck tried to win over the liberals by suggesting that with military force at its disposal, Prussia could lead German unification. But the liberals resisted, and the parliament voted against the military reforms. Unphased, Bismarck carried out the military measures anyway and ordered the collection of the necessary taxes. (See the box "Reading Sources: Bismarck Lectures Parlia-ment on Royal Prerogatives.") The citizens acquiesced, and paid to upgrade their army.

German liberals faced a dilemma: Which did they value more: the goal of nationhood or the principles of liberty? Fellow liberals elsewhere lived in existing nation-states in which statehood had preceded the development of liberalism. And in Italy, unification had been led by the liberal state of Piedmont. That was not the case in Germany, where the natural leader, Prussia, had a long tradition of militarism and authoritarianism. To oppose Bismarck effectively, German liberals knew they would have to join with the working classes, but they feared them and forestalled such an alliance. Germany appeared embarked on an illiberal course.

Bismarck's genius was to exploit the growing desire for German unification. During the Franco-Austrian War of 1859 that launched Italian unification, Germans had feared that the French would attack across the Rhine River. Many came to believe that only a strong, united Germany could give its inhabitants security. Economically a united Germany was developing under Prussian leadership with the *Zollverein*, a customs union of most German states, excluding Austria. Founded in 1834, the customs union had become more extensive with the passage of time; even states that were politically hostile to Prussia joined to protect their economic interests. Germans began to think in all-German terms. Professional and cultural organizations now often extended beyond a single state to the wider, "national" context: the German Commercial Association, the Congress of German Jurists, and the German Sharpshooters League, for example. Although it had yet to find much resonance among the lower classes, the idea of a united Germany had gained a substantial audience by the 1860s.

### ■ Prussian Wars and German Unity

Having established the supremacy of royal power in Prussia, Bismarck was ready to enlarge Prussia's role in Germany at the expense of Austria. A crisis over Schleswig-Holstein° (see Map 22.2) gave him an opening. These two provinces, ethnically and linguistically German (except for northern Schleswig), were ruled by the king of Denmark. Historically and by previous treaty agreements, Schleswig and Holstein were legally inseparable. When in 1863 the Danish king, contrary to earlier treaty obligations, attempted to annex Schleswig to Denmark, Holstein felt threatened. Holstein was a member of the German Confederation, so it called on the confederation for protection. Acting on behalf of the confederation, Prussia and Austria intervened, sending troops that won a quick, cheap victory. Prussia occupied Schleswig, and Austria took Holstein.

Prussia and Austria continued to be bitter rivals for domination of Germany. Bismarck believed war was the only means to win this contest, and conflicts over the administration of Schleswig and Holstein served as a pretext. With no declaration of war, Prussia attacked Austrian-administered Holstein in June 1866. The Austro-Prussian War lasted a scant seven weeks. The de-

cisive victory of the new, reformed Prussian army was the Battle of Sadowa° on July 3. With a much more advanced industry than Austria, Prussia had equipped its soldiers with the new breech-loading rifles, known as needle guns; their advantage was that troops could fire from a prone position, while the Austrians, with their muzzle loaders, had to stand up to shoot. Prussia's superiority in arms and Moltke's superb military leadership defeated Austria, forcing it to accept peace on Prussian terms.

Prussia annexed its smaller neighbors who had supported Austria, creating a contiguous state linking Prussia with the Rhineland. In Bismarck's scheme this enlarged Prussia would dominate the newly formed North German Confederation, comprising all the states north of the Main° River. From now on, Austria was excluded from German affairs.

The triumph of Sadowa made Bismarck a popular hero. Elections held on the day of the battle returned a conservative pro-Bismarck majority to the Prussian parliament. The legislature, including a large number of liberals mesmerized by the military victory, voted to legalize retroactively the illegal taxes that had been levied since 1862 to upgrade the military. Enthusiastic at the prospect of achieving German unity at last, most liberals compromised their principles. They rationalized that national unity ought to be gained first, with liberal constitutional institutions secured later. Their optimism proved to be a miscalculation.

The unification of Germany, like that of Italy, was facilitated by a favorable international situation. The Crimean War had estranged Russia from Austria. In 1850 Austrian resistance to Prussian attempts to lead Germany had been backed by Russia, but by the time the Austro-Prussian War broke out in 1866, Austria stood alone. Although it would have been opportune for France to intervene on the Austrian side, the French emperor was indecisive and in the end did nothing. He also had been lulled into inaction by vague Prussian promises of support for French plans to annex Luxembourg. Once the war was won, Bismarck reneged on these promises. France was left with the problem of a strong, enlarged Prussia on its eastern border, which threatened France's position as a Great Power. British leaders likewise did not intervene in the unification process. Disillusioned by the results of the Crimean War, they were in an isolationist mood. Moreover, Britain's government was sympathetic to the rise of a fellow Protestant power.

Bismarck's design was almost complete. Only the southern German states remained outside the North

---

**Schleswig** (SHLES-vik)    **Holstein** (HOLL-shteyn)        **Sadowa** (SAH-doe-wah)    **Main** (MINE)

**Map 22.2    The Unification of Germany, 1866–1871**    A series of military victories made it possible for Prussia to unite Germany under its domain.

German Confederation. He obliged them to sign a military treaty with Prussia and established a customs parliament for all the members of the Zollverein (the customs union), including the southern German states. The southern states, which were Catholic and sympathetic to Austria, were reluctant to see German unity advance any further. Only some dramatic event could remove their resistance.

### ■ The Franco-Prussian War and Unification, 1870–1871

French leaders were also determined to prevent German unity. They feared the loss of influence in the southern German states that had traditionally been France's allies. Moreover, since the mid-seventeenth century, French security had relied on a weak and divided Germany.

Both Berlin and Paris anticipated war. And war came soon enough, precipitated by a crisis over the Spanish succession. In 1868 a military coup had overthrown the Spanish queen Isabella, and the provisional government offered the throne to a Catholic member of the Hohenzollerns°, the reigning Prussian monarch's family. The French viewed this candidacy as an unacceptable expansion of Prussian power and influence. Fearing a two-front war with Prussia in the east and Spain in the south, they insisted the Hohenzollerns refuse the proffered throne. As passions heated, Bismarck was elated at the prospect of war. But King Wilhelm was not. On July 12, 1870, he engineered the withdrawal of the young prince's candidacy, removing the cause for war. Bismarck was bitterly disappointed.

Not content with this diplomatic victory, the French pushed their luck further. On July 13 the French ambassador met the king of Prussia at Ems and demanded guarantees that no Hohenzollern would ever again be a candidate for the Spanish throne. Unable to provide any more concessions without a serious loss of prestige, the Prussian king refused the French petition.

Wilhelm telegraphed an account of his meeting to Chancellor Bismarck. The chancellor immediately seized the opportunity this message provided. He edited what became known as the Ems dispatch, making the exchange between king and ambassador seem more curt than it actually had been; then he released it to the press. As he hoped, the French interpreted the report as a deliberate snub to their ambassador and overreacted. Napoleon III was deluged with emotional demands that he avenge the imagined slight to French national honor; on July 15 he declared war.

The Prussians led a well-planned campaign. An army of 384,000 Prussians was rushed by rail to confront a force of 270,000 Frenchmen. The French had the advantage of better rifles, but the Prussians were equipped with heavier cannon, which could pulverize French positions from a distance. Within a few weeks, Prussia won a decisive victory at Sedan°, taking the French emperor prisoner on September 2. The French continued the struggle, despite difficult odds. Infuriated by the continuation of the war, the Prussians resorted to extreme measures. They took hostages and burned down whole villages, and they laid siege to Paris, starving and bombarding its beleaguered population.

Throughout Germany the outbreak of the war aroused general enthusiasm for the Prussian cause. Exploiting this popular feeling, Bismarck called on leaders of the southern German states to accept the unification of Germany under the Prussian king. Reluctant princes, such as the king of Bavaria, were bought off with bribes. On January 18, 1871, the German princes met in the Hall of Mirrors at the Versailles palace, symbol of past French greatness, and acclaimed the Prussian king as German emperor, Kaiser Wilhelm I.

In May 1871 the Treaty of Frankfurt established the peace terms (see Map 22.1). France was forced to give up the provinces of Alsace and Lorraine and to pay Germany a heavy indemnity of 5 billion francs. These harsh terms embittered the French, leading many to desire revenge and establishing a formidable barrier to future Franco-German relations.

### ■ The Character of the New Germany

German unity had been won through a series of wars—against Denmark in 1864, Austria in 1866, and France in 1870. The military had played a key role in forging German unity, and it remained a dominant force in the new nation. Italian unity had been sanctioned by plebiscites and a vote by an elected assembly accepting the popular verdict. The founding act of the new German state, as the opening illustration to this chapter shows, was the acclamation of the German emperor by German rulers on the soil of a defeated neighbor. Thus the rulers placed themselves above elected assemblies and popular sanction.

On the surface the constitution of the new Germany was remarkably democratic. It provided for an upper, appointed house, the *Bundesrat*°, representing the individual German states, and a lower house, the *Reichstag*°, which was elected by universal manhood suffrage. The latter might seem a surprising concession from Bismarck, the authoritarian aristocrat. But he knew the liberals lacked mass support and gambled that, with appropriate appeals, he would be able to create majorities that could be manipulated for his purposes.

The dominant state in the new Germany was, of course, Prussia, which was home to two-thirds of its population. The king of Prussia occupied the post of emperor, and the chancellor and other cabinet members were responsible not to parliament but to him. Only the emperor could make foreign policy and war, command the army, and interpret the constitution. The authoritarianism of Prussia had been projected onto all of Germany.

The emergence of a strong, united Germany shattered the European balance of power. In February 1871

---

**Hohenzollerns** (HO-en-tsoll-ernz)    **Sedan** (seh-DAEN)

**Bundesrat** (BOON-tes-raht)    **Reichstag** (RYSH-stak)

the British political leader Benjamin Disraeli observed that the unification of Germany was a "greater political event than the French revolution of last century.... There is not a diplomatic tradition which has not been swept away. You have a new world.... The balance of power has been entirely destroyed."[2] Germany had become the dominant power on the Continent.

# PRECARIOUS EMPIRES

THE three large empires of central and eastern Europe, battered by aggressive behavior from other European states and challenged by internal tensions, attempted to weather the endless crises they confronted. The Austrian, Ottoman, and Russian Empires labored to fortify their regimes with political reforms, restructuring their institutions, but only Austria tried to accommodate democratic impulses by establishing a parliament. The Ottoman sultans and the Russian tsars clung tenaciously to their autocratic traditions.

## ■ The Dual Monarchy in Austria-Hungary

Emperor Franz Joseph (r. 1848–1916) had come to the throne as an 18-year-old in that year of crisis, 1848. He was a well-meaning monarch who took his duties seriously. His upbringing was German, he lived in German-speaking Vienna, and he headed an army and a bureaucracy that was mostly German, but Franz Joseph was markedly cosmopolitan. He spoke several of his subjects' languages and thought of himself as the emperor of all his peoples. A much-loved, regal figure, Franz Joseph provided a visible symbol of the state. He lacked imagination, however, and did little more than try to conserve a disintegrating empire coping with the modern forces of liberalism and nationalism.

After the war with Piedmont and France (see page 746), Austrian statesmen sensed the vulnerability of their empire. To give the government credibility, in February 1861, Franz Joseph issued what became known as the February Patent, which guaranteed civil liberties and provided for local self-government and an elected parliament.

The need to safeguard the remaining territories was clear. By 1866 the Austrian Habsburgs were no longer a German or Italian power (Venetia had been handed over to a united Italy). The strongest challenge to Habsburg rule came from Hungary, where the Magyars insisted on self-rule, a claim based on age-old rights and Vienna's

initial acceptance of autonomy in 1848. Since Magyar cooperation was crucial for the well-being of the Habsburg Empire, the government entered into lengthy negotiations with Magyar leaders in 1867. Empress Elizabeth, sympathetic to the Magyars, helped convince the emperor to take a conciliatory stance. The outcome was "the Compromise of 1867," creating new structures for the empire that lasted until 1918. The agreement divided the Habsburg holdings into Austria in the west and Hungary in the east (see Map 22.3). Each was independent, but they were linked by the person of the emperor of Austria, Franz Joseph, who was also king of Hungary. Hungary had full internal autonomy and participated jointly in imperial affairs—state finance, defense, and foreign relations. The new state created in 1867 was known as the dual monarchy of Austria-Hungary.

The compromise confirmed Magyar dominance in Hungary. Although numerically a minority, Magyars controlled the Hungarian parliament, the army, the bureaucracy, and other state institutions. They opposed self-rule by the Croats, Serbs, Slovaks, Romanians, and others in the kingdom and attempted a policy of Magyarization—teaching only Magyar in the schools, conducting all government business in Magyar, and giving access to government positions only to those fully assimilated in Magyar culture. This arrangement created frustrations and resistance among the various nationalities under their rule.

The terms of the compromise also gave the Hungarians a voice in imperial foreign policy. Magyars feared that Slavic groups outside the empire, who planned to form independent states or had already done so, would inspire fellow Slavs in Austria-Hungary to revolt. To prevent that, the Hungarians favored an expansionist foreign policy in the Balkans, which the monarchy embraced (see Map 22.3). Having lost its influence in Germany, Austria-Hungary saw the Balkans as an area in which to assert itself. The policy was fraught with risks and, by bringing more discontented Slavs into the empire, led to hostility with other states.

## ■ The Ailing Ottoman Empire

At midcentury the Ottoman Empire was still one of the largest European powers, but it faced unrest within its borders and threats from the expansionist designs of its neighbors. The ailing empire was commonly referred to as "the sick man of Europe." Over the next twenty-five years, the empire shed some of its territory and modernized its government, but nothing could save it from decline in the face of nationalist uprisings in its Balkan possessions.

**Map 22.3  Austria-Hungary in 1878**  A multinational state, the Austro-Hungarian Empire occupied Bosnia in 1878, bringing more dissatisfied peoples under its rule. Tensions in the Balkans would lead to the outbreak of world war in 1914.

As early as the 1840s, the Ottoman Empire had begun various reform movements to bring more security to its subjects. Known as the *Tanzimat*°, these changes were initiated by Sultan Abdul Mejid° (r. 1839–1861), with the help of his able prime minister, Reshid Mustafa Pasha° (1800–1858). Reshid had served as the Ottoman ambassador in London and Paris and was familiar with Western institutions, which he admired and wished to emulate. The reforms introduced security of property, equity in taxation, and equality before the law regardless of religion. Government officials—who previously had been free to collect taxes arbitrarily, sending the required amount to the central government and keeping the rest—were given fixed salaries and subjected to regular inspections.

These reforms were strengthened after the Crimean War by further imperial edicts. Contacts with the West encouraged Turks to think of transforming their empire into a more modern, Westernized state. Many young intellectuals were impatient with the pace of change, however, and critical of the sultan. Unable freely to express their opinions at home, some went into exile in the late 1860s to Paris and London. Their hosts called them the "Young Turks," an expression that became synonymous with activists for change and improvement.

Alarmed by challenges to its authority, the central government began to turn away from reform, and in 1871 the sultan decided to assert his personal rule. His inability successfully to wage war and hold onto the empire led to dissatisfaction, and in the spring of 1876 rioters demanded and won the establishment of constitutional government. Within a year, however, the new sultan, Abdul Hamid II (r. 1876–1909), dismissed the constitutional government and reverted to personal rule.

Part of the administration's problem was financial. The Crimean War had forced the empire to borrow money abroad. The easy terms of foreign credit lured the sultan into taking out huge loans to finance extravagant projects. By 1875 more than half the annual income of the empire went to pay the interest on the debt. In spite of a drought and famine, the authorities raised taxes, fostering widespread discontent.

Opposition to the government increased, fueled by nationalist fervor. The empire tolerated religious diversity and did not persecute people because of their religion. But the central administration had lost control over its provincial officials, who were often corrupt and tyrannical. Christians, the majority population in the Balkans, blamed their suffering on Islamic rule, and many were inspired by the 1821 Greek war of independence and the revolutions of 1848 to seek their own independence.

The Romanians, who lived mainly in the adjoining provinces of Moldavia in the north and Wallachia° in the south, began to express nationalist sentiments in the late eighteenth century. These sentiments were nurtured by Western-educated students, who claimed for their countrymen illustrious descent from Roman settlers of antiquity. News of revolution in Paris in 1848 helped trigger a revolt in both provinces demanding unification and independence. This uprising was quickly crushed by the Turks.

In 1856 the Congress of Paris removed Russia's right of protection over Moldavia and Wallachia and provided for a referendum to determine their future. In 1859 the two provinces chose a local military officer, Alexander Cuza° (r. 1859–1866), as ruler of each territory. In 1862, the Ottoman Empire recognized the union of the two principalities in the single, autonomous state of Romania. At the Congress of Berlin in 1878, Romania's full independence was recognized. Thus, in less than a quarter-century, two provinces of the Ottoman Empire had gained full sovereignty.

The path to independence was much more violent for the Bulgarians. Influenced by neighboring Serbia and encouraged by the Russians, revolutionary committees spread propaganda and agitated against Ottoman rule. An uprising in Bulgaria broke out in May 1876. The Christian rebels attacked not only symbols of Ottoman authority but also peaceable Turks living in their midst. The imperial army, aided by local Turk volunteers, quickly re-established Ottoman authority. Incensed by the massacre of fellow Muslims, the volunteers resorted to mass killing, looting, and burning of Christian villages. The "Bulgarian horrors" shocked Europe and made the continuation of Turkish rule unacceptable.

The Bulgarian crisis was resolved by the Balkan wars of 1876–1878, which were provoked by the uprising of the westernmost Ottoman provinces of Bosnia and Herzegovina. Since many of the inhabitants of these two provinces were Serbs, they had the sympathy of Serbia, which hoped to unify the southern Slavs. Together with the neighboring mountain state of Montenegro, Serbia declared war on the Ottoman Empire. They were savagely defeated by the Turks.

Russia, which saw itself as the protector of the Slavic peoples, reacted to the Bulgarian horrors by declaring

Tanzimat (tan-zee-MAT)    Abdul Mejid (Ab-DOOL med-JEED)
Reshid Mustafa Pasha (ray-SHEED moo-STAH-fah PAH-shah)

Wallachia (vall-AK-yah)    Cuza (KOO-sah)

**Nationalistic Uprising in Bulgaria**    In this 1879 lithograph, Bulgaria is depicted in the form of a maiden—protected by the Russian eagle, breaking her chains, and winning liberty from the Ottoman Empire.    *(St. Cyril and Methodius National Library, Sofia)*

the autonomy of Bulgaria. The British insisted on being allowed to administer the island of Cyprus in the eastern Mediterranean as an outpost for checking further Russian challenges to the existing balance of power.

Thus Turkey was plundered, not only by its enemies but also by powers that had intervened on its behalf. When France complained that it received no compensation, it was given the chance to grab Tunisia, another land under Ottoman rule. Russia, which had signed an alliance with Romania and promised to respect its territorial integrity, ignored its obligations and took southern Bessarabia from its ally. The devious work of the congress reflected the power politics that now characterized international affairs. Statesmen shamelessly used force against both foe and friend for the aggrandizement of their own states. Neither morality nor international law restrained ambition.

### ■ Russia and the Great Reforms

Russia's defeat in the Crimean War and its distrust of the Western powers forced the tsar to consider ways of strengthening Russia by restructuring its institutions. Beginning in 1861, a series of measures known collectively as the Great Reforms began to change the face of Russia.

Already by the 1840s, concern about the archaic nature and structure of Russian government was mounting. Many officials lamented the tendency of a timid bureaucracy to lie to and mislead the public. Defeat in the Crimean War widened the critique of Russian institutions. Calls for *glasnost*—greater openness—became the leading motif in the Great Reforms. The chief problem that needed resolution was serfdom. Educated opinion had long denounced serfdom as immoral, but conscience was not the principal reason for its abolition. Serfdom was abolished because it presented clear disadvantages in both the domestic and international domains. The new tsar, Alexander II (r. 1855–1881), feared that if serfdom was not abolished from above, it would be overthrown from below—by a serf rebellion that would sweep away everything in its path, including the autocracy itself.

Serfdom also held Russia back in its competition with the rest of the world. Defeat in the Crimean War by Britain and France suggested that soldiers with a stake in their society fought harder than men bound to lifetime servitude. In addition, the victorious Western states had won in part because their industrial might translated into more and better guns, ammunition, and transportation. Industrial progress required a mobile labor force,

war on the empire in April 1877. At first progress was slow; then the Russians broke through the Turkish lines and forced the sultan to sue for peace. The resulting Treaty of San Stefano, signed in March 1878, created a huge, independent Bulgaria as essentially a Russian protectorate.

The British, Austrians, and French were shocked at the extent to which the San Stefano treaty favored Russia. Under their pressure, the European powers met in Berlin in 1878 to reconsider the treaty. The Congress of Berlin reduced the size of the Bulgarian territory, returning the rest to the Ottomans. Bosnia and Herzegovina were removed from Ottoman rule, henceforth to be administered by Austria-Hungary (see Map 24.4 on page 837). The sultan was forced to acknowledge the legal independence of Serbia, Montenegro, and Romania and

## 📖 READING SOURCES

### The Tsar Demands the Freeing of the Serfs

*In January 1861, Tsar Alexander II addressed the Council of State, an advisory body that he had asked four years earlier to prepare a draft law emancipating the serfs. After this forceful speech, a workable proposal emerged that was implemented six weeks later. Notice that the council's opinion is only advisory; the tsar is indicating his "absolute will." While he gives lip service to the serfs' interests, the power of Russia and the future of the tsarist regime are Alexander's prime concerns.*

The matter of the liberation of the serfs, which has been submitted for the consideration of the State Council, I consider to be a vital question for Russia, upon which will depend the development of her strength and power. . . . [T]his matter cannot be postponed . . . I repeat—and this is my absolute will—that this matter should be finished right away. . . .

[Y]ou will assure yourselves that all that can be done for the protection of the interests of the nobility has been done . . . but I ask you only not to forget that the basis of the whole work must be the improvement of the life of the peasants—an improvement not in words alone or on paper but in actual fact. . . .

My predecessors felt all the evils of serfdom and continually endeavored, if not to destroy it completely, to work toward the gradual limitation of the arbitrary power of the estate owners.

Already in 1856, before the coronation, while in Moscow I called the attention of the leaders of the nobility of the Moscow *guberniia* [region] to the necessity for them to occupy themselves with improving the life of the serfs, adding that serfdom could not continue forever and that it would therefore be better if the transformation took place from above rather than from below. . . .

I have the right to demand one thing from you: that you, putting aside all personal interests, act not like estate owners but like imperial statesmen invested with my trust. Approaching this important matter I have not concealed from myself all those difficulties that awaited us and I do not conceal them now.

*Source:* Speech of January 28, 1861, in George Vernadsky et al., eds., *A Sourcebook for Russian History from Early Times to 1917,* vol. 3. Copyright © 1972. Reprinted by permission of the publisher, Yale University Press.

not one tied to the soil by serfdom. With a free labor force, rural populations, as in the West, could become the abundant labor supply that drove industrial production. Many educated Russians felt that the defeat in the Crimea had revealed Russia's general backwardness. To catch up with the West, they argued, Russia needed to shed its timeworn institutions, particularly serfdom.

In April 1861 Alexander II issued a decree freeing the serfs. (See the box "Reading Sources: The Tsar Demands the Freeing of the Serfs.") At one stroke, he emancipated 22 million people from a system that allowed them to be bought and sold, separated from their families, and treated in the cruelest ways imaginable. Emancipation represented a compromise with the gentry, which had re-

luctantly agreed to liberate its serfs but insisted on compensation. As a result, the newly liberated peasants had to reimburse the government with mortgage payments lasting fifty years. The peasants received some land, but its value was vastly overrated and its quantity insufficient for peasant families. To make ends meet, most freed peasants continued working for their former masters.

The mortgage payments and taxes imposed on the peasants by the central government were handled by the local commune, the *mir°*. The mir determined how the land was to be used, and it paid collectively for the mortgage and taxes on the land. As a consequence,

---

**mir** (MEER)

**A Critique of Russian Serfdom**   The French artist Gustave Doré reveals how landowners viewed their serfs as mere property that could be won and lost with a draw of the cards. *(Miriam and Ira D. Wallach Division of Art, Prints and Photographs, The New York Public Library, Astor, Lenox and Tilden Foundations)*

the commune was reluctant for the peasants to leave the land, and they could do so only with its permission. Freed from serfdom, the peasants still suffered many constraints. In fact, the emancipation declaration was accompanied by massive peasant uprisings that had to be put down by force.

The tsar and his advisers feared the large mass of uneducated peasants as a potential source of anarchy and rebellion. They depended on the mir to preserve control even though the commune system had some inherent economic disadvantages. Since increased productivity benefited the commune as much as the individual peasant, there was little incentive for peasants to improve their land, and agricultural yields remained low.

Alexander, lauded as the "tsar emancipator" by his contemporaries, remained wedded to the principles of autocracy. His aim in abolishing serfdom and introducing other reforms was to modernize and strengthen Russia and stabilize his divinely mandated rule. Like most Russians, Alexander believed that only the firm hand of autocracy could hold together a large, ethnically diverse

country. The peasant uprisings that accompanied emancipation only confirmed his beliefs. Clearly, however, the sudden freedom of 22 million illiterate peasants threatened to overwhelm existing institutions, and some changes had to be made. Although he surrendered no powers, Alexander did institute a number of reforms, altering the government and the judicial and military systems so they could deal more effectively with the totally remodeled Russian society.

Government reform had paramount importance. Between 1800 and 1850, the Russian population had increased from 36 to 59 million, and it had become more and more difficult to administer this vast country. Overcentralized, with a poorly trained civil service, the government was unable to cope effectively with the problems of its people. Emancipation of the serfs greatly exacerbated this situation. Thus in 1864 a law was passed providing for local governments, or *zemstvos*°, at

---

**zemstvos** (SEMST-vose)

the village and regional levels, giving Russians the authority and the opportunity to use initiative in local matters.

The zemstvos were largely controlled by the gentry and not particularly democratic. They were forbidden to debate political issues, and their decisions could be overridden or ignored by local officials appointed by the tsar. Some hoped that zemstvos could become the basis for self-government at the national level and looked for the creation of an all-Russian zemstvo, but such hopes were firmly squelched by the tsar, who jealously insisted on undivided and undiminished autocracy. Nonetheless, the zemstvos were a viable attempt to modernize an overburdened central government.

The tsar also created an independent judiciary that ensured equality before the law, public jury trials, and uniform sentences. Russian political leaders recognized that public confidence in the judiciary and the rule of law was a prerequisite for the development of commerce and industry. Businessmen would no longer fear arbitrary intervention by capricious officials and could develop enterprises in greater security.

In addition, censorship of the press was abolished. Under the previous tsar, Nicholas I, all ideas that did not conform to government policy were censored. Such censorship prevented the central government from being well informed about public opinion or about the effects of its policies on the country. Under Alexander, openness in the press was viewed as a remedy for corruption and misuse of power. People could be punished only for specific violations after publication, and they would face trial in an independent court.

Reform also extended to the Russian army. Its structure and methods became more Western. Military service, previously limited to peasants, became the obligation of all Russian men. All men submitted to a lottery, and those with an "unlucky" number entered the service. In an effort to make military service more attractive, the length of service was drastically cut and corporal punishment was abolished. Access to the officer corps was to be by merit rather than by social connection. The Ministry of War also improved the system of reserves, enabling Russia to mobilize a larger army with more modern weapons in case of war.

The Great Reforms represented considerable change for Russia. Serfdom had been abolished, self-government was established on the local level, the rule of law was adopted, and army service was made more humane. But above the change, the tsarist regime remained autocratic and repressive, flexible only to the degree that its rulers had the will and wisdom to be.

## THE EMERGENCE OF NEW POLITICAL FORMS IN THE UNITED STATES AND CANADA, 1840–1880

**A**CROSS the seas a new power emerged in these years, the United States. It enlarged its territories, strengthened its national government, and broadened its democracy by including a large category of people previously excluded from the political process—African Americans. But these achievements were the result of the bloodiest conflict in all of American history, the Civil War.

### ■ Territorial Expansion and Slavery

In the early years of its existence, the United States was confined to the land east of the Mississippi River, but in the nineteenth century it gained much territory through westward expansion (see Map 22.4). In 1803 President Thomas Jefferson secured the Louisiana Purchase from the French, which nearly doubled the size of the United States. In 1819 Florida was acquired from Spain. Some Americans looked even farther westward. Some began to insist that the United States had a "manifest destiny" to occupy the whole North American continent from coast to coast.

The U.S. government used the settlements of American citizens in Mexican- and British-held territories as pretexts for expansion. In 1845 Congress voted to annex Texas, which had gained independence from Mexico in 1836. As a result of negotiation with Britain, the United States in 1846 acquired Oregon country south of the forty-ninth parallel. Declaring war on Mexico in the same year, and quickly winning, the United States added California and the Southwest in 1848. Manifest destiny or not, the United States now spanned the continent from the Atlantic to the Pacific.

Beginning in the 1820s the United States saw serious sectional clashes between east and west as well as north and south. The latter were more important. Many issues divided the two regions, notably a conflict between the industrial interests of the North and the agrarian interests of the South. What sharpened this divide, however, was the issue of slavery. As the United States annexed new territories, the question of whether they would be slave or free divided the nation. The North opposed the extension of the "peculiar institution," while much of the South favored it. Southerners believed that if the new areas were closed to slavery, the institution would weaken in the South; slaveholding would eventually disappear, and with it southern prosperity. They would then be unable to withstand the political and economic pressure of an economically richer and more populous North, unsympathetic to slavery.

The issue of slavery was passionately debated for decades. Some Americans wanted slavery abolished throughout the United States; if that could not be done, some of the most committed abolitionists, especially in New England, advocated the secession of free states from the Union. On the other side, southerners threatened that if their way of life—meaning a society based on slavery—were not assured, then the South would secede. The threat of secession was lightly and frequently made by partisans of various causes for many decades.

In November 1860 Illinois Republican Abraham Lincoln (1809–1865) was elected president in a highly contested four-way race. Lincoln opposed the spread of slavery beyond its existing borders and hence appeared to threaten its future in the South itself. For many southerners his election to the highest office was the final blow.

Beginning in December 1860 most southern state legislatures voted to secede from the Union, forming in February 1861 the Confederate States of America. The South defined its cause as defending states' rights, claiming that the people of each state had the right to determine their destiny, free from what they viewed as the tyranny of the national government. Southern states seized federal funds and property, and in April 1861 the Confederates bombarded federally held Fort Sumter. Lincoln, inaugurated in March 1861, was determined to preserve the Union and to put down the insurrection. The long-dreaded civil war had begun.

**Map 22.4  U.S. Expansion Through 1853**  In eight short years, from 1845 to 1853, the United States increased its territorial size by a third. The principle of manifest destiny appeared to be fulfilled, as the United States now stretched from the Atlantic to the Pacific.

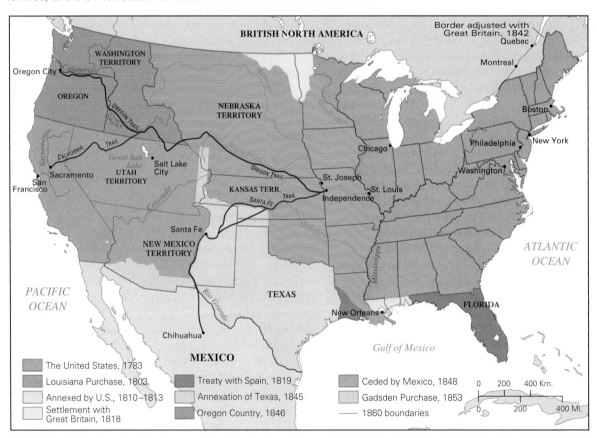

## ■ Civil War and National Unity, 1861–1865

The North had many advantages. It had nearly three times as many people as the South, a strong industrial base that could supply an endless stream of weapons, and a far more extensive rail system for transporting men and materiel to the front. Although blue and gray armies clashed in a number of important military engagements, the North effectively blockaded the South, leading it toward the end of the war to be desperately short of men, money, and supplies.

During the war, Lincoln's government took measures that centralized power in Washington, changing the nation from a loose federation of states to a more centrally governed entity. As one historian has noted, the United States changed from "they" to "it." The federal government intruded into areas of life from which it had before been absent. With the National Banking Act of 1863, state banks were driven out of business and replaced by a uniform national banking system. The federal government provided massive subsidies for a national railroad system. Lincoln established the National Academy of Sciences to advise him on scientific matters. The word *national* came into increasing use. Senator John Sherman of Ohio declared during the war that "the policy of this country ought to be to make everything national as far as possible."

When the main Confederate army surrendered in 1865, the principle of state sovereignty, proclaimed by the South, was roundly defeated. With the passage of the Thirteenth Amendment to the U.S. Constitution the same year, slaves, previously considered property, were declared to be free. The North occupied the South in an attempt to "reconstruct" it. Reconstruction included efforts to root out the Confederate leadership and ensure full civil and political rights for the newly emancipated African Americans. The government also embarked on a short-lived campaign to provide freed slaves with enough land to ensure them a livelihood—another example of federal authority at work. At the end of Reconstruction, federal power retreated and many states with impunity denied African Americans their rights. But certainly the nation was more centralized, and its citizens were more enfranchised, after the Civil War than before.

## ■ The Frontiers of Democracy

One of the major transformations in the United States from the 1820s through the 1860s was the inclusion of an ever greater number of people in the political process. By the late 1820s, under the impact of popular pressure, states abandoned restrictions on voting, and most adult white men received the vote. Symbolic of this new "age of the common man" was the election of Andrew Jackson as U.S. president in 1828. All his predecessors had been men of education and property—some were even described as "Virginia aristocrats"—but Jackson represented himself as a self-made man, a rugged frontiersman. State legislatures had in the past elected members to the presidential Electoral College, but in response to public calls for change, state legislatures altered the system so that Electoral College members were selected by direct popular vote.

National presidential campaigns became rough-and-tumble affairs, with emotional appeals to the public. Scurrilous attacks, many untrue, were mounted against opponents. In 1828, for instance, during President John Quincy Adams's re-election campaign, his opponents charged him with corruption, although once he was defeated, they admitted he had been one of the nation's most honest officeholders. Campaigns began to revolve around easily grasped symbols, and when William Henry Harrison ran for president in 1840 he was depicted as a simple frontiersman. His supporters wore log-cabin badges, sang log-cabin songs, and dragged log-cabin replicas on floats in parades. Such paraphernalia became a common sight in American elections. If some contemporary observers, such as the Frenchman Alexis de Tocqueville (1805–1859), were disappointed at the lack of a thoughtful and deliberate process in choosing political leaders, they recognized that democracy was nowhere in the world as fully developed as in the United States, where it foreshadowed the future of other societies.

When Abraham Lincoln was elected U.S. president in 1860, nobody of his social standing occupied an equivalent position in Europe. At the news of his assassination in 1865, workmen and artisans, seeing in the dead president a kindred spirit, stood for hours in line outside the U.S. legation in London and the consul general's office in Lyon (France) to sign a book of condolence to express their sorrow. It was also a form of tribute to the nation that had elected a backwoodsman, born in a log cabin, to its highest office.

The frontiers of democracy appeared to have widened after the Civil War when amendments to the U.S. Constitution granted African Americans full equality with whites. Slavery was forbidden throughout the United States, and regardless of "race, color, or previous

**Bingham: The Verdict of the People** In George Caleb Bingham's 1855 painting set in the American West, voters await election results. Unlike in Europe, where religious and property barriers to suffrage continued throughout the nineteenth century, many U.S. states had universal white male suffrage by the 1820s. *(From the Art Collection of NationsBank)*

condition of servitude," all Americans were declared to be citizens. During the first few years of Reconstruction, whites who had supported the Confederacy were deprived of the right to vote, and African Americans represented a voting bloc in the South. As a result, for the first time the United States saw the election of blacks to positions as varied as lieutenant governor, U.S. senator, congressman, postmaster, and innumerable county and town offices. After the end of military occupation of the South, however, local white power reasserted itself and the rights of African Americans were sharply curtailed. Yet, compared with their status before the Civil War, African Americans had advanced significantly. They were no longer slaves but citizens, they were free to move

where they wanted, and in some places they were able to participate in the political process.

By 1880 the United States not only had seen four decades of territorial expansion but had been transformed by the ordeal of the Civil War, which brought about the extension of federal authority and—however hesitatingly—of the rights of citizenship to new groups. A large, powerful democracy had arisen in the North American continent.

### ■ The Northern Neighbor: Canada

Just north of the United States, in Canada, some similar processes unfolded during the 1800s that also resulted

**Map 22.5     Dominion of Canada, 1873**     By 1873 Canada had become a vast territory with the addition of the western territories. Like the United States, Canada reached from the Atlantic to the Pacific.

in a larger, freer, and more centralized society. Though Canada was spared a civil war, a popular uprising did occur as citizens chafed under the oligarchical grip of British colonial rule, in which authority was in the hands of a few families. Lord Durham, the new governor, suggested in 1839 a series of reforms (see pages 727–728) that in the end were implemented, uniting Upper and Lower Canada, and providing for an elected assembly and a government responsible to it. The British North America Act in 1867 created a federal system of government, with each province exercising considerable autonomy. With the purchase of the Northwest Territories from the private Hudson Bay Company in 1869 and the gradual attachment of other provinces, Canada gained in size; by 1871, the country stretched from the maritime provinces in the east to the Pacific (see Map 22.5). The building of a transcontinental railroad in the 1880s helped unite the huge nation. By the end of the nineteenth century, Canada was virtually self-governing, having full control over all its affairs, except for defense and foreign affairs.

# THE DEVELOPMENT OF WESTERN DEMOCRACIES

 N the generation after 1850, Britain, France, and several smaller states in northern Europe made major strides forward in creating democratic political systems and cultures. Although universal manhood suffrage had been instituted only in France, all these countries' governments were responsible to elected representatives of the voters. Lincoln had spoken of the United States enjoying "government of the people, by the people, for the people." As a result of a series of political reforms, this goal was in the process of being attained in many European countries.

## ■ Victorian Britain

The mid-nineteenth century was a period of exceptional wealth and security for Britain, as the population as a whole began to share in the economic benefits of

⊕ G L O B A L   E N C O U N T E R S

## A Japanese View of the British Parliament

*In 1862 the Japanese government sent its first diplomatic mission to Europe. Accompanying the delegation was its young translator, Fukuzawa Yukichi (1835–1901). Intrigued by what he saw and eager to interest his fellow Japanese in the West, Fukuzawa published several books. In fact, all books about the West in Japan came to be known as "Fukuzawa-bon." Toward the end of his life in his* Autobiography, *he described how, while in London, he had tried to understand the workings of the British Parliament.*

Of political situations at that time, I tried to learn as much as I could from various persons that I met in London . . . though it was often difficult to understand things clearly as I was as yet unfamiliar with the history of Europe. . . . A perplexing institution was representative government. When I asked a gentleman what the "election law" was and what kind of an institution the Parliament really was, he simply replied with a smile, meaning I suppose that no intelligent person was expected to ask such questions. But these were the things most difficult of all for me to understand. In this connection, I learned that there were different political parties—the Liberal and the Conservative—who were always "fighting" against each other in the government.

For some time it was beyond my comprehension to understand what they were "fighting" for, and what was meant, anyway, by "fighting" in peace time. "This man and that man are 'enemies' in the House," they would tell me. But these "enemies" were to be seen at the same table, eating and drinking with each other. I felt as if I could not make much out of this. It took me a long time, with some tedious thinking, before I could gather a general notion of these separate mysterious facts. In some of the more complicated matters, I might achieve an understanding five or ten days after they were explained to me. But all in all, I learned much from this initial tour of Europe.

*Source: The Autobiography of Fukuzawa Yukichi,* trans. Eiichi Kiyooka (Tokyo: Hokuseida Press, 1948), pp. 138, 143–144.

 **For additional information on this topic, go to http://college.hmco.com.**

industrialization. Britain enjoyed both social and political peace. The political system was not challenged as it had been in the generation after the Napoleonic Wars. A self-assured, even smug, elite—merchants, industrialists, and landowners—developed a political system reflecting liberal values.

Although suffrage was still very restricted, the parliamentary system was firmly established, with a government clearly responsible to the electorate. The importance of Parliament was symbolized by the new building in which it met, finished in 1850 on the site of previous parliamentary buildings but of unprecedented splendor and size. The form of government developed in its halls after midcentury aroused the curiosity and envy of much of the world. (See the box "Global Encounters: A Japanese View of the British Parliament.")

In the twenty years after 1846, five different political parties vied for power. Depending on the issue, parties and factions coalesced to support particular policies. After 1867, however, a clear two-party system emerged: Liberal and Conservative (Tory), both with strong leadership. This development gave the electorate a distinct choice. The Conservatives were committed to preserving traditional institutions and practices, whereas the Liberals were more open to change.

Heading these parties were the two strong-minded individuals who dominated British political life for over a generation: William E. Gladstone (1809–1898), a Liberal, and Benjamin Disraeli° (1804–1881), a Conservative. Gladstone came from a family of industrialists and married into the aristocracy; Disraeli was the son of a Jewish man of letters who had converted to Christianity. His father's conversion made his career possible—before the 1850s Jews were barred from Parliament. Prior to heading their parties, Gladstone and Disraeli both served in important cabinet positions. They were master debaters; Parliament and the press hung on their every word. Each was capable of making speeches lasting five hours or more and of conducting debates that kept the house in session until 4 A.M. The rivalry between the two men thrilled the nation and made politics a popular pastime.

The Conservatives' electoral base came from the landed classes, Anglicans, and from England, rather than the rest of the United Kingdom. The Liberals' base came from the middle classes, from Christian groups other than the Church of England, and from Scotland and Wales. In the House of Commons both parties had a large number of members from the landed aristocracy, but cabinet members were increasingly chosen for political competence rather than family background. Aristocratic birth was no longer a requirement for reaching the pinnacle of power, as Gladstone and Disraeli so clearly illustrated.

The competition for power between the Liberals and Conservatives led to an extension of suffrage in 1867. The Second Reform Bill lowered property qualifications, extending the vote from 1.4 to 2.5 million people out of a population of 22 million, and gave new urban areas better representation by equalizing the electoral districts—henceforth the same size population was required for each district sending a member to Parliament. Although some in Parliament feared that these changes would lead to the masses capturing political power—"a leap into the dark," one member called it—in fact no radical change ensued. Extending the vote to clerks, artisans, and other skilled workers made them feel more a part of society, and thus bolstered the existing system. John Stuart Mill, then a Member of Parliament, championed the cause of women's suffrage, but he had few allies and that effort failed.

As the extension of voting rights increased the size of the electorate, parties became larger and stronger. Strong party systems meant alternation of power between the Liberals and the Conservatives. With an obvious majority and minority party, the monarch could no longer play favorites in choosing a prime minister. The leader of the majority party had to be asked to form a government. Thus, even though Queen Victoria (r.

Disraeli (diz-RAY-lee)

**Disraeli and Gladstone: Victorian Political Rivals**    This 1868 cartoon from *Punch* magazine captures the politicians' personalities. Disraeli was known as vain and theatrical, while Gladstone was dour and moralistic.    *(Mary Evans Picture Library)*

1837–1901) detested Gladstone, she had to ask him to form governments when the Liberals won parliamentary elections. (See the feature "Weighing the Evidence: An Engraving of the British Royal Family" on pages 772–773.)

The creation of a broad-based electorate also meant that politicians had to make clear appeals to the public and its interests. In the past, oratory had been limited to the halls of Parliament, but after the electoral reforms, it occurred in the public arena as well. Public election campaigns became part of the political scene in Britain. The democratic, "American" style of campaigning appealed to the common man. Also borrowed from across the seas was the "Australian ballot"—the secret ballot—adopted in 1872. This protected lower-class voters from intimidation by their employers, landowners, or other social superiors. In 1874 the first two working-class members of Parliament were elected, sitting as Liberals.

Although their victory represented a very modest gain for workers' representation, it presaged the increasingly democratic turn England was to take.

## ■ France: From Empire to Republic

Unlike Britain, which was transformed gradually into a parliamentary democracy, France took a more tumultuous path. Revolutions and wars overthrew existing political systems and inaugurated new ones. Each time the French seemed to have democracy within reach, the opportunity slipped away.

The constitution of the Second French Republic provided for a single four-year presidential term. Frustrated by this limitation of power, Louis Napoleon by a coup d'état extended his presidency to a ten-year term in 1851. The following year, he called for a plebiscite to confirm him as Napoleon III (r. 1852–1870), emperor of the French. Both of these moves were resisted in the countryside, particularly in the south, but the resistance was put down by massive repression.

In the rest of the country, huge majorities of voters endorsed first the prolonged presidency and then the imperial title. The new emperor seemed different from his predecessors. He believed in the principle of popular sovereignty (he maintained universal male suffrage, introduced in 1848), he did not pretend to reign by divine right, and he repeatedly tested his right to rule by an appeal to the popular vote. He seemed to combine order and authority with the promises of the Revolution—equality before the law, careers open to talent, and the abolition of hereditary rights.

The mid-nineteenth century was a period of prosperity for most Frenchmen, including urban workers and peasants. Louis Napoleon, in his youth the author of a book on pauperism, introduced measures congenial to labor. On the one hand, workers were required to keep a booklet in which employers recorded their conduct; on the other hand, workers were granted limited rights to strike, and labor unions were virtually legalized. The emperor expressed his desire to improve the workers' lot, and the government initiated a few concrete measures, such as providing some public housing. Although slum clearance during the rebuilding of Paris drove many from their homes to the outskirts of the city, it did provide healthier towns for those who stayed behind, and the ambitious urban projects provided work for many (see page 791). Other public works projects, such as ports, roads, railroads, and monumental public buildings, also created jobs. Railroad mileage in France increased tenfold, enabling peasants to market their harvests more widely. If some peasants had initially opposed Louis Napoleon, most supported him once he was in power. Not only were they a cautious group, preferring stable authority, but they saw in the emperor—the heir to the great Napoleon—an incarnation of national glory.

Not all the French supported the emperor; many republicans could not forget that he had usurped the constitution of 1848. In protest, some had gone into exile, including the poet Victor Hugo. Trying to win over the opposition, Napoleon made some concessions in 1860, easing censorship and making his government more accountable to the parliament. Instead of winning him new support, however, liberalization allowed the expression of mounting opposition. A coordinated republican opposition strongly criticized the economic policies of the empire, notably the decision to sign a free-trade treaty with England. Free trade helped wine and silk exporters, but it left iron and textile manufacturers unprotected. Businessmen in these fields rallied their workers against the imperial regime.

A number of other issues—including widespread hostility to the influence of the Catholic Church and the desire for more extensive freedoms of expression and assembly—also helped forge a republican alliance of the middle classes and workers. This alliance was strongest in the large cities and in some southern regions notorious for their opposition to central government control. Republicanism was better organized than in earlier years and had a more explicit program. Moreover, its proponents were now better prepared to take over the government, if the opportunity arose.

By 1869 the regime of Napoleon III, which declared itself a "liberal empire," had evolved into a constitutional monarchy, responsible to the Legislative Corps, the lower house of the parliament. In a plebiscite in May 1870, Frenchmen supported the liberal empire by a vote of five to one. It might have endured had Napoleon III not rashly declared war against Prussia two months later in a huff over the supposedly insulting Ems dispatch (see page 754). Defeat at the hands of Bismarck brought down the empire. In September, at news of the emperor's capture, the republican opposition in the Legislative Corps declared a republic. It continued the war but had to sign an armistice in January 1871.

The leader of the new government was an old prime minister of Louis Philippe, Adolphe Thiers° (1797–1877). Before signing a definitive peace, the provisional government held elections. The liberals, known as republicans since they favored a republic, were identified with con-

Thiers (tee-YAIR)

tinuing the war; the conservatives, mostly royalists, favored peace. Mainly because of their position on this issue, the royalists won a majority from a country discouraged by defeat.

The new regime had no time to establish itself before a workers' uprising in the spring of 1871 shook France, while reminding the rest of Europe of revolutionary dangers. The uprising was called the Paris Commune, a name that harked back to 1792–1794, when the Paris crowds had dictated to the government. The Commune insisted on its right to home rule. Radicals and conservatives greeted the Commune as a workers' revolt intended to establish a workers' government. Marx described it as the "bold champion of the emancipation of labor." To an even larger degree than during the revolution of 1848, women took an active part, fighting on the barricades, pouring scalding water on soldiers, posting revolutionary broadsides. The main woman's leader was Louise Michel (1830–1905), a schoolteacher, who while agitating for both socialism and women's rights, took an active part in the fighting.

Although labor discontent played a role in the Paris Commune, other forces also contributed, notably the Prussian siege of Paris during the Franco-Prussian War. Paris had become radicalized during the siege: the rich had evacuated the city, leaving a power vacuum quickly filled by the lower classes. Parisians suffered much because of the siege, and angered that their economic needs went unmet and their courage against the Prussians unnoticed, they rose up against the new French government. Food was the paramount issue sparking the massive women's participation in the uprising. The Commune, composed largely of artisans, now governed the city.

In March 1871 the Commune declared itself free to carry out policies independent of the central government in Versailles. Its goals were quite moderate: it sought free universal education, a fairer taxation system, a minimum wage, and disestablishment of the official Catholic Church. But this was too radical for the conservative French government, which sent in the army. It suppressed the Commune, massacring 25,000 people, arresting 40,000, and deporting several thousand more.

The crushing of the Paris Commune and some of its sister communes in southern France, which had also asserted local autonomy, signified the increasing power of the centralized governments. One mark of the emerging modern state was its capacity to squelch popular revolts that, in the past, had constituted serious threats. Western Europe would not again witness a popular uprising of this magnitude.

**Napoleon III**    This is an example of official art glorifying the emperor. The emperor is framed by a Roman statue on his right and the imperial eagle on his left, both symbols of strength and glory.    *(Giraudon/Art Resource, NY)*

Despite its brutality, the suppression of the Commune reassured many Frenchmen. "The Republic will be conservative, or it will not be," declared Thiers. The question now at hand was what form the new government would take. The monarchist majority offered the throne to the Bourbon pretender. However, he insisted he would become king only if the *tricouleur*—the flag of the Revolution, which long since had become a cherished national symbol—were discarded and replaced by the white flag of the house of Bourbon. This was unacceptable, so France remained a republic. The republic, as Thiers put it, "is the regime which divides us the least."

By 1875 the parliament had approved a set of basic laws that became the constitution of the Third Republic. Ironically, a monarchist parliament had created a liberal, democratic parliamentary regime. A century after the French Revolution, the republican system of government in France was firmly launched.

### ■ Scandinavia and the Low Countries

France and especially Britain served as models of parliamentary democracy for the smaller states in northern Europe. Norway, Sweden, Denmark, Belgium, and Holland recast their political institutions at midcentury. Several of the states were affected by the 1848 revolutions: Stockholm saw minor riots, Denmark a peaceful protest demanding enlarged political participation (see page 736) , and in Holland, the king feared that his country would be affected by revolution as in the neighboring German states. In Copenhagen King Frederick VII (r. 1848–1863), who had no stomach for a confrontation, yielded and accepted a constitution providing for parliamentary government. "Now I can sleep as long as I like," he is reputed to have said.

Sweden's parliamentary system, established in the Middle Ages, had representation by estates—noble, clergy, burgher, and peasant. The 11,000 nobles were weighted in the same manner as the 2.5–3 million peasants. After the riots of 1848, liberal aristocrats recognized that abolition of the estates system would best preserve their privileges, removing the major issue that had provoked popular resentments. With some delays, this conviction, born in 1848, was finally carried out in 1866. The estates were replaced by a parliament with two houses; the upper was restricted to the wealthiest landowners and the lower to men of property, providing the vote to 20 percent of adult men. While the king was not constitutionally obligated to choose a government reflecting parliamentary currents, desiring to avoid conflict, he usually did.

Norway had been joined to Sweden in 1814 under the Swedish king , but it had a separate parliament and made its own laws. Swedish rule rankled the Norwegians, however, and their Liberal Party in the 1850s began to insist that the king should not have the final word in governance, but rather parliament, representative of the Norwegian people, should be supreme. In 1883 the principle that government officials are responsible to parliament won out. In 1905 Norway peacefully separated from Sweden and became an independent state.

In the Netherlands as a result of the revolutions of 1848, the king recognized the need to strengthen support for his crown by acceding to liberals' demands for parliamentary government. By midcentury, government in the Netherlands was responsible to parliament, rather than the king. A new constitution guaranteed the principles of freedom of speech, assembly, and religion.

Belgium had enjoyed a liberal constitution from the time it became an independent state in 1830, but because no strong party system materialized, the king was able to appoint to government whom he pleased. In the 1840s the liberals organized, and the king, reluctantly, had to invite them to govern in 1848. The new government reduced property qualifications for voting, thus increasing the electorate.

Unlike the reforms that had followed the revolutions of 1848, only to be rolled back in conservative backlashes, these sweeping reforms in northern European states became the basis for their evolution into full democracies.

For full democracy, the electorate had to be broadened. These years witnessed much agitation for universal male suffrage. Property qualifications, wherever they were instituted, were questioned and resisted. For instance, in Sweden the stipulation that a man had to earn 800 crowns a year to be a voter unleashed a pamphlet war: What if a man earned only 799 crowns? Did that make him less qualified? What if a man qualified one year, but through no fault of his own, for instance a natural disaster, did not earn that much the following year? Should he then be barred from voting? Belgium in the 1880s saw a mass movement in favor of universal suffrage; the letters "SU," standing for universal suffrage in French, became emblematic of the hopes for the masses for a better life. While suffrage remained as yet limited in these countries, it was only a matter of time before democracy would be achieved.

## Summary

 OVEL configurations of power appeared on the West's chessboard in the period from about 1850 to 1880 as new or enlarged states were created through warfare or the threat of force. Liberal nationalists in the early nineteenth century had believed that Europe would be freer and more peaceful if each people had a separate nation, but they were now proved wrong. The Crimean War and its aftermath replaced the congress system, which had sought a balance of power among partners, with a system of rival states in pursuit of their own self-interest. The international order was severely shaken as Italy and Germany emerged from the center of Europe and as Romania and Bulgaria were carved out of the Ottoman Empire in the east.

Both new and existing states faced a choice between federalism and centralized rule. In the process of unification, Italy and Germany could have opted for a loose federal union, but both Piedmont and Prussia chose central control. And the crushing of the Paris Commune spelled the doom of those who wanted a France of decentralized self-governing units. Strong, centralized governments increasingly became the norm. That was also the case across the ocean in the United States, where North and South fought a bloody Civil War over the issues of slavery and state sovereignty, and the victorious federal government imposed its will on the rebellious states. Canada became a large state, stretching across the continent, and acquired self-government.

To achieve legitimacy, however, governments had to appear to be enjoying the consent of their peoples. Hence all European rulers except those of the Ottoman and Russian Empires found it necessary to have a parliament. France, Britain, and several northern European states became increasingly democratic in these years, answerable to a growing electorate. In other states parliaments had only limited powers, but once they were in place, it could be argued—and was—that more power should be shifted toward them and that they should be chosen by an expanded electorate. In the United States whites already enjoyed freer and more open institutions than existed anywhere else, and the post–Civil War era marked a further enlargement of political participation when African American men were granted the right to vote.

Two major changes that liberals in 1848 had agitated for had become reality: freer political institutions and the organization of nation-states. Although neither of these was fully implemented everywhere, both appeared to have been successfully established. Many Europeans could easily believe they were living in an age of optimism.

## ■ Notes

1. Quoted in Otto Pflanze, *Bismarck and the Development of Germany,* vol. 1 (Princeton: Princeton University Press, 1990), p. 184.
2. Quoted in William Flavelle Monypenny and George Earle Buckle, *The Life of Benjamin Disraeli: Earl of Beaconsfield,* vol. 2 (London: John Murray, 1929), pp. 473–474.

## ■ Suggested Reading

Alter, Peter. *The German Question and Europe. A History.* 2000. Explains the international context within which German unity was possible and its impact on European diplomacy.

Blackbourn, David. *The Long Nineteenth Century—A History of Germany, 1780–1918.* 1998. Particularly strong on the social aspects and consequences of German unification.

Jelavich, Charles and Barbara. *The Establishment of the Balkan National States, 1804–1920.* 1977. Traces the emergence of independent states from the Ottoman Empire.

Lincoln, W. Bruce. *Great Reforms.* 1990. Shows the reforms to be part of a general program of modernization.

Matthew, Colin, ed. *The Nineteenth Century: The British Isles, 1815–1901.* 2000. An up-to-date collection of articles on major themes in British history.

**For a searchable list of additional readings for this chapter, go to http://college.hmco.com.**

# An Engraving of the British Royal Family

Why were Queen Victoria and her family depicted in the manner shown in this popular engraving? The illustration might well have been of an upper-middle-class family. Note the family's attire. The queen is plainly dressed; her husband, Prince Albert, wears a dark business suit; the children are clothed in simple outfits. The image extends from the royal family to the rest of England, depicted as a quaint farm, some cottages, and a grouping of common people. Notice the crown hovering over this idyllic scene. Victoria's reign was the longest of any British monarch; the manner in which she conducted herself, and her subjects' image of her, shaped the monarchy and people's expectations of it.

Illustrations of this type familiarized the British with their monarch. Surrounded by her husband and children, the queen seemed to have an endearing common touch. In the past representations of the monarchy had suggested power and intimidation. The aura of the close-knit, nuclear royal family, not unlike the families of the queen's middle-class subjects, suggested a serenity that was reassuring to those subjects.

Victoria cultivated the image of herself as contented mother, but in reality she resented much about motherhood. She complained of the extent to which her pregnancies interfered with her daily routines, preventing her from traveling and from being with her beloved Albert as much as she would have liked. She described childbearing as an "annoyance" that made her feel "so pinned down—one's wings clipped." She also refused to romanticize birthing, seeing it as an animal-like act, reducing a woman to "a cow or a dog." Biology put women in an inauspicious position; "I think our sex a most unenviable one," she lamented. And Victoria continued viewing the children, once they were no longer babies, as a burden, describing them as "an awful plague and anxiety for which they show one so little gratitude very often!" But such views were expressed strictly privately, and the public never suspected Victoria's ambivalence toward her role as mother.

Whatever her complaints about children, Victoria's family life was in strong contrast to that of her predecessors, projecting a new image of the monarchy. Her grandfather George III (r. 1760–1820) had been plagued with bouts of insanity. Her uncle George IV (r. 1820–1830) was a notorious philanderer. George IV and his brothers, the duke of Clarence (later to be William IV [r. 1830–1837]) and the duke of Kent (Victoria's father), were bigamists. They fathered a large brood of illegitimate children and were implicated in numerous public scandals.

The character of Victoria's three predecessors and of the various other men in line to the throne had strengthened opposition to the monarchy. Public outrage at their excesses had led to a call for the abolition of the institution. When the 18-year-old Victoria came to the throne, it would have been difficult to imagine that she would on her death leave the monarchy considerably strengthened.

The image of Victoria shown here intentionally contrasts her reign with those of her predecessors. Victoria is surrounded by four of her children (eventually she would have nine). Her predecessors had died leaving no legitimate direct heirs and thus endangering the regular succession to the throne. The engraving announces that the royal line is assured. English people wary of a female ruler can find solace in knowing that Victoria would be succeeded by one of her sons. Later, Victoria's children and their progeny would intermarry with the rest of Europe's royalty, and by the end of her reign most of Europe's crowned heads would be related to one another.

Although Victoria's uncles and father were wastrels and bankrupts, the queen and her husband lived frugally by royal standards and conducted an exemplary family life. Under the wise administration of Prince Albert, royal wealth increased; he carefully administered various royal estates and investments. Instead of being subject to various debtors, the British royal house became one of the wealthiest landowners in Great Britain, achieving financial independence and winning social prestige. Among the large landowning magnates of Britain, the royal house became the most prominent.

The model royal family appealed to the growing middle class of Victorian society. Consider how the simple terms in which the monarch is depicted here and in many other illustrations reflect the increasingly democratic

Illustration from *A Book of English Song*

spirit of the era. The ruler and her family appear in a common scene. Victoria is queen, but she also is a mother and wife. There is no sign here of pomp and ceremony.

Given the disrepute into which the monarchy had fallen and the rise of republican sentiment, the coming to the throne of a woman in 1837 may have substantially lessened antimonarchical sentiment. The last woman to rule England, Elizabeth I (r. 1558–1603), had been one of its greatest monarchs, one who had provided stability and brought glory to her kingdom. A young, seemingly frail woman coming to the throne lent a certain gallantry to the royal household. Also, because of her gender Victoria was seen as less of a threat to constitutional liberties.

Under Victoria's rule, Britain completed the process of becoming a constitutional monarchy. Although Victoria's predecessors had been openly partisan, the queen cultivated the image of being above party, a symbol of national unity and the state. Fellow monarchs in central and eastern Europe exercised greater power, but after World War I they were all toppled. In Britain, monarchy in its constitutional form endured. Victoria established a pattern of public and private behavior by which members of subsequent generations of the British royal family were to be judged.

 **For additional information on this topic, go to** http://college.hmco.com.

# The Age of Optimism 1850–1880

T HE first department store in Paris, which served as a model for others in France and abroad, *Le Bon Marché* (the "good buy") opened its doors in the 1850s. The store bought goods in mass quantities and thus could sell them at low prices. Constructed of glass and iron, Le Bon Marché represented the new, modern age. It combined under one roof a large range of products that previously had been available only in separate specialty shops—a time-saving convenience in an increasingly harried age. The store also had a large catalog sales department for customers too busy or distant to shop in person. Filled with toys, bed linens, furniture, crystal, and other items, the department store was a symbol of the new opulence of the middle classes.

This new type of store would not have been possible in an earlier age. It serves as a summary of the various technological and social changes that the more prosperous regions of the West experienced as industrialization advanced in the second half of the nineteenth century. Industrial innovation had lowered the price of glass and steel, so that these new, huge commercial emporiums could be built at reasonable cost. Railroads brought into the city large quantities of increasingly mass-produced goods, as well as out-of-town customers. In town, trams and omnibuses transported shoppers to the store. The penny press provided advertising for the department store, which in turn supported the emergence of this new medium. The expansion of the postal system facilitated catalog sales and the mailing of parcels to customers. And the higher incomes available to many people allowed them to purchase more than just the necessities. A phenomenon

Felix Valloton, *Le bon marché.*
(Private Collection/Edimedia)

began that would become predominant in the West a century later—the consumer society.

As industrialization spread throughout western Europe, rising productivity brought greater wealth to more social groups and nations. This wealth not only led to more consumer spending but also contributed to a change in attitudes. The second half of the nineteenth century was an era shaped to a large extent by the growing middle classes, who were filled with optimism and convinced they were living in an age of progress. John Stuart Mill proclaimed that in his era "the general tendency is and will continue to be . . . one of improvement—a tendency towards a better and happier state." Across the Channel in France, the social thinker Auguste Comte° (1798–1857) concurred, confidently stating, "human development brings . . . an ever growing amelioration." The successful application of science and technology to social problems gave many men and women confidence in the human ability to improve the world. People controlled their environments to a degree never before possible. On farms they increased the fertility of the soil; to the burgeoning cities they brought greater order. Scientists used new methods to study and combat disease. Public authorities founded schools, trained teachers, and reduced illiteracy. Transportation and communication rapidly improved.

In reality, not all of society benefited from the fruits of progress. The new wealth was far from equally shared. Eastern and southern Europe changed little, and even in the western regions a large part of the population still lived in great misery. If some cities carried out ambitious programs of urban renewal, others continued to neglect slums. Public sanitation programs did not affect the majority of Europeans who lived in rural areas. Despite spectacular advances in science, much of the population maintained a traditional belief in divine intervention. Many intellectuals strongly denounced the materialism and smugness of the age, stressing the meanness and ignorance that lay just beneath the surface.

Still, the tone of the age was set by the ascendant middle classes in western Europe, which embraced change and believed that the era was heading toward even more remarkable improvements. Their optimism was all the greater because the ultimate effects of the social and technological changes taking place in Europe were not yet known. Of the major processes that unfolded between 1850 and 1880, many were still in their infancy in 1880. What lay beyond the horizon would certainly be even more wonderful.

---

**QUESTIONS TO CONSIDER**

■ What technological changes led to the expansion of the European economy after the mid-nineteenth century?

■ How did the economic expansion affect the various social classes, and city versus rural areas, differently?

■ In what ways did the state increasingly intervene in people's daily lives?

■ How did Charles Darwin both reflect and shape the intellectual trends of his era?

---

**TERMS TO KNOW**

| | |
|---|---|
| second industrial revolution | impressionism |
| bourgeois century | Darwinism |
| professionalization | Social Darwinism |
| Victorian morality | |
| separate spheres | |
| solidarism | |
| social Catholics | |
| positivism | |

---

**Auguste Comte** (oh-GOOST KONT)

# INDUSTRIAL GROWTH AND ACCELERATION

**B**EGINNING in the 1850s, western Europe experienced an unprecedented level of economic expansion. Manufacturers created new products and harnessed new sources of energy. An enlarged banking system provided more abundant credit to fund this expansion. Scientific research was systematically employed to improve methods of manufacture. A revolution in transportation speedily delivered goods and services to distant places. For many Europeans, daily life was profoundly changed by technological innovations.

## ■ The "Second Industrial Revolution"

The interrelated cluster of economic changes that began in the generation after 1850 is often called the "second industrial revolution." It was characterized by a significant speedup in production and by the introduction of new materials such as mass-produced steel, synthetic dyes, and aluminum. Manufacturers replaced the traditional steam engine with stronger steam-powered turbines or with machines powered by new forms of energy—petroleum and electricity.

The invention of new products and methods of manufacture spurred this industrial expansion. The second half of the nineteenth century has often been called the "age of steel." Up to then, steel production had been limited by the expense involved in its manufacture, but in 1856, Sir Henry Bessemer (1813–1898) discovered a much cheaper method, which produced in twenty minutes the same amount of steel previously produced in twenty-four hours. Ten years later, William Siemens° (1823–1883) in England and Pierre Martin (1824–1915) in France developed an even more efficient technique of steel production, the open-hearth process. The Thomas-Gilchrist method, invented in 1878, made possible the use of phosphor-laden iron ore, which previously had been economically unfeasible.

The results were dramatic. In Great Britain steel production increased fourfold, and the price of steel fell by more than 50 percent between the early 1870s and the following decade. Greater steel production made possible the expansion of the rail system, the creation of a steamship fleet, and an explosive growth in the building industry. No longer was steel a rare alloy used only for the

**CHRONOLOGY**

| | |
|---|---|
| **1818** | Gas street lamps in London |
| **1820s** | Omnibuses introduced in France |
| **1829** | Stephenson runs the *Rocket* |
| **1830** | Lyell founds the principles of modern geology |
| **1831** | Faraday discovers electromagnetic induction |
| **1833** | Telegraph invented |
| **1840** | Penny stamp introduced |
| **1848** | Europe's first public health system, in England |
| **1850s** | Age of clipper ships |
| | Trams added to public transportation systems |
| **1851** | Crystal Palace |
| **1852–1870** | Rebuilding of Paris |
| **1859** | Darwin, *On the Origin of Species* |
| **1863** | Europe's first underground railroad, in London |
| **1864** | Pope Pius IX issues *Syllabus of Errors* |
| **1865** | Transoceanic telegraph cable installed |
| | Lister initiates antiseptic surgery |
| | University of Zurich admits women |
| **1869** | Opening of Suez Canal |
| | Mendeleev produces periodic table of elements |
| **1874** | Impressionist exhibition |
| **1875** | Bell invents telephone |
| | Electric lights in Paris |
| **1881** | Pasteur proposes germ theory of disease |
| **1891** | Pope Leo XIII issues *Rerum novarum* |

**Siemens** (SEE-menz)

**The Suez Canal**    Opened in 1869, the canal significantly shortened the voyage by ship from Europe to East Asia. The Suez Canal exemplified the speeding up of transportation and communication in the second half of the nineteenth century.    *(AKG London)*

finest swords and knives; it became the material that defined the age.

Significant changes in the supply of credit further stimulated economic expansion. Discovery of gold in California and Australia led to the inflow of huge amounts of the precious metal to Europe, expanding the supply of money and credit. This led to the establishment of the modern banking system.

Each advance made possible additional changes. Increased wealth and credit accelerated further expansion of industrial plants and the financing of an ambitious infrastructure of roads, railroads, and steamships, which in turn boosted trade. Between 1800 and 1840, the value of world trade had doubled. In the twenty years following 1850, it increased by 260 percent.

By the 1880s important scientific discoveries fueled industrial improvements. Electricity began to be more widely used, replacing coal as a source of energy. Synthetic dyes revolutionized the textile industry, as did alkali in the manufacture of soap and glass. Dynamite, invented by the Swedish chemist Alfred Nobel° (1833–1896) in the 1860s, made it possible to level hills and blast tunnels through mountains, facilitating construc-

tion. Five years after Nobel's death, his will established a prestigious prize named after its donor, to honor significant contributions to science and peace.

### ■ Transportation and Communications

The rail system grew dramatically in the middle decades of the nineteenth century. When the English engineer Robert Stephenson (1803–1859) demonstrated the feasibility of his steam locomotive, the *Rocket*, in 1829, it ran at 5 miles per hour on a track that was 1½ miles long. By 1880 total European railroad mileage was 102,000 (see Map 23.1). In 1888 the Orient Express line opened, linking Constantinople to Vienna and thus to the rest of Europe. Distance was conquered by speed as well: by midcentury, trains ran 50 miles per hour, ten times as fast as when they were invented. The cost of rail transport steadily decreased, allowing for its greater use. Between 1850 and 1880 in Germany, the number of rail passengers increased tenfold and the volume of goods eightyfold. In France and Great Britain, the increases were nearly as impressive.

Ocean transportation was also revolutionized. In 1869 the French built the Suez Canal across Egyptian territory, linking the Mediterranean to the Red Sea and the Indian Ocean. The canal reduced by 40 percent the

---

**Nobel** (no-BELL)

**Map 23.1    European Rails, 1850 and 1880**    During the mid-nineteenth century, European states built railroads at an increasing rate, creating a dense network by the 1880s.    *(Adapted from Norman J. G. Pounds,* An Historical Geography of Europe, 1800–1914 *[New York: Cambridge University Press, 1985].)*

thirty-five-day journey between London and Bombay. More efficient ships were developed; by midcentury, the so-called clipper ship could cross the Atlantic in fourteen days, half the previous length of time. Steamships were also built, although they did not dominate ocean traffic until the 1890s. By 1880 European shipping carried nearly three times the cargo it had thirty years earlier.

The optimism born of conquering vast distances was reflected in a popular novel by the French writer Jules Verne° (1828–1905), *Around the World in Eighty Days*

(1873). The hero, Phineas Fogg, travels by balloon, llama, and ostrich, as well as by the modern steam locomotive and steamship to accomplish in eighty days a feat that, only thirty years earlier, would have taken at least eleven months. In 1889 the New York newspaper *The World* in a publicity gambit to increase readership sent its reporter Nellie Bly (1867–1922) on an around-the-world trip to see if she could beat Phineas Fogg's record. Readers breathlessly kept up with reports of her progress. She circled the globe in 72 days, 6 hours, 11 minutes, and 14 seconds. Such was the impact of the steamship, the locomotive, the Suez Canal—and the newspaper.

**Jules Verne** (DJOOL VAIRN)

# The Telegraph

The telegraph radically altered the speed with which information could be collected and spread around the world. In 1793 two young Frenchmen, Claude Chappe (1763–1805) and his brother, Ignace (1760–1829), built a device with large wooden arms that, by their location, designated letters of the alphabet in a pre-arranged code. A lookout, equipped with a telescope and stationed on a tower mounted on a tall building or a hill, would take down the message and relay it to the next lookout, as far as 6 miles away. The system was called the *telegraph,* meaning "far, or long-distance writing" in Greek. This system was cumbersome, depending as it did on the messengers' ability to read and retransmit the signals. It could obviously not be used at night or in bad weather.

The Chappes' invention was to be replaced by something more powerful and functional, but that retained the name telegraph. In the 1830s the American Samuel F. B. Morse (1791–1872) surmised that electricity could be used to send messages over long distances. With funding from Congress, in 1844 he built a line 40 miles long from Washington, D.C., to Baltimore. Morse sent electrical impulses in combinations representing letters of the alphabet—sequences of "dots" and "dashes" that became known as the Morse code. A clerk would transcribe the signals into the alphabetical letters they represented, spelling out a message, and have it delivered to the recipient.

In England two events popularized the telegraph, showing its benefits. In 1844, forty minutes after the palace announced that Queen Victoria had given birth to her second son, the *Times* was able to share the happy news with the nation. The following year, a John Tawell murdered his mistress in Slough. Fleeing the police, he took the train for London. Alerted by telegraph, the police arrested the murderer as he got off the train in Paddington Station. The utility of the telegraph had been convincingly demonstrated.

Telegraph wires were rapidly expanded. In the 1850s the telegraph in Britain crossed the English Channel. The following decade the telegraph spread across the North American continent and connected it in turn with Europe via the transatlantic cable. From a few dozen miles in the 1840s, telegraph lines thirty years later were 650,000 miles long, connecting twenty thousand towns and villages across the world to one another.

Newspapers prided themselves on being "wired" and so able to give their readers the latest news fast; many a newspaper adopted a name such as the *Daily Telegraph.* In the 1840s newspapers had printed news from overseas that was often obsolete, or at best outrageously outdated. News from Cape Town, South Africa, in the *London Times* was eight weeks old, from Brazil six weeks old. A couple of decades later, thanks to the telegraph, international news had happened only yesterday.

Governments found the telegraph useful in collecting information and issuing orders to subordinates. Imperial authority over distant territories was now better assured. In the 1840s it had taken ten weeks for a message and a reply to go from London to Bombay and back; thirty years later, the exchange took four minutes.

The telegraph was also a tool of warfare. The first war in which the telegraph played a crucial role was the Crimean; the British and French high commands in London and Paris were able to communicate with their officers in the Crimea, directing operations from afar. In the Austro-Prussian War the Prussians directed their pincer attack leading to the victory at Sadowa by telegraph. Battle plans could be modified quickly as the telegram informed commanders of how the fighting was developing. The telegraph was widely used in the American Civil War, helping shape many a battle; during that conflict 6 million telegrams were sent.

The most common early use for the telegraph was to coordinate the railroads. Still in their infancy, most rail lines had single tracks, and collisions were frequent. One station could inform another by telegram of a train's departure, so that managers could decide which train had the right of way

Along with the new speed, advances in refrigeration changed food transport. Formerly, refrigeration could be achieved only with natural ice, cut from frozen ponds and lakes, but this changed in the 1870s with the introduction of mechanical ice-making machines. By the 1880s dairy products and meat were being transported vast distances by rail and even across the seas by ship. Thanks to these advances, the surplus food of the Americas and Australia, rich in grasslands, could offer Europe a cheaper and far more varied diet.

Regular postal service was also a child of the new era of improved transportation. In 1840 Britain instituted a postage system based on standard rates. Replacing the earlier practice in which the recipient paid for the delivery of a letter, the British system enabled the sender to buy a stamp—priced at just one penny—and drop and take appropriate precautions. The telegraph spread with the rail lines, usually built alongside them. Train travel became safer and more speedy, for with good communications between stations, trains could be more readily dispatched.

Even so, railroads found it impossible to schedule trains traveling across large nations properly because each area had its own local time. The setting of a standard time was facilitated by the telegraph: at a given moment a telegraphic message indicated the exact time to the second, and every town along the line was able to set its time accordingly.

Until the advent of the telegraph it was difficult for merchants to know trade conditions in distant lands. With the new device, business people could collect market information, such as the cheapest price of commodities, and offer their wares competitively to potential buyers around the world. The telegraph brought instant information to merchants, allowing them to expand their markets and lower their costs, thus fostering the development of the consumer society.

Used by governments and businesses, the telegram also became a means for frequent and immediate communication between individuals. Lovers sent each other messages, parents proudly announced children's births, people shared the sad news of a death in the family. Telegraph operators in the dead of night when there was no traffic on the wires would share jokes or play chess. With greater use, the cost of sending telegrams went down; by 1885 in Britain, a short message was priced at 6 pence, an amount within reach of most people. Lower cost allowed for greater use. Within half a century after 1851, the number of telegrams sent each year in Britain rose from 100,000 to over 90 million.

The telegraph was one of the technological advances of the nineteenth century that, along with the train and steamship, conquered distances. Charles Dickens described the telegraph as "of all our modern wonders the most wonderful." Even more than improved transportation, it transformed the world into an instant, global village. As the governor of New York said at a commemorative event a generation after Samuel Morse's invention, "Men speak to one another now, though separated by the width of the earth, with lightning's speed and as if standing face to face."

the letter into a mailbox. It was collected, transported speedily by the new railroads, and delivered. The efficiency and low cost of mail led to a huge increase in use.

The post combined with transoceanic telegraphs and the invention of the telephone to transform the world of information. In the late 1830s the telegraph was invented, and by 1864, 80,000 miles of telegraph wire had been laid on the European continent. (See the feature "Information Technology: The Telegraph.") In 1875 the American inventor Alexander Graham Bell (1847–1922) invented a machine capable of transmitting the human voice by electrical impulses; in 1879 the first telephones were installed in Germany; two years later they appeared in France. At first a curiosity, used to listen to a musical or theatrical production at a distance, the phone began to be installed in homes for people to communicate with each other.

781

# CHANGING CONDITIONS AMONG SOCIAL GROUPS

NDUSTRIAL advances transformed the traditional structure of European society. Fewer people worked the land; more worked in industry. The social and political influence of the landed aristocracy waned as wealth became far less dependent on property ownership. To varying degrees, this influence now had to be shared with the growing middle classes. Generally, life for both industrial and farm workers improved in this period. However, great disparities persisted, and many people continued to suffer from profound deprivation.

## ■ The Declining Aristocracy

Always a small, exclusive group, the European aristocracy in the nineteenth century represented less than 1 percent of the population. Many of those of noble birth were quite poor and economically indistinguishable from their non-noble neighbors. Others owned vast estates and were fabulously wealthy.

Some ennoblements were of recent origin. In England, most titles were less than a hundred years old, having originally been conferred on individuals in recognition of service to the state, the arts, or the economy. In France both Napoleons had bestowed titles on persons they wished to honor. In Germany Chancellor Otto von Bismarck ennobled the Jewish banker Gerson Bleichröder° (1822–1893) for helping finance the wars of the Prussian state and for relieving the German chancellor of personal financial worries by making profitable investments for him. Distinctions between aristocrats and members of the upper middle class became increasingly blurred. Noble families in financial straits often married their children to the offspring of wealthy merchants. And many nobles who previously had shunned manufacture participated in the new economy by becoming industrialists and bankers. Idle members of the nobility were now somewhat rare. Although many aristocrats still enjoyed a lavish lifestyle, others had adopted the habits of successful business people.

Despite the theories of egalitarianism sweeping Europe in the aftermath of the French Revolution and the rapidly changing social structure engendered by industrialization, the power of the aristocracy did not disappear altogether. In Prussia some of the wealthiest industrialists came from the highest aristocracy. The heavily aristocratic officer corps played an important role in running the Prussian state and unified Germany. In France about 20 to 25 percent of officers and many diplomats were aristocrats. In Britain officers, diplomats, and high-ranking civil servants were usually of noble birth. In Austria and Russia, aristocratic origin was the norm for government service.

Nonetheless, nobles no longer asserted privileges based exclusively on birth. In most European states, such claims had become anachronisms.

## ■ The Expanding Middle Classes

Up to the eighteenth century, society had been divided into legally separate orders on the basis of birth. In the nineteenth century, it became more customary to classify people by their economic functions. The "middle class" belonged neither to the nobility nor to the peasantry nor to the industrial working class. It included such people as wealthy manufacturers, country physicians, and bank tellers. Given this diversity, it has become common to use the plural and think of all these people as forming the "middle classes." Another term frequently used to describe these people is *bourgeois.*

The nineteenth century has often been described as "the bourgeois century." Although such a label may be too broad, after the midcentury mark it is appropriate enough to use as a shorthand term to describe the dominance of the bourgeois elites. This situation was especially prevalent in western Europe, where the middle classes helped fashion much of society.

The middle classes expanded dramatically in the wake of industrialization. More trade and manufacture meant more entrepreneurs and managers, while the increasingly complex society called for more engineers, lawyers, accountants, and bankers. New standards of comfort and health demanded more merchants and doctors. Urban improvements in the generation after 1850 created a need for architects and contractors, among other professionals.

The middle and lower levels of middle-class society grew most rapidly as business, the professions, and government administration created more jobs. In the 1870s about 10 percent of urban working-class people reached lower-middle-class status by becoming storekeepers, lower civil servants, clerks, or salespeople. Faster growth occurred for white-collar workers than for their blue-collar counterparts. As industries matured, the increasing use of machinery and better industrial organization

---

**Bleichröder** (BLY-shro-der)

meant a need for fewer additional laborers and more clerks and bureaucrats. Large import-export businesses, insurance companies, and department stores provided opportunities of this kind. So did the expansion of government services.

The social impact of job growth was great. The men and women staffing these new positions often came from modest backgrounds. For the son or daughter of peasants to become village postmaster, schoolteacher, or clerk in a major firm signified social ascension, however modest. And for the family, such a position, even more than income, meant joining the lower stratum of the middle classes. Accessibility to its ranks was certainly one of the strengths of the bourgeoisie, an ever growing group whose promise of social respectability and material comfort exercised a compelling force of attraction over the lower classes.

A widening subgroup of the middle classes consisted of members of the professions, those whose prestige rested on the claim of exclusive expertise in a particular field. In the early nineteenth century, requirements for exercising a profession varied, depending on the country. In France and Prussia, for example, government regulation stipulated the necessary qualifications to practice medicine; while in England only the Royal Colleges did. Medicine in the United States was unregulated by either governmental or medical schools. As the professions attempted to create a monopoly for themselves and eliminate rivals, they established stricter standards. Medical doctors, for instance, began requiring specialized education to distinguish themselves from herbalists, midwives, bone-setters, healers, and other competitors, and they insisted on their exclusive right to exercise their profession. The medical profession controlled access to its ranks by establishing powerful professional associations—for example, the British Medical Association (1832) and the German Medical Association (1872).

Although the professionalization of medicine did not create better doctors immediately, as the science of medicine taught at universities improved, so did the preparation and expertise of doctors. Similarly, in other professions, such as law, architecture, and engineering, common standards and requirements encouraged professional practice and expertise. By midcentury either professional associations or the state itself accredited members of the professions. Women had limited access to these professions; typically their opportunities were confined to lower teaching positions. After the Crimean War, as a result of Florence Nightingale's efforts (see page 743), nursing became an increasingly popular profes-

**Interior of a Danish Middle-Class Home**   With its stuffed furniture, lace curtains and tablecloths, and gilt-edged framed paintings, this living room provided a comfortable and pleasing escape from the grimy exterior of the industrial city. *(National Museum of Denmark)*

sion for women. But the dominant view in the middle classes was to discourage women from all employment.

The growing role of the state in society led to bureaucratic expansion. More and more, civil servants were selected by merit rather than through patronage. By the eighteenth century, Prussia had instituted a civil service examination system. After the Revolution, France instituted educational requirements for certain government corps, and by the 1880s it established civil service exams for all government positions. Beginning in 1870, Britain introduced the civil service examination and eliminated patronage.

## ■ Middle-Class Lifestyles

The standard of living of the growing middle classes varied considerably, from the wealthy entrepreneur who bought a château, or built one, to the bourgeois who dwelled in a modest apartment. But they all lived in new standards of comfort. Their homes had running water, upholstered furniture, and enough space to provide separate sleeping and living quarters. They owned several changes of clothing and consumed a varied diet that included meat and dairy products, sugar, coffee, and tea. They read books and subscribed to newspapers and journals. Having at least one servant was a requisite for anyone who wished to be counted among the middle classes in the mid-nineteenth century.

By 1900 servants were still common among bourgeois households, but they were fewer in proportion to the population as a whole. As service industries developed, the need for servants decreased. With the growth of cab services, for instance, a family could dispense with a coachman and groom. And many families went without servants. Toward the end of the century, domestics' wages rose as competing forms of employment vied for their service, and only the upper layers of the bourgeoisie still employed domestic help.

In some areas suburban living became fashionable. The wealthy lived in large, imposing houses; the less well-off lived in smaller houses with a garden for privacy and quiet. Some owned two homes—one in the city and one in the countryside, providing a respite from the hectic urban environment.

For further relief from the crowded cities, visits to resorts became popular. Throughout Europe, resort towns sprang up, devoted principally to the amusement of the well-off. It became fashionable to "take the waters"—to bathe in hot springs and drink the mineral waters thought to have special attributes—and gamble in resorts such as Baden-Baden in Germany and Vichy in France. For the first time, tourism became big business. Thomas Cook (1808–1892), an Englishman, organized tours to the Crystal Palace exhibition of 1851 in London, the largest world exposition, which highlighted industrial accomplishments. Discovering the large market for guided travel, Cook began running tours in England and

**The Crystal Palace**    Built in 1851, this building was the largest glass and steel structure of its time. Site of the first great international exposition, the Crystal Palace displayed the inventiveness and opulence of the age.    *(Courtesy of the Trustees of the British Museum)*

on the Continent. In the eighteenth century the European tour had been a custom of the aristocracy, but now many members of the middle classes demanded this experience as well.

New wealth and leisure time led as well to more hotels, restaurants, and cafés. In 1869 Paris had 20,000 cafés and 4,000 hotels and lodging houses; the largest hotel offered 700 well-appointed rooms to discriminating guests. Vienna's National Hotel, with 300 rooms, had steam heat, spring water on every floor, and an icehouse providing cool drinks. For the traveler's convenience, many hotels, such as the monumental Charing Cross Hotel in London, were located next to train stations. At home or away, the bourgeois valued comfort.

The middle classes shared certain attitudes about the conduct of their lives. They believed their successes were due not to birth but to talent and effort. They wanted to be judged by their merits, and they expected their members to abide by strict moral principles. Their lives were supposed to be disciplined, especially with regard to sex and drink. The age was called "Victorian" because the middle classes in Britain saw in the queen who reigned for two-thirds of the century a reflection of their own values. (See the feature "Weighing the Evidence: An Engraving of the British Royal Family" in Chapter 22, on pages 772–773.) "Victorian morality," widely preached but not always practiced, was often viewed as hypocritical by social critics. Yet as the middle classes came to dominate society, their values became the social norms. Public drunkenness was discouraged, and anti-alcohol movements vigorously campaigned against drinking. Public festivals were regulated, making them more respectable and less rowdy.

In spite of their differences in education, wealth, and social standing, most of the bourgeoisie resembled one another in dress, habits of speech, and deportment. Bourgeois men dressed somberly, in dark colors, avoiding any outward signs of luxury. Their clothing fit closely and eschewed decoration—an adjustment to the machine age, in which elaborate dress hampered activity. It also reflected a conscious attempt to emphasize the frugal and achievement-oriented attitudes of the bourgeoisie in contrast to what was seen as the frivolous nobility.

Bourgeois conventions regarding women's dress were less reserved. Extravagant amounts of colorful fabrics used to fashion huge, beribboned hoop dresses reflected the newfound wealth of the middle classes and confirmed their view of women as ornaments whose lives were to be limited to the home and made easier by servants. This era was dominated by domesticity, by the ideal of the home. While the man was out in the secular

**Josephine Grey Butler**    An important Victorian reformer, Butler agitated for several causes, most notably abolition of the Contagious Diseases Act. This act empowered the police to arrest any woman it suspected of prostitution and to force her to be examined for venereal disease. Largely as a result of Butler's efforts, this act was repealed in 1886.
*(Fawcett Library/Mary Evans Picture Library)*

world earning a living and advancing his career, the bourgeois woman was to run her household, providing her family with an orderly, comfortable shelter from the storms of daily life. (See the box "Reading Sources: Advice on Running the Middle-Class Household.") She decorated the rooms, changed curtains with the seasons and the styles, supervised the servants, kept the accounts, oversaw the children's homework and religious education, and involved herself in charitable works. In the decades around midcentury, the notion of two separate spheres—one male and public, the other female and private—reached its height.

In spite of the relatively passive role assigned to women, many bourgeois women were very active. Some took up philanthropic causes, helping the sick and the poor. In England, Josephine Grey Butler (1828–1906), a member of a family of reformers, fought for the spread of education to impoverished women. She also waged a fierce battle against prostitution. Many bourgeois women helped their husbands or fathers in the office, the business, or the writing of scientific treatises. Others

ε**ʚ READING SOURCES**

## Advice on Running the Middle-Class Household

*In 1861 Isabella Mary Mayson Beeton, a London housewife, published* Mrs. Beeton's Book of Household Management, *which in Britain was outsold only by the Bible. Her popular book provided British middle-class women with advice on running their households and reflected their values concerning discipline, frugality, and cleanliness.*

As with the commander of an army, or the leader of an enterprise, so is it with the mistress of a house. Her spirit will be seen through the whole establishment; and just in proportion as she performs her duties intelligently and thoroughly, so will her domestics follow in her path. Of all those acquirements, which more particularly belong to the feminine character, there are none which take a higher rank, in our estimation, than such as enter into a knowledge of household duties; for on these are perpetually dependent the happiness, comfort, and well-being of a family. . . .

Early rising is one of the most essential qualities which enter into good Household Management, as it is not only the parent of health, but of innumerable other advantages. Indeed, when a mistress is an early riser, it is almost certain that her house will be orderly and well-managed. . . .

Cleanliness is indispensable to health, and must be studied both in regard to the person and the house, and all that it contains. . . .

Frugality and economy are home virtues, without which no household can prosper. . . .

Charity and benevolence are duties which a mistress owes to herself as well as to her fellow-creatures; and there is scarcely any income so small, but something may be spared from it. . . . Great ad-

vantages may result from visits paid the poor, for there being, unfortunately, much ignorance, generally amongst them with respect to all household knowledge, there will be opportunities for advising and instructing them in a pleasant and unobtrusive manner, in cleanliness, industry, cookery, and good management. . . .

A housekeeping account-book should invariably be kept, and kept punctually and precisely. . . .

. . . The treatment of servants is of the highest possible moment as well to the mistress as to the domestics themselves. On the head of the house the latter will naturally fix their attention; and if they perceive that the mistress's conduct is regulated by high and correct principles, they will not fail to respect her. If, also a benevolent desire is shown to promote their comfort, at the same time that a steady performance of their duty is exacted, then their respect will not be unmingled with affection, and they will be more solicitous to continue to deserve her favour.

*Source:* Isabella Mary Mayson Beeton, *Mrs. Beeton's Book of Household Management* (London: S. O. Beeton, 1861), pp. 1–6.

 **For additional information on this topic, go to http://college.hmco.com.**

achieved success on their own terms, running their own businesses, writing, painting, teaching.

The expectation that middle-class women would be married and taken care of by their husbands led to the provision of inferior education for girls and young women. Even bright and intellectually curious young girls could not receive as good an education as their brothers, nor as

a consequence pursue as interesting a career—a situation that had prevailed for centuries.

Various liberal movements in the nineteenth century insisted on legal equality among men, removing disabilities aimed against members of a particular social class or religion. Such discrimination, many had insisted, should also not be based on gender. Proponents

**Ladies' Bicycling Fashion**    This new mode of transportation suggested possibilities for female emancipation. Free, on her bicycle, the young woman is contrasted with a man, who rides only a tricycle.    *(From Karin Helm [ed.],* Rosinen aus der Gartenlaube *[Gutersloh: Signum Verlag, n.d.]. Reproduced with permission.)*

**Telephone Operators in London**    New technologies opened up new employment opportunities for women. Telephone operators formed a completely feminized profession.    *(Boyer-Viollet)*

of women's rights demanded equal access to education and the professions. Slowly, secondary and university education was made available to young women. In Europe the University of Zurich in Switzerland was the first university to admit women in 1865. Although British universities admitted women, the University of London did not grant them degrees until after 1878; and the most prestigious British institutions, Oxford and Cambridge, did not grant degrees to women until after World War I. In spite of discriminatory laws, harassment by male students, and initial obstruction by professional and accrediting groups, a few female doctors and lawyers practiced in England by the 1870s and on the Continent in the following decades.

Women more easily penetrated lower levels of middle-class occupations. Expanding school systems, civil services, and businesses provided new employment opportunities for women. By the 1890s, two-thirds of primary school teachers in England and half the post office staff in France were women; by 1914 nearly half a million women worked as shop assistants in England. Some new technologies created jobs that became heavily feminized, such as the positions of typist and telephone operator.

■ **The Workers' Lot**

The increased prosperity and greater productivity of the period gradually improved the conditions of both female and male workers in the generation after 1850. Their wages and standards of living rose, and they enjoyed more job security. In Britain the earning power of the average worker rose by one-third between 1850 and 1875. For the first time, workers were able to put money aside to tide them over in hard times.

The workers' increased income permitted a better diet. In France the average number of calories consumed per adult male increased by one-third between 1840 and

1890. In Britain, between 1844 and 1876, per capita consumption of tea tripled, and that of sugar quadrupled. The quality of food as well as the amount also improved: people consumed more meat, fish, eggs, and dairy products.

Legislation gradually reduced the length of the workweek. The British workweek, typically 73 hours in the 1840s, was reduced to 56 hours in 1874. In France it was reduced to 10 hours a day, in Germany to 11. But these improvements were accompanied by an increased emphasis on efficiency at the workplace. Fewer informal breaks were allowed as industrialists insisted on greater worker productivity. New machines increased the tempo of work, frequently leading to exhaustion and accidents.

As workers had more time and more money, their leisure patterns changed. Some leisure activities that previously had been limited to the upper classes became available to workers. The introduction of rail connections to resort towns such as Brighton in England or Trouville and Dieppe in France enabled workers to visit such places. New music and dance halls, popular theaters, and other forms of public entertainment sprang up to claim workers' increased spending money.

Although most workers believed their lot had improved, they were also aware that a vast gulf remained between them and the middle and upper classes. In the 1880s in the northern French industrial city of Lille, the combined estate of twenty thousand workers equaled that of one average industrialist. Life expectancies still varied dramatically according to income; in Bordeaux in 1853, the life expectancy of a male bourgeois was twenty years greater than that of a male laborer.

The disparity between rich and poor was especially striking in the case of domestics. Most servants were female, and they led tiring and restricted lives under the close supervision of their employers. Their hours were overly long: a six-and-one-half-day week was not uncommon. Housed in either the basement or the attic, servants experienced extremes of cold, heat, and humidity. Sometimes they were subjected to physical or sexual abuse by the master of the house, his sons, or the head of the domestic staff. And yet, for impoverished rural women with little chance of finding better work, domestic service was a risky but often necessary option. It provided free housing, food, and clothing and allowed the servant to save an annual sum equivalent to an amount between one-third and one-half of a worker's yearly wages. These savings often served as a dowry and allowed the young woman to make an advantageous match. Two out of five female wage earners in England were in domestic employ in 1851.

Although a few members of the working class managed to enter the lower levels of the middle classes, most remained mired in the same occupations as their grandparents. Poverty was still pervasive. In the 1880s about one-third of Londoners were living at or below the subsistence level. Industrial and urban diseases, such as tuberculosis, were common among workers. Compared with the healthier, better-fed, and better-housed middle classes, the workers continued living in shabby and limited circumstances.

## ■ The Transformation of the Countryside

Before the nineteenth century, the countryside had hardly changed at all, but beginning at midcentury it was radically transformed. Especially in western Europe, an increasing number of people left the land. In 1850, 20 percent of the population of Britain were agricultural workers; by 1881 only 11 percent were. The decrease of the agricultural population led in many places to labor shortages and therefore higher wages for farm hands.

Agriculture became increasingly efficient, and the food supply grew significantly. More land was put under the plow. Not only was more land cultivated but the yield per acre increased. In 1760 an agricultural worker in England could feed himself and one other person; by 1841 he could feed himself and 2.7 others. The population of Europe nearly doubled between 1800 and 1880, and yet it was nourished better than ever before.

Higher yields were the result of an increased use of manure, augmented in the 1870s by saltpeter imported from Chile and, beginning in the 1880s, by chemical fertilizers manufactured in Europe. Innovations in tools also improved productivity. The sickle, which required the laborer to crouch to cut grass or wheat, was replaced by the long-handled scythe, which allowed the field hand to stand and use the full weight of the body to swing the instrument through the grain. This new method increased efficiency fourfold. In the 1850s steam-driven threshing machinery was introduced in some parts of western Europe. Organizational techniques borrowed from industrial labor, including specialization and regular schedules, also contributed to greater productivity on the land.

Improved roads and dramatically expanded rail lines enabled farmers to extend their markets. No longer did they need to produce only for the local area; they could depend on a national market and beyond for customers.

While the prices of farm products rose, those of industrial products fell, allowing farmers to purchase machinery to work the land as well as items providing personal convenience such as cast-iron stoves. Owners of medium and large farms did particularly well. For the first time, many qualified for credit, and the availability of fire and weather insurance buffered some from the unpredictability of farming.

Life in the countryside became less insular. Not only did rail lines connect farms to cities, but national school systems brought teachers into the villages. Local dialects and in some cases even distinct languages that peasants had spoken for generations were replaced by a standardized national language. Local provincial costumes became less common as styles fashionable in the cities spread to the countryside via mail order catalogs. The farm girls who went to the cities as maids to work in middle-class homes returned to their villages with urban and middle-class ideals. The military draft brought the young men of the village into contact with urban folk and further spread urban values to the countryside.

Even so, the rural world remained very distinct from urban society. Many of the forces seen as contributing to modernity actually aggravated rural conditions. The expansion of manufacturing in cities contributed to the decline of cottage industry in rural areas, where agricultural workers had relied on the putting-out system to provide supplementary income. Thus farm workers were idle during slack seasons, and rural unemployment grew. In many cases railroads bringing goods made elsewhere wiped out some of the local markets on which these cottage industries had depended. The steamship lowered the cost of transporting freight, including grain from distant Canada and Argentina, which often undersold wheat grown in Europe. The resultant crisis, worsened by a rural population explosion, led to the emigration of millions, who left the land for towns and cities or even migrated across the seas to the Americas and Australia (see page 820). Although this process was painful for large segments of the rural population, for those who were able to remain on the land, the situation eventually improved.

These trends had a striking effect in the rural areas of western Europe. Eastern Europe, in contrast, was hardly touched by them. In Russia agriculture remained backward; the average yield per acre in 1880 was one-quarter that of Great Britain. The land sheltered a large surplus population that was underemployed and contributed little to the rural economy. In the Balkans, most peasants were landless and heavily indebted.

**Steam-Powered Thresher**    This image shows the thresher being operated in the French countryside in 1860. It would be decades before this kind of technology became a common sight in Europe, but it was a harbinger of the change coming to the rural world.    *(Bibliothèque Nationale de France)*

**Pissarro: L'avenue de l' Opéra, Sunlight, Winter Morning**   Camille Pissarro, one of the leading impressionists, portrayed the broad new avenue designed by Baron Haussmann. The avenue leads to the new opera, in background, also planned during the Second Empire.   *(Musée Saint-Denis, Reims/Giraudon/Art Resource, NY)*

# URBAN PROBLEMS AND SOLUTIONS

B Y 1851 the majority of English people lived in cities; by 1891 the majority of Germans did as well. To cope with urban growth and its attendant problems—epidemics, crowding, traffic jams—cities developed public health measures and introduced planning and rebuilding programs. They adapted the new technologies to provide such urban amenities as streetlights, public transportation, water and sewer systems, and helped make the city safer by establishing large, more efficient police forces. Cities gradually became safer and more pleasant places to live, although for a long time city dwellers continued to suffer high mortality rates.

## ■ City Planning and Urban Renovation

Most of Europe's cities had begun as medieval walled cities and had grown haphazardly into major industrial centers. Their narrow, crooked streets could not accommodate the increased trade and daily movement of goods and people, and traffic snarls were common. City

**Map 23.2  Haussmann's Paris, 1850–1870**   During the reign of Napoleon III, Baron Georges Haussmann reshaped the city of Paris, replacing its narrow medieval streets with a system of broad avenues and public parks and encircling the city with a railway.

officials began to recognize that broad, straight avenues would help relieve the congestion and also bring sunlight and fresh air into the narrow and perpetually dank lanes and alleys. In the 1820s, London saw the first ambitious street-widening initiative. On Regency Street, old hovels were torn down and replaced with fancy new houses; the poor were displaced. Later projects followed this pattern. (See the feature "Weighing the Evidence: The Modern City and Photography" on pages 806–807.)

The most extensive program of urban rebuilding took place in midcentury Paris. Over a period of eighteen years, Napoleon III and his aide, Baron Georges Haussmann (1809–1891), transformed Paris from a dirty medieval city to a beautiful modern one (see Map 23.2). Haussmann and his engineers carved broad, straight avenues through what had been dingy slums. They built elegant houses on the new tree-lined avenues. Public monuments and buildings, such as the new opera house, enhanced the city. The tremendous costs of this ambitious scheme kept the city of Paris in debt for decades. In addition, the slum-removal program drove tens of thousands of the poorest Parisians to the outskirts of the city, leading to greater social segregation than had previously existed.

Haussmann's extensive work in Paris served as a model for other cities, and although none was rebuilt as extensively, many underwent significant improvements. The cities of Europe began to display an expansive grace and sense of order, supporting the belief of the middle classes that theirs was an age of progress.

## ■ The Introduction of Public Services

Beginning at midcentury, government at the central and local levels helped make cities more livable by legislating sanitary reforms and providing public transportation and lighting. Medical practitioners in the 1820s had observed that disease and higher mortality were related to dirt and lack of clean air, water, and sunshine. Since diseases spreading from the poorer quarters of town threatened the rich and powerful, there was a general interest in improving public health by clearing slums, broadening streets, and supplying clean air and water to the cities.

Reform began in England, where the lawyer and civil servant Edwin Chadwick (1800–1895) drafted important plans for reform that became the basis for legislation. The Public Health Bill of 1848 established national standards for urban sanitation and required cities to regulate the installation of sewers and the disposal of refuse. The 1875 Health Act mandated certain basic health standards for water and drainage. Armed with these laws, cities and towns took the initiative: Birmingham cleared 50 acres of slums in the 1870s, for example.

London was also a leader in supplying public water, a service later adopted by Paris and many other cities. Berlin had a municipal water system in 1850, but it took several decades before clean water was available in every household. As late as the 1870s, Berlin's sewage was carried in open pipes. In Paris, which typically led France in innovations, 60 percent of the houses had running water in 1882. The French capital did not have a unitary sewer system until the 1890s, however.

As running water in the home became a standard rather than a luxury, bathing became more common. The English upper classes had learned the habit of daily baths from their colonial experience in India; on the Continent it did not become the custom until about the third quarter of the nineteenth century. The French artist

Edgar Degas° (1834–1917) frequently painted bath scenes, portraying the new European habit.

All these changes had a direct impact on the lives of city dwellers. Life became healthier, more comfortable, and more orderly. Between the 1840s and 1880, London's death rate fell from 26 per thousand to 20 per thousand. In Paris for the same period the decline was from 29.3 to 23.7 per thousand. The decline in the incidence of diseases associated with filthy living conditions was even more immediate. Improved water supplies provided a cleaner environment and reduced the prevalence of waterborne diseases such as cholera and typhoid.

Other improvements also contributed to a better quality of life. With the introduction of urban transportation, city dwellers no longer had to live within walking distance of their workplaces. An early example of public transportation was the French omnibus service of the 1820s—a system of horse-drawn carriages available to the public on fixed routes. In the 1850s the tram was introduced. A carriage drawn on a rail line by horses, a tram could pull larger loads of passengers faster than the omnibus. Because of the many rail stations in London and the difficulty of getting from one station to another in time to make a connection, London built an underground railway in 1863, the predecessor of the subway system. Technological improvements made the bicycle a serious means of transportation for some city dwellers. By the mid-1880s, nearly 100,000 bicycles were being pedaled around Great Britain, and a decade later, 375,000 in France—rising to a million by 1900.

Improvements in public transportation enabled workers to move out of the inner city into the less dense and less expensive suburbs. This trend in turn led to a decrease in urban population density and eventually helped make the city a healthier place to live.

Gaslights also improved city life, making it easier and safer to be outside at night. (Prior to gaslights, city dwellers depended mainly on moonlight or, rarely, expensive and time-consuming oil lamps—which had to be lit one at a time.) In 1813 London was the first city to be illuminated by gas; Berlin followed in 1816. Electrical lights were introduced in Paris in 1875, although they were not common until the end of the century.

Cities also significantly expanded police forces to impose order, to control criminal activity, and to discourage behavior deemed undesirable, such as dumping garbage on the street, relieving oneself in public, or carousing late at night. In 1850 London was the best-policed city in Europe with a 5,000-man force. Paris had around 3,000 police officers.

---

**Degas** (DAY-gah)

# SOCIAL AND POLITICAL INITIATIVES

EW institutions and groups emerged to tackle the unequal distribution of wealth and critical urban problems that followed in the wake of economic growth. The state intervened in the economy in new ways. Private charitable groups sprang up. Socialist political parties, exclusively dedicated to improving the workers' lot, gained in numbers and strength.

## ■ State Intervention in Welfare

The difficult conditions industry imposed on workers led to debates in several countries about the need for the state to protect the workers. The growing militancy of organized labor also forced the established authority to consider ways to meet the workers' needs. While some rejected government intervention in the free operation of market forces, others argued that the laws of supply and demand had caused the exploitation of many who ought to have been protected—especially very young children and pregnant women. Britain led the way with Factory Acts regulating child and female labor; similar acts were passed later in Prussia and France. In much of Europe, however, the state did little to improve the welfare of the working class. In eastern Europe, where industry was still in its infancy, workers had no protection.

Fear of social upheaval and the rising strength of socialist political parties prompted some governments to act. In France moderate bourgeois liberals attempted to defuse class war by advocating "solidarism." With the motto "Every man, his neighbor's debtor," solidarism insisted on the mutual responsibility of classes and individuals for one another's well-being. Guided by such sentiments, French Republicans passed a number of laws toward the end of the century that improved the lot of the working class. In newly unified Germany, the government wanted to impress workers with state benefits so they would abandon the growing Socialist Party and back the kaiser's authoritarian government. Chancellor Otto von Bismarck embarked on a deliberate program to tame the workers and win their support for the existing political and economic institutions. Thus, in the 1880s the new German government provided a comprehensive welfare plan that included health insurance and old-age pensions. In addition to the welfare initiatives by state and city governments, middle and upper classes also worked to better the workers' lot. Concern among these groups and individuals arose from a mixture of pity for workers' conditions, religious teachings about their responsibilities for the less fortunate, and fear of the consequences of unrelieved misery.

Women participated heavily in volunteer charity work. By the end of the nineteenth century, as many as half a million English women contributed their time to provide charity to the less fortunate. In Sweden by the 1880s, women had founded refuges for the destitute, old-age homes, a children's hospital, an asylum for the mentally handicapped, and various societies to promote female industry.

In Catholic and Protestant countries, the Christian churches traditionally had identified with the rights of employers and seemed to ignore the lot of the workers. However, a number of Christians, lay and clerical, began to emphasize the church's need to address social issues. Pope Leo XIII (r. 1878–1903) reflected this trend and reinforced it among Catholics when in 1891 he issued his encyclical *Rerum novarum* ("Of New Things"), which defined society's responsibility for the well-being of the poor. His message was taken up in France, Italy, and Spain among what became known as "social Catholics." (See the box "Reading Sources: Leo XIII Calls for Concern for the Working Classes.") In England, Protestants' concern for the poor was evidenced by the founding of the Salvation Army in 1878. Religious groups also hoped they could win converts among the less privileged by alleviating their plight.

Increasingly, municipalities, volunteer groups, and churches accepted responsibility for the well-being of others. Among their many activities, private charitable groups furnished cheap housing for the poor, church groups visited them, providing advice and some monetary assistance, municipalities opened free medical dispensaries. In many cases these pioneering efforts in aiding the poor were later taken over by the state, which, in amplified form, led to the development—in much of twentieth-century Europe—of the welfare state.

## ■ Educational and Cultural Opportunities

At the beginning of the nineteenth century, governments took little responsibility for providing education. Some upper-class children were educated with private tutors, and others attended elite schools. All schools were segregated by social class and all but a few charity schools for the poor charged tuition. In England the education of the masses became a national responsibility after the Second Reform Bill of 1867. This legislation extended the vote to the artisan classes and prompted a movement to ensure that the new voters were educated. In 1870 the

❧ R E A D I N G   S O U R C E S

## Leo XIII Calls for Concern for the Working Classes

*In his 1891 encyclical* Rerum Novarum (Of New Things), *Pope Leo XIII called on the propertied classes and the state to show concern for the poor. Leo reminded his readers of the central Christian message: charity. Note also how he appears to present the church as a solution to the growing class conflicts of the late nineteenth century.*

The momentous seriousness of the present state of things just now fills every mind with painful apprehension . . . and there is nothing which has a deeper hold on public attention. . . .

. . . There is nothing more powerful than religion (of which the Church is the interpreter and guardian) in drawing rich and poor together, by reminding each class of its duties to the other, and especially of the duties of justice. Thus religion teaches the labouring man and the workman to carry out honestly and well all equitable agreements freely made; never to injure capital, or to outrage the person of an employer. . . . Religion teaches the rich man and the employer that their work people are not their slaves; that they must respect in every man his dignity as a man and as a Christian. . . . [T]he employer must never tax his work people beyond their strength, nor employ them in work unsuited to their sex or age. . . . [R]ich men and masters should remember this—that to exercise pressure for the sake of gain upon the indigent and the destitute and to make one's profit out of the need of another is condemned by all laws, human and divine. To defraud anyone of wages that are his due is a crime which cries to the avenging anger of Heaven.

Rights must be religiously protected wherever they are found; and it is the duty of the public authority to prevent and punish injury, and to protect each one in the possession of his own. Still, when there is question of protecting the rights of individuals, the poor and helpless have a claim to special consideration. The richer population have many ways of protecting themselves, and stand less in need of help from the State; those who are badly off have no resources to fall back upon, and must chiefly rely upon the assistance of the State. And it is for this reason that wage-earners, who are undoubtedly among the weak and necessitous, should be specially cared for and protected by the commonwealth.

*Source:* Francesco Nitti, *Catholic Socialism,* trans. Mary Mackintosh (New York: Macmillan & Co., 1895), pp. 404, 409, 415.

---

English government began to provide significant subsidies for education, to set educational standards, and to establish a national inspection system to enforce them. England and France initiated mandatory primary school education in the 1880s.

Public education included not only reading, writing, and arithmetic but other skills as well. By insisting on punctuality and obliging students to carry out repetitive tasks such as copying letters, words, or sentences, schools encouraged people to fit into the emerging industrial society. The obedience and respect for authority learned at school shaped the soldiers and factory workers of the future. And regardless of political inclination, each regime took advantage of its control of the educational system to inculcate in the young the love of country and of its form of government.

Secondary education was, on the whole, available only to the privileged few in the upper middle classes. It confirmed their social status and won them access to the universities and the professions. For a very small number from the lower middle classes, secondary school attendance provided the means to ascend socially. The lower middle class was sparsely represented in universities, and the children of workers and peasants were totally absent.

Public education spread from the schools to other institutions, which made culture available to the masses in new ways. Between 1840 and 1880, the number of large libraries in Europe increased from 40 to 500. The French national public library, the *Bibliothèque Nationale,* was established in Paris in the 1860s. This iron and glass building, radical for its time, was an impressive monument to the desire to make reading available to an expanded public. Many provincial cities, as well as the glittering capitals of Europe, were endowed with new libraries. Less grandiose, but probably more important for mostly rural populations, were the traveling libraries.

Museums and art galleries, which in the previous century had been open to only a select few, gradually became accessible to the general public. The first museum to open to the public was the Louvre in Paris after the French Revolution. Other European countries lagged behind in making their cultural heritages available to the masses, but in the later part of the century even the poorer classes gained access to these temples of culture.

## CULTURE IN AN AGE OF OPTIMISM

THE improving economic and material conditions of the second half of the nineteenth century buoyed European thinkers. Many believed that men and women were becoming more enlightened, and they expressed faith in humankind's ability to transform the world with a parade of scientific and technological breakthroughs. The world seemed knowable and perfectible. This faith advanced secularism while it undermined the certainties of traditional religion. The arts reflected these new values, emphasizing realism and science—as well as an underlying foreboding about the dark side of this "age of optimism."

### ■ Darwin and Evolution

By midcentury most thinkers accepted the notion of change and transformation of society—and, by analogy, of the natural environment. The French thinker Comte championed the notion that human development—human history—proceeded through distinct and irreversible stages. Human progress, inscribed in the laws of nature, leads inexorably upward to the final and highest stage of development, the positive—or scientific—stage. Widely read throughout Europe and Latin America, Comte's writings helped bolster the era's faith in science, and the very progress science made seemed to confirm its precepts. Comte's philosophy, known as positivism, dominated the era. While the romantics had emphasized feeling, positivists upheld the significance of the measurable, the palpable, the verifiable. Scientific methods, the positivists were confident, would ensure the continued progress of humanity. Hadn't science already proved that the world was evolving to ever higher forms?

**Charles Darwin, Proponent of Evolution** This portrait was made in 1840, when the young scientist was wrestling with the meaning of the evidence he had collected in the Galápagos Islands. His observations there became the basis for *On the Origin of Species by Means of Natural Selection* (1859), the most important scientific work of the nineteenth century. *(Down House/The Bridgeman Art Library, London and New York)*

In the field of geology, the Englishman Charles Lyell (1797–1875) maintained that the earth was far older than the biblical story of Genesis suggested. He argued that its geological formations—the mountains, valleys, and seas—were subject to natural forces that, over hundreds of thousands, even millions, of years, had shaped them. Most educated people accepted his theory, which led many to wonder if it might also be true that the animal kingdom had evolved gradually over long periods of time.

Although evolution in the biological realm had been suggested as early as the end of the eighteenth century, Charles Darwin (1809–1882) was the first to offer a plausible explanation of the process. As the naturalist on an official British scientific expedition in the

## 🞉 READING SOURCES

## Darwin's Basic Laws of Evolution

*Writing in an age of vast transformations, Darwin could imagine the mutability of all nature, including species, over time. And like his contemporaries, he could imagine that evolution would lead to improvement, to increasing "perfection" of various species. A religious man who lost much of his faith as a result of his scientific investigations, Darwin was anxious to reassure Christians, hence his attempt to portray evolution as part of God's divine plan.*

Nothing at first can appear more difficult to believe than that the more complex organs and instincts have been perfected, not by means superior to, though analogous with, human reason, but by the accumulation of innumerable slight variations, each good for the individual possessor. Nevertheless, this difficulty, though appearing to our imagination insuperably great, cannot be considered real if we admit the following propositions, namely, that all parts of the organisation and instincts offer, at least, individual differences—that there is a struggle for existence leading to the preservation of profitable deviations of structure or instinct—and, lastly, that gradations in the state of perfection of each organ may have existed, each good of its kind. The truth of these propositions cannot, I think, be disputed. . . .

As geology plainly proclaims that each land has undergone great physical changes, we might have expected to find that organic beings have varied under nature, in the same way as they have varied under domestication. And if there has been any variability under nature, it would be an unaccountable fact if natural selection had not come into play. . . .

There is grandeur in this view of life, with its several powers, having been originally breathed by the Creator into a few forms or into one; and that, whilst this planet has gone cycling on according to the fixed law of gravity, from so simple a beginning endless forms most beautiful and most wonderful have been, and are being evolved.

*Source:* Charles Darwin, *On the Origin of Species by Means of Natural Selection,* 6th ed., vol. 2 (1872; reprint, New York: Appleton, 1923), pp. 267–268, 279, 305–306.

1830s, he had visited the Galápagos Islands off the western coast of South America. On these islands he found species similar to but different from those on the mainland and even different from one another. Could they be the results of separate creations? Or was it more likely that in varying environments they had adapted differently? Darwin proposed that closely related species compete for food and living space. In this struggle, those in each species that are better adapted to the environment have the advantage over the others and hence are more likely to survive. In the "struggle for existence," only the fittest endure. Those surviving, Darwin surmised, pass on the positive traits to their offspring. He called the mechanism that explained the evolution and development of new species "natural selection," a process that he proposed was imperceptible but continuous. (See the box "Reading Sources: Darwin's Basic Laws of Evolution.")

Darwin's theory of the inevitability of evolution in nature echoes the era's confidence in change and its conviction that the present represented a more developed stage of the past. His work was seen as confirming the notion that societies—like species—were preordained to evolve toward progressively higher stages. Darwin at first avoided the question of whether human beings, too, were affected by the laws of evolution. To do so would be to question humanity's uniqueness, its separation from the rest of creation by its possession (in the

Christian view) of a soul. But in *The Descent of Man* (1871), Darwin did confront this issue, clearly stating his belief that humanity, too, was subject to these natural laws. The recognition that human beings were members of the animal kingdom like other species disturbed him, and the admission, he wrote, "is like confessing a murder." Nonetheless, for Darwin scientific evidence took precedence over all other considerations.

Many Christians were shocked by these assertions, and some denounced the new scientific findings. Some argued that science and faith belonged to two different worlds. Others claimed that there was no reason why God could not have created the world through natural forces. In the long run, however, Darwinism seemed to undermine the certainties of religious orthodoxies by showing their incompatibility with scientific discovery.

Some contemporaries applied Darwin's theories to human society. Social Darwinists argued that human societies evolved in the same way as plants and animals. Just as species, so some human societies—races, classes, nations—were destined to survive, while others were condemned to fade away. And from these harsh laws a better humanity would evolve. The British social theorist Herbert Spencer (1820–1903), who coined the expression "survival of the fittest," believed that society should be established in such a way that the strongest and most resourceful would survive. The weak, poor, and improvident were not worthy of survival, and if the state helped them survive—for instance by providing welfare—it would only perpetuate the unfit. Poverty was a sign of biological inferiority, wealth a sign of success in the struggle for survival. In Europe and the United States (where Spencer was extremely popular, selling hundreds of thousands of books), Social Darwinism was thus used to justify callousness toward the poor at home and imperial conquest abroad. Since in the colonizing game the white races were the subjugators of Africans and Asians and not vice versa, whites were clearly superior, argued Social Darwinists. People of color were seen as inferior, poorly endowed to compete in the race for survival (see Chapter 24).

### ■ Physics, Chemistry, and Medicine

Dramatic scientific breakthroughs occurred in the nineteenth century, confirming the prevalent belief that human beings could understand and control nature. Since the seventeenth century, scientists had attempted to study nature by careful observation, by seeking regularities in nature, and by developing theories to explain what they had observed. Scientific truths had their own rules, independent of the investigator, who had to remain impartial and objective. The scientific method yielded major breakthroughs in the nineteenth century. In physics, laws regarding electricity and magnetism were articulated by Michael Faraday (1791–1867) and James Clerk Maxwell (1831–1879) in the 1830s and 1850s, respectively. Their work established the field of electrical science. In the 1840s, Hermann von Helmholtz (1821–1894) in Germany and James Joule (1818–1889) in Great Britain defined the nature of energy in the laws of thermodynamics. In chemistry, new elements were discovered almost every year, and individual findings contributed to the understanding of larger patterns. In 1869 Russian chemist Dmitri Mendeleev° (1834–1907) developed the periodic table, in which the elements are arranged by their atomic weight. He left blank spaces for elements still unknown but that he was confident existed. Within ten years, three of these elements were discovered, affirming the belief that scientific knowledge not only can be experimentally tested but also has predictive value. Such triumphs further enhanced science's prestige.

Prolific research yielded discoveries in one field of knowledge that could be transferred to another. For example, chemists produced new color dyes, enabling biologists to stain slides of microorganisms and better study their evolution. Scientific breakthroughs also led to technical achievements; for instance, inventions in chemistry led to the development of the first artificial fertilizers in 1842, while in physics the discovery of electromagnetism formed the basis of the telegraph and later the commercial uses of electricity.

Science also became increasingly specialized. In the eighteenth century, the scientist had been a learned amateur practicing a hobby. In the nineteenth century, as the state and industry became more involved in promoting scientific research, the scientist became a professional employed by a university, a hospital, or some other institution. New theories and discoveries were disseminated by scientific journals and at meetings of scientific associations and congresses. Around the mid-century mark, a number of important breakthroughs occurred in medicine. Before the development of anesthesia, surgical intervention was limited. With only alcohol to dull the patient's pain, even the swiftest surgeons could perform only modest surgical procedures. In the

---

**Mendeleev** (men-del-LAY-ef)

1840s, however, the introduction of ether and then chloroform allowed people to undergo more extensive surgery. It also was used to relieve pain in more routine procedures and in childbirth; Queen Victoria asked for chloroform when in labor.

Increasingly, the experimental method in science was applied to medicine, and as a result physicians became concerned not simply with treating diseases but with discovering their origins. Louis Pasteur (1822–1895) achieved notable breakthroughs when he discovered that microbes, small organisms invisible to the naked eye, cause various diseases. Pasteur found that heating milk to a certain temperature kills disease-carrying organisms. This process, called pasteurization, reduced the incidence of certain diseases that were particularly harmful to children. Pasteur initiated other advances as well in the prevention of disease. Vaccination against smallpox had started in England in the eighteenth century, but Pasteur invented vaccines for other diseases and was able to explain the process by which the body, inoculated with a weak form of bacilli, developed antibodies that successfully overcame more serious infections. In England the surgeon Joseph Lister (1827–1912) developed an effective disinfectant, carbolic acid, to kill the germs that cause gangrene and other infections in surgical patients. Lister's development of germ-free procedures transformed the science of surgery. By reducing the patient's risk, more ambitious surgery could be attempted. Eventually, midwives and doctors, by washing their hands and sterilizing their instruments, began to reduce the incidence of the puerperal, or "childbed," fever that killed so many women after childbirth. The increasingly scientific base of medicine and its visible success in combating disease improved its reputation.

Science was now fashionable. In 1869 Empress Eugénie in France had Louis Pasteur come to tea, draw blood from her finger, and examine it under a microscope, all to the astonishment of her guests. Some frogs, brought in for experimentation, escaped down palace corridors. The spectacle of science as the chic entertainment of an empress was a reminder of the increasing authority it commanded in the later nineteenth century.

## ■ Birth of the Social Sciences

The scientific method, so dramatically effective in uncovering the mysteries of nature, was also applied to the human enterprise. Just as the secrets of nature were unlocked, the workings of society, it was thought, could be understood in a scientific manner.

No field in the human sciences flourished as much in the nineteenth century as history. In an era undergoing vast transformations, many people became interested in change over time. They were eager to employ the methods of the scientist to explore their past. The father of modern historical writing is the German Leopold von Ranke° (1795–1886). Departing from the tradition of earlier historians, who explained the past as the ongoing fulfillment of an overarching purpose—divine will, the liberation of humanity, or some other goal—Ranke insisted that the role of the historian was to "show how things actually were." Like a scientist, the historian must be objective and dispassionate. By viewing humankind of all eras and environments on their own terms, and not those of others, historians could arrive at a better understanding of humanity.

This perspective transformed the study of history into a discipline with recognizable common standards of evidence. Historians studied and interpreted original (or "primary") sources; they collected and published their findings; they founded professional organizations and published major journals.

Other social sciences also developed in this period. Anthropology, the comparative study of people in different societies, had been the subject of speculative literature for hundreds of years. Increased contacts with non-European societies in the nineteenth century—the effect of burgeoning trade, exploration, and missionary activities—stimulated anthropological curiosity. In 1844 the Society of Ethnology was founded in Paris, followed by the Anthropological Society (1859). London, Berlin, and Vienna quickly followed suit, establishing similar societies in the 1860s. Consisting of medical doctors, biologists, and travelers, these societies speculated on the causes of the perceived differences among human races, mainly attributing the variations to their physical structures. Anthropologists gave apparent "scientific" backing to the era's racism, explaining that non-Europeans were condemned to an existence inferior to the white races.

In Britain, the main anthropological theorist was Edward Tylor (1832–1917), the son of a brass manufacturer. Through his travels, Tylor came into contact with non-European peoples, who aroused his curiosity. Strongly influenced by the evolutionary doctrines of his day, Tylor believed that the various societies of humankind were subject to discoverable scientific laws. Tylor posited that if one could travel back in time, one would find humankind increasingly unsophisticated; so,

---

**von Ranke** (fon RANG-key)

too, the farther one traveled from Europe, the more primitive humankind became. The contemporary African was at a level of development similar to that of Europeans in an earlier era.

Tylor was not technically a racist, since he argued that the conditions of non-Europeans were not due to biology but rather were a function of their institutions. Eventually, they would "evolve" and become akin to Europeans. Like racists, however, evolutionists believed in the superiority of the European over other races. Anthropology gave "scientific" sanction to the idea of a single European people, sharing either a similar biological structure or a common stage of social development, which distinguished them from non-Europeans.

Anthropology gradually gained recognition and legitimacy as a profession. In 1872 in France, Paul Broca founded a journal devoted to physical anthropology. In 1876 he founded a school of anthropology with six chaired professors. In 1884 Tylor—who was so closely identified with anthropology it was called "Mr. Tylor's science"—was appointed to the first university chair in anthropology in Britain.

The term *sociology* was coined by Auguste Comte. A number of ambitious thinkers, among them the English "social philosopher" Herbert Spencer (see page 797), had considered how individuals are affected by the society in which they live. In the 1840s various social reformers published detailed statistical investigations revealing relationships between, for instance, income and disease and death rates. A few decades later, the theoretical principles underlying sociology were spelled out. Among the first researchers to do so was Emile Durkheim° (1858–1917), who insisted that sociology was a verifiable science. He occupied the first chair of sociology at a French university in 1887. A few years later he founded a journal of sociology and mentored a corps of disciples who ensured the success of sociology as a professionalized discipline.

Whereas in the past, history, anthropology, and sociology were the purview of amateurs, now professional historians, anthropologists, and sociologists were engaged full-time in research and teaching at universities or research institutes. The professionalization that had occurred in medicine and physics also transformed the social sciences. Professionalization and specialization led to significant advances in several disciplines, but it also led to the fragmentation and compartmentalization of knowledge. People of broad learning and expertise became far less common.

**Durkheim** (DIRK-hime)

## ■ The Challenge to Religion

The scientific claims of the era seemed to clash with the traditions of religion. A number of scientists, including Darwin himself, found their Christian faith undermined by theories on evolution. Although most Europeans continued to be strongly influenced by traditional religious beliefs, they appeared less confident than in earlier eras.

After the revolutions of 1848, religion was seen as a bulwark of order. In France Napoleon III gave the Catholic Church new powers over education, and the bourgeoisie flocked to worship. In Spain moderates who had been anticlerical (opposed to the clergy) began to support the church, and in 1851 they signed a concordat (an agreement with the papacy) declaring Roman Catholicism "the only religion of the Spanish nation." In Austria in 1855, the state surrendered powers it had acquired in the 1780s, returning to bishops full control over the clergy, the seminaries, and the administration of marriage laws.

In 1848 the papacy had been nearly overthrown by revolution, and in 1860 it lost most of its domains to Italy. Thus Pope Pius IX became a sworn enemy of liberalism, and in 1864, in the *Syllabus of Errors,* he condemned a long list of perceived errors, among them "progress," "liberalism," and "modern civilization." To establish full control over the clergy and believers, the Lateran Council in 1870 issued the controversial doctrine of papal infallibility, declaring that the pope, when speaking officially on matters of faith and morals, was incapable of error. This doctrine became a target of anticlerical opinion.

The political alliance the Catholic Church struck with reactionary forces meant that when new political groups came to power, they moved against the church. In Italy, since the church had discouraged national unification, conflict raged between the church and the new state. In Germany, Catholics had either held on to their regional loyalties or favored unification under Austrian auspices. When Protestant Prussia unified Germany, Chancellor Bismarck viewed the Catholics with suspicion as unpatriotic and launched a campaign against them, the *Kulturkampf*° ("cultural struggle"). Bismarck expelled the Jesuits and attempted to establish state control over the Catholic schools and appointment of bishops. Not satisfied, he seized church property and imprisoned or exiled 1,800 priests.

In France the republicans, who finally won the upper hand over monarchists in 1879, bitterly resented the church's support of the monarchist party. They were also

**Kulturkampf** (KOOL-toor-kampf)

strongly influenced by Comte's ideas of positivism, believing that France would not be a free country until the power of the church was diminished and its nonscientific or antiscientific disposition was overcome. The republican regime reduced the role of the church in education as well as some other clerical privileges.

Greater religious tolerance, or perhaps indifference to religion in general, led to more acceptance of religious diversity. In 1854 and 1871 England opened university admission and teaching posts at all universities to non-Anglicans. Anti-Catholicism, at times a popular and virulent movement, declined in the 1870s. In France, too, the position of religious minorities improved. Some of the highest officials of the Second Empire were Protestants, as were some early leaders of the Third Republic and some important business leaders and scientists.

Legal emancipation of Jews, started in France in 1791, subsequently spread to the rest of the Continent. England removed restrictions on Jews when the House of Commons, in 1858, and the House of Lords the following decade allowed Jews to hold parliamentary seats. In the 1860s Germany and Austria-Hungary granted Jews the rights of citizenship. Social discrimination continued, however, and Jews were not accepted as social equals in most of European society. Although some Jews occupied high office in France and Italy, in Germany and Austria-Hungary they had to convert before they could aspire to such positions. In other fields, access was easier. Some of the major European banking houses were founded by Jews—the Rothschilds in France, Britain, and Germany, and the Warburgs in Germany, for instance.

In the expanding economy of western Europe, where the condition of most people was improving, the enhanced opportunity of a previously despised minority aroused relatively little attention. In other parts of Europe, Jews were not so fortunate. When they seized economic opportunities in eastern Europe and moved into commerce, industry, and the professions, they were resented. Outbreaks of violence against them, called *pogroms,* occurred in Bucharest, capital of Romania, in 1866 and in the Russian seaport of Odessa in 1871. Although economic rivalries may have fueled anti-Jewish feelings, they do not completely explain it. In most cases anti-Jewish sentiment occurred in the areas of Europe least exposed to liberal ideas of human equality and human rights.

The emphasis on science and reason transformed religion in the nineteenth century, but, as the continued anti-Semitism demonstrates, it by no means always led to increased tolerance or weakened religious fervor. On the contrary, in certain cases religiosity grew. French people reported frequent sightings of the Virgin Mary. In 1858 a shepherd girl claimed to have seen and spoken with her at Lourdes°, which became an especially important shrine whose waters were reputed to heal the lame and the sick. In 1872 construction of a rail line allowed 100,000 people a year to visit the town.

Church attendance continued to be high, especially in rural areas. In England villagers usually attended church, many twice or more each Sunday. Children dutifully attended Sunday schools. Advances in printing made it possible to distribute large quantities of inexpensive religious tracts to a sizable and avid readership. The faithful eagerly funded proselytizing, sending large numbers of missionaries into all corners of the globe.

## ■ Culture in the Age of Material Change

The era's admiration of technology and science, and its idolization of progress, were reflected in the arts. Some artists optimistically believed they could more accurately portray reality by adopting the methods of the scientist, coolly depicting their subjects. A minority, however, were disillusioned by the materialism of the age and warned against its loss of values.

Photography had a direct impact on painting. Various experiments in the late eighteenth century, plus the inventions of the Frenchman Louis Daguerre° (1789–1851), made the camera relatively usable by the 1830s. It was still a large, cumbersome object, however, until the dry plate and the miniature camera were introduced in the 1870s. Twenty years later, with the invention of celluloid film, the camera came into wide use, the best-known mass-produced version being the Kodak camera invented by the American George Eastman (1854–1932). Unlike painting and sculpture, photography was affordable for the public. Photographic services were in high demand; by the 1860s, thirty thousand people in Paris made a living from photography and allied fields. Many Europeans became amateur photographers—Queen Victoria and Prince Albert had a darkroom at Windsor Castle (see the feature "Weighing the Evidence: The Modern City and Photography").

The ability of photography to depict a scene with exactitude had a significant impact on art. On the one hand, it encouraged many artists to be true to reality, to reproduce on the canvas a visual image akin to that of a photograph. On the other hand, other artists felt that such realism was no longer necessary in their sphere. However, the great majority of the public, which now

---

**Lourdes** (LOORD)   **Daguerre** (dah-GAIR)

**Courbet: The Stone Breakers**   This realistic 1849 painting depicts the rough existence of manual laborers. The bleakness of the subject matter and the style in which it was carried out characterized much of the realist school of art.   *(Staatliche Kunstsammlungen, Dresden/The Bridgeman Art Library, London and New York)*

had wide access to museum exhibitions, was accustomed to photographic accuracy and desired art that was representative and intelligible. Realistic works of art met this need, at least superficially.

Discarding myths and symbols, many artists portrayed the world as it actually was, or at least as it appeared to them—a world without illusions, everyday life in all its grimness. The realist painter Gustave Courbet° (1819–1877) proclaimed himself "without ideals and without religion." His fellow Frenchman, Jean-François Millet° (1814–1875), held a similar opinion. Instead of romanticizing peasants in the manner of earlier artists, he painted the harsh physical conditions under which they labored. In England the so-called pre-Raphaelites took as their model the painters of Renaissance Italy prior to Raphael, who presumably had depicted the realistic simplicity of nature. In painting historical scenes,

these artists emphasized meticulous research of the landscape, architecture, fauna, and costumes of their subjects. To paint the Dead Sea in *The Scapegoat,* English artist Holman Hunt (1827–1910) traveled all the way to Palestine to guarantee accurate portrayal of the site.

In the past, artists had been concerned about composition and perspective. But under the influence of photography, they began to paint incomplete, off-center pictures. *Orchestra of the Paris Opera* by French artist Edgar Degas looks as if it has been cropped, with only half a musician showing on each edge and the top half of the ballet dancers missing.

On April 15, 1874, six French artists—Edgar Degas (1834–1917), Claude Monet° (1840–1926), Camille Pissarro (1830–1903), Auguste Renoir° (1840–1919), Alfred Sisley (1839–1899), and Berthe Morisot° (1841–1895)—

---

Courbet (koor-BAY)   Millet (mil-LAY)

Monet (moh-NAY)   Renoir (ren-WOIR)
Morisot (mor-ee-SO)

opened an exhibition in Paris that a critic disparagingly called "impressionist," after the title of one of Monet's paintings, *Impression: Sunrise.* The impressionists were influenced by new theories of physics that claimed images were transmitted to the brain as small light particles that the brain then reconstituted. The impressionists wanted their paintings to capture what things looked like before they had been "distorted" by the brain. In their search for realism, impressionist painters ceased painting in their studios and increasingly went outdoors to paint objects exactly as they looked when light hit them at a certain angle. Monet, for example, emphasized outdoor painting and the need for spontaneity—for reproducing subjects without preconceptions about how earlier artists had depicted them—and seeking to show exactly how the colors and shapes struck the eye. Monet was particularly interested in creating multiple paintings of the same scene—from different viewpoints, under different weather conditions, at different times of day—to underscore that no single "correct" depiction could possibly capture a subject.

The school of realism also influenced literature, especially the novel. In realist novels, life was not glorified or infused with mythical elements; the stark existence of daily life was seen as a suitable subject. Charles Dickens (1812–1870), who came from a poor background and had personally experienced the inhumanity of the London underworld, wrote novels depicting the lot of the poor with humor and sympathy. The appalling social conditions he described helped educate his large middle-class audience on the state of the poor. He also provided numerous examples of individuals who by hard work were able to rise above their circumstances. In fact, the income from Dickens' many novels provided him with a comfortable income; by the pen he was able to join the middle class himself.

Another realist, the French novelist Gustave Flaubert° (1821–1880), consciously debunked the romanticism of his elders. His famous novel, *Madame Bovary°*, describes middle-class life as bleak, boring, and meaningless. The heroine seeks to escape the narrow confines of provincial life by adulterous and disastrous affairs.

Emile Zola (1840–1902), another Frenchman, belonged to the naturalist school of literature. The writer, he declared, should be like a surgeon or chemist, providing a scientific cause and record of human behavior; his work, in Zola's words, is similar to "the analysis that surgeons make on cadavers." (See the box "Reading Sources: Emile Zola on the Novelist as Scientist.") In his Rougon-Macquart° series, which describes in detail the experience of several generations of a family, Zola's major theme is the impact of environment and heredity on his characters' lives of degradation and vice. His characters seem locked in a Darwinian struggle for survival: some are doomed by the laws of biology to succeed, others to succumb.

The Russian novelist Leo Tolstoy (1828–1910) brought a new perspective to the historical novel in *War and Peace.* Instead of a heroic approach to battle, he showed individuals trapped by forces beyond their control. Small and insignificant events as well as major ones seemed to govern human destiny. Another Russian novelist often associated with the realist school, Feodor Dostoyevsky (1821–1881), aimed to portray realistically the psychological dimensions of his characters in novels such as *Crime and Punishment* (1866), *The Idiot* (1868), and *The Brothers Karamazov* (1879–1880).

In music, realism was less evident. Johannes Brahms (1833–1897), while not sympathetic to some of the romantic composers, himself wrote music that evoked folk themes, such as his *Hungarian Dances* or his *Love Songs,* just as the romantics had done. The major musician whose work might be labeled as paralleling the realist movement in the other arts is the Russian Modest Mussorgsky (1839–1881), whose music was consciously realistic. Mussorgsky attempted to capture the accents of natural speech, gestures, and the sound of crowds in piano pieces such as *Pictures at an Exhibition* and the opera *Boris Godunov.*

Although this era generally celebrated material progress, a number of intellectuals reacted against it. They were alarmed by the prospect of the popular masses achieving political power through winning the vote and by mass production and consumption. They denounced the smug and the self-satisfied, who saw happiness in acquisition and consumption. Some condemned the age in severe terms. Dostoyevsky railed against the materialism and egotism of the West, branding its civilization as driven by "trade, shipping, markets, factories." In Britain—the nation that seemed to embody progress—the historian Thomas Carlyle (1795–1881) berated his age as one not of progress but of selfishness. Parliamentarism he saw as a sham, and he called for a strong leader to save the nation from endless debates and compromises. Unlike most of his contemporaries, who saw in material plenty a sign of progress, Carlyle saw the era as one of decline, bereft of spiritual values.

---

**Flaubert** (flo-BEAR)  **Bovary** (bo-vah-REE)

**Rougon-Macquart** (roo-ZHON–mah-KAR)

## ❧ R E A D I N G   S O U R C E S

---

### Emile Zola on the Novelist as Scientist

*Emile Zola believed that the novelist should act like a scientist, experimenting with characters' reactions to differing circumstances in order to determine the laws that govern thought and emotion. Zola wanted to be the literary equivalent of the great French scientist, Claude Bernard (1813–1878), one of the founders of experimental science. The title of this essay, "The Experimental Novel," published in 1880, echoes the title of Bernard's* Introduction to Experimental Medicine *(1865).*

Here you have scientific progress. In the last century, a more exact application of the experimental method creates chemistry and physics which free themselves from the irrational and the supernatural. Profound studies lead to the discovery that there are established laws; phenomena are mastered. Then a fresh step is taken. Living bodies, in which the vitalists still admitted a mysterious influence, are in their turn reduced to the general mechanism of matter.

Science proves that the conditions of life of all phenomena are the same in matter and in living bodies; hence, physiology gradually acquires the same certitude as chemistry and physics. But will we stop at that? Evidently not.

When we have proved that the body of man is a machine, which we shall one day be able to take to pieces and put together again at the experimenter's will, then it will be time to pass on to the sentimental and intellectual activities of man. This means that we should enter a realm which, until now, belonged wholly to philosophy and literature; it will be the decisive victory of science over the hypotheses of philosophers and writers. We already have experimental chemistry and physics; we are going to have experimental physiology; and then, later, we shall have the experimental novel. This is a necessary progression, and one whose end can easily be foreseen today. Everything is related, one had to start from the determinism of matter to arrive at the determinism of living bodies. . . . The same determinism must rule the stones in the roadway and the brains of man. . . .

It follows that science already enters our domain—the domain of writers like us, who are at the moment the students of man in his private and social activities. By our observations, by our experiments, we carry forward the work of the physiologist who had continued that of physicists and chemists.

*Source:* Eugen Weber, ed. and trans., *Paths to the Present* (New York: Dodd, Mead & Co., 1960), p. 170.

---

Another Englishman, John Ruskin (1819–1900), looked back to the Middle Ages as an ideal era in human history. People then did not produce with machines but exercised a fine sense of craftsmanship. People then supposedly had a better sense of community and labored for the common good. Ruskin was one of the founders of the arts and crafts movement, which aimed to produce goods for daily use with an eye for beauty and originality. "Industry without art is brutality," Ruskin warned.

In France republicans saw in the ostentation of the Second Empire a sign of depravity and decline. Defeat in war in 1870 and the outbreak of the Commune furthered a mood of pessimism among many intellectuals. Flaubert detested his own age, seeing it as petty and mean. The characters in Zola's Rougon-Macquart novels slide steadily downward as each generation's mental faculties, social positions, and morals degenerate. And some abroad were also unimpressed with developments in Europe. (See the box "Global Encounters: A Chinese Official's Views of European Material Progress.")

Not all were optimistic in this age of optimism. If many people celebrated what they viewed as an age of progress, others claimed that under the outer trappings of material comfort lay a frightening ignorance of aesthetic, moral, and spiritual values.

## A Chinese Official's Views of European Material Progress

*Educated in European universities, Ku Hung-Ming rose to become a high official in the Chinese court. His essays were penned under the impact of the European military intervention in China during the Boxer Rebellion in 1900. Ku denounced European notions of superiority over Asia, arguing that material progress was an inappropriate measure of a civilization's value.*

In order to estimate the value of a civilization, it seems to me, the question we must finally ask is not what great cities, what magnificent houses, what fine roads it has built and is able to build; what beautiful and comfortable furniture, what clever and useful implements, tools and instruments it has made and is able to make; no, not even what institutions, what arts and sciences it has invested: the question we must ask, in order to estimate the value of a civilization,—is, what type of humanity, what kind of men and women it has been able to produce. In fact, the man and woman,— the type of human beings—which a civilization produces, it is this which shows the essence, the personality, so to speak, the soul of that civilization. Now if the men and women of a civilization show the essence, the personality and soul of that civilization, the language which the men and women in that civilization speak, shows the essence, the personality, the soul of the men and women of that civilization. . . .

To Europeans, and especially to unthinking practical Englishmen, who are accustomed to take what modern political economists call "the standard of living" as the test of the moral culture of or civilization of a people, the actual life of the Chinese and of the people of the East at the present day, will no doubt appear very sordid and undesirable. But the standard of living by itself is not a proper test of the civilization of a people. The standard of living in America at the present day, is, I believe, much higher than it is in Germany. But although the son of an American millionaire, who regards the simple and comparatively low standard of living among the professors of a German University, may doubt the value of the education in such a University, yet no educated man, I believe, who has travelled in both countries, will admit that the Germans are a less civilized people than the Americans.

*Source:* Ku Hung-Ming, *The Spirit of the Chinese People,* 2d ed. (Beijing: Commercial Press, 1922), pp. 1, 144–145.

## SUMMARY

URING the second half of the nineteenth century, advances in industry created for many westerners an era of material plenty, providing more riches and comforts to a larger population than ever before. This self-confident age believed in progress and anticipated further improvements in its material and intellectual environment. It appeared to be an age of unbounded optimism.

Economic changes transformed the class structure of many European countries, and middle-class values and tastes defined the second half of the century. The new wealth and technologies led to improvements in both the countryside and the cities; in both, life became more comfortable and safer. Governments provided new services such as public education, cultural facilities, and expanded welfare services.

The material changes in society were reflected in intellectual currents. Change and evolution were embraced as an explanation for the origin of species. A new confidence in scientific research led to many scientific and technological breakthroughs. Novelists and painters aimed to dissect like scientists the world around them, adopting realism in the arts. Some intellectuals, however, were repulsed by the crass self-satisfaction of the bourgeoisie, and they despised their age's worship of industry and materialism.

Progress, as Europeans were to learn in a later era, was two-edged: the very forces that improved life for many also threatened it. The same breakthroughs in chemistry that led to the development of artificial fertilizers also provided more powerful military explosives. The expansion of education and reduction of illiteracy meant an end to ignorance but also the creation of a public that could more easily absorb messages of hate against a rival nation or against religious or ethnic minorities at home. Material progress and well-being continued, but there were new forces in the shadows that would ultimately undermine the comforts, self-assurance, and peace of this age.

## ■ Suggested Reading

Auerbach, Jeffrey A. *The Great Exhibition of 1851*. 1999. Brings alive the great exhibition.

Cannadine, David. *The Rise and Fall of Class in Britain*. 1999. Reveals the importance of class in nineteenth-century British society.

Clark, Linda L. *The Rise of Professional Women in France*. 2000. A fine study delineating the increasing role of women in the professions, especially public administration.

Goodman, David, and Colin Chant, eds. *European Cities and Technology Reader*. 1999. Emphasizes the importance of technological breakthroughs in the modernization of cities.

Hobsbawm, Eric J. *The Age of Capital, 1848–1875*. 1979. Particularly strong on social and economic developments.

Nord, Philip. *Impressionists and Politics*. 2000. Sets the French impressionists in their political and social contexts.

Standage, Tom. *The Victorian Internet*. 1998. A brief, popular history of the telegraph.

 **For a searchable list of additional readings for this chapter, go to http://college.hmco.com.**

# The Modern City and Photography

This photo of Piccadilly Center in Manchester was taken in 1886. It documents the modernization of the nineteenth century city and at the same time conveys the sense of immediacy that a new means of representation, the photograph, provided.

Manchester in the nineteenth century became a wealthy textile city, manufacturing and marketing textiles to the rest of Britain and the world. The first rail lines in Britain were built in Manchester; by 1840 six rail lines connected it to the rest of the kingdom. The city grew dramatically, from 43,000 in 1774 to 271,000 in 1831. By 1900 it had reached the 600,000 mark.

Piccadilly, the commercial center of Manchester, had warehouses and offices where buyers purchased textiles that they would in turn sell to retail consumers. Fancy stores were also located here, and in some cases elegant dwellings were situated in the upper floors. Piccadilly was a large open square allowing for the easy movement of pedestrians and wagons. City planners in the nineteenth century created squares and broad, straight avenues, such as those gracing Piccadilly, by tearing down old slums and narrow alleys. These broad avenues eased the flow of traffic and admitted fresh air and sunlight, which diminished exposure to killer diseases such as cholera and tuberculosis.

As it grew, Manchester needed public transportation to move people quickly on the broad new avenues. Notice the rails for the horse-drawn tramways. Horse-drawn carriages called omnibuses, which had been introduced in the 1820s, were the first means of mass transportation within the city. Trams ran on rails that reduced friction and allowed a horse to pull a far greater load; in this case the tram, located in the center of the photo, is a double-decker.

An industrial town, Manchester was not a particularly pleasant city to live in. Visitors complained of its grime, pollution, and foul smells. Many members of the commercial classes lived in wealthy suburbs and commuted by tram to work in the center with little waste of time. Sometime after this picture was taken, the horse-drawn tram was replaced by the electrical tram, which could transport more people faster than its predecessor. Its lower cost also meant that it was accessible even to most workers. With the advent of the electrical tram, workers too began to move to the suburbs, making the center less crowded.

The large modern city required ease of communication at night as well as in the daytime. Street lighting provided that convenience, as well as making the streets more secure by discouraging crime. Street lamps became the norm in large cities, especially in the better neighborhoods. The elegant gas lights that adorn the square were replaced a few years later by electrical ones that were cheaper to operate and allowed for the spread of city lighting. In lighting, public transport, police, sanitation, and other municipal services, it was quite common to discriminate in favor of the richer neighborhoods, while neglecting the poorer ones. The latter were usually the last to be served. By the 1880s, when the franchise was enlarged, municipalities became more sensitive to the needs of new voters of every class. In Manchester, as in many British cities, public services such as lighting, water supplies, and the tram system were municipalized, thus reducing the cost of these amenities and making them available to a larger proportion of the citizenry.

This photo,* taken in the 1880s, is also evidence of the great progress that had taken place in photography since its invention half a century earlier. In 1839 Louis Daguerre publicized the method of fixing an image on silvered copperplate. At first, the cameras and equipment were so cumbersome that photography was confined to studios; photographers could not take pictures anywhere else. Thus the only images were portraits of people, or the occasional still life. As the camera became simpler, photographers could leave the studio and take pictures outdoors. Improvements in film, most significantly the introduction of the dry plate method in the 1870s, made it far more sensitive to light, reducing exposure time to a fraction of a second. Now a photograph could capture movement without reducing it to a blur, as in this bustling city scene.

*The advice of Thomas Prasch in the choice of this photo is gratefully acknowledged.

Originally, photography had been regarded as a more exact, and less expensive, form of illustration and so was influenced by the conventions of painting. Most early photographs, even outdoor shots, were staged. Given the slowness of taking pictures and the obvious presence of the photographer with all the equipment, it could hardly have been different. But soon thereafter, thanks to technical innovations, photographers could capture a scene even without the cooperation of the subject. None of the subjects in this photo has eye contact with the camera. In fact, they seem unaware of the presence of the photographer as they go about their daily business.

If the modern photograph was different from a painting, photography still adhered to some of the traditions of painting—notably composition. The photographer has composed this image, has made choices as to what to put in the foreground. We get a sense of the harried merchant crossing the well-ordered street with its backdrop of amenities.

The new chemical and optical breakthroughs that made the camera such an effective new tool were implemented by inventors in cities such as London, Paris, Berlin. Photographers, in turn, took pictures of some of the great technical feats of their era. The modern aspects of the city, such as this scene, were frequent subjects for the photographer's lens. With a modern device, the camera, the photographer captured the new modern metropolis that was so much more efficient—and exciting—than its predecessor.

**Piccadilly Square, Manchester, ca. 1886** *(Topham Picturepoint/The Image Works)*

# CHAPTER 24

# Escalating Tensions 1880–1914

I N April 1912, the *Titanic*, the largest and most technologically advanced passenger ship ever built, sailed from Southampton, England, for New York. Its owners, the White Star Line, boasted that the building of this majestic vessel testified to "the progress of mankind" and would "rank high in the achievements of the twentieth century." Hailed as "virtually unsinkable," the *Titanic* struck an iceberg on the night of April 12, south of Newfoundland, and rapidly did sink. More than 1,500 of the 2,100 people aboard perished in the icy North Atlantic waters. The overconfident captain had not taken warnings of icebergs in the ship's path seriously enough.

Two years later European society was hit by a major disaster, the outbreak of a world war. That such a disaster would end the era called by contemporaries the *belle époque*°, "the beautiful epoch," was as unimaginable as *Titanic*'s fate. The booming economy had been expanding opportunities for many. The arts flourished and were celebrated. Parliamentary government continued to spread, and more nations seemed to be adapting to democracy as suffrage was extended. Yet hand in hand with these trends of apparent progress appeared troubling tendencies. Under the surface were forces threatening the stability of European society. There was peace, but in 1914 a lone assassin's bullet set off a series of reactions that ultimately led to war and the crash of the pre-1914 world.

In many societies, governing became more complex as populations increased. The population of Europe jumped from 330 million in 1880 to 460 million by 1914. A larger population coupled with extended

---

**belle époque** (BELL eh-POK)

The *Titanic* proudly announces its maiden voyage.
(Corbis)

suffrage meant that more people participated in the political system, but it became harder to reach consensus. The example of democracy in some countries led to discontent in the autocratic ones at their failure to move toward freer institutions. In the same way that prosperity and economic growth aroused resentment in those who did not share in the benefits, some groups became frustrated at their exclusion from the political system.

Intellectuals revolted against what they viewed as the smug self-assuredness of earlier years. They no longer felt certain that the world was knowable, stable, or subject to comprehension and, ultimately, to mastery by rational human beings. Some jettisoned rationality, imagining that they had made strides in sophistication by glorifying emotion, irrationality, and in some cases violence. The works of painters and writers seemed to anticipate the impending destruction of world order.

The anxieties and tensions that beset many Europeans took a variety of forms. Ethnic minorities became targets of hatred. European states embarked on a race for empire throughout the world, forcibly putting non-Europeans under white domination. On the Continent, states felt increasingly insecure, worried that they would be subject to attack. They established standing armies, shifted alliances, drafted war plans, and, in the end, went to war.

---

### QUESTIONS TO CONSIDER

- **What were the main motivations for European imperialism?**

- **In what ways did the world-view of intellectuals living in the *belle époque* differ from that of a generation earlier?**

- **In what ways did British and Russian political institutions reveal an inability to resolve the issues facing society?**

- **To what extent did social problems undermine the Russian regime?**

- **What responsibility did each of the Great Powers have for the outbreak of war in 1914?**

---

### TERMS TO KNOW

| | |
|---|---|
| "new imperialism" | suffragists |
| Second International | *Weltpolitik* |
| anti-Semitism | Bolshevik |
| Zionism | Triple Alliance |
| Sigmund Freud | Triple Entente |
| avant-garde | |

---

## THE NEW IMPERIALISM AND THE SPREAD OF EUROPE'S POPULATION

 ART of Europe's self-confidence during the period from the 1880s to 1914 was based on the unchallenged sway it held over the rest of the globe. Europeans brought under political control large swathes of land across the seas and also marked the globe by massive migrations.

The age of empire building that started in Europe in the sixteenth century seemed to have ended by 1750. Then, in the 1880s, the European states launched a new era of expansionism, conquering an unprecedented amount of territory. In only twenty-five years, Europeans subjugated 500 million people—one half of the world's non-European population. European expansion was also manifest in a massive movement of people: between 1870 and 1914, 55 million Europeans moved overseas, mainly to Australia, the United States, Canada, and Argentina.

This era of ambitious conquest is often called the "new imperialism" to differentiate it from the earlier stage of empire building. Whereas the earlier imperialism focused on the Americas, nineteenth-century imperialism centered on Africa and Asia. And unlike the colonizing of the earlier period, the new imperialism occurred in an age of mass participation in politics and was accompanied by expressions of popular enthusiasm.

## ■ Economic and Social Motives

The hope of profit overseas was crucial in the dynamic of the new imperialism. Most of these hopes were illusory, but the desire for huge markets was instrumental in stirring an interest in empire. Colonies, it was believed, would provide eager buyers for European goods that would stimulate production at home. "Colonial policy is the daughter of industrial policy," declared French prime minister Jules Ferry° in 1884. Yet colonies did not represent large markets for the mother countries. In 1914 France's colonies represented only 12 percent of its foreign trade. Great Britain's trade with its colonies represented a considerable one-third of its foreign trade, but most of that was with the settlement colonies, such as Canada and Australia, not those acquired in the era of the new imperialism. As for Germany, colonial trade represented less than 1 percent of its exports. Even protective tariffs imposed on colonies by no means secured monopoly of trade. Far more than their colonies, France, Germany, and Great Britain continued to be one another's best customers.

Some proponents of empire, known as social imperialists, argued that possession of an empire could resolve social as well as economic issues. An empire could be an outlet for a variety of domestic frustrations, especially for those nations concerned about overpopulation. German and Italian imperialists often argued that their nations needed colonies in which to resettle their multiplying poor. Once the overseas territories were acquired, however, few found them attractive for settlement.

## ■ Nationalistic Motives

To a large extent, empire building was triggered by the desire to assert national power. At the end of the nineteenth century, two major powers emerged, Russia and the United States. Compared with these giants, western European nations seemed small and insignificant, and many of their leaders believed that to compete effectively on the world stage they needed to become large territorial entities. Empires would enable them to achieve that goal.

The British Empire, with India as its crown jewel, constituted the largest, most powerful, and apparently the wealthiest of all the European domains. It was the envy of Europe. Although the real source of Britain's wealth and power was the country's industrial economy,

Ferry (feh-REE)

## CHRONOLOGY

| | |
|---|---|
| **1873** | Three Emperors' League |
| **1882** | Britain seizes Egypt |
| | Triple Alliance of Germany, Italy, and Austria-Hungary |
| **1884** | Three Emperors' League renewed |
| **1890** | Kaiser Wilhelm II dismisses Bismarck as chancellor |
| **1894** | Franco-Russian Alliance |
| | Beginning of the Dreyfus affair |
| **1900** | King of Italy assassinated |
| **1903** | Emmeline Pankhurst founds the Women's Social and Political Union |
| **1904** | Anglo-French Entente |
| **1905** | Einstein proposes theory of relativity |
| | Revolution in Russia |
| **1907** | Anglo-Russian Entente |
| **1908** | Young Turk rebellion in Ottoman Empire |
| **1911** | Italy grabs Libya |
| | Second Moroccan crisis |
| **June 28, 1914** | Archduke Franz Ferdinand is assassinated |
| **August 4, 1914** | With the entry of Britain, Europe is at war |

many people believed possession of a vast empire explained Britain's success. And so the British example stimulated other nations to carve out empires. Their activities, in turn, triggered British anxieties. Britain and France unleashed a scramble for Africa and Asia; in Asia Britain also competed with Russia.

France, defeated by Prussia in 1870, found in its colonies proof that it was still a Great Power. Germany and Italy, which formed their national identities relatively late, cast a jealous eye on the British and French empires and decided that if they were to be counted as

Great Powers, they too would need overseas colonies. Belgium's King Leopold II (r. 1876–1909) spun out various plans to acquire colonies to compensate for his nation's small size. And Britain, anxious at the emergence of rival economic and political powers in the late nineteenth century, found in its colonies a guarantee for the future.

In the race for colonies, worldwide strategic concerns stimulated expansion. Because the Suez Canal ensured the route to India, the British established a protectorate over Egypt in 1882. Beginning in the next decade, fearing that a rival power might threaten their position by encroaching on the Nile, they established control over the Nile Valley all the way south to Uganda (see Map 24.1). Russian expansion southward into central Asia toward Afghanistan was intended to avert a British takeover of this area, while the British movement northwestward to Afghanistan had the opposite intention—to prevent Russia from encroaching on India. The "great game" played by Russia and Britain in central Asia lasted the entire nineteenth century, ending only in 1907, with the signing of the Anglo-Russian Entente.

Much of this expansion was driven by the desire to control the often turbulent frontiers of newly acquired areas. Once those frontiers had been brought under control, there were, of course, again new frontiers that had to be subdued. As a Russian foreign minister said of such an incentive for expansion, "The chief difficulty is to know where to stop." The imperial powers rarely did.

The bitter rivalry among the Great Powers helps explain the division of the globe, but it also protected some regions from falling under European domination. In an effort to contain their rivalry in southeast Asia, Britain and France established Siam (now Thailand) as a buffer state. Russia seriously violated China's sovereignty by usurping large chunks of territory as it moved southward and eastward. The Western powers seized Chinese "treaty ports" and insisted on the right of their merchants and missionaries to move freely through the country. Yet most of China survived because the European powers held one another's ambitions in check. No state alone could conquer all of China; none would allow the others to do so either.

### ■ Other Ideological Motives

In addition to the search for profit and nationalistic pride, Europeans used a strong sense of mission to rationalize imperialism. Because Europeans had gained technological and scientific know-how, many imperialists believed it was Europe's duty to develop Africa and Asia for the benefit of colonizer and colonized. Railroads, telegraphs, hospitals, and schools would transform colonial peoples by opening them to what were seen as the beneficent influences of Europe. If necessary, these changes would be realized by force.

At the same time that Europeans were making substantial material progress as a result of industrialization, their wide-scale expansion overseas brought them into contact with Africans and Asians who had not created an industrial economy. They assumed that the dramatic disparity between their own material culture and that of colonial peoples was proof of their own innate superiority. Africans and Asians were seen as primitive, inferior peoples, still in their evolutionary "infancy." (See the feature "Weighing the Evidence: The Layout of the British Museum" on pages 840–841.)

Influenced by Darwin and his theory of the struggle for survival (see pages 795–797), many argued that just as competition among species existed in nature, so did groups of humans struggle for survival. Dubbed "Social Darwinists," these thinkers envisioned a world of fierce competition. They believed that the most serious struggle was among the races and, further, that the outcome was predetermined: the white race was destined to succeed, the nonwhites to succumb.

Many Europeans paternalistically believed they had a duty to "develop" these "infant" peoples. The British bard of imperialism, Rudyard Kipling (1865–1936), celebrated this view in his poem "White Man's Burden" (1899):

> Take up the White Man's burden—
> Send forth the best ye breed—
> Go bind your sons to exile
> To serve your captives' need.

Each nation was certain that providence had chosen it for a colonial mission. France, its leaders announced, had a civilizing mission to fulfill in the world; Prime Minister Ferry declared it the duty of his country "to civilize the inferior races." Although European states were colonial rivals, they also believed they were engaged in a joint mission overseas. Empire building underscored the belief in a common European destiny, as opposed to the ascribed savagery and backwardness of non-Europeans.

**Map 24.1   Africa in 1914**   European powers in the late nineteenth century conquered most of Africa. Only Liberia and Ethiopia were left unoccupied at the start of the war.

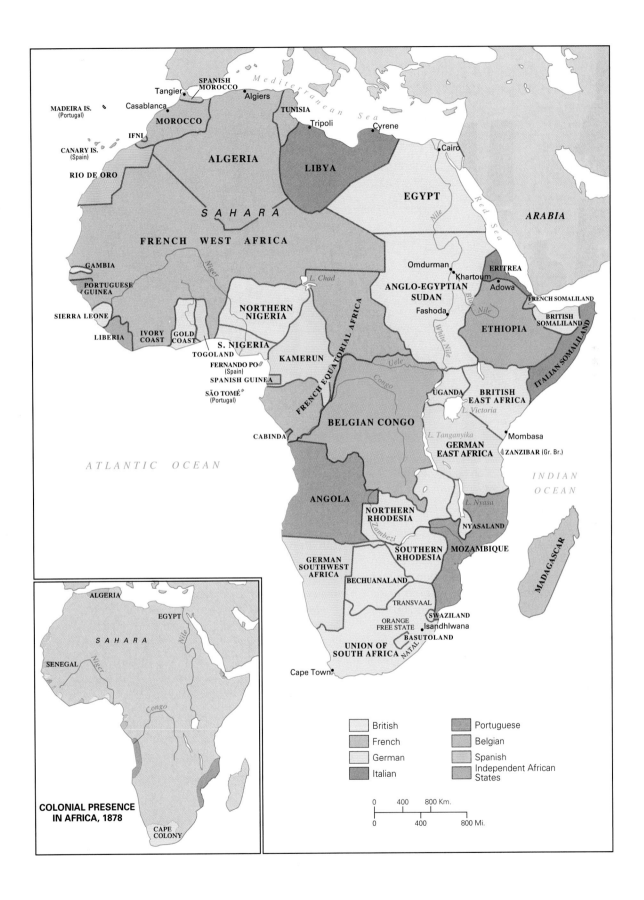

MADEIRA IS.
(Portugal)

SPANISH
MOROCCO

Tangier

Casablanca

MOROCCO

IFNI

CANARY IS.
(Spain)

RIO DE ORO

Algiers

TUNISIA

Tripoli

Cyrene

*Mediterranean Sea*

Cairo

ALGERIA

LIBYA

EGYPT

*ARABIA*

*Red Sea*

*S A H A R A*

*Nile*

FRENCH   WEST   AFRICA

GAMBIA

PORTUGUESE
GUINEA

SIERRA LEONE

LIBERIA

IVORY
COAST

GOLD
COAST

TOGOLAND

*Niger*

*L. Chad*

NORTHERN
NIGERIA

S. NIGERIA

FERNANDO PO
(Spain)

SPANISH GUINEA

SÃO TOMÉ
(Portugal)

KAMERUN

FRENCH EQUATORIAL AFRICA

Omdurman

Khartoum

ANGLO-EGYPTIAN
SUDAN

Fashoda

ERITREA

Adowa

FRENCH SOMALILAND

BRITISH
SOMALILAND

ETHIOPIA

*White Nile*

*Blue Nile*

ITALIAN SOMALILAND

*Uele*

*Congo*

BELGIAN CONGO

UGANDA

BRITISH
EAST
AFRICA

*L. Victoria*

*L. Tanganyika*

Mombasa

GERMAN
EAST AFRICA

ZANZIBAR (Gr. Br.)

CABINDA

*ATLANTIC   OCEAN*

*INDIAN
OCEAN*

ANGOLA

NORTHERN
RHODESIA

*L. Nyasa*

NYASALAND

*Zambezi*

SOUTHERN
RHODESIA

MOZAMBIQUE

MADAGASCAR

GERMAN
SOUTHWEST
AFRICA

BECHUANALAND

TRANSVAAL

SWAZILAND

ORANGE
FREE STATE

Isandhlwana

BASUTOLAND

NATAL

UNION OF
SOUTH AFRICA

Cape Town

## COLONIAL PRESENCE
## IN AFRICA, 1878

ALGERIA

EGYPT

*S A H A R A*

*Nile*

SENEGAL

*Niger*

*Congo*

CAPE
COLONY

| | British | | Portuguese |
|---|---|---|---|
| | French | | Belgian |
| | German | | Spanish |
| | Italian | | Independent African States |

0   400   800 Km.

0   400   800 Mi.

**Dutch Colonial Officials in the Dutch East Indies**    In this club in an outpost of empire (in present-day Indonesia), the comforts of European bourgeois life were lovingly re-created. Absent from this photo are the countless Indonesian servants who were part of the colonial officials' lives.    *(Royal Tropical Institute, Amsterdam)*

Pointing to historical antecedents, imperialists colored their activities with a hue of heroism. Many Europeans took satisfaction in the idea that their country performed feats akin to those of ancient Rome or the Crusaders, spreading "civilization" to far-flung empires. Colonial literature celebrated white men of action who, by their heroism, conquered and administered what had been large kingdoms or empires in Africa and Asia. Even novelists such as Kipling who tried to be sympathetic to "natives" nonetheless portrayed them as simple, almost childlike people, thus reinforcing European superiority.

Colonial acquisitions triggered public support for further expansion of the empire—support that was expressed by the founding of various colonial societies. Britain's Primrose League, which lobbied for empire as well as other patriotic goals, had 1 million members. The German Colonial Society, founded in 1888, had 43,000 members by 1914. The French and Italian groups were limited in size but had influential contacts with policymakers. Colonial societies generally drew their membership from the professional middle classes—civil servants, professors, and journalists—who were quite open to nationalist arguments. These societies produced a steady stream of propaganda favoring empire building.

Much of the literature celebrating empire building described it in masculine terms. European men were seen as proving their virility by going overseas, conquering, and running empires. They contrasted their manliness with the supposed effeminacy of the colonial peoples. And in building empires, Europeans asserted their manliness in comparison with their wives, sisters, or mothers. Women were to stay home; if later they came overseas, it was as helpmates to male colonial officials. A few women heroically explored distant lands; the Englishwoman Mary Kingsley (1862–1900) went on two exploration trips into Africa. (See the box "Reading Sources: Mary Kingsley Decries Racism but Defends Imperialism.") Her books were popular and focused British interest on overseas territories, but they in no way shook the established view that empire was a man's enterprise.

## ⁂ READING SOURCES

### Mary Kingsley Decries Racism but Defends Imperialism

*Mary Kingsley belonged to a small but hardy group of women who, despite the Victorian ideal of the woman as homebody, went exploring overseas. In two separate expeditions she visited the western part of Africa. Her observations of Africans represent a mixture of views: if she believes that Africans are different from Europeans, and even inferior in some respects, she also sees them as excelling in other fields. Kingsley bases her views on differences of culture, rather than of biology. She suggests that because Africans are less developed than Europeans, Britain has a special duty and obligation to them.*

I openly and honestly own I sincerely detest touching on this race question. For one thing, Science has not finished with it; for another, it belongs to a group of enormous magnitude, upon which I have no opinion, but merely feelings, and those of a nature which I am informed by superior people would barely be a credit to a cave man of the paleolithic period. . . . I am often cornered for the detail view, whether I can reconcile my admiration for Africans with my statement that they are a different kind of human being to white men. Naturally I can, to my own satisfaction, just as I can admire an oak tree or a palm; but it is an uncommonly difficult thing to explain. All that I can say is, that when I come back from a spell in Africa, the thing that makes me proud of being one of the English is not the manners of customs up here, certainly not the houses or the climate; but it is the thing embodied in a great railway engine. I once came home on a ship with an Englishman who had been in South West Africa, for seven unbroken years; he was sane and in his right mind. But no sooner did we get ashore at Liverpool, than he rushed at and threw his arms round a postman, to that official's embarrassment and surprise. Well, that is how I feel about the first magnificent bit of machinery I come across: it is the manifestation of the superiority of my race.

In philosophic moments I call superiority difference, from a feeling that it is not mine to judge the grade in these things. Careful scientific study has enforced on me, as it has on other students, the recognition that the African mind naturally approaches all things from a spiritual point of view. . . . [H]is mind works along the line that things happen because of the action of spirit upon spirit. . . . We think along the line that things happen from action of matter upon matter. . . . This steady sticking to the material side of things, I think, has given our race its dominion over matter; the want of it has caused the African to be notably behind us in this. . . .

This seems to me simply to lay upon us English for the sake of our honour that we keep clean hands and a cool head, and be careful of Justice; to do this we must know what there is we wish to wipe out of the African, and what there is we wish to put in, and so we must not content ourselves by relying materially on our superior wealth and power, and morally on catch phrases. All we need to look to is justice.

*Source:* Mary H. Kingsley, *West African Studies* (London: Macmillan, 1899), pp. 329–331.

### ■ Conquest, Administration, and Westernization

Industrialization gave Europeans the means to conquer overseas territories. They manufactured rapid-fire weapons. Their steam-driven gunboats and ocean-going vessels effectively projected power overseas. Telegraphic communications tied the whole world into a single network, allowing Europeans to gather information and coordinate military and political decision making. (See the feature "Information Technology: The Telegraph" in Chapter 23, pages 780–781.) Such advantages made Europeans virtually invincible in a colonial conflict. One remarkable exception was the defeat of the Italians in Adowa in 1896 at the hands of an Ethiopian force that was not only superior in numbers but better armed.

Conquest was often brutal. In September 1898, British-led forces at the Battle of Omdurman slaughtered 20,000 Sudanese. From 1904 to 1908, an uprising in southwest Africa against German rule led to the killing of an estimated 60,000 of the Herero people. The German general, who had expressly given an order to exterminate the whole population, was awarded a medal by Kaiser Wilhelm II.

Colonial governments could be brutally insensitive to the needs of the indigenous peoples. (See the box "Global Encounters: Chief Montshiwa Petitions Queen Victoria.") To save administrative costs in the 1890s, France put large tracts of land in the French Congo under the control of private rubber companies, which systematically and savagely coerced the local people to collect the sap of the rubber trees. When the scandal broke in Paris, the concessionary companies were abolished and the French state re-established its control. The most notorious example of exploitation, terror, and mass killings was connected with the Belgian Congo. Leopold II of Belgium had acquired it as a personal empire: it was his private domain, and he was not accountable to anyone for his actions there. To his shame, Leopold mercilessly exploited the Congo and its people. An international chorus of condemnation finally forced the king to surrender his empire and put it under the administration of the Belgian government, which abolished some of the worst features of Leopold's rule.

Brutal and abusive, imperialism spread Western technologies, institutions, and values. By 1914 Great Britain had built 40,000 miles of rail in India—nearly twice as much as in Britain. In India and Egypt, the British erected hydraulic systems that irrigated previously arid lands. Colonials built cities often modeled on the European grid system. In some cases they were graced with large, tree-lined avenues, and some neighborhoods were equipped with running water and modern sanitation. Schools, patterned after those in Europe, taught the imperial language and spread Western ideas and scientific knowledge—though only to a small percentage of the local population.

The European empire builders created political units that had never existed before. Although there had been many efforts in the past to join the whole Indian subcontinent under a single authority, the British were the first to accomplish this feat (see Map 24.2). Through a common administration, rail network, and trade, Britain gave Indians the sense of a common condition, leading in 1885 to the founding of the India Congress Party. The Congress Party platform included the demand for constitutional government, representative assemblies, and the rule of law—concepts all based on Western theory and practice. While initially demanding reforms within the British colonial system, eventually the Congress Party became India's major nationalist group.

In contact with the colonizers, intellectuals in colonial societies adopted a European ideology, nationalism. Nationalism was one of the major values Europeans successfully exported to its overseas possessions. In India, it

**Empire and Advertising**  Empire had become so much a part of European life that advertisements for biscuits included colonial scenes. Media such as advertisement made colonial domination seem normal, part of the natural order of things.  *(The Robert Opie Collection)*

## Chief Montshiwa Petitions Queen Victoria

*In 1885 Bechuanaland in southern Africa became a British protectorate. The Bechuana leaders saw British protection as a means to prevent takeover by the Boers, Dutch-speaking white settlers who were aggressively expanding in South Africa. The British were cavalier about their responsibilities, however, and a few years later allowed the British South Africa Company, a particularly exploitive enterprise, to take control of Bechuanaland. In protest, Chief Montshiwa (1815–1896), a major chief of the Baralong people, petitioned Queen Victoria for redress. His petition was supported by missionary lobbying, and most of Bechuanaland was saved from the clutches of the company.*

Mafeking, 16 August, 1895

To the Queen of England and Her Ministers:

We send greetings and pray that you are all living nicely. You will know us; we are not strangers. We have been your children since 1885.

Your Government has been good, and under it we have received much blessing, prosperity, and peace. . . .

We Baralong are very astonished because we hear that the Queen's Government wants to give away our country in the Protectorate to the Chartered Company; we mean the B[ritish] S[outh] A[frica] Company.

Our land there is a good land, our fathers lived in it and buried in it, and we keep all our cattle in it. What will we do if you give our land away? My people are increasing very fast and are filling the land.

We keep all the laws of the great Queen; we have fought for her; we have always been the friends of her people; we are not idle; we build houses; we plough many gardens; we sow. . . .

Why are you tired of ruling us? Why do you want to throw us away? We do not fight against your laws. We keep them and are living nicely.

Our words are No: No. The Queen's Government must not give my people's land in the Protectorate to the Chartered Company. . . .

Peace to you all, we greet you;

Please send a good word back.

I am etc,

Montshiwa

*Source:* S. M. Molema, *Montshiwa, 1815–1896* (Cape Town: G. Struik, 1966), pp. 181–182.

---

was those Indians who had been most exposed to British influence, by having studied in British schools or visited Britain, who were most likely to be nationalists. They founded a movement, known as Young India, harking back to Young Italy and other European nationalist movements founded in Mazzini's lifetime (see Chapter 21). Similarly, in French Algeria before World War I a movement named Young Algerians sprang up.

It was to be several decades before nationalism successfully challenged the European empires. In the meantime, Europeans took great satisfaction in their achievements overseas, confirming their sense of themselves as agents of progress, building a new and better world. Europeans arrogantly believed they knew what was best for other people; and they accepted force as a means of implementing their ideas. Such attitudes may also have colored the increasingly caustic relations between European states.

The ties of empire affected metropolitan cultures. The Hindi word for *bandit* became the English word *thug;* the Hindi number five, denoting the five ingredients necessary for a particular drink, became *punch.* Scenes from the colonial world often were the themes of European art, such as Paul Gauguin's° paintings of Tahiti and advertising

---

**Gauguin** (go-GEYN)

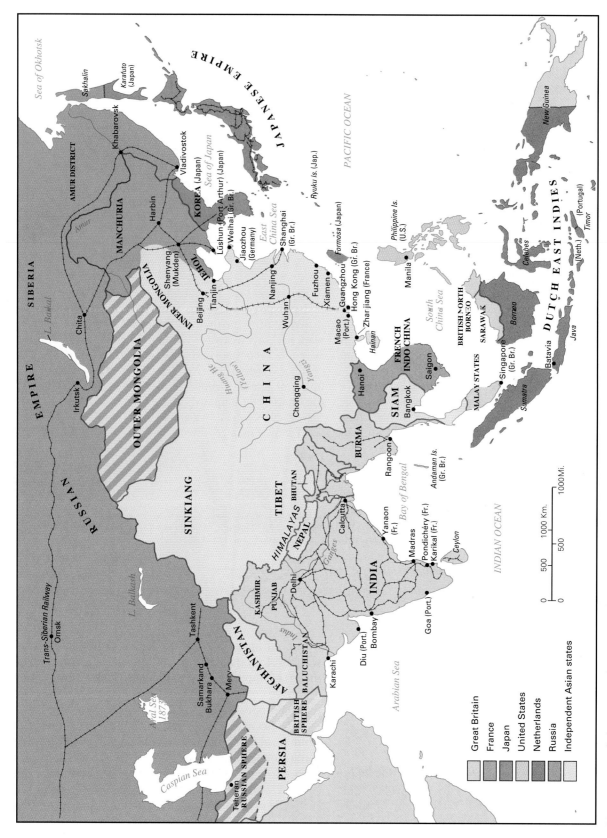

**Map 24.2  Asia in 1914**  China, Siam (Thailand), and a portion of Persia were the only parts of Asia still independent after the Great Powers, including the United States and Japan, subjugated the continent to alien rule.

**Map 24.3    European Migrations, 1820–1910**    Throughout the nineteenth century, millions of Europeans left home for overseas; most headed for the United States.    *(Source: Reproduced from* The Times Atlas of World History, *3d ed., by kind permission of Times Books. Some data from Eric Hobsbawm,* The Age of Empire, 1875–1914 *[New York: Pantheon, 1987].)*

posters for products as different as soap and whiskey. After the turn of the century, Pablo Picasso's° cubism reflected his growing familiarity with African art. In running the largest empire in the world, the British emphasized the need to develop masculine virtues. They cultivated competitive sports and stern schooling, which, they believed, would develop "character" and leadership. To administer their overseas colonies, Europeans developed sophisticated means of gathering and managing information that benefited metropolitan societies. A growing number of people from the colonies also came to live in European

cities. By 1900 some former colonial subjects, despite various forms of discrimination, had become full participants in the lives of their host countries; two East Indians won election to the British Parliament in the 1890s.

### ■ Overseas Migrations and the Spread of European Values

The nineteenth century saw a phenomenal expansion in European overseas migrations, adding to Europe's impact on other societies (see Map 24.3). Europeans had always migrated. They left villages for towns or, in the case of migrant farm laborers, traveled from village to village

**Picasso** (pih-KAH-so)

**Petersen: Emigrants Preparing to Depart**   Edward Petersen's 1890 painting depicts Danish emigrants readying to leave their homeland. Between 1860 and 1914, 300,000 people emigrated from the small country of Denmark, most of them to the United States.   *(Courtesy of the Aarhus Kunstmuseum. Reproduced with permission of Thomas, Poul, and Ole Hein Pedersen, Aarhus.)*

as the seasons changed and different crops needed to be harvested. With the expansion of European power abroad beginning in the sixteenth century, Europeans migrated overseas; between the sixteenth and eighteenth centuries around 6 million people left Europe. These numbers pale, however, when compared with the nineteenth-century figures: between 1870 and 1914, 55 million Europeans left the Continent for the Americas, Australia, and New Zealand.

Certain European groups migrated to specific areas. Scandinavians settled in the upper midwestern United States, Italians in Argentina, Germans in Paraguay, Britons in South Africa, Portuguese in Brazil, each group leaving its imprint on its adopted land. The upper Midwest was known as "the great desert," but Scandinavians used farm techniques from their homelands to cultivate these dry lands. German Mennonites settled in Kansas and brought with them a strain of wheat that became the basis of the state's prosperity. Immigrants made similar impacts on urban sites. Durban in South Africa

looks like an English city, and some towns in Paraguay resemble Alpine villages of southern Germany. The Germans who came to Milwaukee, Wisconsin, made it a city of beer and strong socialist convictions, reminiscent of home.

Emigration scattered peoples and extended cultures overseas. By 1914 nearly half of all Irish and Portuguese lived outside Europe. The settlers consumed many European goods and in turn produced for the European market, increasing the centrality of Europe in the world economy. The migrations across the globe reinforced imperial conquest, further imprinting Europe's stamp on peoples and societies abroad.

If Europe appeared triumphant, its supremacy rested on frail foundations—mainly force. From the start, local resistance and even expressions of proto-nationalist sentiments challenged Europe's supremacy. Imperial powers, worried that their European rivals or their colonial subjects might cause trouble, looked to force to assure the future of their empires.

# FROM OPTIMISM TO ANXIETY: POLITICS AND CULTURE

ANY of the beliefs and institutions that had seemed so solid in the "age of optimism" found themselves under attack in the next generation. Forces hostile to liberalism became increasingly vocal. In the arts and philosophy, the earlier confidence was replaced by doubt, relativism, and a desire to flee the routines of everyday life.

## ■ The Erosion of the Liberal Consensus

In 1850 liberalism appeared to be the ascendant ideology, and liberals assumed that with the passage of time more and more people would be won over to their world-view. By 1900, however, liberalism faced serious challenges. Principles eroded within the liberal camp, and in addition, various ideas and movements—some new, some rooted in the past—chipped away at the liberal consensus. Prominent among these were socialism, anarchism, a new political right, racism, and anti-Semitism.

The undermining of the liberal consensus began among liberals themselves, who, in the face of changing circumstances, retreated from some of their basic tenets. For example, one of the principal emphases of liberalism had always been free trade. But under the pressure of economic competition, liberals supported tariffs at home and created closed markets for the mother country overseas in the empire.

Historically, liberals had typically stood for an expansion of civil liberties, yet several groups were denied their rights. Power remained an exclusively male domain, and liberal males saw nothing wrong or inconsistent in continuing to deny women both the vote and free access to education and professional advancement. In the face of labor agitation, many liberals no longer unconditionally supported civil liberties for workers and favored instead the violent crushing of strikes.

Similarly, liberals had always upheld the sanctity of private property, but under the pressure of events, they abandoned this principle as an absolute goal. To ensure workers' safety, they placed limits on employers by passing legislation on working conditions. In some countries, some supported progressive income taxes, which other liberals perceived as a serious invasion of private property. When it became clear that a free market was unable to meet many human needs, welfare programs were instituted in several countries. These reforms were intended to strengthen the state by winning support from the masses. But because they reflected the liberals' willingness to breach fundamental principles, these measures also revealed the apparent inability of liberal ideology to deal with the real-life problems of the day.

## ■ The Growth of Socialism and Anarchism

Among the groups challenging the power and liberal ideology of the middle classes were the socialist parties, both Marxist and non-Marxist, whose goal was to win the support of workers by espousing their causes. Socialists varied in their notions of how their goals should be achieved: some favored pursuing objectives gradually and peacefully; others were dedicated to a violent overthrow of capitalist society.

In Britain, where the Liberal Party was more open to the needs of workers than in other European states, a separate socialist party, the Independent Labour Party, was established relatively late, in 1893. Not until the 1920s did this party gain any particular electoral success. More influential in the late nineteenth century was the Fabian Society, founded in 1884 and named after the Roman general Fabian, who was noted for winning by avoiding open, pitched battles. The Fabians criticized the capitalist system as inefficient, wasteful, and unjust. They believed that by gradual, democratic means, Parliament could transfer factories and land from the private sector to the state, which would manage them for the benefit of society as a whole. Socialism was a desirable system that would replace capitalism because it was more efficient and more just. It would come into being not through class war but through enlightened ideas. This gradualist approach became the hallmark of British socialism, shaping the ideology of the Labour Party.

In Germany various strands of socialism came together when a single united party was formed in 1875. But within a few years a debate that was to break out in most socialist parties rent the German party: Could socialism come about by gradual democratic means, or, as Marx had contended, would it require a violent revolution? The German socialist leader, Eduard Bernstein° (1850–1932), who had visited England and had soaked up the influence of the Fabians, argued for gradualism in a book with the telling English title *Evolutionary Socialism* (1898). Marx had been wrong, said Bernstein, to suggest that capitalism necessarily led to the increasing wretchedness of the working class. The capitalist economy had in fact expanded and been able to provide for steadily improved conditions. Workers would not need to seize power by some cataclysmic act. Rather, by piecemeal democratic action they could win more

Bernstein (BURN-stine)

**Jean Jaurès**    An ideological moderate, the French socialist leader Jean Jaurès (1859–1914) was a firebrand as a speaker, one of France's greatest orators. Much of his socialism was based on ethical notions about social justice, rather than on Marxist doctrine. Here Jaurès addresses a socialist gathering in 1913.    *(Roger-Viollet)*

power and legislate on behalf of their interests. Since he argued for a revision of Marxist theory, Bernstein was labeled a "revisionist." Opposing him in this great debate was the party theoretician Karl Kautsky° (1854–1938). Kautsky insisted that nothing short of a revolution would institute socialism.

Like most other socialists in Europe, the German socialists rejected revisionism and claimed to embrace the doctrine of a violent proletarian revolution, but in fact pursued revisionist policies. Socialists in practice had become another parliamentary party that hoped to reach its goals through legislation.

Another movement that sought to liberate the downtrodden was anarchism, which proclaimed that humans could be free only when the state had been abolished. According to anarchist theory, in a stateless society people would naturally join together in com-

munes and share the fruits of their labor. Some anarchists believed they could achieve their goal by educating people. Others were more impatient and hoped to speed up the process by making direct attacks on existing authority. The Russian nobleman Michael Bakunin° (1814–1876), frustrated at the authoritarianism of his homeland, became a lifelong anarchist. He challenged tsarism at home and participated in the 1848 revolutions throughout Europe. He viewed all governments as repressive and declared unilateral war on them: "The passion for destruction is also a creative passion." His ideas were particularly influential in Italy, Spain, and parts of France, especially among the artisan classes.

Many anarchists of this period wanted to bring about the new society by "propaganda of the deed." An attack on the bastions of power, these anarchists believed, could bring about the dissolution of the state. They formed secret terrorist organizations that assassinated heads of state or those close to them. Between 1894 and 1901, anarchists killed a president of France, a prime minister of Spain, an empress of Austria, a king of Italy, and a president of the United States. These murders fixed the popular image of anarchism as a violence-prone ideology. More important, such manifestations of the "propaganda of the deed" produced no particular improvement in the lives of the working-class people on whose behalf these deadly campaigns had supposedly been launched.

Without accepting the anarchists' methods, some in the labor movement shared their hostility toward parliamentary institutions. A working-class program, labor activists argued, could be implemented only by a pure workers' movement, such as unionization. Workers should shun the political arena and concentrate on direct action. According to this line of thought, known as "syndicalism°" (after the French word for unions), workers should amass their power in unions, and at the right moment carry out a general strike, crippling capitalist society and bringing it down. Syndicalism was particularly popular in Mediterranean countries, where its more militant form, anarcho-syndicalism, radicalized labor and made a sizable number of workers hostile to parliamentarism.

European socialism also attempted an international presence. In 1864 Marx had participated in the founding of the International Workers' Association, which fell prey to internal dissension and dissolved after a few years. Known as the First International, it was followed by a more robust organization, the Second International, in 1889. The International met yearly and debated issues of

---

**Kautsky** (KOUT-skee)

**Bakunin** (bah-KOO-neen)    **syndicalism** (SIN-dih-ka-lizm)

concern to socialists in general, including the worsening relations among European states. As early as 1893 the International urged European states to resolve their conflicts by mandatory arbitration. In 1907, sensing impending war, the International called on the workers to strike and refuse military service in case of international conflict. The International saw itself as a bulwark of peace; it did not realize that once war broke out, Europeans, including socialists, would be swept up in nationalist fervor and would willingly go to war. Although most socialists advocated peace at home and abroad, many had contributed to a militant discourse with their class war rhetoric.

### ■ The New Right, Racism, and Anti-Semitism

The traditional opponents of liberalism on the political right were the conservatives, wedded to preserving the existing order. Beginning in the 1880s, however, a "new right" emerged that was populist and demagogic. Although conservatives had been wary of nationalism, the new right embraced it. Alienated by industry, democracy, and social egalitarianism, many in this new right rejected doctrines of human equality and embraced racist ideologies.

Racist thinking was common in the nineteenth century. Many Europeans believed human races were not only different physiologically but also—as a result of these biological variations—differently endowed in intelligence and other qualities (see pages 798–799). Europeans were often ethnocentric, convinced they were the epitome of humankind, whereas members of other races belonged to lesser groups. In midcentury the Frenchman Arthur de Gobineau° (1816–1882) published his *Essay on the Inequality of Human Races,* declaring that race "dominates all other problems and is the key to it." Biologists and early anthropologists made similar statements, thus giving racism a "scientific" aura. Throughout the second half of the nineteenth century, race was thought to be the principal explanation for the differences that were discovered among human groupings.

These racist ideas helped fuel anti-Semitism. For centuries Jews had been the object of suspicion and bigotry. Originally, the basis of the prejudice was religious. As early as the Middle Ages, however, the argument emerged that "Jewish blood" was different. And with the popularization of pseudoscientific racist thinking in the nineteenth century, Jews were commonly viewed as a separate, inferior race, unworthy of the same rights as the majority of the population.

Historically, Christians had relegated the Jews in their midst to marginal positions. In the Middle Ages, when land was the basis of wealth and prestige, Jews had been confined to such urban trades as cattle trading and moneylending. They incurred high risks by lending money: they often were not paid back and faced unsympathetic courts when they tried to collect their debts. To counteract these risks, Jewish moneylenders charged high interest rates that earned them their unpopular reputation as usurers.

The emancipation of the Jews, which began in France with the Revolution and spread to Germany and Austria by the 1860s, provided them opportunities they had not had before. Some members of society found it hard to adjust to the prominence a few Jews gained. Because their increased social standing and success were concurrent with the wrenching social transformations brought by industrialization and urbanization, anti-Semites pointed to the Jews as the perpetrators of these unsettling changes.

Many people perceived Jews as prototypical of the new capitalist class. Although most Jews were of modest means, resentment of the rich often was aimed at Jews. Earlier in the century, many anti-Semites were socialists, speaking on behalf of the working class. Later they came from among the petty bourgeois—small shopkeepers and artisans—who felt threatened by economic change.

Political movements based on anti-Semitism were founded in the 1880s. They depicted Jews as dangerous and wicked and called for their exclusion from the political arena and from certain professions. In some cases proponents suggested that Jews be expelled from the state. Karl Lueger (1844–1928) was elected mayor of Vienna, on an anti-Semitic platform. In Berlin the emperor's chaplain, Adolf Stöcker° (1835–1909), founded an anti-Semitic party, hoping to make political inroads among the working-class supporters of socialism. In France Edouard Drumont (1844–1917) published one of the best-sellers of the second half of the nineteenth century, *Jewish France,* in which he blamed all the nation's misfortunes on the Jews.

In Russia organized *pogroms,* or mass attacks, on Jews killed two thousand in the 1880s and one thousand in 1905, frightening 2 million Jews into exile, mostly to the United States. Russian Jews lived under social as well as legal disabilities; condemned to second-class citizenship, they won full emancipation only with the Bolshevik Revolution of 1917.

In the face of growing hostility, some Jews speculated that they would be safe only in their own nation. The

---

**Gobineau** (go-bee-NO)

**Stöcker** (SHTOE-kur)

## ❧ R E A D I N G   S O U R C E S

### Nietzsche Declares God to Be Dead

*By pronouncing God dead, Nietzsche believed he had liberated people from tradition and conventions. Fully free, they can explore all the potentialities of human existence, test the boundaries of what is possible—if, indeed, there are any boundaries. Consider the deliberate shock value of Nietzsche's formulation.*

The greatest recent event—that "God is dead," that the belief in the Christian God has ceased to be believable—is even now beginning to cast its first shadows over Europe. For the few, at least, whose eyes, whose *suspicion* in their eyes, is strong and sensitive enough for this spectacle, some sun seems to have set just now. . . . In the main, however, this may be said: the event itself is much too great, too distant, too far from the comprehension of the many even for the tidings of it to be thought of as having *arrived* yet, not to speak of the notion that many people might know what has really happened here, and what must collapse now that this belief has been undermined—all that was built upon it, leaned on it, grew into it; for example our European morality.

Indeed, we philosophers and "free spirits" feel as if a new dawn were shining on us when we receive the tidings that "the old god is dead"; our heart overflows with gratitude, amazement, anticipation, expectation. At last the horizon appears free again to us, even granted that it is not bright; at last our ships may venture out again, venture out to face any danger; all the daring of the lover of knowledge is permitted again; the sea, *our* sea, lies open again; perhaps there has never yet been such an "open sea."

*Source:* Walter Kaufmann, ed., *The Portable Nietzsche* (New York: Viking Press, 1954), pp. 447–448.

---

Austrian Jewish journalist Theodore Herzl° (1860–1904), outraged by the Dreyfus affair in France, in which a Jewish officer was imprisoned on trumped-up charges of treason (see page 828), founded the Zionist movement. He advocated establishing a Jewish state in the Jews' ancient homeland of Israel. In the beginning, the Zionist movement won a following only in eastern Europe, where the Jews were particularly ill-treated, but by 1948, Zionism culminated in the creation of the state of Israel.

Various manifestations of anti-Semitism revealed the vulnerability of tolerance, one of the basic ideas of liberalism. It became eminently clear that racism, with its penchant for irrationality and violence, could easily be aroused.

### ■ Irrationality and Uncertainty

In contrast to the confidence in reason and science that had prevailed at midcentury, the era starting in the 1880s wrestled with the issues of irrationality and uncer-

tainty—in philosophy, in science, in the arts, even in religion. The positivism of the earlier era had emphasized surface reality of "progress" but neglected inner meaning and ignored the emotional and intuitive aspects of life. By the 1890s a neoromantic mood, emphasizing emotion and feeling, stirred major intellectual movements. The spotlight was no longer on reason, but on instinct.

In philosophy the tension between reason and emotion was vividly expressed in the work of the German philosopher Friedrich Nietzsche° (1844–1900), who proclaimed that rationality had led humankind into a meaningless abyss. Reason would not resolve human problems, nor would any preconceived ideas. "God is dead," Nietzsche announced. With no God, humankind was free of all outside constraints, free to overthrow all conventions. (See the box "Reading Sources: Nietzsche Declares God to Be Dead.") Nietzsche admonished his readers to challenge existing institutions and accepted truths and to create new ones.

---

**Herzl** (HER-tsl)

**Friedrich Nietzsche** (FREED-reesh NEET-sheh)

The French philosopher Henri Bergson° (1859–1940) argued that science—and indeed life—must be interpreted not rationally but intuitively. "Science," Bergson declared, "can teach us nothing of the truth; it can only serve as a rule of action." Humans could best understand meaningful truths—such as the truth of religion, literature, and art—by relying on their feelings.

Various disciplines of knowledge subscribed to the notion that humans were often irrational, motivated by deep-seated instinctive forces. The Austro-Hungarian Sigmund Freud° (1856–1939) founded psychoanalysis, a method of treating psychic disorders by exploring the unconscious. Freud believed that people were motivated not only by observed reality but also by their unconscious feelings and emotions. Whereas earlier physicians had described the mental condition of "hysteria" as a physical ailment, Freud saw its roots as psychological, the result of unresolved inner conflicts. Although Freud's work was influenced by rational methods, he stressed that irrational forces played a significant role in human behavior.

The social theorist Gaetano Mosca (1858–1941) in his book *Elements of Political Science* (1891) posited that in all societies—even democratic ones—an elite minority rules over the majority. The desire to dominate is a basic part of human nature; even in democratic or socialist societies, this thirst for power is never slaked. Beneath slogans touting the public good lies selfish ambition. Thus, as did Freud, Mosca suggested that surface appearances are deceptive and at heart humans are guided by irrational forces.

The scientists of this period seemed to underscore the conclusions of contemporaries who questioned the knowableness of the world through reason. In 1905 Albert Einstein (1879–1955) proposed the theory of relativity, which undermined the certainties of Newtonian physics. Einstein's theory demonstrated that time and space are not absolute but exist relative to the observer. Much of the research in atomic theory also revealed variations and unexplained phenomena. For example, the work of German physicist Max Planck (1858–1947) upset fundamental theories about the nature of the atom with his quantum theory. Planck showed that energy in the form of electrons is absorbed or emitted not continuously, as previously assumed, but rather discontinuously. A subatomic particle such as an electron could be in two places at the same time, until measured. The stability of nature was questioned; waves could be particles, but particles could also be waves; causes were not necessarily linked to effects. Some scientists no longer shared

**Bergson** (BERK-sohn)   **Freud** (FROYD)

**Freud in 1909**   Although much of Sigmund Freud's career still lay ahead of him, he already had established a reputation as the founder of modern psychology.   *(Sigmund Freud Copyrights/ Mary Evans Picture Library)*

the self-confidence that their colleagues had maintained half a century earlier, finding it increasingly difficult to believe in absolute certainties.

In the arts, the idea of being *avant-garde*—French for "forefront"—took hold among creative people. Breaking the taboos of society and the conventions of one's craft seemed to be signs of artistic creativity. Artistic movements proclaimed idiosyncratic manifestos and constantly called for the rejection of existing forms of expression and the creation of new ones. The symbolists in France and Italy, the expressionists in Germany, the futurists in Italy, and the secessionists in Austria all reflected the sense that they were living through a fractured period.

In protest against the mass culture of their day, artists focused on images that were different and unique. Unlike earlier art, which had a clear message, the art of this era did not. Many artists no longer believed their role was to portray or spread ideals. Rather, they tended to be introspective and even self-absorbed. The public at

Austrian artist Egon Schiele° (1890–1918) and the Norwegian painter Edvard Munch° (1863–1944) emphasized scenes of violence, fear, and sheer horror.

Musicians too stretched the traditional forms of their art. Claude Debussy° (1862–1918) defied established rules of tone and harmony of Western music and its usage of orchestral instruments in works such as *Prelude* and *Afternoon of a Faun* (1894) and his opera *Pelléas and Mélisande* (1902). Rather than being cerebral, he insisted, his work was instinctive.

Religion, too, felt the effects of intellectual challenge. Although large numbers of people still held traditional religious beliefs and followed traditional practices, indifference to organized religion spread. In urban areas of western Europe, church attendance declined; as these regions urbanized, they became increasingly secular. But with the decline of traditional Christian practices, various forms of mysticism became more widespread. Some people were attracted to Eastern religions such as Buddhism and Hinduism and to other mystical beliefs. These attitudes may have reflected a loss of faith in Western culture itself. As the century came to an end, a number of intellectuals argued that their culture, like the century, was destined for decline.

**Munch: The Scream** Painted in 1893, this work reflects the fear and horror that some intellectuals experienced at the end of the nineteenth century. *(Edvard Munch,* The Scream, *1893. Tempera and oil pastel on cardboard. 91 × 73.5 cm. Photo: J. Lathion, Nasjonalgalleriet, Oslo. Copyright Munch Museum, Oslo, 1993)*

large found it difficult to decipher the meaning of the new art, but bewildered or not, a number of patrons supported the avant-garde artists' talent and insight.

Unlike the realists who preceded them, artists in the 1890s surrendered to neoromanticism, trying to investigate and express inner forces. As the French painter Paul Gauguin (1848–1903) noted, the purpose of painting was to communicate not how things looked but the emotions they conveyed. The Russian Wassily Kandinsky° (1866–1944) asked viewers of his art to "look at the picture as a graphic representation of a mood and not as a representation of objects." Artists appeared to be examining the hidden anxieties of society. The Frenchman Gustave Moreau° (1826–1898) displayed monsters, creations of nightmare, byproducts of the unconscious. The

## VULNERABLE DEMOCRACIES

**B**Y the end of the nineteenth century, most of Europe's political systems floundered in crisis. The major powers with democratic institutions—Great Britain, France, and Italy—confronted volatile public opinion and had difficulty winning a broad consensus for their policies. They struggled with new challenges emerging from an expanded electorate that was at times frustrated by the failure of the system to respond to its demands. Turning away from the democratic precept of resolving differences through the ballot and legislation, many people—both in government and out—were willing to resort to extraparliamentary means, including violence, to see their interests prevail.

### ■ Great Britain

In Great Britain the Reform Bill of 1884 transformed the political landscape by giving the vote to two of every three adult men, doubling suffrage to 5 million. The appeal of this enlarged electorate tempted politicians to

---

**Wassily Kandinsky** (vass-IH-lee kan-DIN-skee)
**Moreau** (mo-RO)

**Egon Schiele** (EYE-gohn SHE-lee)   **Munch** (MOONGK)
**Debussy** (day-bew-SEE)

make demagogic promises, which were often broken later, to the exasperation of their constituents. It was also more difficult to reach compromises in a Parliament that no longer consisted of a fairly limited class of people with common interests and values. The British political system was faced with issues it was unable to resolve peacefully, and it was obliged—uncharacteristically—to resort to force or the threat of force.

As in earlier periods, Ireland proved to be a persistent problem. The political consciousness of the Irish had risen considerably, and they seethed under alien rule. In an attempt to quell Irish opposition in 1886, Prime Minister William Gladstone° proposed autonomy, or "home rule," for Ireland. There were many objections to such a plan, the most serious being that if Ireland, a predominantly Catholic country, ruled itself, the local Protestant majority in Ulster, the northeast part of the island, would be overwhelmed and likely to fall under Catholic control. "Home rule is Rome rule," chanted the supporters of Ulster Protestantism. Among Gladstone's own Liberals, many opposed changing the existing relationship between England and its neighboring possession. They seceded from the Liberals and formed the Unionist Party, which, in coalition with the Conservatives, ruled the country from 1886 to 1905. When the Liberals returned to power in 1906, they again proposed home rule. In 1911 the House of Commons finally passed a home rule bill, but it was obstructed in the House of Lords and was not slated to go into effect until September 1914.

In the process of wrangling over the Irish issue, many segments of British society showed they were willing to resort to extralegal and even violent means. Fearing Catholic domination, Protestants in northern Ireland armed themselves, determined to resist home rule. In the rest of Ireland, Catholic groups took up arms, too, insisting on the unity of the island; they were ready to fight for home rule for the whole of Ireland. The Conservative Party in Britain, which opposed home rule, called on Ulster to revolt. British officers threatened to resign their commissions rather than fight Ulster. The behavior of the Conservatives and the army indicated a breakdown of order and authority, a disregard for tradition by two of its bulwarks. Only the outbreak of world war in 1914 delayed a showdown over Ireland, and then by only a few years.

Once back in power in 1906, the Liberals committed themselves to an impressive array of social reforms but were frustrated by the difficulty of getting their program through the House of Lords. The feisty Liberal chancellor of the exchequer, David Lloyd George (1863–1945), ex-

Gladstone (GLAD-sten)

pressed his outrage that the will of the people was being thwarted by a handful of magnates in the House of Lords, sitting there not by election but by hereditary right.

The Liberals' social reform program included old-age pensions. To finance them, Lloyd George proposed raising income taxes and death duties and levying a tax on landed wealth. A bill with these measures easily passed the House of Commons in 1909 but was stymied in the upper chamber, where many members were prominent landowners. The House of Lords technically had the power to amend or reject a bill passed by Commons, but for nearly 250 years it had been tacitly understood that the Lords did not have the right to reject a money bill. Nonetheless, motivated by economic self-interest and personal spite against the Liberals, a majority in the House of Lords disregarded convention and voted against the bill. This decision provoked a major constitutional crisis.

The Liberal government wanted not only to pass its bill but also to reduce the power of the Lords. In 1911 it sponsored a bill, quickly passed by the House of Commons, to limit the House of Lords to a suspensive veto. This would mean that a bill defeated in the House of Lords could be prevented from going into effect for only a predetermined period—in this case, two years. The House of Lords refused at first to pass such a law. But at the request of the government, the king threatened to appoint four hundred new lords. Reluctantly, the House of Lords passed the bill.

During the debate over the bill, Conservatives—the representatives of British traditionalism and the upholders of decorum—resorted to brawling and refused to let the prime minister speak. It was the first time in British parliamentary history that such breach of conduct had occurred. The British Parliament, considered the model for supporters of free institutions, had shown itself unable to resolve issues in a civil manner.

Violence also appeared in another unlikely place: the women's suffrage movement. Most liberal males, when speaking of the need to extend human liberty, had excluded women. Toward the end of the nineteenth century, that bastion, too, was under siege. Women began to organize into groups devoted to winning the vote but had little initial success. In 1903 Emmeline Pankhurst (1858–1928) and her two daughters founded the Women's Social and Political Union, whose goal was immediate suffrage.

Angered and frustrated by their lack of progress, in 1906 the suffragists (often referred to by contemporaries as "suffragettes"), led by the Pankhursts, began a more militant program of protest—disturbing proceedings in

**A Suffragist Attempts to Chain Herself to the Gates of Buckingham Palace, London, 1914** In their effort to win the vote, women resorted to public protests and the police often violently intervened. *(Popperfoto/Archive Photos)*

Parliament, breaking windows at the prime minister's residence, slashing canvases at the National Gallery, burning down empty houses, dropping acid into mailboxes, and throwing bombs. They even threatened the lives of the prime minister and the king. Suffragists who were arrested often engaged in hunger strikes. Fearing they would die, the authorities force-fed the women—a painful and humiliating procedure. Female protesters were also physically attacked by male thugs. (See the box "Reading Sources: Pankhurst Testifies on Women's Rights.") That women would resort to violence, and that men in and outside of the government would retaliate in kind, demonstrated how widespread the cult of force had become.

### ■ France

The Third French Republic, founded in 1870 after France's humiliating military defeat at the hands of the Prussians, also struggled with an ongoing series of crises. Challenged by enemies on the political left and right

who continually called for the abolition of democracy, the regime found itself buffeted from all sides.

The French government itself contributed to the unstable political situation by its lack of strong leadership. The need to build coalitions among the several parties in the parliament rewarded those politicians who had moderate programs and were flexible. Thus there was little premium on firm ideas and commitments, and the prime minister was often more a conciliator than a leader. Further, lackluster leadership appealed to republicans, who continued to fear that a popular leader might—as Louis Napoleon had in 1851—exploit his support to make himself dictator.

The regime seemed to lurch from scandal to scandal. The most notorious was the Dreyfus affair. In October 1894, Captain Alfred Dreyfus° (1859–1935) of the French army was arrested and charged with passing military secrets to the German embassy. Dreyfus seems to have attracted suspicion because he was the only Jewish

---

**Dreyfus** (DRY-fooss)

## ❧ READING SOURCES

---

### Pankhurst Testifies on Women's Rights

*In 1908 the suffragists, led by Emmeline Pankhurst, issued a handbill calling on the people of London to "rush" Parliament and win the vote for women. The legal authorities interpreted their action as a violation of the peace, and several suffragists, including Pankhurst, were put on trial. They put up a spirited defense, in which Pankhurst movingly explained her motives for leading the suffragist cause.*

---

I want you to realise how we women feel; because we are women, because we are not men, we need some legitimate influence to bear upon our lawmakers. Now, we have tried every way. We have presented larger petitions than were ever presented for any other reform, we have succeeded in holding greater public meetings than men have ever had for any reform, in spite of the difficulty which women have in throwing off their natural diffidence, that desire to escape publicity which we have inherited from generations of our foremothers; we have broken through that. We have faced hostile mobs at street corners, because we were told that we could not have that representation for our taxes which men have won unless we converted the whole of the country to our side. Because we have done this, we have been misrepresented, we have been ridiculed, we have had contempt poured upon us. The ignorant mob at the street corner has been incited to offer us violence, which we have faced unarmed and unprotected by the safeguards which Cabinet Ministers have. We know that we need the protection of the vote even more than men have needed it. . . .

We believe that if we get the vote it will mean better conditions for our unfortunate sisters. We know what the condition of the woman worker is . . . and we have been driven to the conclusion that only through legislation can any improvement be effected, and that that legislation can never be effected until we have the same power as men have to bring pressure to bear upon our representatives and upon Governments to give us the necessary legislation. . . .

I should never be here if I had the same kind of power that the very meanest and commonest of men have—the same power that the wife-beater has, the same power that the drunkard has. I should never be here if I had that power, and I speak for all the women who have come before you and other magistrates. . . .

If you had power to send us to prison, not for six months, but for six years, for sixteen years, or for the whole of our lives, the Government must not think that they can stop this agitation. It will go on. . . .

We are here not because we are law-breakers; we are here in our efforts to become lawmakers.

*Source:* F. W. Pethick Lawrence, ed. *The Trial of the Suffragette Leaders* (London: The Women's Press, 1909), pp. 21–24.

---

officer on the general staff. The evidence was flimsy—a handwritten letter that some thought Dreyfus had penned, although other experts testified that the handwriting was not that of the young officer.

This letter, and materials that later turned out to be forged, led the French army to court-martial Dreyfus and sentence him to life imprisonment on Devil's Island off the coast of South America. By March 1896, the general staff had evidence that another officer, Major Esterhazy, was actually the spy. But to reopen the case would be to admit the army had made an error, and that the general staff refused to do.

By late 1897, when the apparent miscarriage of justice became widely known, French society split over "the affair." The political left, including many intellectuals, argued for reopening the case. For them it was crucial that justice be carried out. The army and its supporters, right-wing politicians, royalists, and zealous Catholics, argued that the decision should stand. As the bulwark against internal and foreign threats, the army should be above challenge, and the fate of a single man—guilty or innocent—was immaterial.

The affair unleashed a swirl of controversy and rioting, which led the government to order a retrial in 1899.

**Riots in Italian Parliament** Party strife and conflicts between individuals in the Italian parliament were so severe that often they degenerated into fisticuffs. This illustration catches a particularly violent moment of a parliamentary debate. *(Madeline Grimoldi)*

But the court again found Dreyfus guilty—this time with "extenuating circumstances" and the recommendation that he be pardoned. Finally, in 1906, Dreyfus was fully exonerated. He ended his days as a general in the army that had subjected him to so much suffering.

The strong encouragement many Catholics gave to those who supported the original verdict confirmed the republicans' belief that the church was a menace to the regime. The Radical Party, the staunchest backers of Dreyfus, won the elections in 1898. Despite its title, the Radical Party backed moderate social reforms. It was uncompromising, however, in its anticlericalism, determined to wreak vengeance on Catholics and end the influence of the church once and for all. In 1905 the parliament passed a law separating church and state, thus ending the privileged position the Catholic Church had enjoyed. Violent language and physical confrontations on both sides accompanied this division. Catholics trying to prevent state officials from entering churches to take required inventories sometimes resorted to force, using weapons or, in one case, a bear chained to the church. Armed soldiers broke down church doors and dragged priests away.

Labor problems also triggered repeated confrontations with the government. Increased labor militancy produced long, drawn-out strikes, which in 1904 alone led to the loss of 4 million workdays. There was agitation in the countryside, too, particularly in 1907 in the Midi, the south of France. This region suffered from a crisis in the wine industry caused by a disease that attacked the vines, competition from cheap foreign wines, and fraud. More important, the region witnessed increased rural proletarianization as population grew and larger landholdings were concentrated in fewer hands. Rural militancy led to revolt in 1907. Troops were sent in, killing dozens and winning for the Radical regime the title "government of assassins."

## ■ Italy

The third major power in Europe to adopt parliamentary government also had grave problems. Although unification took place in 1860, Italy found genuine unity elusive. The country was plagued by regionalism, social strife, and an unrepresentative political system. As in the past, the south especially challenged the central government. Assertive regionalism, crime, and poverty made this area resistant to most government programs.

The parliamentary system established in 1860 was far from democratic. Property qualifications limited suffrage to less than 3 percent of the population. And as a result of the persistence of *trasformismo* (see Chapter 22)—the practice by which government corrupted and co-opted the opposition—electoral choice was short-circuited.

Between 1870 and 1890 the Italian government introduced some important reforms, but it was difficult to improve the general standard of living for a people undergoing rapid population growth. In the fifty years after unification, the population increased from 25 to 35 million, and the country had limited resources to deal with such growth. In the south, a few wealthy landowners held large *latifundia*°, or private estates, while the majority of the peasants were landless and forced to work the land for minimum wages. In the north, industrialization had started, but the region was not rich in coal or iron. To be competitive, industry paid very low wages, and the workers lived in abject misery.

---

**latifundia** (lah-tee-FOON-dya)

Conditions on the land and in the factory led to widespread protests, followed by stern government repression. In 1893 a Sicilian labor movement won the adherence of 300,000 members, who seized land and attacked government offices. The government responded with massive force and declared martial law. In 1896, with unrest spreading throughout the peninsula, the government placed half of the provinces under military rule. A cycle of violence and counterviolence gripped the nation. In this turbulent atmosphere, an anarchist killed King Umberto I on July 29, 1900.

After the turn of the century, a new prime minister, Giovanni Giolitti° (1842–1928), tried to bring an end to the upheaval. He used government force more sparingly and showed a spirit of cooperation toward the workers. Seeking to broaden his popularity by an appeal to nationalist fervor, Giolitti launched an attack on Libya in 1911, wresting it from the ailing Ottoman Empire. The territory was arid and bereft of economic promise, but its conquest was championed as a test of national virility and the foundation of national greatness. The imperialists proudly proclaimed force the arbiter of the nation's future.

Domestically, the nation also returned to force. A wave of workers' discontent seized the nation again, and in June 1914 a national strike led to rioting and workers' seizing power in several municipalities. In the Romagna, in northern Italy, an independent workers' republic was proclaimed. It took 100,000 government troops ten days to restore order. The workers' restlessness and brazen defiance led some nationalist right-wing extremists to form groups of "volunteers for the defense of order," anticipating the vigilante thugs who were to make up the early bands of Italian fascism.

## AUTOCRACIES IN CRISIS

 OUR major autocracies dominated central and eastern Europe: Germany, Austria-Hungary, the Ottoman Empire, and Russia. If the democracies encountered difficulties in these years, the autocracies faced even more vehement opposition. Although many groups in the parliamentary regimes grew impatient at the slowness of change, theoretically at least they could believe that someday their goals would be realized. Not so in the autocracies. In authoritarian states, the demands for more democracy were growing louder; opponents sought by all means, including violence, to challenge the existing order. Governments in turn were willing to use violence to maintain themselves.

The severity of autocratic rule varied from state to state, ranging from the absolutism of the Ottoman Empire to the semiparliamentary regime of Germany, but the ruler had the final political say in all of them. Resistance to the autocracies included broad popular challenges to the German imperial system, the reduction of Austria-Hungary into a nearly ungovernable empire, and revolution in the Russian and Ottoman Empires.

### ■ Germany

Although Germany had a parliament, the government was answerable to the kaiser, not the people's electoral representatives. And in the late nineteenth century, Prussia, the most reactionary part of the country, continued to dominate.

To rule effectively, Chancellor Otto von Bismarck maneuvered and intrigued to quell opposition. In the face of socialist growth, he used an attempt to assassinate the emperor as the excuse to ban the Socialist Party in 1879. He succeeded in simultaneously winning over conservative agrarian and liberal industrial interests by supporting tariffs on both imported foodstuffs and industrial goods. He also turned against the Catholics, who were lukewarm toward Protestant Prussia, persecuting them and their institutions. These measures, however, did not prevent the growth of the Socialist and Catholic Center Parties.

Unfortunately for Bismarck, whose tenure in office depended on the goodwill of the emperor, Wilhelm I died in 1888, to be succeeded first by his son Friedrich, who ruled only a few months, and then by his grandson, Wilhelm II (r. 1888–1918). The young Kaiser Wilhelm intended to rule as well as reign, but he was ill fit to govern. Convinced of his own infallibility, he bothered to learn very little. Born with a crippled hand, Wilhelm seemed to want to compensate for this infirmity by appearing forceful, even brutal. He hated any hints of limitation to his powers, announcing, "There is only one ruler in the Reich and I am he. I tolerate no other." A restless individual, Wilhelm changed uniforms eight times daily and traveled ceaselessly among his seventy-five castles and palaces. Dismayed by Bismarck's proposals of reprisals against the socialists and the chancellor's unwillingness to take on a clearly pro-Austrian and anti-Russian foreign policy, the kaiser dismissed him. But he also did so to rid himself of a formidable, intimidating individual.

Wilhelm II was determined to make Germany a world power whose foreign policy would have a global

---

**Giovanni Giolitti** (jo-VAH-nee jo-LEE-tee)

**Wilhelm II** The German emperor liked to be viewed in a heroic and military posture. His crippled left hand is turned away from the viewer. *(Landesbildstelle, Berlin)*

impact. He wanted Germany to have colonies, a navy, and major influence among the Great Powers. This policy, *Weltpolitik,* or "world politics," greatly troubled Germany's neighbors, partly because they already worried about a new, assertive power in central Europe and partly because German moves were accompanied by the kaiser's bombastic threats. Within Germany, however, *Weltpolitik* won support. Steel manufacturers and shipbuilders received lucrative contracts; workers, in some industries at least, seemed assured of employment.

Although the nationalist appeals impressed many Germans, the nation could not be easily managed. The emperor's autocratic style was challenged, and his behavior was increasingly viewed as irresponsible. In the elections of 1912, one-third of all Germans voted for Socialist Party candidates. Thus the largest single party in the Reichstag was at least rhetorically committed to the downfall of the capitalist system and autocracy. Labor militancy also reached new heights. In 1912, 1 million workers—a record number—went on strike. More and

more Germans pressed for a parliamentary system with a government accountable to the people's elected representatives.

The emperor could not tolerate criticism of his behavior. He had come to Bismarck's conclusions and frequently talked about using the military to crush socialists and the parliament. These violent thoughts were echoed in the officer corps and in government circles. To some observers it seemed likely that the days of German autocracy were numbered—or that the army and the people would come to blows.

### ■ Austria-Hungary

The neighboring Austro-Hungarian Empire was also wracked by a series of crises. In an age of intense nationalism, a multinational empire was an anomaly, as the emperor Franz Joseph (r. 1848–1916) himself acknowledged. Although the relationship between the two halves of the empire was regulated by the Compromise of 1867 (see page 755), the agreement did not prevent conflict between Austria and Hungary, particularly over control of their joint army. The insistence on separate Hungarian interests had developed to such a degree that, had it not been for the outbreak of the world war, Hungary probably would have broken loose from the dual monarchy.

In the Hungarian half of the empire, the Magyars found it increasingly difficult to maintain control. Other nationalities opposed Magyarization—the imposition of the Magyar language and institutions—and insisted on the right to use their own languages in their schools and administrations. The Hungarian government resorted to censorship and jailings to silence nationalist leaders. In the Austrian half of the empire, the treatment of nationalities was less harsh, but the government was equally strife-ridden.

There were no easy solutions to the many conflicts the empire faced. Since much of the national agitation was led by middle-class intellectuals, the Habsburg government introduced universal male suffrage in 1907 in an effort to undercut their influence. However, the result was an empire even more difficult to govern. It became nearly impossible to find a workable majority within a parliament that included thirty ethnically based political parties.

The virulence of debate based on nationality and class divisions grew to unprecedented extremes. Within the parliament, deputies threw inkwells at each other, rang sleigh bells, and sounded bugles. Parliament ceased to be relevant. By 1914 the emperor had dissolved it and several regional assemblies. Austria was being ruled by decree. Emperor Franz Joseph feared the empire would not survive him.

## ■ Ottoman Empire

In the generation before 1914, no political system in Europe suffered from so advanced a case of dissolution as the Ottoman Empire, undermined by both secessionist movements within its own borders and aggression from other European powers. Sultan Abdul Hamid° II (r. 1876–1909) ruled the country as a despot and authorized mass carnage against those who contested his rule, earning him the title "the Great Assassin."

Young, Western-educated Turks—the so-called Young Turks—disgusted at one-man rule and the continuing loss of territory and influence, overthrew Abdul Hamid in a coup in July 1908. They set up a government responsible to an elected parliament. The Young Turks hoped to stem the loss of territory by establishing firmer central control, but their efforts had the opposite effect. The various nationalities of the empire resented the attempts at "Turkification," the imposition of Turkish education and administration. Renewed agitation broke out in Macedonia, in Albania, and among the Armenians. The government carried out severely repressive measures to end the unrest, killing thousands of Armenians.

For foreign powers, the moment seemed propitious to plunder the weakened empire. In 1911 Italy occupied Libya, an Ottoman province. Greece, Bulgaria, and Serbia—impatient to enlarge their territories—formed an alliance, the Balkan League, which in 1912 prosecuted a successful war against the empire. Albania became independent, and Macedonia was partitioned among members of the league. Thus, except for the capital, Constantinople, and a narrow strip of surrounding land, the empire was stripped of most of its European possessions.

## ■ Russia

Through the Great Reforms of the 1860s, the Russian autocracy had attempted to resolve many of the problems troubling its empire and people. But the reforms and the major social changes of the period unleashed new forces, making it even more difficult for the tsars to rule.

The needs of a modernizing country led to an increase in the number of universities and students. The newly educated Russian youths almost instantly began an ardent, sustained critique of autocracy. In the absence of a large group upholding liberal, advanced ideas, university students and graduates, who came to be known as the *intelligentsia*, saw it as their mission to transform Russia.

In the 1870s, university youths by the thousands organized a populist movement, hoping to bring change to the countryside. These young idealists intended to educate the peasants and make them more politically aware. But they met with suspicion from the peasantry and repression by the government. Large numbers of populists were arrested and put on trial. Frustrated at the difficulty of bringing about change from below by transforming the people, disaffected radicals formed the People's Will, which turned to murdering public officials to hasten the day of revolution.

Although the regime intensified repression, it also sought to broaden its public support. In 1881 Tsar Alexander II decided to create an advisory committee that some thought would eventually lead to a parliamentary form of government. In March 1881, as he was about to sign the decree establishing this committee, the tsar was assassinated by members of the People's Will.

The new ruler, Tsar Alexander III (r. 1881–1894), who had witnessed the assassination, blamed his father's leniency for his death. By contrast, he was determined to uphold autocracy firmly. He sought to weaken his father's reforms, reducing local self-rule in the process.

When Alexander's son, Nicholas II (r. 1894–1917), succeeded his father on the throne in 1894, he declared he would be as autocratic as his father. However, he lacked the methodical, consistent temperament such a pledge required. A pleasant man, he wanted to be liked, and he lacked the forcefulness to establish a coherent policy for his troubled country.

Since the Great Reforms, serious problems had accumulated that threatened the stability of the regime. In the countryside the situation worsened steadily as the population exploded and pressure on the land increased. The provisions that had accompanied the freeing of the serfs left considerable discontent. The peasants were not free to come and go as they pleased; they had to have the permission of the village council. Agriculture remained inefficient, far inferior to that of western Europe. Hence the allotted land was insufficient to feed the peasants, creating a constant demand for more land.

Although Russia remained largely agrarian, pockets of industrial growth sprang up. Some factories and mining concerns were unusually large, with as many as six thousand employees. When workers grew incensed at their condition and insistent on winning the same rights and protection as their counterparts in western Europe, they engaged in massive strikes that crippled industry.

Political dissatisfaction with the autocracy grew. Members of the expanding middle classes began to clamor that, like their contemporaries in western Europe, they should be given the opportunity to participate in governance. Increasingly, aristocrats also demanded a right to political participation.

---

**Abdul Hamid** (ab-DOOL ah-MEED)

## ❧ READING SOURCES

> # Lenin Urges a Conspiratorial Revolutionary Party

*The Russian Socialist Party was wracked by internal debates over the direction and means by which a socialist revolution could be created. The majority favored a broad-based party, but in his 1902 essay, "What Is to Be Done?" Lenin explained why revolution in Russia could succeed only if it were led by a cadre of professional revolutionaries, organized into a tightly knit conspiratorial group. As Lenin presses for a tightly organized party, notice the practical reasons he enumerates as well as the self-serving nature of his argument.*

We must have a committee of professional revolutionaries . . . irrespective of whether they are students or working men. I assert: 1) That no movement can be durable without a stable organization of leaders to maintain continuity; 2) that the more widely the masses are drawn into the struggle and form the basis of the movement, the more necessary it is to have such an organization and the more stable it must be—otherwise it is much easier for demagogues to sidetrack the more backward sections of the masses; 3) that the organization must consist chiefly of persons engaged in revolution as a profession; 4) that in a country with a despotic government, the more we restrict the membership of this organization to persons who are engaged in revolution as a profession and who have been professionally trained in the art of combating the political police, the more difficult will it be to catch the organization; and 5) the wider will be the circle of men and women of the working class or of other classes of society able to join the movement and perform active work in it. . . .

It is . . . argued against us that the views on organization here expounded contradict the "principles of democracy."

Ponder a little over the real meaning of the high-sounding phrase . . . and you will realize that "broad democracy" in party organization, amidst the gloom of autocracy and the domination of the gendarmes, is nothing more than a useless and harmful toy. It is a useless toy, because as a matter of fact, no revolutionary organization has ever practiced broad democracy, nor could it, however much it desired to do so.

The only serious organizational principle the active workers of our movement can accept is: Strict secrecy, strict selection of members and the training of professional revolutionists.

*Source:* Vladimir Ilich Lenin, "What Is to Be Done?" *Collected Works*, vol. 4 (New York: International Publishers, 1929), pp. 198–199, 210–213.

 **For additional information on this topic, go to http://college.hmco.com.**

Various revolutionary groups committed to socialism continued to flourish. The heirs to the People's Will were the Social Revolutionaries, who emerged as a political force in the 1890s. They believed that the peasants would bring socialism to Russia. In 1898 the Russian Social Democratic Party was founded; a Marxist party, it promoted the industrial working class as the harbinger of socialism. In 1903 that party split into the Menshevik and the Bolshevik factions. The Mensheviks insisted that Russia had to go through the stages of history Marx had outlined—to witness the full development of capitalism

and its subsequent collapse before socialism could come to power. The Bolsheviks, a minority group, were led by Vladimir Ilich Lenin (1870–1924), a zealous revolutionary and Marxist. Rather than wait for historical forces to undermine capitalism, he insisted that a revolutionary cadre could seize power on behalf of the working class. Lenin favored a small, disciplined, conspiratorial party, like the People's Will, while the Mensheviks favored a more open, democratic party. (See the box "Reading Sources: Lenin Urges a Conspiratorial Revolutionary Party.")

**Workers' Demonstration in Moscow, 1905** In 1905 workers as well as peasants protested against the Russian autocracy. To bring the revolution under control, Nicholas II was obliged to grant several concessions. *(Novosti)*

At the turn of the century these groups were still quite small and played a limited role in the mounting opposition to tsarism. But popular opposition soon grew in the face of Russian military ineptitude in the war against Japan, which had broken out in February 1904 in a dispute over control of northern Korea. Antagonism to the tsarist regime escalated as a result of social tensions, heightened by an economic slowdown.

Beginning in January 1905, a series of demonstrations, strikes, and other acts of collective violence erupted. Together, they were dubbed "the revolution of 1905." One Sunday in January 1905, 400,000 workers seeking redress of their grievances gathered in front of the tsar's St. Petersburg palace. Rather than hear their protests, officials ordered soldiers to fire on them, resulting in 150 deaths and hundreds more wounded. "Bloody Sunday" inflamed the populace. The tsar, instead of being viewed as an understanding, paternal authority, had become the murderer of his people. Unrest spread to most of the country. As reports reached Russia of more defeats in the war with Japan, the regime's prestige deteriorated

further. By September 1905, Russia had to sue for peace and admit defeat. Challenged in the capital, where independent workers' councils called *soviets* had sprung up, the government also lost control over the countryside, the site of widespread peasant uprisings.

Fearing for his regime, Nicholas hoped to disarm the forces challenging tsarism by meeting the demands for parliamentary government and granting major constitutional and civil liberties, including freedom of religion, speech, assembly, and association. At the end of October, the tsar established an elective assembly, the Duma, with restricted male suffrage and limited political power. It was far from the Western-style parliament that Russian liberals had desired, but it quickly became the arena for criticism of autocracy. Wanting to create a more pliant instrument, the tsar suspended the assembly, changing its electoral base and its rules of operations. Even many conservatives were disillusioned with the tsar's backtracking and his breach of the promise he had made in 1905 to establish constitutionalism and parliamentarism.

The government reduced the peasants' financial obligations; the power of the commune, or *mir* (see pages 759–760), was weakened; and local self-rule was extended to the peasants. But these changes did little to alleviate a worsening relationship between population and land. Between emancipation and 1914, the peasant population grew by 50 percent, but it acquired only 10 percent more land. Rural poverty was widespread; in 1891 famine broke out in twenty provinces, killing a quarter of a million people. Rural discontent was deep and widespread.

Labor unrest also mounted among industrial workers. In 1912, walkouts had involved 725,000 strikers, but by the first half of 1914, that number had doubled. When the French president visited St. Petersburg on the eve of the outbreak of the First World War, barricades were rising in the workers' neighborhoods.

Internally, the authoritarian states of Europe were fighting strong challenges. It was unclear how long they could maintain their respective grips.

## THE COMING WAR

 NSTABILITY and upheaval characterized international relations in the years between 1880 and 1914. But the outbreak of war was by no means inevitable. Good common sense dictated against it, and some intelligent people predicted that in the new modern era, war would become so destructive that it would be unthinkable. Finally, no European state wanted a war, although the Great Powers carried on policies that brought them to its brink.

### ■ Power Alignments

Germany enjoyed an unchallenged position in the international order of the 1870s and 1880s. It was united in an alliance with the two other eastern conservative states—Russia and Austria-Hungary—in the Three Emperors' League, formed in 1873 and renewed by treaty in 1884. And it was part of the Triple Alliance with Austria and Italy. France stood alone, without allies. Britain, with little interest in continental affairs, appeared to be enjoying a "splendid isolation."

However, Germany's alliance system was not free from problems. Two of its allies, Austria-Hungary and Russia, were at loggerheads over control of the Balkans. How could Germany be the friend of both? Wary of apparent German preference for Austria, Bismarck signed the Reinsurance Treaty in 1887, assuring Russia that Germany would not honor its alliance with Austria if the latter attacked Russia. After Bismarck's resignation in 1890, Kaiser Wilhelm allowed the Reinsurance Treaty to lapse. Alarmed, the Russians turned to France and, in January 1894, signed the Franco-Russian Alliance, by which each side pledged to help the other should either be attacked by Germany.

The Great Powers on the Continent were now divided into two alliances, the Triple Alliance and the Franco-Russian Alliance. Britain formally belonged to neither, but if it favored any side, it would be the German-led alliance. Britain's strongest competitors in the 1880s and 1890s were France and Russia. Both rivaled Britain for influence in Asia, while France vied with Britain for control of Africa.

By its actions in the 1890s Germany lost British goodwill. Launching his *Weltpolitik*, Wilhelm II built up the German navy. Over the years, Britain had developed a navy second to none. An island nation, dependent on international trade for its economic survival, Britain saw a strong navy as a necessity, the German naval buildup as a threat to its security.

In the face of what they viewed as a mounting German menace, Britain and France decided to resolve their difficulties overseas: in 1904 they signed an understanding, or *entente*, resolving their rivalries in Egypt. In 1907 Great Britain and Russia regulated their competition for influence in Persia (present-day Iran) with the Anglo-Russian Entente. Europe was still loosely divided into two groups, but now according to a different configuration: the Triple Alliance of Germany, Austria-Hungary, and Italy, and the Triple Entente of Great Britain, France, and Russia.

### ■ The Momentum Toward War

Only through a series of crises did these alignments solidify to the point where their members were willing to go to war to save them. France's attempts to take over Morocco twice led to conflict with Germany. In 1905 Germany insisted that an international conference discuss the issue and deny France this kingdom adjacent to its colony of Algeria. When France grabbed Morocco anyway, in 1911, Germany accepted the situation only after extorting compensation from the French, who deeply resented what they viewed as German bullying.

The heightened international rivalry forced the European states to increase their arms expenditures, which added in turn to their sense of insecurity. In 1906 Britain introduced a new class of ships with the launching of the *Dreadnought*. Powered by steam turbines, it was the fastest ship afloat; heavily armored, it could not be sunk easily; and its ten 12-inch guns made it a menace on the seas. The British had thought the Germans could not build equivalent ships, but they did, wiping out British supremacy—older British ships could easily be sunk by German dreadnoughts. No longer able to depend on its past supremacy, Britain was feeling less secure than at any time since the Napoleonic Wars, and it continued an expensive and feverish naval race with Germany.

In Germany the growing war-making capacity of Russia created great anxieties. The Japanese defeat of the tsarist empire in 1905 revealed the Russian military to be inferior—a lumbering giant, slow to mobilize and maneuver. As a result Germany had not been particularly afraid of its eastern neighbor. But stung by its humiliation in 1905, Russia quickly rebuilt its army and planned an extensive rail network in the west. To many in Germany, their country now appeared encircled by a hostile Russia to the east and an equally unfriendly France to the west. Germany became genuinely worried, and beginning in 1912 many in the military and within the government started thinking about a preventive war. If war was inevitable, many Germans argued, it should occur before Russia became even stronger. Fear of the future military balance made some of the highest policymakers see the crisis that broke out in the summer of 1914 as an opportunity to go to war and throttle Russia.

Many political leaders viewed the escalating arms race as a form of madness. Between 1904 and 1913, French and Russian arms expenditures increased by 80 percent; those of Germany by 120 percent; those of Austria-Hungary by 50 percent; and those of Italy by 100 percent. British foreign secretary Sir Edward Grey (1862–1933) warned that if the arms race continued, "It will submerge civilization." But no way was found to stop it.

On the whole warfare was not feared. Except for short victorious colonial wars, the Western powers had not experienced a major conflict since the Crimean War. Russia had successfully warred against the Ottoman Empire in 1876. Its war against Japan in 1905 had been a calamity, but Russia refused to believe that such a disaster would happen again. Most policymakers believed that the next war would be short. The wars that had so dramatically changed the borders of European states in the second half of the nineteenth century, notably the Austro-Prussian War of 1866 and the Franco-Prussian War of 1870, had been decided within a few short weeks. Few imagined that the next war, if it came, would be very brutal or very lengthy. And therefore many of Europe's leaders did not dread war enough to make a major effort to prevent or avoid it.

It was the territorial rivalry between Austria and Russia that triggered international disaster. For decades

**Map 24.4    The Balkans in 1914**   By 1914 the Ottoman Empire was much diminished, containing virtually no European territory. Political boundaries did not follow nationality lines. Serbia was committed to unite all Serbs at the expense of the Austro-Hungarian Empire.

enmity had been growing between the two empires over control of the Balkans (see Map 24.4). In 1903, following a bloody military coup that killed the king and queen of Serbia, a pro-Russian party took control of the Serbian government. In 1908 Russia, still not recovered from its defeat in 1905, was surprised when Austria unilaterally declared the annexation of the province of Bosnia (which it had administered since the Congress of Berlin in 1878; see page 758). The annexation appeared to spell an end to Serbia's dream of annexing Bosnia, which had many Serb inhabitants. Fearing war, Russia had to accept diplomatic defeat and abandoned its ally, Serbia. But Russia determined it would not cave in again.

Undeterred, Serbia spread anti-Austrian propaganda and sought to unify under its banner Slavs living

**The Shot Heard 'Round the World**
The young Serb nationalist Gavril Princip shoots Franz Ferdinand, the heir to the Austro-Hungarian throne, and his consort. The assassination unleashed the outbreak of World War I. *(Österreichische Nationalbibliothek, Vienna)*

in the Balkans, including those under Austrian rule. As a result, many Austrian officials were convinced that the survival of the Austro-Hungarian Empire required the destruction of Serbia. Talk of an attack on Serbia filled the Austrian court in 1914.

On June 28, 1914, the heir to the Habsburg throne, Archduke Franz Ferdinand, visited Sarajevo in Austrian-ruled Bosnia. A young Bosnian-Serb nationalist hostile to Austrian rule, who had been trained and armed by a Serb terrorist group called the Black Hand, assassinated the archduke and his wife.

The assassination of the heir to the throne provided Austria with an ideal pretext for military action. The German kaiser, fearing that failure to support Vienna would lead to Austrian collapse and a Germany bereft of any al-

lies, urged Austria to attack Serbia. On July 23, Austria issued an ultimatum to Serbia, deliberately worded in such a way as to be unacceptable. When Serbia refused the ultimatum, Austria declared war on July 28.

Perceived self-interest motivated each state's behavior in the ensuing crisis. Although in the past Russia had failed to protect Serbia, now it was resolved to help. Russia's status as a Great Power demanded that it not allow its client state to be humiliated, much less obliterated. In the past the French government had acted as a brake on Russian ambitions in the Balkans. On the very eve of the war in 1914, France counseled restraint, but it did not withhold its aid. Since 1911, France had increasingly feared isolation in the face of what it perceived as growing German aggression. Its only ally on the Continent was Russia. To remain a Great Power, France needed to preserve its friendship with Russia and help that country maintain its own Great Power status.

Germany could not allow Austria, its only ally, to be destroyed. Its leaders may also have seen the crisis as a propitious moment to begin a war that was going to occur sooner or later anyway. The Germans no doubt also thought it expedient to strike before the entente powers, especially Russia, became stronger. As the German prime minister put it, his country was about to take "a leap in the dark," and he declared war on Russia. Assuming that France would come to the aid of Russia, Germany invaded France through Belgium. The British, concerned by the threat to their ally France, and outraged by the violation of Belgian neutrality to which all the Great Powers had been signatories since 1839, declared war on Germany. Events had hurtled forward between the Austrian declaration of war on Serbia on July 28 and the British decision on August 4. Europe was at war. Eventually so would be much of the world.

# SUMMARY

ON the surface, the years from 1880 to 1914 seemed comfortable. More people than ever before enjoyed material advantages and improved standards of living. Literacy spread. Death rates went down. Life expectancy rose.

Europe appeared to dominate the globe. In their relations with Africa and Asia, Europeans resorted to force to an unprecedented degree, conquering most of the African and much of the Asian continents. Europe intended to exploit the new empires as new sources of wealth, trade, and the trappings of power. But colonial rivals and subjects challenged the future of these empires, leading to various anxieties.

With improved conditions in Europe, a revolution of rising expectations had been created. People grew more demanding, insisting in sometimes violent ways on their political and economic rights. Although mass movements such as socialism and the women's suffrage movement generally used peaceful means in their campaigns to change society, some of their members advocated and employed force. Anarchism appeared to stalk Europe. In turn, states did not hesitate to use force in efforts to quell various protest movements, even resorting to martial law.

Reflecting these trends, intellectuals such as Freud and Bergson and artists such as Munch and Moreau suggested that a hidden, irrational dimension of life lurked beneath the tranquil surface appearances. Behind the façade of security and conformity lay many disturbing impulses such as racism, anti-Semitism, and tyranny.

Although most Europeans were confident and optimistic about their futures, such self-assuredness was not universally shared. Intellectuals spoke of decadence and decline. Policymakers worried about the future of their countries and, anxious to avoid the threat of decline, resorted to extreme measures such as empire building overseas and armed competition in Europe. Among European thinkers and leaders, force had become widely accepted as the means to an end; some leaders—notably those of Austria-Hungary and Germany—favored war over negotiation in July 1914.

The major powers—except Britain, confident in its naval dominance—built up large standing armies with millions of men and lethal modern equipment. Europe's network of alliances led inexorably to the larger conflict. If some leaders still feared war, more dreaded the consequences of not fighting, believing that war would save their regimes from the internal and external challenges they faced. Few could foresee the dire consequences of such a choice.

## ■ Suggested Reading

Burrow, J. W. *The Crisis of Reason: European Thought, 1848–1914.* 2000. Strong emphasis on individual intellectuals and their contributions.

Carrère d'Encausse, Hélène. *Nicholas II.* 2000. A biography of the tsar, set within the context of an increasingly difficult country to govern.

Hobsbawm, Eric. *The Age of Empire, 1875–1914.* 1987. A fine survey, emphasizing social change, by a leading British historian.

Hochschild, Adam. *King Leopold's Ghost.* 1998. A dramatic account of Leopold II's brutal rule over the Congo.

Jay, Mike, and Michael Neve, eds. *1900. A fin de siècle Reader.* 1999. A rich collection of documents on how people imagined the new century.

Johnson, Martin P. *The Dreyfus Affair.* 1999. A brisk review of the major events shaping the affair.

Joll, James. *The Origins of the First World War.* 1984. A clear, concise, readable history tracing how strategic interests and nationalist passions led to the outbreak of the war.

Schorske, Carl E. *Fin de Siècle Vienna—Politics and Culture.* 1980. A critically acclaimed work on the arts and social and political thought in the Habsburg capital at the turn of the century.

 **For a searchable list of additional readings for this chapter, go to http://college.hmco.com.**

# The Layout of the British Museum

The British Museum was founded in the mid-eighteenth century when the government acquired some private collections. The museum increased the size of its collections, largely through donations, bringing in objects from around the world. In its early years the museum was located in a converted private mansion; then in 1847, to house its growing collection, the museum moved into a monumental building with a neo-classical façade. Until the 1830s public access was limited to the upper classes, mainly the learned. By the mid-nineteenth century, however, a million people a year were visiting the museum. Displays of materials gathered from non-European cultures drew particularly large audiences.

Consider how the exhibits reflected British imperialism. In the first half of the nineteenth century, objects from Oceania, reflecting British activities in the Pacific, were acquired. African materials became more plentiful with the British conquest of much of Africa after the 1880s; the British military expedition to Nigeria in 1897 led to the acquisition of the fabulous Benin bronzes.

While imperial adventures were shaping the museum collection, the museum in turn was supporting imperialism. Museum officials declared that increased knowledge about regions overseas would fuel enthusiasm for the imperial venture and make the British people better fit to rule their new subjects.

**Plan of the Upper Floor of the British Museum, ca. 1880**   *(Based on map in Henry C. Shelley,*
*The British Museum: Its History and Treasures [Boston: L. C. Page, 1911], pp. 274–275.)*

1   Anglo-Saxon Room
2   Waddesdon Bequest Room
3   Mediaeval Room
4   Asiatic Saloon
5 to 9   Ethnographical Gallery
10   North East Landing
11   American Room
12   First Egyptian Room
13   Second Egyptian Room
14   Third Egyptian Room
15   Fourth Egyptian Room
16   Babylonian and Assyrian Room

The manner in which the British Museum displayed some of its possessions reflected the intellectual currents of the times. In the late eighteenth and early nineteenth centuries the museum grouped its non-European objects with "natural history"; non-Europeans were associated with nature, with the beasts of the earth. Running out of space, the museum moved the natural history collection to a separate Natural Museum in South Kensington, and in the 1880s ethnography, the branch of anthropology devoted to human cultures, constituted a separate collection.

The late-nineteenth-century plan of the upper floor of the museum shown here reflects the racial views of imperial Britain. After climbing the stairs from the ground floor, we start at the room labeled 1, the Anglo-Saxon Room, which celebrates England's early history. Then comes the Waddesdon Bequest Room, which houses various artifacts of ancient and medieval English and European history (the room is named after the Rothschild mansion, where the collection was previously housed). Next we arrive at the Mediaeval Room itself. Using the route most visitors would then take, we come to the Asiatic Saloon, filled with pottery, porcelain, and other works of art from Japan, China, Persia, and India.

What is the significance of this juxtaposition of rooms? The British and other Europeans had developed an ethnocentric view of the human races, believing that the white race was by far superior to all others. This belief seemed confirmed by the material accomplishments of Europeans, especially impressive in the nineteenth century. Of the non-Europeans, Asians had won the grudging respect of the British and other Europeans. China, with its thousands of years of recorded history and sophisticated government structures, was one of several Asian societies that impressed them. Because many African societies lacked a written culture and had government and religious systems dramatically different from the Europeans', the British and other Europeans often considered Africans ignorant and primitive.

Biologists, anthropologists, and others speculating about the human races offered two different explanations for racial variations. These hypotheses competed with each other for public acceptance. According to the first, biology determined the level of civilization of each people. According to the second, different peoples were at different levels of development. In this view, Europeans were most developed, Africans least; but eventually Asians and Africans would progress and reach a level similar to that of Europeans. In the meantime non-Europeans illustrated European life at earlier stages of development.

It is interesting that the Asiatic Saloon, with its swords, shields, and other elaborate Asian objects, was next to the Mediaeval Room. The positioning invites consideration that some nineteenth-century Asian societies were at a level of development akin to medieval England.

An empty corridor separated this part of the museum from the Ethnographical Gallery, giving visitors the sense that what they would view was separate from medieval England and selected Asian societies. The Ethnographical Gallery displayed objects from Asia, Oceania, Africa, and the Americas. They tended to be objects of daily life such as household wares, weapons, and clothing. The stress was on their simplicity and primitiveness—presumably reflections of the primitive culture of their makers. The objects were not differentiated chronologically; pre-Columbian artifacts from the Americas were displayed beside modern African crafts. Ethnographic items were seldom dated, implying that the peoples who created them did not develop and had no history. The museum guidebook invited nineteenth-century viewers to consider how close the development of these peoples was to that of the earliest Europeans.

After passing through the Ethnographical Gallery, a visitor would arrive at the North East Landing and then enter the American Room. It contained items from Eskimos, Native Americans, and other peoples whom Victorians considered "primitives," but it also included artifacts from the Aztecs and Incas, whom the British considered to have been highly developed.

The Aztec and Inca collections abutted the room devoted to two ancient civilizations with monumental architecture, the Babylonian and Assyrian Room. Next came four Egyptian rooms. In the nineteenth century the greatness of ancient Egyptian culture was recognized. The British Museum allotted ancient Egypt ample space far removed from what were seen as the "primitive" peoples represented in the Ethnographical Gallery.

In 1972 the ethnographic collection was moved out of the Brtitish Museum and now constitutes the Museum of Mankind. With the loss of empire and the decline of confidence in the superiority of the white race, the old uses for the objects collected overseas had become obsolete.*

---

* The author is grateful to Thomas Prasch, Washburn University, for his help and advice and for making available two of his unpublished papers on this subject.

# CHAPTER 25

# War and Revolution 1914–1919

**M**UD. It was not what soldiers had in mind when they headed off to war in August 1914 amid visions of glory, gallantry—and quick victory. But after heavy rain and constant shelling, mud was a fact of life for those fighting on the western front—Belgium and northern France—during the fall of 1917. The mud was so pervasive, in fact, that soldiers literally drowned in it. These Canadian troops are holding the line on November 14, 1917, at the end of the Battle of Passchendaele°, a British-led assault that began late in July. That assault pushed the Germans back a mere 5 miles—at the cost of 300,000 lives. There was no end to the war in sight.

Some had thought a major war impossible in rational, civilized Europe. Others had devoutly wished for war—precisely to break out of the stifling bourgeois conventions of rational, civilized Europe. When war actually began early in August 1914, the European mood was generally enthusiastic, even festive. No one was prepared for what this war would bring, including the hellish scenes of mud, smoke, artillery craters, blasted trees, decaying bodies, and ruined buildings that came to frame the daily experience of those on the western front. A far wider and more destructive war would follow within a generation, but it was World War I, known to contemporaries as "the Great War," that shattered the old European order, with its comfortable assumptions of superiority, rationality, and progress. After this war, neither Westerners nor non-Westerners could still believe in the privileged place of Western civilization in quite the same way.

**Passchendaele** (PAH-shun-dale)

**The Unforeseen Stalemate, 1914–1917**

**The Experience of Total War**

**Two Revolutions in Russia: March and November 1917**

**The New War and the Allied Victory, 1917–1918**

**The Outcome and the Impact**

Passchendaele, Belgium, 1917
(By courtesy of the Trustees of the
Imperial War Museum)

The war that began in August was supposed to be over by Christmas. The British government promised "business as usual." But the fighting bogged down in a stalemate during the fall of 1914, then continued for four more years. By the time it ended, in November 1918, the war had strained the whole fabric of life, affecting everything from economic organization to literary vocabulary, from journalistic techniques to the role of women.

Partly because the war grew to become the first "world war," it proved the beginning of the end of European hegemony. The intervention of the United States in 1917 affected the military balance and seemed to give the war more idealistic and democratic purposes. The geographic reach of the war was itself unprecedented, especially after the intervention of the Ottoman Empire spread the fighting to the Middle East. Because of European colonial networks, the war also involved many other non-Europeans in combat or support roles. Although the old colonialism continued into the postwar era, the war nourished the forces that would later overthrow it.

Because of all the strains it entailed, the war had many unintended consequences. Revolutions dramatically changed the political landscape first in Russia, then in Germany. The Habsburg and Ottoman Empires collapsed. So when the victors met early in 1919 to shape the peace, they confronted a situation that could not have been foreseen in 1914. And their effort to determine the contours of the postwar world, and thus the immediate meaning of the war, left much unresolved.

### QUESTIONS TO CONSIDER

- How did geography affect the shape and outcome of World War I?

- Why did this prove a total war, making necessary new forms of socioeconomic coordination and even systematic propaganda?

- What was the relationship between the war and the two revolutions in Russia in 1917?

- What factors shaped the peace settlement that the victors imposed on Germany in 1919?

### TERMS TO KNOW

| | |
|---|---|
| Sacred Union | Vladimir Lenin |
| British blockade | Wilson's "Fourteen |
| total war | Points" |
| Kriegsrohstoffabteilung | Treaty of Brest-Litovsk |
| (KRA), war raw | "stab in the back" myth |
| materials office | Treaty of Versailles |
| Petrograd Soviet | League of Nations |
| provisional government | |

# THE UNFORESEEN STALEMATE, 1914–1917

 HEN the war began in August 1914, enthusiasm and high morale, based on expectations of quick victory, marked both sides. But fighting on the crucial western front led to a stalemate by the end of 1914, and the brutal encounters of 1916 made it clear that this was not the sort of war most had expected. By early 1917 the difficulties of the war experience brought to the surface underlying questions about what all the fighting was for—and whether it was worth the price.

### ■ August 1914: The Domestic and Military Setting

Although some, including Helmuth von Moltke° (1848–1916), chief of the German general staff, worried that this would prove a long, destructive war testing the very fabric of Western civilization, the outbreak of fighting early in August produced a wave of euphoria and a remarkable degree of domestic unity. To many, war came almost as a relief; at last, the issues that had produced tension and intermittent crisis for the past decade would find a definitive solution. Especially among educated young

**Moltke** (MOLT-kuh)

people, this settling of accounts seemed to offer the prospect of renewal, even a kind of redemption, for themselves and their societies. The war promised an escape from the stifling bourgeois world and, in response to the common danger, an end to the bickering and divisiveness of everyday politics. (See the box "Reading Sources: The Joys of August 1914.")

An unexpected display of patriotism from the socialist left reinforced the sense of domestic unity and high morale. Forgetting their customary rhetoric about international proletarian solidarity, members of the socialist parties of the Second International rallied to their respective national war efforts almost everywhere in Europe. To socialists and workers, national defense against a more backward aggressor seemed essential to the eventual creation of socialism. French socialists had to defend France's democratic republic against autocratic and militaristic Germany; German socialists had to defend German institutions, and the strong socialist organizations that had proven possible within them, against repressive tsarist Russia. When, on August 4, the German Socialist delegation in the Reichstag voted with the other parties to give the government the budgetary authority to wage war, it was clear that the Second International had failed in its long-standing commitment to keep the workers of Europe from slaughtering each other.

In France, the government had planned, as a precaution, to arrest roughly one thousand trade union and Socialist leaders in the event of war, but no such arrests were necessary. The order of the day was "Sacred Union," which meant that French leaders from across the political spectrum agreed to cooperate for the duration of the war. Rather than seek to sabotage the war, Socialist leaders joined the new government of national defense. Germany enjoyed a comparable "Fortress Truce," including an agreement to suspend labor conflict during the war, although no Socialist was invited to join the war cabinet.

In 1914 the forces of the Triple Entente outnumbered those of Germany and Austria-Hungary. Russia had an army of over 1 million men, the largest in Europe, and France had 700,000. Britain, which did not introduce conscription until 1916, had about 250,000. Germany led the Central Powers with 850,000; Austria-Hungary contributed 450,000. Though outnumbered, the Central Powers had potential advantages in equipment, coordination, and speed over their more dispersed adversaries. The outcome was hardly a foregone conclusion in August 1914.

After the fighting began, a second group of nations intervened one by one, expanding the war's scope and complicating the strategic alternatives. In November 1914 the Ottoman Empire, fearful of Russia, joined the Central

## CHRONOLOGY

| | |
|---|---|
| **August 1914** | Fighting begins |
| **September 1914** | French forces hold off the German assault at the Marne |
| **August–September 1914** | German victories repel Russian invasion on eastern front |
| **May 1915** | Italy declares war on Austria-Hungary |
| **February–December 1916** | Battle of Verdun |
| **July–November 1916** | Battle of the Somme |
| **January 1917** | Germans resume unrestricted submarine warfare |
| **March 1917** | First Russian revolution: fall of the tsar |
| **April 1917** | U.S. declaration of war |
| **July 1917** | German Reichstag war-aims resolution |
| **November 1917** | Second Russian revolution: the Bolsheviks take power |
| **March 1918** | Treaty of Brest-Litovsk between Germany and Russia |
| **March–July 1918** | Germany's last western offensive |
| **June 1918** | Initial outbreak of "Spanish flu" |
| **July 1918** | Second Battle of the Marne |
| **November 1918** | Armistice: fighting ends |
| **January 1919** | Paris Peace Conference convenes |
| **June 1919** | Victors impose Treaty of Versailles on Germany |

Powers, thereby extending the war along the Russo-Turkish border and on to Mesopotamia and the approaches to the Suez Canal in the Middle East. For Arabs disaffected with Ottoman Turkish rule, the war presented an opportunity to take up arms—with the active

**Map 25.1  Major Fronts of World War I**  Although World War I included engagements in East Asia and the Middle East, it was essentially a European conflict, encompassing fighting on a number of fronts. A vast territory was contested in the east, but on the western front, which proved decisive, fighting was concentrated in a relatively small area.

## ♨ READING SOURCES

### The Joys of August 1914

*In an autobiography published in 1943, writer Stefan Zweig (1881–1942) recalled the remarkable enthusiasm that accompanied the outbreak of war in his native Vienna in 1914. The popular mood reflected a naive faith, yet Zweig sensed that something more troubling was at work as well.*

[I]n Vienna I found the entire city in a tumult. The first shock at the news of war—the war that no one, people or government, had wanted—the war which had slipped, much against their will, out of the clumsy hands of the diplomats who had been bluffing and toying with it, had suddenly been transformed into enthusiasm. There were parades in the streets, flags, ribbons, and music burst forth everywhere, young recruits were marching triumphantly, their faces lighting up at the cheering. . . .

And to be truthful, I must acknowledge that there was a majestic, rapturous, and even seductive something in this first outbreak of the people from which one could escape only with difficulty. And in spite of all my hatred and aversion for war, I should not like to have missed the memory of those first days. As never before, thousands and hundreds of thousands felt what they should have felt in peace time, that they belonged together. A city of two million, a country of nearly fifty million, in that hour felt that they were participating in world history, in a moment which would never recur, and that each one was called upon to cast his infinitesimal self into the glowing mass, there to be purified of all selfishness. All differences of class, rank, and language were flooded over at that moment by the rushing feeling of fraternity. Strangers spoke to one another in the streets, people who had avoided each other for

years shook hands. . . . [T]he clerk, the cobbler, had suddenly achieved a romantic possibility in life; he could become a hero, and everyone who wore a uniform was already being cheered by the women. . . . But it is quite possible that a deeper, more secret power was at work in this frenzy. So deeply, so quickly did the tide break over humanity that, foaming over the surface, it churned up the depths, the subconscious primitive instincts of the human animal—that which Freud so meaningfully calls "the revulsion from culture," the desire to break out of the conventional bourgeois world of codes and statutes, and to permit the primitive instincts of the blood to rage at will.

. . . [T]he people had unqualified confidence in their leaders; no one in Austria would have ventured the thought that the all-high ruler Emperor Franz Josef, in his eighty-third year, would have called his people to war unless from direct necessity, would have demanded such a sacrifice of blood unless evil, sinister, and criminal foes were threatening the peace of the Empire.

*Source:* Stefan Zweig, *The World of Yesterday: An Autobiography* (New York: Viking, 1943), pp. 223–225.

 **For additional information on this topic, go to http://college.hmco.com.**

---

support of Britain and France. Italy, after dickering with both sides, committed itself to the Entente in the Treaty of London of April 1915. This secret agreement specified the territories Italy would receive—primarily the Italian-speaking areas still within Austria-Hungary—in the event of Entente victory. In September 1915 Bulgaria entered the war on the side of the Central Powers, seeking territorial advantages at the expense of Serbia, which

had defeated Bulgaria in the Second Balkan War in 1913. Finally, in August 1916, Romania intervened on the side of the Entente, hoping to gain Transylvania, then part of Hungary.

Thus the war was fought on a variety of fronts (see Map 25.1). This fact, combined with uncertainties about the role of sea power, led to ongoing debate among military decision makers about strategic priorities. Because

**No Trenches in Sight** Spirits were high early in August 1914, as soldiers like these in Paris marched off to war. None foresaw what fighting this war would be like. None grasped the long-term impact the war would have. *(Archives Larousse-Giraudon)*

of the antagonism that the prewar German naval buildup had caused, some expected that Britain and Germany would quickly be drawn into a decisive naval battle. Britain promptly instituted an effective naval blockade on imports to Germany, but the great showdown on the seas never materialized. Even the most significant naval encounter between them, the Battle of Jutland in 1916, was inconclusive. Despite the naval rivalry of the prewar years, World War I proved fundamentally a land war.

Germany faced not only the long-anticipated two-front war against Russia in the east and France and Britain in the west; it also had to look to the southeast, given the precarious situation of its ally Austria-Hungary, which was fighting Serbia and Russia, then also Italy and Romania as well. On the eastern front, Germany was largely successful, forcing first Russia, then Romania, to seek a separate peace by mid-1918. But it was the western front that proved decisive.

### ■ Into the Nightmare, 1914

With the lessons of the wars of German unification in mind, both sides had planned for a short war based on rapid offensives, a war of movement. According to the Schlieffen° Plan, drafted in 1905, Germany would concentrate first on France, devoting but one-eighth of its forces to containing the Russians, who would need longer to mobilize. After taking just six weeks to knock France out of the war, Germany would then concentrate on Russia. French strategy, crafted by General Joseph Joffre° (1852–1931), the commander-in-chief of the French forces, similarly relied on rapid offensives. The boys would be home by Christmas—or so it was thought.

Although German troops encountered more opposition than expected from the formerly neutral Belgians, they moved swiftly through Belgium into northern France during August. By the first week of September they had reached the Marne River, threatening Paris and forcing the French government to retreat south to Bordeaux°. But French and British troops under Joffre counterattacked September 6–10, forcing the Germans to fall back and begin digging in along the Aisne° River. By holding off the German offensive at this first Battle of the Marne, the Entente had undercut the Schlieffen Plan—and with it, it turned out, any chance of a speedy victory by either side.

---

**Schlieffen** (SHLEE-fyn) **Joffre** (JOFF-ruh)
**Bordeaux** (bor-DOH) **Aisne** (ENN)

**Trench Warfare** Grim though they were, the trenches proved effective for defensive purposes. Here a British soldier guards a trench at Ovillers, on the Somme, in July 1916. *(Trustees of the Imperial War Museum)*

During the rest of the fall of 1914, each side tried—unsuccessfully—to outflank the other. When, by the end of November, active fighting ceased for the winter, a military front of about 300 miles had been established, all the way from Switzerland to the coast of the North Sea in Belgium (see Map 25.2 on page 864). This line failed to shift more than 10 miles in either direction over the next three years. So the result of the first six weeks of fighting on the western front was not a gallant victory but a grim and unforeseen stalemate.

Virtually from the start, the war took a fiercely destructive turn. In northern France in September 1914, the Germans fired on the cathedral at Reims°, severely damaging its roof and nave, because they believed—apparently correctly—that the French were using one of its towers as an observation post. If such a catastrophe could happen to one of the great monuments in Europe, what else might this war bring?

The two sides were forced to settle into a war of attrition relying on an elaborate network of defensive trenches. Although separated by as much as 5 miles in some places, enemy trenches were sometimes within shouting distance, so there was occasionally banter back and forth, even attempts to entertain the other side. But the trenches quickly became almost unimaginably gruesome—filthy, ridden with rats and lice, noisy and smoky from artillery fire, and foul-smelling, partly from the odor of decaying bodies.

As defensive instruments, however, the trenches proved quite effective. Each side quickly learned to take advantage of barbed wire, mines, and especially machine guns to defend its positions. A mass of barbed wire, 3 to 5 feet high and 30 yards wide, guarded a typical trench. The machine gun had been developed before the war as an offensive weapon; few foresaw the decided advantage it would give the defense. But with machine guns, soldiers could defend trenches even against massive assaults—and inflict heavy casualties on the attackers.

In 1916 the British sent the first shipment of tanks to France as an antidote to the machine gun, but, as skeptics had warned, tanks proved too ungainly and unreliable to be widely effective. Although the French used them to advantage in the decisive Allied offensive in 1918, tanks were not crucial to the outcome of the war.

Though the defensive trenches had formidable advantages, neither side could give up the vision of a decisive offensive to break through on the western front.

Reims (RAANZ)

## ❧ READING SOURCES

### Into the Trenches

*As the initial offensives on the western front turned into stalemate, ordinary soldiers on both sides began to experience unprecedented forms of warfare in an eerie new landscape. Writing home to his family from France in November 1914, a young German soldier, Fritz Franke (1892–1915), sought to convey what this new war was like. He was killed six months later.*

Yesterday we didn't feel sure that a single one of us would come through alive. You can't possibly picture to yourselves what such a battle-field looks like. It is impossible to describe it, and even now, when it is a day behind us, I myself can hardly believe that such bestial barbarity and unspeakable suffering are possible. Every foot of ground contested; every hundred yards another trench; and everywhere bodies—rows of them! All the trees shot to pieces; the whole ground churned up a yard deep by the heaviest shells; dead animals; houses and churches so utterly destroyed by shellfire that they can never be of the least use again. And every troop that advances in support must pass through a mile of this chaos, through this gigantic burial ground and the reek of corpses.

In this way we advanced on Tuesday, marching for three hours, a silent column, in the moonlight, toward the Front and into a trench as Reserve, two to three hundred yards from the English, close behind our own infantry.

There we lay the whole day, a yard and a half to two yards below the level of the ground, crouching in the narrow trench on a thin layer of straw, in an overpowering din which never ceased all day or the greater part of the night—the whole ground trem-bling and shaking! There is every variety of sound—whistling, whining, ringing, crashing, rolling . . . [ellipses in the original] the beastly things pitch right above one and burst and the fragments buzz in all directions, and the only question one asks is: "Why doesn't one get me?" Often the things land within a hand's breath and one just looks on. One gets so hardened to it that at the most one ducks one's head a little if a great, big naval-gun shell comes a bit too near and its grey-green stink is a bit too thick. Otherwise one soon just lies there and thinks of other things. . . .

One just lives from one hour to the next. For instance, if one starts to prepare some food, one never knows if one may'nt have to leave it behind within an hour. . . .

. . . Above all one acquires a knowledge of human nature! We all live so naturally and unconventionally here, every one according to his own instincts. That brings much that is good and much that is ugly to the surface.

*Source:* A. F. Wedd, ed., *German Students' War Letters*, translated and arranged from the original edition of Dr. Philipp Witkop (London: Methuen, 1929), pp. 123–125.

Thus the troops were periodically called on to go "over the top" and then across "no man's land" to assault the dug-in enemy. Again and again, however, such offensives proved futile, producing incredibly heavy casualties: "Whole regiments gambled away eternity for ten yards of wasteland."[1]

For the soldiers on the western front the war became a nightmarish experience in a hellish landscape. Bombardment by new, heavier forms of artillery scarred the terrain with craters, which became muddy, turning the landscape into a near swamp. (See the box "Reading Sources: Into the Trenches.") Beginning early in 1915, tear gas, chlorine gas, and finally mustard gas found use on both sides. Although the development of gas masks significantly reduced the impact of this menacing new chemical warfare, the threat of poison gas added another nightmarish element to the experience of those who fought the war.

The notions of patriotism, comradeship, duty, and glory that had been prevalent in 1914 gradually dissolved as soldiers experienced the horrors of warfare. A French soldier, questioning his own reactions after battle in

1916, responded with sarcasm and irony: "What sublime emotion inspires you at the moment of assault? I thought of nothing other than dragging my feet out of the mud encasing them. What did you feel after surviving the attack? I grumbled because I would have to remain several days more without *pinard* [wine]. Is not one's first act to kneel down and thank God? No. One relieves oneself."[2]

Although the Germans had been denied their quick victory in the west, by the end of 1914 they occupied much of Belgium and almost one-tenth of France, including major industrial areas and mines producing most of France's coal and iron. On the eastern front, as well, the Germans won some substantial advantages in 1914—but not a decisive victory.

The first season of fighting in the east suggested that the pattern there would not be trench warfare but rapid movement across a vast but thinly held front. When the fighting began in August, the Russians mustered more quickly than anticipated, confronting an outnumbered German force in a menacing, if reckless, invasion of East Prussia. But by mid-September German forces under General Paul von Hindenburg (1847–1934) and his chief of staff General Erich Ludendorff (1865–1937) repelled the Russian advance, taking a huge number of prisoners and seriously demoralizing the Russians.

As a result of their victory in East Prussia, Hindenburg and Ludendorff emerged as heroes, and they would play major roles in German public life thereafter. Hindenburg, the senior partner, became chief of staff of the entire German army in August 1916, and the able and energetic Ludendorff remained at his side. Ludendorff proved to be the key figure as this powerful duo gradually assumed undisputed control of the whole German war effort, both military and domestic.

## ■ Seeking a Breakthrough, 1915–1917

After the campaigns of 1915 proved inconclusive, German leaders decided to concentrate in 1916 on a massive offensive against the great French fortress at Verdun, intending to inflict a definitive defeat on France. To assault the fortress, the Germans gathered 1,220 pieces of artillery for attack along an 8-mile front. Included were thirteen "Big Bertha" siege guns, weapons so large that nine tractors were required to position each of them; a

**Paul von Hindenburg and Erich Ludendorff**
The talents of Hindenburg (*left*) and Ludendorff meshed effectively to carry them from success on the eastern front in 1914 to a predominant role in the German war effort. They are shown here at a reception in honor of Hindenburg's seventieth birthday in October 1917.   (*AKG London*)

crane was necessary to insert the shell, which weighed over a ton. The level of heavy artillery firepower that the Germans applied at Verdun was unprecedented in the history of warfare.

German forces attacked on February 21, taking the outer defenses of the fortress, and appeared poised for victory. The tide turned, however, when General Philippe Pétain° (1856–1951) assumed control of the French defense at Verdun. Pétain had the patience and skill necessary to organize supply networks for a long and difficult siege. Furthermore, he proved able, through considerate treatment, to inspire affection and confidence among his men. By mid-July the French army had repelled the German offensive, although only in December did the French retake the outer defenses of the fortress. The French had held firm in what would prove the war's longest, most trying battle—one that killed over 700,000 men on both sides. For the French the Battle of Verdun would remain the epitome of the horrors of World War I.

To relieve pressure on Verdun, the British led a major attack at the Somme River on July 1, 1916. On that day alone the British suffered almost 60,000 casualties, including 21,000 killed. Fighting continued into the fall, but the offensive proved futile in the end. One-third of those involved, or over 1 million soldiers, ended up dead, missing, or wounded.

Dominated by the devastating battles at Verdun and the Somme, the campaigns of 1916 finally extinguished the high spirits of the summer of 1914. Both sides suffered huge losses—apparently for nothing. By the end of 1916, the front had shifted only a few miles from its location at the beginning of the year.

In light of the frustrating outcome so far, the French turned to new military leadership, replacing Joffre as commander-in-chief with Robert Nivelle (1856–1924), who promptly sought to prove himself with a new offensive during the spring of 1917. Persisting even as it became clear that this effort had no chance of success, Nivelle provoked increasing resistance among French soldiers, some of whom were refusing to follow orders by the end of April.

With the French war effort in danger of collapse, the French government replaced Nivelle with General Pétain, the hero of the defense of Verdun. Pétain reestablished discipline by adopting a conciliatory approach—improving food and rest, visiting the troops in the field, listening, offering encouragement, urging patience, even dealing relatively mercifully with most of the resisters themselves. To be sure, many of the soldiers who had participated in this near-mutiny were court-martialed, and over 3,400 were convicted. But of the 554 sentenced to death, only 49 were executed.

After the failure of the Nivelle offensive, the initiative fell to the British under General Douglas Haig (1861–1928), who was convinced, despite skepticism in the British cabinet, that Nivelle's offensive had failed simply because of tactical mistakes. Beginning near Ypres° in Belgium on July 31, 1917, and continuing until November, the British attacked. As before, the effort yielded only minimal territorial gains—about 50 square miles—at a horrifying cost, including 300,000 British and Canadian casualties. Known as the Battle of Passchendaele, the British offensive of 1917 ranks with the Battles of Verdun and the Somme as the bloodiest of the war.

## ■ 1917 as a Turning Point

Meanwhile, the Germans decided to concentrate on the eastern front in 1917 in an effort to knock Russia out of the war. This intensified German military pressure helped spark revolution in Russia, and in December 1917 Russia's new revolutionary regime asked for a separate peace (see page 862). The defeat of Russia freed the Germans at last to concentrate on the west, but by this time France and Britain had a new ally.

On April 6, 1917, the United States entered the war on the side of the Entente, in response to Germany's controversial use of submarines. Germany did not have enough surface ships to respond to Britain's naval blockade, whether by attacking the British fleet directly or by mounting a comparable blockade of the British Isles. So the Germans decided to use submarines to interfere with shipping to Britain. Submarines, however, were too vulnerable to be able to surface and confiscate goods, so the Germans had to settle for sinking suspect ships with torpedoes. In February 1915 they declared the waters around the British Isles a war zone and served notice that they would torpedo not only enemy ships but also neutral ships carrying goods to Britain.

The German response was harsh, but so was the British blockade, which violated a number of earlier international agreements about the rights of neutral shipping and the scope of wartime blockades. The British had agreed that only military goods such as munitions and certain raw materials, not such everyday goods as food and clothing, were to be subject to confiscation. Yet in blockading Germany, the British refused to make this distinction, prompting the sarcastic German quip that Britannia not only rules the waves but waives the rules.[3]

**Pétain** (puh-TANH)

**Ypres** (EE-pray)

In May 1915 a German sub torpedoed the *Lusitania*, a British passenger liner, killing almost 1,200 people and producing widespread indignation. Partly because 128 of those killed were Americans, U.S. president Woodrow Wilson issued a severe warning, which contributed to the German decision in September 1915 to pull back from unrestricted submarine warfare. But as German suffering under the British blockade increased, pressure mounted on Berlin to put the subs back into action.

The issue provoked bitter debate. Chancellor Theobald von Bethmann-Hollweg° and the civilian authorities opposed resumption out of fear it would provoke the United States to enter the war. But Ludendorff and the military finally prevailed, partly with the argument that even if the United States did intervene, U.S. troops could not get to Europe in sufficient numbers, and in sufficient haste, to have a major impact. Germany announced it would resume unrestricted submarine warfare on January 31, 1917, and the United States responded with a declaration of war on April 6.

Many on both sides doubted that U.S. intervention would make a pivotal difference; most assumed—correctly—that it would take at least a year for the American presence to materialize in force. Still, the entry of the United States gave the Entente at least the promise of more fighting power. And the United States seemed capable of renewing the sense of purpose on the Entente side, showing that the war had a meaning that could justify the unexpected costs and sacrifice.

## THE EXPERIENCE OF TOTAL WAR

S the war dragged on, the distinction between the military and civilian spheres blurred. Suffering increased on the home front, and unprecedented governmental mobilization of society proved necessary to wage war on the scale that had come to be required. Because it became "total" in this way, the war decisively altered not only the old political and diplomatic order, but also culture, society, and the patterns of everyday life.

### ■ Hardship on the Home Front

The war meant food shortages, and thus malnutrition, for ordinary people in the belligerent countries, although Britain and France, with their more favorable geographic positions, suffered considerably less than

**Bethmann-Hollweg** (BETT-mahn–HOHL-veg)

others. Germany was especially vulnerable, and the British naval blockade exacerbated an already dire situation. With military needs taking priority, the Germans encountered shortages of the chemical fertilizers, farm machinery, and draft animals necessary for agricultural production. The government began rationing bread, meat, and fats during 1915. The increasing scarcity of food produced sharp increases in diseases such as rickets and tuberculosis and in infant and childhood mortality rates.

The need to pay for the war produced economic dislocations as well. Government borrowing covered some of the cost for the short term, but to underwrite the rest, governments all over Europe found it more palatable to inflate the currency, by printing more money, than to raise taxes. The notion that the enemy would be made to pay once victory had been won seemed to justify this decision. But this way of financing the war meant rising prices and severe erosion of purchasing power for ordinary people all over Europe. In France and Germany, the labor truces of 1914 gave way to increasing strike activity during 1916.

With an especially severe winter in 1916–1917 adding to the misery, there were serious instances of domestic disorder, including strikes and food riots, in many parts of Europe during 1917. In Italy, major strikes developed in Turin and other cities over wages and access to foodstuffs. The revolution that overthrew the tsarist autocracy in Russia that same year began with comparable protests over wartime food shortages.

The strains of war even fanned the flames in Ireland, where an uneasy truce over the home-rule controversy accompanied the British decision for war in 1914. Partly because of German efforts to stir up domestic trouble for Britain, unrest built up again in Ireland, culminating in the Easter Rebellion in Dublin in 1916. The brutality with which British forces crushed the uprising intensified demands for full independence—precisely what Britain would be forced to yield to the Irish Republic shortly after the war.

Moreover, new technologies made civilians ever less immune to wartime violence. Although bombing from aircraft began with an immediate military aim—to destroy industrial targets or to provide tactical support for other military units—it quickly became clear that night bombing, especially, might demoralize civilian populations. In 1915 German airplanes began bombing English cities, provoking British retaliation against cities in the German Ruhr and Rhineland areas. These raids had little effect on the course of the war, but they showed that new technologies could make warfare more destructive even for civilians.

## ■ Domestic Mobilization

Once it became clear that the war would not be over quickly, leaders on both sides also realized that the outcome would not be determined on the battlefield alone. Victory required mobilizing all of the nation's resources and energies. So World War I became a total war, involving the entire society.

The British naval blockade on Germany, which made no distinction between military and nonmilitary goods, was a stratagem characteristic of total war. The blockade would not affect Germany's immediate strength on the battlefield, but it could damage Germany's long-term war-making capacity. The blockade was effective partly because Germany had not made adequate preparations—including stockpiling—for a protracted war of attrition.

In peacetime, Germany had depended on imports of food, fats, oils, and chemicals, including the nitrates needed for ammunition. With the onset of war, these goods were immediately in short supply, as was labor. Thus Germany seemed to need stringent economic coordination and control. By the end of 1916, the country had developed a militarized economy, with all aspects of economic life coordinated for the war effort. Under the supervision of the military, state agencies, big business, and the trade unions were brought into close collaboration. The new system included rationing, price controls, and compulsory labor arbitration, as well as a national service law enabling the military to channel workers into jobs deemed vital to the war effort.

The Germans did not hesitate to exploit the economy of occupied Belgium, requisitioning foodstuffs even to the point of causing starvation among the Belgians themselves. They forced 62,000 Belgians to work in German factories under conditions of virtual slave labor. By the time this practice was stopped in February 1917, nearly a thousand Belgian workers had died in German labor camps.

The body coordinating Germany's war economy was the Kriegsrohstoffabteilung° (KRA), or war raw materials office. Led initially by the able Jewish industrialist Walther Rathenau° (1867–1922), this agency came to symbolize the unprecedented coordination of the German economy for war. Recognizing that Germany lacked the raw materials for a long war, Rathenau devised an imaginative program that included the development of synthetic substitute products and the creation of new

mixed (private and government) companies to allocate raw materials. The KRA's effort was remarkably successful—a model for later economic planning and coordination in Germany and elsewhere.

Although Germany presented the most dramatic example of domestic coordination, the same pattern was evident everywhere. In Britain, the central figure was David Lloyd George (1863–1945), appointed to the newly created post of minister of munitions in 1915. During his year in that office, ninety-five new factories opened, soon overcoming the shortage of guns and ammunition that had impeded the British war effort until then. His performance made Lloyd George seem the one person who could organize Britain for victory. Succeeding Herbert Asquith as prime minister in December 1916, he would direct the British war effort to its victorious conclusion.

## ■ Accelerating Socioeconomic Change

Everywhere the war effort quickened the long-term socioeconomic change associated with industrialization. Government orders for war materiel fueled industrial expansion. In France, the Paris region became a center of heavy industry for the first time. The needs of war spawned new technologies—advances in food processing and medical treatment, for example—that would carry over into peacetime.

With so many men needed for military service, women were called on to assume new economic roles—such as running farms in France, or working in the new munitions factories in Britain. (See the box "Reading Sources: Domestic Mobilization and the Role of Women.") During the course of the war, the number of women employed in Britain rose from 3.25 million to 5 million. In Italy, 200,000 women had war-related jobs by 1917. Women also played indispensable roles at the front, especially in nursing units.

The expanded opportunities of wartime intensified the debate over the sociopolitical role of women that the movement for women's suffrage had stimulated. The outbreak of war led some antiwar feminists to argue that women would be better able than men to prevent wars, which were essentially masculine undertakings. Women should have full access to public life, not because they could be expected to respond as men did but because they had a distinctive—and valuable—role to play. At the same time, by giving women jobs and the opportunity to do many of the same things men did, the war undermined the stereotypes that had long justified restrictions on women's political roles and life choices.

---

**Kriegsrohstoffabteilung** (kreegs-ROH-stoff-AHB-ty-loong)
**Rathenau** (RAT-un-ow)

## ✒ READING SOURCES

## Domestic Mobilization and the Role of Women

*Early in 1917, British writer Gilbert Stone published a remarkable collection of statements intended to illuminate the new experiences that British women were encountering in the workplace. The following passage by Naomi Loughnan, a well-to-do woman who worked in a munitions factory, makes it clear that the new work experience during the war provoked new questions about both gender and class.*

Engineering mankind is possessed of the unshakable opinion that no woman can have the mechanical sense. If one of us asks humbly why such and such an alteration is not made to prevent this or that drawback to a machine, she is told, with a superior smile, that a man has worked her machine before her for years, and that therefore if there were any improvement possible it would have been made. As long as we do exactly as we are told and do not attempt to use our brains, we give entire satisfaction, and are treated as nice, good children. Any swerving from the easy path prepared for us by our males arouses the most scathing contempt in their manly bosoms. . . . Women have, however, proved that their entry into the munitions world has increased the output. Employers who forget things personal in their patriotic desire for large results are enthusiastic over the success of women in the shops. But their workmen have to be handled with the utmost tenderness and caution lest they should actually imagine it was being suggested that women could do their work equally well, given equal conditions of training—at least where muscle is not the driving force. This undercurrent of jealousy rises to the surface rather often, but as a general rule the men behave with much kindness, and are ready to help with muscle and advice whenever called upon. If eyes are very bright and hair inclined to curl, the muscle and advice do not even wait for a call.

The coming of the mixed classes of women into the factory is slowly but surely having an educative effect upon the men. "Language" is almost unconsciously becoming subdued. There are fiery exceptions who make our hair stand up on end under our close-fitting caps, but a sharp rebuke or a look of horror will often bring to book the most truculent. . . . It is grievous to hear the girls also swearing and using disgusting language. Shoulder to shoulder with the children of the slums, the upper classes are having their eyes pried open at last to the awful conditions among which their sisters have dwelt. Foul language, immorality, and many other evils are but the natural outcome of overcrowding and bitter poverty. If some of us, still blind and ignorant of our responsibilities, shrink horrified and repelled from the rougher set, the compliment is returned with open derision and ribald laughter. . . . On the other hand, attempts at friendliness from the more understanding are treated with the utmost suspicion, though once that suspicion is overcome and friendship is established, it is unshakable.

*Source:* Naomi Loughnan, "Munition Work," in Gilbert Stone, ed., *Women War Workers: Accounts Contributed by Representative Workers of the Work Done by Women in the More Important Branches of War Employment* (New York: Thomas Y. Crowell, 1917), pp. 35–38.

For many women, doing a difficult job well, serving their country in this emergency situation, afforded a new sense of accomplishment, as well as a new taste of independence. Women were now much more likely to have their own residences and to go out on their own, eating in restaurants, even smoking and drinking. Yet while many seized new opportunities and learned new skills, women frequently had to combine paid employment with housework and child rearing, and those who left home—to serve in nursing units, for example—often felt guilty about neglecting their traditional family roles.

**Working Women and the War**    All over Europe, governments recruited women to work in munitions factories. This Russian government poster uses an image of working women to rally support for the war. The text reads, "Everything for the war effort! Subscribe to the war loans at 5½ percent."

*(Eileen Tweedy, The Art Archive)*

### ■ Propaganda and the "Mobilization of Enthusiasm"

Because the domestic front was crucial to sustaining a long war of attrition, it became ever more important to shore up civilian morale as the war dragged on. The result was what the historian Elie Halévy called the "mobilization of enthusiasm"—the deliberate manipulation of collective passions by national governments on an unprecedented scale. Every country instituted extensive censorship, even of soldiers' letters from the front. Because of concerns about civilian morale, the French press carried no news of the Battle of Verdun, with its horrifying numbers of casualties. In addition, systematic propaganda included not only patriotic themes but also attempts to discredit the enemy, even through outright falsification of the news. British anti-German propaganda helped draw the United States into the war in 1917.

At the outset of the war, the brutal behavior of the German armies in Belgium made it easy for the French and the British to demonize the Germans. Having expected to pass through neutral Belgium unopposed, the Germans were infuriated by the Belgian resistance they encountered. At Louvain late in August 1914 they responded to alleged Belgian sniping by shooting a number of hostages and setting the town on fire, destroying the famous old library at the university. This notorious episode led the *London Times* to characterize the Germans as "Huns," a reference to the central Asian tribe that began invading Europe in the fourth century. Stories about German soldiers eating Belgian babies began to circulate.

**Devastation at Louvain**    Unexpected destruction at the outset of the war fanned the flames of hatred and changed the stakes of the conflict. Located in the path of the first German advance, the Belgian city of Louvain was particularly hard hit.    *(Trustees of the Imperial War Museum)*

In October 1914 ninety-three German intellectuals, artists, and scientists signed a manifesto, addressed to "the World of Culture," justifying Germany's conduct in Belgium and its larger purposes in the war. As passions heated up, major intellectuals on both sides—from the German theologian Adolf von Harnack (1851–1930) to the French philosopher Henri Bergson (1859–1941)—began denigrating the culture of the enemy and claiming a monopoly of virtue for their own sides.

As the war dragged on, some came to believe that real peace with an adversary so evil, so abnormally different, was simply not possible. There must be no compromise but rather total victory, no matter what the cost. At the same time, however, war-weariness produced a countervailing tendency to seek a "white peace," a peace without victory for either side. But in 1917, as Europeans began earnestly debating war aims, the Russian Revolution and the intervention of the United States changed the war's meaning for all the belligerents.

# TWO REVOLUTIONS IN RUSSIA: MARCH AND NOVEMBER **1917**

**S**TRAINED by war, the old European order cracked first in Russia in 1917. Initially the overthrow of the tsarist autocracy seemed to lay the foundations for parliamentary democracy. But by the end of the year, the Bolsheviks, the smallest and most extreme of Russia's major socialist parties, had taken power, an outcome that was hardly conceivable when the revolution began.

### ■ The Wartime Crisis of the Russian Autocracy

The Russian army performed better than many had expected during the first year of the war. As late as June 1916, it mounted a successful offensive against Austria-Hungary. Russia had industrialized sufficiently by 1914 to sustain a modern war, at least for a while, and the country's war production increased significantly by 1916. But Russia suffered from problems of leadership and organization—in transportation, for example—that made it less prepared for a long war than the other belligerents. Even early in 1915, perhaps a fourth of Russia's newly conscripted troops were sent to the front without weapons; they were told to pick up rifles and supplies from the dead.

In August 1915, Tsar Nicholas II (1868–1918) assumed personal command of the army, but his absence from the capital only accelerated the deterioration in government and deepened the divisions within the ruling clique. With the tsar away, the illiterate but charismatic Siberian "holy man" Grigori Rasputin (ca. 1872–1916) emerged as the key political power within the circle of the German-born Empress Alexandra (1872–1918). He won her confidence because of his alleged ability to control the bleeding of her hemophiliac son, Alexis, the heir to the throne. Led by Rasputin, those around the empress made a shambles of the state administration. Many educated Russians, appalled at what was happening, assumed—incorrectly—that pro-German elements at court were responsible for the eclipse of the tsar and the increasing chaos in the government. Asked one Duma deputy of the government's performance, "Is this stupidity, or is it treason?"

Finally, late in December 1916, Rasputin was assassinated by aristocrats seeking to save the autocracy from these apparently pro-German influences. This act indicated how desperate the situation was becoming, but eliminating Rasputin made little difference.

By the end of 1916, the difficulties of war had combined with the strains of rapid wartime industrialization to produce a revolutionary situation in Russia. The country's urban population had mushroomed, and now, partly because of transport problems, the cities faced severe food shortages. Strikes and demonstrations spread from Petrograd (the former St. Petersburg, whose name was abandoned as too German at the start of the war) to other cities during the first two months of 1917. In March renewed demonstrations in Petrograd, spearheaded by women protesting the lack of bread and coal, led to revolution.

### ■ The March Revolution and the Fate of the Provisional Government

At first, the agitation that began in Petrograd on March 8, 1917, appeared to be just another bread riot. Even when it turned into a wave of strikes, the revolutionary parties (see page 834) expected it to be crushed by the government troops stationed at the Petrograd garrison. But

when they were called out to help the police break up the demonstrations, the soldiers generally avoided firing at the strikers. Within days, they were sharing weapons and ammunition with the workers; the garrison was going over to what was now becoming a revolution.

Late in the afternoon of March 12, leaders of the strike committees, delegates elected by factory workers, and representatives of the socialist parties formed a *soviet,* or council, following the example of the revolution of 1905, when such soviets had first appeared. Regiments of the Petrograd garrison also began electing representatives, soon to be admitted to the Petrograd Soviet, which officially became the Council of Workers' and Soldiers' Deputies. This soviet was now the ruling power in the Russian capital. It had been elected and was genuinely representative—though of a limited constituency of workers and soldiers. Following the lead of Petrograd, Russians elsewhere promptly began forming soviets, so that over 350 local units were represented when the first All-Russian Council of Soviets met in Petrograd in April. The overwhelming majority of their representatives were Mensheviks and Socialist Revolutionaries; about one-sixth were Bolsheviks.

On March 14 a committee of the Duma, recognizing that the tsar's authority had been lost for good, persuaded Nicholas to abdicate, then formed a new provisional government. This government was to be strictly temporary, paving the way for an elected constituent assembly, which would write a constitution and establish fully legitimate governmental institutions.

Considering the strains in the autocratic system that had produced the revolution of 1905 after the Russo-Japanese War, it was hardly surprising that the system would shatter now, in light of this far more trying war and the resulting disarray within the tsarist government. Russia had apparently experienced, at last, the bourgeois political revolution necessary to develop a Western-style parliamentary democracy. Even from an orthodox Marxist perspective, the immediate priority was to help consolidate the new democratic order, which would then provide the framework for the longer-term pursuit of socialism.

Although the fall of the tsarist order produced widespread relief, Russia's new leaders faced difficult questions about priorities. Should they focus their efforts on revitalizing the Russian war effort? Or, given the widespread war-weariness in the country, should they focus on domestic political reform? For now, the Petrograd Soviet was prepared to give the provisional government a chance to govern. But the soviet was a potential rival for power if the new government failed to address Russia's immediate problems.

**Lenin as Leader**  Although he was in exile during much of 1917, Lenin's leadership was crucial to the Bolshevik success in Russia. He is shown here addressing a May Day rally in Red Square, Moscow, on May 1, 1919. *(ITAR-TASS/Sovfoto)*

The provisional government took important steps toward Western-style liberal democracy, establishing universal suffrage, civil liberties, autonomy for ethnic minorities, and labor legislation, including provision for an eight-hour workday. But the government failed in two key areas, fostering discontents that the Bolsheviks soon exploited. First, it persisted in fighting the war. Second, it dragged its feet on agrarian reform.

The provisional government's determination to renew the war effort stemmed from genuine concern about Russia's obligations to its allies, about the country's national honor and position among the great powers. The long-standing goal of Russian diplomacy—an outlet to the Mediterranean Sea through the Dardanelles Strait—seemed within reach if Russia could continue the war and contribute to an Entente victory. The educated, well-to-do Russians who led the new government expected that ordinary citizens, now free, would fight with renewed enthusiasm, like the armies that had grown from the French Revolution over a century before. These leaders failed to grasp how desperate the situation of ordinary people had become.

Although the March revolution began in the cities, the peasantry soon moved into action as well, seizing land, sometimes burning the houses of their landlords. By midsummer, a full-scale peasant war seemed to be in the offing in the countryside, and calls for radical agrarian reform became increasingly urgent. Partly from expediency, partly from genuine concern for social justice, the provisional government promised a major redistri-bution of land. But it insisted that the reform be carried out legally—not by the present provisional government, but by a duly elected constituent assembly.

Calling for elections would thus seem to have been the first priority. The new political leaders kept putting it off, however, waiting for the situation to cool before giving up power to a newly elected assembly. But playing for time was a luxury they could ill afford. As unrest grew in the countryside, the authority of the provisional government diminished and the soviets gained in stature. But what role were the soviets to play?

## ■ The Bolsheviks Come to Power

In the immediate aftermath of the March revolution, the Bolsheviks had not seemed to differ substantially from their rivals within the socialist movement, at least on matters of immediate concern—the war, land reform, and the character of the revolution itself. But the situation began to change in April when Lenin, assisted by the German military, returned from exile in Switzerland. The Germans assumed—correctly, it turned out—that the Bolsheviks would help undermine the Russian war effort. Largely through the force of Lenin's leadership, the Bolsheviks soon took the initiative within the still-developing revolution in Russia.

Lenin (1870–1924), born Vladimir Ilich Ulianov, came from a comfortable upper-middle-class family. He was university-educated and trained as a lawyer. But after an older brother was executed in 1887 for participating in a plot against the tsar's life, Lenin followed him into revolutionary activity. Arrested for the first time in 1895, he was confined to Siberia until 1900. He then lived in exile abroad for almost the entire period before his return to Russia in 1917.

The Bolshevik Party was identified with Lenin from its beginning in 1903, when it emerged from the schism in Russian Marxist socialism. Because of his emphases, Bolshevism came to mean discipline, organization, and a special leadership role for a revolutionary vanguard. Lenin proved effective because he was a stern and somewhat forbidding figure, disciplined, fiercely intelligent, sometimes ruthless. As a Bolshevik colleague put it, Lenin was "the one indisputable leader . . . a man of iron will, inexhaustible energy, combining a fanatical faith in the movement, in the cause, with an equal faith in himself."[4]

Still, Lenin's reading of the situation when he returned to Petrograd in April astonished even many Bolsheviks. He argued that the revolution was about to pass from the present bourgeois-democratic stage to a socialist phase, involving dictatorship of the proletariat in the form of government by the soviets. So the Bolsheviks should begin actively opposing the provisional government, especially by denouncing the war as fundamentally imperialist and by demanding the distribution of land from the large estates to the peasants. This latter measure had long been identified with the Socialist revolutionaries; most Bolsheviks had envisioned collectivization and nationalization instead.

As Lenin saw it, under the strains of war, all of Europe was becoming ripe for revolution. A revolution in Russia would provide the spark to ignite wider proletarian revolution, especially in Germany. He did not envision backward Russia seeking to create socialism on its own. Although some remained skeptical of Lenin's strategy, he promptly won over most of his fellow Bolsheviks. And thus the Bolsheviks began actively seeking wider support by promising peace, land, and bread.

In April 1917 moderate socialists still had majority support in the soviets, so the Bolsheviks sought to build support gradually, postponing any decisive test of strength. But events escaped the control of the Bolshevik leadership in mid-July when impatient workers, largely Bolshevik in sympathy, took to the streets of Petrograd on their own. The Petrograd Soviet refused to support the uprising, and the provisional government had no difficulty getting military units to put it down, killing two hundred in the process. Though the uprising had developed spontaneously, Bolshevik leaders felt compelled to offer public support, and this gave the government an excuse to crack down on the Bolshevik leadership. Lenin

managed to escape to Finland, but a number of his colleagues were arrested and jailed.

With the Bolsheviks on the defensive, counterrevolutionary elements in the Russian military decided to seize the initiative with a march on Petrograd in September. To resist this attempted coup, the provisional government, now led by the young Socialist revolutionary Alexander Kerensky (1881–1970), had to rely on whoever could offer help, including the Bolsheviks. And thanks to Bolshevik propaganda, the soldiers under the command of the counterrevolutionaries refused to fight against the upholders of the revolution in Petrograd. Thus the coup was thwarted. Within days, the Bolsheviks won their first clear-cut majority in the Petrograd Soviet, then shortly gained majorities in most of the other soviets as well.

During the fall of 1917, the situation became increasingly volatile, eluding control by anyone. People looted food from shops; peasants seized land, sometimes murdering their landlords. Desertions and the murder of officers increased within the Russian military.

With the Bolsheviks now the dominant power in the soviets, and with the government's control diminishing, Lenin, from his hideout in Finland, urged the Bolshevik central committee to prepare for armed insurrection. Although some found this step too risky, the majority accepted Lenin's argument that the provisional government would continue dragging its feet, inadvertently giving right-wing officer cadres time for another coup.

Because Lenin remained in hiding, the task of organizing the seizure of power fell to Leon Trotsky (1870–1940), who skillfully modified Lenin's aggressive strategy. Lenin wanted the Bolsheviks to rise in their own name, in opposition to the provisional government, but Trotsky linked the insurrection to the cause of the soviets and played up its defensive character against the ongoing danger of a counterrevolutionary coup. With the political center at an impasse, the only alternative to such a coup seemed to be a Bolshevik initiative to preserve the Petrograd Soviet, by now the sole viable institutional embodiment of the revolution and its promise. Trotsky's interpretation led people who wanted simply to defend the Soviet to support the Bolsheviks' initiative.

During the night of November 9, armed Bolsheviks and regular army regiments occupied key points in Petrograd, including railroad stations, post offices, telephone exchanges, power stations, and the national bank. Able to muster only token resistance, the provisional government collapsed. Kerensky escaped and mounted what quickly proved a futile effort to rally troops at the front for a counterattack against the Bolsheviks. In contrast to the March revolution, which had taken about a week, the Bolsheviks took over the

### ❧ READING SOURCES

## The Bolsheviks in Power, November 1917

*John Reed (1887–1920), an American journalist and communist leader from Portland, Oregon, was in Russia during the fall of 1917, when the second revolution began. His enthusiastic firsthand account, which drew the praise of Lenin himself, conveys the drama and excitement of the revolution. In the following passage, Reed provides a sense of the emergency, improvisation, and revolutionary enthusiasm that marked the Bolsheviks' first days in power.*

Having settled the question of power, the Bolsheviki turned their attention to problems of practical administration. First of all, the city, the country, the Army must be fed. Bands of sailors and Red Guards scoured the warehouses, the railway terminals, even the barges in the canals, unearthing and confiscating thousands of *poods* [a *pood* equals 36 pounds] of food held by private speculators. Emissaries were sent to the provinces, where with the assistance of the Land Committees they seized the storehouses of the great grain dealers. Expeditions of sailors, heavily armed, were sent out in groups of five thousand to the South, to Siberia, with roving commissions to capture cities still held by the White Guards, establish order and *get food* [italics in the original]. . . .

Towards the end of November occurred the "wine-pogrom"—looting of the wine cellars—beginning with the plundering of the Winter Palace vaults. For days there were drunken soldiers on the streets. In all this was evident the hand of the counterrevolutionists, who distributed among the regiments plans showing the location of the stores of liquor. The Commissars of Smolny began by pleading and arguing, which did not stop the growing disorder, followed by pitched battles between soldiers and Red Guards. Finally the Military Revolutionary Committee sent out companies of sailors with machine-guns, who fired mercilessly upon the rioters, killing many; and by executive order the wine cellars were invaded by Committees with hatchets, who smashed the bottles—or blew them up with dynamite.

. . . In all quarters of the city small elective Revolutionary Tribunals were set up by the workers and soldiers to deal with petty crime. . . .

Alert and suspicious, the working class of the city constituted itself a vast spy system, through the servants prying into bourgeois households, and reporting all information to the Military Revolutionary Committee, which struck with an iron hand, unceasing. In this way was discovered the Monarchist plot led by a former Duma-member Purishkevich and a group of nobles and officers, who had planned an officers' uprising. . . .

Still the strike of the Ministries went on, still the sabotage of the old officials, the stoppage of normal economic life. Behind Smolny was only the will of the vast, unorganized popular masses; and with them the Council of People's Commissars dealt, directing revolutionary mass action against its enemies. In eloquent proclamations, couched in simple words and spread over Russia, Lenin explained the Revolution, urged the people to take the power into their own hands, by force to break down the resistance of the propertied classes, by force to take over the institutions of Government. Revolutionary order! Revolutionary discipline! Strict accounting and control! No strikes! No loafing!

*Source:* John Reed, *Ten Days That Shook the World* (London: Penguin, 1977), pp. 244–246.

capital, overthrowing the Kerensky government, literally overnight, and almost without bloodshed.

But though the Bolsheviks enjoyed considerable support in the network of soviets, it was not clear that they could extend their control across the whole Russian Empire. (See the box "Reading Sources: The Bolsheviks in Power, November 1917.") Moreover, from their own perspective, the revolution's immediate prospects, and its potential wider impact, were bound up with the course of the war. Would the Bolshevik Revolution in Russia prove the spark for revolution elsewhere in war-weary Europe, as Lenin anticipated?

### ■ The Russian Revolution and the War

Having stood for peace throughout the revolution, the Bolsheviks promptly moved to get Russia out of the war, agreeing to an armistice with Germany in December 1917. They hoped that Russia's withdrawal would speed the collapse of the war effort on all sides and that this, in turn, would intensify the movement toward revolution elsewhere in Europe. The Russian Revolution was but a chapter in this larger story. As Lenin noted to Trotsky, "If it were necessary for us to go under to assure the success of the German revolution, we should have to do it. The German revolution is vastly more important than ours." Indeed, said Lenin to the Bolsheviks' party congress of March 1918, "It is an absolute truth that we will go under without the German revolution."[5]

After assuming control in November, the Bolsheviks published the tsarist government's secret agreements specifying how the spoils were to be divided in the event of a Russian victory. They hoped to inflame revolutionary sentiment elsewhere by demonstrating that the war had been, all along, an imperialist offensive on behalf of capitalist interests. This Bolshevik initiative added fuel to the controversy already developing in all the belligerent countries over the war's purpose and significance.

## THE NEW WAR AND THE ALLIED VICTORY, 1917–1918

**B**ECAUSE the stakes of the war changed during 1917, the outcome, once peace finally came in November 1918, included consequences that Europeans could not have foreseen in 1914. German defeat brought revolution against the monarchy and the beginning of a new democracy. Austro-Hungarian defeat brought the collapse of the Habsburg monarchy and thus the opportunity for its national minorities to form nations of their own. As the old European order fell, grandiose new visions competed to shape the postwar world.

### ■ The Debate over War Aims

The French and British governments publicly welcomed the March revolution in Russia, partly because they expected Russia's military performance to improve under new leadership, but also because the change of regime seemed to have highly favorable psychological implications. With Russia no longer an autocracy, the war could be portrayed—and experienced—as a crusade for democracy. At the same time, the March revolution

could only sow confusion among the many Germans who had understood their own war effort as a matter of self-defense against reactionary Russia. But the November revolution required a deeper reconsideration for all the belligerents.

Allied war aims agreements, such as the Treaty of London that brought Italy into the war in 1915, had remained secret until the Bolsheviks published the tsarist documents. Products of old-style diplomacy, those agreements had been made by a restricted foreign policy elite within the governing circles of each country; even members of the elected parliaments generally did not know their contents. The debate over war aims that developed in 1917 thus became a debate over decision making as well. Many assumed that a more democratic approach to foreign policy would minimize the chances of war since the people would not agree to wars for dynastic or business interests. In addition, there were exhortations for all the parties in the present war to renounce annexations and settle for a white peace. It was time to call the whole thing off and bring the soldiers home.

Seeking to counter such sentiments, especially the Russian contention that the war was not worth continuing, the idealistic U.S. president, Woodrow Wilson (1856–1924), insisted on the great potential significance of an Allied victory. First in his State of the Union speech of January 1918, and in several declarations thereafter, Wilson developed the "Fourteen Points" that he proposed should guide the new international order. Notable among them were open diplomacy, free trade, reduced armaments, self-determination for nationalities, a league of nations, and a recasting of the colonial system to ensure for the indigenous populations rights equal to those of the colonizers.

Lenin and Wilson, then, offered radically different interpretations of the war, with radically different implications for present priorities. Yet, compared with the old diplomacy, they had something in common. Together, they seemed to represent a whole new approach to international relations—and the possibility of a more peaceful world. Thus, they found an eager audience among the war-weary peoples of Europe.

Despite the strains of the war, Sacred Union in France did not weaken substantially until April 1917, with General Nivelle's disastrous offensive. But then, as near-mutiny began to develop within the army, rank-and-file pressures forced Socialist leaders to demand clarification, and perhaps revision, of French war aims. Suddenly the French government was under pressure to suggest that the war had idealistic and democratic purposes. Doubts about the government's goals were threatening to turn into active opposition to the war.

The same pressures were at work in Germany. Antiwar sentiment grew steadily within the Social Democratic Party (SPD) until the antiwar faction split off and formed the Independent Socialist party (USPD) in April 1917. A large-scale debate on war aims, linked to considerations of domestic political reform, developed in the Reichstag by the summer of 1917. On July 19, a solid 60 percent majority passed a new war aims resolution, which affirmed that Germany's purposes were solely defensive, that Germany had no territorial ambitions. Germany too seemed open to a white peace.

But just as the dramatic events of 1917 interjected new pressures for moderation and peace, pressures in the opposite direction also mounted as the war dragged on. It seemed to some that this war was only the beginning of a new era of cutthroat international competition; the old rules would no longer apply. War aims grew more grandiose as nations tried to gain the leverage for success in the postwar world. The present war offered a precious opportunity to secure advantages for that more contentious world, which would surely entail further war before long.

The shape of the current war convinced top German officials that Germany's geography and dependence on imports made it especially vulnerable in a long war. So Germany had to seize the present opportunity to conquer the means to fight the next war on a more favorable footing. Responding in February 1918 to calls for a white peace, General Ludendorff stressed that "if Germany makes peace without profit, it has lost the war." Germany, insisted Ludendorff, must win the military and economic basis for future security—to "enable us to contemplate confidently some future defensive war."[6] Many German officials believed that Germany could achieve parity with Britain, and thus the basis for security and peace, only if it maintained control of the Belgian coast. German expansion into Russian Poland and up the Baltic coast of Lithuania and Latvia seemed essential as well.

When, in response to the Russian request for an armistice, Germany was able to dictate the peace terms, as specified in the Treaty of Brest-Litovsk of March 1918, it became clear how radically annexationist Germany's war aims had become. European Russia was to be largely dismembered, leaving Germany in direct or indirect control of 27 percent of Russia's European territory, 40 percent of its population, and 75 percent of its iron and coal. All the Reichstag parties except the Socialists accepted the terms of the treaty, which, in fact, produced a renewed determination to push on to victory after the disillusionment that had led to the Reichstag war aims resolution of July 1917.

France, less vulnerable geographically than Germany, tended to be more modest. But news of the terms the Germans had imposed at Brest-Litovsk inflamed the French, reinforcing their determination to fight on to an unqualified victory. Only thus could France secure the advantages necessary to ward off an ongoing German menace.

### ■ The Renewal of the French War Effort

The domestic division in France that followed the failure of Nivelle's offensive reached its peak during the fall of 1917. In November, with pressures for a white peace intensifying and France's ability to continue fighting in doubt, President Raymond Poincaré° called on Georges Clemenceau° (1841–1929) to lead a new government. The 76-year-old Clemenceau was known as a "hawk"; his appointment portended a stepped-up prosecution of the war. His message was simple as he appeared before the Chamber of Deputies on November 20, 1917: "If you ask me about my war aims, I reply: my aim is to be victorious." For the remainder of the war, France was under the virtual dictatorship of Clemenceau and his cabinet.

Clemenceau moved decisively on both the domestic and military fronts. By cracking down on the antiwar movement—imprisoning antiwar leaders, suppressing defeatist newspapers—he stiffened morale on the home front. Understanding that lack of coordination between French and the British military leaders had hampered the Allied effort on the battlefield, Clemenceau persuaded the British to accept the French general Ferdinand Foch° (1851–1929) as the first supreme commander of all Allied forces in the west. In choosing Foch, known for his commitment to aggressive offensives, Clemenceau was pointedly bypassing Pétain, whom he found too passive, even defeatist. After some initial friction, Clemenceau let Foch have his way on the military level, and the two proved an effective leadership combination.

### ■ The German Gamble, 1918

As the military campaigns of 1918 began, Germany seemed in a relatively favorable position: Russia had been knocked out of the war, and American troops were yet to arrive. Moderates in Germany wanted to seize the opportunity to work out a compromise peace while there was still a chance. But the military leadership persuaded Kaiser Wilhelm II that Germany could win a definitive victory on the western front if it struck quickly,

---

**Poincaré** (PWAN-cah-RAY)    **Clemenceau** (KLEM-ahn-SOH)
**Foch** (FOHSH)

before U.S. help became significant. Since Germany would be out of reserves by summer, the alternative to decisive victory in the west would be total German defeat.

The German gamble almost succeeded. From March to June 1918, German forces seized the initiative with four months of sustained and effective attacks. By May 30 they had again reached the Marne, where they had been held in 1914. Paris, only 37 miles away, had to be evacuated again (see Map 25.2). As late as mid-July, Ludendorff remained confident of victory, but by mid-August it was becoming clear that Germany lacked the manpower to exploit the successes of the first several months of 1918.

Those successes had caused mutual suspicion between the French and the British at first, but under Foch's leadership the Western allies eventually managed fuller and more effective coordination. By mid-1918 American involvement was also becoming a factor. On June 4, over a year after the U.S. declaration of war, American troops went into action for the first time, bolstering French forces along the Marne. This was a small operation, in which the Americans' performance was amateurish when compared with that of their battle-seasoned allies. But as the Allied counterattack proceeded, 250,000 U.S. troops were arriving per month, considerably boosting Allied morale and battlefield strength.

By June 1918 Europe was experiencing the first outbreak of a virulent new influenza virus, promptly dubbed the "Spanish flu" though it had originated in South Africa. Because of their inferior diets, German soldiers proved far more susceptible to the disease than their adversaries, a fact that significantly affected Germany's combat performance during the crucial summer of 1918.

Germany lost the initiative for good during the second Battle of the Marne, which began on July 15 with yet another German attack. Foch launched a sustained counterattack on July 18, using tanks to good advantage, and maintained the momentum thereafter. By early August the whole western front began to roll back. With astonishing suddenness, the outcome was no longer in doubt, although most expected the war to drag on into 1919. Few realized how desperate Germany's situation had become.

Meanwhile, Germany's allies began falling one by one. In the Balkans an Allied offensive broke through the German-Bulgarian line in September, prompting the Bulgarians to ask for an armistice. The Turkish military

**Map 25.2   Stalemate and Decision on the Western Front**
On the western front, in northern France and Belgium, trench warfare developed and the best known battles of the war were fought. Notable sites include Verdun, Passchendaele, and the Marne and Somme Rivers.

effort collapsed in October. With the defeat of Russia in 1917, the Habsburg Empire of Austria-Hungary redoubled its effort on the Italian front, inflicting a devastating defeat on the Italians at Caporetto late in 1917. But the Italians held, resisted, and then began driving the Austrians back. The Italian victory at Vittorio Veneto forced Austria's unconditional surrender on November 3, 1918. But by this point the armies of the Habsburg Empire, a central pillar of the old European order, were disintegrating along nationality lines. And the impending collapse of this centuries-old empire gave its various national minorities the chance to form states of their own.

## ■ Military Defeat and Political Change in Germany

By late September it was clear to Ludendorff that his armies could not stop the Allied advance. On September 29 he informed the government that to avoid invasion, Germany would have to seek an immediate armistice. Hoping to secure favorable peace terms and to foist responsibility for the defeat onto the parliamentary politicians, Hindenburg and Ludendorff asked that a government based on greater popular support be formed. A leading moderate, Prince Max von Baden° (1867–1929), became chancellor, and he promptly replaced Ludendorff with General Wilhelm Groener° (1867–1939), who seemed more democratic in orientation. By now it was clear that ending the war could not be separated from the push for political change in Germany, especially because it was widely assumed that a more democratic Germany could expect more favorable peace terms.

After securing a written request for an armistice from Hindenburg, Prince Max sent a peace note to President Wilson early in October, asking for an armistice based on Wilson's Fourteen Points. During the month that followed, Prince Max engineered a series of measures, passed by the Reichstag and approved by the emperor, that reformed the constitution, abolishing the three-class voting system in Prussia and making the chancellor responsible to the Reichstag. At last Germany had a constitutional monarchy. Not completely satisfied, President Wilson encouraged speculation that Germany could expect better peace terms if Wilhelm II were to abdicate and Germany became a republic.

But a far more radical outcome seemed possible during late 1918 and early 1919. As negotiations for an armistice proceeded in October, the continuing war effort produced instances of mutiny in the navy and breaches of discipline in the army. By early November workers' and soldiers' councils were being formed all over Germany, just as in Russia the year before. On November 7, antiwar socialists in Munich led an uprising of workers and soldiers that expelled the king of Bavaria and proclaimed a new Bavarian republic. Its provisional government promptly sought its own peace negotiations with the Allies. On November 9, thousands of workers took to the streets of Berlin to demand immediate peace, and the authorities could not muster enough military resources to move against them.

The senior army leadership grew concerned that the collapse of government authority would undermine the ability of officers even to march their troops home. So Hindenburg and Groener persuaded the emperor to abdicate. Having lost the support of the army, Wilhelm II accepted the inevitable and left for exile in the Netherlands.

With the German right, including the military, in disarray, and with the centrist parties discredited by their support for what had become an annexationist war, the initiative passed to the socialists. They, at least, had been in the forefront of the movement for peace. But the socialists had divided in 1917, mostly over the question of response to the war. The mainstream of the SPD, by supporting the war for so long, had irrevocably alienated the party's leftist socialist wing. The most militant of these leftist socialists, led by Karl Liebknecht (1871–1919) and Rosa Luxemburg (1870–1919), envisioned using the workers' and soldiers' councils as the basis for a full-scale revolution, more or less on the Bolshevik model.

The SPD, on the other hand, clung to its reformist heritage and insisted on working within parliamentary institutions. Party leaders argued that a Bolshevik-style revolution was neither appropriate nor necessary under the circumstances. So SPD moderates proclaimed a parliamentary republic on November 9, just hours before the revolutionaries proclaimed a soviet-style republic. The next day the soldiers' and workers' councils in Berlin elected a provisional executive committee, to be led by the moderate socialist Friedrich Ebert° (1871–1925). As the new republic sought to consolidate itself, the radical leftists continued to promote further revolution. For Germany the end of the war meant a leap into an unfamiliar democratic republic, which had to establish itself in conditions not only of military defeat and economic hardship but also of incipient revolution on the extreme left.

Birth from military defeat was especially disabling for the new republic because the German people were so little prepared for defeat when it came. Vigorous censorship had kept the public in the dark about Germany's

---

**Baden** (BAH-dyn)    **Groener** (GREU-nur)

**Ebert** (A-bairt)

real situation, so the request for an armistice early in October came as a shock. At no time during the war had Germany been invaded from the west, and by mid-1918 the German army had seemed on the brink of victory. It appeared inconceivable that Germany had lost a military decision, plain and simple. Thus the "stab in the back" myth, the notion that political intrigue and revolution at home had sabotaged the German military effort, developed to explain what otherwise seemed an inexplicable defeat. This notion would prove a heavy burden for Germany's new democracy to bear.

## THE OUTCOME AND THE IMPACT

FTER the armistice officially ended the fighting on November 11, 1918, it was up to the war's four victors—France, Britain, Italy, and the United States—to establish the terms of peace and, it was to be hoped, a new basis for order at the same time. But the peacemakers had to deal with a radically new political and territorial situation. Revolution had undermined, or threatened to undermine, the old political order in much of Europe. And the war had come to involve non-European powers and peoples in unprecedented ways. After all that had happened since August 1914, it was not clear what a restoration of peace and order would require. But it was evident that Europe would no longer dominate world affairs in quite the way it had.

### ■ The Costs of War

Raw casualty figures do not begin to convey the war's human toll, but they afford some sense of the magnitude of the catastrophe that had befallen Europe and much of the world. Estimates differ, but it is generally agreed that from 10 to 13 million military men lost their lives, with another 20 million wounded. In addition, between 7 and 10 million civilians died as a result of the war and its hardships. In the defeated countries especially, food shortages and malnutrition continued well after the end of the fighting. Thus the Spanish flu that had affected the balance on the battlefield early in the summer of 1918 returned with particularly devastating results during the fall. The influenza pandemic killed perhaps 30 million people worldwide.

Germany suffered the highest number of military casualties, but France suffered the most in proportional terms. Two million Germans were killed, with another 4 million wounded. Military deaths per capita for France

were roughly 15 percent higher than for Germany—and twice as severe as for Britain. Of 8 million Frenchmen mobilized, over 5 million were killed or wounded. Roughly 1.5 million French soldiers, or 10 percent of the active male population, were killed—and this in a country already concerned about demographic decline. The other belligerents suffered less, but still in great numbers. Among the military personnel killed were 2 million Russians, 500,000 Italians, and 114,000 Americans.

Economic costs were heavy as well. In addition to the privations suffered during the years of war, Europeans found themselves reeling from inflation and saddled with debt, especially to the United States, once the war was over. Although the immediate transition to a peacetime economy did not prove as difficult as many had feared, the war and its aftermath produced an economic disequilibrium that lingered, helping to produce a worldwide depression by the 1930s.

### ■ The Search for Peace in a Revolutionary Era

The war had begun because of an unmanageable nationality problem in Austria-Hungary, and it led not simply to military defeat for Austria-Hungary but to the breakup of the Habsburg system (see Map 25.3). In east-central Europe, the end of the war brought bright hopes for self-determination to peoples like the Czechs, Slovaks, Poles, Serbs, and Croats. Even before the peacemakers opened deliberations in January 1919, some of these ethnic groups had begun creating a new order on their own. For example, a popular movement of Czechs and Slovaks established a Czechoslovak republic on October 29, 1918, and a new Yugoslavia and an independent Hungary similarly emerged from indigenous movements. Czechoslovakia and Yugoslavia were made up of different ethnic groups that found cooperation advantageous now but that might well disagree in the future. Moreover, many of these countries lacked traditions of self-government, and they had reason to feud among themselves. With the Habsburg system no longer imposing one form of stability, a power vacuum seemed likely in this potentially volatile part of Europe.

**Map 25.3   The Impact of the War: The Territorial Settlement in Europe and the Middle East**   The defeat of Russia, Austria-Hungary, Germany, and Ottoman Turkey opened the way to major changes in the map of east-central Europe and the Middle East. A number of new nations emerged in east-central Europe, while in the Arab world the end of Ottoman rule meant not independence but new roles for European powers.

Boundaries of German, Russian, and
Austro-Hungarian empires in 1914

Areas lost by Austro-Hungarian Empire

Areas lost by Russian Empire

Areas lost by German Empire

Areas lost by Bulgaria

Areas lost by Ottoman Empire

Demilitarized Zones

Boundaries of 1926

Areas controlled under mandates from
the League of Nations, 1920

Murmansk

NORWAY

Oslo

SWEDEN

FINLAND

Helsinki

Stockholm

Leningrad
(St. Petersburg)

Tallinn

ESTONIA

North
Sea

GREAT
BRITAIN

DENMARK

Copenhagen

Baltic Sea

Riga   LATVIA

Memel

RUSSIAN
EMPIRE
(Became Union of Soviet
Socialist Republics, 1922)

Volga

NETHERLANDS

Amsterdam

LITHUANIA

Vilnius

Danzig
POLISH
CORRIDOR

EAST
PRUSSIA

Brussels

BELGIUM

RUHR

Cologne

GERMANY

Berlin

POLAND

Warsaw

Paris

LUX.

Rhine

Weimar

Frankfurt

Elbe

Oder

Vistula

Kiev

Don

FRANCE

LORRAINE

ALSACE

Strasbourg

Prague

CZECHOSLOVAKIA

GALICIA

Seine

Loire

Geneva

Bern

SWITZ.

Vienna

AUSTRIA

Budapest

Dnieper

Rhône

Locarno

S.
TYROL

HUNGARY

Milan

Venice

Po

Trieste

Zagreb

ROMANIA

BESSARABIA

Genoa

Rapallo

CROATIA

Belgrade

Corsica

ITALY

YUGOSLAVIA

Bucharest

Caspian
Sea

Rome

Danube

Black Sea

SERBIA

MONTENEGRO
(To Yugoslavia 1921)

BULGARIA

Sofia

Sardinia

Naples

ALBANIA

Batum

Baku

GREECE

Istanbul
(Constantinople)

Kars

Sicily

Ankara

TURKEY

Tabriz

Athens

Izmir
(Smyrna)

PERSIA
(IRAN)

Mediterranean

Sea

Crete

Cyprus
(Gr. Br.)

Annexed
by Turkey
1939

Aleppo

SYRIA
(French Mandate)

Tigris

Euphrates

Baghdad

TUNISIA
(French)

Beirut

Damascus

IRAQ
(MESOPOTAMIA)
(British Mandate)

Kut el Amara

PALESTINE
(British Mandate)
Jerusalem

Amman

Basra

KUWAIT
(Gr. Br.)

TRANSJORDAN
(British Mandate)

NEUTRAL
ZONES

Cairo

Suez Canal

LIBYA
(Italian)

EGYPT
(Independent 1922)

NEJD
(SAUDI ARABIA)

Nile

Red Sea

Riyadh

Medina

0    200    400 Km.

0    200    400 Mi.

The Bolshevik Revolution in Russia immeasurably complicated the situation. The unsettled conditions in Germany and the former Habsburg territories in the wake of defeat seemed to invite the spread of revolution—precisely according to Lenin's script. Shortly after taking power, Lenin and his party had begun calling themselves "communists," partly to jettison the provincial Russian term *bolshevik,* but especially to underline their departure from the old reformist socialism of the Second International. In adopting "communism," they wanted to make it clear that they stood for a revolutionary alternative, and they actively sought to inspire revolution elsewhere.

Outside Russia, the greatest communist success in the wake of the war was in Hungary, where a communist regime under Béla Kun (1885–1937) governed Budapest and other parts of the country from March to August 1919, when it was put down by Allied-sponsored forces. At about the same time, communist republics lasted for months in the Slovak part of Czechoslovakia and in the important German state of Bavaria. Even in Italy, which had shared in the victory, Socialists infatuated with the Bolshevik example claimed that the substantial labor unrest that developed during 1919–1920 was the beginning of full-scale revolution.

Meanwhile, fears that the Russian Revolution might spread had fueled foreign intervention in Russia itself beginning in June 1918, when 24,000 French and British troops landed at Murmansk, in northern Russia. As long as the war with Germany lasted, military concerns helped justify this course, but after the armistice of November 1918, the intervention became overtly anticommunist, intended to help topple the new regime and undercut its effort to export revolution.

Further complicating the postwar situation were the defeat and dissolution of the Turkish Ottoman Empire, which had controlled much of the Middle East in 1914. The Arab revolt against the Turks that developed in the Arabian peninsula in 1916 did not achieve its major military aims, though it endured, causing some disruption to the Turkish war effort. Its success was due partly to the collaboration of a young British officer, T. E. Lawrence (1888–1935), who proved an effective military leader and an impassioned advocate of the Arab cause. The support that Britain had offered the Arabs suggested that independence, perhaps even a single Arab kingdom, might follow from a defeat of the Ottoman Empire.

But British policy toward the Arabs was uncertain and contradictory. Concerned about the Suez Canal, the British government sought to tighten its control in Egypt by declaring it a protectorate in 1914, triggering increased anti-British sentiment in the region. The secret Sykes-Picot Agreement of May 1916, named for the British and French diplomats who negotiated it, projected a division of the Ottoman territories of the Middle East into colonial spheres of influence. France would control Syria and Lebanon, while Britain would rule Palestine and Mesopotamia, or present-day Iraq.

Potentially complicating the situation in the region was Zionism, the movement to establish a Jewish state in Palestine. Led by Chaim Weizmann (1874–1952), a remarkable Russian-born British chemist, the Zionists reached an important milestone when British foreign secretary Arthur Balfour (1848–1930) cautiously announced, in the Balfour Declaration of November 1917, that the British government "looked with favor" on the prospect of a "Jewish home" in Palestine. At this point, British leaders sympathetic to Zionism saw no conflict in simultaneously embracing the cause of the Arabs against the Ottoman Turks; indeed, Arabs and Jews, each seeking self-determination, could be expected to collaborate.

In the heat of war, the British established their policy for the former Ottoman territories without careful study. Thus, they made promises and agreements that were not entirely compatible. After the war, the victors' effort to install a new order in the Middle East would create fresh conflicts.

## ■ The Peace Settlement

The peace conference took place in Paris, beginning in January 1919. Its labors led to five separate treaties, with each of the five defeated states, known collectively as the Paris peace settlement. The first and most significant was the Treaty of Versailles with Germany, signed in the Hall of Mirrors of the Versailles Palace on June 28, 1919. Treaties were also worked out, in turn, with Austria, Bulgaria, Hungary, and finally Turkey, in August 1920.

This was to be a dictated, not a negotiated, peace. Germany and its allies were excluded, as was renegade Russia. The passions unleashed by the long war had dissolved the possibility of a more conciliatory outcome, a genuinely negotiated peace. Having won the war, France, Britain, the United States, and Italy were to call the shots on their own, with the future of Europe and much of the world in the balance. However, spokesmen for many groups—from Slovaks and Croats to Arabs, Jews, and pan-Africanists—were in Paris as well, seeking a hearing for their respective causes. Both the Arab Prince Faisal (1885–1933), who would later become king of Iraq, and Colonel T. E. Lawrence were on hand to plead for an independent Arab kingdom. (See the box "Global Encounters: Prince Faisal at the Peace Conference.") The African American leader W. E. B. Du Bois° (1868–1963), who took his Ph.D. at Harvard in 1895, led a major pan-African congress in Paris concurrently with the peace conference.

The fundamental challenge for the peacemakers was to reconcile the conflicting visions of the postwar world that had emerged by the end of the war. U.S. President Wilson represented the promise of a new order that could give this terrible war a lasting meaning. As he toured parts of Europe on his way to the peace conference, Wilson was greeted as a hero. Clemenceau, in contrast, was a hard-liner concerned with French security and dismissive of Wilsonian ideals. Since becoming prime minister in 1917, he had stressed that only permanent French military superiority over Germany, and not some utopian league of nations, could guarantee a lasting peace. The negotiations at Paris centered on this fundamental difference between Wilson and Clemenceau. Although Britain's Lloyd George took a hard line on certain issues, he also sought to mediate, helping engineer the somewhat awkward compromise that resulted. When, after the peace conference, he encountered criticism for the outcome, Lloyd George replied, "I think I did as well as might be expected, seated as I was between Jesus Christ and Napoleon Bonaparte."[7]

**Du Bois** (doo BOYS)

**The Victors and the Peace**  In June 1919 the leaders of the major victorious powers exude confidence after signing with Germany the Treaty of Versailles, the most important of the five treaties that resulted from the Paris Peace Conference. From the left are David Lloyd George of Britain, Georges Clemenceau of France, and Woodrow Wilson of the United States.  *(Corbis-Bettmann)*

⊕ G L O B A L   E N C O U N T E R S

## Prince Faisal at the Peace Conference

*With the war nearing its end in October 1918, British authorities, in line with provisions of the Sykes-Picot agreement, permitted Faisal ibn-Husayn (1885–1933) to set up a provisional Arab state, with its capital at Damascus. As head of a delegation from this area to the Paris Peace Conference, Faisal claimed to speak for all Arab Asia, but some in the Arabian peninsula challenged his claim. In the memorandum of January 1919 that follows, he outlined the Arab position, mixing pride and assertiveness with a recognition that the Arabs would continue to need the support and help of Western powers. After the peace was concluded, Faisal found himself caught up in British and French rivalries as he was installed as king first of Syria, then of Iraq. But his efforts were central to the eventual achievement of Arab independence in the Middle East.*

We believe that our ideal of Arab unity in Asia is justified beyond need of argument. If argument is required, we would point to the general principles accepted by the Allies when the United States joined them, to our splendid past, to the tenacity with which our race has for 600 years resisted Turkish attempts to absorb us, and, in a lesser degree, to what we tried our best to do in this war as one of the Allies. . . .

The various provinces of Arab Asia—Syria, Irak, Jezireh, Hedjaz, Nejd, Yemen—are very different economically and socially, and it is impossible to constrain them into one frame of government.

We believe that Syria, an agricultural and industrial area thickly peopled with sedentary classes, is sufficiently advanced politically to manage her own internal affairs. We feel also that foreign technical advice and help will be a most valuable factor in our national growth. We are willing to pay for this help in cash; we cannot sacrifice for it any part of the freedom we have just won for ourselves by force of arms.

. . . The world wishes to exploit Mesopotamia rapidly, and we therefore believe that the system of government there will have to be buttressed by the men and material resources of a great foreign Power. We ask, however, that the Government be Arab, in principle and spirit, the selective rather than the elective principle being necessarily followed in the neglected districts, until time makes the broader basis possible. . . .

In Palestine the enormous majority of the people are Arabs. The Jews are very close to the Arabs in blood, and there is no conflict of character between the two races. In principles we are absolutely at one. Nevertheless, the Arabs cannot risk assuming the responsibility of holding level the scales in the clash of races and religions that have, in this one province, so often involved the world in difficulties. They would wish for the effective super-position of a great trustee, so long as a representative local administration commended itself by actively promoting the material prosperity of the country. . . .

In our opinion, if our independence be conceded and our local competence established, the natural influences of race, language, and interest will soon draw us together into one people; but for this the Great Powers will have to ensure us open internal frontiers, common railways and telegraphs, and uniform systems of education. To achieve this they must lay aside the thought of individual profits, and of their old jealousies. In a word, we ask you not to force your whole civilisation upon us, but to help us to pick out what serves us from your experience. In return we can offer you little but gratitude.

Source: J. C. Hurewitz, *Diplomacy in the Near and Middle East: A Documentary Record: 1914–1956* (Princeton, N.J.: D. Van Nostrand, 1956), vol. 2, pp. 38–39.

In Article 231 of the final treaty, the peacemakers sought to establish a moral basis for their treatment of Germany by assigning responsibility for the war to Germany and its allies. On this basis, the Germans were required to pay reparations to reimburse the victors for the costs of the war, although the actual amount was not established until 1921. The determination to make the loser pay for what had ended up a fabulously expensive war was one of the factors militating against a compromise peace on both sides by 1917.

Germany was also forced to dismantle much of its military apparatus. The army was to be limited to a hundred thousand men, all volunteers. The treaty severely restricted the size of the German navy as well, and Germany was forbidden to manufacture or possess military aircraft, submarines, tanks, heavy artillery, or poison gas.

France took back Alsace and Lorraine, the provinces it had lost to Germany in 1871 (see Map 25.3). But for France, the crucial security provision of the 1919 peace settlement was the treatment of the adjacent Rhineland section of Germany itself. For fifteen years Allied troops were to occupy the west bank of the Rhine River in Germany—the usual military occupation of a defeated adversary. But this would only be temporary. The long-term advantage for France was to be the permanent demilitarization of all German territory west of the Rhine and a strip of 50 kilometers along its east bank. Germany was to maintain no troops on this part of its own soil; in the event of hostilities French forces would be able to march unopposed into this economically vital area of Germany.

French interests also helped shape the settlement in east-central Europe. Wilsonian principles called for self-determination, but in this area of great ethnic complexity, ethnic differences were not readily sorted out geographically. This made it easier for the French to bring their own strategic concerns to bear on the situation. To ensure that Germany would again face potential enemies from both the east and the west, French leaders envisioned building a network of allies in east-central Europe. The first was the new Poland, created from Polish territories formerly in the German, Russian, and Austro-Hungarian Empires. That network might come to include Czechoslovakia, Yugoslavia, and Romania as well. These states would be weak enough to remain under French influence but, taken together, strong enough to replace Russia as a significant force against Germany.

Partly as a result of French priorities, Poland, Czechoslovakia, Yugoslavia, and Romania ended up as large as possible, either by combining ethnic groups or by incorporating minorities that, on ethnic grounds, be-

**Map 25.4   Ethnicity in East-Central Europe, 1919**
Ethnic diversity made it hard to create homogeneous nation-states in east-central Europe. The new states that emerged after World War I mixed ethnic groups, and ethnic tensions would contribute to future problems.

longed with neighboring states. The new Czechoslovakia included not only Czechs and Slovaks but also numerous Germans and Magyars. Indeed, Germans, mostly from the old Bohemia, made up 22 percent of the population of Czechoslovakia. On the other hand, Austria, Hungary, and Bulgaria, as defeated powers, found themselves diminished (see Map 25.4). What remained of Austria, the German part of the old Habsburg Empire, was prohibited from choosing to join Germany, an obvious violation of the Wilsonian principle of self-determination.

Desires to contain and weaken communist Russia were also at work in the settlement in east-central Europe. A band of states in east-central Europe, led by

France, could serve not only as a check to Germany but also as a shield against the Russian threat. Romania's aggrandizement came partly at the expense of the Russian Empire, as did the creation of the new Poland. Finland, Latvia, Estonia, and Lithuania, all part of the Russian Empire for over a century, became independent states (see Map 25.3).

The territorial settlement cost Germany almost 15 percent of its prewar territory, but German bitterness over the peace terms stemmed above all from a sense of betrayal. In requesting an armistice, German authorities had appealed to Wilson, who had not emphasized war guilt and reparations. He seemed to be saying that the whole prewar international system, not one side or the other, had been responsible for the current conflict. Yet the peacemakers placed the primary blame on Germany, so for Germans the terms of the peace greatly intensified the sting of defeat.

Wilson had been forced to compromise with French interests in dealing with east-central Europe, but he achieved a potentially significant success in exchange—the establishment of a League of Nations, embodying the widespread hope for a new international order. According to the League covenant worked out by April, disputes among member states were no longer to be settled by war but by mechanisms established by the new assembly. Other members were to participate in sanctions, from economic blockade to military action, against a member that went to war in violation of League provisions.

How could Wilsonian hopes for a new international order be squared with the imperialist system, which seemed utterly at odds with the ideal of self-determination? Elites among the colonial peoples had tended to support the war efforts of their imperial rulers, but often in the hope of winning greater autonomy or even independence. The Indian leader Mohandas Gandhi (1869–1948), who had been educated in the West and admitted to the English bar in 1889, even helped recruit Indians to fight on the British side. But his aim was to speed Indian independence, and he led demonstrations that embarrassed the British during the war. (See the box "Global Encounters: Gandhi Advocates Nonviolence" in Chapter 27 on page 919.)

Colonial peoples participated directly in the war on both sides. In sub-Saharan Africa, for example, German-led Africans fought against Africans under British or French command. France brought colonial subjects from West and North Africa into front-line service during the war. But the resulting expansion of political consciousness led more of those subject to European imperialism to question the whole system.

The hope that support for the Western powers in wartime would eventually be rewarded led China and Siam (now Thailand) to associate with the Allied side in 1917, in an effort to enhance their international stature. Each was seeking to restore full sovereignty in the face of increasing Western influence. China sent 200,000 people to work in France to help ease France's wartime labor shortage.

At the peace conference, spokesmen for the non-Western world tended to be moderate in their demands. And prodded by Wilson, the peacemakers made some concessions. German colonies and Ottoman territories were not simply taken over by the victors, in the old-fashioned way, but were placed under the authority of the League. The League then assigned them as mandates to one of the victorious powers, which was to report to the League annually on conditions in the area in question. Classes of mandates varied, based on how prepared for sovereignty the area was judged to be. In devising this system, the Western powers formally recognized for the first time that non-Western peoples under Western control had rights and interests of their own and that, in principle, they were progressing toward independence.

Still, the mandate approach to the colonial question was a halting departure at best. Although Britain granted considerable sovereignty to Iraq in 1932, the victorious powers generally operated as before, assimilating the new territories into their existing systems of colonial possessions. After the hopes for independence raised in the Arab world during the war, this outcome produced a sense of betrayal among Arab leaders.

The Chinese similarly felt betrayed. Despite China's contribution to the Allied war effort, the victors acquiesced in special rights for Japan in China, causing a renewed sense of humiliation among Chinese elites and provoking popular demonstrations and a boycott of Japanese goods. Although Western leaders were allowing a non-Western power, Japan, access to the imperial club, they were hardly departing from imperialism. For Chinese, Arabs, and others, the West appeared hypocritical. Those whose political consciousness had been raised by the war came to believe not only that colonialism should end, but that the colonial peoples would themselves have to take the lead in ending it.

The incongruities of the postwar settlement prompted Marshal Foch to proclaim, "This is not peace. It is an armistice for twenty years."[8] Would the principal victors have the resolve, and the capacity, to preserve the new order they had solidified at Paris? Debate over the American role promptly developed in the United States as President Wilson sought Senate ratification of the Versailles treaty, which entailed U.S. membership in the League of Nations as well as commitments to France and Britain. Wilson's opponents worried that League membership would compromise U.S. sovereignty, but other nations managed to overcome such concerns and join the new organization. American reluctance stemmed especially from the isolationist backlash that was developing against the U.S. intervention in the European war. Late in 1919, at the height of the debate, Wilson suffered a disabling stroke. The Senate then refused to ratify the peace treaty, thereby keeping the United States out of the League of Nations.

American disengagement stemmed partly from the doubts about the wisdom of the peace settlement that quickly developed in both Britain and the United States. During the peace conference, a member of the British delegation, the economist John Maynard Keynes° (1883–1946), resigned to write *The Economic Consequences of the Peace* (1920), which helped undermine confidence in the whole settlement. Keynes charged that the shortsighted, vindictive policy of the French, by crippling Germany with a punishing reparations burden, threatened the European economy and thus the long-term peace of Europe. For some, then, the challenge was not to enforce the Versailles treaty but to revise it. This lack of consensus about the legitimacy of the peace made it especially hard to anticipate the longer-term consequences of the war.

## ■ The Cultural Impact of the Great War

The war touched virtually everyone, but it marked for life those who had experienced the nightmare of the trenches. At first, traditional notions of glory, heroism, and patriotic duty combined with images of fellowship and regeneration to enable the soldiers to make a certain sense of their wartime experience. But as the war dragged on, such sentiments gradually eroded, giving way, in many cases, to resignation and cynicism. (See the feature "Weighing the Evidence: The Poetry of World War I" on pages 876–877.) But others, such as the young German soldier and writer Ernst Jünger (1895–1998), lauded the war as the catalyst for a welcome new era of steel, hardness, discipline, organization, and machine precision.

After the war, many of those who had fought it felt a sense of ironic betrayal; their prewar upbringing, the values and assumptions they had inherited, had not

equipped them to make sense of what they had lived through. But the effort to find meaning involved not only the survivors but also the families and friends of those killed or maimed. There was much effort to recast traditional, often-religious categories and images for the near-universal experience of bereavement, which transcended national and class divisions.

Beginning in the late 1920s a wave of writings about the war appeared. Many were memoirs, such as *Goodbye to All That* by the English writer Robert Graves (1895–1985) and *Testament of Youth* by Vera Brittain (1893–1970), who had served as a British army nurse at the front. But easily the most famous retrospective was the novel *All Quiet on the Western Front* (1929) by the German Erich Maria Remarque (1898–1970), which sold 2.5 million copies in twenty-five languages in its first eighteen months in print. Remarque provided a gripping portrait of the experience of ordinary soldiers on the western front, but his book also reflected the disillusionment that had come to surround the memory of the war by the late 1920s. Not only were many friends dead or maimed for life, but all the sacrifices seemed to have been largely in vain, a sentiment that fueled determination to avoid another war in the future.

The novel forms of warfare introduced during World War I intensified fears of renewed war. Thanks to modern technology, which had been central to the West's confident belief in progress, Europeans had now experienced machine-gun fire, poison gas attacks, and the terror-bombing of civilians from airplanes. A generation later, to be sure, the advent of the nuclear age occasioned a measure of terror hardly imaginable earlier, but the experience of World War I was the turning point, the end of an earlier innocence.

What followed from the war, most fundamentally, was a new sense that Western civilization was neither as secure nor as superior as it had seemed. The celebrated French poet Paul Valéry (1871–1945), speaking at Oxford shortly after the war, observed that "we modern civilizations have learned to recognize that we are mortal like the others. We had heard . . . of whole worlds vanished, of empires foundered. . . . Elam, Nineveh, Babylon were vague and splendid names; the total ruin of these worlds, for us, meant as little as did their existence. But France, England, Russia . . . these names, too, are splendid. . . . And now we see that the abyss of history is deep enough to bury all the world. We feel that a civilization is as fragile as a life."[9] Valéry went on to warn that the coming transition to peace would be even more difficult and disorienting than the war itself. So traumatic might be the convulsion that Europe might lose its leadership and

---

**Keynes** (KAINZ)

**Severini: Armoured Train** In this painting from 1915, the Italian futurist Gino Severini (1883–1996) conveys the hard, steel-like imagery and the sense of disciplined modern efficiency that became associated with war, making it attractive to some young Europeans. *(Richard S. Zeisler Collection, New York/The Bridgeman Art Library, London and New York)*

be shown up for what it was in fact—a pathetically small corner of the world, a mere cape on the Asiatic landmass. Astounding words for a European, yet even Valéry, for all his foresight, could not anticipate what Europe would experience in the decades to follow.

## SUMMARY

THE war that began in August 1914 was supposed to be over in a few months, but it quickly bogged down in stalemate in the west, which proved the decisive military front. Germany had to fight a two-front war, and it almost immediately began suffering under Britain's naval blockade. But the Germans defeated Russia in 1917 and then, in 1918, mounted a last-ditch offensive in the west that came

close to succeeding as well. By 1918, however, lack of food, provisions, and manpower was fatally weakening the German effort, and U.S. intervention gave the anti-German coalition the long-term advantage in any case. Though it entailed a far greater effort than anyone had expected at the outset, the war reached a definitive outcome with the defeat of Germany and its allies by November 1918.

So great were the strains of the war that radical political changes accompanied military defeat, first in Russia, then in Turkey, Austria-Hungary, and Germany. In destroying the Habsburg Empire and the imperial regime in Germany, that outcome addressed the problems that seemed to have caused the war in the first place. But with so many pillars of the old order falling in the wake of the war, the future remained uncertain indeed even after the major provisions of the peace settlement were established in 1919.

Because it proved so much longer and more difficult than expected, this first "world war" proved a total war, calling forth new forms of socioeconomic coordination and even systematic propaganda. Partly as a result, the war accelerated processes, from technological development to women's suffrage, that many deemed progressive. But coming after a century of relative peace and apparent progress, this unexpectedly long and brutal war ended up shaking Europe's social and cultural foundations. The number of casualties, the advent of terrifying new weapons, the destruction of famous old monuments—all gave the war an apocalyptic aura that heightened its psychological impact. So despite a widespread desire to return to normal once the war was over, many were plagued by a deeper sense that the world could never be the same again. Troubling new uncertainties mixed with exciting new possibilities as Europe and the West looked to the future.

## ■ Notes

1. Thus wrote the German poet Ivan Goll in 1917; quoted in Modris Eksteins, *Rites of Spring: The Great War and the Birth of the Modern Age* (Boston: Houghton Mifflin, 1989), p. 144.
2. The remarks of Raymond Joubert, as quoted in John Ellis, *Eye-Deep in Hell: Trench Warfare in World War I* (Baltimore: Johns Hopkins University Press, 1989), p. 104.
3. Brian Bond, *War and Society in Europe, 1870–1970* (New York: Oxford University Press, 1986), p. 114.
4. By A. N. Potresov, as quoted in Richard Pipes, *The Russian Revolution* (New York: Random House, Vintage, 1991), p. 348.
5. Both statements are quoted in Koppel S. Pinson, *Modern Germany: Its History and Civilization*, 2d ed. (New York: Macmillan, 1966), p. 337.
6. Quoted in Arno J. Mayer, *Political Origins of the New Diplomacy, 1917–18* (New York: Random House, Vintage, 1970), p. 135.
7. Quoted in Walter Arnstein, *Britain Yesterday and Today: 1830 to the Present*, 6th ed. (Lexington, Mass.: D. C. Heath, 1992), p. 266.
8. Quoted in P. M. H. Bell, *The Origins of the Second World War* (London and New York: Longman, 1986), p. 14.
9. Paul Valéry, *Variety*, 1st series (New York: Harcourt, Brace, 1938), pp. 3–4.

## ■ Suggested Reading

Chickering, Roger. *Imperial Germany and the Great War, 1914–1918.* 1998. A balanced, comprehensive introduction to the German war effort and experience, especially good on the interpenetration of military and sociopolitical concerns.

Ellis, John. *Eye-Deep in Hell: Trench Warfare in World War I.* 1989. A compelling account of life and death in the trenches, covering topics from trench construction to eating, drinking, and sex; includes striking photographs.

Figes, Orlando. *A People's Tragedy: The Russian Revolution, 1891–1924.* 1997. A lengthy, comprehensive but gripping account of the revolutionary trajectory, from the famine of 1891 to the death of Lenin in 1924. Seeks to reveal the complexity of the whole process, its many episodes and forms of agency.

Fitzpatrick, Sheila. *The Russian Revolution, 1917–1932.* 2d ed. 1994. An ideal introductory work that places the events of 1917 in the sweep of Russian history.

Keegan, John. *The First World War.* 1999. A comprehensive and accessible study by a widely read military historian.

Robbins, Keith. *The First World War.* 1985. An accessible, balanced, and comprehensive treatment, covering everything from military operations to the domestic impact of the war.

Sharp, Alan. *The Versailles Settlement: Peacemaking in Paris, 1919.* 1991. A brief, clear, and balanced overview that seeks to do justice to the magnitude of the task the peacemakers faced.

Wall, Richard, and Jay Winter, eds. *The Upheaval of War: Family, Work and Welfare in Europe, 1914–1918.* 1988. A series of essays that sheds much new light on the war's domestic impact, from nutrition and standards of living to social and labor policy.

Winter, J. M. *The Experience of World War I.* 1989. A beautifully illustrated work that proceeds via concentric circles from politicians to generals to soldiers to civilians, then to the war's longer-term effects.

Winter, Jay. *Sites of Memory, Sites of Mourning.* 1995. Using an effective comparative approach, a leading authority argues that Europeans relied on relatively traditional means of making sense of the bloodletting of World War I.

 **For a searchable list of additional readings for this chapter, go to http://college.hmco.com.**

# The Poetry of World War I

We don't normally think of poetry and war together, and World War I, with its unexpected brutality and severe hardship, may seem the least poetic of wars. Yet even during the war, soldiers like Englishmen Rupert Brooke (1887–1915) and Wilfred Owen (1893–1918) sought to shape their experiences into poetic imagery. What does such poetry tell us about what the war meant to those who fought it? How has poetic testimony affected our understanding of the place of World War I in the Western experience?

In Brooke's wartime poetry what strikes us first is his gratitude that his generation had come of age at this dramatic historical moment:

Now, God be thanked Who has matched us with
   His hour,
And caught our youth, and wakened us from
   sleeping

But why would a young man like Brooke welcome war? He seemed to envision release, deliverance—but from what?

When the war broke out, Brooke promptly volunteered, even pulling strings to get into a combat unit. Seeing action for the first time, in Belgium in October 1914, he was excited by the intensity of battle and pleased by his own calm self-control. Back in England for further training shortly thereafter, he wrote several sonnets, including "Peace," the one reproduced here, expressing his feelings about the war. But he died of blood poisoning on the way to battle in April 1915—without ever fully experiencing trench warfare.

Although most of the young Englishmen who took up arms with such enthusiasm in 1914 assumed that their country was in the right, that Germany was at fault, they gave little thought to the purposes of the war or the larger historical impact it might have. Brooke understood that the war would not accomplish all that was claimed for it, but he was grateful for the personal experience it made possible. Somehow it meant "peace," as the title of his sonnet suggests, and even cleanliness:

To turn, as swimmers into cleanness leaping,
   Glad from a world grown old and cold and weary

Brooke's sense of deliverance responded to personal frustrations, yet he spoke for others of his generation who also were finding it difficult to assume a place in

**Rupert Brooke (1887–1915)**  *(Mansell/Time Inc.)*

PEACE

Now, God be thanked Who has matched us with His hour,
   And caught our youth, and wakened us from sleeping,
With hand made sure, clear eye, and sharpened power,
   To turn, as swimmers into cleanness leaping,
Glad from a world grown old and cold and weary,
   Leave the sick hearts that honour could not move,
And half-men, and their dirty songs and dreary,
   And all the little emptiness of love!

Oh! we, who have known shame, we have found release there,
   Where there's no ill, no grief, but sleep has mending.
      Naught broken save this body, lost but breath;
Nothing to shake the laughing heart's long peace there
   But only agony, and that has ending;
      And the worst friend and enemy is but Death.

*Rupert Brooke*

**Wilfred Owen (1893–1918)**   *(© Hulton Getty/Corbis)*

## ANTHEM FOR DOOMED YOUTH

What passing-bells for these who die as cattle?
　　—Only the monstrous anger of the guns.
　　Only the stuttering rifles' rapid rattle
Can patter out their hasty orisons.
No mockeries now for them; no prayers nor bells;
　　Nor any voice of mourning save the choirs,—
The shrill, demented choirs of wailing shells;
　　And bugles calling for them from sad shires.

What candles may be held to speed them all?
　　Not in the hands of boys but in their eyes
Shall shine the holy glimmers of goodbyes.
　　The pallor of girls' brows shall be their pall;
Their flowers the tenderness of patient minds,
And each slow dusk a drawing-down of blinds.

　　　　　　　　　　　　　　*Wilfred Owen*

adult society at that particular time. Though they came from educated, upper-middle-class families, they were contemptuous of the routines and compromises of the respectable, everyday world to which they were expected to adjust. Thus Brooke welcomed the chance to

> Leave the sick hearts that honour could not move,
> And half-men, and their dirty songs and dreary

Yet those of Brooke's generation were equally troubled by their own uncertainty about values and commitments—to marriage, career, a place in society. Thanks to the overwhelming, inescapable reality of the war, values that had seemed empty—honor, country, duty, fellowship—now seemed meaningful after all. To his surprise and relief, Brooke found that he himself was capable of courage, commitment, and sacrifice. With its promise of cleanliness and renewal, the war was worth even its highest price, which was merely death.

Unlike Brooke, Wilfred Owen hated the war from the start. He was quickly struck by its sheer ugliness, as manifested in the landscape, the noise, the coarse language of the soldiers themselves. Yet he served with distinction, was decorated for bravery, and was killed by machine-gun fire just one week before the armistice in November 1918.

Owen, then, experienced the reality of World War I in a way that Brooke did not. The sonnet here, "Anthem for Doomed Youth," was written during September and October 1917, after the war had come to entail a terrible bloodletting. Thus Owen sought to shape sentiments very different from Brooke's—a sense of waste, of loss, of incongruity between suffering endured and results achieved. Whereas Brooke had brushed aside the possi-

bility of death, Owen saw death as relentless, carrying off a generation of innocent youth, dying like cattle.

In a sense, even the dignity of death had become a casualty of the war. Thus Owen mixed funeral images with the new horror that this war had brought forth: the only mourning was "The shrill, demented choirs of wailing shells." Mocking the ongoing effort to sweeten the reality of death at the front through reference to nobility and sacrifice, Owen drowned out his initial suggestion of bells with the new and awful sounds of machine-gun fire:

> —Only the monstrous anger of the guns.
> Only the stuttering rifles' rapid rattle

Quite apart from its military and political outcome, World War I has assumed a particular place in our collective memory, thanks partly to those like Brooke and Owen who managed to frame their wartime experiences in the memorable language of poetry. At first, Brooke's poetry helped to justify the alarming slaughter to those who began questioning the war's purpose as it claimed the lives of their sons. Yet by now we find it hard to grasp the ideals that inspired his poetic testimony, for they were in one sense consumed by the war and the era of violence that it began. We still live in the world that emerged from that war, so Owen, with his tragic cynicism, is far more our contemporary. Brooke may still reveal for us something of the innocence that was lost, but it is especially through Owen's way of conveying the tragedy, the sense of betrayal and lost innocence, that World War I has continued to haunt the memory of Western civilization.

# CHAPTER 26

# The Illusion of Stability 1919–1930

I N 1925 Josephine Baker (1906–1975), a black entertainer from St. Louis, moved from the chorus lines of New York to the bistros of Paris, where she quickly became a singing and dancing sensation. Also a favorite in Germany, she was the most famous of the African American entertainers who took the cultural capitals of Europe by storm during the 1920s. After the disillusioning experience of war, many Europeans found a valuable infusion of vitality in Baker's jazz music, exotic costumes, and "savage," uninhibited dancing (see the photo on page 897).

The European attraction to African Americans as primitive, vital, and sensual reflected a good deal of racial stereotyping, but there really *was* something fresh and uninhibited about American culture, especially its African American variant. And even as they played to those stereotypes, black performers like Baker had great fun ironically subverting them. Many realized they could enjoy opportunities in parts of Europe that were still denied them in the United States. Baker herself was a woman of great sophistication who became a French citizen in 1937, participated in progressive causes, and was decorated for her secret intelligence work in the anti-Nazi resistance during World War II.

The prominence of African Americans in European popular culture was part of a wider infatuation with things American as Europeans embraced the new during the 1920s. Lacking the cultural baggage of Europe, America seemed to offer revitalization and modernity at the same time. With so many old conventions shattered by the war, the ideal of being "modern" became widespread among Europeans, affecting everything from sex education to furniture design. "Modern" meant no-nonsense efficiency, mass production, and a vital popular culture, expressed in jazz, movies, sport, and even advertising. (See the feature "Weighing the Evidence: Advertising" on pages 910–911.)

Kees van Dongen, *Au cabaret nègre* (detail).
(Collection Christie's/Edimedia)

## The West and the World After the Great War

## Communism, Fascism, and the New Political Spectrum

## Toward Mass Society

## Weimar Germany and the Trials of the New Democracies

## The Search for Meaning in a Disordered World

But Europeans themselves had pioneered modernism in many areas of the arts and sciences, and innovation continued after the war. Paris held its own as an international cultural center, hosting a decorative arts exhibition in 1925 that produced art deco, the sleek, "modernistic" style that helped give the decade its distinctive flavor. And in the unsettled conditions of postwar Germany, Berlin emerged to rival Paris for cultural leadership during what Germans called "the Golden Twenties." Innovations ranged from avant-garde drama to a sophisticated cabaret scene with a prominent homosexual dimension.

Still, something dizzying, even unnerving, marked the eager embrace of the new during the 1920s. Some European cultural observers saw the vogue of black American entertainers as a symptom of decadence that would only undermine further the best of European civilization. Even in embracing the new, many were seeking a new basis for order and security, but where their efforts would lead remained unclear.

Although the immediate disruptions of wartime carried over to 1923, a more hopeful era of relative prosperity and international conciliation followed, continuing until 1929. But there was much that called into question the ideal of a "world safe for democracy" that had surrounded the end of the war. Revolutionary Russia remained an uncertain force, even as it began seeking to build socialism on its own. In Italy, the democracy that had emerged in the nineteenth century gave way to the

first regime to call itself fascist, and some of the new democracies in east-central Europe did not survive the decade. The postwar efforts at economic restabilization, apparently successful for a while, masked growing strains in the international economy. In one sphere after another, postwar restabilization was fragile—and could quickly unravel.

### QUESTIONS TO CONSIDER

- How did the differing priorities of Britain and France affect international relations during the 1920s?

- How and why did the priorities of the Russian communist regime change from 1919 to 1930?

- Why did Italy turn from parliamentary democracy to fascism even after sharing in the victory in World War I?

- What were the sources of the political instability that made the future of the new German democracy so uncertain during the 1920s?

### TERMS TO KNOW

Maginot Line
fascism
Benito Mussolini
Comintern (Third, or Communist, International)
New Economic Policy (NEP)

Joseph Stalin
Matteotti murder
corporative state, corporativism
Gustav Stresemann
Treaty of Locarno
surrealism
Bauhaus

## THE WEST AND THE WORLD AFTER THE GREAT WAR

ALTHOUGH the United States and Japan were becoming important, the major international players before 1914 had been the European powers, who had apportioned much of the non-Western world in imperial networks. But the war and the peace

had weakened—and to some extent discredited—the belligerent countries of Europe, who now found themselves saddled with foreign debts and unbalanced economies. Though the United States pulled back from a direct political role in Europe in 1919, it became far more active in world affairs, helping to engineer major conferences on arms limitation and international economic relations during the 1920s. But in crucial respects, the shape of the postwar international order still depended on Europeans. And colonial concerns continued to affect the balance of power in Europe, where it fell to the two major victors in the war, France and Britain, to enforce the controversial peace settlement.

## ■ The Erosion of European Power

Emerging from the war as the principal power in East Asia was a non-Western country, Japan, whose claims to the German bases in the region and to special rights in China were formally recognized at the Paris Peace Conference. With the Washington treaty of 1922, Japan won naval parity with Britain and the United States in East Asia. The Western nations were recognizing Japan as a peer, a great power—even a threat. Aspects of the Washington agreements were intended to block Japanese expansion in East Asia. If a new international system was to emerge, it would not be centered in Europe to the extent the old one had been.

After the slaughter of the war and the hypocrisy of the peace, Europeans could no longer claim to embody civilization with the same arrogance. And as the old Europe lost prestige, President Wilson's ideals of self-determination and democracy were greeted enthusiastically outside the West—in China, for example. At the same time, the Russian revolutionary model appealed to those in the colonial world seeking to understand the mainsprings of Western imperialism—and the means of overcoming it. To some Chinese intellectuals by the early 1920s, Leninism was attractive because it showed the scope for mass mobilization by a revolutionary vanguard.

Non-Western elites were learning to pick and choose from among the elements of the Western tradition. In the 1920s, ever greater numbers of colonial subjects were traveling to western Europe, often for education. Paris was a favored destination, partly because France made an effort to assimilate its colonial peoples. Although those educated in Europe were subject to Westernization, that did not necessarily make them more supportive of Western rule. Many began not only to question colonialism but also to take a fresh look at their own traditions, asking how they might serve the quest for a postcolonial order.

By the 1920s, a generation of anticolonialist, nationalist intellectuals was emerging to lead the non-Western world. Some were more radical than others, but most agreed that the challenge was to learn from the West and to modernize, but without simply copying the West and losing distinctive cultural identities. It was imperative to sift through tradition, determining what needed to be changed and what was worth preserving. The pioneering

### CHRONOLOGY

| | |
|---|---|
| **March 1919** | Founding of the Italian fascist movement |
| **November 1920** | Russian civil war ends |
| **March 1921** | New Economic Policy announced at Russian Communist Party congress |
| **October 1922** | Mussolini becomes Italian prime minister |
| **January 1923** | French-led occupation of the Ruhr |
| **November 1923** | Peak of inflation in Germany |
| **January 1924** | First Labour government in Britain |
| | Death of Lenin |
| **August 1924** | Acceptance of the Dawes Plan on German reparations |
| **October 1925** | Treaty of Locarno |
| **May 1926** | Pilsudski's coup d'état in Poland |
| | Beginning of general strike in Britain |
| **May 1927** | Lindbergh completes first transatlantic solo flight |
| **January 1929** | Stalin forces banishment of Trotsky from Soviet Union |
| **April 1929** | Soviets adopt first economic Five-Year Plan |
| **August 1929** | Acceptance of the Young Plan on German reparations |
| **October 1929** | Death of Stresemann |

Chinese nationalist Sun Yixien (Sun Yat-sen, 1866–1925) was typical in recognizing the need to adopt the science and technology of the West. But China, he insisted, could do so in its own way, without sacrificing its unique cultural and political traditions. (See the box "Global Encounters: Sun Yixien on Chinese Nationalism.")

As the greatest imperial power, Britain was especially vulnerable to the growing anticolonial sentiment. The struggle to hang on to its empire drew British energies away from the problems of Europe after the peace settlement.

## GLOBAL ENCOUNTERS

### Sun Yixien on Chinese Nationalism

*Sun Yixien (Sun Yat-sen), widely regarded as the father of modern China, founded the Guomindang (Kuomintang), the Chinese nationalist movement, in 1912. Educated by Western missionaries in China, he lived in the United States for extended periods and came to admire the West in important respects. But he insisted that China, to make the best use of what the West offered, had to reconnect with its own unique traditions. Variations on this argument would be heard for decades as the rest of the world sought to come to terms with the seemingly more advanced West. The following passages are from an influential series of lectures that Sun Yixien presented in China in the early 1920s.*

What is the standing of our nation in the world? In comparison with other nations we have the greatest population and the oldest culture, of four thousand years' duration. We ought to be advancing in line with the nations of Europe and America. But the Chinese people have only family and clan groups; there is no national spirit. Consequently, in spite of four hundred million people gathered together in one China, we are in fact but a sheet of loose sand. We are the poorest and weakest state in the world, occupying the lowest position in international affairs; the rest of mankind is the carving knife and the serving dish, while we are the fish and the meat. Our position now is extremely perilous; if we do not earnestly promote nationalism and weld together our four hundred millions into a strong nation, we face a tragedy—the loss of our country and the destruction of our race. To ward off this danger, we must espouse Nationalism and employ the national spirit to save the country. . . .

But even if we succeed in reviving our ancient morality, learning, and powers, we will still not be able, in this modern world, to advance China to a first place among the nations. . . . [W]e will still need to learn the strong points of Europe and America before we can progress at an equal rate with them. Unless we do study the best from foreign countries, we will go backward. With our own fine foundation of knowledge and our age-long culture, with our own native intelligence besides, we should be able to acquire all the best things from abroad. The strongest point of the West is its science. . . .

As soon as we learn Western machinery we can use it anytime, anywhere; electric lights, for example, can be installed and used in any kind of Chinese house. But Western social customs and sentiments are different from ours in innumerable points; if, without regard to customs and popular feelings in China, we try to apply Western methods of social control as we would Western machinery—in a hard and fast way—we shall be making a serious mistake. . . .

. . . For the governmental machinery of the United States and France still has many defects, and does not satisfy the desires of the people nor give them a complete measure of happiness. So we in our proposed reconstruction must not think that if we imitate the West of today we shall reach the last stage of progress and be perfectly contented. . . .

Only in recent times has Western culture advanced beyond ours, and the passion for this new civilization has stimulated our revolution. Now that the revolution is a reality, we naturally desire to see China excel the West and build up the newest and most progressive state in the world. We certainly possess the qualifications necessary to reach this ideal, but we must not merely imitate the democratic systems of the West.

*Source:* Sun Yat-sen, *San Min Chu I: The Three Principles of the People* (Taipei, Taiwan: China Cultural Service, 1953), pp. 5, 46, 109–113, 136, 138–139.

In light of the strong Indian support for the British war effort, the British government promised in 1917 to extend the scope for Indian involvement in the colonial administration in India. Growing expectations as the war was ending provoked episodes of violence against the British, whose troops retaliated brutally in April 1919, firing indiscriminately into an unarmed crowd. This Amritsar Massacre helped galvanize India's independence movement, even though the British, seeking conciliation in the aftermath, extended self-rule by entrusting certain less essential government services to Indians. Another milestone was reached in 1921, when Mohandas Gandhi, the British-educated leader of the Indian independence movement, shed his European clothes in favor of simple Indian attire. But it was on the basis of Western egalitarianism, not some indigenous value, that Gandhi demanded political rights for the "untouchables," the lowest group in India's long-standing caste system.

In Egypt a full-scale anti-British insurrection broke out in 1919. After British troops suppressed the rebellion, British authorities offered to grant moderate concessions, as in India. But Egyptian nationalists demanded independence, which was finally granted in 1922. Egypt gradually evolved into a constitutional monarchy, with representative government and universal suffrage. But Britain retained a predominant influence in Egypt until the nationalist revolution of 1952 (see Chapter 29).

At the same time, nationalism was growing among West Africans who had studied in England. In March 1919 Western-educated Africans in the Gold Coast asked the British governor to establish representative institutions so that Africans could at least be consulted about governmental affairs. The West African National Congress, formed in 1920, made similar demands. The British agreed to new constitutions for Nigeria in 1923 and the Gold Coast in 1925 that took significant steps in that direction. They also agreed to build more schools, though they tended to promote practical education, including African languages and agriculture, whereas the African leaders wanted students to learn the Western classics that "made gentlemen." Such conflicting priorities indicate the complexities of the relationships between colonial rulers and the emerging elites among the colonized peoples.

**Anticolonialism in the Middle East** Syria became a League of Nations mandate under French control after World War I. Friction began immediately between the French and Arab nationalists, who had wanted independence. A major nationalist uprising during the fall of 1925 produced the destruction shown here and forced the French to grant concessions. After long negotiations, the French agreed to a treaty granting autonomy for Syria in 1936. *(Topham Picturepoint/The Image Works)*

## ■ Enforcing the Versailles Settlement

It was up to France and Britain to make sure the new international order worked, but it was not clear that either had the will and resources to do so. Cooperation between them was essential, yet sometimes their differences—in geography, in values, and in perceptions—seemed to doom them to work at cross-purposes.

France was the dominant power on the European continent after World War I, and until well into the 1930s it boasted the strongest army in the world. Yet even in the early 1920s a sense of hollowness, artificiality, tarnished France's image of strength—and thus the shrillness and the defensiveness that came to mark French thinking and French policy.

In light of Germany's larger population and stronger industrial base, France's long-term security seemed to require certain measures to tip the scales in its favor. By imposing German disarmament and the demilitarization of the Rhineland, the Versailles treaty gave France immediate military advantages. Yet how long could these measures be maintained, once the passions of war had died down and Germany no longer seemed such a threat? France had hoped for British help in enforcing the treaty, but Britain was pulling back from the Continent to concentrate on its empire, just as it had after other major European wars.

In particular, the British wanted to avoid getting dragged into the uncertain situation in east-central Europe, where vital national interests did not seem to be at stake. Yet the French, to replace their earlier link with Russia, promptly developed an alliance system with several of the new or expanded states of the region, including Poland, Czechoslovakia, Romania, and Yugoslavia. France's ties to east-central Europe made the British especially wary of binding agreements with the French.

At first, France felt confident enough to take strong steps even without British support. In response to German foot-dragging in paying reparations, Prime Minister Raymond Poincaré decided to get tough in January 1923. Declaring the Germans in default, he sent French troops at the head of an international force to occupy the Ruhr industrial area and force German compliance. But the move backfired. The Germans adopted a policy of passive resistance in response, and the costs of the occupation more than offset the increase in reparations that France received. The French government ended up having to raise taxes to pay for the venture. Moreover, the move alienated the British, whose lack of support bordered on active hostility.

British leaders now viewed French policy as unnecessarily vindictive and bellicose, and they increasingly saw the Versailles treaty as counterproductive. Instead, they placed great store in the League of Nations and in the international arms reduction effort gaining momentum by the later 1920s. So France found itself with ever less support from its wartime allies as it sought to enforce the peace settlement. The Ruhr occupation of 1923 proved the last time the French dared to go it alone.

From that point on, France gradually lost the advantages it had gained by defeating Germany, and self-confidence gave way to defensiveness and resignation. The defensive mentality found physical embodiment in the Maginot° Line, a system of fortifications on the country's eastern border. Remembering the defensive warfare of World War I and determined to preclude the sort of invasion France had suffered in 1914, the military convinced France's political leaders to adopt a defensive strategy based on a fortified line. Construction began in 1929, and the Maginot system reached preliminary completion in 1935, when it extended along France's border with Germany from Switzerland to the border with Belgium.

This defensive system was not consistent with the other major strands of French policy, especially its alliances with states in east-central Europe. If France emphasized defense behind an impregnable system of forts, what good were French security guarantees to such new allies as Poland and Czechoslovakia?

Still, the situation remained fluid during the 1920s. In France, as in Britain, national elections in 1924 produced a victory for the moderate left, ending a period of conservative nationalist dominance since the war. In each country, international relations became a major issue in the elections, and the outcome forecast a more conciliatory tack, especially in relations with Germany. If democracy was taking root in Germany, then perhaps France's fears about the European power balance were misguided.

# COMMUNISM, FASCISM, AND THE NEW POLITICAL SPECTRUM

 N making their revolution in 1917, the Russian Bolsheviks had expected to spark wider revolution, and hopes—and fears—that the revolution would spread were palpable in the immediate postwar period. The Russian communists initially enjoyed extraordinary prestige on the European left; but as

**Maginot** (MAH-zhih-noh)

the nature of Leninist communism became clearer, some Marxists grew skeptical or hostile, and the Russian model eventually produced a damaging split in international socialism. By the end of the 1920s revolution elsewhere was nowhere in sight, and it seemed that, for the foreseeable future, the communist regime in Russia would have to go it alone.

By then, a new and unexpected political movement had developed in Italy, expanding the political spectrum in a different direction. The groundswell was fascism, which brought Benito Mussolini to power in 1922. Emerging directly from the war, the fascist movement was violent and antidemocratic—and thus disturbing to many. Stressing national solidarity and discipline, the fascists were hostile not only to liberal individualism and the parliamentary system, but also to Marxist socialism, with its emphasis on class struggle and the special role of the working class. Claiming to offer a modern alternative to both, Italian fascism quickly attracted the attention of those in other countries who were disillusioned with parliamentary politics and hostile to the Marxist left. The interplay of communism and fascism, as new political experiments, added to the uncertainties of novel postwar world.

## ■ Changing Priorities in Communist Russia, 1918–1921

Even after leading the revolution that toppled the provisional government in November 1917, the Bolsheviks could not claim majority support in Russia. When the long-delayed elections to select a constituent assembly were held a few weeks after the revolution, the Socialist Revolutionaries won a clear majority while the Bolsheviks ended up with fewer than one-quarter of the seats. But the Bolsheviks' new Red Army simply dispersed the assembly when it met in January 1918. And over the next three years the Communists, as the Bolsheviks renamed themselves, gradually consolidated their power, establishing a centralized and nondemocratic regime. Power lay not with the soviets, nor with some coalition of socialist parties, but solely with the Communist Party.

During its first years, the new communist regime encountered a genuine emergency that seemed to require a monopoly of power. During 1918–1920, in what became a brutal civil war, the communist "Reds" battled counterrevolutionary "Whites," people who had been dispossessed by the revolution or who had grown disillusioned with the Communists. Appointed People's Commissar for War in April 1918, Leon Trotsky forged a loyal and disciplined Red Army. The Whites drew support from foreign intervention and from separatist senti-

ment, as several of the non-Russian nationalities of the old Russian Empire sought to free themselves from Russian and communist control.

A series of thrusts, involving troops from fourteen countries at one time or another, struck at Russia from a variety of points along its huge border. The Whites and the foreign troops never forged a coordinated strategy, but the dogged counterrevolutionary assault seriously threatened the young Communist regime and the territorial basis of the state it had inherited from the tsarist autocracy. In the final analysis, however, the Whites proved unable to rally much popular support. Peasants feared, plausibly enough, that a White victory would mean a restoration of the old order, including the return of their newly won lands to the former landlords. By the end of active fighting in November 1920, the Communist regime had not only survived but regained most of the territory it had lost early in the civil war (see Map 26.1).

The need to launch the new communist regime in this way, fighting counterrevolutionaries supported by foreign troops, inevitably affected Communist perceptions and priorities. Separatist sentiment might continue to feed counterrevolutionary efforts, so the new regime exerted careful control over the non-Russian nationalities. Thus, when the Union of Soviet Socialist Republics (USSR) was organized in December 1922, it was only nominally a federation of autonomous republics; strong centralization from the Communists' new capital in Moscow was the rule from the start.

In the midst of the civil war the Russian communists founded the Third, or Communist, International—commonly known as the Comintern—in March 1919, to make clear their break with the seemingly discredited strategies of the Second International. Through the Comintern, the Russian communists expected to translate their success in Russia into leadership of the international socialist movement. However, many old-line Marxists elsewhere were not prepared to admit that the leadership of European socialism had passed to the Bolshevik rulers of backward Russia. (See the box "Reading Sources: A Marxist Critique of Communism.")

From its founding in March 1919 until the spring of 1920, as a wave of leftist political agitation and labor unrest swept Europe, the Comintern actively promoted the wider revolution that Lenin had envisioned. Seeking to win mass support, the organization accented leftist solidarity and reached out to the rank and file in the labor unions. By the spring of 1920, however, it seemed clear that further revolution was not imminent. Thus, Comintern leaders began concentrating on improving organization and discipline for a more protracted revolutionary struggle.

Boundary of the Russian Empire 1914
Boundary of area controlled by the Bolsheviks August 1918
Boundary of area controlled by the Bolsheviks October 1919
Boundary of Soviet territory March 1921
Boundary of area controlled by the anti-Bolshevik forces May 1920
White Russian armies
Non-Russian anti-Bolshevik forces

Entente fleet

NORWAY

SWEDEN

Murmansk
BRITISH
FRENCH
CANADIANS
ITALIANS
SERBS

CANADIANS
AMERICANS

Archangel

BRITISH
FRENCH

FINLAND
(Independent)
1917

FINNS

Helsinki

Kronstadt

British fleet

Yudenich
1918-20

Petrograd (Leningrad)

ESTONIA

Pskov

BOLSHEVIK   RUSSIA

Perm

Baltic Sea

LATVIA

Riga

LETTS

BALTIC
GERMANS

Volga

Kazan

Kolchak 1918-19

CZECHS

LITHUANIA

Moscow

Nizhniy-
Novgorod

GERMANY
(E. PRUSSIA)

Minsk

Smolensk

Samara

Orenburg

Warsaw

Vistula

Brest-
Litovsk

Mogilev

Kaluga

Penza

Ural

POLAND

POLES

Gomel

Orel

Tambov

Saratov

Zhitomir

Kiev

Voronezh

Don

CZECHOSLOVAKIA

UKRAINE

Denikin
1919

Kharkov

Poltava

Dnieper

Tsaritsyn
(Stalingrad)

Volga

COSSACKS
1918-20

HUNGARY

ROMANIANS

BESSARABIA

Dniester

FRENCH

Yekaterinoslav

Rostov-on-
Don

Novocherkassak

Astrakhan

ROMANIA

Odessa

Cossacks

YUGOSLAVIA

Danube

Simferopol

FRENCH

Novorossiysk

BRITISH

BULGARIA

Entente
fleet

Batum

Tiflis

BRITISH

Baku

Krasnovodsk

GREECE

Kars

BRITISH

BRITISH

Tabriz

1918-19

TURKEY

PERSIA

0      200      400 Km.

0      200      400 Mi.

## A Marxist Critique of Communism

*Karl Kautsky (1854–1938) was the leading spokesman for orthodox Marxism within the German Social Democratic Party, the most influential Marxist party in the world during the era of the Second International. Thus it is striking that he harshly criticized Leninist Bolshevism, or communism, as a heretical departure that could lead only to disaster. Kautsky's* Terrorism and Communism, *written in 1919, was central to a volley of charges and countercharges that pitted him first against Lenin, then against Trotsky.*

The hereditary sin of Bolshevism has been its suppression of democracy through a form of government, namely, the dictatorship, which has no meaning unless it represents the unlimited and despotic power, either of one single person, or of a small organization intimately bound together. . . . It is as easy to begin a dictatorship as it is to begin war, if one has the State power under control. But when once such steps have been taken, it is as difficult at will to stop the one as the other. . . .

. . . [W]herever Socialism does not appear to be possible on a democratic basis, and where the majority of the population rejects it, its time has not yet fully come. Bolshevism, on the other hand, argues that Socialism can only be introduced by being forced on a majority by a minority. . . . The Bolsheviks are prepared, in order to maintain their position, to make all sorts of possible concessions to bureaucracy, to militarism, and to capitalism, whereas any concession to democracy seems to them to be sheer suicide. And yet that alone offers any possibility . . . of leading Russia along paths of economic progress and prosperous development towards some higher form of existence. . . .

. . . [S]ince the rise of the Soviet Republic, a new wedge has been driven through the Socialist ranks of Germany by Bolshevik propaganda, which has demanded that our Party should relinquish the essential claims of democracy. . . .

. . . It was only after long and bitter struggle that the proletariat succeeded in acquiring universal and equal suffrage—a perfectly well-known fact, which, however, all communists and their friends seem to have completely forgotten. Democracy, with its universal equal suffrage, is the method to transform the class-struggle out of a hand-to-hand fight into a battle of intelligence, in which one particular class can triumph only if it is intellectually and morally on a level with its opponent. Democracy is the one and only method through which the higher form of life can be realised. . . .

*Source:* Karl Kautsky, *Terrorism and Communism: A Contribution to the Natural History of Revolution* (Westport, Conn.: Hyperion Press, 1973), pp. 217–218, 220–222, 226, 229, 231.

**Map 26.1    Foreign Intervention and Civil War in Revolutionary Russia, 1918–1920**    By mid-1918 the new communist regime was under attack from many sides, by both foreign troops and anticommunist Russians. Bolshevik-held territory shrank during 1919, but over the next year the Red Army managed to regain much of what had been lost and to secure the new communist state. Anton Deniken, Alexander Kolchak, and Nicholas Yudenich commanded the most significant counterrevolutionary forces.
*(Source: Adapted from* The Times Atlas of World History, *3d ed., by kind permission of Times Books.)*

The Russians felt that poor organization and planning had undermined the wider revolutionary possibility in Europe during 1919 and 1920. The Comintern would therefore cut through all the revolutionary romanticism to show what the Leninist strategy, or communism, meant in fact. The Russians themselves would have to call the shots because what communism meant, above all, was tight organization and discipline.

The second Comintern congress, during the summer of 1920, devised twenty-one conditions for Comintern affiliation. Most notably, any socialist party seeking membership had to accept the Comintern's authority, adopt a centralized organization, and purge its reformists. By early 1921, the Comintern's aggressive claim to leadership had split the international socialist movement, for the Comintern attracted some, but not all, of the members of the existing socialist parties. Those who now called themselves "communists" accepted the Leninist model and affiliated with the Comintern. Those who retained the "socialist" label rejected Comintern leadership; they still claimed to be Marxists but declined to embrace the Bolshevik strategy for taking power.

At first, many European socialists had difficulty assessing the Comintern objectively. The Russian communists enjoyed great prestige because they had made a real revolution, while elsewhere socialists had talked and compromised, even getting swept up in wartime patriotism. When the French Socialist Party debated Comintern membership at its national congress in December 1920, about 70 percent of the delegates voted to join and agreed to the twenty-one points, while a minority walked out to form a new socialist party. But as the implications of Comintern membership became clearer over the next few years, the balance shifted in favor of the socialists. Membership in the French Communist Party, which stood at 131,000 in 1921, declined to 28,000 by 1932.

Late in 1923 the Comintern finally concluded that revolution elsewhere could not be expected any time soon. The immediate enemy was not capitalism or the bourgeoisie, but the socialists, the communists' rivals for working-class support. The communists' incessant criticism of the socialists, whom they eventually dubbed "social fascists," demoralized and weakened the European left, especially in the face of the growing threat of fascism by the early 1930s. The schism on the left remained an essential fact of European political life for half a century.

## ■ From Lenin to Stalin, 1921–1929

To win the civil war, the communist regime had adopted a policy of "war communism," a rough-and-ready controlled economy in which food and supplies were commandeered for the Red Army. At the beginning of 1921, the economy was in crisis. Industrial production equaled only about one-fifth the 1913 total, workers in key factories went on strike, and peasants were resisting further requisitions of grain. In March 1921 sailors at the Kronstadt naval base near Petrograd mutinied, suffering considerable loss of life as governmental control was re-established.

With the very survival of the revolution in question, Lenin replaced war communism with the New Economic Policy (NEP) in March 1921. Although transport, banking, heavy industry, and wholesale commerce remained under state control, the NEP restored considerable scope for private enterprise, especially in the retail sector and in agriculture. Peasants could again sell some of their harvest. The economy quickly began to revive and by 1927 was producing at prewar levels.

But what about the longer term? If revolution elsewhere was not on the immediate horizon, could the Soviet Union—relatively backward economically and scarred by over a decade of upheaval—build a genuinely socialist order on its own? Certain measures were obvious: The new regime engineered rapid improvements in literacy, for example. But the Marxist understanding of historical progress required industrialization, and so debate focused on how to promote industrial development under Soviet conditions. That Soviet industrialization was somehow bound up with the creation of socialism was taken for granted.

This debate about priorities became intertwined with questions about the leadership of the new regime. Lenin suffered the first of a series of strokes in May 1922 and then died in January 1924, setting off a struggle among his possible successors. Leon Trotsky, an effective organizer and powerful thinker, was by most measures Lenin's heir apparent. Although he favored tighter economic controls to speed industrial development, Trotsky insisted that the Soviet Union's top priority should be spreading the revolution to other countries.

In contrast, Nikolai Bukharin (1888–1938) wanted to concentrate on the gradual development of the Soviet Union, based on a more open and conciliatory strategy than Trotsky envisioned. Rather than tightening controls to squeeze a surplus from agricultural producers, the government should promote purchasing power by allowing producers to profit. By the time of his death Lenin had apparently begun thinking along the same lines. And he had come to have considerable misgivings about the man who would win this struggle to direct the fragile new Soviet regime, Joseph Stalin (1879–1953).

Stalin was born Josef Djugashvili into a lower-class family in Georgia, in the Caucasus region. As an ethnic Georgian, he did not learn to speak Russian until he was 11 years old. From the position of party secretary, which he had assumed in 1922, Stalin established his control within the Soviet system by 1929. Though he lacked Trotsky's charisma and knew little of economics, he was highly intelligent and proved a master of backstage po-

**Rivals for the Soviet Leadership**   In July 1926 in Moscow, Soviet leaders carry the coffin of Feliks Dzerzhinsky, the first head of the secret police. Among them are Trotsky (*with glasses, center left*), Stalin (*right foreground*), and Bukharin (*with mustache, at far right*), rivals for the Soviet leadership after Lenin's death. The winner, Stalin, would eventually have his two competitors killed. *(David King Collection)*

litical maneuvering. Stalin first outmaneuvered Trotsky and his allies, removing them from positions of power and forcing Trotsky himself into exile in 1929. Bitterly critical of Stalin to the end, Trotsky was finally murdered by Stalin's agents in Mexico in 1940. Stalin's victory over those like Bukharin was more gradual, but ultimately just as decisive. And his victory proved decisive for the fate of Soviet communism.

By the latter 1920s, those who believed in the communist experiment were growing disillusioned with the compromises of the NEP. It was time for the Soviet Union to push ahead to a new order, leaving capitalism behind altogether. Even if revolution was not imminent elsewhere, the Soviet Union could seize the lead and build "socialism in one country." And genuine enthusiasm greeted the regime's turn to centralized economic planning in 1927, and its subsequent adoption of the first Five-Year Plan early in 1929. Central planning led to a program of crash industrialization, favoring heavy industry, by the end of that year. But this new, more radical direction was not fully thought through, and it soon caused incredible suffering.

To buy the necessary plants and equipment, the state seemed to require better control of agricultural output than had been possible under the New Economic Policy. The key was to squeeze the agricultural surplus from the peasantry on terms more favorable to the government. By forcing peasants into large, state-controlled collective farms, government leaders could more readily extract the surplus, which would then be sold abroad, earning the money to finance factories, dams, and power plants.

Stalin's effort to mobilize society for the great task of rapid industrialization affected the whole shape of the regime—including cultural and artistic policy. During the 1920s, the possibility of building a new socialist society in the Soviet Union had attracted a number of modernist artists, who assumed that artistic innovation went hand in hand with the radical socioeconomic transformation the communists were seeking to engineer. These artists wanted to make art more socially useful and more central to the lives of ordinary people. With Soviet cultural officials welcoming their experiments, such Soviet artists as Vladimir Tatlin (1885–1956) and Kasimir Malevich (1878–1935) developed striking new cultural forms.

But in 1929 Soviet officials began mobilizing the cultural realm to serve the grandiose task of building socialism in one country. No longer welcoming experiment and innovation, they demanded "socialist realism," which portrayed the achievements of the ongoing Soviet

**Tatlin: Monument to the Third International** Vladimir Tatlin created this model for a monument to the Third International, or Comintern, during 1919 and 1920. He envisioned a revolving structure, made of glass and iron, and twice as tall as the later Empire State Building. Although the monument was never built, Tatlin's bold, dynamic form symbolized the utopian aspirations of the early years of the communist experiment in Russia. *(David King Collection)*

revolution in an inspiring, heroic light. Modernism, in contrast, they denounced as decadent and counterrevolutionary.

In retrospect, it is clear that a Stalinist revolution within the Soviet regime began in 1929, but where it was to lead was by no means certain—not even to Stalin himself. Still, the Soviet Union was pulling back, going its own way by the end of the 1920s. For the foreseeable future, the presence of a revolutionary regime in the old Russia would apparently be less disruptive for the rest of Europe than it had first appeared.

### ■ The Crisis of Liberal Italy and the Creation of Fascism, 1919–1925

Fascism emerged directly from the Italian experience of World War I, which proved especially controversial because the Italians could have avoided it altogether. No one attacked Italy in 1914, and the country could have received significant territorial benefits just by remaining neutral. Yet it seemed to many, including leading intellectuals and educated young people, that Italy could not stand idly by in a European war, especially one involving Austria-Hungary, which still controlled significant Italian-speaking areas. To participate in this major war would be the test of Italy's maturity as a nation. In May 1915 Italy finally intervened on the side of the Triple Entente. The government's decision stemmed not from vague visions of renewal but from the commitment of tangible territorial gains that France and Britain made to Italy with the secret Treaty of London in April.

Despite the near collapse of the Italian armies in October 1917, Italy lasted out the war and contributed to the victory over Austria-Hungary. Supporters of the war felt that this success could lead to a thoroughgoing renewal of Italian public life. Yet many Italians had been skeptical of claims for the war from the outset, and the fact that it proved so much more difficult than expected hardly won them over. To socialists, Catholics, and many left-leaning liberals, intervention itself had been a tragic mistake. Thus, despite Italy's participation in the victory, division over the war's significance immensely complicated the Italian political situation after the war was over.

Their skepticism was only confirmed when Italy did not secure all the gains it sought at the Paris Peace Conference. Italy got most of what it had been promised in the Treaty of London, but appetites increased with the dissolution of the Austro-Hungarian Empire. To some Italians, the disappointing outcome of the peace conference simply confirmed that the war had been a mistake, its benefits not worth the costs. But others were outraged at what seemed a denigration of the Italian contribution by France, Britain, and the United States. The outcome fanned resentment not only of Italy's allies but also of the country's political leaders, who seemed too weak to deliver on what they had pledged.

The established leaders of Italy's parliamentary democracy also failed at the task of renewing the country's political system in light of the war experience. To be sure, in a spirit of democratic reform, Italy adopted proportional representation to replace the old system of small, single-member constituencies in 1919. The new system meant a greater premium on mass parties and party discipline at the expense of the one-to-one bargaining that had characterized the earlier *trasformismo*. But the new multiparty system quickly reached an impasse—partly because of the stance of the Italian Socialist Party.

In contrast to the French and German parties, the Italian Socialists had never supported the war, and they did not accept the notion that the war experience could yield political renewal in the aftermath. So rather than reaching out to idealistic but discontented war veterans,

Socialist leaders talked of imitating the Bolshevik Revolution. And the Italian situation seemed at least potentially revolutionary during 1919 and 1920, when a wave of national strikes culminated in a series of factory occupations. But despite their revolutionary rhetoric, Italy's Socialist leaders did not understand the practical aspects of Leninism and did not carry out the planning and organization that might have produced an Italian revolution.

The established parliamentary system was at an impasse, and the Socialist Party seemed at once too inflexible and too romantic to lead some sort of radical transformation. It was in this context that fascism emerged, claiming to offer a third way. It was bound to oppose the Socialists and the socialist working class because of conflict over the meaning of the war and the kind of transformation Italy needed. And this antisocialist posture made fascism open to exploitation by reactionary interests. By early 1921 landowners in northern and central Italy were footing the bill as bands of young fascists drove around the countryside in trucks, beating up workers and burning down socialist meeting halls. But fascist spokesmen claimed to offer something other than mere reaction—a new politics that all Italians, including the workers, would eventually find superior.

At the same time, important sectors of Italian industry, which had grown rapidly thanks to government orders during the war, looked with apprehension toward the more competitive international economy that loomed now that the war was over. With its relative lack of capital and raw materials, Italy seemed to face an especially difficult situation. Nationalist thinkers and business spokesmen questioned the capacity of the present parliamentary system to provide the vigorous leadership that Italy needed. Prone to short-term bickering and partisanship, ordinary politicians lacked the vision to pursue Italy's international economic interests and the will to impose the necessary discipline on the domestic level. Thus the government's response to the labor unrest of 1919 and 1920 was hesitant and weak. (See the box "Reading Sources: Toward Fascism: Alfredo Rocco on the Weakness of the Liberal Democratic State.")

Postwar Italy, then, witnessed widespread discontent with established forms of politics, but those discontented were socially disparate, and their aims were not entirely compatible. Some had been socialists before the war, others nationalists hostile to socialism. While some envisioned a more intense kind of mass politics, others thought the masses already had too much power. Still, these discontented groups agreed on the need for an alternative to both conventional parliamentary politics

🞂 R E A D I N G   S O U R C E S

## Toward Fascism: Alfredo Rocco on the Weakness of the Liberal Democratic State

*As Italy's minister of justice from 1925 to 1932, the Italian legal scholar Alfredo Rocco (1875–1935) spearheaded the construction of the new fascist state. Speaking in November 1920, he revealed why he would seek to replace parliamentary democracy with a new, stronger form of government. Rocco was troubled, most immediately, by the apparent weakness of the liberal state in the face of strikes by unions, or syndicates, of public service employees. But the deeper problem he saw was liberal individualism, linked to shortsighted pursuit of personal advantage.*

There is a crisis within the state; day by day, the state is dissolving into a mass of small particles, parties, associations, groups and syndicates that are binding it in chains and paralysing and stifling its activity: one by one, with increasing speed, the state is losing its attributes of sovereignty. . . . The conflict of interests between groups and classes is now being settled by the use of private force alone. . . . The state stands by impassively watching these conflicts which involve countless violations of public and private rights. This neutrality which, in liberal doctrine, was intended to allow free play for economic law in the clash of interests between the classes is now being interpreted as allowing the state to abandon its essential function of guardian of public order and agent of justice. . . .

. . . The eighteenth-century reaction against the state . . . came to a head politically in the explosion of the French Revolution. . . . From that time onwards, the claims of individualism knew no bounds. The masses of individuals wanted to govern the state and govern it in accordance with their own individual interests. The state, a living organism with a continuous existence over the centuries that extends beyond successive generations and as such the guardian of the immanent historical interests of the species, was turned into a monopoly to serve the individual interests of each separate generation. . . .

Now there can be no doubt that one of the most serious consequences of liberal agnosticism was the emergence of syndicalism, a syndicalism that was at once violent, subversive, and opposed to the state.

. . . The state must return to its traditions, interrupted by the triumph of liberal ideology, and treat the modern syndicates exactly as it treated the medieval corporations. It must absorb them and make them part of the state. . . . On the one hand, syndicates must be recognized as essential and on the other they must be placed firmly beneath the control of the state. . . . But above all, it is necessary to change them from aggressive bodies defending particular interests into a means of collaboration to achieve common aims.

*Source:* Adrian Lyttelton, ed., *Italian Fascisms from Pareto to Gentile* (New York: Harper & Row, Harper Torchbooks, 1975), pp. 269, 273–275, 278–280.

and conventional Marxist socialism. And all found the germs of that alternative in the Italian war experience.

The person who seemed able to translate these aspirations into a new political force was Benito Mussolini (1883–1945), who had been a prominent socialist journalist before the war. Indeed, he was so talented that he was made editor of the Socialist Party's national newspaper in 1912, when he was only 29 years old. At that point many saw him as the fresh face needed to revitalize Italian socialism.

His concern with renewal made Mussolini an unorthodox socialist even before 1914, and he was prominent among those on the Italian left who began calling for Italian intervention once the war began. The fact that socialists in France, Germany, and elsewhere had immediately rallied to their respective national war efforts

**Benito Mussolini**    The founder of fascism is shown with other fascist leaders in 1922, as he becomes prime minister of Italy. Standing at Mussolini's right (*with beard*) is Italo Balbo, later a pioneering aviator and fascist Italy's air force minister.    *(Corbis)*

raised new questions about conventional socialism, based on international proletarian solidarity. But the Italian Socialist Party refused to follow his call for intervention, remaining neutralist and aloof, so Mussolini found himself cut off from his earlier constituency.

However, through his new newspaper, *Il popolo d'Italia (The People of Italy)*, Mussolini helped rally the disparate groups that advocated Italian participation in the war. He saw military service once Italy intervened, and after the war he seemed a credible spokesman for those who wanted to translate the war experience into a new form of politics. Amid growing political unrest, he founded the fascist movement in March 1919, taking the term *fascism* from the ancient Roman *fasces,* a bundle of rods surrounding an ax that guards carried at state occasions as a symbol of power and unity.

But fascism was not a major force at first. And even as it gathered force in violent reaction against the socialist labor organizations by 1921, the movement's direc-

tion was something of a mystery. Although young fascist militants wanted to replace the established parliamentary system with a new political order, Mussolini seemed ever more prone to use fascism as his personal instrument to achieve power within the existing system. When his maneuvering finally won him the prime minister's post in October 1922, it was not at all clear that a change of regime, or a one-party dictatorship, was at hand.

At that point, Mussolini, like most Italians, emphasized normalization and legality. Fascism had apparently been absorbed within the political system, perhaps to provide an infusion of youthful vitality after the war. With Mussolini as prime minister, there would be changes, but not revolutionary changes. Government would become more vigorous and efficient; the swollen Italian bureaucracy would be streamlined; the trains would run on time. But those who had envisioned more sweeping change were frustrated that nothing more had come of fascism than this.

A crisis in 1924 forced Mussolini's hand. In June the moderate socialist Giacomo Matteotti° rose in parliament to denounce the renewed fascist violence that had accompanied recent national elections. His murder by fascist thugs shortly thereafter produced a great public outcry, though the responsibility of Mussolini and his government was unclear. Many establishment figures who had tolerated Mussolini as the man who could keep order now deserted him. A growing chorus called for his resignation.

Mussolini sought at first to be conciliatory, but more radical fascists saw the crisis as an opportunity to end the compromise with the old liberal order and to begin creating a whole new political system. The crisis came to a head on December 31, 1924, when thirty-three militants called on Mussolini to demand that he make up his mind. In their view, the way out of the crisis was not to delimit the scope of fascism but to expand it. Mussolini was not an ordinary prime minister but the leader of fascism, *Il Duce*°. In that role he would have to accept responsibility even for his movement's violent excesses and finally begin implementing a full-scale fascist revolution.

Mussolini committed himself to this more radical course in a speech to the Chamber of Deputies a few days later, on January 3, 1925. Defiantly claiming the "full political, moral, and historical responsibility for all that has happened," including "all the acts of violence," he promised to accelerate the transformation that he claimed to have initiated with his agitation for intervention in 1914 and 1915.[1] And now began the creation of a new fascist state, although the compromises continued and the direction was never as clear as committed fascists desired.

## ■ Innovation and Compromise in Fascist Italy, 1925–1930

Early in 1925, the fascist government began to undermine the existing democratic system by imprisoning or exiling opposition leaders and outlawing nonfascist parties and labor unions. But fascism was not seeking simply a conventional monopoly of political power; the new fascist state was to be totalitarian, all-encompassing, limitless in its reach. Under the old liberal regime, the fascists charged, the state had been too weak to promote the national interest, and Italian society had been too fragmented to achieve its full potential. So Mussolini's regime both expanded the state's sovereignty and mobilized the society to create a deeper sense of national identity and shared purpose. To settle labor disputes, a new system of labor judges replaced the right to strike, which, the fascists claimed, had fostered neither productivity nor long-term working-class interests. And the Fascist Party founded new organizations—for youth, for women, for leisure-time activities—that would make possible new forms of public participation.

The centerpiece of the new fascist state was corporativism, which entailed mobilizing people as producers, through organization of the workplace. Groupings based on occupation, or economic function, were gradually to replace parliament as the basis for political participation and decision making. Beginning in 1926, corporativist institutions were established in stages until a Chamber of Fasces and Corporations at last replaced the old Chamber of Deputies in 1939.

Especially through this corporative state, the fascists claimed to be fulfilling their grandiose mission and providing the world with a third way, beyond both outmoded democracy and misguided communism. The practice of corporativism never lived up to such rhetoric, but the effort to devise new forms of political participation and decision making was central to fascism's self-understanding and its quest for legitimacy. And that effort attracted much attention abroad, especially with the Great Depression of the 1930s.

Despite the commitment to a new regime, however, fascism continued to compromise with pre-existing elites and institutions. The accommodation was especially evident in the arrangements with the Catholic Church that Mussolini worked out in 1929, formally ending the dispute between the church and the Italian state that had festered since national unification in 1870. With the Lateran Pact, Mussolini restored a measure of sovereignty of the Vatican; with the Concordat, he conceded to the church autonomy in education and supremacy in marriage law.

This settlement of an old and thorny dispute afforded Mussolini a good deal of prestige among nonfascists at home and abroad. But compromise with the church could only displease committed fascists, who complained that giving this powerful, autonomous institution a role in Italian public life undermined the totalitarian aspirations of fascism. Such complaints led to a partial crackdown on Catholic youth organizations in 1931, as Mussolini continued trying to juggle traditionalist compromise and revolutionary pretension.

---

**Matteotti** (mah-tay-OH-tee)　**Il Duce** (eel DOO-chay)

By the end of the 1920s, then, it remained unclear whether Italian fascism was a form of restoration or a form of revolution. It had restored order in Italy, overcoming the labor unrest of the immediate postwar years, but it was order on a new, antidemocratic basis. Yet the fascists claimed to be implementing a revolution of their own at the same time. Fascism could be violent and disruptive, dictatorial and repressive, but Mussolini seemed dynamic and creative. Though its ultimate direction remained nebulous, fascism attracted those elsewhere who were discontented with liberal democracy and Marxist socialism. It thus fed the volatility and ideological polarization that marked the European political order after World War I.

# TOWARD MASS SOCIETY

AFTER a few years of wild economic swings just after the war, Europe was enjoying renewed prosperity by the later 1920s. Common involvement in the war had blurred class lines and accelerated the trend toward what contemporaries began to call "mass society." As the new prosperity spread the fruits of industrialization more widely, ordinary people increasingly set the cultural tone, partly through new mass media such as film and radio. To some, the advent of mass society portended a welcome revitalization of culture and a more authentic kind of democracy, whereas others saw only a debasement of cultural standards and a susceptibility to populist demagoguery. But though the contours of mass society now became evident, social change did not keep up with the promise of—and the requirements for—democratic politics.

## ■ Economic Readjustment and the New Prosperity

In their effort to return to normal, governments were quick to dismantle wartime planning and control mechanisms. But the needs of war had stimulated innovations that helped fuel the renewed economic growth of the 1920s. The civilian air industry, for example, developed rapidly during the decade by taking advantage of wartime work on aviation for military purposes. More generally, newer industries such as chemicals, electricity, and advanced machinery led the way to a new prosperity in the 1920s, which significantly altered patterns of life in the more industrialized parts of the West. The automobile, a luxury plaything for the wealthy before the war, began to be mass-produced in western Europe. In France, automobile production shot up dramatically, from 40,000 in 1920 to 254,000 in 1929.

But the heady pace masked problems that lay beneath the relative prosperity of the 1920s, even in victorious Britain and France. While new industries prospered, old ones declined in the face of new technologies and stronger foreign competition. In Britain, the industries responsible for Britain's earlier industrial pre-eminence—textiles, coal, shipbuilding, and iron and steel—were now having trouble competing. Rather than investing in new technologies, companies in these industries demanded government protection and imposed lower wages and longer hours on their workers. At the same time, British labor unions resisted the mechanization necessary to make these older industries more competitive.

Rather than realistically assessing Britain's prospects in the more competitive international economy, British leaders sought to return to the prewar situation, based on the gold standard, with London the world's financial center. For many Britons, the government's announcement in 1925 that the British pound was again freely convertible to gold at 1914 exchange rates was the long-awaited indication that normality had returned at last. Yet the return to 1914 exchange rates overvalued the pound relative to the U.S. dollar, making British goods more expensive on export markets and making it still more difficult for aging British industries to compete. Further, Britain no longer had sufficient capital to act as the world's banker. By trying to do so, Britain became all the more vulnerable when the international economy reached a crisis in 1929.

The structural decline of older industries was clearest in Britain, but inflation and its psychological impact was most prominent in Germany and France. By the summer of 1923, Germany's response to the French occupation of the Ruhr had transformed an already serious inflationary problem, stemming from wartime deficit spending, into one of the great hyperinflations in history. At its height in November, when it took 4.2 trillion marks to equal a dollar, Germans were forced to cart wheelbarrows of paper money to stores to buy ordinary grocery items. By the end of 1923, the government managed to stabilize prices through currency reform and drastically reduced government spending—a combination that elicited greater cooperation from the victors. But the rampant inflation, and the readjustment necessary to control it, had wiped out the life savings of ordinary people while profiting speculators and those in debt, including some large industrialists. This inequity left scars that remained even as Germany enjoyed a measure of prosperity in the years that followed.

Inflation was less dramatic in France, but there, too, it affected perceptions and priorities in significant ways. For over a century, from the Napoleonic era to the outbreak of war in 1914, the value of the French franc had remained stable. But the war started France on an inflationary cycle that shattered the security of its many small savers—those, such as teachers and shopkeepers, who had been the backbone of the Third Republic. To repay war debts and rebuild war-damaged industries, the French government continued to run budget deficits,

and thereby cause inflation, even after 1918. Runaway inflation threatened during 1925 and 1926, but the franc was finally restabilized in 1928, though at only about one-fifth its prewar value.

On the international level, war debts and reparations strained the financial system, creating problems with the financing of trade. But in the course of the 1920s, experts made adjustments that seemed to be returning the international exchange system to equilibrium. Only in retrospect, after the international capitalist system fell into crisis late in 1929, did it become clear how potent those strains were—and how inadequate the efforts at readjustment.

**The Legacy of Inflation in Germany**
Packets of worthless old banknotes serve as children's building blocks in November 1923. The German government had just introduced a new currency in an effort to check a price inflation that had reached 2,500 percent a month. Although the inflation was brought under control by the end of the year, it produced lasting scars. Many ordinary Germans found their savings wiped out entirely.   *(© Hulton-Deutsch Collection/Corbis)*

## ■ Work, Leisure, and the New Popular Culture

The wartime spur to industrialization produced a large increase in the industrial labor force all over Europe, and a good deal of labor unrest accompanied the transition to peacetime. Some of that agitation challenged factory discipline and authority relationships. Seeking to re-establish authority on a new basis for the competitive postwar world, business leaders and publicists fostered a new cult of efficiency and productivity, partly by adapting Taylorism and Fordism, influential American ideas about mass production. On the basis of his "time-and-motion" studies of factory labor, Frederick W. Taylor (1856–1915) argued that breaking down assembly-line production into small, repetitive tasks was the key to maximizing worker efficiency. In contrast, Henry Ford (1863–1947) linked the gospel of mass production to mass consumption. In exchange for accepting the discipline of the assembly line, the workers should be paid well enough to be able to buy the products they produced—even automobiles. Sharing in the prosperity that mass production made possible, factory workers would be loyal to the companies that employed them. Not all Europeans, however, welcomed the new ideas from America. In the new cult of efficiency and mass production, some saw an unwelcome sameness and a debasement of cultural standards.

In light of the major role women had played in the wartime labor force, the demand for women's suffrage proved irresistible in Britain, Germany, and much of Europe, though not yet in France or Italy. In Britain, where the call for women's suffrage had earlier met with controversy (see page 827), the right to vote was readily conceded in 1918, though at first only to women over 30. By now women no longer seemed a threat to the political system. And in fact British women, once they could vote, simply flowed into the existing parties, countering earlier hopes—and fears—that a specifically feminist political agenda would follow from women's suffrage.

Although female employment remained higher than before the war, many women were willing to return home, yielding their jobs to the returning soldiers. The need to replace the men killed in the war lent renewed force to the traditional notion that women served society, and fulfilled themselves, by marrying and rearing families. Still, the spirit of innovation brought into the public arena subjects with significant implications for gender roles—subjects largely taboo before the war. The desire to be "modern" produced, for example, a more open, unsentimental, even scientific discussion of sexuality and reproduction.

**The Sensational Josephine Baker**    A native of St. Louis, the African American Josephine Baker moved to Paris in 1925 and quickly created a sensation in both France and Germany as a cabaret dancer and singer. Playing on the European association of Africa with the wild and uninhibited, she featured unusual poses and exotic costumes.    *(Hulton Getty/Liaison)*

The new "rationalization of sexuality" fed demands that governments provide access to sex counseling, birth control, and even abortion as they assumed ever greater responsibilities for promoting social health. This trend was especially prominent in Germany, although German innovators learned from experiments in the new Soviet Union and from the birth control movement that Margaret Sanger (1883–1966) was spearheading in the United States.

The more open and tolerant attitude toward sexuality affected popular entertainment. Thus, for example, Josephine Baker's dancing and costumes—unthinkable before the war. Another result was the emergence of a more visible gay subculture, prominent especially in the vibrant cabaret scene in Berlin during the 1920s.

**Weimar Cinema**   This poster advertises Fritz Lang's film *Metropolis*, which explored the dehumanization and exploitation of the modern city.   *(Schulz-Neudamm, Metropolis, 1926. Lithograph, 83" × 36½". The Museum of Modern Art, New York. Gift of Universum Film Aktiengesellschaft.)*

Mass consumption followed from the mass production that created the new prosperity of the 1920s. As it became possible to mass-produce the products of the second industrial transformation, more people could afford automobiles, electrical gadgets such as radios and phonographs, and clothing of synthetic fabrics, developed through innovations in chemistry. First came rayon, produced in small quantities since 1891 but mass-produced beginning in the 1920s. In this new artificial form, silk, long one of the trappings of wealth, was now within the means of ordinary people.

With the eight-hour workday increasingly the norm, growing attention was devoted to leisure as a positive source of human fulfillment—for everyone, not just the wealthy. European beach resorts grew crowded as more people had the time, and the means, to take vacations. An explosion of interest in soccer among Europeans paralleled the growth of professional baseball and college football in the United States. Huge stadiums were built across Europe.

The growth of leisure was linked to the development of mass media and mass culture. During the early 1920s radio became a commercial venture, reaching a mass audience in Europe, as in the United States and Canada. Although movies had begun to emerge as vehicles of popular entertainment even before the war, they came into their own during the 1920s, when the names of film stars became household words for the first time.

The rapid development of film showed that new, more accessible media could nurture extraordinary innovation. Germany led the way with such films as *The Cabinet of Dr. Caligari* (1920), *Metropolis* (1927), and *The Blue Angel* (1930), but the Russian Sergei Eisenstein (1898–1948) became perhaps the most admired film maker of the era with *Battleship Potemkin* (1925), his brilliant portrayal of the Russian revolution of 1905. In some spheres, however, America was beginning to outdo both Paris and Berlin. Marlene Dietrich (1901–1992), famous as Lola Lola in *The Blue Angel,* was among a number of German film celebrities who went to Hollywood.

Exploiting the new popular fascination with air travel, the American Charles Lindbergh (1902–1974) captured the European imagination in 1927 with the first solo flight across the Atlantic. Lindbergh's feat epitomized the affirmative side of the decade—the sense that there were new worlds to conquer and that there still were heroes to admire, despite the ironies of the war and the ambiguities of the peace.

## ■ Society and Politics in the Victorious Democracies

France and Britain seemed the best positioned of the major European countries to take advantage of renewed peace and stability to confront the sociopolitical problems of the postwar era. And during the 1920s, each seemed to return to normal. But was normal good enough, in light of the rupture of the war and the challenges of the emerging mass society?

Victory in the Great War seemed to belie France's prewar concerns about decadence and decline. In the immediate aftermath of the war, Clemenceau and other French leaders were confident in dealing with radical labor unrest and aggressive in translating the battlefield victory into a dominant position on the European continent. But the tremendous loss of French lives had produced a new fear—that France could not withstand another such challenge. The renewed confidence thus proved hollow.

Although some in prewar France had worried about falling behind rapidly industrializing Germany, victory seemed to have vindicated France's more cautious, balanced economy, with its blend of industry and agriculture. Thus the prewar mistrust of rapid industrial development continued. Rather than foster a program of economic modernization that might have promoted genuine security, the French pulled back even from the measure of state responsibility for the economy that had developed during the war.

To be sure, in France, as elsewhere, the 1920s was a decade of relative prosperity. Led by the oil and electricity industries, the economy grew at an annual rate of 4.6 percent between 1923 and 1929, double the prewar rate. Industrial production by 1929 was 40 percent higher than it had been in 1913. But, with the exception of Britain, other Western economies grew more rapidly during the 1920s, and the opportunity that growth afforded to modernize the French economy was not seized. Although government grants helped reconstruct almost eight thousand factories, most were simply rebuilt as they had been before the war. Moreover, the working class benefited little from the relative prosperity of the 1920s. Housing remained poor, wages failed to keep up with inflation, and France continued to lag other countries in social legislation.

Britain, too, made certain adjustments after the war but missed the chance to make others. The government's handling of the Easter Rebellion in Ireland in 1916 (see page 853) intensified anti-British feeling and fed further

violence. But the British finally forged at least a provisional resolution. The first step was to partition Ireland, creating a separate Ulster, or Northern Ireland, from those counties with Protestant majorities. Ulster then remained under the British crown when a new independent Republic of Ireland was established in the larger, majority Catholic part of the island in 1922.

The British political system remained stable between the wars, although the Labour Party supplanted the Liberals to become the dominant alternative to the Conservatives by the early 1920s. The Labour Party even got a brief taste of power when Ramsay MacDonald (1866–1937) formed Britain's first Labour government in January 1924. The coming of Labour to power resulted in a significant expansion of the governmental elite to incorporate those, like MacDonald himself, with genuinely working-class backgrounds.

The rise of Labour was striking, but it was the Conservative leader, Stanley Baldwin (1867–1947), who set the tone for British politics between the wars in three stints as prime minister during the years from 1923 to 1937. Although the wealthy son of a steel manufacturer, Baldwin deliberately departed from the old aristocratic style of British Conservative politics. More down-to-earth and pragmatic than his predecessors, he was the first British prime minister to use radio effectively, and he made an effort to foster good relations with workers. Yet Baldwin's era was one of growing social tension.

With exports declining, unemployment remained high in Britain throughout the interwar period, never falling below 10 percent. The coal industry, though still the country's largest employer, had become a particular trouble spot in the British economy. As coal exports declined, British mine owners became ever more aggressive in their dealings with labor, finally, in 1926, insisting on a longer workday and a wage cut of 13 percent to restore competitiveness. The result was a coal miners' strike in May that promptly turned into a general strike, involving almost all of organized labor—about 4 million workers—in the most notable display of trade-union solidarity Britain had ever seen. For nine days the economy stood at a virtual standstill. But threats of arrest and a growing public backlash forced the union leadership to accept a compromise. The miners continued the strike on their own, but they finally returned to work six months later at considerably lower wages.

Although for somewhat different reasons, Britain and France both failed during the 1920s to take advantage of what would soon seem, in retrospect, to have been a precious opportunity to adjust their economies, heal social wounds, and create more genuinely democratic political systems. The lost opportunity would mean growing social tensions once the relative prosperity of the decade had ended.

## WEIMAR GERMANY AND THE TRIALS OF THE NEW DEMOCRACIES

HE war was supposed to have paved the way for democracy, and the fall of the monarchies in Russia, Germany, and Austria-Hungary seemed almost made-to-order invitations. But events quickly overwhelmed the new democracy in Russia in 1917. After the war was over, circumstances seemed more favorable in Germany, Poland, and elsewhere in central Europe, but almost everywhere the new democracies led tortured lives and soon gave way to more authoritarian forms of government. So the postwar decade did not see the extension and consolidation of the political democracy that optimistic observers associated with the emerging mass society.

The most significant test took place in Germany, which adopted its first fully democratic constitution in 1919, as the new Weimar Republic emerged from the provisional revolutionary republic proclaimed in November 1918. But the Weimar democracy had great difficulty establishing its legitimacy, and it was suffering serious strains by 1930.

### ■ Democracy Aborted in East-Central Europe

New democracies were established in much of central and eastern Europe after the war, but except in Czechoslovakia and Finland the practice of parliamentary government did not match the initial promise. Democracy seemed divisive and ineffective, so one country after another adopted a more authoritarian alternative during the 1920s and early 1930s.

Poland offers the most dramatic example. Although its democratic constitution of 1921 established a cabinet responsible to a parliamentary majority, the parliament fragmented into so many parties that instability proved endemic from the start. Poland had fourteen different ministries from November 1918 to May 1926, when Marshal Josef Pilsudski led a coup d'état that replaced parliamentary government with an authoritarian regime stressing national unity. This suppression of democracy came as a relief to many Poles—and was welcomed even

by the trade unions. After Pilsudski's death in 1935, a group of colonels ruled Poland until the country was conquered by Nazi Germany in 1939.

Democracy proved hard to manage in east-central Europe partly because of the economic difficulties resulting from the breakup of the Habsburg system. New national borders meant new economic barriers that disrupted long-standing economic relationships. Industrial centers such as Vienna and Budapest found themselves cut off from their traditional markets and sources of raw materials. In what was now Poland, Silesians had long been oriented toward Germany, Galicians toward Vienna, and those in eastern Poland toward Russia. Thus the new Polish nation-state was hardly a cohesive economic unit.

The countries of east-central Europe remained overwhelmingly agrarian, and this, too, proved unconducive to democracy. Land reform that accompanied the transition to democracy made small properties the norm in much of the region. But because these units were often too small to be efficient, agricultural output actually decreased after land was redistributed, most dramatically in Romania and Yugoslavia. When agricultural prices declined in the late 1920s, many peasants had no choice but to sell out to larger landowners. What had seemed a progressive and democratic reform thus failed to provide a stable agrarian smallholder base for democracy.

### ■ Germany's Cautious Revolution, 1919–1920

Meanwhile, in Germany, the Weimar Republic began under particularly difficult circumstances. Born of military defeat, it was promptly forced to take responsibility for the harsh and dictated Treaty of Versailles in 1919. During its first years, moreover, the regime encountered severe economic dislocation, culminating in the hyperinflation of 1923, as well as ideological polarization that threatened to tear the country apart.

Although Germany had strong military and authoritarian traditions, the initial threat to the new democracy came not from the right, disoriented and discredited, but from the left, stimulated by the Russian example. Those seeking further revolution, and those who feared it, could easily equate the proclamation of a German republic with the first revolution in Russia; as in Russia, the new, more democratic order could prove a mere prelude to communist revolution.

Spearheaded by Karl Liebknecht and Rosa Luxemburg in Berlin, revolutionary unrest reached its peak in Germany during December 1918 and January 1919. But even after Liebknecht and Luxemburg were captured and murdered in January, a serious chance of further revolution persisted through May 1919, and communist revolutionary agitation continued to flare up until the end of 1923.

As it turned out, there was no further revolution, partly because the parallel between Germany and Russia carried only so far. The new German government had made peace, whereas the leaders of the provisional government in Russia had sought to continue the war. Furthermore, those who ended up controlling the councils that sprang up in Germany during the fall of 1918 favored political democracy, not communist revolution, and therefore they supported the provisional government.

Even so, the revolutionary minority constituted a credible threat. And the new government made repression of the extreme left a priority—even if it meant leaving in place some of the institutions and personnel of the old imperial system. In November 1918, at the birth of the new republic, the moderate socialist leader Friedrich Ebert had agreed with General Wilhelm Groener, the new army leader, to preserve the old imperial officer corps to help prevent further revolution. But when the regular army, weakened by war and defeat, proved unable to control radical agitation in Berlin in December, it seemed the republic would have to take extraordinary measures to defend itself from the revolutionary left. With the support of Ebert and Groener, Gustav Noske (1868–1946), the minister of national defense, began to organize "Free Corps," volunteer paramilitary groups to be used against the revolutionaries. Noske, who was a socialist, but one long supportive of the military, noted that "somebody will have to be the bloodhound—I won't shirk the responsibility."[2]

During the first five months of 1919, the government unleashed the Free Corps to crush leftist movements all over Germany, often with wanton brutality. In relying on right-wing paramilitary groups, the republic's leaders were playing with fire, but the immediate threat at this point came from the left. In 1920, however, the government faced a right-wing coup attempt, the Kapp Putsch. The army declined to defend the republic, but the government managed to survive thanks largely to a general strike by leftist workers. The republic's early leaders had to juggle both extremes because, as one of them put it, the Weimar Republic was "a candle burning at both ends."

Though sporadic street fighting by paramilitary groups continued, the republic survived its traumatic birth and achieved an uneasy stability by 1924. But Germany's postwar revolution had remained confined to the political level. There was no program to break up the car-

tels, with their concentrations of economic power. Even on the level of government personnel, continuity was more striking than change. There was no effort to build a loyal republican army, and no attempt to purge the bureaucracy and the judiciary of antidemocratic elements from the old imperial order. When right-wing extremists assassinated prominent leaders, such as the Jewish industrialist Walther Rathenau in 1922, the courts often proved unwilling to prosecute those responsible. In general, those who ran the new government day to day were often skeptical of democracy, even hostile to the new regime.

In light of the republic's eventual failure, the willingness of its early leaders to leave intact so much from the old order has made them easy targets for criticism. It can be argued, however, that the course they followed—heading off the extreme left, reassuring the established elites, and playing for time—was the republic's best chance for success. The new regime might establish its legitimacy by inertia, much like the Third Republic in France, which had similarly been born of defeat. Even lacking the sentimental fervor that had earlier surrounded democratic ideals, Germans might gradually become "republicans of reason," recognizing that this regime could be a framework for prosperity and renewed German prominence in international affairs. In the event of an early crisis, however, a republic consolidating itself in this cautious way might well find fewer defenders than opponents.

Elections in January 1919 produced a constituent assembly that convened in Weimar, a town associated with what seemed the most humane German cultural traditions, to draft a democratic constitution. The elections took place before the peace conference had produced the widely detested Treaty of Versailles. When the first regular parliamentary elections finally were held in June 1920, the three moderate parties that had led the new government, and that had been forced to accept the treaty, suffered a major defeat, dropping from 76 to 47 percent of the seats. These were the parties most committed to democratic institutions, but they were never again to achieve a parliamentary majority.

The 1920 elections revealed the problems of polarization and lack of consensus that would bedevil, and eventually ruin, the Weimar Republic. Because the electorate found it difficult to agree, or even to compromise, Germany settled into a multiparty system that led to unstable coalition government. And the strength, or potential strength, of the extremes immeasurably complicated political life for those trying to make the new democracy work. On the left, the Communists constantly criticized

**Hopes for Peace**   Foreign ministers Aristide Briand (*left*) of France and Gustav Stresemann of Germany spearheaded the improved international relations that bred optimism during the later 1920s.   *(Corbis)*

the more moderate Socialists for supporting the republic. On the right, the Nationalist Party (DNVP) played on nationalist resentments and fears of the extreme left—but the result was similarly to dilute support for the new republic. To the right even of the Nationalists were Adolf Hitler's National Socialists, or Nazis, who were noisy and often violent, but they attracted little electoral support before 1930.

### ■ Gustav Stresemann and the Scope for Gradual Consolidation, 1920–1929

All was not necessarily lost for the republic when the three moderate, pro-Weimar parties were defeated in 1920. Germans who were unsupportive or hostile at first might be gradually won over. After the death of President Ebert in 1925, Paul von Hindenburg, the emperor's field marshal, was elected president. Depending on the circumstances, having a conservative military leader from the old order in this role could be advantageous, or

damaging, for the future of democracy. As long as scope for consolidation remained, Hindenburg's presidency suggested to skeptics that the new regime was legitimate and a worthy object of German patriotism. But when crisis came by 1930, Hindenburg was quick to give up on parliamentary government—with devastating results.

The individual who best exemplified the possibility of winning converts to the Weimar Republic was Gustav Stresemann° (1878–1929), the leader of the German People's Party (DVP), a conservative party that did not support the republic at the outset. But it was relatively flexible and offered at least the possibility of broadening the republic's base of support. As chancellor, and especially as foreign minister, Stresemann proved the republic's leading statesman.

Stresemann's background and instincts were not democratic, but by the end of 1920 Germany's postwar

---

**Stresemann** (STRAY-zuh-mahn)

political volatility had convinced him that if the new republic should go under, the outcome would not be the conservative monarchy he preferred but the triumph of the extreme left. Moreover, it had become clear that the new democratic republic was not likely to be revolutionary on the socioeconomic level. It made sense, then, to work actively to make the new regime succeed. From within this framework Germany could pursue its international aims, negotiating modifications of the Versailles treaty and returning to great power status.

Stresemann became chancellor in August 1923, when inflation was raging out of control. Within months his government managed to get the German economy functioning effectively again, partly because the French agreed that an international commission should review the reparations question, specifying realistic amounts based on Germany's ability to pay. During the summer of 1924, a commission led by the American financier Charles G. Dawes produced the Dawes Plan, which remained in force until 1929. The plan worked well by pinpointing revenue sources, lowering payments, providing loans, and securing the stability of the German currency. With the expiration of the Dawes Plan in 1929, the Young Plan, conceived by American businessman Owen D. Young, removed Allied controls over the German economy and specified that Germany pay reparations until 1988. The annual amount was less than Germany had been paying, so it was expected that this plan constituted a permanent, and reasonable, settlement.

Quite apart from the immediate economic issue, Stresemann understood that better relations with the victors, starting with France, had to be a priority if Germany was to return to the councils of the great powers. French foreign minister Aristide Briand° (1862–1932) shared Stresemann's desire for improved relations, and together they engineered a new, more conciliatory spirit in international affairs. Its most substantial fruit was the Treaty of Locarno of 1925. France and Germany accepted the postwar border between the two countries, which meant that Germany gave up any claim to Alsace-Lorraine. France, for its part, renounced the sort of direct military intervention in Germany that it had attempted with the Ruhr invasion of 1923 and agreed to begin withdrawing troops from the Rhineland ahead of schedule. On the other hand, Germany freely accepted France's key advantage, the demilitarization of the Rhineland, and Britain and Italy now explicitly guaranteed the measure.

By accepting the status quo in the west, Stresemann was freeing Germany to concentrate on eastern Europe,

**Briand** (bree-AHN)

where he envisioned gradual but substantial revision in the territorial settlement that had resulted from the war. Especially with the creation of Poland, that settlement had come partly at Germany's expense. Stresemann, then, was pursuing German interests, not subordinating them to some larger European vision. But he was willing to compromise and, for the most part, to play by the rules as he did so.

With the Locarno treaty, the victors accepted Germany as a diplomatic equal for the first time since the war. Germany's return to good graces culminated in its entry into the League of Nations in 1926. The new spirit of reconciliation was widely welcomed. Indeed, Stresemann and Briand were joint winners of the Nobel Peace Prize for 1926.

Still, those to the right in Germany continually exploited German resentments by criticizing Stresemann's compromises with Germany's former enemies—in accepting the Dawes and Young plans, for example. Even when successful from Stresemann's own perspective, these negotiations continually cost his party electoral support. The controversy that surrounded Stresemann, a German conservative pursuing conventional national interests, indicates how volatile the German political situation remained, even with the improved economic and diplomatic climate of the later 1920s. Still, Stresemann's diplomatic successes were considerable, and his death in October 1929, at the age of 51, was a severe blow to the republic.

## ■ An Uncertain Balance Sheet

Although Weimar Germany was considerably better off in 1929 than it had been in 1923, the political consensus remained weak, the political party system remained fragmented, and unstable coalition government remained the rule. Although the immediate threat from the extreme left had been overcome by 1923, many German conservatives continued to fear that the unstable Weimar democracy would eventually open the way to a socialist or communist regime.

The Weimar Republic epitomized the overall European situation during the 1920s. As long as prosperity and international cooperation continued, the new democracy in Germany might endure, even come to thrive. But the new institutions in Germany, like the wider framework of prosperity and stability, were fragile indeed. At the first opportunity, antidemocratic elites, taking advantage of their access to President Hindenburg, would begin plotting to replace the Weimar Republic with a more authoritarian alternative.

# THE SEARCH FOR MEANING IN A DISORDERED WORLD

OR all its vitality, the new culture of the 1920s had something brittle about it: the frenetic pace masked a deeper sense that things had started to come apart and might well get worse. The war had accelerated the long-term modernization process toward large industries, cities, and bureaucracies, and toward mass politics, society, and culture. That process was positive, even liberating, in certain respects, but it was also disruptive and disturbing. So the postwar sense of release and excitement combined with an anxious longing for stability, for a return to order. And thus the emphases of intellectuals and artists differed dramatically in the 1920s.

## ■ Anxiety, Alienation, and Disillusionment

Concern about the dangers of the emerging mass civilization was especially clear in the *Revolt of the Masses* (1930), by the influential Spanish thinker José Ortega y Gasset (1883–1955). In his view, contemporary experience had shown that ordinary people were incapable of creating standards and content with the least common denominator. Communism and fascism indicated the violent, intolerant, and ultimately barbaric quality of the new mass age. But Ortega found the same tendencies in American-style democracy. Much of Europe seemed to be moving toward the mass politics and culture of the United States, but, as far as Ortega was concerned, that was a symptom of the deeper problem, not a solution.

Concern with cultural decline was part of a wider pessimism about the condition of the West, which stood in stark contrast to the belief in progress, and the attendant confidence in Western superiority, that had been essential to Western self-understanding before 1914. The German thinker Oswald Spengler (1880–1936) made concern with decline almost fashionable with his bestseller of the immediate postwar years, *The Decline of the West* (1918), which offered a cyclical theory purporting to explain how spirituality and creativity were giving way to a materialistic mass-based culture in the West.

To Sigmund Freud, the eruption of violence and hatred during the war and afterward indicated a deep, instinctual problem in the human makeup. In his gloomy essay *Civilization and Its Discontents* (1930), Freud suggested that the progress of civilization requires individuals to bottle up their aggressive instincts, which are directed inward as guilt but may erupt in violent outbursts. This notion raised fundamental questions not only about the scope for continued progress but also about the plausibility of the Wilsonian ideals that had surrounded the end of the war. Perhaps, with civilization growing more complex, the Great War had been only the beginning of a new era of hatred and violence. (See the box "Reading Sources: Probing the Limits of Civilization and Progress.")

The sense that something incomprehensible, even nightmarish, haunted modern civilization, with its ever more complex bureaucracies, technologies, and cities, found vivid expression in the work of the Czech Jewish writer Franz Kafka (1883–1924), most notably in the novels *The Trial* and *The Castle*, published posthumously in the mid-1920s. In a world that claimed to be increasingly rational, Kafka's individual is the lonely, fragile plaything of forces utterly beyond reason, comprehension, and control. In such a world, the quest for law, or meaning, or God, is futile, ridiculous.

Especially in the unsettled conditions of Weimar Germany, the anxiety of the 1920s tended to take extreme forms, from irrational activism to a preoccupation with death. Suicides among students increased dramatically. Youthful alienation prompted the novelist Jakob Wassermann (1873–1934) to caution German young people in 1932 that not all action is good simply because it is action, that feeling is not always better than reason and discipline, and that youth is not in itself a badge of superiority.

## ■ Recasting the Tradition

Expressions of disillusionment revealed something about human experience in the unsettled new world, but they were sometimes morbid and self-indulgent. Other cultural leaders sought to be more positive; the challenge was not to give vent to new anxieties but to find antidotes to them. One direction was to recast traditional categories—in the arts, in religion, in politics—to make them relevant to contemporary experience. Although not all were optimistic about human prospects, many found such a renewal of tradition to be the best hope for responding to the disarray of the postwar world.

Among artists, even those who had been prominent in the modernist avant-garde before the war now pulled back from headlong experimentation and sought to pull things back together, though on a new basis. In music, composers as different as Igor Stravinsky (1882–1971) and Paul Hindemith (1895–1963) adapted earlier styles, although often in a somewhat ironic spirit, as they sought to weave new means of expression into familiar

## ❧ READING SOURCES

# Probing the Limits of Civilization and Progress

*Writing at the end of the 1920s, Sigmund Freud, the founder of psychoanalysis, sought to probe the sources, and the wider implications, of the violence and aggressiveness that had been unleashed by the war and that had continued into the 1920s. His account of the wellsprings of violence challenged the long-standing Western belief in continued progress based on human rationality.*

[Human beings] are not gentle creatures who want to be loved, and who at the most can defend themselves if they are attacked; they are, on the contrary, creatures among whose instinctual endowments is to be reckoned a powerful share of aggressiveness. As a result, their neighbor is for them not only a potential helper or sexual object, but also someone who tempts them to satisfy their aggressiveness on him, to exploit his capacity to work without compensation, to use him sexually without his consent, to seize his possessions, to humiliate him, to cause him pain, to torture and kill him. . . . Anyone who calls to mind the atrocities committed during the racial migrations or the invasion of the Huns, . . . or at the capture of Jerusalem by the pious Crusaders, or even, indeed, the horrors of the recent World War—anyone who recalls these things to mind will have to bow humbly before the truth of this view.

. . . In consequence of this primary mutual hostility of human beings, civilized society is perpetually threatened with disintegration. The interest of work in common would not hold it together; instinctual passions are stronger than reasonable interests. Civilization has to use its utmost efforts in order to set limits to man's aggressive instincts and to hold the manifestations of them in check. . . .

The communists believe that they have found the path to deliverance from our evils. According to them, man is wholly good and is well-disposed to his neighbor; but the institution of private property has corrupted his nature. . . . I have no concern with any economic criticisms of the communist system. . . . But I am able to recognize that the psychological premises on which the system is based are an untenable illusion. In abolishing private property we deprive the human love of aggression of one of its instruments, . . . but we have in no way altered the differences in power and influence which are misused by aggressiveness, nor have we altered anything in its nature. Aggressiveness was not created by property. It reigned almost without limit in primitive times, when property was still very scanty, and it already shows itself in the nursery. . . .

. . . [I]t is precisely communities with adjoining territories, and related to each other in other ways as well, who are engaged in constant feuds and in ridiculing each other—like the Spaniards and the Portuguese, for instance, the North Germans and South Germans, the English and Scotch, and so on. I gave this phenomenon the name of "the narcissism of minor differences." . . . We can now see that it is a convenient and relatively harmless satisfaction of the inclination to aggression, by means of which cohesion between the members of a community is made easier.

. . . We may expect gradually to carry through such alterations in our civilization as will better satisfy our needs and will escape our criticisms. But perhaps we may also familiarize ourselves with the idea that there are difficulties attaching to the nature of civilization which will not yield to any attempt at reform.

*Source:* Sigmund Freud, *Civilization and Its Discontents*, trans. James Strachey (New York: W. W. Norton, 1961), pp. 68–72, 74.

forms. The overall tendency toward neoclassicism during the period was an effort to give musical composition a renewed basis of order.

One of the most striking responses to the anxieties of this increasingly secular age was a wave of neo-orthodox religious thinking, most prominent in Protestants like the German-Swiss theologian Karl Barth (1886–1968). In his *Epistle to the Romans* (1919), Barth reacted against the liberal theology, the attempt to marry religious categories to secular progress, that had become prominent by the later nineteenth century. The war, especially, had seemed to shatter the liberal notion that the hand of God was at work in history, and Barth emphasized the radical cleft between God and this, the human world of history, sunken in sin. Recalling the arguments of Augustine and Luther, he portrayed humanity as utterly lost, capable only of a difficult relationship with God, through faith, grace, and revelation.

With democracy faring poorly in parts of Europe, and with fascism and communism claiming to offer superior alternatives, some sought to make new sense of the democratic tradition. In Italy, Benedetto Croce° (1866–1952) agreed with critics that the old justifications for liberal democracy, based on natural law or utilitarianism, were deeply inadequate, but he also became one of Europe's most influential antifascists. He insisted that the most significant innovations in modern thought show us why democratic values, institutions, and practices are still appropriate. We human beings are free, creative agents of a history that we make as best we can, without quite understanding what will result from what we do. Humility, tolerance, and equal access to political participation are essential to the process whereby the world is endlessly remade.

The new political challenges also stimulated fresh thinking within the Marxist tradition. By showing that Marxism could encompass consciousness as well as economic relationships, the Hungarian Georg Lukács (1885–1971) invited a far more sophisticated Marxist analysis of capitalist culture than had been possible before. Lukács accented the progressive role of realistic fiction and attacked the disordered fictional world of Kafka, which seemed to abandon all hope for human understanding of the forces of history. Though more eclectic, the Institute for Social Research, founded in Frankfurt, Germany, in 1923, gave rise to an influential tradition of criticism of capitalist civilization in what came to

be known as the Frankfurt School. These innovations helped give the Marxist tradition a new lease on life in the West, even as it was developing in unforeseen ways in the Soviet Union.

## ■ The Search for a New Tradition

While some intellectuals sought renewal from within the European tradition, others insisted that a more radical break was needed—but also that the elements for a viable new cultural tradition were available.

Reflecting on the situation of women writers in 1928, the British novelist Virginia Woolf (1882–1941) showed how women in the past had suffered from the absence of a tradition of writing by women. By the 1920s, women had made important strides, but Woolf suggested that further advance required a more self-conscious effort by women to develop their own tradition. Most basically, women needed greater financial independence so that they could have the time for scholarship, the leisure of cultivated conversation, and the privacy of "a room of one's own." Woolf also envisioned a new sort of historical inquiry, focusing on how ordinary women lived their lives, that could show contemporary women where they came from—and thus deepen their sense of identity. (See the box "Reading Sources: Tradition and Women: The Conditions of Independence.")

A very different effort to establish a new tradition developed in Paris, where the poet André Breton (1896–1966) spearheaded the surrealist movement in literature and the visual arts. Surrealism grew directly from Dada, an artistic movement that had emerged in neutral Zurich, Switzerland, and elsewhere during the war. Radically hostile to the war, Dada artists developed shocking, sometimes nihilistic forms to deal with a reality that now seemed senseless and out of control. Some made collages from gutter trash; others indulged in nonsense or relied on chance to guide their art. By the early 1920s, however, the surrealists felt it was time to create a new and deeper basis of order after the willful disordering of Dada. Having learned from Freud about the subconscious, they sought to adapt Dada's novel techniques—especially the use of chance—to gain access to the subconscious mind, which they believed contains a deeper truth, without the overlay of logic, reason, and conscious control.

But other artists, seeking to embrace the modern industrial world in a more positive spirit, found surrealism merely escapist. Among them was Walter Gropius

---

**Croce** (CROH-chay)

**❧ READING SOURCES**

# Tradition and Women:
## The Conditions of Independence

*Speaking in 1928 about the situation of women writers, British novelist Virginia Woolf raised questions that were relevant to all women seeking the opportunity to realize their potential. Indeed, her reflections about the value of difference, and the need for particular traditions, inspired those seeking equal opportunity for decades to come. And her question about why we know so little about women's lives in the past helped stimulate later historians to investigate the experiences of ordinary people.*

Woman . . . pervades poetry from cover to cover; she is all but absent from history. . . .

Occasionally an individual woman is mentioned, an Elizabeth, or a Mary; a queen or a great lady. But by no possible means could middle-class women with nothing but brains and character at their command have taken part in any one of the great movements which, brought together, constitute the historian's view of the past. . . . What one wants . . . is a mass of information; at what age did she marry; how many children had she as a rule; what was her house like; had she a room to herself; did she do the cooking; would she be likely to have a servant? All these facts lie somewhere, presumably, in parish registers and account books; the life of the average Elizabethan woman must be scattered about somewhere, could one collect it and make a book of it. It would be ambitious beyond my daring, I thought, looking about the shelves for books that were not there, to suggest to the students of those famous colleges that they should re-write history, though I own that it often seems a little queer as it is, unreal, lopsided. . . .

But whatever effect discouragement and criticism had upon their writing—and I believe they had a very great effect—that was unimportant compared with the other difficulty which faced them (I was still considering those early nineteenth-century novelists) when they came to set their thoughts on paper—that is that they had no tradition behind them,

or one so short and partial that it was of little help. For we think back through our mothers if we are women. It is useless to go to the great men writers for help, however much one may go to them for pleasure. . . .

. . . [W]omen have sat indoors all these millions of years, so that by this time the very walls are permeated by their creative force, which has, indeed, so overcharged the capacity of bricks and mortar that it must needs harness itself to pens and brushes and business and politics. But this creative power differs greatly from the creative power of men. And one must conclude that it would be a thousand pities if it were hindered or wasted, for it was won by centuries of the most drastic discipline, and there is nothing to take its place. It would be a thousand pities if women wrote like men, or lived like men, or looked like men. . . . Ought not education to bring out and fortify the differences rather than the similarities?

*Source:* Virginia Woolf, *A Room of One's Own* (San Diego: Harcourt Brace Jovanovich, Harvest/HBJ, 1989), pp. 43–45, 76, 87–88.

 **For additional information on this topic, go to http://college.hmco.com.**

**The Bauhaus Building, Dessau** The Bauhaus, an influential but controversial German art school, was established in Weimar in 1919 and then moved to Dessau in 1925. Walter Gropius, its founding director, spearheaded the design of its new headquarters building, constructed in 1925–1926. The building immediately became a symbol of the Weimar modernism that some admired and others detested. *(Vanni/Art Resource, NY)*

(1883–1969), a pioneering modernist architect and leader of an influential German art school, the Bauhaus, during the 1920s. Gropius held that it was possible to establish new forms of culture, even a new tradition, that could be affirmative and reassuring in the face of the postwar cultural disarray. Rather than putting up familiar neoclassical or neo-Gothic buildings, "feigning a culture that has long since disappeared," we must face up to the kind of civilization we have become—industrial, technological, efficient, urban, democratic, mass-based. If we pick and choose carefully from among the elements of our new machine-based civilization, we can again have a culture that works, an "integrated pattern for living."[3]

This "constructive," promodern impulse was particularly prominent in Germany, but it could be found all over—in the modernists of the Russian Revolution, in the French painter Fernand Léger° (1881–1955), in the Swiss architect Le Corbusier° (1887–1965). Whereas many of their contemporaries were at best ambivalent about the masses, these artists sought to bring high art and mass society together in the interests of both. And they welcomed the new patterns of life that seemed to be emerging in the modern world of mass production and fast-paced cities.

**Léger** (leh-ZHAY)  **Le Corbusier** (luh cor-BOO-zee-ay)

# SUMMARY

HE 1920s proved a contradictory period of vitality and despair, pacifism and violence, restabilization and instability. The era began with bright hopes for democracy, yet the outcome of the democratic experiment in central and eastern Europe was disappointing. In Germany, the improved economic and diplomatic situation by 1924 enhanced the prospects for democracy, but the new Weimar Republic remained fragile, unstable, and on the defensive. Even Italy, heir to a respectable tradition of democracy, gave rise to the troubling new phenomenon of fascism. A hopeful new spirit of international conciliation drew France and Germany closer together by the end of 1925, but France and Britain seemed to drift apart as the British, preoccupied with colonial concerns, distanced themselves from politics on the Continent.

Still, Europe seemed on its way to restabilization by early 1929. Of the three most volatile and potentially disruptive of the major countries, Italy and Germany seemed to be settling down, and the Soviet Union, though embarking on an unprecedented experiment in socioeconomic engineering, was by now looking inward rather than seeking to export revolution. When the decade is taken on its own terms, it is clear that the vitality, the renewed prosperity, and the diplomatic goodwill were all real. But so also were the unresolved problems that made the 1920s a prelude to the more difficult 1930s, when the notion that Europe had returned to normal came to seem but a fairy tale.

## ■ Notes

1. Benito Mussolini, speech to the Italian Chamber of Deputies, January 3, 1925, from Charles F. Delzell, ed., *Mediterranean Fascism, 1919–1945* (New York: Harper & Row, 1970), pp. 59–60.

2. Quoted in Robert G. L. Waite, *Vanguard of Nazism: The Free Corps Movement in Postwar Germany, 1918–1923* (New York: W. W. Norton, 1969), pp. 14–15.

3. Walter Gropius, *Scope of Total Architecture* (New York: Collier Books, 1962), pp. 15, 67.

## ■ Suggested Reading

Gay, Peter. *Weimar Culture: The Outsider as Insider.* 1970. An influential study providing a good sense of the conflicting impulses—the embrace of modernity, the nostalgia for wholeness, the sense of foreboding—that made German culture so intense and vital during the 1920s.

Gentile, Emilio. *The Sacralization of Politics in Fascist Italy.* 1996. Engaging account of the rituals, symbols, and myths that, beginning in Italy during the 1920s, fed the first overtly totalitarian experiment.

Kitchen, Martin. *Europe Between the Wars: A Political History.* 1988. A clear narrative of international and domestic political developments from a leftist perspective.

Kolb, Eberhard. *The Weimar Republic.* 1988. Provides a good overall survey, then pinpoints the recent trends in research and the questions at issue among historians of the period.

Morgan, Philip. *Italian Fascism, 1919–1945.* 1995. A good introductory survey.

Pedersen, Susan. *Family, Dependence, and the Origins of the Welfare State: Britain and France, 1914–1945.* 1993. An effective comparative study showing how concerns about gender roles and family relations helped shape discussion and policy as government assumed greater responsibility for social welfare. Detailed but readable, a landmark in the new gender history.

Peukert, Detlev. *The Weimar Republic: The Crisis of Classical Modernity.* 1992. Accessible interpretive study, accenting the strains stemming from the rapid modernization of the 1920s. Stresses the loss of political legitimacy even before the onset of Depression.

Stites, Richard. *Revolutionary Dreams: Utopian Visions and Experimental Life in the Russian Revolution.* 1989. A vivid account of the utopian aspirations that gave the new communist regime emotional force from 1917 to 1930.

Tucker, Robert C. *Stalin as Revolutionary, 1879–1929: A Study in History and Personality.* 1973. A pioneering account of Stalin's early years and rise to power, probing the sources of the elements of character and personality that helped shape his subsequent rule.

**For a searchable list of additional readings for this chapter, go to http://college.hmco.com.**

# Advertising

A sleek new automobile. A stylish "new woman" who'd adore a Christmas gift of jewelry. These images from the 1920s catch our eye even today, but why? The designs look "modern" somehow, and they convey particular messages about efficiency and the good life. What do such advertisements tell us about the changes at work in Western cultures after World War I?

Advertising in one form or another is as old as civilization itself. But the advent of printing expanded possibilities, and the second industrial revolution led to a big boost in advertising by the 1890s, as ads for new products like bicycles and sewing machines appeared in newspapers and magazines. But it was during the 1920s that modern advertising came into its own. As mass consumption grew, advertising budgets expanded dramatically, and professional ad agencies emerged to study tastes and determine how to shape the desires of consumers. Moreover, the advent of commercial radio in 1920 opened a whole new set of possibilities, including the scope for musical jingles.

Mass consumption required advertising to show people what to want. And during the 1920s, ad agencies began offering images of the good life, seeking to define the popular sense of what it meant to be "modern." They often drew from the United States, which stood for efficiency and a fast-paced life of fun, pleasure, and consumerist abundance. So eager were the Germans to follow the U.S. lead in advertising that they adopted the term *sex appeal*, leaving it untranslated.

The new products featured in the print and broadcast media ran the gamut from the automobile to cosmetics, from rayon apparel to chewing gum. When the Wrigley Company of Chicago opened a factory in Germany in 1925, chewing gum quickly became associated with Americanization—and its use increased dramatically. But luxury goods were prominent as well, as in elegant ads such as the two shown here. Even for the many who could not afford expensive jewelry or the six-cylinder Opel, images of the good life stimulated the desire to buy less costly versions. Automobile consumption rose sharply during the 1920s, thanks also to the new techniques of mass production that Henry Ford had pioneered in the United States.

Although advertising served the economic interests of business by stimulating consumption, many began to view it as an art form as well. Far more attention was paid to its design, so the advertising "look" of the 1920s differed dramatically from anything seen before. As in the examples here, the new ads were often self-consciously modern, using simplified typefaces and stylized images suggesting the sleek efficiency and precision of the new machine age. The jewelry ad features an elegant contemporary typeface, and the German automobile ad of 1928 relies on crisp, bold forms and a clean, modern design.

The new prominence of advertising raised issues that were debated all over, but especially in Weimar Germany, where conditions remained unsettled even as a measure of prosperity returned by 1924. From cultural standards to gender roles, much was being called into question, and the wider implications of advertising were central to the "culture wars" of the period.

At an international advertising congress in Berlin in 1929, critics charged that advertising was furthering the debasement of standards already associated with mass culture and Americanization. Defenders countered that advertising was rejuvenating the mainstream culture, which had grown either stale and conventional or overblown and elitist. The fact that advertising served a commercial purpose need not have to mean cultural debasement. On the contrary, they argued, this new meshing of the best design with popular culture was healthy. In 1928 G. F. Hartlaub, a leading German art dealer, summed up a widespread view when he observed that advertising was a "truly social, collective, mass art: the only one we now have. It shapes the visual habits of that anonymous collectivity: the public. Little by little an artistic attitude is hammered into the mass soul by billboards."[*]

A particular advertising target was the "new woman," with her liberated lifestyle, bobbed hair, and short skirts. But the image of women in advertisements was controversial, especially in Weimar Germany. Partly because of the simplification of female attire, images of

---

[*]Quoted in John Willett, *Art and Politics in the Weimar Period: The New Sobriety, 1917–1933* (New York: Pantheon, 1978), p. 137. Translation modified slightly.

the new woman in popular magazines provoked much concern about the "masculinization" of women by the mid-1920s. Some men found such images aggressive, even threatening.

Yet at the same time advertising often assumed women to be master consumers—or perhaps merely mindless shoppers. In the holiday advertisement here, the woman is chic and liberated in one sense, but she is urged to drape herself with jewelry—to indulge in conventional ornament. This was also an age that claimed to value efficiency purified of ornament, as with the stripped-down typeface in the automobile ad. So though

gender differentiation and women's roles were very much at issue in advertising, the relationship between portrayals of the new woman and genuine liberation remained uncertain.

Despite tensions and contradictions, advertising helped bring new issues to center stage after World War I. Although the ads of the 1920s assumed a prosperity that proved fleeting, the cultural change proved enduring. Eye-catching images of the sleek, the chic, the new—all bathed in "sex appeal"—became the staples of twentieth-century advertising, bound up with the new culture of mass consumption.

**Advertising the Six-Cylinder Opel, 1928** *(From Bärbel Schrader and Jürgen Schebera, The "Golden" Twenties: Art and Literature in the Weimar Republic [New Haven: Yale University Press, 1990]. Reproduced with permission.)*

**Jewelry for the New Woman**
*(AKG London)*

# CHAPTER 27

# The Tortured Decade 1930–1939

"THEY shall not pass," proclaimed the charismatic Spanish communist Dolores Ibarruri° (1895–1989), whose impassioned speeches and radio broadcasts helped inspire the heroic defense of Madrid during the civil war that gripped Spain, and captured the attention of the world, during the later 1930s. Known as *La Pasionaria*—the passion flower—Ibarruri became a living legend for her role in defending the Spanish republic against the antidemocratic nationalists seeking to overthrow it. But the Republican side lost, and she spent thirty-eight years in exile before returning to Spain in 1977, after the end of the military dictatorship that had resulted from the Spanish civil war.

In her effort to rally the Republican side, Ibarruri stressed the political power of women, and indeed women were prominent in the citizen militias defending Madrid and other Spanish cities. Women fought for the republic partly because it seemed to open new opportunities for them, especially as it became more radical by 1936. But just as some women welcomed the new direction, others became politically active on the opposing Nationalist side—to support the church, to combat divorce, to defend a separate sphere for women as the guardians of private life and family values.

The ideological polarization that characterized the Spanish civil war reflected the expanding reach of politics in the 1930s, when economic depression and the challenge from new, antidemocratic governments immeasurably complicated the European situation. The mechanisms used to realign the international economy after World War I had seemed effective for most of the 1920s, but by 1929, they

**Ibarruri** (ee-bah-RUHR-ee)

**¡No pasarán!** ("They shall not pass"): Defending the democratic republic during the Spanish civil war. (Biblioteca Nacional, Madrid)

## The Great Depression

## The Stalinist Revolution in the Soviet Union

## Hitler and Nazism in Germany

## Fascist Challenge and Antifascist Response, 1934–1939

## The Coming of World War II, 1935–1939

were beginning to backfire, helping to trigger the Great Depression. During the early 1930s the economic crisis intensified sociopolitical strains all over the Western world—and even beyond, heightening anti-Western feeling. In Germany the Depression helped undermine the Weimar Republic and opened the way for the new Nazi regime under Adolf Hitler, whose policies led through a series of diplomatic crises to a new European war.

German Nazism paralleled Italian fascism in its reliance on a single charismatic leader, its willingness to use violence, and its hostility to both parliamentary democracy and Marxist socialism. But Nazism emphasized racism and anti-Semitism in a way that Italian fascism did not, and it more radically transformed its society.

At the same time, Stalin's communist regime in the Soviet Union seemed to converge, in some ways, with these new fascist regimes—especially with German Nazism. So though they expressed widely different aims, Stalinism and Nazism are sometimes lumped together as instances of "totalitarianism." Both apparently sought control over all aspects of society, partly through the use of secret police agencies. But on closer inspection, the forms of coercion and violence in the Soviet and the German regimes by the later 1930s were quite different, and the extent to which each can be understood as an instance of totalitarianism remains controversial.

Fascism, Nazism, and communism seemed able to sidestep—or surmount—the ills of the Depression, yet they stood opposed to the parliamentary democracy that had long seemed the direction of progressive political change. So the democratic movement appeared to lose its momentum in the face of the political and economic challenges of the 1930s. The defeat, by early 1939, of the democratic republic in Spain by the authoritarian Nationalists seemed to exemplify the political direction of the decade.

**QUESTIONS TO CONSIDER**

■ **How did the new international economic interdependence after World War I help produce the Great Depression?**

■ **Why did the Stalinist attempt to build "socialism in one country" lead to the "terror-famine" of 1932–1933 and the "great terror" of 1937–1938?**

■ **Through what measures did the Nazi regime claim to be improving the quality of the German population?**

■ **Why did the other major countries not stop Hitler's Germany before it was strong enough to start a new European war in 1939?**

**TERMS TO KNOW**

collectivization
gulag
show trials
Adolf Hitler
National Socialist
    (Nazi) Party
*Schutzstaffel* (SS)

"euthanasia" program
popular front
Rome-Berlin Axis
remilitarization of the
    Rhineland
appeasement
Nazi-Soviet Pact

## THE GREAT DEPRESSION

 A LTHOUGH the stock market crash of October 1929 in the United States helped usher in the world economic crisis of the early 1930s, it had this effect only because the new international economic order after World War I was extremely fragile. By October 1929, in fact, production was already declining in all the major Western countries except France.

The economies of Germany and the states of east-central Europe remained particularly vulnerable after World War I, and in the increasingly interdependent economic world, their weaknesses magnified problems that started elsewhere. The crash of the U.S. stock market led to a restriction of credit in central Europe, which triggered a more general contraction in production and trade. Facing cruel dilemmas, policymakers proved unable to master the situation for the first few years of the crisis. The consequences—both human and political—were profound.

## ■ Sources of the Economic Contraction

Certain economic sectors, especially coal mining and agriculture, were already suffering severe problems by the mid-1920s, well before the stock market crash of 1929. British coal exports fell partly because oil and hydroelectricity were rapidly developing as alternatives. Unemployment in Britain was never less than 10 percent even in the best of times between the wars. In agriculture high prices worldwide during the war produced oversupply, which, in turn, led to a sharp drop in prices once the war was over. During the later 1920s, bumper harvests of grain and rice in many parts of the world renewed the downward pressure on prices. The result of low agricultural prices was a diminished demand for industrial goods, which impeded growth in the world economy.

Throughout the 1920s, finance ministers and central bankers had difficulty juggling the economic imbalances created by the war, centering on war debts to the United States and German reparations obligations to France, Britain, and Belgium. The strains in the system finally caught up with policymakers by 1929, when an international restriction of credit forced an end to the international economic cooperation that had been attempted throughout the decade.

The shaky postwar economic system depended on U.S. bank loans to Germany, funneled partly by international agreements but also drawn by high interest rates. By 1928, however, U.S. investors were rapidly withdrawing their capital from Germany in search of the higher returns that could be made in the booming U.S. stock market. This shift tightened credit in Germany. And then the crash of the overpriced U.S. market in October 1929 deepened the problem by forcing suddenly strapped American investors to pull still more of their funds out of Germany. This process continued over the next two years, weakening the major banks in Germany and the other countries of central Europe, which were closely tied to the German economy. In May 1931 the bankruptcy of Vienna's most powerful bank, the Credit-Anstalt, made it clear that a crisis of potentially catastrophic proportions was in progress.

Despite attempts at adjustment on the international level, fears of bank failure or currency devaluation led to runs on the banks and currencies of Germany and east-central Europe. To maintain the value of the domestic currency in world markets, and thereby to resist the withdrawal of capital, government policymakers raised

## CHRONOLOGY

| | |
|---|---|
| October 1929 | U.S. stock market crash helps trigger Great Depression |
| December 1929 | Forced collectivization in Soviet agriculture begins |
| June 1930 | Smoot-Hawley Tariff Act (U.S.) |
| May 1931 | Bankruptcy of Vienna's Credit-Anstalt |
| January 1933 | Hitler becomes German chancellor |
| December 1934 | Assassination of Kirov |
| March 1935 | Hitler announces rearmament |
| October 1935 | Italy invades Ethiopia |
| March 1936 | Germany remilitarizes the Rhineland |
| May 1936 | Blum becomes French popular front prime minister |
| July 1936 | Spanish civil war begins |
| March 1938 | Third Moscow show trial; Bukharin and others convicted and executed |
| March 1938 | Anschluss: Germany absorbs Austria |
| September 1938 | "Appeasement": Munich conference ends Sudetenland crisis |
| November 1938 | Crystal Night pogrom |
| March 1939 | Dismemberment of Czechoslovakia |
| May 1939 | Pact of Steel binds fascist Italy and Nazi Germany |
| August 23, 1939 | Nazi-Soviet nonaggression pact |
| September 1, 1939 | German invasion of Poland |
| September 3, 1939 | Britain and France declare war on Germany |

**Unemployment in Britain**
The Depression hit Britain hard—and its effects continued to be felt throughout the 1930s. These unemployed shipyard workers from Jarrow, in northeastern England, are marching to London in 1936 to present a protest petition. *(Hulton Getty/ Liaison)*

interest rates. This measure was not sufficient to stem the capital hemorrhage, but by restricting credit still more, it further dampened domestic economic activity.

Finally, the Germans seemed to have no choice but to freeze foreign assets—that is, to cease allowing conversion of assets held in German marks to other currencies. In this atmosphere, investors seeking the safest place for their capital tried to cash in currency for gold— or for British pounds, which could then be converted to gold. Europe's flight to gold, however, soon put such pressure on the British currency that Britain was forced to devalue the pound and sever it from the gold standard in September 1931. This proved the definitive end of the worldwide system of economic exchange based on the gold standard that had gradually crystallized during the nineteenth century.

The absence of a single standard of exchange, combined with various currency restrictions, made foreign trade more difficult and uncertain, thereby diminishing it further. So did the scramble for tariff protection that proved a widespread response to the developing crisis. Crucial was the U.S. Smoot-Hawley Tariff Act of June 1930, which raised taxes on imports by 50 to 100 percent, forcing other nations to take comparable steps. Even Britain, long a bastion of free trade, adopted a peacetime tariff for the first time in nearly a century with the Import Duties Act of 1932, which imposed a 10 percent tax on most imports.

The decline of trade spread depression throughout the world economic system. By 1933 most major Euro-

pean countries were able to export no more than two-thirds, and in some cases as little as one-third, of the amount they had sold in 1929. At the same time, losses from international bank failures contracted credit and purchasing power and furthered the downward spiral, until by 1932 the European economies had shrunk to a little over half their 1929 size. This was the astonishing outcome of the short-lived prosperity of the 1920s.

### ■ Consequences and Responses

The Depression was essentially a radical contraction in economic activity; with less being produced and sold, demand for labor declined sharply. In Germany industrial production by early 1933 was only half what it had been in 1929, and roughly 6 million Germans, or one-third of the labor force, were unemployed.

Although its timing and severity varied, the Depression profoundly affected the lives of ordinary people throughout the Western world and beyond. (See the box "Reading Sources: Working-Class Life During the Great Depression.") Unemployment produced widespread malnutrition, which led, in turn, to sharp increases in such diseases as tuberculosis, scarlet fever, and rickets. The decline in employment opportunities helped produce a backlash against the ideal of "the new woman," working outside the home, which had been a prominent aspect of the new freedom of the 1920s in Germany and elsewhere. Even those men and women who hung on to jobs

## 🐚 R E A D I N G   S O U R C E S

---

### Working-Class Life During the Great Depression

*During the Depression, the Left Book Club, an important movement of left-leaning British intellectuals, commissioned George Orwell (1903–1950) to write a report on the conditions of unemployed miners in the north of England. Published in 1937, Orwell's study of responses to the Depression offered pioneering insights into the dynamics of relative poverty in the modern world. The P.A.C. to which he refers is the British Public Assistance or welfare system.*

---

. . . It is noticeable everywhere that the anomalous position created by unemployment—the man being out of work while the woman's work continues as before—has not altered the relative status of the sexes. . . . Practically never . . . will you see the man doing a stroke of the housework. Unemployment has not changed this convention, which on the face of it seems a little unfair. The man is idle from morning to night but the woman is as busy as ever—more so, indeed, because she has to manage with less money. Yet so far as my experience goes the women do not protest. I believe that they, as well as the men, feel that a man would lose his manhood if, merely because he was out of work, he developed into a "Mary Ann."

But there is no doubt about the deadening, debilitating effect of unemployment on everybody, married or single, and upon men more than women. . . .

I remember the shock of astonishment it gave me, when I first mingled with tramps and beggars, to find that a fair proportion, perhaps a quarter, of these beings whom I had been taught to regard as cynical parasites, were decent young miners and cotton-workers gazing at their destiny with the same sort of dumb amazement as an animal in a trap. They simply could not understand what was happening to them. They had been brought up to work, and behold! it seemed as though they were never going to have the chance of working again. In their circumstances it was inevitable, at first, that they should be haunted by a feeling or personal degradation. That was the attitude toward unemployment in those days: it was a disaster which happened to *you* as an individual and for which *you* were to blame. . . .

. . . When people live on the dole for years at a time they grow used to it, and drawing the dole, though it remains unpleasant, ceases to be shameful. . . . In the back streets of Wigan and Barnley I saw every kind of privation, but I probably saw less *conscious* misery than I should have seen ten years ago. The people have at any rate grasped that unemployment is a thing they cannot help. It is not only Alf Smith who is out of work now; Bert Jones is out of work as well, and both of them have been "out" for years. It makes a great deal of difference when things are the same for everybody.

So you have whole populations settling down, as it were, to a lifetime on the P.A.C. And what I think is admirable, perhaps even hopeful, is that they have managed to do it without going spiritually to pieces. . . . [T]hey realize that losing your job does not mean that you cease to be a human being. So that in one way things in the distressed areas are not so bad as they might be. Life is still fairly normal, more normal than one really has the right to expect. Families are impoverished, but the family-system has not broken up. The people are in effect living a reduced version of their former lives. . . .

But they don't necessarily lower their standards by cutting out luxuries and concentrating on necessities; more often it is the other way about—the more natural way, if you come to think of it. Hence the fact that in a decade of unparalleled depression, the consumption of all cheap luxuries has increased. The two things that have probably made the greatest difference of all are the movies and the mass-production of cheap smart clothes since the war. . . . You may have three halfpence in your pocket and not a prospect in the world, and only the corner of a leaky bedroom to go home to; but in your new clothes you can stand on the street corner, indulging in a private daydream of yourself as Clark Gable or Greta Garbo, which compensates for a great deal.

---

*Source:* George Orwell, *The Road to Wigan Pier* (New York: Berkley Medallion, 1961), pp. 77–78, 81–83.

suffered from growing insecurity. In his aptly titled *Little Man, What Now?* (1932), the German novelist Hans Fallada (1893–1947) explored the effects of the Depression on members of the lower middle class—store clerks, shop owners, civil servants. Such people were first resentful, then resigned, as their dreams of security, of "order and cleanliness," fell apart.

During the first years of the Depression, central bankers everywhere sought to balance budgets in order to reassure investors and stabilize currencies. With economies contracting and tax revenues declining, the only way to balance the budget was to sharply reduce government spending. In addition, governments responded to the decline in exports by forcing wages down, seeking to enhance competitiveness abroad. But by cutting purchasing power at home, both these measures reinforced the slowdown in economic activity.

Economic policymakers based their responses on the "classical" economic model that had developed from the ideas of Adam Smith in the eighteenth century (see page 717). According to this model, a benign "invisible hand" ensured that a free-market price for labor, for capital, and for goods and services would produce an ongoing tendency toward economic equilibrium. A downward turn in the business cycle was a normal and necessary adjustment; government interference would only upset this self-adjusting mechanism.

By 1932, however, it was clear that the conventional response was not working, and governments began seeking more actively to stimulate the economy. Strategies varied widely. In the United States, Franklin D. Roosevelt (1882–1945) defeated the incumbent president, Herbert Hoover, in 1932 with the promise of a New Deal—a commitment to increase government spending to restore purchasing power. In fascist Italy, a state agency created to infuse capital into failing companies proved a reasonably effective basis for collaboration between government and business. In Germany, economics minister Hjalmar Schacht (1877–1970) mounted an energetic assault on the economic problem after Hitler came to power in 1933. Government measures sealed off the German mark from international fluctuations, stimulated public spending, partly on rearmament, and kept wages low. By 1935 Germany was back to full employment. This success added tremendously to Hitler's popularity.

High unemployment in Norway, Sweden, and Denmark helped social democrats win power in all three of these Scandinavian countries by the mid-1930s. The new left-leaning governments responded to the economic crisis not by a frontal assault on capitalism but by pioneering the "welfare state," providing such benefits as health care, unemployment insurance, and family al-

lowances. To pay for the new welfare safety net, the Scandinavian countries adopted a high level of progressive taxation and pared military expenditures to a minimum. The turn to a welfare state in Scandinavia eased the immediate human costs of the Depression and helped restore production by stimulating demand. At the same time, the Scandinavian model attracted much admiration as a "third way" between free-market capitalism and the various dictatorial extremes.

In the other European democracies the Depression proved more intractable. Although Britain saw some recovery by the mid-1930s, it was especially the rearmament of the later 1930s, financed by borrowing, or deficit spending, that got the British economy growing again. France, less dependent on international trade, experienced the consequences of the world crisis only gradually. But by the early 1930s, France, too, was suffering its effects, which lingered to the end of the decade, helping to poison the political atmosphere.

The Depression also had a major impact on the non-Western world and its relations with the West. The radical restriction of international trade meant a sharp decline in demand for the basic commodities that colonial and other regions exported to the industrialized West. Economic strains fed nationalist, anti-Western sentiments in colonial nations. The increase in misery among rural villagers in India, for example, spread the movement for national independence from urban elites to the rural masses. In this context Mohandas Gandhi°, who had become known by 1920 for advocating noncooperation with the British, became the first leader to win a mass following throughout the Indian subcontinent. Encouraging villagers to boycott British goods, Gandhi accented simplicity, self-reliance, and an overall strategy of nonviolent civil disobedience based on Indian traditions. (See the box "Global Encounters: Gandhi Advocates Nonviolence.")

In Japan, the strains of the Great Depression helped produce precisely the turn to imperialist violence that Gandhi sought to counter. Densely populated yet lacking raw materials, Japan was particularly dependent on international trade and thus reacted strongly as increasing tariffs elsewhere cut sharply into Japanese exports. Led by young army officers who were already eager for their country to embrace a less subservient form of Westernization, Japan turned to aggressive imperialism, seeking to justify its course by claiming to spearhead a wider struggle to free East Asia from Western imperialism. Attacking in 1931, Japanese forces quickly reduced Manchuria to a puppet state, but the Japanese met stubborn resistance

**Gandhi** (GAHN-dee)

# Gandhi Advocates Nonviolence

*Mohandas Gandhi, a successful English-educated lawyer, emerged as a major force in the movement for Indian independence just after World War I. Calling first for a strategy of noncooperation with the British colonial overlords, Gandhi gradually developed a philosophy of nonviolent civil disobedience, which won widespread sympathy for the cause of Indian independence. The following excerpts from articles published in 1935 and 1939—years notable for outbreaks of violence elsewhere— explain the significance of nonviolence to Gandhi's overall strategy.*

Non-violence to be a creed has to be all-pervasive. I cannot be non-violent about one activity of mine and violent about others. That would be a policy, not a life-force. That being so, I cannot be indifferent about the war that Italy is now waging against Abyssinia. . . . India had an unbroken tradition of non-violence from times immemorial. But at no time in her ancient history, as far as I know it, has it had complete non-violence in action pervading the whole land. Nevertheless, it is my unshakeable belief that her destiny is to deliver the message of non-violence to mankind. . . .

. . . India as a nation is not non-violent in the full sense of the term. . . . Her non-violence is that of the weak. . . . She lacks the ability to offer physical resistance. She has no consciousness of strength. She is conscious only of her weakness. If she were otherwise, there would be no communal problems, nor political. If she were non-violent in the consciousness of her strength, Englishmen would lose their role of distrustful conquerors. We may talk politically as we like and often legitimately blame the English rulers. But if we, as Indians, could but for a moment visualize ourselves as a strong people disdaining to strike, we should cease to fear Englishmen whether as soldiers, traders or administrators, and they to distrust us. Therefore if we became truly non-violent we should carry Englishmen with us in all we might do. In other words, we being millions would be the greatest moral force in the world, and Italy would listen to our friendly word. . . .

. . . [W]hen society is deliberately constructed in accordance with the law of non-violence, its structure will be different in material particulars from what it is today. But I cannot say in advance what the government based wholly on non-violence will be like.

What is happening today is disregard of the law of non-violence and enthronement of violence as if it were an eternal law. The democracies, therefore, that we see at work in England, America and France are only so called, because they are no less based on violence than Nazi Germany, Fascist Italy or even Soviet Russia. The only difference is that the violence of the last three is much better organized than that of the three democratic powers. Nevertheless we see today a mad race for outdoing one another in the matter of armaments. And if and when the clash comes, as it is bound to come one day, the democracies win, they will do so only because they will have the backing of their peoples who imagine that they have a voice in their own government whereas in the other three cases the peoples might rebel against their own dictatorships.

Holding the view that without the recognition of non-violence on a national scale there is no such thing as a constitutional or democratic government, I devote my energy to the propagation of non-violence as the law of our life—individual, social, political, national and international. I fancy that I have seen the light, though dimly. I write cautiously, for I do not profess to know the whole of the Law. If I know the successes of my experiments, I know also my failures. But the successes are enough to fill me with undying hope. I have often said that if one takes care of the means, the end will take care of itself. Non-violence is the means, the end for every nation is complete independence.

*Source:* Raghavan Iyer, ed., *The Essential Writings of Mahatma Gandhi* (Delhi: Oxford University Press, 1991), pp. 245–247, 262–263.

**Collectivization in Soviet Agriculture**   At the "New Life" collective farm, not far from Moscow, women stand for the morning roll call. The Soviet collectivization effort of the 1930s rested in important measure on the forced mobilization of peasant women. *(Endeavor Group UK)*

when they began seeking to extend this conquest to the rest of China in 1937.

Japanese pressure indirectly advanced the rise of the Chinese communist movement, led by Mao Zedong (Mao Tse-tung; 1893–1976). Securing a base in the Yanan district in 1936, Mao began seeking to apply Marxism-Leninism to China through land reform and other measures to link the communist elite to the Chinese peasantry. Mao was notable among those adapting Western ideas to build an indigenous movement that would at once overcome Western imperialism and create an alternative to Western liberal capitalism.

The Depression, and the halting responses of the democracies in dealing with it, enhanced the prestige of the new regimes in the Soviet Union, Italy, and Germany. These three despotic powers appeared either to have avoided the economic crisis or to be dealing with it more creatively. But each of these new regimes was an experiment, and the innovations of each added to the uncertainties of the decade.

# THE STALINIST REVOLUTION IN THE SOVIET UNION

HOUGH it won the admiration of some, the Soviet Union, in particular, experienced a decade of unprecedented upheaval during the 1930s. Seeking to build "socialism in one country," Joseph Stalin led the Soviet Union during the 1930s

through an astounding transformation that mixed achievement with brutality and terror in often tragic ways. The resulting governmental system, which gave Stalin unprecedented power, proved crucial to the outcome of the great experiment that had begun with the Russian Revolution of 1917. But whether the fateful turn of the 1930s had been implicit in the Leninist revolutionary model all along, or stemmed mostly from unforeseen circumstances and Stalin's idiosyncratic personality, remains uncertain.

## ■ Crash Industrialization and Forced Collectivization

Stalin's program of rapid industrialization based on forced collectivization in agriculture began in earnest at the beginning of 1930. It entailed an assault on the better-off peasants, or *kulaks,* who were often sent to labor camps in Siberia while their lands were taken over by the government. The remaining peasants were herded into new government-controlled collective farms. So unpopular was this measure that many peasants simply killed their livestock or smashed their farm implements rather than have them collectivized. During the first two months of 1930, as many as 14 million head of cattle were slaughtered, resulting in an orgy of meat eating and a shortage of draft animals. By 1934 the number of cattle in the Soviet Union was barely half what it had been in 1928.

Collectivization served, as intended, to squeeze from the peasantry the resources needed to finance industrialization, but it was carried out with extreme brutality.

## Carrying Out the Stalinist Revolution

*Lev Kopelev (b. 1912), who came from a middle-class Jewish family, was an enthusiastic communist as a young man. Believing that the Soviet Communist Party embodied the progressive movement of history, he eagerly assisted in the forced collectivization drive of the early 1930s, which caused such suffering and death in his native Ukraine. But after World War II, he became critical of Soviet communism, and he was finally exiled from the Soviet Union in 1980.*

Our great goal was the universal triumph of Communism, and for the sake of that goal everything was permissible.... And to hesitate or doubt about all this was to give in to "intellectual squeamishness" and "stupid liberalism," the attributes of people who "could not see the forest for the trees."

...I saw what "total collectivization" meant—how ... mercilessly they stripped the peasants in the winter of 1932–33. I took part in this myself, scouring the countryside, searching for hidden grain, testing the earth with an iron rod for loose spots that might lead to buried grain. With the others, I emptied out the old folks' storage chests, stopping my ears to the children's crying and the women's wails. For I was convinced that I was accomplishing the great and necessary transformation of the countryside; that in the days to come the people who lived there would be better off for it; that their distress and suffering were a result of their own ignorance or the machinations of the class enemy; that those who sent me—and I myself—knew better than the peasants how they should live, what they should sow and when they should plow.

In the terrible spring of 1933 I saw people dying from hunger. I saw women and children with distended bellies, turning blue, still breathing but with vacant, lifeless eyes....

Nor did I lose my faith. As before, I believed because I wanted to believe. Thus from time immemorial men have believed when possessed by a desire to serve powers and values above and beyond humanity....

That was how we thought and acted—we, the fanatical disciples of the all-saving ideals of communism. When we saw the base and cruel acts that were committed in the name of our exalted notions of good, and when we ourselves took part in those actions, what we feared most was to lose our heads, fall into doubt or heresy and forfeit our unbounded faith....

... The concepts of conscience, honor, humaneness we dismissed as idealistic prejudices, "intellectual" or "bourgeois," and, hence, perverse.

*Source:* Lev Kopelev, *No Jail for Thought* (London: Secker & Warburg, 1977), pp. 11–13.

---

What was being squeezed was not merely a surplus—the state's extractions cut into subsistence. So while Soviet agricultural exports increased after 1930, large numbers of peasants starved to death. The great famine that developed during 1932–1933 resulted in between 5 and 6 million deaths, over half of them in Ukraine. This "terror-famine" went unrecorded in the Soviet press, and the Soviets refused help from international relief agencies. (See the box "Reading Sources: Carrying Out the Stalinist Revolution.")

By 1937 almost all Soviet agriculture took place on collective farms—or on state farms set up in areas not previously under agriculture. However, restrictions on private plots and livestock ownership were eased slightly

after 1933, and partly as a result, agriculture rebounded and living standards began to rise. By the late 1930s, moreover, significant increases in industrial output had established solid foundations in heavy industry, including the bases for military production.

In pursuing this program, Stalin played up the great historical drama surrounding the Soviet experiment, with its incredible targets and goals. Suggestions by some that the pace could not be maintained only proved grist for Stalin's mill: "No, comrades," he told a workers' conference early in 1931, "the tempo must not be reduced. On the contrary, we must increase it as much as is within our powers and capabilities.... To slow the tempo would mean falling behind. And those who fall behind get beaten. . . . Do you want our socialist fatherland to be beaten and to lose its independence? . . . We are fifty or a hundred years behind the advanced countries. We must make good this distance in ten years. Either we do this or they will crush us."[1]

Soviet propaganda, including art in the official socialist realist style, glorified the achievements of the new Soviet industrial and agricultural workers. "Stakhanovism°," named for a coal miner who had heroically exceeded his production quota in 1935, became the term for the prodigious economic achievements that the regime valued as it proclaimed the superiority of the communist system. Indeed, the fact that in the Soviet Union state management seemed to produce results while much of the world languished in depression helps explain the prestige that communism developed among intellectuals, in both the Western and non-Western worlds, during the 1930s.

But, whatever its successes, this forced development program created many inefficiencies and entailed tremendous human costs. The Soviet Union could probably have done at least as well, with much less suffering, through other strategies of industrial development. Moreover, Stalin's program departed from certain socialist principles—egalitarianism in wages, for example—that the regime had taken very seriously during the late 1920s. By 1931, bureaucratic managers, concerned simply with maximizing output, were openly favoring workers in certain industries. Collective bargaining and the right to strike had vanished from the workers' arsenal.

### ■ From Opposition to Terror, 1932–1938

Stalin's radical course, with its brutality and uncertain economic justification, quickly provoked opposition. During the summer of 1932, a group centered around M. N. Ryutin° (1890–1937) circulated among party leaders a two-hundred-page tract calling for a retreat from Stalin's economic program and a return to democracy within the party. It advocated readmitting those who had been expelled—including Stalin's archenemy, Leon Trotsky. Moreover, the document strongly condemned Stalin personally, describing him as "the evil genius of the Russian Revolution, who, motivated by a personal desire for power and revenge, brought the Revolution to the verge of ruin."[2]

Stalin promptly had Ryutin and his associates ousted from the party, then arrested and imprisoned. But especially as the international situation grew menacing dur-

ing the 1930s, Stalin became ever more preoccupied with the scope for further opposition. Both Germany and Japan exhibited expansionist aims that might threaten Soviet territories. Trotsky from exile might work with foreign agents and Soviet dissidents to sabotage the Soviet development effort.

In December 1934 the assassination of Sergei Kirov° (1888–1934), party leader of Leningrad (the former Petrograd), gave Stalin an excuse to intensify the crackdown against actual and potential opponents. The eventual result was a series of bizarre show trials, deadly purges, and, ultimately, a kind of terror, with several categories of Soviet citizens vulnerable to arbitrary arrest by the secret police. By the time it wound down, early in 1939, this "great terror" had significantly changed the communist regime—and Soviet society. But though the bare facts are clear, what to make of them is not.

In the three Moscow show trials, which took place during a twenty-month period from 1936 to 1938, noted Bolsheviks including Nikolai Bukharin and major functionaries such as Genrikh Yagoda, recently removed as chief of the secret police, confessed to a series of sensational trumped-up charges: that they had been behind the assassination of Kirov, that they would like to have killed Stalin, that they constituted an "anti-Soviet, Trotskyite center," spying for Germany and Japan and preparing to sabotage Soviet industry in the event of war. Almost all the accused, including Bukharin and others who had been central to the 1917 revolution, were convicted and executed. Soviet authorities did not dare risk public trial for the few who refused, even in the face of torture, to play their assigned roles and confess. Among them was Ryutin, who was shot in secret early in 1937.

During 1937 a purge wiped out much of the top ranks of the army, with half the entire officer corps shot or imprisoned in response to unfounded charges of spying and treason. The Communist Party underwent several purges, culminating in the great purge of 1937 and 1938. Of the roughly two thousand delegates to the 1934 congress of the Communist Party, over half were shot during the next few years. The most prominent were especially vulnerable. Indeed, 114 of the 139 central committee members elected at the 1934 party congress had been shot or sent to a forced labor camp by 1939.

The first such camps were established under Lenin in 1918, during the civil war, but the camp system expanded exponentially under Stalin during the 1930s,

---

**Stakhanovism** (stah-KAH-nov-izm)   **Ryutin** (ree-YOU-tin)   **Kirov** (KIH-roff)

coming to play a major economic role. This network of forced labor camps—there were eventually at least 476 of them—became known as the *gulag,* originally an acronym for "main camp administration."

Although considerable controversy remains over the number of victims of the gulag, and of the Stalinist revolution more generally, the totals were clearly staggering. According to one influential high-end estimate, 8.5 million of the approximately 160 million people in the Soviet Union were arrested during 1937 and 1938, and of these perhaps 1 million were executed by shooting. Half the total membership of the Communist Party—1.2 million people—were arrested; of these, 600,000 were executed, and most of the rest died in gulag camps. Altogether, the terror surrounding the several purges resulted in approximately 8 million deaths. Estimates of the death toll from all of Stalin's policies of the 1930s, including the forced collectivizations, range as high as 20 million.

## ■ Communism and Stalinism

What was going on in this bizarre and lethal combination of episodes? Obviously Stalinism was one possible outcome of Leninist communism, but was it the logical, even the inevitable, outcome? Leninism had accented centralized authority and the scope for human will to force events, so it may have created a framework in which Stalinism was likely to emerge. Yet Stalin's personal idiosyncrasies and growing paranoia seem to have been crucial for the Soviet system to develop as it did. But though he ended up the regime's undisputed leader, Stalin was part of a wider dynamic.

It was long assumed that Stalin was pursuing a coordinated policy of terror to create a system of total control. Yet recent research has shown that he was often merely improvising, responding to a situation that had become chaotic, out of control, as the communists tried to carry through a revolution in a backward country. No one had ever attempted this sort of forced industrialization based on a centrally planned economy. At once idealistic, inexperienced, and suspicious, the regime's leaders really believed that failures must be due to sabotage—that "wreckers" were seeking to undermine the heroic Soviet experiment. Moreover, though Stalin tended to blow them out of proportion, there were genuine threats to the Soviet regime and his own leadership by the mid-1930s.

Whereas the terror was long viewed as almost random, it is now clearer that those in the upper and middle reaches of the Soviet system were the most vulnerable.

Top officials encouraged ordinary workers to provide information about plant managers and local party officials who seemed incompetent or corrupt. And although some workers did so to serve the revolution, others to vent personal resentments, they often took the initiative in denouncing their superiors, thereby playing important roles in the dynamic that developed.

But what explains the "confessions" that invariably resulted from the bizarre show trials? The accused sometimes succumbed to torture, and to threats to their families. But some, at least, offered false confessions because they believed that in doing so they were still serving the communist cause. All along, the revolution had required a willingness to compromise personal scruples, including "bourgeois" concerns about personal honor and dignity. Even though false, these confessions could help the communist regime ward off the genuine dangers it faced. So in confessing, the accused would be serving the long-term cause, which they believed to be bigger than Stalin and the issues of the moment. What some could not see—or admit—was that the triumph of Stalinism was fatally compromising the original revolutionary vision.

Surrounded by great propaganda, the show trials were central to the unending talk of foreign intrigues, assassination plots, and "wrecking" by the later 1930s. And all the talk had its effect, leading many ordinary citizens to believe that a vast conspiracy was indeed at work, responsible for the shortages and economic misfortunes that had accompanied the crash industrialization program.

Although much was unplanned and even out of control, Stalin's ultimate responsibility for the lethal dynamic of the later 1930s is undeniable. At the height of the terror, he personally approved lists for execution, and he took advantage of the chain of events to crush all actual or imagined opposition. By 1939 Stalin loyalists constituted the entire party leadership.

In a sense, the outcome was the triumph of Stalin over the Communist Party, which had held to the original Bolshevik ideal of collective leadership by a revolutionary vanguard. But even this outcome did not snuff out the revolutionary idealism that had helped carry the communist regime through the upheavals of the 1930s. Though some turned away in disillusionment or despair, others found the regime's ruthlessness in rooting out its apparent enemies evidence of its ongoing revolutionary purpose. And whereas Stalin was not a charismatic leader like Hitler or Mussolini, he was coming for many to embody the ongoing promise of the communist experiment.

# HITLER AND NAZISM IN GERMANY

ESET with problems from the start, the Weimar Republic lay gravely wounded by 1932. Various antidemocratic groups competed to replace it. The winner was the Nazi movement, led by Adolf Hitler, who became chancellor in January 1933. It was especially Hitler's new regime in Germany that made the 1930s so tortured, for Hitler not only radically transformed German society but fundamentally altered the power balance in Europe.

Nazism took inspiration from Italian fascism, but Hitler's regime proved more dynamic—and more troubling—than Mussolini's. Nazism was not conventionally revolutionary, in the sense of mounting a frontal challenge to the existing socioeconomic order. Some of its themes were traditionalist and even antimodernizing. But in the final analysis Nazism was anything but conservative. Indeed, it constituted a direct assault on what had long been held as the best of Western civilization.

## ■ The Emergence of Nazism and the Crisis of the Weimar Republic

The National Socialist German Workers' Party (NSDAP), or Nazism, emerged from the turbulent situation in Munich just after the war. A center of leftist agitation, the city also became a hotbed of the radical right, nurturing a number of new nationalist, militantly anticommunist political groups. One of them, a workers' party founded under the aegis of the right-wing Thule Society early in 1919, attracted the attention of Adolf Hitler, who soon gave it his personal stamp.

Adolf Hitler (1889–1945) had been born not German but Austrian, the son of a middling government official. As a young man he had gone to Vienna, hoping to become an artist, but he failed to gain admission to the Viennese Academy of Fine Arts. By 1913 he had become a German nationalist hostile to the multinational Habsburg Empire, and he emigrated to Germany to escape service in the Austrian army. He was not opposed to military service per se, however, and when war broke out in 1914, he immediately volunteered for service in the German army.

Corporal Hitler experienced firsthand the fighting at the front and, as a courier, performed bravely and effectively. Indeed, he was in a field hospital being treated for gas poisoning when the war ended. Although his fellow soldiers considered him quirky and introverted, Hitler found the war experience crucial; it was during the war, he said later, that he "found himself."

Following his release from the hospital, Hitler worked for the army in routine surveillance of extremist groups in Munich. In this role he joined the infant German Workers' Party late in 1919. When his first political speech at a rally in February 1920 proved a resounding success, Hitler began to believe he could play a special political role. From this point, he gradually developed the confidence to lead a new nationalist, anticommunist, and anti-Weimar movement.

But Hitler jumped the gun in November 1923 when, with Erich Ludendorff at his side, he led the Beer Hall Putsch in Munich, an abortive attempt to launch a march on Berlin to overthrow the republic. On trial after this effort failed, Hitler gained greater national visibility as he denounced the Versailles treaty and the Weimar government. Still, *Mein Kampf* (My Battle), the political tract that he wrote while in prison during 1924, sold poorly. To most, Hitler was simply a right-wing rabble-rouser whose views were not worth taking seriously.

His failure in 1923 convinced Hitler that he should exploit the existing political system, but not challenge it directly, in his quest for power on the national level. Yet Hitler did not view the NSDAP as just another political party, playing by the same rules as the others within the Weimar system. Thus, most notably, the Nazi Party maintained a paramilitary arm, the *Sturmabteilung* (SA), which provoked a good deal of antileftist street violence. Still, the Nazis remained confined to the margins of national politics in 1928, when they attracted only 2.6 percent of the vote in elections to the Reichstag.

The onset of the economic depression by the end of 1929 produced problems that the Weimar democracy could not handle—and that radically changed the German political framework. The pivotal issue was unemployment insurance, which became a tremendous financial burden for the government as unemployment grew. The governing coalition fell apart over the issue in March 1930, and this proved to be the end of normal parliamentary government in Weimar Germany.

President Paul von Hindenburg called on Heinrich Brüning (1885–1970), an expert on economics from the Catholic Center Party, to become chancellor. Brüning was to spearhead a hard-nosed, deflationary economic program intended to stimulate exports by lowering prices. Like most of the German middle classes, Brüning feared inflation, disliked unemployment insurance, and believed that Germany could not afford public works projects to pump up demand—the obvious alternative to his deflationary policy. But when he presented his program to the Reichstag, he encountered opposition not only from those on the left but also from conservatives, eager to undermine the republic altogether. As a result, Brüning

**The Coming of Nazism** The last years of the Weimar Republic saw accelerating street violence between the SA, the Nazi Party's paramilitary arm, and the Communist and trade-unionist left. When the Nazis came to power in January 1933, they immediately cracked down on their leftist enemies. Here SA members line up leftist political prisoners at gunpoint. *(Mary Evans Picture Library)*

could get no parliamentary majority. Rather than resigning or seeking a compromise, he invoked Article 48, the emergency provision of the Weimar constitution, which enabled him to govern under presidential decree.

When this expedient provoked strenuous protests, Brüning dissolved the Reichstag and scheduled new elections for September 1930. At this point there was still some chance that a more conciliatory tack would have enabled the chancellor to build a new parliamentary majority—and save parliamentary government. The Socialists were seeking to be more cooperative in the face of the deepening economic crisis and the prospect of new parliamentary elections, which, under these difficult circumstances, seemed to invite trouble. However, Brüning persisted, believing the electorate would vindicate him.

In fact, the outcome of the elections of September 1930 was disastrous—for Brüning, and ultimately for Germany as well. While two of the democratic, pro-Weimar parties lost heavily, the two extremes, the Communists and the Nazis, improved their totals considerably. Indeed, this was a major breakthrough for the Nazis, whose share of the vote jumped from 2.6 percent to 18.3 percent of the total.

Brüning continued to govern, still relying on President Hindenburg and Article 48 rather than majority support in the Reichstag. But his program of raising taxes and decreasing government spending failed to revive the economy. Meanwhile, the growth of the political extremes helped fuel an intensification of the political violence and street fighting that had bedeviled the Weimar Republic from the beginning. As scuffles between Nazis and Communists sometimes approached

pitched battles, the inability of the government to keep order further damaged the prestige of the republic. And as the crisis deepened in 1932, conservative fears of a Marxist outcome played into Hitler's hands.

By this point, conservatives close to Hindenburg sensed the chance to replace the fragmented parliamentary system with some form of authoritarian government. A new, tougher regime would not only attack the economic crisis but also stiffen governmental resistance against the apparent threat from the extreme left. In May 1932 those advisers finally persuaded Hindenburg to dump Brüning, and two of them, Franz von Papen° (1878–1969) and General Kurt von Schleicher° (1882–1934), each got a chance to govern in the months that followed. But neither succeeded, partly because of the daring strategy Hitler adopted.

When, following the ouster of Brüning, new elections were held in July 1932, the Nazis won 37.3 percent of the vote and the Communists 14.3 percent. Together, the two extremes controlled a majority of the seats in the Reichstag. Hitler, as the leader of what was now the Reichstag's largest party, refused to join any coalition—unless he could lead it as chancellor. Meanwhile, the authoritarian conservatives around President Hindenburg wanted to take advantage of the Nazis' mass support for antidemocratic purposes. Finally, in January 1933, with government at an impasse, Papen lined up a new coalition that he proposed to Hindenburg to replace Schleicher's government. Hitler would be chancellor, Papen himself vice-chancellor, and Alfred Hugenberg (1865–

**Papen** (PAH-pin)   **Schleicher** (SHLY-shur)

1951), the leader of the Nationalist Party, finance minister. For months, Hindenburg had resisted giving Hitler a chance to govern, but he felt this combination might work to establish a parliamentary majority, to box out the left—and to contain Nazism. So Hindenburg named Hitler Germany's chancellor on January 30, 1933.

It became clear virtually at once that the outcome of the crisis was a dramatic change of regime, the triumph of Hitler and Nazism. But though the Nazis had always wanted to destroy the Weimar Republic, they were not directly responsible for overthrowing it. The rise of Nazism was more a symptom than a cause of the crisis of Weimar democracy.

In one sense, the Weimar Republic collapsed from within, largely because the German people disagreed fundamentally about priorities after the war—and then again with the onset of the Depression. Thus the new democracy produced unstable government based on multiparty coalitions, and it fell into virtual paralysis when faced with the economic crisis by 1930. At the same time, however, those around Hindenburg were particularly quick to begin undercutting democratic government in 1930, as the economic crisis seemed to intensify the threat from the extreme left.

As unemployment grew during the first years of the 1930s, both the Nazis and the Communists gained electoral support, but the Germans voting for the Nazis were not simply those most threatened economically. Nor did the Nazi Party appeal primarily to the uneducated or socially marginal. Rather, the party served as a focus of opposition for those growing alienated from the Weimar Republic itself. Although the Nazis did relatively poorly among Catholics and industrial workers, they put together a broad, fairly diverse base of electoral support, ranging from artisans and small shopkeepers to university students and civil servants. But though Hitler was clearly anti-Weimar, anticommunist, and anti-Versailles, his positive program remained vague, so those who voted for the Nazis were not clear what they might be getting. In light of economic depression and political impasse, however, it seemed time to try something new.

### ■ The Consolidation of Hitler's Power, 1933–1934

When Hitler became chancellor, it was not obvious that a change of regime was beginning. Like his predecessors, he could govern only with the president's approval, and governmental institutions like the army, the judiciary, and the diplomatic corps, though hardly bastions of democracy, were not in the hands of committed Nazis.

But even though an element of caution and cultivated ambiguity remained, a revolution quickly began, creating a new regime, the Third Reich.

On February 23, just weeks after Hitler became chancellor, a fire engulfed the Reichstag building in Berlin. It was set by a young Dutch communist acting on his own, but it seemed to suggest that a communist uprising was imminent. This sense of emergency gave the new Hitler government an excuse to restrict civil liberties and imprison leftist leaders, including the entire Communist parliamentary delegation. Even in this atmosphere of crisis the Nazis could not win a majority in the Reichstag elections of March 5. But support from the Nationalists and the Catholic Center Party enabled the Nazis to win Reichstag approval for an enabling act granting Hitler the power to make laws on his own for the next four years, bypassing both the Reichstag and the president.

Although the Weimar Republic was never formally abolished, the laws that followed fundamentally altered government, politics, and public life in Germany. The other parties were either outlawed or persuaded to dissolve, so that in July 1933 the Nazi Party was declared the only legal party. When President Hindenburg died in August 1934, the offices of chancellor and president were merged, and Germany had just one leader, Adolf Hitler, holding unprecedented power. Members of the German armed forces now swore loyalty to him personally.

During this period of power consolidation, Hitler acted decisively but carefully, generally accenting normalization. To be sure, his methods occasionally gave conservatives pause, most notably when he had several hundred people murdered in the "blood purge" of June 30, 1934. But this purge was directed especially against the SA, led by Ernst Röhm (1887–1934), who had had pretensions of controlling the army. His removal seemed evidence that Hitler was taming the radical elements in his own movement. In fact, however, this purge led to the ascendancy of the *Schutzstaffel*, or SS, the select Nazi elite, led by Heinrich Himmler (1900–1945). Linked to the Gestapo, the secret political police, the SS became the institutional basis for the most troubling aspects of Nazism.

### ■ Hitler's World-View and the Dynamics of Nazi Practice

In achieving the chancellorship and in expanding his power thereafter, Hitler showed himself an adept politician, but he was hardly a mere opportunist, seeking to amass power for its own sake. Power was only the instrument for the grandiose transformation he believed necessary. And what most troubles us about Nazism, from personal dictatorship to the eventual effort to exterminate the Jews of Europe, stemmed from an overall vision of the world that radiated from Hitler himself.

Hitler acted on the basis of a world-view that coalesced by about 1924—and that remained extremely important to him. This is not to say that he was an original thinker or that his ideas were true—or even plausible. But he sought to make systematic sense of things, and the most disturbing features of his political activity stemmed directly from the resulting world-view. His most committed followers shared certain of his ideas, although fanatical loyalty to Hitler himself was more important for some of them. The central components of Hitler's thinking—geopolitics, biological racism, anti-Semitism, and Social Darwinism—were by no means specifically German. They could be found all over the Western world by the early twentieth century.

Geopolitics claimed to offer a scientific understanding of world power relationships based on geographical determinism. In his writings of the 1920s, Hitler warned that Germany faced imminent decline unless it confronted its geopolitical limitations. To remain fully sovereign in the emerging new era of global superpowers like the United States, Germany would have to act quickly to expand its territory. Otherwise it would end up like Switzerland or the Netherlands.

For decades German imperialists had argued about whether Germany was better advised to seek overseas colonies or to expand its reach in Europe. As Hitler saw it, Germany's failure to make a clear choice had led to its defeat in World War I. Now choice was imperative, and current geopolitical thinking suggested the direction for expansion. Far-flung empires relying on naval support were said to be in decline. The future lay with land-based states—unified, geographically contiguous, with the space necessary for self-sufficiency. By expanding eastward, into Poland and the Soviet Union, Germany could conquer the living space, or *Lebensraum,* necessary for agricultural-industrial balance—and ultimately for self-sufficiency.

Though limited and mechanistic, this geopolitical way of thinking is at least comprehensible, in light of the German vulnerabilities that had indeed surfaced during World War I. The other three strands of Hitler's world-view were much less plausible, though each had become prominent during the second half of the nineteenth century. Biological racism insisted that built-in racial characteristics determine what is most important about any individual. Anti-Semitism went beyond racism in claim-

ing that Jews have played, and continue to play, a special and negative role in history. The fact that the Jews were dispersed and often landless indicated that they were different—and parasitical. Finally, Social Darwinism, especially in its German incarnation, accented the positive role of struggle—not among individuals, as in a prominent American strand, but among racial groups.

The dominant current of racist thinking labeled the "Aryans" as healthy, creative, superior. Originally the Sanskrit term for "noble," *Aryan* gradually came to indicate the ancient language assumed to have been the common source of the modern Indo-European languages. An Aryan was simply a speaker of one of those languages. By the late nineteenth century, however, the term had become supremely ill defined. In much racist thinking, Germanic peoples were somehow especially Aryan, but race mixing had produced impurity—and thus degeneration. Success in struggle with the other races was the ultimate measure of vitality, the only proof of racial superiority for the future.

Hitler brought these themes together by emphasizing that humanity is not special, but simply part of nature, subject to the same laws of struggle and selection as the other animal species. Humanitarian ideals are thus dangerous illusions. As he put it to a group of officer cadets in 1944:

> Nature is always teaching us . . . that she is governed by the principle of selection: that victory is to the strong and that the weak must go to the wall. She teaches us that what may seem cruel to us, because it affects us personally or because we have been brought up in ignorance of her laws, is nevertheless often essential if a higher way of life is to be attained. Nature . . . knows nothing of the notion of humanitarianism, which signifies that the weak must at all costs be protected and preserved even at the expense of the strong.
>
> Nature does not see in weakness any extenuating reasons . . . on the contrary, weakness calls for condemnation.[3]

To Hitler, the Jews were not simply another of the races involved in this endless struggle. Rather, as landless parasites, they embodied the principles—from humanitarianism to class struggle—that were antithetical to the healthy natural struggle among unified racial groups. "Jewishness" was bound up with the negative, critical intellect that dared suggest things ought to be not natural but just, even that it was up to human beings to change the world, to make it just. The Jews were the virus keeping the community from a healthy natural footing. Marxist communism, embodying divisive class struggle as well as utopian humanitarian ideals, was fundamentally Jewish.

The central features of Nazism in practice, from personal dictatorship to the extermination of the Jews, followed from Hitler's view of the world. First, the racial community must organize itself politically for this ceaseless struggle. Individuals are but instruments for the success of the racial community. Parliamentary democracy, reflecting short-term individual interests, fostered selfish materialism and division, thereby weakening that community. The political order must rest instead on a charismatic leader, united with the whole people through bonds of common blood.

**Hitler and Children**    Adolf Hitler was often portrayed as the friend of children. This photograph accompanied a story for an elementary school reader that described how Hitler, told it was this young girl's birthday, picked her from a crowd of well-wishers to treat her "to cake and strawberries with thick, sweet cream."    *(From* Jugend um Hitler, *Heinrich Hoffman © "Zeitgeschichte" Verlag und Vertriebs-Gesellschaft Berlin. Reproduced with permission. Photo courtesy Wiener Library, London)*

## ■ Nazi Aims and German Society

Although Hitler's world-view provided the underlying momentum for the Nazi regime, it did not specify a consistent program that could be implemented all at once. Moreover, the regime sometimes found it necessary to adopt short-term expedients that conflicted with its long-term aims. Thus it was possible for Germans living under Nazi rule in the 1930s to embrace aspects of Nazism in practice without seeing where it was all leading.

Hitler's special leadership function was based on a charismatic relationship with the German people, a nonrational bond resting on common race. But to create a genuine racial community, or *Volksgemeinschaft,* it was necessary to unify society and instill Nazi values, thereby making the individual feel part of the whole— and ultimately an instrument to serve the whole. This entailed more or less forced participation in an array of Nazi organizations, from the Women's Organization to the Hitler Youth, from the Labor Front to the Strength Through Joy leisure-time organization.

Common participation meant shared experiences such as weekend hikes and a weekly one-dish meal. Even the most ordinary, once-private activities took on a public or political dimension. Moreover, the Nazis devised unprecedented ways to stage-manage public life, using rituals like the Hitler salute, symbols like the swastika, new media like radio and film, and carefully orchestrated party rallies—all in an effort to foster this sense of belonging. (See the feature "Weighing the Evidence: Film as Propaganda" on pages 944–945.)

Hitler's regime enjoyed considerable popular support, but even after Hitler was well entrenched in power, most Germans did not grasp the regime's deeper dynamic. Certainly some welcomed the sense of unity, the feeling of belonging and participation, especially after what had seemed the alienation and divisiveness of the Weimar years. Moreover, Hitler himself was immensely popular, partly because of his personal charisma, partly because his apparently decisive leadership was a welcome departure from the near paralysis of the Weimar parliamentary system. But most important, before the coming of war in 1939, he seemed to go from success to success, surmounting the Depression and repudiating the major terms of the hated Versailles treaty.

Hitler's propaganda minister, Joseph Goebbels (1897–1945), played on these successes to create a "Hitler myth," which made Hitler seem at once heroic and a man of the people, even the embodiment of healthy German ideals against the corruptions of the Nazi Party. This myth became central to the Nazi regime, but it merely provided a façade behind which the real Hitler could pursue hidden, longer-term aims. These aims were not publicized directly because the German people did not seem ready for them. In this sense, then, support for Hitler and his regime was broad but shallow during the 1930s.

Moreover, resistance increased as the regime became more intrusive. Youth gangs actively opposed the official Hitler Youth organization as it became more overbearing and militaristic by the late 1930s. But people resisted especially by minimizing their involvement with the regime, retreating into the private realm, in response to the Nazi attempt to make everything public.

Did such people feel constantly under threat of the Gestapo, the secret police? In principle, the Gestapo could interpret the will of the *Führer*, or leader, and decide whether any individual citizen was "guilty" or not. And the Gestapo was not concerned about due process; on occasion it simply bypassed the regular court system. But the Gestapo did not terrorize Germans at random. Its victims were generally members of specific groups, people suspected of active opposition, or people who protected those the Gestapo had targeted.

Moreover, changes and contradictions in Nazi goals allowed considerable space for personal choice. During the struggle for power, the Nazis had emphasized the woman's role as wife and mother and deplored the ongoing emancipation of women. Once Hitler came to power, concerns about unemployment reinforced these views. (See the box "Reading Sources: The Nazi Revolution and the Role of Women.") Almost immediately Hitler's government began offering interest-free loans to help couples set up house if the woman agreed to leave the labor force. Such efforts to increase the German birthrate reinforced the emphasis on child rearing in Nazi women's organizations. Nonetheless, the size of the family continued to decrease in Germany as elsewhere in the industrialized world during the 1930s.

Beginning in 1936, when rapid rearmament began to produce labor shortages, the regime did an about-face and began seeking to attract women back to the workplace, especially into jobs central to military preparation. These efforts were not notably successful, and by 1940 the military was calling for conscription of women into war industries.

Further, the Nazis valued the family only insofar as it was congruent with the "health" of the racial community, and efforts to promote that health also compromised traditional family values. The regime regulated marriage and sought actively to eliminate the "unhealthy," those deemed unfit. Just months after coming to power in 1933, Hitler brushed aside the objections of Vice Chancellor Franz von Papen, a Catholic, and engineered a law mandating the compulsory sterilization of persons suffering from certain allegedly hereditary diseases. Medical personnel sterilized some 400,000, the vast majority of them "Aryan" Germans, during the Nazi years.

Hitler's regime also began immediately to single out the Jews, although Nazi Jewish policy remained an improvised hodgepodge prior to World War II. Within weeks after Hitler became chancellor in 1933, new restrictions limited Jewish participation in the civil service, in the professions, and in German cultural life—and quickly drew censure from the League of Nations. The Nuremberg Laws, announced at a party rally in 1935, included prohibition of sexual relations and marriage between Jews and non-Jewish Germans. Beginning in 1938, the Jews had to carry special identification cards and to add "Sarah" or "Israel" to their given names.

But though Hitler and other Nazi leaders claimed periodically to be seeking a definitive solution to Germany's "Jewish problem," the dominant objective during the 1930s was to force German Jews to emigrate. About 60,000 of Germany's 550,000 Jews left the country during 1933 and 1934, and perhaps 25 percent had gotten out by 1938. The fact that the regime stripped emigrating Jews of their assets made emigration more difficult. Potential host countries, concerned about unemployment during the Depression, were especially unwilling to take in substantial numbers of Jews if they were penniless.

On November 9, 1938, using the assassination of a German diplomat in Paris as a pretext, the Nazis staged the *Kristallnacht* (Crystal Night) pogrom, during which almost all the synagogues in Germany and about seven thousand Jewish-owned stores were destroyed. Between 30,000 and 50,000 relatively prosperous Jews were arrested and forced to emigrate after their property was confiscated. Although the German public had generally acquiesced in the earlier restrictions on Jews, this pogrom, with its wanton violation of private property, shocked many Germans.

Concentration camps—supplementary detention centers—had become a feature of the Nazi regime virtually at once, but prior to 1938 they were used primarily to hold political prisoners. As part of the Crystal Night pogrom, about 35,000 Jews were rounded up and sent to the camps, but most were soon released as long as they could document their intention to emigrate. When World War II began in 1939, the total camp population was about 25,000. The systematic physical extermination of the Jews began only during the war, in newly constructed death camps.

*ɩ̀♣* R E A D I N G   S O U R C E S

## The Nazi Revolution and the Role of Women

*Hitler and the Nazis trumpeted a highly traditionalist conception of women's roles. In doing so, they were reacting sharply against the emancipation of women that had been a hallmark of the 1920s, especially in Germany. Although a shortage of labor would force some compromise later in the decade, Hitler made the official Nazi view of women unmistakably clear in a speech to the women's section of the Nazi Party on September 8, 1934.*

. . . The slogan "Emancipation of women" was invented by Jewish intellectuals and its content was formed by the same spirit. In the really good times of German life the German woman had no need to emancipate herself. She possessed exactly what nature had necessarily given her to administer and preserve; just as the man in his good times had no need to fear that he would be ousted from his position in relation to the woman.

In fact the woman was least likely to challenge his position. Only when he was not absolutely certain in his knowledge of his task did the eternal instinct of self and race-preservation begin to rebel in women. There then grew from this rebellion a state of affairs which was unnatural and which lasted until both sexes returned to the respective spheres which an eternally wise providence had preordained for them.

If the man's world is said to be the State, his struggle, his readiness to devote his powers to the service of the community, then it may perhaps be said that the woman's is a smaller world. For her world is her husband, her family, her children, and her home. But what would become of the greater world if there were no one to tend and care for the smaller one? . . . [O]nly on the basis of this smaller world can the man's world be formed and build up. The two worlds are not antagonistic. They complement each other, they belong together just as man and woman belong together.

We do not consider it correct for the woman to interfere in the world of the man, in his main sphere. We consider it natural if these two worlds remain distinct. To the one belongs the strength of feeling, the strength of the soul. To the other belongs the strength of vision, of toughness, of decision, and of the willingness to act. In the one case this strength demands the willingness of the woman to risk her life to preserve this important cell and to multiply it, and in the other case it demands from the man the readiness to safeguard life.

The sacrifices which the man makes in the struggle of his nation, the woman makes in the preservation of that nation in individual cases. What the man gives in courage on the battlefield, the woman gives in eternal self-sacrifice, in eternal pain and suffering. Every child that a woman brings into the world is a battle, a battle waged for the existence of her people. And both must therefore mutually value and respect each other when they see that each performs the task that Nature and Providence have ordained. And this mutual respect will necessarily result from this separation of the functions of each.

It is not true, as Jewish intellectuals assert, that respect depends on the overlapping of the spheres of activity of the sexes; this respect demands that neither sex should try to do that which belongs to the sphere of the other. It lies in the last resort in the fact that each knows that the other is doing everything necessary to maintain the whole community. . . .

So our women's movement is for us not something which inscribes on its banner as its programme the fight against men, but something which has as its programme the common fight together with men. For the new National Socialist national community acquires a firm basis precisely because we have gained the trust of millions of women as fanatical fellow-combatants, women who have fought for the common life in the service of the common task of preserving life, who in that combat did not set their sights on the rights which a Jewish intellectualism put before their eyes, but rather on the duties imposed by nature on all of us in common.

*Source:* J. Noakes and G. Pridham, *Nazism: A History in Documents and Eyewitness Accounts, 1919–1945*, vol. 1 (New York: Schocken, 1990), pp. 449–450.

However, the killing of others deemed superfluous or threatening to the racial community began earlier, with the so-called euthanasia program initiated under volunteer medical teams in 1939. Its aim was to eliminate chronic mental patients, the incurably ill, and people with severe physical handicaps. Those subject to such treatment were overwhelmingly ethnic Germans, not Jews or foreigners. Although the regime did all it could to make it appear the victims had died naturally, a public outcry developed, especially among relatives and church leaders. Thus the program was discontinued in 1941, but by then it had claimed 100,000 lives—and seems essentially to have achieved its initial objectives.

This "euthanasia" program was based on the sense, fundamental to radical Nazism, that war was the norm and readiness for war the essential societal imperative. In war, societies send individuals to their deaths and, on the battlefield, make difficult distinctions among the wounded, letting some die in order to save those most likely to survive and return to battle. Struggle necessitates selection, which requires overcoming humanitarian scruples—especially the notion that "weakness" calls for special protection. Thus it was desirable to kill even ethnic Germans who were deemed unfit, as "life unworthy of life."

Preparation for war was the core of Nazism in practice. The conquest of living space in the east would make possible a more advantageous agricultural-industrial balance. The result would be not only the self-sufficiency necessary for sovereignty but also the land-rootedness necessary for racial health. Such a war of conquest would strike not only the Slavic peoples of the region but also communism, centered in the Soviet Union.

The point of domestic reorganization was to marshal the community's energies and resources for war. Because German business interests generally seemed congruent with Nazi purposes, Nazi aims did not appear to require some revolutionary assault on business elites or the capitalist economy. But the Nazis had their own road to travel, and beginning in 1936 they proved quite prepared to bend the economy, and to coordinate big business, to serve their longer-term aims of war-making.

The Nazi drive toward war during the 1930s transformed international relations in Europe. The other European powers sought to understand Hitler's Germany in terms of the increasingly polarized political context of the period. Before considering the fortunes of Hitler's foreign policy, we must consider fascism as a wider phenomenon—and the efforts of the democracies, on the one hand, and the Soviet Union, on the other, to come to terms with it.

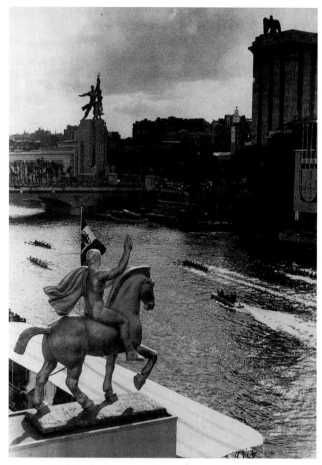

**Ideological Confrontation**   At a major international exhibition in Paris in 1937, the new antidemocratic political regimes of the interwar period made bold propaganda statements. With a sculpture from fascist Italy's pavilion in the foreground, we look across the Seine River to a classic representation of the ideological warfare of the 1930s: the Soviet Pavilion, on the left, facing the German Pavilion, on the right. *(AP/Wide World Photos)*

# FASCIST CHALLENGE AND ANTIFASCIST RESPONSE, 1934–1939

COMMUNISM, fascism, and Nazism all repudiated the parliamentary democracy that had been the West's political norm. Each seemed subject to violence and excess, yet each had features that some found attractive, especially in light of the difficult socioeconomic circumstances of the 1930s. Yet communists and adherents of the various forms of fascism were bitterly hostile to each other, and the very presence of these new political systems caused polarization all over Europe.

Beginning in 1934 communists sought to join with anyone who would work with them to defend the democratic framework, and thus a role for communist parties, against further fascist assaults. This effort led to new antifascist coalition governments in Spain and France. In each case, however, the Depression restricted maneuvering room, and these governments ended up furthering the polarization they were seeking to avoid. By mid-1940, democracy had fallen in Spain, after a brutal civil war, and even in France, in the wake of military defeat.

## ■ European Fascism and the Popular Front Response

Although fascism attracted some of those elsewhere who were disaffected with democracy and hostile to communism, the line between fascism and conservative authoritarianism blurred in the volatile political climate of the 1930s. To some, any retreat from democracy appeared a step toward fascism.

In east-central Europe, political distinctions became especially problematic. Movements like the Arrow Cross in Hungary and the Legion of the Archangel Michael in Romania modeled themselves on the Italian and German prototypes, but they never achieved political power. Those who controlled the antidemocratic governments in Hungary and Romania, as in Poland, Bulgaria, and Yugoslavia, were authoritarian traditionalists, not fascists. Still, many government leaders in the region welcomed the closer economic ties with Germany that Hitler's economics minister, Hjalmar Schacht, engineered. The difference between authoritarianism and fascism remained clearest in Austria, where Catholic conservatives undermined democracy during 1933 and 1934. They were actively hostile to the growing pro-Nazi agitation in Austria, partly because they wanted to keep Austria independent.

In France various nationalist, anticommunist, and anti-Semitic leagues gathered momentum during the early 1930s. They covered a spectrum from monarchism to outspoken profascism, but together they constituted at least a potential threat to French democracy. In February 1934, right-wing demonstrations against the Chamber of Deputies provoked a bloody clash with police and forced a change of ministry. As it began to seem that even France might be vulnerable, those from the center and left of the political spectrum began to think about collaborating to resist fascism. The Communists, espe-

cially, took the initiative by promoting "popular fronts" of all those seeking to preserve democracy.

This was a dramatic change in strategy for international communism. Even as Hitler was closing in on the German chancellorship in the early 1930s, German Communists, following Comintern policy, continued to attack their socialist rivals rather than seek a unified response to Nazism. From the communist perspective, fascism represented the crisis phase of monopoly capitalism, so a Nazi government would actually be useful to strip away the democratic façade hiding class oppression in Germany. But by 1934 the threat of fascism seemed so pressing that the Communists began actively promoting electoral alliances and governing coalitions with Socialists and even liberal democrats to resist its further spread. From 1934 until 1939, Communists everywhere consistently pursued this "popular front" strategy.

But by the 1930s it was becoming ever harder to be sure what was fascist, what was dangerous, what might lead where. As fears intensified, perceptions became as important as realities. Popular front governments, intended to preserve democracy against what appeared to be fascism, could seem, to conservatives, to be leaning too far to the left. Ideological polarization made democracy extraordinarily difficult. The archetypal example proved to be Spain, where a tragedy of classical proportions was played out.

## ■ From Democracy to Civil War in Spain, 1931–1939

Spain became a center of attention in the 1930s, when its promising new parliamentary democracy, launched in 1931, led to civil war in 1936 and the triumph of a repressive authoritarian regime in 1939. An earlier effort at constitutional monarchy had fizzled by 1923, when King Alfonso XIII (1886–1941) supported a new military dictatorship. But growing opposition led first to the resignation of the dictator in 1930 and then, in April 1931, to the end of the monarchy and the proclamation of a republic. The elections for a constituent assembly that followed in June produced a solid victory for a coalition of liberal democrats and Socialists, as well as much hope for substantial reform.

A significant agrarian reform law was passed in 1932, but partly because of the difficult depression economic context, the new government was slow to implement it. Feeling betrayed, Socialists and agricultural workers became increasingly radical, producing growing upheaval in the countryside. Radicalism on the left made it harder for the moderates to govern and, at the same time, stimulated conservatives to become more politically active.

A right-wing coalition known as the CEDA, led by José Maria Gil Robles° (1898–1980), grew in strength, becoming the largest party in parliament with the elections of November 1933. In light of its parliamentary strength, the CEDA had a plausible claim to a government role, but it was kept from participation in government until October 1934. It seemed to the left, in the ideologically charged atmosphere of the time, that the growing role of the CEDA was a prelude to fascism. To let the CEDA into the government would be to hand the republic over to its enemies.

A strong Catholic from the traditional Spanish right, Gil Robles refused to endorse the democratic republic as a form of government, but he and the CEDA were willing to work within it. So the Spanish left may have been too quick to see the CEDA as fascist—and to react when the CEDA finally got its government role. However, Mussolini and Hitler had each come to power more or less legally, from within parliamentary institutions. The German left had been criticized for its passive response to the advent of Hitler; the Spanish left wanted to avoid the same mistake.

Thus, when the CEDA finally got a role in the government, the left responded during the fall of 1934 with quasi-revolutionary uprisings in Catalonia and Asturias, where a miners' commune was put down only after two weeks of heavy fighting. In the aftermath, the right-leaning government of 1935 began undoing some of the reforms of the left-leaning government of 1931–1933, though still legally, within the framework of the parliamentary republic.

In February 1936 a popular front coalition to ward off fascism won a narrow electoral victory, sufficient for an absolute majority in parliament. As would be true in France a few months later, electoral victory produced popular expectations that went well beyond the essentially defensive purposes of the popular front. Hoping to win back the leftist rank and file and head off what seemed a dangerous attempt at revolution, the new popular front government began to implement a progressive program, now including the land reform that had been promised but not implemented earlier. But it was too late to undercut the growing radicalization of the masses.

A wave of land seizures began in March 1936, followed by the most extensive strike movement in Spanish history, which by June was becoming clearly revolutionary in character. To many, the government's inability to keep order had become the immediate issue. By the early summer of 1936, leaders of the democratic republic had become isolated between the extremes of left and right, each preparing an extralegal solution.

Finally, in mid-July, several army officers initiated a military uprising against the government. Soon led by General Francisco Franco (1892–1975), these Nationalist insurgents took control of substantial parts of Spain. Elsewhere they failed to overcome the resistance of the Republican Loyalists, those determined to defend the republic. So the result was not the intended military takeover but a brutal civil war (see Map 27.1). The substantial Italian fascist and Nazi German intervention on the Nationalist side by the end of 1936 intensified the war's ideological ramifications. At the same time, the remarkable, often heroic resistance of the Loyalists captured the imagination of the world. Indeed, forty thousand volunteers came from abroad to fight to preserve the Spanish republic.

It proved a war of stunning brutality on both sides. Loyalist anticlericalism led to the murder of twelve bishops and perhaps one-eighth of the parish clergy in Spain. On the other side, the German bombing of the Basque town of Guernica° on a crowded market day in April 1937, represented unforgettably in Pablo Picasso's painting, came to symbolize the violence and suffering of the whole era.

Republican Loyalists assumed that Franco and the Nationalists represented another instance of fascism. In fact, however, Franco was no fascist, but rather a traditional military man whose leadership role did not rest on personal charisma. He was an authoritarian emphasizing discipline, order, and Spain's Catholic traditions.

Still, in their effort to rally support during the civil war, Franco's forces found it expedient to take advantage of the appeal of the Falange°, a genuinely fascist movement that had emerged under the leadership of the charismatic young José Antonio Primo de Rivera (1903–1936). Although extremely weak at the time of the elections in February 1936, the Falange grew rapidly in opposition to the leftist radicalism that followed the popular front victory. As street fighting between left and right intensified that spring, the republic arrested José Antonio, as he was called, and he was in prison when the civil war began.

José Antonio decided his best hope was alliance with the military. Although he was contemptuous of their

---

**Gil Robles** (heel ROH-blayce)

**Guernica** (gher-NEE-kah, in Spanish; GWAIR-nee-kah, as customarily rendered in English)    **Falange** (fah-LAHN-hay)

**Map 27.1   The Spanish Civil War, 1936–1939**   The Nationalist insurgents quickly took over most of northern and eastern Spain in 1936 and then gradually expanded their territory. The fall of Madrid early in 1939 marked the end of fighting. The revolutionary effort of 1936–1937 within the Republican zone was centered in Barcelona.   *(Source: Adapted from* The Times Atlas of World History, *3d ed., by kind permission of Times Books.)*

shortsighted conservatism, he felt their very absence of ideas afforded an opening for the Falange to provide direction, a genuine alternative. But it worked out the other way. In November 1936, José Antonio was tried and executed for conspiring to overthrow the republic, and the Nationalists promptly began using the trappings of the Falange, including the memory of José Antonio, to increase their popular appeal.

Meanwhile, the Republicans had to fight a civil war while dealing with continuing revolution in their own ranks. Developing especially in Catalonia from the uprisings of 1936, that revolution was not communist but anarchist and syndicalist in orientation. The Communists, true to popular front principles, insisted that this was no time for such "infantile leftist" revolutionary experiments. What mattered, throughout the Republican zone, was the factory discipline necessary to produce essential war materiel. So the Communists, under Stalin's orders, were instrumental in putting down the anarchist revolution in Catalonia in June 1937.

Under these extraordinary circumstances, the Communists, at first a distinct minority on the Spanish left, gradually gained the ascendancy on the Republican side, partly because they were disciplined and effective, partly because Soviet assistance enhanced their prestige. However, this single-minded prosecution of the civil war did not prove enough to defeat the military insurgency, despite the considerable heroism on the Loyalist side. The war ended with the fall of Madrid to the Nationalists in March 1939. General Franco's authoritarian regime governed Spain until his death in 1975.

In Spain, as in Weimar Germany, the initial lack of consensus in a new republic made parliamentary democracy difficult, and the wider ideological framework magnified the difficulties. With the political boiling point so low, the left and the right each saw the other in

**Picasso: Guernica**    Created for the Spanish Pavilion at the famed 1937 Paris Exhibition, Picasso's painting conveyed horror and outrage—his response to the German bombing of Guernica on a crowded market day in 1937, during the Spanish civil war. Picasso's stark, elemental imagery helped define this era of violence and suffering for the generations that followed.    *(Pablo Picasso, Guernica [1937, May–early June]. Oil on canvas. © Art Resource, NY. © ARS, NY)*

extreme terms and assumed that extraordinary response to the other was necessary. Thus the left tended to view even conservatives operating within a parliamentary framework as "fascist." And each side was relatively quick to give up on a democratic republic that seemed to be tilting too far in the other direction.

### ■ France in the Era of the Popular Front

In France, as in Spain, concern to arrest the spread of fascism led to a popular front coalition, here including Socialists, Communists, and Radicals, that governed the country from 1936 to 1938. Although it did not lead to civil war, the popular front was central to the French experience of the 1930s, producing polarization and resignation, and undermining confidence in the Third Republic.

Beginning in 1934, the French Communists took the initiative in approaching first the Socialists, then the Radicals, to develop a popular front coalition against fascism. In reaching out to the Radicals, the Communists stressed French patriotism and made no demand for significant economic reforms. Stalin gave this effort a major push in 1935 when, in a stunning change in the commu-

nist line, he stressed the legitimacy of national defense and explicitly endorsed French rearmament.

In the elections of April and May 1936, the popular front won a sizable majority in the Chamber of Deputies, putting the Socialists' leader, Léon Blum (1872–1950), in line to become France's first Socialist prime minister. The Communists pledged full support of the new Blum government but, to avoid fanning fears, they did not participate directly. However, despite the popular front's moderate and essentially defensive aims, the situation quickly began to polarize after the elections.

Fearing that the new Blum government would be forced to devalue the French currency, and thereby diminish the value of assets denominated in francs, French investors immediately began moving their capital abroad. At the same time, the popular front victory produced a wave of enthusiasm among workers that escaped the control of popular front leaders and culminated in a spontaneous strike movement, the largest France had ever seen. By early June it had spread to all major industries nationwide. Although the workers' demands—for collective bargaining, a forty-hour week, and paid vacations—were not extraordinary, the movement involved sit-down strikes as well as the normal

**Léon Blum**    The French Socialist leader appears in an enthusiastic moment after the popular front victory in 1936. He was about to become France's first Socialist prime minister, but in that role he encountered one dilemma after another. By 1938, the high spirits of 1936 had dissolved.    *(Archives Ringart)*

creases as a direct result of Matignon, then a forty-hour week and paid vacations in a reform package promptly passed by parliament.

In the enthusiasm of the summer of 1936, other reforms were enacted as well, but after that the popular front was forced onto the defensive. Two problems undermined its energy and cohesion: the noncooperation of French business and the Spanish civil war. The cautious response of Blum, the Socialist prime minister, is striking in each case, but he faced a situation with little maneuvering room.

From the outset Blum stressed that he had no mandate for revolution, and as France's first Socialist prime minister, he felt it essential to prove that a Socialist could govern responsibly. Thus, Blum did not respond energetically to the capital flight, even though it produced serious currency and budgetary difficulties. Perhaps, as critics suggest, he should have acted more aggressively to overhaul the French banking and credit system. But Blum shied away from any such drastic measures, both to prove he could be moderate and to avoid antagonizing business.

Blum was also uncertain as he faced the dilemmas surrounding the Spanish civil war. The key question was whether the French government should help the beleaguered Spanish republic, at least by sending supplies. Although he initially favored such help, Blum changed his mind under pressure from three sides. The Conservative government of Stanley Baldwin in Britain was against it. So was the French right; some even suggested that French intervention would provoke civil war in France as well. Moreover, the Radicals in his own coalition were generally opposed to helping the Spanish republic, so intervention would jeopardize the cohesion of the popular front itself.

Thus, rather than help supply the Spanish republic, Blum promoted a nonintervention agreement among the major powers, including Italy and Germany. Many Socialists and Communists within the popular front disliked Blum's cautious policy, however, especially as it became clear that Mussolini and Hitler were violating their hands-off pledges. As Blum stuck to nonintervention, the moral force of the popular front dissolved.

In 1938 a new government under the Radical Edouard Daladier° (1884–1970), still nominally a creature of the popular front, began dismantling some of the key gains of 1936, even attacking the forty-hour week. Citing productivity and national security concerns, Daladier adopted probusiness policies and succeeded in at-

walkouts and thus seemed quasi-revolutionary in character. The major trade union confederation, the Communists, and most Socialists, including Blum himself, saw the strikes as a danger to the popular front, with its more modest aims of defending the republic, and eagerly pursued a settlement.

That settlement, the Matignon° Agreement of June 8, 1936, was a major victory for the French working class. Having been genuinely frightened by the strikes, and now reassured that the popular front government would at least uphold the law, French industrialists were willing to make significant concessions. So the workers got collective bargaining, elected shop stewards, and wage in-

---

**Matignon** (mah-tin-YAWN)

**Daladier** (dah-lah-dee-YAY)

tracting capital back to France. But workers, watching the gains they had won in 1936 slip away, felt betrayed. At the same time, businessmen and conservatives began blaming the workers' gains—such as the five-day week—for slowing French rearmament. Although such charges were not entirely fair, they indicated how poisoned the atmosphere in France had become in the wake of the popular front.

As France began to face the possibility of a new war, the popular front was widely blamed for French weakness. When war came at last, resignation and division were prevalent, in contrast with the patriotic unity and high spirits of 1914. It was partly for that reason that France was so easily defeated by Germany in 1940. And when France fell, the democratic Third Republic fell with it.

# THE COMING OF WORLD WAR II, 1935–1939

VEN as the Great Depression added to their burdens, Western leaders faced the challenge of maintaining the peace during the 1930s. But despite the promising adjustments of the 1920s, many of the problems that accompanied the World War I peace settlement were still in place when Hitler came to power. And Hitler had consistently trumpeted his intention to overturn that settlement. What scope was there for peaceful revision? Could Hitler be stopped by threat of war? By the last years of the 1930s, these questions tortured the Western world as Hitler went from one success to another, raising the possibility of a new and more destructive war. And the power balance rested on the responses not only of the Western democracies, but of fascist Italy and the communist Soviet Union as well.

## ■ The Reorientation of Fascist Italy

During its first decade in power, Benito Mussolini's fascist regime in Italy concentrated on domestic reconstruction, especially the effort to mobilize people through their roles as producers within a new corporative state (see page 894). But though corporativist institutions were gradually constructed, with great rhetorical fanfare, they bogged down in bureaucratic meddling. Corporativism proved more the vehicle for regimentation than for a more genuine kind of participation. Mussolini offered assurances that, despite the necessary compromises, fascism's corporativist revolution was

continuing, but many committed fascists were sharply critical of the new system. Fascism seemed to have stalled, partly as the result of compromise with prefascist elites and institutions, and partly as the result of its own internal contradictions.

Mussolini was never merely the instrument of the established elites, but neither was he a consistent ideologue like Hitler. By the early 1930s, he sometimes seemed satisfied with ritual, spectacle, and the cult of his own infallibility as he juggled the contending forces in fascist Italy. But the limitations he had encountered on the domestic level increasingly frustrated him. On the international level, in contrast, the new context after Hitler came to power offered some welcome space for maneuver. So as the fascist revolution in Italy faltered, Mussolini concentrated increasingly on foreign policy.

Though Italy, like Germany, remained dissatisfied with the territorial status quo, it was not obvious that fascist Italy and Nazi Germany had to end up in the same camp. For one thing, Italy was anxious to preserve an independent Austria as a buffer with Germany, whereas many Germans and Austrians favored the unification of the two countries. Such a greater Germany might then threaten the gains Italy had won at the peace conference at Austria's expense. When, in 1934, Germany seemed poised to absorb Austria, Mussolini helped stiffen the resistance of Austria's leaders and played a part in forcing Hitler to back down. Mussolini even warned that Nazism, with its racist orientation, posed a significant threat to the best of European civilization.

As it began to appear that France and Britain might have to work with the Soviet Union to check Hitler's Germany, French and British conservatives pushed for good relations with Mussolini's Italy to provide ideological balance. So Italy was well positioned to play off both sides as Hitler began shaking things up on the international level after 1933. In 1935, just after Hitler announced significant rearmament measures, unilaterally repudiating provisions of the Versailles treaty for the first time, Mussolini hosted a meeting with the French and British prime ministers at Stresa, in northern Italy. In an overt warning to Hitler's Germany, the three powers agreed to resist "any unilateral repudiation of treaties which may endanger the peace of Europe."

However, Mussolini was already preparing to extend Italy's possessions in East Africa to encompass Ethiopia (formerly called Abyssinia). He assumed that the French and British, who needed his support against Hitler, would not offer significant opposition. Ethiopia had become a League of Nations member in 1923—sponsored by Italy, but opposed by Britain and France because it still practiced slavery. After a border incident in December 1934, Italian troops invaded in October 1935, prompting the League to announce sanctions against Italy.

These sanctions were applied haphazardly, largely because France and Britain wanted to avoid irreparable damage to their longer-term relations with Italy. In any case, the sanctions did not deter Mussolini, whose forces prevailed through the use of aircraft and poison gas by May 1936. But they did make Italy receptive to German overtures in the aftermath of its victory. And the victory made Mussolini more restless. Rather than seeking to play again the enviable role of European balancer, he sent Italian troops and materiel to aid the Nationalists in the Spanish civil war, thereby further alienating democratic opinion elsewhere.

Conservatives in Britain and France continued to push for accommodation with Italy, hoping to revive the "Stresa front" against Hitler. Some even defended Italian imperialism in East Africa. But Italy continued its drift toward Germany. Late in 1936 Mussolini spoke of a new Rome-Berlin Axis for the first time. During 1937 and 1938 he and Hitler exchanged visits. Finally, in May 1939, Italy joined Germany in an open-ended military alliance, the Pact of Steel, but Mussolini made it clear that Italy could not be ready for a major European war before 1943.

To cement this developing relationship, fascist Italy adopted anti-Semitic racial laws, even though Italian fascism had not originally been anti-Semitic. Indeed, the party had attracted Jewish Italians to its membership in about the same proportion as non-Jews. Although the imperial venture in Ethiopia had been popular among the Italian people, the increasing subservience to Nazi Germany displeased even many committed fascists. Such opposition helped keep Mussolini from intervention when war broke out in September 1939.

### ■ Restoring German Sovereignty, 1935–1936

During his first years in power, through 1936, Hitler could be understood as merely restoring German sovereignty, revising a postwar settlement that had been misconceived in the first place. However uncouth and abrasive he might seem, it was hard to find a basis for opposing him. Yet in commencing German rearmament in 1935, and especially in remilitarizing the Rhineland in March 1936, Hitler fundamentally reversed the power balance established in France's favor at the peace conference.

France's special advantage had been the demilitarization of the entire German territory west of the Rhine River and a 50-kilometer strip on the east bank. The measure had been reaffirmed at Locarno in 1925, now with Germany's free agreement, and it was guaranteed by Britain and Italy. Yet on a Saturday morning in March 1936, that advantage disappeared as German troops moved into the forbidden area. The French and British acquiesced, uncertain of what else to do. After all, Hitler was only restoring Germany to full sovereignty.

But Hitler was not likely to stop there. As a result of the war and the peace, three new countries—Austria, Czechoslovakia, and Poland—bordered Germany (see Map 27.2). In each, the peace settlement had left trouble spots involving the status of ethnic Germans; in each, the status quo was open to question.

### ■ Austria, Czechoslovakia, and Appeasement

As early as 1934, Hitler had moved to encompass his homeland, Austria, but strenuous opposition from Italy led him to back down. The developing understanding with Italy by 1936 enabled Hitler to focus again on Austria—initiating the second, more radical phase of his prewar foreign policy. On a pretext in March 1938, German troops moved into Austria, which was promptly incorporated into Germany. This time Mussolini was willing to acquiesce, and Hitler was genuinely grateful.

The Treaty of Versailles had explicitly prohibited this *Anschluss,* or unity of Austria with Germany, though that prohibition violated the principle of self-determination. It was widely believed in the West, no doubt correctly, that most Austrians favored unity with Germany now that the Habsburg Empire had broken up. The Anschluss could thus be justified as revising a misconceived aspect of the peace settlement.

Czechoslovakia presented quite a different situation. Although it had preserved democratic institutions, the country included restive minorities of Slovaks, Magyars, Ruthenians, Poles, and—concentrated especially in the Sudetenland, along the German and Austrian borders—about 3.25 million Germans. After having been part of the dominant nationality in the old Habsburg Empire, those Germans were frustrated with their minority status in the new Czechoslovakia. Worse, they seemed to suffer disproportionately from the Depression. Hitler's agents actively stirred up their resentments.

Leading the West's response, when Hitler began making an issue of Czechoslovakia, was Neville Chamberlain (1869–1940), who followed Stanley Baldwin as Britain's prime minister in May 1937. An intelligent, vigorous, and public-spirited man from the progressive wing of the Conservative party, Chamberlain has long been derided as the architect of the "appeasement" of Hitler at the Munich conference of 1938, which settled

**Map 27.2  The Expansion of Nazi Germany, 1936–1939**  Especially with the remilitarization of the Rhineland in 1936, Hitler's Germany began moving, step by step, to alter the European power balance. In September 1939 the Soviet Union also began annexing territory, capitalizing on its agreement with Germany the month before.

the crisis over Czechoslovakia. Trumpeted as the key to peace, the Munich agreement proved but a step to the war that broke out less than a year later. Yet though it failed, Chamberlain's policy of appeasement stemmed not from cowardice or mere drift, and certainly not from some unspoken pro-Nazi sentiment.

Rather than let events spin out of control, as seemed to have happened in 1914, Chamberlain sought to master the difficult international situation through creative

bargaining. The excesses of Hitler's policy resulted from the mistakes of Versailles; redo the settlement on a more realistic basis, and Germany would behave responsibly. The key, Chamberlain felt, was to pinpoint the sources of Germany's frustrations and, as he put it, "to remove the danger spots one by one."

Moreover, in Britain as elsewhere, there were some who saw Hitler's resurgent Germany as a bulwark against communism, which might spread into east-central

**The Illusion of Peace** Neville Chamberlain, returning home to Britain from Munich to a hero's welcome, waves the peace declaration that was supposed to have brought "peace in our time." This was late September 1938. Less than a year later, Europe was again at war. *(Hulton Getty/Liaison)*

Europe—especially in the event of another war. Indeed, the victor in another war might well be the revolutionary left. To prevent such an outcome was worth a few concessions to Hitler.

The Czechs, led by Eduard Beneš° (1884–1948), made some attempt to liberalize their nationality policy. But by April 1938 they were becoming ever less sympathetic to Sudeten German demands for autonomy, especially as German bullying came to accompany them. Tensions between Czechoslovakia and Germany mounted, and by late September 1938 war appeared imminent, despite Chamberlain's efforts to mediate. (See the box "Reading Sources: Toward Appeasement: The Longing for Peace.") Both the French and the British began mobilizing, with French troops manning the Maginot Line for the first time.

A 1924 treaty bound France to come to the aid of Czechoslovakia in the event of aggression. Moreover, the Soviet Union, according to a treaty of 1935, was bound to assist Czechoslovakia if the French did so. And throughout the crisis, the Soviets pushed for a strong stand in de-

fense of Czechoslovakia against German aggression. For both ideological and military reasons, however, the British and French were reluctant to line up for war on the side of the Soviet Union. The value of the Soviet military was uncertain, at best, at a time when the Soviet officer corps had just been purged.

By September, Hitler seemed eager to smash the Czechs by force, but when Mussolini proposed a four-power conference, he was persuaded to talk again. At Munich late in September, Britain, France, Italy, and Germany settled the matter, with Czechoslovakia—and the Soviet Union—excluded. Determined not to risk war over what seemed Czech intransigence, the British ended up agreeing to what Hitler had wanted all along—not merely autonomy for the Sudeten Germans but German annexation of the Sudetenland.

The Munich agreement specified that all Sudeten areas with German majorities be transferred to Germany. Plebiscites were to be held in areas with large German minorities, and Hitler pledged to respect the sovereignty of the now diminished Czechoslovak state. Chamberlain and his French counterpart, Edouard Daladier, each returned home to a hero's welcome, having transformed

**Beneš** (BAY-naish)

## ◈ READING SOURCES

---

# Toward Appeasement: The Longing for Peace

*Late in September 1938, the crisis that developed over Germany's demands on Czechoslovakia produced an emotional roller coaster for Europeans. Central to the continuing effort to preserve the peace was the British prime minister, Neville Chamberlain, who flew to Germany twice to meet with Hitler before the crisis reached its climax. At first, Chamberlain thought he had found a formula for peace, but then Hitler upped his demands. Thus, Chamberlain's tone was somber when he addressed the British people by radio shortly after his second trip, on September 27, at what proved the height of the crisis.*

---

First of all I must say something to those who have written to my wife or myself in these last weeks to tell us of their gratitude for my efforts and to assure us of their prayers for my success. Most of these letters have come from women—mothers or sisters of our own countrymen. But there are countless others besides—from France, from Belgium, from Italy, even from Germany, and it has been heartbreaking to read of the growing anxiety they reveal. . . .

If I felt my responsibility heavy before, to read such letters has made it seem almost overwhelming. How horrible, fantastic, incredible it is that we should be digging trenches and trying on gas masks here because of a quarrel in a far-away country between people of whom we know nothing. It seems still more impossible that a quarrel which has already been settled in principle should be the subject of war.

I can well understand the reasons why the Czech Government have felt unable to accept the terms which have been put before them in the German memorandum. Yet I believe after my talks with Herr Hitler that, if only time were allowed, it ought to be possible for the arrangements for transferring the territory that the Czech government has agreed to give to Germany to be settled by agreement under condi-

tions which would assure fair treatment to the population concerned. . . .

However much we may sympathise with a small nation confronted by a big and powerful neighbor, we cannot in all circumstances undertake to involve the whole British Empire in war simply on her account. If we have to fight it must be on larger issues than that. . . . [I]f I were convinced that any nation had made up its mind to dominate the world by fear of its force, I should feel that it must be resisted. . . . But war is a fearful thing, and we must be very clear, before we embark on it, that it is really the great issues that are at stake. . . .

For the present I ask you to await as calmly as you can the events of the next few days. As long as war has not begun, there is always hope that it may be prevented, and you know that I am going to work for peace to the last moment. Good night.

---

*Source:* Neville Chamberlain, *In Search of Peace: Speeches (1937–1938)* (London: Hutchinson, 1939), pp. 274–276.

 **For additional information on this topic, go to http://college.hmco.com.**

---

what had seemed certain war to, in Chamberlain's soon-to-be-notorious phrase, "peace in our time."

Rather than settle the nationality questions bedeviling Czechoslovakia, the Munich agreement only provoked further unrest. Poland and Hungary, eager to exploit the new weakness of Czechoslovakia, agitated successfully to annex disputed areas with large numbers of their respective nationalities. Then unrest stemming from Slovak separatism afforded a pretext for Germany to send troops into Prague in March 1939. The Slovak areas were spun off as a separate nation, while the Czech areas became the Protectorate of Bohemia and Moravia.

Less than six months after the Munich conference, most of what had been Czechoslovakia had landed firmly within the Nazi orbit (see Map 27.2). It was no longer possible to justify Hitler's actions as an effort to unite all Germans in one state.

## ■ Poland, the Nazi-Soviet Pact, and the Coming of War

With Poland, the German grievance was still more serious, for the new Polish state had been created partly at German expense. Especially galling to Germans was the Polish corridor, which cut off East Prussia from the bulk of Germany in order to give Poland access to the sea. The city of Danzig (now Gdansk), historically Polish but part of Germany before World War I, was left a "free city," supervised by the League of Nations.

Disillusioned by Hitler's dismemberment of Czechoslovakia, and angered by the Germans' menacing rhetoric regarding Poland, Chamberlain announced to the House of Commons on March 31, 1939, that Britain and France would intervene militarily should Poland's independence be threatened. Chamberlain was not only abandoning the policy of appeasement; he was making a clear commitment to the Continent, of the sort that British governments had resisted since 1919. He could do so partly because Britain was rapidly rearming. By early 1940, in fact, Britain was spending nearly as large a share of its national income on the military as Germany was.

Chamberlain's assertive statement was not enough to deter Hitler, who seems to have been determined to settle the Polish question by force. In an effort to localize the conflict, however, Hitler continued to insist that German aims were limited and reasonable. Germany simply wanted Danzig and German transit across the corridor; it was the Polish stance that was rigid and unreasonable. Hitler apparently believed that Polish stubbornness would alienate the British and French, undercutting their support. And as the crisis developed by mid-1939, doubts were increasingly expressed, on all sides, that the British and French were really prepared to aid Poland militarily—that they had the will "to die for Danzig."

Although they had been lukewarm to Soviet proposals for a military alliance, Britain and France began to negotiate with the Soviet Union more seriously during the spring and summer of 1939. But reservations about the value of a Soviet alliance continued to gnaw at Western leaders. For one thing, Soviet troops could gain access to Germany only by moving through Poland or Romania. But each had territory gained at the expense of Russia in the postwar settlement, so the British and French, suspicious of Soviet designs on both, were reluctant to insist that Soviet troops be allowed to pass through them.

Even as negotiations between the Soviet Union and the democracies continued, the Soviets came to their own agreement with Nazi Germany on August 23, 1939, in a pact that astonished the world. Each side had been denouncing the other, and although Hitler had explored the possibility of Soviet neutrality in May, serious negotiations began only that August, when the Soviets got the clear signal that a German invasion of Poland was inevitable. It now appeared that no Soviet alliance with Britain and France could prevent war. Under these circumstances, a nonaggression pact with Germany seemed better to serve Soviet interests than a problematic war on the side of Britain and France. So the Soviets agreed with the Germans that each would remain neutral in the event that either became involved in a war with some other nation.

The Soviet flip-flop stemmed partly from disillusionment with the British and French response to the accelerating threat of Nazism. The democracies seemed no more trustworthy, and potentially no less hostile, than Nazi Germany. Moreover, a secret protocol to the Nazi-Soviet Pact apportioned major areas of east-central Europe between the Soviet Union and Germany. As a result, the Soviets soon regained much of what they had lost after World War I, when Poland, Finland, and other states had been created or aggrandized with territories that had formerly been part of the Russian Empire.

The Nazi-Soviet Pact seemed to give Hitler the free hand he wanted in Poland. With the dramatic change in alignment, the democracies were surely much less likely to intervene. But Chamberlain, again determined to avoid the hesitations of 1914, publicly reaffirmed the British guarantee to Poland on August 25. Britain would indeed intervene if Germany attacked. And after Hitler ordered the German invasion of Poland on September 1, the British and French responded with declarations of war on September 3.

With each step on the path to war, Hitler had vacillated between apparent reasonableness and wanton aggressiveness. Sometimes he accented the plausibility of his demands in light of problems with the postwar settlement; sometimes he seemed to be actively seeking war. Even in invading Poland, he may still have hoped to localize hostilities. But he was certainly willing to risk a more general European war, and the deepest thrust of his policy was toward an all-out war of conquest—first against Poland, but ultimately against the Soviet Union. War was essential to the Nazi vision, and only when the assault on Poland became a full-scale war did the underlying purposes of Nazism become clear.

# Summary

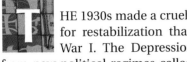

HE 1930s made a cruel mockery of the hopes for restabilization that had followed World War I. The Depression and the challenges from new political regimes called both capitalism and democracy into question. Hitler's Germany, especially, presented an unprecedented challenge to the European order, but the leading democracies, Britain and France, were slow to respond. Eagerness to avoid another war affected their reactions, as did the ideological polarization of the decade. Led by Britain, the democracies began seriously resisting the Nazi challenge only in 1939.

During the 1930s the democracies had to respond to three novel regimes—Italian fascism, German Nazism, and Stalinist communism—that did not play by the expected rules. Although their originating purposes differed, each was totalitarian in seeking the total political mobilization of the population, so that even leisure-time activities took on a public or political dimension. And each claimed to be superior partly because of its capacity to mobilize people for great collective projects as democratic regimes could not. But though they did involve ordinary people in new ways, each of the three regimes concentrated power in the hands of dictators. Thus they were at once dynamic and unpredictable— and thus, in part, the hesitancy and uncertainty of the democracies in dealing with them.

At the same time, the hesitations of the democracies during the 1930s tended to confirm the view of the three dictators that democracy was weak, decadent, passé. Such contempt inclined Mussolini and Hitler to ever greater recklessness, and persuaded Stalin finally to make his own deal with the Nazis in August 1939. When he invaded Poland on September 1, Hitler seriously believed the democracies would let him have his way. It was hardly clear that this would end up another European war, let alone the most destructive, cataclysmic war the world had ever seen.

## ■ Notes

1. Quoted in Martin McCauley, *The Soviet Union Since 1917* (London and New York: Longman, 1981), pp. 72–73.
2. Quoted in Robert Conquest, *The Great Terror: A Reassessment* (New York: Oxford University Press, 1990), p. 24.
3. Quoted in Helmut Krausnick et al., *Anatomy of the SS State* (New York: Walker, 1968), p. 13.

## ■ Suggested Reading

Bell, P. M. H. *The Origins of the Second World War in Europe.* 2d ed. 1997. A well-organized and fair-minded survey.

Boffa, Giuseppe. *The Stalin Phenomenon.* 1992. An invaluable historiographical survey—thorough, balanced, and accessible.

Burleigh, Michael, and Wolfgang Wippermann. *The Racial State: Germany 1933–1945.* 1991. Influential, thoroughly researched study of the Nazi quest for "race hygiene."

Fischer, Klaus P. *Nazi Germany: A New History.* 1995. Comprehensive and well researched, this is perhaps the best one-volume treatment of Nazism in English.

Fitzpatrick, Sheila. *Everyday Stalinism, Ordinary Life in Extraordinary Times: Soviet Russia in the 1930s.* 1999. An engaging, balanced account of urban life in the Soviet Union in the context of the upheavals of the 1930s.

Kershaw, Ian. *Hitler,* Vol. 1: *1889–1936, Hubris,* and Vol. 2: *1936–1945, Nemesis.* 1999, 2000. A thorough, very readable biography by a leading authority on Nazism.

Payne, Stanley G. *A History of Fascism, 1914–1945.* 1995. A comprehensive account with historical and interpretive sections, as well as an epilogue on the scope for neofascism.

Watt, Donald Cameron. *How War Came: The Immediate Origins of the Second World War, 1938–1939.* 1989. Detailed but readable narrative account, based on thorough research.

Weber, Eugen. *The Hollow Years: France in the 1930s.* 1994. A lively account of French life and manners during a decade that led to humiliation and defeat.

 **For a searchable list of additional readings for this chapter, go to http://college.hmco.com.**

# Film as Propaganda

One of the extraordinary pieces of evidence from the Nazi period is *Triumph of the Will,* a documentary film on the sixth Nazi Party rally, which took place September 4–10, 1934, in the historic city of Nuremberg, by this time the official site for such party rallies. Directed by a talented young woman, Leni Riefenstahl (b. 1902), *Triumph of the Will* has long been recognized as one of the most compelling propaganda films ever made. What can we learn from this film about how the Nazis understood and used propaganda? What was the Nazi regime trying to convey in sponsoring the film, with the particular images it contained?

A sense of the scope for political propaganda was one of the defining features of the Nazi movement virtually from its inception. In his quest for power Hitler allotted an especially significant role to his future propaganda minister, Joseph Goebbels. Both Hitler and Goebbels saw that new media and carefully orchestrated events might be used to shape the political views of masses of people.

The Nazi Party held the first of what would become annual conventions in Nuremberg in 1927. From the start, these meetings were rallies of the faithful, intended to give the Nazi movement a sense of cohesion and common purpose; but they increasingly became carefully staged propaganda spectacles, with banners and searchlights, parades and speeches. When, by 1934, the regime had completed the task of immediate power consolidation, it seemed time to seize the potential of the film medium to carry the spectacle beyond those present in Nuremberg. The intention to make a film thus influenced the staging of the 1934 rally. Film would transform the six-day event into a single potent work of art.

When Hitler came to power, Goebbels, as propaganda minister, assumed control of the German film industry, and he was particularly jealous of his prerogatives in this sphere. If there was to be a film of one of the Nuremberg rallies, he assumed that he would be in charge. So he objected strenuously when Hitler decided that Riefenstahl, who was not even a party member, should film the 1934 rally.

Already popular as an actress, Riefenstahl had established her own film-making company in 1931, before she turned 30. Her first film won the admiration of Hitler, who sought her out and eventually proposed that she di-rect the film of the party rally. Although she was an artist with no special interest in politics, Riefenstahl, like many Germans, believed at this point that Hitler might be able to revive Germany's fortunes. So despite considerable reluctance, she bowed to Hitler's persistence and agreed to do the film—though only after she was guaranteed final control over editing. Her relations with Goebbels remained strained, but Hitler continued to support her as she made *Triumph of the Will.*

Riefenstahl developed the 107-minute film by editing sixty-one hours of footage that covered everything from Hitler's arrival and motorcade to the closing parades and speeches. As depicted on film, the party rally does not convey an overt ideological message. We hear Hitler not attacking Jews or glorifying conquest but simply trumpeting German renewal. What strikes us in Riefenstahl's portrayal are the unity and epic monumentality that Nazism had apparently brought to Germany thanks to Hitler's leadership.

The film opens as Hitler emerges from dramatic cloud formations to arrive by airplane, descending from the sky like a god. He appears throughout the film as an almost superhuman figure, even, as in the shot shown here, as inspired, possessed, uncanny. Above all, he is a

As seen in *Triumph of the Will,* the Leader . . .

**. . . and the Disciplined, Tightly Knit Community of Followers** *(Both photos from the Museum of Modern Art/Film Stills Archive)*

creator who shapes reality by blending will and art, forging masses of anonymous individuals into one people, one racial community, ready for anything. Those individuals seem, from one perspective, to lose their individuality in a monolithic mass, as in the shot of the parade grounds. But their sense of involvement in grandiose purposes charges them emotionally, even gives them a kind of ecstasy. The symbols, the massed banners, the ritualistic show of conformity, all strengthened this sense of participation in the new people's community. But unity and community were not ends in themselves; the film exalted military values and depicted a disciplined society organized for war.

*Triumph of the Will* extended participation in the spectacle to those who were not actually present in Nuremberg. The film chiseled the sprawling event into a work of art, so seeing the film was in some ways more effective than being there. The Nazis looked for every means possible to involve the whole society in ritualistic spectacles that could promote a sense of belonging and unity. In addition to film, they made effective use of radio, even subsidizing the purchase of radio sets, or "people's receivers." Such new media were to help ordinary Germans feel a more meaningful kind of belonging than possible under the democracy of the Weimar Republic. But this was only an emotional involvement, not the active participation of free citizens invited to make rational choices.

*Triumph of the Will* had its premiere in March 1935, with Hitler in the audience. It won several prizes in Germany and abroad but enjoyed only mixed success with the German public, especially outside the large cities. For some, it was altogether too artistic, and the Nazi regime did not use it widely for overt propaganda purposes. Still, the Nazis commissioned no other film about Hitler, for *Triumph of the Will* captured the way he wanted to be seen. Indeed, Hitler praised the film as an "incomparable glorification of the power and beauty of our Movement."

---

 **For additional information on this topic, go to http://college.hmco.com.**

# CHAPTER 28

# The Era of the Second World War 1939–1949

THE effects could well be called unprecedented, magnificent, beautiful, stupendous and terrifying. No manmade phenomenon of such tremendous power had ever occurred before. . . . Thirty seconds after the explosion came first, the air blast pressing hard against the people and things, to be followed almost immediately by the strong, sustained, awesome roar which warned of doomsday and made us feel that we puny things were blasphemous to dare tamper with the forces heretofore reserved to The Almighty."[1]

So wrote Brigadier General Thomas F. Farrell, who had just witnessed the birth of the atomic age. On July 16, 1945, watching from a shelter 10,000 yards away, Farrell had seen the first explosion of an atomic bomb at a remote, top-secret U.S. government testing ground near Alamogordo, New Mexico. Such a weapon had been little more than a theoretical possibility when World War II began, and it required a remarkable concentration of effort, centered first in Britain, then in the United States, to make possible the awesome spectacle that confronted General Farrell. Exceeding most expectations, the test revealed a weapon of unprecedented power and destructiveness.

Within weeks, the United States dropped two other atomic bombs—first on Hiroshima, then on Nagasaki—to force the surrender of Japan in August 1945. Thus ended the Second World War, the conflict that had begun six long years earlier with the German invasion of Poland. At first Germany enjoyed remarkable success, prompting Italy to intervene—and encouraging Japanese aggressiveness as well. But Britain held on even after its ally, France, fell to Germany in 1940. Then

Atomic bombing of Nagasaki, August 9, 1945. When this photo was taken, from an observation plane 6 miles up, thirty-five thousand people on the ground had already died.
(By courtesy of the Trustees of the Imperial War Museum)

the war changed character in 1941 when Germany attacked the Soviet Union and Japan attacked the United States.

Britain, the United States, and the Soviet Union quickly came together in a "Grand Alliance," which spearheaded the victorious struggle against the Axis powers, Germany, Italy, and Japan. In Europe, the Soviet victory in a brutal land war with Germany proved decisive. In East Asia and the Pacific, the Americans gradually prevailed against Japan. The American use of the atomic bomb to end the war was the final stage in an escalation of violence that made World War II the most destructive in history. What the advent of this terrifying new weapon would mean for the future remained unclear in the war's immediate aftermath.

The ironic outcome of the Second World War was a new cold war between the two major victors, the United States and the Soviet Union. Emerging from the war with far greater power and prestige, each assumed a world role that would have been hard to imagine just a few years earlier. By the end of the 1940s, these two new superpowers had divided Europe into competing spheres of influence. Indeed, the competition between the United States and the Soviet Union almost immediately became global in scope, creating a bipolar world. And the cold war between them was especially terrifying because, seeking military advantage, they raced to stockpile ever more destructive nuclear weapons. Thus the threat of nuclear annihilation helped define the cold war era.

World War II led to the defeat of Italy, Germany, and Japan and in this sense resolved the conflicts that had caused it. But the experience of this particular war changed the world forever. Before finally meeting defeat, the Nazis were sufficiently successful to begin implementing their "new order" in Europe, especially in the territories they conquered to the east. As part of this effort, in what has become known as the Holocaust, they began systematically murdering Jews in extermination camps, eventually killing as many as 6 million. The most destructive of the camps was at Auschwitz°, in what had been Poland. Often paired after the war, Auschwitz and Hiroshima came to stand for the incredible new forms of death and destruction that the war had spawned—and that continued to haunt the world long after it had ended, posing new questions about the meaning of Western civilization.

## QUESTIONS TO CONSIDER

- How did the Allies manage to defeat Germany in World War II, after Germany's remarkable successes during the war's first two years?

- Does it make sense to link the Holocaust and the atomic bombing of Japan as radically new forms of violence emerging from the Second World War, or are they better seen as fundamentally dissimilar?

- What are the arguments for and against the Allied policy of forcing Nazi leaders to stand trial after Germany's military defeat?

- What was the relationship between the Allied victory in World War II and the coming of the cold war?

## TERMS TO KNOW

| | |
|---|---|
| Vichy France | United Nations |
| Winston Churchill | Potsdam conference |
| Auschwitz-Birkenau | Nuremberg trials |
| Stalingrad | cold war |
| "the Great Patriotic War" | Truman Doctrine |
| Franklin Delano Roosevelt | |
| lend-lease | |
| D-Day | |
| Yalta conference | |

**Auschwitz** (OWSH-vits)

# THE VICTORY OF NAZI GERMANY, 1939–1941

NSTEAD of the enthusiasm evident in 1914, the German invasion of Poland on September 1, 1939, produced a grim sense of foreboding, even in Germany. Well-publicized incidents such as the German bombing of civilians during the Spanish civil war and the Italian use of poison gas in Ethiopia suggested that the frightening new technologies introduced in World War I would now be used on a far greater scale. The new conflict would be a much uglier war, more directly involving civilians.

Still, as in 1914, there were hopes that this war could be localized and brief—that it would not become a "world war." Hitler and the Germans envisioned a *Blitzkrieg*, or "lightning war," and the initial outcome seemed to confirm these expectations. Poland fell quickly, and Hitler publicly offered peace to Britain and France, seriously thinking that might be the end of it. The British and French refused to call off the war, but from 1939 through 1941 the Nazis won victory after victory, establishing the foundation for their new order in Europe.

## ■ Initial Conquests and "Phony War"

The Polish army was large enough to have given the Germans a serious battle. But in adapting the technological innovations of World War I, Germany had developed a new military strategy based on rapid mobility. This Blitzkrieg strategy employed swift, highly concentrated offensives based on mobile tanks covered with concentrated air support, including dive-bombers that struck just ahead of the tanks. In Poland this strategy proved decisive. The French could offer only token help, and the last Polish unit surrendered on October 2, barely a month after the fighting had begun. The speed of the German victory stunned the world.

Meanwhile, the Soviets began cashing in on the pact they had made with Nazi Germany a few weeks before. It offered a precious opportunity to undo provisions of the World War I settlement that had significantly diminished the western territories of the former Russian Empire. On September 17, with the German victory in Poland assured, Stalin sent Soviet forces westward to share in the spoils. Soon Poland was again divided between Germany and Russia, just as most of it had been before 1914. The Baltic states of Estonia, Latvia, and Lithuania soon fell as well.

## CHRONOLOGY

| | |
|---|---|
| September 1, 1939 | Germany invades Poland |
| 1939–1940 | Soviets wage "Winter War" against Finland |
| 1940 | Germany attacks Denmark and Norway (April) |
| | Germany attacks the Netherlands, Belgium, and France (May 10) |
| 1941 | Germany attacks the Soviet Union (June 22) |
| | Churchill and Roosevelt agree to the Atlantic Charter (August) |
| December 7, 1941 | Japan attacks Pearl Harbor |
| August 1942–February 1943 | Battle of Stalingrad |
| November 1942 | Allied landings in North Africa |
| April–May 1943 | Warsaw ghetto revolt |
| 1943 | Soviet victory in Battle of Kursk-Orel (July) |
| | Allied landings in Sicily; fall of Mussolini; Italy asks for an armistice (July) |
| | Teheran conference (November) |
| June 6, 1944 | D-Day: Allied landings in Normandy |
| February 1945 | Yalta conference |
| May 7–8, 1945 | Germany surrenders |
| June 1945 | Founding of the United Nations |
| July–August 1945 | Potsdam conference |
| August 6, 1945 | U.S. atomic bombing of Hiroshima |
| August 14, 1945 | Japan surrenders |
| March 1947 | Truman Doctrine |
| June 1948–May 1949 | Berlin blockade and airlift |
| August 1949 | First Soviet atomic bomb |
| September 1949 | Founding of the Federal Republic in West Germany |

**Map 28.1  World War II: European Theaters**  Much of Europe saw fighting during World War II, although different fronts were important at different times. What proved decisive was the fighting that ensued in the vast expanse of the Soviet Union after the Germans invaded in June 1941.

When Finland proved less pliable, the Soviets invaded in November 1939. In the ensuing "Winter War," the Finns held out bravely, and only by taking heavy casualties did the Soviets manage to prevail by March 1940. These difficulties seemed to confirm suspicions that Stalin's purge during the mid-1930s had substantially weakened the Soviet army. Still, by midsummer 1940 the Soviet Union had regained much of the territory it had lost during the upheavals surrounding the revolution of 1917.

In the west, little happened during the strained winter of 1939–1940, known as the "Phony War." Then, on April 9, 1940, the Germans attacked Norway and Denmark in a surprise move to preempt a British and French scheme to cut off the major route for the shipment of Swedish iron ore to Germany. Denmark fell almost at once, while the staunch resistance in Norway was effectively broken by the end of April. The stage was set for the German assault on France.

## ■ The Fall of France, 1940

The war in the west began in earnest on May 10, 1940, when the Germans attacked France and the Low Countries. They launched their assault on France through the Ardennes Forest, above the northern end of the Maginot Line—terrain so difficult the French had discounted the possibility of an enemy strike there (see page 884). As in 1914, northern France quickly became the focus of a major war pitting French forces and their British allies against invading Germans. But this time, in startling contrast to World War I, the Battle of France was over in less than six weeks, a humiliating defeat for the French.

The problem for France was not lack of men and materiel, but strategy: how men and materiel were used. For example, Germany had only a slight numerical advantage in tanks. But in France, as in Poland, Germany took advantage of mobile tanks and dive-bombers to mount rapid, highly concentrated offensives. Germany achieved the essential breakthrough partly because the French command underestimated the speed with which the German army could move through Belgium.

Anticipating another long, defensive war, France had dispersed its tanks among infantry units along a broad front. Once the German tank column broke through the French lines, it quickly cut through northern France toward the North Sea. France's poor showing convinced the British that rather than commit troops and planes to a hopeless battle in France, they should get out and regroup for a longer global war. Finally, 200,000 British troops—as well as 130,000 French—escaped German encirclement and capture through a difficult evacuation at Dunkirk early in June (see Map 28.1).

By mid-June, Germany had won a decisive victory. As the French military collapsed, the French cabinet resigned, to be replaced by a new government under Marshal Philippe Pétain, who had led the successful French effort in the Battle of Verdun during World War I. Pétain's government first asked for an armistice and then engineered a change of regime. The French parliament voted by an overwhelming majority to give Pétain exceptional powers, including the power to draw up a new constitution. So ended the parliamentary democracy of the Third Republic, which seemed responsible for France's weakness. The republic gave way to the more authoritarian Vichy° regime, named after the resort city to which the government retreated as the Germans moved into Paris. The end of the fighting in France resulted in a kind of antidemocratic revolution, but one in which the French people, stunned by military defeat, at first acquiesced.

According to the armistice agreement, the French government was not only to cease hostilities but also to collaborate with the victorious Germans. French resistance began immediately, however. In a radio broadcast from London on June 18, Charles de Gaulle° (1890–1970), the youngest general in the French army, called on French forces to rally to him to continue the fight against Nazi Germany. The military forces stationed in the French colonies, as well as the French troops that had been evacuated at Dunkirk, could form the nucleus of a new French army. Under the circumstances of military defeat and political change, de Gaulle's appeal seemed quixotic at best, and most French colonies went along with what seemed the legitimate French government at Vichy. For the new Vichy government, de Gaulle was a traitor. Yet a new Free French force grew from de Gaulle's remarkable appeal, and its subsequent role in the war helped overcome the humiliation of France's quick defeat in 1940.

What next for Hitler and the Germans, who seemed virtually invincible after their conquest of France? Ultimately decisive would be the assault on the Soviet Union in June 1941, but two chains of events after the Battle of France influenced the timing of the assault—perhaps in crucial ways. Britain proved a more implacable foe, and Italy a more burdensome friend, than Hitler had expected.

---

**Vichy** (VEE-shee)    **de Gaulle** (duh GOHL)

## ■ Winston Churchill and the Battle of Britain

With the defeat of France, Hitler seems to have expected that Britain, now apparently vulnerable to German invasion, would come to terms. And certainly some prominent Britons did question the wisdom of remaining at war. But the British war effort found a new and effective champion in Winston Churchill (1874–1965), who replaced Neville Chamberlain as prime minister on May 10, when the German invasion of western Europe began. Although Churchill had been prominent in British public life for years, his career to this point had not been noteworthy for either judgment or success. He was obstinate, difficult, something of a curmudgeon. Yet he rose to the wartime challenge, becoming one of the notable leaders of the modern era. In speeches to the House of Commons during the remainder of 1940, he inspired his nation with some of the most memorable words of the war. Though some found a negotiated settlement with Germany even more sensible in light of the outcome in

France, Churchill's dogged promise of "blood, toil, tears, and sweat" helped rally the British people, so that later he could say, without exaggeration, that "this was their finest hour."

After the fall of France, Churchill's Britain promptly moved to full mobilization for a protracted war. Indeed, Britain developed the most thoroughly coordinated war economy of all the belligerents, producing more tanks, aircraft, and machine guns than Germany did between 1940 and 1942. The National Service Act of 1941 subjected men aged 18 to 50 and women aged 20 to 30 to military or civilian war service. The upper age limits were subsequently raised to meet the demand for labor. Almost 70 percent of the 3 million people added to the British work force during the war were women.

Britain, then, intended to continue the fight even after France fell. Hitler weighed his options and decided to attack. In light of British naval superiority, he hoped to rely on aerial bombardment to knock the British out of the war without an actual invasion. The ensuing Battle of

**British Resistance**    At the height of the German bombing of Britain in 1940, Winston Churchill surveys the damage in London.    *(Hulton Getty/Tony Stone Images)*

Britain culminated in the nightly bombing of London from September 7 through November 2, 1940, killing fifteen thousand and destroying thousands of buildings. But the British held. Ordinary people holed up in cellars and subway stations, while the fighter planes of the Royal Air Force fought back effectively, inflicting heavy losses against German aircraft over Britain.

Although the bombing continued into 1941, the British had withstood the worst the Germans could deliver, and Hitler began looking to the east, his ultimate objective all along. In December 1940 he ordered preparations for Operation Barbarossa, the assault on the Soviet Union. Rather than continuing the attack on Britain directly, Germany would use submarines to cut off shipping—and thus the supplies the British needed for a long war. Once Germany had defeated the Soviet Union, it would enjoy the geopolitical basis for world power, while Britain, as an island nation relying on a dispersed empire, would sooner or later be forced to come to terms.

### ■ Italian Intervention and the Spread of the War

Lacking sufficient domestic support, and unready for a major war, Mussolini could only look on as the war began in 1939. But as the Battle of France neared its end, it seemed safe for Italy to intervene, sharing in the spoils of what appeared certain victory. Thus in June 1940 Italy entered the war, expecting to secure territorial advantages in the Mediterranean, starting with Corsica, Nice, and Tunisia at the expense of France. Italy also hoped eventually to supplant Britain in the region—and even to take the Suez Canal.

Although Hitler and Mussolini got along reasonably well, their relationship was sensitive. When Hitler seemed to be proceeding without Italy during the first year of the war, Mussolini grew determined to show his independence and finally, in October 1940, ordered Italian forces to attack Greece. But the Greeks mounted a strong resistance, thanks partly to the help of British forces from North Africa.

Meanwhile, Germany had established its hegemony in much of east-central Europe without military force, often by exploiting grievances over the outcome of the peace conference in 1919. In November 1940 Romania and Hungary joined the Axis camp, and Bulgaria followed a few months later. But in March 1941, just after Yugoslavia had similarly committed to the Axis, a coup overthrew the pro-Axis government in Yugoslavia, and the new Yugoslav government prepared to aid the Allies.

By this point Hitler had decided it was expedient to push into the Balkans with German troops, both to reinforce the Italians and to consolidate Axis control of the area. As the war's geographic extent expanded, its stakes increased, yet the Germans continued to meet every challenge. By the end of May 1941 they had taken Yugoslavia and Greece (see Map 28.1).

At the same time, the war was spreading to North Africa and the Middle East because of European colonial ties. The native peoples of the area sought to take advantage of the conflict among the Europeans to pursue their own independence. Iraq and Syria became involved as Germans operating from Syria, administered by Vichy France, aided anti-British Arab nationalists in Iraq. But most important proved to be North Africa, where Libya, an Italian colony since 1912, lay adjacent to Egypt, where the British presence remained strong.

In September 1940 the Italian army drove 65 miles into Egypt, initiating almost three years of fighting across the North African desert. A British counteroffensive from December 1940 to February 1941 drove the Italians back 340 miles into Libya, prompting Germany to send some of its forces from the Balkans into North Africa. Under General Erwin Rommel (1891–1944), the famous "Desert Fox," Axis forces won remarkable successes in North Africa from February to May 1941. But successful though they had been to this point, the German forays into the Balkans and North Africa had delayed the crucial attack on the Soviet Union.

## THE ASSAULT ON THE SOVIET UNION AND THE NAZI NEW ORDER

GERMAN troops invaded the Soviet Union on June 22, 1941, initiating what proved the decisive confrontation of World War II. Although the Nazis enjoyed the expected successes for a while, the Soviets eventually prevailed, spearheading the Allied victory in Europe. Supplies from their new Allies—Britain and eventually the United States—aided the Soviet cause, but the surprising strength of the Soviet military effort was the most important factor in the eventual outcome. In the process, though, the Soviets suffered incredible casualties, and after they gained the initiative, they proceeded with particular brutality as they forced the invading Germans back into Germany.

In doing so, the Soviets were responding to the unprecedented form of warfare that the Nazis had unleashed. In preparing for the attack on the Soviet Union, Hitler had made it clear to the Nazi leadership that this was to be no ordinary military engagement but a war of racial-ideological extermination. And the Germans penetrated well into the Soviet Union, reaching the apex of

954

**Map 28.2 The Nazi New Order in Europe, 1942** At the zenith of its power in 1942, Nazi Germany controlled much of Europe. Concerned most immediately with winning the war, the Nazis sought to coordinate the economies of their satellite states and conquered territories. But they also began establishing what was supposed to be an enduring new order in eastern Europe. The inset shows the location of the major Nazi concentration camps and of the six extermination camps the Nazis constructed in what had been Poland.

**Forgive me, comrade . . .** On June 23, 1941, the day after Nazi Germany attacked the Soviet Union, the London *Daily Mail* published this cartoon depicting Hitler's betrayal of his 1939 pact with Stalin. *(Daily Mail, London, 23 June 1941. Reprinted with permission of Solo Syndication Limited)*

their power late in 1942. German conquests by that point enabled Hitler to begin constructing the new, race-based European order he had dreamed of. Although in western Europe the Nazis generally sought the collaboration of local leaders, in the Soviet Union, as in Poland, the new order meant brutal subjugation of local populations. As part of this process, the Nazis began systematically killing Jews, first by shooting, then by mass gassing in specially constructed death camps.

### ■ An Ambiguous Outcome, 1941–1942

In ordering preparations for Operation Barbarossa in December 1940, Hitler decided to risk attacking the Soviet Union before knocking Britain out of the war. Then he invaded the Balkans and North Africa in what may

have been an unnecessary diversion. In retrospect, it is easy to pinpoint that combination as his fatal mistake. But in light of the Soviet purges of the 1930s and what seemed the poor performance of the Soviet army against Finland, Hitler had reason to believe the Soviet Union would crack relatively easily. Western military experts had come to similar conclusions, estimating that German forces would need but six weeks to take Moscow. And if Germany were to defeat the Soviet Union with another Blitzkrieg, it could gain control of the oil and other resources required for a longer war against Britain and, if necessary, the United States.

Attacking the Soviet Union on June 22, 1941, German forces achieved notable successes during the first month of fighting, partly because Stalin was so unprepared for this German betrayal. Ignoring warnings of an impending German assault, he had continued to live up to his end of the 1939 bargain with Hitler, even supplying the Germans with oil and grain. After the attack, Russia's defenses were at first totally disorganized, and by late November, German forces were within 20 miles of Moscow.

But the Germans were ill equipped for Russian weather, and as an early and severe winter descended, the German offensive bogged down. In December the Soviets mounted a formidable surprise counterattack near Moscow. The German Blitzkrieg, which had seemed a sure thing in July, had failed; Germany might still prevail, but a different strategy would be required.

Although their initial assault had stalled, the Germans still had the advantage. German forces failed to take the key city of Leningrad in 1941, but they cut it off by blockade and, until early 1944, kept it under siege with relentless bombing and shelling. And during the summer of 1942, they mounted another offensive, moving more deeply into the Soviet Union than before, reaching Stalingrad in November. But this proved the deepest penetration of German forces—and the zenith of Nazi power in Europe.

### ■ Hitler's New Order

By the summer of 1942, Nazi Germany dominated the European continent as no power ever had before (see Map 28.2). German military successes allowed the Nazi regime to begin building a new order in the territories under German domination. Satellite states in Slovakia and Croatia, and client governments in Romania and Hungary, owed their existence to Nazi Germany and readily adapted themselves to the Nazi system. Elsewhere in the Nazi orbit, some countries proved eager collaborators; others did their best to resist; still others were given no opportunity to collaborate but were ruthlessly subjugated instead.

The Nazis' immediate aim was simply to exploit the conquered territories to serve the continuing war effort. Precisely as envisioned, access to the resources of so much of Europe made Germany considerably less vulnerable to naval blockade than it had been during World War I. France proved a particularly valuable source of raw materials; by 1943, for example, 75 percent of French iron ore went to German factories.

But the deeper purposes of the war were also clear in the way the Nazis treated the territories under their control, especially in the difference between east and west. Western Europe experienced plenty of atrocities, but Nazi victory there still led to something like conventional military occupation. The Germans tried to enlist the cooperation of local authorities in countries like Denmark, the Netherlands, and France, though with mixed results. And though the Nazis exploited the economy of France, for example, it never became clear what role France might play in Europe after a Nazi victory. However, in Poland and later in the conquered parts of the Soviet Union, there was no pretense of cooperation, and it was immediately clear what the Nazi order would entail.

After the conquest of Poland, the Germans annexed the western part of the country outright and promptly executed, jailed, or expelled members of the Polish elite—professionals, journalists, business leaders, and priests. The Nazis prohibited the Poles from entering the professions and restricted even their right to marry. All the Polish schools and most of the churches were simply closed.

In the rest of Poland, known as the General Government, Nazi policy was slightly less brutal at first. Most churches remained open, and Poles were allowed to practice the professions, but the Nazis closed most schools above the fourth grade, as well as libraries, theaters, and museums as they sought to root out every expression of Polish culture. Some Poles in this area were forced into slave labor, but a final decision as to whether the Polish population was to be exterminated, enslaved, or shipped off to Siberia was postponed—to be made after the victory. (See the box "Reading Sources: Toward the Nazi New Order.")

With the conquest of Poland, Nazi leaders proclaimed that a new era of monumental resettlement in eastern Europe had begun for Germany. Germans selected for their racial characteristics were now resettled in the part of Poland annexed to Germany. Most were ethnic Germans who had been living outside Germany. During the fall of 1942, Heinrich Himmler's *Schutzstaffel*

(SS), the select Nazi elite, began to arrest and expel peasants from the rest of Poland to make way for further German resettlement. By 1943 perhaps 1 million Germans had been moved into what had been Poland.

After the assault on the Soviet Union, Hitler made it clear that eastern Europe as far as the Ural Mountains was to be opened for German settlement. War veterans were to be given priority, partly because the German settlers would have to be tough to resist the Slavs, who would be concentrated east of the Urals. To prepare for German colonization, Himmler told SS leaders that Germany would have to exterminate 30 million Slavs in the Soviet Union. After the German invasion, the SS promptly began executing prisoners of war, as well as any Soviet leaders they could find. However, the Nazis expected that several generations would be required for the resettlement of European Russia.

## ■ The Holocaust

Conquest of the east also opened the way to a more radical solution to the "Jewish problem" than the Nazis had ever contemplated before. Under the cover of war, they began actually killing the Jews within their orbit. Thus began the process, and the experience, that has come to be known as the Holocaust.

When and why this radical policy was chosen remains controversial. Although prewar Nazi rhetoric occasionally suggested the possibility of actual physical extermination, talk of a "final solution to the Jewish problem" seemed to mean forced emigration. Although the precise chain of events that led to a more radical approach will no doubt remain uncertain, it was surely bound up with the fortunes of the war.

The conquest of Poland, with a Jewish population of 3.3 million, gave the Nazis control over a far greater number of Jews than ever before. In 1940, as part of their effort to create a new order, the Nazis began confining Polish Jews to ghettos set up in Warsaw and five other cities. Although much brutality, and many deaths, accompanied this process, the Nazis had not yet adopted a policy of systematic killing. Indeed, at first no one knew what was to become of these Jews. At this point the Nazis were concentrating on removing, or even killing, non-Jewish Poles to make way for German resettlement into former Polish lands. The fate of the Jews would be decided later.

After the defeat of France, Himmler and the SS made tentative plans to develop a kind of superghetto for perhaps 4 million Jews on the island of Madagascar, at that point still a French colony, once the war had been won. However, as the Polish ghettos grew more crowded and

## ✿ READING SOURCES

### Toward the Nazi New Order

*After Nazi Germany conquered much of Poland in 1939, the SS assumed major responsibility for creating a new Nazi order in the conquered territories. In a memorandum dated May 15, 1940, and endorsed by Hitler, the SS leader Heinrich Himmler offered "some thoughts on the treatment of the alien population in the east." The passages that follow make clear the racist basis of Nazi wartime policy.*

In our treatment of the foreign ethnic groups in the east we must . . . fish out the racially valuable people from this mishmash, take them to Germany and assimilate them there.

. . . The non-German population of the eastern territories must not receive any education higher than that of elementary school with four forms [grades]. The objective of this elementary school must simply be to teach: simple arithmetic up to 500 at the most, how to write one's name, and to teach that it is God's commandment to be obedient to the Germans and to be honest, hard-working, and well-behaved. I consider it unnecessary to teach reading.

There must be no schools at all in the east apart from this type of school. Parents who wish to provide their children with a better education both in the elementary school and later in a secondary school, must make an application to the higher SS and Police Leader. . . . If we recognize such a child as being of our blood then the parents will be informed that the child will be placed in a school in Germany and will remain in Germany indefinitely. . . .

The parents of these children of good blood will be given the choice of either giving up their child . . . or they would have to agree to go to Germany and become loyal citizens there. . . .

Apart from the examination of the petitions which parents put forward for a better education, all 6–10 year olds will be sifted each year to sort out those with valuable blood and those with worthless blood. Those who are selected as valuable will be treated in the same way as the children who are admitted on the basis of the approval of the parents' petition.

. . . [T]he moment the children and parents arrive in Germany they should not be treated in school and life as outcasts but—after changing their names and despite being treated with vigilance—should be integrated into German life on the basis of trust. The children must not be made to feel rejected; for, after all, we believe in our own blood, which through the mistakes of German history has flowed into a foreign nation, and are convinced that our ideology and ideals will find an echo in the souls of these children which are racially identical to our own. . . . Abusive expressions such as "Polack" or "Ukrainian" and such like must be out of the question. . . .

After these measures have been systematically implemented during the next ten years, the population of the General Government will inevitably consist of an inferior remnant. . . . This population will be available as a leaderless laboring class and provide Germany with migrant and seasonal labor for special work projects (road-building, quarries, construction); even then they will get more to eat and have more from life than under Polish rule.

*Source:* J. Noakes and G. Pridham, *Nazism, 1919–1945: A Documentary Reader,* vol. 3: *Foreign Policy, War and Racial Extermination* (Exeter: University of Exeter Press, 1988).

---

difficult to manage, Nazi officials in Poland began pressing for a more immediate solution.

At the same time, Hitler made it clear, in preparing for the invasion of the Soviet Union, that Barbarossa would be an escalation—a racial-ideological war of annihilation. And accompanying the military forces were specially trained SS units, essentially mobile killing squads, assigned to get rid of Communist Party officials and adult male Jews. But some were soon murdering Jewish women and children as well. By late November 1941, the Nazis had killed 136,000 Jews, most by shooting, in the invaded Soviet territories. But this mode of

**The End of the Warsaw Ghetto**    In April 1943 the sixty thousand Jews remaining in the Warsaw ghetto revolted rather than face shipment to the extermination camps. Many died in the ensuing fighting; others perished as the Germans set fire to the ghetto. Almost all the rest were captured and sent to their deaths at Treblinka. Before it was put down in May, the uprising killed at least three hundred Germans.    *(AP/Wide World Photos)*

killing proved both inefficient and psychologically burdensome—even for these specially trained killers. Their experience in the Soviet Union combined with the problems in the Polish ghettos to lead Nazi leaders to begin seeking a more systematic and impersonal method of mass extermination by late summer 1941.

The most likely scenario is that Hitler settled on physical extermination of the Jews in the thrill of what seemed impending victory over the Soviet Union. At the end of July 1941, Reinhard Heydrich of the SS began developing a detailed plan, and by fall the Nazis were sending German and Austrian Jews to the ghettos in Poland and actively impeding further Jewish emigration from Europe.

Heydrich explained his plan for the extermination of the Jews in January 1942 at a conference of high-ranking officials at Wannsee, a suburb of Berlin. The conference had been postponed from November, and by now the operation had already begun. The Nazis took advantage of the personnel and the methods, and especially the

deadly Zyklon-B gas, that had proven effective during the "euthanasia" campaign of 1939 through 1941 in Germany (see page 931). By March 1942 they had constructed several extermination camps with gas chambers and crematoria, intended to kill large numbers of Jews and dispose of their bodies as efficiently as possible. And now they began full-scale mass killing, targeting first the Polish Jews who had already been confined to ghettos. The Nazis brutally suppressed attempts at resistance, like the Warsaw ghetto uprising of April and May 1943.

During the course of the war the Nazis constructed six full-scale death camps, although not all were operating at peak capacity at the same time. All six were located in what had been Poland (see inset, Map 28.2). Horrifying though they were, the concentration camps in Germany, such as Dachau, Buchenwald, and Bergen-Belsen, were not extermination camps, although many Jews died in them late in the war.

The largest of the six death camps was the Auschwitz-Birkenau complex, which became the principal extermination center in 1943. The Nazis shipped Jews from all over Europe to Auschwitz, which was killing about twelve thousand people a day at the height of its operation in 1944. Auschwitz was one of two extermination camps that included affiliated slave-labor factories, in which Jews most able to work were literally worked to death. Among the companies profiting from the arrangement were two of Germany's best known, Krupp and IG Farben.

The Jews typically arrived at one of the camps crammed into cattle cars on special trains. SS medical doctors subjected new arrivals to "selection," picking some for labor assignments and sending the others, including most women and children, to the gas chambers. Camp personnel made every effort to deceive the Jews who were about to be killed, to lead them to believe they were to be showered and deloused. Even in camps without forced-labor factories, Jews were compelled to do much of the dirty work of the extermination operation. But under the brutal conditions of the camps, those initially assigned to work inevitably weakened; most were then deemed unfit and put to death.

The Nazis took every precaution to hide what was going on in the death camps. The SS personnel involved were sworn to silence. Himmler insisted that if secrecy was to be maintained, the operation would have to be quick—and total, to include women and children, "so that no Jews will remain to take revenge on our sons and grandsons." Indeed, Himmler constantly sought to accelerate the process, even though it required labor and transport facilities desperately needed for the war effort. Indeed, as the fortunes of war turned against Germany, the extermination of the Jews became a kind of end in itself.

Himmler and the other major SS officials, such as Rudolf Höss°, the commandant at Auschwitz, or Adolf Eichmann°, who organized the transport of the Jews to the camps, cannot be understood simply as sadists who enjoyed humiliating their victims. Rather, they took satisfaction in doing what they believed was their duty without flinching, without signs of weakness. Addressing a group of SS members in 1943, Himmler portrayed the extermination of the Jews as a difficult "historical task" that they, the Nazi elite, must do for their racial community: "Most of you know what it means to see a hundred corpses piled up, or five hundred, or a thousand. To have gone through this and—except for cases of human weakness—to have remained decent, that has made us tough. This is an unwritten, never to be written, page of glory in our history."[2]

Höss (HOESS)    Eichmann (IKE-mahn)

**Children at Auschwitz**    Images from the Nazi camps haunted the decades that followed the Second World War. The Auschwitz-Birkenau complex proved the largest and most destructive of the camps that the Nazis created specifically for mass killing. The overwhelming majority of those sent to these camps were Jews, most of whom were killed by gassing shortly after their arrival. Those deemed fit for work might be spared, at least for a while, but children were typically killed at once.    *(Hulton Getty/Liaison)*

However, as Himmler's casual reference to "cases of human weakness" suggests, a minority of camp guards and others failed to live up to this image and indulged in wanton cruelty, toward their helpless victims. For some, the extermination process became the occasion to act out sadistic fantasies. But though this dimension is surely horrifying, the bureaucratic, factorylike nature of the extermination process has seemed still more troubling in some respects, for it raises questions about the nature of modern rationality itself. The mass killing of Jews required the expertise of scientists, doctors, and lawyers; it required the bureaucratic organization of the modern state—all to provide the most efficient means to a monstrous end.

Despite the overriding emphasis on secrecy, reports of the genocide reached the West almost immediately in 1942. At first, however, most tended to discount them as wartime propaganda of the sort that had circulated during World War I, when stories about Germans eating Belgian babies whipped up war fever. Skepticism about extermination reports was easier because there were a few concentration camps, like Theresienstadt° in the former Czechoslovakia, that housed Jews who had been selected for special treatment. These camps were not used for extermination and were not secret; the Red Cross was even allowed to inspect Theresienstadt several times. Those outside, and the German people as well, were led to believe that all the Jews were being interned, for the duration of the war, in camps like these, much as Japanese-Americans were being interned in camps in the western United States at the same time. But even as the evidence grew, Allied governments, citing military priorities, refused pleas from Jewish leaders in 1944 to bomb the rail line into Auschwitz.

The Nazis' policy of actually murdering persons deemed undesirable or superfluous did not start with, and was not limited to, the Jews. First came the "euthanasia" program in Germany, and the war afforded the Nazis the chance to do away with an array of other "undesirables," including Poles, Sinti and Roma ("Gypsies"), communists, homosexuals, and vagrants. So the most radical and appalling aspect of Nazism did not stem from anti-Semitism alone. This must not be forgotten, but neither must the fact that the Jews constituted by far the largest group of victims—perhaps 5.7 to 6 million, almost two-thirds of the Jews in Europe. (See the feature "Weighing the Evidence: Holocaust Testimony" on pages 982–983.)

■ **Collaboration in Nazi Europe**

In rounding up Jews for extermination, and in establishing their new order in Europe, the Nazis found willing collaborators among some of the countries within their orbit. Several of them found collaboration with the victorious Nazi regime the best way to pursue their own nationalist agendas. Croatia, earlier part of the new state of Yugoslavia, was eager to round up Jews and Gypsies, as well as to attack Serbs, as part of its effort to establish itself as a nation-state. But national circumstances varied across Europe, and so did degrees of collaboration. In Denmark, Norway, and the Netherlands, the Nazis

thought racial kinship would matter, but they never found sufficient support to make possible genuinely independent collaborationist governments. Denmark did especially well at resisting the German effort to round up Jews, as did Italy and Bulgaria.

Vichy France was somewhere in the middle, and thus it has remained particularly controversial. When the Vichy regime was launched during the summer of 1940, Marshal Pétain, its 84-year-old chief of state, enjoyed widespread support. Pétain promised to maximize French sovereignty and shield his people from the worst aspects of Nazi occupation. At the same time, the Vichy government claimed to be implementing its own "national revolution," returning France to authority, discipline, and tradition after the shambles of the Third Republic. Vichy's revolution was anti-Semitic and hostile to the left, so it seemed compatible, up to a point, with Nazism. And at first Germany seemed likely to win the war. Thus, Pétain's second-in-command, Pierre Laval (1883–1945), was willing to collaborate actively with the Nazis. The Vichy regime ended up doing much of the Nazis' dirty work for them—rounding up workers for forced shipment to German factories, hunting down members of the anti-German resistance, and picking up Jews to be sent to the Nazi extermination camps.

After the war, Pétain, Laval, and others were found guilty of treason by the new French government. Because of his advanced age, Pétain was merely imprisoned, while Laval and others were executed. But the shame of Vichy collaboration continued to haunt the French, deepening the humiliation of the defeat in 1940.

■ **Toward the Soviet Triumph**

The import of what happened elsewhere in Europe depended on the outcome of the main event, the German invasion of the Soviet Union. Although the German Sixth Army, numbering almost 300,000 men, reached Stalingrad by late 1942, the Germans could not achieve a knockout. The Soviets managed to defend the city in what was arguably the pivotal military engagement of World War II. While some Soviet troops fought street by street, house by house, others counterattacked, encircling the attacking German force. Hitler refused a strategic retreat, but his doggedness backfired. By the end of January 1943, the Soviets had captured what remained of the German force, about 100,000 men, very few of whom survived to return to Germany. Perhaps 240,000 German soldiers died in the Battle of Stalingrad or as prisoners afterward. But the price to the Soviets for their victory was far greater: a million Soviet soldiers and civilians died at Stalingrad.

---

**Theresienstadt** (teh-REZ-ay-en-shtat)

Although the Germans resumed the offensive on several fronts during the summer of 1943, the Soviets won the tank battle of Kursk-Orel in July, and from then on Stalin's Red Army moved relentlessly westward, forcing the Germans to retreat. By February 1944 Soviet troops had pushed the Germans back to the Polish border, and the outcome of the war was no longer in doubt (see Map 28.1).

The Soviet victory on what proved the decisive front of World War II was incredible, in light of the upheavals of the 1930s and the low esteem in which most held the Soviet military in 1941. Portraying the struggle as "the Great Patriotic War" for national defense, Stalin managed to rally the Soviet peoples as the Germans attacked. Rather than emphasize communist themes, he recalled the heroic defenses mounted against invaders in tsarist times, including the resistance to Napoleon in 1812. But though the Soviets ultimately prevailed, the cost in death, destruction, and suffering was almost unimaginable. For example, by the time Soviet forces finally broke the siege of Leningrad in January 1944, a million people in the city had died, most from starvation, freezing, or disease. And the Soviets won on the battlefield partly by taking incredible numbers of casualties.

The invading Germans gained access to major areas of Soviet industry and oil supply, and by the end of 1941 the country's industrial output had been cut in half. Yet the Soviet Union was able to weather this blow and go on to triumph. Outside help contributed, but only 5 to 15 percent of Soviet supplies came from the West. Between 1939 and 1941, Soviet leaders had begun building a new industrial base east of the Urals. And when the Germans invaded in 1941, the plant and equipment of 1,500 enterprises were dismantled and shipped by rail for reassembly farther east, out of reach of German attack. Then, beginning in 1942, thousands of brand-new factories were constructed in eastern regions as well.

Moreover, the earlier purges of the armed forces proved to have done less long-term damage than outside observers had expected. If anything, the removal of so many in the top ranks of the military hierarchy made it easier for talented young officers like Georgi Zhukov (1896–1974), who would become the country's top military commander, to rise quickly into major leadership positions.

When the United States entered the war in December 1941, the Soviets were fighting for survival. They immediately began pressuring the United States and Britain to open another front in Europe, preferably by landing in northern France, where an Allied assault could be expected to have the greatest impact. But the Allies did not invade northern France and open a major second front until June 1944. By then the Soviets had turned the tide in Europe on their own.

**Stalingrad, November 1942**    From September 1942 until the German surrender early in February 1943, this city on the Volga River saw some of the heaviest fighting of World War II. The Soviet victory, in the face of incredible casualties, was arguably the turning point in the war in Europe.    *(Sovfoto/Eastfoto)*

# A Global War, 1941–1944

WORLD War II proved unprecedented in its level of violence partly because it eclipsed even World War I in its geographical reach. The European colonial presence quickly drew the war to North Africa and the Middle East. But the war's early results in Europe also altered the power balance in East Asia and the Pacific, where the Russians and the Japanese had long been antagonists. During the 1930s, the United States had also become involved in friction with Japan. By 1941 President Franklin Roosevelt was openly favoring the anti-Axis cause, though it took a surprise attack by the Japanese in December 1941 finally to bring the United States into the war.

## ■ Japan and the Origins of the Pacific War

As a densely populated island nation lacking the raw materials essential for industry, Japan had been especially concerned about foreign trade and spheres of economic influence as it modernized after 1868. By the interwar period, the Japanese had become unusually reliant on exports of textiles and other products. During the Depression of the 1930s, when countries all over the world adopted protectionist policies, Japan suffered from increasing tariffs against its exports. This situation tilted the balance in Japanese ruling circles from free-trade proponents to those who favored a military-imperialist solution.

To gain economic hegemony by force, Japan could choose either of two directions. The northern strategy, concentrating on China, would risk Soviet opposition as well as strong local resistance. The southern strategy, focusing on southeast Asia and the East Indies, would encounter the imperial presence of Britain, France, the Netherlands, and the United States.

Japan opted for the northern strategy in 1931, when it took control of Manchuria, in northeastern China. But the Japanese attempt to conquer the rest of China, beginning in 1937, led only to an impasse by 1940. Japanese aggression in China drew the increasing hostility of the United States, a strong supporter of the Chinese nationalist leader Jiang Jieshi (Chiang Kai-shek) (1887–1975), as well as the active opposition of the Soviet Union. Clashes with Soviet troops along the border between Mongolia and Manchuria led to significant defeats for the Japanese in 1938 and 1939. The combination of China and the Soviet Union seemed more than Japan could handle.

By 1941, Germany's victories in Europe had seriously weakened Britain, France, and the Netherlands, the major European colonial powers in southeast Asia and the East Indies. The time seemed right for Japan to shift to a southern strategy. To keep the Soviets at bay, Japan agreed to a neutrality pact with the Soviet Union in April 1941. Rather than worry about China and the areas of dispute with the Soviet Union, the Japanese would seek control of southeast Asia, a region rich in such raw materials as oil, rubber, and tin—precisely what Japan lacked.

Japan had already joined with Nazi Germany and fascist Italy in an anticommunist agreement in 1936. In September 1940, the three agreed to a formal military alliance. For the Germans, alliance with Japan was useful to help discourage U.S. intervention in the European war. Japan, for its part, could expect the major share of the spoils of the European empires in Asia. However, diplomatic and military coordination between Germany and Japan remained minimal.

The United States began imposing embargoes on certain exports to Japan in 1938, in response to the Japanese aggression in China. After Japan had assumed control of Indochina, nominally held by Vichy France, by the summer of 1941, the United States imposed total sanctions, and the British and Dutch followed, forcing Japan to begin rapidly drawing down its oil reserves. Conquest of the oil fields of the Dutch East Indies now seemed a matter of life and death to the Japanese.

These economic sanctions heightened the determination of Japanese leaders to press forward aggressively now, when the country's likely enemies were weakened or distracted. But the Japanese did not expect to achieve a definitive victory over the United States in a long, drawn-out war. Rather, they anticipated, first, that their initial successes would enable them to grab the resources to sustain a longer war if necessary, and, second, that Germany would defeat Britain, leading the United States to accept a compromise peace allowing the Japanese what they wanted—a secure sphere of economic hegemony in southeast Asia.

Some Japanese leaders—diplomats, businessmen, naval officers, and even the emperor and some of his circle—were dismayed by the prospect of war with the United States. But as the influence of the military grew during the 1930s, it became ever more difficult for those opposing Japan's new imperialist direction to make themselves heard. By 1941, a conformist confidence in victory was demanded, and dissenters dared not speak out for fear of being labeled traitors.

**Map 28.3    The War in East Asia and the Pacific**    After a series of conquests in 1941 and 1942, the Japanese were forced gradually to fall back before advancing U.S. forces. When the war abruptly ended in August 1945, however, the Japanese still controlled much of the territory they had conquered.

The Japanese finally provoked a showdown on December 7, 1941, with a surprise attack on Pearl Harbor, a U.S. naval base in Hawaii. The next day, Japanese forces seized Hong Kong and Malaya, both British colonies, and Wake Island and the Philippines, both under U.S. control. The United States promptly declared war; in response, Hitler kept an earlier promise to Japan and declared war on the United States. World War II was now unprecedented in its geographic scope (see Map 28.3).

Much like their German counterparts, Japanese forces got off to a remarkably good start. By the summer of 1942, Japan had taken Thailand, the Dutch East Indies, the Philippines, and the Malay Peninsula. Having won much of what they had been seeking, the Japanese began devising the Greater East Asia Co-Prosperity Sphere, their own new order in the conquered territories. (See the box "Global Encounters: Japan's 'Pan-Asian' Mission.")

⊕ G L O B A L   E N C O U N T E R S

## Japan's "Pan-Asian" Mission

*With the coming of war against the Western powers in 1941, the Japanese could claim to be freeing Asians from Western imperialism and establishing a new economic order in East Asia and the Pacific. This selection from an essay entitled "Our Present War and Its Cultural Significance," written just after the bombing of Pearl Harbor by the well-known author Nagayo Yoshio (1888–1961), accents Japan's anti-Western mission in the region. Yoshio understood, especially from his country's recent experience in China, that Asians might find Japanese hegemony just as oppressive as Western domination. Although it served Japan's own economic interests and was often applied brutally, Japanese "Pan-Asianism" helped fuel the reaction against Western imperialism in Asia and the Pacific, with lasting results after the war.*

Whenever Japan has faced a powerful enemy it has been the *yamato damashii* [Japanese national spirit] which provided the basis of our courage. Now that we can talk in retrospect of the Sino-Japanese War, I am afraid our national spirit has not been given a proper chance to be aroused, due to the deplorable fact that we had to fight with China, our sister nation, with no foreseeable conclusion to look forward to. . . . While desperately fighting with a country which we made our enemy only reluctantly we were trying to find out a principle, an ethic based upon a new view of the world, which would justify our course of action. . . . The China incident was not only insufficient to fulfill this goal but also met with insurmountable obstacles. Consequently, time and opportunity ripened to declare war against the United States and England. . . .

. . . We would have nothing to say for ourselves if we were merely to follow the examples of the imperialistic and capitalistic exploitation of Greater East-Asia by Europe and the United States. . . .

. . . It is true that the science of war is one manifestation of a nation's culture. But from this time on we have to realize the increasing responsibility on our part if we are to deserve the respect of the people of East-Asian countries as their leaders, in the sphere of culture in general (not only the mere fusion and continuance of Western and Oriental cultures but

something surpassing and elevating them while making the most out of them) such as the formation of national character, refinement, intellect, training to become a world citizen, etc. . . .

The sense of awe and respect with which the Orientals have held the white race, especially the Anglo-Saxons, for three hundred years is deep-rooted almost beyond our imagination. It is our task to realize this fact and deal this servility at its root, find out why the white people became the objects of such reverence. It goes without saying that we cannot conclude simplemindedly that their shrewdness is the cause. Also we have to be very careful not to impose the *hakko ichiu* [the gathering of the whole world under one roof] spirit arbitrarily upon the Asians. If we make this kind of mistake we might antagonize those who could have become our compatriots and thus might also blaspheme our Imperial rule. . . .

To sum up, we have finally witnessed the dawn of a new principle which we had been searching for over ten years. . . . [T]he phrase "Greater East-Asian Coprosperity Sphere" is no longer a mere abstract idea.

*Source:* William H. McNeill and Mitsuko Iriye, eds., *Modern Asia and Africa* (New York: Oxford University Press, 1971), pp. 232–236.

## ■ The United States in Europe and the Pacific

During the first years of the war in Europe, the United States did not have armed forces commensurate with its economic strength; in 1940, in fact, its army was smaller than Belgium's. But the United States could be a supplier in the short term, and, if it chose to intervene, a major player over the longer term. With the Lend-Lease Act of March 1941, intended to provide war materiel without the economic dislocations of World War I, the United States lined up on the side of Britain against the Axis powers. In August 1941 a meeting between Churchill and Roosevelt aboard a cruiser off the coast of Newfoundland produced the Atlantic Charter, the first tentative agreement about the aims and ideals that were to guide the anti-Axis war effort. The Americans extended lend-lease to the Soviet Union the next month.

But though President Roosevelt was deeply committed to the anti-Axis cause, isolationist sentiment remained strong in the United States. The Japanese attack on Pearl Harbor in December inflamed American opinion and enabled Roosevelt at last to bring his country into the war as an active belligerent. By May 1942 the United States had joined with Britain and the Soviet Union in a formal military alliance against the Axis powers.

The two democracies had joined with Stalin's Soviet Union in a marriage of expediency, and mutual suspicions marked the relationship from the start. Initially, Britain and the United States feared that the Soviet Union might even seek a separate peace, as Russia had in World War I. The Soviets, for their part, worried that these newfound allies, with their long-standing anti-communism, might hold back from full commitment or even seek to undermine the Soviet Union.

In response to pressure from Stalin, Britain and the United States agreed to open a second front in Europe as soon as possible. But the Nazis dominated the Continent, so opening such a front required landing troops from the outside. It proved far more difficult to mount an effective assault on Europe than either Churchill or Roosevelt anticipated in 1942. The resulting delays furthered Stalin's suspicions that his allies were only too eager to have the Soviets do the bulk of the fighting against Nazi Germany—and weaken themselves in the process.

The United States agreed with its new allies to give priority to the war in Europe. But because it had to respond to the direct Japanese assault in the Pacific, the United States was not prepared to act militarily in Europe right away. What it could do, however, was supply the British with the ships needed to overcome German submarines, which seriously threatened shipping to Britain by 1942.

In the Pacific theater, in contrast, it was immediately clear that the United States would bear the brunt of the fighting against Japan. Although the Japanese went from one success to another during the first months of the war, they lacked the long-term resources to exploit their initial victories. In May 1942 the Battle of Coral Sea—off New Guinea, north of Australia—ended in a stalemate, stopping the string of Japanese successes. Then in June, the United States defeated the Japanese navy for the first time in the Battle of Midway, northwest of Hawaii. After the United States stopped attempted Japanese advances in the Solomon Islands and New Guinea early in 1943, U.S. forces began steadily advancing across the islands of the Pacific toward Japan (see Map 28.3).

## ■ The Search for a Second Front in Europe

As the Soviet army fought the Germans in the Soviet Union, the United States and Britain tried to determine how they could help tip the scales in Europe, now an almost impregnable German fortress. Stalin kept urging a direct assault across the English Channel, which, if successful, would have the greatest immediate impact. Churchill, however, advocated attacking the underbelly of the Axis empire by way of the Mediterranean, which would first require winning control of North Africa. And it was that strategy that the Allies tried first, starting in 1942.

By May 1943, step one of Churchill's plan had succeeded, but North Africa was valuable only as a staging ground for an Allied attempt to penetrate Europe from the south (see Map 28.1). Meeting at the Moroccan city of Casablanca in January 1943, Churchill and Roosevelt agreed that British and American forces would proceed from North Africa to Sicily and on up through Italy. The Soviets, still pushing for an invasion across the English Channel into France, objected that the Germans could easily block an Allied advance through the long, mountainous Italian peninsula.

Crossing from North Africa, Allied troops landed in Sicily in July 1943, leading to the arrest of Mussolini and the collapse of the fascist regime. Supported by King Victor Emmanuel III, the Italian military commander, Pietro Badoglio°, formed a new government to seek an armistice. Meanwhile, Allied forces moved on to the Italian mainland, but the Germans quickly occupied much of Italy in response. They even managed a daring rescue of Mussolini and promptly re-established him as puppet

---

**Badoglio** (bah-DOHL-yo)

**D-Day, 1944**    Allied forces land at Normandy, early in the morning of June 6, 1944, at last opening a major second front in Europe.    *(National Archives, Washington)*

leader of a new rump republic in northern Italy, now under German control. Just as the Soviets had warned, the Germans sought to block the Italian peninsula, and it was only nine months later, in June 1944, that the Allies reached Rome. So Churchill's strategy of assaulting Europe from the south proved less than decisive.

Only when Churchill, Roosevelt, and Stalin met for the first time, at Teheran, Iran, in November 1943, did they agree that the next step would be to invade western Europe from Britain. Preparations had been underway since early 1942, but the operation was complex and hazardous in the extreme. Finally, Allied troops crossed the English Channel to make an amphibious landing on the beaches of Normandy, in northern France, on June 6, 1944, known to history as D-Day. And partly by deceiving the Germans seeking to defend the area, they were quickly able to consolidate their positions.

The success of the D-Day invasion opened a major second front in Europe at last. Now American-led forces from the west and Soviet forces from the east worked systematically toward Germany. The one substantial German counterattack in the west, the Battle of the Bulge in December 1944, slowed the Allies' advance, but

on March 7, 1945, Allied troops crossed the Rhine River (see Map 28.1).

By June 1944, when Allied forces landed at Normandy, Soviet forces had already crossed the 1939 border with Poland as they moved steadily westward. But in August the Soviets stopped before reaching Warsaw, and the major Soviet thrust began cutting south, through Romania, which surrendered in August, and on into the Danube valley in Hungary and Yugoslavia during the fall. The Soviets resumed their advance westward through Poland and toward Germany only in January 1945.

Now, with the defeat of Germany simply a matter of time, Allied concern shifted to the postwar order. Churchill, especially, worried about the implications of the Soviet advances in east-central Europe and the Balkans. As a supplement to the D-Day landings, he wanted to strike from Italy through Yugoslavia into east-central Europe. But the Americans resisted; Churchill's priorities, they felt, reflected old-fashioned concerns over spheres of influence that were no longer appropriate. So the Allies concentrated instead on a secondary landing in southern France in August 1944. This assault, in which Free French forces were prominent, led quickly to the liberation of Paris.

But because the Allies made both their landings in France, and not in southeastern Europe, the Western democracies were involved only in the liberation of western Europe. It was the Soviets who drove the Germans from east-central Europe and the Balkans. This fact, and the resulting geographic distribution of military strength, fundamentally affected the postwar order in Europe.

# THE SHAPE OF THE ALLIED VICTORY, 1944–1945

HE leaders of the Soviet Union, Britain, and the United States sought to mold that postwar order at two notable conferences in 1945. Even as they brought different aspirations for the postwar world, they had to deal together with the legacy of a war of unprecedented violence and destruction. At the same time, they also had to face the hard military realities that had resulted from the fighting so far: each country had armies in certain places but not in others. The result was an informal division of Europe into spheres of influence among the victors.

The most serious question the Allies faced concerned Germany, which was widely held responsible for the two world wars, as well as for Nazism with all its atrocities—including the concentration and extermination camps, discovered with shock and horror by the advancing Allied armies in 1945. Germany was to be forced to surrender unconditionally; there would be no negotiation or armistice. But what should be done with the country over the longer term?

In the Pacific theater, as in Europe, the way the war ended had major implications for the postwar world. The United States decided to use the atomic bomb, a weapon so destructive that it forced a quick Japanese surrender. The suddenness of the ending helped determine the fate of the European empires in Asia.

### ■ The Yalta Conference: Shaping the Postwar World

When Stalin, Roosevelt, and Churchill met at Yalta, a Soviet Black Sea resort, in February 1945, Allied victory was assured, and the three leaders accomplished a great deal. Yet controversy has long surrounded the Yalta conference. Western critics have charged that the concessions made there to Stalin consigned east-central Europe to communist domination and opened the way to the dangerous cold war of the next forty years. At the time, however, the anticipation of victory produced a relatively cooperative spirit among the Allies. Thus, they firmed up plans for military occupation of Germany in separate zones, for joint occupation of Berlin, and for an Allied Control Council, composed of the military

**The Big Three at Yalta**   With victory over Nazi Germany assured, Churchill, Roosevelt, and Stalin were in reasonably good spirits when they met at Yalta, a Black Sea resort in the Soviet Union, in February 1945. Important sources of friction among them were evident at the meeting, but the differences that led to the cold war did not seem paramount at this point. The Yalta conference proved to be the last meeting of the three leaders.
*(F.D.R. Library)*

968

**Map 28.4   The Impact of World War II in Europe**   As a result of World War II the Soviet Union expanded its western borders and Poland shifted westward at the expense of Germany. Territorial changes added to the wartime disruption and produced a flood of refugees. The cold war division of Europe did not depend on immediate territorial changes, but soon Germany itself came to be divided along east-west lines.

commanders-in-chief, which would make policy for all of Germany by unanimous agreement.

Each of the Allies had special concerns, but each got much of what it was seeking at Yalta. Roosevelt was eager for Soviet help against Japan as soon as possible, and he won Soviet commitment to an agreement tentatively worked out earlier. In exchange for territorial concessions in Asia and the Pacific, Stalin agreed to declare war on Japan within three months of the German surrender.

Churchill, meanwhile, worried about the future of Europe in light of the American intention, which Roosevelt announced at Yalta, to maintain occupation troops in Europe for only two years after the war. To help balance Soviet power on the Continent, Churchill felt it essential to restore France as a great power. To this end, he urged that France be granted a share in the occupation of Germany and a permanent seat on the Security Council of the proposed new international organization, the United Nations (see page 975). Roosevelt agreed, even though he had little use for Charles de Gaulle or what he viewed as the pretensions of the French.

It seemed to the Americans that both Britain and the Soviet Union remained too wedded to traditional conceptions of national interest as they sought to shape the postwar world. Hence, one of Roosevelt's major priorities was to secure British and Soviet commitment to the United Nations before the three allies began to disagree over particular issues. He won that commitment at Yalta, but only by giving in to Churchill on the sensitive matter of British colonies.

Because anti-imperial sentiment worked to Japan's advantage in Asia, the United States had pestered Britain on the colonial issue since early in the war. Roosevelt even asked Churchill in 1941 about British intentions in India. So prickly was Churchill that he proclaimed in 1942, "I have not become the King's First Minister in order to preside over the liquidation of the British Empire." The parties agreed at Yalta that the British Empire would be exempt from an anticipated measure to bring former colonies under United Nations trusteeship after the war.

Although it was not the only question on the table, the future of the former Axis territories was central to the seaside deliberations. By the time of the conference, those territories were already being divided into spheres of influence among the Allies, and in light of the location of Allied troops, the eventual alignment was probably inevitable. In Italy, where U.S. and British troops held sway, the two democracies had successfully resisted Stalin's claim for a share in the administration. In east-central Europe, however, the Soviet army was in control. Still, the United States, with its vision of a new world order, objected to spheres of influence and insisted that democratic principles be applied everywhere. At Yalta this American priority led to an awkward compromise over east-central Europe: the new governments in the area were to be both democratic and friendly to the Soviet Union.

Most important to the Soviets was Poland, with its crucial location between Russia and Germany. Although the Soviets insisted that Communists lead the new Polish government at the outset, they compromised by allowing a role for the noncommunist Polish government-in-exile in London and by promising free elections down the road. The Allies agreed that Poland would gain substantial German territory to its west to make up for what it would lose to the USSR to its east (see Map 28.4).

In addition, the United States and Britain were to have a role in committees set up to engineer the transition to democracy in the rest of east-central Europe. However, only the Soviets had troops in the area, and those committees proved essentially powerless. But though the sources of future tension were already at work at Yalta, they generally remained hidden by the high spirits of approaching victory.

## ■ Victory in Europe

Although the tide had turned in 1943, Germany managed to continue the war by exploiting its conquered territories and by more effectively allocating its domestic resources for war production. Thanks partly to the efforts of armaments minister Albert Speer, war production grew sharply between 1941 and 1944, so Germany had plenty of weapons even as the war was ending. The Germans even proved able to withstand the systematic bombing of cities that the British, especially, had thought might prove decisive.

Beginning in 1942, British-led bombing attacks destroyed an average of half the built-up area of seventy German cities, sometimes producing huge firestorms. (See the box: "Reading Sources: Waiting Out the War in Berlin.") The bombing of the historic city of Dresden in February 1945 killed at least sixty thousand civilians in the most destructive air assault of the war in Europe. But despite this widespread destruction, such bombing did not undermine morale or disrupt production to the extent expected. Even in the face of steady Allied bombing, Germany increased its war production during 1943 and 1944.

But Germany encountered two crucial bottlenecks that finally crippled its military effort: it was running out of both oil and military personnel. Despite making

## Waiting Out the War in Berlin

*Marie Vassiltchikov (1917–1978) was a member of a noble Russian family that had left Russia in 1919, shortly after the Bolshevik Revolution. Having grown up as a refugee in Germany, France, and Lithuania, she found herself in Germany when the war began in 1939. Though not a German citizen, she was able to find employment in Berlin thanks to her linguistic skills and Germany's labor shortage. She immediately began writing a diary in English, which she had learned as a child. By November 1943, when these excerpts were written, she was working in the information department of the German Foreign Ministry. Her diary is especially vivid in chronicling the later years of the war, as civilians in Germany coped with Allied bombing.*

*Tuesday, 23 November*   Last night the greater part of central Berlin was destroyed.

. . . I was rushing down the stairs to go home when the hall porter interrupted me with the ominous words "Luftgefahr 15" ["air-raid danger 15"]. This meant that large enemy formations were on their way. I took the stairs back two at a time to warn those of my colleagues who lived far away to stay put, since they might otherwise be caught out in the open. . . .

The streets were full of people. Many just stood around, for the visibility was so poor on account of the rain that nobody expected the raid to last long or cause much damage. . . . As one does now in such cases, I . . . packed a few things in a small suitcase. . . .

I had just finished packing when the *flak* opened up. It was immediately very violent. Papa emerged with his pupils and we all hurried down to the half-basement behind the kitchen, where we usually sit out air-raids. We had hardly got there when we heard the first approaching planes. They flew very low and the barking of the *flak* was suddenly drowned by a very different sound—that of exploding bombs, first far away and then closer and closer, until it seemed as if they were falling literally on top of us. At every crash the house shook. The air pressure was dreadful and the noise deafening. . . .

The all-clear came only half an hour after the last planes had departed, but long before that we were called out of the house by an unknown naval officer. The wind, he told us, thus far non-existent, had suddenly risen and the fires, therefore, were spreading. We all went out into our little square and, sure enough, the sky on three sides was blood-red. This, the officer explained, was only the beginning; the greatest danger would come in a few hours' time, when the fire storm really got going. Maria had already given each of us a wet towel with which to smother our faces before leaving the house—a wise precaution, for our square was already filled with smoke and one could hardly breathe.

. . . [T]he electricity, gas and water no longer worked and we had to grope our way around with electric torches [flashlights] and candles. Luckily we had had time to fill every available bath tub, wash basin, kitchen sink, and pail. By now the wind had increased alarmingly, roaring like a gale at sea. When we looked out of the window we could see a steady shower of sparks raining down on our and the neighbouring houses and all the time the air was getting thicker and hotter, while the smoke billowed in through the gaping window frames. . . .

*Wednesday, 24 November* . . . At first our Woyrsch-strasse did not look too bad; but one block away, at the corner of Lützowstrasse, all the houses were burnt out. As I continued down Lützowstrasse the devastation grew worse; many buildings were still burning and I had to keep to the middle of the street, which was difficult on account of the numerous wrecked trams. There were many people in the streets, most of them muffled in scarves and coughing, as they threaded their way gingerly through the piles of fallen masonry. At the end of Lützowstrasse, about four blocks away from the office, the houses on both sides of the street had collapsed and I had to climb over mounds of smoking rubble, leaking water pipes and other wreckage to get across to the other side.

*Source:* Marie Vassiltchikov, *Berlin Diaries, 1940–1945* (New York: Alfred A. Knopf, 1987), pp. 105–110.

**The Soviet Victory in Europe** After forcing the Germans back for almost two years, Soviet troops reached Berlin in April 1945. Although it required a day of heavy fighting and bombardment, the Soviets took the Reichstag building, in the heart of the now devastated German capital, on April 30. Here two Soviet sergeants, Yegorov and Kantariya, plant the Soviet flag atop the Reichstag, symbolizing the Soviet victory in the decisive encounter of World War II in Europe. *(ITAR-TAS/Sovfoto)*

effective use of synthetics, the Nazi war machine depended heavily on oil from Romania. Late in August 1944, however, Soviet troops crossed into Romania, taking control of the oil fields. And though the terror bombing of cities did not have the anticipated impact, the more precisely targeted bombing favored by U.S. strategists significantly affected the outcome. In May 1944 the United States began bombing oil fields in Romania and refineries and synthetic oil plants in Germany. Soon Germany lacked enough fuel even to train pilots. So serious were the bottlenecks by 1945 that the German air force could not use all the aircraft that German industry was producing.

Soviet troops moving westward finally met U.S. troops moving eastward at the Elbe River in Germany on April 26, 1945. With his regime now thoroughly defeated and much of his country in ruins, Hitler committed suicide in his underground military headquarters in Berlin on April 30, 1945. The war in Europe finally ended with the German surrender to General Dwight D. Eisenhower (1890–1969) at Reims, France, on May 7 and to Marshal Zhukov at Berlin on May 8. The world celebrated the end of the fighting in Europe, but an element of uncertainty surrounded the Allied victory. East-West differences were increasingly coming to the fore within the anti-German alliance.

## ■ The Potsdam Conference and the Question of Germany

The immediate question for the victorious Allies was the fate of Germany, which they confronted at the last of their notable wartime conferences, at Potsdam, just outside Berlin, from July 17 to August 2, 1945. The circumstances were dramatically different from those at Yalta just months before. With Hitler dead and Germany defeated, no common military aim provided unity. And of the three Allied leaders who had been at Yalta, only Stalin remained. President Roosevelt had died in April, so his successor, Harry Truman (1884–1972), represented the United States. In Britain, Churchill's Conservatives lost the general election during the first days of the conference, so Clement Attlee (1883–1967), the new Labour prime minister, assumed the leadership of the British delegation.

At Potsdam the Allies had to determine how to implement their earlier agreements about Germany, which, devastated by bombing and devoid of a government, depended on the Allied occupying forces even for its day-to-day survival. For a time, U.S. policymakers had even considered destroying Germany's industrial capacity in perpetuity. However, cooler heads understood that the deindustrialization, or "pastoralization," of Germany would not be in anyone's economic interests. Moreover, as the democracies grew increasingly suspicious about Soviet intentions, an economically healthy Germany seemed necessary to help in the balance against the Soviet Union.

For their part, the Soviets had reason to take a much harder line against Germany. Having been ravaged by invading German forces twice within living memory, the Soviet Union wanted to weaken Germany both territorially and economically. And of the three victors, the Soviets had suffered a greatly disproportionate share of the wartime destruction and economic loss, so they also sought to exploit the remaining resources of Germany by exacting heavy reparations. Moreover, the British and the Americans accepted the Soviet proposal that Germany's eastern border with Poland be shifted substantially westward, to the line formed by the Oder and Neisse° Rivers. But just as Poland gained at the expense of Germany, the Soviet Union kept a substantial slice of what had been eastern Poland (see Map 28.4).

Each of the three Allies had responsibility for administering a particular zone of occupation, but they were supposed to coordinate their activities in a common policy toward Germany. This effort was to include de-Nazification, demilitarization, and an assault on concentrations of economic power—to root out what seemed the sources of Germany's antidemocratic and aggressive tendencies. But East-West disagreements over economic policy soon undermined the pretense of joint government.

### ■ The Atomic Bomb and the Capitulation of Japan

In the Pacific, Japan had been forced onto the defensive by September 1943, and though it mounted two major counterattacks during 1944, the Japanese navy was crippled by shortages of ships and fuel by the end of the year. However, as the situation grew more desperate for Japan, Japanese ground soldiers battled ever more fiercely, often fighting to the death, or taking their own lives, rather than surrendering. Beginning late in 1944, aircraft pilots practiced *kamikaze*°, suicidally crashing planes filled with explosives into U.S. targets. The Japanese used this tactic especially as the Americans sought to take Okinawa in the spring of 1945. The U.S. forces finally prevailed in June, but only after the most bitter combat of the entire Pacific war (see Map 28.3).

In conquering Okinawa, American forces got close enough for air raids on the Japanese home islands. But though the United States was now clearly in control, it seemed likely that an actual invasion of Japan would be necessary to force a Japanese surrender. Some estimated that, because the Japanese could be expected to fight even more desperately to defend their own soil, invasion might well cost the United States 1 million additional casualties. It was especially for this reason that the Americans decided to try to end the war in an altogether different way, by using an atomic bomb.

In 1939 scientists in several countries, including Germany, had started to advise their governments that new, immensely destructive weapons based on thermonuclear fission were theoretically possible. The German economics ministry began seeking uranium as early as 1939, but Hitler promoted jet- and rocket-propelled terror weaponry instead, especially the V-2 rocket bombs that the Germans began showering on England in the fall of 1944. Still, fear that the Nazis were developing atomic weapons lurked behind the Allied effort to produce the ultra-lethal bomb as quickly as possible.

Although the British were the first to initiate an atomic weapons program, by late 1941 the Americans were building on what they knew of British findings to develop their own crash program, known as the Manhattan Project. Constructing an atomic bomb proved far more difficult and costly than most had expected in 1941, and it took a concerted effort by the United States to have atomic weapons ready for use by mid-1945.

The U.S. decision actually to use the atomic bomb on Japanese civilians has been one of the most controversial of modern history. The decision fell to the new president, Harry Truman, who had known nothing of the bomb project when Roosevelt died in April 1945. During the next few months, Truman listened to spirited disagreement among American policymakers. Was it necessary actually to drop the bomb to force the Japanese to surrender? Especially because the ultimate victory of the United States was not in doubt, some argued that it would be enough simply to demonstrate the new weapon to the Japanese in a test firing.

By July, when the Allies met at Potsdam, the United States was prepared to use the bomb. But President Truman first warned Japan that if it did not surrender at once, it would be subjected to destruction immeasurably greater than Germany had just suffered. The Japanese ignored the warning, although the United States had begun area-bombing Japanese cities a few months before. The bombing of Tokyo in March produced a firestorm that gutted one-fourth of the city and killed over 80,000 people. In light of the Japanese refusal to surrender, the use of the atomic bomb could seem the logical next step.

**Neisse** (NYE-suh)    **kamikaze** (kah-mih-KAH-zee)

At 8:15 on the morning of August 6, 1945, from a height of 32,000 feet above the Japanese city of Hiroshima, an American pilot released the first atomic bomb to be used against an enemy target. The bomb exploded after 45 seconds, 2,000 feet above the ground, killing 80,000 people outright and leaving tens of thousands more to die in the aftermath. Three days later, on August 9, the Americans exploded a second atomic bomb over Nagasaki, killing perhaps 50,000 people. Although sectors of the Japanese military held out for continued resistance, Emperor Hirohito° (1901–1989) finally surrendered on August 15. The bombing of civilians had discredited the Japanese military, which not only had proved unable to defend the country but had systematically misled the Japanese people about their country's prospects.

The war in the Pacific ended more suddenly than had seemed possible just a few months earlier (see Map 28.3). This worked in favor of the various national liberation or decolonization movements that had developed in Asia during the war, for the Europeans had little opportunity to re-establish their dominance in the colonial territories they had earlier lost to the Japanese. In the Dutch East Indies, the Japanese had encouraged anticolonial sentiment, even helping local nationalists create patriotic militias. After the war, the Dutch were never able to reassert their control against this Indonesian nationalist movement. But though the war had severely weakened the old Western imperialism in Asia and the Pacific, what would replace it remained unclear.

## ■ Death, Disruption, and the Question of Guilt

World War II left as many as 60 million people dead—three times as many as World War I. About that same number were left homeless for some length of time, or found themselves forced onto the mercies of others as refugees. The Soviet Union and Germany suffered by far the highest casualty figures; for each, the figure was considerably higher than in World War I. An appalling 23 million Soviet citizens died, of whom 12 to 13 million were civilians. Germany lost 5 to 6 million, including perhaps 2 million civilians.

In contrast, casualty rates for Italy, Britain, and France were lower than in World War I. Italy suffered 200,000 military and 200,000 civilian deaths. Total British losses, including civilians, numbered 450,000, to which must be added 120,000 from the British Empire. Despite its quick defeat, France lost more lives than Britain because of the ravages of German occupation: the 350,000

deaths among French civilians considerably exceeded the British figure, closer to 100,000.

The United States lost 300,000 servicemen and 5,000 civilians. Figures for Japan are problematic, partly because the Japanese claim that 300,000 of those who surrendered to the Soviets in 1945 have remained unaccounted for. Apart from this number, 1,740,000 Japanese servicemen died from 1941 to 1945, more from hunger and disease than from combat, and 300,000 civilians died in Japan, most from U.S. bombing.

During the war, Jews, Poles, and others deemed undesirable by the Nazis had been rounded up and shipped to ghettos or camps, where the great majority had died. Of those Jews who were still alive when the Nazi camps were liberated, almost half died within a few weeks. Even those who managed to return home sometimes faced pogroms during the difficult months that followed; forty Jews were killed in the worst of them, at Kielce°, Poland, in 1946.

Late in the war, as German forces in the east retreated, ethnic Germans living in Poland, Czechoslovakia, Hungary, and elsewhere in east-central Europe began seeking refuge in Germany. They were fleeing the Soviet advance but also seeking to escape the growing wave of anti-German resentment in those countries. Once the war was over, the Poles began expelling ethnic Germans from the historically German areas that were now to become Polish. These Germans were sometimes sent to detention camps, and when they were shipped out, it was often in cattle cars. According to some estimates, as many as 2 million died in the process. In Czechoslovakia the government expelled 3.5 million Germans from the Sudetenland area by 1947. All tolled, at least 7 million German refugees moved west, into the shrunken territory of the new Germany, by 1947. They were among the 16 million Europeans who were permanently uprooted and transplanted during the war and its immediate wake. And the process continued at a diminished rate thereafter. By 1958 perhaps 10 million Germans had either left or been forced out of the new Poland, leaving only about 1 million Germans still living there.

As the end of the war approached, Europeans began attempting to assess guilt and punish those responsible for the disasters of the era. In the climate of violence, resistance forces in France, Italy, and elsewhere often subjected fascists and collaborators to summary justice, sometimes through quick trials in ad hoc courts. In Italy this process led to 15,000 executions, in France 10,000. French women accused of sleeping with German soldiers were shamed by having their heads shaved.

---

**Hirohito** (hee-roh-HEE-toh)

**Kielce** (KYEL-tsuh)

**Reconstruction Begins**
Shortly after the end of the war, women in Berlin pass pails of rubble along a line to dump. Wartime bombing had severely damaged cities throughout much of Europe, although destruction was greatest in Germany.    *(Hulton Getty/Liaison)*

The most sensitive confrontation with the recent past took place in Germany, where the occupying powers imposed a program of de-Nazification. In the western zones, German citizens were required to attend lectures on the virtues of democracy and to view the corpses of the victims of Nazism. In this context, the Allies determined to identify and bring to justice those responsible for the crimes of Hitler's regime. This effort led to the Nuremberg trials of 1945 to 1946, the most famous of a number of war crimes trials held in Germany and the occupied countries after the war.

Although Hitler, Himmler, and Goebbels had committed suicide, the occupying authorities apprehended for trial twenty-four individuals who had played important but very different roles in Hitler's Third Reich. All but three were convicted of war crimes and "crimes against humanity." Twelve were sentenced to death; of those, two committed suicide, and the other ten were executed.

Questions about their legitimacy dogged the Nuremberg trials from the start. To a considerable extent the accused were being judged according to law made after the fact. The notion of "crimes against humanity" remained vague. Moreover, even insofar as a measure of international law was in force, it was arguably binding only on states, not individuals. But in light of the unprecedented atrocities of the Nazi regime, there was widespread agree-

ment among the victors that the Nazi leaders could not be treated simply as defeated adversaries.

## INTO THE POSTWAR WORLD

EVEN after the fighting stopped in 1945, remarkable changes continued as the forces unleashed by the war played themselves out. In a number of war-torn countries, the legacies of wartime resistance movements helped shape the political order and priorities for beginning anew. At the same time, differences between the Soviets and the Western democracies began to undermine the wartime alliance, soon producing the division of Germany and a bipolar Europe. Thus the conclusion of World War II led directly to the danger of a third world war, which might involve nuclear weapons and threaten the very survival of human life.

In addition to the dramatic changes in Europe, the wider effects of the war brought to the forefront a whole new set of issues, from anticolonialism to the Arab-Israeli conflict to the spread of communism within the non-Western world. These issues would remain central for decades. By 1949, however, it was already possible to discern the contours of the new postwar world, a world with new sources of hope but also with conflicts and dangers hardly imaginable ten years earlier.

## ■ Resistance and Renewal

Though the Nazis had found some willing collaborators, the great majority of those living under German occupation came to despise the Nazis as their brutality became ever clearer. Nazi rule meant pillage, forced labor in Germany, and the random killing of hostages in reprisal for resistance activity. In one extreme case, the Germans destroyed the Czech village of Lidice°, killing all its inhabitants, in retaliation for the assassination of SS security chief Reinhard Heydrich in 1942.

Clandestine movements of resistance to the occupying Nazi forces gradually developed all over Europe. In western Europe, resistance was especially prominent in France and, beginning in 1943, northern Italy, which was subjected to German occupation after the Allies defeated Mussolini's regime. But the anti-German resistance was strongest in Yugoslavia, Poland, and the occupied portions of the Soviet Union, where full-scale guerrilla war against the Germans and their collaborators produced the highest civilian casualties of World War II. The Polish resistance achieved some notable successes in sabotaging roads and railroads, although it met disastrous defeat when it sought to tackle the Germans head-on in Warsaw in 1944.

The role of the resistance proved most significant in Yugoslavia, where the Croatian Marxist Josip Broz, taking the pseudonym Tito (1892–1980), forged the opponents of the Axis powers into a broadly based guerrilla army. Its initial foe was the inflated Croatian state that the Germans, early in 1941, carved from Yugoslavia and entrusted to the pro-Axis Croatian separatist movement, the Ustashe°. But Tito's forces soon came up against a rival resistance movement, led by Serb officers, that tended to be pro-Serb, monarchist, and anticommunist. By 1943 Tito led 250,000 men and women in what had become a vicious civil war, one that deepened ethnic divisions and left a legacy of bitterness. Tito's forces prevailed, enabling him to create a communist-led government in Yugoslavia late in the war.

In France and Italy as well, communists played leading roles in the wartime resistance movements. As a result, the Communist Party in each country overcame the disarray that followed from the Nazi-Soviet Pact of 1939, and after the war each enjoyed a level of prestige that would have been unthinkable earlier.

Lidice (LIH-dyit-seh)    Ustashe (oo-STAH-zhiy)

In the French case, the indigenous resistance, with its significant communist component, generally worked well with de Gaulle and the Free French, operating outside France until August 1944. Still, de Gaulle took pains to cement his own leadership in the overall struggle. Among the measures to this end, he decreed women's suffrage for France, partly because women were playing a major role in the resistance. After the liberation of France in 1944, he sought to control a potentially volatile situation by disarming the resistance as quickly as possible.

The western European resistance movements are easily romanticized, their extent and importance overstated. Compared with regular troops, resistance forces were poorly trained, equipped, and disciplined. In France fewer than 30 percent of the nearly 400,000 active resisters had firearms in 1944. But though the Allies never tried to use them in a systematic way, the resistance movements made at least some military contribution, especially through sabotage. And they boosted national self-esteem for the longer term, helping countries humiliated by defeat and occupation make a fresh start after the war.

## ■ Conflicting Visions and the Coming of the Cold War

Starting with the Atlantic Charter conference of 1941, Roosevelt had sought to ensure that the common effort against the Axis powers would lead to a firmer basis for peace, to be framed through a new international organization after the war. At a conference at Dumbarton Oaks in Washington in September 1944, the United States proposed the structure for a new "United Nations" organization. Meeting in San Francisco from April to June 1945, delegates from almost fifty anti-Axis countries translated that proposal into a charter for the new United Nations. As Roosevelt had envisioned, the major powers were given a privileged position in the organization as permanent members of the Security Council, each with veto power. To dramatize its departure from the Geneva-based League of Nations, which the United States had refused to join, the United Nations was headquartered in New York. In July 1945 the American Senate approved U.S. membership in the international body almost unanimously.

By the end of the war, several international meetings had used the United Nations title. In July 1944 the United Nations Monetary and Financial Conference at Bretton Woods, New Hampshire, brought together delegates from forty-four nations to deal with problems of currency and exchange rates. Although it produced only recommendations subject to ratification by the individual states, the conference indicated a new determination to cooperate on the international level after the failures of the interwar period. And the outcome of the conference, the Bretton Woods Agreement, laid the foundation for international economic exchange in the noncommunist world for the crucial quarter-century of economic recovery after the war. In addition, the conference gave birth to the International Monetary Fund and the International Bank for Reconstruction and Development, which played major roles in the decades that followed.

Whereas the United States envisioned a world order based on the ongoing cooperation of the three victors, the Soviet Union had a different agenda. Its top priority was to create a buffer zone of friendly states in east-central Europe, especially as a bulwark against Germany. While seeking this sphere of influence in east-central Europe, Stalin gave the British a free hand to settle the civil war between communists and anticommunists in Greece, and he did not push for revolution in western Europe. The strong communist parties that had emerged from the resistance movements in Italy and France were directed by Moscow to work within broad-based democratic fronts rather than try to take power. Although no formal deal was made, Stalin saw this moderate position in western and southern Europe as a tacit exchange with the West for a free hand in east-central Europe.

### ■ The Division of Germany

The site of greatest potential stress between the Soviets and the democracies was Germany. At first, the Western Allies were concerned especially to root out the sources of Germany's antidemocratic, aggressive behavior, but that concern faded as communism, not Nazism, came to seem the immediate menace. And it was especially conflict over Germany that cemented the developing division of Europe. Neither the democracies nor the Soviets lived up to all their agreements concerning Germany, but in light of the fundamental differences in priorities, cooperation between the two sides was bound to be difficult at best.

Disagreements over economic policy proved the major source of the eventual split. At Potsdam, the West had accepted Soviet demands for German reparations, but rather than wait for payment, the Soviets began removing German factories and equipment for reassembly in the Soviet Union. To ensure that they got their due, the Soviets wanted access to the economic resources not simply of the Russian occupation zone but of the whole of Germany. The United States and Britain, in contrast, gave priority to economic reconstruction and quickly began integrating the economies of the Western zones for that purpose.

Friction developed from 1945 to 1948 as the West insisted on reduced reparations and a higher level of industrial production than the Soviets wanted. Finally, as part of their effort to spur economic recovery, the United States and Britain violated inter-Allied agreements by introducing a new currency without Soviet consent. Stalin answered in June 1948 by blockading the city of Berlin, cutting its western sectors off from the main Western occupation zones, almost 200 miles west (see Map 28.4). The Western Allies responded with a massive airlift that kept their sectors of Berlin supplied for almost a year, until May 1949, when the Soviets finally backed down.

By 1948 two separate German states began emerging from the Allied occupation zones. The Western occupying powers had begun restoring local government immediately after the war, to create the administrative framework necessary to provide public utilities and food distribution. Gradually a governing structure was built from the ground up in the Western zones, which were increasingly coordinated.

With Allied support, a "parliamentary council" of West German leaders met during 1948 and 1949 and produced a document that, when ratified in September 1949, became the "Basic Law" of a new Federal Republic of Germany, with its capital at Bonn. This founding document was termed simply the Basic Law, as opposed to the constitution, to emphasize the provisional character of the new West German state. To create a state limited to the west was not to foreclose the future reunification of Germany. But as it became clear that a new state was being created in the Western zones, the Soviets settled for a new state in their zone, in eastern Germany. Thus the Communist-led German Democratic Republic, with its capital in East Berlin, was born in October 1949.

### ■ The "Iron Curtain" and the Emergence of a Bipolar World

In east-central Europe, only Yugoslavia and Albania had achieved liberation on their own, and the communist leaders of their resistance movements had a plausible claim to political power. Elsewhere, the Soviet army had provided liberation, and the Soviet military presence remained the decisive political fact as the war ended. In much of the region, authoritarianism and collaboration had been the rule for a decade or more, so there was no possibility of returning to a clearly legitimate prewar political order. To be sure, each country had local political groups, some representing former governments in exile, that now claimed a governing role, but their standing in relation to the Soviet army was uncertain.

## Discerning the Iron Curtain

*Winston Churchill, out of office and touring the United States, sought to explain the postwar international situation in a speech at Westminster College in Fulton, Missouri, on March 5, 1946. To characterize the developing division of Europe, Churchill referred to "an iron curtain," a term that attracted immediate attention and dramatically affected public opinion in both the United States and western Europe. Some have suggested that Churchill was overdramatizing the situation in an effort to keep the United States engaged in Europe.*

A shadow has fallen upon the scenes so lately lighted by the Allied victory. Nobody knows what Soviet Russia and its Communist international organization intend to do in the immediate future, or what are the limits, if any, to their expansive and proselytizing tendencies. . . . We understand the Russian need to be secure on her western frontiers by the removal of all possibility of German aggression. We welcome her to her rightful place among the leading nations of the world. . . . It is my duty, however, to place before you certain facts. . . .

From Stettin in the Baltic to Trieste in the Adriatic, an iron curtain has descended across the Continent. Behind that line lie all the capitals of the ancient states of central and eastern Europe. Warsaw, Berlin, Prague, Vienna, Budapest, Belgrade, Bucharest, and Sofia, all these famous cities and the populations around them lie in what I must call the Soviet sphere, and all are subject in one form or another, not only to Soviet influence but to a very high and, in many cases, increasing measure of control from Moscow. Athens alone—Greece with its immortal glories—is free to decide its future at an election under British, American and French observation. The Russian-dominated Polish Government has been encouraged to make enormous and wrongful inroads upon Germany, and mass expulsions of millions of Germans on a scale grievous and undreamed-of are now taking place. The Communist parties, which were very small in all these Eastern States of Europe, have been raised to pre-eminence and power far beyond their numbers and are seeking everywhere to obtain totalitarian control. . . .

If now the Soviet Government tries, by separate action, to build up a pro-Communist Germany in their areas, this will cause new serious difficulties in the British and American zones, and will give the defeated Germans the power of putting themselves up to auction between the Soviets and the Western Democracies. Whatever conclusions may be drawn from these facts—and facts they are—this is certainly not the Liberated Europe we fought to build up. Nor is it one which contains the essentials of permanent peace. . . .

. . . I do not believe that Soviet Russia desires war. What they desire is the fruits of war and the indefinite expansion of their power and doctrines. But what we have to consider here to-day while time remains, is the permanent prevention of war and the establishment of the conditions of freedom and democracy as rapidly as possible in all countries. . . .

From what I have seen of our Russian friends and allies during the war, I am convinced that there is nothing they admire so much as strength, and there is nothing for which they have less respect than for weakness, especially military weakness.

*Source: Winston S. Churchill: His Complete Speeches, 1897–1963*, vol. VII, *1943–1949*, ed. Robert Rhodes James (New York: Chelsea House, 1974), pp. 7290–7292.

**For additional information on this topic, go to http://college.hmco.com.**

Under these circumstances, the Soviets were able to work with local communists to install new communist-led regimes friendly to the Soviet Union in most of east-central Europe. But though Churchill warned as early as 1946 that "an iron curtain" was descending from the Baltic to the Adriatic, the process of Soviet power consolidation was not easy, and it took place gradually, in discrete steps over several years. (See the two boxes "Reading Sources: Discerning the Iron Curtain" and "Reading Sources: Churchill as Warmonger: Stalin's Response to the 'Iron

# Churchill as Warmonger: Stalin's Response to the "Iron Curtain" Speech

*Soviet leader Joseph Stalin was quick to respond to Churchill's speech. In an interview in the official Soviet newspaper* Pravda *eight days later (March 13, 1946), he accused Churchill of calling for war on the Soviet Union. But Stalin also revealed the more subtle concerns that were causing the divergence between the Soviets and their former allies, Britain and the United States. The three countries had joined forces against Hitler, but the Soviets' geographical situation and recent historical experience contrasted sharply with U.S. and British circumstances. These dissimilarities, perhaps even more than ideological differences, led Stalin to his antithetical interpretation of the outcomes and lessons of the recent war.*

*Question:* How do you appraise Mr. Churchill's latest speech in the United States of America?

*Answer:* I appraise it as a dangerous act, calculated to sow the seeds of dissension among the Allied states and impede their collaboration. . . .

. . . Mr. Churchill now takes the stand of the warmongers. . . .

. . . The German race theory led Hitler and his friends to the conclusion that the Germans, as the only superior nation, should rule over other nations. The English race theory leads Mr. Churchill and his friends to the conclusion that the English-speaking nations, as the only superior nations, should rule over the rest of the nations of the world. . . .

*Question:* How do you appraise the part of Mr. Churchill's speech in which he attacks the democratic systems in the European states bordering upon us, and criticizes the good neighborly relations established between these states and the Soviet Union?

*Answer:* This part of Mr. Churchill's speech is compounded of elements of slander and elements of discourtesy and tactlessness. . . .

. . . [T]he following circumstances should not be forgotten. The Germans made their invasion of the U.S.S.R. through Finland, Poland, Rumania, Bulgaria, and Hungary. The Germans were able to make their invasion through these countries because, at the time, governments hostile to the Soviet Union existed in these countries. As a result of the German invasion the Soviet Union has lost irretrievably in the fighting against the Germans, and also through the German occupation and the deportation of Soviet citizens to German servitude, a total of about seven million people. In other words, the Soviet Union's loss of life has been several times greater than that of Britain and the United States of America put together. Possibly in some quarters an inclination is felt to forget about these colossal sacrifices of the Soviet people which secured the liberation of Europe from the Hitlerite yoke. But the Soviet Union cannot forget about them. And so what can there be surprising about the fact that the Soviet Union, anxious for its future safety, is trying to see to it that governments loyal in their attitude to the Soviet Union should exist in these countries? How can anyone, who has not taken leave of his wits, describe these peaceful aspirations of the Soviet Union as expansionist tendencies on the part of our state? . . .

Mr. Churchill comes somewhere near the truth when he speaks of the increasing influence of the Communist parties in eastern Europe. It must be remarked, however, that he is not quite accurate. The influence of the Communist parties has grown not only in eastern Europe, but in nearly all the countries of Europe which were previously under fascist rule . . . or which experienced German, Italian, or Hungarian occupation. . . .

The increased influence of the Communists cannot be considered fortuitous. It is a perfectly logical thing. The influence of the Communists has grown because, in the years of the rule of fascism in Europe, the Communists showed themselves trusty, fearless, self-sacrificing fighters against the fascist regime for the liberty of the peoples.

*Source:* Josef Stalin, "Churchill's Speech Is a Call for War on Russia," in Walter LaFeber, ed., *The Origins of the Cold War, 1941–1947* (New York: Weber), pp. 139–143.

Curtain' Speech.") The Communist-led government of Poland held elections in January 1947—but rigged them to guarantee a favorable outcome. In Czechoslovakia the communists anticipated serious losses in upcoming elections and so finally took power outright in 1948. By 1949 communist governments, relying on Soviet support, controlled Poland, Czechoslovakia, East Germany, Hungary, Romania, and Bulgaria, with Yugoslavia and Albania also communist but capable of a more independent line.

Communism might have spread still farther in Europe, and perhaps beyond, but the West drew the line at Greece. There, as in Yugoslavia, an indigenous, communist-led resistance movement had become strong enough to contend for political power by late 1944. But when it sought to oust the monarchical government that had just returned to Greece from exile, the British intervened, helping the monarchy put down the leftist uprising. Although Stalin gave the Greek communists little help, communist guerrilla activity continued, thanks partly to support from Tito's Yugoslavia. In 1946 a renewed communist insurgency escalated into civil war.

As the cold war developed, both the Soviet Union and the United States began taking a more active interest in the Greek conflict, though Soviet intentions remained uncertain. After the financially strapped Labour government in Britain reduced its involvement early in 1947, the United States stepped in to support the Greek monarchy against the communists. American policymakers feared that communism would progress from the Balkans through Greece to the Middle East. Thus, in March 1947, President Truman announced the Truman Doctrine, which committed the United States to the "containment" of communism throughout the world. American advisers now began re-equipping the anticommunist forces in Greece. Faced with this determined opposition from the West, Stalin again pulled back, but the Greek communists, with their strong indigenous support, were not defeated until 1949.

Thus the wartime marriage of expediency between the Soviet Union and the Western democracies gradually fell apart in the war's aftermath. Only in Austria, jointly occupied by the Soviets and the Western democracies, were the former Allies able to arrange the postwar transition in a reasonably amicable way. The Soviets accepted the neutralization of a democratic Austria as the occupying powers left in 1955. Elsewhere, Europe was divided into two antagonistic power blocs.

The antagonism between the two superpowers became more menacing when the Soviets exploded their first atomic bomb in August 1949, intensifying the postwar arms race. By then, in fact, the United States was on its way to the more destructive hydrogen bomb. The split

between these two nations, unmistakable by 1949, established the framework for world affairs for the next forty years.

## ■ The West and the New World Agenda

At the same time, other dramatic changes around the world suggested that, with or without the cold war, the postwar political scene would be hard to manage. Events in India in 1947, in Israel in 1948, and in China in 1949 epitomized the new hopes and uncertainties that were the offspring of World War II.

Although the British, under U.S. pressure, had reluctantly promised independence for India in order to

**Gandhi and Anticolonialism**    An apostle of nonviolence, Mohandas Gandhi became one of the most admired individuals of the century as he spearheaded the movement for Indian independence. He is pictured (*center*) in December 1942 with the British statesman Sir Stafford Cripps (*left*), who had come to India to offer a plan for Indian self-government. Despite the good spirit evident here, Cripps's mission failed; Gandhi and his movement held out for full independence. *(Corbis)*

**Map 28.5   The Proposed Partition of Palestine and the Birth of the State of Israel**   In November 1947 the United Nations offered a plan to partition the British mandate of Palestine, but complications immediately arose. The Jews of the area won their own state, Israel, but the Palestinian Arabs did not. Thus tensions continued in the area.

elicit Indian support during the war, British authorities and Indian leaders had continued to skirmish. Mohandas Gandhi was twice jailed for resisting British demands and threatening a massive program of nonviolent resistance to British rule. But by 1946 the British lacked the will and the financial resources to maintain their control on the subcontinent. Thus Britain acquiesced as the new independent states of India and Pakistan emerged on August 15, 1947. Allowing independence to India, long the jewel of the British Empire, raised questions about Britain's role in the postwar world and portended a wider disintegration of the European colonial system. There would be new countries, many of them poor—and resentful of Western imperialism. What would that mean for the new world order, centering on the United Nations, that Roosevelt had envisioned?

Questions about the fate of the Jews, who had suffered so grievously during World War II, were inevitable as well. Almost two-thirds of the Jews of Europe had been killed, and many of the survivors either had no place to go or had decided that they could never again live as a minority in Europe. Many concluded that the Jews must have a homeland of their own. For decades such Zionist sentiment (see page 824) had centered on the biblical area of Israel, in what had become, after World War I, the British mandate of Palestine. Jewish immigration to the area accelerated during the interwar period, but it caused increasing friction between Jews and the Palestinian Arabs.

Concerned about access to Middle Eastern oil, the British sought to cultivate good relations with the Arab world after the war. Thus they opposed further immigration of Jews to Palestine, as well as proposals to carve an independent Jewish state from the area. The United States, however, was considerably more sympathetic to the Zionist cause. As tensions built, Jewish terrorists blew up the British headquarters in Jerusalem, and the British decided to abandon what seemed a no-win situation. In September 1947 they announced their intention to withdraw from Palestine, leaving its future to the United Nations. In November the UN voted to partition Palestine, creating both a Jewish and a new Arab Palestinian state (see Map 28.5).

Skirmishing between Jews and Arabs became full-scale war in December, and in that context the Jews declared their independence as the new state of Israel on May 14, 1948. When fighting ended in 1949, the Israelis had conquered more territory than had been envisioned in the original partition plan, and the remaining Arab territories fell to Egypt and Jordan, rather than forming an independent Palestinian state. Thus was born the new state of Israel, partly a product of the assault on the Jews during World War II. Yet it was born amid Arab hostility and Western concerns about oil, and so its long-term prospects remained uncertain.

In 1949 the communist insurgency in China under Mao Zedong (Mao Tse-tung) (see page 920) finally triumphed over the Chinese Nationalists under Jiang Jieshi (Chiang Kai-shek), who fled to the island of Taiwan. During the war, the Communists had done better than the Nationalists at identifying themselves with the Chinese cause against both Japanese and Western imperialism. And after their victory, the Chinese Communists enjoyed great prestige among other "national liberation" movements struggling against Western colonialists. To many in the West, however, the outcome in China by 1949 simply intensified fears that communism was poised to infect the unsettled postwar world.

# SUMMARY

THE war that began in Europe in 1939 gradually spread to become by far the widest and most destructive in history. Driven by expansionist aims, the aggressors—first Germany and then Japan—won impressive victories at the start. Then a Grand Alliance of Britain, the Soviet Union, and the United States gradually came together and won the war in both Europe and Asia by August 1945. But the war brought unprecedented death and destruction and troubling new forms of violence, from factorylike genocide to the nuclear bombing of civilians.

As a result of the war, the two major fascist powers collapsed and fascist forms of politics, with their hostility to democracy and their tendencies toward violence and war, stood discredited. But it was not clear whether Germany and Italy, and, for that matter, much of the rest of Europe, would be able to develop effective democratic political systems amid defeat and destruction.

The Soviets had borne the brunt of the war in Europe, and the Soviet Union—and its communist system—emerged with enhanced prestige. At the same time, an overseas war had again drawn the United States, which was prepared in the aftermath, as it had not been after World War I, to play an ongoing leadership role in world affairs. The Soviet Union and the United States offered competing visions of the future, and during the decades that followed, their competition helped shape everything from Italian domestic politics to the decolonization struggle in southern Africa.

By 1949 the division of Europe, the advent of nuclear weapons, and the symptomatic events in India, Israel, and China made it clear that the world's agenda had been radically transformed in the ten years since the beginning of World War II. With the Soviet Union and United States emerging from the war as superpowers, and with the once-dominant European countries weakened and chastened, the center of gravity in the West changed dramatically. Thus the relationship between the West and the world was bound to be radically different.

Whereas there had been, for a while, some illusion of a "return to normal" after World War I, it was obvious after World War II that the old Europe was gone forever. Indeed, much of Europe's proud culture, on the basis of which it had claimed to lead the world, lay in the ruins of war, apparently exhausted. What role could Europe play in Western civilization, and in the wider world, after all that had happened? What lessons had been learned, and what foundations for the future could be found, as the experiment continued?

## ■ Notes

1. From Farrell's full account as related by General Leslie Groves in his "Memorandum to the Secretary of War," dated July 18, 1945, in Philip L. Cantelon, Richard G. Hewlett, and Robert C. Williams, eds., *The American Atom: A Documentary History of Nuclear Policies from the Discovery of Fission to the Present*, 2d ed. (Philadelphia: University of Pennsylvania Press, 1991), pp. 56–57.
2. Quoted in Karl Dietrich Bracher, *The German Dictatorship: The Origins, Structure, and Effects of National Socialism*, trans. Jean Steinberg (New York: Praeger, 1970), p. 423.

## ■ Suggested Reading

Browning, Christopher R. *Ordinary Men: Reserve Police Battalion 101 and the Final Solution in Poland*. With a new afterword. 1998. A case study approach to the role of ordinary Germans in the Holocaust.

Campbell, John, ed. *The Experience of World War II*. 1989. Focusing on the experience of those touched by the war, this collaborative volume covers everything from prisoners of war to the uses of the arts for propaganda purposes; large format, with superb illustrations and maps.

Gaddis, John Lewis. *We Now Know: Rethinking Cold War History*. 1997. Taking advantage of newly available Russian and Chinese documents, a leading authority reassesses the cold war, from its origins to the Cuban missile crisis of 1962.

Hilberg, Raul. *Perpetrators, Victims, Bystanders: The Jewish Catastrophe, 1933–1945*. 1992. The dean of Holocaust historians offers an accessible, compelling account by weaving capsule portraits delineating the many layers of involvement and responsibility at issue in the Holocaust.

Keegan, John. *The Second World War*. 1989. A detailed but readable study featuring military operations; well illustrated.

Overy, Richard J. *Why the Allies Won*. 1995. Denying that the sheer weight of numbers made the outcome inevitable, this account focuses on the differences in political, economic, and even moral mobilization to explain why the Allies defeated the Axis powers.

Parker, R. A. C. *Struggle for Survival: The History of the Second World War*. 1990. This accessible, comprehensive, and well-balanced survey is especially good on debates over strategy and the wider implications of the strategies chosen.

Trachtenberg, Marc. *A Constructed Peace: The Making of the European Settlement, 1945–1963*. 1999. An original work that pushes beyond the long-standing cold war framework to argue that concerns about Germany and nuclear weapons were central to the postwar settlement.

Weinberg, Gerhard L. *A World at Arms: A Global History of World War II*. 1994. An enlightening global approach by a leading historian of the period that stresses the interrelationship among simultaneous events and decisions in the various theaters of the war around the world.

 **For a searchable list of additional readings for this chapter, go to http://college.hmco.com.**

# Holocaust Testimony

There were loud announcements, but it was all fairly restrained: nobody did anything to us. I followed the crowd: "Men to the right, women and children to the left," we had been told. The women and children disappeared into a barrack further to the left and we were told to undress. One of the SS men—later I knew his name, Küttner—told us in a chatty sort of tone that we were going into a disinfection bath and afterwards would be assigned work. Clothes, he said, could be left in a heap on the floor, and we'd find them again later. . . .

The queue began to move and I suddenly noticed several men fully dressed standing near another barrack further back, and I was wondering who they were. And just then another SS man (Miete was his name) came by me and said, "Come on, you, get back into your clothes, quick, special work." That was the first time I was frightened. Everything was very quiet, you know. And when he said that to me, the others turned around and looked at me—and I thought, my God, why me, why does he pick on me? When I had got back into my clothes, the line had moved on and I noticed that several other young men had also been picked out and were dressing. We were taken through to the "work-barrack," most of which was filled from floor to ceiling with clothes, stacked up in layers. . . . You understand, there was no time, not a moment between the instant we were taken in there and put to work, to talk to anyone, to take stock of what was happening . . . [ellipses in the original] and of course never forget that we had no idea at all what this whole installation was for. One saw these stacks of clothing—I suppose the thought must have entered our minds, where do they come from, what are they? We must have connected them with the clothes all of us had just taken off outside . . . [ellipses in the original] but I cannot remember doing that. I only remember starting work at once making bundles.*

*The testimony of Richard Glazar is from Gitta Sereny, *Into That Darkness: An Examination of Conscience* (New York: Random House, Vintage Books, 1983), pp. 176–179, 183.

This is the voice of Richard Glazar, recalling when, as a young Jewish student from Prague, he arrived at the Nazi extermination camp at Treblinka in October 1942. Glazar was telling his story in 1972 to the British journalist Gitta Sereny, who had been covering the trial in Germany of the commandant of the Treblinka camp, Franz Stangl. Seeking to understand Stangl, Sereny tracked down a number of those who had come into contact with him, including survivors like Glazar.

Glazar's recollections are part of a rich body of testimony by Jewish survivors of the Holocaust, testimony that is often moving, gripping, terrifying. Some accounts offer direct personal recollections. Others integrate personal remembrance into literature. Still others use the insights of social psychology in an effort to explain the special features of the camp experience.

Even with all this evidence, we wonder if we can ever really grasp what millions of Jews experienced at the hands of the Nazis in the extermination camps. But listening to witnesses like Glazar, we gain some sense of the uncertainty and fear, the suffering and humiliation, that helped define that experience. And we recognize the determination, the affirmation of life, that marked the Jewish response.

We may be surprised at Glazar's insistence that "we had no idea at all what this whole installation was for." Didn't the Jews understand what the camps held for them? In fact, some Jews had a better idea than others, but in most cases only through rumor, and no one could know the whole story as it was unfolding. Over a year before, Glazar's family had sent him to work in the country, where they assumed he would be safe, so he had been relatively isolated. But what one knew, or could surmise, also depended on what one was prepared to believe was possible, what the world could hold. Some simply could not believe the rumors.

Once they were in the camps, however, the Jews could only come to terms with the unprecedented situation as best they could. Let us listen further to Glazar, whose insights into the minds of the SS overseers help us better to grasp the terrible capriciousness of the situation:

One must not forget their incredible power, their autonomy within their narrow and yet, as far as we were concerned, unlimited field; but also the isolation created by their unique situation and by what they—and hardly anyone else even within the German or Nazi community—had in common. Perhaps if this isolation had been the result of good rather than evil deeds, their own relationship towards each other would have been different. As it was, most of them seemed to hate and despise each other and do anything—almost anything—to "get at" each other. Thus, if one of them selected a man out of a new transport for work, in other words to stay alive at least for a while, it could perfectly easily happen . . . that one of his rivals . . . would come along and kill that man just to spite him. . . . All this created a virtually indescribable atmosphere of fear. The most important thing for a prisoner at Treblinka, you see, was not to make himself conspicuous.

But what, then, can be said about the human attributes that such conditions called forth—and that enabled some, at least, to survive?

Our daily life? It was in a way very directed, very specific. . . . [I]t was essential to fill oneself completely with a determination to survive; it was essential to create in oneself a capacity for dissociating oneself to some extent from Treblinka; it was important not to adapt completely to it. . . .

It wasn't *ruthlessness* that enabled an individual to survive—it was an intangible quality, not peculiar to educated or sophisticated individuals. Anyone might have it. It is perhaps best described as an overriding thirst—perhaps, too, a talent for life, and a faith in life.

Glazar, of course, was speaking thirty years later, and despite the engaging spontaneity of his testimony, he may have forgotten things, or the experiences of the intervening years may have colored his memory. Moreover, he could only tell what he recalled through the categories of language, which may be inadequate to convey, to those who were not there, what it was like to be sent to Nazi extermination camps. Perhaps survivors called upon, years later, to put their recollections into words are bound to impose too much order, even to romanticize, by using categories their listeners can understand—or want to hear. Glazar was clearly stretching to find the words. Does "talent for life" ring true? We will continue to wonder.

As for Glazar himself, he escaped from Treblinka in an uprising in August 1943, and then made his way to Germany, where he managed to survive the war disguised as a foreign laborer. When Sereny reached him in 1972, he was living in Switzerland, working as an engineer.

**Arrival at the Auschwitz Extermination Camp**

(*Corbis*)

# CHAPTER 29

# An Anxious Stability: The Age of the Cold War 1949–1989

THE atmosphere was festive, euphoric. Those who came to celebrate could hardly believe it was happening, for it had been unthinkable just a few months before. Yet happening it was, one of the defining events of the twentieth century, live on television. This was November 1989, and the Berlin Wall was coming down.

Erected to stop emigration from communist East Germany to the West in 1961, the wall had become an all-too-tangible symbol of the division of Europe, and much of the world, for more than four decades after World War II. The two superpowers that had emerged from the war, the Soviet Union and the United States, had settled into a cold war marked by ideological competition, an arms race, and nuclear stalemate.

As a physical barrier of concrete and barbed wire, the Berlin Wall had divided families and caused much human suffering. Indeed, 191 people died and 5,000 were arrested trying to cross it. But the East German government, by 1989 desperate to preserve its legitimacy, opened the wall on November 9—and began dismantling it within days. However, it proved too late. The communist regime in East Germany collapsed as part of a wider anticommunist revolution that finally enveloped even the Soviet Union in 1991. The anxious cold war era was suddenly over; virtually no one had foreseen its abrupt ending.

Although Berlin had been a particular hot spot, the cold war was global in scope. It seemed that confrontation between the Soviet Union and the United States might take place almost anywhere, sparking the cold war into a hot war threatening nuclear annihilation. And indeed confrontation came closest not over Berlin but over Soviet missiles in Cuba in 1962. That crisis was surmounted, and

East Germans (*backs to camera*) stream through the dismantled Berlin Wall into West Berlin.
(Lionel Cironneau/AP/Wide World Photos)

**The Search for Cultural Bearings**

**Prosperity and Democracy in Western Europe**

**The Communist Bloc: From Consolidation to Stagnation**

**Europe, the West, and the World**

**The Collapse of the Soviet System, 1975–1991**

East-West relations alternately warmed and cooled during the quarter century that followed.

Both halves of Europe had to operate within the bipolar framework, but the Western and Soviet blocs confronted different challenges and evolved in different ways. The countries of western Europe adjusted to a diminished international role as they recognized their dependence on U.S. leadership and gradually lost their overseas colonies. The change in scale led many politicians and intellectuals to advocate some form of European union, which might eventually enable the western Europeans to deal with the superpowers on a more equal basis. On the domestic level, the immediate postwar situation was so unsettled that few western European countries could simply return to the prewar norm. Postwar reconstruction rested on a new consensus that government must play a more active role in promoting economic growth and social welfare. By the 1960s the promise of shared prosperity was realized to a remarkable extent. But changing circumstances by the early 1970s threatened the consensus that postwar prosperity had made possible.

Although the Soviet Union had suffered immensely in winning World War II, the communist regime emerged from the war with renewed legitimacy. During the 1950s and 1960s, the Soviet system achieved some significant successes, but its efforts to outgrow its Stalinist framework were halting. By 1980 the system was becoming rigid and stagnant. And thus the dramatic changes in the Soviet bloc that came to a head in 1989, leading to the opening of the Berlin Wall and, by 1991, to the end of communism in Europe. Only as it was ending, more than four decades after World War II, did observers realize that the anxious cold war era had been one of relative stability and peace.

## Questions to Consider

- What factors led to the surprisingly rapid restoration of democracy in much of continental western Europe after World War II?

- How did decolonization and the beginnings of European integration reflect the changing status of western Europe in world affairs during the cold war era?

- What caused the new sociopolitical discontents evident in western Europe by the end of the 1960s?

- What led to the collapse of the communist system in the Soviet Union and its satellite states?

## Terms to Know

| | |
|---|---|
| existentialism | Prague Spring |
| welfare state | Suez crisis |
| North Atlantic Treaty Organization (NATO) | European Economic Community (EEC) |
| Warsaw Pact | Helsinki Accords |
| Konrad Adenauer | Solidarity |
| Willy Brandt | Mikhail Gorbachev |

## THE SEARCH FOR CULTURAL BEARINGS

 HE events from World War I to the cold war added up to an unprecedented period of disaster for Europe. Europeans were bound to ask what had gone wrong, and what could be salvaged from the ruins of a culture that had made possible the most destructive wars in history, as well as fascism, totalitarianism, and the Holocaust. With so much discredited or called into question, Europeans faced an unprecedented period of experiment.

The cold war framework crucially shaped responses all over the Western world. Some embraced the Soviet Union or sought a renewed Marxism. Opposition to communism helped stimulate others to return to religious or classical traditions or to embrace new ideas associated with America's recent successes. In western Europe, at least, this effort to take stock led promptly to the renewed determination and fresh ideas that helped produce the dramatically successful reconstruction of the postwar years. But the anxieties stemming from superpower rivalry, and especially the nuclear arms race, were bound to temper any renewed optimism.

## ■ Absurdity and Commitment in Existentialism

The postwar mood of exhaustion and despair found classic expression in the work of the Irish-born writer Samuel Beckett (1906–1989), especially in his plays *Waiting for Godot* (1952) and *Endgame* (1957). Through Beckett's characters, we see ourselves going through the motions, with nothing worth saying or doing, ludicrously manipulating the husks of a worn-out culture. The only redeeming element is the comic pathos we feel as we watch ourselves.

The same sense of anxiety and despair led to the vogue of existentialism, a movement that marked philosophy, the arts, and popular culture from the later 1940s until well into the 1950s. Existentialism developed from the ideas of the German thinker Martin Heidegger (1889–1976), especially *Being and Time* (1927), one of the most influential philosophical works of the century. Though it was a philosophy of sorts, existentialism was most significant as a broader cultural tendency, finding expression in novels and films. The existentialists explored what it means to be a human being in a world cast adrift from its cultural moorings, with no mutually accepted guideposts, standards, or values.

The most influential postwar existentialists were the Frenchmen Jean-Paul Sartre° (1905–1980) and Albert Camus° (1913–1960), each of whom had been involved in the French resistance, Camus in a particularly central role as editor of an underground newspaper. For both, an authentic human response to a world spinning out of control entailed engagement, commitment, responsibility—even though every action is fraught with risk.

Rather than accept the bleak, ludicrously comic vision of Beckett's plays, Camus sought to show how we might go on living in a positive, affirmative spirit, even in a world that seemed simply absurd in one sense, especially after the recent disasters in Europe. Conventional values like friendship and tolerance could be made usable again, based on the simple fact that we human beings are all caught up in this unmasterable situation together. People suffer and die, but as we come together to help as best we can, we might at least learn to stop killing one another.

Camus split from Sartre in a disagreement over the ongoing value of Marxism and the communist experiment

**Sartre** (SAH-truh)  **Camus** (kah-MOO)

## CHRONOLOGY

| | |
|---|---|
| **1947** | India and Pakistan achieve independence |
| | Marshall Plan announced |
| **1949** | Formation of NATO |
| **1951** | Formation of the European Coal and Steel Community |
| **1953** | Death of Stalin |
| | Workers' revolt in East Germany |
| **1955** | West Germany joins NATO |
| | Warsaw Pact |
| **1956** | Khrushchev de-Stalinization speech |
| | Suez crisis |
| | Hungarian reform movement crushed |
| **1957** | *Sputnik I* launched |
| | Common Market established |
| **1958** | Beginning of Fifth Republic in France |
| **1959** | Bad Godesberg congress: reorientation of German socialism |
| **1961** | Berlin Wall erected |
| **1962** | Algerian independence from France |
| | Cuban missile crisis |
| **1964** | Ouster of Khrushchev |
| **1968** | Days of May uprising in France |
| | Prague Spring reform movement crushed |
| **1969** | Brandt becomes West German chancellor |
| **1973** | First OPEC oil crisis |
| **1975** | North Vietnamese victory and reunification of Vietnam |
| **1979** | Election of Pope John Paul II |
| **1980** | Formation of Solidarity in Poland |
| | Formation of independent Zimbabwe from Southern Rhodesia |
| **1982** | Death of Brezhnev |
| **1985** | Gorbachev comes to power in the Soviet Union |
| **1986** | Chernobyl disaster |
| **1989** | Collapse of communism in east-central Europe |
| **1991** | Collapse of communism in the Soviet Union |
| | Dissolution of the Soviet Union |

**Sartre and de Beauvoir** Among the most influential intellectual couples of the century, Jean-Paul Sartre and Simone de Beauvoir emerged as leaders of French existentialism by the later 1940s. See the box on page 994. *(Giansant/Sygma)*

in the Soviet Union. Though never an orthodox communist, Sartre found potential for human liberation in the working class, in communist parties, even in the Soviet Union itself, which he saw as the strongest alternative to U.S. imperialism. By the 1950s he was portraying existentialism as fundamentally a way to revitalize Marxism.

By contrast, Camus, who had started as a communist in the 1930s, had grown disillusioned with communism even before the war, and his major political tract, *The Rebel* (1951), was partly an attack on Marxism and communism. Establishing new bases for human happiness and solidarity meant recognizing limits to what human beings could accomplish, limits even to our demands for freedom and justice. These were precisely the limits that the new political movements of the century had so disastrously overstepped. Communism, like fascism, was part of the problem, not the solution.

### ■ Marxists and Traditionalists

Sartre was among the many European intellectuals who believed that Marxism had won a new lease on life from the wartime resistance. As they saw it, Marxism could be revamped for the West, without the Stalinist excesses of the Soviet Union. Marxism remained a significant strand in Western political culture throughout the cold war era, but it also attracted periodic waves of denunciation.

In Italy, as in France, the communists' major role in the resistance enhanced their prestige, preparing the way for the extraordinary posthumous influence of Antonio

Gramsci° (1891–1937), a founder of the Italian Communist Party who had spent most of the fascist period in prison. His *Prison Notebooks,* published during the late 1940s, became influential throughout the world and helped make Marxism a powerful force in postwar Italian culture. Seeking to learn the lessons of the fascist triumph in Italy, Gramsci pointed Marxists toward a flexible political strategy, attuned to the special historical circumstances of each country. Thanks partly to Gramsci's legacy, Italy had the most innovative and important communist party outside the communist world for several decades after the war.

Loosely Marxist ideas were central to the renewal of political activism in the West by the later 1960s, although Marxism proved more effective as a critique of capitalism than as a blueprint for change. The best-known spokesman for a renewed radicalism on both sides of the Atlantic during the late 1960s and early 1970s was the German-born social thinker Herbert Marcuse° (1898–1979), who explored the cultural mechanisms through which capitalism perpetuates itself in *One-Dimensional Man* (1964).

Even during the late 1940s, however, others, like Camus, denied that any recasting could overcome the inherent flaws in Marxism. Damaging revelations about the excesses of Stalinism during the 1930s seemed to confirm this view. Such writers as the Hungarian-born Arthur Koestler° (1905–1983) who had believed in communism during the 1930s now denounced it as "the God that failed." Whatever its initial promise, Marxism anywhere would inevitably lead to the kind of tyranny that had developed in the Soviet Union. In his futuristic novel *Nineteen Eighty-Four,* published in 1949, the British intellectual George Orwell, long a partisan of leftist causes, chillingly portrayed the dehumanization that totalitarianism—and by association, communism—conjured up.

By the mid-1970s, the disturbing portrait of the Soviet gulag, or forced-labor-camp system, by the exiled Soviet writer Alexander Solzhenitsyn° (b. 1918) stimulated another wave of anticommunist thinking. And whether or not Marxism was necessarily Stalinist and repressive in implication, its relevance to the increasingly prosperous industrial democracies of western Europe was open to question. By the early 1980s, many had come to believe that the Marxist understanding of capitalism and class relations was simply passé.

Those hostile to Marxism often insisted that the West had to reconnect with older traditions if it was to avoid further horrors like those it had just been through.

---

**Gramsci** (GRAHM-she)  **Marcuse** (mar-KOO-zuh)
**Koestler** (KEST-lur)  **Solzhenitsyn** (soul-zhen-IT-sin)

**Dubuffet: Spinning Round**
Seeking to depart from the European tradition of sophisticated, well-made art, Jean Dubuffet developed imagery that was at once crude and primitive, playful and whimsical.    *(Dubuffet, Jean,* Spinning Round, *1961. ARS Tate Gallery, London/Art Resource, NY)*

Especially in the first years after the war, many, like the French Catholic thinker Jacques Maritain° (1882–1973), held that only a return to religious traditions would suffice. For the American-born British writer T. S. Eliot (1888–1965), the essential return to tradition had to embrace family and locality, as well as religion. Without a return to tradition, Eliot warned, the West could expect more excesses such as fascism and totalitarianism in the future.

### ■ The Intellectual Migration and Americanism

The extraordinary migration of European artists and intellectuals to the United States to escape persecution during the 1930s and 1940s profoundly affected the cultural life of the postwar period. An array of luminaries arrived on American shores, from the composer Igor Stravinsky to the theoretical physicist Albert Einstein, from the architect Walter Gropius to the radical social theorist Herbert Marcuse.

Before this cross-fertilization, American culture had remained somewhat provincial, sometimes proudly and self-consciously so. All the direct contact with the Euro-

peans by the 1940s helped propel the United States into the Western cultural mainstream. No longer could "Western" culture be identified primarily with Europe. In some spheres—painting, for example—Americans were now confident enough to claim the leadership for the first time.

With the abstract expressionism of the later 1940s, American painters began creating visual images the likes of which had never been seen in Europe. In comparison with the raw, energetic painting of Jackson Pollock (1912–1956), the work of the Europeans seemed merely "pretty"—and the newly brash Americans were not shy about telling them so. Now New York began to supplant Paris as the art capital of the Western world.

But the American achievement owed something to European existentialism, and it became possible only because so many of the most innovative European painters had come to New York, where the Americans had been able to learn their lessons at first hand. At the same time, European painters such as Jean Dubuffet° (1901–1985) in France and Francis Bacon (1910–1992) in Britain created new forms of their own—sometimes playful, sometimes brutal—as they sought the startling

**Maritain** (mar-eh-TAHN)

**Dubuffet** (doo-boo-FAY)

new visual imagery that seemed appropriate to Western culture after the era of fascism and war. Even in the United States, artists began reacting against the deep seriousness of abstract expressionism during the mid-1950s. One new direction led by the early 1960s to "pop art," which was "American" in a different sense, featuring the ordinary objects and mass-produced images of modern consumerist culture. (See the feature "Weighing the Evidence: Pop Art" on pages 1020–1021.)

Some Europeans were eager to embrace what seemed distinctively American because America had remained relatively free of the political ideologies that seemed to have led Europe to totalitarianism and ruin. By the 1950s, there was much talk of "the end of ideology," with America pointing the way to a healthier alternative, combining technology, value-free social science, and scientific management. Whereas the old European way led either to mere theorizing, to political extremism, or to polarization and impasse, the American approach got results by tackling problems one at a time, so that they could be solved by managerial or technical experts.

Such Americanism fed the notion that Europe needed a clean break based on technological values. If such a break was necessary, however, what was to become of the European tradition, for centuries the center of gravity of the West, and until recently dominant in the world? Did anything distinctively European remain, or was Europe doomed to lick its wounds in the shadow of America? These questions lurked in the background as Europeans faced the difficult task of economic and political restoration.

# PROSPERITY AND DEMOCRACY IN WESTERN EUROPE

Y 1941 democracy seemed to be dying on the European continent, yet it quickly revived in western Europe after World War II, taking root more easily than most had thought possible. The bipolar international framework helped. The United States actively encouraged democracy, and Europeans nervous about communism and the Soviet Union were happy to follow the American lead. Success at economic reconstruction was important as well. Not only was there greater prosperity, but governments could afford to deliver on promises of enhanced security, social welfare, and equal opportunity. It also mattered that western Europeans learned from past mistakes.

## ■ Economic Reconstruction and the Atlantic Orientation

It is hard to imagine how desperate the situation in much of western Europe had become by 1945. Major cities like Rotterdam, Hamburg, and Le Havre lay largely in ruins, and normal routines suffered radical disruption. Production had declined to perhaps 25 percent of the prewar level in Italy, to 20 percent in France, and to a mere 5 percent in southern Germany. Cigarettes, often gained through barter from American soldiers, served widely as a medium of exchange.

Although the U.S. commitment to assist European reconstruction was not originally a cold war measure, the developing cold war context made it seem all the more necessary for the United States to help the Europeans get their economies running again. The key was the Marshall Plan, which U.S. secretary of state General George Marshall outlined in 1947, and which channeled $13.5 billion in aid to western Europe by 1951.

Cold war concerns deepened the partnership in April 1949, when the United States spearheaded a military alliance, the North Atlantic Treaty Organization (NATO), that included much of western Europe. The Soviets were tightening their grip on their satellite states in east-central Europe, and the NATO alliance was intended to check any Soviet expansion westward. The Soviets had considerable superiority in conventional forces, which had ready access to western Europe, but U.S. nuclear superiority provided a balance. Indeed, the American nuclear guarantee to western Europe was the cornerstone of the NATO alliance. Thus it seemed crucial for the United States to maintain its superiority in nuclear weapons, a fact that fueled the continuing arms race and nuclear buildup.

On the economic level, the west Europeans quickly proved worthy partners. So impressive was the recovery in continental western Europe by the 1950s that some dubbed it an "economic miracle." West Europeans took advantage of the need to rebuild by adopting up-to-date methods and technologies, though economic strategies differed from one country to the next. The new German government cut state aid to business and limited the longstanding power of cartels—organizations of private businesses that regulate the production, pricing, and marketing of goods. The state was permitted to intervene in the economy only to ensure free competition. In France, by contrast, many were determined to use government to modernize the country, thereby overcoming the weakness that had led to defeat. So France adopted a flexible, pragmatic form of government-led economic planning.

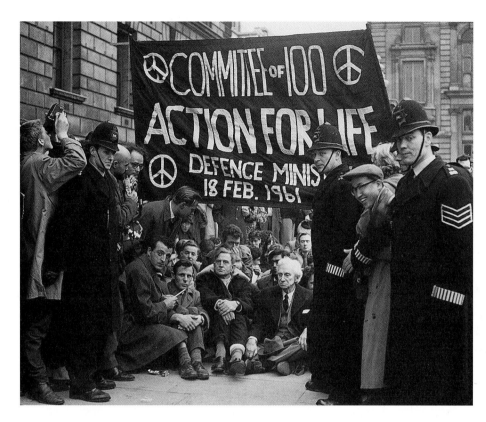

**Ban the Bomb**   As nuclear tension escalated during the 1950s, some built air-raid shelters; others took to the streets in antinuclear protests. The protest movement was especially prominent in Britain, where the noted philosopher Bertrand Russell (1872–1970) played a central role. Here, seated at right, he awaits arrest during a sit-in demonstration outside the British Defense Ministry.
*(Hulton Getty/Liaison)*

In 1946 Jean Monnet° (1888–1979) launched the first of the French postwar economic plans, which brought government and business leaders together to agree on production targets. Economic planning enabled France to make especially effective use of the capital that the Marshall Plan provided. French industrial production returned to its prewar peak by 1951, and by 1957 it had risen to twice the level of 1938.

Strong and sustained rates of economic growth were achieved throughout much of western Europe until the later 1960s. From 1953 to 1964, annual rates of growth averaged 6 percent in Germany, 5.6 percent in Italy, and 4.9 percent in France. Britain, however, lagged considerably, averaging only 2.7 percent growth annually during that same period.

As part of the new postwar consensus, labor was supposed to be brought more fully into economic decision making. Thus, for example, the trade unions participated in the planning process in France. In Germany the codetermination law of 1951 provided for labor participation in management decisions in heavy industry, and labor representatives were given access to company books and full voting memberships on boards of direc-

tors. This measure ultimately made little difference in the functioning of the affected firms, but it helped head off any return to trade-union radicalism.

During the first years of rapid economic growth, the labor movement remained fairly passive in western Europe, even though wages stayed relatively low. After an era of depression, fascist repression, and war, workers were grateful simply to have jobs, free trade unions, and at least the promise of greater prosperity in the future. By the 1960s, however, it seemed time to redeem that promise; labor began demanding—generally with success—to share more fully in the new prosperity. Now, rather abruptly, much of western Europe took on the look of a consumer society, with widespread ownership of automobiles, televisions, and other household appliances.

■ **Social Welfare and the Issue of Gender**

Western governments began to adopt social welfare measures on a large scale late in the nineteenth century (see page 793), and by the 1940s some degree of governmental responsibility for unemployment insurance, workplace safety, and old-age pensions was widely accepted. Some Europeans, seeking renewal after the war, found attractive models in Sweden and Denmark, where

**Monnet** (moh-NAY)

the outlines of a welfare state had emerged by the 1930s. Sweden, especially, drew attention as a "middle way" that avoided the extremes of either Soviet Marxism, with its coercive statism, or American-style capitalism, with its brash commercialism and selfish individualism.

Sweden's economy remained fundamentally capitalist, based on private ownership; even after World War II, its nationalized, or government-run, sector was not large by European standards. But the system of social insurance in Sweden was the most extensive in Europe, and the government worked actively with business to promote full employment and to steer the economy in directions deemed socially desirable. Moreover, the welfare state came to mean a major role for the Swedish trade unions, which won relatively high wages for workers and even enjoyed a quasi-veto power over legislation.

At the same time, the Swedish government began playing a more active role in spheres of life that had formerly been private, from sexuality to child rearing. Thus, for example, drugstores were required to carry contraceptives beginning in 1946. Sweden was the first country to provide sex education in the public schools; optional from 1942, it became compulsory in 1955. By 1979 the Swedes were limiting corporal punishment—the right to spank—and prohibiting the sale of war toys. This deprivatization of the family stemmed from a sense, especially pronounced in Sweden, that society is collectively responsible for the well-being of its children.

Although the Swedish model was extreme in certain respects, most of western Europe moved in the same direction in an effort to restore consensus and establish the foundations for democratic renewal after the war. Even Britain, one of the war's major victors, quickly began constructing a welfare state, dumping Winston Churchill in the process.

Early in the war most Britons began to take it for granted that major socioeconomic changes would follow from victory. Greater collective responsibility for the well-being of all British citizens seemed appropriate in light of the shared hardships the war had imposed. Moreover, the successes of government planning and control during the wartime emergency suggested that once the war was over, government could assume responsibility for the basic needs of the British people, guaranteeing full employment and providing a national health service. But the Labour Party, led by Clement Attlee (1883–1967), seemed better equipped to deliver on that promise than the Conservatives, whose leader, Churchill, was in fact quite hostile to welfare state notions. So when Britain held its first postwar elections, in July 1945, Churchill's Conservatives suffered a crushing

**Social Welfare in Sweden**   With the state playing a major role, Sweden proved a pioneer in responding to the family and children's issues that became increasingly prominent after World War II. Here children play at a day-care center in Stockholm in 1953.   *(Roland Janson/Pressens Bild, Stockholm)*

loss to Labour, which promptly began creating the British welfare state.

Although some expected, and others feared, that the result would be a form of socialism, the new direction did not undermine the capitalist economic system. The Labour government nationalized some key industries, but 80 percent of the British work force remained employed in private firms in 1948. Moreover, even under Labour, the British government did not seek the kind of economic planning role that government was playing in France. Much like the United States, Britain relied on monetary and fiscal policy to coordinate its economy.

The core of the British departure was a set of government-sponsored social welfare measures that significantly affected the lives of ordinary people. These included old-age pensions; insurance against unemployment, sickness, and disability; and allowances for pregnancy, child rearing, widowhood, and burial. The heart of the system was free medical care, to be provided by a National Health Service, created in November 1946 and operating by 1948.

In Britain as elsewhere, gender roles were inevitably at issue as government welfare measures were debated and adopted. Were married women to have access to the welfare system as individual citizens, or as members of a family unit, responsible for child rearing and dependent on their husbands as breadwinners? Should government seek to enable women to be both mothers and workers, or should government help make it possible for mothers not to have to work outside the home? Women themselves did not always agree on priorities, and some instructive differences in accent were evident across national boundaries.

As during the First World War, the percentage of women in the work force had increased significantly during World War II, but both women and men proved eager to embrace the security of traditional domestic patterns once the war was over. So the war did not change gender patterns of work even to the extent that World War I had done. In Britain women made up about 30 percent of the labor force in 1931, 31 percent in 1951. The percentage of women in the U.S. work force increased from 26 to 36 percent during the war years, but by 1947 it had returned to 28 percent. Thus the embrace of welfare measures took place at a time of renewed conservatism in conceptions of gender roles.

British feminists initially welcomed provisions of the British welfare state that recognized the special role of women as mothers. The government was to ease burdens by providing family allowances, to be paid directly to mothers of more than one child to enable them to stay home with their children. This seemed a more progressive step than the perpetual British trade union demand for a "family wage," sufficient to enable the male breadwinner to support a family so that his wife would not have to work. But though women were now to be compensated directly for their role as mothers, the assumptions about gender roles remained essentially the same.

In France, which had refused even to grant women the vote after World War I, the very different situation after 1945 stimulated an especially innovative response to gender and family issues. After the experience of defeat, collaboration, and resistance, the French were determined to pursue both economic dynamism and individual justice. But they also remained concerned with population growth, so they combined incentives to encourage large families with measures to promote equal opportunity and economic independence for women.

As they expanded the role of government after the war, the French tended more than the British to assume that paid employment for women was healthy and desirable. New laws gave French women equal access to civil service jobs and guaranteed equal pay for equal work. However, the French recognized at the same time both that women had special needs as mothers and that husbands shared the responsibility for parenting. So the French system provided benefits for women during and after pregnancy but also family allowances that treated the two parents as equally essential. At the same time, the system viewed women as individual citizens, regardless of marital or economic status. Thus all were equally entitled to pensions, health services, and job-related benefits.

Although female participation in the paid labor force declined just after the war, it began rising throughout the West during the 1950s, then accelerated during the 1960s, reaching new highs in the 1970s and 1980s. Thanks partly to the expansion of government, the greatest job growth was in the service sector—in social work, health care, and education, for example—and many of these new jobs went to women. From about 1960 to 1988, the percentage of women aged 25 to 34 in the labor force rose from 38 to 67 in Britain, from 42 to 75 in France, and from 49 to 87 in Germany.

These statistics reflected significant changes in women's lives, but even as their choices expanded in some respects, women became more deeply aware of enduring limits to their opportunities. Thus a new feminist movement emerged by the early 1970s, drawing intellectual inspiration from *The Second Sex*, a pioneering work published in 1949 by the French existentialist Simone de Beauvoir (1908–1986). (See page 999 and the box "Reading Sources: Human Freedom and the Origins of a New Feminism.")

## ꝅ READING SOURCES

### Human Freedom and the Origins of a New Feminism

*The renewed feminism that emerged during the later 1960s took inspiration from* The Second Sex, *a pioneering work by the French existentialist Simone de Beauvoir that was first published in 1949. Even while valuing sexual difference, she showed the scope for opening the full range of human choices to women.*

[T]he nature of things is no more immutably given, once for all, than is historical reality. If woman seems to be the inessential which never becomes the essential, it is because she herself fails to bring about this change. . . .

To decline to be the Other, to refuse to be a party to the deal—this would be for women to renounce all the advantages conferred upon them by their alliance with the superior caste. Man-the-sovereign will provide woman-the-liege with material protection and will undertake the moral justification of her existence; thus she can evade at once both economic risk and the metaphysical risk of a liberty in which ends and aims must be contrived without assistance. Indeed, along with the ethical urge of each individual to affirm his subjective existence, there is also the temptation to forgo liberty and become a thing. . . .

If a caste is kept in a state of inferiority, no doubt it remains inferior; but liberty can break the circle. Let negroes vote, and they become worthy of having the vote; let woman be given responsibilities and she is able to assume them. . . .

. . . [T]here will be some to object that . . . when woman is "the same" as her male, life will lose its salt and spice. . . .

. . . And it is true that the evolution now in progress threatens more than feminine charm alone: in beginning to exist for herself, woman will relinquish the function as double and mediator to which she owes her privileged place in the masculine universe. . . . There is no denying that feminine dependence, inferiority, woe, give women their special character; assuredly woman's autonomy, if it spares men many troubles, will also deny them many conveniences; assuredly there are certain forms of the sexual adventure which will be lost in the world of tomorrow. But this does not mean that love, happiness, poetry, dream, will be banished from it.

. . . New relations of flesh and sentiment of which we have no conception will arise between the sexes; already, indeed, there have appeared between men and women friendships, rivalries, complicities, comradeships—chaste or sensual—which past centuries could not have conceived. . . .

. . . [T]here will always be certain differences between man and woman; her eroticism, and therefore her sexual world, have a special form of their own and therefore cannot fail to engender a sensuality, a sensitivity, of a special nature. . . .

. . . To emancipate women is to refuse to confine her to the relations she bears to man, not to deny them to her; let her have her independent existence and she will continue none the less to exist for him *also:* mutually recognizing each other as subject, each will yet remain for the other an *other*. . . . [W]hen we abolish the slavery of half of humanity, together with the whole system of hypocrisy that it implies, then the "division" of humanity will reveal its genuine significance and the human couple will find its true form.

*Source:* Simone de Beauvoir, *The Second Sex* (New York: Random House, Vintage, 1989), pp. xxv, xxvii, 728–731.

### ■ The Restoration of Democracy

Much of continental western Europe faced the challenge of rebuilding democracy after defeat and humiliation. With the developing cold war complicating the situation, the prospects for democracy were by no means certain in the late 1940s. Although the division of Germany weakened communism in the new Federal Republic, in France and Italy strong Communist Parties had emerged from the wartime resistance and claimed to point the way beyond conventional democracy altogether.

The new Federal Republic of Germany held its first election under the Basic Law in August 1949, launching what proved a stable and successful democracy. Partly to counter the Soviet Union, but also to avoid what seemed the disastrous mistake of the harsh peace settlement after World War I, the victors sought to help get West Germany back on its feet as quickly as possible. At the same time, West German political leaders, determined to avoid the mistakes of the Weimar years, now better understood the need to compromise, to take responsibility for governing the whole nation.

To prevent the instability that had plagued the Weimar Republic, the creators of the new government strengthened the chancellor in relation to the Bundestag, the lower house of parliament. In the same way, the Basic Law helped establish a stable party system by discouraging splinter parties and by empowering the courts to outlaw extremist parties. And the courts found reason to outlaw both the Communist Party and a Neo-Nazi Party during the formative years of the new German democracy.

The West German republic proved more stable than the earlier Weimar Republic partly because the political party system was now considerably simpler. Two mass parties, the Christian Democratic Union (CDU) and the Social Democratic Party (SPD), were immediately predominant, although a third, the much smaller Free Democratic Party (FDP), proved important for coalition purposes.

Konrad Adenauer (1876–1967), head of the CDU, the largest party in 1949, immediately emerged as postwar Germany's leading statesman. A Catholic who had been mayor of Cologne under Weimar, he had withdrawn from active politics during the Nazi period, but he re-emerged after the war to lead the council that drafted the Basic Law. As chancellor from 1949 until 1963, he oriented the new German democracy toward western Europe and the Atlantic bloc, led by the United States.

The new bipolar world confronted West Germany with a cruel choice. By accepting the bipolar framework, the country could become a full partner within the Atlantic bloc. But by straddling the fence instead, it could keep open the possibility that Germany could be reunified as a neutral and disarmed state. When the outbreak of war in Korea in 1950 intensified the cold war, the United States pressured West Germany to rearm and join the Western bloc. Although some West Germans resisted, Adenauer prevailed, committing the Federal Republic to NATO in 1955. Adenauer was eager to anchor the new Federal Republic to the West, partly to buttress the new democracy in West Germany, but also to cement U.S. support in the face of what seemed an ongoing Soviet threat to German security.

By the late 1950s the West German economy was recovering nicely, and the country was a valued member of the Western alliance. Adenauer's CDU seemed so potent that the other major party, the SPD, appeared to be consigned to permanent—and sterile—opposition. Frustrated with its outsider status, the SPD began to shed its Marxist trappings in an effort to widen its appeal. Prominent among those pushing in this direction was Willy Brandt (1913–1992), who became mayor of West Berlin in 1957, and who would become the party's leader in 1963. At its watershed national congress at Bad Godesberg in 1959, the party officially gave up talk of the class struggle and adopted a more moderate program.

Adenauer stepped down in 1963 at the age of 87, after fourteen years as chancellor. The contrast with Weimar, which had known twenty-one different cabinets in a comparable fourteen-year period, could not be more striking. The Adenauer years proved to Germans that democracy could mean effective government, economic prosperity, and foreign policy success. Still, Adenauer had become somewhat authoritarian by his later years, and it was arguable that West Germany had become overly reliant on him and his party.

During the years from 1963 to 1969, the CDU proved it could govern without Adenauer, and the SPD came to seem ever more respectable, even joining as the junior partner in a government coalition with the CDU in 1966. Finally, in October 1969, new parliamentary elections brought Brandt to the chancellorship, and the SPD became responsible for governing West Germany for the first time since the war.

Brandt sought to provide a genuine alternative to the CDU without undermining the consensus that had developed around the new regime since 1949. He wanted especially to improve relations between West Germany and the Soviet bloc, but this required a more independent foreign policy than Adenauer and his successors had followed. Under Adenauer, the Federal Republic had refused to deal with East Germany at all. So Brandt's opening to the East, or *Ostpolitik*°, was risky for a socialist chancellor seeking to prove his respectability. But he pursued it with skill and success.

In treaties with the Soviet Union, Czechoslovakia, and Poland during the early 1970s, West Germany accepted the main lines of the postwar settlement. This was to abandon any claim to the former German territory east of the Oder-Neisse° line, now in Poland. Brandt also managed to improve relations with East Germany. After the two countries finally agreed to mutual recognition, each was admitted to the United Nations in 1973. Brandt's overtures made possible closer economic ties between them, and even broader opportunities for

---

**Ostpolitik** (OST-po-luh-teek)   **Oder-Neisse** (OH-dur–NYE-suh)

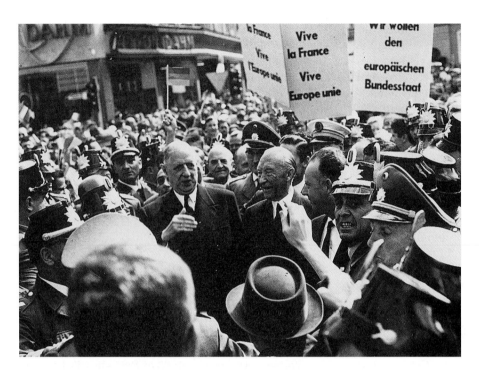

**Franco-German Cooperation**
French president Charles de Gaulle (*left*) and West German chancellor Konrad Adenauer (*right*) draw an enthusiastic crowd in Bonn in September 1963. De Gaulle was in the West German capital for the first formal meeting after France and West Germany had signed a friendship treaty in January. Each of the two leaders strongly advocated the new cooperation between their countries, and that cooperation proved a cornerstone of the unprecedented peace and prosperity in western Europe after World War II. (*AKG London*)

ordinary citizens to interact across the east-west border. His *Ostpolitik* was widely popular and helped deepen the postwar consensus in West Germany.

In France and Italy, unlike West Germany, communists emerged powerful from major roles in wartime resistance movements. Indeed, in either nation they might conceivably have made a bid for power as the war was ending. But Moscow called for the moderate route of participation in coalitions instead, at least partly because the presence of Western troops in these countries gave the leverage to noncommunists. And the United States intervened persistently to minimize the communists' role as new democracies took root in both nations after 1945. In France support for the communists continued to grow until 1949. Thereafter, the French Communist Party settled into a particularly doctrinaire position, maintaining strict subservience to the Soviet Union—and found itself increasingly marginalized.

As the leader of the French resistance effort, Charles de Gaulle immediately assumed the dominant political role after the liberation of France in August 1944. But he withdrew, disillusioned, from active politics early in 1946, as the new Fourth Republic returned to the unstable multiparty coalitions that had marked the later years of the Third. Still, governmental decision making changed significantly as the nonpolitical, technocratic side of the French state gained power in areas such as economic planning. And government technocrats survived the fall of the Fourth Republic in 1958, when de Gaulle returned to politics at a moment of crisis, stemming from France's war to maintain control of Algeria (see page 1007).

Although de Gaulle became prime minister within the Fourth Republic, it was clear that his return signified a change of regime. The French legislature promptly gave his government full powers for six months. Taking up the mandate, the regime drafted a new constitution, which was then approved by referendum in the fall of 1958. The result was the new Fifth Republic, which featured a stronger executive—and soon a president elected directly by the people and not dependent on the Chamber of Deputies. It was only in 1958, with the return of de Gaulle and the advent of the Fifth Republic, that government in postwar France began to assume definitive contours.

Italy's political challenge, after more than twenty years of fascism, was even more dramatic than France's. Shortly after the war, the Italians adopted a new democratic constitution and voted to end the monarchy, thereby making modern Italy a republic for the first time. But much depended on the balance of political forces, which quickly crystallized around the Christian Democratic party (DC), oriented toward the Catholic Church, and the strong Communist Party. Many Italian moderates with little attachment to the church supported the Christian Democrats as the chief bulwark against communism. And though they consistently had to work with smaller parties to attain a parliamentary majority, the

Christian Democrats promptly assumed the dominant role, which they maintained until the early 1990s.

The Communists continued to offer the major opposition, typically winning 25–35 percent of the vote in national elections. Taking their cue from Gramsci's writings, they adopted a proactive strategy to make their presence felt in Italian life and to demonstrate the superiority of their diagnoses and prescriptions. And they found considerable success as they organized profit-making cooperatives for sharecroppers, ran local and regional governments, and garnered the support of intellectuals, journalists, and publishers. But though they had proven capable of operating constructively within a democratic framework, their longer-term role remained unclear into the 1970s. What were the Communists trying to accomplish on the national level, and how long was it supposed to take? Could a Communist Party function as part of a majority governing coalition within a democratic political system?

By the 1960s the new democracies in Germany, France, and Italy seemed firmly rooted, and during the 1970s Greece, Spain, and Portugal also established workable democracies after periods of dictatorial rule. Following the death of Francisco Franco in 1975, almost forty years after his triumph in the Spanish civil war, democracy returned to Spain more smoothly than most had dared hope. Franco ordained that a restoration of the monarchy would follow his death, and King Juan Carlos (b. 1938; r. 1975– ) served as an effective catalyst in the transition to democracy. The new constitution of 1978 dismantled what was left of the Franco system so that, for example, Catholicism was no longer recognized as the official religion of the Spanish state.

### ■ New Discontents and New Directions

Even as democracy seemed to be thriving in western Europe, political disaffection began to threaten the consensus in the more established democracies by the late 1960s. Such frustration deepened in the more difficult economic environment of the 1970s, when Britain, for example, began finding it could no longer afford its welfare state. But when disaffection first emerged, in the late 1960s, western Europe was at the height of the new prosperity, and so the discontent did not stem from immediate economic circumstances alone. And it produced a sudden eruption of political radicalism.

The most dramatic instance of radical protest was the "Days of May" uprising of students and workers that shook France during May and June of 1968. The movement's aims were amorphous or utopian, and cooperation between students and workers proved sporadic. But the episode gave vent to growing discontent with the aloofness of the technocratic leaders and the unevenness

**Days of May**    French students use garbage-can covers as shields just minutes before a violent confrontation with police near the Gare de Lyon in Paris on May 25, 1968. The student-led protest movement revealed a reservoir of resentment that had built up in French society despite the democracy and prosperity of the postwar period.    *(Marc Riboud/Magnum Photos)*

**READING SOURCES**

## Students and Revolution: The "Days of May" in Paris, 1968

*As part of the radical demonstrations in Paris in May 1968, the Sorbonne, the most famous university on the European continent, became the focus of student demonstrations. Despite a series of arrests, students took over and occupied the university on May 13. A month later, on June 13, the Occupation Committee of the Sorbonne issued a manifesto reviewing what had happened and specifying the course for the future. The police retook the Sorbonne three days later, but the interplay of frustrations and aspirations evident in this manifesto continued to shape debate and influence policy thereafter.*

It was during the evening of 13 May after a week of fighting that we finally reoccupied the Sorbonne. We then realised more than ever that things would never again be as they had been. From that day onwards a new era had begun for the university. During the general strike and factory occupations, hundreds of thousands of students occupied their faculties, transforming them into red centres of support for the workers' struggle and for reflection on the future of the university.

Today, now that the majority of workers have, for the time being, returned to work, where has it all got us? Assemblies and committees have discussed the reforms for the university, the principles of university administration and teaching. We have witnessed the collapse of the academic authorities, the disappearance of rectors. We have heard the professors, the former landlords, shout about their sudden willingness for dialogue! . . .

Everyone knows that in the present circumstances a pure and simple reform of the university structures will by no means suffice. By calling the Sorbonne the "People's University," we have simply said that before changing the internal structures of the university, we must be sure for whom and with what aim it will be used. It took five centuries for the priests and then the bourgeoisie to build their university. It is therefore to be expected that in one month we cannot transform their university into one for the workers. . . .

. . . The Sorbonne should be called "the University at the Service of the Revolution":

a. Not only university reform, but also the political atmosphere which conditions it, should be examined during the six-month study programme. All problems concerning society will be examined, studied and discussed. Seminars will be arranged, enquiries carried out. Reports will be prepared. At the Sorbonne, we will talk about social living conditions, about the power of management, about underdevelopment, as well as imperialistic wars, advertising and immigrant workers. . . .

d. It should be an open forum for workers, farm workers, employees, all those wishing to give their opinion on the university of tomorrow. The Sorbonne could be used to help them in their struggle in their factory or profession against capitalism. . . .

THE FORMER REGIME IS DEAD, HELP US TO BUILD A NEW ORDER!

*Source:* Vladimir Fišera, *Writing on the Wall: May 1968: A Documentary History* (New York: St. Martin's Press, 1979), pp. 245–247.

of the modernization effort in de Gaulle's France. Despite the impressive economic growth, many ordinary people were coming to feel left out as public services were neglected and problems worsened in such areas as housing and education. French universities were a particular target, drawing protests and even full-scale takeovers by radical students. (See the box "Reading Sources: Students and Revolution: The 'Days of May' in Paris, 1968.")

Enrollment in French universities more than doubled between 1939 and 1960, then more than doubled again between 1960 and 1967. Apart from a few highly selective *grandes écoles,* the institutions of the state-run university system were open to anyone who passed a standard examination. To limit enrollments by restricting access did not seem politically feasible. Instead, the government tried to build to keep up with demand—thereby creating vast, impersonal institutions with professors increasingly inaccessible to students. But overcrowding persisted, and the value of a university degree diminished, leaving graduates with uncertain job prospects.

In Italy frustration with the stagnation of the political system bred radical labor unrest by 1969 and then a major wave of terrorism during the 1970s. By this time many radical young people found the Communists too caught up in the system to be genuinely innovative, yet still too weak to break the Christian Democrats' lock on power. Because the Italian Communists, unlike the German Social Democrats, never established their credibility as a national governing party, the Christian Democrats grew ever more entrenched, becoming increasingly arrogant and corrupt.

In Germany the Green movement formed by peace and environmental activists during the late 1970s took pains to avoid acting like a conventional party. Concerned that Germany, with its central location, would end up the devastated battleground in any superpower confrontation, the Greens opposed deployment of additional U.S. missiles on German soil and called for an alternative to the endless arms race. The SPD, as the governing party in an important NATO state, seemed unable to confront this issue and lost members as a result.

Prominent among the new political currents emerging by the early 1970s was the renewed feminist movement, which recalled the earlier movement for women's suffrage. This movement for "women's liberation" sought equal opportunities for women in education and employment. It was striking, for example, that despite major steps toward equal educational opportunity in postwar France, the country's prestigious engineering schools were still not admitting women in the late 1960s—and would begin doing so only during the 1980s. But feminists also forced new issues onto the political stage as they worked, for example, to liberalize divorce and abortion laws.

At the same time, women faced new questions after a generation of experience with the activist postwar state. In Britain, where government had sought to free mothers from the necessity of employment outside the home, feminists increasingly blamed the welfare state for their ongoing second-class status. But the tradeoffs were complex, and discussion continued, making gender issues central to public policy and personal choice all over the Western world by the last two decades of the century.

# THE COMMUNIST BLOC: FROM CONSOLIDATION TO STAGNATION

Y the late 1950s, policymakers in the West were increasingly concerned that the Soviet Union, though rigid and inhumane in important respects, might have significant advantages in the race with the capitalist democracies. Westerners worried especially about producing enough scientists and engineers to match the Soviets. With the Great Depression still in memory, some economists argued that central planning might prove more efficient, and certainly more equitable, than capitalism. The Soviet effort constituted a highly visible chapter in the continuing experiment in the West, and it was not clear what the outcome might be. The sense that the communist system offered formidable competition added to the anxieties in the U.S.-led Atlantic bloc.

Nonetheless, the flawed political and economic order that had emerged under Stalin continued in the Soviet Union. And when it was imposed on the countries within the Soviet orbit after the war, it produced widespread resentment—and new dilemmas for Soviet leaders. Efforts to make communism more flexible after Stalin's death in 1953 proved sporadic at best. The Soviet suppression of the reform movement in Czechoslovakia during the "Prague Spring" of 1968 seemed to prove the inherent rigidity of the Soviet system.

## ■ Dilemmas of the Soviet System in Postwar Europe, 1949–1955

Even in victory, the Soviet Union had suffered enormously in the war with Nazi Germany. Especially in the more developed western part of the country, thousands of factories and even whole towns lay destroyed, and there were severe shortages of everything from labor to housing. Yet the developing cold war seemed to require that military spending remain high.

At the same time, the Soviet Union faced the challenge of solidifying the new system of satellite states it had put together in east-central Europe. Most of the region had no desirable interwar past to reclaim, and thus there was widespread sentiment for significant change. Even in Czechoslovakia, which had been the most prosperous and democratic state in the region, considerable nationalization of industry was completed even before the communist takeover in 1948. And whatever integration into the new Soviet bloc might mean politically, it was not clear in the late 1940s

**Map 29.1  Military Alliances and Multinational Economic Groupings, 1949–1989**  The cold war split was reflected especially in the two military alliances: NATO, formed in 1949, and the Warsaw Pact, formed in 1955. Each side also had its own multinational economic organization, but the membership of the EEC, or Common Market, was not identical to that of NATO. Although communist, Yugoslavia remained outside Soviet-led organizations, as did Albania for part of the period.

that it had to be economically disadvantageous over the long term. The Soviet system seemed to have proved itself in standing up to the Nazis, and many believed that a socialist economic system could be made to work.

Partly in response to U.S. initiatives in western Europe, the Soviets sought to mold the new communist states into a secure, coordinated bloc of allies. In the economic sphere, the Soviets founded a new organization, COMECON, as part of their effort to lead the economies of the satellite states away from their earlier ties to the West and toward the Soviet Union (see Map 29.1). In the military-diplomatic sphere, the Soviets countered NATO in 1955 by bringing the Soviet bloc countries together in a formal alliance, the Warsaw Pact, which provided for a joint military command and mutual military assistance. The Warsaw Pact established a new basis for the continuing presence of Soviet troops in the satellite states, but the tensions within the Soviet-dominated system in east-central Europe soon raised questions about what the pact meant.

From the start, Yugoslavia had been a point of vulnerability for the Soviet system. Communist-led partisans under Josip Tito had liberated Yugoslavia from the Axis on their own, and they had not needed the Red Army to begin constructing a new communist regime (see page 975). Tito was willing to work with the Soviets, but because he had his own legitimacy, he could be considerably more independent than those elsewhere whose power rested on Soviet support. Thus the Soviets deemed it essential to bring Tito to heel, lest his example encourage too much independence in the other communist states. When Soviet demands became intolerably meddlesome from the Yugoslav point of view, Tito broke with the Soviet Union altogether in 1948. Yugoslavia then began developing a more flexible socialist economic system, with greater scope for local initiatives.

Stalin's response to Tito's defection was a crackdown on potential opponents throughout the Soviet bloc. Though the terror did not approach the massive scale of 1937–1938 (see page 922), again the secret police executed those suspected of deviation, inspiring fear even among the top leadership. But as such repression proceeded in the satellite states, opposition strikes and demonstrations developed as well, finally reaching a crisis point in East Germany in 1953.

In East Berlin a workers' protest against a provision to increase output or face wage cuts promptly led to political demands, including free elections and the withdrawal of Soviet troops. Disturbances soon spread to the other East German cities. Though this spontaneous uprising was not well coordinated, Soviet military forces had to intervene to save the East German communist regime. But the East German protest helped stimulate strikes and antigovernment demonstrations elsewhere in the Soviet bloc as well, convincing Soviet leaders that something had to be done. However, at this point the leadership of the Soviet Union was again being sorted out, for Stalin had died early in 1953, a few months before the crisis in East Germany came to a head.

## ◼ De-Stalinization Under Khrushchev, 1955–1964

Although a struggle for succession followed Stalin's death, the political infighting involved a reasonable degree of give and take, as opposed to terror and violence. To be sure, the contestants quickly ganged up on the hated secret police chief, who was tried and executed within months, but this stemmed from their prior agreement to limit the role of the secret police. Moreover, although one of the eventual losers was sent to Siberia to run a power station and the other was made ambassador to Outer Mongolia, it was a major departure that the winner, Nikita Khrushchev° (1894–1971), ordered neither of them exiled or executed.

Slightly crude, even something of a buffoon, Khrushchev outmaneuvered his rivals by 1955 partly because they repeatedly underestimated him. Although his period of leadership was brief, it was eventful indeed—and in some ways the Soviet system's best chance for renewal.

At a closed session of the Soviet Communist Party's twentieth national congress in February 1956, Khrushchev made a dramatic late-night speech denouncing the criminal excesses of the Stalinist system and the "cult of personality" that had developed around Stalin himself. (See the box "Reading Sources: Khrushchev Denounces the Crimes of Stalinism.") Khrushchev's immediate aim was to undercut his hard-line rivals, but he also insisted that key features of Stalinism had amounted to an unnecessary deviation from Marxism-Leninism. So the advent of Khrushchev suggested there might be liberalization and reform.

At the same time, however, the growing popular discontent in the satellite states placed the whole system in crisis. In the face of the East German uprising of 1953, the Soviets backed off from hard-line Stalinism, making room for more moderate communists they had previously shunned, such as the Hungarian Imre Nagy° (1896–1958). Khrushchev even sought to patch things up

**Khrushchev** (KROOSH-choff)    **Nagy** (NAHZH)

## ❧ READING SOURCES

---

# Khrushchev Denounces the Crimes of Stalinism

*In his speech to the Soviet Communist Party's national congress in 1956, Nikita Khrushchev repeatedly contrasted Stalin with Lenin, seeking to show that Stalinism had been an unfortunate and unnecessary deviation, not the logical outcome of the communist revolution. Khrushchev's denunciation of Stalin produced considerable commotion in the hall.*

[I]t is impermissible and foreign to the spirit of Marxism-Leninism to elevate one person, to transform him into a superman possessing supernatural characteristics akin to those of a god. . . .

Such a belief about a man, and specifically about Stalin, was cultivated among us for many years. . . .

While ascribing great importance to the role of the leaders and organizers of the masses, Lenin at the same time mercilessly stigmatized every manifestation of the cult of the individual. . . .

Stalin originated the concept "enemy of the people." This term . . . made possible the usage of the most cruel repression, violating all norms of revolutionary legality, against anyone who in any way disagreed with Stalin, against those who were only suspected of hostile intent, against those who had bad reputations. This concept, "enemy of the people," actually eliminated the possibility of any kind of ideological fight or the making of one's views known on this or that issue, even those of a practical character. In the main, and in actuality, the only proof of guilt used, against all norms of current legal science, was the "confession" of the accused himself; and, as subsequent probing proved, "confessions" were acquired through physical torture against the accused. . . .

Arbitrary behavior by one person encouraged and permitted arbitrariness in others. Mass arrests and deportations of many thousands of people, execution without trial and without normal investigation created conditions of insecurity, fear and even desperation. . . .

Lenin used severe methods only in the most necessary cases, when the exploiting classes were still in existence and were vigorously opposing the revolution, when the struggle for survival was decidedly assuming the sharpest forms, even including a civil war. Stalin, on the other hand, used extreme methods and mass repressions at a time when the revolution was already victorious, when the Soviet state was strengthened, when the exploiting classes were already liquidated. . . . It is clear that here Stalin showed in a whole series of cases his intolerance, his brutality and his abuse of power. . . .

*Source: The Anti-Stalin Campaign and International Communism: A Selection of Documents, edited by the Russian Institute, Columbia University (New York: Columbia University Press, 1956), pp. 2, 4, 12–14, 17, 20–21.*

 **For additional information on this topic, go to http://college.hmco.com.**

---

with Tito, exchanging visits with him in 1955 and 1956. In his speech to the party congress in 1956, Khrushchev suggested that different countries might take different routes to communism.

But could liberalization be contained within the larger framework of Soviet leadership, or were openness and innovation bound to threaten the system itself? The test case proved to be Hungary, where reformers led by the moderate communist Nagy had taken advantage of the liberalizing atmosphere by mid-1956 to begin dismantling collective farms and moving toward a multiparty political system. They even called for Soviet troops to withdraw, to enable Hungary to leave the Warsaw Pact and become neutral. These were not changes within the system, but challenges to the system itself. So when a democratic coalition government was set up by November, the Soviets used tanks to crush the Hungarian reform movement. Thousands were killed during the fighting or subsequently executed, and 200,000 Hungarians fled to the West.

Yet even the crackdown in Hungary did not mean a return to the old days of Stalinist rigidity in the Soviet bloc. The Soviets understood that the system had to become more palatable, but liberalization was to be contained within certain limits. Above all, it could not challenge communist monopoly rule and the Warsaw Pact. So after 1956 the satellites were granted greater leeway, and showed greater diversity, than had previously seemed possible. Hungary's new leader, János Kádár, collectivized agriculture more fully than before, but he also engineered a measure of economic decentralization, allowing scope for local initiatives and market mechanisms.

In East Germany, in contrast, Walter Ulbricht (1893–1973) concentrated on central planning and heavy industry in orthodox fashion. But the East German economy became the most successful in the Soviet bloc, primarily because here the new communist regime fell heir to a skilled industrial labor force. Still, that economic growth was built on low wages, so East German workers were tempted to emigrate to West Germany as the West German economic miracle gleamed ever brighter during the 1950s. The special position of Berlin, in the heart of East Germany yet still divided among the occupying powers, made such emigration relatively easy, and 2.6 million East Germans left for the West between 1950 and 1962. With a population of only 17.1 million, East Germany could not afford to let this hemorrhaging continue. Thus, in August 1961 the Ulbricht regime erected the Berlin Wall, an ugly symbol of the cold war division of Europe.

## ■ From Liberalization to Stagnation

As a domestic leader, Khrushchev proved erratic, but he was an energetic innovator, willing to experiment. He jettisoned the worst features of the police state apparatus, including some of the infamous forced labor camps, and offered several amnesties for prisoners. He also liberalized cultural life and gave workers greater freedom to move from one job to another. The economic planning apparatus was decentralized somewhat, affording more scope for local initiatives and placing greater emphasis on consumer goods. The government expanded medical and educational facilities and, between 1955 and 1964, doubled the nation's housing stock, substantially alleviating a severe housing shortage.

Though living standards remained relatively low, Khrushchev's reforms helped improve the lives of ordinary people. Even his claim in 1961 that the Soviet Union would surpass the Western standard of living within twenty years did not seem an idle boast. The Soviets had launched *Sputnik I* in 1957, assuming the lead in the ensuing space race, and they sent the first human into space in 1961. Such achievements suggested that even ordinary Soviet citizens had reason for optimism. More generally, the communist regimes throughout the Soviet bloc entered the 1960s with confidence after having achieved excellent rates of economic growth during the 1950s.

Yet Khrushchev had made enemies with his erratic reform effort, and this led to his forced retirement in October 1964. After the unending experiment in the economy, his opponents wanted to consolidate, to return to stability and predictability. But not until 1968 did it become clear that the liberalization and innovation of the Khrushchev era were over.

By early 1968 a significant reform movement had developed within the Communist Party in Prague, the capital of Czechoslovakia. Determined to avoid the fate of the Hungarian effort in 1956, the reformers emphasized that Czechoslovakia was to remain a communist state and a full member of the Warsaw Pact. But within that framework, they felt, it should be possible to invite freer cultural expression, democratize the Communist Party's procedures, and broaden participation in public life.

However, efforts to reassure the Soviets alienated some of the movement's supporters, who stepped up their demands. As earlier in Hungary, the demand for change seemed to outstrip the intentions of the movement's organizers. Finally, in August 1968, Soviet leaders decided to crack down, sending Soviet tanks into Prague to crush the reform movement. This end of the "Prague Spring" closed the era of relative flexibility and cautious innovation in the Soviet bloc that had begun in 1953.

A period of relative stagnation followed under Leonid Brezhnev° (1906–1982), a careful, consensus-seeking bureaucrat. In dealing with the United States, Brezhnev helped engineer significant moves toward arms control and easing tensions. But despite this *détente*, the "Brezhnev doctrine" specified in no uncertain terms that the Soviet Union would intervene as necessary to help established communist regimes remain in power. For the Soviet satellite states, there seemed to be no further hope of reform from within. But even as resignation marked the first years after 1968, forces soon emerged that undermined the whole communist system.

---

**Brezhnev** (BREZH-nef)

**The End of the Prague Spring**   Moving tanks into Prague in August 1968, Soviet leaders ended the widely admired reform movement in Czechoslovakia. Though there were protests, as shown here on August 20, the outcome was a foregone conclusion once the Soviets decided to intervene. Although life soon returned to "normal" in the Czechoslovak capital, the ending of the Prague Spring proved a watershed for the fate of communism in Europe.   *(Josef Kondelka/Magnum Photos)*

## EUROPE, THE WEST, AND THE WORLD

BY the early 1950s, the old Europe seemed dwarfed by the two superpowers and, for the foreseeable future, divided by the conflict between them. The colonial networks that had manifested European predominance unraveled rapidly at the same time. One obvious response was some form of European integration. A unified Europe might eventually become a global superpower in its own right. Although the first steps toward European unity did not go so far as visionaries had hoped, a new group of leaders established lasting foundations by the late 1950s. Still, the cold war framework limited the new union's geographical extent and the scope of its activity for decades.

## ■ The Cold War Framework

The most intense phase of the cold war ended with Stalin's death in 1953. In his speech to the twentieth party congress in 1956, Khrushchev repudiated the previous Soviet tenet that the very existence of Western capitalist imperialism made a military showdown with the communist world inevitable. During a visit to the United States in 1959, he stressed that the ongoing competition between the two sides could be peaceful. However, despite summit conferences and sporadic efforts at better relations, friction between the Soviet Union and the United States continued to define the era.

Indeed, a new peak of tension was reached in October 1962 when the Soviets began placing missiles in

Cuba, just 90 miles from the United States. Cuba had developed close ties with the Soviet Union after a 1959 revolution led by Fidel Castro (b. 1926). With Castro beginning to develop a communist system, a U.S.-supported force of Cuban exiles sought to invade Cuba and foment insurrection against the new regime in April 1961. This particular effort proved a fiasco, but it demonstrated to the Soviets that the new Cuban regime was vulnerable to overthrow from the United States.

Although the United States had placed offensive missiles in NATO-member Turkey, adjacent to the Soviet Union, the Soviet attempt to base missiles in Cuba seemed an intolerable challenge. U.S. president John F. Kennedy (1917–1963) responded with a naval blockade of Cuba, and for several days, the superpowers seemed on the verge of military confrontation. But the Soviets agreed to withdraw their missiles in exchange for a U.S. promise not to seek to overthrow the communist government in Cuba. The Americans also agreed informally to remove their offensive missiles from Turkey. Khrushchev's willingness to retreat antagonized hardliners in the Soviet military and contributed to his ouster from power two years later. Yet Khrushchev himself viewed the outcome in Cuba as a victory. By challenging the United States with missiles, the Soviets had helped secure the survival of the Cuban communist regime, which was now less vulnerable to overthrow by the United States. The long-term significance of the outcome was not clear in 1962, but the Cuban missile crisis produced anxiety on all sides. This was the closest the superpowers came to armed confrontation during the cold war period.

At the same time, it became increasingly clear that international communism was not the monolithic force it had once seemed. The most dramatic indication was the Sino-Soviet split, which developed during the 1950s as the communists under Mao Zedong solidified their regime in China. In the long struggle that led to their victory in 1949, the Chinese communists had often had no choice but to go their own way, and during the 1940s, especially, Stalin had been willing to subordinate any concern for their cause to Soviet national interests. After taking power in 1949, the Chinese communists pursued their own path to development without worrying about the Soviet model. Not without reason, the Soviets feared that the independent, innovative Chinese might be prepared to challenge Soviet leadership in international communism. By the early 1960s, the communist Chinese path had become appealing especially in the non-Western world, though it attracted dissident communists in the West as well.

## The Varieties of Decolonization

The advent of a new world configuration, with a circumscribed place for Europe, found dramatic expression in the rapid disintegration of the European colonial empires after World War II (see Map 29.2). The war itself had been a major catalyst for independence movements throughout the world. In southeast Asia and the Pacific, quick Japanese conquests revealed the tenuous hold of France, the Netherlands, and Britain on their domains. And it was not colonial reconquest that marked the end of the war, but the atomic bomb and the victory of the United States, which took a dim view of conventional European colonialism.

The effort of the Netherlands to regain control of the Dutch East Indies led to four years of military struggle against the Indonesian nationalist insurgency. Although most independent observers felt they could not win, the Dutch were reluctant to relinquish control of the East Indies, which had been in Dutch hands since the seventeenth century. Especially after the humiliations of defeat and occupation during World War II, many of the Dutch took pride in their imperial role. The struggle lasted from 1945 to 1949, when the Dutch finally had to yield as their former colony became independent Indonesia.

Unlike the Netherlands, Britain was still a great power in the twentieth century, and its empire had long seemed essential to its stature. But the structure of the British Empire had been evolving for decades before World War II. With the Statute of Westminster, passed by the British Parliament in 1931, such dominions as Canada, Australia, New Zealand, and South Africa became truly independent, controlling their own foreign policies and joining the League of Nations. This statute was essentially the founding document of the British Commonwealth of Nations. Though it initially encompassed only former British possessions dominated by people of European origin, the commonwealth provided the basis for relatively orderly decolonization after World War II.

In granting independence to India and Pakistan in 1947, the British understood that traditional colonial arrangements were ending, but they envisioned playing an ongoing leadership role by incorporating their former colonies into the British Commonwealth. However, the commonwealth idea proved to have little appeal for those winning independence, and the British Commonwealth proved little more than a voluntary cooperative association. Still, Britain proved the most realistic of the European colonial powers, grasping the need to compromise and work with emerging national leaders.

**Map 29.2   Decolonization, 1945–1980**   During a thirty-five-year period after World War II, the European empires in Africa, Asia, and the Pacific gradually came apart as the former colonies became independent nations.

Date is year independence was achieved.
Shading indicates former colonial power.

- Great Britain
- France
- Netherlands
- Italy
- Belgium
- Portugal
- Spain
- United States

JAPAN

NORTH KOREA
1948
SOUTH KOREA
1948
From Japan

PHILIPPINES
1946

INDONESIA
1949

BRUNEI 1984
From Great Britain

NORTH VIETNAM
1954

Unified 1974

SOUTH VIETNAM
1954

CAMBODIA
1954

MALAYSIA 1963

SINGAPORE
1965

LAOS
1949

MYANMAR
(BURMA)
1947

PAKISTAN 1947
BANGLADESH 1973

INDIA
1947

SRI LANKA
(CEYLON)
19-8

PAKISTAN
1947

KUWAIT
1961

BAHRAIN 1971
QATAR 1971
UNITED ARAB
EMIRATES 1971

YEMEN P.D.R. OF YEMEN 1967
DJIBOUTI
1977

SOMALIA
1960

IRAQ
1932

SYRIA
1944

JORDAN
1946

CYPRUS
1960
LEBANON 1944
ISRAEL 1948

ETHIOPIA
1941

KENYA
1963

UGANDA
1962

MADAGASCAR
1960

MAURITIUS
1968
From Great Britain

EGYPT
1922

SUDAN
1956

TANZANIA
1964

MALAWI
1964

MOZAMBIQUE
1974

SWAZILAND
1968

LESOTHO
1966

TUNISIA
1957

MALTA 1964
From Great Britain

LIBYA
1951

CHAD
1960

CENTRAL AFRICAN
REPUBLIC 1960

DEM. REP.
OF CONGO
1960

RWANDA
1962

BURUNDI
1962

ZAMBIA
1964

ZIMBABWE
1980

BOTSWANA
1966

SOUTH AFRICA
(Republic 1961)

GREAT
BRITAIN

NETHERLANDS

BELGIUM

FRANCE

ITALY

SPAIN

PORTUGAL

WESTERN SAHARA
(Morocco)
1975

MOROCCO
1956

ALGERIA
1962

NIGER
1960

NIGERIA
1960

CAMEROON
1960

GABON
1960

EQUATORIAL GUINEA
1968

REPUBLIC OF CONGO
1960

ANGOLA
1975

NAMIBIA 1985
From South Africa

MAURITANIA
1960

MALI
1960

BURKINA FASO
1960

BENIN 1960

TOGO
1960

GHANA
1957

SENEGAL 1960
GAMBIA 1965
GUINEA-BISSAU
1974
GUINEA
1958
SIERRA LEONE
1961
LIBERIA
1820s

CÔTE
D'IVOIRE
1960

PACIFIC
OCEAN

INDIAN OCEAN

ATLANTIC
OCEAN

0    500    1000    1500 Km.

0    500    1000    1500 Mi.

Nevertheless, even Britain decided to resist in 1956, when it provoked an international crisis over the status of the Suez Canal in Egypt (see Map 28.1 on page 950). Once a British protectorate, Egypt had remained under heavy British influence even after nominally becoming sovereign in 1922. But a revolution in 1952 produced a new government of Arab nationalists, led by the charismatic Colonel Gamal Abdel Nasser (1918–1970). In 1954 Britain agreed with Egypt to leave the Suez Canal zone within twenty months, though the zone was to be international, not Egyptian, and Britain was to retain special rights there in the event of war. In 1956, however, Nasser announced the nationalization of the canal, partly so that Egypt could use its revenues to finance public works projects.

Led by the Conservative Anthony Eden (1897–1977), Britain decided on a showdown. Eden won the support of Israel and France, each of which had reason to fear the pan-Arab nationalism that Nasser's Egypt was now spearheading. Israel had remained at odds with its Arab neighbors since its founding in 1948, and Nasser was helping the Arabs who were beginning to take up arms against French rule in Algeria.

Late in 1956 Britain, Israel, and France orchestrated a surprise attack on Egypt. After the Israelis invaded, the British and French bombed military targets, then landed troops to take the canal. But the troops met stubborn Egyptian resistance, and the British and French encountered decisive defeat in the diplomatic maneuvering that accompanied the outbreak of fighting. Both the United States and the Soviet Union opposed the Anglo-French-Israeli move, as did world opinion. The old European powers had sought to act on their own, by the old rules, but the outcome of this Suez crisis demonstrated how limited their reach had become.

Still, the 1956 debacle did not convince France to abandon its struggle to retain Algeria. And that struggle proved the most wrenching experience that any European country was to have with decolonization. For the French the process started not in North Africa but in Indochina, in southeast Asia, during World War II.

Led by the communist Ho Chi Minh (1890–1969), the Indochinese anticolonialist movement gained strength resisting the Japanese during the war. Then, before the French could return, Ho established a political base in northern Vietnam in 1945. Although the French re-established control in the south, negotiations between the French and the Vietnamese nationalists seemed at first to be moving toward some form of self-government for Vietnam. But in 1946 French authorities in Indochina deliberately provoked an incident to undercut negotiations and start hostilities. Eight years of difficult guerrilla war followed, creating a major drain on the French economy.

With its strongly anticolonialist posture, the United States was unsympathetic to the French cause at first. But the communist takeover in China in 1949 and the outbreak of war in Korea in 1950 made the French struggle in Indochina seem a battle in a larger war against communism in Asia. By 1954 the United States was covering 75 percent of the cost of the French effort in Indochina. Nonetheless, when the fall of the fortified area at Dien Bien Phu in May 1954 signaled a decisive French defeat, the United States decided to pull back and accept a negotiated settlement. Partly at the urging of its European allies, the United States had concluded that the Soviet threat in Europe must remain its principal concern.

France worked out the terms of independence for Vietnam in 1955. The solution, however, entailed a north-south partition to separate the communist and anticommunist forces, pending elections to unify the country. The anticommunist regime the United States sponsored in the south resisted holding the elections, so the country remained divided (see Map 29.2). Only in 1975, after defeating the United States, would the communist heirs of those who had fought the French assume the leadership of a unified Vietnam.

In France the defeat in Indochina left a legacy of bitterness, especially among army officers, many of whom felt that French forces could have won had they not been undercut by politicians at home. When the outcome in Indochina emboldened Arab nationalists in North Africa to take up arms against the French colonial power, the French army was anxious for a second chance—and the French government was willing to give it to them. Algeria had been under French control since 1830, and it had a substantial minority of ethnic Europeans, totaling over a million, or 10 percent of the population.

Although France gradually committed 500,000 troops to Algeria, the war bogged down into what threatened to become a lengthy stalemate, with increasing brutality on both sides. As it drained French lives and resources, the war became a highly contentious political issue in France. The situation came to a head during the spring of 1958 when the advent of a new ministry, rumored to favor a compromise settlement, led to violent demonstrations, engineered by the sectors of the French army in Algeria. Military intervention in France itself seemed likely to follow—and with it the danger of civil war.

It was at this moment of genuine emergency that Charles de Gaulle returned to lead the change to the Fifth Republic. Those determined to hold Algeria welcomed him as their savior. But de Gaulle fooled them, working out a compromise with the nationalist rebels that ended the war and made Algeria independent in 1962. Only de Gaulle could have engineered this outcome without provoking still deeper political division in France.

By the end of the 1950s, the colonialist impulse, which had still been significant immediately after World War II, was waning noticeably all over Europe. But resistance remained, through considerable variation, as the colonies of sub-Saharan Africa continued to move toward independence. Outcomes depended on several factors: the number and intransigence of European settlers; the extent to which local elites had emerged; and the confidence of the Europeans that they could retain their influence if they agreed to independence. Of the major imperial powers in the region, Britain had done best at preparing local leaders for self-government and proved the most willing to work with indigenous elites. The two smaller countries, Belgium and Portugal, were less certain they could maintain their influence, and they proved the most reluctant to give up their imperial status.

The transition was smoothest in British West Africa, where the Gold Coast achieved independence as Ghana, first as a commonwealth dominion in 1957, then as a fully independent republic in 1960. Few British settlers lived in that part of Africa, and the small, relatively cohesive African elite favored a moderate transition, not revolution. Where British settlers were relatively numerous, however, the transition to independence proved much more difficult. The very presence of Europeans had impeded the development of cohesive local elites, so movements for independence in those areas tended to become more radical, threatening the expropriation of European-held property. In Southern Rhodesia, unyielding European settlers resisted the British government's effort to promote a compromise. A white supremacist government declared its independence from Britain in 1965, fueling a guerrilla war. The Africans won independence as Zimbabwe only in 1980.

The process of decolonization led to a remarkable transformation in the thirty-five years after World War II. Forms of colonial rule that had been taken for granted before World War I stood discredited, virtually without defenders, by the late twentieth century. Europeans were now accepting the principle of national self-determination for non-Europeans. But decolonization hardly offered a neat and definitive solution. In formerly colonial territories, new political boundaries often stemmed from the way Europeans had carved things up, rather than from indigenous ethnic or national patterns. Moreover, questions remained about the longer-term economic relationships between the Europeans and their former colonies.

The reaction against Eurocentrism that accompanied the turn from colonialism was not confined to those who had been subjected to European imperialism. Westerners themselves were intrigued with the work of Frantz Fanon (1925–1961), a black intellectual from Martinique who became identified especially with the cause of the Algerian rebels. In *The Wretched of the Earth* (1961), Fanon found the West spiritually exhausted and called on the peoples of the non-Western world to go their own way, based on their own values and traditions. (See the box "Global Encounters: The Legacy of European Colonialism.")

## ■ Economic Integration and the Origins of the European Union

As the old colonialism increasingly fell into disrepute, many found in European unity the best prospect for the future. Although hopes for full-scale political unification were soon frustrated, the movement for European integration achieved significant successes in the economic sphere, especially through the European Economic Community (EEC), or Common Market, established in 1957.

The impetus for economic integration came especially from a new breed of "Eurocrats"—technocrats with a supranational, or pan-European, outlook. A notable example was Robert Schuman (1886–1963), a native of Lorraine, which had passed between France and Germany four times between 1870 and 1945. After serving as a German officer in World War I, he was elected to the French Chamber of Deputies in 1919 just after Lorraine was returned to France. As French foreign minister after World War II, Schuman was responsible for a 1950 plan to coordinate French and German production of coal and steel. The Schuman Plan quickly encompassed Italy, Belgium, the Netherlands, and Luxembourg to become the European Coal and Steel Community (ECSC) in 1951. Working closely with Schuman was Jean Monnet, who served as the ECSC's first president. From this position, he pushed for more thoroughgoing economic integration. The successes of the ECSC led the same six countries to agree to a wider "Common Market," officially known as the European Economic Community (EEC), in 1957.

After the merger of the governing institutions of the several European supranational organizations in 1967, the term *European Community* (EC) and later *European Union* (EU) came to indicate the institutional web that had emerged since the launching of the European Coal

# The Legacy of European Colonialism

*In the following passage from* The Wretched of the Earth *(1961), Frantz Fanon probes the negative consequences of colonialism—for both colonizers and colonized— and tries to show why a radical, even violent break from colonialism was necessary.*

The violence which has ruled over the ordering of the colonial world, which has ceaselessly drummed the rhythm for the destruction of native social forms and broken up without reserve the systems of reference of the economy, the customs of dress and external life, that same violence will be claimed and taken over by the native at the moment when, deciding to embody history in his own person, he surges into the forbidden quarters. . . .

. . . In the colonial context the settler only ends his work of breaking in the native when the latter admits loudly and intelligibly the supremacy of the white man's values. In the period of decolonization, the colonized masses mock at these very values, insult them, and vomit them up.

. . . All that the native has seen in his country is that they can freely arrest him, beat him, starve him: and no professor of ethics, no priest has ever come to be beaten in his place, nor to share their bread with him. As far as the native is concerned, morality is very concrete; it is to silence the settler's defiance, to break his flaunting violence—in a word, to put him out of the picture. . . .

. . . The colonialist bourgeoisie, in its narcissistic dialogue, expounded by the members of its universities, had in fact deeply implanted in the minds of the colonized intellectual that the essential qualities remain eternal in spite of all the blunders men may make: the essential qualities of the West, of course. . . . Now it so happens that during the strug-

gle for liberation, at the moment that the native intellectual comes into touch again with his people, . . . [a]ll the Mediterranean values—the triumph of the human individual, of clarity, and of beauty . . . are revealed as worthless, simply because they have nothing to do with the concrete conflict in which the people is engaged.

Individualism is the first to disappear. . . . The colonialist bourgeoisie had hammered into the native's mind the idea of a society of individuals where each person shuts himself up in his own subjectivity, and whose only wealth is individual thought. Now the native who has the opportunity to return to the people during the struggle for freedom will discover the falseness of this theory. The very forms of organization of the struggle will suggest to him a different vocabulary. Brother, sister, friend—these are words outlawed by the colonialist bourgeoisie, because for them my brother is my purse, my friend is part of my scheme for getting on. The native intellectual . . . will . . . discover the substance of village assemblies, the cohesion of people's committees, and the extraordinary fruitfulness of local meetings and groupments. Henceforward, the interests of one will be the interests of all, for in concrete fact *everyone* will be discovered by the troops, *everyone* will be massacred—or *everyone* will be saved.

*Source:* Frantz Fanon, *The Wretched of the Earth* (New York: Grove, 1968), pp. 40–47.

and Steel Community in 1951. Meanwhile, its membership gradually expanded, encompassing Denmark, Ireland, and Britain in 1973, Greece in 1981, Spain and Portugal in 1986, and Austria, Finland, and Sweden in 1995 (see Map 29.1). For newly democratic countries like Spain, Portugal, and Greece, Common Market membership became a pillar of the solidifying democratic consensus.

The immediate aim of the original EEC was to facilitate trade by eliminating customs duties between its member countries and by establishing common tariffs on imports from the rest of the world. For each member of the EEC, tariff reduction meant access to wider markets abroad, but also the risks of new competition in its own domestic market. So it was hard to be sure who might gain and who might lose from the move. However, the EEC proved advantageous to so many that tariff reduction proceeded well ahead of schedule. By 1968 the last internal tariffs had been eliminated.

With tariffs dropping, trade among the member countries nearly doubled between 1958 and 1962. French exports of automobiles and chemicals to Germany increased more than eightfold. Partly because the increasing competition stimulated initiative and productivity, industrial production within the EEC increased at a robust annual rate of 7.6 percent during those years.

Despite these successes, vigorous debate accompanied the development of the EEC during the 1960s. To enable goods, capital, and labor to move freely among the member countries, some coordination of social and economic policy was required. Thus state sovereignty became an important issue. To what extent was the Common Market to be a new whole, greater than the sum of its parts, as opposed to a mere commercial federation of existing states?

In the mid-1960s French president de Gaulle forced some of the underlying uncertainties to the fore. Though he had willingly turned from the old colonialism, de Gaulle was not prepared to compromise French sovereignty, and he was not persuaded that supranational integration offered the best course for postwar Europe. With the end of the Algerian war in 1962, France began playing an assertively independent role in international affairs. Thus, for example, de Gaulle developed an independent French nuclear force, curtailed the French role in NATO, and recognized the communist People's Republic of China.

This determination to assert France's sovereignty led to friction between de Gaulle and the supranational Eurocrats of the Common Market. Matters came to a head in 1965 when a confrontation developed over agricultural policy. The immediate result was a compromise, but de Gaulle's tough stance served to check the increasing supranationalism evident in the EEC until then. As the economic context became more difficult during the 1970s, it became still harder to maintain the EEC's cohesion. So though the Common Market proved an important departure, it did not overcome traditional national sovereignty or give western Europe a more muscular world role during the first decades after World War II.

## ■ The Energy Crisis and the Changing Economic Framework

As the political situation in western Europe became more volatile by the early 1970s, events outside Europe made it clear how interdependent the world had become—and that the West did not hold all the trump cards. In the fall of 1973, Egypt and Syria attacked Israel, seeking to recover the losses they had suffered in a brief war in 1967. Although the assault failed, the Arab nations of the oil-rich Middle East came together in the aftermath to retaliate against the Western bloc for supporting Israel. By restricting the output and distribution of the oil its members controlled, the Arab-led Organization of Petroleum Exporting Countries (OPEC) produced a sharp increase in oil prices and a severe economic disruption all over the industrialized world.

**Oil, the West, and the World**
Led by several oil-rich Arab states, OPEC drove up world oil prices by restricting production during the 1970s. The power of the oil cartel made it clear that decisions by non-Westerners could vitally affect the industrialized West. OPEC delegates are shown here in Algiers in 1975. *(Sygma)*

Western Europe, which was heavily dependent on Middle Eastern oil, was especially hard hit. By January 1975 the price of oil was six times what it had been in 1973, before the embargo, and this increase remained a source of inflationary pressure throughout the Western world until the early 1980s.

The 1970s proved to be an unprecedented period of "stagflation"—sharply reduced rates of growth combined with inflation and rising unemployment. The economic miracle was over, partly because the process soon to be known as globalization was now taking off. The European economies were subject to growing competition from non-Western countries, most notably Japan. In light of increasing global competition and rising unemployment, the labor movement was suddenly on the defensive throughout the industrialized West. And the changing circumstances inevitably strained the social compact that had enabled western Europe to make a fresh start after the war.

# THE COLLAPSE OF THE SOVIET SYSTEM, 1975–1991

I N the Soviet Union economic stagnation and even crisis were increasingly apparent during the 1970s, finally producing a major reform effort by the mid-1980s. Its leaders actively encouraged liberalization in the satellite states, where new forms of opposition had developed after the crushing of the Prague reform movement in 1968. But the liberalization effort unleashed forces that led to the unraveling of the satellite system in 1989, then even to the collapse of the Soviet Communist regime in 1991.

The disintegration of the communist system stunned Western observers, who had come to take the anxious stability of the cold war framework for granted. But that framework rested on a kind of balance between the superpowers, with their parallel, even competing experiments. By the 1980s those experiments had produced radically different results. Thus the balance was lost, and the framework of anxious stability dissolved.

## ■ Economic Stagnation in the Soviet Bloc

The impressive rates of economic growth achieved in the Soviet Union and several of the satellite states continued into the 1960s. However, much of that success came from adding labor—women and underemployed peasants—to the industrial work force. By the end of the 1960s that process was reaching its limits, so increasingly the challenge for the Soviet bloc was to boost productivity through technological innovation.

By the late 1970s, however, the Soviets were falling seriously behind the West as a new technological revolution gathered force. The state-directed Soviet economy had proven quite capable of technological leadership when marshaling resources for a particular task was required. Thus the Soviets led the way in space travel, for example. But continuing development in high technology demanded the freedom to experiment and exchange ideas and the flexibility to anticipate innovation and shift resources. In these areas, the Soviet system, with its direction from the top, proved too rigid to compete with the free-market systems of the Atlantic bloc. Moreover, as the Soviet system bogged down, the expense of the arms race with the United States dragged ever more seriously on the Soviet economy. Ordinary Soviet citizens grew increasingly frustrated as the communist economy proved erratic in providing the most basic consumer goods. Yet major functionaries enjoyed access to special shops and other privileges.

In satellite countries such as Poland and Hungary, the communist governments managed for a while to win mass support by borrowing from foreign banks to provide meat and other consumer goods at artificially low prices. "Sausage-stuffing," some called it. But as the lending banks came to realize, by the end of the 1970s, that such loans were not being used to foster modernization and productivity, these governments found it much harder to borrow. Thus they began having to impose greater austerity.

Throughout the Soviet bloc, frustration grew especially among women, who seemed to bear a disproportionate share of the burdens. Women were more likely to be employed outside the home in the communist countries than in the West. About 90 percent of adult women in the Soviet Union and East Germany had paid jobs outside the home by 1980. In 1984, 50 percent of the East German work force was female, compared with 39 percent in West Germany. Yet not only were these women concentrated in jobs with low pay and prestige, but they also still bore the major responsibility for child care, housework, and shopping. They had few of the labor-saving devices available in the West, and they often had to spend hours in line to buy ordinary consumer items. Dissatisfaction among women fed a new underground protest movement that began developing in the Soviet bloc in the mid-1970s—an indication of the growing strains in the overall system.

**Women's Work in the Soviet Union**
This cartoon adapts the caryatid form from ancient sculpture to depict the special burdens that were coming to wear more heavily on women as the Soviet economy bogged down. Intended to commemorate International Women's Day, the image appeared in the Soviet magazine *Krokodil* in 1984.
*(Krokodil Magazine, March 1984)*

## ■ The Crisis of Communism in the Satellite States

For many intellectuals in the Soviet bloc, the Soviet suppression of the Prague Spring in 1968 ended any hope that communism could be made to work. The immediate outcome was a sense of hopelessness, but by the mid-1970s a new opposition movement had begun to take shape, especially in Hungary, Poland, and Czechoslovakia. It centered initially on underground (or *samizdat*) publications, secretly produced and privately circulated writings—sometimes mimeographed in as few as five or six copies—that enabled dissidents to share ideas critical of the regime.

In one sense, these dissidents realized, intellectuals and ordinary people alike were powerless in the face of heavy-handed communist government. But they came to believe they could make a difference simply by "living the truth," ceasing to participate in the empty rituals of communist rule. And mere individual honesty could have political potential especially because of the Helsinki Accords on human rights that the Soviet bloc countries had accepted in 1975.

The meeting of thirty-five countries in Helsinki, Finland, in 1975 was one of the most important fruits of the *Ostpolitik*, or opening to the East, that Willy Brandt began pursuing after becoming West Germany's chancellor in 1969 (see page 995). Eager to grasp the chance that

Brandt's policy offered to regularize the status of East Germany and to confirm the western border of Poland, the Soviet bloc found it expedient to accept a detailed agreement on human rights that came to be known as the Helsinki Accords.

Though merely symbolic in one sense, that agreement proved a touchstone for initiatives that would help bring the whole Soviet system crashing down. Through various "Helsinki Watch" groups monitoring civil liberties, anticommunists in the satellite states managed to assume the moral leadership. By demanding that the communist governments live up to their agreements, by noting the gap between idealistic pretense and grim reality, opposition intellectuals began to cast doubts on the very legitimacy of the communist regimes.

The most significant such group was Charter 77, which emerged in Czechoslovakia in response to the arrest of a rock group called "The Plastic People of the Universe." Long-haired and anti-establishment like their counterparts in the West, the Plastic People were deemed filthy, obscene, and disrespectful of society by the repressive Czechoslovak regime. In 1977, protesting the crackdown on the group, 243 individuals signed "Charter 77"—using their own names and addresses, living the truth, acting as if they were free to register such an opinion.

A leader in Charter 77 was the writer Václav Havel° (b. 1936), who noted that after 1968 the notion of reforming the communist system through direct political action was dead. (See the box "Reading Sources: Power from Below: Living the Truth.") Hopes for change depended on people organizing themselves, outside the structures of the party-state, in diverse, independent social groupings. Havel and a number of his associates were in and out of jail as the government sought to stave off this protest movement. And despite their efforts, government remained particularly repressive and ordinary people relatively passive in Czechoslovakia until the late 1980s. For quite different reasons, Hungary and Poland offered greater scope for change.

Even after the failed reform effort of 1956, Hungary proved the most innovative of the European communist countries. Partly because its government allowed small-scale initiatives outside the central planning apparatus, Hungary was able to respond more flexibly to the growing economic stagnation. By the mid-1980s various alternative forms of ownership were responsible for one-third of Hungary's economic output.

This openness to economic experiment enabled reformers within the Hungarian Communist Party to gain the upper hand. Amid growing talk of "socialist pluralism," the Hungarian elections of 1985 introduced an element of genuine democracy. Increasingly open to a variety of viewpoints, the Hungarian communists gradually pulled back from their long-standing claim to a monopoly of power.

The reform effort that built gradually in Hungary stemmed especially from aspirations within the governing elite. More dramatic was the course of change in Poland, where workers and intellectuals, at odds even as recently as 1968, managed to come together during the 1970s. When Polish workers struck in 1976, in response to a cut in food subsidies, intellectuals formed a committee to defend them. This alliance had become possible because dissident intellectuals were coming to emphasize the importance of grass-roots efforts that challenged the logic of the communist system without attacking it directly.

But an extra ingredient from an unexpected quarter also affected the situation in Poland, perhaps in a decisive way. In 1978 the College of Cardinals of the Roman Catholic Church departed from long tradition and, for the first time since 1522, elected a non-Italian pope. But even more startling was the fact that the new pope was from Poland, behind the iron curtain. He was Karol Cardinal Wojtyla° (b. 1920), the archbishop of Kracow, who took the name John Paul II.

After World War II, the Polish Catholic Church had been unique among the major churches of east-central Europe in maintaining and even enhancing its position. It worked just enough with the ruling communists to be allowed to carve out a measure of autonomy. For many Poles, the church thus remained a tangible institutional alternative to communism and the focus of national self-consciousness in the face of Soviet domination. Thus the new pope's visit to Poland in 1979 had an electrifying effect on ordinary Poles, who took to the streets by the millions to greet him—and found they were not alone. This boost in self-confidence provided the catalyst for the founding of a new trade union, Solidarity, in August 1980.

Led by the remarkable shipyard electrician Lech Walesa° (b. 1944), Solidarity emerged from labor discontent in the vast Lenin shipyard in Gdansk, on the Baltic Sea (see Map 29.1). Demanding the right to form their own independent unions, seventy thousand workers took over the shipyards, winning support both from their intellectual allies and from the Catholic Church. Support for Solidarity grew partly because the government, facing the crisis of its "sausage-stuffing" strategy, was cutting

---

**Havel** (HA-vul)

**Wojtyla** (voy-TILL-ah)    **Walesa** (va-WEN-sah)

## ❧ READING SOURCES

### Power from Below: Living the Truth

*Considering the scope for change in the communist world by the late 1970s, Václav Havel imagines a conformist grocer who routinely puts a sign in his window with the slogan "Workers of the world, unite!" simply because it is expected. That same grocer, says Havel, has the power to break the system, which rests on innumerable acts of everyday compliance.*

[T]he real meaning of the greengrocer's slogan has nothing to do with what the text of the slogan actually says. Even so, this real meaning is quite clear and generally comprehensible because the code is so familiar: the greengrocer declares his loyalty . . . in the only way the regime is capable of hearing; that is, by accepting the prescribed *ritual*, by accepting appearances as reality, by accepting the given rules of the game. In doing so, however, he has himself become a player in the game, thus making it possible for the game to go on, for it to exist in the first place. . . .

Let us now imagine that one day something in our greengrocer snaps and he stops putting up the slogans merely to ingratiate himself. He stops voting in elections he knows are a farce. He begins to say what he really thinks at political meetings. . . . He rejects the ritual and breaks the rules of the game. He discovers once more his suppressed identity and dignity. . . .

. . . He has shown everyone that it *is* possible to live within the truth. Living within the lie can constitute the system only if it is universal. The principle must embrace and permeate everything. There are no terms whatsoever on which it can coexist with

living within the truth, and therefore everyone who steps out of line *denies it in principle and threatens it in its entirety.* . . .

And since all genuine problems and matters of critical importance are hidden beneath a thick crust of lies, it is never quite clear when the proverbial last straw will fall, or what that straw will be. This . . . is why the regime prosecutes, almost as a reflex action preventively, even the most modest attempts to live within the truth.

. . . [T]he crust presented by the life of lies is made of strange stuff. As long as it seals off hermetically the entire society, it appears to be made of stone. But the moment someone breaks through in one place, when one person cries out, "The emperor is naked!"—when a single person breaks the rules of the game, thus exposing it as a game—everything suddenly appears in another light and the whole crust seems then to be made of a tissue on the point of tearing and disintegrating uncontrollably.

*Source:* Václav Havel et al., *The Power of the Powerless: Citizens Against the State in Central-Eastern Europe* (Armonk, N.Y.: M. E. Sharpe, 1985), pp. 31, 37, 39–40, 42–43.

---

subsidies and raising food prices. But the new union developed such force because it placed moral demands first—independent labor organizations, the right to strike, and freedom of expression. Reflecting the wider opposition thinking in east-central Europe, Solidarity was not to be bought off with lower meat prices, even had the government been able to deliver them.

After over a year of negotiation, compromise, and broken promises, the tense situation came to a head in December 1981, when the government under General

Wojciech Jaruzelski° (b. 1923) declared martial law and outlawed Solidarity, imprisoning its leaders. Strikes in protest were crushed by military force. So much for that, it seemed: another lost cause, another reform effort colliding with inflexible communist power in east-central Europe, as in 1953, 1956, and 1968. But this time, it was different, thanks especially to developments in the Soviet Union.

---

**Jaruzelski** (yah-roo-SHELL-skee)

**Lech Walesa and Solidarity**    A shipyard electrician, Walesa spearheaded the dissident Polish trade union, Solidarity, formed in 1980, and then emerged from prison to lead the movement that eventually toppled the communist regime in Poland in 1989. Here he addresses a rally during a strike at the Lenin shipyard in Gdansk in August 1988.    *(Sygma)*

## ■ The Quest for Reform in the Soviet Union

The death of Leonid Brezhnev in 1982 paved the way for a concerted reform effort that began in earnest when Mikhail Gorbachev° (b. 1931) became Soviet Communist Party secretary in 1985. Gorbachev's effort encompassed four intersecting initiatives: arms reduction; liberalization in the satellite states; *glasnost*°, or "openness" to discussion and criticism; and *perestroika*°, or economic "restructuring." This was to be a reform within the Soviet system. There was no thought of giving up the Communist Party's monopoly on power or embracing a free-market economy. The reformers still took it for granted that communism could point the way beyond Western capitalism, with its shallow consumerism, its illegal drugs, its widespread crime. So a measure of idealism guided the reformers' efforts. But they had to make communism work.

Gorbachev understood that "openness" was a prerequisite for "restructuring." The freedom to criticize was essential to check abuses of power, which, in turn, was

Gorbachev (GOR-ba-choff)    glasnost (GLAHZ-nost)
perestroika (pair-es-TROY-kah)

necessary to overcome the cynicism of the workers and improve productivity. Openness was also imperative to gain the full participation of the country's most creative people, whose contribution was critical if the Soviet Union was to become competitive in advanced technology.

The main thrust of perestroika was to depart from the rigid economic planning mechanism by giving local managers more autonomy. The alternative did not have to entail privatization or a return to free-market capitalism. It could mean, for example, letting workers elect factory managers. But any restructuring was bound to encounter resistance, especially from those with careers tied to the central planning apparatus. And Gorbachev's program made only partial headway in this crucial sector.

## ■ The Anticommunist Revolution in East-Central Europe

Meanwhile, in Poland, Walesa remained a powerfully effective leader even from prison. He was able to keep his heterogeneous movement together as the ideas of Solidarity continued to spread underground. Then the advent of Gorbachev in 1985 changed the overall framework, for Gorbachev was convinced that restructuring of the Soviet system required reform in the satellites as well. So as the Polish economy, already in difficulty by 1980, reached a crisis in 1987, Solidarity began stepping up its efforts.

When proposed price increases were rejected in a referendum, the Polish government imposed them by fiat. Strikes demanding the relegalization of Solidarity followed during the spring of 1988. The government again responded with military force, but Solidarity-led strikes in August forced government leaders to send signals that they might be prepared to negotiate. With the economy nearing collapse, the government recognized that it could no longer govern on its own.

The negotiations that followed early in 1989 proved pivotal. When they began, Walesa and his advisers wanted primarily to regain legal status for Solidarity within the communist-dominated system, still under Jaruzelski. In exchange, they assumed they would have to help legitimate a rigged election to approve painful but necessary economic measures. But as these "Round Table" negotiations proceeded, the government gave ever more in exchange for Solidarity's cooperation. Not only did it consent to legalize Solidarity, but it agreed to make the forthcoming elections free enough for the opposition genuinely to participate.

The elections of June 1989 produced an overwhelming repudiation of Poland's communist government. Even government leaders running unopposed failed to win election as voters crossed out their names. In the aftermath of the elections, President Jaruzelski was forced to give Solidarity a chance to lead. Not all members of the opposition felt it wise to accept government responsibility under such difficult economic circumstances, but finally Tadeusz Mazowiecki° (b. 1927), Walesa's choice and one of the movement's most distinguished intellectuals, agreed to form a government.

The chain of events in Poland culminated in one of the extraordinary events of modern history—the negotiated end of communist rule. That a communist government might give up power voluntarily had been utterly unforeseen. It happened partly because the Soviet Union under Gorbachev was seeking reform and thus had become much less likely to intervene militarily. It also helped that the Polish Catholic Church was available to act as mediator, hosting meetings, reminding both sides of their shared responsibilities in the difficult situation facing their country. By some accounts, General Jaruzelski, who seemed for most of the 1980s to be just another military strongman and Soviet lackey, had proven a national hero for his grace, perhaps even ingenuity, in

yielding power to the opposition. But most important was the courage, the persistence, and the vision of Solidarity itself.

Although the Hungarians were already breaking out of the communist mold, it was especially the Polish example that suggested to others in the Soviet bloc that the whole system was open to challenge. During 1989, demands for reform and, increasingly, for an end to communist rule spread through east-central Europe by means of the domino effect that had preoccupied the Soviets from the start. By the end of that year, the Soviet satellite system was in ruins (see Map 30.1 on page 1026).

A marked increase in illegal emigration from East Germany to the West had been one manifestation that the system was starting to unravel. During 1989 the reform-minded Hungarian communists decided to stop impeding East Germans, many of whom vacationed in Hungary, from emigrating to the West at the Hungarian border with Austria. If the communist reformers in East Germany were to have any chance of turning the situation around, they had to relax restrictions on travel and even grant the right to emigrate. Thus they immediately began preparing legislation to both ends, amid a host of reforms intended to save the system. On November 9, 1989, the East German communist regime did the unthinkable and opened the Berlin Wall, which was promptly dismantled altogether. Germans now traveled freely back and forth between East and West. Although the fate of the Soviet Union itself remained uncertain, the opening of the wall signaled the end of the cold war. It was no longer a bipolar world.

This liberalization effort proved too late, however. By now, discontented East Germans envisioned not simply reforming the communist system but ending it altogether. Within weeks it was clear that the rhythm of events was beyond the control of East Germany's reform communists, who opened the way for German reunification in 1990. Despite some nervousness, the four postwar occupying powers—the United States, Britain, France, and the Soviet Union—gave their blessing as the Federal Republic simply incorporated the five East German states. The communist system in East Germany had simply dissolved.

Although some in West Germany were hesitant about immediate reunification, especially because of the economic costs that seemed likely, West German chancellor Helmut Kohl° (b. 1930) sought to complete the process as quickly as possible. By early 1990 the emigration of East Germans to the West had become a flood.

---

**Mazowiecki** (maz-oy-YES-key)

**Kohl** (KOLE)

West German law treated these Germans as citizens, entitled to social benefits, so their arrival in such numbers presented a considerable financial burden. It seemed imperative for West Germany to regularize the situation as quickly as possible, assuming responsibility for the east and restoring its economy.

The division of Germany, symbolized by the Berlin Wall, had been the central fact of the bipolar cold war world. Now Germany was a unified country for the first time since Nazism and the Second World War. What would it mean?

### ■ The End of the Soviet Union

Meanwhile, in the Soviet Union, what began as a restructuring of the communist system became a struggle for survival of the system itself. The much-trumpeted glasnost produced greater freedom in Soviet culture and politics, but Gorbachev sought to avoid alienating hard-line

communists, so he compromised, watering down the economic reforms essential to perestroika. The result proved a set of half-measures that only made things worse. Because so little was done to force the entrenched Soviet bureaucracy to go along, the pace of economic reform was lethargic. The essential structures of the command economy weakened, but free-market forms of exchange among producers, distributors, and consumers did not emerge to replace them.

In 1986 an accidental explosion at the Soviet nuclear power plant at Chernobyl, in Ukraine (see Map 29.3), released two hundred times as much radiation as the atomic bombs dropped on Hiroshima and Nagasaki combined. The accident contaminated food supplies and forced the abandonment of villages and thousands of square miles of formerly productive land. The radioactivity released would eventually hasten the death of at least 100,000 Soviet citizens. Despite his commitment to openness, Gorbachev reverted to old-fashioned

**Map 29.3    The Dissolution of the Soviet Union**    As crisis gripped the Soviet system by the late 1980s, the republics of the Soviet Union began declaring first their sovereignty, then their independence. Most of the fifteen republics that had made up the Soviet Union became part of a much looser confederation, the Commonwealth of Independent States, in 1991 and 1992.

Soviet secrecy for several weeks after the accident, in an effort to minimize what had happened. As a result, the eventual toll was far greater than it need have been. The accident and its aftermath seemed stark manifestation of all that was wrong with the Soviet system—its arrogance and secrecy, its premium on cutting corners to achieve targets imposed from above.

By the end of the 1980s, Soviet citizens felt betrayed by their earlier faith that Soviet communism was leading to a better future. A popular slogan spoke sarcastically of "seventy years on the road to nowhere." The economic situation was deteriorating, yet people were free to discuss alternatives as never before. As the discussion came to include once unthinkable possibilities such as privatization and a market economy, it became clear that the whole communist system was in jeopardy.

By mid-1990, moreover, the union of Soviet republics itself tottered on the verge of collapse. Lithuania led the way in calling for outright independence. But the stakes were raised enormously when the Russian republic, the largest and most important in the USSR, followed Lithuania's lead. In June 1990 the newly elected chairman of Russia's parliament, Boris Yeltsin (b. 1931), persuaded the Russian republic to declare its sovereignty. Yeltsin had grown impatient with the slow pace of economic and political change, and by threatening that Russia might go its own way, he hoped to force Gorbachev's reform effort beyond the present impasse. As a further challenge to Gorbachev, Yeltsin dramatically resigned from the Communist Party during its televised national congress in July 1990. When, in June 1991, free elections in the Russian republic offered the first clear contest between communists determined to preserve the system and those seeking to replace it, the anticommunist Yeltsin was elected the republic's president by a surprising margin.

After tilting toward the hard-liners late in 1990, Gorbachev sought a return to reform after Yeltsin's dramatic election as Russia's president in June 1991. He even engineered a new party charter that jettisoned much of the Marxist-Leninist doctrine that had guided communist practice since the revolution. In August the hard-liners struck back with a coup that forced Gorbachev from power—but only for a few days. Yeltsin, supported by ordinary people in Moscow, stood up to the conspirators, while the secret police refused to follow orders to arrest Yeltsin and other opposition leaders. The coup quickly fizzled, but the episode galvanized the anticommunist movement and radically accelerated the pace of change.

Although Gorbachev was restored as head of the Soviet Union, the winner was Yeltsin, who quickly mounted an effort to dismantle the party apparatus before it could regroup. Anticommunist demonstrations across much of the Soviet Union toppled statues of Lenin and dissolved local party networks. In a referendum in December 1991, Ukraine, the second most populous Soviet republic, overwhelmingly voted for independence. Not only the communist system but the Soviet Union itself was simply disintegrating. Late in December, Gorbachev finally resigned, paving the way for the official dissolution of the Soviet Union on January 1, 1992 (see Map 29.3). The European map again included Russia, as well as, in a matter of months, fourteen other sovereign states from what had been the Soviet Union.

One of the notable experiments in the history of the West, nourished by the hopes and ideals of generations, the communist regime in the Soviet Union had proved a resounding failure.

## SUMMARY

N the decades that followed World War II, a bipolar framework, dominated by the United States and the Soviet Union, shaped world affairs. The states of western Europe declined in influence, even losing their remaining colonial possessions. They had to follow the U.S. lead, especially in matters of national security. From within that framework, however, they were able to achieve remarkable prosperity and significant steps toward multinational integration.

In the Soviet bloc, Stalin's death in 1953 brought an end to the most repressive features of the communist system. Under his successor, Nikita Khrushchev, the Soviet Union seemed able to compete with the United States in areas from education to space travel. But the experiment with various forms of central planning in the Soviet bloc proved ever less successful. At the same time, the crushing of a series of opposition and reform efforts, from East Berlin in 1953 to Prague in 1968, made it clear that the Soviets intended to keep their European satellites on a tight leash.

In western Europe, the shared experience of wartime led to a new social compact based on greater government responsibility for economic well-being and social welfare. By 1968, however, strains began to appear in the Western democracies, and the slowdown in economic growth during the 1970s only made them worse. Though the economic improvement remained remarkable, many western Europeans came to feel left out as the key decisions fell to party leaders or technocratic planners. Still, western Europe had come to take for granted a substantial measure of prosperity and political legitimacy, while in the communist countries of eastern Europe, growing economic stagnation fueled a much deeper form of political disaffection during the 1970s and 1980s. The parallel experiments were turning out very differently. Discontent in the Soviet bloc produced forces for change that led the whole communist system to unravel by the end of 1991.

Thus ended the cold war era. The immediate response in the West was euphoria, for the anxieties that had resulted from the rivalries and mutual suspicions of the superpowers seemed to vanish almost overnight. But what would follow remained unclear. Reformers in the former communist countries claimed to want individual freedom, political democracy, and free-market capitalism, but it would be necessary to build these on the ruins of the now-discredited communist system, a task never confronted before. And what sort of international order might replace the dangerous but stable bipolar framework that had stood since World War II?

## ■ Suggested Reading

Bark, Dennis L., and David R. Gress. *A History of West Germany,* Vol. 1: *From Shadow to Substance, 1945–1963,* and Vol. 2: *Democracy and Its Discontents, 1963–1991.* 2d ed. 1993. A favorable account of West Germany's democracy and its Atlantic and European roles in the face of ongoing suspicion and criticism.

Chamberlain, M. E. *Decolonization: The Fall of the European Empires.* 2d ed. 1999. An updated edition of a highly regarded overview.

Crockatt, Richard. *The Fifty Years' War: The United States and the Soviet Union in World Politics, 1941–1991.* 1995. A balanced history of U.S.-Soviet relations, showing the global impact of their cold war rivalry.

Dedman, Martin J. *The Origins and Development of the European Union, 1945–95: A History of European Integration.* 1996. A concise and accessible introductory work.

Garton Ash, Timothy. *The Magic Lantern: The Revolution of '89 Witnessed in Warsaw, Budapest, Berlin, and Prague.* 1990. Firsthand testimony on the fall of communism by a British intellectual with close contacts among anticommunists in east-central Europe.

Laqueur, Walter. *Europe in Our Time: A History, 1945–1992.* 1992. A comprehensive, well-balanced survey by a leading authority on twentieth-century Europe.

Marwick, Arthur. *The Sixties: Cultural Revolution in Britain, France, Italy, and the United States, c. 1958–c. 1974.* 1998. A lengthy but gripping portrait of a pivotal decade.

Morgan, Kenneth O. *The People's Peace: British History, 1945–1990.* 1992. A thorough survey that seeks to avoid overemphasis on decline and pessimism; accents the relative peace and stability of the period.

Schulze, Max-Stephan, ed., *Western Europe: Economic and Social Change Since 1945.* 1999. A superior collection of essays accenting economic change; some treat individual countries, others overarching topics.

Stokes, Gale. *The Walls Came Tumbling Down: The Collapse of Communism in Eastern Europe.* 1993. Dramatic and comprehensive, the first standard account of the dissolution of communism in east-central Europe.

 **For a searchable list of additional readings for this chapter, go to http://college.hmco.com.**

# Pop Art

Hamburgers, comic strips, soup-can labels, familiar images of entertainment icons—such was the stuff of "pop art," which burst onto the New York art scene in the early 1960s and came to exert a widespread cultural influence. Indeed, with their imaginative renderings of familiar images and whimsical sculptures of everyday objects, artists like Andy Warhol (1928–1987), Roy Lichtenstein (b. 1923), and Claes Oldenburg (b. 1929) helped shape the experience of the later twentieth century. But was this serious art—or simply a joke, a parody, a put-on? Were the pop artists poking fun at the triviality of modern society, or were they deepening our encounter with defining aspects of contemporary culture? Whatever their intent, what does this striking new art form tell us about the direction of Western culture in the decades after World War II?

The term *pop art* was coined in England in the later 1950s, when a group of artists and critics became interested in bridging the cultural gap between "fine art" and the emerging popular culture of mass media and machine-produced images, of advertising and automobiles. Like everyone else, they associated that consumerist mass culture with America—the America of Hollywood, Detroit, and Madison Avenue. And they found it more vital than the conventional fine art of the period. The American pop artists were similarly fascinated by the impersonal, mass-produced, often expendable quality of the objects and images that have come to surround us.

Pop art was part of a wider reaction against the deeply serious abstract expressionist painting that emerged in New York just after the Second World War. By the early 1950s, abstract expressionists like Jackson Pollock and Mark Rothko had created images of unprecedented power, whether seeking to forge an artistic identity in the face of nothingness, or to transcend selfhood in a cosmic wholeness. In the mid-1950s, however, younger artists "tired of the stink of artists' egos" began reacting against the self-importance of abstract expressionism. For these younger artists, art did not have to be a vehicle for the psychological expression of the artist or a quest for "the tragic and timeless." Although the reaction took several forms, pop art proved the most influential. The pop movement emerged especially in the United States, and it interested Europeans as typically American, fresh and fascinating or garish and vulgar, depending on one's point of view.

Whereas the abstract expressionists had sought to rise above the everyday world, Claes Oldenburg's sculptures played with the scale and context of the most ordinary objects—a mixer, a three-pronged plug, a lipstick, a hamburger—to deepen our involvement with the everyday things that surround us. In this sense, the aim of pop art was not simply to parody or satirize, but to affirm our relationship with the trappings of ordinary life. Hollywood, Detroit, and Madison Avenue were all right after all; indeed, they had become the centers of Western culture by the later twentieth century.

Though anonymous and impersonal, the modern world of mass production, mass consumption, and mass media is "popular" because its images and objects are accessible to us all. In fact, they bombard us from all directions, giving shared shape and definition to our everyday lives. This is our world, the pop artists were saying, and they were creating the art appropriate to our time. They invite us to relax and enjoy that world, but they also enhance our experience by making art from it, thereby awakening us to its novelty and vitality.

**Oldenburg: Floor Burger, 1962** *(Claes Oldenburg [American, b. 1929], Floor Burger, 1962. Canvas filled with foam rubber and cardboard boxes, painted with acrylic paint. 132.1 × 213.4 cm. Art Gallery of Ontario, Toronto.)*

**Warhol: Marilyn Diptych, 1962**   *(© Copyright ARS, NY. Tate Gallery, London/Art Resource, NY)*

But some viewers have found an element of melancholy, nostalgia, even tragedy just beneath pop art's eye-catching surface. In a world of mass media and reproduced images, more of our experience becomes secondhand and literally superficial. Likewise, pop subjects, from fast food to billboards, have no deeper meaning, no expressive personal agenda. With his multiplied image of Marilyn Monroe, Andy Warhol dealt not with the actress herself but with the obsessive familiarity of her image. He cultivated a deadpan, detached style that reflected the machine-made quality of his subject matter—the quality that made the images he started with so familiar in the first place. But even as, on one level, he embraced aspects of the new mass culture, Warhol was exploring precisely the emotional detachment—and the accompanying trivialization of emotion—at work in the culture that had produced the images he adapted. Especially in his paintings treating impersonal newspaper images of disaster and death, Warhol bore witness to our indifference—and perhaps to a cosmic meaninglessness as well. One expert has noted that "in Warhol's pictures of the material objects and other false idols that most of us worship, the pain lies just below the bright surfaces of the images and waits passively to engage us."*

The advent of pop art provoked a series of questions that remain unanswered: Is the embrace of the mass-produced and commercial, at the expense of traditional "fine-art" values, a symptom of exhaustion or a healthy affirmation of contemporary popular culture, so bound up with the commercial world? Or is pop art perhaps a valuable comment on the emptiness of that culture, with its impersonal conformity, garish commercialism, and mechanical repetition? In the final analysis, were the pop artists abandoning the artist's lofty mission and giving in to the ordinary? Or were they the first to show us what "Western civilization" had come to mean by the late twentieth century?

---

*Eric Shanes, *Warhol* (New York: Portland House, 1991), p. 41.

 **For additional information on this topic, go to http://college.hmco.com.**

# CHAPTER 30

# The West and the World Since 1989

**D**URING the fall of 1989, three teenaged Muslim girls were suspended from a public school near Paris because they insisted on wearing the headscarves traditional for Islamic women. School authorities cited a law barring religious displays in France's secular, state-run school system. The three girls protested that Islamic teaching required women to cover their heads in public as a sign of modesty. Yet in the eyes of some westerners, that practice simply reflected the second-class status of women in Islamic civilization. The leader of France's largest teachers union contended that "this flaunting of a clear symbol of women's subordination negates the teaching of human rights in schools." Thus, when the French minister of education defended the students' right to wear the scarves, he was widely criticized for condoning the oppression of women in Islam.

In fact, the education minister was not seeking to defend Islamic tradition or cultural diversity, let alone the oppression of women. He simply wanted to keep these girls—and the many others like them—in public schools, to expose them to secular influence and to promote their assimilation into French culture.

In 1989 Muslims made up 5 percent of the French population, or 2.7 million people, and this episode prompted many of them to demonstrate for greater pluralism and tolerance in France. Some of France's non-Muslim majority joined in, even wearing scarves in solidarity. Others, in contrast, called for stepped-up efforts to assimilate immigrants and those with foreign backgrounds into the common French civilization.

The Search for a New International Order

Economy and the Political Order in the Mature Democracies

The Postcommunist Experiment

Lifestyles and Identities in the West

The West in a Global Age

Conclusion: Learning from Western Civilization in a Postmodern World

"The hijab [headscarf] is our honor": Muslim women and girls demonstrate in Paris, October 1989. (AP/Wide World Photos)

France's prestigious Council of State soon ruled that the scarves did not violate the constitutional separation of church and state, as long as they were not worn in an effort to flaunt religion or to proselytize. The council left it to local school authorities to decide each case. But the riddles of citizenship, assimilation, and cultural diversity at issue in this "affair of the scarves" kept coming up in France and elsewhere by the early twenty-first century, as contact between the West and other parts of the world took new forms.

Such questions came to center stage partly because of the end of the cold war, which had overshadowed all else for four decades after World War II. With the collapse of communism, "the West" was no longer divided into rival power blocs representing competing experiments. The former communist countries scrambled to institute Western-style democratic capitalism, and several even joined NATO by the end of the 1990s. So there was now a single West, but it was ragged, diverse, and lacking an inner compass. What role would it play in the world? Confronted with post–cold war chaos, NATO proved willing to intervene in Europe to counter massive human rights violations. But whether the West was prepared to act comparably on the wider world stage remained unclear as the new century began.

Largely as the result of unprecedented economic and technological change, even the established Western democracies encountered new questions about immigration, environmental protection, and the role of the state. Such issues intersected to challenge the political consensus that had crystallized since World War II. At the same time, the European Union spread its reach even as new questions arose about Europe's relationship with the United States.

---

**QUESTIONS TO CONSIDER**

■ Why, and how, did the relationship between western Europe and the United States change with the end of the cold war?

■ What can we learn from the experience of post-communist Russia, in light of ongoing questions facing the West and the world?

■ Why were issues surrounding immigration, citizenship, assimilation, and cultural diversity increasingly central all over the Western world by the beginning of the twenty-first century?

■ What obstacles emerged as the West began playing a more active leadership role in confronting global trouble spots during the 1990s?

**TERMS TO KNOW**

European Union
Maastricht agreement
euro
"ethnic cleansing"
Kosovo
information technology (IT)

social market economy
Chechnya
digital divide
nongovernmental organizations (NGOs)

---

## THE SEARCH FOR A NEW INTERNATIONAL ORDER

HE disintegration of the Soviet system during 1989–1991 meant the swift, unexpected end of the bipolar cold war framework that had defined the era since World War II. Terrifying, potentially catastrophic though it had been at the time, that framework had provided a measure of order and security for over four decades. What sort of international configuration was to follow? What international roles might the Western democracies be prepared to play now that resisting communism was no longer the central preoccupation? And what place would the former communist countries assume in the new order?

The end of the cold war division of Europe expanded the possibilities for European integration, and the European Union made notable strides during the 1990s. But the capacity of the EU to respond to wider international issues on its own, independently of the United States, remained uncertain. Indeed, the series of wars in what had been Yugoslavia raised questions about the ability of any international body to assure stability in the post–cold war world. At the same time, however, the response of the NATO alliance to the Yugoslav situation by the end of the 1990s suggested the scope for new forms of multinational cooperation—and perhaps a new, more peaceful international order.

## ■ The West and the Uncertain International Framework

The end of the cold war left the United States "the world's only superpower," but its international role was less certain in a world without the perceived menace of international communism (see Map 30.1). As the potential threat from the Soviet Union dissolved, American support no longer seemed essential for European security. The NATO alliance, formed to check Soviet expansion in Europe, almost inevitably became less cohesive.

With the end of the Soviet Union, it made sense for western Europeans to rethink their security needs and military priorities. This reconsideration led in several directions, not all of them compatible. Some suggested that under the new circumstances, each nation would be well advised to look after its own defense. France even resumed nuclear testing in the South Pacific in 1995, though promptly ceased in light of the resulting international protest. Ten leading members of the European Union began developing a common defense mechanism but it remained tied to NATO. Problems that arose when NATO intervened in the fighting in Yugoslavia (see page 1032) prompted deeper consideration of the scope for an independent European force, but it remained uncertain what role the Europeans might play on their own.

Although its role was less clear with the end of the Soviet threat, NATO remained prominent. It even expanded in 1999 as membership was extended to the former Soviet bloc countries Poland, Hungary, and the Czech Republic. (Czechoslovakia divided peacefully into two nations, the Czech Republic and Slovakia, on January 1, 1993.) Further eastward expansion seemed likely. To these countries, NATO membership meant the definitive repudiation of the cold war division of Europe. But others worried that NATO expansion was a needless provocation to Russia, now, in its postcommunist guise, an especially uncertain player on the international scene.

Whereas the collapse of communism meant renewed pride and independence for the former satellite states, Russia quickly felt humiliated in world affairs. The one-time superpower was now poor, diminished in size,

## CHRONOLOGY

| | |
|---|---|
| **1979** | Thatcher becomes prime minister of Britain |
| | First direct elections to European parliament |
| **1981** | Mitterrand elected president of France |
| **1990** | Reunification of Germany |
| **1991** | Beginning of fighting in Yugoslavia |
| | Maastricht agreement expands scope of European Union |
| **1996** | Peace in Bosnia |
| | Yeltsin re-elected as president of Russia |
| **1997** | Blair becomes prime minister of Britain |
| **1998** | Financial crisis in Russia |
| | UN establishes international criminal court in The Hague |
| | Socialist-led coalition under Schröder replaces Kohl's conservative government in Germany |
| **1999** | Euro launched as currency of European Union |
| | NATO bombing of Serbia in response to Serb policies in Kosovo |
| | Renewal of Russia's war with Chechnya |
| | Protests at WTO meeting in Seattle |
| **2000** | Putin elected president of Russia |
| | Kostunica defeats Milosevic, becomes president of Yugoslavia |

apparently ignored. Hard-liners began proposing that the now-collapsed "Soviet Union" be revived as a military alliance. Some even favored selling nuclear technology to such countries as Iran, Iraq, and Algeria—to put pressure on the West, especially the United States, which many Russians blamed for their problems.

The most obvious beneficiary of the end of the cold war was Germany, which promptly reunified as communism collapsed in the East. Some—Germans and non-Germans alike—were eager to have Germany assume a major diplomatic role—and thus the responsibilities commensurate with its economic strength. But reunification also prompted anxiety about the role the new Germany might seek to play. Because 30 percent of the

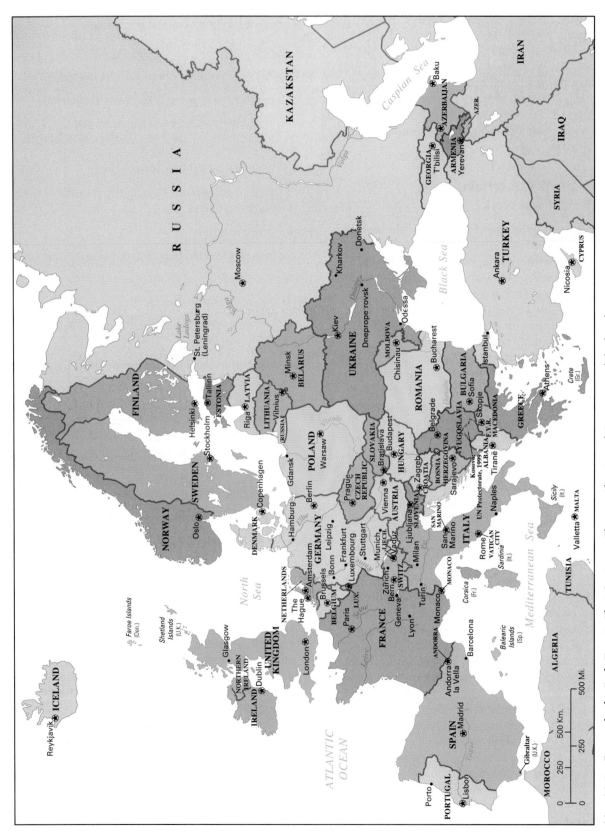

**Map 30.1  Europe in the Early Twenty-First Century**  The reunification of Germany and the breakup of the Soviet Union, Yugoslavia, and Czechoslovakia fundamentally altered the map of Europe during the 1990s.

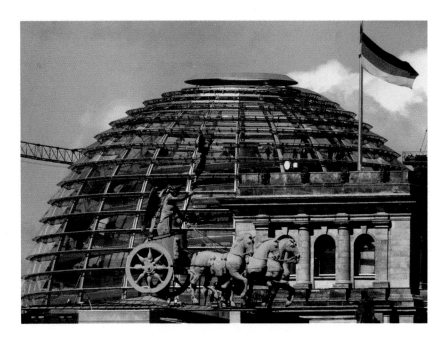

**The Democratic Reichstag, Berlin**
The centerpiece of the renovation of the German parliament building, completed in 1999, was the addition of a glass dome, shown here with the sculpture atop the Brandenburg Gate in the foreground. The dome was to manifest the openness of Germany's democracy as its capital moved from Bonn to Berlin. *(AP/Wide World Photos)*

territory of present-day Poland had been taken from Germany after World War II, the Poles were especially concerned. The German government, however, remained eager to prove its good intentions by pressing for further European integration. Some worried that the European Union would itself become a vehicle for German domination, but the Germans took care to offer reasoned, cautious leadership into the new century.

The Federal Republic officially moved its capital from quiet, provincial Bonn to Berlin in 1999, when the costly makeover of the old parliament (Reichstag) building by a British architect had been completed. (See the box "Reading Sources: Reconstructing Berlin: The New German Capital After the Cold War.") But the return to the traditional German capital, and even the original building, worried some in light of Germany's earlier aggressiveness. As it happened, precisely as the refurbished Reichstag building was opened, German forces were involved in their first combat roles since World War II. This time, however, they were participating in NATO air strikes against a state, Yugoslavia, charged with genocidal aggression. German chancellor Gerhard Schröder, a socialist, insisted that Germany could not turn away but indeed had a particular responsibility to respond, in light of its recent history.

Many Germans still remained reluctant to support an expanded international military role. But as the rich countries of the West seemed expected to respond more widely to an increasingly volatile world, the United States pressured Germany to step up its military spend-

ing, which in 1998 amounted to but 1.5 percent of its economy, compared with 3.2 percent in the United States, and 2.8 percent in both Britain and France. However, German leaders, like those elsewhere in Europe, were reluctant to commit more resources to military spending at a time when budget pressures on the welfare state were already straining the social compact.

## ■ The European Union

With Europe no longer divided, the scope for European integration was suddenly much wider. The former Soviet bloc countries were eager to join the European club. At the same time, the EU was expanding its scope and developing a still more complex institutional network. Thus new questions accompanied the steps toward fuller integration in the decade after the end of the cold war.

From the start, proponents had envisioned that the Common Market would gradually promote greater uniformity in areas such as tax policy and business law, where national differences constituted barriers to economic activity across national borders. Although a full customs union had been achieved by the late 1960s, national governments continued to compromise the open market, especially by favoring certain companies to give them an advantage in international competition. For domestic political reasons, governments sometimes bought only from national firms or gave subsidies to domestic producers, enabling them to offer artificially lower prices to compete with foreign firms.

## ⚜ R E A D I N G   S O U R C E S

---

# Reconstructing Berlin:
# The New German Capital After the Cold War

*Berlin was a city like none other in modern history. Associated with Prussian mili-
tarism, then with German nationalism, and finally with the worst features of Nazi
aggression, the city ended up divided by the cold war—and the Wall—then restored
as capital of reunified Germany in 1999. How could the democratic Federal Republic, modestly headquartered in provincial Bonn since its inception in 1949, best embrace Berlin, with all its historical connotations? Jane Kramer, one of the most
authoritative journalistic analysts of contemporary Europe, conveyed what Berlin
was like in 1999 as it remade itself to be the capital of an established democracy.*

---

One morning in Berlin this spring, on my way to an
interview with a city planner, I stopped at the new
Galeries Lafayette, in the east of the city on
Friedrichstrasse, to pick up a croissant at the basement supermarket. By then, I had been in Berlin for
at least a week. I had tried counting the construction
cranes—seven hundred of them, the papers said—
dipping over the born-again capital of a united Germany. I had prowled the sites of that construction,
tracing the path of a wall and a no man's land that
only ten years ago had split the city down its center.
I had toured the Chancellery and some of the other
new government buildings going up around the
Reichstag, itself restored with a new glass dome. I
had been through the Potsdamer Platz, where Sony
and DaimlerChrysler were hosting a real-estate-
development potlatch on twenty-eight acres of what
used to be bombed-out desert. And I had seen the
Schlossplatz, in East Berlin, where people were still
arguing about the fate of an immense and incon-
testably ugly building called the Palace of the Republic, which until November of 1989, when the Wall
came down, had housed the East German parliament. I had dug up the figures: five thousand six
hundred and forty architects practicing in Berlin; a
hundred and thirty thousand workers officially rebuilding Berlin (and no one knows how many un-
registered foreign crews still bunking in converted
shipping-container dormitories on the big sites); six
thousand bureaucrats drawing salaries to (depending
on who's talking) contribute to or complicate the
process. I had heard all about "the architecture of the

European city," "the architecture of the Berlin Republic," "the architecture of civil society," "the architecture
of public space," and "the architecture of democratic
transparency." I had spent so much time looking at
buildings, thinking about buildings, listening to people
whose job it was to try to redeem or redefine or rein-
vent "Germanness" through the new buildings of the
capital, that my trip to the Galeries Lafayette was the
first time I had actually used any of those buildings in
what for me could be considered a normal way. . . .

. . . [I]t's safe to say that only in Berlin will you
hear that a middle-sized, medium-priced department
store with seventeen brands of tights and fresh
breakfast pastries in the basement is a field of battle
for nothing less than the soul of Germany—and not
even because of its assault on your pocketbook (Germans call it "consumer terrorism") but because of a
cone-shaped glass-and-steel atrium that a planner
found "authoritarian," and not the "agora" he had
hoped for.

The change in Berlin over the past few years has
been astonishing, and, with this sort of architectural
anguish (it's endemic now), the most astonishing
part may be that anything gets built at all.

. . . Every city creates a market in its own obses-
sions, and right now in Berlin the obsession is architecture—or, more accurately, how to make a credible
Berlin out of a city with no consensual idea of itself,
and no common history beyond a negative one. . . .

---

*Source:* Jane Kramer, "Living with Berlin," *The New Yorker*, July
5, 1999, pp. 50–52. Reprinted by permission of the author.

After the oil crises of the 1970s, and amid increasing concern about "Eurosclerosis," or lack of innovation and competitiveness, the European Community's twelve members committed themselves in 1985 to creating a true single market with genuinely free competition by the end of 1992. Goods, services, and money would circulate freely among the member countries; manufacturing would conform to uniform product standards; and equal competition for government contracts would apply.

Meeting at Maastricht, in the Netherlands, in 1991, leaders of the member countries agreed to the Treaty on European Union. The treaty provided for a common policy on workers' rights and committed members to a common currency, the *euro,* and a common central banking structure by 1999. The subsequent ratification debates in each country proved more divisive than expected. Some feared German domination; others argued that faceless bureaucrats in foreign cities would now be making the vital decisions for domestic economies. Although the EU's members eventually ratified most of the Maastricht agreements, there were exceptions. Citing the danger of terrorism and drug smuggling, France essentially opted out of a provision for the free movement of people within the Union, a provision Germany found indispensable. And several members, including Britain, remained outside the common currency mechanism.

Moreover, the creation of an internal customs union, benign though it seemed, did not commit the EU to freer trade with nonmember countries such as the United States. Indeed, half the EU budget at the end of the 1990s went to farm subsidies—to protect farmers from outside competition. The possibility that the French government would lower agricultural supports, partly in response to pressures from the United States, led to several massive demonstrations by French farmers during the 1990s. By the late 1990s, EU quotas restricting the import of bananas from Central America produced serious friction with the United States. Such quotas favored former European colonies but thereby hurt American multinational fruit companies. Disputes erupted over the import of American hormone-enhanced beef and over governmental subsidies to the competing aircraft manufacturing giants, Europe's Airbus and America's Boeing.

The most controversial, and potentially most significant, of the Maastricht agreements was the provision for an Economic and Monetary Union (EMU), based on the euro. Especially by eliminating the costs of currency exchange, use of the euro promised to boost trade and economic interaction among the member countries. And it would simplify economic relations with non-EU countries as well. But a common currency required coordina-

tion of fiscal policy, and a number of the countries involved had to reduce their budget deficits substantially by cutting spending or raising taxes. Moreover, any budget deficits thereafter could not exceed a specified, relatively low figure. So whereas this deeper economic integration promised greater prosperity in the long term, it required immediate sacrifices that crashed against the social compact, already under pressure, that had produced high government spending for social welfare measures in the first place.

Although four of the fifteen members of the EU chose to remain outside the mechanism at this point, the euro was launched with much fanfare, and right on schedule, on January 1, 1999. National currencies remained temporarily in use for ordinary transactions, but the euro was used for major governmental and institutional transactions and traded on international currency exchanges. The common currency lived up to its promise, even facilitating a notable increase in supranational mergers and takeovers—a trend that threatened some but promised greater efficiency and international competitiveness for European firms. (See the feature "Weighing the Evidence: The Euro" on pages 1062–1063.)

The EU was more visible than ever. And as countries from Estonia and Poland to Turkey and Cyprus clambered to join, the EU insisted on strict membership criteria, including democratic institutions and alignment with EU laws and procedures in advance. The lure of membership sometimes strengthened democracy in the candidate states. When an apparent drift toward authoritarianism in Slovakia during the mid-1990s prompted EU warnings, Slovak voters ousted their present government in favor of a pro-EU alternative in 1998.

But as the roles and potential geographical reach of EU institutions expanded, long-standing questions about their structure and functioning became more pressing. For though it made democracy a condition for membership, the EU itself was only indirectly democratic in character. With major decisions made by an unelected policy elite, the EU's own "democratic deficit" seemed contradictory, and unacceptable. The issue of openness and accountability was complex, however, because the functioning of each particular EU institution, its relative importance, and the relationships among the institutions were all at issue.

By 2000 the European Union included a network of five interlocking core institutions, variously seated in Brussels, Strasbourg, Luxembourg, and Frankfurt. The executive branch was the Commission in Brussels, consisting of twenty appointed members, but with a professional staff of sixteen thousand. Charged to pursue the

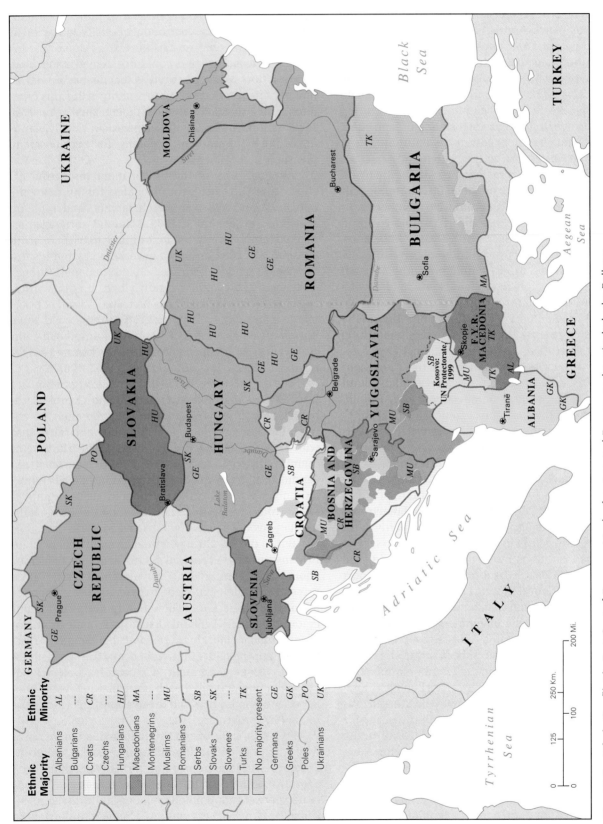

**Map 30.2  Ethnic Conflict in East-Central Europe**  Much of east-central Europe, and particularly the Balkans, has long been an area of complex ethnic mixture. The end of communist rule opened the way to ethnic conflict, most tragically in what had been Yugoslavia. This map shows ethnic distribution in the region in the mid-1990s.

wider interests of the community, not to represent national interests, the commission had considerable power to initiate and enforce EU legislation. The question was whether these unelected Eurocrats had too much power.

The legislative branch of the EU was the Council of Ministers, composed of ministers from the governments of the member countries. On routine matters, the Council voted by majority, weighted by the size of each country's population. But more sensitive issues required unanimity; thus each member country had veto power. Reformers wanted to expand the role of majority rule and minimize the scope for veto. The British, citing concerns about national sovereignty, led resistance to change.

EU membership clearly entailed some loss of sovereignty, thanks especially to the increasingly powerful role of the judicial branch, the European Court of Justice, headquartered in Luxembourg. In a landmark 1988 case, the court struck down a German law on beer purity, which it judged an instance of disguised protectionism. EU agreements took precedence over national legislation, and the court was increasingly willing to interpret EU treaties in ways that had sweeping implications.

In contrast, the power of the European Parliament, which had developed from the assembly of the European Coal and Steel Community, and which divided its time between Strasbourg and Brussels, was more potential than actual. Though it had some oversight over budget and expanding powers to block or amend legislation, the parliament remained much the weakest of the core EU institutions by 2001. So despite the genuinely democratic character of this body, voters in the member countries demonstrated little interest in the elections of its members.

The fifth core institution, the European Central Bank, headquartered in Frankfurt, was born with the commitment to a common monetary policy and currency in 1991. Like central banks everywhere, its chief role was to regulate the money supply. And also like other central banks, this one faced political controversy over priorities. Citing inflation concerns, the bank adopted tight credit policies in the late 1990s, but politicians were quick to blame these policies for Europe's stubbornly high unemployment. Skeptics suggested that the elected politicians appreciated having a scapegoat for policies that were necessary, though not immediately popular.

Through gradual, incremental change over more than fifty years, the EU had become an established and powerful entity by the early twenty-first century, though it was an experiment still very much in progress. By now

"Europe" was a hybrid, at once a genuinely supranational entity and a collection of sovereign states. There had never been anything quite like it before. In such spheres as trade, agriculture, and the environment, the EU was dominant; national governments had little freedom of action. But other spheres, such as defense, taxation, and criminal justice, remained mostly national prerogatives. And though concerns about its "democratic deficit" were widely heard, the EU was successful enough to enjoy broad public support. Many sensed that whereas more democracy was desirable in principle, it would make the EU more beholden to short-sighted, parochially national concerns—and thus less successful.

## ■ Ethnic Conflict and the Wars of Yugoslav Secession

As the members of the European Union struggled to create a supranational entity, forces in the opposite direction—subnational, religious, ethnic, tribal—grew more powerful in parts of Europe, sometimes producing violent conflict. Beginning in 1969, the British had to use troops in Northern Ireland to keep order in the face of ongoing threats from Irish Catholics seeking the end of British rule and unification with the Republic of Ireland. The result was three decades of conflict between Protestants and Catholics that eluded definitive solution into the twenty-first century. In Czechoslovakia, which had been widely admired for its peaceful, civilized departure from communism in 1989, the Slovak minority broke away to form an independent republic at the beginning of 1993. In Belgium, antagonism between Flemish-speaking Flemings and French-speaking Walloons deepened during the 1990s. And the movement to separate French-speaking Quebec from the rest of Canada almost achieved success in 1995.

Most dramatic was the situation in Yugoslavia, where ethnic and religious conflict led to the disintegration of the country in a series of brutal wars among Serbs, Croats, Bosnian Muslims, and ethnically Albanian Kosovars (see Map 30.2). Defining events of the 1990s, these wars proved a major challenge for the new international order that was emerging, haltingly, after the cold war.

Although much was made of ancient ethnic and religious differences once Yugoslavia began falling apart, the area had long traditions of pluralism and tolerance. But ethnic relations had been poisoned by recent events—especially the civil war during World War II (see page 975). The situation had remained reasonably stable under Josip Tito's independent communist regime, which insisted on Yugoslav unity while affording some

**Refugees from Kosovo, 1999** Kosovo, long a potential trouble spot within the Yugoslav Confederation, finally became the focal point of Slobodan Milosevic's Serb nationalism in 1999. The Serb campaign of ethnic cleansing forced many Kosovars to flee, primarily to neighboring Macedonia or Albania, where most had to survive in primitive camps. Here a mass of Kosovar refugees seeks to crowd onto a train to Macedonia. *(Roger Lemoyne/Liaison)*

measure of regional autonomy. But Tito was himself a Croat, and the state structure he devised angered some Serbs. Within a few years of Tito's death in 1980, intellectuals concerned for cultural distinctiveness began demanding cultural autonomy, thereby undermining the Yugoslav identity that Tito had sought to foster. A 1986 manifesto of leading Serb writers and intellectuals charged that Tito had allowed Kosovar genocide against Serbs and had pursued economic policies that favored Slovenes and Croats.

Insofar as this emphasis on ethnic identity pointed simply toward self-determination, it might prove benign, but each region of Yugoslavia harbored minority enclaves. Thus to accent ethnic identity, and grievance, carried the potential for trouble. After the fall of communism, Slovenia and Croatia declared themselves independent of Yugoslavia in May 1991. Led by the nationalist Franjo Tudjman°, Croatia adopted a constitution for a new "state of the Croat people" that left the 600,000 Serbs living in Croatia, most for generations, suddenly a vulnerable minority.

At the same time, the Serb leader of the remaining Yugoslavia, Slobodan Milosevic° (b. 1941), moved to center stage, becoming one of the key figures of the 1990s. A former communist, Milosevic embraced Serb national-

ism at least partly to maintain his own power. His aim was to unite all the Serbs, 2 million of whom lived outside Serbia proper, mostly in Croatia and Bosnia-Herzegovina. He would start by taking over the substantial parts of Croatia with Serb majorities, then divide Bosnia-Herzegovina with Croatia.

Starting in 1991 Milosevic proceeded with extreme brutality, fostering "ethnic cleansing"—forced relocation or mass killing to rid the territory in question of its non-Serb inhabitants. Through his government's control of the media, he encouraged a sense of victimization that incited hatred among the Serbs. And each in the series of wars that followed seemed to open the way to worse atrocity and deeper bitterness.

The Serb assault in Bosnia by 1995 especially brought home to the world the depth of the tragedy at work (see Map 30.2). In the Bosnian capital, Sarajevo, a culturally diverse city long known for its tolerant, cosmopolitan atmosphere, more than 10,000 civilians, including 1,500 children, were killed by shelling and sniper fire during a Serb siege from 1992 to early 1996.

When a Serb mortar killed thirty-seven civilians in a marketplace in Sarajevo in August 1995, NATO forces responded with air strikes that led to peace accords and the end of fighting by early 1996. But though the peace agreement envisioned a unified Bosnian state, the contending Serbs, Croats, and Bosnian Muslims quickly began carving out separate spheres, violating agreements about repatriation and the rights of minorities. By 2001 Bosnia remained an ethnically divided international protectorate, its peace dependent on the foreign troops stationed there.

The next phase of the Yugoslav tragedy centered on the province of Kosovo, which Serbs viewed as the cradle of their nationhood (see Map 30.2). For complex historical reasons, however, Serbs had long constituted only a minority of its population. The majority were ethnically Albanian, and by the late 1980s, they were talking independence—and sometimes mistreating the minority Serbs. As part of his effort to foster Serb nationalism, Milosevic countered by suspending autonomy for Kosovo within the Yugoslav confederation in 1991. The fissuring of Yugoslavia over the next few years emboldened the Kosovars, who counted on Serb intransigence to justify a demand for full independence, as opposed to mere autonomy.

When Milosevic struck against the Kosovars in the spring of 1999, ruthlessly pursuing ethnic cleansing, the Western powers again intervened, first convening a meeting with Serb and Kosovar leaders on Kosovo's future. When the Serb-led remnant of Yugoslavia refused to sign, NATO made good on threats to bomb Serbia in re-

---

**Tudjman** (TOODCH-mahn)  **Milosevic** (mih-LO-suh-vitch)

taliation. The bombing, concentrated on such economic targets as bridges and power stations, continued for eleven weeks later in 1999.

Critics argued that it set a dubious precedent to attack Serbia for refusing a settlement that would have ceded territory and opened the rest of Serbia to quasi-occupation by NATO. No one could deny that Kosovo was part of Serbia, so the NATO action was an overt interference in the internal affairs of a sovereign state. Under what authority was NATO acting, and according to what criteria? Did it claim the right to bomb any state pursuing policies not to its liking? What about the likely damage to NATO's relations with Russia, long close to Serbia, and now hypersensitive in light of its declining influence in world affairs?

Even the claim that the operation was a humanitarian response to genocide seemed hypocritical to some, who asked why the international community had done nothing in response to the manifestly more systematic genocide in Rwanda in 1994, when 800,000 people had been killed in a hundred days. Defenders countered that it was partly because of the soul-searching in the aftermath of Rwanda that the advanced countries of the West were now changing the rules and taking responsibility for concerted action. But on what basis was NATO the appropriate multinational agent? The response of the Western alliance to Kosovo's plight seemed something of a turning point, but what it would mean for the future remained unclear.

Once the NATO bombing began, the Serbs intensified their ethnic cleansing of Kosovo, burning homes, forcing 800,000 refugees to flee into neighboring Macedonia and Albania. But the bombing finally led both the Serbs and the Kosovars to pull back from their more extreme demands, and Russia agreed to join in the multinational peacekeeping force in Kosovo in the aftermath.

Still, the outcome bore little relationship to the multi-ethnic pluralism NATO had been seeking. The Kosovars clearly dominated the now-ravaged territory. Thirsting for revenge, younger Kosovars engaged in their own ethnic cleansing, targeting not only Serbs but also Roma ("Gypsies") and Bosnian Muslims. The resulting violence sickened even older Kosovars, who remembered years of peaceful coexistence with the Serbs. With many having fled, Serbs constituted only 10 percent of the population, confined to the region adjacent to Serbia proper, by 2000. So in Kosovo, as in Bosnia, fighting resulted in near-complete ethnic separation, with some form of partition likely.

Ethnic cleansing by the Kosovars was but one aspect of the wider anarchy that followed the fighting. Six months after the bombing stopped, the area had no working government and was essentially run by armed gangs. Beset by domestic political pressures, national rivalries, and problems of coordination, the outside peacekeepers found it difficult to play any meaningful role.

Though he was the first sitting head of state to be indicted for war crimes, Milosevic proved resilient, initially surviving his defeat in Kosovo in 1999, just as he had survived a major protest movement in 1996–1997. In addition to the recent bombing, ongoing economic sanctions hurt ordinary Serbs, arousing a sense of victimization and resentment against the West. But opposition continued as well, and in September 2000, Vojislav Kostunica° defeated Milosevic in Yugoslavia's presidential election. Although a moment of carefully orchestrated violence after the election was needed to force Milosevic from power, the transition to democracy in Yugoslavia was far smoother than most had thought possible. Milosevic was the last of the former communists to continue in power, and some saw his fall as the definitive end of the cold war era. (See the box "Reading Sources: The Fall of Milosevic as the Last Revolution.")

# ECONOMY AND THE POLITICAL ORDER IN THE MATURE DEMOCRACIES

B Y the 1980s democracy had become the unchallenged norm in western Europe, where the radical right remained largely discredited and the left seemed to have been domesticated for good. In important respects, in fact, conservatives and social democrats sounded more and more alike. But at the same time the postwar consensus about governmental responsibility for social and economic well-being began to fade as new questions arose about the reach of the state.

Many of the trends important in western Europe by the 1980s were visible in the United States and Canada as well. All over the Western world, organized labor weakened, more women entered in the work force, and issues from child-care to pension costs moved to center stage. But there were some instructive differences in the ways the various nations of the West dealt with these matters.

## ■ Rethinking the Welfare State

Government welfare measures had helped establish the new political consensus in western Europe since World War II. Although much publicity surrounded the British welfare state, the percentage of the British economy

---

**Kostunica** (kohs-TOO-nih-kah)

# The Fall of Milosevic as the Last Revolution

*Slobodan Milosevic was the key player in the brutal wars in the former Yugoslavia that produced massive civilian suffering during the 1990s. Despite defeat in Kosovo in 1999, he seemed fully in control of the Serb-dominated remnant of Yugoslavia—until an extraordinary election in September 2000. Milosevic was defeated, but an element of violence was required to oust him during the weeks that followed. In this passage, the noted British historian and journalist Timothy Garton Ash analyzes the chain of events and considers the outcome in light of the end of the cold war.*

The last revolution was also the strangest.

On Thursday, October 5, as Serbs stormed the parliament in Belgrade, waving flags from its burning windows, and seized the headquarters of state television, which an opposition leader had once christened "TV Bastille," it looked like a real, old-fashioned European revolution. The storming of the Winter Palace! The fall of the Bastille! . . .

. . . [L]ate on the evening of Friday, October 6, Milosevic appeared on another national television channel to make the kind of gracious speech conceding election defeat that one expects from an American president or a British prime minister. He had just received the information, he said, that Vojislav Kostunica had won the presidential election. (This from the man who had spent the last eleven days trying to deny exactly that, by electoral fraud, intimidation, and manipulation of the courts.)

. . . He stood stiffly beside the Yugoslav flag, with his hands crossed very low in front of him, like a schoolboy who had been caught cheating. Or like a penitent before the priest that his father once aspired to be. Sorry, father, I've cheated in the elections, ruined my country, caused immeasurable bloodshed and misery to our neighbors—but I'll be a good boy now. It was incongruous, surreal, ridiculous in the pretense that this was just an ordinary, democratic change of leader. . . .

. . . What happened between about three and seven o'clock on the afternoon of Thursday, October 5, changed everything. Led by a man in a red shirt, defying police batons and tear gas, a crowd stormed the parliament. Soon thereafter, the nearby state television headquarters was trashed and set alight. A handful of other key media outlets, including the state television studio and transmission center, and Veran Matic's B92 radio, were more peacefully taken over. Kostunica cried, "Good evening, liberated Serbia," to an ecstatic crowd, and they celebrated in the streets.

These events invite a moment's reflection on the relationship between image and reality. Those who stormed the parliament created an unforgettable image of liberation—an image that CNN and the BBC sent around the world. This image then became reality. Taking over the state television was itself another compelling television image: the "TV Bastille" in flames. But it also meant that the opposition now controlled the place that made the images. And that, not the army or police, is the very heart of power in modern politics. . . .

. . . There was . . . a brief moment of 1917: a deliberate yet limited use of revolutionary violence. It is hard to imagine the breakthrough coming without it. But the remarkable thing is how limited it was, and how quickly the country returned to new-style, peaceful revolution. Within a week, Otpor activists were organizing an action to encourage people to return the goods they had looted from the shops. . . .

. . . If the Solidarity revolution in Poland was the beginning of the end of communism, this was the end of the end of communism. It was the last of a twenty-year chain of new-style, Central and East European revolutions, each learning from the previous one but also adding new ingredients and variations. And not just in Europe. There are echoes here of the Philippines or Indonesia. And messages, one hopes, for other countries. In a now globalized politics, we have moved beyond the old 1789 and 1917 models of revolution. If it could happen in Serbia, why not in Burma? Why not in Cuba? . . .

. . . [A]fter the fall of Milosevic there is no longer any external obstacle to our building a liberal community not just of fifteen but of thirty democratic nation-states.

*Source:* Timothy Garton Ash, "The Last Revolution," *The New York Review of Books,* November 16, 2000, pp. 8, 11–12, 14.

devoted to public expenditure for welfare, housing, and education by the early 1970s—18.2 percent—was about average for the industrialized nations of the West. Sweden had the highest figure at 23.7 percent. But the welfare state began to encounter strains with the more difficult economic circumstances of the 1970s. Globalization and technological change threatened the postwar prosperity, and what government should try to do, could afford to do, became central to the agenda in the West.

Pressures on the welfare state were especially striking in Sweden. By the early 1970s, 40 percent of Sweden's national income was devoted to taxes to finance the system—the highest rate of taxation in the world. At the same time, Sweden found itself less competitive, both because its wages were high and because it was not keeping abreast of technological developments. In Sweden, as elsewhere, opinion-makers grew increasingly doubtful that a welfare state could nurture the initiative and productivity needed for success in the increasingly competitive global economy. By 1980 unemployment and efforts to cut government spending led to the most severe labor unrest the country had experienced since the war. Even on the level of everyday life, more Swedes were coming to believe that the Swedish model entailed excessive governmental intrusion in the private sphere.

In Britain a dramatic assault on the welfare state began developing at the same time, especially because the British economy, having lagged the others of the industrialized West, suffered especially during the 1970s. Between 1968 and 1976, the country lost 1 million manufacturing jobs. By the mid-1970s this economic decline threatened to shatter Britain's postwar consensus around the welfare state as the British people could not agree on how to apportion the pain of the necessary austerity measures.

During the 1970s each of Britain's two major political parties made a serious effort to come to grips with the situation, but neither succeeded, especially because neither could deal effectively with Britain's strong trade unions. But when the militantly conservative Margaret Thatcher (b. 1925) became prime minister in 1979, it was clear that Britain was embarking on a radically different course.

Thatcher insisted that Britain could reverse its economic decline only by fostering a new "enterprise culture," restoring the individual initiative that had been sapped, as she saw it, by decades of dependence on government. Thatcher took it for granted that the free market, undistorted by government intervention, produced optimum economic efficiency and thus, in the long term, the greatest social benefit.

Abandoning its paternalistic tendencies and aristocratic vestiges, the Conservative Party now appealed especially to the upwardly mobile, entrepreneurial

**Thatcher's Conservative Revolution**    As British prime minister from 1979 to 1990, Margaret Thatcher led an assault on the welfare state and a renewed embrace of free-market economics in Britain. Together with U.S. president Ronald Reagan, who greatly admired her, she came to symbolize the retreat from government that marked the 1980s. Thatcher is shown here at a political rally in London in 1987.   *(D. Hudson/Sygma)*

middle class. But in light of the socioeconomic difficulties Britain faced by the late 1970s, Thatcher's message had broad appeal across the social spectrum. With Labour increasingly isolated, identified with decaying inner cities and old industrial regions, Thatcher easily won re-election in 1983 and 1987.

Three immediate priorities followed directly from Thatcher's overall strategy. First, her government made substantial cuts in taxes and corresponding cuts in spending for education, national health, and public housing. Second, the government fostered privatization, selling off an array of state-owned firms from Rolls Royce to British Airways. The government even sold public housing to tenants, at as much as 50 percent below market value, a measure that helped Thatcher win considerable working-class support. Third, Thatcher curbed the power of Britain's labor unions, which were already on the defensive in this period of high unemployment.

Several new laws curtailed trade-union power, and Thatcher refused to consult with union leaders as her predecessors had done since the war. A showdown was reached with the yearlong coal miners' strike of 1984 and 1985, one of the most bitter and violent European strikes of the twentieth century. The strike's failure in the face of government intransigence further discredited the labor movement and enhanced Thatcher's prestige. Still, the

# The Internet

In the late 1960s the U.S. Department of Defense commissioned some bright graduate students to develop a way to share information on computers with university researchers. The program they devised enabled computers to use existing telephone lines to send files from one machine to another. The resulting protocol, or set of rules, included the little-used "at" symbol—@—which soon became the pivot in every electronic mail (e-mail) address in the world.

Thus was born the Internet—not in some Silicon Valley garage but at the U.S. defense department, which made the new program freely available to universities to facilitate research. At first the impact was limited. Computers were big, clunky machines, and only governments, universities, and large businesses could afford them. All of this changed during the 1980s when IBM began marketing the small, affordable personal computer (PC). The potential to share information on computers was now available to individuals—in their professional or working roles, but also as consumers, correspondents, hobbyists, political activists, or simply as human beings curious about their world. Anyone could put information on a computer that others might want to access. The potential magnitude of such sharing became clear only gradually, but by the end of the 1990s the Internet had taken definite form, encompassing an array of possibilities from e-mail to the World Wide Web.

The Internet seemed to overcome physical distance by opening a whole new "cyberspace"—a term derived from cybernetics, coined in 1948 to indicate the comparative study of control systems, from the brain to the computer. Since Antiquity people had been able to go to physical places—libraries—to access physical objects containing information. But as the Internet made possible access to all networked computers, and as more people found it advantageous to make more information available, Internet users could find a great deal of information more quickly than ever before. Thus, for example, stock markets became more open and democratic, and interactive learning across physical distance became possible. And though much hype ballyhooed the "new economy," centered around young "high-tech" companies, the Internet revolution offered long-established companies the chance to improve productivity through more efficient procurement and inventory control.

The growth of the Internet was bound up with globalization—or Americanization. By 2000 English was the language of 78.3 percent of webpages worldwide; only 1.7 percent were in Spanish and 1.2 percent in French. However, as Internet access came to seem essential for success in an increasingly competitive world, many worried about the growing "digital divide" between those with and those without such access.

Some suggested that the Internet made possible greater democracy by bypassing the "gatekeepers" in journalism, publishing, or academics, but others grew anxious about quality as the Internet made ever more unedited information available. So much was available that it was easy to get caught up in the technical means; following links threatened to become more important than actually reading content. Moreover, commerce seemed ever more intrusive by the early twenty-first century. With its blinking advertisements, even the website of the once staid Encyclopedia Bri-

---

violent encounters between police and picketing strikers, carried nationwide on television, indicated the cracks in the relative social harmony that Britain had long enjoyed.

In addition, riots by unemployed youths broke out in several major industrial cities in 1981 and again in 1985. On one issue, however, the Thatcher government managed a meeting of the minds with discontented city dwellers. Even before Thatcher took office, increasing immigration from Britain's former colonies was being blamed for a variety of social ills, from unemployment to urban crime. Taking a hard line on the issue, Thatcher's Conservatives sponsored the Nationality Act of 1982, which restricted immigration from the former British colonies.

With her nationalist bent, Thatcher resisted the growing power of the multinational European Union. But her stance on the EU, coupled with what seemed an increasingly arrogant, strident tone, provoked growing opposition even within her own party, which finally ousted her as party leader, and thus as prime minister, in 1990.

Even critics admitted that Thatcher's policies, especially her willingness to curb the unions, had produced a significant change in British attitudes in favor of enterprise and competition. Privatization found increasing approval, while the number of new businesses reflected a revival of entrepreneurship—apparently the basis for better economic performance during the 1990s. But the gap between rich and poor widened, and the old industrial regions of the north were left ever further behind.

Still, even as the welfare state receded in Sweden and Britain, the reach of government expanded elsewhere. In

**An Internet Café** With the sudden popularity of the Internet by the mid-1990s, "Internet cafés" emerged all over the world. They offered Internet access, along with coffee, to those who did not own personal computers. London's Cyberia café, shown here in 1995, was typical.
*(Martyn Hayhow/SIPA Press)*

tannica recalled some nineteenth-century carnival. Still, Britannica was not a public service but a profit-making company, which had to be compensated for making its information available.

As a new way of delivering information, the Internet raised complex intellectual property issues, which came dramatically to a head in 2000 over access to recorded music. Through the website of Napster Inc., 10 million people were downloading recorded music from a network of fellow users, bypassing traditional methods of distribution and remuneration. The recording industry filed suit to recover millions in lost compact disk sales, but record companies scrambled to find new ways to distribute music over the Internet at the same time. The Internet was opening new ways for users to compensate the creators of music and other forms of intellectual property.

As they became ever more dependent on the Internet, organizations and individuals also became more vulnerable—and concerned about privacy and security. Third parties could keep track of sites accessed and purchases made

and then develop a profile of interests, buying habits, health concerns—whether for marketing or some less elevated purpose. By the early twenty-first century, critics suggested that tough decisions through the political process were necessary to govern the further development of the Internet. Otherwise, with commercial considerations dominant, the outcome would be less democracy, less free speech, less privacy.

Sheer volume was increasingly a concern as well. By 2000 the number of Internet users reached 300 million people worldwide, and the figure was projected to exceed 1 billion by 2005. The amount of information traveling across the Internet was doubling every three months—prompting concerns that even as high-tech companies devised ever more sophisticated routers and switchers, innovations in hardware could not keep up with mushrooming demand. Some experts predicted gigantic cyber traffic jams, even gridlock. But there was no turning back. The ongoing Internet revolution had become central to the continuing information technology experiment.

---

Italy reforms during the 1970s made available a wider range of state services than ever before, from kindergarten and medical care to sports and recreational facilities. In France by the mid-1990s, five-week paid vacations were mandatory, with the government sometimes subsidizing the cost of transportation to seaside or mountain resorts. Government subsidies kept the costs of cultural events affordable to ordinary workers. Accustomed to a strong government role in society, Europeans had difficulty understanding how measures such as government-sponsored health care could cause such controversy among Americans. But as global economic competition intensified during the last decades of the century, France and Italy found it more difficult to pay for all the benefits their governments had gradually come to promise.

## ■ An Uncertain Affluence

As the Soviet bloc economies bogged down during the 1980s, the democratic countries of the West enjoyed renewed affluence. One driving force was the technological change that, during the late twentieth century, produced a "third industrial revolution." Though it encompassed everything from robotics to fiber optics, it was based especially on the computer, or what soon came to be summed up as "information technology" (IT). The advent of these new technologies in a context of increasing global competition affected patterns of employment in ways that damaged some, but also produced new opportunities and new winners. (See the feature "Information Technology: The Internet.")

Some new firms were able to exploit such technologies to start from scratch, without the problems of redundant workers or outmoded plants and equipment that older competitors often faced. A good example was Benetton, an Italian clothing firm founded in 1964 that pioneered the use of computer technology in all aspects of its operation. But Benetton proved a notable success partly because it needed fewer workers. Manufacturing jobs, especially, tended to be lost as competition forced the industrial sector to become more efficient through computers and automation. In the German steel industry, which had spearheaded a remarkable industrial transformation a century before, over half the jobs disappeared during the 1970s and 1980s.

Changing labor patterns reinforced the decline of organized labor, which was decidedly on the defensive throughout western Europe and the United States by the 1980s. In France, for example, the organized labor movement was at once divided and relatively small, encompassing fewer than 10 percent of French workers. The increasing danger of unemployment undercut the leverage of the unions. And as the economy grew more complex, workers were ever less likely to think of themselves as members of a single, unified working class.

So the renewed prosperity of the 1980s was in some ways brittle and uncertain, especially because unemployment reached levels not seen since the Great Depression. Even after solid growth resumed by 1983, unemployment hovered stubbornly at around 10 percent throughout much of western Europe, with 13 percent the norm in some older industrial areas. These figures would have seemed unimaginable fifteen years before and were much higher than the rates of 5 to 7 percent typical in the United States during the same period. Even as unemployment declined to postwar lows in the United States during the 1990s, elevated levels persisted in much of western Europe.

Most attributed the higher European rate to the structure of labor markets and, more generally, to the greater agility and flexibility of the American economy. The relationship was paradoxical because as a result of laws, labor agreements, and the postwar consensus now in place, those European workers who had jobs were more secure than their American counterparts. But, as the other side of the coin, European employers were less able to adapt to changing conditions by laying off workers or hiring new ones with different skills. During the 1980s, American firms were more likely to restructure or downsize in response to technological change and increasing global competition. But thus the American economy proved better at creating new jobs as new opportunities emerged during the 1990s.

In fact, it was increasingly clear that two models of capitalism were at work—and in competition. The U.S. model, increasingly shared by Britain, placed greater emphasis on free enterprise, whereas continental western Europe had evolved a "social market economy," with greater commitment to security, consensus, and communitarian values. (See the box "Reading Sources: The Varieties of Liberal Capitalism.") But was the European model sustainable if it obstructed adaptability and consistently yielded high unemployment, especially among young people?

The continental model was increasingly on the defensive during the 1990s, a period of remarkable prosperity for the United States, which forcefully asserted its leadership in the "new economy" revolving around information technology. Said one executive of Intel, a leading American high tech firm, "If France were a stock, I'd sell it."[1] But the European model provided a more substantial safety net—in health care, for example—as well as a stronger commitment to public goods like transportation and day care. The question by the early twenty-first century was clear. Could Europe maintain and even extend its more socially oriented model while becoming more economically competitive? Or, in light of globalization and the third industrial revolution, was Europe bound to adapt the lean and mean American model?

## ■ Left, Right, and the Democratic Consensus

Although the timing varied from country to country, the western European democracies tended toward some form of two-party political system after World War II. The domestication of the socialist left was essential to that process. After Willy Brandt became chancellor in 1969, the West German Socialists led the government for thirteen years, finally meeting electoral defeat in 1982. By that point, Socialists and Conservatives agreed on the essentials, squabbling only about degrees. The Socialists had completed the turn to moderation that they began in the late 1950s, leaving Germany with essentially a two-party system.

But the political mainstream seemed to offer fewer choices; the resulting frustration fed the new radicalism evident by the early 1970s. As the established Marxist left seemed unable to deal persuasively with contemporary concerns, new coalitions developed around newly politicized issues like abortion and the environment. The successes of this new left fed hopes for more systematic change in socioeconomic relations. And during the early 1980s, revitalized socialist parties in France, Spain, and Italy marginalized the communists and, for a time, seemed poised to reorient government, even to spearhead that systematic change.

## ❧ READING SOURCES

# The Varieties of Liberal Capitalism

*The collapse of communism during 1989–1991 meant the triumph of capitalism, but it also brought to center stage the choices and tradeoffs at work within the advanced capitalist world. Postwar West Germany had achieved remarkable success with its "social market economy," but as renewed under Ronald Reagan and Margaret Thatcher during the 1980s, the more individualistic, entrepreneurial capitalism of the United States and Britain attracted increasing support. Writing in 1991, the French industrialist and government leader Michel Albert offered a spirited critique of Anglo-American capitalism and advocated that France embrace the German "Rhine model" within a more fully integrated European Union.*

The rich need no longer feel ashamed of their wealth. Where they once shunned any hint of ostentation, they now display it with an immodesty that the French used to consider shockingly vulgar when they witnessed it in Americans. And this wealth increasingly rubs shoulders with a new poverty of the kind that is flourishing in the USA. France, too, now has its zones of urban blight, dumping-grounds populated by a growing army of the unemployed, those whose benefit has run out, young people seeking their first job, and immigrants—illegal or otherwise. . . .

The Rhine model . . . embodies, on the one hand, capitalism which can provide social security, and on the other, a system in which the company is seen not just as a heap of capital but a group of people. This is exactly what France badly needs. . . .

. . . If the aim is to harness capitalism without impairing its efficiency, it is no longer to the nation state that we must look, but to Europe. And Europe must produce both powerful financial structures . . . and political institutions. . . .

. . . [A] whole new ideology of capitalism had come to power:

[T]he market is good, the state is bad; social welfare provision, once a sign of progress, is blamed for encouraging laziness; taxation, once an indispensable means for reconciling economic development and social justice, is accused (not without reason) of discouraging talent and initiative. . . . Where the nineteenth century saw capitalism challenge the state, but with no thought of replacing it in such areas as health, education or the media . . . , the late twentieth century now proposes to substitute market forces for the state. . . . [I]n the majority of developed countries, more and more services, from broadcasting to rubbish collection and from the water supply to the post office, are being transferred from the public to the private sector. . . .

We Europeans are, more than anyone else on the planet, faced with the question of which sacrifices we shall make, and for which gains. The European Community is the main battleground on which the conflict of capitalism against capitalism will be fought. . . .

1. Either Europeans will fail to understand what is really at stake, and so will not press their leaders to make the imaginative leap towards true political union: in which case, the Single Market will begin to fray and disintegrate before it has begun; the possibility of unity will recede ever further under a cloud of permanent Euro-pessimism; the slide towards the neo-American model will accelerate as the zones of decay and deprivation already staked out on the periphery of our cities continue to swell. . . .

2. Or we will actually begin to build the United States of Europe: in which case, we will have all the means at our disposal to choose the best possible socioeconomic system, that which has already proven its mettle within one part of the continent and which will become the "European model" of capitalism.

*Source:* Michel Albert, *Capitalism Against Capitalism* (London: Whurr, 1993), pp. 238–240, 244, 247, 253–254, 260.

 **For additional information on this topic, go to http://college.hmco.com.**

The pivotal case was France, where François Mitterrand° (1916–1996) was elected president in 1981, promising to create the first genuinely democratic socialism. But despite a vigorous start he gradually abandoned any talk of socialism in the face of economic and political pressures. By the end of the 1980s, he was questioning the relevance of long-standing socialist tenets and playing up the virtues of entrepreneurship, the profit mechanism, and free-market competition. Mitterrand realized that France, like the other industrial democracies, had to operate in an increasingly competitive international economy.

As French socialism seemed to lose its sense of direction, some leading Socialists got caught up in corruption scandals, and the party met massive defeat at the polls in 1993 and 1995. But they had proven they could work within the system, and a socialist-led coalition regained the parliamentary majority in 1997. Much like Germany, France seemed to have settled into a two-party system, which meant stability, but also a narrowing of discussion and choice. Even Italy, long notorious for the surface instability of its government, seemed to settle into a system of alternating left-leaning and right-leaning coalitions after major scandals during the early 1990s undermined the longstanding political establishment.

Although the socialist left had won reforms that were now central to the consensus around democratic capitalism, by the 1990s it had abandoned much of what it had stood for—from class struggle and revolution to state ownership and a centrally planned economy. It could apparently serve only as the mildly left-leaning alternative within the framework of capitalist democracy. When Labour returned to power in Britain in 1997, the popular new prime minister, Tony Blair, did not offer a bold new program or reverse the key Thatcherite measures like privatization.

With the decline of socialism as a political alternative, a new right, associated especially with anti-immigrant sentiment at first, gained prominence by the mid-1990s. Although differing considerably in priorities, respectability, and success, such leaders as Jean-Marie LePen in France, Jörg Haider° in Austria, and Gianfranco Fini° in Italy tapped into political frustration and economic uncertainty.

But what did it mean to be "right wing" or conservative by the late twentieth century? In Italy and Austria, new right politicians criticized the prevailing understanding of the recent past—the era of fascism and the Second World War—playing up the patriotic, anticom-munist thrust of the interwar right. But because Haider seemed to have played down Nazi atrocities, a major international outcry developed when his party was invited to join Austria's governing coalition in 1999.

As far as present priorities were concerned, conservatives sometimes differed sharply among themselves. In Britain the Thatcher government had tamed the labor unions and sold state-owned industries, but conservative critics pointed out that it had expanded centralized control over local government, health care, and education. With its ideological agenda, the Thatcher government had been activist and interventionist, not cautious, gradualist, and pragmatic—not truly conservative. In addressing economic anxieties, the new right sometimes articulated problems that mainstream politicians ignored, but it seemed unable to come up with viable solutions. Its proponents even disagreed over the relative merits of free trade and protectionism. So though some new right politicians could be noisy, they failed to offer a systematic alternative.

Although democratic capitalism rested on broad and solid support by the 1990s, the questions about the quality of democracy that began surfacing in the late 1960s remained on the table. Indeed, as technological change and globalization added up to unprecedented revolution by the 1980s, concerns deepened that key decisions were increasingly being made by multinational corporations or supranational organizations not directly subject to democratic control. As global competition intensified, the logic of capitalism, or the market, seemed increasingly to overwhelm the capacities of democratic politics.

Even on the domestic political level, the increasingly obvious role of money—needed to finance campaigns and win elections—raised doubts about the capability of democratically elected governments to pursue some common interest. In Italy the quest for such political money bred systematic corruption that finally came to light in 1992, discrediting the Christian Democrats and the whole entrenched political class. By the end of the 1990s, even former German chancellor Helmut Kohl, long one of Europe's most respected leaders, stood partly discredited for accepting illegal campaign contributions.

The need for money to finance electioneering and political patronage seemed to keep even a democratic political system on the edge of corruption. And thus, in part, national governments sometimes seemed to lack the muscle or the will to address the pressures following from the third industrial revolution. By the 1990s, declining voter turnout suggested growing political cynicism all over the Western world.

---

**Mitterrand** (MEE-tuh-rahn)   **Haider** (HY-dur)   **Fini** (FEE-nee)

# THE POSTCOMMUNIST EXPERIMENT

WHATEVER the uncertainties in the capitalist democracies, the former communist countries scrambled to join the Western mainstream after the anticommunist revolutions of 1989–1991. A number of them sought to join NATO and the European Union. But the area had little experience with the give-and-take of democratic politics, and the fragile new political systems found themselves responsible for the difficult transition from a command to a free-market economy. Indeed, political prospects clearly depended in large part on the success of the economic transition. And though several of the countries of east-central Europe made notable progress during the decade that followed, the region lagged dramatically in per capita gross domestic product (GDP). (See Map 30.3.) And Russia, still the major power in the region, experienced wave after wave of difficulty.

With the disintegration of the Soviet bloc, it became clear that the years of communism had produced environmental degradation on an appalling scale. The Stalinist determination to industrialize quickly had combined with the Marxist faith in progress to produce this result, and those who came after were left to clean up as best they could. In many cases, improvement had to wait because jobs or energy sources depended on the old polluting patterns. Ukraine could not afford to replace the remaining nuclear reactors at Chernobyl, despite safety and environmental risks that the 1986 accident had only worsened (see page 1017). International aid finally enabled the country to close the plant in 2000.

## ■ Success and Uncertainty in East-Central Europe

The economies in the former communist satellite states were close to chaos as the transition began, and their attempts to construct market economies brought on unemployment, inflation, and widespread corruption. No longer could ordinary people count on the subsidized consumer goods or the welfare safety net the communist regimes had provided. While many suffered great hardship, some former communist functionaries quickly got rich by taking over state-owned companies. Still, by the mid-1990s the transition to a market economy seemed to be working, though the pattern of change and the degree of success varied considerably from one country to the next.

Some of the postcommunist governments concentrated on privatizing existing state-owned concerns, while others sought especially to foster entrepreneurship and innovation. In Poland privatization lagged, but a buoyant new private sector emerged as the Poles proved adept at starting new businesses. Privatization was greatest in the Czech Republic under the forceful leadership of Václav Klaus, a passionate partisan of market economics. Each country had a reasonably stable, outward-looking market economy by the mid-1990s. Within a few years, Poland was attracting outside investment at a remarkable rate, and its capital, Warsaw, was emerging as a significant European financial center.

In the political sphere, the former communist countries tended first toward political fragmentation—a multiplicity of parties in a weak, divided parliament—which in turn encouraged reliance on a strong leader. Postcommunist Poland's first parliamentary elections in October 1991 produced a legislature splintered among twenty parties, none commanding more than 12 percent of the vote. This situation seemed to open the way to an ever more authoritarian approach from the president, who, beginning in December 1990, was Lech Walesa, the Solidarity leader who had spearheaded the defeat of communism (see page 1013). Although Walesa, during his five years as president, never became the authoritarian some feared, he was sometimes bullying and intolerant, and his dominant role reinforced concerns about the viability of the new democracies in the face of parliamentary fragmentation.

Throughout the formerly communist part of Europe, most politicians were eager to jettison the communist label at first. But by 1992 those in power in Lithuania, Romania, Bulgaria, and the dominant Serbian part of Yugoslavia were former communists whose long-term commitment to democracy remained suspect. And economic dislocations produced growing support for former communists by the mid-1990s. But some one-time communists were more reformed than others, and their electoral successes did not mean the same thing everywhere.

In Poland and Hungary, maturing politically, the election of former communists during the mid-1990s did not compromise democracy or the market economy. When a charismatic young ex-communist, Alexander Kwasniewski°, defeated Walesa in a watershed presidential election in Poland in 1995, the outcome was not a repudiation of the anticommunist revolution. It was arguable, in fact, that Walesa was no longer a progressive

---

**Kwasniewski** (kvazh-NEV-skee)

**Map 30.3  GDP per Capita in Europe, 2000**  Gross domestic product (GDP) per capita is a widely recognized measure of national economic success. By 2000, this measure varied dramatically among the European countries, revealing the wide disparity in economic well-being across the Continent. The former communist countries continued to lag, even as some were growing at impressive rates. The U.S. figure was $33,900, and Canada's was $23,300.

force. His vote came largely from traditionalist, rural, strongly Catholic parts of Poland, whereas Kwasniewski attracted Poles interested in expanding the market economy and developing closer ties with western Europe.

Although economic reconstruction was paramount, the end of communism opened up divisive new questions across the former Soviet bloc. It quickly became clear that political freedom did not necessarily bring wider rights and liberties. For example, the eclipse of communism in Poland initially promised a major role for the Roman Catholic Church, but angry debate followed when, in 1990, the government ordered that children be taught the Catholic religion in school and the head of the Polish church called for an end to the "communist-inspired" separation of church and state. An effort to pass a strong anti-abortion bill in time for a visit by Pope John Paul II in 1991 caused more heated debate; public opinion polls indicated that a majority of Poles favored abortion rights.

Abortion was similarly a major issue when the former East Germany was incorporated into the Federal Republic of Germany. Abortion law had been more liberal in the communist east than in the west, and East Germany was considerably more generous in providing maternity leaves and day care. Though some East German feminists, by the mid-1980s, were accenting gender differences to enable women to pull back from the workplace, they feared that the transition to capitalism could mean diminished employment opportunities for women. A compromise was worked out on the abortion issue, but as the differences in priorities between West and East German feminists made clear, the end of communism was no panacea.

## ■ The Yeltsin Years in Russia, 1991–1999

In Russia, communism had far deeper roots than elsewhere in the former Soviet bloc. It had not been imposed by foreigners, and it had been in power far longer. And thus the course that Russia took after the fall of communism was especially uncertain and dramatic.

Boris Yeltsin had emerged from the anticommunist revolution a hero. As Russia's president during the first postcommunist years, he seemed a committed reformer—surely the best hope for an orderly transition to democracy and a market economy. So he enjoyed widespread support from the Western democracies, even when his policies produced a certain messiness in both the political and economic spheres.

In 1993 the elected parliament, which included many communists or former communists opposed to Yeltsin's free-market reforms, challenged the president's authority within the new political system. Yeltsin put down the challenge by force and did much of his governing by presidential decree. His approach seemed especially necessary as the anti-reform backlash by 1995 threatened a return to communism or authoritarianism. At the same time, radical nationalists played provocatively on frustrations with Russia's suddenly diminished stature in world affairs. The danger of anti-Western extremism reinforced the support that Yeltsin enjoyed in the West—even as it increased pressure at home to take an independent foreign policy line.

Although privatization proceeded rapidly in Russia—two-thirds of formerly state-owned industry had been redistributed by 1994—its fairness was disputed from the start. In certain sectors, especially natural resources and energy, the process included much insider dealing. As a result, privatization in Russia, even more than elsewhere, benefited former Communist Party functionaries, some of whom became instant multimillionaires.

By the mid-1990s, Russia had evolved a kind of "crony capitalism," with a small group of economic oligarchs exploiting the nation's resources for their own advantage. They often hid or laundered profits abroad—with Cyprus the favored destination—and they paid no taxes. To be sure, anyone could start a business, but those who did so required the protection of the oligarchs, who manipulated much of the economy through dubious banking practices and outright extortion. With government tax collection lax at best, state employees went many months at a time without being paid. Much of society depended on a barter economy. The combination of economic stringency and governmental weakness also produced a chilling increase in street crime, from mugging to auto theft.

Under the circumstances, disenchantment with reform and nostalgia for the stability of communism grew among ordinary Russians. In 1995, when Russia's second postcommunist parliamentary elections took place, the communists, led by Gennady Zyuganov° (b. 1944), won a plurality of seats, thanks to the support of workers and pensioners. Zyuganov seemed poised to win the presidency the following year. But his economic platform was riddled with contradictions, and it was hardly clear what a communist victory would have meant.

After trailing badly in the polls, Yeltsin defeated Zyuganov to win re-election in July 1996. This highly visible election was Russia's fullest experience of democracy

**Zyuganov** (zhoo-GAH-noff)

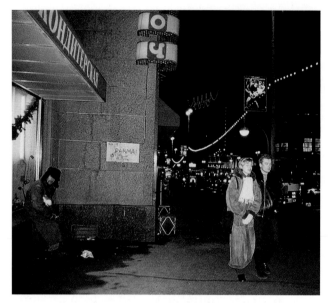

**Postcommunist Russia**   Images of the new extremes of wealth and poverty became commonplace as postcommunist Russia sought to join the Western mainstream.
*(Star-Tass/Sovfoto/Eastfoto)*

to date, and optimists saw it as a turning point in the consolidation of a democratic order. But Yeltsin survived because of the heavy financial support of the oligarchs, to whom he was increasingly beholden. Even reform-minded Yeltsinites like Anatoly Chubais° felt that working with the oligarchs was the lesser of evils, the best hope for evolution toward the Western model in light of the "red-brown" menace—the combined danger from communists and nationalists.

However, the imbalances in the economy finally produced a major financial crisis in August 1998, when a collapse of the banking system led the government to default on its domestic debt and deflate the currency. The economy recovered somewhat thereafter, but Yeltsin, in poor health and increasingly erratic, was by now deeply unpopular. Meanwhile, dozens of journalists, politicians, and business leaders were murdered gangland style, with the killers never apprehended. Particularly appalling to Russians was the death of Galina Starovoitova°, a widely admired liberal legislator and potential presidential candidate who was gunned down outside her St. Petersburg apartment in November 1998.

Shrinking every year after the fall of communism, the Russian economy had decreased by perhaps half after ten years. The results inevitably included a sharp decline in living standards and the decay of the infrastructure, in-

cluding roads, schools, and hospitals. But especially sobering were the demographic effects. Russians were dying young and having few children; the population dropped to 143 million—a decline of 6 million people in ten years.

### ■ Chechnya and the Rise of Vladimir Putin

As it sought to engineer the transition to democratic capitalism, the Yeltsin government had to deal with the attempted defection of Chechnya°, a small, largely Muslim republic located in the Caucasus (see Map 29.3 on page 1017). Long the thorn in Russia's control of the region, the Chechens began demanding independence after the collapse of the Soviet Union in 1991, finally provoking war with Russia in 1994. Yeltsin and Chechen leaders agreed to a compromise settlement in 1996 that was essentially a defeat for Russia, though determination of the precise status of Chechnya was postponed. But in the aftermath Chechen hard-liners oppressed the Russian minority, kidnapping and enslaving some, and even killed journalists and international aid workers. When Islamic militants began spreading the anti-Russian message from Chechnya to adjacent Dagestan, Russia renewed full-scale war with Chechnya in 1999.

This renewed confrontation made possible the rise of Vladimir Putin°, who had been virtually unknown in political circles, though he had been director of Russia's secret police. Calling for a tough stance on Chechnya, Putin was Yeltsin's choice for prime minister in 1999, and he immediately delivered on his promise to clear Dagestan of Chechen terrorists. Whereas most Russians had disliked the earlier confrontation with Chechnya, by now they had had enough—not only of Chechen defiance but also of Russia's weakness. Putin's popularity soared as he talked tough and acted tougher.

In September 1999 a mysterious series of explosions in apartment buildings in several Russian cities killed almost three hundred people. The explosions were immediately blamed on Chechen terrorists, though no conclusive evidence was presented. Some suspected—or took it for granted—that the government had planted the bombs as an excuse for renewing the war against Chechnya. In any case, the explosions inflamed Russian public opinion, buttressing support for the brutal Russian assault that left much of Chechnya, especially the capital, Grozny, in ruins in the months that followed.

Yeltsin resigned at the end of 1999, essentially to make way for Putin, who was elected president early in 2000. Some felt that Putin would prove but a tool of the oligarchical faction that had promoted his rise to power.

---

**Chubais** (choo-BYE-eess)   **Starovoitova** (STAH-ro-VOY-to-vah)     **Chechnya** (CHECH-nyah)   **Putin** (POO-tin)

His police background and harsh rhetoric also caused alarm. But for six years during the postcommunist transition, he had worked closely with the reform-oriented democratic mayor of St. Petersburg. Perhaps he had, or could develop, the stature to break the cycle of criminality and corruption that was wrecking Russia's experiment in democracy.

By the early twenty-first century, some noted signs of progress in Russia, including improved tax collection and the emergence of some undeniably well-run companies. But international observers worried that even should Putin engineer the reforms to create legitimate capitalism, his political leadership portended renewed nationalism and authoritarianism, not a more genuinely democratic culture. He represented a new generation coming into positions of power around 2000. He and his cohorts were bold and dynamic, but cynical; they sensed that it was time for postcommunist Russia to start over, without illusions, no longer bound to some Western developmental model.

Putin's inauguration in May 2000 prompted much soul-searching in the West, amid a growing sense that a precious opportunity had been lost, that it was too late to bring Russia into the Western democratic mainstream. Some, including the prominent financier and philanthropist George Soros, began asking, "Who lost Russia?" Recalling the Marshall Plan after World War II (see page 990), Soros suggested that postcommunist Russia could have become not only prosperous and democratic but a true friend of the United States—just like West Germany after Nazism. But it had not happened.

Soros blamed the conservative governments in the United States and Britain for failing to offer Russia sufficient help at the initial stages of the transition, when the scope for Western influence was great. But such influence required a proactive stance, and real money, to help establish the cultural framework, whereas these conservative Western governments, viewing the free market as a panacea, assumed that Russia could simply be turned loose. When the outcome began to entail corruption, crime, and capital flight, Western leaders tended to look the other way. Thus, by the end of the 1990s, the Russians were increasingly resentful of the West, especially the United States, whose free-market gospel was now identified with the graft and greed of the oligarchy. Some came to believe that the United States had simply been seeking to weaken Russia all along.

When Russia's communist experiment ended in failure in 1991, the world had reason to hope for a smooth transition, since Russia was now seeking to embrace the democratic capitalism of the West, not claiming to point the way beyond it. But the effort to move from communism to democratic capitalism was also an unprecedented experiment, the results of which could not be foreseen. And it was hard even to find the words for what had emerged in Russia by the early twenty-first century. Some spoke of "primitive gangster capitalism" or "infantile capitalism run amok," but even these characterizations did not quite get at it, for they still reflected the earlier assumption that Russia was on a predictable course of development.

In fact, the new Russian capitalism was not merely primitive or infantile but often sophisticated. Russia's oligarchs were not babes in the woods doing their best to behave like real capitalists; they could extort and launder money as well as anyone in history. And in doing so they revealed that under certain circumstances, even the experiment with freedom and a market economy could yield something unforeseen and brutal.

But though the juxtaposition of freedom, capitalism, and democracy was no cure-all, it had not always led to these results, so the Russian experience invited a deeper understanding of the institutional and cultural conditions necessary for a happier outcome. If democracy and a market economy were to be socially beneficial, more was required—in particular, a consensus around civic responsibility and the rule of law. People had to be willing to pay taxes. And the state had to be strong enough to collect taxes, to limit corruption, and to sustain genuinely open markets and an orderly banking system. "Negative liberty," getting government out of the way, was not sufficient. Indeed, this second Russian experiment demonstrated that a single-minded accent on negative liberty was no less utopian than Soviet Russia's single-minded insistence on central planning and command from above.

## LIFESTYLES AND IDENTITIES IN THE WEST

POSTWAR economic growth had created a secular, consumerist society throughout much of the West by the mid-1960s, establishing patterns of life that continued into the twenty-first century, when cell phones and personal computers were commonplace. Changing lifestyles brought new sources of identity—but also new challenges, as greater egalitarianism and affluence yielded new choices. Thus conflict was also commonplace, over issues from education to gender roles to the environment.

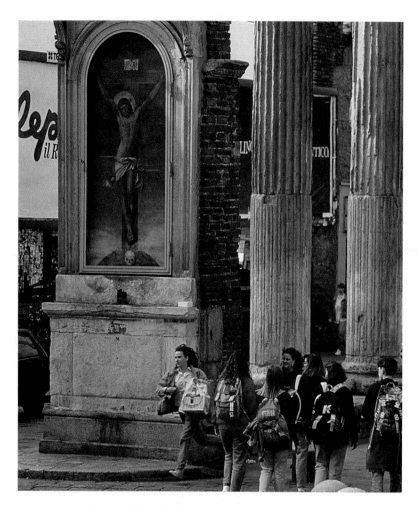

**Old and New in Contemporary Europe**
Especially with the transformation of Europe since World War II, new styles of life intersect with living artifacts from the past to form sometimes ironic combinations. Here, in a neighborhood in Milan, Italy, teenagers wearing blue jeans and backpacks seem oblivious to the legacies of Roman antiquity and Christianity that are prominent around them.    *(© 1993 George Steinmetz)*

By the early twenty-first century, this newly secular, consumerist society had become one of the defining aspects of the West. It was what many nonwesterners hoped to achieve and sought to emulate. Thus, in part, the increased immigration from the non-Western world to the more developed countries of the West. But immigrants often retained aspects of their non-Western cultural identities, prompting new questions about diversity, assimilation, and community in the West. Moreover, important groups of nonwesterners rejected Western secular consumerism altogether. For the various forms of Islamic fundamentalism, it was nothing less than an abomination.

### ■ The Challenges of Affluence

The impact of rapid economic growth on the European landscape and cityscape provoked ever greater concern by the last third of the twentieth century. The number of automobiles in western Europe increased from 6 million

in 1939 to 16 million by 1959 to 42 million by 1969. Almost overnight, traffic and air pollution fundamentally changed the face of Europe's old cities. In 1976 five statues that had supported the Eastern Portico of the Erectheum Temple on the Acropolis in Athens since the fifth century B.C. had to be replaced by replicas and put in a museum to save them from the rapid decay that air pollution was causing. There was talk of the "melancholy of progress" as the dimensions of the conflict between economic prosperity and the tangible monuments of Europe's history became clear.

The natural setting proved just as vulnerable. By the early 1980s acid rain had damaged one-third of the forests of West Germany, including the famous Black Forest of the southwest. Water pollution was a major problem from the Rhine to the Mediterranean to the Black Sea.

A major source of environmental concern was nuclear power, which solved certain environmental problems while posing the risk of still more serious ones. By the 1990s the West's greatest proponent of nuclear energy was France, which was getting 80 percent of its electricity from nuclear plants and was striving for 100 percent. In the United States and Britain the comparable figure was only 20 percent—and shrinking. The French boasted that they had experienced no major safety problems and that by using nuclear power they were avoiding the hazards associated with fossil fuels, from acid rain to global warming.

Much of Europe, however, moved decisively away from nuclear power, even before the Soviet nuclear accident at Chernobyl in 1986. In Germany the environmentalist Greens led demonstrations in 1977 that forced the government drastically to decrease its plans for nuclear power. In 2000, amid growing concerns about nuclear waste disposal, and with the Greens now junior partners in the socialist-led governing coalition, the German government worked out an agreement with the nuclear power industry to phase out all use of atomic energy over a twenty-year period.

Just as it posed unforeseen threats to the environment, the new affluence challenged traditional sources of personal identity in sometimes unexpected ways. Although religion remained a potent force, its reach contracted. In assuming responsibility for social welfare, the state had taken over much of the charitable role that the churches had long played. Regular church attendance dropped steadily, and popular culture revolved less around religious festivals and holy days.

Seeking to change with the times, the Catholic Church undertook a notable modernization effort under the popular Pope John XXIII (r. 1958–1963). But under his more conservative successors, the church became caught up in controversy, especially over issues such as abortion that women had forced to the fore. By the 1990s, its conservative social policy had put the Catholic Church on the defensive.

In traditionally Catholic countries like France, Italy, and Spain, many people considered themselves "cultural Catholics" and ignored church rulings they found inappropriate, especially those concerning sexuality, marriage, and gender roles. The easier availability of contraception—especially the birth control pill, widely obtainable by the late 1960s—fostered a sexual revolution that was central to the new secular lifestyle. In referenda in 1974 and 1981, two-thirds of Italians defied the Vatican by voting to legalize divorce and approve abortion rights. Even in heavily Catholic Ireland, the electorate narrowly approved the legalization of divorce in 1995, after defeating it overwhelmingly in a referendum just nine years before.

In western Europe, as in the United States, a remarkable baby boom had followed the end of the war and carried into the early 1960s. The birthrate declined rapidly thereafter, however, so that family size diminished markedly by 1990. In Italy, where changes in lifestyle accompanying the new prosperity were especially dramatic, the number of births in 1987 was barely half the number in 1964, when the postwar baby boom reached its peak. By 1995 the population was not sustaining itself in a number of European countries (see Map 30.4).

Increasing affluence and egalitarianism led to rising expectations and demands for still wider opportunity. Such pressure focused especially on access to government-supported higher education, the chief vehicle for upward mobility based on merit. In France, university admission required passing the *baccalauréat* exam at the end of secondary school. The percentage of the age group that reached this threshold grew from 1 percent in 1900 to 5 percent in 1949, then rose to 23 percent by 1974. In Italy the number of university students increased sixfold from the late 1930s to the late 1960s, partly the result of an open enrollment policy. In West Germany, higher education was still restrictive, elitist, and authoritarian at the end of the 1960s, but under pressure from the left the university system quadrupled in size by 1975.

The development of a mass-based university system produced new dilemmas. In France, demands for reform of higher education had been central to the uprising of 1968, but subsequent government efforts to decentralize the system produced widespread opposition from students and faculty by the 1980s. The government's proposal to give individual universities the right to choose their own students provoked protests and strikes, the most notable of which, in 1986, involved 400,000 demonstrators and violent clashes with police. Such opposition forced the government to abandon much of its academic reform effort.

The resistance to reform reflected the reverse side of social mobility—the considerable status anxiety among students and faculty, especially those in the humanities and social sciences. As French universities had become institutions of mass education, the market value of the state diploma had declined, as had the prestige of the faculty. For those who opposed reform, fear of loss outweighed the possibility of gain from a more competitive system. The French experience with university reform made it clear that mobility and security, equality and excellence, opportunity and merit meshed uneasily in the democratic societies of the West.

**Map 30.4    World Population Growth**    This map shows both current populations and rates of population growth throughout the world. In the developed countries of the West, populations are relatively high but growing slowly, if at all. Most of the world's population growth is occurring in the less developed countries outside the West.    *(National Geographic Maps 1998/10 Map Supplement, Population Growth. Used by permission of National Geographic Society.)*

## ■ The Significance of Gender

The feminist movement that had re-emerged in the late 1960s gradually expanded its focus beyond the quest for formal equality of opportunity. Examining subtle cultural obstacles to equality led feminists to the more general issue of gender—the way societies make sense of sexual difference and allocate social roles. There was much interest in the ideas of the French existentialist Simone de Beauvoir, who had raised in 1949 precisely the issues that came to the fore during the 1980s. (See the box "Reading Sources: Human Freedom and the Origins of a New Feminism" on page 994.) And as debate expanded from "women's issues" to gender roles, the self-understanding of men was inevitably at issue as well.

Insofar as gender roles are "constructed" by particular societies, "gendering" had always been central to the socialization process whereby young people learn how to function in their societies. But the gender roles dictated by society had usually been taken as natural, so gender was only rarely as controversial as it became in the late twentieth century. By the 1990s the gender issue was central not only to public policy but also to private relationships and to decisions about life choices in much of the Western world.

It was increasingly recognized that, at least implicitly, debates about the welfare state had often centered on gender from the beginning. After World War II, concerns about labor shortages in both East and West led to conflicting impulses in policy discussions and decisions. Should women be encouraged to work or to concentrate on rearing the children who would be the workers of the future? In western Europe immigration helped ease the labor shortage, so it was especially in the Soviet bloc that this tension was evident in shifting public policy. In 1981, for example, the Soviet Union reversed course by increasing child-care payments and adopting measures to reduce the hours that mothers worked outside the home.

The dramatic slowdown in population growth in western Europe after the mid-1960s revived fears about shortages of labor. At the same time, the feminist movement, seeking equal opportunity, sought measures such as government-subsidized day care that would enable women to combine paid employment with raising a family. By the 1970s, these impulses had come together in much of western Europe. Seeking to enhance both equality of opportunity and economic vigor, governments sought measures that would combine productive working parents with effective childhood development.

Setting the pace was France, where the government began making quality day care available to all during the 1980s. Government subsidies kept costs within reach for ordinary working families. In addition, 95 percent of French children aged 3 to 6 were enrolled in the free public nursery schools available by the early 1990s. Comparable figures for Italy (85 percent) and Germany (65 to 70 percent) were also high, although Britain lagged at 35 to 40 percent.

As some saw it, the increasing reliance on child-care at once reflected and reinforced a decline in the socializing role of the traditional family. Concerns about "latchkey children," or the decline of "quality time" for families, became prominent in the popular press. But the social changes at work were complex, and their longer-term implications for the well-being of parents, children, and society itself remained unclear. Some studies showed that an early day-care experience enhanced the socialization of children. Others cautioned against romanticizing the traditional nuclear family, which had been less prevalent than widely believed—and not always successful in any case. Moreover, the responsibilities of parenting did not have to fall primarily on mothers. The biological difference in childbearing and nursing remained, however, and even committed feminists disagreed about whether parenting entailed a special role for women and about the implications for public policy. The interrelationship of family, gender, and personal self-realization, never static, was evolving in new ways—a crucial aspect of the ongoing experiment in the West.

Though much remained contested or uncertain, the scope for greater sharing of parental responsibilities and the need for equal career opportunities across gender lines were widely recognized by the 1990s. The French model seemed to work well in combining child support with equal opportunity for paid employment. Moreover, in France social services were delivered with less paperwork and intrusiveness than elsewhere. French family policy was widely popular; the question by 2000 was simply whether France could still afford the costs it required.

The concern with gender equality brought new scrutiny to female political participation during the 1990s. Patterns had come to differ markedly even among the members of the European Union. In 2000, the percentage of women in national legislative bodies ranged from a high of 45 percent in Sweden to under 9 percent in France. Comparable figures included 30 percent in Germany and 17 percent in Britain.

The relative dearth of female officeholders in France prompted much discussion by the mid-1990s.

The outcome was a constitutional amendment in 1999 specifying the right of French women to equal access to public office. On that basis, a law passed in 2000 mandated "parity": political parties had to include women in 50 percent of their slates of nominees to maintain their full share of government campaign funding. This measure did not guarantee that women would be elected, only that voters would have the option of choosing women from among the party nominees.

The issue was discussed elsewhere as well, but by 2000 only Belgium had adopted a comparable quota system—though it mandated not one-half but one-third as the minimal share for women among party nominees. In Germany, Austria, and Spain, individual parties voluntarily established quotas for female representation on their slates of candidates.

It remained to be seen whether these innovative measures would boost the percentage of female office-holders. Moreover, whatever their eventual outcome, such measures offended some who were not otherwise conservative. In France a number of female intellectuals opposed the parity law on what they saw as humanistic and universalist grounds: in their view women had no distinctive way of thinking and did not need special protections. Some pointed out that people of North African origin were not represented at all in the French assembly. Gays objected that the parity law took one basis of human differentiation as privileged at the expense of others. But supporters countered that numerous progressive changes—universal elementary education, for example—would not have occurred without the force of law.

## Immigration, Assimilation, and Citizenship

With immigration growing sharply in western Europe by the 1980s, questions about citizenship became politically central, giving a new twist to the interaction with the non-Western world that had helped define "the West" from the beginning. The problem grew more complex by the 1990s when refugees from various trouble spots, especially the former Yugoslavia, sought homes in new countries. The claims of immigrants and refugees forced all the Western democracies to wrestle with the meaning of citizenship. And as economic pressures grew during the 1980s and 1990s, the tensions surrounding immigrants and foreigners especially threatened the political consensus in western Europe. For example, increased immigration from disintegrating Yugoslavia made immigration a central issue in Austria, contributing to the growing popularity, and by 1999 the controversial governmental role, of Jörg Haider's ultra-right Freedom Party.

By 1995, 11 million legal resident immigrants were living in the countries of the European Union—including, as the largest contingent, 2.6 million Turks (see Map 30.5). There were also as many as 4 million illegals. At issue throughout Europe was not only new immigration, but the status of immigrant families already resident, in many cases for several generations since World War II. Some of those raising questions were not seeking simply to preserve economic advantages by limiting access. Rather, they were concerned about community, diversity, and national identity—about what it meant to belong. Because of differences in tradition, individual countries tended to conceive the alternatives differently.

Germany had actively recruited foreign workers during the decades of economic boom and labor shortage that followed the war. By 1973 noncitizens constituted 2.6 million workers, or 11.9 percent of the work force. At first these "guest workers" were viewed not as immigrants but as temporary, almost migrant, workers. But as they remained in Germany, their family patterns came to approximate those of the rest of the country, though their birthrates were considerably higher. By the 1980s, Germany had a large and increasingly settled population of non-Germans, many of them born and educated there.

In addition, the German Federal Republic had adopted a generous asylum law in an effort to atone for the crimes of the Nazi period. With the turmoil surrounding the end of communism in the Soviet bloc, the newly reunified Germany found sixty thousand new arrivals seeking asylum every month by 1993. At that point Germany had a large foreign population of 6.4 million.

The law governing citizenship for immigrants and their descendants had originated in 1913 and reflected a long-standing German assumption that citizenship presupposed German ethnicity—or at least full assimilation. Thus ethnic Germans—over a million of whom moved to Germany from the former Soviet bloc between 1988 and 1991—were immediately accorded German citizenship. But the many Turks, for example, who had been born in Germany could not become citizens. Precisely because citizenship entailed full assimilation, some Germans opposed that status for such "foreigners" out of respect for cultural diversity.

But as the new wave of immigration from the east swelled the "foreign" population in Germany, more mundane motives came to the fore. Germans subject to economic pressures felt that immigrants and asylum-seekers were getting a better deal than ordinary citizens such as themselves. Resentments simmered, and sometimes boiled over. Two thousand attacks on foreigners, some of them fatal, were reported in 1992 alone. As reaction against refugees and foreign workers grew, the German parliament voted in 1993 to restrict the right of asylum.

But questions of immigration and citizenship remained politically central. After Helmut Kohl's conservatives lost the parliamentary elections in 1998, the new governing coalition of Socialists and Greens promptly voted, in 1999, to shelve the 1913 law. Citizenship was now available to almost everyone born in Germany or whose parents who had resided and worked in Germany for at least eight years. Still, controversy and even violence continued. During 2000, right-wing attacks on foreigners and synagogues reached levels not seen since the early 1990s. On November 9, the anniversary of the Crystal Night pogrom of 1938 and several other major events in recent German history, 200,000 Germans marched in Berlin to protest the violence and demand equal rights.

Controversy also raged in France by the 1980s as the country attracted rising numbers of immigrants, especially from Algeria and the other Islamic countries of North Africa. French law accorded citizenship automatically to second-generation immigrants, assuming that these offspring would be readily assimilated. But critics such as Jean-Marie LePen, leader of the right-wing National Front, charged that many recent immigrants did not want to assimilate. Whereas the French left defended cultural diversity and its compatibility with citizenship, the right complained that citizenship was being devalued as a mere convenience, requiring no real commitment to the national community. This difference in perspective helps explain the contentious "affair of the scarves" that gripped France in 1989.

Although some remained nervous about immigrants from outside countries, the fifteen members of the European Union were growing ever more comfortable with the free movements of EU-member peoples across national borders. Indeed, changes in EU rules during the 1990s made dual citizenship easier for the Union's increasingly mobile population. As many began to feel themselves citizens of the European Union itself, even notions of "foreign" began to change.

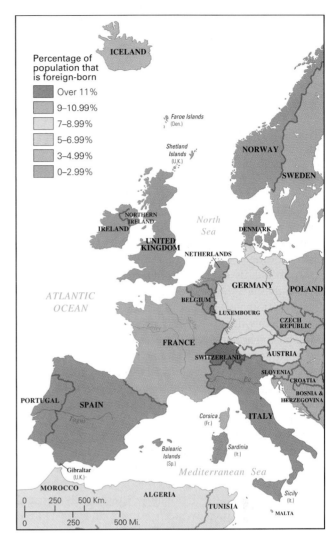

**Map 30.5    Foreign-Born Population in Western Europe**
Increasing immigration prompted resentment against foreigners and concerns about assimilation in much of western Europe during the 1980s and 1990s. This map indicates the percentage of the population that was foreign-born in each of the countries of western Europe as of 1997.    (*Source:* New York Times, *September 24, 2000. Copyright © 2000 by the New York Times Co. Reprinted by permission.*)

## ■ Subnational and Supranational Identities

The growing prominence of the supranational EU, and doubts about the import of national politics, nourished a renewed premium on subnational identities in such distinctive European regions as Flanders, Corsica, Scotland, and Catalonia. Flemings and Corsicans, Scots and Catalans actively sought to preserve some measure of their distinct cultures and languages in the face of standardization pressures stemming from globalization, Americanization, or even the EU itself. In Britain the Labour government of Tony Blair fostered the "devolution" of powers from the central government in London to Scottish and Welsh assemblies by 2000. There was a growing recognition that the existing nations were not natural, given, but largely historical constructions. But the resulting weakening of national loyalties could lead to political fragmentation. The breakup of Yugoslavia afforded a particularly tragic example.

Much less dramatic, but also instructive, was the example of Italy, whose movement for national unification had drawn the enthusiasm of the world in the nineteenth century (see pages 745–750). But by the 1990s, disillusionment with national politics made many Italians particularly eager to embrace the EU, while others turned in the other direction, renewing their identification with region or locality. Resentful of the national government's ties to the less prosperous south, a new political movement, the Northern League, pushed for the north to break from Italy and become an independent state. Though some doubted the seriousness of such separatism, the Northern League's persistent strength suggested that "Italian" was becoming less important as a basis of individual identity.

National identities were weakening in much of Europe partly because a generally unspoken, mostly friendly, rivalry with the United States led Europeans increasingly to think of themselves *as* European, rather than some particular nationality. The broadly cultural relationship between western Europe and the United States had been tricky since World War II. For decades the Europeans seemed to have no choice but to follow the U.S. lead. But such subservience was troubling, so a kind of love-hate relationship with the United States had developed in western Europe.

Even after Europe's postwar economic recovery, the United States was clearly setting the pace in high-technology industries, prompting renewed concerns by the 1960s that Europe was becoming a mere economic satellite of the United States. Europe seemed to be caught in a dilemma: to retain its distinctiveness over the long term, it had to become more competitive—which apparently meant becoming more like America in the short term. The French writer Jean-Jacques Servan-Schreiber° (b. 1924) made this case in 1967 in *The American Challenge,* the classic statement of postwar Europe's ambivalent attitude toward Americanization.

Haunted by the decline of earlier civilizations, Servan-Schreiber warned that if Europeans failed to become sufficiently dynamic to compete with the Americans, Europe would gradually sink into decadence without ever understanding why it had happened.

By the 1980s much of western Europe had caught up with the United States in standard of living, and the western Europeans set the pace in confronting some of the new problems that resulted from ongoing socioeconomic change. The French day-care system was one example. The size of the EU economy was about equal to that of the United States by the end of the 1990s, and the Europeans proved quite competitive in certain fields. For example, Europe's Airbus did well in head-to-head competition with American aircraft manufacturer Boeing.

But by the 1990s, as America assumed a decisive lead in the new information technology, and as the American model came to seem better at fostering innovation and competitiveness, the western Europeans again worried about falling behind, even as they also sought to preserve European distinctiveness in the face of Americanization. The dilemma that Servan-Schreiber had noted in the 1960s was still very much at issue.

In light of the countervailing pressures at work, the European relationship with America was bound to remain complex. By the late 1980s consumerism and the widening impact of American popular culture—from blue jeans and American TV to shopping malls and theme parks—suggested a growing homogenization in the capitalist democracies. A Euro-Disneyland opened in France in 1992 and, after a slow start, proved increasingly popular. Though they adopted some European ways, even serving beer and wine, American fast-food chains like McDonald's satisfied hungry locals in cities all over Europe.

But as the fall of communism both ended the division of Europe and removed the common adversary, the ties that had helped bind western Europe to the United States inevitably loosened. In 2000 France charged that the United States was using its satellite surveillance capacity, still in place from the cold war, for industrial espionage to the disadvantage of European firms.

Even what counted as "the West" became more uncertain. Especially when the East Asian economies were booming, America liked to see itself as a Pacific power. Moreover, Americans began stressing the multiple sources of their culture: it was not necessarily superior, but neither was it simply an offshoot of European culture. This reorientation was to place less emphasis on the common "Western heritage." Though they were trading partners, Europe and America were also economic

---

**Servan-Schreiber** (SAIR-vahn–SHRY-bay)

and cultural rivals, and they might increasingly drift apart. In this continuing experiment, even something so apparently solid as "the Western Alliance" or "the Atlantic orientation" was not cut in stone.

# THE WEST IN A GLOBAL AGE

B Y the early twenty-first century, the West was part of a world that, in one sense, was dramatically less Eurocentric than it had been a century before, when European imperialism was at its peak. Events in the West competed for attention with the India-Pakistan nuclear rivalry, OPEC oil prices, Chinese trade issues, or the struggle against warlords in parts of Africa. Decisions vitally affecting, or demanding the response of, the industrialized countries of the West might be made anywhere. A planetary culture, a threatened environment, an interdependent economy, and an increasing sense of international responsibility required people to think in global terms as never before.

## ■ Differentiation and Collaboration in the "Global Village"

By the last decades of the twentieth century, as information and capital flowed instantaneously, a kind of global culture was beginning to emerge for the first time. But as cultural contact increased, it took diverse forms. "Americanization," appealing to some, appalling to others, made products like Coca-Cola and McDonald's burgers and fries familiar worldwide and nourished a common urban youth style. But many spheres, from food to popular music, were marked by fusion, as elements from diverse cultures interpenetrated and enriched each other. At the same time, there was also increasing appreciation of diversity. The British tourist board declared Indian curry to be the official British dish, testimony to the number of Indian restaurants in Britain—itself testimony to the enduring cultural interchange between Britain and its former colony. But even as cultural contact deepened and talk of a single "global village" became commonplace, cultural boundaries loomed larger in some respects—as the controversy in France over the Islamic headscarves makes clear.

Cultural convergence stemmed especially from the process known as modernization, or "Westernization," which entailed, above all, participation in the competitive global market economy that had spread from Europe. Beginning especially in the 1970s, western Europe and North America encountered formidable economic competition first from Japan, and later from other countries of the East Asian Pacific rim. What increasingly mattered, from this perspective, was the difference between the industrialized, relatively affluent "North" and the less developed "South," including much of Africa, Latin America, southern Asia, and the Middle East.

Indeed, "North-South" tensions, resulting from demographic and economic patterns, quickly moved to center stage to replace the East-West tensions that had ended with the cold war. World population reached 6 billion in 1999, having more than doubled in forty years. This was the fastest rate of world population growth ever, and by the 1990s virtually all of the growth was in Africa, Asia, and Latin America. The population of Europe was growing at only 0.2 percent per year (see Map 30.4).

As the population exploded in the less developed world, the gap between rich and poor nations widened. One aspect, producing much concern by 2000, was the growing "digital divide"—the disparity in access to the computing and Internet technologies that seemed essential to compete in the global economy. New technologies were not bridging but widening the gap between the haves and the have-nots.

At the same time, growing concern with the global environment intensified the sense of world interdependence and pointed to the need for international cooperation. Such problems as global warming, the loss of biodiversity, and the deterioration of the ozone layer were inherently supranational in scope. Yet environmental concerns complicated relations between the industrialized nations and the rest of the world. Countries seeking to industrialize encountered environmental constraints that had not been at issue when the West industrialized. The challenge for the West was to foster protection of the environment in poorer regions of the globe without imposing unfair limitations on economic growth.

## ■ The Controversy over Economic Globalization

A variety of supranational entities, apart from the European Union, wielded increasing clout by the late twentieth century, making decisions that deeply affected the lives of ordinary people. Most obvious were multinational corporations, but the World Bank and the International Monetary Fund (IMF) also played increasingly visible—and controversial—roles. Developing from the Bretton Woods agreement near the end of World War II (see page 976), these institutions had long drawn praise for helping to keep the world economy stable and growing. Also central, especially in promoting free trade, was the World Trade Organization (WTO), which grew from a multilateral trade agreement in 1947. These organizations were major vehicles for the influence of the wealthy nations, centered in the West, on those from eastern Europe to southern Africa that were trying to catch up. In that role they often swayed domestic policies—by refusing, for example, to lend to countries spending heavily on armaments.

During the 1990s these agencies became the focal points for growing concerns about the new economic globalization—its costs and the distribution of its benefits. Meetings of the WTO in Seattle in 1999 and of the World Bank and IMF in Washington in 2000 drew large demonstrations. Those protesting were often naive about economics and the uses of free trade. But their protests raised genuine questions about wages, working conditions, environmental impact, and international financial arrangements that were not always adequately addressed in the prevailing economic models.

Should a consumer in the United States be free to purchase a cheaper garment made by low-wage workers in Honduras or Bangladesh? Or should that consumer have to pay more to protect the jobs of American workers? Perhaps buying the cheaper product was to support sweatshop conditions and pollution in the interests of multinational corporations and international bankers. But those workers in Honduras or Bangladesh might be eager for such jobs, in light of the even less fortunate alternatives available. It could be argued that it was up to consumers to decide, but even when such choices were

available, consumers rarely had the information to know what they were choosing, how conditions of labor had affected price.

The question was whether it made sense to foster free trade and globalization without greater uniformity in social and environmental policy. In the absence of common standards, free trade was arguably not fair trade. But lines were not easily drawn, and these issues, playing on the North-South divide, promised to remain central—and especially contentious.

Prominent among European critics of globalization by the early twenty-first century was José Bové, the outspoken leader of France's small farmers. When he stood trial in 2000 for vandalizing a McDonald's restaurant, thirty thousand turned up to demonstrate in his support. His book *The World Is Not for Sale* became a bestseller at the same time.

Typically equating globalization with Americanization, Bové articulated a widespread concern for French distinctiveness and identity in the face of U.S. "cultural imperialism." France seemed increasingly overrun with American films, television, music, even novels in French translation. Such uneasiness over diversity and conformity was more pronounced in Latin and southern Europe than in Britain and the North. The Italian film industry, among the most innovative and important in the world for several decades after the war, had largely disappeared by 2000.

Early in 2001, a serious outbreak of foot-and-mouth disease, a highly contagious illness affecting especially

**Protesting Globalization at McDonald's**
Led by José Bové's association of small farmers, protesters vandalize a McDonald's restaurant in southern France in August 1999. Bové's trial a year later stimulated comparable protests. The American fast-food chain had come to symbolize the two-sided force of globalization and Americanization.
*(Frances/Markow/Corbis Sygma)*

cows, pigs, and sheep, spread throughout Britain and even to other EU countries. Much of the rest of the world banned livestock imports from the EU. This crisis, too, dramatized the reverse side of the new interconnectedness in a global world. Capital and information flowed more quickly than ever across national borders, but so could epidemic diseases.

## ■ The West and the Question of Global Responsibility

If people were forced to think in global terms as never before, how far did global responsibility extend in a world that remained divided into sovereign nation-states? The series of brutal, sometimes genocidal conflicts from Yugoslavia to Rwanda to Chechnya to East Timor that helped to define the 1990s fostered a growing sense of collective responsibility in what was increasingly referred to as "the international community." Amorphous though it was, that entity, or community, seemed to take on real existence by the end of the decade. But who or what constituted it, and the conditions under which it should act, remained uncertain.

Of course a prominent international organization was already in place—the United Nations, the fruit of the hopes for a better world in light of World War II. But though it achieved significant successes in such areas as nutrition, health, and education, the UN frequently found difficulty when called on to restore or maintain peace. Its forces were often overburdened as they took on the sometimes incompatible objectives of peace-keeping and humanitarian relief—sometimes in areas where there was no real peace to keep. And its members, especially its leaders on the Security Council, were often divided about what should be done. When Serbs in a UN "safe area" around Srebrenica°, in Bosnia, massacred as many as twenty thousand people in 1995, torturing or burying alive a number of the victims, the Security Council refused the UN secretary-general's pleas for additional troops.

But the UN remained an important, or potentially important, player even as long-standing questions of national sovereignty continued to compromise its ability to act. Ad hoc UN war crimes tribunals dealt with atrocities in the Balkans and in Rwanda, and in 1998 the UN established a permanent international criminal court in The Hague. Its charge was to bring to justice those responsible for war crimes or crimes against humanity. While an overwhelming majority—120 nations—voted in favor of

**Diseases and Borders**    The outbreak of foot-and-mouth disease early in 2001 raised questions about globalization and strained relations within the European Union. Here a Spanish border official sprays disinfectant on the wheels of a French truck in March 2001, as part of the European effort to keep the disease from spreading.    *(Reuters/STR/Archive Photos)*

the measure, seven opposed it, including the United States, China, Israel, Iraq, and Libya. As efforts to establish the court followed, the United States sought an exemption for itself because it worried that American peacekeepers might be especially tempting targets for false accusations of war crimes. Such concerns were not groundless, and they indicated the unique problems the United States faced as the world's undisputed superpower. But these U.S. reservations also indicated how hard it was to come to meaningful international agreement in light of the different circumstances the nations of the world faced.

An ad hoc international criminal tribunal was already dealing with the crimes against humanity that had occurred during the wars accompanying the breakup of Yugoslavia of the 1990s. The court proved more aggressive than many had expected when it was set up in 1993, but it had difficulty apprehending major figures among

**Srebrenica** (shreb-reh-NEET-sah)

# The Question of Western Responsibility

*As clashes between warlords and peacekeepers became prominent during the 1990s, some called for a more coherent and effective Western role, whereas others worried that the West was becoming overextended. Brian Urquhart, born in Britain in 1919, was long a senior official of the United Nations. Here he offers a pointed analysis of the issues facing the Western-led "international community" by the turn of the century.*

What is to be done when hundreds of thousands of people in a hitherto little-known region of the world are hounded from their homes, massacred, or starved to death in a brutal civil war, or even in a deliberate act of genocide? To our credit, we no longer turn away from the face of evil, but we still don't know how to control it. As the new century dawns, one of the biggest problems for international organizations and their member governments is to learn how to react to the great human emergencies that still seem to occur regularly in many parts of the world. . . .

The so-called "international community" is anything but a constitutional system. As far as it is organized at all, it is an institutional arrangement, unpredictable and slow to act. It usually responds only when disaster has already struck and when its members, usually in the UN Security Council, can agree to take action. Even then, since the UN has no standing forces or substantial resources of its own, its action, if it can be agreed upon, is likely to be too little and too late.

In his opening address to the General Assembly on September 20, 1999, Secretary-General Kofi Annan made an impassioned plea for UN intervention in cases of gross violations of human rights. The reactions of governments to Annan's remarks showed very clearly how far the world still has to go before evil can be systematically dealt with internationally. Most comments on Annan's speech were critical and stressed the paramount importance of national sovereignty; some even saw humanitarian intervention as a cloak for American or Western hegemony or neocolonialism. Only a small minority of Western countries supported Sweden's position that the collective conscience of mankind demands action.

A new idea of "human security" has now taken its place alongside the much older concept of "international peace and security." It has emerged as the result of a vaguely defined and fitful international conscience on the part of the liberal democracies, and it has been encouraged both by the prodigious growth of nongovernmental organizations and by the communications revolution. However, the rules and the means for protecting human security are still tentative and controversial, not least because virtually any situation threatening human security is likely to raise questions of national sovereignty. No government wants to set up a system which may, at some point in the future, be invoked against itself.

Humanitarian action as it emerged in the aftermath of World War II was principally concerned with refugee resettlement and the reconstruction of war-shattered countries. In those innocent days, humanitarian relief was seen as a nonpolitical activity, dictated by the needs of the afflicted and by the resources and expertise available to meet them. . . . That relatively nonpolitical concept of humanitarianism has come to a brutal end with the rising importance of warlords and the conflicts within states of the post–cold war world. The international sponsors of humanitarian aid are no longer dealing with more or less responsible governments. . . .

. . . In the new situation of 1990s peacekeeping, humanitarian assistance still saved hundreds of thousands of lives but it could also provide warlords with the means to continue and expand the conflict. . . .

. . . "The whole aid community has been overtaken by a new reality," the IRC [International Rescue Committee] stated. "Humanitarianism has become a resource . . . and people are manipulating it as never before. Sometimes we just shouldn't show up for a disaster." . . .

In the 1990s, humanitarian workers were in the front line as never before and were increasingly dealing with factions, warlords, and thugs who had no respect for international personnel or organizations. For the first time, aid workers were more at risk than military forces, and the death toll rose alarmingly all over the world.

*Source:* Brian Urquhart, "In the Name of Humanity," *The New York Review of Books,* April 27, 2000, pp. 19–21.

the accused. The most conspicuous was Slobodan Milosevic himself, indicted in 1999 while still president of what remained of Yugoslavia. Even after his defeat in 2000, friction persisted between the tribunal and Yugoslav leaders. While the tribunal's chief prosecutor, the former Swiss attorney general Carla Del Ponte, energetically pursued Milosevic's extradition, the new president, Vojislav Kostunica, insisted that the Yugoslavs would make their own accounting with Milosevic and other top officials of his regime.

Whatever its center of gravity, the international community rested on the commitment and initiative of the rich Western countries, because they had the means to act globally, in response to natural or human-made disasters. Supplementing the efforts of governments was a network of nongovernmental organizations (NGOs), such as the Red Cross, Amnesty International, and Doctors Without Borders, that had gradually emerged to deal with humanitarian relief or human rights issues. Collectively they were a major presence on the international scene by the dawn of the twenty-first century—and central to the international community.

A succession of disasters challenged that community during the 1990s, as ethnic conflict erupted and tyrants terrorized civilian populations in hot spots around the world. Concurrent with the ongoing tragedies in Chechnya and the former Yugoslavia, a series of crises erupted in Africa—natural disasters from famine to flooding, but also civil wars that spawned ethnic massacre, slave trading, and rule by violent warlords. Such horrors spawned an increasing sense by the later 1990s that it was up to the Western-led international community to "do something." But do what—and at what cost? What aims were realistic?

Corruption and theft bedeviled efforts to get even nonpolitical humanitarian aid to the ordinary people who become victims. There was often no responsible government to deal with. Instead, those seeking to provide aid or maintain peace were forced to deal with semi-criminal elements who diverted humanitarian aid to buy weapons and who took peacekeepers and aid workers hostage—or even killed them. In 1994, for the first time, more UN civilian aid workers (twenty-four) than peacekeeping soldiers were killed in the line of duty. And the death toll for aid workers rose rapidly during the decade. In Chechnya a widely admired American relief worker, Fred Cuny, disappeared in 1995.

The rich countries of the West felt a responsibility to deal with such situations, but they were reluctant to supply the means, to take the risks, even to suffer the casualties necessary to do so effectively. Still, how could the leaders of those nations ask for such sacrifice in situations that perhaps could not be brought under control—at least not without permanent occupation and a return to semi-colonial status? As one crisis followed another, those in the West felt a sense of overload. Some even began to suggest that half-measures only made things worse, so perhaps it was better to stay away altogether. Such was "the new world order" that had emerged in the decade after the end of the cold war. (See the box "Reading Sources: The Question of Western Responsibility.")

## ■ Old and New, Modern and Beyond

Although the shadow of fascism and war remained, Europe had experienced a radical transformation in the half-century since World War II, a transformation that in some ways had cut Europeans off from their own tradition. Tangible reminders of Europe's distinctive past survived, but the growing "heritage industry" in Britain and elsewhere suggested that they were merely commodities to be packaged like any other. At the same time, Europe's increasingly uncertain, even ironic relationship to its own tradition, including its difficult recent past, found striking expression in architecture and painting by the last decades of the twentieth century.

During the first two decades after World War II, modernist architecture, turning from tradition to embrace the modern industrial age, had triumphed at last, transforming cities throughout the world. By the 1980s, however, architects were turning from modernism to postmodernism, a glitzy way of building with ambiguous or ironic references to a tradition that was still present, even if those living within it were not quite sure what to make of it.

This uneasy contemporary relationship with the past, especially the traumatic past of the earlier twentieth century, took more pointed form in the neoexpressionist painting prominent in Germany and Italy by the 1980s. For a generation after World War II, German artists, especially, had been unsure of their direction—or had settled for following the latest fashion from New York. But by the late 1960s, the new generation that included such artists as the German Anselm Kiefer (b. 1945) and the Italian Sandro Chia (b. 1946) sought to confront the recent past—and thus the meaning of a tradition that now included fascism, total war, and the Holocaust. Through art, they felt, we might deepen our relationship with our own recent history. Kiefer and Chia created striking images, but they offered no clear message. Rather, they conveyed the paradox and ambiguity that we encounter as we engage our multifaceted, seemingly contradictory cultural tradition.

**Kiefer: Osiris and Isis**   The German artist Anselm Kiefer combined unusual materials to create haunting images that often suggested the horrors of recent history. In this work from 1985–1987, the interpenetrating layers of human culture include images of ruin and death, hope and resurrection.   *(Anselm Kiefer,* Osiris und Isis, *1985–87. Mixed media on canvas, 150" × 220½" × 6½". San Francisco Museum of Modern Art. Purchased through a gift of Jean Stein by exchange, the Mrs. Paul L. Wattis Fund, and the Doris and Don Fisher Fund. Photo: Ben Blackwell)*

## CONCLUSION: LEARNING FROM WESTERN CIVILIZATION IN A POSTMODERN WORLD

N what sense was that tradition still to be understood as "Western" by the early twenty-first century, when talk of globalization and cultural fusion was rampant? Was "the West" still a meaningful category at all?

The geographical contours of Western civilization had never been precise, and the center of gravity of "the West" had shifted many times. Moreover, the West had always been involved in dynamic interaction with others, not closed and self-contained. But its contours had become especially uncertain with the dramatic changes that followed World War II. The cold war had

split Europe, and western Europe had found itself dependent on the United States. So the United States became, in one sense, the new center of the West, though the Soviet Union offered an alternative, based on different strands of the Western tradition. At the same time, European colonial networks unraveled, leaving "Westernization" as a very mixed legacy in formerly colonial areas.

By the 1990s, Europe was reuniting and the Soviet-style alternative stood discredited. Meanwhile, the United States was considering itself more multicultural and less European. The accelerating sense of globalization bred deeper uncertainty about what was specifically Western. In one sense, to be sure, globalization essentially *meant* Westernization to many advocates and critics alike. But what did that process entail, and what did it say about the meaning of the Western tradition by the early twenty-first century?

Led by businessmen in conservative Western dress, postwar Japan developed the world's second largest economy. Skyscrapers in booming Asian cities proved indistinguishable from skyscrapers elsewhere. Cultural distinctions remained, but they became more subtle and harder to define. The distinctions obviously were bound up with differences in shared experience—in history and memory, in heroes and villains, in art, even in values. But efforts to pin down such cultural differences became problematic as the long-standing Western assumption of superiority came to seem dubious at best.

During the last third of the twentieth century, bitter debate erupted in the West over the significance of Western civilization—even its legitimacy as a concept. Some critics highlighted the geographical imprecision of "the West" and claimed that the words *Western* and *civilization* had been juxtaposed simply to justify conquest and domination. Even among those who recognized a distinctive Western cultural tradition, some found it elitist and limiting. In their view, Western culture had defined itself around a group of artifacts—writings, paintings, monuments—that reflected the experience of a very restricted circle.

Others countered that imperialism and assumptions of superiority had not been confined to the West. Moreover, they continued, the West had been the source of ideas—the "rights of man," the scope for eliminating exploitation—that were now being eagerly embraced in the non-Western world. Even charges of cultural elitism stemmed from a democratic impulse that had itself grown from within the Western tradition. By the last decades of the twentieth century, that impulse was prompting historians to focus on ordinary people and cultural interpreters to expand the "canon"—the body of works considered worthy of our attention.

Questions about the Western tradition and its contemporary relevance were bound up with the advent of *postmodernism,* a term widely used by the early 1990s for a cultural orientation that had been gathering force for decades. Postmodernists question claims of certainty, objective truth, and intrinsic meaning in language, in works of art, and ultimately in all cultural expressions. From their perspective, such claims are assertions of privilege in what is essentially a political struggle for power—the power to set the wider social agenda. Postmodernism reflected a certain conception of what *modernism* had meant, even a sense that modernism had defined an era that was now ending. But what was it that was ending—and how was it bound up with the debate over Western civilization?

Postmodernism emerged partly as confidence in the scope for a neutral, objective social science began to decline during the 1960s. That confidence had reflected the belief in reason that had emerged from the Scientific Revolution and the Enlightenment. Reason had seemed universal, not limited to any particular culture, and it was assumed to be applicable to the human as well as the natural world.

To apply reason seemed "modern," and the West, having progressed by applying reason, had long understood itself to be in the forefront of modernity. Everyone else was scrambling to catch up through the universal process of modernization or Westernization. Such was the "master narrative" through which the West had understood its place in the world as it set the agenda during the modern era. It had indeed been that conception of the world, and the sense of superiority underlying it, that had seemed to justify Western imperialism.

Even as Westernization continued during the later twentieth century, Western thinkers retreated from this long-standing master narrative. There was no question that capitalism had spread from Europe, but the West was not necessarily the model, the standard of development. Indeed, a growing interest in the non-Western world and an increasing respect for its diverse traditions marked Western culture during the last quarter of the twentieth century. At the same time, Edward Said°, a scholar of Palestinian origin teaching in the United States, showed how Western images of the non-Western world had been constructed, and become stereotypes, reinforcing assumptions of Western superiority. (See the box "Global Encounters: The Case of 'Orientalism.'")

Especially in the United States, the postmodernist reaction led by the 1980s to the vogue of the French philosopher and historian Michel Foucault° (1926–1984), who showed that the power to specify what counts as knowledge was the key to social or political power. Since all knowledge was suspect, Foucault's accents invited mistrust and disruption. An array of equally innovative thinkers, from the German Jürgen Habermas to the American Richard Rorty, sought a more constructive orientation based on a renewed, no longer arrogant understanding of Western traditions, including the place of reason and democracy.

For those embracing this more constructive approach, the point was not to celebrate Western civilization but simply to understand it—as the framework that continued to shape the West and, less directly, the world. That tradition included much that might be criticized, and its present outcome entailed much that might be changed. Habermas, in particular, was a persistent and often radical critic of what he saw as the disparity

---

**Said** (sy-EED)    **Foucault** (foo-KOH)

⊕ G L O B A L   E N C O U N T E R S

## The Case of "Orientalism"

*In his influential book* Orientalism, *published in 1978, the Palestinian-American scholar Edward Said explored the process through which Westerners had constructed the "Middle East"—as different from the West. Though critical of the West, Said appealed to our common humanity in an effort to overcome the ongoing tendency, which was not confined to the West, to understand oneself as superior by stereotyping others. In the final analysis, he suggested, we all need to learn from one another.*

The Orient is not only adjacent to Europe; it is also the place of Europe's greatest and richest and oldest colonies, the source of its civilizations and languages, its cultural contestant, and one of its deepest and most recurring images of the Other. In addition, the Orient has helped to define Europe (or the West) as its contrasting image, idea, personality, experience. . . .

. . . The relationship between Occident and Orient is a relationship of power, of domination, of varying degrees of a complex hegemony. . . . There is very little consent to be found, for example, in the fact that Flaubert's encounter with an Egyptian courtesan produced a widely influential model of the Oriental woman; she never spoke of herself, she never represented her emotions, presence, or history. *He* spoke for and represented her. He was foreign, comparatively wealthy, male, and these were historical facts of domination that allowed him not only to possess Kuchuk Hanem physically but to speak for her and tell his readers in what way she was "typically Oriental." . . .

. . . [T]here is no avoiding the fact that even if we disregard the Orientalist distinctions between "them" and "us," a powerful series of political and ultimately ideological realities inform scholarship today. No one can escape dealing with, if not the East/West division, then the North/South one, the have/have-not one, the imperialist/anti-imperialist one, the white/colored one. We cannot get around them all by pretending they do not exist; on the contrary, contemporary Orientalism teaches us a great deal about the intellectual dishonesty of dissembling on that score, the result of which is to intensify the divisions and make them both vicious and permanent. Yet an openly polemical and right-minded "progressive" scholarship can very easily degenerate into dogmatic slumber, a prospect that is not edifying either.

. . . [E]nough is being done today in the human sciences to provide the contemporary scholar with insights, methods, and ideas that could dispense with racial, ideological, and imperialist stereotypes of the sort provided during its historical ascendancy by Orientalism. I consider Orientalism's failure to have been a human as much as an intellectual one; for in having to take up a position of irreducible opposition to a region of the world it considered alien to its own, Orientalism failed to identify with human experience, failed also to see it as human experience. . . . I hope to have shown my reader that the answer to Orientalism is not Occidentalism. No former "Oriental" will be comforted by the thought that having been an Oriental himself he is likely—too likely—to study new "Orientals"—or "Occidentals"—of his own making. If the knowledge of Orientalism has any meaning, it is in being a reminder of the seductive degradation of knowledge, of any knowledge, anywhere, at any time. Now perhaps more than before.

*Source:* Edward W. Said, *Orientalism* (New York: Random House, Vintage, 1979), pp. 1–2, 4–8, 327–328.

between Western democratic ideals and contemporary social and political practices. But effective criticism had to rest on free inquiry and rational understanding, as opposed to prejudice or wishful thinking. The invitation to think freely about the Western tradition, to criticize and change it, rested on precisely that tradition; indeed, the scope for such criticism and change had been central to the Western belief in reason. That openness remained perhaps the West's most fundamental legacy. The debate over Western civilization was itself testimony to the openness and freedom of that tradition.

The influential novelist V. S. Naipaul (b. 1932) confronted some of the most sensitive of these issues in a lecture in 1990. Born and raised in Trinidad, in a family of Indian Hindu background, he had experienced Western racism and imperialism firsthand. But that experience, he suggested, enabled him better to appreciate what he found the West's extraordinary attempt to accommodate the rest of the world since World War II. And the world was reciprocating, eagerly embracing Western ideals, which Naipaul grouped around the pursuit of happiness: "It implies a certain kind of society, a certain kind of awakened spirit. . . . So much is contained in it: the idea of the individual, responsibility, choice, the life of the intellect, the idea of vocation and perfectibility and achievement. It is an immense human idea."[2] So Naipaul, from his cross-cultural perspective, did not hesitate to insist that specifically Western values were proving universal in appeal and significance.

As the twenty-first century began, concerns about diversity and assimilation throughout the West suggested that controversy would continue over the significance of the Western tradition. There seemed ever less agreement about what an educated Westerner should know—about the West, or about the other cultures of the world. Within the framework of globalization, what was best understood as "Westernization," as opposed to cultural fusion, or ongoing diversity? Insofar as the Western element could be pinpointed, was it liberating or did it involve cultural imperialism and renewed exploitation?

The continuing debate made it clear that historical study had become more relevant than ever in this era of rapid cultural cross-fertilization. But, not surprisingly, it had also become more contested, as the ultimate court of appeal. The danger was that historical inquiry would become too politicized to allow us genuinely to learn from it. Such learning is crucial not to enable us to celebrate "who we are," but to deepen our understanding, even to make us more self-critical. As we continue the experiment, we may thereby act more effectively—and possibly create a better future.

## ■ Notes

1. As quoted in Thomas L. Friedman, *The Lexus and the Olive Tree,* as quoted in *Europe,* no. 391 (Nov. 1999): 47.
2. V. S. Naipaul, "Our Universal Civilization," in *The New York Review of Books,* January 31, 1991, pp. 22, 25.

## ■ Suggested Reading

Ardagh, John. *France in the New Century: Portrait of a Changing Society.* 1999. An updated edition of a lively, perceptive survey of the remarkable changes in French life since World War II.

Brubaker, Rogers. *Citizenship and Nationhood in France and Germany.* 1992. A lucid comparative study showing how very different conceptions of citizenship emerged in these two countries as a result of their contrasting historical experiences over the past two centuries.

Garton Ash, Timothy. *In Europe's Name: Germany and the Divided Continent.* 1993. A searching essay on Germany's place in Europe and the world, from the years of division, to reunification, to the post–cold war order.

Guttman, Robert J., ed. *Europe in the New Century: Visions of an Emerging Superpower.* 2001. An assessment of Europe's strengths and weaknesses by leading European politicians and journalists, who also seek to envision what the new century will bring.

Ignatieff, Michael. *Virtual War: Kosovo and Beyond.* 2000. An innovative exploration of the 1999 war over Kosovo, arguing that the use of technology to maintain distance transformed the idea of war.

Judah, Tim. *Kosovo: War and Revenge.* 2000. An authoritative account of the origins and unfolding of the Kosovo tragedy of the late 1990s.

Keane, John. *Václav Havel: A Political Tragedy in Six Acts.* 2000. A masterful political biography of the Czech anticommunist who became president of postcommunist Czechoslovakia— and one of the world's most respected moral and political leaders.

McCormick, John. *Understanding the European Union: A Concise Introduction.* 1999. A clear introduction to the history, structure, and functioning of the central institutions of the EU.

Shawcross, William. *Deliver Us from Evil: Peacekeepers, Warlords, and a World of Endless Conflict.* 2000. Accents the limits and contradictions of the Western response to crises in areas lacking an indigenous political class.

Steele, Jonathan. *Eternal Russia: Yeltsin, Gorbachev, and the Mirage of Democracy.* 1994. Places events before and after the fall of communism in useful historical perspective, while criticizing the preoccupation with privatization and the corresponding failure to foster a culture of democracy.

 **For a searchable list of additional readings for this chapter, go to http://college.hmco.com.**

# The Euro

**Front and Back of 10 Euro Note**

Since ancient times, cities and empires have minted coins to facilitate commerce and trade. Over time, images of gods and symbolic plants and animals gave way to stylized depictions of rulers. The study of coins—numismatics—has long provided insights into how rulers saw themselves and how they displayed their power at home and abroad.

When national banks and governments took over the production of paper money from commercial banks in the nineteenth and twentieth centuries, states gained a much bigger canvas on which to display their national symbols. Monarchies typically featured the current ruler on the face of the note, while republics picked a gallery of national heroes. Take a couple of bills out of your pocket, and you will see this is still the case in North America today: in the United States, the bills honor presidents and the first secretary of the Treasury, Alexander Hamilton. In Canada, Queen Elizabeth II still graces the $20 bill.

In 1991 member countries of the European Union agreed at Maastricht to the creation of a unified currency, to be called the *euro*, to replace their existing currencies (see page 1029). A competition was launched to choose appropriate designs. Two examples of the winning designs, by Robert Kalina of the Austrian National Bank, appear on the right. What can we learn by examining these notes?

First, it would be helpful to know what constraints the European Monetary Institute (the judging body) imposed on the designers. The seven bills (ranging from 5 to 500 euros) were to illustrate the "ages and styles of Europe," specifically Classical, Romanesque, Gothic, Renaissance, Baroque and Rococo, the age of iron and glass architecture, and modern twentieth-century architecture. The European flag was to be included on each bill. The criteria for selecting the winner were "creativity, aesthetics, style, functionality, likely public perception and acceptability (in particular the avoidance of any national bias and the achievement of a proper balance between the number of men and the number of women portrayed)."

You will notice right away that the design avoids the problem of equitably representing men and women by not including any people at all. Featured instead are architectural elements—windows on the front of the bills, bridges on the back. According to the designer, the windows symbolize "the spirit of openness and cooperation

in the European Union," while the bridges are "a metaphor for communication both among the people of Europe, and also between Europe and the rest of the world." Depicted on the back of the bills, with the bridges, is a map of the entire continent of Europe, including not just eastern Europe and western Russia, but parts of Turkey and North Africa. (Notice also how the bills differ: as is customary with European currency, the euro bills are different sizes and colors to help the visually impaired distinguish among them.)

Look first at the 10 euro note, illustrating the Romanesque style. Does the window look familiar? It may, if you have seen pictures of early medieval European churches. What about the bridge? It may remind you of the bridge in the French children's song "On the Bridge of Avignon." But if you were to compare the images with real monuments, you would quickly see that they are not the same. Indeed, unlike the White House on the U.S. $20 bill or countless other buildings shown on currency around the world, the windows and bridges on the euro are not labeled. The reason is simple: the architectural features are supposed to be generic and "European," and not reproduce any real monument. In fact, the initial designs of many of the notes, especially the bridges, were returned to Kalina for modification because they were "too recognizable."

**Front and Back of 500 Euro Note**

**Austrian 2 Euro Coin (Back)**
*(Courtesy of the Oesterreichische Nationalbank [Austrian National Bank], Vienna, Austria)*

**French 5 Eurocent Coin (Back)**

There were few such problems with the 500 euro note, illustrating twentieth-century architecture. The modernist style, originating in Europe in the 1920s (see page 908), had spread by the end of the century to virtually every corner of the world. The glass-and-steel buildings on the front of the note could just as well be in Tokyo, Singapore, or Nairobi, and the bridge recalls any number of modern suspension bridges around the world.

Notice how little writing appears on the bills. The word *euro* appears in the bottom corners in both the Latin and Greek alphabets (Greece joined the original eleven participants in the Eurozone on January 1, 2001). By indicating the issuing authority—the European Central Bank (ECB)—only by its initials, the notes have to include only five variants (BCE, ECB, EZB, EKT, EKP) to cover all the languages spoken in the European Union.

The coins were developed in a different way from the bills. Although the "heads" are uniform, each country could choose the design of the "tails" for the coins it produced at its national mint. All euro coins are legal tender in every Eurozone country, regardless where they were minted. Because there are eight coins, ranging in value from one eurocent to two euros, each country has eight opportunities to display its national symbols. The twelve countries took widely varying approaches. France features Marianne, a symbol of the French Republic since the time of the Revolution, on three of its coins. Marianne first appeared on French coins during the Revolution and is a traditional figure of French political art.

The remaining five French coins were divided among just two designs, *La Semeuse* (a woman sowing seeds, another traditional symbol of France) and a tree of life surrounded by the revolutionary motto "Liberty, Equality, Fraternity." None of the nineteenth- and twentieth-century figures currently on French notes—Paul Cézanne or Gustave Eiffel or Marie Curie—were selected. The choice of symbolic figures instead makes clear the continuing centrality of the French Revolution in France's national identity.

Austria, on the other hand, decided on eight different images. The smallest three coins feature different floral motifs; the next three, well-known Austrian buildings. The two largest coins are devoted to individuals whom the designers decided were Austria's most important figures: Mozart—known throughout the world—and Bertha Suttner—barely known anywhere outside Austria. Suttner was a writer and pacifist who is credited with persuading Alfred Nobel to establish the Nobel prizes. She herself was awarded the Nobel Peace Prize in 1905. No one could question the choice of Mozart—but why Suttner? Suttner had been a mainstay of Austrian currency for decades, appearing on the 1,000 schilling note until the mid-1980s. Reviving her somewhat antiquated image on the 2 euro coin may reflect Austria's renewed desire to project itself as a peace-loving, neutral nation that was not a willing partner in Nazi aggression but its first victim.

# GLOSSARY

**This Glossary covers the complete text, Chapters 1 through 30.**

**absolutism**  Extraordinary concentration of power in royal hands, achieved particularly by the kings of France, most notably **Louis XIV,** in the seventeenth century. Proponents argued that hereditary monarchy was the divinely ordained form of government. *(Ch. 16)*

**Act of Supremacy (1534)**  Act of the English Parliament during the Protestant Reformation that finalized the break with the Catholic Church by declaring the king to be head of the Church of England. Henry VIII required a public oath supporting the act, which Sir **Thomas More** refused to take; More was then executed for treason. *(Ch. 14)*

**Adenauer, Konrad (1876–1967)**  Leading statesman of post–World War II Germany. As chancellor (1949–1963), he oriented the country toward western Europe and the United States and proved to Germans that democracy could mean effective government, economic prosperity, and foreign policy success. *(Ch. 29)*

**agricultural revolution**  Dramatic increase in food production from the sixteenth to eighteenth centuries, brought about by changes in agricultural practices, cultivation of new crops, greater availability of animal manure, and introduction of the nutrient-rich potato from the Americas. *(Ch. 18)*

**Alexander the Great (356–323 B.C.)**  King of **Macedon** (r. 336–323) and conqueror of the **Persian Empire.** Son of **Philip II** of Macedon, Alexander was an ingenious warrior who, in the course of his conquests, spread Greek civilization to western Asia, Egypt, and India. His despotism and ruler-worship set a precedent for later monarchs, including many Roman emperors. *(Ch. 4)*

**Alexandria**  Mediterranean seaport in northern Egypt founded by **Alexander the Great** in 332 B.C. It was a thriving Hellenistic city with great harbors, marketplaces, banks, inns, courts, shipbuilding facilities, and a renowned library. *(Ch. 4)*

**Amarna reform**  Term for the ancient Egyptian king Amenhotep IV's seizure of power from temple priests by replacing the god Amun-Re with Aten and renaming himself Akhenaten. After Akhenaten's death, the Amun-Re cult regained power. *(Ch. 1)*

**Anabaptists**  Radical religious reformers in Germany and Switzerland during the Reformation. They rejected the practice of infant baptism, believing that baptism should occur only after confession of sin. They also believed that Christians should live apart in communities of the truly redeemed. Mennonites and Hutterites are their modern descendants. *(Ch. 14)*

**Antigonids**  Dynasty of Macedonian rulers founded in 276 B.C. by Antigonus Gonatas, grandson of Antigonus the One-Eyed, a general of **Alexander the Great.** The Antigonid dynasty lasted about 140 years, until the Roman conquest. *(Ch. 4)*

**Antioch**  Greatest of the cities founded by Seleucus, a general of **Alexander the Great.** Located near the present-day Turkish-Syrian border, it became one of the wealthiest and most luxurious of all eastern Mediterranean cities. *(Ch. 4)*

**anti-Semitism**  Centuries-old prejudice against and demonization of Jews. Anti-Semitism became virulent in Europe in the 1880s with the emergence of the ultranationalist and racist

"New Right" ideologies and political movements. An essential part of the Nazi world-view, it led to the Holocaust. *(Ch. 24)*

**appeasement**  The term for the policy employed by Britain's prime minister, Neville Chamberlain, to defuse the 1938 crisis with Germany's **Adolf Hitler.** Chamberlain acquiesced to Hitler's demands to annex the Sudetenland portion of Czechoslovakia, which proved a giant step toward the war that broke out less than a year later. *(Ch. 27)*

**Aquinas, Thomas (1225–1274)**  Dominican friar and theologian. In his two most famous works, *Summa Contra Gentiles* and *Summa Theologiae,* he distinguished between natural truth, or what a person could know by reasoning, and revealed truths, which can be known only through faith in God's revelation. No one before him had so rigorously followed the dialectical method of reasoning through a whole field of knowledge. *(Ch. 10)*

**Archaic Greece**  Period of ancient Greek history from around 700 to 500 B.C. Archaic Greece was characterized by artistic achievement, increased individualism amid communal solidarity, and a moving away from divine and toward abstract, mechanistic explanations. The Western philosophical tradition began during this period. *(Ch. 3)*

**Arianism**  Popular heresy advocated by the priest Arius (ca. 250–336), emphasizing that Jesus was the "first born of all creation." It sought to preserve and purify Christianity's monotheism by making Jesus slightly subordinate to the Father. It was condemned by the **Council of Nicaea.** *(Ch. 7)*

**Aristotle (384–322 B.C.)**  Ancient Greek philosopher, student of **Plato** and tutor of **Alexander the Great.** Aristotle emphasized the goal (*telos* in Greek) of change; in his view the entire cosmos is teleological, and every one of its parts has an essential purpose. Aristotle's scientific writings were the most influential philosophical classics of Greek and Roman civilization and remained so during the Middle Ages. *(Ch. 3)*

**Armada (1588)**  Massive fleet of Spanish warships sent against England by **Philip II** but defeated by the English navy and bad weather. The tactics used by the English helped set the future course of naval warfare. *(Ch. 15)*

**Assyrians**  Warlike people who ruled the ancient Near East during the first millennium B.C. Their innovations included using cavalry as their main striking force and having weapons and armor made of iron. *(Ch. 2)*

**Augsburg Confession (1532)**  Document written by Philip Melanchthon (1497–1560), with the approval of **Martin Luther,** that became the most widely accepted statement of the Lutheran faith. It constitutes part of the creedal basis for today's Lutheran churches. *(Ch. 14)*

**Augustine (354–430)**  North African bishop and one of the most influential Christian thinkers. Augustine wrote that all people were sinners in need of God's redemption, that history is the struggle between those who call on divine grace and those who sin, and that learning was useful only to the extent that it equipped individuals to read and understand the Bible's message of salvation. *(Ch. 7)*

**Augustus (63 B.C.–A.D. 14)** Honorific title of Gaius Julius Caesar Octavianus, grandnephew of Julius **Caesar** and first Roman emperor. After defeating Mark Antony and Cleopatra at the Battle of Actium (31 B.C.), Augustus ruled the empire for forty-five years. His rule laid the foundations of two hundred years of prosperous Roman peace. See also **Principate.** *(Ch. 6)*

**Auschwitz-Birkenau** The largest and principal extermination center of Nazi Germany's six death camps, all of which were located in what had been Poland. The Nazis shipped Jews from all over Europe to Auschwitz, which killed about twelve thousand people a day at the height of its operation in 1944. *(Ch. 28)*

**avant-garde** French for "forefront," the term refers to early-twentieth-century artists who, inspired by novel or unconventional techniques, considered themselves precursors of new styles. Avant-garde movements proclaimed idiosyncratic manifestos and constantly called for the rejection of existing forms of expression and the creation of new ones. *(Ch. 24)*

**Aztecs** Amerindian people that dominated central Mexico from the fourteenth through the sixteenth centuries from their capital Tenochtitlán (present-day Mexico City). Weakened by exposure to virulent Old World diseases, they were conquered in 1521–1523 by Spanish forces led by **Hernán Cortés.** *(Ch. 13)*

**Bacon, Francis (1561–1626)** England's lord chancellor during the reign of James I and author of a utopian essay extolling science's benefits for a peaceful society and human happiness. His influential works encouraged the empirical method and inductive reasoning. See also **empirical reasoning.** *(Ch. 17)*

**barbarian kingship** Central institution in a succession of kingdoms (ca. 300–600) ruled by barbarian (non-Roman) leaders, which evolved from former Roman provinces. Most such kings had been political or military leaders under Roman authority before becoming independent rulers. *(Ch. 7)*

**baroque** Style of European art and architecture popular from the late sixteenth to early eighteenth century. Baroque artists, such as Peter Paul Rubens, modified Renaissance techniques, adding dynamism and emotional energy. Baroque painting used light to portray dramatic illusion, and baroque churches were both impressively grand and emotionally engaging. *(Ch. 15)*

**Bauhaus** An influential German art school, founded in 1919, that sought to adopt contemporary materials to develop new forms of architecture, design, and urban planning in response to the cultural uncertainty that followed World War I. Though it arguably failed in its immediate German context, the Bauhaus helped shape the whole idea of "the modern" in the West and throughout the world for decades to come. *(Ch. 26)*

**Bernard of Clairvaux (1090–1153)** Monk, church reformer, and influential adviser to kings and popes. Bernard believed that faith and divine inspiration were more important than dialectical reasoning. He was instrumental in the success of the Cistercian religious order. *(Ch. 10)*

**Bismarck, Otto von (1815–1898)** Nineteenth-century German statesman. A Prussian aristocrat, Bismarck was the autocratic architect who, through a series of aggressive wars, united Germany and served as the nation's first chancellor. He administered an emperor-controlled country that became the dominant power in Europe. See also **Realpolitik.** *(Ch. 22)*

**Black Death (1348–1351)** First of a series of epidemics, probably bubonic plague, that raged in Europe and western Asia for three centuries. The Black Death killed about 60 percent of those infected. The huge population decline fueled the economic and social transformations of the late Middle Ages. *(Ch. 11)*

**Bolsheviks** Members of a faction of the Russian Socialist Party led by **Vladimir Ilich Lenin** (1870–1924), a zealous Marxist who insisted that a revolutionary cadre could seize power on behalf of the working class. The Bolsheviks gained control of Russia in November 1917. *(Ch. 24)*

**Bonaparte, Napoleon.** See **Napoleon Bonaparte.**

**bourgeois century** Characterization of the nineteenth century, especially the latter half. In western Europe, the bourgeois elites (middle classes), which had expanded dramatically in the wake of industrialization, helped fashion much of society. *(Ch. 23)*

**Brandenburg-Prussia** Group of German territories ruled by the Hohenzollern family that became one of Europe's most powerful states in the seventeenth century. Its military strength was supported by its hereditary landowners, who were granted autonomy in their territories. *(Ch. 16)*

**Brandt, Willy (1913–1992)** Socialist West German chancellor (r. 1969–1974). Brandt's widely popular policy of opening to the East, or *Ostpolitik*, made possible closer economic ties between West and East Germany and broader opportunities for ordinary citizens to interact across the east-west border. *(Ch. 29)*

**Brest-Litovsk, Treaty of (1918)** Treaty in which Russia accepted its defeat by Germany and its allies in World War I. The treaty forced the Russians to cede much of European Russia to Germany. After Germany's defeat by the Allies later in the year, the **Bolsheviks** recaptured Ukraine and the Caucasus region. *(Ch. 25)*

**British blockade** Britain's naval blockade of Germany during World War I. By means of this tactic, which cut off supplies to Germany but which also violated several provisions of international law, the British seriously impeded the German war effort. *(Ch. 25)*

**Caesar, Gaius Julius (100–44 B.C.)** Roman general gifted at war and politics. Named dictator in 49 B.C., he was assassinated by the members of the **senate** in 44 B.C. He introduced to Europe the calendar of 365¼ days. He was succeeded as ruler by his grandnephew Octavian (**Augustus**). Later Roman emperors were also called *caesar*. *(Ch. 5)*

**Caliphate** Arab empire established by the successors of **Muhammad**; *caliph* means "successor to the prophet." The Umayyad caliphate, with its capital in Damascus, ruled from 661 to 750; the Abbasid caliphate, based in Baghdad, from 750 to 1258. *(Ch. 8)*

**Calvin, John (1509–1564)** Franco-Swiss theologian and founder of the Reformed Church in Geneva. Calvin's theological writings, most notably *Institutes of the Christian Religion* (1536), were widely disseminated and hugely influential. Calvin stressed the absolute power of God and the need for moral reform of the Christian community. *(Ch. 14)*

**canon law** Collection of orderly rules for the government of the Catholic Church, based on papal decrees and decisions of church councils. In 1140 the monk Gratian published the *Decretum*, the first systematic collection of canon law. *(Ch. 10)*

**Carlowitz, Treaty of (1699)** Treaty imposed by the European allies on a weakening Ottoman Empire. The Habsburgs, Venetians, Russians, and Poles gained territory and power at the Turks' expense. *(Ch. 16)*

**Carolingian Renaissance**  Major revival of learning, combined with reform of religious and political institutions, that occurred under **Charlemagne** and his successors. The revival encompassed the founding of schools in religious institutions, production of textbooks, dissemination of early church teachings and of **canon law,** as well as secular reforms such as regularization of royal estates. *(Ch. 8)*

**Catherine the Great (r. 1762–1796)**  Empress of Russia. Through an astute policy of wars and alliances, Catherine expanded her country's borders south to the Black Sea and west into Europe. An "enlightened despot," she advanced the westernizing reforms begun by **Peter the Great.** *(Ch. 18)*

**Cato the Elder (234–149 B.C.)**  Marcus Portius Cato, Roman general and statesman. Known as Cato the Censor because he denounced luxury goods, he was the first Roman historian to write in Latin. *(Ch. 5)*

**Charlemagne**  Frankish king (r. 768–814), crowned emperor in 800. He carried out a program of legal and ecclesiastical reform, patronized learning, and revitalized the western Roman Empire. See also **Carolingian Renaissance.** *(Ch. 8)*

**Charles V (r. 1519–1558)**  Holy Roman emperor and, as Charles I, king of Spain. His empire included Spain, Italy, the Low Countries, and Germany. Though he vigorously opposed the spread of Protestantism during the Reformation, he was forced to sign the Religious Peace of Augsburg in 1555, which acknowledged the right of German princes to choose the religion to be practiced in their territories, Lutheran or Catholic. Charles abdicated his imperial and royal titles the next year, ceding the empire to his brother Ferdinand and his Spanish possessions to his son **Philip II.** *(Ch. 14)*

**Chartism**  Nineteenth-century British political movement whose goal was to transform Britain from an oligarchy to a democracy. The Chartists' demands were contained in the 1838 "people's charter," which called for universal male suffrage, electoral districts with equal population, salaries and the abolition of property qualifications for Members of Parliament, the secret ballot, and annual general elections. The movement failed, but most of its measures eventually became law. See also **Second Reform Bill.** *(Ch. 21)*

**Chechnya**  Small, largely Muslim republic in the Caucasus region of Russia that attempted to declare independence in 1991. Russia intervened in the resulting civil war in 1994. After the Chechens won a substantial measure of autonomy, fighting resumed in 1999. *(Ch. 30)*

**chivalry**  Initially, a medieval code of conduct for mounted warriors, focusing on military prowess, open-handed generosity, and earning a glorious reputation. Later it evolved into an elaborate set of rules governing relations between men and women. *(Ch. 10)*

**Christianity**  Sect originally rooted in Judaism that emerged as a fully separate religion by around A.D. 200. Emphasizing belief in one God and the mission of his son, **Jesus of Nazareth,** as savior, Christianity offered salvation in the next world and a caring community in the present one. A messianic religion, Christianity emphasized Christ's return, leading to the beginning of a heavenly kingdom on earth. *(Ch. 6)*

**Churchill, Winston (1874–1965)**  British prime minister (1940–1945; 1951–1955). As the leader of his country during World War II, Churchill's courage, decisiveness, memorable words, and boundless energy made him widely seen as one of Britain's greatest leaders of the twentieth century. See also **Yalta conference**.

**Cicero, Marcus Tullius (106–43 B.C.)**  Philosopher, writer, and statesman who was Rome's greatest orator. He was crucial in making the Latin language a vessel for the heritage of Greek thought. *(Ch. 5)*

**city-state**  State consisting of an independent city and the surrounding territory under its control. Early examples were the Sumerian city-states in the third millennium B.C. *(Ch. 1)*

**civic humanism**  An ideology, championed by Florentine writers and public officials during the Renaissance, that emphasized their city's classical republican virtues and history. They argued that a moral and ethical value was intrinsic to public life. *(Ch. 12)*

**Civil Code**  Law code established under Napoleon in 1804 that included limited acceptance of revolutionary gains, such as a guarantee of equality before the law and taxation of all social classes. Also known as the Napoleonic Code, it enshrined modern forms of property ownership and civil contracts, enhanced paternal control of families, outlawed divorce in most circumstances, and placed women under the legal domination of fathers and husbands. *(Ch. 19)*

**Classical Greece**  Period of ancient Greek history from about 480 to 323 B.C. Classical Greek culture emphasized public life as the central theme of art and literature, and its sculpture was the most anatomically precise yet. Classical Greece set many standards for modern Western culture. See also **demokratia**. *(Ch. 3)*

**Cluny (Cluniacs)**  A spiritual reform begun in 910 in central France. The movement emphasized strict adherence to the Benedictine Rule, as well as the ideas that the church should pray for the world without being deeply involved in it and must be free from lay control. *(Ch. 10)*

**cold war**  The hostile standoff between the Soviet Union and the United States that began after World War II, when communist governments, relying on Soviet support, took control of most of east-central Europe. The Soviets' first atomic bomb explosion in 1949 intensified the conflict, which shaped world affairs for the next forty years. *(Ch. 28)*

**collectivization**  The program that reshaped agriculture in the Soviet Union under **Joseph Stalin** during the early 1930s. By forcing peasants into government-controlled collective farms, the Soviet regime sought to take control of agricultural production in order better to finance rapid industrialization. *(Ch. 27)*

**Columbian Exchange**  Historians' term for the blending of cultures between the Old World and the New after Christopher Columbus's arrival in the New World in 1492. The Spanish and other Europeans brought their plants, domesticated animals, and diseases to the Americas. The Americas contributed New World crops, most notably maize (corn) and potatoes, transforming the Old World diet. *(Ch. 13)*

**Comintern (Third, or Communist, International)**  An association founded in March 1919 by the communists (formerly **Bolsheviks)** to translate their success in Russia into leadership of the international socialist movement. Its program of tight organization and discipline under Russian leadership produced a schism between communists and socialists in Europe and throughout the world. *(Ch. 26)*

**communes**  Form of government in Italian towns that rose in the eleventh century. Despite numerous local variations, communes involved common decision making by local notables, including both landed aristocrats and wealthy merchants or industrialists. *(Ch. 9)*

**Compromise of 1867**  Agreement that divided the Habsburg Empire into Austria in the west and Hungary in the east, a dual monarchy under Emperor Franz Joseph called Austria-Hungary. The compromise confirmed Magyar dominance in Hungary. *(Ch. 22)*

**congress system**  System of European international relations in the first half of the nineteenth century in which the major European states cooperated to preserve the balance of power. This system disappeared as political leaders increasingly used force to pursue their narrow interests. *(Ch. 22)*

**Congress of Vienna (1814–1815)**  Conference called by the victorious powers—Austria, Great Britain, Prussia, and Russia—who defeated Napoleon. Guided by the Austrian foreign minister, Prince Metternich, the Great Powers drew new territorial boundaries advantageous to themselves. They also attempted to provide long-term stability on the European continent and restored some of the rulers who had been overthrown. See also **congress system.** *(Ch. 20)*

**conservatism**  Ideology underlying the order established in Europe in 1815. Conservatives emphasized resistance to change and preservation of the existing order of monarchy, aristocracy, and an established church. *(Ch. 20)*

**Copernicus, Nicholas (1473–1543)**  Polish astronomer who initiated the Scientific Revolution by proposing that the earth and other planets orbit the sun, a theory called the heliocentric, or sun-centered, system. See also **heliocentrism**. *(Ch. 17)*

**corporative state, corporativism**  The system established in fascist Italy beginning in 1926 that sought to involve people in public life not as citizens but as producers, through their roles in the economy. A system based on such occupational groupings eventually replaced parliament as the basis of political representation in fascist Italy. *(Ch. 26)*

**Cortés, Hernán (1485–1546)**  Spanish commander who conquered the **Aztecs** and claimed the Valley of Mexico for Spain. Cortés had only five hundred men but was aided by an outbreak of smallpox and the help of Amerindian peoples eager to end Aztec control. *(Ch. 13)*

**Council of Constance (1414–1418)**  Assembly convened by Holy Roman Emperor Sigismund to heal deep religious and civil divisions. The council declared that its rulings were binding even on the pope. Its selection of Pope Martin V ended the **Great Schism**. *(Ch. 11)*

**Council of the Indies**  Body established by the king of Spain in 1524 to oversee Spain's colonial possessions. Located at court, eventually in Madrid, it supervised all legal, administrative, and commercial activity in the colonies until the early eighteenth century. *(Ch. 13)*

**Council of Nicaea (325)**  History's first ecumenical, or "all-church," council, convened by the emperor Constantine. The council condemned **Arianism** and proclaimed key elements of the Nicene Creed, especially the doctrine that Christ was "one in being with the Father," co-equal and co-eternal. *(Ch. 7)*

**Council of Trent (1545–1563)**  Ecumenical council of the Roman Catholic Church during the Reformation. Though rejecting many Protestant positions, the council reformed and reorganized the church partly in response to Protestant criticisms. Its decrees reaffirmed and defined the basic tenets of Roman Catholicism for the next four hundred years. *(Ch. 14)*

**covenant**  As told in the Hebrew Bible, the pact God made with Abraham, the first patriarch of **Israel**. In return for the land of Canaan and the promise of becoming a great nation, the Israelites agreed to worship no other gods. *(Ch. 2)*

**Cromwell, Oliver (1599–1658)**  English Puritan general and statesman. A military genius and leader in the English Civil War, Cromwell governed as Lord Protector during the Interregnum from 1653 to 1658. *(Ch. 16)*

**Crusades (1095–1270)**  A series of largely unsuccessful wars waged by western European Christians to recapture the Holy Land from the Muslims and ensure the safety of Christian pilgrims to Jerusalem. Later, the term came to designate any military effort by Europeans against non-Christians. *(Ch. 9)*

**cuneiform**  First writing system in Mesopotamia, consisting of wedge-shaped impressions in soft clay. Named from the Latin word for "wedge-shaped," it was developed about 3500–3100 B.C. *(Ch. 1)*

**Darwinism**  Profoundly influential theory of biological evolution, first put forth by Charles Darwin (1809–1882). He proposed that all forms of life continuously develop through natural selection, whereby those that are better adapted to the environment have the advantage and are more likely to survive and pass on their beneficial traits to their offspring. *(Ch. 23)*

**D-Day**  The complex Allied amphibious landings in Normandy, France, on June 6, 1944, that opened a second major European front in World War II. In the aftermath of this invasion, American-led forces in the west began moving toward Germany, completing the Soviet effort, which was already forcing the Germans back on the eastern front. *(Ch. 28)*

**Decembrists**  Group of Russian military officers who led the December 1825 rebellion after the death of Tsar Alexander I, seeking to install a constitutional monarchy with Alexander's eldest brother, Constantine, as tsar. They were defeated and executed by Constantine's younger brother, Nicholas. The Decembrists were seen as martyrs by later Russian revolutionaries. *(Ch. 21)*

**Declaration of the Rights of Man and the Citizen (1789)**  Document issued by the **National Assembly** of France in August 1789. Modeled on the U.S. Constitution, the declaration set forth the basis for the new French government and asserted "the natural, inalienable and sacred rights of man." *(Ch. 19)*

**demokratia**  Term coined in Athens in the fifth century B.C. to describe the city's system of direct government. It means "the power *(kratos)* of the people *(demos)*." Athenian society pioneered today's key democratic principles, including freedom, equality, universal citizenship, and the rule of law. *(Ch. 3)*

**Descartes, René (1596–1650)**  French philosopher, scientist, and mathematician. Descartes emphasized skepticism and deductive reasoning in his most influential treatise, *Discourse on Method*. He offered the first alternative physical explanation of matter after the Copernican revolution. *(Ch. 17)*

**digital divide**  A term for the disparity in access to the computing and Internet technologies that seemed essential to compete in the twenty-first-century global economy. It was one way that new technologies were widening the gap between the world's haves and have-nots. *(Ch. 30)*

**Directory**  French revolutionary government from 1795 to 1799, consisting of an executive council of five men chosen by the upper house of the legislature. It was overthrown in a coup led by **Napoleon Bonaparte.** *(Ch. 19)*

**Dominic**  Dominic de Guzman (1170–1221), Spanish priest and founder of the spiritually influential Dominican mendicant order. The order was known for the irreproachable life of its members, its learning, and its desire to emulate the apostolic life of the early church by poverty and preaching. *(Ch. 10)*

**Dutch East India Company** Commercially innovative Dutch company formed in 1602 that combined government management of trade with both public and private investment. The formation of the company created a permanent pool of capital to sustain trade and resulted in a dramatic expansion of commerce with Asia. *(Ch. 16)*

**Edict of Milan (313)** Proclamation issued primarily by Emperor Constantine that made Christianity a legal religion in the Roman Empire. Constantine promoted the Christian church, granting it tax immunities and relieving the clergy of military service. *(Ch. 7)*

**Edict of Nantes (1598)** Edict of Henry IV granting France's Protestants (**Huguenots**) the right to practice their faith and maintain defensive garrisons. They were also guaranteed access to schools, hospitals, royal appointments, and separate judicial institutions. The edict was revoked by **Louis XIV** in 1685. *(Ch. 15)*

**Elizabeth I (r. 1558–1603)** First woman to occupy the English throne successfully. Elizabeth's adroit rule brought stability to England after the turmoil of previous reigns. She firmly established Protestantism in England, encouraged English commerce, defended the nation against the Spanish **Armada**, and fostered the English Renaissance in poetry and drama. *(Ch. 15)*

**empirical reasoning** Philosophical view developed by the seventeenth-century English philosophers **Francis Bacon** and **John Locke**, asserting that all knowledge is based on observation and experimentation and that general principles should be derived from particular facts. *(Ch. 17)*

*encomienda* A Spanish royal grant of protectorship over a group of Amerindians. The receivers of the grants (*encomenderos*) were obliged to Christianize the people under their charge, but instead most forced the natives to work as virtual slaves in mines and on Spanish lands. See also **Bartolomé de Las Casas**. *(Ch. 13)*

**enlightened despotism** Term for the reform-oriented rule of eighteenth-century monarchs such as **Frederick the Great**, Joseph II of Austria, and **Catherine the Great**. Enlightened despots applied Enlightenment remedies to economic problems, encouraged education and legal reform, and improved agricultural productivity by enabling some peasants to own the land they worked. *(Ch. 18)*

**Epicureans** Adherents of the Athenian philosopher Epicurus (341–270 B.C.), who taught that the soul is made up of atoms that do not exist after death. Epicureans emphasized the avoidance of pain and the pursuit of intellectual pleasure. *(Ch. 4)*

**Erasmus, Desiderius (1466–1536)** Prominent Dutch humanist during the Renaissance, best known for his satire *Praise of Folly*. Erasmus's works reinterpreted Greek and Roman wisdom and emphasized tolerance, reason, and faith in the goodness and educability of the individual. *(Ch. 12)*

**"ethnic cleansing"** A term describing attempts to remove an unwanted ethnic group from an area, which can include forced relocation and mass killing. Beginning in 1991, this tactic was implemented by Yugoslavian ruler Slobodan Milosevic (b. 1941) to unite all Serbs, many of whom lived in neighboring Croatia, Bosnia-Herzegovina, and **Kosovo**. *(Ch. 30)*

**Etruscans** Inhabitants of twelve loosely confederated city-states north of Rome in Etruria that flourished in the seventh to sixth centuries B.C. They were conquered by the Romans by the early third century B.C. *(Ch. 5)*

**euro** The common currency launched by the **European Union** in 1999 to eliminate the cost of currency exchange and boost trade and economic interaction. As of January 1, 2002, it replaced the national currencies of the participating countries (the "Eurozone"). *(Ch. 30)*

**European Economic Community (EEC) (1957–1967)** Common market formed by Belgium, France, West Germany, Italy, Luxembourg, and the Netherlands to promote free trade. The EEC was replaced by the European Community (EC) in 1967. *(Ch. 29)*

**European Union (EU)** New name for the European Community after the **Maastricht agreement** of 1991. By 2001 the European Union had nine members in addition to the original six members of the **European Economic Community:** Britain, Denmark, Ireland (joined 1973); Greece (joined 1981); Portugal, Spain (joined 1985); and Austria, Finland, Sweden (joined 1995). See also **euro**. *(Ch. 30)*

**"euthanasia" program** The Nazi program of systematically killing people, overwhelmingly ethnic Germans, whom the Nazis deemed superfluous or threatening to the German racial health. Victims included chronic mental patients, the incurably ill, and people with severe physical handicaps. Initiated in 1939, the program had claimed 100,000 lives by the time it was discontinued in 1941. *(Ch. 27)*

**existentialism** A philosophical and cultural movement, influential from the late 1940s into the 1950s, that explored life in a world cast adrift from its cultural moorings. Highly influential were the Frenchmen Jean Paul Sartre (1905–1980) and Albert Camus (1913–1960), for whom an authentic human response to an apparently meaningless universe entailed commitment and responsibility. *(Ch. 29)*

**factories** Centralized workplaces where a number of people cooperate to mass-produce goods. The first factories of industrializing Europe were made possible by the development of the **steam engine** as a central power source. The mechanized production of factories led to huge productivity increases in the nineteenth century. See also **industrialization, mass production**. *(Ch. 20)*

**fascism** A violent, antidemocratic movement founded by **Benito Mussolini** in Italy in 1919. The term is widely used to encompass Hitler's Nazi regime in Germany and other movements stressing disciplined national solidarity and hostile to liberal individualism, the parliamentary system, and Marxist socialism. *(Ch. 26)*

**February Patent (1861)** Enactment issued in February 1861 by the Austrian emperor Franz Joseph (r. 1848–1916) that established a constitutional monarchy in the old Austrian Empire. The patent guaranteed civil liberties and provided for local self-government and an elected parliament. *(Ch. 22)*

**feudal revolution** The societal change in tenth-century France from prince-dominated territories with loyal, reliable, but few vassals to the advent of many locally powerful magnates with numerous vassals whose fidelity was uncertain and who primarily provided military service. *(Ch. 9)*

**Five Pillars of Islam** The basic teachings of Islam: (1) the profession of faith, "There is no God but Allah and **Muhammad** is His Prophet"; (2) individual prayer five times daily, plus group prayers at noon on Friday; (3) the sunup-to-sundown fast during the month of Ramadan; (4) giving generous alms to the poor; and (5) pilgrimage to Mecca at least once in a person's lifetime. *(Ch. 8)*

**Flavians** Dynasty of the Roman emperors Vespasian (r. 69–79), Titus (r. 79–81), and Domitian (r. 81–96), whose rule was a time of relative peace and good government. Unlike the Julio-Claudians, the Flavians descended from Italian landowners, not old Roman nobility. Domitian persecuted the nobility and was assassinated. *(Ch. 6)*

**Fourteen Points** Proposals by U.S. president Woodrow Wilson (1856–1924) to guide the new international order that would follow an Allied victory in World War I. Specifics included open diplomacy, free trade, reduced armaments, self-determination for nationalities, and a league of nations. *(Ch. 25)*

**Francis of Assisi (1181–1226)** Italian monk and founder of a new order of friars ("brothers," from the Latin *fratres*). Francis was born wealthy but adopted a life based on the scriptural ideals of poverty, preaching, and service. His apostolate to the urban poor was highly popular. *(Ch. 10)*

**Frankfurt Assembly (1848–1849)** Popularly elected national assembly that attempted to create a unified German state. The assembly drew up a constitution and offered the German throne to Friedrich Wilhelm IV, king of Prussia, who declined, fearing a war with Austria and not wanting an office offered by representatives of the people. *(Ch. 21)*

**Frederick the Great (r. 1740–1786)** Autocratic king of Prussia who transformed the country into a major military power, acquired Polish Prussia, and waged three wars against Austria. He participated in and encouraged the study of philosophy, history, poetry, and French literature. *(Ch. 18)*

**Freud, Sigmund (1856–1939)** Austrian founder of psychoanalysis, a method of treating psychic disorders by exploring the unconscious. Freud believed that people were motivated in part by their unconscious feelings and drives. He helped call attention to the concept that irrational forces play a significant role in human behavior. *(Ch. 24)*

**friendly societies** Nineteenth-century organizations formed by workers; members pooled their resources to provide mutual aid. Combining business activity with feasts, drinking bouts, and other social functions, friendly societies promoted group solidarity and a sense of working-class identity. *(Ch. 20)*

**Galileo Galilei (1564–1642)** Italian physicist and astronomer who provided evidence supporting the heliocentric theory of **Nicholas Copernicus** and helped develop the physics of mechanics. His publication of his astronomical observations and his subsequent condemnation by the Catholic Church spurred popular debate and greatly influenced the future of science. *(Ch. 17)*

**gentry** Class of wealthy, educated, and socially ambitious families in western Europe, especially England, whose political and economic power was greatly enhanced during the sixteenth century. They shared with traditional old-family warrior-aristocrats certain legal privileges, security of landownership, and a cooperative relationship with the monarchy. See also **price revolution.** *(Ch. 15)*

**Girondins** Political faction during the French Revolution. Republicans and members of the Jacobin Club, the Girondins dominated the French Legislative Assembly when it began to meet in 1791. They favored an activist government but were less radical than other members of the club, called the **Jacobins**. The Girondins were purged from the National Con-

vention in 1793, and many were executed during the **Terror**. *(Ch. 19)*

**glasnost** Russian term meaning "greater openness." Glasnost was the leading motif in the Great Reforms begun in 1861 by Tsar Alexander II (r. 1855–1881), who sought to strengthen Russia by restructuring its institutions in the wake of defeat in the Crimean War. Glasnost was also part of the reform efforts of **Mikhail Gorbachev** in the Soviet Union during the 1980s. *(Ch. 22)*

**Glorious Revolution (1688)** Bloodless English revolution in which Parliament replaced the Catholic King James II with William (of Orange) and his wife Mary (James's Protestant daughter). Parliament imposed on the new sovereigns a Bill of Rights that confirmed Parliament's power and protected freedom of speech. *(Ch. 16)*

**Golden Bull of 1356** Edict of Holy Roman Emperor Charles IV establishing the method of electing a new emperor. It acknowledged the political autonomy of Germany's seven regional princes. *(Ch. 11)*

**Gorbachev, Mikhail (b. 1931)** The Soviet Communist Party secretary who, beginning in 1985, attempted to reform the Soviet communist system through arms reduction; liberalization in the satellite states; *glasnost,* or "openness" to discussion and criticism; and *perestroika,* or economic "restructuring." Though widely admired in the West, these measures failed, and Gorbachev ended up presiding over the end of the Soviet communist regime. *(Ch. 29)*

**Gothic** Period in European architecture, sculpture, and painting from the twelfth to early sixteenth centuries. Gothic architecture was distinguished by the pointed arch, ribbed vault, and point support, which produced a building characterized by verticality and translucency. Examples are the Cathedral of Notre-Dame of Paris and the royal portal at Chartres Cathedral. *(Ch. 10)*

**Gracchi** Ancient Roman faction led by Tiberius Sempronius Gracchus (163–133 B.C.) and later his brother, Gaius (153–121 B.C.), both of whom were killed by their political opponents. They challenged the conservative **senate** on behalf of the poor. *(Ch. 5)*

**Great Northern War (1700–1721)** War between Sweden and Russia over control of Baltic territories. **Peter the Great** secured Livonia and Estonia as well as the territory on which he built Russia's new capital, St. Petersburg. Russia became the pre-eminent power on the Baltic. *(Ch. 16)*

**"the Great Patriotic War"** Term for World War II devised by **Joseph Stalin** to rally Soviet citizens against the German invasion. Stalin appealed to Russian nationalism and recalled past heroic defenses of Russia rather than communist themes. *(Ch. 28)*

**Great Reform Bill (1832)** British law that broadened the franchise and provided parliamentary seats for new urban areas that had not previously been represented. The bill was a major victory for the government and middle classes over the aristocracy. *(Ch. 21)*

**Great Schism (1378–1417)** Period during which two, then three, rival popes claimed to rule the Christian Church. The schism ended when the **Council of Constance** deposed all three competing previous popes and elected Martin V as the new pope. *(Ch. 11)*

**guilds** Merchant groups and associations of crafts and trades established in European cities and towns beginning in the thirteenth century. Guilds expanded greatly during the later

Middle Ages. They provided economic benefits, fostered a sense of community, and served as mutual assistance societies. *(Ch. 9)*

**gulag** Network of 476 forced labor camps for political prisoners in the Soviet Union. The *gulag* (an acronym for "main camp administration") was first used by Lenin in 1918 but was greatly expanded by **Joseph Stalin** in the 1930s. *(Ch. 27)*

**Gutenberg, Johann (ca. 1399–1468)** German inventor of movable metal type. His innovations led to the publication of the first printed book in Europe, the Gutenberg Bible, in the 1450s. Printed books and broadsheets played a critical role in disseminating the ideas of the Renaissance and the Reformation. *(Ch. 12)*

**Hagia Sophia** Largest Christian church ever built, constructed in Constantinople from 532 to 537 for the Roman emperor **Justinian.** The church consists of two intersecting rectangular basilicas that incorporate arches; the whole is surmounted by a huge dome. *(Ch. 7)*

**Hanseatic League** Late medieval association of over a hundred trading cities, centered on the German city of Lübeck. The league dominated coastal trade in northern Europe from the fourteenth to the fifteenth centuries, until Dutch, English, and south German merchants finally gained shares of the wool, grain, and fur trades. *(Ch. 11)*

**heliocentrism** Theory advanced by **Nicholas Copernicus** that the earth and other planets orbit the sun. Supported by the scientific and mathematical discoveries of **Johannes Kepler** and **Galileo Galilei**, heliocentrism, which means "sun-centered," won acceptance by the end of the seventeenth century. *(Ch. 17)*

**Hellenism** Term used to designate ancient Greece's language, culture, and civilization, especially after **Alexander the Great** spread them to other parts of the Mediterranean, western Asia, and North Africa. *(Ch. 4)*

**Helsinki Accords (1975)** Agreements signed by thirty-five countries in Helsinki, Finland, that committed the signatories to recognize existing borders, to increase economic and environmental cooperation, and to promote freedom of expression, religion, and travel. Dissidents in Soviet bloc countries soon fastened on these provisions to highlight the lack of human rights and to discredit the ruling communist governments. *(Ch. 29)*

**Henry IV (r. 1589–1610)** First Bourbon king of France, who converted to Catholicism to restore that nation's peace. His **Edict of Nantes** granted rights to the persecuted French Protestants, and he strengthened finance, agriculture, and commerce. *(Ch. 15)*

**Henry "the Navigator" (1394–1460)** Portuguese prince and director of Portugal's exploration and colonization of Africa's western coast. The Portuguese quickly established trading stations in the region, laying the foundations for their overseas empire. *(Ch. 13)*

**Herodotus (ca. 485–425 B.C.)** Ancient Greek historian; with **Thucydides,** a founder of history-writing in the West. The word *history* comes from a word used by Herodotus, *historiai*, meaning "inquiries" or "research." In his history of the Persian Wars, Herodotus saw the fall of the Persian Empire as part of a perpetual cycle of the rise and fall of empires. *(Ch. 3)*

**Hildegard of Bingen (1098–1179)** German abbess who was perhaps the most profound psychological thinker of her age. More than anyone before her, Hildegard opened up for discussion the feminine aspects of divinity. She was also adept in music and biblical studies. *(Ch. 10)*

**Hitler, Adolf (1889–1945)** The German dictator who, after being legally named chancellor in 1933, militarized Germany and started World War II in 1939, leading the country to defeat in 1945. His enforcement of state-sponsored **anti-Semitism** and racial purity among German people led to the murder of millions of Jews, Gypsies, and Slavic peoples. *(Ch. 27)*

**Hobbes, Thomas (1588–1679)** English philosopher. In his treatise *Leviathan*, Hobbes asserted that people are made up of mechanistic appetites and so need a strong ruler to hold them in check. However, he also envisioned citizens as potentially equal and constrained neither by morality nor by natural obedience to authority. *(Ch. 17)*

**Homer** Greatest ancient Greek poet, credited as the author of the epics the *Iliad* and the *Odyssey*, both written during the eighth century B.C. His dramatic stories inspired, moved, and educated the Greeks. *(Ch. 2)*

**hominids** The primate family *Hominidae*, which includes humans. The modern human being, *Homo sapiens sapiens*, is the only species of this family still in existence. *(Ch. 1)*

**hoplite phalanx** Battlefield tactic of **Archaic Greece** that relied on a tightly ordered unit of heavily armed, pike-bearing infantrymen. It was the dominant military force in western Asia and the Mediterranean region until 197 B.C. *(Ch. 3)*

**Huguenots** French Protestants, followers of the teachings of **John Calvin.** Huguenots battled Catholics throughout the sixteenth and seventeenth centuries. Many emigrated to other western European countries and England's American colonies, especially after the revocation of the **Edict of Nantes.** French Protestants gained full religious freedom in the nineteenth century. *(Ch. 15)*

**humanism** Western European literary and cultural movement of the fourteenth and fifteenth centuries. Humanists emphasized the superiority of ancient Greek and Roman literature, history, and politics, and focused on learning and personal and public duty. See also **Desiderius Erasmus, Francesco Petrarch, Thomas More.** *(Ch. 12)*

**Hundred Years' War (1337–1453)** Series of conflicts between the ruling families of France and England over territory in France and the succession to the French crown. Sporadic raids and battles devastated the French countryside and checked population growth. The inspirational leadership of **Joan of Arc** contributed to France's eventual success in expelling the English from nearly all of the disputed land. *(Ch. 11)*

**hunter-gatherers** Food-collecting society in which people live by hunting, fishing, and gathering fruits and nuts, with no crops or livestock being raised for food. During the **Neolithic Revolution**, some hunter-gatherers developed agriculture. *(Ch. 1)*

**Hus, Jan (ca. 1370–1415)** Czech religious reformer who strongly attacked clerical power and privileges and advocated reform of church practice. His execution for heresy at the **Council of Constance** provoked a civil war in Prague and Bohemia. *(Ch. 11)*

**iconoclasm** Rejection of, or even the destruction of, religious images in worship. Iconoclasm was the official policy of the Byzantine Empire from 726 to 843 and played a role in the continuing estrangement of Byzantium from the West. *(Ch. 8)*

**impressionism** Late-nineteenth-century style of painting pioneered by the French artists Degas, Monet, Pissarro,

Renoir, Sisley, and Morisot. Influenced by new theories that images were transmitted to the brain as small light particles, which the brain then reconstituted, the impressionists sought to capture what things looked like before they were "distorted" by the brain. *(Ch. 23)*

**Inca**  A flourishing sixteenth-century empire administered from the mountains of Peru and extending from modern Ecuador to Chile. It was conquered for Spain by Francisco Pizarro (1470–1541), aided by a smallpox epidemic and native peoples seeking to end Inca domination. *(Ch. 13)*

***Index of Prohibited Books***  A list of books banned by the Roman Catholic Church because of moral or doctrinal error. First announced in 1559, it was only sporadically enforced and had little effect. The Index was suppressed in 1966. *(Ch. 14)*

**industrialization**  Beginning in Britain in the later eighteenth century, a system of **mass production** of goods in which specialization and mechanization made manufacturing efficient and profitable. Early industrialization enabled Britain to become the dominant world power in the nineteenth century. See also **factories.** *(Ch. 20)*

**information technology (IT)**  Term for the revolution in information availability and communications resulting from the late-twentieth-century development of personal computers and the Internet. See also **digital divide.** *(Ch. 30)*

**Interregnum (1649–1660)**  Literally "between reigns," the period in English history from the execution of Charles I to the restoration of Charles II. During these years England was a republic—a Commonwealth—ruled by **Oliver Cromwell,** who became Lord Protector in 1653. *(Ch. 16)*

**Israel**  People who settled on the eastern shore of the Mediterranean around 1200 B.C., or perhaps earlier. Their belief in one God directly influenced the faith of Christians, Muslims, and modern Jews. See also **monotheism.** *(Ch. 2)*

**Jacobins**  In revolutionary France, a political club named for a monastic order. One of the most radical of republican groups, the Jacobins purged the **Girondins,** originally fellow members of the club, from the National Convention in 1793. Leaders of the **Terror,** such as **Maximilien Robespierre,** came from their ranks. *(Ch. 19)*

**Jesus of Nazareth (ca. 4 B.C.–A.D. 30)**  Founder of **Christianity.** A forceful preacher and reformer who, to his followers, was Christ, "the anointed one" (from the Greek *Christos*), foretold in the Hebrew Bible as the redeemer of Israel who would initiate the kingdom of heaven. The dynamism and popularity of his teachings led to a clash with Jewish and Roman authorities in Jerusalem and to his crucifixion by the Romans. *(Ch. 6)*

**Joan of Arc (d. 1431)**  Charismatic French military leader during the **Hundred Years' War.** A late medieval mystic, Joan heard "voices" telling her to assist in driving the English from France. She was captured and burned as a heretic by the English. Later she was canonized as Saint Joan, patron saint of France. *(Ch. 11)*

**Julio-Claudians**  Dynasty of Roman emperors founded by **Augustus** and ruling from A.D. 14 to 68. The succession consisted of Augustus's stepson Tiberius, great-grandson Caligula, grandnephew Claudius, and great-great-grandson Nero. For elite Romans, this era was one of decadence and scandal; for ordinary people, it was a time of stability and peace. *(Ch. 6)*

**July Revolution (1830)**  Uprising in Paris in July 1830 that forced King Charles X to abdicate and signaled a victory for constitutional reform over an absolute monarchy. The liberal Louis Philippe was proclaimed "King of the French," with limited powers, by the chamber of deputies. The revolution sparked democratic uprisings in Belgium, Germany, Italy, and Russian Poland and helped persuade British peers to vote for the **Great Reform Bill.** *(Ch. 21)*

**justification by faith**  Doctrine professed by **Martin Luther** that Christians can be saved (justified) only by faith, a free gift of God, and not by penitential acts or good works. Luther's doctrine directly challenged the authority and fundamental practices of the Roman Catholic Church. *(Ch. 14)*

**Justinian (r. 527–565)**  One of the greatest of all Rome's emperors. His comprehensive collection of Roman law is the most influential legal collection in human history. He built **Hagia Sophia,** reformed the imperial administration, and fought constant wars to expand the empire. *(Ch. 7)*

**Kepler, Johannes (1571–1630)**  German astronomer. Kepler developed the three laws of planetary motion, known as Kepler's Laws, which are still accepted, and mathematically confirmed the Copernican heliocentric hypothesis. *(Ch. 17)*

**Kosovo**  Yugoslav province, viewed by Serbs as the cradle of their nationhood but populated overwhelmingly by ethnic Albanians. After Slobodan Milosevic launched a campaign of **"ethnic cleansing"** there in 1999, NATO bombing forced him to agree to allow a UN peacekeeping force to administer the province. *(Ch. 30)*

**Kriegsrohstoffabteilung (KRA)**  The "War Raw Materials Office" that coordinated Germany's World War I economy. The KRA produced synthetic substitute products and created new mixed (private and government) companies to allocate raw materials. This body served as a model for later economic planning and coordination in Germany and elsewhere. *(Ch. 25)*

**laissez faire**  French term meaning "to leave alone," it was applied to the economic doctrine put forward by **Adam Smith** in 1776. Smith advocated freeing national economies from the fetters of the state and allowing supply and demand to shape the marketplace. Laissez-faire ideas contributed to the drive to lower tariffs in the nineteenth century. See also **liberalism.** *(Ch. 21)*

**Las Casas, Bartolomé de (1474–1566)**  First bishop of Chiapas, in southern Mexico. A former *encomendero*, Las Casas passionately condemned the brutality of the Spanish conquests. In 1542 King Charles accepted Las Casas's criticisms, abolishing Indian slavery and greatly restricting the transfer of **encomiendas.** *(Ch. 13)*

**Latin**  Indo-European language of ancient Rome and its empire, from which today's Romance languages developed. *(Ch. 5)*

**laws of motion**  The natural laws of gravity, planetary motion, and inertia first laid out in the seventeenth century by **Isaac Newton.** Newton demonstrated that these laws apply to the solar system and could be used to predict the existence of an as-yet-unseen planet. *(Ch. 17)*

**lay investiture**  Control of church appointments by laymen. Emperor Henry IV (1066–1106) and Pope Gregory VII (1073–1085) disputed who should have this authority in the Christian world. The 1122 Concordat of Worms stipulated that bishops could be invested by kings only after a free church election. *(Ch. 9)*

**League of Nations (1919–1946)**  An international alliance established at the end of World War I without the membership of the United States. Though its covenant called for the peaceful settlement of disputes among member states and for sanctions against a member that went to war in violation of League provisions, it failed to prevent the escalating violence that culminated in World War II. *(Ch. 25)*

**legion**  Innovative and highly successful ancient Roman battle formation. The legion included many flexible, adaptable, and semi-independent groups that broke their enemies' order with javelins at long range, then charged with sword and shield. *(Ch. 5)*

**Lend-Lease Act (1941)**  Act by the U.S. Congress authorizing President **Franklin Roosevelt** to lend or lease weapons or other aid to countries the president designated. A major declaration of American support for the threatened British, lend-lease was later extended to several other countries. *(Ch. 28)*

**Lenin, Vladimir Ilyich (1870–1924)**  Russian revolutionary. Leader of the **Bolsheviks** since 1903, he launched the November 1917 revolution that overthrew the **provisional government**. He concluded the **Treaty of Brest-Litovsk** with Germany and began the establishment of communism in the Soviet Union. See also **New Economic Policy**. *(Ch. 25)*

**liberalism**  Nineteenth-century economic and political theory that called for reducing government powers to a minimum. Liberals worked to impose constitutional limits on government, establish the rule of law, eliminate state regulation of the economy, and ensure a voice in government for men of property and education. *(Ch. 21)*

**linear perspective**  Revolutionary technique developed by early-fifteenth-century Florentine painters for representing three-dimensional objects on a two-dimensional plane. The technique is based in part on the observation that as parallel lines recede, they appear to converge. *(Ch. 12)*

**Livia (58 B.C.–A.D. 29)**  Wife of **Augustus** and mother of Tiberius, his successor. As one of Augustus's main advisers, she intrigued to secure the succession for Tiberius and was suspected of poisoning several family members, including Augustus himself. *(Ch. 6)*

**Locarno, Treaty of (1925)**  Treaty that introduced a new, more conciliatory spirit in international affairs. France and Germany accepted the postwar border between them, and Germany was again accepted as a diplomatic equal and entered the League of Nations in 1926. *(Ch. 26)*

**Locke, John (1632–1704)**  English philosopher. In his influential *Two Treatises on Government,* Locke asserted that the state arises from a contract that individuals freely endorse. Therefore, because sovereignty resides with the people, rebellion against abuse of power is justified—a revolutionary vision of a political society based on human rights. See also **empirical reasoning**. *(Ch. 17)*

**Louis XIV (r. 1643–1715)**  Longest-reigning ruler in European history, who imposed absolute rule on France and waged several wars attempting to dominate Europe. He was known as the Sun King, and his reign marked a great flowering of French culture. *(Ch. 16)*

**Loyola, Ignatius (1491–1556)**  Spanish nobleman and founder of the Society of Jesus, or Jesuits, which has been called the vanguard of the Catholic reform movement. After papal approval of the order, the Jesuits focused primarily on educating Catholics and reconverting Protestants. *(Ch. 14)*

**Luther, Martin (1483–1546)**  German theologian and religious reformer. Luther began the Protestant Reformation in 1517 with the publication of his *Ninety-Five Theses*, which challenged indulgences and Catholic teachings on penitential acts. His translation of the Bible into German in 1522 standardized the modern German language. See also **Augsburg Confession**, **justification by faith**, **sola scriptura**. *(Ch. 14)*

**Maastricht agreement (1991)**  Agreement among twelve European Community countries at Maastricht, the Netherlands, to form the **European Union**. The member states agreed to expand cooperation on social, foreign, judicial, and security matters and adopted a timetable for a common policy on workers' rights, a common currency (the **euro**), and a common central banking structure. *(Ch. 30)*

**Maccabees**  Traditionalist Jews led by the Hasmonean family, who in 168 B.C. revolted against Hellenizing laws and influences. Their success is celebrated today during the Jewish holiday of Hanukkah. *(Ch. 4)*

**Macedon**  Weaker, less culturally advanced state on Greece's northern border. It was unified and led to power by **Philip II** and **Alexander the Great**, who became rulers of Greece. *(Ch. 4)*

**Machiavelli, Niccolò (1469–1527)**  Florentine politician and political theorist. His most famous work, *The Prince*, describes the methods a prince can use to acquire and maintain power. Often misunderstood as a defender of despotism, Machiavelli emphasized that a successful ruler needed to anticipate and consider the consequences of his actions. *(Ch. 12)*

**Magellan, Ferdinand (1480?–1521)**  Portuguese-born Spanish explorer who led the first expedition to sail around the world. After finding the South American passage to the Pacific Ocean, he sailed to the Philippines, where he was killed by natives. Survivors on one of his ships completed the circumnavigation. *(Ch. 13)*

**Maginot Line**  A 200-mile system of elaborate permanent fortifications on France's eastern border, named for war minister André Maginot, and built primarily during the 1930s. It was a defense against German frontal assault; in 1940 the Germans invaded by flanking the line. *(Ch. 26)*

**Magna Carta (1215)**  Momentous document that England's barons forced King John to sign. It required the king to respect the rights of feudal lords, not abuse his judicial powers, and consult the barons—in essence, it put the king under the law, not above it. *(Ch. 9)*

**manifest destiny**  Term coined in 1845 for the belief that the expanding United States was destined to occupy the North American continent from coast to coast. The rhetoric of manifest destiny was invoked to justify war with Mexico in 1846 and the acquisition of California and the southwest from Mexico in 1848. *(Ch. 22)*

**manor**  In western Europe, a type of estate that developed under the Carolingians. One-quarter to one-half of the land was set aside as a reserve (or demesne), to be worked on behalf of the landlord; the remainder was divided into tenancies worked by individual peasants for their own support. *(Ch. 8)*

**Maria Theresa (r. 1740–1780)**  Habsburg archduchess of Austria and queen of Hungary and Bohemia. After successfully defending her right to the Austrian throne against attacks by **Frederick the Great** and others, she reformed and centralized the administration of her Austrian and Bohemian lands. *(Ch. 18)*

**Marxism**  Political and economic theories of the two German philosophers and revolutionaries, Karl Marx (1818–1883) and Friedrich Engels (1820–1895), which they called scientific **socialism** and which gave birth to modern communism. Marxism argued that the oppressed working class should and inevitably would rebel against the capitalist owners and build a communist society. *(Ch. 21)*

**mass production**  System in which great numbers of people work in centralized, mechanized **factories** to produce large quantities of goods; an essential feature of **industrialization**. A series of eighteenth-century inventions, culminating in the **steam engine**, enabled Britain to mass-produce textiles and benefit from the resulting increases in productivity. *(Ch. 20)*

**Matteotti murder**  The 1924 killing by fascist thugs of Italian moderate socialist Giacomo Matteotti after he denounced the fascist violence accompanying national elections. The public outcry following the murder eventually led **Mussolini** to commit to a more radical direction, which included the creation of a new fascist state. *(Ch. 26)*

**mechanistic world-view**  Seventeenth-century philosophical view that saw the world as a machine that functions in strict obedience to physical laws, without purpose or will. Experience and reason were regarded as the standards of truth. *(Ch. 17)*

**Mehmed II (r. 1451–1481)**  Ottoman sultan who completed the conquest of the Byzantine Empire by capturing Constantinople in 1453. Mehmed established Constantinople as the Ottoman capital and repopulated the city with a mix of Greek, Armenian, Jewish, and Muslim communities. *(Ch. 11)*

**mercantilism**  Economic policy pursued by western European states in the seventeenth and eighteenth centuries, stressing self-sufficiency in manufactured goods, tight government control of trade to foster the domestic economy, protectionist policies, and the absolute value of bullion. *(Ch. 16)*

**Minoans**  Society that flourished between 2000 and 1375 B.C. on the Aegean island of Crete, where Greece's first civilization appeared. Their sophisticated culture and economy were administered from their magnificent palaces. See also **Mycenaeans.** *(Ch. 2)*

**mir**  Russian peasant commune. After Tsar Alexander II freed the serfs in 1861, the mir determined land use and paid the government mortgages and taxes. Peasants could leave the land only with the mir's permission. *(Ch. 22)*

**monasticism**  Ascetic way of life. Christian monasticism was founded by an Egyptian layman, Anthony (d. 356), who renounced all worldliness and pursued a life of prayer in the desert. A more communal form of monasticism was created by Pachomius (290–346), who wrote the first monastic Rule—a code for daily living in a monastic community. Monasticism quickly spread throughout the Christian world. *(Ch. 7)*

**monophysitism**  Fifth-century theological doctrine emphasizing the divine nature of **Jesus of Nazareth.** The Council of Chalcedon condemned monophysitism and pronounced that Christ had two authentic natures—he was true God and true man. *(Ch. 7)*

**monotheism**  Belief that there is only one God. The Hebrew Bible places this belief as originating about 2000–1500 B.C., when God commanded Abraham to give up Mesopotamian polytheism for belief in one God. *(Ch. 2)*

**More, Thomas (1478–1535)**  Chancellor of England under Henry VIII. More's best-known work, *Utopia*, was highly critical of contemporary European kingdoms. It describes a fictional land of peace and harmony that has outlawed private property and all forms of wealth. More was executed when he refused to take an oath to support the **Act of Supremacy.** See also **humanism.** *(Ch. 12)*

**Muhammad (570–632)**  Prophet and founder of Islam. In 610 he began to receive revelations commanding him to teach all people a new faith that called for an unquestioned belief in one god, Allah, and a deep commitment to social justice for believers. Before his death, he had converted most of Arabia. See also **Five Pillars of Islam, Quran.** *(Ch. 8)*

**Mussolini, Benito (1883–1945)**  Italian fascist dictator. Mussolini founded the fascist movement in 1919 and took power in 1922. He replaced Italy's parliamentary democracy with a **corporative state** and pursued an expansionist foreign policy. He concluded the Pact of Steel with **Adolf Hitler** in 1939 and took Italy into World War II in 1940. Deposed in 1943, he was killed by partisans in 1945. *(Ch. 26)*

**Mycenaeans**  Militaristic people from the Greek mainland who conquered the **Minoans** around 1550–1375 B.C. Mycenaean civilization was a center of Bronze Age culture until its destruction around 1100 B.C. *(Ch. 2)*

**mystery religions**  Popular Hellenistic cults featuring the initiation of worshipers into secret doctrines. Mystery religions replaced the traditional Greek religion of the Olympian gods. Some ancient Egyptian cults were recast as mystery religions, influencing early Christianity. *(Ch. 4)*

**Napoleon Bonaparte (1769–1821)**  Emperor of the French (r. 1804–1815). A French general who took part in a coup in 1799 against the **Directory**, Napoleon consolidated power as first consul and proclaimed himself emperor with the approval of a national plebiscite in 1804. His military conquests exported French revolutionary reforms to the rest of Europe. He was finally defeated and exiled in 1815. *(Ch. 19)*

**National Assembly (1789–1791)**  Legislative body formed in France in 1789 after the Third Estate insisted on being certified as members of the Estates General as a whole. The National Assembly drafted the **Declaration of the Rights of Man and the Citizen** and a constitution that called for a constitutional (not absolute) monarchy. *(Ch. 19)*

**National Socialist (Nazi) Party**  The political party that grew from the movement that German dictator **Adolf Hitler** made his vehicle to power. Originating from the radical right in Munich in 1919, the Nazi Party won voting support during the early 1930s, paving the way for Hitler to be named German chancellor in 1933. *(Ch. 27)*

**nationalism**  Belief arising in the eighteenth century that people derive their identity from their nation and owe it their primary loyalty. The criteria for nationhood typically included a common language, religion, and political authority, as well as common traditions and shared historical experiences. Nationalism was a major force in most of the revolutions of 1848 and in the subsequent unification of Italy and of Germany. *(Ch. 20)*

**Nazi-Soviet Pact (1939)**  Surprise agreement between the Soviet Union and Nazi Germany in August 1939 that each would remain neutral if either got into a war with some other nation. The pact freed Germany to attack Poland a few days later without fear of Soviet reprisal. *(Ch. 27)*

**Neo-Babylonians**  Rulers of western Asia between 612 and 539 B.C. who elaborately rebuilt Babylon, creating the famous Hanging Gardens. They destroyed Jerusalem, deporting many Judeans in what is known as the Babylonian Captivity. *(Ch. 2)*

**Neolithic Revolution**  Human discovery and spread of agriculture, between about 13,000 and 5000 B.C. People first domesticated dogs and other animals and then learned how to cultivate crops. *(Ch. 1)*

**New Economic Policy (NEP) (1921–1928)** A Russian economic liberalization measure aimed at reviving an economy in crisis. The NEP restored considerable scope for private enterprise and allowed peasants to sell some of their harvest. After initial economic success, it was eventually considered a threat to the socialist state and was replaced by state-controlled central planning. *(Ch. 26)*

**new imperialism** Era of European overseas expansion launched in the 1880s. In the following decades, Europeans subjugated 500 million people in Africa and Asia—one half of the world's non-European population. *(Ch. 24)*

**Newton, Isaac (1643–1727)** English physicist, mathematician, and natural philosopher. Newton's mathematical computation of the laws of gravity and planetary motion, which he combined with a fully developed theory of inertia, completed the explanation for motion initiated by **Nicholas Copernicus.** See also **laws of motion.** *(Ch. 17)*

**nongovernmental organizations (NGOs)** A network of organizations unaffiliated with governments but central to the international community, such as the Red Cross, Amnesty International, and Doctors Without Borders, that had gradually emerged by the early twenty-first century to deal with humanitarian relief and human rights issues. *(Ch. 30)*

**North Atlantic Treaty Organization (NATO)** An alliance for regional defense, created in 1949 by the United States, Canada, and western European nations, whose members agree to defend one another from attack by nonmember countries. Its original aim was to contain the Soviet Union. *(Ch. 29)*

**Nuremberg trials** The war crimes trials conducted in Nuremberg, Germany. Most of the twenty-four defendants were convicted of war crimes and "crimes against humanity." *(Ch. 28)*

***On the Donation of Constantine*** Work by Lorenzo Valla (1407–1457) proving that the *Donation of Constantine* was not written at the time of the emperor Constantine. The forged *Donation* purported to record Constantine's transfer to the pope of jurisdiction over Rome and the western half of the empire. Valla's work undermined the papacy's claim to political rule in central Italy. *(Ch. 12)*

**Orthodoxy** The Catholic Christian faith of Byzantium. It differed from Roman Catholicism by its use of Greek instead of Latin, the inclusion of icons in worship, an adherence to the Greek church fathers, some differences in basic theology, and many differences in customs and practices. *(Ch. 8)*

**papacy** Name for the institution ruled by the bishop of Rome who, in Roman Catholic tradition, is the successor to Peter, the most prominent apostle. Since Peter was believed to be the leader of the original followers of Christ, his successors, the popes (from *papa* by the fourth century), were believed to be the leaders of the whole church. *(Ch. 7)*

**papal monarchy** Period during the twelfth and thirteenth centuries when the power of the Catholic Church was increasingly expanded and centralized in the hands of the popes, as papal policy focused on recovering lost lands and rights in central Italy. *(Ch. 9)*

**Papal States** Beginning in the eighth century, territories held by the popes in central Italy under the protection of the Frankish kings. *(Ch. 8)*

**papyrus** Paperlike writing material used by the ancient Egyptians, Greeks, and Romans. Made primarily in Egypt from the papyrus plant, it was durable, flexible, and easy to write on. *(Ch. 1)*

**Paris Commune (1871)** Parisian workers' uprising intended to establish a workers' government under home rule. Stemming from labor discontent and the radicalization of workers during the siege of Paris in the Franco-Prussian War, the commune was suppressed by the army of the conservative French government. *(Ch. 22)*

**Parliament** English legislative institution whose ancestors were the royal courts that met in 1265 and 1295. The king considered the courts a device to win support for royal agendas; the barons viewed them as opportunities to play a real policymaking role in government. *(Ch. 9)*

**paterfamilias** Oldest living male in an ancient Roman family, who had supreme legal power within the household. Only the paterfamilias could own property free and clear. *(Ch. 5)*

**Paul of Tarsus (d. ca. 67)** Christian apostle and saint. A Jew from Anatolia and a Roman citizen, Paul first persecuted the Christians but became a believer around A.D. 36. Paul taught that the life and resurrection of **Jesus of Nazareth** offered all humanity the hope of salvation through faith. Under Paul, **Christianity** began its complete separation from Judaism. *(Ch. 6)*

**pax Romana** Latin for "Roman peace," the term refers to the period of peace and prosperity in the Roman Empire from A.D. 69 to 180. During this time the emperors emphasized extending citizenship and spreading prosperity throughout the provinces, and Italy was no longer the tyrant of the Mediterranean. See also **Flavians.** *(Ch. 6)*

**Peace of Westphalia (1648)** Treaty that ended the **Thirty Years' War.** The principalities within the Holy Roman Empire were recognized as virtually autonomous, severely weakening the power of the emperor. Calvinism joined Catholicism and Lutheranism as tolerated faiths within the empire, and the treaty closed the age of religious wars. *(Ch. 15)*

**Pericles** Leader of fifth-century-B.C. Athens when **demokratia** became entrenched as the government and way of life. Distinguished for his oratory and honesty, he established Athens as a great center of art and literature as well as a great empire. *(Ch. 3)*

**Persian Empire** Vast, prosperous, and law-abiding West Asian empire, from about 550 B.C. to its conquest by **Alexander the Great** around 330 B.C. The relatively tolerant rule of the Persian emperors represented the greatest success yet of a universal kingship. The Persians also built the first great navy. *(Ch. 2)*

**Peter the Great (r. 1682–1725)** Russian tsar. Brilliant, energetic, and tyrannical, Peter revolutionized Russian society by his determined efforts to westernize his nation culturally, economically, and politically. He modernized the army and navy, secured seaports, and made Russia into a great power. See also **Great Northern War.** *(Ch. 16)*

**Petrarch, Francesco (1304–1374)** Influential Italian poet, biographer, and humanist during the Renaissance. Petrarch advocated imitating the actions, values, and culture of the ancient Romans to reform the excesses of the present world. *(Ch. 12)*

**Petrograd Soviet** The *soviet* (council) of leaders of strike committees and army regiments elected in March 1917, when Petrograd's workers protested in response to severe wartime food and coal shortages. Central to the Bolshevik Revolution of 1917, the soviet eventually became the ruling power in the Russian capital—but only temporarily. *(Ch. 25)*

**pharaoh**  Ancient Egyptians' title for their king, an absolute, all-powerful, and all-providing ruler. It was believed that the ruler represented the ancestors and guaranteed the fertility of the soil. *(Ch. 1)*

**Philip II (382–336 B.C.)**  King of **Macedon.** A brilliant soldier and statesman, Philip conquered the Greek world. He developed a well-trained, professional year-round army and mastered the technology of siegecraft. He was succeeded by his son, **Alexander the Great.** *(Ch. 4)*

**Philip II (r. 1556–1598)**  King of Spain, son of **Charles V.** An avid Roman Catholic, he ruled Spain at the height of its influence. Philip dispatched the ill-fated **Armada** to invade England and attempted to quash the revolt of the Netherlands. *(Ch. 15)*

**philosophes**  Influential group of eighteenth-century French intellectuals, including **Voltaire** and Diderot, who argued that people have natural rights and that governments exist to guarantee and protect those rights. While not advocating violent revolution, they severely criticized the regime's abuses of power. *(Ch. 18)*

**Phoenicians**  Canaanites whose civilization flourished about 1000–750 B.C. in present-day coastal Syria, where they established major trading ports. Master sailors, they planted colonies around the Mediterranean, many of which, including Carthage, became independent states. The Phoenicians exported the civilization of western Asia—including the Phoenician alphabet, derived from **Ugarit**—to the Mediterranean world. *(Ch. 2)*

**plantation system**  Agricultural practices developed by the fifteenth-century Portuguese to produce sugar on their island colonies in the Atlantic using involuntarily transported slaves from Africa. Portugal's prototype—wealthy absentee landlords and masses of forced labor producing cash crops on vast tracts of land—was the model for the New World plantation system. In seventeenth- and eighteenth-century French and English colonies in the Caribbean, large sugar plantations owned by wealthy, often absentee, landlords replaced smaller-scale independent farming. *(Chs. 13, 16)*

**Plato (427–348 B.C.)**  Ancient Greek philosopher, student of **Socrates.** One of Western philosophy's greatest exponents of idealism, Plato believed that the senses are misleading and that truth can therefore be attained only by training the mind to overcome commonsense evidence. In the *Republic,* Plato describes an ideal state in which philosophers rule as kings, benevolently and unselfishly. *(Ch. 3)*

**polis**  Term for an ancient Greek city-state, a system that reached its height around 700–300 B.C. The ideological and political organization of the polis emphasized equality and a shared community life for all citizens, not just the elite. *(Ch. 3)*

**popular front**  A term for antifascist electoral alliances and governing coalitions that communists promoted from 1934 until 1939 to resist the further spread of fascism. Popular front coalitions won control of government in both Spain and France during 1936. *(Ch. 27)*

**positivism**  Philosophy of the French thinker Auguste Comte (1798–1857). Comte asserted that human history progressed through distinct and irreversible stages, leading inexorably upward to the final and highest stage of development, the positive—or scientific—stage. Positivism and its optimistic outlook for human progress were influential in both Europe and Latin America during the nineteenth century. *(Ch. 23)*

**Potsdam conference**  A July–August 1945 meeting held at Potsdam, Germany, between the USSR, the United States, and Great Britain to implement their earlier agreements concerning the treatment of defeated Germany. Many of the agreements reached were later abandoned amid growing hostility between the USSR and the Western democracies. *(Ch. 28)*

**Prague Spring**  The attempt by Czechoslovakian reformers in 1968 to gain freer cultural expression, democratization of Communist Party procedures, and broader participation in public life within the framework of a communist state. The forcible suppression of the movement by Soviet leaders seemed to signal the end of any hope for flexibility and openness within the Soviet sphere. *(Ch. 29)*

**price revolution**  Steady rise in prices in the sixteenth and seventeenth centuries, resulting from population growth and the influx of precious metals from Spain's New World territories. As wages lost one-tenth to one-fourth of their value, people sought new work, protested against taxes, and attacked scapegoats. The price revolution concentrated wealth in fewer hands and contributed to the rise of a new **gentry** class. *(Ch. 15)*

**Principate**  The constitutional monarchy of the Early Roman Empire, from 31 B.C. to A.D. 192. The term comes from *Princeps,* or "first citizen," an old title of respect used in the **senate.** See also **Augustus, Flavians.** *(Ch. 6)*

**professionalization**  Establishment in the nineteenth century of common standards and requirements, especially in medicine, law, architecture, and engineering. Professionalization brought either government or self-regulation to vocations whose prestige rested on the claim of exclusive expertise in their fields. *(Ch. 23)*

**proletariat**  Term used by Karl Marx to describe the new class of industrial workers who owned none of the means of production and were totally dependent on factory owners for their livelihoods. In Marxist thought, capitalists were destined to be overthrown by the proletariat. See also **Marxism.** *(Ch. 20)*

**provisional government**  The body that ruled Russia from March to November 1917, in the wake of the revolution that overthrew the tsarist regime. Originally intended to be a temporary step to an elected constituent assembly, its policies caused discontents that the **Bolsheviks** were quick to exploit. *(Ch. 25)*

**Ptolemies**  Dynasty of Egyptian kings who ruled from 304 to 30 B.C., founded by Ptolemy I, a Macedonian general of **Alexander the Great.** It was the wealthiest, most sophisticated, and longest lasting of the Hellenistic kingdoms. See also **Alexandria.** *(Ch. 4)*

**Punic Wars (264–146 B.C.)**  Three wars during which the Roman Empire eventually destroyed Carthage. The Romans later adopted the Carthaginians' plantation system using massive numbers of slaves. *(Ch. 5)*

**Puritans**  Radical Protestants in late-sixteenth- and seventeenth-century England. Puritans emphasized Bible reading, preaching, private scrutiny of conscience, and de-emphasized institutional ritual and clerical authority. Puritans became a majority in Parliament during the reign of Charles I and led the campaign against the king during the English Civil War. *(Ch. 15)*

**putting-out system**  The production in country homes of thread and cloth by spinners and weavers for an entrepreneur who bought raw materials and "put them out" to be finished by individual workers. This cottage industry system expanded in eighteenth-century Europe as increased numbers of agricultural laborers needed more nonfarm work in off-seasons. *(Ch. 18)*

**Quran** Islamic sacred writings, which **Muhammad** communicated in the form of "recitations," insisting that he was transmitting a direct revelation from Allah. After Muhammad's death, his followers arranged the recitations into 114 *Suras*, or chapters, containing legal and wisdom literature and moral teaching. *(Ch. 8)*

**rabbinic Judaism** Main form of Judaism, which emerged during the first century A.D. under the leadership of the rabbis, the spiritual descendants of the Pharisees. Rabbinic Judaism amplified and interpreted the Hebrew Bible to clarify Jewish practice, elevated the oral law to equal authority with the written **Torah**, and enabled Judaism to evolve flexibly. *(Ch. 6)*

**Realpolitik** Style of governing that uses all means, including war, to expand the influence and power of a state. The best-known practitioner of Realpolitik was Prussian chancellor **Otto von Bismarck.** *(Ch. 22)*

**Reconquista** Wars of reconquest in the Iberian Peninsula from the eleventh to fifteenth centuries. Spanish and Portuguese rulers seized territories from the weakening Muslim regime. By awarding reconquered lands to their nobles, Christian kings enhanced their own status and power. *(Ch. 9)*

**remilitarization of the Rhineland** The reoccupation of Germany's Rhineland territory by German troops in March 1936, in clear violation of the **Treaty of Versailles.** When the French and British did not resist the German move, **Adolf Hitler** was emboldened to additional acts of aggression elsewhere. *(Ch. 27)*

*res publica* Romans' concept of their republic, which uniquely influenced Western political institutions. *Res publica* is Latin for "public thing," as opposed to *res privata*, "private thing," as the Romans characterized monarchy. *(Ch. 5)*

**revisionism** Late-nineteenth-century argument that **socialism** could and should come about by gradual, democratic means. This idea was a "revision" of Marx's contention that socialism would require a violent revolution. Most European socialists claimed to reject revisionism while at the same time pursuing revisionist policies. *(Ch. 24)*

**risorgimento** Italian term, beginning in the late eighteenth century, for the political and cultural renewal of Italy. It later came to describe the political and military events that led to the unification of Italy in 1861. *(Ch. 22)*

**Robespierre, Maximilien (1758–1794)** French lawyer and revolutionary leader. A **Jacobin** who joined the Committee of Public Safety in 1793, Robespierre called for the **Terror** to suppress internal dissent. *(Ch. 19)*

**Romanesque** Meaning "in the Roman style," this nineteenth-century term characterized the transitional architecture and painting of the period between the waning of Carolingian art and the full emergence of **Gothic** art in the twelfth century. Distinctive features of Romanesque churches are their exuberant decoration and ornament. *(Ch. 10)*

**romanticism** Artistic movement, prevalent from the 1760s to 1840s, that rebelled against rationalism. Writers, painters, and composers rejected the Enlightenment and its rationalist values, instead praising emotion and sensitivity, and worshiping nature for its inherent beauty. *(Ch. 20)*

**Rome-Berlin Axis** Alliance between Hitler's Nazi Germany and Mussolini's fascist Italy. Beginning as an informal understanding by 1936, it was cemented by an anti-Comintern agreement and eventually by an open-ended military alliance, the Pact of Steel, in 1939. *(Ch. 27)*

**Roosevelt, Franklin Delano (1882–1945)** U.S. president who served from 1933 to 1945, through the Great Depression of the 1930s and World War II. His New Deal program, including large public works projects, was an innovative response to the Depression. *(Ch. 28)*

**Rousseau, Jean-Jacques (1712–1778)** French writer and philosopher. In his 1762 work, *The Social Contract*, Rousseau depicted a hypothetical state with direct democracy in which citizens have inalienable rights to wide-ranging liberties. He was influential as a critic of an elite society still dominated by status, patronage, and privilege. *(Ch. 18)*

**salons** Regular gatherings in eighteenth-century Parisian private homes, where **Voltaire** and other **philosophes** read and discussed their works in progress, with the exchange of ideas facilitated by female *salonnières* (salon leaders). Anyone with appropriate manners could participate as an equal, enabling conversation to shift from maintaining the status quo to questioning it. *(Ch. 18)*

**sans-culottes** Ordinary citizens of revolutionary Paris, whose derisive nickname referred to their inability to afford fashionable knee pants ("culottes"). Because of their effective political organization, they were able to influence the direction of the French Revolution through pressure on the government as well as direct action, such as to overthrow the monarchy in August 1792. *(Ch. 19)*

**Sappho (fl. ca. 625 B.C.)** Ancient Greek poet from the island of Lesbos. Sappho wrote odes, wedding songs, and hymns expressing intimate feelings, including love for other women. She wrote of female sexuality in a male-dominated culture. *(Ch. 3)*

**second industrial revolution** Interrelated economic changes that resulted in a significant speedup in production in western Europe after 1850. Key factors were the introduction of new products, new methods of manufacture, and new materials such as mass-produced steel, synthetic dyes, and aluminum. *(Ch. 23)*

**Second International** International socialist organization founded in 1889 that met yearly to debate issues of broad concern. Beginning in 1907, it called for workers to strike and to refuse military service in case of international conflict. *(Ch. 24)*

**Second Reform Bill (1867)** British legislation that extended suffrage by lowering property qualifications and set equal population requirements for all parliamentary districts. The legislation bolstered the existing system, as the newly enfranchised clerks, artisans, and other skilled workers felt more a part of society. *(Ch. 22)*

**Seleucids** Dynasty of rulers of Asia Minor from 312 to 64 B.C. Founded by Seleucus (ca. 358–281 B.C.), a general of **Alexander the Great**, the kingdom spread **Hellenism** by establishing seventy colonies throughout the Near East. *(Ch. 4)*

**senate** In the ancient Roman Republic and Empire, the powerful council of elders that advised the monarchs (Latin: *senatus*, from *senex*, "old man"). Romans spoke of the senate's *auctoritas*, a quasi-religious prestige. *(Ch. 5)*

**separate spheres** Notion, especially prevalent in the mid-nineteenth century, of two distinct sets of roles—one male and public, the other female and private. While the man was out in the world advancing his career, the bourgeois woman was to run her home, providing her family with an orderly, comfortable shelter. *(Ch. 23)*

**show trials**  Trials staged for ideological and propaganda reasons in the USSR. In the most famous, orchestrated by **Joseph Stalin** from 1936 to 1938, major communist figures were made to confess to trumped-up charges and executed. These trials helped persuade Soviet citizens that a high-level conspiracy was responsible for the USSR's economic woes. *(Ch. 27)*

**Sistine Chapel**  Chapel at the Vatican Palace commissioned by Pope Sixtus IV in 1475, best known for Michelangelo's magnificent paintings of the Creation and Last Judgment. The monument vividly captures the cultural, religious, and ideological program of the papacy. *(Ch. 12)*

**Smith, Adam (1723–1790)**  Scottish economist who developed the doctrine of **laissez faire.** In his treatise *The Wealth of Nations* (1776), Smith argued that an economy regulates itself better without interference by government and without monopolies and other economic privileges. Smith suggested that people's economic activities are often "led by an invisible hand" to benefit society as a whole. *(Ch. 18)*

**social Catholics**  Catholics in western Europe who believed that society bore responsibility for the well-being of the poor. They were following the ideas set out in 1891 by Pope Leo XIII (r. 1878–1903) in his encyclical *Rerum novarum* ("Of New Things"). *(Ch. 23)*

**Social Darwinism**  Theory of social evolution first articulated by Herbert Spencer (1820–1902). According to Social Darwinists, human societies evolve in the same way as plants and animals, and the weak, poor, and improvident are not worthy of survival. Social Darwinism was used to justify callousness toward the poor at home and imperialist conquest abroad. See also **Darwinism.** *(Ch. 23)*

**social market economy**  The late-twentieth-century socially-oriented model of capitalism practiced in continental western Europe, providing a substantial safety net in health care and a commitment to public services such as transportation and day care. It competed with the U.S. model, shared by Britain, which emphasized free enterprise. *(Ch. 30)*

**socialism**  Nineteenth-century economic and social doctrine and political movement that opposed private ownership and control of the means of production. Socialists believed that the "social" or state ownership of property, unlike private ownership, would benefit society as a whole, creating a more just system. *(Ch. 21)*

**Society of Revolutionary Republican Women**  In revolutionary France, a powerful political club that represented the interests of female **sans-culottes.** The society was included in a general ban on political participation by women that the Committee of Public Safety instituted in October 1793. *(Ch. 19)*

**Socrates (469–399 B.C.)**  Ancient Greek philosopher, a founder of the Western philosophical tradition. Socrates changed the emphasis of philosophy from the natural world to human ethics. He believed that no one who truly understood goodness would ever choose to do evil. Accused of being an atheist and corrupting the young, Socrates was executed in 399. Socrates' teachings were recorded and transmitted by his students, including **Plato.** *(Ch. 3)*

**sola scriptura**  Doctrine put forward by **Martin Luther** in *On the Babylonian Captivity of the Church* (1520) that church authority had to be based on biblical teachings. In particular he argued that the sacraments of the Catholic Church—other than baptism and communion—were not found in the Bible. *(Ch. 14)*

**solidarism**  Late-nineteenth-century policy of conservative and liberal parties to blunt the appeal of socialism. Solidarism emphasized the mutual responsibility of classes and individuals for one another's well-being and led to the passage of laws and benefits to improve the lot of the working class. *(Ch. 23)*

**Solidarity**  A trade union formed from a movement of shipyard workers in communist Poland in 1980. It became the nucleus of widespread demands for change—including independent labor organizations, the right to strike, and freedom of expression. Though forced underground in 1981, the movement eventually proved crucial to the downfall of the communist regime in Poland. *(Ch. 29)*

**Solon (ca. 630–560 B.C.)**  Statesman of early Athens. Appointed to a one-year term as sole archon in 594 B.C., Solon transformed Greek society through mediation, moderation, respect for law, and measures that liberated the poor and downtrodden. His economic reforms sparked a commercial boom. *(Ch. 3)*

**Spanish Inquisition**  Church court that began in 1478 when King Ferdinand and Queen Isabella obtained papal approval to control the grand inquisitor. The Spanish Inquisition investigated and condemned many former Jews and Muslims who were believed to have insincerely converted to Christianity. It became an important and lucrative instrument to expand state power. *(Ch. 11)*

**SS (*Schutzstaffel*)**  Nazi elite troops, led by Heinrich Himmler. Linked to the Gestapo, the secret political police, the SS specialized in institutionalized terror tactics and were responsible for some of the worst atrocities of the Nazi regime. *(Ch. 27)*

**"stab in the back" myth**  The notion, widely held among Germans after their unexpected loss in World War I, that political intrigue and revolution at home had sabotaged the German military effort. It helped alienate Germans from their new democratic government. *(Ch. 25)*

**Stalin, Joseph (1879–1953)**  Soviet dictator. Secretary of the Communist Party since 1922, Stalin outmaneuvered his rivals after the death of Lenin to take control of the Soviet government by 1929. Stalin jettisoned the **New Economic Policy** and instituted a program of crash industrialization and agricultural **collectivization.** He concluded the **Nazi-Soviet Pact** in 1939 but joined the Allies after the German invasion of the Soviet Union in 1941. Victorious in World War II, Stalin sponsored the takeover of governments in eastern Europe by communist regimes, contributing to the development of the **cold war.** See also **"the Great Patriotic War," gulag, Potsdam conference, show trials, Yalta conference.** *(Ch. 26)*

**Stalingrad (1942–1943)**  Decisive World War II battle. The Soviet Union, at immense cost in lives, launched repeated counterattacks on Germany's Sixth Army, stopping it from advancing farther and finally forcing it to surrender. The battle is often considered the turning point of World War II in Europe. *(Ch. 28)*

**steam engine**  Machine invented in England in its modern form by James Watt in 1777. The steam engine provided mechanized power for manufacturing and made **factories** and **mass production** possible. *(Ch. 20)*

**Stoics**  Believers in a philosophical system begun in Athens by Zeno (335–263 B.C.). Stoicism emphasized the pursuit of wisdom, the reliability of sensory experience, and freedom from all passion. Stoics focused on intentions as well as the results of actions. *(Ch. 4)*

**Streseman, Gustav (1878–1929)** German statesman of the Weimar Republic. Leader of the conservative German People's Party, Streseman served briefly as chancellor in 1923, then as foreign secretary from 1923 to 1929. He secured a reduction of Germany's reparations payments and negotiated the **Treaty of Locarno,** paving the way for Germany's entry to the League of Nations in 1926. His death in 1929 was a blow to hopes for the development of democracy in Germany and peace in Europe. *(Ch. 26)*

**Suez crisis (1956)** Crisis prompted by Egypt's nationalization of the British-owned Suez Canal. The effort of Britain, France, and Israel to seize the canal prompted a strong negative reaction in world opinion, forcing them to withdraw. The episode demonstrated the newly limited reach of the western European powers in world affairs. *(Ch. 29)*

**suffragists** Activists who, beginning in the late nineteenth century, organized to win the vote for women. Adopting increasingly violent tactics, English suffragists (often referred to by contemporaries as "suffragettes") endured attacks by male thugs, were arrested, engaged in hunger strikes, and were force-fed. *(Ch. 24)*

**Sumerians** Dominant inhabitants of Mesopotamia in the third millennium B.C. They established the world's first civilization, thirty flourishing city-states with a common culture, commerce, and tendency to make war on one another. *(Ch. 1)*

**summa** An encyclopedic compendium of carefully arrayed knowledge on a particular subject. Examples are the two most famous works of **Thomas Aquinas,** the *Summa Contra Gentiles* and the *Summa Theologiae. (Ch. 10)*

**surrealism** A movement in literature and the visual arts that emerged in Paris in the early 1920s. Though indebted to dada and its mocking defiance of convention, surrealism sought to find something positive by exploring the realm of the subconscious, partly by following some of **Sigmund Freud**'s insights about access to the subconscious. *(Ch. 26)*

**Tacitus, Cornelius (ca. A.D. 55–120)** Roman historian of the "Silver Age." Tacitus lauded the simple virtues of the German tribes and expressed nostalgia for the Republic. His greatest works were *The Histories,* on the civil wars of A.D. 69, and *The Annals,* chronicling the emperors from Tiberius through Nero. *(Ch. 6)*

**Tanzimat** Turkish term, meaning "restructuring," for the reform movements in the Ottoman Empire beginning in 1839. Reforms included security of property, equity in taxation, and equality before the law regardless of religion. Government officials were given fixed salaries and subjected to regular inspections. *(Ch. 22)*

**Tennis Court Oath (1789)** Pledge signed by all but one Third Estate deputy of the Estates General of France on June 20, 1789. The deputies swore to continue to meet until a constitution was drafted. *(Ch. 19)*

**Terror (1793–1794)** Systematic repression of internal enemies undertaken by revolutionary tribunals across France at the urging of **Maximilien Robespierre.** Approximately fourteen thousand people were executed, including aristocrats, **Girondins,** and **sans-culottes.** The Terror ended with the arrest and execution of Robespierre in July 1794. *(Ch. 19)*

**tetrarchy** Government ruled by four leaders. Emperor Diocletian established a tetrarchy in about 293 to address the Roman Empire's political instability, huge size, and complexity, as well as to promote experienced men and provide an orderly imperial succession. *(Ch. 7)*

**third-century crisis** Period from A.D. 235 to 284, when the Roman Empire suffered barbarian invasions, domestic economic problems, plague, assassinations, and urban decline. Attempting to fend off invasions at opposite fronts, the emperors devalued the currency, leading to massive inflation. *(Ch. 6)*

**Third Estate** In France, the common people, as distinct from the nobles (First Estate) and clergy (Second Estate). In the Estates General in 1789, it was presumed that the votes of the First and Second Estates would overrule those of the Third Estate, although the commoners vastly outnumbered the nobles and clergy. *(Ch. 19)*

**Thirty Years' War (1618–1648)** Destructive war, involving most European countries but fought in Germany, resulting from sixteenth-century religious tensions, regionalism versus centralizing forces, and dynastic and strategic rivalries between rulers. See also **Peace of Westphalia.** *(Ch. 15)*

**Thucydides (ca. 455–397 B.C.)** Ancient Greek historian; with **Herodotus,** a founder of history-writing in the West. A failed Athenian general, Thucydides made a careful study of the Peloponnesian War and prided himself on the accuracy of his account of the prolonged conflict. *(Ch. 3)*

**Torah** First five books of the Bible. Accepted as sacred by the Hebrews around 425 B.C., it relates the working out of God's pact, or **covenant**, with the Hebrews, his chosen people. *(Ch. 2)*

**total war** The concept, first associated with World War I, that war requires the mobilization of all a nation's resources and energies. The unexpected need to wage total war during World War I accelerated social and economic processes, from technological development to women's suffrage. *(Ch. 25)*

**Toussaint-Louverture, François (1743–1803)** Former slave who governed the island of Saint Domingue (Haiti) as an independent state after the slave revolt of 1791. In 1802 French forces captured Toussaint-Louverture, who died in prison. *(Ch. 19)*

**trading-post empire** Commercial system developed by Portugal in the sixteenth century to dominate trade in the Indian Ocean through fortified, strategically placed naval bases. All merchants were expected to acquire export licenses and ship products through Portuguese ports. *(Ch. 13)*

**tragedy** Serious play with an unhappy ending. Greek tragedy emerged and reached its height in the fifth century B.C. in the works of Aeschylus, Sophocles, and Euripides. The essence of Greek tragedy is the nobility in the spectacle of a great man or woman failing because of a "fatal flaw," but learning from failure. *(Ch. 3)*

**trasformismo** System of political manipulation used by Count Camillo di Cavour (1810–1861), Piedmont's prime minister, to create majorities in parliament to support his cabinet. The practice of using cajolery and bribery to transform foes into supporters would continue to characterize Italian government in the late nineteenth century. *(Ch. 22)*

**Triple Alliance** Military alliance established in 1882 among Germany, Austria-Hungary, and Italy to counter the Franco-Russian Alliance (later the **Triple Entente**). The system of rival alliances contributed to the escalation of international tensions. *(Ch. 24)*

**Triple Entente** Military alliance between Great Britain, France, and Russia, completed in 1907, countering the

**Triple Alliance.** The system of rival alliances eventually brought all of Europe into World War I. *(Ch. 24)*

**triumph** Elaborate procession through the streets of ancient Rome. Triumphs were voted by the **senate** to salute a general's victory over a foreign army. *(Ch. 5)*

**Truman Doctrine** The U.S. policy of containment, or limiting communist expansion, as outlined by President Harry Truman in 1947. Intended most immediately to deter any communist designs on Greece or Turkey, the doctrine was used thereafter to support any country that the United States considered threatened by communism during the **cold war.** *(Ch. 28)*

**Ugarit** Cosmopolitan port on northern Syria's Mediterranean coast that was a thriving trading center, especially around 1400–1200 B.C. The alphabet invented by Ugaritic scribes is the source of today's widely used Roman alphabet. *(Ch. 1)*

**United Nations** International organization of nations founded in 1945 to encourage peace, cooperation, and recognition of human rights. The major powers—China, France, Great Britain, the Soviet Union, and the United States—were given a privileged position as permanent members of the Security Council, each with veto power. *(Ch. 28)*

**utilitarianism** Political theory of Jeremy Bentham (1748–1832). Bentham argued that the purpose of government is to provide "the greatest happiness of the greatest number" and that the test of government is its usefulness. Democracy was implicit in Bentham's philosophy: the greatest number could ensure its own happiness only by voting for its rulers. *(Ch. 21)*

**Vasco da Gama (1460?–1524)** Pioneering Portuguese explorer and trader whose voyage from 1497 to 1499 around the Cape of Good Hope to Mozambique and India inaugurated a four-hundred-year-long Portuguese presence in the Indian Ocean region. *(Ch. 13)*

**vassal** Drawing on both Roman and Germanic customs, vassalage linked two men—lord and vassal—in an honorable, reciprocal bond based on loyalty and service. Eventually leading nobles and their vassals formed a social and political elite. *(Ch. 8)*

**Versailles, Treaty of (1919)** Peace treaty between the victorious Allies and defeated Germany after World War I. The harsh terms of this dictated peace produced a sense of bitterness and betrayal in Germany. *(Ch. 25)*

**Vichy France** The term for the repressive French government that followed the Third Republic after France's defeat by Nazi Germany in 1940. Headquartered in the resort town of Vichy, the government collaborated with the victorious Germans, who occupied Paris. *(Ch. 28)*

**Victorian morality** Nineteenth-century ethos wherein the values of the dominant middle class, which emphasized strict moral principles, especially regarding sex and drink, became the social norms. In Queen Victoria, who reigned for two-thirds of the century, the middle classes saw a reflection of their own values. *(Ch. 23)*

**Virgil** Roman poet whose works contributed to the Augustan renewal. In the *Eclogues,* Virgil (Publius Vergilius Maro, 70–19 B.C.) describes the blessings of peace under **Augustus**; in the *Georgics,* he glorifies Italian agriculture. His *Aeneid* mythologizes Rome and describes both the burden and glory of empire. *(Ch. 6)*

**Visigoths** Germanic people who served as allied troops for the Romans. When threatened by the Huns, the Visigoths crossed the Danube and settled in the Balkans. Eventually they sacked Rome in 410 and expanded their rule to parts of Spain and southern France. *(Ch. 7)*

**Voltaire (François-Marie Arouet, 1694–1778)** Prolific French writer, critic, and reformer who believed that literature should bring about social change. His satires and philosophical critiques targeted Christianity, intolerance, and tyranny. He embodied the spirit of eighteenth-century rationalism: its confidence, its increasingly practical bent, its wit and sophistication. *(Ch. 18)*

**Vulgate Bible** Latin version of new translations of the Hebrew Scriptures and Greek New Testament written by Jerome (331–420) for Pope Damasus. It was called the Vulgate because it was the Bible for the "people" (*vulgus*), whose language was Latin. *(Ch. 7)*

**Warsaw Pact (1955–1991)** Military-diplomatic alliance of Soviet bloc countries, created to counter NATO. The pact established a joint military command and mutual military assistance, as well as a new basis for the continuing presence of Soviet troops in the satellite states. See also **cold war.** *(Ch. 29)*

**welfare state** The concept, especially prevalent in western countries after World War II, that government should adopt large-scale social welfare measures, while maintaining a primarily capitalistic economy. Among the welfare measures usually adopted were a national health service, old-age pensions, and insurance against unemployment, sickness, and disability. *(Ch. 29)*

***Weltpolitik*** Meaning "world politics," the term describes the policy pursued by Kaiser **Wilhelm II** (r. 1888–1918) to make Germany a world power, with colonies, a navy, and major influence among the Great Powers. The kaiser implemented his ambitious agenda with nationalistic appeals and bombastic threats. *(Ch. 24)*

**Wilhelm II (r. 1888–1918)** German kaiser (emperor) whose aggressive diplomatic, commercial, and military policies helped trigger World War I. His pursuit of *Weltpolitik* severely aggravated international tensions. See also ***Weltpolitik.*** *(Ch. 24)*

**Yalta conference** The meeting in February 1945 at Yalta, a Soviet Black Sea resort, between Stalin, Roosevelt, and Churchill. With Allied victory assured, they began outlining plans for the postwar order, including the military occupation of Germany. See also **Potsdam conference.** *(Ch. 28)*

**Young Turks** Term describing the young intellectuals who wanted to transform the Ottoman Empire into a more modern, Westernized state. Self-exiled in the late 1860s in Paris and London, they overthrew the sultan and seized power in 1908. The expression has subsequently come to designate any group of activists pushing for political change. *(Ch. 22)*

**Zionism** Nationalist Jewish movement. In the late nineteenth century, faced with growing **anti-Semitism**, some Jews argued that they would be safe only in their own nation. Zionism advocated establishing a Jewish state in the Jews' ancient homeland of Palestine, an idea that became reality with the creation of Israel in 1948. *(Ch. 24)*

**Zoroastrianism** Religion founded about 1000–550 B.C. by the Persian prophet Zarathustra (*Zoroaster* in Greek). Zoroastrians believe in a supreme deity and a cosmic contest between good and evil within each individual. *(Ch. 2)*

# CREDITS

**Chapter 15:** **Page 512:** "Secret Dispatches from the Venetian Ambassador in Spain" from *Pursuit of Power: Venetian Ambassador's Reports* by James C. Davis, Editor & Translator. English translation copyright © 1970 by James C. Davis. Reprinted by permission of HarperCollins Publishers, Inc. **Page 515:** "A Justification of Rebellion Against the King" from Laski: *A Defense of Liberty Against Tyrants*, Peter Smith Publisher, Inc., Gloucester, Mass., 1963. **Page 530:** "Montaigne Discusses Barbarity in the New World and the Old" from *The Complete Essays of Montaigne* translated by Donald M. Frame, Stanford University Press, 1948. Reprinted by permission of the publisher. **Page 531:** Lines 40–50 from *Richard II,* Act II, Scene I, in *The Riverside Shakespeare,* edited by G. Blakemore Evans. Copyright © 1997 by Houghton Mifflin Company. Reprinted by permission of the publisher.

**Chapter 16:** **Page 544:** "A Courtier Criticizes the King" from Louis, duc de Saint-Simon, *Versailles, the Court and Louis XIV,* ed. Lucy Norton (New York : Harper and Row, 1966), pp 248–251. **Page 550:** "The Putney Debates" from "The Levellers" in *The English Revolution,* edited by G.E. Aylmer (Cornell University Press 1975). Copyright Thames & Hudson Ltd. Reprinted by permission of Doubleday, a division of Random House, Inc. **Page 565:** "Global Encounters: Journal of a Dutch Slave Ship" from *New Netherlands Documents,* v. 17 edited by Charles T. Gehring and J.A. Schiltkamp. Used by permission from the *New Netherland Project,* The New York State Library.

**Chapter 17:** **Page 581:** "Galileo Reassures a Patron" from *Discoveries and Opinions of Galileo* by Galileo Galilei, translated by Stillman Drake, copyright © 1957 by Stillman Drake. Used by permission of Doubleday, a division of Random House, Inc. **Page 595:** "Jesuits and Astronomy in China" from *China in the Sixteenth Century* by Matthew Ricci, translated by Louis J. Gallagher, S.J., copyright 1942, 1953 and renewed 1970 by Louis J. Gallagher, S.J. Used by permission of Random House, Inc.

**Chapter 18:** **Page 607:** "Voltaire on Britain's Commercial Success" from *Philosophical Letters: Voltaire,* edited and translated by Ernest Dilworth. Copyright © 1961. Reprinted by permission of Prentice-Hall, Inc., Upper Saddle River, N.J. **Page 610:** "Rousseau Discusses the Benefits of Submitting to the General Will" from *The Social Contract* by Jean-Jacques Rousseau, translated by Maurice Cranston. Reprinted by permission of PFD on behalf of The Estate of Maurice Cranston. Copyright © 1968 by Maurice Cranston.

**Chapter 19:** **Pages 649, 655:** "Lists of Grievances for the Estates-General" and "Declaration of the Rights of Woman" from *The French Revolution: A Document Collection* by Laura Mason and Tracey Rizzo. Copyright © 1999 Houghton Mifflin Company. Reprinted by permission. **Page 659:** "Robespierre Justifies the Terror" from *Robespierre,* edited by George Rudé. Copyright © 1967 by Prentice-Hall, Inc., renewed 1995 by George Rudé. Reprinted by permission of Simon & Schuster. **Page 668:** "A Napoleonic Soldier Recounts the Horrors of the Russian Campaign" from Jakob Walter, *The Diary of a Napoleonic Footsoldier,* ed. Marc Raeff (New York:

Penguin Books, 1993), pp. 83–86. **Page 671:** "A Planter's Wife on the Haitian Slave Revolt" from *Une Correspondance familiale au temps des troubles de Saint-Domingue* by M. E. McIntosh and B. C. Weber (Paris: Société de l'Histoire des Colonies Françaises et Librairie Larose, 1959). Translated by Kristen B. Neuschel. Reprinted by permission of Kristen B. Neuschel.

**Chapter 21:** **Page 712:** "A Spanish Carlist Appeals to the Peasantry" from "La Primera Guerra Carlista" by A. Bullon de Mendoza, translated and edited by Michael Broers in *Europe after Napoleon— Revolution, Reaction, and Romanticism, 1814–1848* (Manchester: Manchester University Press, 1996). Reprinted with permission from Dr. Michael Broers. **Page 714:** "Franz Liszt, Passionate Piano Virtuoso" from "Allgemeine musikalische Zeitung" (May 1838), trans. and ed. by Pierro Weiss and Richard Taruskin, eds., *Music in the Western World—A History in Documents,* Schirmer Books, 1984. **Page 727:** "A Moroccan Describes French Freedom of the Press" from *Disorienting Encounters: Travels of a Moroccan Scholar in France in 1845–1846,* translated and edited by Susan Gilson Miller. Copyright © Regents of the University of California. Reprinted by permission of the University of California Press.

**Chapter 22:** **Page 748:** "Cavour Outlines a Deal with Napoleon III" from *Plombieres: Secret Diplomacy and the Rebirth of Italy,* edited by Mack Walker, copyright © 1968 by Oxford University Press, Inc. Used by permission of Oxford University Press, Inc. **Page 751:** "Bismarck Lectures Parliament on Royal Prerogatives" from *Europe in the Nineteenth Century—A Documentary Analysis of Change and Conflict,* Vol. I by Eugene N. Anderson, Stanley Pincetl, Jr., and Donald Ziegler, eds. Copyright © 1964. Reprinted by permission of Pearson Education, Inc., Upper Saddle River, NJ 07458. **Page 759:** "The Tsar Demands the Freeing of the Serfs" from "Speech of January 28, 1861" in *A Sourcebook for Russian History from Early Times to 1917,* vol. 3, edited by George Vernadsky. Copyright © 1972 by Yale University Press.

**Chapter 23:** **Page 803:** "Emile Zola on the Novelist as Scientist" from *Movements, Currents, Trends: Aspects of European Thought in the Nineteenth and Twentieth Centuries* by Eugen Weber. Copyright © 1992 by D.C. Heath and Company. Reprinted by permission of Houghton Mifflin Company.

**Chapter 25:** **Page 847:** "The Joys of August 1914" from *The World of Yesterday* by Stefan Zweig, translated by Helmut Ripperger, copyright 1943 by the Viking Press, Inc. Used by permission of Viking Penguin Putnam, Inc. **Page 850:** "Into the Trenches" from *German Students' War Letters* edited by A. F. Wedd. Translated and arranged from the original edition of Dr. Philipp Witkop (London: Methuen, 1929). **Page 861:** "The Bolsheviks in Power, November 1917" from *Ten Days That Shook the World* by John Reed (London: Penguin, 1977). **Page 870:** "Encounters: Prince Faisal at the Peace Conference" from J.C. Hurewitz, *Diplomacy in the Near and Middle East: A Documentary Record: 1914–1956.* D. Van Nostrand, 1956; reprinted by Archive Editions, UK, 1987.

# INDEX

# BEST PRACTICE
**THE PROS ON ADOBE ILLUSTRATOR**